POLITICAL GEOGRAPHY

AMS International Studies

No. 1

ISSN 1058-2371

POLITICAL GEOGRAPHY

A Comprehensive Systematic Bibliography

B.L. Sukhwal and Lilawati Sukhwal

AMS PRESS

New York

Library of Congress Cataloging-in-publication Data

Sukhwal. B. L., 1929-
  Political geography : a comprehensive systematic bibliography /B.L. Sukhwal and Lilawati Sukhwal.
    (AMS international studies ; no. 1)
    Includes indexes.
    ISBN 0-404-63151-7 (hardcover: acid-free)
    1. Political geography—Bibliography. I. Sukhwal, Lilawati.
  II. Title. III. Series.
  Z.6004.P7S85 1996
  (JC319)
  016.3201'2—dc20

91-57956
CIP

AMS Press, Inc.
56 East 13th Street
New York, N.Y. 10003

MANUFACTURED IN THE UNITED STATES OF AMERICA

DEDICATION

This bibliography is respectfully dedicated to the devoted scholars, researchers, teachers, and students of political geography who have established the discipline as an important branch of geography through their dedication and hard work.

TABLE OF CONTENTS

PREFACE

The main aim of this bibliography is to gather the literature of political geography written in English in one comprehensive volume. Important material in European and other languages has also been included to cover the field in its entirety. Some of the foreign language material contains either a translation or an abstract in English.

The field of political geography dates back to Aristotle's model of an ideal state. Since then, it has faced ups and downs as a branch of geography. Between World Wars I and II, the discipline became less attractive to researchers and scholars because of general opposition to German Geopolitik. As Richard Muir put it, "Political geography is simultaneously one of the most retarded and most underdeveloped branches of geography, and one that offers the greatest potential for both theoretical and practical advances." During the period between World Wars I and II, however, many geographers, such as Halford J. Mackinder, Alfred T. Mahan, Jean Gottman, Derwent Whittlesey, Richard Hartshorne, Isaiah Bowman, S. Whittmore Boggs, and others continued their quest for improving the discipline. Since the late 1950s, several new trends emerged as a result of the works published by such political geographers as: A.E. Moodie, Eric Fisher, Stephen B. Jones, Kevin Cox, Harm J. deBlij, Roger Kesperson, Robert McColl, Richard Muir, Edward Soja, Lewis M. Alexander, Norman J.G. Pounds, G. Etzel Pearcy, Samuel Van Valkenberg, Saul B. Cohen, and many others. In recent years, along with the above-mentioned geographers, other political geographers vigorously worked to establish the field as an important branch of geography. Chief among them are Julian V. Minghi, W.A. Douglas Jackson, J.R.V. Prescott, Martin Ira Glassner, Peter J. Taylor, R.J. Johnston, Richard Morrill, Stanley Brunn, David Knight, Fred M. Shelly, P.P. Karan, George Hoffman, and K.W. Robinson, and Andrew Kirby. Presently, geographers are realizing the importance of political geography. As a result, its status among the branches of geography has steadily improved.

The interest in compiling this bibliography developed as the authors conducted research on various topics in political geography and advised graduate students on their research papers. They soon found that there was no systematic way to locate material on the subject. Although there were adequate geography bibliographies published in other branches of geography, none existed for political geography. Andre-Louis Sanguin's *Geographie Politique: Bibliographie International* and Martin Ira Glassner's *Bibliography on Land-Locked States* are the only major references.

The authors took a great deal of time compiling the material in the final form, with a complete index. The material was collected from more than 270 journals, periodicals, and bibliographies of various political geography books. The Current Geographical Publications, and the American Geographical Research Catalog are important sources. An open letter was also sent to all political geographers requesting a list of their published work and many of them were receptive to the request. The inclusion of theses and dissertations enhance the usefulness of this bibliography. The listings of theses and dissertations are compiled from issues of the Professional Geographer and University Microfilm, Ann Arbor, Michigan.

The bibliography has been compiled almost wholly first-hand; virtually all the items listed have been personally examined in the original sources. Secondary sources were avoided because of their incompleteness. The authors apologize for any unintentional omissions, but they are happy to see the work completed. It is hoped that this work may prove an important tool to professional geographers, researchers, teachers, and students of geography.

ACKNOWLEDGEMENT

The authors wish to express sincere thanks to those political geographers who sent their publications list for the compilation of this bibliography. Miriam Kerndt, In Charge, Geography Library, University of Wisconsin-Madison, Judith Moriarity and Myrt Weber, Acquisition Department and Polly Myers, Inter-Library Loan/Periodicals, Karrmann Library, University of Wisconsin-Platteville deserve special thanks for their generous assistance in acquiring pertinent material for this book. The authors are also indebted to their daughter, Archna Sukhwal, who devoted not hours, but days, weeks, and months helping them during the preparation of this manuscript.

INTRODUCTION

This bibliography is divided into seventeen chapters. Each chapter is further divided into: (A) General and Theoretical works and (B) Political Geography of regions, which include: 1) Africa, 2) Americas, 3) Asia, 4) Australia, Oceania, and Antarctica, and 5) Europe. These divisions are further subdivided into a) books and b) journals. Books, theses, dissertations, reports, government publications, monographs, atlases, and pamphlets are included in the book section. If a work is published by a government agency such as, The Geographer, U.S. Department of State, or U. S. Department of State, Office of the Geographer, it has been credited to the government agency. If a particular work has more than one author, all names are listed separately in the author index. All corporate entries (entries without an author) are listed under the author index as the subject or organization, such as Washington, D.C., Pakistan Embassy, or Pakistan Embassy, Washington, D.C.

The journal sections contain all material published on a periodical basis, for example: monthly, quarterly, bi-annually, or annually. Book reviews, newspaper articles, papers presented in national or international conferences are excluded due to the lack of space. The journal section also includes a chapter on books or articles in an edited book.

The division of sections by type of material (books, journals) is followed throughout the manuscript, except in smaller sections containing relatively few entries. In this case, books and journals have been combined. In some cases, books, journals, and regions have been combined to avoid very small sections.

The classification used to place entries in sections is based on the compilers' judgment; in some cases, entries may not be placed according to the views of the original writers of the articles. In some cases, information may be overlooked because a listed item deals with two or more aspects or interests. In quoting volumes, Arabic rather than Roman numerals have been used to facilitate easier use. Some entries have been used more than once because they cover more than one category. In the case of authors who spell their names in more than one way, the form preferred or most frequently used has been adopted. In the scheme of categorization, some topics overlap, such as Chapter II - Political Geography and Geopolitics and Chapter XVII C - Strategic Aspects of the Oceans. In such cases, duplicated entries have to be retained to facilitate search by readers. Other examples include: Chapter IV D - Power of a Nation-State, Chapter XV E - Geopolitics of Resources, and Chapter XVII D - Exploration and Control Over Resources of the Oceans. Annotations are excluded, due to the limitations of the size of the volume. The arrangement of chapters is as follows:

Chapter I deals with general works on political geography, including development of political geographic thoughts, textbooks, and basic works. Chapter II, Historical development of the field of political geography. Some pure historical geographic material have also been included in this chapter because the development of political geography is based on historical geography.

Chapter III, Political geography and geopolitics, includes the historical basis of geopolitics, power politics, and the status of nation-states. The evolutionary approach has been adopted in this chapter. Chapter IV contains several subdivisions interrelated to the organization of political territory and the nation-state. For example, a nation state: its size, shape, location, and formation deals with the establishment of various nation-states; B - Demographic aspects of a territory deals with population requirements of a nation; C - Organization of a territory lists the governmental structure and functioning of the government; D - Power of a nation-state includes resources and the viability of a nation; E - Core areas and capital cities are comprised of core regions and capital cities of the nation-state; and F - Regionalism and nationalism which contains regionalistic and nationalistic material pertaining to a nation.

Chapter V, Categories of nation-states, encompasses theoretical aspects of a nation-state's political organization, unitary/central or Federal type of structure of governments. Chapter VI, Political geography and administrative areas, includes the local and municipal government, urbanization, and structure of politically organized spaces. Chapter VII, Politics of management of resources, lists the material related to the development of resources and imbalance created among regions by governmental policies in a nation-state. National self-sufficiency and stockpiling references are included in this chapter. Chapter VIII, Civilizations and cultures, include races and tribes, peoples and ethnic groups, languages and religions and their affect on the political organization of space.

Chapter IX deals with frontiers, boundaries, and land-locked states. This chapter is subdivided into seven sub-categories including: A - Boundary Concepts and Theories; B - Boundary Classification and Demarcation; C - Boundary Problems in the Contemporary World; D - Frontiers; E - Land-locked States and Access to Sea; F - Buffer Zones and Territories, and G - Enclaves and Exclaves. There is a great deal of material on this topic, so subheadings have been created.

Chapter X includes electoral geography. The region of the United States has been expanded, as it includes a large number of Ph.D. dissertations. Substantial work has been done on the electoral geography, especially in democratic nations of Western Europe, North America, Asia, and Australia.

Chapters XI, XII, XIII and XIV deal with various aspects of international relations, such as international rivers and bays, supernationalism, power blocs, global structure, colonies and colonialism. Chapter XV also deals with international aspects of political geography; however, its eight subdivisions have been broken down to show various aspects of international politics. In order to avoid small sections, all regions have been combined under the subdivisions of books and journals. Chapter XVI, Military Geography and Geostrategy, is expanded to include large numbers of entries written by political geographers in recent years. Chapter XVII, Political Geography of the Oceans, has been subdivided into four subsections: A - General and Theoretical Aspects of Oceans; B - Continental Shelf and Territorial Sea; C - Strategic Aspects of the Oceans; and D - Exploration and Control of the Resources of the Oceans. Finally, the author index was prepared to facilitate search for relevant entries and easy access. A subject index with entry numbers assists readers in finding entries for their particular subject.

CHAPTER I

GENERAL WORKS ON POLITICAL GEOGRAPHY

GENERAL AND THEORY

Books

1 **Alexander, Lewis M.** *World Political Patterns.* 2nd ed. Chicago: Rand McNally, 1963.

2 **Ante, Ulrich.** *Politische Geographie.* Braunscheweig: Westerman, 1981.

3 **Argenbright, Robert Thomas.** *Bowman's New World: World Power and Political Geography.* Berkeley: University of California, Master's Thesis, 1984.

4 **Barbag, Jozef.** *Geografia Polityczna Ogolna (General Political Geography).* 3rd ed. Warszawa: Panstwowe Wydawn, Naukowe, 1978.

5 **Barnett, J. Ross,** and **Mercer, John.** *Urban Political Analysis and New Directions in Political Geography.* Iowa City: University of Iowa, Department of Geography, 1973.

6 **Bergman, Edward Fisher.** *Modern Political Geography.* Dubuque, Iowa: Brown Publishing, 1975.

7 **Blomley, Nicholas K.** *Law, Space, and the Geographies of Power.* New York: Guilford Publications, Inc., 1994.

8 **Board, I.C.; Charley, R.J.; Haggett, P.; and Stoddard, D.R.,** eds. *Progress in Geography.* London: Edward Arnold, 1969.

9 **Boesch, Martin.** Engagierte Geographie: zur Rekonstruktion der Raumwissenschaft als politik-orientierte Geographie. Stuttgart: Franz Steiner Verlag, 1989.

10 **Boesler, Klaus-Achim.** *Politische Geographie.* Stuttgart: B. G. Teubner, 1983.

11 **Bornschier, Volker,** and **Lengyel, Peter,** eds. *Waves, Formations and Values in the World System.* New Brunswick: Transaction Publishers, 1992.

12 **Bowman, Isaiah.** *The New World: Problems in Political Geography.* New York: World Book, 1928.

13 **Brecher, Michael.** *Crises in World Politics.* New York: Elsevier Science, 1993.

14 **Brunhes, Jean.** *Etude de Geographie Humaine.* Paris: Naud, 1902.

15 **Brunhes, Jean.** "Geographie Dite Politique." *La Geographie Humaine.* Paris: Presses Universitaries de France, 1956.

16 **Brunhes, Jean.** et **Vallaux, Camille.** *La Geographie de l'Histoire: Geographie de la paix et de la guerre sur terre et sur mer.* Paris: Felix Alcan, 1921.

17 **Brunner, H.R.A.** *Friedrich Ratzels Politische Geographie und Staat.* Zurich: Diss, 1977.

18 **Buckholts, Paul.** *Political Geography.* New York: Ronald Press, 1966.

19 **Burnett, Alan D.,** and **Taylor, Peter J.,** eds. *Political Studies from Spatial Perspectives: Anglo-American Essays on Political Geography.* New York: John Wiley & Sons, 1981.

20 **Busteed, M.A.,** ed. *Developments in Political Geography.* London: Academic Press, 1983.

21 **Butler, D.** *The Study of Political Behavior.* London: Hutchinson University, 1966.

22 **Carlson, Lucile.** *Geography and World Politics.* Englewood Cliffs, New Jersey: Prentice-Hall, 1960.

23 **Carvalho, Carlos Miguel Delgado de.** *Introducao a Geographia Politica.* Rio de Janeiro: liv. Francisco Alves, 1929.

24 **Carvalho, Carlos Miguel Delgado de.** *Geographia Humana, Politica Economica.* Rio de Janeiro: Editora Nacional, 1935.

25 **Christensen, Kathleen Elizabeth.** *Geography as a Human Science: A Philosophical Approach.* University Park: Pennsylvania State University, Ph.D., 1981.

26 **Cohen, Saul B.** *Geography and Politics in a World Divided.* 2nd ed. New York: Oxford University Press, 1973.

27 **Cole, John P.** *Geography of World Affairs.* 6th ed. London and New York: Penguin Books, 1981.

28 **Cox, Kevin R.** *Location and Public Problems: A Political Geography of the Contemporary World.* New York: Maaroufa Press, 1979.

29 Crick, B. *The Defense of Politics*. Chicago, Illinois: University of Chicago Press, 1972.

30 Crone, Gerald R. *Background to Political Geography*. Chester Springs, Pennsylvania: Defour, 1967.

31 Derruau, Max. "Nou Veau," *Precis de Geographie Humaine*. Paris: Armand Colin, 1969.

32 Dikshit, R.D. *Political Geography: A Contemporary Perspective*. New Delhi: Tata McGraw-Hill, 1982.

33 Dix, Arthur. *Politische Geographie: Weltpolitisches Handbuch*. Munchen, Berlin: Oldenburg, 1923.

34 Dix, Arthur. *Geografia Politica*. Barcelona: Ed. Labor, 1929.

35 Dorpalen, Andreas. *The New World*. Yonkers-on-Hudson, New York: World Book, 1921.

36 Dove, K. *Allgemeine Politische Geographie*. Berlin, Leipzig: e Gruyter, 1920.

37 East, W. Gordon, and Moodie, A.E. *The Changing World: Studies in Political Geography*. New York: World Book, 1956.

38 East, W. Gordon; Moodie, A.E.; and Prescott, J.R.V. *Our Fragmented World: An Introduction to Political Geography*. London: Macmillan, 1975.

39 East, W. Gordon; Moodie, A.E.; Prescott, J.R.V; and Wooldridge, S.W. *The Spirit and Purpose of Geography*. New York: Capricorn Books, 1967.

40 Easton, David. *A Framework for Political Analysis*. New York: Prentice-Hall, 1965.

41 Easton, David. *The Political System*. New York: Knopf, 1953.

42 Easton, David. *A Systems Analysis of Political Life*. New York: John Wiley & Sons, 1965.

43 Ekins, Paul. *A New World Order: Grassroots Movement for Global Change*. London: Routledge, 1992.

44 Entricksin, J. Nicholas, and Brunn, Stanley D., eds. *Reflections on Richard Hartshorne's The Nature of Geography*. Washington, D.C., Occasional Publications of the Association of American Geographers, 1989.

45 Fairgrieve, James. *Geographic und Weltmacht*. Berlin: Vowinckel, 1925.

46 Febvre, Lucien. *La Terre et l'Evolution Humaine, Introduction Geographique a l'Histore*. Paris: Albin Michel, 1970.

47 Fifield, Russell H., and Pearcy, G. Etzel. *World Political Geography*. 2nd ed. New York: Thomas Y. Crowell, 1957.

48 Fisher, Charles A. *Essays in Political Geography*. London: Methuen, 1968.

49 Freeman, T.W. *The Geographer's Craft*. Manchester: Manchester University Press, 1967.

50 Fried, Morton H. *The Evolution of Political Society*. New York: Random House, 1967.

51 Gaile, Gary L., and Willmott, Cort J., eds. *Geography in America*. Columbus, Ohio: Merrill Publishing, for the Association of American Geographers, 1989.

52 Garry, Robert. *Geographie Politique*. Montreal: Presses de l'Universite de Montreal, 1968.

53 Glassner, Martin Ira. *Political Geography*. New York: John Wiley & Sons, Inc., 1993.

54 Glassner, Martin I., and de Blij, Harm J. *Systematic Political Geography*. 4th ed. New York: John Wiley & Sons, 1988.

55 Goblet, Y.M. *Political Geography and the World Map*. New York: Praeger, 1955.

56 Gottmann, Jean. *La Politique des Etats et leur Geographie*. Paris: Armand Colin, 1952.

57 Gurdon, Charles, ed. *The Horn of Africa*. London: University College Londno Press, 1994.

58 Hayford, Alison Margaret. *The Territory of Struggle: A Political Geography of Revolution*. Ann Arbor: University of Michigan, Ph.D., 1981.

59 Haring, L. Lloyd, and Norris, Robert E. *Political Geography*. Columbus, Ohio: Charles Merrill Publishing, 1980.

60 Harris, Keith Donald, and Brunn, Stanley D. *The Geography of Laws and Justice: Spatial Perspectives on the Criminal Justice System*. New York: Praeger, 1978.

61 Hartshorne, Richard. *Perspective on the Nature of Geography*. Chicago: Rand McNally, 1959.

62 Hoggart, Keith, and Kofman, Eleanor, eds. *Politics, Geography and Social Stratification*. Croom Helm; Series in Geography and Environment. London: Croom Helm, 1986.

63 Horrabin, J.F. *An Outline of Political Geography*. New York: Knopf, 1942.

64 Huber, Wilhelm. *Politische Geographie*. Munich: Oldenbourg, 1927.

65 **Hunter, James M.** *Perspective on Ratzel's Political Geography.* Lanham, Maryland: University Press of America, 1983.

66 **Jackson, W.A. Douglas.** *Politics and Geographic Relationships: Readings on the Nature of Political Geography.* 2nd ed. Englewood Cliffs: Prentice-Hall, 1971.

67 **Jackson, W.A. Douglas, and Bergman, Edward Fisher.** *A Geography of Politics.* Dubuque, Iowa: Brown Publishing, 1973.

68 **Jackson, W.A. Douglas, and Samuels, Marwyn S.,** eds. *Politics and Geographic Relationships; Toward a New Focus.* Englewood Cliffs, New Jersey: Prentice-Hall, 1971.

69 **Jackson, W.A. Douglas, and Shoichi, Yokoyama.** *Modern Political Geography (Seiji-Chirigaku - in Japanese).* Tokyo: Taimeido, 1979.

70 **James, Preston E.** *One World Divided; A Geographer Looks at the Modern World.* New York: Blaisdell Publishing, 1964.

71 **James, Preston E., and Jones, Clarence F.,** eds. *American Geography: Inventory and Prospect.* Syracuse, New York: Syracuse University Press, 1954.

72 **Johnston, R.J.,** ed. *The Future of Geography.* London: Methuen, 1985.

73 **Johnston, R.J.,** ed. *Geography and Geographers.* London: Edward Arnold, 1979a.

74 **Johnston, R.J.,** ed. *Geography and the State: An Essay in Political Geography.* London: Macmillan, 1982.

75 **Johnston, R.J., and Taylor, P.J.,** eds. *A World in Crisis: Geographical Perspectives.* Cambridge, Massachusetts: Basil Blackwell, 1989.

76 **Jones, Steven B., and Murphy, M.F.** *Geography and World Affairs,* 3rd ed. Chicago: Rand McNally, 1971.

77 **Kasperson, Roger E.** *Frontiers of Political Geography.* Englewood Cliffs, New Jersey: Prentice-Hall, 1974.

78 **Kasperson, Roger E, and Minghi, J.V.** *The Structure of Political Geography.* London: University of London Press, 1969.

79 **Keohane, R.O.** *After Hegomony.* Princeton, New Jersey: Princeton University Press, 1984.

80 **Kidron, Michael, and Segal, Ronald.** *The New State of the World Atlas.* New York: Simon and Schuster, 1984.

81 **Kliot, Nurit.** *The Political Geography of Conflict and Peace.* New York: John Wiley and Sons, 1993.

82 **Kliot, Nurit.** *The Political Landscape: A Geographical Analysis of the Impact of Ideology on the Landscape.* Worchester, Massachusetts: Clark University, Ph.D., 1978.

83 **Kohn, Clyde F.,** ed. *The United States and the World Today: An Appraisal of Geographic Learnings for Educational Programs.* Chicago: Rand McNally, 1958.

84 **Kriesel, Karl Marcus.** *Spatial Patterns and the Hierarchy of Interlocal Cooperation in Metropolitan Southeast Michigan: An Application of the Central Place Theory in Political Geography.* Ann Arbor: University of Michigan, Ph.D., 1970.

85 **Londono, Julio.** *Fundamentos de la Geografia Politia.* Bogota: imp. y pub. de las Fuerzas Armadas, 1965.

86 **Loth, J.** *Geografia Polityczna (Political Geography).* Krakov: Academie Polonaise des Sciences, 1925.

87 **Mackinder, Halford J.** *Democratic Ideals and Reality: A Politics of Reconstruction.* New York: Holt, Rinehart & Winston, 1942 and New York: W.W. Norton, 1962.

88 **Marchi, Luigi de.** *Fondamenti di geografia politica.* Milan-Padoue: s.e., 1929.

89 **Matznetter, Josef.** *Politische Geographie.* Darmstadt: Wissenschaftliche Buchgesellschaft, 1977.

90 **Maull, Otto.** *Geografia Politica.* Barcelona: Ediciones Omega S.A., 1960.

91 **Maull, Otto.** *Politische Geographie.* Berlin: Safari, 1956.

92 **Mendlovitz, Saul H.,** ed. *On the Creation of a Just World Order: Preferred Worlds for the 1990's.* New York: The Free Press, 1975.

93 **Merton, R.K.** *Social Theory and Social Structure: Towards a Codification of Theory and Research.* Glencoe, Illinois: The Free Press, 1949.

94 **Migliorini, E.** *La terra e gli Stati. Lezioni di geografia politica.* Napoli: s.e., 1966.

95 **Mirheydar, Dorreh.** *Principles of Political Geography* (in Persian). Tehran: Tehran University Press, 1968.

96 **Mirheydar, Dorreh.** *Recent Development in Political Geography.* Translated in Persian from English of the Political Geography by J. Prescott. Tehran: Tehran University Press, 1979.

97 **Moodie, A.E.** *Geography Behind Politics.* London: Hutchinson University, 1947.

98 **Muir, Richard.** *Modern Political Geography.* 2nd ed. London: Macmillan, 1981.

99 **Muir, Richard, and Paddison, Ronan.** *Politics, Geography and Behaviour.* London: Methuen, 1981.

100 **National Academy of Sciences.** *Studies in Political Geography.* Washington, D.C.: Committee on Geography, 1965.

101 **Norris, Robert E.** *Spatial Interaction and the Politicization of Individuals.* Iowa City: University of Iowa, Department of Geography, Ph.D., 1970.

102 **Pacione, M.,** ed. *Progress in Political Geography.* London: Croom Helm, 1985.

103 **Peet, Richard,** ed. *Radical Geography: Alternative Viewpoints on Contemporary Social Issues.* Chicago: Maroufa Press, 1977.

104 **Pounds, Norman J.G.** *Political Geography.* New York: McGraw-Hill, 1972.

105 **Prescott, J.R.V.** *Political Geography.* New York: St. Martin's Press, 1972.

106 **Pye, Lucian W.,** ed. *Political Science and Area Studies: Rival or Partners?* Bloomington: Indiana University Press, 1975.

107 **Raffestin, Claude.** *Pour une Geographie du Pouvoir.* Paris: Litec, 1980.

108 **Ratzel, Friedrich.** *Erdenmacht und Volkerschicksal.* Ed. Karl Hauschofer. 2nd ed. Stuttgart: A. Kroner, 1940.

109 **Ratzel, Friedrich.** *Der Staat und Sein Boden, Geographisch Betrachteb.* Leipzig: S. Hirzel, 1896.

110 **Ratzel, Friedrich.** *Politische Geographie: Oder, die Geographie der Staaten, des Verkehres, und des Krieg.* Munchen: Oldenbourg, 1897.

111 **Ratzel, Friedrich.** *Politische Geographie.* 3rd ed. Munich and Berlin: R. Oldenbourg, 1923.

112 **Ray, James Lee.** *Global Politics.* 4th ed. Boston: Houghton Mifflin Company, 1990.

113 **Reclus, Elisee.** *L'homme et la Terre.* Paris: Librairie Universelle, 1905.

114 **Renner, G.T.** *Political Geography and Its Point of View.* New York: Thomas Y. Crowell, 1948.

115 **Reparez, Gonzalo de.** *Geografia y Politica.* Barcelona: Muentora, 1929.

116 **Roletto, Georgio, et Massi, Ernesto.** *Lineamenti di Geografia Politica.* Trieste: Publications Institut de Geographie, 1931.

117 **Rosenau, James N.,** ed. *Linkage Politics: Essays on the Convergence of National and International Systems.* New York: The Free Press, 1969.

118 **Russett, Bruce M.** *International Regions and the International System: A Study in Political Ecology.* Chicago: Rand McNally, 1967.

119 **Russett, Bruce M.** *Trends in World Politics.* New York: Macmillan, 1965.

120 **Russett, Bruce M.; Alker, Hayward R.; Deutsch, Karl W., Lasswell, Harold D.; and others.** *World Handbook of Political and Social Indicators.* New Haven, Connecticut: Yale University Press, 1964.

121 **Rustow, Dankwart A.** *A World of Nations: Problems of Political Modernization.* Washington, D.C.: Brookings Institution, 1967.

122 **Samatar, Ahmed I.,** ed. *The Somali Challenge: From Catastrophe to Renewal?* Boulder: Lynne Rienner Publishers, 1994.

123 **Sanchez, Pedro C.** *Geografia Politica.* Mexico: Ed. Tacubaya, 1938.

124 **Sandoval, R. Rodolfo.** *Compendio Geografico Politico, Elaborado Para Auxiliar a la Ensinanza de la Geografia Politica.* Mexico: Ed. Periodisca, 1966.

125 **Sanguin, Andre-Louis.** *Geographie Politique: Bibliographie Internationale.* Montreal: Les Presses de l'universite du Quebec, 1976.

126 **Santos, M.** *Por uma Geografia Nova. Da critica da Geografia a uma Geografia critica.* Sao Paulo: Editora Hucitec, 1980.

127 **Saxena, H.M.** *Political Geography* (in Hindi). Meerut, India: Rastogi Publications, 1982.

128 **Schone, Emil.** *Politische Goegraphie.* Leipzig: B. G. Teubner, 1911.

129 **Semple, Ellen Churchill.** *Influences of Geographic Environment: On the Basis of Ratzel's System of Anthropo-Geography.* New York: Holt, Rinehart & Winston, 1911.

130 **Short, John Rennie.** *An Introduction to Political Geography.* 2nd ed. London: Routledge, 1993.

131 **Smith, D.M.** *Human Geography: A Welfare Approach.* London: Edward Arnold, 1977.

132 **Soja, Edward W.** *A Paradigm for the Geographical Analysis of Political Systems.* Evanston, Illinois: Northwestern University, 1969.

133 **Soja, Edward W.** *The Political Organization of Space.* Washington, D.C.: Association of American Geographers, Resource Paper No. 8, 1971.

134 **Sprout, Harold H.,** and **Sprout, Margaret.** *Foundations of International Politics.* Princeton, New Jersey: Van Nostand, 1962.

135 **Sprout, Harold H.,** and **Sprout, Margaret.** *Man-milieu Relationships Hypotheses in the Context of International Politics.* Princeton, New Jersey: Center of International Studies, Princeton University, 1956.

136 **Sprout, Harold H.,** and **Sprout, Margaret.** *Toward A Politics of the Planet Earth.* New York: Van Nostrand, 1971.

137 **Supan, Alexander.** *Leitlinen der Allgemeinen Politischen Geographie. Naturlehre des Staates.* Berlin-Leipzig, Walter De Gruyter Co., 1922.

138 **Taylor, Peter.** *Political Geography of the Twentieth Century: A Global Analysis.* New York: John Wiley and Sons, Inc., 1994.

139 **Taylor, Peter.** *Political Geography: World Economy, Nation-State and Locality.* 3rd ed. New York: John Wiley and Sons, Inc., 1993.

140 **Taylor, Peter J.** *Political Geography: World Economy, Nation State and Locality.* 2nd ed. London: Longman, 1989.

141 **Taylor, Peter J.,** and **House, J.W.,** eds. *Political Geography: Recent Advances and Future Directions.* London: Croom Helm, 1984.

142 **Vallaux, Camille.** *Le sol et l'Etat.* Paris: Doin, 1911.

143 **Vallaux, Camille,** et **Brunhes, Jean.** *La Geographie de l'Histoire.* Paris: Presses Universitaires de France, 1921.

144 **Van Valkenburg, Samuel,** et **Stotz, Carl L.** *Elements of Political Geography.* Englewood Cliffs, New Jersey: Prentice-Hall, 1954.

145 **Vogel, Walther.** *Politische Geographie.* Leipzig-Berlin: B.G. Teubner, 1922.

146 **Wallerstein, I.** *The Modern World System,* 2 vols. New York: Academic Press, 1981.

147 **Wanklyn, Harriet Grace.** *Friedrich Ratzel: A Bibliographical Memoir and Bibliography.* Cambridge: Cambridge University Press, 1961.

148 **Weigert, Hans Werner,** et al. *Principles of Political Geography.* New York: Appleton-Century-Crofts, 1957.

149 **Weigert, Hans Werner; Stefansson, Wilhjalmer;** et **Harrison, Richard E.** *New Compass of the World: A Symposium on Political Geography.* New York: Macmillan, 1949.

150 **Whitbeck, R.H.,** and **Thomas, O.J.** *The Geographic Factor, Its Role in Life and Civilization.* New York: Century, 1932.

151 **Whiteley, P.** *Models of Political Economy.* London: Sage Publications, 1980.

152 **Whittlesey, Derwent.** *The Earth and the State: A Study of Political Geography.* New York: Henry Holt, 1944.

153 **Williams, Colin,** ed. *The Political Geography of the New World Order.* London: Belhaven Press, 1993.

154 **Zaidi, Iqtidar H,** ed. *Readings in Political Geography.* Lahore: Punjab University Press, 1965.

Journals

155 **Ackerman, Edward A.** "Where Is a Research Frontier." *Annals of the Association of American Geographers,* 53, No. 4 (December, 1963), 429-440.

156 **Agnew, J. A.** "The Return of Time and the Need for a New Materialism," *Political Geography,* 12, No. 1 (January, 1993), 84-86.

157 **Alexander, Lewis M.** "Major Trends in the World Political Pattern." *Institute of Indian Geographers (Bihar),* 1 (1954), 6-12.

158 **Allison, L.** "Review of 'Politics, Geography and Behavior'." *Political Geography Quarterly,* 1, No. 2 (April, 1982), 109-112.

159 **Almagia, Roberto.** "La Geografia Politica," *l'Universo,* 4, No. 5 (September-October, 1923), 751-760.

160 **Ante, Ulrich.** "Ansatze fur Zeitgensassische Politische Geographie." *Zeitschrift fur Wirschaftsgeographie* (Frankfurt am Main), 30 Jahr Heft 2 (1986), 10-14.

161 **Archer, J. Clark.** "Political Geography." *Progress in Human Geography,* 4, No. 2 (June, 1980), 255-264; and 6, No. 2 (June, 1982), 231-241.

162 **Archer, J. Clark,** and **Shelley, Fred M.** "Theory and Methodology in Political Geography." In *Progress in Political Geography.* London: Croom Helm, 1984.

163 **Auburtin, Jean.** "La Geographie Politique."
Sciences Politiques, 52° annee, No. 5 (Decembre,
1937), 482-487.

164 **Baker, J.N.L.**, "Geography and Politics: The
Geographical Doctrine of Balance," *Transactions of
the Institute of British Geographers*, No. 13 (May,
1947), 1-15.

165 **Barbag, Jozef.** "O Miejesce Geographii
polityzcenej w Sustemie Nauk o Ziemi" (Position de
la geographie politique dans l'ensemble des sciences
naturelles), *Czas. Geogr*, No. 3-4 (1964), 355-370.

166 **Barbag, Jozef.** "Wspolczesne Problemy Geografii
Politycznej." *Przeglad Geograficzny*, 40 Zeszyt 1
(1968), 67-90.

167 **Bassin, Mark.** "Imperialism and the Nation State in
Friedrich Ratzel's Political Geography." *Progress
in Human Geography*, 11, No. 4 (December, 1987),
473-495.

168 **Blacksell, Mark; Watkins, Charles; and
Economides, Kim.** "Human Geography and Law:
A Case of Separate Development in Social Science."
Progress in Human Geography, 10, No. 3
(September, 1986), 377-396.

169 **Blomley, Nicholas K., and Clark, Gordon L.**
"Law, Theory, and Geography." *Urban Geography*
[Silver Spring], 11, No. 5 (September-October,
1990), 433-446.

170 **Boesler, Klaus-Achim.** "Gedanken zum Konzept
der Politischen Geographie." *Die Erde*, 105 Jahrg,
Heft 1 (1974) 7-33.

171 **Boesler, Klaus-Achim.** "Geographie und
Raumordnung." *Geographie und Schule*, 4 (1980)
4-12.

172 **Boggs, S. Whittemore.** "Geographic and Other
Scientific Techniques for Political Science."
American Political Science Review, 42, No. 2
(April, 1948), 223-238.

173 **Bonetti, E.** "La Struttura Della Geografia Politica."
Rivista di Geografia Italiana, 77, No. 4 (1970) 435-
443.

174 **Bowen, E.G.** "The Geography of Nations."
Geography, 48, Part 1, No. 218 (January, 1963), 1-
17.

175 **Brecher, M. and Wilkenfeld, J.** "Crises in World
Politics." *World Politics*, 34, No. 2 (April, 1982),
380-417.

176 **Brown, Chris.** "'Really Existing Liberalism' and
International Order." *Millennium* [London], 21, No.
3 (Winter, 1992), 313-328.

177 **Brown, Seyom.** "Explaining the Transformation of

World Politics." *International Journal* [Toronto],
46, No. 2 (Spring, 1991), 207-219.

178 **Brunn, Stanley D., and Yanarella, Ernie.**
"Towards a Humanistic Political Geography."
Studies in Comparative Internal Development, 22,
No. 2 (Summer, 1987), 3-49.

179 **Burghardt, Andrew F.** "The Dimensions of
Political Geography: Some Recent Texts." *The
Canadian Geographer*, 9 No. 4 (Winter, 1965),
229-233.

180 **Burnett, Alan D.** "The Application of Alternative
Theories in Political Geography: The Case of
Political Participation. *Political Geography: Recent
Advances and Future Directions*. (P.J. Taylor and
J. House, eds.). London: Croom Helm, 1984, 25-
49.

181 **Campbell, Craig S.** "The Second Nature of
Geography: Hartshorne as Humanist." *The
Professional Geographer*, 46. No. 4 (November,
1994), 411-417.

182 **Camu, Pierre.** "Jacques Ancel et la Geographie
Politique." *Revue Canadienne de Geographie*, 1,
Nos. 2-3 (Juin-Septembre, 1947), 28-31.

183 **Chaudhuri, Manoranjan.** "Evolution of Ideas in
Political Geography." *Calcutta Geographical
Review*, 9, No. 1-4 (1947), 23-31.

184 **Clark, Gordon L.** "Law and the Interpretive Turn
in the Social Sciences." *Urban Geography*, 10, No.
3 (May-June, 1989), 209-228.

185 **Claval, Paul.** "Le Renouveau de la Geographie
Politique." *Bulletin de l'Association de Geographes
Francais*, 60, No. 493 (1983), 87-98.

186 **Claval, Paul.** "Les Aspects Modernes de la
Geographie Politique." *Travaux de l'Institut de
Geographie de Reims*, 29-30 (1977), 11-29.

187 **Claval, Paul.** "Us Cadres Conceptvels de l'analyse
des situations de conflit en geographie politique."
L'Espace geographique, 16, No. 4
(Octobre/Decembre, 1987), 269-276.

188 **Clozier, Rene.** "La Geographie Politique et
l'Enseignement du Second Degre." *Etudes
Rhodaniennes*, No. 4 (1948), 5.

189 **Clozier, Rene.** "La Geographie Politique."
Information Geographique, 35, No. 4 (July-August,
1971) 159-162.

190 **Clozier, Rene.** "Toward a Geography of Policy."
Economic Geography, 42, No. 1 (January, 1966).
Guest editorial for January.

191 **Clozier, Rene, et Rosenthal, Lewis D.** "A Geographical Model for Political Systems Analysis." *Geographical Review*, 61, No. 1 (January, 1971), 5-31.

192 **Coldren, Fanny A., and Cook, Jean E.**, Comps. "Political Geography: A Bibliography." *The Journal of Geography*, 41, No. 9 (December, 1942), 336-340.

193 **Cole, John P.** "What is Political Geography?" *Profile* (The Geographical Journal published by St. Paul's and St. Mary's Colleges of Education Geographical Society, Cheltenham), 5, No. 14, Pt. 2 (March 1973), 57-73.

194 **Corbridge, S.** "Political Geography of Contemporary Events v. Crisis, What Crisis? Monetarism, Brandt II and the Geopolitics of Debt." *Political Geography Quarterly*, 3, No. 4 (October, 1984), 331-345.

195 **Cox, Kevin R.** "A Spatial Interactional Model for Political Geography." *The East Lake Geographer*, 4 (December, 1968) 58-76.

196 **Curry, M.** "On Possible Worlds: From Geographies of the Future to Future Geographies." In *Geography and Humanistic Knowledge. Waterloo Lectures in Geography*. L. Guelke, ed., 11, Series No. 25. Waterloo, Ontario, Canada: University of Waterloo, Department of Geography, 1986, 87-101.

197 **Czajka, Willi.** "Die Wissenschaftlichkeit der Politischen Geographie." *Taschenworterbuch und Jahrweiser zur Landeskunde*, (1961), 464-487.

198 **De Blig, Harm.** "Political Geography of the Post Cold War World. *The Professional Geographer* [New York], 44, No. 1 (February, 1992, 16-19.

199 **Dear, Michael J.** "Research Agendas in Political Geography--A Minority View." *Political Geography Quarterly*, 1, No. 2 (April, 1982), 197-180.

200 **Demangeon, Albert.** "Geographie Politique." *Annales de Geographie*, 41, No. 1 (January, 1932), 22-31.

201 **Desserteaux, Marc.** "Droit Compare et Geographie Humaine." *Annales de Geographie*, 56, No. 302 (Avril-Juin, 1947), 81-93.

202 **Devi, Sunita.** "Nature of Political Geography." In *Recent Trends and Concepts in Geography*. Ram Bahadur Mandal and Vishwanath Prasad Sinha, eds. New Delhi: Concept Publishing, 1980, 319-336.

203 **Dikshit, R.D.** "The Retreat from Political Geography." *Area*, 9, No. 4 (December, 1977), 234-239.

204 **Dikshit, R.D.** "Time-lag in Political Geography." *Area*, 11, No. 1 (March, 1979), 92-93.

205 **Dikshit, R.D.** "Toward a Generic Approach in Political Geography." *Tijdschrift voor Economische en Sociale Geographie*, 61, No. 4 (July-August, 1970), 242-245.

206 **Dikshit, S.K., and Giri, H.H.** "Methodology and Approaches in Political Geography; Geographical Note 1." *Geographical Review of India*, 49, No. 3 (September, 1987), 75-76.

207 **Douglas, J.N.H.** "Geography and Political Problems." In: *Geography at Aberystwyth*. E.G. Bowen, Harold Carter, James A. Taylor, eds. Cardiff: University of Wales Press, 1968, 196-204.

208 **Drake, Christine, and Horton, June.** "Comment on Editorial Essay: Sexist Bias in Political Geography." *Political Geography Quarterly*, 2, No. 4 (October, 1983), 329-37.

209 **Duncan, C.J. and Epps, W.R.** "Comments: GIS and the Role of the state 'down under'." *Political Geography*, 12, No. 1 (January, 1993), 3-7.

210 **Dwivedi, R.L.** "The Applied Political Geography as an Applied Geography Field." *National Geographer*, 6 (1971), 9-12.

211 **East, W. Gordon.** "The Nature of Political Geography." *Politica*, 2, No. 1 (March, 1937), 259-286.

212 **Fillip, K.** Politischer Geographleunterricht. Eine Traditionsauslegung als Beitrrag der Geographie didaktik. *Aus polifik und zeitgeschichte*, Beilage zur Wochenzeitschrift das Parlament), Baud 32, Heft 2 (Februar, 1978), 33-117.

213 **Fleming, Dan B., and Morrill, Robert W.** "Contemporary Textbook Treatment of Political Geography." *Social Studies* (Washington, D.C.), 73, No. 3 (May/June, 1982), 106-109.

214 **Gallusser, Werner A.** "Umweltpolitik als Moderner Problembereich der Politischen Geographie." *Zeitschrfit fur Wirtschaftsgeographie*, 30 Jahr, Heft 2 (1986), 15-22.

215 **Glassner, Martin Ira.** "A Geographer Among Diplomats." The Geographical Review (April, 1977). Reprinted in Nepali in *Roop Rekha* (November, 1977), 236-237.

216 **Glatz, Hans, and Scheer, Gunter.** "Regionalpolitik in Osterreich: Anstaze zu neuen strategien." *Geographische Rundschau*, Jahr 39, Heft 10 (October, 1987), 554-562.

217 **Goertz, Gary.** "Contextual Theories and Indicators in World Politics." *International Interactions* [Philadelphia], 17, No 4 (1992), 285-303.

218 **Gorbatsevich, R.A.** "Political Geography and Its Problems." *Soviet Geography: Review and Translation*, 13, No. 4 (April, 1972), 220-227.

219 **Gottmann, Jean.** "The Basic Problem of Political Geography: The Organization of Space and the Search for Stability." *Tijdschrift voor economic en sociale geografie*, 73, No. 6 (November-December, 1982), 340-349.

220 **Gottmann, Jean.** "La Politique et le concret." *Politique Etrangere*, 28, Nos. 4-5 (1963), 273-302.

221 **Gottmann, Jean.** "Mer et terre, esquisse de geographie politique." *Annales, Economies, Societes, Civilisations*, 4 anne, No. 1 (Janvier-Mars, 1949), 10-22.

222 **Gottmann, Jean.** "The Political Partitioning of our World, An Attempt at Analysis." *World Politics*, 4, No. 4 (July, 1952), 512-519.

223 **Hartshorne, Richard.** "The Functional Approach in Political Geography." *Annals of the Association of American Geographers*, 40, No. 2 (June, 1950), 95-130.

224 **Hartshorne, Richard.** "Political Geography of the Modern World." *Journal of Conflict Resolution*, 4, No. 1 (March, 1960), 52-66.

225 **Hartshorne, Richard.** "Political Geography." In James, Preston E., et Jones, C.F. *American Geography: Inventory and Prospects*. Syracuse, New York: Syracuse University Press, 1954, 167-225.

226 **Hartshorne, Richard.** "The Politico-Geographic Pattern of the World." *Annals of the American Academy of Political and Social Science*, 218 (November, 1941), 45-57.

227 **Hartshorne, Richard.** "Recent Developments in Political Geography." *American Political Science Review*, 29, No. 5 (October, 1935), 785-804.

228 **Heffernan, Michael.** "On Geography and Progress: Turgot's *Plan D'un Ouvrage Sur la Geographie Politique* (1751) and the Origins of Modern Progressive Thought." *Political Geography*, 13, No. 4 (July, 1994), 328-343.

229 **Heske, H.** "Political Geographers of the Past III: German Geographical Research in the Nazi Period: A Content Analysis of the Major Geography Journal, 1925-1945." *Political Geography Quarterly*, 5, No. 3 (July, 1986), 267-281.

230 **Hassert, Kurt.** "Die anthropogeographische und politisel-geographische Bedenntung der Flusse." *Zeitschrift fur Gervasserk*, 2 (1899), 189-219.

231 **Holdich, Thomas H.** "Some Aspects of Political Geography." *Geographical Journal*, 34, No. 6 (December, 1909), 584-607.

232 **Hollist, W. Ladd,** and **Rosenau, James N.** "World Systems Debates." *International Studies Quarterly*, 25, No. 1 (March, 1981), 1-176.

233 **Honey, Rex D.** "Political Geography: A Behavioral Framework." *Geographical Perspectives*, 37, No. 1 (Spring, 1976), 3-11.

234 **Ibragimov, A. I.** "Regional Politico-Geographical Aspects of Developing Countries." *Moskovskii Universitet. Vestnik. Serita 5. Geografiia* [Moskva], No. 4 (Iiun-Avgust, 1992), 73-77.

235 **Iwata, Kozo.** "The Recent Trend of Political Geography." *The Human Geography*, The Jimban Chiri, 8, No. 3 (1956), 165-175.

236 **Jackson, W.A. Douglas.** "Whither Political Geography?" *Annals of the Association of American Geographers*, 48, No. 2 (June, 1958) 178-183.

237 **Jenkins, A.M.** "Independencia: A Simulation in Political Geography." *Teaching Geography*, 3, No. 2 (April, 1977), 27-29.

238 **Jenkins, A.M.,** and **McEvoy, D.** "Teaching Political Geography." *Area*, 9, No. 1 (March, 1977), 60-61.

239 **Johnston, R.J.** "The Challenge of a Rapidly Changing World Political Map." *Fennia*, 172, No. 2 (1994), 87-96.

240 **Johnston, R.J.** "Political Geography: Improving the Theoretical Base; Review Essay I." *Political Geography Quarterly*, 4, No. 3 (July, 1985), 251-255.

241 **Johnston, R.J.** "Political Geography with Dogma." *Progress in Human Geography*, 5, No. 4 (December, 1984), 595-598.

242 **Johnston, R.J.** "Political Geography Without Politics." *Progress in Human Geography*, 4, No. 3 (September, 1980), 439-446.

243 **Johnston, R.J.** "'Real' Political Geography: Some Comments Engendered by a Review of Andrew Sayer's Method in Social Science." *Political Geography*, 12, No. 5 (September, 1993), 473-480.

244 **Jones, Stephen B.** "Field Geography and Postwar Political Problems." *Geographical Review*, 33 (July, 1943), 446-456.

245 **Jones, Stephen B** "A Unified Field Theory of Political Geography." *Annals of the Association of American Geographers*, 44, No. 1 (March, 1954), 111-123.

246 **Jones, Stephen B** "Views of the Political World." *The Geographical Review*, 45, No. 3 (July, 1955), 309-326.

247 **Kick, Edward L.** "World System Properties and Mass Political Conflict Within Nations: A Theoretical Framework." *Journal of Political & Military Sociology*, 8, No. 2 (Fall, 1980), 175-190.

248 **Kirby, Andrew.** "Pseudo-random Thoughts on Space, Scale and Ideology in Political Geography." *Political Geography Quarterly*, 4, No. 1 (January, 1985) 5-18.

249 **Kliot, Nurit.** "Recent Themes in Political Geography--A Review." *Tijdschrift voor Economische en Sociale Geografie* (Amsterdam), 73, No. 5 (September-October, 1982), 270-279.

250 **Korchak, J.** "Ustredni problem politicke geografic." (Central concept of political geography), *Sbornik CSZ Spol. zeniepisne*, 73 (1968), 266-277.

251 **Kriesel, Karl Marcus.** "Montesquieu: Possibilistic Political Geographer." *Annals of the Association of American Geographers*, 58, No. 3 (September, 1968), 557-574.

252 **Latella, Francesco.** "Regioni Arretrate e Politiche Communitarie." *Finisterra* [Lisboa], 24, No. 48 (1989), 219-249.

253 **Lauria, Mickey.** "Political Geography: Improving the Theoretical Base: Review Essay II." *Political Geography Quarterly*, 4, No. 3 (July, 1985), 255-257.

254 **Lavin, Jose Domingo.** "Commentario a la Conferencia, influencia de los avances de la tecnica en los conceptos de la geografia politica." *Boletin de la Sociedad Mexicana de geografia y Estadisca*, 94 (December, 1963) 27-49.

255 **Lavin, Jose Domingo.** "Influncia de los advances de la tecnica en los conceptos de la geografia Politica." *Boletin de la Sociedad Mexicana de Geografia y Estadistica*, (September, 1963), 137-189.

256 **Loen, Ernst Van.** "Geopolitik oder Imperialismus." *Zeitschrift fur Geopolitik*, Jahrg 27, Heft 2 (February, 1956), 19-24.

257 **Lyman, Brad.** "Urban Primacy and World-System Position." *Urban Affairs Quarterly* [Newbury Park], 28, No. 1 (September, 1992), 22-37.

258 **MacDonald, Gerald U., and O'Hara, John T.** "Political Geographers of the Past VII: Samuel van Valkenburg: Politics and Regional Geography." *Political Geography Quarterly*, 7, No. 3 (July, 1988), 288-291.

259 **Mackinder, Halford J.** "The Physical Basis of Political Geography." *Scottish Geographical Magazine*, 6, No. 2 (February, 1980), 78-84.

260 **MacLaughlin, James.** "State-centered Political Science and the Anarchist Critique: Ideology in Political Geography. *Antipode*, 18, No. 1 (April, 1986), 11-38.

261 **Magistris, L.F. de.** "Geografia politica e coloniale." *Rivista Geografica Italiana*, 38 (1931), 135-152.

262 **Maull, Otto.** "Entwicklung, Sinn und Aufgaben der Politischen Geographie." *Zeitschrift fur Wintschaftsgeographie*, 1, No. 2 (February, 1957) 37-42.

263 **Mashbits, Ya. G.** "The Nature of Political Geography and Ways of Increasing its Geographical Content." *Soviet Geography*, 30, No. 8 (October, 1989), 650-656.

264 **McColl, Robert W.** "Political Geography as Political Ecology." *Professional Geographer*. 28, No. 3 (May, 1966), 143-145.

265 **Means, Margaret.** "International Problems: A Study in Political Geography." *Journal of Geography*, 34, No. 5 (May, 1935), 187-192.

266 **Minghi, Julian V.** "Teaching Political Geography." *Journal of Geography*, 65, No. 8 (November, 1966), 362-370.

267 **Minghi, Julian V.; Rumley J.; and Grimm, F.** "The Content of Ratzell's Politische Geographie." *Professional Geographer*, 25, No. 3 (August, 1973), 271-277.

268 **Mojumdar, K.K.** "A Case for Specific Studies in Political Geography." *The Geographical Observer* (Meerut), 5, No. 1 (March, 1969), 50-61.

269 **Mookerjee, Sitanshu.** "A Review of Politial Geography." *Geographical Review of India*, 18, No. 1 (March, 1956), 34-36.

270 **Mookerjee, Sitanshu.** "A Trend in Political Geography." *Deccan Geographer*, 10, No. 2 (July-December, 1972), 80-89.

271 **Morrill, Robert W.** "Political Geography, Sketch Maps, and Introductions in Dyads." *Journal of Geography in Higher Education*, 4, No. 2 (Autumn, 1980), 27-29.

272 **Neville, J., and Douglas, Henry H.** "Political Geography: From Comprehensive Empiricism to Tentative Theory." *Progress in Human Geography*, 8, No. 3 (September, 1984), 418-423.

273 **Nomura, Shoshichi.** "Methodology by Hartshorne's Political Geography." *The New Geography,* 5, No. 4 (March, 1957), 31-61.

274 **O'Loughlin, John.** "Political Geography: Bringing the Context Back." *Progress in Human Geography,* 12, No. 1 (January, 1988), 121-137.

275 **O'Loughlin, John.** "Political Geography: Marching to the Beats of Different Drummers." *Progress in Human Geography,* 11, No. 2 (June, 1987), 247-263.

276 **O'Loughlin, John.** "Political Geography: Tilling the Fallow Field." *Progress in Human Geography,* 10, No. 1 (March, 1986), 69-84.

277 **O'Loughlin, John.** "Political Geography: Attempting to Understand a Changing World Order." *Progress in Human Geography* [London], 14, No. 3 (1990), 420-437.

278 **O'Loughlin, John.** "Political Geography: Returning to Basic Conceptions." *Progress in Human Geography* [London], 15, No. 3 (September, 1991), 322-339.

279 **Ossenbrugge, Jurgen.** "Recent Developments in Political Geography in West Germany: A Historical Reflection of the Past, A Political Analysis of the Present, and Possibilities for the Future." *Political Geography Quarterly,* 2, No. 1 ((January, 1983) 71-80.

280 **O'Tuathail, Gearoid.** "Political Geographers of the Past VIII: Putting Mackinder in His Place: Material Transformation and Myth." *Political Geography,* 11, No. 1 (January, 1992), 100-118.

281 **Passarge, Siegfried.** "Aufgaben und Methoden der politischen Geographie." *Zeitschrift fur Politik,* 21 (August, 1932), 443-460.

282 **Patrick, Richard A.** "Problems of Definition and Origination in Political Geography." In *Political Geography and the Cyprus Conflict, 1963-1971.* Waterloo, Ontario, Canada: Department of Geography. Faculty of Environmental Studies, University of Waterloo, 1976, 372-379.

283 **Peet, Richard.** "Political Geographers of the Past VI: 2 Wittfogel on the Nature-Society Dialectic." *Political Geography Quarterly,* 7, No. 1 (January, 1988), 81-85.

284 **Perry, Peter J.** "Political Geographers of the Past VI: 1. Thirty Years on: Or Whatever Happened to Wittfogel." *Political Geography Quarterly,* 7, No. 1 (January, 1988), 75-81.

285 **Perry, Peter J.** "Real World and Real time Political Geography." *New Zealand Geographers* (Christchurch), 43, No. 1 (April, 1987), 33-34.

286 **Prescott, J.R.V.** "Political Geography." *Australian Geographical Studies,* 26, No. 1 (April, 1988), 149-156.

287 **Prescott, J.R.V., and Hajdu, Joseph.** "A Review of Some German Post-war Contributions to Political Geography." *Australian Geographical Studies,* 2, No. 1 (April, 1964), 35-46.

288 **Pue, W. Wesley.** "Wrestling With Law: (Geographical) Specificity vs. (Legal) Abstraction." *Urban Geography* [Silver Spring], 11, No. 6 (November-December, 1990), 566-585.

289 **Renner, George T.** "Maps for a New World." Excerpt: *Collier's,* 109, No. 23 (June 6, 1942), 14-16, and 28.

290 **Reynolds, David R.** "Political Geography: Closer Encounters with the State, Contemporary Political Economy, and Social Theory." *Progress in Human Geography* [Sevenoaks], 17, No. 3 (September, 1993), 389-403.

291 **Reynolds, David R.** "Political Geography: Thinking Globally and Locally." *Progress in Human Geography* [London], 16, No. 3 (September, 1992), 393-405.

292 **Reynolds, David R.** "Spatial Contagion in Political Influence Processes." In *Locational Approaches to Power and Conflict.* New York: Sage Publications, 1974, 233-274.

293 **Reynolds, Philip A.** "The World of States or the State of the World." *Review of International Studies* [Cambridge], 18, No. 3 (July, 1992), 261-269.

294 **Riggs, Fred W.** "The Theory of Political Development." In *Contemporary Political Analysis,* James C. Charlesworth, ed. New York: The Free Press, 1967, 317-349.

295 **Robinson, K.W.** "Diversity, Conflict and Change--The Meeting Place of Geography and Politics." *Australian Geographical Studies,* 8, No. 1 (April, 1970), 1-15.

296 **Rubio Y Munoz-Bocanegra, Angel.** "Visiones geografico-politicas mundiales." *Revista Geografica,* 20, No. 46 (1 Semestre, 1957), 112-125.

297 **Rumley, Dennis.** "Conflict and Compromise: Political Geography at the IGU Congress in Sydney, Australia, August 1988." *Political Geography Quarterly,* 8, No. 2 (April, 1989), 197-200.

298 **Rumley, Dennis.** *"On the Relevance of Context as a Dimension in Political Geography."* In W.P. Adams and F. M. Helleiner, eds., International Geography 1972. Toronto: University of Toronto Press, 1 (1972), 509-511.

299 Russett, Bruce M. "Delineating International Regions." In *Quantitative International Politics*, J. David Singer, ed., New York: The Free Press, 1967, 317-374.

300 Russett, Bruce M. "Is There a Long-run Trend Toward Concentration in the International System?" *Comparative Political Studies*, 1, No. 1 (April, 1968), 103-122.

301 Sanguin, Andre-Louis. "L'evolution et le renouveau de la geographie politique." *Annales de Geographie*, 84 annee No. 463 (Maii-Juin, 1975), 275-296.

302 Shaudys, Vincent K. "Geographic Consequences of Establishing Sovereign Political Units." *Professional Geographer*, 14, No. 2 (March, 1962), 16-20.

303 Schat, P. "Political Geography: A Review." *Tidjschrift voor Economische en Sociale Geographie*, 60, No. 4 (July-August, 1969), 255-260.

304 Scholler, Peter. "Das Ende der Politischen Geographie Ohne sozial-geographie Bindung." *Erdkunde*, Band 12, Heft 12 (Dezembre, 1958), 313-316.

305 Schwalm, Eberhardt. "Im Blickpunkt: Politische Geographie." *Geolit*, 5 (1981), 107-110.

306 Schwind, M. "Die Aufgaben einer politischen Geographie in neuer Sicht." *Geographische Rundschau*, Jahrg 22, Heft 3 (Marz, 1970), 97-103.

307 Sevrin, Robert. "Political Geography Around the World IV. Research Themes in Political Geography: A French Perspective." *Political Geography Quarterly*, 4, No. 1 (January, 1985), 67-68.

308 Short, John R. "Political Geography." *Progress in Human Geography* (London), 7, No. 1 (March, 1983), 122-125; 8, No. 1 (January, 1984), 127-156; and 9, No. 1 (January, 1985), 115-118.

309 Smith, Neil. "Bowman's New World and the Council on Foreign Relations." *The Geographical Review*, 76, No. 4 (October, 1986), 438-460.

310 Solch, Johann. "Zur politische-geographischen Terminologie." *Zeitschrift fur Erdkunde*, (1917), 497-529 et (1918), 48-69.

311 Sprout, Harold H. "Political Geography as a Political Science Field." *American Political Science Review*, 25, No. 2 (April, 1931), 442.

312 Sprout, Harold H., and Sprout, Margaret T. "Geography and International Politics in an Era of Revolutionary Change." *Journal of Conflict Resolution*, 4, No. 1 (March, 1960), 145-161.

313 Stanislawski, Dan. "Tarascan Political Geography." *American Anthropologist*, 49, No. 1 (January-March, 1947), 46-55.

314 Stanley, Eugene. "The Myth of Continents." *Foreign Affairs*, 19, No. 3 (April, 1941), 481-494.

315 Stevenson, I. "Don't Shoot the Coachman: A Rejoinder to Andrew Kirby." *Political Geography*, 12, No. 2 (March, 1993), 99-102.

316 Sugimura, Oaki. "Spatial Concepts of 'Continent' and 'World'." *Political Geography*, 1 (1960), 59-99.

317 Sukhwal, B.L. "Changing Dimensions in Political Geography." *Bhoodarshan*, 13, No. 1 (January-March, 1980), 1-9.

318 Sukhwal, B.L. "Modern Political Geography: An Appraisal." *The Geography Teacher*, 6, No. 3 (April-May, 1971), 106-116.

319 Swyngedouw, Erik A. "Political Space and Social Thought." *Revue Belge de Geographie*, 112e annee. Fasc. 1-2 (1988), 49-60.

320 Takagi, Akihiko. "The World-Systems Analysis and New Trends in Political Geography." *Geographical Review of Japan* [Tokyo], 64, Series A, No. 12 (December, 1991), 839-858.

321 Taylor, E.G.R. "Whither Geography? A Review of Some Recent Geographical Texts." *Geographical Review*, 27, No. 1 (January, 1937), 129-135.

322 Taylor, Peter J. "Editorial Essay: Political Geography Research Agendas for the Nineteen Eighties." *Political Geography Quarterly*, 1, No. 1 (January, 1982), 1-17.

323 Taylor, Peter J. "Political Geography Within World-Systems Analysis." *Farnand Braudel Center Review*, 14, No. 3 (Summer, 1991), 387-402.

324 Taylor, Peter J. "World System Analysis and Regional Geography." *Professional Geographer*, 40, No. 3 (August, 1988), 259-265.

325 Taylor, Peter J. "A Materialist Framework for Political Geography." *Transactions of the Institute of British Geographers* (new series), 7, No. 1 (January, 1982), 15-34.

326 Taylor, Peter J. "The Question of Theory in Political Geography." In *Pluralism and Political Geography*. N. Kliot and S. Waterman, eds. Beckenham, United Kingdom: Croom Helm, 1983, 9-18.

327 Taylor, Peter J. "Review of 'The Modern World System II'." *Progress in Human Geography*, 7, No. 2 (June, 1983) 300-303.

328 **Thrift, N.J.** Editorial. (Special Issue on Industrial Geography and Political Geography.) *Environment and Planning,* A 14, No. 4 (December, 1982), 1565-1569.

329 **Thrift, N.J., and Forbes, D.K.** "A Landscape with Figures: Political Geography with Human Conflict." *Political Geography Quarterly,* 2, No. 3 (July, 1983), 247-263.

330 **Toschi, Umberto.** "L'ogetto centrale di studio della geografia politica." *Rivista Geografica Italiana,* 56 (1949), 81-89.

331 **Van Valkenburg, S.** "A Political Geographer Looks at the World." *Professional Geographer,* 12, No. 4 (July, 1960), 6-8.

332 **Van Vorys, Karl,** ed. "New Nations: The Problem of Political Development." *The Annals of the American Academy of Political and Social Science,* 358, No. 1 (March, 1965), 1-179.

333 **Vickers, G.** "The Regulation of Political Systems." *Yearbook of the Society for General Systems Research,* 12 (1967), 60.

334 **Whittlesey, Derwent.** "Political Geography: A Complex Aspect of Geography." *Education,* 55, No. 5 (January, 1935), 293-298.

335 **Wright, John K.** "Training for Research in Political Geography." *Annals of the Association of American Geographers,* 34, No. 4 (December, 1944), 190-201.

336 **Yag'ya, V.S.** "The Main Periods in Forming of World Political Map." *Izvestiyavsesoyuzhogo Grograficheskogo Obschehstva,* 119, No. 4 (1987), 306-313.

337 **Yang, J.** "Geography and Politics." *Transactions of the Institute of British Geographers,* 12, No. 4 (1987), 391-397.

338 **Yokoyama, Shoichi.** "The Focus on Political Geography." *Chiiki,* Tokoyo: Taimeido, 1 (1979), 153-160.

339 **Yokoyama, Shoichi.** "Review on the Development of the American Political Geography." *Human Geography,* 29, No. 4 (August, 1977) 32-61.

340 **Zaidi, Iqtidar H.** "The World Pattern of Political-areal Functional Cohesiveness." *International Geography,* (1972), 515-516.

341 **Zelinsky, Wilbur.** "Beyond the Expotentials: The Role of Geography in the Great Transition." *Economic Geography,* 46, No. 3 (July, 1970), 498-535.

POLITICAL GEOGRAPHY OF REGIONS

AFRICA

Books and Journals

342 **Berg-Schlosser, Dirk.** "African Political Systems: Typology and Performance." *Comparative Political Studies,* No. 1 (April, 1984), 121-151.

343 **Boateng, E.A.** *A Political Geography of Africa.* Cambridge, England: Cambridge University Press, 1978.

344 **de Blij, Harm J.** "Africa's Geomosaic Under Stress." *Journal of Geography,* 90, No. 1 (January-February, 1991), 2-10.

345 **Delgado de, Carvalho Carlos, et De Castro, Therezinha.** *Africa: geographia social, economica e politica.* Rio de Janeiro: IBGE, 1963.

346 **Drysdale, Alasdair Duncan, and Blake, Gerald H.** *The Middle East and North Africa: A Political Geography.* New York and Oxford: Oxford University Press, 1985.

347 **Fordham, Paul.** *The Geography of African Affairs.* Pelican: Harmondsworth, 1968.

348 **Hamdan, G.** "The Political Map of the New Africas." *The Geographical Review,* 53, No. 3 (July, 1963), 418-439.

349 **Harbeson, John W., and Rothchild, Donald,** eds. *Africa in World Politics.* Boulder, CO: Westview Press, 1991.

350 **Khadduri, Majid.** *Modern Libya: A Study in Political Development.* Baltimore, Maryland: Johns Hopkins University Press, 1963.

351 **Kingsbury, Robert C.** "The Changing Map of Africa." *The Journal of Geography,* 59, No. 5 (May, 1960), 220-224.

352 **Le Roux, Gabriel A.** *A Political Geography of Southern Africa.* Worcester, Massachusetts: Clark University, Ph.D., 1947.

353 **McKay, Vernon.** *Africa in World Politics.* New York: Harper & Row, 1962.

354 **Noon, John A.** "Political Developments in East Africa." In *Africa in the Modern World,* Lord Hailey and Others. Chicago: University of Chicago Press, 1955, 182-203.

355 "Political Africa." *The Geographical Magazine,* 37, No. 3 (July, 1964), 169-174.

356 "Political Divisions of Africa." *The Department of State Bulletin*, 43, No. 1104 (August 22, 1960), 283-286.

357 **Pollock, Norman Charles.** "The Political Geography of Nigeria." *Bulletin of Oxford* (1968), 195-199.

358 **Prescott, J.R.V.** "La geographie politique du Cameroun septentrionnal sous mandat britannique." *Annales de Geographie*, 70, No. 377 (Janvier-Fevrier), 1961, 86-90.

359 **Sommers, John Willis Jr.** *The Sudan: A Study in Political Geography*. Boston, Massachusetts: University of Boston, Ph.D., 1968.

AMERICAS

Books and Journals

360 **Aguiar, Jose.** "Antecedentes para la determinacion geografico-politica de la republica Oriental del Uruaguay." *Revista Nacional*, (Julio, 1939), 200-201.

361 **Belov, A.L.** "Political Geography of Canada: Main Contemporary Problems." *Voesoyuznoe Geograficheskoe Obshchestvo, Izvestiia*, Tom 115, Vyp. 4 (1983), 363-368.

362 **Benhart, John E., and Ford, John J.** "The Political Process and Geography in South Central Pennsylvania." *The Pennsylvania Geographer*, 17, No. 1 (March, 1979), 1-6.

363 **Blanksten, George I.** "Bibliography of Latin American Politics and Government." *Inter-American Review of Bibliography*, 4, No. 3 (July-September, 1954), 191-214.

364 **Blaut, J. M.** "Political Geography Debates No. 3: On the Significance of 1492:1. Fourteen Ninety-Two." *Political Geography* [Oxford], 11, No. 4 (July, 1992), 355-389.

365 **Brunn, Stanley D.** *Geography and Politics in America*. New York: Harper and Row, 1974.

366 **Brunn, Stanley D.** "Geography and Politics of the United States in the Year 2000." *Journal of Geography*, 72, No. 4 (April, 1973), 42-49.

367 **Brunn, Stanley D.; Ford, John J.; and McIntosh, Terry L.** "The State of Political Geography Research in Latin America." In *Geographic Research on Latin America: Benchmark 1970, Proceedings of the Conference of Latin Americanist Geographers*, Vol. 1 by Barry Lentnek, Robert L. Carmin, and Tom L. Martinson, eds. Muncie, Indiana: Ball State University, 1971, 265-287.

368 **Campo, Wilson J.** del. *Geografia politica de America*. Buenos Aires: Ed. Virtus, 1920.

369 **Condon, Kevin Paul.** *A Subjective Tradition in American Geography: From Geosophy to Geometaphysics*. Lawrence: University of Kansas, Ph.D., 1981.

370 **Crist, Raymond E.** "Politics and Geography: Some Aspects of Centrifugal and Centripetal Forces in Operating in Andean America. *The American Journal of Economics and Sociology*, 25, No. 4 (October, 1966), 349-358.

371 **Danbaugh, Veva Kathern.** *Newfoundland: A Study in Political Geography*. Worcester, Massachusetts: Clark University, Ph.D., 1949.

372 **De Dubnic, Vladimir Reisky.** *Political Trends in Brazil*. Washington, D.C.: Public Affairs Press, 1968.

373 **Dobles Segreda, Luis.** *Indice bibliografico de Costa Rica*, Tomo 7: Politica y derecho desde 1831 hasta 1921. San Jose, Costa Rica: Lehmann & Cia, 1935.

374 **Farmer, Paul.** *The Uses of Haiti*. Monroe, ME: Common Courage Press, 1994.

375 **Flynn, P.** *Brazil: A Political Analysis*. Boulder, Colorado: Westview Press, 1978.

376 **Glusa, Rudolf.** *Zur politischen geographie westindiens*. Munster: Max Kramer, 1962.

377 **Haring, L. Lloyd.** "A Suggested Study Model for an Internal Political Geography of the United States." *California Geographer*, 5 (1964), 17-21.

378 **Haushofer, Albrecht.** "Zur Politischen Geographie der Grenzen in Nordamerika." *Zeitschrift fur Geopolitik*, 5, No. 7-12 (Juli-Dec., 1928) 769-779.

379 **Huck, Susan.** *British Honduras: A Problem in Political Geography*. Worcester, Massachusetts: Clark University, Ph.D., 1962.

380 **Hudson, Tim W..** "Six Approaches to Political Geography: The Case of Belize." *Geographical Perspectives*, 50, No. 3 (Fall, 1982), 19-29.

381 **James, Preston E.** "Forces for Union and Disunion in Brazil: On Essay in Political Geography." *Journal of Geography*, 38, No. 7 ((October, 1939), 260-266.

382 **Jones, Stephen B., and Mehnert, Klaus.** "Hawaii and the Pacific: A Survey of Political Geography." *Geographical Review*, 30, No. 3 (July, 1940), 358-75.

383 **Kuhn, Arthur.** "Zum Begriff der 'Westlichen Hemisphare'. Ein Beitrag zur Politischen Geographie." *Zeitschrift der Gesellschaft fur Erdkunde zu Berlin,* 5/6 (August, 1941), 222-238.

384 **Magalhaes, J. Cezar de.** "Algumas Nocoes Sobre Geografia Politica." *Revista Brasileira de Geografia,* 20, No. 2 (April-June, 1958), 230-238.

385 **Manrique, Gustavo.** "Influenca de la Geografia en la Historia Polityca y Administrativa de America." *Boletin de la Real Sociedad Geografica (Madrid),* 68 (1928), 342-350.

386 **Meisel, J.** *Working Papers on Canadian Politics.* Montreal, Province of Quebec, Canada: McGill-Queen's University Press, 1972.

387 **Natunewicz, Henry.** "Political Geography of the Colony and State of Connecticut." New York: Colombia Teachers College, Ph.D., 1954.

388 **Nicholson, Norman L.** "Some Aspects of Political Geography of the District of Keewatin." *Canadian Geographer,* 1, No. 3 (Fall, 1953), 73-83.

389 **O'Loughlin, John, and Grant, Richard.** "The Political Geography of Presidential Speeches, 1946-87. *Association of American Geographers. Annals* [Washington, D.C.], 80, No. 4 (December, 1990), 504-530.

390 **Ossenbrugge, Jurgen.** "Zwischen Lokalpolitik Regionalismus und internationalen Konflikten: Neuentwicklungen in der Anglo-Amerikanischer Politischen Geographie." *Geographische zeitschrift,* (Title in English: "New Directions in Anglo American Political Geography.") Weisbaden, Jahr. 72, Hef. 1, (Quartall, 1984), 22-23.

391 **Pineda, Salvador.** "America, Geografia, Politica." *Cuadernos,* 19 (Julio-Agosto, 1956), 91-94.

392 **Revert, Eugene.** "Geographie Politique der Monde Caraibe. *Annales de Geographie,* 60, No. 318 (Janvier-Fevrier, 1951), 34-47.

393 **Rodrigues, Mendoza Emilio.** "Algo Sobre Geografia Politica Sudamericanna, Chili y la Argentina." *Atena,* 115, No. 346-347 (1954), 122-142.

394 **Roys, R.L.** *The Political Geography of the Yucatan Maya.* Washington, D.C.: Carnegie Institution of Washington, 1957.

395 **Sapper, Karl.** "Mittelamerika and Westindien Ein Beitrag Zur Politischen Geographie Kleiner und Kleinster Raume." *Zeitschrift fur Geopolitik.* 4, No. 1-6 (Januar-Juni, 1927), 334-344, et 4, No. 7-12 (September-December, 1927), 448-461.

396 **Scheman, L. Ronald.** "Rhetoric and Reality: The Inter-American System's Second Century." *Journal of Interamerican Studies and World Affairs,* 29, No. 3 (Fall, 1987), 1-31.

397 **Sternberg, H. O'Reilly.** "The Status of Geography in Brazil." *Professional Geographer,* 3, No. 3 (July, 1951), 23-29.

398 **Sutton, Imre.** "The Political Geography of Indian Country: An Introduction." *American Indian Culture and Research Journal* [Los Angeles], 15, No. 2 (1991), 3-35.

399 **Temer, Franz.** "Die Eithischen Grundlagen der Politischen Geographie von Mittelamerika." *Zeitschrift der Gesellschaft fur Erdkunde.* No. 3-4 (August, 1943), 148-171.

400 **Thomas, Benjamin E.** *Political Geography of Idaho.* Cambridge, Massachusetts: Harvard University, Ph.D., 1947.

401 **Ullman, Edward L.** "Political Geography in the Pacific North-West." *The Scottish Geographical Magazine,* 54, No. 4 (July, 1938), 236-239.

ASIA

Books and Journals

402 **Ajami, Fouad.** *The Arab Predicament: Arab Political Thought and Practice Since 1967.* Updated edition. Cambridge: Cambridge University Press, 1992.

403 **Al-Barbar, Aghil.** *Political Development in the Arab World: A Bibliography.* Monticello, Illinois: Vance Bibliographies. Public Administration Series, 1980.

404 **Atwell, Donald L.** *East Pakistan: A Study in Political Geography.* Worcester, Massachusetts: Clark University, Ph.D., 1958.

405 **Baldoria, Pedro L.** "Political Geography of the Philippines." *Philippine Geographical Journal,* 1, No. 1 (January, 1953), 15-23.

406 **Brecher, Michael.** *The New States of Asia: A Political Analysis.* New York: Oxford University Press, 1966.

407 **Callard, Keith B.** *Pakistan: A Political Study.* New York: Macmillan, 1958.

408 **Cressey, George.** *Asia's Lands and Peoples.* New York: McGraw-Hill, 1951.

409 **Daoud, Mahmoud A.** "Political Geography of Aden and Protectorate." *Iraqi Geographical Journal,* 1 (1962), 1-14.

410 Ditcher, A. *Pakhtunistan: A Study in Political Geography*. Worcester, Massachusetts: Clark University, M.A., 1960.

411 Dening, B.H. "Greater Syria, A Study in Political Geography." *Geography*, 35, No. 168, Part 2 (June, 1950), 110-123.

412 Fisher, Charles A. "The Changing Political Geography of British Malaysia." *Professional Geographer*. 7, No. 2 (March, 1955), 6-9.

413 Fisher, Charles A. *Southeast Asia--A Social, Economic and Political Geography*, 2nd ed. London: Methuen, 1966.

414 Ginsburg, Norton S. "China's Changing Political Geography." *The Geographical Review*, 42, No. 1 (January, 1952), 102-117.

415 Gopalkrishnan, Ramamorthy. *Geography and Politics of Afghanistan*. New Delhi: Concept, 1982.

416 Graz, Liesl. *The Turbulent Gulf: People, Politics and Power*. London: I.B. Tauris & Co., Ltd, 1992.

417 Janaki, V.A. *Some Aspects of the Political Geography of India*. Baroda: The Maharaja Sayajirao University of Baroda, Geography Series No. 8, 1977.

418 Jurika, Stephen Jr. *The Political Geography of the Philippines*. Stanford, California: Stanford University, Ph.D., 1962.

419 Karan, Pradyumna Prasad, and Jenkins. W.M. *The Himalayan Kingdoms: Bhutan, Sikkim, and Nepal*. Princeton, New Jersey: Van Nostrand, 1963.

420 Kliot, N., and Waterman, S. "The Political Impact on Writing the Geography of Palestine/Israel." *Progress in Human Geography* [London], 14, No. 2 (June 1990), 237-260.

421 Lattimore, Owen. "The New Political Geography of Inner Asia." *The Geographical Journal*, 119, No. 1 (March, 1953), 17-32.

422 Leach, E.R. *Political Systems of Highland Burma*. Boston: Beacon Press, 1968.

423 Lee, Yong Leng. *Southeast Asia: Essays in Political Geography*. Singapore: Singapore University Press, 1982.

424 Maley, William. "Political Legitimacy in Contemporary Afghansitan." *Asian Survey*, 27, No. 6 (June, 1987), 705-725.

425 Maniruzzaman, Talukdar. *Political Development in Pakistan, 1955-1958*. Kingston, Ontario, Canada: Queen's University at Kingston, 1966.

426 McColl, Robert W. "A Political Geography of Revolution: China, Vietnam and Thailand." *Journal of Conflict Resolution*. 11, No. 2 (June, 1967), 153-167.

427 McCune, George M. "Recent Political Developments in Korea." *India Quarterly*, 4, No. 2 (April-June, 1948), 138-152.

428 McDonald, A. H. "Political Development in Southeast Asia." *The Australian Outlook*, 1, No. 4 (December, 1947), 6-13.

429 McGee, T.G. "Aspects of the Political Geography of Southeast Asia." *Pacific Viewpoint*, 1, No. 1 (March, 1960), 39-58.

430 Melamid, Alexander. "Political Geography of Trucial 'Oman and Qatar." *The Geographical Review*, 43, No. 2 (April, 1953), 194-206.

431 *The Middle East--A Political and Economic Survey*. London: Royal Institute of International Affairs, 1950.

432 Newell, Richard S. *The Politics of Afghanistan*. Ithaca, New York: Cornell University Press, 1972.

433 Palmerlee, Albert E. *Viet Cong Political Geography*. Saigon: United States Mission in Vietnam, 1968.

434 Park, Richard L. *India's Political System*. Englewood Cliffs, New Jersey: Prentice-Hall, 1967.

435 Park, Richard L., and de Mesquita, B.B. *India's Political System*. Englewood Cliffs, New Jersey: Prentice-Hall, 1979.

436 Rose, Saul, ed. *Politics in Southeast Asia*. London: Oxford University Press, 1963.

437 Shabad, Theodore. *China's Changing Map: A Political and Economic Geographic of the Chinese People's Republic*. New York: Praeger, 1956.

438 Shreevasatava, M.P. "Political Problems of India; A Functional Approach." *The Indian Geographical Journal*, 37, No. 2 (April-June, 1962), 35-44.

439 Singh, Govind Saran. *Political Geography of India*. Allahabad: Central Book Depot, 1968.

440 Sukhwal, B.L. *India: A Political Geography*. New Delhi: Allied Publishers, 1971.

441 Sukhwal, B.L. *Modern Political Geography of India*. New Delhi: Sterling Publishers, 1985.

442 **Sukhwal, B.L.** *Political Geography of the Indian Republic: An Evaluation of Changing Patterns Since Independence.* Norman: University of Oklahoma, Ph.D., 1969.

443 **Sukhwal, B.L.** *A Systematic Geographic Bibliography on Bangladesh.* Illinois: Council of Planning Libraries, Exchange Bibliographies, No. 455, 1973.

444 **Sukhwal, B.L.** *Theses and Dissertations in Geography on South Asia.* Monticello, Illinois: Council of Planning Libraries, Exchange Bibliographies, No. 438, 1973.

445 **Sukhwal, B.L.** *South Asia: A Systematic Geographic Bibliography.* Metuchen, New Jersey: Scarecrow Press, 1974.

446 **Tayyab, Ali.** *Pakistan: A Political Geography.* 2nd ed. London: Oxford University Press, 1972.

447 **Tinker, Hugh.** *India and Pakistan: A Political Analysis.* New York: Praeger, 1962.

448 **Tschirgi, Dan, ed.** *The Arab World Today.* Boulder: Lynne Rienner Publishers, 1994.

449 **Van Valkenburg, Samuel.** "Current Political Geographical Problems of Jordania." *Professional Geographer.* 5, No. 6 (November, 1953), 18.

450 **Wilkinson, J.C.** "The Oman Question: A Background Study to the Political Geography of South-East Arabia." *Geographical Journal,* 137, Part 3 (September, 1971), 361-371.

AUSTRALIA, OCEANIA AND ANTARCTICA

Books and Journals

451 **Botts, Adelbert K.** "Some Problems in New Zealand's Political Geography." *The Scientific Monthly,* 53, No. 6 (December, 1941), 503-518.

452 **Cunningham, J.K.** "Maori Pakeha Conflict, 1858-1885: A Background to Political Geography." *New Zealand Geographer,* 12, No. 1 (April, 1956), 12-31.

453 **Knight, David B.** "Changing Orientations: Elements of New Zealand's Political Geography." *The Geographical Bulletin,* 1, No. 1 (August, 1970), 21-30.

454 **Riesco, Jaramillo R.** "Fundamentos de geografia politica y sus proyecciones futuras en las relaciones de podes en la oceano-pacifico. II. Parte. (the Fundamentals of Political Geography and Its Future Projections in the Power Relations of the Pacific Ocean Basin)." *Revista Chilena de Geopolitica,* 2 (1), (1985), 126-148.

455 **Robinson, K.W.** "The Political Influence in Australian Geography." *Pacific Viewpoint,* 3, No. 2 (September, 1962), 73-86.

456 **Sanguin, Andre-Louis.** "Transformation et signification de la Geographie Politique du Pacifique sud." *The Canadian Geographer,* 20, No. 2 (Summer, 1976), 233-239.

457 **Shaudys, Vincent K.** "The External Political Geography of Dutch New Guinea." *Oriental Geography,* 5, No. 2 (July, 1961), 145-160.

EUROPE

Books and Journals

458 **Ancel, J.** *Manuel Geographique de Politique Europeene,* 2nd ed. Paris: Armand Colin, 1937.

459 **Ante, Ulrich.** *Zur Grundlegung des Gegenstandbereiches der Politische Geographie: Uber das 'Politische' in der Geographie.* Stuttgart: Steiner-Verlag Wiesbaden, 1985.

460 **Blacksell, Mark.** *Post-war Europe: A Political Geography,* 2nd ed. London: Hutchinson, 1981.

461 **Boesler, Klaus-Achim.** "Die Behandlung der Auberen Sicherheit in der Politischen Geographie. Einfuhrende Bemerkungen." *Geographische Zeitschrift* [Sstuttgart], 81, Heft 4 (1993), 199-203.

462 **Buckholts, Paul.** *A Political Geography of the Federal Republic of Germany.* Cambridge, Massachusetts: Harvard University, Ph.D, 1957.

463 **Budge, Ian, and McKay, David, eds.** *The Developing British Political System: The 1990s.* London: Longman, 1993.

464 **Buleon, Pascal.** "The State of Political Geography in France in the 1970s and 1980s." *Progress in Human Geography* [London], 16, No. 1 (March, 1992), 24-40.

465 **Burghardt, Andrew F.** *The Politial Geography of Burgenland.* Madison: University of Wisconsin, Ph.D, 1958.

466 **Demangeon, Albert.** "Geographie politique a propos de l'Allemagne." *Annales de Geographie,* 48 Annee, No. 272 (15 Mars 1939), 113-119.

467 **Dowlah, A.F.** *Soviet Political Economy in transition: From Lenin to Gorbachev.* New York: Greenwood Press, 1992.

468 **Fawcett, C.B.** *A Political Geography of the British Empire.* London: Hazell, Watson and Viney, 1933.

469 Fitzgerald, Walter. *The New Europe: An Introduction to its Political Geography*, 2nd ed., revised. Published in England in 1945. New York: Harper & Brothers, 1946.

470 Gay, F.J. "A Legacy of Andre Siefried: Political Geography of Normandy." *Etudes Normandes*, 4 (1987), 5-8.

471 Goblet, Y.M. *La transformation de la geographie politique de l'Irlande au XVIIe siecle*. Nancy: Berger-Levraault, 1930.

472 Goodey, Brian R. "Recent Change in West Europe's Internal Political Geography." *North Dakota Quarterly*, 35, No. 4 (Autumn, 1967), 119-125.

473 Hartshorne, Richard. "The Tragedy of Austria-Hungary: A Post-Mortem in Political Geography." *Annals of the Association of American Geographers*, 28, No. 1 (March, 1938), 49-50; idem. "The Concepts of 'Raison de'Etre' and 'Maturity' of States," 40, No. 1 (March, 1940), 59-60.

474 Hauser, Henri. "La position geographique de la Suisse, etude de geographie politique." *Annales de Geographie*. 25 Annee, No. 138 (15 Novembre, 1916), 413-428.

475 Hoffman, George W. "East Europe: A Study in Political Geography." *Texas Quarterly*, 2, No. 3 (1959) 57-88.

476 Hoffman, George W. "The Netherlands Demands on Germany: A Post-War Problem in Political Geography." *Annals of the Association of American Geographers*, 42, 2 (June, 1952), 129-152.

477 Hoffman, George W. "The Political Geography of a Neutral Austria." *Geographical Studies*, 3, No. 1 (January, 1956), 12-32.

478 Hunt, Lynn. "The Political Geography of Revolutionary France." *Journal of Interdisciplinary History* (Cambridge, Massachusetts), 14, No. 3 (Winter, 1984), 535-559.

479 Iimoto, Nobuyuki. "Political and Economic Geography of Belgium." *Journal of Geography, Tokyo Geographical Society*, 52, No. 619 (September, 1940) 406-421.

480 Kish, George. *The Danube Basin: Patterns in Political Geography*. Ann Arbor: University of Michigan, Ph.D., 1945.

481 Kish, George. "Some Aspects of the Political Geography of the Hungarian Basin." *The Journal of Geography*, 41, No. 2 (February, 1942), 69-72.

482 Kish, George. "Some Aspects of the Regional Political Geography of Italy." *Annals of the Association of American Geographers*, 43, No. 2 (June, 1953), 178.

483 Kolosov, V.A. "Political Geography in the USSR." *Soviet Geography*, 30, 8 (October 1989), 635-649.

484 Konarek, J. "Main Elements of Slovakia's Political Geography: An Historical Survey." *Laurentian University Review*, 2, No. 3 (1970), complete issue.

485 Kostanick, Huey Louis. *Macedonia: A Study in Political Geography*. Worcester, Massachusetts: Clark University, Ph.D., 1948.

486 Leimbruber, W. "Politische Willensausserung und politische Geographie gedanken zu einem Buch von Jean Vanlaer." [The Expression of Political Will and Politicay Geography, Europe.] *Cahiers-Institit de Geographie de4 Fribarg*, 3 (1985), 19-26.

487 Le Lannon, Maurice. "La Venetie Julienne; etude geographie politique." *Annales de geographie*, 56° annee, No. 301 (Janvier-Mars, 1947), 13-35.

488 Lichtenberger, E. "The Impact of Political Systems Upon Geography: The Case of the Federal Republic of Germany and the German Democratic Republic." *Professional Geographer*, 31, No. 2 (May, 1979), 201-211.

489 Lucas, John. "The Soviet State at 65." *Foreign Affairs*, 65, No. 1 (Fall, 1986), 21-36.

490 Lunden, Thomas. "Political Geography Around World VI: Swedish Contribution to Political Geography. *Political Geography Quarterly*, 5, No. 2 (April, 1986), 181-186.

491 Meyer, H.C. "Mitteleuropa in German Political Geography." *Annals of the Association of American Geographers*, 36, No. 2 (June, 1946), 178-194.

492 O'Loughlin, John. *New Political Geography of Eastern Europe*. New York: John Wiley and Sons, Inc., 1993.

493 Olson, Ralph E. "The Grand Duchy of Luxembourg." *Annals of the Association of American Geographers*, 37, No. 1 (March, 1947), 56-57.

494 Olson, Ralph E. *Luxembourg: A Study in Political Geography*. Worcester, Massachusetts: Clark University, Ph.D., 1946.

495 Otok, Stanislaw. "Political Geography Around the World V: Poland." *Political Geography Quarterly*, 4, No. 4 (October, 1985), 321-327.

496 Parker, Geoffrey. *A Political Geography of Community Europe*. London: Butterworths, 1983.

497 Platt, Rutherford H. "Berlin: Island of Detente." *Journal of Geography*, New Series, 22, No. 1 (March, 1987), 1-24.

498 **Ramsaur, Robert T.** *Directed Studies in the Political Geography of Europe and the Near East.* New York: Columbia Teachers College, Ph.D., 1954.

499 **Ramm, Agatha.** "Great Britain and the Planting of Italian Power in the Red Sea, 1868-1885." Excerpt: *The English Historical Review,* 59, No. 234 (May, 1944), 211-236.

500 **Randall, Richard R.** "Political Geography of the Klagenfurt Basin." *The Geographical Review,* 47, No. 3 (July, 1957), 406-419.

501 **Robertson, Patrick, ed.** *Reshaping Europe in the Twenty-First Century.* Houndmills: Macmillan, 1992.

502 **Roeder, Philip G.** *Red Sunset: The Failure of Soviet Politics.* Princeton: Princeton University Press, 1993.

503 **Sanguin, Andre-Louis.** "La Geographie Politique et son Heritage Francais." *Revue Belge de Geographie,* 109° Anne, Fasc. 2 (1981), 33-57.

504 **Sanguin, Andre-Louis.** "Political Geography Around the World II: Whither the Geography of Power Among French Geographers." *Political Geography Quarterly* (Guilford), 2, No. 4 (October, 1983), 319-327.

505 **Schultze, J.H.** "Die Geographie als politische Wissenschaft. Der Dienst der Geographie am Deutschen Volk." *Zeitschrift fur Erdkunde,* 4, No. 1 (Januar, 1936), 104-112.

506 **Shabad, Theodore.** "Recent Changes in the Political Geography of the Soviet Union." *The American Review on the Soviet Union,* 7, No. 2 (February, 1946), 26-34.

507 **Shaudys, Vincent K.** "The External Aspects of the Political Geography of Five Diminutive European States." *Journal of Geography,* 41, No. 1 (January, 1962), 20-31.

508 **Smith, G.; Patterson, W.E.; Merkl, P.H.; and Padgett, S.** *Development in German Politics.* London: Macmillan, 1992.

509 **Solly, Marion B.** "Yugoslavia: A Case Study in Political Geography." New Zealand Geographical Society. *Proceedings of the First Geography Conference, Auckland, 1955,* (1956), A3/61-66.

510 **Strang, David.** "Anomaly and Commonplace in European Political Expansion: Realist and Institutional Accounts." *International Organization* [Cambridge], 45, No. 2 (Spring, 1991), 143-162.

511 **Tatham, George.** "Political Geography of Southeastern Europe." *Canadian Geographical Journal,* 23, No. 6 (December, 1941), 265-282.

512 **Troll, Carl.** "Geographic Science in Germany During the Period 1933-1945; A Critique and Justification." *Annals of the Association of American Geographers,* 39, No. 2 (June, 1949), 99-137. The complete German paper is published in *Erdkunde,* Band 1, Lfg. 1-3 (Ausgegeben-Mai, 1947), 3-48.

513 **Turnock, David.** *Eastern Europe: An Economic and Political Geography.* New York: Routledge, 1989.

514 **Wackermann, Gabriel.** "Der Wandel der Geographie in der Behandlung der Auberen Sicherheit. Neue Wege der Politischen Geographie." *Geographische Zeitschrift* [Stuttgart], 81, Heft 4 (!993), 204-209.

515 **Young, J.** "Geography and Politics." *Transactions of the Institute of British Geographers,* (New Series), 12, No. 4 (November, 1987), 391-397.

CHAPTER II

HISTORICAL OVERVIEW OF POLITICAL GEOGRAPHY

GENERAL AND THEORY

Books

516 Barbera, Henry. *Rich Nations and Poor in Peace and War: Continuity and Change in the Development Hierarchy of Seventy Nations from 1913 through 1952*. Lexington, Massachusetts: Lexington Books/D.C. Heath, 1973.

517 Barker, Ernest. *The Politics of Aristotle*. Oxford: Clarendon Press, 1946.

518 Blum, Yehuda Z. *Historic Titles in International Law*. The Hague: Martinus Nijhoff, 1965.

519 Chatterjee, S.P., and Das Gupta, S.P., eds. *Historical and Political Geography*. Calcutta: National Committee for Geography, 1972.

520 Dilloway, James. *Is World Order Evolving: An Adventure Into Human Potential*. Oxford: Pergamon Press, 1986.

521 Febvre, Lucien. *A Geographical Introduction to History*. London: Kegan Paul, 1925.

522 Fillip, K. *Geographie im historisch-politischen Zusammenhang. Aspekte und Materialien zum goegraphischen Gesellschaftsbzug*. Neuwied/Berlin: Luchterhand, 1975.

523 Fillip, K. *Geographie und Erziehung. Zur erslehungswissenschaftlichen Grundlegung der geographiedidaktik*. Munchen: Ehrenwirth, 1978a.

524 Fox, E.W. *History in Geographic Perspective: The Other France*. New York: W.W. Norton, 1975.

525 Freeman, T.W. *One Hundred Years of Geography*. Chicago: Aldine, 1961.

526 George, H.B. *The Relations of Geography and History*. Oxford: Clarendon Press, 1901.

527 Gurevich, Avon. *Medieval Popular Culture: Problems of Belief and Perception*. Cambridge: Cambridge University Press, 1988.

528 Hayes, Carleton J.H. *The Historical Evolution of Modern Nationalism*. New York: Richard Smith, 1931.

529 Huntington, Ellsworth. *Climate and Civilization*. New Haven, Connecticut: Yale University Press, 1915.

530 Huntington, Ellsworth. *Civilization and Climate*. New Haven, Connecticut: Yale University Press, 1924.

531 James, Preston E., and Martin, G. *All Possible Worlds: A History of Geographical Ideas*. New York: John Wiley & Sons, 1981.

532 Kevenhorster, P., ed. *Lakoale Politik unter exekutiven Fubrerschaft*. Meisenheim: Sozialwissenschaftliche studien zur stadtund regional politik. 1, Hain, 1977.

533 Kirk, William. *Geographical Pivots of History; An Inaugural Lecture Delivered in the University of Leicester, 24 November, 1964*. Leicester: Leicester University Press, 1965.

534 Kirk, William. *Historical Geography and the Concept of the Behavioural Environment*. Madras: Indian Geographical Society, Silver Jubilee Edition, 1951.

535 Lorton, David Marvin. *The Juridical Terminology of International Relations in Egyptians Texts through Dynasty XVIII*. Baltimore, Maryland: Johns Hopkins University, Ph.D., 1972.

536 MacPherson, Anne Margaret. *The Human Geography of Alexander von Humboldt*. Berkeley: University of California, Ph.D., 1972.

537 Malin, James C. *The Contriving Brain as the Pivot of History*. Lawrence: University of Kansas Press, 1959.

538 Popper, K.R. *The Poverty of Historicism*. London: Routledge, 1957.

539 Reparez, Gonzalo de. *Geografia y politic. Los fundamentos naturales de la historia humana*. Buenos Aires: ed. Americalee, 1943.

540 Ritter, Karl. *Comparative Geography*. Philadelphia: Lippincott, 1864.

541 Schwab, George, and Friedlander, Henry, eds. *Detente in Historical Perspective*. New York: Cyrco Press, 1975.

542 Seymour, Charles. *Geography, Justice, and Politics at the Paris Conference of 1919*. New York: American Geographical Society, 1951.

543 **Strabo**. *The Geography of Strabo*, trans. H.C. Hamilton & W. Falconer, I London: Bohn, 1854-57.

544 **Taylor, Griffith**. *Geography in the Twentieth Century*. London: Methuen, 1951.

545 **Thomas, J. Oliver**. *History of Ancient Geography*. Cambridge: Cambridge University Press, 1948.

546 **Toynbee, Arnold J.** *A Study of History*. New York: Oxford University Press, 1951.

547 **Walsh, Edmund A.** *Total Power; A Footnote to History*. Garden City, New York: Doubleday, 1948.

Journals

548 **Alker, Jr.; Hayward, R.; and Biersteker, Thomas J.** "The Dialectics of World Order: Notes for a Future Archaeologist of International Savoir Faire." *International Studies Quarterly*, 28, No. 2 (June, 1984), 121-142.

549 **Arques, Enrique**. "Las Fronteras de Marruecos en su Geografia Historica." *Africa*, 15, No. 199 (July, 1958), 304-306.

550 **Beck, H.** "Zue Geschichte der Geographie und des Erkundeunterrichts 1799 bis 1980--Grundlinien und Einblicke. In *Theorie und Geschichte des geographischen Unterrichts*. W. Sperling, ed. Braunschweig: Westermann, 1981, 61-83.

551 **Buck, N.** "The Analysis of State Intervention in Nineteenth Century Cities." In *Urbanization and Planning in Capitalist Societies*. New York: Methuen, 1981, 501-534.

552 **Dalby, S.** "(Re)reading Fukuyama: Political Geography at 'The End of History.'" *Political Geographer*, 12, No. 1 (January, 1993), 87-90.

553 **DeVries, Jan**. "The Rise and Decline of Nations in Historical Perspective." *International Studies Quarterly*, (Guilford) 27, No. 1 (March, 1983), 11-16.

554 **Field, Stephen B.** "Field Geography and Postwar Political Problems." *The Geographical Review*, 33, No. 3 (July, 1943), 446-456.

555 **Galtung, Johan; Heistad, Tore; and Rudeng, Erik.** "On the Decline and Fall of Empires: The Roman Empire and Western Imperialism Compared." *Review*, 4, No. 1 (Summer, 1980), 91-153.

556 **Kohler, F.** "125 Jahrgange von Petermanns Geographischen Mitteilungen: Wandlungen im Profilder Zeitschrift." *Petermanns Geographische Mitteilungen*, 125, Heft 1 (Marz, 1981), 1-10 and

Heft 2 (June, 1981), 109-115.

557 **Kruszewski, Charles**. "The Pivot of History." *Foreign Affairs*, 32, No. 3 (April, 195), 388-401.

558 **Mackinder, Halford J.** "The Geographical Pivot of History." *Geographical Journal*, 23, No. 2 (April, 1904), 421-444.

559 **Packenham, Robert A.** "Approaches to the Study of Political Development." *World Politics*, 17, No. 1 (October, 1964) 108-120.

560 **Pearson, M.N.** "Premodern Muslin Political Systems." *American Oriental Society New Haven Journal*, 102, No. 1 (January-March, 1982), 47-58.

561 **Peet, Richard**. "The Social Origins of Environmentral Determinism." *Annals of the Association of American Geographers*, 75, No. 3 (September, 1985), 309-333.

562 **Post, John D.** "A Study of Meteorological and Trade Cycle History: The Economic Crisis following the Nepoleonic Wars." *The Journal of Economic History*, 34, No. 2 (June, 1974), 315-349.

563 **Pounds, Norman J.G.** "History and Geography: A Perspective of Partition." *Journal of International Affairs*, 18, No. 2 (Fall, 1964), 161-172.

564 **Pred, A.** "Place as Historically Contingent Process: Structuration and the Time-geography of Becoming Places." *Annals of the Association of American Geographers*, 74, No. 2 (June, 1984), 279-297.

565 **Sanguin, Andre-Louis**. "Political Geographers of the Past II: Andre Slegfried, An Unconventional French Political Geographer." *Political Geography Quarterly*, 4, No. 1 (January, 1985), 79-83.

566 **Sayer, A.** "Review of 'A Contemporary Critique of Historical Materialism'." *Environment and Planning*, D, No. 1 (March, 1983), 109-114.

567 **Schoeller, P.** "Nachtrang zu: Wege und Irrwege der Politischen Geographie." *Politische Geographie*, Darmstadt: Wege der Forschung 431, Wissenschaftliche Buchgesellschaft, (1977), 295-302.

568 **Semple, Ellen Churchill**. "The Operation of Geographic Factors in History." *Bulletin of the American Geographic Society*, 41, No. 7 (July, 1909), 422-439.

569 **Singh, Basant**. "Political Journey Towards Sarvatantra: Some Geo-historical Trends and Problems." In *International Geography*, 1972, Edited by W. Peter Adams and Frederick M. Helleiner. Toronto: University of Toronto Press, 1972, 512-515.

570 **Smith, Neil.** "Political Geographers of the Past. Isaiah Bowman: Politic Geography and Geopolitics." *Political Geography Quarterly*, 3, No. 1 (January, 1984), 69-76.

571 **Soja, Edward W.** "Regions in Context-Spatially, Periodicity, and the Historical Geography of the Regional Question." *Society and Space*, 3 (1985), 175-190.

572 **Soja, Edward W.** "Review of 'A Contemporary Critique of Historical Materialism'." *Environment and Planning*, A15, No. 4 (December, 1983), 1267-1272.

573 **Spate, O.H.K.** "Toynbee and Huntington: A Study in Determinism." *Geographical Journal*, 118, Part 4 (December, 1952), 406-428.

574 **Taylor, Peter J.** "History's Dialogue: An Exemplification from Political Geography." *Progress in Human Geography*, Vol. 12, No. 1 (March, 1988), 1-14.

575 **Traverton, Gregory F.** "Finding an Analogy for Tomorrow." *Orbis* [Greenwich, CT], 37, No. 1 (Winter, 1993), 1-20.

576 **Volz, W.** "Die nationalen Aufgaben der Geographie." *Mitteilungen des Vereins der Geographen an der Universitat Leipzig*, 13 (1934), 1-11.

POLITICAL GEOGRAPHY OF REGIONS

AFRICA

Books and Journals

577 **Ardrey, Robert.** *African Genesis.* London: Fontana, 1961.

578 **Crush, Jonathan S., and Rogerson, C.** "New Wave African Historiography and African Historical Geography." *Progress in Human Geography*, 7, No. 2 (June, 1983), 203-231.

579 **DuBois, W.E. Burghardt.** *The World and Africa; An Inquiry into the Part Which Africa Has Played in World History.* New York: Viking Press, 1947.

580 **Floyd, Barry N.** "Gambia: A Case Study of the Role of Historical Accident in Political Geography." *The Bulletin; The Journal of the Sierra Leone Geographical Association*, 10 (1966), 22-38.

581 **Garlake, P.S.** "Prehistory and Ideology in Zimbabwe." *Africa*, 42, No. 3 (March, 1982), 1-19.

582 **Hopkins, A.** *An Economic History of West Africa.* London: Longman, 1973.

583 **Howe, Russell Warren.** *Along the Africa's Shore: An Historical Review of Two Centuries of U.S.-African Relations.* New York: Barnes and Noble, 1975.

584 **Karis, Thomas, and Carter, Gwendolen M.** eds. *From Protest to Challenge: A Documentary History of African Politics in South Africa, 1882-1964.* Challenges and Violence, 1953-1964. 3 Volumes. Stanford, California: Stanford University, Hoover Institution Press, 1977.

585 **Kirchherr, Eugene C.** *Abyssinia to Zona al sur del Draa: An Index to the Political Units of Africa in the Period 1951-1967.* Kalamazoo: Western Michigan University, 1968.

586 **Kirchherr, Eugene C.** "Towards an Explanation of the Transitionary Nature of the Political Map of Africa in the Period 1950-1978." *Africa Quarterly*, 21, Nos. 2-4 (July-September to January-Marhc, 1982) 5-22.

587 **McKee, Jessee O.** "An Application of the Jones Field Theory to Rhodesia and the Concept of the Historical Time Period." *The Virginia Geographer*, 6, No. 1 (Spring-Summer, 1971), 11-14.

588 **Murdock. G.P.** *Africa: Its Peoples and Their Cultural History.* New York: McGraw-Hill, 1959.

589 **Murray, C.** "From Granary to Labour Reserve: An Economic History of Lesotho." *South African Labour Bulletin*, 6, No. 4 (November, 1980), 3-20.

590 **Pike, John G.** *Malawi: A Political and Economic History.* New York: Praeger, 1968.

591 **Saul, John S., and Gelb, Stephen.** *The Crisis in South Africa.* Rev. ed. New York: Monthly Review Press, 1986.

592 **Ruytjens, E.** *Historisch Ontstaan der grens van de Onafhankelighe Congostaat en de Portuguese Bezittingen in Neder-Congo Tussen 1885-1894.* Bruxelles: Academic Royale des Sciences Colonieles, 1959.

593 **Turner, Henry Ashby, Jr.** *The Two Germanies Since 1945.* New Haven, Connecticut: Yale University Press, 1987.

AMERICAS

Books and Journals

594 **Adkins, Howard Glenn.** *The Historical Geography of Extinct Towns in Mississippi.* Knoxville: University of Tennessee, Ph.D., 1972.

595 **Allen, John Logan.** *The Geographical Images of the American Northwest, 1673 to 1806: An Historical Geosophy,* Worchester, Massachusetts: Clark University, Ph.D., 1969.

596 **Ayala-Vallejo, Reynolds.** *An Historical Geography of Parras de la Fuente, Coahvila-Mexico, or the Changing Man-Land Relationship in Parras de la Fuente, Coahvila-Mexico.* Carbondale: Southern Illinois University, Ph.D., 1971.

597 **Bemis, Samuel Flagg.** *A Diplomatic History of the United States.* New York: Henry Holt, 1950.

598 **Bemis, Samuel Flagg.** *The Latin American Policy of the United States; An Historical Interpretation.* New York: Harcourt Brace, 1943.

599 **Blaut, James M.** *The National Question: Decolonizing the Theory of Nationalism.* London: Zed Books, 1987.

600 **Blood, Richard Wallace.** *A Historical Geography of the Economic Activities of the Jesuit Colegio Maximo de San Pedro Y San Pable in Colonial Mexico, 1572-1767.* Minneapolis: University of Minnesota, Ph.D., 1922.

601 **Brigham, Albert Perry.** *Geographic Influences in American History.* Boston: Ginn, 1903.

602 **Brown, Ralph H.** *Historical Geography of the United States.* New York: Harcourt Brace, 1948.

603 **Calmon, Pedro.** *Brasil e America; historia d'uma politica.* Rio de Janeiro: Livraria J. Olympio, editora, 1943.

604 **Corkran, Robert Slaymaker.** *Rail Route Selection in the Northern Rocky Mountains, 1853-1890,* Chicago, Illinois: University of Chicago, Ph.D., 1969.

605 **Costeloe, Michael P.** *The Central Republic in Mexico, 1835-1846: Hombres de Bien in the Age of Santa Anna.* Cambridge: Cambridge University Press, 1993.

606 **Craig, Beatrice.** "Agriculture and the Lumberman's Frontier in the Upper St. John Valley, 1800-70." *Journal of Forest History,* 32, No. 3 (July, 1988), 125-187.

607 **Crowl, Philip A.** *Maryland During and After the Revolution: A Political and Economic Study.* (The John Hopkins University Studies in Historical and Political Science, Series 61, No. 1.) Baltimore, Maryland: Johns Hopkins University, 1943.

608 **Fatzinger, Dale Roger.** *Historical Geography of Lead and Zinc Mining in Southwest Wisconsin 1820-1920: A Century of Change.* East Lansing: Michigan State University, Ph.D., 1971.

609 **Gilderhus, Mark T.** *Pan American Visions Woodrow Wilson in the Western Hemisphere 1913-1921.* Tucson: University of Arizona Press, 1986.

610 **Grantham, Dewey W.** "The Live and Detah of Solid South: A Political History. Lexington: University Press of Kentucky, 1988.

611 **Head, Clifford Grant.** *The Changing Geography of Newfoundland in the Eighteenth Century.* Madison: University of Wisconsin, Ph.D., 1971.

612 **Heidenreich, Conrad Edmund.** *The Historical Geography of Huronia in the First Half of the Seventeenth Century.* Hamilton, Ontario, Canada: McMaster University, Ph.D., 1971.

613 **Hertel, F.M.** *Sea Power in American History.* Chicago: Rand McNally, 1967.

614 **Hewlett, S.A.** *The Cruel Dilemmas of Development: Twentieth Century Brazil.* New York: Basic Books, 1980.

615 **Hoffman, George W.** "Nineteenth Century roots of American Power Relations: A Study in Historical Political Geography." *Political Geography Quarterly,* 1 (July, 1982), 279-292.

616 **Jackson, Richard H.** *Myth and Reality: Environmental Perception of the Mormons, 1840-1865, An Historical Geography.* Worchester, Massachusetts: Clark University, Ph.D., 1970.

617 **Johnson, Hildegard Binder.** "Zur historischen und rechtlichen Problematik von Grenze und Flussgebiet in Nordamerika." *Forschungen zu Staat und Verfassung,* Festgabe fur Fritz Hartung, Duncker & Humblot, Berlin, January, 1958, 307-324.

618 **Keenleyside, Hugh L.** *Canada and the United States; Some Aspects of Their Historical Relations.* New York: Alfred A. Knopf, 1952.

619 **Kelly, K.** "An Explanation of the Great North-South Extent of the Inca Empire in 1532 and of the Position of Its Eastern Boundary Through Peru and Bolivia." *The Journal of Tropical Geography,* 28, No. 1 (June, 1969), 57-63.

620 **Kennedy, Kathleen.** "Loyalty and Citizenship in the Wisconsin Women's Suffrage Association, 1917-1919." *Mid-America,* 76, No. 2 (Spring/Summer, 1994), 109-131.

621 **Kixmiller, Patricia Elaine.** *Anastasia Island, Florida: A Case Study in Historical Perception of Resources and Resistances.* Boca Raton: Florida Atlantic University, M.A., 1973.

622 **Koschnik, Albrecht.** "Political Conflict and Public Contest: Rituals of National Celebration in Philadelphia, 1788-1815." *The Pennsylvania Magazine of History and Biography*, 118, No. 3 (July, 1994), 209-248.

623 **Lalande, Jeff.** "A 'Little Kansas' in Southern Oregon: The Course and Character of Populism in Jackson county, 1890-1900." *Pacific Historical Review* [Berkeley], 63, No. 2 (May, 1994), 149-176.

624 **Lipset, Seymour M.** *The First New Nation: The United States in Historical and Comparative Perspective.* New York: Basic Books, 1963.

625 **Lobb, Charles Gary.** *The Historical Geography of the Cattle Regions Along Brazil's Southern Frontier.* Berkeley: University of California, Ph.D., 1970.

626 **Lopez, George A., and Stohl, Michael,** eds. *Liberalization and Redemocratization in Latin America.* New York: Greenwood Press, 1987.

627 **McNeil, W.H.** *The Rise of the West.* Chicago, Illinois: University of Chicago Press, 1963.

628 **Meinig, Donald W.** *The Shapping of America: A Geopolitical Perspective on 500 Years of History.* New Haven, Connecticut: Yale University Press, 1986.

629 **Merrill, Gordon C.** *The Historical Geography of Saint Kitts and Nevis.* Berkeley: University of California, Ph.D., 1957.

630 **Mitchell, Robert Davis.** *The Upper Shenandoah Valley of Virginia During the Eighteen Century: A Study in Historical Geography.* Madison: University of Wisconsin, Ph.D., 1969.

631 **Moodie, Donald Wayne.** *An Historical Geography of Agriculture Patterns, and Resource Appraisals in Rupert's Land, 1670-1974.* Edmonton, Alberta, Canada: University of Alberta, Ph.D., 1972.

632 **Moore, Conrad Taylor.** *Man and Fire in the Central North American Grassland 1535-1890: A Documentary Historical Geography.* Los Angeles: University of California, Ph.D., 1972.

633 **Moore, Harriet.** "American Relations with the Russian Empire and the USSR; A Reference Review, with Chronology and Bibliography." *The American Quarterly on the Soviet Union*, 3, No. 2-3 (November, 1940), 3-26.

634 **Nowell, Charles Edward.** "The Treaty of Tordesillas and the Diplomatic Background of American History." In *Greater America;* Essays in Honor of Herbert Eugene Bolton (1945), 1-18.

635 **Paden, John.** "Several and Many Grievances of Very Great Consequences": North Carolina's Political Factionalism in the 1720s." *The North Carolina Historical Review* [Raleigh], 71, No. 3 (July, 1994), 285-305.

636 **Paulin, C.O.** *Atlas of the Historical Geography of the United States.* John K. Wright (ed.). New York and Washington, D.C.: American Geographical Society and Carnegie Institution, 1932.

637 **Peet, R.** "The End of Prehistory and the First Human." *Political Geography*, 12, No. 1 (January, 1993), 91-95.

638 **Pohl, Thomas Walter.** *Seattle 1851-1861: A Frontier Community.* Seattle: University of Washington, Ph.D., 1970.

639 **Powell, William Earl.** *The Historical Geography of the Impact of Coal Mining Upon the Cherokee-Crawford Coal Field of Southeastern Kansas.* Lincoln: University of Nebraska, Ph.D., 1970.

640 **Quesada y Miranda, Gonzalo de.** *Archivo de Gonzalo de Quesada: Documentos historicos. . .* La Habana: Editorial de la Universidad de la Habana, 1965.

641 **Radell, David Richard.** *An Historical Geography of Western Nicaragua: The Spheres of Influence of Leon, Granada, and Managua, 1519-1965.* Berkeley: University of California, Ph.D., 1969.

642 **Ratzel, Friedrich.** *Anthropogeographie.* Stuttgart: J. Engelhorn, 1882.

643 **Ray, Arthur Joseph, Jr.** *Indian Exploitation of the Forest-grassland Transition Zone in Western Canada, 1650-1860: A Geographical View of Two Centuries of Change.* Madison: University of Wisconsin, Ph.D., 1971.

644 **Rees, Peter William.** *Route Inertia and Route Competition: An Historical Geography of Transportation Between Mexico City and Veracruz.* Berkeley: University of California, Ph.D., 1972.

645 **Rowles, Ruth A. and Martis, Kenneth C.** "Mapping Congress: Developing a Geographic Understanding of American Political History." *Prologue* , 16, No. 1 (Spring, 1984), 5-21.

646 **Santer, Richard Arthur.** *A Historical Geography of Jackson, Michigan: A Study on the Changing Character of an American City, 1829-1969.* East Lansing: Michigan State University, Ph.D., 1970.

647 **Santiso Galvez, Gustavo.** *El caso de Belice a la luza de la historia y el derecho internacional. la condicion resolutoria tacita por incumplimiento en los tratados internacionales.* Guatemala: La Tipografia Nacional, 1941.

648 **Semple, Ellen Churchill.** *American History and Its Geography Conditions.* Boston-New York: Houghton Mifflin, 1903.

649 **Sheck, Ronald Calvin.** *An Historical Geography of Quito, Ecuador.* Eugene: University of Oregon, Ph.D., 1969.

650 **Solomon, Susan Gross,** ed. *Beyond Sovietology: Essays in Politics and History.* Armonk: M. E.Sharpe, 1993.

651 **Stein, Gregory Paul.** *Lake Minnetonka: Historical Perceptions of an Urban Lake.* Minneapolis: University of Minnesota, Ph.D., 1971.

652 **Sternberg, Rolf.** "The Historical-Political Geography of the Humid Pampa to 1850." *Excerpts: The Monclair Journal of Social Sciences and the Humanities,* Fall (1974), 97-125.

653 **Turner, F.J.** "Geographical Influences in American Political History." *Bulletin of the American Geographical Society,* 46, No. 8 (August, 1914), 591-595.

654 **Upchurch, John Calhoun.** *'Middle Florida': An Historical Geography of the Area Between the Apalachicola and Suwannee Rivers.* Knoxville: University of Tennessee, Ph.D., 1971.

655 **Valentine, Rodney J.** "Pioneer Settler's Abuse of Land Laws in the Nineteenth Century: The Case of the Boise River Valley, Idaho." *Agricultural History* [Berkeley], 67, No. 3 (Summer, 1993), 47-65.

656 **Vila Lalera, Oscar.** *Historio y geografico de la Antartica chilena.* Santiago: Tegualda, 1948.

657 **Wishart, David John.** *An Historical Geography of the Fur Trade on the Upper Missouri, 1807-1843.* Lincoln: University of Nebraska, Ph.D., 1971.

658 **Wright, John K.** "Geographical Sections and American Political History as Illustrated by Certain Maps in the Atlas of the Historical Geography of the United States." *C.R., Warsaw,* Tome 4 (1934), 103-107.

ASIA

Books and Journals

659 **Arfa, H.** *The Kurds: An Historical and Political Study.* London, Oxford University Press, 1966.

660 **Aziz-ur-Rahman, Mian.** "Evolution of the Sahiwal District; A Case in Historical Geography." *Pakistan Geographical Review,* 22, No. 2 (July, 1967), 95-108.

661 **Chew, Ernest C.T.** "The Fall of the Burmese Kingdom in 1885: Review and Reconsideration." *Journal of Southeast Asian Studies,* (Singapore) 10, No. 2 (September, 1979), 372-380.

662 **Cobban, James L.** *The City of Java: An Essay on Historical Geography.* Berkeley: University of California, Ph.D., 1970.

663 **Efrat, Elisha.** *Geography and Politics in Israel Since 1967.* Totowa, New Jersey: Frank Cass, 1988.

664 **Fawaz, Leila.** "The City and the Mountain: Beirut's Political Radius in the Nineteenth Century as Revealed in the Crisis of 1860." *International Journal of Middle East Studies,* 16, No. 4 (November, 1984), 489-495.

665 **Gellner, Charles E.** *The Palestine Problem; An Analysis, Historical and Contemporary.* (U.S. Library Congress, Legislative Reference Service, Public Affairs, Bulletin, No. 50) Washington, D.C.: U.S. Library of Congress, 1947.

666 **Hag, S. Moinul.** "Ideological Basis of Pakistan in Historical Perspective (III)." *Pakistan Historical Society Journal,* 28, Part 1 (January, 1980), 1-32.

667 **International Geographical Congress,** 21st [New Delhi] India, 1968. *Selected Papers,* Vol. 3: Population and Settlement Geography, Political and Historical Geography. Calcutta, National Committee for Geography, 1971.

668 **Johnson, Douglas Leslie.** *Jabal Al-Akhdar, Cyrenaica: An Historical Geography of Settlement and Livelihood.* Chicago, Illinois: University of Chicago, Ph.D., 1972.

669 **Lattimore, Owen.** "The Geographical Factor in Mongol History." *Geographical Journal,* 91, No. 1 (January, 1938), 1-20.

670 **McFadden, John H.** "Civil-Military Relations in the Third Turkish Republic. *The Middle East Journal,* 39, No. 1 (Winter, 1985), 69-85.

671 **Milivojevic, Marko.** "The Resurrection of Genghis Kahn." *Geographical Magazine* [London], 63, No. 7 (July, 1991), 36-38.

672 **Mostyn, Trevor.** *Major Political Events in Iran, Iraq and the Arabian Peninsula, 1945-1990.* New York: Facts on File, 1991.

673 **Murton, Brian Joseph.** *Man, Mind, and Land: A Peasant Production System in Late Eighteenth Century South India.* Minneapolis: University of Minnesota, Ph.D., 1970.

674 **Pannikar, K.M.** *Geographical Factors in Indian History.* Bombay: Bhartiya Vidhya Bhawan, 1955.

675 **Perlmutter, Amos.** *Israel: The Partitioned State: A Political History Since 1900.* New York: Charles Scribner's Sons, 1985.

676 **Pipes, Daniel.** "The Year the Arabs Discovered Palestine." *Middle East Review*, 21, No. 4 (Summer, 1989), 37-44.

677 **Popkin, S.L.** *The Rational Peasant. The Political Economy of Rural Society in Vietnam.* Berkeley: University of California Press, 1979.

678 **Rabinovich, Itamar.** "Historiography and Politics in Syria." *Asian Affairs*, 9 (Old Series, Vol. 65), Pt. 1 (February, 1978), 57-66.

679 **Rodzinski, Witold.** *The People's Republic of China: A Concise Political History.* New York: The Free Press, 1988.

680 **Sayigh, Rosemary.** *Palestinians: From Peasants to Revolutionaries: A People's History.* London: Zed Press *Middle East Series.* No. 3, 1979.

681 **Schwartzberg, Joseph E.** *A Historical Atlas of South Asia.* Association for Asian Studies Reference Series No. 2. Chicago, Illinois: University of Chicago Press, 1978.

682 **Stanley, Richard J.** *Asiatic Interests in American History: Study Guide and Source Unit.* Hartford, Connecticut: State Department of Education, 1943.

683 **Van Valkenburg, Samuel.** *Whose Promised Lands? A Political Atlas of the Middle East and India.* (Headline Series, No. 57) New York: Headline Series, 1946.

AUSTRALIA, OCEANIA AND ANTARCTICA

Books and Journals

684 **Golovin, N., et Bubnov, A.D.** *The Problem of the Pacific in the Twentieth Century.* New York: Charles Scribner's Sons, 1922.

685 **Gueffroy, Edna Mae.** *Historical Geography of New Zealand.* Seattle: University of Washington, Ph.D., 1950.

686 **Logan, W.S.** *Post-Convergence Political Geography: Death or Transfiguration?* Australia: Department of Geography, Monash University, Monash Publications in Geography, No. 18, 1978.

687 **Peoples, James G.** "Political Evolution in Micronesia." *Ethnology* [Pittsburgh], 32, No. 1 (Winter, 1993), 1-17.

688 **Verosta, Stephan.** "History: The Australians and Their State." *Australia Today,* 4 (Autumn, 1978), 8-19.

689 **Zavatti, Silvio.** "L'Antartide; Aspetti generali e questioni politiche." *L'Universo,* Anno 31, N. 5 (Septembre-Octobre, 1951), 645-659.

EUROPE

Books and Journals

690 **Ahmad, Nafis.** "Changing Map of Europe." *The Journal of the Madras Geographical Association,* 15, No. 4 (October-December, 1940), 371-379.

691 **Akino, Yutaka.** "Soviet Policy in Eastern Europe, 1943-1948: A Geopolitical Analysis." *East European Quarterly,* (Boulder) 17, No. 3 (September, 1983), 257-266.

692 **Bartlett, Robert.** "The Impact of Royal Government in the French Ardennes: The Evidence of the 1247 Enquete." *Journal of Medieval History,* 7, No. 1 (March, 1981), 83-96.

693 **Black, Jeremy.** *Natural and Necessary Enemies: Anglo-French Relations in the Eighteenth Century.* London: Duckworth, 1986.

694 **Burghardt, Andrew F.** *Borderland, A Historical and Geographical Study of Burgenland* (Austria). Madison: University of Wisconsin Press, 1962.

695 **Calender, Geoffrey.** *The Naval Side of British History.* London: Christopher's, 1924.

696 **Chirot, Daniel, and Barkey, Karen.** "States in Search of Legitimacy: Was there Nationalism in the Balkans in the Early Nineteenth Century?" *International Journal of Comparative Sociology,* 24, Nos. 1-2 (January-April, 1983), 30-46.

697 **Collins, David N.** "Russia's Conquest of Siberia: Evolving Russian and Soviet Historical Interpretations." *European Studies Review,* 12, No. 1 (January, 1982), 17-44.

698 **East, Roger.** *Revolutions in Eastern Europe.* London: Pinter Publishers, 1992.

699 **East, W. Gordon.** *An Historical Geography of Europe.* London: Methuen, 1967.

700 **Fahlbusch, M.; Roessler, M.; and Siegrist, D.** *Conservatism, Ideology and Geography in Germany 1920-45.* Hamburg: University of Hamburg, Geographisches Institut, Unpublished paper,1986.

701 **Fahlbusch, M.; Roessler, M.; and Siegrist, D.** "Conservatism, Ideology and Geography in Germany, 1920-1950." *Political Geography Quarterly,* 8, No. 4 (October, 1989), 353-367.

702 Fischer, F. *Griff nach der Weltmacht. Die Kriegszielpolitik des Kaiserlichen Deutchlands 1914/18.* Dusseldorf: Droste, 1961.

703 Freeman, Edward A. *The Historical Geography of Europe,* 3rd ed. London: Longmans, 1974.

704 "Germany and Poland 1919-1939. A Historical and Political Study." *Volkerbund,* 8th year, No. 16-17 (May 15-June 1, 1939), 205-232.

705 Gorban, N.V. "From the History of the Construction of Forts in the South of Western Siberia: The New Ishim Fortified Line." *Soviet Geography,* (Silver Spring) 25, No. 3 (March, 1984), 177-194. (Translated from: *Voprosy geografi,* No. 31 (1953), 206-277.

706 Grada, Carmac. *Ireland Before and After the Famine: Explorations in Economic History, 1800-1925.* Manchester: Manchester University Press, 1988.

707 Hardy, D. *Alternative Communities in Nineteenth Century England.* Harlow: Longmans, 1979.

708 Heske, Jenning. "Political Geographers of the Past III: German Geographic Research in the Nazi Period--A Content Analysis of the Major Geography Journals." *Political Geography Quarterly,* 5, No. 2 (July, 1986), 267-282.

709 Himka, John-Paul. "Hope in the Tsar: Displaced Naive Monarchism Among the Ukrainian Peasants of the Habsburg Empire." *Russian History,* 7, Parts 1-2 (1980), 125-138.

710 Inglehart, Ronald. "An End to European Integration?" *American Political Science Review,* 61, No. 1 (March, 1967), 91-105.

711 Jarry, Eugene. *Provinces et pays de France; essai de geographie historique.* Paris: Librairie des Anciennes provinces, C. Poisson, 1943.

712 Johnson, John J. "Early Relations of the United States with Chile." *The Pacific Historical Review,* 13, No. 3 (September, 1944), 260-270.

713 Knafou, Remy. "L'evolution de la Politique de la Montagne en Fance." *L'Information Geographique,* (Paris) 49, No. 2 (1985), 53-62.

714 Konarek, J. *Territorial Dynamics in the Western Dinarics Before 1881 with Special Reference to the Vogna Krajina of Croatia.* London, Ontario, Canada: University of Western Ontario, Ph.D., 1975.

715 Konovalov, Serge, ed. *Russo-Polish Relations; An Historical Survey.* Princeton, New Jersey: Princeton University Press, 1945.

716 Kos, Milko. *Historical Development of the Slovene Western Frontier.* Ljubljana: Research Institute, Section for Frontier Questions, 1946.

717 Kost, Klaus. "The Conception of Politics in Political Geography and Geopolitics in Germany Until 1945." *Political Geography Quarterly,* 8, No. 4 (October, 1989), 369-385.

718 Kost, Klaus. *Die Einflusse der Geopolitik auf Forschung und Theorie der Politischen Geographic von ihren Anfangen bis 1945.* Bonn: Bonner Geographische Abhandlungen 76, 1988.

719 Kostelski, Z. *The Yugoslavs: The History of the Yugoslavs and Their States to the Creation of Yugoslavia.* New York: Philosophical Library, 1952.

720 Krause, E.; Huber, L.; and Fischer, H., eds. *Hochschulalltag im Dritten Reich Die Hamburger universitat, 1933-1945.* Berlin: D. Reimer, 1989.

721 Lobotka, Vojtech. "Historical Changes in the Structure of Interregional Relations of the East-Slovak Territory from the Half of the 19th Century till World War II." *Acta Geographica Universitatis Comenianae,* Economico-Geographica. Nr. 8 (1968), 289-307.

722 Low, D.H. "The Kingdom of Serbia: Her People and Her History." *Scottish Geographical Magazine,* 31, No. 6, (June, 1915), 303-315.

723 Lynch, Donald F. *The Historical Geography of New Russia.* New Haven, Connecticut: Yale University, Ph.D., 1964.

724 McCauley, Martin, and Waldron, Peter. *The Emergence of the Modern Russian State.* Totowa, New Jersey: Barnes and Noble, 1987.

725 Mommsen, Hans. "History and National Identity: The Case of Germany." *German Studies Review,* 6, No. 3 (October, 1983), 559-582.

726 Mommsen, Wolfgang J., ed. *The Long Way to Europe: Historical Observations from a Contemporary View.* Chicago: Edition Q, Inc., 1994.

727 Ossenbrugge, Jurgen. "Territorial Ideologies in West Germany 1945-1985: Between Geopolitics and Regionalist Attitudes." *Political Geography Quarterly,* 8, No. 4 (October, 1989), 387-399.

728 Parker, W.H. *An Historical Geography of Russia.* London: University of London Press, 1969.

729 Pounds, Norman J.G. "France and 'Les Limites Naturelles' from the Seventeenth to the Twentieth Centuries." *Annals of the Association of American Geographers,* 44, No. 1 (March, 1954), 51-62.

730 **Pugh, Martin.** *State and Society: British Political and Social History, 1870-1992.* London: Edward Arnold, 1994.

731 **Rennier, G.J.** *The Dutch Nation: An Historical Study.* London: Allen & Unwin, 1944.

732 **Roberts, Geoffrey.** "A Soviet Bid for Coexistence with Nazi Germany, 1935-1937: The Kandelaki Affair." *The International History Review,* 16, No. 3 (August, 1994), 466-490.

733 **Sandner, Gerhard.** "Introduction to Special Issue: Historical Studies of German Political Geography." *Political Geography Quarterly,* 8, No. 4 (October, 1989), 311-314.

734 **Sandner, Gerhard.** "Die 'Geographische Zeitschrift' 1933-1944: eine Dokumentation uber Zensur, Selbstzensur und Anpassungsdruk bein wissenschaftlichen Zeitschriften im Dritten Reich." *Geographische Zeitschrift,* 71 (1983), 65-87, 127-149.

735 **Sandner, Gerhard.** "Recent Advances in the History of German Geography, 1918-1945: A Progress Report for the Federal Republic of Germany." *Geographische Zeitschriff,* 76, 120-133.

736 **Sandner, Gerhard.** "The Germania Triumphaus Syndrome and Passages is Erdkundliche Weltanschauung: The Roots and Effects of German Political Geography Beyond Geopolik." *Political Geography Quarterly,* 8, No. 4 (October, 1989), 341-351.

737 **Schnapper, Bernard.** "Pour und Geographie des Mentalites Judiciaires: La Litigiosite un France ai XIX° Siecle." *Annales Economics, Societes, Civilisations,* 34° annee, No. 2 (Febrier-Mars, 1979), 399-419.

738 **Scholler, Peter.** "The Division of Germany: Based on Historical Geography?" *Erdkunde,* Band 19, Heft 2 (June, 1965), 161-164.

739 **Schultz, Hans-Dietrich.** "Fantasies of Mitte: Mittellage and Mitelleuropa in German Geographical Discussion in the 19th and 20th Centuries." *Political Geography Quarterly,* 8, No. 4 (October, 1989), 315-339.

740 **Schultz, Hans-Dietrich.** *Die Geographie als Bildungsfach in Kaiserreich.* Osnabruck: Selbstverlag des Fachbereichs 2 der Universitat Osnabruch, Osnabrucher Studien tur Geographie 10, 1989.

741 **Semple, Ellen Churchill.** "The Barrier Boundary of the Mediterranean Basin and Its Northern Reaches as Factors in History." *Annals of the Association of American Geographers.* 5, No. 1 (March, 1915), 27-59.

742 **Senn, A.E.,** ed. *Readings in Russian Political and Diplomatic History.* Homewood, Illinois: Dorsey Press, 1966.

743 **Shirer, William L.** *Rise and Fall of the Third Reich: A History of Nazi Germany.* New York: Simon and Schuster, 1960.

744 **Stachura, Peter D.** *Political Leaders in Weimar Germany, A Biographical Study.* New York: Simon & Schuster, 1993.

745 **Stokes, Gale,** ed. *From Stalinism to Pluralism: A Documentary History of Eastern Europe Since 1945.* New York: Oxford University Press, 1991.

746 **Svarlien, Oscar.** *The Eastern Greenland Case in Historical Perspective.* Gainesville: University of Florida Press, 1964.

747 **Symmons-Symonolewicz, Konstantin.** "National Consciousness in Medieval Europe: Some Theoretical Problems." *Canadian Review of Studies in Nationalism,* (Charlottetown, Prince Edward Island), 8, No. 1 (Spring, 1981), 151-166.

748 **Verdery, Katherine.** "On the Nationality Problem in Transylvania until WW I: An Overview." *East European Quarterly,* 19, No. 1 (Spring, 1985), 15-30.

749 **Wehler, H.U.** *Entsorgung der deutschen Vergangenheit? Ein Polemischer Essay zum Historikerstreit.* Munchen: C. H. Beck, 1988.

CHAPTER III

POLITICAL GEOGRAPHY AND GEOPOLITICS

GENERAL AND THEORY

Books

750 **Ancel, Jacques**. *Geopolitique*. Paris: Librarie Delagrave, 1936.

751 **Atencio, Jorge E.** *Que es la geopolitica?* Buenos Aires: Ed. Pleamar, 1966.

752 **Bloomfield, Jack.** *Focus on--Maps of World Crisis.* Dobbs Ferry, New York: Oceana Publications, 1962.

753 **Blouet, Brian W.** *Halford Mackinder: A Bibliography.* College Station: Texas A & M, 1987.

754 **Blouet, Brian W.** *Sir Halford Mackinder, 1861-1947: Some New Perspectives.* Oxford: University School of Geography, Research Paper No. 13, May, 1975.

755 **Bonasera, F.** *Geopolitica.* Palermo: Herbita, 1982.

756 **Boyd, Andrew K.H.** *An Atlas of World Affairs.* New York: Methuen, 1983.

757 **Brecher, Michael.** *Crises in World Politics: Theory and Reality.* Oxford: Pergamon Press, 1993.

758 **Brzezinski, Zbigniew.** *Out of Control: Global Turmoil on the Eve of the Twenty-First Century.* New York: Charles Scribuer's Sons, 1993.

759 **Butts, Kent Hughes.** *The Geopolitics of Southern Africa: South Africa as Regional Superpower.* Boulder, Colorado: Westview Press, 1986.

760 **Canetti, E.** *Crowds and Power.* Rev. ed. London: Penguin Books, 1973.

761 **Castro, Josue de.** *The Geopolitics of Hunger.* New York: Monthly Review Press, 1977.

762 **Castro, Josue de.** *Geopolitique de la Faim.* Paris:

Les Editions Ouvrieres, 1971.

763 **Cattaneo, Atilio E.** *Geopolitica Imperialista y la Nueva Argentina.* Buenos Aires: Talleres Graficos "Denbigh", 1948.

764 **Cavalla, A.; Chateaus, J.; and Revista 'Principios'.** *La Geopolitica y el Fascismo Dependiente.* Mexico City: Casa de Chile, 1977.

765 **Celerier, Paul.** *Geopolitique et geostrategie.* Paris: Presses Universitaires de France, 1964.

766 **Chaliand, Gerard., and Rageau, J.P.** *Atlas strategique: Geopolitique des Rapports de Forces dans le Monde.* Paris: Fayard, 1983.

767 **Chavenatto, J.J.** *Geopolitica, Arma do Fascismo.* Sao Paulo: Global Editora, 1981.

768 **Cleveland, Harlan.** *Birth of a New World: An Open Moment for International Leadership.* San Francisco: Jossey-Bass Publishers, 1993.

769 **Cline, R.S.** *World Power Assessment, 1977: A Calculus of Strategic Drift.* Boulder, Colorado: Westview Press, 1977.

770 **Comblin, J.** *The Church and the National Security State.* Maryknoll, New York: Orbis Books, 1979.

771 *Countries of the World: Official background notes of the U.S. Department of State covering contemporary political and economic conditions, government policies and personnel, political parties, religion, history, education, press, radio and T.V., and other characteristics of each nation.* Detroit, Michigan: Gale Research Company, 1974.

772 **Couto E Silva, Golbery Do.** *Planejamento Estrategico.* Rio de Janeiro: Biblioteca do Exercito, 1955.

773 **Dean, Vera Micheles.** *The Struggle for World Order.* (Headline books, No. 32) New York: Foreign Policy Association, 1941.

774 **Demko, George, and Wood, William B.** *Reordering the World: Geopolitical Perspective on the Twenty-First Century.* Boulder, CO: Westview Press, 1994.

775 **DeSeVersky, Alexander P.** *America: Too Young to Die.* New York: McGraw-Hill, 1961.

776 **Deudney, Daniel.** *Whole Earth Security: A Geopolitics of Peace.* (Worldwatch Paper No. 55) Washington, D.C.: Worldwatch Institute, 1983.

777 **Deutsch, Karl W., et al.** *International Political Communities.* Garden City: Anchor Books, 1966.

778 **Dorpalen, Andreas.** *The World of General Haushofer; Geopolitics in Action.* New York: Farrar & Rinehart, 1942.

779 **Emeny, Brooks.** *Mainsprings of World Politics.* New York: Foreign Policy Association, 1956.

780 **Enggass, Peter M.** *Geopolitics: A Bibliography of Applied Political Geography.* Monticello, Illinois: Vance Bibliographies, May, 1984.

781 **English, J.S.** *Halford Mackinder, 1861-1947.* London: Gainsborough, 1974.

782 **Erfurt, Werner.** *Die Sowjetrussische Deutschland politik 1945-1955; Eine Studie zur Zeitgeschichte.* Esslingen: Bechtle, 1956.

783 **Escalona Ramos, Alberto.** *Geopolitica mundial y geo-economica, dinamica mundial, historica y contemporana.* Mexico: Ediciones "Ateneo", 1959.

784 **Fairgrieve, James.** *Geography and World Power.* 8th and rev. ed. New York: Dutton, 1941.

785 **Falk, Richard.** *Explorations at the Edge of Time: Prospects for World Order.* Philadelphia: Temple University Press, 1992.

786 **Farrell, John C. and Smith, Asa P.,** eds. *Image and Reality in World Politics.* New York City: Columbia University Press, 1967.

787 **Fifield, Russell H., and Pearcy, G. Etzel.** *Geopolitics in Principle and Practice.* Boston: Ginn, 1944.

788 **Fonseca, Jr. Leopoldo Nery de.** *Geopolitica.* Rio de Janeiro: Bedeschi, 1940.

789 **Frankel, Joseph.** *International Politics; Conflict and Harmony.* London: Penguin Books, 1969.

790 **Freud, Arthur.** *The World Without Nations.* Cynthiana, Kentucky: Hobson Book Press, 1943.

791 **Fucks, Wilhelm.** *Formeln zur Macht: Prognosen Uber Volker, Wirtschaff, Potentiale.* Stuttgart: Deutsche Verlags-Anstalt, 1965.

792 **Gilbert, Edmund W.** *Sir Halford Mackinder 1861-1947: An Appreciation of His Life and Work.* London: G. Bell, 1961.

793 **Girot, Pascal and Kofman, Eleanor,** ed. and trans. *International Geopolitical Analysis: A Selection from Herodota.* London: Croom Helm, 1987.

794 **Grabonsky, A.** *Raum als Schicksal. Das Problem der Geopolitik.* Berlin: Heymann, 1933.

795 **Graca, Jayme Ribeiro da.** *A geografia na politica externa.* Rio de Janeiro: Biblioteca do Excercito, 1951.

796 **Gray, Colin S.** *The Geopolitics of Superpower.* Lexington: University of Kentucky Press, 1988.

797 **Gray, Colin S.** *The Geopolitics of the Nuclera Era: Heartland, Rimlands, and the Technological Revolution.* New York: Crane, Russak, 1977.

798 **Griffith, William E.** *The World and the Great-Power Triangles.* Cambridge: Massachusetts Institute of Technology Press, 1975.

799 **Griggs, Richard Allen.** *The Role of Fourth World Nations and Synchronous Geopolitical Factors in the Breakdown of States.* Berkeley: Ph.D. Dissertation, University of California, 1993.

800 **Grimm, Hans.** *Volk ohne Raum.* Munchen: A.Langen, 1926.

801 **Gyorgy, Andrew.** *Geopotics, The New German Science.* Berkeley: University of California Press, 1944.

802 **Harbeck, K.H.** *Die Zeitschrift fur Geopolitik.* Kiel: Diss, 1963.

803 **Haushofer, Albrecht.** *Allgemeine politische geographie und geopolitik.* Heidelberg: Kurt Vowinckel, 1951.

804 **Haushofer, Karl.** *Bausteine zur Geopolitik.* Berlin: Kurt Vowinckel, 1928.

805 **Haushofer, Karl.** *Geographie und Weltmacht: Eine ein fuhrung in die geopolitik.* Berlin: Kurt Vowinckel Verlag, 1925.

806 **Haushofer, Karl.** *Geopolitik der selbstbestimmung.* Berlin: Kurt Vowinckel, 1923.

807 **Haushofer, Karl.** *Grenzen in ihrer geographischen und politischen bedeutung.* Berlin-Gruenwald: Kurt Vowinckel, 1927 and 1939.

808 **Haushofer, Karl.** *Jenseits der grossmachte; erganzungsband zur neubearbeitung der grossmachte Rudolph Kjellens, unter mitwirkung von W. Geisler, A. Grabowsky, H. Lautensach (U.A.)...herausgegeben vod dr. Karl Kaushofer...Mit 100 Kartenskizzen und graphischen darstellungen.* Leipzig und Berlin: B.G. Teubner, 1932.

809 **Haushofer, Karl.** *Macht und Erde.* 3 vols. Leipzig: B.G. Teubner, 1930-1934.

810 **Haushofer, Karl.** *Politische Erkunde und Geopolitik.* Munchen: Kurt Vowinckel, 1925.

811 **Haushofer, Karl.** *Raumuberwindende Machte.* Leipzig: B.G. Teubner, 1934.

812 **Haushofer, Karl.** *Wehr-geopolitik; geographische grundlagen eine Wehrkunde.* Berlin: Junker and Dunnhaupt, 1932.

813 **Haushofer,** *p485XWadmure und Weltmachte.* Berlin: Zeitgeschichte Verlag, 1937.

814 **Haushofer, Karl.** *Weltpolitik von Heute.* Berlin: Zeitgeschichte Verlag, 1934.

815 **Haushofer, Karl.** *Zur geopolitik der selb-bestimmung.* Munchen und Leipzig: Rosl, 1923.

816 **Haushofer, Karl, mit Obst, Eric; Lautensauch, Herman; und Maull, Otto.** *Bausteine zur geopolitik.* Berlin: Kurt Vowinckel, 1928.

817 **Haushofer, Karl, mit Obst, Eric; Lautensauch, Herman, Maull, Otto; et Kjellen, Rudolf.** *Jenseits der Grossmachte.* Berlin: Kurt Vowinckel, 1932.

818 **Hayes, John D.** *Peripheral Strategy—Mahan's Doctrine Today.* Norfolk, Virginia: United States Naval Institute Proceedings, 1953.

819 **Hennig, Richard.** *Geopolitik: Die Lehre vom staats als Lebenswesen.* Leipzig: B.G. Teubner, 1928.

820 **Hennig, Richard, et Korholz, G.** *Introduccion a la geopolitica.* La Plata: Talleres Graficos de Guerra Naval, 1941.

821 **Hennings, W., and Rhode-Juchtern, T.** *Geopolitik 2000. Der Politisch-Geographische Alltag Unserer Erde.* Stuttgart: J.B. Metzlersche Verlagsbuchhandlung, 1985.

822 **Hershwy, Burnet.** *The Air Future: A Primer of Aeropolitics.* New York: Duel, Sloan and Pearce, 1943.

823 **Heyden, G.** *Kritik der deutschen geopolitik.* Berlin: Dietz, 1958.

824 **Hinsley, F.H.** *Sovereignty.* New York: Basic Books, 1966.

825 **Hitler, Adolph.** *Mein Kampf.* New York: Stackpole Publishers, 1939.

826 **Huntington, Ellsworth.** *World Power and Evolution.* New Haven, Connecticut: Yale University Press, 1920.

827 **Jacob, Philip E., and Toscano, James V., eds.** *The Integration of Political Communities.* Philadelphia: Lippincott, 1964.

828 **Jacobsen, H.A.** *Karl Haushofer. Leben und Wrk.* 2 vols. Boppard Am Rhein: Harald Boldt Verlag, 1979.

829 **Jas, Marianne.** *The Phenomenology of Geopolitics: The Case of the 1971 Bangladesh Crisis.* Syracuse, New York: Syracuse University, M.A., 1984.

830 **Jasson, Jorge Edmund, et Perlinger, Luis.** *Geopolitica: Origen, Evolucion, Principales Fundamentos del Poder.* Buenos Aires: Biblioteca del official, Circulo Militar, 1948.

831 **Jeffries, William W.** *Geography and National Power.* Annapolis, Maryland: U.S. Naval Institute, 1967.

832 **Jenkins, Ronald W.** *Coalition Defense Versus Maritime Strategy: A Critical Examination Illustrating a New Approach to Geopolitical Analysis.* University Park: Pennsylvania State University, Ph.D., 1985.

833 **Jezowa, Kazimiera.** *Politische Propaganda in der deutschen geographie.* Danzig: Torwarzystwo Przyjaciol Naukii Sztuki, 1933.

834 **Jones, Stephen B.** *Theoretical Studies of National Power.* New Haven, Connecticut: Yale University Press, 1955.

835 **Joshua, Wynfred, and Hahn, Walter F.** *Nuclear Politics: America, France, and Britain.* Beverly Hills, California: Sage Publications, 1973.

836 **Kalijarvi, Thorsten V., ed.** *Modern World Politics*, 3rd ed. New York: Thomas Y. Crowell, 1974.

837 **Kaplan, Morton A., ed.** *New Approaches to International Relations.* New York: John Wiley & Sons, 1968.

838 **Keohane, R.O., and Nye, J.S.** *Power and Interdependence: World Politics in Transition.* Boston: Little Brown, 1977.

839 **Kidd, Benjamin.** *The Science of Power.* 4th ed. London: Methuen, 1918.

840 **Kieffer, John E.** *Realities of World Power.* New York: D. McKay, 1952.

841 **Kirby, Andrew.** *The Politics of Location.* New York: Methuen, 1982.

842 **Kjellen, Rudolf.** *Der staat als lebensform.* Leipzig: S. Hirzel Velag, 1917; Berlin: Kurt Vowinckel, 1924.

843 **Kjellen, Rudolf.** *Die Grossmachte der Geganwart.* Ubersetzt von C. Koch. Leipzig und Berlin: B.G. Teubner, 1914.

844 **Kjellen, Rudolf.** *Die grossmachte vor und nach dem wltkriege: Zweiundzwanzigste auflage der grossmachte Rudolf Kjellans. Herausgegeben von Dr. Karl Haushofer.* Leipzig/Berlin: B.G. Teubner, 1930.

845 **Kjellen, Rudolf.** *Die politische probleme des weltkrieges. Ubersetzt von Dr. Friedrich Stieve.* Leipzig: B.G. Teubner, 1916.

846 **Konrad, G., and Szelenyi I.** *The Intellectuals on the Road to Class Power.* New York: Harcourt Brace Jovanovich, 1979.

847 **Kuczynski, Robert Rene.** *"Living-Space" and Population Problems.* Oxford Pamphlets on World Affairs, No. 8. New York: Farrar and Rinehart, 1939.

848 **Lanchans-Ratzeburg, Manfred.** *Geopolitik und geojurisprudenz.* Iena: Buchlandlung, 1932.

849 **Lassell, H.D., et Kaplan, Abraham.** *Power and Society: A Framework for Political Inquiry.* New Haven, Connecticut: Yale University Press, 1950.

850 **Laves, Walter H.C., ed.** *The Foundations of a More Stable World Order.* Chicago, Illinois: University of Chicago Press, 1941.

851 **Lacoste, Yves.** *Dictionnaire de Geopolitiue.* Paris: Flammarion, 1993.

852 **Lima, Miguel Alves de.** *Geopolitica, Conceito Fundamentais.* Rio de Janeiro: Escola Superior de Guerra, 1959.

853 **Lima, Miguel Alves de.** *O poder nacional: seus fundamentos geograficos.* Rio de Janeiro: Escola Superior de Guerra, 1958.

854 **Lincoln, George A.** *Economics of National Security.* Englewood Cliffs, New Jersey: Prentice-Hall, 1954.

855 **Litwak, R.S.** *Detente and the Nixon Doctrine.* Cambridge: Cambridge University Press, 1984.

856 **Lowe, James Trapier.** *Geopolitics and War: Mackinder's Philosophy of Power.* Washington, D.C.: University Press of America, 1981.

857 **Lukas, G.** *Geopolitik und Politische Geographie.* Gratz: Hammerling, 1929.

858 **Lyon, Thoburn C.** *Air Geography, a Global View.* New York: Van Nostrand, 1951.

859 **Mackinder, Halford J.** *Britain and the British Seas.* New York: Appleton, 1902.

860 **Mahan, Alfred Thayer.** *The Influence of Sea Power upon the French Revolution and Empire, 1793-1812.* Boston: Little Brown, 1892.

861 **Mahan, Alfred Thayer.** *The Influence of Sea Power Upon History. 1600-1783.* Boston: Little Brown, 1890.

862 **Mahan, Alfred Thayer.** *The Interest of America in Sea Power, Present and Future.* Boston: Little Brown, 1897.

863 **Mahan, Alfred Thayer.** *Letters and Papers of Alfred Thayer Mahan, V. 1-3,* edited by Robert Seager II and Doris D. Maguire. Annapolis, Maryland: Naval Institute Press, 1975.

864 **Massialas, Byron G., et Zevin, Jack.** *Political Systems.* Chicago: Rand McNally, 1969.

865 **Matern, R.** *Karl Haushofer und seine Geopolitik in den Jahren der Weimarer Republik und des Dritten Reichese.* Karlsruhe: Diss., 1978.

866 **Mattern, Johannes.** *Geopolitik: Doctrine of National Self-Sufficiency and Empire.* Baltimore, Maryland: Johns Hopkins University Press, 1942.

867 **Maull, Otto.** *Das politische Erbild der Gegenwart.* Berlin: De Gruyter, 1931.

868 **Maull, Otto.** *Das Wesen der Geopolitik.* Leipzig: B.G. Teubner, 1936.

869 **Maull, Otto.** *Die Vereinigten Staaten als Grossreich.* Leipzig: De Gruyter, 1940.

870 **Maull, Otto.** *Politische Grenzen: Weltpolitische Bucherei,* Vol. III. Berlin: Zentral-Verlag, 1928.

871 **McGrenner, Patrick R.** *Mental Geopolitics: National Images and the Geographer's role in the Formation of Global Consciousness.* Bellingham: Western Washington University, M.A., 1984.

872 **Meira Mattos, C. de.** *A Geopolitica e as Projecoes.* Rio de Janeiro: Jose y Olympio, 1977.

873 **Meira Mattos, C. de.** *Geopolitica e Tropicos.* Rio de Janeiro: Biblioteca do Exercito, 1984.

874 **Miller, Lynn H.** *Global Order: Values and Power in International Politics.* Boulder, Colorado: Westview Press, 1985.

875 **Mills, Charles W.** *Power, Politics and People.* New York: Oxford University Press, 1963.

876 **Montague, M.F.A.** *Man and Aggression.* New York: Oxford University Press, 1968.

877 **Morgenthau, H.J., and Thompson, Kenneth W.** *Politics Among Nations: The Struggle for Power and Peace.* 6th Edition. New York: Knopf, 1985.

878 **Navarro Andrade, Ulpiano.** *El determinismo geografico de la historia: la Sociografia y la geopolitica. Ritter, Ratzel, Spencer, Humboldt, Toynbee,* Quito: C.C. Liebmanns, 1957.

879 **Nijman, Jan.** *The Geopolitics of Power and Conflict: Superpowers in the International System, 1945-1992.* London: Belhaven Press, 1993.

880 **Nye, J.S., et al.** *International Regionalism.* Boston: Little Brown, 1968.

881 **Organski, Katherine, et A.F.K.** *Population and World Power.* New York: Knopf, 1961.

882 **O'Loughlin, John, ed.** *Dictionary of Geopolitics.* Westport: Greenwood Press, 1994.

883 **O'Sullivan, Patrick.** *Geopolitics.* Beckenham: Croom Helm, 1986

884 **O'Tuathail, Gearoid.** *Critical Geopolitics: The Social Construction of Space and Place in the Practice of State Craft.* Syracuse, New York: Syracuse University, Ph.D., 1988.

885 **Paddison, Ronan.** *The Fragmented State: The Political Geography of Power.* New York: St. Martin's Press, 1983.

886 **Page, Stanley W.** *The Geopolitics of Leninism.* Columbia, New York City: East European Monographs, Columbia University Press, 1982.

887 **Panten, Donald, ed.** *Current Affairs Atlas.* New York: Facts on File, 1979.

888 **Parker, Geoffrey.** *Western Geopolitical Thought in the Twentieth Century.* London: Croom Helm, 1985.

889 **Parker, W.H.** *Mackinder: Geography as an Aid to Statecraft.* London: Clarendon Press, 1982.

890 **Pearcy, G. Etzel.** *Geopolitics and Foreign Relations.* Washington, D.C.: U.S. Department of State, 1964.

891 **Pearcy, G. Etzel, ed.** *Many Nations: A Survey of the Countries of the World.* Chicago: Rand McNally, 1967.

892 **Pearcy, G. Etzel.** *World Sovereignty.* Fullerton, California: Plycon Press, 1977.

893 **Pearcy, G. Etzel, and Stoneman, Elvyn Arthur.** *A Handbook of New Nations.* London: Van Nostrand, 1968.

894 **Pinochet, Augusto.** *Geopolitica.* Santiago, Chile: Editorial Andres Bello, 1974.

895 **Poulsen, Thomas M.** *Nations and States: A Geographic Background to World Affairs.* Englewood Cliffs, NJ: Prentice-Hall, 1995.

896 **Renner, George T., and Others.** *Global Geography.* New York: Thomas Y. Crowell, 1944.

897 **Rona, Thomas.** *Our Changing Geo-Political Premises.* New Brunswick, New Jersey: Transaction Books, 1982.

898 **Rosecrance, Richard N.** *Action and Reaction in World Politics.* Boston: Little Brown, 1963.

899 **Rosenau, James N., ed.** *In Search of Global Patterns.* New York: The Free Press, 1976.

900 **Rosenau, James N.** *The Study of Global Interdependence: Essays on the Transnationalization of World Affairs.* New York: Nichols Publishing, 1980.

901 **Rosenau, James N.** *Turbulence in World Politics: A Theory of Change and Continuity.* Princeton: Princeton University Press, 1990.

902 **Roucek, Joseph S., ed.** *Contemporary Political Ideologies.* New York: Philosophical Library, 1961.

903 **Russell, B.** *Power: A New Social Analysis.* London: Allen & Unwin, 1938.

904 **Schatz, Gerald S.** *Science, Technology and Sovereignty in the Polar Regions.* Lexington, Massachusetts: Lexington Books/D.C. Heath, 1974.

905 **Schilling, P.** *El Expansionismo Brasileno.* Buenos Aires: El Cid, 1978.

906 **Schmidt-Haack.** *Geopolitischer Typenatlas.* Gotha: Perthes, 1929.

907 **Schnitzer, E.W.** *German Geopolitics Revised: A Survey of Geopolitical Writings in Germany Today.* Santa Monica, California: The Rand Corporation, 1954.

908 **Schurmann, Franz H.** *The Logic of World Power: An Inquiry into the Origins, Currents and Contradictions of World Politics.* New York: Pantheon, 1974.

909 **Schwartzberg, Joseph E.** *Global Interdependence.* Minnesota: World Affairs Center, 1976.

910 **Schwarzenberger, Georg.** *Power Politics.* 2nd edition. London: Stevens, 1964.

911 **Scott, A.M.** *The Functioning of the International Political System.* New York: Macmillan, 1967.

912 **Segal, Gerald.** *The World Affairs Companion: The Essential One-Volume Guide to Global Issues.* Rev. ed. London: Simon and Schuster Ltd., 1993.

913 **Semjonow, Juri.** *Die faschistische Geopolitik im Dienste des amerikanischen Imperialismus.* Translated by J. Harhammer from original 1952 Russian edition. East Berlin: Dietz Verlag, 1955.

914 **Sen, D.K.** *Basic Principles of Geopolitics and History.* Delhi: Concept Publishing, 1975.

915 **Senghaas, D.** *Weltwirtschaftsordnung und Entwicklungspolitik. Pladoger fur Dissozation.* Frankfurt: Suhrkamp, 1977.

916 **Seversky, A.P.** *Victory through Air Power.* New York, 1942.

917 **Short, Ernest H.** *Esqisse de geopolitique.* Paris: Payot, 1936.

918 **Short, Ernest H.** *Handbook of Geopolitics.* London: Allen & Unwin, 1935.

919 **Singer, M.** *Weak States in a World of Powers.* New York: The Free Press, 1972.

920 **Singh, Govind Saran.** *World Regions of Political Power.* Dharwar: Karnatak University, 1965.

921 **Slater, Robert O.; Schutz, Barry M.; and Dorr, Steven R.,** eds. *Global Transformation and the Third World.* Boulder, CO: Lynne Rienner Publishers, 1993.

922 **Smith, Anthony D.** *The Geopolitics of Information: How Western Culture Dominates the World.* London: Faber, 1980.

923 **Sombart, Werner,** ed. *Volk und Raum.* Hamburg: Hanseatische Verlagsanstalt, 1928.

924 **Sprout, Harold H., and Sprout, Margaret,** eds. *Foundations of National Power; Readings on World Politics and American Security,* 2nd ed. Princeton, New Jersey: Princeton University Press, 1951.

925 **Spykman, Nicholas J.** *America's Strategy in World Politics: The United States and the Balance of Power.* New York: Harcourt Brace, 1942.

926 **Spykman, Nicholas J.** *The Geography of the Peace.* Edited by Helen R. Nicholl. New York: Harcourt Brace, 1944.

927 **U.S. Department of State.** *Status of the World's Nations.* Washington, D.C.: Geographic Bulletin No. 2. Bureau of Intelligence and Research, U.S. Department of State, 1964.

928 **Steinmetzler, Johanned.** *Die Anthropogeographie dur Friedrich Ratzel und Ihre ideengeschichtlicher Wurzeln.* Bonn: Im Selbsteurlag des Geographoschen Instituts der Universitat Bonn, 1956.

929 **Stoll, Richard J. and Ward, Michael D.,** eds.

Power in World Politics. Boulder, Colorado: Lynne Rienner Publishers, 1988.

930 **Strack, Conrad William.** *Foundations of Geographic Analysis.* University Park: Pennsylvania State University, Ph.D., 1971.

931 *Strategy for Peace, 14th Conference Report.* Airlie House, Warrenton, Virginia, October 11-14, 1973. Muscatine, Iowa: The Stanley Foundation, 1973.

932 **Strausz-Hupe, Robert.** *Axis America: Hitler Plans our Future.* New York: Putnam, 1941.

933 **Strausz-Hupe, Robert** *The Balance of Tomorrow; Power and Foreign Policy in the United States.* New York: Putnam, 1945.

934 **Strausz-Hupe, Robert** *Geopolitics; The Struggle for Space and Power.* New York: Putnam, 1942.

935 **Tapinos, Georges, and Piotrow, Phyllis T.** *Six Billion People: Demographic Dilema and World Politics.* New York: McGraw-Hill, 1978.

936 **Taylor, C.L. and Jodice, D.A.** *World Handbook of Political and Social Indicators.* 3rd edition, Vol. 1. *Cross-National Attributes and Rates of Change.* New Haven, Connecticut: Yale University Press, 1983.

937 **Taylor, Griffith.** *Our Evolving Civilization: An Introduction to Geopacifics; Geographial Aspects of the Path Toward World Peace.* Toronto: University of Toronto Press, 1946.

938 **Taylor, Peter J.** *Geopolitics Revived.* Newcastle-upon-Tyne: University of Newcastle-upon-Tyne, Department of Geography, Seminar Papers, No. 53, 1988.

939 **Toal, Gerard J.P.** *Geo-Politics: The Politics of Writing Spaces and Places.* Syracuse, New York: Syracuse University, Ph.D., 1988.

940 **Tosevic, Dimitri J.** *The World Crisis in Maps.* New York: Funk, 1954.

941 **Ultee, Marteen,** ed. *Adapting to Conditions: War and Society in the Eighteenth Century.* Birmingham: University of Alabama, 1986.

942 **United Nations.** Library. *List of Countries and Territories of the World. March, 1959.* New York: United Nations, 1959.

943 **U.S. Army War College.** *Power Analysis of the Nation-State.* Discussion Topic 2-B. Pennsylvania: Carlisle Barracks, 1960.

944 **United States.** Congress. Office of Technology Assessment. *Global Models, World Futures, and Public Policy: A Critique.* Washington, D.C.: U.S. Government Printing Office, 1982.

945 **United States**. *Major Political Entities of the World*. Rev. Washington, D.C.: U.S. Department of State, 1962.

946 **Van Houtte, J.A.** *Geopolitique. Introduction aux facteurs geographiques de l'histoire et de la politique*. Bruxelles: Le Pennon, 1946.

947 **Verba, S., Nie, N.H., and Kim, J.O.** *Participation and Political Equality: A Seven-Nation Comparison*. Cambridge: Cambridge University Press, 1978.

948 **Vicenes, J.** *Tratado General de geopolitica*. Barcelona: Teida, 1950.

949 **Visintin, L.** *Atlante geopolitico universale*. Novare: Institut Agostini, 1947.

950 **Vivo Escoto, Jorge A.** *Guia de Estudio de geopolitica*. Mexico: Univ. Nacional Autonoma de Mexico, 1960.

951 **Vivo Escoto, Jorge A.** *La Geopolitica*. Mexico: El colegio de Mexico, Centro de Estudios sociales, 1943.

952 **Wallerstein, Immanuel.** *Geopolitics and Geoculture: Essays on the Changing World-System*. Cambridge: Cambridge University Press, 1991.

953 **Walsh, Edmund A.** *An Essay on Geopolitics. Origin, Meaning and Value*. Washington, D.C.: Georgetown University, School of Foreign Service, 1942.

954 **Walsh, Edmund A.** *The Politics of the World-Economy*. Cambridge: Cambridge University Press, 1984.

955 **Warntz, William.** *Geography Now and Then, Some Notes on the History of Academic Geography in the United States*. New York: American Geographical Society, Research Series No. 25, 1964.

956 **Weigert, Hans Werner.** *Generals and Geographers: The Twilight of Geopolitics*. New York: Oxford University Press, 1942.

957 **Weigert, Hans Werner.** *German Geopolitics*. London: Oxford University Press, 1941.

958 **Wesson, Robert G.** *The Russian Dilemma: A Political and Geopolitical View*. New Brunswick, New Jersey: Rutgers University Press, 1974.

959 **Wittfogel, Karl A.** *Oriental Despotism; A Comparative Study of Total Power*. New Haven, Connecticut: Yale University Press, 1957.

960 **Whittlesey, Derwent S. with Charles C. Colby; and Richard Hartshorne.** *German Strategy of World Conquest*. New York: Farrar and Rinehart, 1942.

961 **Zoppo, C.E., and Zorgbibe, C., eds.** *On Geopolitics: Classical and Nuclear*. Dordrecht, Netherlands: Martinus Nijhoff, 1985.

Journals

962 **Abdel-Malik, Anonar.** "Geopolitics and National Movements: An Essay on the Dialectics of Imperialism." In *Radical Geography: Alternative Viewpoints on Contemporary Social Issues*. Richard Peck, ed. Chicago: Maaronfa Ress, 1977, 293-307.

963 **Agnew, John A.** "Sociologizing the Geographical Imagination: Spatial Concept in the World-System Perspective." *Political Geography Quarterly*, 1, No. 2 (April, 1982), 151-166.

964 **Alexander, Lewis M.** "The New Geopolitics: A Critique." *Journal of Conflict Resolution*, 5, No. 4 (December, 1961), 407-410.

965 **Almond, Gabriel A.** "A Developmental Approach to Political Systems." *World Politics*, 17, No. 2 (January, 1965), 183-215.

966 **Ancel, Jacques.** "Geopolitik et Geographie politique." *Revue d'Allemagne*. 6, No. 57 (July 15, 1932), 672-691.

967 **Ashley, R.** "The Geopolitics of Geopolitical Space: Toward a Critical Social Theory of International Politics." *Alternatives*, 12, No. 4 (December, 1987), 403-434.

968 **Atencio, Jorge E.** "Influencia geopolitica do mar." *A Defesa Nacional*. No. 463 (1953), 83-87; No. 464 (1953), 103-107; et No. 465 (1953), 71-76.

969 **Azved, Arnoldo de.** "A geografia a servico da politica." *Boletin Paulista de geografia*, (1955), 42-68.

970 **Backheuser, Everardo.** "Aspectos geopoliticos do mar." *A Defesa Nactional*, 538 (Maio, 1959), 131-138, and 539 (Junho, 1959), 83-86.

971 **Backheuser, Everardo.** "Geopolitica e geografia politica." *Boletin do Ministerio do Trabalho industria e comercio (Rio de Janeiro)*, 9, No. 98 (Outubro, 1942), 315-328.

972 **Backheuser, Everardo.** "Geopolitica e geografia politica." *A Defesa Nacional*, 541 (Agosto, 1959), 111-126.

973 **Backheuser, Everardo.** "Geopolitica e geografia politica." *Revista Brasileira de Geografia*, 4, No. 1 (Jan-Marco, 1942), 21-23.

974 Backheuser, Everardo. "Leis geopoliticas da evolucao dos estados. *Boletin Geografico*, 8, No. 88 (Julho, 1950), 419-430.

975 Backheuser, Everardo. "A politica e geopolitica, segundo Kjellen." *Boletim Geografico*, 10, No. 110 (Set.-Oct., 1952), 534-539.

976 Bailly, Antoines. "Une Geo-politique de la Regio Genevensis." *Geographica Helvetica*, 42 Jahr, Heft 3 (1987), 191-202.

977 Baldwin, David A. "Interdependence and Power: A Conceptual Analysis." *International Organization*, 34, No. 4 (Autumn, 1980), 471-506.

978 Bassin, Mark. "Race Contra Space: The Conflict Between Geopolitik and National Socialism." *Political Geography Quarterly*, 6, No. 2 (April, 1987), 115-134.

979 Baumann, M. "Geopolitik und Geschichte." *Zeitschrift fur geopolitik.* 9 (1934), 586.

980 Billeb, Eberhard. "The Airplane as a Geopolitical Force." In *The World of General Haushofer*, Andreas Dorpalen, ed. New York: Farrar and Rinehart, 1942, 124-134.

981 Billeb, Eberhard. "Geopolitische Auswirkungen der Luftfahrt." *Zeitschrift fur Geopolitik*, 14, Jahrg, Heft 12 (Dezember, 1937), 996-1004.

982 Blouet, Brian W. "Halford Mackinder's Heartland Thesis: Formation Influences." *Great Plains-Rocky Mountain Geographical Journal*, 5, No. 1 (December, 1976), 2-6.

983 Blouet, Brian W. "The Maritime Origins of Mackinder's Heartland Thesis." *Great Plains-Rocky Mountain Geographical Journal*, 4 (1973), 6-11.

984 Blouet, Brian W. "Sir Halford Mackinder as British High Commissioner to South Russia, 1919-1920." *Geographical Journal.* 142, Part 2 (July, 1976), 228-236.

985 Borgese, G.A. "Geopolitical Front." *Nation*, 155, No. 11 (September 12, 1942), 206-209.

986 Bowman, Isaiah. "Commanding Our Wealth." *Science*, 100, No. 2594 (September 15, 1944), 229-241.

987 Bowman, Isaiah. "Geography vs. Geopolitics." *Geographical Review*, 32, No. 4 (October, 1942), 646-658.

988 Bowman, Isaiah. "Political Geography of Power." *Geographical Review*, 32, No. 2 (April, 1942), 349-352.

989 Brams, Steven J. "Transaction Flows in the International System." *American Political Science Review*, 60, No. 1 (December, 1966), 880-898.

990 Bravo Bravo, L. "Vision Geopolitica Mundial. (A World Geopolitical View)." *Revista Cltilens de Geopolitica*, 2, No. 2 (1986), 5-22.

991 Brown, Lester R. "Human Needs and the Security of Nations." *Headline Series*, 238, No. 2 (February, 1978), 3-63.

992 Brucan, Silviu. "The Global Crisis." *International Studies Quarterly*, 28, No. 1 (March, 1984), 97-109.

993 Brunn, Stanley D., and Mingst, K.A. "Geopolitics." In *Progress in Political Geography*. Beckenham: Croom Helm, 1985, 41-76.

994 Buehrig, Edward H. "The International Pattern of Authority." *World Politics*, 17, No. 3 (April, 1965), 369-385.

995 Bundy, William P. "Elements of Power." *Foreign Affairs*, 56, No. 1 (October, 1977), 1-26.

996 Cahnman, Werner J. "Methods of Geopolitics." *Social Forces*, 21, No. 2 (December, 1942), 147-154.

997 Carr, E.H. "The Forms of Political Power." In *Foundations of National Power*, H.H. Sprout and M. Sprout (eds.). Princeton, New Jersey: Princeton University Press. 1945, 31-38.

998 Champier, Laurent. "La Sarre; Essai d'interpretation geopolitique." *Arbeiten aus dem Geographischen Institut, Universitat des Saarlandes*, 1 (1956), 3-74.

999 Chaudhuri, Manoranjan. "Geopolitical Aspects of World Population." *Calcutta Geographical Review*, 11, No. 3-4 (September-December, 1949), 48-54.

1000 Chubb, Basil. "Geopolitics." *Irish Geography*, 3, No. 1 (1954), 15-25.

1001 Clark, Ian. "Autonomy and Dependence in Recent Indo-Soviet Relations." *Australian Outlook*, 31, No. 1 (April, 1977), 147-164.

1002 Claval, Paul. "Frankreich und das globale geopolitische Gleichgewicht." *Geographische Rundschau* [Braunschweig] Jahr, 46, Heft 1 (Januar, 1994), 4-10.

1003 Clokie, H. McD. "Geopolitics--New Super-Science or Old Art?" *Canadian Journal of Economics and Political Science*, 10, No. 4 (November, 1944), 492-502.

1004 Cochran, C. "Mackinder's Heartland Theory: A Review." *Association of the North Dakota Geographers Bulletin*, 24 (1972), 29-31.

1005 **Cohen, Saul B.** "Global Geopolitical Change in the Post-Cold War Era." *Association of American Geographers Annals* [Washington, D.C.], 81, No. 4 (December 1991), 551-580.

1006 **Cohen, Saul B.** "Policy Prescriptions for the Post Cold War World." *The Professional Geographer* [New York], 44, No. 1 (February, 1992), 13-16.

1007 **Cohen, Saul B.** "The Contemporary Geopolitical Setting: A Proposal for Global Geopolitical Equilibrium." In *Essays in Political Geography*, Charles A. Fisher, ed. London: Methuen, 1968, 61-74.

1008 **Cohen, Saul B.** "The World Geopolitical System in Retrospect and Prospect." *Journal of Geography*, 89, No. 1 (January-February, 1990), 2-12.

1009 **Cohen, Saul B.** "A New Map of Global Geopolitical Equilibrium: A Developmental Approach. *Political Geography Quarterly*, 1, No. 3 (July, 1982), 223-242.

1010 **Coker, Christopher.** "Post-Modernity and the End of the Cold War: Has War Been Disinvented?" *Review of International Stsudies* [Cambridge], 18, No. 3 (July, 1992), 189-198.

1011 **Collins, Randall.** "Does Modern Technology Change the Rules of Geopolitics?" *Journal of Political and Military Sociology*, 9, No. 2 (Fall, 1981), 163-177.

1012 **Cortes Alonso, Vicenta.** "Geopolitica del sureste de los Estados Unidos (1750-1800)." *Revista de Indias*, Ano 12, Num. 47 (Enero-Marzo, 1952.) 23-47.

1013 **Croisat, Victor J.** "O Mundo Estavel de Halford Mackinder." *A Defesa Nacional*, 547 (February, 1960), 125-130.

1014 **Cunha, Ruy Vieira da.** "A historia, a geografia e o poder nacional." *A Defesa Nacional*, 624 (Marco-Abril, 1969), 57-74.

1015 **Dalby, S.** "Critical Geopolitics: Discourse, Difference and Dissent." *Environment and Planning D: Society and Space*, 9 (1991), 261-283.

1016 **de Diaz Villegas, Jose.** "Lecciones geopoliticas de la guerra actual." *Boletin de la Real sociedad geografica*, Tomo 78, Num. 4-6 (Abril-Junio, 1942), 203-233.

1017 **DeBres, Karen.** "Political Geographers of the Past IV: George Renner and the Great Map Scandal of 1942." *Political Geography Quarterly*, 5, No. 4 (October, 1986), 385-394.

1018 **Delgado de Carvalho, Carlos, and de Castro,**

Therezinha. "Geografia Politica e Geopolitica: Estudos e ensaios." *Boletim Geografico*, 14, No. 133 (July-August, 1956), 382-391.

1019 "Problemas de geopolitica." *Boletin de la Sociedad Argentina de estudios geograficos GAEA*, 24 (Julio, 1947), 37-46.

1020 **Dharamdasani, M.D.** "The Problem of General Theory in International Politics." *International Review of History and Political Science*, 20, No. 3 (August, 1983), 66-75.

1021 **Diner, D.** "'Grunbuch des Planeten'. Zur Geopolitik Karl Haushofers." *Vierteljahreshefte fur Zeitgeschichte*, 32 (1984), 1-28.

1022 **Dittrich, E.** "Raumordmung, Raumordnungspolitik and Gesellschaftspolitik." *Informationen*, 14 (1966), 417-446.

1023 **Djordjevic, J.** "Progres technique et systemes politiques." *Revue internationale de sciences sociales*, 2 (1960), 202-214.

1024 **Domschke, W., and Drexl, A.** "Location and Layout Planning: An International Bibliography." *Lecture Notes in Economics*, 238 (1955), 1-134.

1025 **Doran, Ronald J.** "Changing Geopolitical Views." *Journal of Geography*, 58, No. 1 (January, 1959), 32-33.

1026 **Dow, Roger.** "Proster; A Geographical Study of Russia and the United States." *Russian Review*, 1, No. 1 (November, 1941), 6-19.

1027 **Dryer, Charles R.** "Mackinder's 'World Island' and Its American 'Satellite'." *Geographical Review*, 9, No. 1 (March, 1920), 205-207.

1028 **Dugan, Arthur Butler.** "Mackinder and His Critics Reconsidered." *Journal of Politics*, 24, No. 2 (May, 1962), 241-257.

1029 **Dumont, Maurice E.** "Geographie Politique et Geopolitique." *L'Information Geographique*, 19, No. 4 (July-August, 1955), 151-159.

1030 **Dumont, Maurice E.** "Politicke Aardrykskunde en Geopolitick." *Bulletin de la Societe Belge d'Etudes Geographiques*, 25, No. 1 (1956), 187-209.

1031 **Dupon, Jean-Francois.** "Frankreich im Pazifik-- Gegen Alle Widerstande." *Geographische Rundschau* [Braunschweig], Jahr. 46, Heft 1 (Januar, 1994), 28-34.

1032 **East, W. Gordon.** "How Strong is the Heartland?" *Foreign Affairs*, 29, No. 1 (October, 1950), 78-93, and 31, No. 4 (July, 1953), 619-633.

1033 **Ehrnorn, Irmgard**. "Ist Geopolitik 'Neo-Nazismus'?" *Zeitschrift fur Geopolitik*, Jahrg 24, Heft 7/8 (Juli-August, 1953), 438-440.

1034 **Fairgrieve, James**. "Geography and World Power." *Journal of Geography*, 21, No. 8 (November, 1922), 285-294.

1035 **Faucher, Daniel**. "Espace vital et geographie." *Bulletin de l'Universite de Toulouse*, 68, No. 4 (1940), 121-141.

1036 **Fawcett, C.B.** "Marginal and Interior Lands of the Old World." *Geography*, 32, No. 155, Part 1 (March, 1947), 1-12.

1037 **Fischer, Eric**. "A German Geographer Reviews German Geography." *Geographical Review*, 38, No. 2 (April, 1948), 307-310.

1038 **Fischer, Eric**. "German Geographical Literature, 1940-1945." *Geographical Review*, 36, No. 1 (January, 1946), 92-100.

1039 **Fischer, M.** "Haushofer's Geopolitical Theories." *Commonweal*, 37, No. 7 (February 19, 1943), 446-447.

1040 **Fitzgerald, Walter**. "Geography and International Settlement." *Nature*, 152, No. 3864 (November 20, 1943), 589-591.

1041 **Fleig, Hans**. "Die Geopolitische Erbschaft der Sieger." *Zeitscchrift fur Geopolitik*, Jahrg 24, Heft 3 (Marz, 1953), 129-130.

1042 **Freeman, Otis W.** "Teaching Geographic Relationships in World Problems." *Journal of Geography*, 35, No. 3 (March, 1936), 90-98.

1043 **Frey, Hans**. "Geographie, Krieg, Geopolitik." *Der Schweizer Geograph*, 20, Jahrg, Heft 1/2 (Februar, 1943), 3-9.

1044 **Furniss, Edgar S.** "The Contribution of Nicholas John Spykman to the Study of International Politics." *World Politics*, 4, No. 3 (April, 1952), 382-401.

1045 **Gardner, Gerard**. "Le Valeur Strategique du Grand-Nord." *L'Actualite Economique*, 29, No. 3 (October-December, 1953), 525-547.

1046 **German, F. Clifford**. "A Tentative Evaluation of World Power." *Journal of Conflict Resolution*, 4, No. 1 (March, 1960), 138-144.

1047 **Giblin-Delvallet, Beatrice**. "Geopotitique des regions Francaisses." *Herodote*, 40 (Janvier-Mars, 1986), 32-51.

1048 **Giblin-Delvallet, Beatrice**. "'La Communaute Nationale en Question' et le Debat Sur L'amenagement du Terroire: Une Operation Geopolitique." *Herodote*, No. 72/73 (Janvier-Juin, 1994), 9-21.

1049 **Giblin-Delvallet, Beatrice**. "L'immigration et la nation: Un Probleme Geopolitique." *Herodote* [Paris], No. 69/70 (Avril-Septembre, 1993), 9-29.

1050 **Gicouate, Moises**. "A Geopolitica no estudo da geografica e da historia." *Revista Brasileira de Estodos Pedagogicos*, 6, No. 17 (November, 1945), 213-229.

1051 **Gilbert, Edmund W.** "The Right Honourable Sir Halford J. Mackinder, P.C., 1861-1947." *Geographical Journal*, 110, Nos. 1-3 (July-September, 1947), 94-99 and 127, No. 1 (March, 1961), 27-29.

1052 **Gilbert, Edmund W., and Parker, W.H.** "Mackinder's 'Democratic Ideals and Reality' After 50 Years." *Geographical Journal*, 135, No. 2 (June, 1969), 228-231.

1053 **Glassner, Martin Ira**. "Political Geography of Contemporary Events VII: The View From the Near North-South Americans View Antarctica and the Southern Ocean Geopolitically." *Political Geography Quarterly*, 4, No. 4 (October, 1985), 329-342.

1054 **Gordejuela, Amando**. "Geopolitica o geografia politica. Su posible contenido." *Estudios Geograficos*, 2 (1941), 5-33.

1055 **Gottmann, Jean**. "The Background of Geopolitics." *Military Affairs*, 6 (1942), 197-205.

1056 **Gottmann, Jean**. "Vauban and Modern Geography." *Geographical Review*, 34, No. 1 (January, 1944), 120-128.

1057 **Graham, J.** "The Ego-Politics of Nixon: Is His Journey Really Necessary." *Spectator*, 225, No. 7423 (3 October, 1970), 356-357.

1058 **Greenwood, Thomas**. "Der Geist der Geopolitik." *Zeitschrift fur Geopolitik*, 23, No. 10 (October, 1952), 576-581.

1059 **Greenwood, Thomas**. "O Espirito da Geopolitica." *A Defesa Nacional*, 539 (Junho, 1959), 151-156.

1060 **Grigg, D.B.** "The Logic of Regional Systems." *Annals of the Association of American Geographers*, 55, No. 4 (December, 1965), 465-491.

1061 **Griswold, A. Whitney**. "Paving the Way for Hitler." *Atlantic Monthly*, 167, No. 3 (March, 1941), 314-321.

1062 **Guardia, Ernesto de la.** "Consideraciones geopoliticas." *Revista del instituto de Derecho Internacional*, 2, No. 9-10 (September-October, 1949), 1667-1673.

1063 **Guerra, Antonio Teixeira.** "A regiao geografica e sua importancia para o poder nacional." *Revista Brasileira de geografia*, 26, No. 3 (Julho-Septembro, 1964), 459-463.

1064 **Gyorgy, Andrew.** "The Application of German Geopolitics: Geosciences." *American Political Science Review*, 37, No. 4 (August, 1943), 677-686.

1065 **Gyorgy, Andrew.** "Geopolitics: The New German Science." *International Relations*, 3, No. 3 (May, 1944), 141-304.

1066 **Gyorgy, Andrew.** "On Systems and International Regions." *World Politics*, 27, No. 2 (January, 1975), 147-174.

1067 **Halkin, J.** "Geopolitique et geographie politique." *Cercle des Geographes Liegeois*, (1929), 1-20.

1068 **Hall, Arthur R.** "Mackinder and the Course of Events." *Annals of the Association of American Geographers*, 45, No. 2 (June, 1955), 109-126.

1069 **Hall, Henrique R.** "Geopolitica." *Naco Armada*, 1 (1939), 32-33.

1070 **Haltenberger, Michael.** "Das geopolitische Steigen und Sinken der Staatsmacht und der geopolitische Zyklus." *Petermans Mittellungen*, 71, Heft 2 (Juni, 1925), 110-111.

1071 **Haltenberger, Michael.** "Territorialkurven und geopolitische Zylenkurven." *Petermans Mittellungen*, 73, Heft 1 (Marz, 1927), 33.

1072 **Hannah, Norman B.** "The Five Worlds of Detente: A Strategic Apercu." *National Review*, 29, No. 18 (May 13, 1977), 541-545.

1073 **Harvey, David W.** "The Geopolitics of Capitalism." In *Social Relations and Spatial Structures*, D. Gregory and J. Urry, eds. London: Macmillan, 1985a, 128-163.

1074 **Harper, Lawrence A.** "Geopolitics and Mercantilism." *American Historical Association, Annual Report, 1942*, 3 (1944), 111-121.

1075 **Harrison, Richard E.** "The Face of One World: Five Perspectives for an Understanding of the Air Age." *Saturday Review of Literature*, 27, No. 27 (July 1, 1944), 5-6.

1076 **Hassert, Kurt.** "Friedrich Ratzel: Sein Leiben and Wirken." *Geographische Zeitschrift*, 11 Jahrg, Heft 6 (Juin, 1905), 305-325 et Heft 7 (Juli, 1905), 361-380.

1077 **Hassinger, H.** "Der Staat als Landschaftsgestalter." *Zeitschrift fur Geopolitik*, 9, Heft 2-3 (Februar-Marz, 1932), 117-122 et 182-187.

1078 **Hatfield, H.W.** "Haushoferism." *New Republic*, 108, No. 5 (No. 1470) (February 1, 1943), 155-156, 158.

1079 **Haushofer, Karl.** "Geopolitik in den Handbuchern des Wissens." *Zeitschrift fur Geopolitik*, Jahrg 11, Heft 8 (August, 1934), 525-526.

1080 **Haushofer, Karl** "Geopolitik in den Handbuchern des Wissens." *Zeitschriftfur Geopolitik*, Jahrg 12, Heft 1 (Januar, 1935), 56-57.

1081 **Haushofer, Karl** "Hochbilb als Helfer der Geopolitik." *Zeitschrift fur Geopolitik*, Jahrg 12, Heft 1 (Januar, 1935), 48-54.

1082 **Haushofer, Karl** "Pflicht und Anspruch der Geopolitik als Wissenschaft." *Zeitschrift fur Geopolitik*, Jahrg 12, Heft 1 (Juli, 1935), 443-448.

1083 **Haushofer, Karl.** "Zwei Jahrzehnte Geopolitik." *Zeitschrift fur Geopolitik*, Jahrg 20, Heft 4 (April, 1943), 183-184.

1084 **Hecker, Edgar Mahn.** "Algunas consideraciones sobre la geopolitica." *Economia*, 8, No. 24-25 (Nobembre de, 1947), 45-56.

1085 **Henning, Von R.** "Das Wasser Als Geopolitischer Faktor." *Geographische Zietschrift*, Jahrg 35, Heft 1 (Januar,1929), 5-12.

1086 **Henrikson, Alan K.** "The Emanation of Power." *International Security*, 6, No. 1 (Summer, 1981), 152-164.

1087 **Henrikson, Alan K.** "The Moralist as Geopolitician." *The Fletcher Forum: A Journal of Studies in International Affairs*, 5, No. 2 (1981), 391-414.

1088 **Henske, Henning.** "Karl Haushofer: His Role in German Geopolitics and the Nazi Politics." *Political Geography Quarterly*, 6, No. 2 (April, 1987), 135-144.

1089 **Herausgeber, Der.** "Existenz, Geopolitik als Weltverantwortung." *Zeitshrift fur Geopolitik*, Jahrg 38, Heft 1 (Januar-Februar-Marz, 1967), 1-4.

1090 **Herb, G. Henrik.** "Persuasive Cartography in Geopolitik and National Socialism." *Political Geography Quarterly*, 8, No. 3 (July, 1989), 289-304.

1091 **Herold, David.** "Political Geography" und "Geopolitics." *Die Erde*, 105, Jahrg, Heft 2 (1974), 200-213.

1092 **Herrick, Francis H.** "World Island and Heartland--The Strategical Theories of Sir Halford John Mackinder." *South Atlantic Quarterly*, 43, No. 3 (July, 1944), 248-255.

1093 **Hettner, Von Alfred.** "Die Geopolitik und die Politische Geographie." *Geographische Zeitschrift*, 35 Jahrg, Heft 6 (June, 1929), 332-336.

1094 **Hinder, Rolf.** "Eine neue herzland-Theorie." *Zeitschrift fur geopolitik*, 39, No. 2 (Marz-April, 1968), 52-55.

1095 **Hinder, Rolf.** "Geopolitik als Weg Zur Weltbefriedung." *Zeitshcrift fur Geopolitik*, Jahrg 29, Heft 4 (April, 1958), 23-24.

1096 **Hinder, Rolf.** "Vom Sinn der Modernen Geopolitik." *Zeitschrift fur Geopolitik*, Jahrg 29, Heft 1 (Januar, 1958), 35-38.

1097 **Hinder, Rolf.** "Wahre anstatt 'legitime' Geopolitik." *Zeitschrift fur Geopolitik*, Jahrg 24, Heft 7/8 (Juli-August, 1953), 440-443.

1098 **Hinrichs, Emil.** "Geopolitische und wehregeographische Betrachtungen in Erdkundeunterricht." *Zeitschrift fur Erdkunde*, 10, Jahrg, Heft 11 (November, 1942), 654-665.

1099 **Horlings, Albert.** "Who Rules Russia Rules the World." *New Republic.* (An account of Karl Haushofer's geopolitics) 105, No. 1 (July 7, 1941), 11-13.

1100 **Horrabin, J.F.** "Os fatores geograficos na historia dos povos." *A Defesa Nacional*, 419 (1949), 149-153.

1101 **Huet, Rafael.** "Geopolitica y objectivos nacionales." *Dinamica Social*, 14, No. 145 (Abril, 1963), 23-24.

1102 **Hutchinson, P.** "The Father of Geopolitics." *Christian Century*, 59, No. 40 (October 7, 1942), 1216-1217.

1103 **Hutchinson, P.** "Geopolitical Balance Sheet." *Christian Century.* (A Review of H.W. Weigert's Generals and Geographers) 60, No. 1 (January 6, 1943), 16-17.

1104 **Jackson, W.A. Douglas.** "Mackinder and the Communist Orbit." *Canadian Geographer.* 6, No. 1 (Spring, 1962), 12-21.

1105 **Jacobsen, Hans-Adolf.** "'Kampf um Lebenstraum': Karl Haushofer's 'Geopolitik' und der Nationalsocialismus. Aus Politik und Zeitgeschichte." (Supplement to *Das Parlament*), B34-35(79), 17-29.

1106 **Jacobsen, Hans-Adolf.** "Kampfun Lebenstraum zur rolle des geopolitikers Karl Haushofer im Dritten Reich." *German Studies Review*, 4, No. 1 (February, 1981), 79-104.

1107 **Jay, Peter.** "Regionalism as Geopolitics." *Foreign Affairs*, 58, No. 3 (Spring, 1980), 485-514.

1108 **Jelden, Helmut.** "Geopolitik in der Ranmschule des Krieges." *Zeitschrift fur Geopolitik.* Jahrg 20, Heft 3 (Marz, 1943), 107-110.

1109 **Jessop, R.** "Recent Theories of the Capitalist State." *Cambridge Journal of Economics*, 1, No. 4 (December, 1977), 353-373.

1110 **Jones, Stephen B.** "Global Strategic Views." *Geographical Review*, 45, No. 4 (October, 1955), 492-508.

1111 **Jones, Stephen B.** "The Power Inventory and National Strategy." *World Politics*, 6, No. 4 (July, 1954), 421-452.

1112 **Joyner, Christopher C.** "Polar Politics in the 1980's: Some Preliminary Thoughts on Polar Contrasts and Geopolitical Considerations." *International Studies Notes*, 411(3) (1985), 1-4.

1113 **Kearns, G.** "Closed Space and Political Practice: Frederick Jackson Turner and Halford Mackinder." *Environment and Planning D: Society and Space*, D1, No. 1 (March, 1984), 23-34.

1114 **Kelly, Philip L.** "Geopolitical Themes in the Writings of General Carlos de Meira Mattos of Brazil." *Journal of Latin American Studies*, 16, Part 2 (1984), 439-461.

1115 **Kish, George.** "Geografia politica na geo-politica." *Revista Brasileira de geografia*, 4, No. 4 (Out.-Dez., 1942), 853-862.

1116 **Kish, George.** "Global Strategic Views." *Geographical Review.* 45, No. 4 (Octber, 1955), 492-508.

1117 **Kish, George.** "Political Geography into Geopolitics; Recent Trends in Germany." *Geographical Review*, 32, No. 4 (October, 1942), 632-645.

1118 **Knight, David B.** "Self-Determination as a Geopolitical Force." *Journal of Geography*, 82, No. 4 (July-August, 1983), 148-152.

1119 **Korinman, Michael.** "Naissance et renaissance d'un project geopolitique." *Herodote*, No. 46 (Janvier-Mars, 1988), 19-35.

1120 **Kost, Klaus.** "Begriffe und Macht-Die Funktion der Geopolitik als Ideologie (Terms and Power: The function of Geopolitics as an Ideology.)" *Geographische Zeitschrift*, 74 Jahr, Heft 1 (Januar, 196), 14-30.

1121 **Kristof, Ladis K.D.** "The Origins and Evolution of Geopolitics." *Journal of Conflict Resolution*, 4, No. 1 (March, 1960), 15-51.

1122 **Kruszewski, Charles.** "The Pivot of History. *Foreign Affairs*, 32, No. 3 (April, 1954), 388-401.

1123 **LaCoste, Yves.** "Democratie et Geopolitique." *Herodote* [Paris], No. 69/70 (Avril-Septembre, 1993), 3-8.

1124 **LaCoste, Yves.** "Geographicite et Geopolitique: Elisee Reclus." *Herodote*, 22, 3ᵉ Trimestre (Juillet-Septembre, 1981), 14-55.

1125 **LaCoste, Yves.** "Geopolitique das Islams, Editorial." *Herodote*, 35, 4ᵉ Trimestre (Octobre-Decembre, 1984), 3-18.

1126 **Lange, K.** "Der Terminus 'Lebenstraum' in Hitler's 'Mein Kampf'." *Vierteljahreshefte fur Zeitgeschichte*, 13 (1965), 426-437.

1127 **Legum, Colin.** "The Soviet Union, China and the West in Southern Africa." *Foreign Affairs*, 54, No. 4 (July, 1976), 745-62.

1128 **Leiblinger, Walter Francisco.** "Estructura de Fronteras y Organismo Estatal; (Un Analisis Geopolitico)." *Revista del Instituto de Geografia*, Universidad Nacional Major de San Marcos, Lima, 4 (1957), 54-59.

1129 **Leiblinger, Walter Francisco.** "Contribucion al deserrallo de la consciecia geopolitica." *Revista del Instituto de Geografia*, Universidad Mayor de San Marcos, 3 (1957), 35-39.

1130 **Lepotier, A.** "Geopolitica e geoestrategia." *A Defesa Nacional*, 548 (Marco, 1960), 135-138 et 549 (Abril, 1960), 173-180.

1131 **Lin, Yutang.** "Geopolitics: Law of the Jungle." *Asia and the Americas*, 43, No. 4 (April, 1943), 199-202.

1132 **Lipschutz, Ronnie D.** "Reconstructing World Politics: The Emergence of Global Civil Society." *Millennium* [London], 21, No. 3 (Winter, 1992), 389-420.

1133 **Livingston, Dennis.** "Global Equilibrium and the Decentralized Community." *Ekistics*, 42, No. 250 (September, 1976), 173-176.

1134 **Loewenstein, Karl.** "Sovereignty and International Co-operation." *American Journal of International Law*, 48, No. 2 (April, 1954), 222-244.

1135 **Lopez Imizcoz, Danul.** "Acotaciones o geopolitica?" *Boletin del museo social Argentino*, 43, No. 326 (1966), 5-12.

1136 **Lyons, Roy.** "The USSR, China and the Horn of Africa." *Review of African Political Economy*. 11, No. 2 (May-August), 5-30.

1137 **Maass, G.** "Geopolitik als Nationale Staatswissenschaft." *Zeitschrift fur Geopolitik*, Jahrg 10, Heft 9 (September, 1933), 559-564.

1138 **Magalhaes, Joao Batista.** "Geopolitica, imperialismo e guerra." *A Defesa Nacional*, 416 (1949), 109-125.

1139 **Malin, James C.** "The Contriving Brain as the Pivot of History. Sea, Landmass and Air Power: Some Bearings of Cultural Technology Upon the Geography of International Relations." In *Issues and Conflicts: Studies in Twentieth Century Diplomacy*, George LaVerne Anderson, ed. Lawrence: University of Kansas Press, 1959.

1140 **Malin, James C.** "Space and History: Reflections on Closed-Space Doctrines of Turner and Mackinder and the Challenge of Those Ideas by the Air Age." *Agricultural History*, 18, No. 2 (April, 1944), 107-126.

1141 **Marcal, Heitor.** "As teorias geopoliticas." *Boletin Geografico*, 24, No. 185 (1965), 258-267.

1142 **Martin, Geoffrey J.** "Political Geography and Geopolitics." *Journal of Geography*, 58, No. 9 (December, 1959), 441-444.

1143 **Marull, Bermudez, Federico.** "Geopolitica." *Revista Geografica de Chile, Terra Australio*, Ano 1970, No. 21 (1971), 31-50.

1144 **Marz, Josef.** "Karl Haushofer und Sudostasien." *Zeitshcrift fur Geopolitik*, Jahrg 24, Heft 12 (Dez., 1953), 637-639.

1145 **Marz, Josef.** "Unbekannte Geopolitik." *Zeitschrift fur Geopolitik*, (1943), 126.

1146 **Mattern, Johannes.** "If the Geopolitians Have Their Way." *Commonwealth*, 30 (April 28, 1939), 6-9.

1147 **Mattern, Johannes.** "From Geopolitik to Political Relativism." In *Essays in Honor of Westel Woodbury Willoughby*. Baltimore, Maryland: Johns Hopkins University Press, 1937, 125-172.

1148 **Mattusch, Kurt R.** "Geopolitics - 'Science' of Power Politics." *Amerasia*, 6, No. 5 (July, 1942), 236-243.

1149 **Maull, Otto.** "Politische Geographie und Geopolitik." *Geographische Anzeiger*, 27 (1926), 245-253.

1150 **McColl, Robert W.** "Geopolitics, National Policies and International Behavior." *USA Today*, 107, No. 2402 (November, 1978), 40-42.

1151 **Meinig, Donald W.** "Cultural Blocs and Political Blocs: Emergent Patterns in World Affairs." *Western Humanities Quarterly*, 10, No. 3 (Spring, 1956), 203-222.

1152 **Meinig, Donald W.** "Heartland and Rimland in Eurasian History." *Western Political Quarterly*, 9, No. 3 (September, 1956), 553-569.

1153 **Meira Mattos, C. de.** "Desinformaco historica e seguranca nacional." *A Defesa Nacional*, 66, No. 684 (1979), 61-65.

1154 **Michaels, Daniel W.** "Formulas for Power: A Review of 'Formeln zur Macht'." *Professional Geographer*, 18, No. 5 (September, 1966), 305-310.

1155 **Migvens, A. Pires.** "Geopolitical Influences of Itaipu." *Revista Chilena de Geopolitica*, 2, No. 3 (1986)P 31-46.

1156 **Moll, Kenneth L.** "A.T. Mahan, American Historian." *Military Affairs*, 27 (1963), 131-140.

1157 **Moodie, Michael, and Cottrell, Alvin J.** "Geopolitics and Maritime Power." In *Washington Papers, 9, No. 87.* Beverly Hills: Sage Publications for the Center for Strategic and International Studies, 1981.

1158 **Moro, R.O.** "Geopolitica transpolar." *Geopolitica*, 2, No. 9/10 (Diciembre, 1977), 7-12.

1159 **Most, B.A., and Starr, Harvey.** "Diffusion, Reinforcement, Geopolitics and the Spread of War." *American Political Science Review*, 74, No. 4 (December, 1980), 932-946.

1160 **Muller-Wille, Wilhelm.** "Politische-Geographischer Leitbilder, reale Lebensraume und Globale Spannungsfelder." *Geographische Zeitschrift*, 54, Heft 1 (Januar, 1966), 13-38.

1161 **Myers, Ramon H.** "Political Theory and Recent Political Developments in the Republic of China." *Asian Survey*, 27, No. 9 (September, 1987), 1003-1022.

1162 "Mysteries of Geopolitics." *Time*, 41, No. 2 (January 11, 1943), 92-96.

1163 **Neumann, Franz L.** "Approaches to the Study of Political Power." *Political Science Quarterly*, 65, No. 2 (June, 1950), 161-180.

1164 **Neumann, Sigmund.** "Fashions in Space (Geopolitics)." *Foreign Affairs*, 21, No. 2 (January, 1943), 276-288.

1165 "The New Geopolitics." *Carribbean Review*. 11, No. 2 (1982), theme issue.

1166 **Nowak, Robert.** "Bohmen und Mahren; eine geopolitischer Uberblick von 1918 bis heute." *Zeitschrift fur Geopolitik*, 16, Jahrg, Heft 4 (April, 1939), 249-257.

1167 **Oglivie, A.G.** "Isaiah Bowman: An Appreciation." *Geographical Journal*, 115, Nos. 4-6 (April-June, 1950), 226-230.

1168 **Olague, Ignacio.** "La geopolitique contemporaine et le cadre geographique." *Diogne*, 27 (1959), 29-47.

1169 **O'Loughlin, John.** "Political Geography: Coping with Global Restructuring." *Progress in Human Geography*, 13, No. 3 (September, 1989), 412-426.

1170 **Osterud, O.** "The Uses and Abuses of Geopolitics." *Journal of Peace Research*, 25, No. 3 (July, 1988), 191-199.

1171 **Ott, George.** "Geopolitics for an uncertain era." *Air University Review*, 33, No. 6 (September-October, 1982), 29-35.

1172 **Otauthall, G.** "The Language and Nature of the 'New Geopolitics'--The Case of US-El Salvador Relations." *Political Geography Quarterly*, 5, No. 1 (January, 1986), 73-85.

1173 **O'Tuathail, Gearoid.** "Problematizing Geopolitics: Survey, Statesmanship and Strategy." *Institute of British Geographers. Transactions*, 19, No. 3 (1994), 259-272.

1174 **O'Tuathail, Gearoid.** "The Critical Reading/Writing of Geopolitics: Re-Reading/Writing Wittfogel, Bowman and Lacoste." *Progress in Human Geography,* 18, No. 3 (September, 1994), 313-332.

1175 **Overbeck, Hermann.** "Das Politischgeographische Lehrgebaude von Friedrich Ratzel in der Scht Unserer Zeit." *Die Erde*, 88 Jahrg, Heft No. 3-4 (Ausgegeben im Dezember, 1957), 169-192.

1176 **Parker, Geoffrey.** "French Geopolitical Thought in the Inter-War Years and the Emergence of European Idea." *Political Geography Quarterly*, 6, No. 2 (April, 1987), 145-150.

1177 **Passarge, Siegfried.** "Politische Geographie und Geopolitik." *Petermans Mitteilungen*, 81, Heft 4 (Dezember, 1935), 185-189.

1178 **Pauly, W.F.** "Writings of Halford Mackinder Applied to the Evolution of Soviet Naval Power." *Pennsylvania Geographer*, 12 (1962), 3-7.

1179 **Pavic, Radovan.** "Problem: Geopolitickih Deformacija." *Geografski Pregled-Revue de Geographie*, 8-9 (1964-1965), 109-129.

1180 **Pearcy, G. Etzel.** "Geopolitics and Foreign Relations." *U.S. Department of State Bulletin*, 50, No. 1288 (March 2, 1964), 318-330.

1181 **Peterson, J.H.** "German Geopolitics Reassessed." *Political Geogrpahy Quarterly*, 6, No. 2 (April, 1987), 107-114.

1182 **Poole, Sidman P.** "Geopolitik-Science or Magic." *Journal of Geography*, 43, No. 1 (January, 1944), 1-12.

1183 **Prevelakis, Georges.** "Isaiah bowman, Adversaire de la *Geopolitik*." *L'Espace Geographique*, 23, No. 1 (1994), 78-88.

1184 **Price, David Lynn.** "Nambiquarra Geopolitical Organization." *Man*, New Series, 22, No. 1 (March, 1987), 1-24.

1185 **Rakowska-Harmstone, Teresa.** "Baltic Nationalism and the Soviet Armed Forces." *Journal of Baltic Studies*, 17, No. 3 (Fall, 1986), 179-193.

1186 **Ratzel, Friedrich.** "Der Lebensraum: eine biogeographische Studie." In *Festgaben fur Albert Schaffle*. Tubingen: Laupp. 1901, 103-189.

1187 **Ratzel, Friedrich** "Die Gesetze des Raumlichen Wachstums der Staaten ein Beitrag zur Wissenschaftlichen politischen Geographie." *Peterman Mitteilungen*, 42, Heft 5 (Mai, 1896), 97-107.

1188 **Ratzel, Friedrich.** "Politische-geographische Ruckblicke." *Geographische Zeitschrift*, 4, Heft 3 (Marz, 1898), 143-156; Heft 4 (April, 1898), 211-244; and Heft 5 (Mai, 1898), 268-274.

1189 **Ratzel, Friedrich.** "Studien uber politische Raume." *Geographische Zeitschrift*, 1 Jahrg, Heft 4 (April, 1895), 163-182 et Heft 5 et 6 (Mai-Juni, 1895), 286-302.

1190 **Ratzel, Friedrich.** "Le sol, la societe et l'Etat." *L'annee sociologique*, 3 (1898-1899), 1-14.

1191 **Raup, Henry F.** "Geopolitics." *Education*, 63, No. 5 (January, 1943), 266-272.

1192 **Redler, Richard.** "How the Geopolitician Looks at Our World." *Canadian Geographical Journal*, 29, No. 1 (July, 1944), 4-9.

1193 **Riad, Mohamed.** "Geopolitics and Politics in the Arab Gulf States (GCC)." *GeoJournal*, 13, No. 3 (October, 1986), 201-210.

1194 **Richards, I.A.** "Psychopolitics: A New Study and a Name for It, More Pertinent to Our Problem Than Geopolitics." *Fortune*, 26, No. 9 (September, 1942), 108-109+.

1195 **Rodrigues, Lysias A.** "Geopolitica: Novo Conceito da Heartland." *Revistado institudo de geografia e historia militar do Brasil*, 15 (1949), 25-44.

1196 **Rosenau, James N.** "The State in an Era of Cascading Politics: Wavering Concept, Widening Competence, Withering Colossus, or Weathering Change?" *Comparative Political Studies*, 21, No. 1 (April, 1988), 13-44.

1197 **Ross, Douglas A.** "Middlepowers as Extra-Regional Balancer Powers: Canada, India, and Indochina, 1954-62." *Pacific Affairs*, 55, No. 2 (Summer, 1982), 185-209.

1198 **Roucek, Joseph S.** "The New Pseudoscience of Geopolitics." In *Modern World Politics*, 3rd ed., T.B. Kalijarvi, ed. New York: Thomas Y. Crowell, 1974, 609-635.

1199 **Ruiz de Gordejuela, Amando Melon.** "Geopolitica o geografia politica; su posible contenido." *Estudios geograficos*, 2, No. 2 (Febrero, 1941), 5-33.

1200 **Russell, W.H.** "Amphibious Doctrines of Alfred Thayer Mahan." *Marine Corps Gazette*, 40, No. 2 (1956), 34-42.

1201 **Schaefer, E.** "Exceptionalism in Geogrpahy." *Annals of the Association of American Geographers*, 43, No. 2 (June, 1953), 226-249.

1202 **Schafer, Otto.** "20 Jahre tschechischer Politik und Geopolitik." *Geographischer Anzeiger*, 39 Jahrg, Heft 16 (1938), 365-376; Heft 17 (1938), 394-398.

1203 **Schafer, Otto.** "Zur geopolitischen Lage." *Geographischer Anzeiger*, 43, Jahrg, Heft 17-18 (September, 1942), 305-311.

1204 **Schlesinger, James R.** "The Geopolitics of Energy." *Washington Quarterly*, 2, No. 3 (Summer, 1979), 3-7.

1205 **Schmidt, C.** "Schulung, Schule und Geopolitik." *Zeitschrift fur Geopolitik*, Jahrg 12, Heft 5 (Mai, 1935), 318-320.

1206 **Schnitzer, Ewald W.** "Geopolitics as an Element in Social Education." *Harvard Educational Review*, 8, No. 4 (October, 1938), 507-516.

1207 **Scholler, Peter.** "Die Geopolitik in Weltbild des Historischen Materialismus." *Erdkunde*, 13, No. 2 (May, 1959), 88-98.

1208 **Scholler, Peter.** "Die Rolle Karl Haushofers fur Entwicklung und Ideologic Nationalsozialistischer Geopolitik." *Erdkunde* (Bonn), Baund 36, Heft 3 (September, 1982), 160-167.

1209 **Scholler, Peter.** "Geopolitik als Raumideologie?
Eine Entgeznung." *Zeitschrift fur Geopolitik*, Jahrg
26, Heft 4 (April, 1958), 21-23.

1210 **Scholler, Peter.** "Wege und Irrwege der
Politischen Geographie und Geopolitik."
Erdkunde. 11, No. 1 (February, 1957), 1-20.

1211 **Schrepfer, Von Hans.** "Geopolitik und
Erdkunde." *Zeitschrift fur Erdkunde*, 4 Jahrg, Heft
17/18 (1936), 919-925 and Heft 22 (1936),
966-969.

1212 **Schumacher, Rupert Von.** "Zur Theorie des
Raumes." *Zeitschrift fur Geopolitik*, Jahrg 11, Heft
9 (September, 1934), 573-580.

1213 **Schumacher, Rupert Von.** "Zur Theorie der
Raumstrategie." *Zeitschrift fur Geopolitik*, Jahrg
11, Heft 12 (Dez., 1934), 779-788.

1214 **Schumacher, Rupert Von.** "Zur Theorie der
Geopolitischen Signatur." *Zeitschrift fur
Geopolitik*, Jahrg 12, Heft 4 (April, 1935),
246-265.

1215 **Schumacher, Rupert Von.** "Der Sudostraum in
der Konzeption Mitteleuropas 1: Die
Voraussetzungen im Sudotsen." *Zeitschrift fur
Geopolitin*, Jahrg 11, Heft 3 (Marz, 1934), 156-
176.

1216 **Schuman, Frederick L.** "Let Us Learn Our
Geopolitics." *Current History.* N.S. 2, No. 9
(May, 1942), 161-165.

1217 **Segal, Gerald.** "Nuclear Strategy: The
Geography of Stability." *Political Geography
Quaterly*, 5, No. 4 Supplement (October, 1986),
S37-S47.

1218 **Semeusky, Boris N.** "La geopolitica como
ideologia del imperialismo." *Universidad de la
Habana*, 28, No. 166-167 (1964), 67-84.

1219 **Semmell, Bernard.** "Sir Halford Mackinder:
Theorist of Imperialism." *Canadian Journal of
Economics and Political Science*, 24, No. 4
(November, 1958), 554-561.

1220 **Sempa, Francis P.** "The Geopolitics of the Post-
Cold War World." *Strategic Review* [Washington,
D.C.]], 20, No. 1 (Winter, 1992), 9-18.

1221 **Sempa, Francis P.** "Why Teach Geopolitics?"
International Social Science Review, 65, No. 1
(Winter, 1990), 16-20.

1222 **Siddiqi, Mohamed Ismail.** "Geopolitical
Perspective and Theoretical Framework of
Geographical Views." *Pakistan Navy Staff College
Review*, (1984), 56-66.

1223 **Sieger, Robert.** "Rudolf Kjellen." *Zeitschrift fur*

Geopolitik, Jahrg 1, Heft 6 (Juni, 1924), 339-345.

1224 **Sillani, Tomaso.** "The New Balance of Power in
the Levant." *Foreign Affairs*, 17, No. 2 (January,
1939), 336-350.

1225 **Couto E Silva, Golbery Do.** "Esboco de um
plano de pesquisa geopolitica." *A Defesa
Nacional*, 549 (Abril, 1960), 147-151; 550 (Maio,
1960), and (Junho, 1960), 109-110.

1226 **Couto E Silva, Golbery Do.** "Geopolitica e
geo-estrategia." *A Defesa Nacional*, 528 (Junho,
1958), 81-84; 529 (Agosto, 1958), 81-87; 530
(Set., 1958), 45-50; 531 (Out., 1958), 95-102;
532-533 (Nov.-Dez., 1958), 95-98.

1227 **Silva, Joao Mendes de.** "Escolas geopoliticas." *A
Defesa Nacional*, 539 (Junho, 1959), 107-128.

1228 **Silva, Paulo Eneas F. da.** "A Geopolitica e a
guerra." *A Defesa Nacional*, 438 (January, 1951),
37-39.

1229 **Simon, Julian L.** "Lebensraum: Paradoxically,
Population Growth May Eventually End Wars."
Journal of Conflict Resolution (Newbury Park),
33, No. 1 (March, 1989), 164-180.

1230 **Slater, David.** "The Geopolitical Imagination and
the Enframing of Development Theory." *Institute
of British Geographers, Transactions* [London], 18,
No. 4 (1993), 419-437.

1231 **Smith, J. Russell.** "Heartland, Grassland, and
Farmland." In *Compass of the World*, W. Weigert
and V. Stefansson, eds. New York: Macmillan,
1943, 148-160.

1232 **Smith, J. Russell.** "Mackinder: 1942." *New
Republic*, 107 (September 14, 1942), 322-323.

1233 **Smith, Neil.** "Isaiah Bowman: Political
Geography and Geopolitics." *Political Geography
Quarterly*, 3, No. 1 (January, 1984), 69-76.

1234 **Smith, Woodruff D.** "Friedrich Ratzel and the
Origins of Lebensraun." *German Studies Review*,
3, No. 1 (February, 1980), 51-68.

1235 **Snyder, Jack.** "Science and Sovietology: Briding
the Methods Gap in Soviet Foreign Policy Studies."
World Politics, 40, No. 2 (January, 1958), 169-
193.

1236 **Sondern, Frederick, Jr.** "Hitler's Scientists."
Current History and Forum, 53, No. 1 (June,
1941), 10-12, 47.

1237 **Sondern, Frederick, Jr.** "Thousand Scientists
Behind Hitler." *Reader's Digest*, 38, No. 6 (June,
1941), 23-27.

1238 **Sonnerfeld, Joseph.** "The Geopolitical Environment as a Perceptual Environment." *Journal of Geography*, 69, No. 7 (October, 1970), 415-419.

1239 **Spencer, Donald S.** "A Short History of Geopolitics." *Journal of Geography*, 87, No. 2 (March-April, 1988), 42-48.

1240 **Spiegel, Henry W.** "The Quest for 'Living Space'." In *The Economics of Total War*. New York: Appleton-Century, 1942, 5-11.

1241 **Springenschmidt, K.** "Geopolitik von der Heimat aus." *Zeitschrift fur Geopolitik*, Jahrg 12, Heft 5 (Mai, 1935), 284-290.

1242 **Sprout, Harold H.** "Geopolitical Hypotheses in Technological Perspective." *World Politics*, 15, No. 2 (January, 1963), 187-212.

1243 **Stevens, A.** "'Lebensraum' Fanciful." *Science News Letter*, 36, No. 11 (September 9, 1939), 66.

1244 **Stevens, P.** "Geopolitics of East and West." *Nation*, 152 (June 28, 1941), 747-750.

1245 **Stieglitz, Robert R.** "The Geopolitics of the Phoenician Littoral in the Early Iron Age." *American Schools of Oriental Research*, Bulletin [Baltimore], No. 279 (August, 1990), 9-12.

1246 **Stone, Adolf.** "Geopolitics as Haushofer taught it." *Journal of Geography*, 52, No. 4 (April, 1953), 167-171.

1247 **Strausz-Hupe, Robert.** "Geopolitics Major General Professor Doktor Karl Haushofer's Sinister Pseudo Science was Inspired by the Monroe Doctrine and Now Rules German Foreign Policy." *Fortune*, 24, No. 5 (November, 1941), 111-119.

1248 **Strausz-Hupe, Robert.** It's Smart to be Geopolitical." *Saturday Review of Literature*, 26, No. 6 (February 6, 1943), 4-5+.

1249 **Strausz-Hupe, Robert.** "Population and Power." Part Two. In *The Balance of Tomorrow*, New York: Putnam, 1945, 39-115.

1250 **Sugimura, Oaki.** "Concepts of Political Geography and Geopolitics, and Border Field of Geography and Political Science." Political Geography, Vol. III. Published by the *Annals of The Japanese Association of Political Geographers*, Tokyo: Kokim-Shoim, 1968, 1-48.

1251 **Sur, Etienne.** "Pacifisme et Geopolitique en Allemagne." *Herodote* [Paris], No. 60-61 (Janvier-Juin, 1991), 91-99.

1252 **Sylvester, John Andrew.** "Mackinder lernte von den Deutschen." *Zeitschrift fur Geopolitik*, Jahrg 39, Heft 2 (Marz-April, 1968), 55-59.

1253 **Tamayo, Jorge L.** "Contenido de la Geografia." *Investigacion Economica* (UNAM, Mexico), 8, No. 1 (1948), 1-28.

1254 **Taylor, Griffith:** "Geographers and World Peace; A Plea for Geo-pacifics." *Australian Geographical Studies*, 1, No. 1 (April, 1963), 3-17.

1255 **Taylor, Peter J.** "The Paradox of Geographical Scale in Marx' Politics." *Antipode*, 19, No. 3 (December, 1987), 287-306.

1256 **Teggart, Frederick J.** "Geography as an Aid to Statecraft; An Appreciation of Mackinder's 'Democratic Ideals and Reality'." *Geographical Review*, 8, Nos. 4-5 (October-November, 1919), 227-242.

1257 **Thermaenius, Edvard.** "Geopolitics and Political Geography." *Baltic and Scandinavian Countries*, 4, No. 2 (May, 1938), 165-177.

1258 **Thies, J.** "Die Eingliederung der Geopolitik in die Deutsche Volksschle." *Geographische Wochenschrift*, 2 (1934), 254-257.

1259 **Thom, William G.** "Trends in Soviet Support for American Liberation." *Air University Review*, 25, No. 5 (July-August), 36-43.

1260 **Thorndike, Joseph J. Jr.** "Geopolitics; The Lurid Career of a Scientific System which a Briton Invented, the Germans Used, and Americans Need to Study." *Life*, 13, No. 25 (December 21, 1942), 106-115.

1261 **Thorndike, Joseph J. Jr** "Geopolitica." *Boletin Geografico*, 1, No. 6 (1943), 15-26.

1262 **Thumerelle, J.** "Migrations Internationales et Changement Geopolitique en Europe." *Annales de Geographie* [Paris] 101e Annee, No. 565 (Mai-Juin, 1992), 289-318.

1263 **Turner, Ralph.** "Technology and Geopolitics." *Military Affairs*, 7, No. 1 (Spring, 1943), 5-15.

1264 **Vagts, Alfred.** "Geography in War and Geopolitics." *Military Affairs*, 7, No. 1 (Spring, 1943), 79-88.

1265 **Vidal de la Blache, Paul.** "La geographie politique a propos des ecrits de M. Frederic Ratzel." *Annales de Geographie*, 7, Annee No. 32 (15 Mars 1898), 97-111.

1266 **Villegas, Osiris Guilhermo.** "America del Sur: Geopolitica de integracion y desarrollo." *Boletim da Sociedade Brasileira de Geografia*, Ano 19, N. 33-34, (Janeiro a Junho, 1970), 7-22.

1267 **Vogel, Walther.** "Politische Geographie und Geopolitik, 1909-1934." *Geographische Jahrbuch*, 49 Band (1934), 79-304.

1268 **Vogel, Walther**. "Rudolf Kjellen, 1864-1922."
Encyclopedia of the Social Sciences, 8 (1932), 576.

1269 **Von Lengercke, Wolfgang B.** "Raum, Volk und
Staat." *Zeitschrift fur Geopolitik*, Jahrg 20, Heft 4
(April, 1943), 185-188.

1270 **Vries Reilingh, H.D. de.** "Kommt die Deutsche
Geopolitik Wieder Hoch?" *Tydschrift van het
Koninkliyk Nederlandsch Aardrijkskundig
Genootschap*, 74, No. 4 (October, 1957), 485-489.

1271 **Wagner, R. Harrison.** "Demkschrift: Geopolitik
als Nationale Staatswissenschaft." *Zeitshcrift fur
Geopolitik*, 10, Heft5 (Mai, 1933), 301-304.

1272 **Wagner, R. Harrison.** "The Theory of Games
and the Balance of Power." *World Politics*, 38,
No. 4 (July, 1986), 546-576.

1273 **Waibel, Leo.** "Determinismo, Geografico e
Geopolitica." *Boletim Geografico*, 19, No. 164
(Setembro-Outubro, 1961), 612-617.

1274 **Walker, R.B.J.** "Realism, Change, and
International Political Theory." *International
Studies Quarterly*, 41, No. 4 (Autumn, 1987), 65-
86.

1275 **Walsh, Edmund A.** "Geopolitica e Moral
Internacional." *Boletin de Geografia*, 12, No. 120
(1954), 304-318.

1276 **Walsh, Edmund A.** "Geopolitics and International
Morals." In *Compass of the World*, H.W. Weigert
and V. Stefansson, eds. New York: Macmillan,
1944, 12-39.

1277 **Wassermann, Felix M.** "Geopolitik und
Unterwasser Erdol." *Zeitschrift fur Geopolitik*,
Jahrg 24, Heft 7/8 (Juli-August, 1953), 420.

1278 **Waters, D.W.** "Seaman, Scientists, Historians,
and Strategy: Presidential Address, 1978. *British
Journal for the History of Science*, 13, Part 3,
No. 45 (November, 1980), 189-210.

1279 **Weigert, Hans Werner.** "German Geopolitics; A
Workshop for Army Rule." *Harpers*, 183
(November, 1941), 586-597.

1280 **Weigert, Hans Werner.** "Heartland Revisited."
In *New Compass of the World*, H.W. Weigert,
V. Stefansson, and R.E. Harrison, eds. New
York: Macmillan, 1949, 80-90.

1281 **Weigert, Hans Werner**, et al. "The Impact of
Location on Strategy and Power Politics." In
Principles of Political Geography, Ch. 8.
New York: Appleton, Century, Crofts, 1957.

1282 **Weigert, Hans Werner.** "Mackinder's
Heartland." *American Scholar*, 15, No. 1 (Winter,
1945-46), 43-54.

1283 **Weigert, Hans Werner.** "Military Implications of
German Geopolitics; The Geographical Pattern of
the War." *Vital Speeches*, 8 (August 15, 1942),
645-647.

1284 **Weigert, Hans Werner.** "Strategic Areas and Life
Lines." In *New Compass of the World*,
H.W. Weigert, V. Stefansson, and R.E. Harrison,
eds. New York: Macmillan, 1949, 219-237.

1285 **Whebell, C.F.J.** "Mackinder's Heartland Theory
in Practice Today." *Geographical Magazine*, 42,
No. 9 (June, 1970), 630-636.

1286 **Whittlesey, Derwent S.** "Haushofer: The
Geopoliticans." In *Makers of Modern Strategy:
Military Thought from Machiavelli to Hitler*,
Edward Mead Earle, ed. Princeton, New Jersey:
Princeton University Press, 1944, 388-414.

1287 **Williams, Maurice.** "Some Reflections on Austro-
Nazis and Their Brand of Nationalism Before and
After Anschluss." *Canadian Reiew of Studies in
Nationalism*, 12, No. 2 (Fall 1985), 285-306.

1288 **Wilms, Douglas C., and Steinbrink, John E.**
"Escalation: A Simulation of Contemporary
Geo-politics." *Journal of Geography*, 70, No. 8
(November, 1971), 492-497.

1289 **Wilson, Curtis M.** "The Geographical Basis of
Rational Power." *Ohio Journal of Science*, 50,
No. 1 (January, 1950), 33-44.

1290 **Winkler, E.** "Karl Haushofer und die deutsche
Geopolitik." *Schweitzer Monatshefte*, 27 Jahr, Heft
1 (April, 1947), 29-35.

1291 **Wittfogel, Karl A.** Geopolitics, Geographical
Materialism and Marxism." *Antipode*, 17, No. 1
(April, 1986), 21-72.

1292 **Wittfogel, Karl A.** "Geopolitik, geographischer
materialismus und Marxismus." *Unter dem Banner
des Marxismus*, 3 (1929), 17-51, 485-522,
698-735.

1293 **Wohl, Paul.** "An American 'Geopolitical
Masterhand'." *Asia*, 41, No. 11 (November,
1941), 601+.

1294 **Wood, William B.** "Ecopolitics: Domestic and
International Linkages." *Acta Universitatis
Carolinae, Geographica* [Praha], 27, No. 1 (1992),
49-54.

1295 **Wrigley, Glady M.** "Isaiah Bowman."
Geographical Review, 41, No. 1 (January, 1951),
7-65.

1296 **Wunderlich, E.** "Neue geopolitische Karten und
Atlanten." *Zeitschrift fur Geopolitik*, Jahr 20, Heft
2 (February, 1943), 81-84 et 316.

1297 **Young, Oran R.** "Professor Russett: Industrious Tailor to a Naked Emperor." *World Politics*, 21, No. 3 (April, 1969), 486-511.

1298 **Yutang, Lin.** "Geopolitics: The Law of the Jungle." *Asia*, 43, No. 4 (April, 1943), 199-202.

1299 **Zanegin, Boris N.** "Beyond the Geopolitical Crash of the 1990s--Towards a New Equilibrium? *Security Dialogue* [Newbury Park], 23, No. 4 (December, 1992), 13-19.

1300 **Zanotti, N.** "Geopolitica e nacionalismo." *Anhembi*, 11, No. 31 (1953), 82-84.

1301 **Zeck, Hans F.** "Was ist Geopolitik?" *Zeitschrift fur Erdkunde*, 4 Jahrg, Heft 21 (1936), 974-977.

1302 **Zeck, Hans F.** "Was ist Geopolitik? Wesen und Wandel des Begriffs." *Geographische Anzeiger*, 38 (1937), 78-80.

1303 **Zeck, Hans F.** "Was will die Geopolitik heute?" *Zeitschrift fur Geopolitik*, Jahrg 24, Heft 4 (April, 1953), 193-201.

1304 **Zumwalt, Jr., Elmo R.** "20th Century Mahan." *U.S. Naval Institute Proceedings*, 100 (November, 1974), 70-73.

POLITICAL GEOGRAPHY OF REGIONS

AFRICA

Books and Journals

1305 **Adam, Heribert.** "Variations of Ethnicity: Afrikaner and Black Nationalism in South Africa." *Journal of Asian and African Studies*, 20, Nos. 3-4 (July-October, 1985), 169-180.

1306 **Aluko, Olajide, and Shaw, Timothy M.,** eds. *Southern Africa in the 1980's*. London: Allen & Unwin, 1985.

1307 **Apter, David E., and Rosberg, Carl G.,** eds. *Political Development and the New Realism in Sub-Saharan Africa*. Charlottesville: University Press of Virginia, 1994.

1308 **Bullier, A.J.** *Geopolitiques de l'Apartheid: Strategie ethnique de Pretoria*. Paris: Presses Universitaires de France, 1982.

1309 **Calvocoressi, Peter.** *Independent Africa and the World*. London: Longman, 1985.

1310 **Dikshit, R.D.** "Uganda: A Geopolitical Study." *Modern Review*, 117, No. 1 (January, 1965), 17-28.

1311 **Hamdan, G.** "The Political Map of the New Africa." *Geographical Review*. 53, No. 3 (July, 1963), 418-439.

1312 **Hesselberg, Jan.** "Botswana and Its Geopolitical Location." *Norsk geografisk tidsskrift*, 38, No. 2 (June, 1984), 77-84.

1313 **Hodgson, Robert D., and Stoneman, Elvyn Arthur.** *The Changing Map of Africa*. 2nd ed. Princeton, New Jersey: Van Nostrand, 1968.

1314 **Innes, D.** *Anglo: Anglo American and the Rise of Modern South Africa*. Johannesburg: Ravan Press, 1984.

1315 **Kouba, Leonard J.** "Africa: A Study in Geopolitical Transition." *Bulletin of the Illinois Geographical Society*. 11, No. 2 (June, 1969, 34-49; 12, No. 3 (December, 1970), 49-63).

1316 **Lycett, Andrew.** "Eastern Africa: Sudan's Growing Significance." *Africa Report*, 22, No. 2 (March-April, 1977), 12-20.

1317 **Lyra Tavares, Aurelio de.** "A geopolitica da Africa do Norte." *Revista do institudo de geografia e historia do Brasil*, 4 (1943), 47-53.

1318 **Odingo, R.S.** "Geopolitical Problems of East Africa." *East Africa Journal*, 2, No. 9 (February, 1966), 17-24.

1319 **Reed, William Cyrus.** "International Politics nad National Liberation: ZANU and the Politics of Contested Sovereignty in Zimbabwe." *African Studies Review* [Atlanta], 36, No. 2 (September, 1993), 31-59.

1320 **Riukin, Arnold.** "The New States of Africa." *Headline Series*. (Foreign Policy Association), 183 (June, 1967), 1-63.

1321 **Roucek, Joseph S.** "The Geopolitics of the Congo." *United Asia*, 14, No. 1 (January, 1962), 81-85.

1322 **Roucek, Joseph S.** "Nigerian Geopolitics." *United Asia*, 14, No. 3 (March, 1962), 182-185.

1323 **Sircar, Parbati K.** "Aspects of African Geopolitics." In *Contemporary Africa*. Bombay: Asia Publishing House, 1960, 1-10.

1324 **Smolansky, O.M.** "Soviet Policy in the Middle East and Africa." *Current History*, 75, No. 440 (October, 1978), 113-116 and 127-138.

1325 **U.S. Department of State.** "The Geographer." *Africa: Pattern of Sovereignty*. Washington, D.C.: U.S. Department of State, 1965.

1326 **U.S. Department of State.** *Political Division of Africa.* Washington, D.C.: U.S. Department of State, 1962.

1327 **Velasco-Erraxriz, C.** "Vision Geopolitica del Sudoeste de Africa (Geopolitical View of Southwest Africa)." *Revista Chilena de Geopolitica*, 267 (1985), 67-102.

1328 **Whittlesey, Derwent S.** "Reshaping the Map of Africa." In *Geographic Aspects of International Relations*, C.C. Colby, ed. Chicago: University of Chicago Press, 1938, 127-159.

AMERICAS

Books

1329 **Anderson, Thomas D.** *Politics in Central America: Guatemala, El Salvador, Honduras, and Nicaragua.* Rev. ed. New York: Praeger, 1988.

1330 **Backheuser, Everardo.** *A Geopolitika geral do Brasil.* Rio de Janeiro: Biblioteca do Exercito, 1952.

1331 **Backheuser, Everardo.** *A Geopolitika geral do Brasil.* Rio de Janeiro: Biblioteca do Exercito, 1952.

1332 **Briano, Justo P.** *Geopolitica y geostrategia Americana.* Buenos Aires: Ed. Pheamar, 1966.

1333 **Careceda, Quezada, Domingo.** *Los imperativos geopoliticos de Chile en relacion con sun desarrollo economico.* Santiago: Ed. Universitaria, 1962.

1334 **Carles, Fernando Jose.** *Algunos aspectos de lageopolitica boliviana.* Buenos Aires: Instituto de Derecho internacional, 1950.

1335 **Cartaxo, Octacilio.** *O Problema geopolitico brasileiro; Teoria e pratica de uma revolucao nacionalista.* Rio de Janeiro: Empresa Grafica Ouvidor, 1965.

1336 **Castro Martinez, P.F.** *Fronteras Abiertas: Expansionismo y Geopolitica en el Brasil Contemporaneo.* Mexico City: Siglo Veintiuno Editores, 1980.

1337 **Child, Jack C.** *Geopolitics and Conflict in South America: Quarrels Among Neighbors.* New York: Praeger, 1985.

1338 **Conteh-Morgan, Earl.** *American Foreign Aid and Global Power Projection: The Geopolitics of Resource Allocation.* Aldershot: Dartmouth, 1990.

1339 **Couto E Silva, Golbery Do.** *Aspectos Geopoliticos do Brasil.* Rio de Janeiro: Biblioteca do Eercito, 1957.

1340 **Couto E Silva, Golbery Do.** *Conjunctura Politica Nacional o Poder Executivo & Geopolitico do Brasil.* Rio de Janeiro: Jose Olympio, 1981.

1341 **Couto E Silva, Golbery Do.** *Geopolitica do Brasil.* Rio de Janeiro: Jose Olympio, 1967.

1342 **da Cunha, Ovidio.** *Fundamentos geopoliticas da communidade lasiada.* Rio de Janeiro: Grafica O limpica, 1969.

1343 **Dalby, Wilfrid Simon.** *American Geopolitics and Soviet Threat.* Burnaby: Simon Fraser University, Ph.D., 1988.

1344 **De Carvalho, C.M. Delgado.** *Le Bresil Meridional.* Paris and Rio de Janeiro: E. Desfosses, 1910.

1345 **de Castro, T.** *Atlas Texto de Geopolitica do Brasil.* Rio de Janeiro: Capemi Editoria, 1982.

1346 **De Meira Mattos, C.** *Brasil: Geopolitica e Destino.* Rio de Janeiro: Jose Olympio, 1975.

1347 **De Meira Mattos, C.** *Uma Geopolitica Pan-Amazonica.* Rio de Janeiro: Jose Olympio, 1980.

1348 **De Meira Mattos, C.** *Projecao Mundial do Brasil.* Sao Paulo: Grafica Leal, 1960.

1349 **de Mendonca, Renato.** *Fronteira em marcha: Essaio de geopolitica brasileira.* Rio de Janeiro: Biblioteca do exercito, 1956.

1350 **Di Tella, Torcuato S.** *Latin American Politics: A Theoretical Framework.* Austin: University of Texas Press, 1990.

1351 **Fagon, Donald O'Connor.** *The Geopolitics of the Caribbean Sea and Its Adjacent Lands.* Washington, D.C.: Catholic University of America, Ph.D., 1973.

1352 **Forman, Brenda.** *America's Place in the World Economy.* New York: Harcourt Brace and World, 1969.

1353 **Gibbons, A.** *The New Map of South America.* New York/London: Century, 1928.

1354 **Hernandez, P.J., and Chitarroni, H.** *Malvinas: Clave Geopolitica.* Buenos Aires: Ediciones Castaneda, 1977.

1355 **Huszar, George B.** *Soviet Power and Policy.* New York: Thomas Y. Crowell, 1955.

1356 **Inman, Samuel Guy.** *Latin America: Its Place in World Life.* Rev. ed. New York: Harcourt Brace, 1942.

1357 **Londono, Julio.** *Geopolitica de Columbia.* Bogota: Imp. del Ministerio de Guerra, 1948.

1358 **Londono, Julio.** *Sudamerica: O la geografia como destino.* Bogota: Imp. del Ministerio de Guerra, 1948.

1359 **Londono, Julio.** *La vision geopolitica de Bolivar.* Bogota: Imp. del Estado Mayor General, 1950.

1360 **Londono, Julio.** *Neuva geopolitica de Columbia.* Bogota: Imp. y pub. de las fuerzas militares, 1965.

1361 **Meneses, Romulo.** *Tres ensayos sobre geopolitica indo-americana.* Lima: Ed. Continente, 1963.

1361.1 **Moneta, C.J.** *Geopolitica y Politica de Poder en el Atlantico Sur.* Buenos Aires: Editorial Pleamar, 1983.

1362 **Mottola, Karid,** ed. *"The Arctic Challenge: Nordic and Canadian Approaches to Security and Cooperation in an Emerging International Region.* Boulder, Colorado: Westview Press, 1988.

1363 **Munoz, Julio H.** *Geopolitica de la provincia de los Rios y del Escado ecuatoriano.* Quito: Ed. "Fray Todoco Ricke," 1953.

1364 **Musso, J.C.** *Antartida Uruguaya.* Montevideo: Documentos 'El Pais', 1970.

1365 **Needler, Martin.** *Latin American Politics in Perspective.* Princeton, New Jersey: Van Nostrand, 1963.

1366 **Oblitas Fernandez, Edgar.** *La geopolitica Chilena y la Guerra del Pacifico.* La Paz: Ed. "Kullasuyo", 1959.

1367 **Old, Colin Campbell.** *The Geopolitics of Quebec's Relations with the International French-Speaking Community.* Ottawa, Ontario, Canada: Carleton University, Master's Thesis, 1983.

1368 **Peffer, Nathaniel.** *America's Place in the World.* New York: Viking Press, 1945.

1369 **Perez Teneiro, Tomas.** *Resumen de geopolitica y nociones de geopolitica venezolana.* Caracas: Imp. Nacional, 1953.

1370 **Pinochet de la Barra, Oscar.** *Chilean Sovereignty in Antarctica.* Santiago de Chile: Edtorial del Pacifico, 1955.

1371 **Pittman, Howard Taylor.** *Geopolitics in the ABC Countries: A Comparison.* Washington, D.C.: American University, Ph.D., 1981.

1372 **Radames Isola, Emilio.** *Introduction a la geopolitica Argentina (las influencias geopoliticas en la formacion de Nuestro Estado).* Buenos Aires: Circulo Militar, 1950.

1373 **Rodrigues, Lysias A.** *Geopolitica do Brasil.* Rio de Janeiro: Biblioteca militar, 1947.

1374 **Ruiz Garcia, Enrique.** *Ensayo geopolitico de Centro-America.* Guatemala: Jose de Pineda i barra, 1961.

1375 **Sandner, Gerhard.** *Zentralamerika und der Ferne Karibische Western. Konjunkturen, Krisen und Konflikte 1503-1984.* Stuttgart: Franz Steiner Verlag Wiesbaden GMbH, 1985.

1376 **Semenov, Ivru Nilolaevich.** *Fashistskaia geopolitika na sluzhbe Amerikanskogo imperializma.* Moskva: Geopolitizdat, 1952.

1377 **Serbin, Andres.** *Caribbean Geopolitics: Toward Security Through Peace?* Translated form the Spanish by Sabeth Ramirex. Boulder, CO: Lynne Rienner Publishers, 1990.

1378 **Sherry, Michael S.** *The Rise of American Air Power: The Creation of Armageddon.* New Haven, Connecticut: Yale University Press, 1987.

1379 **Siegfried, Andre.** *Canada; An International Power.* London: J. Cape, 1949.

1380 **Spadoni, Robert Bernard.** *National Identity Formation and Diffusion in the Commonwealth of the Bahamas: A Politico-Geographic Appraisal.* Greeley: University of Northern Colorado, Ph.D., 1978.

1381 **Stodder, Joseph H.,** and **McCarthy, Kevin F.** *Profiles of the Caribbean Basin in 1960/1980: Changing Geopolitical & Geostrategic Dimensions.* Santa Monica, California: The Rand Corporation. Rand Note No. N-2058-AF, December, 1983.

1382 **Stone, Carl.** *Class, State, and Democracy in Jamaica.* New York: Praeger, 1986.

1383 **Taylor, Griffith.** *Canada's Role in Geopolitics; A Study in Situation and Status.* (Contemporary Affairs, No. 17) Toronto: Ryerson Press, 1942.

1384 **Tickell, Crispin.** *Climatic Change and World Affairs.* Rev. ed. Cambridge, Massachusetts: Harvard University Center for International Affairs, University Press of America, 1986.

1385 **Triska, Jan F.,** ed. *Dominant Powers and Subordinate States: The United States in Latin America and Soviet Union in Eastern Europe.* Durham, North Carolina: Duke University Press, 1986.

1386 **Ulloa, Alberto.** *Posicion internacional del Peru.* Lima: Imprenta Torres Aguirre, 1941.

1387 **U.S. Department of State.** "The Geographer." *States and Regions of Latin America.* Washington, D.C.: U.S. Department of State, 1967.

1388 **Valencia Vega, Alipio.** *Geopolitica del Litoral Boliviano.* La Paz, Boliva: Librera Juventud, 1974.

1389 **Villacres Moscoso, Jorge W.** *Geopolitica del mundo tropical sudamericano y la region Amazonica.* Guayaquil: Univ. de Guayaquil, 1963.

Journals

1390 **Adams, D.K.** "A Note: Geopolitics and Political Geography in the United States Between Wars." *Australian Journal of Politics and History*, 6, No. 1 (May, 1960), 77-82.

1391 **Agnew, John.** "The U.S. Position in the World Geopolitical Order After the Cold War." *The Professional Geographer* [New York], 44, No. 1 (February, 1992), 7-10.

1392 **Anderson, Thomas D.** "Political Power Centers in the Caribbean: Identification and Brief Review." *Ohio Geographers*, 15, (1986), 16-23.

1393 **Anton, Werner.** "Die Wendung in der Brasilianischen auslandsschulden Politik." *Zeitschrift fur Geopolitik*, 16, No. 3 (March 2, 1939), 244-247.

1394 **Atencio, Jorge E.** "Cual debe ser nuestra posicion en geopolitica?" *Revista del Circulo Militar*, 10 (1950), Complete issue.

1395 **Atencio, Jorge E.** "Influencias geopoliticos de la posicion geografica Absoluta de America." *Boletin de Estudios Politicos*, 11 (1961), 218-225.

1396 **Atencio, Jorge E.** "Una perspectiva Argentina del pensamiento geopolitico." *Boletin de Estudios Politicos*, 7 (1957), 107-134.

1397 **Atkeson, Edward B.** "Hemispheric Denial: Geopolitical Imperatives and Soviet Strategy." *Strategic Review*, 4, No. 1 (Spring, 1976), 26-36.

1398 **Backheuser, Everardo.** "Alguns concietos geograficos e geopoliticos." *Boletim Geografico*, 4, No. 40 (Julho, 1946), 403-409.

1399 **Balza, Humberto.** "A Geopolitica: Nova estrategia Mundial from Revista Militar de Bolivia." *A Defense Nacional*, 375 (Ago., 1945), 369-374.

1400 **Beauregard, Ludger.** "La Problematique Geopolitique du Quebec." *Cahiers de Geographie du Quebec*, 24, No. 61 (Avril, 1980), 5-8.

1401 **Becker, Jorg.** "La Geopolitia del Papel para usos Culturales." *Foro Internacional*, 23, No. 2 (Octobre-Diciembre, 1982), 183-205.

1402 **Beesley, J.A.** "Rights and Responsibilities of Arctic Coastal States: The Canadian View." *Artic Circular*, 22, No. 2 (Spring/Summer, 1971), 98-110.

1403 **Benavides Correa, Alphonso.** "Antiguo y nuevo Peru: Esquema para una interpretacion geopolitica." *Revista de America*, 15 (Julio-Agosto, 1948), 115-123.

1404 **Berra, Angel Carlos.** "A provincia do Chaco e o influxo geopolitico do algodao." *A Defesa Nacional*, 467 (Junho, 1953), 78-86.

1405 **Bessone, Juan B.** "Ubicacion geopolitica de la republica Argentina en el Continente Americano y el mundo." *Revista de la facultad de Ciencias economicas, comerciales y politicas*, 62-63 (Mayo-Dic., 1950), 1191-1218.

1406 **Bowman, Isaiah.** "The Geographical Situation of the U.S. in Relation to World Politics." *Geographical Journal*, 112, No. 4-6 (October-December, 1948), 129-145.

1407 **Branchi, Camillo.** "L'Antartide e i Diritti del Cile." *L'Universo*, 34, No. 3 (May-June, 1954), 411-416.

1408 **Bravo Bravo, L.** "Bolivia: Vision personal de u n enigma geopolitical (Bolivia: Personal View of a Geopolitical Enigma)." *Revista Chilena de Geopolitica*, 26, No. 1 (1985), 51-66.

1409 "The British Title to Sovereignty in the Falkland Islands Dependencies." *Polar Record*, 8, No. 53 (May, 1956), 125-151.

1410 **Bryan, Carter R.** "America's Geopolitical Institute." *Foreign Commerce Weekly*, 7, No. 6 (May 16, 1942), 1-3+.

1411 **Buchanan, Daniel.** "The Geopolitical Relationship of Canada to the Rest of the World." In *Institute of Political Geography. Global Politics.* Russell H. Fitzgibbon, ed. Berkeley: University of California Press, 1944, 79-89.

1412 **Bull, Hedley.** "Kissinger: The Primacy of Geopolitics." *International Affairs*, 56, No. 3 (Summer, 1980), 484-487.

1413 **Burnham, James.** "Coming Rulers of the United States." *Fortune*, 24, No. 11 (November, 1941), 100-101+.

1414 **Canas Montalva, Ramon.** "Chile el mas Antartico de los paises del orbe y su responsabilidad continental en el sur Pacifico." *Revista Geografica de Chile*, 3, No. 4 (October, 1950), 23-44.

1415 **Canas Montalva, Ramon.** "Chile en el Pacifico, Argentina en el Atlantico: Factores de estabilidad Continental." *Revista Geografica de Chile*, 14 (1956-1957), 65-94.

1416 **Canas Montalva, Ramon.** "El Pacifico, epicentro de um nuevo mundo en estructuracion." *Revista Geografica de Chile*, 12 (September, 1954), 11-16.

1417 **Canas Montalva, Ramon.** "El Valor Geopolitica de la Posicion Antarctica de Chile." *Revista Geographica de Chile*, 6, No. 9 (Junio, 1953), 11-16.

1418 **Canas Montalva, Ramon.** "Fronteras; La Politica Internacional de Chile Frente a los Imperativos Geopoliticos Desprendidos de su Transcendente Posicion en el Pacifico Sur Antarctica." *Revista Geografica de Chile, Terra Australis*, 17 (1959), 15-36.

1419 **Canas Montalva, Ramon.** "Mision o Dimision di Chile en el Pacifico sur Antarctico? La Doctrina Argentina de la 'Cordillera Libre' Bajo un Disfraz Economico, Persique una Finalidad Politica, Contraria al Destino Historico de Chile in el Pacifico Sur." *Revista Geografica de Chile*, 10 (November, 1953), 9-12.

1420 **Canas Montalva, Ramon.** "Reflexiones Geopoliticas Sobre el Presente y el Futuro de America y de Chile." *Revista Geografica de Chile*, 13 (May, 1955), 7-23.

1421 **Carvalho, Carlos Delgado de.** "Geografiapolitica e geopolitica, estudos e ensaios." *Boletim Geografico*, 14, No. 133 (Julho-Agosto,1956), 382-391.

1422 **Chaunu, Pierre.** "Pour une 'geopolitique' de l'espace americain." In *Jahrbuch fur geschichte von Staat, Wirtschaft und gesellschaft latinamerikas*, 1 (1964), 3-26.

1423 **Chaves, Omar Emir.** "O Sentido geopolitico do descobrimento do Brasil." *A Defesa Nacional*, 532-533 (Nov.-Dez., 1958), 105-113, et 534 (Jan., 1959), 81-86.

1424 **Child, Jack.** "The American Southern Cone: Geopolitics and Conflict." In *Contemporary Issues in Latin America*, Barry Lentnek, ed. Muncie, Indiana: Conference of Latin American Geographers, 1983, 200-213.

1425 **Child, Jack.** "Geopolitical Thinking in Latin America." *Latin American Research Review*, 14, No. 2 (1979), 89-111.

1426 **Child, Jack.** "'Latin Lebensraum': The Geopolitics of Ibero-American Antarctica." *Applied Geography* [Buildford], 10, No. 4 (October, 1990), 287-305.

1427 **Child, Jack.** "South American Geopolitical Thinking and Antarctica." *International Studies Notes*, 11, No. 3 (1985), 23-28.

1428 **Chisolfo Araya, F.** "Influjo Geopolitico de la Isla de Pascua (Geopolitical Influence of Easter Island)." *Revista Chilena de Geopolitica*, 26, No. 1 (1985), 40-50.

1429 **Coelho, Djalma Poli.** "Da geografia Antiga a geopolitica." *Anuario do Servico Geografica de Exercito*, 2 (1949), 99-131.

1430 **Cohen, Saul B., ed.** *Problems and Trends in American Geography.* New York: Basic Books, 1967, 146-173.

1431 **Cortesao, Jaime.** "Cartografia antiga e geo-politica de Goias." *Revista de Imigracao e Colonizacao*, 2, No. 1 (Sem. 1, 1951), 30-44.

1432 **Coutau-Begarie, Herve.** "Geopolitique Theorique et Geopolitique Appliquee en Amerique Latine." *Herodote* [Paris], 57 (Avril-Juin, 1990), 160-179.

1433 **Crist, Raymond E.** "Jungle Geopolitics in Guyana: How a Communist Utopia that Ended in Massacre Came to be Sited." *American Journal of Economic and Sociology*, 40, No. 2 (April, 1981), 107-114.

1434 **Dodds, K. J.** "Geopolitics, Cartography and the State in South America." *Political Geographer*, 12, No. 4 (July, 1993), 361-381.

1435 **Dominguez, Jorge I.** "Cuba in the 1980's." *Foreign Affairs*, 65, No. 1 (Fall, 1986), 118-135.

1436 **Dyer, Brainerd.** "Robert J. Walker on Acquiring Greenland and Iceland." *Mississippi Valley Historical Review*, 27, No. 2 (September, 1940), 263-266.

1437 **Earle, Edward Mead.** "Power Politics and American World Politics." *Political Science Quarterly*, 58, No. 1 (March, 1943), 94-106.

1438 **Ewell, Judith.** "The Development of Venezuelan Geopolitical Analysis Since World War II." *Journal of American Studies*, 24, No. 3 (August, 1982), 295-320.

1439 **Ferreira, O.S.** "La geopolitica y el ejercito brasileno." *Aportes*, 12 (Abril, 1969), 111-132.

1440 **Festa, Aldo.** "La questione della Isole Aland." *Geopolitica*, 1, No. 6 (Guigno 30, 1939), 342-349.

1441 **Fialho, Adalardo.** "Geopolitica do Brasil." *A Defesa Nacional*, 470 (Set., 1953), 93-107.

1442 **Fialho, Adalardo.** "Geopolitica do Brasil." *Revista do institutto de geografia e historia Militar do Brasil*, 26 (1954), 161-168.

1443 **Field, Alexander James.** "Do Legal Systems Matter?" *Explorations in Economic History* [San Diego], 28, No. 1 (January, 1991), 1-35.

1444 **Flanders, Dwight P.** "Geopolitics and American Post-War Policy." *Political Science Quarterly*, 60, No. 4 (December, 1945), 578-585.

1445 **Foresta, Ronald A.** "Amazonia and the Politics of Geopolitics." *The Geographical Review* [New York], 82, No. 2 (April, 1992), 128-142.

1446 **Foucher, Michael.** "Les Antilles, iles de la mediterranee d'amerique: presentation geopolitique." *Notes et etudes documentaires*, 4753 (1984), 33-44.

1447 **Foucher, Michael.** "Le bassin mediterraneen d'Amerique: approches geopolitiques." *Herodote*, 27, 3° Trimestre (Novembre-Decembre, 1982), 16-40.

1448 **Garcia Camarrubias, M.J.** "Analisis Geopolitico del desrarollo del nucleo vital en Chile (Geopolitical Analysis of the Development of the Populated Nucleus of Chile)." *Revista Chilena de Geopolitica*, 21, No. 1 (1985), 23-29.

1449 **Gelber, Lionel.** "Canada's New Stature." *Foreign Affairs*, 24, No. 2 (January, 1946), 277-289.

1450 "La geopolitica: sus falacias y sus realidades." *Revista de la Sociedad geografica de Cuba*, 17, No. 2 (Abril-Junio, 1944), 43-61.

1451 **Gobbi, H.J.** "Problemas Australes Argentino-Chilenos. *Estrategia*, 9, No. 48, Parte 1 (Setiembre-Octumbre, 1977), 27-36.

1452 **Gorman, Stephen M.** "Geopolitics and Peruvian Foreign Policy." *Inter-American Economic Affairs*, 36, No. 2 (Autumn, 1982), 65-68.

1453 **Gorman, Stephen M.** "The High Stakes of Geopolitics in Tierra del Fuego." *Parameters—Journal of the U.S. Army War College*, 8, No. 2 (Summer, 1978), 45-56.

1454 **Grabendorff, Wolf.** "America Centralcomo region de crisis internacional." *Estudios internacionales*, 16, No. 63 (Julio-Septiembere, 1983), 483-497.

1455 **Greno Velasco, J.E.** "La adhesion de Brasil al Tratado Antartico." *Revista de Politica Internacional*, 146, No. 1 (January-February, 1976), 71-89.

1456 **Guglialmelli, J.E.** "Golbery do Couto e Silva, el 'destino manifesto' brasileno y el Atlantico Sur." *Estrategia*, 39, Parte 1 (Marzo-Abril, 1976), 6-24.

1457 **Hartshorne, Richard.** "The United States and the 'Shatter Zone' of Europe." In *Compass of the World*, H.W. Weigert and V. Stefansson, eds. New York: Macmillan, 1944, 203-214.

1458 **Helle, Reijo.** "Spatial Expansion of Oil Prospecting and Geopolitical Balance." *GeoJournal*, 14, No. 2 (March, 1987), 211-216.

1459 **Hepple, Leslie W.** "The Revival of Geopolitics." *Political Geography Quarterly*, 5, No. 4, Supplement (October, 1986), 521-536.

1460 **Herrick, Paul B., and Robins, Robert S.** "Varieties of Latin American Revolutions and Rebellions." *Journal of Developing Areas*, 10, No. 3 (April, 1976), 317-336.

1461 **Hessler, William H.** "A Geopolitics for America." *United States Naval Institute Proceedings*, 70, No. 493 (March, 1944), 245-253.

1462 **Hildebrandt, Walter.** "Geopolitik, das ideologische Werkzeng der Amerikanischen Imperialisten." *Zeitschrift fur Geopolitik*, Jahrg 24, Heft 7/8 (Juli-August, 1953), 439-440.

1463 **Holmes, John W.** "Canada and the United States in World Politics." *Foreign Affairs*, 40, No. 1 (October, 1961), 105-118.

1464 **Holmes, Olive.** "Brazil: Rising Power in the Americas." *Foreign Policy Reports*, 21, No. 15 (October 15, 1945), 210-219.

1465 **Ihl C., Pablo.** "Linea Geopolitica de Chile." *Revista Geografica de Chile*, 6, No. 8 (February, 1953), 25-44.

1466 **Isaac, Barry L.** "The Aztec 'Flowery War': A Geopolitical Explanation." *Journal of Anthropological Research*, 39, No. 4 (Winter, 1983), 415-432.

1467 **James, Preston E.** "Estructuras geopoliticas en America latina." *Boletin de Estudios Geograficos*, 2, No. 7 (2° Trimester, 1950), 151-158.

1468 **James, Preston E.** "Geopolitical Structures in Latin America." *Papers of the Michigan Academy of Science, Arts, and Letters*, 27 (1941), (1942), 369-376.

1469 **Kieffer, John E.** "Principios fundamentais e base da geopolitica da America do Sul e Cuba." *Revista Maritima Brasileira*, 74, No. 4-6 (1954), 201-244.

1470 **Kolliker Frers, Alfredo A.** "A Bolivia uma experiencia geopolitica: Alguns elementos da geopolitica do pivot sulamericano. Antonio de Castro Nascimento." *A Defesa Nacional*, 537 (Abril, 1959), 141-148.

1471 **Kuhn, Franz.** "Die Verteilung der Gemeinden in Siedlungsebiet Argentiniens. Eine geopolitishe Analyse." *Zeitschrift fur Geopolitik*, 3, No. 1 (Jan., 1926), 34-44.

1472 **Krug, Werner G.** "Alaska-Zentrum Polarer Strategie." *Zeitschrift fur Geopolitik*, Jahrg 23, Heft 8 (August, 1952), 458-462.

1473 **Kuniholm, Bruce R.** "Apples and Dominoes: The Northern Tier as Crucible for Postwar America." *Jerusalem Journal of International Relations*, 4, No. 1 (March, 1979), 1-22.

1474 **Levine, B.B.** "Geopolitical and Cultural Competition in the Caribbean--An Introduction: Cuba Versus the United States. In *The New Cuban Presence in the Caribbean*, B.B. Levine, ed. Boulder, Colorado: Westview Press, 1983, 1-17.

1475 **Lukashev, K.I.** "Beurteiling der Amerikanischen Geopolitik durch Sowjetgeographen." *Zeitschrift fur Geopolitik*, Jahrg 23, Heft 10 (October, 1952), 592-604.

1476 **Lukashev, K.I.** "Geostrategicheskie'Kontseptsu' Amerikanskikh Geopolitikov." *Izvestiia Vsesouiznogo Geograficheskogo Obschchestva*, 85, No. 4 (July-August, 1953), 423-433.

1477 **Manley, Michael.** "Overcoming Insularity in Jamaica." *Foreign Affairs*, 49, No. 1 (October, 1970), 100-110.

1478 **Marul Bermudez, F.** "Chile: Geopolitica del Pacifico Sur." *Geopolitica*, 3, No. 5 (Abril-Agosto, 1978), 27-34.

1479 **Massi, Ernesto.** "Aspetti geopolitici del panamericanesimo." *Geopolitica*, 2, No. 8-9 (Agosto-Settembre, 1940), 333-355.

1480 **Mattos, Carlos de Meira.** "Aspectos geopoliticos de nosso territorio." *Boletin geografico*, 10, No. 106 (Jan.-Fev., 1952), 48-49.

1481 **Mattos, Carlos de Meira.** "Aspectos geopoliticos de nosso territorio." *Revista Brasileira dos municipos*, 4, No. 15 (Julho-Set., 1951), 362-363.

1482 **Mattos, Carlos de Meira.** "Consciencia geopolitica brasileira." *Cadernos Brasileiros*, 3, No. 3 (Julho-Set., 1961), 63-65.

1483 **Mattos, Carlos de Meira.** "Consciencia geopolitica brasileira." *A Defesa Nacional*, 558 (Jan., 1961), 141-144.

1484 **Mattos, Carlos de Meira.** "Interpretacao geopolitica do Brasil." *A Defesa Nacional*, 532-533 (Nov.-Dez., 1958), 99-104.

1485 **Mattos, Carlos de Meira.** "Interpretacao geopolitica do Brasil." *Revista do instituto Historico e geografico de Sao Paulo*, 58 (1960), 31-42.

1486 **Mattos, Carlos de Meira.** "Reflexos sobre a geopolitica do Brasil." *Cadernos Brasileiros*, 4, No. 1 (Jan.-Marco, 1962), Complete issue.

1487 **Maull, Otto.** "Brasiliens Geopolitische Struktur." *Zeitschrift fur Geopolitik*, 1, No. 3 (Marz, 1924), 90-100.

1488 **Munita Contreras, Herman.** "Intergracion geopolitica de Chile y Argentina." *Economia y Finanzas*, (Sept., 1948), 5-13.

1489 **O'Reilly, Stenberg H.** "Brazil: Complex Giant." *Foreign Affairs*, 43, No. 2 (January, 1965), 297-311.

1490 **Packenham, Robert A.** "Capitalist Dependency and Socialist Dependency: The Case of Cuba." *Journal of Interamerican Studies and World Affairs*, 28, No. 1 (Spring, 1986), 59-92.

1491 **Pastor, Robert A.** "Does the United States Push Revolution to Cuba: The Case of Grenada." *Journal of Interamerican Studies and World Affairs*, 28, No. 1 (Spring, 1986), 1-34.

1492 **Pittman, Howard Taylor.** "Geopolitics and Foreign Policy in Argentina, Brazil, and Chile." In *Latin American Foreign Policies*, E.G. Ferris and J.K. Lincoln, eds. Boulder, Colorado: Westview Press, 1981.

1493 **Reynolds, Clark G.** "The Sea in the Making of America." *United States Naval Institute Proceedings*, 102, No. 881 (July, 1976), 36-51.

1494 **Rodrigues, Lysias A.** "Estrutura geopolitica da Amozonia brasileira." *A Defesa Nacional*, 458 (Set., 1952), 101-110 et 461 (Dez., 1952), 95-100.

1495 **Rodrigues, Lysias A.** "Estrutura geopolitica da Amozonia brasileira." *Revista do instituto de geografia e historia militar do Brasil*, 19-20 (1951), 87-144.

1496 **Rodrigues, Lysias A.** "O Poligono geopolitico do sul so Brasil." *Revista do instituto de geografia e historia militar do Brasil*, 25 (1954), 33-72.

1497 **Roucek, Joseph S.** "The Geopolitics of the Aleutians." *Journal of Geography*, 50, No. 1 (January, 1951), 24-29.

1498 **Roucek, Joseph S.** "The Geopolitics of the United States." *American Journal of Economics and Sociology*, 14, No. 2 (January, 1955), 185-192; No. 3 (April, 1955), 287-303.

1499 **Samuels, M.A., and Jackson, W.A. Douglas.** "U.S. Political Interests in a World of Party Internationals: How Does the U.S. Promote Democracy?" In *Transnational Parties*. R.M. Goldman, ed. Lanham, Maryland: University Press of America, 1983, 261-292.

1500 **Sandner, Gerhard.** "Politisch-Geographische Raumstrukturen und Geopolitik im Karibischen Raum." *Geographische Zeitschrift*, 69 Jahr, Heft 1 (Januar, 1981), 34-56.

1501 **Sandner, William.** "Sovereignty and Interdependence in the New World; Comments on the Inter-American System." *Department of State Bulletin*, 18, No. 449 (February, 1948), 155-184.

1502 **Schafer, Otto.** "Geopolitik des karibischen Raumes." *Geographischer Anzeiger*, 45 Jahrg, Heft 1-4 (Januar-Februar, 1944), 2-7.

1503 **Schultze, J.H.** "Die politich-geographische Struktur Chiles." *Zeitschrift fur Geopolitik*, 4, No. 7-12 (Juli-Dez., 1927), 707-717.

1504 **Selcher, W.A.** "The National Security Doctrine and Policies of the Brazilian Government." *Parameters: Journal of the U.S. Army War College*, 7, No. 1 (Spring, 1977), 10-24.

1505 **Sharp, J. P.** "Publishing American Identity: Popular Geopolitics, Myth and The Reader's Digest." *Political Geography*, 12, No. 6 (November, 1993), 491-503.

1506 **Tambs, Lewis A.** "Factors geopoliticos en America Latina." *Cultura Boliviana*, 6, No. 33 (1969), 45, et No. 34 (1969), 26-27.

1507 **Tambs, Lewis A.** "Latin American Geopolitics: A Basic Bibliography." *Revista Geografica*, 73 (Dezembro, 1970), 71-105.

1508 **Teal, John J., Jr.** "Alaska, Fulcrum of Power." *Foreign Affairs*, 27, No. 1 (October, 1948), 86-95.

1509 **Torres, James F.** "Concentration of Political Power and Levels of Economic Development in Latin American Countries." *Journal of Developing Areas*, 7, No. 3 (April, 1973), 397-409.

1510 **Tosta, Octavio.** "Everardo Backheuser, O precursor da geopolitica no Brasil." *A Defesa Nacional*, 532-533, (Nov.-Dez., 1958), 139-161.

1511 **Tosta, Octavio.** "Geopolitica do Prata." *A Defesa Nacional*, No. 551 (Junho, 1960), 131-132.

1512 **Tosta, Octavio.** "A geopolitica no Brasil." *A*

Defesa Nacional, 547 (1960), 109-114, et No. 548 (Marco, 1960), 125-127.

1513 **Tuathail, Gearoid O.** "The Language and Nature of the 'New Geopolitics'--The Case of U.S. El Salvador Relations." *Political Geography Quarterly*, 5, No. 1 (January, 1986), 73-86.

1514 **Tuathail, G. O.** "'Pearl Harbour Without Bombs': A Critical Geopolitics of the U.S.-Japan 'FSX' Debate." *Environment and Planning A* [London], 24, No. 7 (July, 1992), 975-994.

1515 **Valladao, Alfredo G.** "Le Bresil: L'adieu a la geopolitica. *Herodote* [Paris], No. 57 (Avril-Juin, 1990), 180-196.

1516 **Vidal, Germano Seidl.** "A Hileia a luz da geopolitica." *A Defesa Nacional*, 432 (Julho, 1950), 77-80.

1517 **Viscarrac.** "Geopolitica boliviana: Bolivia no Continente sudamericano." *A Defesa Nacional*, 487 (Fev., 1955), 83-89.

1518 **Viscarrac.** "Geopolitica boliviana: A Bolivia no Continente sudamericano." *A Defesa Nacional*, 537 (Abril, 1959), 149-156.

1519 **Vitkovskiy, O.V.** "Political Geography and Geopolitics: A Recurrence of American Geopolitics (and reply by A.K. Henrikson). *Soviet Geography, Review and Translation*, 22 (1981), 586-597.

1520 **Wade, William W.** "Canada's New Role in World Affairs." *Foreign Policy Reports*, 27, No. 7 (June, 1951), 74-83.

1521 **Waderley, Alberto.** "Corumba: Um imperativo geopolitico." *A Defesa Nacional*, 488 (Marco, 1955), 77-85.

ASIA

Books

1522 **Adams, Ruth.** *The Chinese View of Their Place in the World*. London: Oxford University Press, 1964.

1523 **Bhagat, G.** *Americans in India 1784-1860*. New York City: New York University Press, 1970.

1524 **Chen, Yi-Fong.** *Geopolitical Context and National Formation in Taiwan*. Columbus: Master's thesis, Ohio State University, 1993.

1525 **Clubb, Oliver E.** *Twentieth Century China*. New York City: Columbia University Press, 1964.

1526 **Cohen, Saul B.** *Jerusalem: Bridging the Four Walls: A Geopolitical Perspective*. New York: Herzl Press, 1977.

1527 **Conway, Timothy.** *From Sideshow to Democratic Kampuchea: The Construction of Cambodia in Geopolitical and Revolutionary Space.* Syracuse, NY: Master's thesis, Syracuse University, 1993.

1528 **Crow, Ralph E.; Grant, Philip; Ibrahim, Saad E., eds.** *Arab Nonviolent Political Struggle in the Middle East.* Boulder, CO: Lynne Rienner Publishers, 1990.

1529 **East, W. Gordon; Spate, O.H.K; and Fisher, Charles A.** *The Changing Map of Asia.* 5th edition. London: Methuen, 1971.

1530 **Esterline, John, and Esterline, Mae H.** *How the Dominoes Fall: Southeast Asia in Perspective.* Lanham, Maryland: Hamilton Press, 1986.

1531 **Friters, Gerard M.** *Outer Mongolia and Its International Position.* Baltimore, Maryland: Johns Hopkins University Press, 1949.

1532 **Fuller, Graham E.** *The "Center of the Universe": The Geopolitics of Iran.* Boulder, CO: Westview Press, 1991.

1533 **Gananathan, V.S.** *Geopolitics and India.* Poona: Poona Municipal Gazette, 1952.

1534 **Gopal, Madan.** *India as a World Power: Aspects of Foreign Policy.* New Delhi: Sasar Publications, 1974.

1535 **Gow, James, ed.** *Iraq, the Gulf Conflict and the World Community.* London: Brassey's, 1993.

1536 **Halderman, J.W.** *The Middle East Crisis: Test of International Law.* Dobbs Ferry, New York: Oceania Publications, 1969.

1537 **Haushofer, Karl.** *Dai Nihon; betrachtungen uber Gross-Japans wehrkraft, weltstellung und zukunft.* Berlin: E.S. Mittler, 1913.

1538 **Haushofer, Karl.** *Der Kontinentalblock Mittleuropa, Eurasien, Japan.* Munchen: F. Eher Nachf, 1941.

1539 **Haushofer, Karl.** *Geopolitik der Pan-Ideen.* Berlin: Zentral-Verlag, 1931.

1540 **Hinton, Harold C.** *Communist China in World Politics.* Boston, Massachusetts: Houghton Mifflin, 1966.

1541 **Horiuchi, Russell Nozomi.** *Chiseigaku: Japanese Geopolitics.* Seattle: University of Washington, Ph.D., 1975.

1542 **Hsiung, James C., ed.** *Asia Pacific in the New World Politics.* Boulder: Lynne Rienner Publishers, 1993.

1543 **Hudson, G.F.** *The Far East in World Politics.* London: Oxford University Press, 1953.

1544 *India and Pacific Region, International Labour Office Paper No. 2.* Quebec, Canada: Institute of Pacific Relations, 1942.

1545 **Jack, Ernest.** *The Rising Crescent; Turkey Yesterday, Today, and Tomorrow.* New York: Farrar & Rinehart, 1944.

1546 **Kyogku, Jun-ichi.** *The Political Dynamics of Japan.* Translated by Nobutaka Ike. Tokyo: University of Tokyo Press, 1987.

1547 **Lenczowski, George.** *The Middle East in World Affairs.* Ithaca, New York: Cornell University Press, 1952.

1548 **Levi, Werner.** *Free India in Asia.* Minneapolis: University of Minnesota Press, 1952.

1549 **Malik, Hafeez, ed.** *Central Asia: Its Strategic Importance and Future Prospects.* New York: St. Martin's Press, 1994.

1550 **Mills, Lennox A.** *Malaya: A Political and Economic Appraisal.* Minneapolis: University of Minnesota Press, 1958.

1551 **Pakistan Embassy.** *Peril and Opportunity in Kashmir: Background Report.* Washington, D.C.: Pakistan Embassy, Information Division, 1961.

1552 **Pannikar, K.M.** *The Future of South-East Asia; An Indian View.* New York: Macmillan, 1943.

1553 **Petrov, V.P.** *China, Emerging World Power.* Princeton, New Jersey: Van Nostrand Searchlight Series, 1967.

1554 **Pye, Lucian W.** *Asian Power and Politics: The Cultural Dimensions of Authority.* Cambridge: The Belknap Press of Harvard University, 1985.

1555 **Quddus, Syed Abdul.** *Afghanistan and Pakistan: A Geopolitical Study.* Lahore, Pakistan: Ferozsons, 1982.

1556 **Rajchman, M.** *An Atlas of Far Eastern Politics.* London: Oxford University Press, 1940.

1557 **Reed, Douglas.** *Somewhere South of Suez; A Further Survey of the Grand Design of the Twentieth Century.* New York: Devin-Adair, 1951.

1558 **Rowe, David Nelson.** *China Among the Powers.* New York: Harcourt Brace, 1945.

1559 **Sidaway, J.** *Geopolitics, Geography and Terrorism in the Middle East.* Reading, U.K.: Reading University, Department of Geography, Discussion Paper No. 7, 1992.

1560 **Singh, Govind Saran.** *Martha Geopolitics and the Indian Nation.* Bombay: Manaktalas, 1966.

1561 **Soon Sun Cho.** *Korea in World Politics, 1940-50.* Berkeley and Los Angeles: University of California Press, 1967.

1562 **Spate, O.H.K., et Learmonth, A.T.A.** *India and Pakistan: Land, People and Economy.* New York: Barnes and Noble, 1972.

1563 **Stalker, John N.** *Power Politics in the Middle East.* Honolulu: University of Hawaii, Occasional Paper No. 59, 1953.

1564 **Tice, Robert D.** *Geopolitics and the Ladakh Boundary.* St. Louis, Missouri: St. Louis University, Ph.D., 1965.

1565 **Tobin, Chester M.** *Turkey, Key to the East.* New York: Putnam, 1944.

1566 **Tsang, Steve, ed.** *In the Shadow of China: Political Developments in Taiwan Since 1949.* Honolulu: University of Hawaii Press, 1993.

1567 **Vandenbosch, Amry, and Butwell, Richard A.** *Southeast Asia Among the World Powers.* Lexington: University of Kentucky Press, 1957.

1568 **Ward, Barbara, and Others.** *Hitler's Route to Baghdad.* London: Allen & Unwin, 1939.

1569 **Whiting, Allen S., and Sheng, Shih-ts'ai.** *Sinkiang: Pawn or Pivot?* East Lansing: Michigan State University Press, 1958.

1570 **Wilcox, Wayne Ayres; Rose, Leo E.; and Boyd, Gavin, eds.** *Asia and the International System.* Cambridge, Massachusetts: Winthrop, 1972.

1571 **Wilson, James N.** *Graphic Exercises in the Geopolitics of Asia.* New York City: Columbia Teachers College, Ph.D., 1950.

Journals

1572 **Alexandrowicz-Alexander, Charles Henry.** "India and the Tibetan Tragedy." *Foreign Affairs*, 31, No. 3 (April, 1953), 495-500.

1573 **Alexandrowicz-Alexander, Charles Henry.** "The Legal Position of Tibet." *American Journal of International Law*, 48, No. 2 (April, 1954), 265-274.

1574 **Alpher, Joseph.** "Israel's Security Concerns in the Peace Process." *International Affairs* [Cambridge], 70, No. 2 (April, 1994), 229-241.

1575 "Aufgaban in Pakistan." *Zeitschrift fur Geopolitik*, Jahrg 31, Heft 7/8 (Juli-August, 1960), 50-52.

1576 **Betts, Richard K.** "Wealth, Power, and Instability: East Asia and the United States after the Cold War." *International Security* [Cambridge, MA], 18, No. 3 (Winter, 1993-94), 34-77.

1577 **Bhattacharyya, N.N.** "Geopolitics of North-East India." *Journal of North-East India Geographical Society*, 21, Nos. 1 and 2 (1989), 71-76.

1578 **Bradsher, Henry S.** "Tibet Struggles to Survive." *Foreign Affairs*, 47, No. 4 (July, 1969), 750-762.

1579 **Broek, Jan O.M.** "Diversity and Unity in Southeast Asia." *Geographical Review*, 34, No. 2 (April, 1944), 175-195.

1580 **Baeler, William M.** "Taiwan: A Problem of International Law or Politics?" *World Today*, 27, No. 6 (June, 1971), 256-266.

1581 **Chandrasekhar, S.** "The New Map of India." *Population Review*, 1, No. 1 (January, 1957), 32-36.

1582 **Chatterjee, S.P.** "The Changing Map of India." *Geographical Review of India*, 19, No. 2 (June, 1957), 1-5.

1583 **Cohen, Saul B.** "The Geopolitical Aftermath of the Gulf War." *Focus* [New York], 41, No. 2 (Summer 1991), 23-26.

1584 **Cohen, Saul B.** "Middle East Geopolitical Transformation: The Disappearance of a Shatterbelt." *Journal of Geography* [Indiana, PA], 91, No. 1 (January/February, 1992), 2-10.

1585 **Das Gupta, Sivaprasad.** "The Changing Map of India." *Geographical Review of India*, 22, No. 3 (September, 1960), 23-33, et No. 4 (1960), 13-32.

1586 **Diettrich, Sigismond De R.** "Some Geopolitical Aspects of the Indo-Pak Sub-Continent." *United Asia*, 15, No. 3 (March, 1963), 227-234.

1587 **Fisher, Charles A.** "Containing China?" *Geographical Journal*, 136, Part 4 (December, 1970), 534-556 and 137, Part 3 (September, 1971), 281-310.

1588 **Fisher, Charles A** "The Expansion of Japan: A Study in Oriental Geopolitics." *Geographical Journal*, 115, Nos. 1-3 (January-March, 1950), 1-19, Nos. 4-6 (April-June, 1950), 179-193.

1589 **Fisher, Charles A** "Southeast Asia: The Balkans of the Orient? A Study in Continuity and Change." *Geography*, 47, Part 4 (November, 1962), 347-367.

1590 "Geopolitics of Southeast Asia." *United Asia*, 15, No. 3 (March, 1963), 217-262.

1591 **Ghisolfo Araya, F.** "Percepcion Asiatica del Pacifico, apuntes para un estudio Geopolitico (Asian Perceptions of the Pacific: The Basis for a Geopolitical Study)." *Revista Chilena de Geopolitica*, 2, No. 2 (196), 56-67.

1592 **Ghosheh, Baher A.** "Making Sense of Middle East Geopolitics." *Focus* [New York], 42, No. 4 (Winter, 1992), 20-24.

1593 **Haggard, M.T.** "North Korea's International Position." *Asian Survey*, 5, No. 8 (August, 1965), 375-388.

1594 **Harary, Frank.** "A Structural Analysis of the Situation in the Middle East in 1956." *Journal of Conflict Resolution*, 5, No. 2 (June, 1961), 167-178.

1595 **Harrigan, Anthony.** "Seapower in History—India and China." *Contemporary Review*, 228, No. 1322 (March, 1976), 132-138.

1596 **Harrison, Selig S.** "Baluch Nationalism and Super Power Rivalry." *International Security*, 5, No. 3 (Winter, 1980-81), 152-163.

1597 **Harrison, Selig S.** "Nightmare in Baluchistan." *Foreign Policy*, 32 (Fall, 1978), 136-160.

1598 **Harrison, Selig S.** "Troubled India and Her Neighbors." *Foreign Affairs*, 43, No. 2 (January, 1965), 312-330.

1599 **Haushofer, Karl.** "Grundzuge der Geopolitik von Gross Sudostazien." *Zeitschrift fur Geopolitik*, Jahrg 20, Heft 9 (Dez., 1943), 328-30.

1600 **Hopkinson, A.J.** "The Position of Tibet." *Journal of the Royal Central Asian Society*, 37, Parts 3-4 (July-October, 1950), 228-239.

1601 **Hulbert, Francois, and Labrecque, Georges.** "Eckstein der Geopolitischen Struktur Kanadas." *Geographische Rundschau* [Braunschweig], 46, Heft 1 (Januar, 1994), 18-26.

1602 "India as a World Power." *Foreign Affairs*, 27, No. 4 (July, 1949), 540-550.

1603 "Indo-China: Gateway to Southeast Asia." *World Today*, 7, No. 6 (June, 1951), 240-248.

1604 **Iyer, Raghavan.** "The Significance and Survival of Tibet." *Journal of the Royal Central Asian Society*, 49, Parts 3-4 (July-October, 1962), 255-265.

1605 **Jain, J.P.** "The Legal Status of Formosa; A Study of British, Chinese, and Indian Views." *American Journal of International Law*, 57, No. 1 (January, 1963), 25-45.

1606 **Karan, Pradyumna Prasad.** "Geopolitical Structure of Bhutan." *India Quarterly*, 19, No. 3 (July-September, 1963), 203-213.

1607 **Karan, Pradyumna Prasad.** "Geopolitical Structure of India." In *Proceedings of the 17th International Geographical Congress, Washington, D.C., 1952.* Washington, D.C.: Annals of the Association of American Geographers, 1957, 524-527.

1608 **Karan, Pradyumna Prasad** "Geopolitics of New India." *Geographer*, 4, No. 2 (December, 1951), 49-56.

1609 **Karan, Pradyumna Prasad** "India's Role in Geopolitics." *India Quarterly*, 9, No. 2 (April-June, 1953), 160-169.

1610 **Khan, Mohammed.** "Pakistani Geopolitics: The Diplomatic Perspective." *International Security*, 5, No. 1 (Summer, 1980), 26-36.

1611 **Kozicki, Richard J.** "India and Israel; A Problem in Asian Politics." *Middle Eastern Affairs*, 9, No. 5 (May, 1958), 162-172.

1612 **Kureisky, Khalil Ullah.** "Strategical Importance of Kashmir to Pakistan." *Pakistan Geographical Review*, 6, No. 2 (1951), 10-18.

1613 **Kuriyan, K.** "The International Status of India: Present and Future." *Asiatic Review*, 38, No. 134 (April, 1942), 113-119. Discussion: 119-124.

1614 **Lattimore, Owen.** "Asia in a New World Order." *Foreign Policy Reports*, 18, No. 12 (September 1, 1942), 150-163.

1615 **Lattimore, Owen.** "Yunnan, Pivot of Southeast Asia." *Foreign Affairs*, 21, No. 3 (April, 1943), 476-493.

1616 **Legorreta, Omar Martinez.** "The Balance of Power and Tensions in Asia and the Pacific Basin: The Role of the Intermediate Powers." *Australian Outlook*, 36, No. 3 (December, 1982), 40-45.

1617 **Levi, Werner.** "Nepal in World Politics." *Pacific Affairs*, 30, No. 3 (September, 1957), 236-248.

1618 **Li, Tieh-Tseng.** "The Legal Position of Tibet." *American Journal of International Law*, 50, No. 2 (April, 1956), 394-404.

1619 **Malik, I. H.** "Beyond Ayodhya: Implications for Regional Security in South Asia." *Asian Affairs* [London], 24, Part 3 (October, 1993), 290-303.

1620 **Mattos, Carlos de Meira.** "Oriente-Medio: punctum dolens da geopolitica mundial." *A Defesa Nacional*, 547-548 (Fev., 1960), 114-124; 548 (Marco, 1960), 129-134.

1621 **McColl, Robert W.** "Geopolitical Themes in Contemporary Asian Revolution." *Geographical Review*, 65, No. 3 (July, 1975), 301-310.

1622 **Menefee, Selden C.** "Japan's Global Conceit." *Asia and the Americas*, 43, No. 6 (June, 1943), 330-332.

1623 **Mylroie, Laurie.** "The Superpowers and the Iran-Iraq War." *American-Arab Affairs*, 21 (Summer, 1987), 15-26.

1624 **Nair, Kusum.** "Where India, China, and Russia Meet (Ladakh)." *Foreign Affairs*, 35, No. 2 (January, 1958), 330-339.

1625 **Nand, Nitya.** "Kashmir: A Geopolitical Analysis." *Geographical Observer*, 2 (March, 1966), 54-61.

1626 **Noorani, A.G.** "Soviet Ambitions in South Asia." *International Security*, 4, No. 3 (Winter, 1979-80), 31-59.

1627 **Palmer, Norman D.** "India's Position in Asia." *Journal of International Affairs*, 17, No. 2 (Fall, 1963), 126-141.

1628 **Panda, B.P.** "Geopolitical Problems of Middle East." *Journal of Geography*, 1, No. 1 (1959), 27-36.

1629 **Pant, A.** "The Challenge of the Himalayas: Geopolitics of Confrontation or Cooperation." *Transactions*, 2, No. 2 (July, 1980), 77-89.

1630 **Pelletier, Philippe.** "Miyake-Jima, ou la Geopolotique Insulaire." *revue Belge de Geographie* [Bruxelles], ll4e Annee, Fasc. 46 (1990), 61-78.

1631 **Polisk, A.N.** "Geopolitics of the Middle East." *Middle Eastern Affairs*, 4, No. 8-9 (August-September, 1953), 271-277.

1632 **Racine, Jean.** "Vers une geopolitique de l'Inde." *Herodote*, 2°-3° Trimestres, 33-34 (1984), 89-116.

1633 **Razvi, Mujtaba.** "Pakistan's Geopolitical Environment and Security." *Pakistan Horizon*, 35, No. 3 (Third Quarter, 1982), 29-43.

1634 **Ross, Colin R.** "Das weltpolitische Vakuum der Erde. Samarkand-Hsinking-Chungking-Lhasa." *Zeitschrift fur Geopolitik*, 17, Jahrg, Heft 1 (Januar, 1940), 6-9.

1635 **Roucek, Joseph S.** "La Geopolitica de Oceano Indico." *Cuadernos Africanos y Orientales*, 37 (1957), 27-39.

1636 **Roucek, Joseph S.** "The Geopolitics of Afghanistan." *Social Studies*, 48, No. 4 (April, 1957), 127-129.

1637 **Roucek, Joseph S.** "Geopolitics of Asia." *United Asia*, 15, No. 4 (April, 1963), 290-296.

1638 **Roucek, Joseph S.** "The Geopolitics of Pakistan." *Social Studies*. 44, No. 7 (November, 1953), 254-258.

1639 **Roucek, Joseph S.** "The Geopolitics of Thailand." *Social Studies*, 45, No. 2 (February, 1954), 57-63.

1640 **Roucek, Joseph S.** "Notes on the Geopolitics of Singapore." *Journal of Geography*, 52, No. 2 (February, 1953), 78-81.

1641 **Russett, Bruce M.** "The Asia Rimland as a 'Region' for Containing China." *Public Policy*, 15, No. 2 (Winter, 1967), 226-249.

1642 **Safir, Al.** "Cartas del oriente medio mosaico geopolitico de una region en crisis (Maps of the Middle East Geopolitical Mosaic of a Region in Crisis)." *Revista Chilena de Geopolitica*, 2, No. 2 (1986), 77-87.

1643 **Safir, Al.** "Cartas del oriente medio mosaico geopolitico de una region en crisis. III Parte: el conflicto Iraq-Iran (Maps of the Middle East. Geopolitical Mosaic of a Region in Crisis. Part 3: The Iraq-Iran Conflict)." *Revista Chilena de Geopolitica*, 2, No. 1 (1985), 103-125.

1644 **Safir, Al.** "Letters from the Middle East: The Geopolitical Mosaic of a Region in Crisis." *Revista Chilena de Geopolitica*, 2 (1985), 96-117.

1645 **Sarwar, Ghulam.** "Pakistan's Geo-Political and Strategic Compulsions--A Review Article." *Pakistan Horizon*, 33, No. 3 (Third Quarter, 1980), 96-100.

1646 **Schafer, Otto.** "Geopolitische Wandlungen im Grossen Ozean und in Ostasien." *Geographischer Anzeiger*, 43, Jahrg, Heft 13-16 (Juli-August, 1942), 272-277.

1647 **Seth, S.P.** "The Indian Sub-Continent: New Power Equations." *Australian Outlook*, 26, No. 3 (December, 1972), 306-314.

1648 **Shimoni, Yaacov.** "Israel in the Pattern of Middle East Politics." *Middle East Journal*, 4, No. 3 (July, 1950), 277-295.

1649 **Singh, Savindra.** "The Naga Problem: A Geopolitical Appraisal." *National Geographer*, 6 (1971), 47-55.

1650 **Soffner, Heinz.** "Geopolitics in the Far East." *Amerasia*, 6, No. 13 (January 25, 1943), 513-521.

1651 **Stauffer, Robert B.** "The Political Importance of China's Northeast." *University of Hawaii: Occasional Paper*, 59 (May, 1953), 112-130.

1652 Stubbs, Richard. "Geopolitics and the Political
      Economy of Southeast Asia." *International
      Journal*, 44, No. 3 (Summer, 1989), 517-540.

1653 Swearingen, Will D. "Geopolitic Origins of the
      Iran-Iraq War." *Geographical Review*, 78, No. 4
      (October, 1988), 405-416.

1654 Takeuchi, Keiichi. "Geographic Research and
      Principles of Geopolitics in Contemporary Japan."
      Rivista Geografica Italiana [Pisa], 99, Fasc. 2
      (Guigno, 1992), 145-165.

1655 Takeuchi, K. "Geopolitics and Geography in
      Japan Reexamined." *Hitotsubashi Journal of
      Social Studies*, 12, No. 1 (1980), 14-24.

1656 Topping, Seymour. "Indo-China on the Razor's
      Edge." *Foreign Affairs*, 29, No. 3 (April, 1951),
      468-474.

1657 "Turkey, a Key State." *Round Table*, 109
      (December, 1937), 110-124.

1658 U.S. Naval Institute. "Pakistan and the
      Himalayas." In *Proceedings of the Naval Institute*,
      by W.H. Hessler. Washington, D.C.:
      Government Printing Office, 80 (1954), 850-857.

1659 Vuoristo, Kai-Veikko. "Geopolitiikan ja
      Geoekonomian Pacific Rim." *Terra*, 106, No. 2
      (1994), 81-88.

1660 Wang, Gungwu. "Greater China and the Chinese
      Overseas." *The China Quarterly* [London], No.
      136 (December, 1993), 926-948.

1661 Wichtendahl M. Raul. "Os fatores geopoliticos e
      a inidade nacional." *A Defesa National*, 538
      (Maio, 1959), 169-172.

1662 Wright, Claudia. "Iraq-New Power in the Middle
      East." *Foreign Affairs*, 58, No. 2 (Winter
      1979/80), 257-277.

1663 Wright, E.O. "The 'Greater Syria' Project in
      Arab Politics." *World Affairs*, 5, No. 3 (July,
      1951), 318-329.

AUSTRALIA AND ANTARCTICA

Books and Journals

1664 Agiulai Navarro, Mariano. "Disputas sobre la
      Antartida." *Estudios Ameicanos*, 3, No. 8 (Enero,
      1951), 121-131.

1665 Andrews, John B. "Antarctic Geopolitics."
      Australian Outlook, 11, No. 3 (September, 1957),
      3-9.

1666 "Antarctic Treaty, Signed at Washington,
      December 1, 1959." *American Journal of

      International Law*, 54, No. 2 (April, 1960),
      447-483.

1667 "Antarctic Treaty Signed by IGY Nations: Polar
      Region Established as Neutral Science Reserve."
      Science, 130, No. 3389 (December 11, 1959),
      1641-1644.

1668 "Antarctica: A War for Frozen Colonies Looms in
      the World's Vastest Wasteland." Excerpt: *Life*, 6,
      No. 24 (June 12, 1939), 42-49.

1669 Archdale, H.E. "Legality in the Antarctic."
      Australian Outlook, 11, No. 3 (September, 1957),
      10-16.

1670 Auburn, F.M. *Antarctic Law and Politics*.
      Canberra: Croom Helm, 1982.

1671 Augur, Helen. "America's Claim to the
      Antarctic." *Travel*, 88, No. 3 (January, 1947),
      4-9+.

1672 Brochu, Michel. "Pour une geopolitique de
      l'Ocean Glacial Arctique." *Revue de Geographie
      de Montreal*, 65, No. 2 (1971), 109-110.

1673 Brown, R.N. Rudmose. "Political Claims in the
      Antarctic." *World Affairs*, N.S., 1, No. 4
      (October, 1947), 393-401.

1674 Canas Montalva, Ramon. "La Antartica;
      Visionaria Apreciacion du General O'Higgins."
      Revista Geografica de Chile, 14 (1956-57), 5-23.

1675 Cant, Gilbert. "Oceania: What to Do About It?"
      Asia and the Americas, 43, No. 12 (December,
      1943), 662-666.

1676 Cardona, Gaetano. "Importanza strategica delle
      zone polari artiche." *L'Universo*, 27, No. 2
      (Marzo-Aprile, 1947), 125-139.

1677 Da Costa, J.F. "Antartida: O problema
      politico." *Revista Brasileira de Politica
      Internacional*, 1 (1958), 41-58.

1678 Da Costa, J.F. *Souverainete sur l'Antarctique*.
      Paris: Librairie Generale de Droit et de
      Jurisprudence, 1958.

1679 Dalby, S. "The 'Kiwi Disease': Geopolitical
      Discourse in Aotearoa/New Zealand and the South
      Pacific." *Political Geography*, 12, No. 5
      (September, 1993), 437-456.

1680 Delgado de Carvalho, Carlos, and de Castro,
      Therezinha. "A Questao da Antartica." *Boletim
      Geografica*, 14, No. 135 (November-December,
      1956), 502-506.

1681 **Doumenge, Francois.** "LaDynamique Geopolitique du Pacifique Sud (1965-1990)." *Les Cahiers d'Outre-Mer* [Bordeaux], 43e, No. 170 (Avril-Juin, 1990), 113-188.

1682 **Fiske, Clarence, and Fiske, Mrs. Clarence.** "Territorial Claims in the Antarctic." *United States Naval Institute Proceedings*, 85, No. 1 (January, 1959), 82-91.

1683 **Fitzpatrick, John.** "The Geopolitics of the Garnaut Report." *Australian Journal of International Affairs* [Canberra], 44, No. 1 (April, 1990), 9-20.

1684 **Forsyth, W.D.** "Stability in the Pacific: Australia's Position." *Pacific Affairs*, 16, No. 1 (March, 1943), 7-18. Comment by P.D. Phillips, 19-20.

1685 **Fraga, J.A.** *El Mar y la Antartida en la Geopolitica Argentina.* Buenos Aires: Instituto de Publicaciones Navales, 1980.

1686 **Francis, Henry S.** "The Third Consultative Meeting of Antartic Treaty Representatives." *Antartic Report*, (August, 1964), 4-12; (September, 1964), 5-14.

1687 **Gentilli, J.** "Note di Geopolitica Australiana." *L'Universo*, 34, No. 3 (May-June, 1954), 359-368.

1688 **Gidel, Gilbert.** *Aspects juridiques de la lutte pour l'Antarctique.* Paris: Academie de Marine, 1948.

1689 **Gould, Laurence M.** *Antarctica in World Affairs.* New York: Foreign Policy Association, 1958.

1690 **Guglialmelli, J.E.** "El area meridional del Atlantico Suroccidental: la geopolitica de Chile y el Laudo del Beagle." *Estrategia*, 9, No. 48, Pat 1 (Septembre-Octubre, 1977), 5-18.

1691 **Haushofer, Karl.** *Geopolitik des Pazifischen Ozeans.* Berlin: Kurt Vowinckel, 1924.

1692 **Haushofer, Karl.** *Geopolitik des Pazifischen Ozeans. Studien uber die Wechselbeziehungen zwischen Geographie und Geschichte.* II. Erganzte Aufl. Heidelberg: Kurt Vowinckel, 1938.

1693 **Haushofer, Karl.** "Wehrgiopolitik im Pazifischen Ozean; wie der Groese Friedens-Ozean (Jaiheiya) zum Kriegsschauplatz wurde." *Petermanns Geographische Mitteillungen*, 88, No. 1 (January, 1942), 1-8.

1694 **Haushofer, Karl.** "Zur Geopolitik der Pazifischen Grossraumfischerei." *Zeitschrift fur Geopolitik*, Jahrg 20, Heft 7 (Juli, 1943), 269.

1695 **Hayton, Robert D.** "The 'American' Antarctic." *American Journal of International Law*, 50, No. 3 (July, 1956), 583-610.

1696 **Hayton, Robert D.** "The Antarctic Settlement of 1959." *American Journal of International Law*, 54, No. 2 (April, 1960), 349-371.

1697 **Hayton, Robert D.** "The Nations and Antarctica." Extract from: "Osterr." *Zeitschrift fur Offentliches Recht*, 10, Heft 3-4 (1960), 368-412.

1698 **Henessian, John.** "The Antarctic Treaty." *International and Comparative Law Quarterly*, 9, No. 3 (July, 1960), 436-480.

1699 **Henessian, John.** "Antarctica; Current National Interests and Legal Realities." *Proceedings of the American Society of International Law*, (1958), 145-164.

1700 **International Court of Justice.** "International Court of Justice, The Hague." *Antarctica Case (United Kingdom v. Argentina).* The Hague, 1956, 12-14.

1701 **Kelly, Philip and Child, Jack,** eds. *Geopolitics of the Southern Cone and Antarctica.* Boulder, Colorado: Lynne Rienner Publishers, 1988.

1702 **Kintner, William R.** "Geopolitica para o soldado." *Boletim Geografico*, 12, No. 119 (Marco-Abril, 1954), 202-206.

1703 **Lepotier, R.** "La Dispute Antarctique." *Geografia*, 49, No. 4 (October, 1955), 2-7.

1704 **Lillie, Harry R.** "The Antarctic in World Affairs." *Canadian Geographical Journal*, 36, No. 6 (June, 1948), 282-295.

1705 **Luard, Evan.** "Who Owns Antarctica?" *Foreign Affairs*, 62, No. 5 (Summer, 1984), 1175-1193.

1706 **Marcus, George E.** "Power on the Extreme Periphery: The Perspective of Tongan Elites in the Modern World System." *Pacific Viewpoint*, 22, No. 1 (May, 1981), 48-64.

1707 **Maricq, Luis S.** *Antarctica: Chile's Claim.* Washington, D.C.: National Defense University, Fort Lesley J. McNair, 1987.

1708 **Mitchell, Barbara.** "Antartica: A Special Case." *Oceans*, 10, No. 3 (May-June, 1977), 56-59.

1709 **Moneta, Carlos J.** "Antarctica, Latin America and the International System in the 1980's: Toward a New Antarctic Order?" *Journal of Interamerican Studies*, 23, No. 1 (February, 1981), 29-68.

1710 **Nathan, R.S.** "Geopolitics and Pacific Strategy." *Pacific Affairs*, 15, No. 2 (June, 1942), 155-163.

1711 **Nice, Bruno.** "La partizione politica dell'Antartide." *Il Polo*, 2 (Marzo-Maggio, 1946), 21-28.

1712 **Orlov, B.** "Russian Antarctic Discoveries of 1821 are Basis of Soviet Claim." *U.S.S.R. Information Bulletin*, 9, No. 9 (May 13, 1949), 296-297.

1713 **Palermo, V.** "El Continente Antartico en el contexto internacional contemporaneo." *Geopolitica*, 3, No. 5 (1978), 35-46.

1714 **Palermo, V.** "Latinoamerica puede mas; geopolitiaca del Atlantico Sur." In *La Atlantartida*, Fernando Milia, ed. Buenos Aires: Ediciones Pleamar, 1978, 163-194.

1715 **Peterson, M.J.** "Antarctica: The Last Great Land Rush on Earth." *International Organization*, 34, No. 3 (Summer, 1980), 377-403.

1716 **Phleger, Herman.** "The Antarctic Treaty." *Department of State Bulletin*, 43, No. 1098 (July 11, 1960), 49-52.

1717 **Pinochet de la Barra, Oscar.** "Evolucion Politico-Juridica Del Problema Antartico." *Estudios Internacionales*, 14, No. 55 (Julio-Septembre, 1981), 380-393.

1718 **Pomeroy, Earl S.** *Pacific Outpost; American Strategy in Guam and Micronesia.* Stanford, California: Stanford University Press, 1951.

1719 **Price, A. Grenfell.** *Geopolitical Transformation of the Pacific and Its Present Significance.* Sydney: Australian Royal Geographical Society, 1951.

1720 **Quagliotti de Bellis, B.** "Estrategia y geopolitica en el Atlantico Sur." *Geopolitica*, 3, No. 5 (1978), 5-14.

1721 "Report of Third Antarctic Treaty Consultative Meeting, Brussels, 1964." *Polar Record*, 12, No. 79 (January, 1965), 453-472.

1722 "Rivalries in Antarctica." *World Today*, 4, No. 4 (April, 1948), 151-159.

1723 **Schafer, Otto.** "Geopolitik des Grossen Ozeans." *Geographischer Anzeiger*, 45 Jahrg, Heft 13-16 (Juli-August, 1944), 185-188.

1724 **Scharpff, Adolf.** "Geopolitik der kleinen Verwaltungsbezirke." *Zeitschrift fur Geopolitik*, Jahrg 24, Heft 11 (Nov., 1953), 634.

1725 **Silva, Michael, and Sjogren, Bertil.** *Europe 1992 and the New World Power Game.* New York: John Wiley & Sons, 1990.

1726 **Taubenfeld, Howard J.** "A Treaty for Antarctica." *International Conciliation*, 531 (January, 1961), 245-322.

1727 **Toma, Peter A.** "Soviet Attitude Towards the Acquisition of Territorial Sovereignty in the Antarctic." *American Journal of International Law*, 50, No. 3 (July, 1956), 611-626.

1728 **Tosta, Octavio.** "A geopolitica e o concurso de Admissao ea Escola de Comando e Estado Maior do exercito." *A Defesa Nacional*, 535 (Fev., 1959), 153-154.

1729 "Twelve Nations Sign Treaty Guaranteeing Non-militarization of Antarctica and Freedom of Scientific Investigation." *Department of State Bulletin*, 41, No. 1069 (December 21, 1959), 911-917.

1730 **U.S. Department of State.** *Antartica: Measures in Furtherance of Principles and Objectives of the Antarctic Treaty. Certain Recommendations Adopted at the Third Consultative Meeting Under Article IX of the Antarctic Treaty; Brussels, June 2-13, 1964.* Washington, D.C.: U.S. Department of State, 1966.

1731 **Weigert, Hans Werner.** "Haushofer and the Pacific: The Future in Retrospect." *Foreign Affairs*, 20, No. 4 (July, 1942), 732-742.

1732 **Wilson, Robert E.** "National Interests and Claims in the Antarctic." *Artic*, 17, No. 1 (March, 1964), 15-32.

EUROPE

Books

1733 **Beer, S.H., et Ulam, A.R.** *Patterns of Government: The Major Political Systems of Europe.* New York: Random House, 1962.

1734 **Borsody, Stephen.** *The New Central Europe.* Boulder: East European Monographs, 1993.

1735 **Brandt, Karl.** *Europe, The Emerging Third Power; Phenomenon and Portent.* New York: City News Publishing, 1958.

1736 **Chadwick, H.M.** *The Nationalities of Europe.* Cambridge, England: Cambridge University Press, 1945.

1737 **Chadwick, H.M.** *Soviet Potentials: A Geographic Appraisal.* Syracuse, New York: Syracuse University Press, 1962.

1738 **Crouch, C., and MarQuand, D., eds.** *Toward Greater Europe? A Continent Without Iron Curtain.* London: Belhaven Press, 1991.

1739 **Dickinson, Robert E.** *The German Lebensraum.* London: Routledge, 1943.

1740 **East, W. Gordon.** *The Political Division of Europe.* London: University of London Press, 1948.

1741 **Gianaris, Nicholas V.** *Greece and Turkey: Economic and Geopolitical Perspectives.* New York: Praeger, 1988.

1742 **Gulick, E.V.** *Europe's Classical Balance of Power.* Ithaca, New York: Cornell University Press, 1955.

1743 **Hatchett, Ronald L.** *The Soviet Union and Eastern Europe: A Geopolitical Perspective.* Austin: University of Texas, Ph.D., 1982.

1744 **Hazan, Barurh, A.** *The East European Political System: Instruments of Power.* Boulder, Colorado: Westview Press, 1985.

1745 **Jantzen, Walther.** *Geopolitik in Kartenbild. Verrat an Europe.* Heidelberg: Kurt Vowinckel, 1943.

1746 **Kantorowicz, H.U.** *The Spirit of British Policy and the Myth of Encirclement of Germany.* New York: Oxford University Press, 1932.

1747 **LaCoste, Yves,** ed. *Geopolitiaues des Regions Francaises. Tome I: La France Septentrionale. Tome II: La Fraoe Occidentale. Tome III: La France du Sud-Est* (Geopolitics of the French Regions. Volume 1, Northern France. Volume II: The Western Frontage. Volume III: Southeast France)." Paris: Fayaro, 1986.

1748 **Ogilvie, Alan Grant.** *Europe and Its Borderlands.* Edinburgh: T. Nelson, 1957.

1749 **Parker, Geoffrey.** *The Geopolitics of Dominion: Territorial Supremacy in Europe and the Mediterranean from the Ottoman Empire to the Superpower.* New York: Routledge, 1988.

1750 **Robson, Charles B.** *Berlin-Pivot of German Destiny.* Chapel Hill: University of North Carolina Press, 1960.

1751 **Roucek, Joseph S.** *The Politics of the Balkans.* New York: McGraw-Hill, 1939.

1752 **Royal Institute of International Affairs.** *Political and Strategic Interests of the United Kingdom.* London: Oxford University Press, 1939.

1753 **Walsh, Edmund A.** *Wahre anstatt falsche Geopolitik fur Deutschland.* Frankfurt: G. Schulte-Bulmke, 1946.

Journals

1754 **Bellquist, Eric C.** "Political and Economic Conditions in the Low Countries." *Foreign Policy Reports,* 24, No. 4 (May 1, 1948), 42-48.

1755 **Bellquist, Eric C.** "Political and Economic Conditions in the Scandinavian Countries." *Foreign Policy Reports,* 24, No. 5 (May 15, 1948), 50-63.

1756 **Bildt, Carl.** "The Baltic Litmus Test." *Foreign Affairs,* 73, No. 5 (September/October, 1994), 72-85.

1757 **Blair, Leon B.** "Mediterranean Geopolitics." *United States Naval Institute Proceedings,* 77, No. 2 (February, 1951), 135-139.

1758 **Boyer, Jean-Claude,** and **Deneux, Jean-Franciois.** "Pour une approache geopolitique de la region parisienne." *Herodote,* 2°-3° Trimestres, Nos. 33-34 (1984), 157-173.

1759 **Broek, Jan O.M.** "The German School of Geopolitics." In *Global Politics,* H. Fitzgibbon, ed. University of California, Los Angeles Institute of Political Geography. Berkeley: University of California Press, 1944, 167-177.

1760 **Carroue, Laurent.** "Siemens: Geopolitique Europeene d'une Firme Allemande de Haute Technologie." *L'information Geographique* [Paris], 54, No. 3 (1990), 94-l02.

1761 **Crcic, M.** "Geopolitical Position of Yugoslavia in the Past and Today." *Zbornik Radova-Prirodno-Matematicki Fakulteta, Univerziteta u Beogradu, Geografski Institut,* 31 (1984), 79-95.

1762 **Crone, Gerald R.** "A German View of Geopolitics." *Geographical Journal,* 101, Nos. 1-3 (January-March, 1948), 104-108.

1763 **Dalby, Wilfrid Simon.** "Geopolitical Discourse: The Soviet Union as Other." *Alternatives,* 13, No. 4 (December, 1988), 415-442.

1764 **Dodds, Klaus-John.** "Geopolitics in the Foreign Office: British Representations of Argentina, 1945-1961." *Institute of British Geographers. Transactions,* 19, No. 3 (1994), 273-290.

1765 **Domaniewski, Zbigniew.** "Die Hauptstadt in der Geopolitik Polens." *Zeitshcrift fur Geopolitik,* 16, Jahrg, Heft 5 (Mai, 1939), 322-334.

1766 **East, W. Gordon.** "The Mediterranean: Pivot of Peace and War." *Foreign Affairs,* 31, No. 4 (July, 1953), 619-633.

1767 **Erickson, Karen.** "The Comparative Soviet Periphery: Iran and Finland." *Survey*, 29, No. 3 (126) (Autumn, 1985), 112-128.

1768 **Fifield, Russell H.** "Geopolitics at Munich." *Department of State Bulletin*, 12, No. 313 (June 24, 1945), 1152-1162.

1769 **Foucher, Michael.** "L'invention des frontieres: un modele geopolitique francais." *Herodote*, 40 (Janvier-Mars, 1986), 54-88.

1770 **Friedmann, Bernhard.** "The Reunification of the Germans as a Security Concept." *Atlantic Community Quarterly*, 25, No. 2 (Summer, 1987), 118-122.

1771 **Geraud, Andre.** "Can France Again Be a Great Power?" *Foreign Affairs*, 26, No. 1 (October, 1947), 24-35.

1772 **Guellec, Jean.** "Les Etats-Unis, Geostrategie de la Super-Puissance." *L'Information Geographique* [Paris], 57, No. 5 (1993), 169-178.

1773 **Gursoy, C.** "The Geographical Position of Cyprus." *Cultural Turcica*, 2, No. 2 (1965), 192-198.

1774 **Hall, Duncan.** "The British Commonwealth as a Great Power." *Foreign Affairs*, 23, No. 4 (July, 1945), 594-608.

1775 **Haupert, J.S.** "The Impact of Geographic Location Upon Sweden as a Baltic Power." *Journal of Geography*, 58, No. 1 (January, 1959), 5-14.

1776 **Haushofer, Karl.** "Geopolitische Breiten und Langsdynamik." *Zeitschrift Geopolitik*, Jahrg 20, Heft 9 (Dezember, 1943), 291-293.

1777 **Haushofer, Karl.** "Der Grossostasiengedanke in der deutschen Geopolitik." *Zeitschrift fur Geopolitik*, Jahrg 20, Heft 1 (Januar, 1943), 1-7.

1778 **Hooson, David J.M.** "The Middle Volga--An Emerging Focal Region in the Soviet Union." *Geographical Journal*, 126, Pt. 2 (June, 1960), 180-190.

1779 **Hooson, David J.M.** "A New Soviet Heartland?" *Geographical Journal*, 128, No. 1 (March, 1962), 19-29.

1780 **Hough, Jerry F.** "The Evolution in the Soviet World View." *World Politics*, 32, No. 4 (July, 1980), 509-530.

1781 **Ingram, Edward.** "The Geopolitics of the First British Expedition to Egypt - I: The Cabinet Crisis of September 1800." *Middle Eastern Studies*, 30, No. 3 (July, 1994), 435-460.

1782 **Ingram, Edward.** "The Geopolitics of the First British Expedition to Egypt - II: The Mediterranean Campaign, 1800-1." *Middle Eastern Studies*, 30, No. 4 (October, 1994), 699-723.

1783 **Jantzen, Walther.** "Geopolitische Reise Durch Sudslawien." *Zeitschrift fur Erdkunde*, 6, Jahrg, Heft 2 (Januar 18, 1938), 49-55.

1784 **Kjellen, Rudolf.** "Geopolitische Betrachtungen uber Skandinavien." *Geographische Zeitschrift*, 11 Jahrg, Heft 12 (Dez., 1905), 657-671.

1785 **Klein, J.** "Reflections on Geopolitics: From Pangermanism to the Doctrines of Living Space and Moving Frontiers." In *On Geopolitics: Classical and Nuclear*. C.E. Zoppo and C. Zorgbibe, eds. Dordrecht, Netherlands: Martinus Nijhoff, 1985, 45-75.

1786 **Kleinschmager, R.** "De la commune suburbaine au Villabe: Aspects de la differenciation geopolitique du vote en Alsace (About the Geopolitical Differenciation in Alsace: The Suburban Communes and Villages)." *Recherches Geographiques a Strasbourg*, 24 (1986), 53-89.

1787 **Klessmann, C.** "Osteuropaforschung und Lebensraumpolitik im Dritten Reich." *Aus Politik und Zeitgeschichte* (supplement to *Das Parlament*), B7/84 (1984), 33-45.

1788 **Korinman, Michael.** "Le congres de Berlin, exercises de geopolitique." *Herodote*, 41 (Avril-Juin, 1986), 76-90.

1789 **Kostanick, Huey Louis.** "The German Plea for Lebensraum." *Current History*, 28, No. 164 (April, 1955), 193-199.

1790 **Kristof, Ladis K.D.** "The Geopolitical Image of the Fatherland: The Case of Russia." *Western Political Quarterly*, 20, No. 4 (December, 1967), 941-954.

1791 **Kristof, Ladis K.D.** "The Russian Image of Russia: An Applied Study in Geopolitial Methodology." In *Essays in Political Geography*. Charles A. Fisher, ed. London: Methuen, 1968, 345-387.

1792 **Kruszewski, Charles.** "Germany's Lebensraum." *American Political Science Review*, 34, No. 5 (October, 1940), 964-975.

1793 **LaCoste, Yves.** "Geopolitiques de la France." *Herodote*, 40 (Janvier-Mars, 1986), 5-31.

1794 **Langen, E.** "Zur juristischen Geopolitik Europas." *Zeitschrift fur Geopolitik*, Jahrg 12, Heft 5 (Mai, 1935), 296-301.

1795 **Legvold, Robert.** "The Nature of Soviet Power." *Foreign Affairs*, 56, No. 1 (October, 1977), 49-71.

1796 **Liebowitz, Ronald D.** "Finlandiszation: An Analysis of the Soviet Union's 'Domination' of Finland." *Political Geography Quarterly*, 2, No. 4 (October, 1983), 275-287.

1797 **Loan, Lambertvan der.** "Caosal Process in Spatial Labour Markets." *Tijdschrift voor economische en sociale geografie*, 78, No. 5 (Septembre-Octobre, 1987), 325-338.

1798 **Lopreno, Dario.** "Une dynastie alpine pour und estin mediterraneen? La geopolitique du fascime italien face a la Maison de Savoie." *LeGlobe*, Tome 125 (1985), 191-205.

1799 **Lydolf, Paul E.** "The New Map of the Soviet Union." *Professional Geographer*, 10, No. 4 (July, 1958), 13-17.

1800 **Masetti, Carla.** "Confini Politici e Confini Etnici. I Presupposti Geopolitici di un Conflitto Armato. Il Caso Della Ex-Iugoslvia." *L'Universo* [Firenze], 73, No. 1 (Gennaio-Febbraio, 1993), 41-58.

1801 **Massi, Ernesto.** "Romische und italienische Mittelmeer-Geopolitik." *Zeitschrift fur Geopolitik*, 16, Jahrg, Heft 8-9 (August-September, 1939), 551-566.

1802 **Maull, Otto.** "Polen-Geopolitische Berichterstattung." *Zeitschrift fur Erdkunde*, 7, Jahrg, Heft 23-24 (3. u. 18. Dezember, 1939), 804-807.

1803 **Mehedinti, S.** "Die geopolitische Lage Rumaniens." *Zeitschrift fur Geopolitik*, 15, Jahrg, Heft 8 (August, 1938), 627-634.

1804 **Mercer, John.** "The Canary Islanders in Western Mediterranean Politics." *African Affairs*, 78, No. 3111 (April, 1979), 159-176.

1805 **Mills, D.R.** "The U.S.S.R." A Reappraisal of Mackinder's Heartland Concept." *Scottish Geographical Magazine*, 72, No. 3 (December, 1956), 144-152.

1806 **Ording, Arne.** "Norway in World Affairs; A Political Survey." *American-Scandinavian Review*, 43, No. 2 (June, 1955), 141-150.

1807 **Paasi, Anssi.** "Political Geography Around the World VIII: The Rise and Fall of Finnish Geopolitics. *Political Geography Quarterly*, 9, No. 1 (January, 1990), 53-66.

1808 **Pechoux, Pierre-Yves.** "Chypre: geopolitique d'une ile fracturee." *Herodote*, No. 48 (Janvier-Mars, 1988), 127-142.

1809 **Perepetchko, Alexandre.** "Les Mutations

Geopolotiques en URSS: De L'echelle Globale a L'echelle Regionale." *Revue Belge de Geographie* [Bruxelles], ll5e, Fascs. 1-3 (1991), 45-50.

1810 **Reguera Rodriquez, Antonio T.** "La Eleccion de Madrid Como Asiento de la Corte y Capital del Estado. Un Caso Practico de Geopolitica Historica." *Estudios Geografico* [Madrid], 54, No. 213 (Octubre-Diciembre, 1993), 655-693.

1811 **Reinold, A.** "Britische Geopolitik, Praxisstatt Theorie." *Zeitschrift fur Geopolitik*, Jahrg 12, Heft 1 (Januar, 1935), 58-59.

1812 **Ripka, Hubert.** "Czechoslovakia--The Key to the Danubian Basin." *Slavonic and East European Review*, 17, No. 49 (July, 1938), 54-72.

1813 **Roucek, Joseph S.** "Central-Eastern Europe." In *Approaches to an Understanding of World Affairs, Twenty-Fifth Yearbook of The National Council for the Social Studies*. Howard R. Anderson, ed. Washington, D.C.: National Council for Social Studies, 1954, 138-56.

1814 **Roucek, Joseph S.** "The Geopolitics of the Adriatic." *American Journal of Economics and Sociology*, 11, No. 2 (January, 1952), 171-178.

1815 **Roucek, Joseph S.** "The Geopolitics of the Balkans." *American Journal of Economic and Sociology*, 5, No. 3 (April, 1946), 365-377.

1816 **Roucek, Joseph S.** "The Geopolitics of the Baltic States." *American Journal of Economics and Sociology*, 8, No. 2 (Janaury, 1949), 171-175.

1817 **Roucek, Joseph S.** "The Geopolitics of Danubia." *American Journal of Economics and Sociology*, 5, No. 2 (January, 1946), 211-230.

1818 **Roucek, Joseph S.** "The Geopolitics of Greenland." *Journal of Geography*, 50, No. 6 (September, 1951), 239-246.

1819 **Roucek, Joseph S.** "The Geopolitics of the Mediteranean." *American Journal of Economics and Sociology*, 12, No. 4 (July, 1953), 346-354; 13, No. 1 (October, 1953), 71-86.

1820 **Roucek, Joseph S.** "Geopolitics of Poland." *American Journal of Economics and Sociology*, 7, No. 4 (July, 1948), 421-427.

1821 **Roucek, Joseph S.** "The Geopolitics of Spain." *Social Studies*, 46, No. 3 (March, 1955), 89-93.

1822 **Roucek, Joseph S.** "The Geopolitics of the U.S.S.R." *American Journal of Economics and Sociology*, 10, No. 1 (October, 1950), 17-26; No. 2 (January, 1951), 153-159.

1823 **Roucek, Joseph S.** "The Geopolitics of Yugoslavia." *Social Studies*, 47, No. 1 (January, 1956), 26-29.

1824 **Roucek, Joseph S.** "German Geopolitics." *Journal of Central European Affairs*, 2, No. 2 (July, 1942), 180-189.

1825 **Sanguin, Andre-Louis.** "Islande ou l'Europe meconnue: survol geopolitique et economique." *Protee*, 1, No. 3 (1971), 19-29.

1826 **Santoro, Carlo Maria.** "Italy and the Southern System." *Italian Journal* [New York], 7, No. 6 (1993), 13-18.

1827 **Schafer, Otto.** "Die geopolitischen Grundlagen der osteuropaischen Stattenbildung." *Zeitschrift fur Geopolitik*, 17, Jahrg, Heft 5 (Mai, 1940), 221-226.

1828 **Schafer, Otto.** "Geopolitik der Niederen Lande." *Zeitschrift fur Geopolitik*, Jahrg 20, Heft 4 (April, 1943), 155-163.

1829 **Scharpff, Adolf.** "Zur Geopolitik Sudwestdeutschlands." *Zeitschrift fur Geopolitik*, Jahrg 20, Heft 7/8 (Juli-August, 1953), 444-446.

1830 **Schlesinger, Philip R.** "Europe's Contradictory Communicative Space." *Daedalus* [Cambridge, MA], 123, No. 2 (Spring, 1994), 25-52.

1831 **Sella, Amnon.** "Soviet Russia as a Land Power." *Jerusalem Journal of International Relations*, 5, No. 2 (June, 1981), 85-99.

1832 **Shercliff, Jose.** "Portugal's Strategic Territories." *Foreign Affairs*, 31, No. 2 (January, 1953), 321-325.

1833 **Sinclair, Sir Archibald.** "Le probleme mediterraneen." *Politique etrangere*, 4e anne, No. 3 (Juin, 1939), 229-238.

1834 **Tibi, Bassam.** "Islam and Modern European Ideologies." *International Journal of Middle East Studies*, 18, No. 1 (February, 1986), 15-29.

1835 **Vigor, P.H.** "The Soviet View of Geopolitics." In *On Geopolitics: Classical and Nuclear*. C.E. Zoppo and C. Zorgbibe, eds. Dordrecht, Netherlands: Martinus Nijhoff, 1985, 131-149.

1836 **Wheeler, Geoffrey.** "Russia and the Middle East." *International Affairs*, 35, No. 3 (July, 1959), 295-304.

1837 **Woolbert, Robert Gale.** "Spain as an African Power." *Foreign Affairs*, 24, No. 4 (July, 1946), 723-735.

1838 **Zeck, Hans F.** "Koln: Geopolitik einer Stadt." *Zeitschrift fur Geopolitik*, Jahrg 12, Heft 5 (Mai, 1935), 291-296.

1839 **Zoppo, C.E.** "Geopolitica, sicurezza Europea e pace mondiale nell'era nucleare." *Rivista Italiana di Scienza Politica*, 12, No. 1 (Aprile, 1982), 45-71.

CHAPTER IV

THE ORGANIZATION OF POLITICAL TERRITORY: THE NATION STATE

TERRITORY, NATION STATE: SIZE, SHAPE, LOCATION & FORMATION

GENERAL AND THEORY

Books

1840 **Adamic, Louis.** *A Nation of Nations.* New York: Harper & Row, 1945.

1841 **Agnew, John A.** *Place and Politics: The Geographical Mediation of State and Society.* Boston: Allen & Unwin, 1987.

1842 **Aitken, H.G.J.,** ed. *The State and Economic Growth.* New York: Social Science Research Council, 1959.

1843 **Appleton, J.H.** *The Experience of Landscape.* Chichester: John Wiley & Sons, 1975.

1844 **Ardrey, Robert.** *The Territorial Imperative.* New York: Atheneum Press, 1966.

1845 **Baylson, Joshua C.** *Territorial Allocation by Imperial Rivalry: The Human Legacy in the Near East.* Chicago, Illinois: University of Chicago, Department of Geography, Research Paper No. 221, 1987.

1846 **Beamish, C.** "Space, State and Crisis: Towards a Theory of the Public City." Hamilton, Ontario, Canada: McMaster University, Department of Geography, M.A., 1981.

1847 **Blair, Patricia Wohlgemuth.** *The Ministate Dilemma.* New York: Carnegie Endowment for International Peace, Occasional Paper No. 6, October, 1967.

1848 **Blair, Patricia Wohlgemuth.** *Le probleme des micro-Etats.* Geneve: Dotation Carnegie Pour la Paix Internationale, 1968.

1849 **Buch-Glucksmann, Christine.** *Gramsci and the State.* London: Lawrence and Wishart, 1980.

1850 **Burdeau, G.** *L'Etat.* Paris: Seuil, 1970.

1851 **Burton, Benedict.** *Problems of Smaller Territories.* London: Athlone Press, 1967.

1852 **Cassirer, Ernst.** *The Myth of the State.* New Haven, Connecticut: Yale University Press, 1946.

1853 **Chabod, F.** *L'idea di nazione.* Bari: Laterza, 1961.

1854 **Chodak, Szymon.** *The New State: Etatization of Western Societies.* Boulder, Colorado: Lynne Rienner Publishers, 1989.

1855 **Chisholm, Michael,** and **Smith, David M.,** eds. *Shared Space: Divided Space; Essays on Conflict and Territorial Organization.* Cambridge: Cambridge University, 1990.

1856 **Clarke, Colin,** and **Payne, Tony,** eds. *Politics, Security and Development in Small States.* London: Allen & Unwin, 1987.

1857 **Claval, Paul.** *Regions, nations, grands espaces.* Paris: Editions Genin, 1968.

1858 **De Jasay, Anthony.** *The State.* Oxford: Basil Blackwell, 1985.

1859 **Dear, M.** and **Wolch, J.,** eds. *The Power of Geography: How Territory Shapes Social Life.* New York: Allen & Urwin, 1989.

1860 **Deutsch, Karl W.,** and **Foltz, William J.** *Nation-Building.* New York: Atherton Press, 1963.

1861 **Dicken, Samuel N.,** and **Pitts, Forrest R.** *Men and Nations: Introduction to Cultural Geography.* Toronto: Xerox College Publishing, 1970.

1862 **Diedesheim, J.** *Les Patries—vers une mutation du mode de penser.* Neuchatel: Beconniere, 1967.

1863 **Dommen, Edward,** and **Hein, Philipp,** eds. *States, Microstates and Islands.* London: Croom Helm, 1985.

1864 **Ehigotz, Hermann.** *Stadtebannkunst.* Leipzig: Quelle und Meyer, 1921.

1865 **Etzioni, Amitai.** *Political Unification: A Comparative Study of Leaders and Forces.* New York: Holt, Rinehart & Winston, 1965.

1866 **Fraser, T.G.** *Partition in Ireland, India and Palestine.* London: Macmillan, 1984.

1867 **Gayle, Dennis John.** *The Small Developing State.* Brookfield, Vermont: Gower Publishing, 1986.

1868 **Geertz, C.,** ed. *Old Societies and New States.* New York: The Free Press, 1963.

1869 **Goad, H.E.** *The Making of the Corporate State.* London: Christophers, 1932.

1870 **Goldwin, Robert A.** *A Nation of States.* Chicago: Rand McNally, 1961.

1871 **Gottmann, Jean.** *The Significance of Territory.* Charlottesville: University Press of Virginia, 1973.

1872 **Hall, J.A.,** ed. *States in History.* London: Basil Blackwell, 1986.

1873 **Halle, Louis J.** *Men and Nations.* Princeton, New Jersey: Princeton University Press, 1965.

1874 **Harden, S.,** ed. *Small is Dangerous: Micro States in a Macro World. A Report from the David Davies Memorial Institute of International Studies.* London: Frances Pinter, 1985.

1875 **Harrigan, Norwell.** *The Inter-Virgin Islands Conference: A Study of a Microstate International Organization.* Gainesville: University Presses of Florida, 1980.

1876 **Hassert, Kurt.** *Die Stadte, Geographisch betrachtet.* Leipzig: B. G. Teubner, 1907.

1877 **Hertz, Frederick.** *Nationality in History and Politics.* London: Kegan Trench Trubner, 1944.

1878 **Herz, John H.** *The Nation-State and the Crisis of World Politics.* New York: David McKay, 1976.

1879 **Holt, Jerry Glenn.** *Physical Multipartitism and the Internal Political Morphology of Micro States.* Boca Raton: Florida Atlantic University, Ph.D., 1983.

1880 **Hoosen, D.,** ed. *Geography and National Identity.* London: Basil Blackwell, 1992.

1881 **Jacobs, Jane.** *The Question of Separation.* New York: Random House, 1980.

1882 **Kirchhoff, Alfred.** *Zur Verstandigung uber nation und Nationalitat.* Verlag der Buchlandlung des Waisenhauser, 1905.

1883 **Kohr, Leopold.** *The Breakdown of Nations.* New York: Holt, Rinehart & Winston, 1957.

1884 **Krader, Lawrence.** *Formation of the State.* Englewood Cliffs, New Jersey: Prentice-Hall, 1968.

1885 **Labasse, Jean.** *L'organisation de l'espace, elements de geographie volontaire.* Paris: Hermann, 1966.

1886 **Lamont, Archie.** *Small Nations.* Glasgow: William MacLellan, 1944.

1887 **Lavergne, Bernard.** *Le principe des nationalites et les guerres. Son application au probleme colonial.* Paris: Felix Alcan, 1921.

1888 **Le Lannou, Maurice.** *Le Demenagement du Territoire, Reveries d'un Geographe.* Paris: Seuil, Collection Esprit, 1967.

1889 **Lee, Su-Hoon.** *State-Building in the Contemporary Third World.* Boulder, Colorado: Westview Press, 1988.

1890 **Leupold, Werner,** and **Rutz, Werner,** eds. *Der staat und sein territorium: Beitrage zur raumsirrksamen tatigkeit des staats.* Weisbaden: Franz Steiner Verlag GmbH, 1976.

1891 **Losch, August.** *The Economics of Location.* New Haven, Connecticut: Yale University Press, 1954.

1892 **Lowie.** *The Origin of the State.* New York: Harcourt Brace, 1927.

1893 **Lubasz, Heinz.** *The Development of the Modern State.* New York: Macmillan, 1964.

1894 **Lyra Tavares, Aurelio de.** *Territorio nacional: Soberania e dominio do Estado.* Rio de Janeiro: Americana, 1955.

1895 **Malmberg, Torsten.** *Human Territoriality: Survey of Behavioural Territories in Man with Preliminary Analysis and Discussion of Meansing.* The Hague: Mouton Publishers. New Babylon Studies in the Social Sciences, No. 33, 1980.

1896 **Mann, Michael,** ed. *The Rise and Decline of the Nation State.* Oxford: Basil Blackwell, 1990.

1897 **Markusen, Ann R.** *Regions: The Economics and Politics of Territory.* Totowa, New Jersey: Rowman and Littlefield, 1987.

1898 **Navari, Cornelia,** ed. *The Condition of States: A Study in International Political Theory.* Milton Keynes: Open University Press, 1991.

1899 **Meller, Roy.** *Nation, State and Territory: A Political Geography.* New York: Routledge, 1989.

1900 **Miller, Perry.** *Nature's Nation.* Cambridge, Massachusetts: Harvard University Press, 1967.

1901 **Morgan, J. De.** *Essai sur les nationalites.* Paris: Berger Levrault, 1917.

1902 **Niebhuhr, Reinhold.** *The Structures of Nations and Empires.* New York: Charles Scribner's Sons, 1959.

1903 **O'Connell, Daniel Patrick.** *The Law of State Succession.* Cambridge: Cambridge University Press, 1965.

1904 **Pal, Leslie A.**, and **Schultze, Rainer-Olaf**, eds. *The Nation-State Versus Continental Integration: Canada in North America—Germany in Europe.* Bochum: Universitatsverlag Brockmeyer, 1991.

1905 **Pellegrini, Giacomo Corna.** *Geografia e political del territorio: Problimi e ricerhe.* Milano: Vita e Pensiero, 1974.

1906 **Pounds, Norman J.G.** *Divided Germany and Berlin.* Princeton, New Jersey: Van Nostrand, 1962.

1907 **Prescott, J.R.V.** *The Geography of State Policies.* Chicago: Aldine Publishing, 1969.

1908 **Ratzel, Friedrich.** *Das Meer als Quelle der Volkergrosse.* Berlin: Oldenbourg, 1911.

1909 **Ratzel, Friedrich.** *Volkerkunde.* Vienne: Bibliographisches Institut, 1894.

1910 **Redslob, Robert.** *Le principe des nationalites.* Paris: Sirey, 1930.

1911 **Robinson, E.A.G.** *Economic Consequences of the Size of Nations.* London: Macmillan, 1960.

1912 **Rokkan, S.**, and **Urwin, D.** *The Politics of Territorial Identity.* Beverly Hills, California: Sage Publications, 1983.

1913 **Romer, E.** *Ziemia i Panstwo: La Terre et l'Etat* (The Earth and the State). Warsaw: Lvov, 1939.

1914 **Rouquie, Alain.** *The Military and the State in Latin America.* Translated by Paul E. Sigmund. Berkeley: University of California Press, 1987.

1915 **Sack, Robert David.** *Human Territoriality: Its Theory and History.* Cambridge: Cambridge University Press, 1986.

1916 **Scott, R.**, ed. *The Politics of New States.* London: Allen & Unwin, 1970.

1917 **Seton-Watson, Hugh.** *Nations and States.* Boulder, Colorado: Westview Press, 1977.

1918 **Sieger, Robert.** *Die Geographie und der Staat.* Graz: Leuchner und Lubensky, 1925.

1919 **Slowe, Peter M.** *Geography and Political Power: The Geography of Nations and States.* London: Routledge, 1990.

1920 **Swanton, John R.** *The Evolution of Nations.* (Smithsonian Institution. War Background Studies, No. 2. Publication 2686) Washington, D.C.: Smithsonian Institute, 1942.

1921 **Touret, Bernard.** *L'amenagement constitutionnel des Etats de peuplement composite.* Quebec: Presses de l'Universite Laval, 1973.

1922 **Urry, J.; Harloe, Michael;** and **Pickvane, Chris,** eds. *Place, Policy and Politics: Do Lacalities Matter?* Winchester, Massachusetts: Unwin & Hyman, 1990.

1923 **U.S. Department of State.** The Geographer. *Newly Independent States*, rev., Washington, D.C.: U.S. Department of State, 1962.

1924 **U.S. Department of State.** *Profiles of Newly Independent States: Rev. April, 1967.* Washington, D.C.: U.S. Department of State, 1967.

1925 **Van Gennep, Arnold.** *Traite Comparatif des Nationalites.* Paris: Payot, 1922.

1926 **Vital, David.** *The Inequality of States.* Oxford: Clarendon Press, 1967.

1927 **Williams, C.H.**, ed. *Natinal Separatism.* Cardiff: University of Wales Press, 1982.

1928 **Wriston, Walter B.** *The Twilight of Sovereignty: How the Information Revolution Is Transforming Our World.* New York: Charles Scribner's Sons, 1992.

Journals

1929 **Abbott, George C.** "The Associated States and Indepencence." *Journal of Interamerican Studies*), 23, No. 1 (February, 1981), 69-94.

1930 **Ake, Claude.** "Political Integration and Political Stability: A Hypothesis." *World Politics*, 19, No. 3 (April, 1967), 486-499.

1931 **Ancel, Jacques.** "Climats nationaux." *Europe Nouvelle*, 15 Anne, No. 731 (Avril 2, 1932), 441-442.

1932 **Ancel, Jacques.** "La Nation et ses facteurs geographiqurs." *Affaires Etrangeres*, (1934), 78-87.

1933 **Arndt, E.M.** "Staat, Volk und Bauer." *Zeitshcrift fur Geopolitik*, Jahrg 11, Heft 11 (Nov., 1934), 655-663.

1934 **Atwood, Wallace W.** "The Increasing Significance of Geographic Conditions in the Growth of Nation-States." *Annales of the Association of American Geographers*, 25, No. 1 (March, 1935), 1-16.

1935 **Baldacci, O.** "I contenuti geografici degli Stati." *Cultura e Scuola*, 6, No. 22 (1967), 178-182.

1936 **Balibar, Etienne.** "The Nation Form: History and Ideology." *Fernand Braudel Center Review* [Binghamton], 13, No. 3 (Summer, 1990), 329-361.

1937 **Balsom, Denis; Madgwick, Peter; and Van Mechelen, Denis**. "The Political Consequences of Welsh Identity." *Ethnic and Racial Studies*, 7, No. 1 (January, 1984), 160-181.

1938 **Bastie, Jean.** "Reflexions Sur L'Amenagement du Territoire." *Acta Geographica,* No. 99 (Septembre, 1994), 3-23.

1939 **Beltran Y rozpide, Ricardo.** "La region geographica y el estado politico." *Bulletin Royal de la Societe de Geographie*, 66 (1926), 32-34.

1940 **Beneditti, Giancarlo.** "Evoluzione territoriale delle strutture politico-amministrative germaniche rel XX secolo." *L'Universo*, 63, No. 6 (Novembre-Dicembre, 1983), 865-912.

1941 **Berry, Brian J.L.** "By What Categories May a State be Characterized." *Economic Development and Cultural Change*, 15, No. 1 (October, 1966), 91-93.

1942 **Berry, C.J.** "Nations and Norms." *Review of Politics*, 43, No. 1 (January, 1981) 78-87.

1943 **Blacksell, Mark.** "A Criminal State." *Geographical Magazine*, 58, No. 6 (June, 1986), 282-287.

1944 **Blomley, Nicholas K.** "Legal Interpretation: The Geography of Law." *Tijdschrift voor economische en Sociale Geografie*, 78, No. 4 (1987), 265-275.

1945 **Boyne, George, and Powell, Martin.** "Territorial Justice: A Review of Theory and Evidence." *Political Geography Quarterly* [Oxford], 10, No. 3 (July, 1991), 263-281.

1946 **Bosch, H.M.J., Van den.** "Staat en Natie in Politick-Geografische Theorievorming." *Geografisch Tijdschrift Nieuwe Ruks*, 15, Nr. 2 (Marz, 1981), 108-115.

1947 **Bothe, Adrian.** "Das System der Kommuralen Steveren: Ein Neulcs Instrument fur die Raumordnungspolitik?" *Geographische Runschau*, Jahr 34, Heft 1 (January, 1982), 25-28.

1948 **Bowen.** "The Geography of Nations." *Geography*, 48, No. 218, Part 1 (January, 1963), 1-17.

1949 **Bowman, Isaiah.** "The Strategy of Territorial Decisions." *Foreign Affairs*, 24, No. 2 (January, 1946), 177-194.

1950 **Brown, Seyom.** "The World Polity and the Nation-State System: An Updated Analysis." *International Journal*, 39, No. 2 (Summer, 1984), 509-528.

1951 **Bruneau, Michel.** "Espaces et Territoires de Diasporas." *L'Espace Geographique*, 23, No. 1 (1994), 5-18.

1952 **Burghardt, Andrew F.** "Nation, State and Territorial Unity: A Trans-ontaonais View." *Cahiers de geographie du Quebec*, 24 (1980), 123-134.

1953 **Burns, Tom.** "Sovereignty, Interests and Bureaucracy in the Modern State." *British Journal of Sociology*, 31, No. 4 (December, 1980), 491-506.

1954 **Busteed, M.A.** "A Country in Search of Identity." *Geographical Magazine*, 49, No. 5 (February, 1977), 317-332.

1955 **Cardoso, Vicente Licinio.** "Da geografia como fator de unificacao nacional." *Boletim Geografico*, 1, No. 6 (Set., 1943), 27-31.

1956 **Carneiro, Robert L.** "A Theory of the Origin of the State." *Science*, 169, No. 3947 (August 21, 1970), 733-738.

1957 **Carpenter, C.R.** "Territoriality: A Review of Concepts and Problems." In *Behavior and Evolution*. New Haven, Connecticut: Yale University Press, 1958.

1958 **Chase-Dunn, Christopher.** "World-State Formation: Historical Processes and Emergent Necessity." *Political Geography Quarterly*, 9, No. 2 (April, 1990), 108-130.

1959 **Cherry, J.F.** "Power in Space: Archaelogical and Geographical Studies in the State." *Landscape and Culture*, (1987), 146-172.

1960 **Chouinard, Vera.** "State Formation and the Politics of Place: The Case of Community Legal Aid Clinics." *Political Geography Quarterly*, 9, No. 1 (January, 1990), 23-38.

1961 **Chouinard, Vera, and Fincher, Ruth.** "State Formation in Capitalist Societies: A Conjunctural Approach." *Antipode*, 19, No. 3 (December, 1987), 329-353.

1962 **Clark, G.L.** "Review of R.J. Johnston, 'Geography of the State'." *Environment and Planning*, A 15, No. 4 (December, 1983b), 1419-1421.

1963 **Cole, K.C.** "Theory of the State as a Sovereign Juristic Person." *American Political Science Review*, 42, No. 1 (February, 1948), 16-31.

1964 **Connor, Walker F.** "Nation-building or Nation-destroying?" *World Politics*, 24, No. 3 (April, 1972), 319-355.

1965 **Conti, Sergio.** "Tecnologia e 'Nuova' Territorialita." *Rivista Geografica Italiana* [Pisa], 100, Fasc. 3 (Settembre, 1993), 671-702.

1966 **Cornell, Jimmy**. "Welcome to Micro-State." *Commonwealth*, 21, No. 6 (December, 1978-January, 1979), 14-15.

1967 **Coverdale, Mark**. "The Rise of Martinique." *Bloombury Geographer*, 13 (1985), 9-11.

1968 **Darby, H.C.** "The Medieval Sea-State." *Scottish Geographical Magazine*, 47, No. 3 (May, 1932), 136-149.

1969 **Dauer, M.J.** "Unrepresentative States." *National Municipal Review*, 44, No. 11 (December, 1955), 571-575 and 587.

1970 **Dear, M.J., and Clark, Gordon L.** "The State and Geographic Process: A Critical Review." *Environment and Planning*, A10, No. 2 (April, 1978), 173-183.

1971 **Deutsch, Karl W.** "The Growth of Nations: Some Recurrent Patterns of Political and Social Integration." *World Politics*, 5, No. 2 (January, 1953), 168-195.

1972 **Di Meo, Guy.** "Les Territoires de la Localite, Origine et Actualite." *L'Espace Geographique* [Paris], 22, No. 4 (1993), 306-317.

1973 **Di Meo, Guy; Castaingts, Jean-Pierre; and Ducournau, Colette.** "Territoire, Patrimoine et Formation Socio-Spatiale" (exemples gascons). *Annales de Geographie* [Paris], l02e, No. 573 (Septembre-Octobre, 1993), 472-502.

1974 **Diehl, Paul F., and Goertz, Gary.** "Territorial Changes and Militarized Conflict." *Journal of Conflict Resolution*, 32, No. 1 (March, 1988), 103-122.

1975 **Dommen, Edward.** "Some Distinguishing Characteristics of Island States." *World Development*, 8, No. 12 (December, 1980), 931-943.

1976 **Dorion, Henri.** "Definition et portee de la conscience territoriale en geographie politique." In *International Geography*, W. Peter Adams and Frederick M. Helleiner, eds. Toronto, Ontario, Canada: University of Toronto Press, 1972, 517-519.

1977 **Duncan, S.S., and Goodwin, M.** "The Local State." *Political Geography Quarterly*, 1, No. 1 (January, 1982), 77-96.

1978 **Dupuy, Gabriel.** "Les Reseaux Techniques Sont-ils des Reseaux Territoriaux." *L'Espace Geographisque*, Tome 16, No. 3 (September, 1987), 175-184.

1979 **Fawcett, C.B.** "Some Geographical Factors in the Growth of the State." *Scottish Geographical Magazine*, 38, No. 3 (December, 1922), 221-232.

1980 **Fincher, Ruth.** "Space, Class and Political Proceses: The Social Relations of the Local State." *Progress in Political Geography*, 11, No. 4 (December, 1987), 496-516.

1981 **Fox, Douglas.** "The Riveirina as a New State: A Geographical Appraisal." *Geography Teacher: Journal of the Geography Teachers' Association of Victoria*, 6, No. 1 (June, 1966), 18-28.

1982 **Geisler, Walter.** "Beitrage zur Stadtgeographie." *Zeitschrift fur Gervasserk*, No. 8-10 (1920), 274-296.

1983 **Godolphim, Waldir da Costa.** "Territorio e dominio." *A Defesa Nacional*, 1959, No. 541 (1928), 127-134.

1984 **Goiten, H.** "Some Problems of Sovereignty." *Transactions Grotins Society*, 13 (1928), 79.

1985 **Gold, John R.** "Territoriality and Human Spatial Behavior." *Progress in Human Geography*, 6, No. 1 (March, 1982), 44-67.

1986 **Hakli, Jouni.** "Territoriality and the Rise of Modern State." *Fennia* [Helsinki], 172, No. 1 (1994), 1-82.

1987 **Hartshorne, Richard.** "The Concept of Raison d'Etre and Maturity of States." *Annals of the Assocation of American Geographers*, 30, No. 1 (March, 1940), 59-60.

1988 **Hartshorne, Richard.** "Morphology of the State Area: Significance for the State." In *Essays in Political Geography* by Charles A. Fisher. London: Methuen, 1968, 27-32.

1989 **Hay, Iain M.** "A State of Mind? Some Thoughts on the State in Capitalist Society." *Progress in Human Geography*, 12, No. 1 (March, 1988), 34-46.

1990 **Herman, Theodore.** "Group Values Towards the National Space." *Geographical Review*, 49, No. 2 (April, 1959), 164-182.

1991 **Herz, John H.** "Rise and Demise of the Territorial State." *World Politics*, 9, No. 4 (July, 1957), 473-493.

1992 **Herz, John H.** "The Territorial State Revisited: Reflections on the Future of the Nation-State." *Polity*, 1 (1968), 11-34.

1993 **Honey, Rex D.** "Conflicting Problems in the Political Organization of Space." *Annals of Regional Sciences*, 10, No. 1 (March, 1976), 45-60.

1994 **Honey, Rex D.** "Form, Process, and the Political Organization of Space." *Professional Geographer*, 29, No. 1 (February, 1977), 14-20.

1995   **Honey, Rex D.** "On the Geography of Jurisdictions." *Geographical Perspectives*, 36, No. 2 (Fall, 1975), 18-29.

1996   **Horowitz, Dan.** "Strategic Limitations of 'A Nation in Arms'." *Armed Forces and Society*, 13, No. 2 (Winter, 1987), 277-294.

1997   **Horowitz, Donald L.** "Irredentas and Secessions: Adjacent Phenomena, Neglected Connections." *International Journal of Comparative Sociology* [Leiden], 33, Nos. 1-2 (January-April, 1992), 118-130.

1998   **Isajiw, Wsevolod W.** "Towards a Theory of Idelogical Movement: Nationalism and Community Change in Quebec and Flanders." *Canadian Review of Studies in Nationalism*, 12, No. 1 (Spring, 1985), 141-160.

1999   **Jacobs, Jane M.** "Understanding the Limitations and Cultural Implications of Aboriginal Tribal Boundary Maps." *Globe*, 25 (1986), 2-12.

2000   **Jacobs, John Boyd, Jr.** "The Consequence of Closed Political Space." *Monadnock*, 42, No. 2 (June, 1968), 15-18.

2001   **James, Preston E.** "Some Fundamental Elements in the Analysis of the Viability of States." In *Essays in Political Geography* by Charels A. Fisher. London: Methuen, 1968, 33-38.

2002   **Johnston, R.J.** "The Territoriality of Law: An Exploration." *Urban Geography* [Silver spring], 11, No. 6 (November-December, 1990), 548-565.

2003   **Johnston, R.J.** "Texts, Actors and Higher Managers: Judges, Bureaucrats, and the Political Organization of Space." *Political Geography Quarterly*, 2, No. 1 (January, 1983), 3-20.

2004   **Jones, B.D.** "Review of 'The Politics of Location'." *Political Geography Quarterly*, 3, No. 4 (October, 1984), 350-351.

2005   **Jones, G.** "Review of R.J. Johnston, 'Geography and the State'." *Government and Policy. Environment and Planning*, 2 (1984), 108-109.

2006   **Katz, Michael.** "Origin of the Institutional State." *Marxist Perpsective*, 1, No. 4 (Winter, 1978), 6-22.

2007   **Kaufmann, John H.** "On the Definitions and Functions of Dominance and Territoriality." *Cambridge Philosophical Study Biological Reviews*, 58, No. 1 (February, 1983), 1-20.

2008   **Kedourie, Elie.** "The Nation-State in the Middle East." *Jerusalem Journal of International Relations*, 9, No. 3 (September, 1987), 1-9.

2009   **Khorev, B.S.** "Geography and Society Territorial Organization Problems." *Vsesoyuznoe Geograficheskoe Obshchestvo Izvestiia*, Tom. 114, Vyp. 6 (1982), 498-503.

2010   **Kliot, Nurit.** "The Collapse of the Lebanese State." *Middle Eastern Studies*, 23, No. 1 (January, 1987), 54-74.

2011   **Kirby, Andrew.** "A Public City: Concepts of Space and the Local State." *Urban Geography*, 4, No. 3 (July-September, 1983), 191-202.

2012   **Knight, David B.** "Identity and Territory: Geographical Perspective on Natinalism and Regionalism." *Annals of the Association of American Geographers*, 72, No. 4 (December, 1982), 514-531.

2013   **Knight, David B.** "Statehood: A Politico-Geographic and Legal Perspective." *GeoJournal* [Dordrecht], 28, No. 3 (November, 1992), 311-318.

2014   **Knight, David B.** "Territory and People or People and Territory? Thoughts on Post-colonial Self-Determination." *International Political Science Review*, 6, No. 2 (April, 1985), 248-272.

2015   **Kratowil, F.** "Of Systems, Boundaries and Territoriality." *World Politics, 39*, No. 1 (October, 1986), 27-52.

2016   **Kristof, Ladis K.D.** "The State-Idea, the National Idea and the Image of the Fatherland." *Orbis*, 11, No. 1 (Spring, 1967), 238-255.

2017   **Kucheida, Jean-Pierre.** "Decentralisation et Amenagement du Territoire." *Herodote* [Paris], No. 62 (Juillet-Septembre, 1991) 64-67.

2018   **Kutschera, K.** "Neue Staatavolker im Werden." *Zeitschrift fur Geopolitik*, Jahrg 12, Heft9 (September, 1935), 533-545 and Heft 10 (October, 1935), 625-634.

2019   **LaFlamme, Alan G.** "The Archipelago State as a Societal Subtype." *Current Anthropoloty*, 24, No. 3 (June, 1983), 361-362.

2020   **Lafuente, G.A.** "Essai de classification des etats." *Bulletin de L'Association de Geographes Francais*, No. 338-339 (Novembre-Decembre, 1965), 53-56.

2021   **Lamb, G.** "Marxism, Access and the State." *Development and Change*, 6, No. 2 (April, 1975), 119-135.

2022   **Langbein, Otto.** "Die jungsten Staaten der Erde. (Zum Problem der Staatwerdung in der politischen Geographie)." *Mitteilunger der Geographischen Gesellschaft in Wien*, Band 81, Nr. 1-2 (1938), 26-37.

2023 **Liebieh, Andre.** "Six States in Search of an Identity." *International Journal*, 43, No. 1 (Winter, 1987-88), 1-17.

2024 **Lima, Steven L.** "Territoriality in Variable Environments: A Simple Model." *American Naturalist*, 124, No. 5 (November, 1984), 641-655.

2025 **Lyman, Stanford, and Scott, Marvin B.** "Territoriality: A Neglected Sociological Dimenension." *Social Problems*, 15, No. 2 (Fall, 1967), 236-249.

2026 **Malmberg, Torsten.** "Water, Rhythm, and Territoriality." *Geografiska Annaler.* Series B: Human Geography, 66 B, No. 2 (April, 1984), 73-89.

2027 **Massam, Bryan H.** "The Site Location Problem." *Operational Geographer*, 5 (1984), 16-19.

2028 **Masters, Roger D.** "The Biological Nature of the State." *World Politics*, 35, No. 2 (January, 1983), 161-193.

2029 **Mattos, Carlos de Meira.** "Formas de expansao." *A Defesa Nacional*, 563-564 (Junho-Julho, 1961), 121-125.

2030 **Mbongo, Nsame.** "Problems Theoriques de la Question Nationale en Afrique." *Presence Africaine*, Nouvelle Serie No. 136, 4° Trim. (1985), 31-67.

2031 **McColl, Robert W.** "The Insurgent State: Territorial Bases of Revolution." *Annals of the Association of American Geographers*, 59, No. 4 (December, 1969), 613-631.

2032 **McNair, A.** "Aspects of State Sovereignty." *British Year Book of Internatinal Law*, 26 (1949), 6-47.

2033 **Melamid, Alexander.** "The Economic Geography of Neutral Territories." *Geographical Review*, 45, No. 3 (July, 1955), 359-374.

2034 **Merelman, Richard M.** "The Political Uses of Territoriality." *Environment and Behavior*, 29, No. 5 (September, 1988), 576-600.

2035 **Merritt, R.L.** "Noncontiguity and Political Integration." In *Linkage Politics*, J.N. Rosenau, ed. New York: The Free Press, 1969, 237-72.

2036 **Mikesell, Marvin W.** "The Myth of the Nation State." *Journal of Geography*, 82, No. 6 (November-December, 1983), 257-260.

2037 **Miszlivetz, Ferenc.** "The Unfinished Revolutions of 1989: The Decline of the Nation-State? *Social Research* [New York], 58, No. 4 (Winter, 1991), 781-804.

2038 **Mitchell, D.** "Iconography and Locational Conflict from the Underside." *Political Geography*, 11, No. 2 (March, 1992), 152-169.

2039 **Neuberger, Benyamin.** "History and African Concepts of Nationhood." *Canadian Review of Studies in Nationalism*, 14, No. 1 (Spring, 1987), 161-179.

2040 **Nijim, Basheer K.** "The Geography of a State." *Iowa Geographer*, 23 (October, 1967), 33-37.

2041 **North, Douglas.** "Locational Theory and Regional Economic Growth." *Journal of Political Economy*, 63, No. 3 (June, 1955), 243-258.

2042 **Nyang'oro, Julius E.** "On the Concept of 'Corporatism' and the African State." *Studies in Comparative International Development*, 21, No. 4 (Winter, 1986-87), 31-54.

2043 **Palmer, Norman D.** "The National Interest-Alone or With Other?" *Annals of the American Academy of Political and Social Science*, 282 (July, 1952), 1-118.

2044 **Perevolotsky, Avi.** "Territoriality and Resource Sharing Among the Bedouin of Southern Sinai: A Sicio-Ecological Interpretaiton." *Journal of Arid Environments*, 13, No. 2 (September, 1987), 153-161.

2045 **Pienaar, P.A.** "Xhosa-Grondeise: Simptome van'n onderliggende Politiek-Geografiese Probleem." *South African Geographer*, 13, No. 2 (September, 1985), 21-28.

2046 **Pirie, Gordon.** "On Spatial Justice." *Environment and Planning*, A 15, No. 3 (August, 1983), 465-473.

2047 **Piveteau, Jean-Luc.** "La Territorialite des Hebreux: L'affaire d'un Petit Peuple Il y a Longtemps, Ou un Cas D'ecole Pour le Ille Millenaire?" *L'Espace Geographique* [Paris], 21, No. 1 (1993), 26-34.

2048 **Pounds, Norman J.G.** "History and Geography: A Perspective on the Politics of Partition." *International Affairs*, 18, No. 2 (Fall, 1964), 161-172.

2049 **Pourtier, Ronald.** "Les geographes et le Partage de l'Afrique." *Herodote*, No. 41 (Avril-Juin, 1986), 91-108.

2050 **Racine, Jean-Luc.** "Rama et les Joueurs de Des: Questions sur la Nation Indienne." *Herodote* [Paris], No. 71 (Octobre-Decembre, 1993), 5-42.

2051 **Raffestin, Claude.** "Territorialit: Concept ou Paradigme de la geographie Sociale." *Geographica Helvetica*, Jahr 41, Heft 2 (1986), 91-96.

2052 Ratzel, Friedrich. "The Laws of the Spatial Growth of States." Translated by Ronald L. Bolin. In *The Structure of Political Geography*, R.E. Kasperson and J.V. Minghi, eds. London: University of London Press, 1970, 17-28.

2053 Ratzel, Friedrich. "The Territorial Growth of States" (an abstract). *Scottish Geographical Magazine*, 12, No. 7 (July, 1896), 351-361.

2054 Ronai, Andras. "Les bases geographiques des territoires des Etats." *Nouvelle Revue de Hongrie*, 30 (1937), 208-217.

2055 Roos, Philip D. "Jurisdiction: An Ecological Concept." *Human Relations*, 21, No. 1 (February, 1968), 75-84.

2056 Rosenberg, Justin. "A Non-Realist Theory of Sovereignty?: Giddens." *The Nation-State and Violence, Millenium* [London], 19, No. 2 (Summer 1990), 249-259.

2057 Rumley, Dennis. "the Political Organisation of Space: A Reformist Conception." *Australian Geographical Studies* [Campbell], 29, No. 2 (October, 1991), 329-336.

2058 Sack, Robert D. "Human Territoriality: A Theory." *Annals of the Association of American Geographers*, 73, No. 1 (March, 1983), 55-74.

2059 Salisbury, Howard Graves III. "The State within a State: Some Comparisons Between the Urban Ghetto and the Insurgent State." *Professional Geographer*, 23, No. 2 (April, 1971), 105-112.

2060 Schwalm, Eberhardt. "Die Politische Karte in der Gemeinschaftskunde." *Geographische Rundschau*, 19, Heft 15 (Mai, 1967), 161-169.

2061 Sebba, Rachel, and Churchman, Arza. "Territories and Territoriality in the Home." *Environment and Behavior*, 15, No. 2 (March, 1983), 191-210.

2062 Smith, Anthony D. "The Myth of the 'Modern Nation' and the Myths of Nations." *Ethnic and Racial Studies*, 11, No. 1 (January, 1988), 1-26.

2063 Smith, Anthony D. "The Origins of Nations." *Ethnic and Racial Studies*, 12, No. 3 (July, 1989), 340-367.

2064 Socini, Roberto. "Le Norme Internazionali Sui Confini Terrestri Degli Stati." *L'Universa*, 36, No. 4 (July-August, 1956), 513-526.

2065 Southall, Aidan. "The Segmentary State in Africa and Asia." *Comparative Studies in Society and History*, 30, No. 1 (January, 1988), 52-82.

2066 Stea, David. "Space, Territoriality and Human Movements." *Landscape*, 15, No. 1 (Autumn, 1965), 13-16.

2067 Strong, Rupert. "Partition in Practice." *Geographical Magazine*, 7, No. 2 (June, 1938), 105-114.

2068 Sukhwal, B.L. "The Nation State: A Myth." *National Geographer*, 11, No. 1 (June, 1976), 1-11.

2069 Sur, Etienne. "L'Allemagne Orientale, d'un Territoire a L'autre." *Herodote* [Paris], No. 62 (Juillet-Septembre, 1991), 150-160.

2070 Talbett, Michael S. "The Legal Landscape: One View of the Terrain." *Papers and Proceedings of Applied Geography Conferences*, 11 (1988), 125-130.

2071 Taylor, Peter J. "The State as Container: Territoriality in the Modern World-System." *Progress in Human Geography* [London], 18, No. 2 (June, 1994), 151-162.

2072 Tiryakian, Edward A. "Quebec, Wales, and Scotland: Three Nations in Search of a State." *International Journal of Comparative Sociology*, 21, No. 1-2 (March-June, 1980), 1-13.

2073 Ueda, Gen. "The Concept of Territoriality and Attachments to Place: A Metageogaphical Investigation." *Human Geography*, 38, No. 3 (June, 1986), 1-19. (Text in Japanese)

2074 Visher, Stephen S. "Territorial Expansion." *Scientific Monthly*, 40, No. 5 (May, 1935), 440-449.

2075 Wade, H.W.R. "Basis of Legal Sovereignty." *Cambridge Law Journal*, (November, 1975), 172-197.

2076 Walker, P.C. Gordon. "The Future of City and Island States." *New Commonwealth*, 29, No. 8 (April, 1955), 369-371.

2077 Waterman, Stanley. "Partioned States." *Political Geography Quarterly*, 6, No. 2 (April, 1987), 151-170.

2078 Weber, Cynthia. "Reconsidering Statehood: Examining the Sovereignty/ Intervention Boundary." *Review of International Studies* [Cambridge], 18, No. 3 (July, 1992), 199-216.

2079 Whebell, C.F.J. "Models of Political Territory." *Proceedings of the Association of American Geographers*, 2 (1970), 152-156.

2080 Williams, C.H., and Smith, Anthony D. "The Natinional Construction of Social Space." *Progress in Human Geography*, 7, No. 4 (December, 1983), 502-518.

2081 Wiskemann, Elizabeth. "Berlin Between East and West." *World Today*, 16, No. 11 (November, 1960), 463-472.

2082 Wolpert, Julian. "The Decision Process in Spatial Context." *Annals of the Association of American Geographers*, 54, No. 4 (December, 1964), 537-558.

2083 Wright, J.K. "Sections and National Growth." *Geographical Review*, 22, No. 3 (July, 1932), 353-360.

2084 Ziemann, W., and Lanzendorfer, M. "The State in Peripheral Societies." *Socialist Register*, (1977), 143-177.

2085 Zuniga, M.A. Guadalupe. "Geohistory of the Territorial Divisions of Morelos State, 1519-1980." *Boletin-Instituto de Geografia, Universidad Nacional Autonoma de Mexico*, 15 (1985), 155-209.

POLITICAL GEOGRAPHY OF REGIONS

AFRICA

Books and Journals

2086 Adejuyigbe, Omolade. "The Problems of Unity and the Creation of States in Nigeria." *Nigerian Geographical Journal*, 11, No. 1 (June, 1968), 11-20.

2087 Aicardi de Saint-Paul, Marc. *Gabon: The Development of a Nation*. Translated by A.F. and T. Palmer. London: Routledge, 1989.

2088 "An African Problem; Three Groups of Territories." *Round Table*, 20, No. 130 (March, 1930), 134-141.

2089 Askew, William C. *Europe and Italy's Acquisition of Lybia, 1911-1912*. Durham, North Carolina: Duke University Press, 1942.

2090 Ballinger, Margaret. "The Outlook for the South African Republic." *International Affairs*, 38, No. 3 (July, 1962), 295-303.

2091 Barbour, K.M. "North-Eastern Nigeria--A Case Study of State Formation." *Journal of Modern African Studies*. 9, No. 1 (May, 1971), 49-71.

2092 Beres, Anemone. "L'archipel des bantovstans." *Herodote*, No. 41 (Avril-Juin, 1986), 12-38.

2093 Best, Alan C.G., and Young, Bruce S. "Homeland Consolidation: The Case of Kwazulu." *South African Geographer*, 4, No. 1 (September, 1972), 63-74.

2094 Blumenfield, Jesmond, ed. *South Africa in Crisis*. Beckenham, United Kingdom: Croom Helm, 1987.

2095 Bonner, P. *Kings, Commoners and Concessionaires: The Evolution and Dissolution of the Nineteenth Century Swazi State*. Cambridge: Cambridge University Press, 1983.

2096 Buo, Sammy Kum. "How United is Cameroon?" *Africa Report*, 21, No. 6 (November-December, 1976), 17-20.

2097 Cameron, Sir Donald. "Native Administration in Nigeria and Tanganyika." *Journal of the Royal African Society*. Extra Supplement. 36 (November, 1937), complete issue.

2098 Cashdan, Elizabeth. "Territoriality Among Human Foragers: Ecological Models and An Application to Four Busman Groups." *Current Antropology*, 24, No. 1 (February, 1983), 47-66.

2099 Chanaiwa, David Shingirai. "The Zulu Revolution: State Formation in a Pastoralist Society." *African Studies Review* , 23, No. 3 (December, 1980), 1-20.

2100 Christopher, A. J. "South Africa: The Case of a Failed State Partition." *Political Geography* [Oxford], 13, No. 2 (March, 1994), 123-136.

2101 Cohen, R. "Editorial: The State in Africa." *Review of African Political Economy*, 5 (1976), 1-3.

2102 Congo Belge. *Organisation Territoriale 1953*. Bruxells: Ministrere des Colonies, 1953.

2103 Cope, John. "South Africa." *Nations of the Modern World*. London: Ernest Benn, 1965.

2104 Crowder, Michael. "Two Cameroons or One?" *Geographical Magazine*, 32, No. 6 (November, 1959), 303-34.

2105 Curtis, Neville. "South Africa: The Politics of Fragmentation." *Foreign Affairs*, 50, No. 2 (January, 1972), 283-296.

2106 Davies, Chief H.O. "The New African Profile." *Foreign Affairs*, 40, No. 2 (January, 1962), 293-302.

2107 Dikshit, R.D. "The River State of Gambia." *Africa Quarterly*, 4, No. 4 (January-March, 1965), 229-239.

2108 Fischer, Julie. *The Political and Social Uses of Territoriality in African Societies*. Madison: University of Wisconsin, M.A., 1984.

2109 Gerteiny, A.G. *Mauritania: A Survey of a New African Nation*. New York: Praeger, 1967.

2110 **Gretton, John.** "A Desert State that Vanished." *Geographical Magazine*, 49, No. 3 (December, 1976), 155-160.

2111 **Grundy, Kenneth.** *The Lands and Peoples of Kenya, Uganda and Tanzania.* New York: Macmillan, 1968.

2112 **Harris, Lillian Craig.** *Libya: Qadhafi's Revolution and the Modern State.* Boulder, Colorado: Westview Press, 1986.

2113 **Hill, Christopher R.** *Bantustems; The Fragmentation of South Africa.* New York: Oxford University Press, 1964.

2114 **Hodder, B.W.** "The Ewe Problem: A Re-assessment." In *Essays in Political Geography,* Charles A. Fisher, ed. London: Methuen, 1968, 271-284.

2115 "Homelands: Constitutional Advances." *Bulletin of the African Institute of South Africa*, 9, No. 8 (September, 1973), 325-333.

2116 **Horrell, M.** *The African Homeland of South Africa.* Johannesburg: South African Institute of Race Relations, 1973.

2117 **Howe, Marvine.** "The Birth of the Moroccan Nation." *Middle East Journal*, 10, No. 1 (Winter, 1956), 1-16.

2118 **Huenu, Codjo.** "La Question de l'Etat et de la nation en Afrique." *Presence Africaine*, 3° et 4° Trimestres, No. 127-128 (1983), 329-347.

2119 **Ingrams, Harold.** *Uganda, A Crisis of Nationhood.* London: Her Majesty's Stationery Office, 1960.

2120 **Jaenen, C.J.** "Whither Somalia?" *Middle Eastern Affairs*, 8, No. 4 (April, 1957), 134-138.

2121 **Jalata, Asafa.** *Oromia and Ethiopia: State Formation and Ethnonational Conflict, 1868-1992.* Boulder: Lynne Rienner Publishers, 1993.

2122 **Kapteijns, Lidwien.** "The Emergence of a Sudanic State: Dar Masalit, 1874-1905." *International Journal of African Historical Studies*, 16, No. 4 (1983), 601-613.

2123 **Kirby, Andrew,** and **Ward, Michael D.** "Modernity and the Process of State Formation: An Examination of 20th Century Africa." *International Interactions* [Philadelphia], 17, No. 1 (1991), 113-126.

2124 **Kirchherr, Eugene C.** *Abyssinia to Zimbabwe: A Guide to the Political Units of Africa in the Period 1947-1978.* 3rd ed. Papers in International Studies; Africa Series, No. 25. Athens: Ohio University Press, 1979.

2125 **Legum, Colin.** "New Hope for Nigeria: The Search for National Unity." *Round Table*, 58, No. 230 (April, 1968), 127-136.

2126 **Laitin, David D.,** and **Samatar, Said S.** *Somalia: Nation in Search of a State.* Boulder, Colorado: Westview Press, 1987.

2127 **Lemarchand, Rene.** "Chad: The Misadvantures of the North-South Dialectic." *African Studies Review*, 29, No. 3 (September, 1986), 27-41.

2128 **Manshard, Walther.** "Die neuen Hauptstadte Tropische-Afrikas." *Zeitschrift fur Wirtschaftsgeographie*, Jahr 30, Heft 3/4 (1986), 1-13.

2129 **Nyongo, Peter Anyang.** *Popular Struggle for Democracy in Africa.* London: Zed Books, 1987.

2130 "One Rhodesia or Two? Some Constitutional Anomalies." *Round Table*, 40, No. 159 (June, 1950), 220-225.

2131 **Pankhurst, E. Sylvia,** and **Pankhurst, Richard.** *Ethiopia and Eritrea; The Last Phase of the Reunion Struggle, 1941-1952.* Woodford Green, Essex: Lalibela House, 1953.

2132 **Perham, Margery.** "The Sudan Emerges into Nationhood." *Foreign Affairs*, 27, No. 4 (July, 1949), 665-677.

2133 **Post, K.W.J.** "Is There a Case for Biafra?" *International Affairs*, 44, No. 1 (January, 1968), 26-39.

2134 **Pourtier, Roland.** "Les Etas et le controle territorial en Afrique centrale; principes et pratiques." *Annales de Geographie*, 98°, No. 547 (Mai-Juin, 1989) 286-301.

2135 **Rothchild, Donald S.** "The Politics of African Separatism." *Journal of International Affairs*, 15, No. 1 (Spring, 1961), 15-28.

2136 **Ruedy, John.** *Modern Algeria: The Origins and Development of a Nation.* Bloomington, IN: Indiana University Press, 1992.

2137 **Samatar, Ahni,** and **Samatar, A.I.** "The Material Roots of the Suspended African State: Arguments from Somalia." *Journal of Modern African Studies*, 25, No. 4 (December, 1987), 669-690.

2138 **Sandbrook, Richard.** "Hobbled Leviathans: Constraints on State Formation in Africa." *International Journal*, 41, No. 4 (Autumn, 1986), 707-733.

2139 **Schatzberg, Michael G.** "Two Facesof Kenya: The Researcher and the State." *African Studies Review*, 29, No. 4 (December, 1986), 1-15.

2140 **Senghor, Leopold.** "West Africa in Evolution." *Foreign Affairs*, 39, No. 2 (January, 1961), 240-246.

2141 **Soja, Edward W.** "Communications and Territorial Integration in East Africa." *East Lakes Geographer*, 4 (1968), 39-57.

2142 **Stark, Frank M.** "Theories of Contemporary State Formation in Africa: A Reassessment." *Journal of Modern African Studies*, 24, No. 2 (June, 1986), 335-347.

2143 **Stein, Howard.** "Theories of the State in Tanzania: A Critical Assessment." *Journal of Modern African Studies*, 23, No. 1 (March, 1985), 105-123.

2144 **Stultz, Newell M.** "Creative Self-Withdrawal in the Transkei; A Factual Report on the Establishment of the First Experimental Bomtustam in the Republic of South Africa." *Africa Report*, 9, No. 4 (April, 1964), 18-23.

2145 **Traore, Bakary.** "De a genese de la Nation et l'Etat en Afrique noire." *Presence Africaine*, 3ᵉ et 4ᵉ Trimestres, No. 127-128 (1983), 149-160.

2146 **Van Heerden, W.** "Why Bantu States?" *Optima*, 12, No. 2 (July, 1962), 59-65.

2147 **Vandewalle, Dirk.** "From the New State to the New Era: Toward a Second Republic in Tunisia." *Middle East Journal*, 42, No. 4 (Autumn, 1988), 602-620.

2148 **Varma, S.N.** "National Unity and Political Stability in Nigeria." *International Studies*, 4, No. 3 (January, 1963), 265-280.

2149 **Wallerstein, I.** "Ethnicity and National Integration in West Africa." *Cahiers d'Etudes Africaines*, 3 (October, 1960), 129-139.

2150 **Walter, Bob J.** *Territorial Expansion of the Nandi of Kenya, 1500-1905.* Athens: Ohio University, Center for International Studies, 1970.

2151 **Watts, Michael J., and Bassett, Thomas J.** "Politics, the State and Agrarian Development: A Comparative Study of Nigeria and Ivory Coast." *Political Geography Quarterly*, 5, No. 2 (April, 1986), 103-126.

2152 **Wilks, Ivor.** *Forests of Gold: Essays on the Akan and the Kingdom of Asante.* Athens: Ohio University Press, 1993.

2153 **Wood, Susan.** *Kenya: The Tension of Progress.* London: Oxford University Press, 1962.

2154 **Young, Crawford and Turner.** *Rise and Decline of the Zairian State.* Madison: University of Wisconsin Press, 1985.

2155 **Young, Crawford.** "Zafire: The Shattered Illusion of the Integral State." *The Journal of Modern African Studies*, 32, No. 2 (June, 1994), 247-263.

2156 **Zartman, William I.** *Government and Politics in Northern Africa.* New York: Praeger, 1963.

AMERICAS

Books

2157 **Alba, Victor.** *The Mexicans: The Making of a Nation.* New York: Praeger, 1967.

2158 **Anderson, James,** ed. *The Rise of the Modern State.* Brighton: Wheatsheaf Books, 1986.

2159 **Backheuser, Everardo.** *A estructura politica do Brazil-l-Notas previas.* Rio de Janeiro: Machado, 1926.

2160 **Bloomfield, Richard J.,** ed. *Puerto Rico: The Search for a National Policy.* Boulder, Colorado: Westview Press, 1985.

2161 **Brown, John Stafford.** *Back to Thirteen States.* New York: Vantage Press, 1972.

2162 **Calvert, Peter.** *Guatemala: A Nation in Turmoil.* Boulder, Colorado: Westview Press, 1985.

2163 **da Fonseca Hermes, J.S.** *A politica geografica do Brasil. Conferencia pronunciada na sessao plenaria de 14 de Setembro de 1940 do IX Congresso brasileiro de geografia, realizado na cidade de Florianopolis em 1940.* Rio de Janeiro: Grafica Laemmert, 1940.

2164 **Daus, Frederico.** *Geografia u unidad argentina.* Buenos Aires: Ed. Nova, 1957.

2165 **de Barros, Jayme.** *A politica exterior do Brasil (1930-1942).* 2a. ed., correta e aumentada. Rio: Z. Valverde, 1943.

2166 **Figueiredo, Jose de Lima.** *A Conquista do Brasil pelos brasileiros.* Rio de Janeiro: Conselho Nacional de Geografia, 1943.

2167 **Garreau, Joel.** *The Nine Nations of North America.* Boston: Houghton Mifflin, 1981.

2168 **Granados, Carlos.** *Place, Politics, and Nation--Building in Costa Rica: 1812-1842.* Syracuse, NY: Ph.D. Dissertation, Syracuse University, 1993.

2169 **Gruening, Earnest.** *The Battle for Alaska Statehood.* College: University of Alaska Press, 1967.

2170 **Hardy, W.G.** *From Sea Unto Sea: Canada 1850 to 1910; The Road to Nationhood.* Garden City, New Jersey: Doubleday, 1960.

2171 **Heine, Jorge, and Manigat, Leslie,** eds. *The Caribbean and World Politics: Cross Currents and Cleavages.* New York: Holmes and Meier, 1988.

2172 **Honderich, John.** *Arctic Imperative: Is Canada Losing the North.* Toronto, Ontario, Canada: University of Toronto Press, 1987.

2173 **Lafeber, W.** *The New Empire: An Interpretation of American Expansion, 1860-1898.* Ithaca, New York: Cornell University Press, 1963.

2174 **Landey, Deborah Lucia Elizabeth.** *Quebec as a Non-State Nation Actor in International Relations.* Ottawa, Ontario, Canada: Carleton University, M.A., 1978.

2175 **Morison, Samuel Eliot and Commager, Henry Steele.** *The Growth of the American Republic.* New York: Oxford University Press, 1950.

2176 **Morrison, William Robert.** *Showing the Flag: The Mounted Policy and Canadian Sovereignty in the North.* Vancouver: University of British Columbia Press, 1985.

2177 **Oliveirdias, Demostheres de.** *Formacao teritorial do Brasil origem e evolucao.* Rio de Janeiro: Loja Carlos Ribeiro, 1956.

2178 **Osborne, Harold.** *Bolivia: A Land Divided.* London: Royal Institute of International Affairs, 1954.

2179 **Palmer, Dave R.** *1794: America, Its Army, and the Birth of a Nation.* Novato, CA: Presidio, 1994.

2180 **Pearcy, G. Etzel.** *United States and Outlying Areas: Geographic Report No. 4.* Washington, D.C.: U.S. Department of State, 1963.

2181 **Perry, Gardner.** *Size as Related to Efficiency in United States Counties.* Seattle: University of Washington, M.A., 1987.

2182 **Poneman, Daniel.** *Argentina: Democracy on Trial.* New York: Paragon House, 1987.

2183 **Pratt, Julius W.** *Expansionist of 1812.* Gloucester, Massachusetts: Peter Smith, 1957.

2184 **Pratt, Julius W.** *Expansionsit of 1898: The Acquisition of Hawaii and the Spanish Islands.* Baltimore, Maryland: Johns Hopkins University Press, 1936.

2185 **Ronaghan, Allen.** *We Are One Nation; A Blueprint for a New and Greater Canada.* New York: Greenwich Book Publishers, 1959.

2186 **Shiels, Archie W.** *The Purchase of Alaska.* College: University of Alaska Press, 1967.

2187 **Shumway, Nicolas.** *The Invention of Argentina.* Berkeley: University of Calaifornia Press, 1991.

2188 **Stefanisch, Juan.** *El Estado Solidarista: Estructuray funciones del Estado en el nuevo sistema continental Americano.* Buenos Aires: Arayee, 1935.

2189 **Teshera, Robert Walter.** *The Territorial Organization of American Internal Governmental Jurisdictions.* Seattle: University of Washington, Ph.D., 1970.

2190 **Travassos, Mario.** *Projecao Continental do Brasil.* Sao Paulo: Comp. Editora Nacional, 1938.

2191 **Troy, Ed Rolla Milton, and Others.** *Early Grants and Origin of the Thirteen Colonies.* Indianapolis, Indiana: G.F. Cram, 1954.

2192 **Wolforth, John Raymond.** *'Dual Allegiance' in the Mackenzie Delta, Northwest Territories--Aspects of the Evolution and Contemporary Spatial Structure of a Northern Community.* Vancouver, British Columbia, Canada: University of British Columbia, Ph.D., 1971.

Journals

2193 **Aubert de la Rue, Philippe.** "Le Quebec et l'avenir du Canada." *Politique Etrangere,* 28, Nos. 4-5 (1963), 330-346.

2194 **Backheuser, Everardo.** "Das politiche konglomerat Brasiliens." *Zeitschrift fur Geopolitik,* 3, No. 7-12 (Juli-Dez., 1926), 625-630.

2195 **Barreto, Flamarion.** "Formacao das nacoes sul-americanas do Pacifico e do Caribe." *A Defesa National,* 578 (Set.-Out., 1962), 47-87.

2196 **Bellavance, Marcel.** "Quelques Elements spatiau x de la Conjoncture Politique Quebecoise en 1867." *Cahiers de Geographie du Quebec,* 24, No. 62 (September, 1980), 225-248.

2197 **Bonner, Thomas.** "Dominujace Wzorce W Amerykanskim Procesie Narodot wor czym." (Title in English: "Recurrent Patterns in the American Nation-building Process.") *Przeglad Polonijny,* Rok 9. z 1 (27), 1983, 49-58.

2198 **Braga Cavalcanti, Filinto Alcino.** "Memorial geografico sobre os limites do Amazonas com o Para." *Congresso brasileiro de geografia,* 9°, Florianopolis, 1940, Anais, 5 (1944), 279-306.

2199 **Caldeira, Aroldo.** "Limites do Estado de Santa Catarina." *Revista do Instituto historico e geografico de Santa Catarina*, 2° semestre (1943), 167-170.

2200 **Chapman, Abraham.** "Hawaii Seeks Statehood." *Far Eastern Survey*, 15, No. 14 (July 17, 1946), 209-213.

2201 **Clark, Gordon L.** "Law, the State, and the Spatial Integration of the United States." *Environment and Planning*, A 13, No. 4 (December, 1981), 1197-1227.

2202 **Clibbon, Peter B.** "The 'Stastical Unit': A Tool for Detailed Geographical Analyses in the Province of Quebec." *Cahiers de Geographie de Quebec*, 16, No. 12 (Avril-Septembre, 1962), 265-269.

2203 **Collburn, Forrest D.** "Class, State and Revolution in Rural Nicaragua: The Case of Los Cafetaleros." *Journal of Developing Areas*, 18, No. 4 (July, 1984), 501-518.

2204 **Commons, A.** "Gestation and Birth of a State: Guerrero." *Boletin Instituto de Geografia, Universidad Nacional Autonoma de Mexico*, 15 (1985), 119-153.

2205 "Convenio preliminar para fixacao de limites entre os estados de Pernambuco e Alagoas." *Revista brasileira de geografia*, 5, No. 4 (Autubro-Dezembro, 1943), 670-672.

2206 **Dale, Edmund H.** "The New International Economic Order: Caribbean Small and Middle States." In *Spotlight on the Caribbean, A Microcosm of the Third World*. Regina, Saskatchua Canada: Regina Geograpical Studies No. 2, Department of Geography, University of Regina, 1977, 1-46.

2207 **Dorion, Henri.** "La geographie politique au Quebec: de l'inventaire a' la reflexion." *Canadian Geographer*, 18, No. 1 (Spring, 1974), 39-54.

2208 **Dumas, Claude.** "Nation et Identite dans le Mexique du XIX\ siede: Essai sur ure variation." *Cashiers du Monde Hispanique et Luso-Bresilien*, 38 (1982), 45-69.

2209 **Enloe, Cynthia.** "The Growth of the State and Ethnic Mobilization: The American Experience." *Ethnic and Racial Studies*, 4, No. 2 (April, 1983), 123-136.

2210 **Falardeau, Jean-Charles.** "French Canada Today." *Geographical Magazine*, 32, No. 3 (July, 1959), 107-120.

2211 **Farias Vlach, Vania Rubia.** "Reflexions sur le Territoire et la Formation de L'Etat-Nation Bresilien." *Herodote*, No. 72/73 (Janvier-Juin, 1994), 180-192.

2212 **Fowler, Don D.** "Uses of the Past: Archaeology in the Service of the State." *American Antiquity*, 52, No. 2 (April, 1987), 229-248.

2213 "French Canada Stays Canadian: the Gaullists Lose the First Round." *Round Table*, 58, No. 229 (January, 1968), 65-70.

2214 **Frenette, Jean-Vianney.** "Divisions administratives et organisations de l'espace au Quebec: Essai d'interpretation." *La Revue de geographie de Montreal*, 28, No. 1 (1974), 41-54.

2215 **Goodwin, M., and Duncan, S.** "The Local State and Local Policy: Political Mobilization or Economic Regeneration." *Capital and Class*, 27 (1986), 14-36.

2216 **Heusinkveld, Harriet M.** "Separatist Tendencies in the Yucatan Peninsula." *Professional Geographer*, 19, No. 5 (September, 1967), 258-260.

2217 **Jefferson, Mark.** "The Problem of the Ecumene: The Case of Canada." *Geografiska Annaler*, Band 16, No. 2 (April, 1934), 146-158.

2218 **Johnston, V.K.** "Canada's Title to the Arctic Islands." *Canadian Historical Review*, 16, No. 1 (March, 1933), 24-41.

2219 **Jost, Isabelle.** "Territorial Evolution of Canada." *Canadian Geogrphical Journal*, 75, No. 4 (October, 1967), 134-141.

2220 **Kessler, Margrit.** "Surinam: Probleme Eines Sudamerikanischkaribischen Staats auf dem wege zur Selbstardigkeit." *Zeitschrift fur Wirtschaft sgeogrphie*, Jahr 28, Hef 1 (1984), 37-46.

2221 **Kleber, Louis C.** "Alaska...Russia's Folly." *History Today*, 17, No. 4 (April, 1967), 229-235.

2222 **Kobayashi, Murehiro.** "Structure of Territorial Organizations in the Basin of Mexico During the Aztec Period." *Human Geography*, 32, No. 2 (April, 1980), 1-25.

2223 **Kratowil, Friedrich.** "Of Systems, Boundaries, and Territoriality: An Inquiry Into the Formation of the State." *World Politics*, 39, No. 1 (October, 1986), 27-52.

2224 **Laria, Salvador Carlos.** "Evolucion de la division departamental del ex-territorio nacional del Rio Negro." *Boletin de estudios Geograficos*, 12, No. 47 (Abril-Junio, 1965), 105-121.

2225 **Lines, Jorge A.** "Integracion de la Provincia de Costa Rica Bajo el Reinado de Don Carlos V." *Instituto Costarricense de Cultura Hispanica*, 2 (1959), 27-60.

2226 **Lingard, C. Cecil.** "Economic Forces Behind the Demand for Provincial Status in the Old North West Territories." *Canadian Historical Review*, 21, No. 3 (September, 1940), 254-267.

2227 **Martin, Walter.** "The Proposed Division of the Territory of Florida." *Florida Historical Quarterly*, 20, No. 3 (January, 1942), 260-276.

2228 **Mayo, H.B.** "Newfoundland's Entry into the Dominion." *Canadian Journal of Economics and Political Science*, 15, No. 4 (November, 1949), 505-522.

2229 **Mendoza, Jaime.** "El factor geografico en la nacionalidad boliviana." *Revista de la Sociedad Geografica*, 23-24-25 (Agosto, 1925), 1-15.

2230 **Morrison, Phoebe.** "Newfoundland: Dominion, Tenth Province, Forty-Ninth State?" *American Perspective*, 1, No. 9 (February, 1948), 575-583.

2231 **Murray, R.** "Two Brazils." *Geographical Magazine*, 25, No. 2 (June, 1952), 94-104 and 25, No. 4 (August, 1952), 157-166.

2232 **Nicholson, Norman L.** "Boundary Adjustment in the Gulf of Saint Lawrence Region." *Newfoundland Quarterly*, 53 (1954), 13-17.

2233 **Oberacker, Karl H.** "Die Brasilianishe Nation." *Zeitschrift fur Geopolitik*, 26, No. 1 (Jan., 1955), 28-41.

2234 **Ochoa Paredes, C.M.** "Historico-Geographical Evolution of the Territorial Divisions of Tlaxcala State, 1519-1980." *Boletin-Instituto de Geografia, Universidad Nacional Autonoma de Mexico*, 15 (1985), 211-253.

2235 **Orbegoso R., Efran.** "Un Nueva Provincia (Ascope) en el Departmento de la Libertad?" *Revista del Instituto de Geografia*, 4 (1951), 68-82.

2236 **Osborne, Thomas J.** "The Main Reason for Hawaiian Annexation in July, 1898." *Oregon Historical Quarterly*, 71, No. 2 (June, 1970), 161-178.

2237 **Oszlak, Oscar.** "The Historical Formation of the State in Latin America: Some Theoretical and Methodological Guidelines for Its Study." *Latin American Research Review*, 16, No. 2 (1981), 3-32.

2238 **Pearcy, G. Etzel.** "A Thirty Eight State U.S.A." *Special Liberies Association. Geography and Map Division, Bulletin No.* 97 (September, 1974), 2-15.

2239 **Pinard, Maurice, and Hamilton, Richard.** "The Class Bases of the Quebec Independence Movement: Conjectures and Evidence." *Ethnic and Racial Studies*, 7, No. 1 (January, 1984),

19-54.

2240 **Polnitz, Albrecht Freihern Von.** "Die nationale Staalenentwicklung in Spanisch-Sudamerika." *Zeitschrift fur Geopolitik*, 4, No. 1-6 (Jan.-Juni, 1926), 163-171 et 259-264.

2241 **Premdas, Ralph R.** "Ethnonationalism, Copper, and Secession in Bougainville." *Canadian Review of Studies in Nationalism*, 4, No. 2 (Spring, 1977), 247-265.

2242 **Pye, N.** "A New Official Map of Peru." *Scottish Geographical Magazine*, 56, No. 3 (November, 1940), 102-108.

2243 **Radames Isola, Emilio.** "As influencias geopoliticas na formacao do Estado Argentino." *A Defesa Nacional*, 540 (Julho, 1959), 131-141.

2244 **Rodrigues, Lysias A.** "Os grandes problemas nacionais." *A Defesa Nacional*, 447 (Out., 1951), 137-140.

2245 **Rodrigues, Lysias A.** "Politica aerea do Brasil." *Revista do instituto de geografia e historia militar do Brasil*, 24 (1953), 125-149.

2246 **Rozo M., Dario.** "El Archipielago de San Andres y Providencia: su Nacionalidad Colombiana." *Boletin de la Sociedad Geografica de Colombia*, 19, 69-70 (1961), 55-60.

2247 **Sanguin, Andre-Louis.** "'Small is not Beautiful': la Fragmentation Politique de la Caraibe." *Cashiers de Geographie du Quebec*, 25, No. 66 (Decembre, 1981), 343-360.

2248 **Sanguin, Andre-Louis.** "The Quebec Question and the Political Geography of Canada." *GeoJournal*, 8, No. 2 (March, 1984), 99-107.

2249 **Seligson, Mitchell A., and Muller, Edward N.** "Democratic Stability and Economic Crisis: Costa Rica, 1978-83." *International Studies Quarterly*, 31, No. 3 (September, 1987), 301-326.

2250 **Sharp, Walter R.** "Brazil 1940 - Whither the 'New State'?" *Inter-American Quarterly*, 2, No. 4 (October, 1940), 5-17.

2251 **Sherrill, Peter T.** "Separatism and Quebec." *Current History*, 79, No. 460 (November, 1980), 134-137 and 144-145.

2252 **Simnett, W.E.** "Outlying Territories of the United States; Their Position in the Pacific War and American Policy in Relation to Them." *Crown Colonist*, 12, No. 124 (March, 1942), 139-143.

2253 **Slater, David.** "State and Territory in Post Revolutionary Cuba: Some Critical Reflections on the Development of Spatial Policy." *International Journal of Urban and Regional Research*, 6, No. 1 (March, 1982), 1-34.

2254 **Strange, Susan.** "Newfoundland--Tenth Province?" *World Affairs*, N.s., 1, No. 4 (October, 1947), 376-383.

2255 **Tambs, Lewis A.** "Marsch nach Western. Geopolitische Aspekte der brasilianischen Expansion." *Zeitschrift fur Geopolitik*, Jahrg 39, Heft 2 (Marz-Abril, 1968), 60-72.

2256 **Tansill, William R.** "Hawaii and Statehood." Washington, D.C.: *U.S. Library of Congress Public Affairs Bulletin*, No. 63 (1948), 1-77.

2257 **Weber, Sylvia, and Dollfus, Oliver.** "Territorialities et conflits dans la Sierra Novada de Santa Marta." *L'espaie Geographique*, 16, No. 4 (Octobre/Decembre, 1987), 295-305.

2258 **Weeks, John.** "An Interpretation of the Central American Crisis." *Latin American Research Review*, 21, No. 3 (1986), 31-53.

2259 **Wells, Merle W.** "The Creation of the Territories of Idaho." *Pacific Northwest Quarterly*, 40, No. 2 (April, 1949), 106-123.

2260 **Zarur, J.** "The New Brazilian Territories." *Geographical Review*, 34, No. 1 (January, 1944), 142-144.

ASIA

Books

2261 **Ahmad, Nafis.** *The Basis of Pakistan.* Calcutta: Thacker, Spink & Co., 1947.

2262 **Antulay, A.R.** *Mahajan Report Uncovered.* New Delhi: Allied Publishers, 1968.

2263 **Ayoob, Mohammed, and Others.** *Bangla Desh: A Struggle for Nationhood.* Delhi: Vikas Publications, 1971.

2264 **Bennis, Phyllis.** *From Stones to Statehood: The Palestinian Uprising.* Brooklyn: Olive Branch Press, 1990.

2265 **Bentwich, Norman.** *Israel Resurgent.* New York: Praeger, 1960.

2266 **Bhargava, G.S.** *Pakistan in Crisis.* Delhi: Vikas Publications, 1969.

2267 **Bouman, J.C., and Others.** *The South Moluccas; Rebellious Province of Occupied State.*" Leyden: S.W. Sythoff, 1960.

2268 *China's Expansionist Drive into India; An Analysis of the Data Available in the Fifth White Paper, Released by the Government of India, Containing the Notes, Memoranda and Letters Exchanged Between the Government of India and China During the Period November, 60-November, 61.* New Delhi: Afro-Asian Council, 1961.

2269 **Chung, Chong-Shikied.** *Korean Unification: Source Materials with an Introduction.* Seoul: Research Center for Peace and Unification, Vol. 2, 1979.

2270 **Clarkson, James D.** *India's North East Frontier Agency.* Chicago, Illinois: University of Chicago, Ph.D., 1963.

2271 **Cohen, Mitchell.** *Zion and State: Nation, Class and the Shaping of Modern Israel.* Oxford: Brasil-Blackwell, 1987.

2272 **Cutshall, Alden.** *The Philippines: Nation of Islands.* Princeton, New Jersey: Van Nostrand, 1964.

2273 **Dehra Dun.** "Survey of India." *Political Map of India.* 3rd ed. Dehra Dun: Survey of India, 1956.

2274 **Demko, George.** *The Russian Colonization of Kazakhstan.* Philadelphia, Pennsylvania: State University, Ph.D., 1964.

2275 **Dow, Maynard Weston.** *Nation Building in Southeast Asia.* Colorado: Pruett Press, 1965.

2276 **Duffett, W.E.; Hicks, A.R.; and Parkin, G.R.** *India Today; The Background of Indian Nationalism.* New York: John Day, 1942.

2277 **Duri, Abad al-Aziz.** *The Historical Formation of the Arab Nation: A Study in Identity and Consciousness.* Translated by Lawrence I. Conrad. London: Croom Helm, 1987.

2278 **Farmer, B.H.** *Ceylon, A Divided Nation.* London: Oxford University Press, 1963.

2279 **Hill, Michael, and Lian, Kwen Fee.** *Politics of Nation-Building and Citizenshp in Singapore.* New York: Routledge Politics in Asia Series, 1994.

2280 **Hudson, G.F., ed.** *Reforms and Resolution in Asia.* London: Allen & Unwin, 1972.

2281 **Fishel, Wesley R.** *The End of Extraterritoriality in China.* Berkeley: University of California Press, 1952.

2282 **Friedman, Harry J.** *Consolidation of India Since Independence: A Comparison and Analysis of Four Indian Territorial Problems--The Portuguese Possessions, the French Possessions, Hyderbad and Kashmir.* Pittsburgh, Pennsylvania: University of Pittsburgh, Ph.D., 1956.

2283 **Goldschmidt, Arthur, Jr.** *Modern Egypt: The Formation of a Nation-State.* Boulder, Colorado: Westview Press, 1988.

2284 **Gordon, D.L.** *Lebanon—The Fragmented Nation.* Beckenham, Kent: Croom Helm, 1980.

2285 **Hadawi, Sami.** *Palestine Partitioned 1947-58.* New York: Arab Information Center, 1959.

2286 **Hyamson, Albert Montefiore.** *Palestine: A Policy.* London: Methuen, 1942.

2287 **India.** Ministry of Home Affairs. *White Paper on Hyderabad.* Delhi: Publication Division, Government of India Press, 1948.

2288 **Jahan, Rounaq.** *Nation-Building in the New States: Pakistan, A Case Study. The Relationship Between East Pakistan and the Central Government of Pakistan, 1958-1968.* Cambridge, Massachusetts: Harvard University, Ph.D., 1970.

2289 **Khalidi, Walid.** *Palestine Reborn.* London: I. B. Tauris & Co., Ltd., 1992.

2290 **Kwak, Tae-Hwan; Kim, Chonghan; and Kim, Hong Nack,** eds. *Korean Reunification: New Perspectives and Approaches.* Seoul: Kyongnam Unius Press, 1984.

2291 **Maddy-Weitzman, Bruce.** *The Crystallization of the Arab State System, 1945-1954.* Syracuse: Syracuse University Press, 1993.

2292 **Mahajan, M.C.** *Accession of Kashmir to India: The Inside Story.* Sholapur: Institute of Public Administration, 1950.

2293 **Mansour, Fawzy.** *The Arab World: Nation, State and Democracy.* Tokyo: United Nations University Press, 1992.

2294 **McAdams, A. James.** *Germany Divided: From the Wall to Reunification.* Princeton: Princeton University Press, 1993.

2295 **McColl, Robert W.** *The Rise of Territorial Communism in China (1921-34): The Geograpy Behind Politics.* Seattle: University of Washington, Ph.D., 1964.

2296 *National Integration: Tibet Issue.* New Delhi: G. Singh, 1964.

2297 **Norman, E. Herbert.** *The Emergence of Japan as a Modern State.* New York: International Secretariat, Institute of Pacific Relations, 1940.

2298 **Ongkili, James P.** *Nation-Building in Malaysia, 1946-1974.* Singapore: Oxford University Press, 1985.

2299 *Our Efforts Toward Peaceful Unification.* Seoul,

Korea: National Unification Board, 1978.

2300 *Pakistan: The Struggle of a Nation.* Washington, D.C.: Gibson Brothers, 1949.

2301 **Qureshi, Ishtiaq Husain.** *The Struggle for Pakistan.* Karachi: Universty of Karachi, 1965.

2302 **Rai, Satya M.** *Partition of the Punjab; A Study of Its Effects on the Politics and Administration of the Punjab, 1, 1947-56.* London: Asia Publishing House, 1965.

2303 **Rana, P.S., and Malla, K.P.,** eds. *Nepal in Perspective.* Kathmandu: CEDA, 1973.

2304 **Rose, Leo E., and Risher, Margaret W.** *The Northeast Frontier Agency of India.* Washington, D.C.: U.S. Department of State. Office of External Research, 1967.

2305 **Rosinger, Lawrence K.** *China's Crisis.* New York: Knopf, 1945.

2306 **Rubinoff, Arthur G.** *India's Use of Force in Goa.* Chicago, Illinois: University of Chicago, M.A., 1966.

2307 **Ryland, Robert Shane.** *The Partition of Bengal and Its Aftermath.* Durham, North Carolina: Duke University, M.A., 1966.

2308 **Sarwar, Hasan K.,** ed. *Genesis of Pakistan.* Karachi: Pakistan Institute of International Affairs, 1950.

2309 **Sayeed, Khalid B.** *Pakistan: The Formative Phase.* Karachi: Pakistan Publishing House, 1960.

2310 **Schofield, Richard N.** *Kuwait and Iraq: Historical Claims and Territorial Disputes.* London: Royal Institute of International Affairs, 1993.

2311 **Segal, Jerome M.** *Creating the Palestinian State: A Strategy for Peace.* Chicago: Lawrence Hill Books, 1989.

2312 **Singh, Ranbir Sardar.** *The Indian States Under the Government of India Act, 1935.* Bombay: D.B. Taraporevala, 1938.

2313 **Singh, Govind Saran.** *An Evaluation of the State of Maharashtra.* Worcester, Massachusetts: Clark University, Ph.D., 1962.

2314 **Symonds, Richard.** *The Making of Pakistan.* London: Faber and Faber, 1950.

2315 **Weeks, Richard V.** *Pakistan: Birth and Growth of a Muslim Nation.* New York: Van Nostrand, 1964.

2316 **Wenner, Manfred W.** *Modern Yeman, 1918-1966*. Baltimore, Maryland: Johns Hopkins University Press, 1964.

2317 **Wilcox, Wayne Ayres.** *Pakistan: The Consolidation of a Nation*. New York: Columbia University Press, 1964.

2318 **Wilcox, Wayne Ayres.** *The Political Assimilation of the Princely States of Pakistan*. New York City: Columbia University, Ph.D., 1960.

2319 **Wilkinson, J.C.** *The Origins of the Oman State; The Arabian Peninsula*. Oxford: The SOAS-Oxford Seminar, 1969.

2320 **Williams, L.F.R.** *The State of Pakistan*. Revised ed. London: Faber, 1966.

2321 **Wright, Denis.** *Bangladesh-Origins and Indian Ocean Relations*. New Delhi: Sterling, 1988.

2322 **Wymond, Richard.** *The Making of Pakistan*. London: Faber and Faber, 1950.

2323 **Zamir, Meir.** *The Formation of Modern Lebanon*. London: Croom Helm, 1985.

2324 **Ziff, William B.** *The Rape of Palestine*. New York: Argus Books, 1946.

Journals

2325 **Adhikari, Sudeepta, and Kumar, Alok.** "India's State-Idea--An Application of the Functional Approach in Political Geography. In *Recent Trends and Concepts in Geography*. Edited by Ram Bahadur Mandal and Vishwa Nath Prasad Sinha. New Delhi: Concept Publishing. Vol. 3 (1980), 399-424.

2326 **Ahmed, Hisham H.** "Palestinian State Formation: Means and Ends." *American-Arab Affairs* [Washington, D.C.], No. 33 (Summer, 1990), 10-34.

2327 **Alavi, Hamza.** "The State in Past-Colonial Societies." In *Imperialism and Revolution in South Asia*, K. Gough and A. Sharma, eds. New York: Monthly Review Press, 1973, 145-173.

2328 **Anderson, Benedict R. O'G.** "Old State, New Society: Indonesia's New Order in Comparative Historical Perspective." *Journal of Asian Studies*, 42, No. 3 (May, 1983), 477-496.

2329 **Babcock, F. Lawrence.** "The Much Promised Land." (Palestine) *Fortune*, 30, No. 10 (October, 1944), 166-172.

2330 **Ballantine, Joseph W.** "The Future of the Ryukuyus." *Foreign Affairs*. 31, No. 4 (July, 1953), 663-675.

2331 **Barnds, William J.** "Pakistan's Disintegration." *World Today*, 27, No. 8 (August, 1971), 319-329.

2332 **Baumgarten, Helga.** "The PLO, Its Struggle for Legitimacy, and the Question of a Palestinian State." *Jerusalem Journal of International Relations*, 9, No. 3 (September, 1987), 99-114.

2333 **Ben Dor, Gabriel.** "Stateness and Ideology in Contemporary Middle Eastern Politics." *Jerusalem Journal of International Relations*, 9, No. 3 (September, 1987), 10-37.

2334 **Bhadraj, Vijai Sen.** "Moscow and the Birth of Bangla Desh." *Asian Survey*, 13, No. 5 (May, 1973), 482-495.

2335 **Bhattacharya, B.K.** "Location Ascendancy of North Bengal." *Geographical Review of India*, 33, No. 4 (December, 1971), 287-294.

2336 **Bhattacharya, B.K.** "Separate Assam Hill State: What Does It Mean?" *Economic and Political Weekly*, 2, No. 9 (March 4, 1967), 491-494.

2337 **Bladen, Wildred A.** "Viability of Asian and Pacific States." *National Geographer*, 9 (1974), 7-13.

2338 **Blanc, Edouard.** "Le partage due Pamir La Convention de Simla avril 1895." *Annales de Geographie*, 5 Annee (October, 1896), 438-441.

2339 **Bleiber, Fritz.** "Afghanistan und Paschtunistan." *Zeitschrift fur Geopolitik*, 24, No. 2 (February, 1955), 88-96.

2340 **Blum, Yehuda Z.** "The Missing Reversioner: Reflections on the Status of Judea and Sumaria." *Israel Law Review*, 3, No. 2 (April, 1968), 279-301.

2341 **Bone, Robert C.** "Will Indonesia Disintegrate?" *Foreign Policy Bulletin*, 36, No. 16 (May 1, 1957), 125-127.

2342 **Bose, N.K.** "Bengal Partition and After." *Calcutta Geographical Review*, 9, Nos. 1-4 (December, 1947, Pub. 1949), 14-22.

2343 **Bradshu, Henry S.** "Tibet Struggles to Survive." *Foreign Affairs*, 47, No. 4 (July, 1969), 750-762.

2344 "Breakdown in Pakistan." *Eastern World*, 12, No. 11 (November, 1958), 19.

2345 **Brecher, Michael.** "Jerusalem: Israel's Political Decision, 1947-1977." *Middle East Journal*, 32, No. 1 (Winter, 1978), 13-34.

2346 **Brecher, Michael.** "Succession in India 1967: The Routinization of Political Change." *Asian Survey*, 7, No. 7 (July, 1967), 423-443.

2347 Breton, R.J.L. "Partages reduction et renovation du Pundjab." *Information Geographique*, 32 Annee, No. 1 (Janvier-Fevier, 1968), 23-36.

2348 Brynen, Rex. "Palestine and the Arab State System: Permeability, State Consolidation and the Intifada." *Canadian Journal of Political Science* [Ottawa], 24, No. 3 (September, 1991), 595-621.

2349 Burghardt, Richard. "The Formation of the Concept of Nation-State in Nepal." *Journal of Asian Studies*, 44, No. 1 (November, 1984), 101-125.

2350 Cervin, Vladimir. "Problem in the Integration of the Afghan Nation." *Middle East Jounral*, 6, No. 4 (Autumn, 1952), 400-416.

2351 Cheng, Tao. "The Dispute Over the South China Sea Islands." *Texas International Law Journal*, 10 (1975), 265-277.

2352 Cheng, Tao. "The Sino-Japanese Dispute Over the Tiao-yu-tai (Senkaku) Islands and the Law of Territorial Acquistion." *Virginia Journal of International Law*, 14, No. 2 (Winter, 1974), 221-266.

2353 Chichekian, Garo. "The Territorial Changes of Armenia Since the Treaty of San Stefano." *Armenian Review*, 23, No. 1 (Spring, 1970), 36-53.

2354 Chiu, Hungdah. "Legal Status of the Paracel and Spratly Islands." *Annals of the Chinese Society of International Law*, 12 (1975), 48-57.

2355 Chiu, Hungdah, and Park, Choon-Ho. "Legal Status of the Paracel and Spratly Islands." *Ocean Development and International Law*, 3, No. 1 (1975), 1-28.

2356 Choudhury, G.W. "Bangladesh: Why It Happened." *International Affairs*, 48, No. 2 (April, 1972), 242-249.

2357 Clark, W.E. Le Gros. "Peoples of Sarawak and the Proposal for Cession." *Crown Colonist*, 16, No. 173 (April, 1946), 231-232.

2358 Clyde, Paul H. "Stepping-Stones to Empire: Japan's Outlying Island Possessions." *Amerasia*, 6, No. 13 (January 25, 1943), 522-529.

2359 "Conflict in Pakhtunistan." *Egyptian Economic and Political Review*, 2, No. 1 (September, 1955), 11-14.

2360 "The Crisis in the Lebanon; A Note on Franco-Lebanese Relations." *Bulletin of International News*, 20, No. 24 (November 27, 1943), 1039-1046.

2361 Dannreuther, Roland. "Creating New States in Central Asia." *Adelphi* [London], Papr No. 288 (March, 1994), 1-83.

2362 Das, Taraknath. "The Status of Hyderabad During and After British Rule in India." *American Journal of International Law*, 43, No. 1 (January, 1949), 57-72.

2363 Dikshit, R.D. "India's Evolution as a Nation State." *Indo-Asian Culture*, 16, No. 4 (October, 1967), 211-226.

2364 Dikshit, R.D. "Maldive Islands: The Harbinger of Cold War in the Indian Realm." *Indian Geographical Journal*, 41, Nos. 1 and 2 (January-March and April-June, 1966,) 29-33.

2365 Dikshit, R.D. "Maldive Islands, the Harbinger of Cold War in the Indian Realm: A Study in Political Geography." *Modern Review*, 114 (November, 1963), 362-366.

2366 Dommen, Arthur J. "Separatist Tendencies of Eastern India." *Asian Survey*, 7, No. 10 (October, 1967), 726-739.

2367 Drake, Christine. "National Integration and Public Policies in Indonesia." *Studies in Comparative International Development*, 15, No. 4 (Winter, 1980), 59-84.

2368 Drake, Christine. "The Spatial Pattern of National Integration in Indoensia." Transactions of the *Institute of British Geographers*, New Series, 6, No. 4 (November, 1981), 471-490.

2369 Drysdale, Alasdair Duncan. "The Succession in Syria." *Middle East Journal*, 39, No. 2 (Spring, 1985), 246-257.

2370 Drysdale, Alasdair Duncan. "Syria's Sectarian Schism and the Struggle for Power." *Middle East Insight*, 43 (1984), 24-29.

2371 Drysdale, Alasdair Duncan. "Syria's Troubled Ba'Thi Regime?" *Current History*, 80, No. 462 (January, 1981), 32-37.

2372 Duncanson, Dennis J. "Cambodia: An Elusive Nationhood." *Asian Affairs*, 11 (Old Series Vol. 67), Part 3 (October, 1980), 254-263.

2373 "The End of Extraterritoriality in China." *Bulletin of International News*, 20, No. 2 (January 23, 1943), 49-56.

2374 Ewing, Thomas E. "Russia, China and the Origins of the Mongolian People's Republic, 1911-1921: A Repraisal." *Slavonic and East European Review*, 58, No. 3 (July, 1980), 399-421.

2375 **Firzterald, C.P.** "Chinese Expansion in Central Asia." *Royal Central Asian Journal*, 50, Parts 3 and 4 (July/October, 1963), 290-294.

2376 **Fryer, Donald W.** "Economic Aspects of Indonesian Disunity." *Pacific Affairs*, 30, No. 3 (September, 1957), 195-208.

2377 **Fuber, Holden.** "The Unification of India, 1947-1951." *Pacific Affairs*, 24, No. 4 (December, 1951), 325-371.

2378 **Gerdes, Dick.** "Regionalismus und Politikissenschaff: Zur Wiederentdeckung von 'Territorialitatals Innenpolitischer Konflikt-dimension'." *Geographische Rundschau*, Jahr 39, Heft 10, (October, 1987), 526-531.

2379 **Grajdanzev, Andrew J.** "Korea Divided." *Far Eastern Survey*, 14, No. 20 (October 10, 1945), 281-283.

2380 **Grant, Christina Phelps.** "Must Palestine Be Partitioned?" *Queen's Quarterly*, 44, No. 4 (Winter, 1937), 455-462.

2381 **Gray, Hugh.** "The Demand for a Separate Telengana State in India." *Asian Survey*, 11, No. 5 (May, 1971), 463-474.

2382 **Guo, Zianzhong.** "From 'Chinese Economic Sphere' to Chinese Unification." *Chinese Economic Studies*, 26, No. 6 (Winter, 1993-94), 25-44.

2383 **Ha, Joseph M., and Luebbert, Gregory M.** "A Korean Settlement: The Prospects and Problems." *Asian Survey*, 17, No. 8 (August, 1977), 735-752.

2384 **Haas, Michael.** "Paradigms of Political Integration and Unification: Applications to Korea." *Journal of Peace Research*, 21, No. 1 (1984), 47-60.

2385 **Hadawi, Sami, ed.** "Palestine Partitioned, 1947-1958." *Arab Informatin Center, Document Collections*, No. 3 (1959). Complete Issue.

2386 **Ha-Lim, F.** "The State in West Malaysia." *Race & Class*, 24, No. 1 (Summer, 1982), 33-45.

2387 **Hall, Robert Burnett.** "Geographic Factors in Japanese Expansion." *Proceedings of the Institute of World Affairs*, 16th Session, (1938), 16 (1939), 46-55.

2388 **Hamilton, Thomas J.** "Partition of Palestine." *Foreign Policy Reports*, 23, No. 23 (February 15, 1948), 286-295.

2389 **Harding, Sir John.** "The Cyprus Problem in Relation to the Middle East." *International Affairs*, 34, No. 3 (July, 1958), 291-296.

2390 **Hassan, Riaz.** "Religion, Society, and the State in Pakistan: Pirs and Politics." *Asian Survey*, 27, No. 5 (May, 1987), 552-565.

2391 **Helin, Ronald A.** "Uniting the Wings of Pakistan: A Matter of Circulation." *Professional Geographer*, 20, No. 4 (July, 1968), 251-256.

2392 **Hennayake, Shanta K., and Duncan, James S.** "A Disputed Homeland: Sri Lanka's Civil War." *Focus*, 37, No. 1 (Spring, 1987), 20-27.

2393 **Holland, Sir Robert.** "Union of India." *International Journal*, 2, No. 3 (Summer, 1947), 187-199.

2394 "India: The Settlement with Hyderabad." *Round Table*, 39, No. 153 (December, 1953), 67-70.

2395 **Inlow, E. Burke.** "Report from Bhutan." *Asian Affairs*, 9 (Old Series, 65), Part 3 (October, 1978), 295-308.

2396 **Jentsch, Georg.** "Kann Tibet Souveran Seit?" *Zeitschrift fur Geopolitik*, Jahrg 31, Heft 1 (Januar, 1960), 21-25.

2397 **Kaplan, Charles H.** "The Palestine Royal Commission and the Proposal for Partition." *Wiener Library Bulletin*, 33, New Series Nos. 51-52 (1980), 30-41.

2398 **Kazziha, Walid.** "The Political Evolution of Transjordan." *Middle Eastern Studies*, 15, No. 2 (May, 1979), 239-257.

2399 **Kearney, Robert N.** "Ethnic Conflict and the Tamil Separatist Movement in Sri Lanka." *Asian Survey*, 25, No. 9 (September, 1985), 898-917.

2400 **Kelly, J.B.** "The Persian Claim to Bahrain." *International Affairs*, 33, No. 1 (January, 1957), 51-70.

2401 **Khalidi, Walid.** "Thinking the Unthinkable: A Sovereign Palestinian State." *Foreign Affairs*, 56, No. 4 (July, 1978), 695-713.

2402 **Koh, B.C.** "Dilemmas of Korean Reunification." *Asian Survey*, 11, No. 5 (May, 1971), 475-495.

2403 **Kruger, Karl.** "Staaten und Landschaften in Indien." *Geographica Helvetica*, Band 6, No. 1 (Janur, 1951), 28-30.

2404 **Lattimore, Owen.** "Sinkiang's Place in the Future of China." *Asia and the Americas*, 44, No. 5 (May, 1944), 197-201.

2405 **Lee, Chong-Sik.** "Korea: Troubles in a Divided State." *Asian Survey*, 5, No. 1 (January, 1965), 25-32.

2406 **Legrain, Jean-Francois.** "Les islamistes palestiniens a l'epreuve du soulevement." *Maghreb Machrek*, No. 121 (Julliet-Aout-Septembre, 1988), 5-42.

2407 **Leiden, Carl.** "Pakistan: The Divided Dominion." *Current History*, 25, No. 148 (December, 1953), 339-343.

2408 **Lieberthal, Kenneth.** "The Future of Hong Kong." *Asian Survey* [Berkley], 32, No. 7 (July, 1992), 666-682.

2409 **Leifer, Michael.** "The Phillippines and Sabah Irredenta." *World Today*, 24, No. 10 (October, 1968), 421-428.

2410 **Lin, Yutang.** "The Birth of a New China." *Asia*, 39, No. 3 (March, 1939), Section 2, 173-188.

2411 **Ling, Trevor.** "Creating a New State: The Bengalis of Bangladesh." *South Asian Review*, 5, No. 2 (April, 1972), 221-230.

2412 **McClellan, Grant S.** "Palestine and America's Role in the Middle East." *Foreign Policy Reports*, 21, No. 8 (July 1, 1945), 98-107.

2413 **MacDougall, J.A.** "Birth of a National: National Identification in Singapore." *Asian Survey*, 16, No. 6 (June, 1976), 510-524.

2414 **Mac Gillivray, Sir Donald.** "Malaya-The New Nation." *International Affairs*, 34, No. 2 April, 1958), 157-163.

2415 **Mansergh, Nicholas.** "The Partition of India in Retrospect." *International Journal*, 21, No. 1 (Winter, 1965-1966), 1-19.

2416 **Mason, Stanley.** "The Problem of East Pakistan." *Pacific Affairs*, 28, No. 2 (June, 1955), 132-144.

2417 **Meile, Pierre.** "Le Probleme Etats Himalayens." *Politique Etrangere*, 17, No. 6 (January, 1953), 470-486.

2418 **Mukerjee, Dilip.** "Assam Reorganization." *Asian Survey*, 9, No. 4 (April, 1969), 297-311.

2419 **Nandan, Ram.** "Jammu and Kasmir." *Focus*, 13, No. 1 (1962), 1-6.

2420 **Newman, Joseph, Jr.** "The Future of Northern Afghanistan." *Asian Survey*, 28, No. 7 (July, 1988), 729-739.

2421 **Nijim, Basheer K.** "Partition of the Punjab, 1947." *Iowa Geographer*, 19 (Fall, 1965), 3-7.

2422 **Oberoi, Harjot S.** "From Punjab to 'Khalistan': Territoriality and Metacommentary." *Pacific Affairs*, 60, No. 1 (Spring, 1987), 26-41.

2423 **Orgels, Bernard.** "Les Raisono d'etre de la Syrie; etude de geographie Politique." *Revue belge de Geographie*, 86, No. 1 (1962), 11-72.

2424 **Park, Richard L.** "East Bengal: Pakistan's Troubled Province." *Far Eastern Survey*, 23, No. 5 (May, 1954), 70-74.

2425 **Pearson, S. Vere.** "The Future of Palestine." *American Journal of Economics and Sociology*, 5, No. 2 (January, 1946), 203-209.

2426 **Perlmann, M.** "The Republic of Lebanon." *Palestine Affairs*, 2, No. 1 (November, 1947), 109-114.

2427 **Perlmutter, Amos.** "A Palestine Entity?" *International Security*, 5, No. 4 (Spring, 1981), 103-116.

2428 **Pillai, R.V., and Kumar, Mahendra.** "The Political and Legal Status of Kuwait." *International and Comparative Law Quarterly*, 11, No. 1 (1962), 108-130.

2429 "The Problem of Palestine." *World Today*, N.s., 1, No. 5 (November, 1945), 195-204.

2430 **Rahman, M. Anisur.** "East Pakistan: The Roots of Estrangement." *South Asian Review*, 3, No. 3 (April, 1970), 235-239.

2431 **Rainero, Romain.** "Pathanistan, Terra Contesa." *L'Universe*, 34, No. 6 (November-December, 1954), 903-910.

2432 **Rashiduzzaman, M.** "Leadership, Organization, Strategies and Tactics of the Bangladesh Movement." *Asian Survey*, 12, No. 3 (March, 1972), 185-200.

2433 **Reid, T.** "Should a Jewish State be Established in Palestine?" *Journal of the Royal Central Asian Society*, 33, Part 2 (April, 1946), 161-177.

2434 **Roberts, Guy.** "Making Malaya a Nation." *Geographical Magazine*, 19, No. 4 (August, 1946), 141-150.

2435 **Roosevelt, Kermit.** "The Partition of Palestine: A Lesson in Pressure Politics." *Middle East Journal*, 2, No. 1 (January, 1948), 1-16.

2436 **Routledge, Paul.** "Putting Politics in Its Place: Baliapal, India, as a Terrain of Resistance." *Political Geography* [Oxford], 11, No. 6 (November, 1992), 588-611.

2437 **Rowley, Gwyn.** "Developing Perspectives upon the Areal Extent of Israel: An Outline Evaluation." *GeoJournal*, 19, No. 2 (September, 1989), 99-111.

2438 **Rowley, Gwyn.** "Divisions in Lebanon." *Geographical Magazine*, 58, No. 7 (July, 1986), 326-327.

2439 **Rupen, Robert A.** "The Mongolian People's Republic: The Slow Evolution." *Asian Survey*, 7, No. 1 (January, 1967), 16-20.

2440 "Russia's Eastern Marches: Sinkiang and Tibet." *Round Table*, 160 (September, 1950), 334-340.

2441 **Schanberg, Sydney H.** "Pakistan Divided." *Foreign Affairs*, 50, No. 1 (October, 1971), 125-135.

2442 **Schmahl, Wolfgang.** "Die Auslandischen Konzessionen in China." *Zeitschrift fur Geopolitik*, Jahrg 20, Heft 5 (Mai, 1943), 212-215.

2443 **Scholz, Fred.** "Politische Probleme Pakistans. Die Gebirgstamme Baluchistans und die Zukunft West-Pakistans hach den Wahlen Vom Dez, 1970." *Geographische Rundschau*, Jahrg 23, Heft 7 (Juli, 1971), 249-259.

2444 **Schweinfurth, Ulrich.** "The Problem of Nagaland." In *Essays in Political Geography*. Charles A. Fisher, ed. London: Methuen, 1968, p. 161-176.

2445 **Searls, Guy.** "Communist China's Border Policy. Dragon Throne Imperialism." *Current Scene*, 2 (April 15, 1963), 1-22.

2446 **Sela, Avraham.** "The Changing Focus of the Arab States' System." *Middle East Review*, 20, No. 3 (Spring, 1988), 41-54.

2447 **Serjeant, R.B.** "The Two Yemens: Historical Perspectives and Present Attitudes." *Asian Affairs: Journal of the Royal Central Asian Society*, 60, N.S. Part 1 (February, 1973), 3-16.

2448 **Shadid, Mohammed, and Seltzer, Rick.** "Political Attitudes of Palestinians in the West Bank and Gaza Strip." *Middle East Journal*, 42, No. 1 (Winter, 1988), 16-32.

2449 **Shwadran, Benjamin.** "Jordan Annexes Arab Palestine." *Middle Eastern Affairs*, 1, No. 4, No. 3 (July, 1950), 277-295.

2450 **Singh, Chetan.** "Centre and Periphery in the Mughal State: The Case of Seventeenth-Century Punjab." *Modern Asian Studies*, 22, Part 2 (May, 1988), 299-318.

2451 **Singh, Kirpal.** "Effects of the partition of the Punjab." *Religion and Society*, 11 (March, 1964), 93-102.

2452 **Smith, C.G.** "The Emergence of the Middle East." *Journal of Contemporary History*, 3 (1968), 3-17.

2453 **Smith, Joseph B.** "The Koreans and Their Living Space: An Attempted Analysis in Terms of Political Geography." *Korean Review*, 2, No. 1 (1949), 45-52.

2454 **Smith, Wilfred Cantwell.** "Hyderabad: Muslim Tragedy." *Middle East Journal*, 4, No. 1 (January, 1950), 27-51.

2455 **Spate, O.H.K.** "The Partition of India and the Prospects for Pakistan." *Geographical Review*, 38, No. 1 (January, 1948), 5-29.

2456 **Spate, O.H.K.** "The Partition of the Punjab and of Bengal." *Geographical Journal*, 110, Nos. 4-6 (April-June, 1947, Pub. 1948), 201-222.

2457 **Spinks, Charles Nelson.** "Origin of Japanese Interests in Manchuria." *Far Eastern Quarterly*, 2, No. 3 (May, 1943), 259-271.

2458 **Srivastava, R.P.** "Politico-Territorial Structure of India During British Period." *National Geographer*, 14, No. 2 (December, 1979), 175-191.

2459 **Stanley, Bruce.** "Fragmentation and National Liberation Movements: The PLO." *Orbis*, 22, No. 4 (Winter, 1979), 1033-1055.

2460 **Stephenson, Glenn V.** "Pakistan: Discontiguity and the Majority Problem." *Geographical Review*, 58, No. 2 (April, 1968), 195-213.

2461 **Stephenson, Sir Hugh.** "Some Problems of a Separated Burma." *Journal of the Royal Central Asian Society*, 25, Part 3 (July, 1938), 400-415.

2462 **Sukhwal, B.L.** "Politico-geographic Analysis of Bifurcation: A Case Study of Punjab and Haryana, India." *Geographical Review of India*, 36, No. 4 (December, 1974), 291-308.

2463 **Symonds, Richard.** "State-Making in Pakistan." *Far Eastern Survey*, 19, No. 5 (March 8, 1950), 45-50.

2464 **Szuluc, Tad.** "Cyprus: A Time of Reckoning." *National Geographic* [Washington, D.C.], 184, No. 1 (July, 1993), 104-130.

2465 **Talbot, Phillips.** "The Rise of Pakistan." *Middle East Journal*, 2, No. 4 (October, 1948), 381-398.

2466 **Thompson, Virginia.** "The New Nation of Burma." *Far Eastern Survey*, 17, No. 7 (April 7, 1948), 81-84.

2467 **Thompson, Virginia.** "Thailand Irredenta-Internal and External." *Far Eastern Survey*, 9, No. 21 (October 23, 1940), 243-250.

2468 **Tregonning, K.G.** "The Partition of Brunei." *Journal of Tropical Geography*, 11 (April, 1958), 84-89.

2469 **Toukan, B.** "The Future Settlement of the Arab Countries." *Journal of the Royal Central Asian Society*, 30, Part 2 (May, 1943), 198-205.

2470 "The United States, Japan, and the Ryukyu Islands." *World Today*, 8, No. 8 (August, 1952), 352-360.

2471 "U.S. Meets U.S.S.R. in Manchuria. China Claims Manchuria By Right and By Need. Roosevelt, Following Historic U.S. Policy, Has Flatly Promised Manchuria to China. But Russia is Silent." *Fortune*, 31, No. 4 (April, 1945) 109-112+."

2472 **Van Der Kroef, Justus M.** "Disunited Indonesia." *Far East Survey*, 27, No. 4 (1958), 49-63 and No. 5, (1958), 73-80.

2473 **Van Der Kroef, Justus M.** "Indonesia: Sources of Disunity." *Orbis*, 2, No. 4 (Winter, 1959), 478-491.

2474 **Venkataraman, V.** "Manchuko: A Study in Political and Economic Geography." *Indian Geographical Journal*, 10, Nos. 1 and 2 (April-July, 1935), 73-110.

2475 **Verghese, B.G.** "No Second Partition." *United Asia*, 17, No. 5 (September-October, 1965), 332-337.

2476 **Waddington (Mary), W.F.** "The Modern State of Iraq." *Indian Geographical Journal*, 14, No. 1 (January-March, 1939), 66-100.

2477 **Webb, B.M.** "The Ancient State of Swat." *Canadian Geographical Journal*, 70, No. 2 (February, 1965), 65-73.

2478 **Whittaker, Arnold.** "The Smaller Provinces of India, 1939 to 1944, with Special Reference to Assam." *International Affairs*, 21, No. 1 (January, 1945), 53-59.

2479 **Wilkinson, J.C.** "Traditional Concepts of Territory in South East Arabia." *Geographical Journal*, 149, Part 3 (November, 1983), 301-315.

2480 **Woodhead, Sir John.** "The Report of the Palestine Partition Commission." *International Affairs*, 18, No. 2 (March-April, 1939), 171-185. Discussion: 185-193.

2481 **Woolbert, Robert Gale.** "Pan Arabism and the Palestine Problem." *Foreign Affairs*, 16, No. 2 (January, 1938), 309-322.

2482 **Wurfel, David.** "Okinawa: Irrendeta on the Pacific." *Pacific Affairs*, 35, No. 4 (Winter, 1962), 353-374.

2483 **Yang, Yun-yuan.** "Controversies Over Tibet: China Versus India, 1947-49." *China Quarterly*, 111 (September, 1987), 407-420.

2484 **Yishai, Yael.** "Israeli Annexation of East Jerusalem and the Golan Heights: Factors and Processes." *Middle Eastern Studies*, 21, No. 1 (January, 1985), 45-60.

2485 **Young, Richard.** "The State of Syria: Old or New?" *American Journal of International Law*, 56, No. 2 (April, 1962), 482-488.

2486 **Zaidi, Iqtidar H.** "Toward a Measure of the Functional Effectiveness of a State: The Case of West Pakistan." *Annals of the Association of American Geographers*, 56, No. 1 (March, 1966), 52-67.

AUSTRALIA, OCEANIA AND ANTARCTICA

Books and Journals

2487 **De Smith, Stanley A.** *Microstates and Micronesia: Problems of America's Pacific Islands and Other Minute Territories.* New York: New York University Press, 1970.

2488 **Deutsch, H.J.** "The Evolution of State and Territorial Boundries in the Inland Empire of the Pacific Northwest." *Pacific Northwestern Quarterly*, 51 (1960), 115-131.

2489 **Dunlop, Eric W., and Pike, Walter.** *Australia...Colony to Nation.* London: Logmans, 1960.

2490 **Grieg, D.W.** "Territorial Sovereignty and the Status of Antartica." *Australian Outlook*, 32, No. 2 (August, 1978), 117-129.

2491 **Fish, Ernest Kelvin, ed.** *New Guinea on the Threshold: Aspects of Social, Political and Economic Development,* with a forward by Sir John Crawford. London: Longmans; Camberra, A.N.V. Press, 1966.

2492 **Jeans, D.N.** "Territorial Divisions and the Locations of Towns in New South Wales 1826-1842." *Australian Geographer*, 10, No. 4 (September, 1967), 243-255.

2493 **Legge, J.D.** "Indonesia After West Irian." *Australian Outlook*, 17, No. 1 (April, 1963), 5-20.

2494 "Nations of the Pacific." *Current History*, 65, No. 387 (November, 1973), 193-223+.

2495 **Rainero, Romain.** "L'Irian Occidentale tra Olanda e Indonesia." *L'Universo*, 36, No. 4 (July-August, 1956), 593-604.

2496 **Stewart, P.J.** "Annexation of the Kermadecs and New Zealand's Policy in the Pacific." *Pacific Historical Review*, 28, No. 1 (February, 1959), 67-71.

2497 **Van der Kroef, Justus M.** *The West New Guinea Dispute.* New York: International Secretariat, Institute of Pacific Relations, 1958.

2498 **Van der Kroef, Justus M.** "West New Guinea: The Uncertain Future." *Asian Survey*, 8, No. 8 (August, 1968), 691-707.

2499 **Woolmington, E.R.** *A Spatial Approach to the Measurement of Support for the Separatist Movement in Northern New South Wales.* Armindale: University of New England Press, 1966.

EUROPE

Books

2500 **Banac, Ivo.** *The National Question in Yugoslavia: Origins, History, Politics.* Ithaca, New York: Cornell University Press, 1984.

2501 **Barker, Elisabeth.** *Macedonia; Its Place in Balkan Power Politics.* London: Royal Institute of International Affairs, 1950.

2502 **Benes, Eduard.** *The Future of Small European Nations.* Address before the Council on Foreign Relations in Chicago, on May 22, 1943. (News flashes from Czechoslovakia under Nazi domination, Release No. 187, May 31, 1943.) Chicago: Czechoslovak National Council of America, 1943.

2503 **Best, Harry.** *The Soviet State and Its Inception.* New York: Philisophical Library, 1950.

2504 **Blum, Douglas W.,** ed. *Russia's Future: Consolidation or Disintegration?* Boulder: Westview Press, 1994.

2505 **Breuilly, John,** ed. *The State of Germany: The National Idea in the Making, Unmaking and Remaking of a Modern Nation-State.* London: Longman Group UK Limited, 1992.

2506 **Bristow, S.,; Kermode, D.; and Mannin, M.** *The Redundant Countries.* Ormskirk: Hesketh, 1984.

2507 **Buday, Laszlo.** *Dismembered Hungary.* London: Grant Richards, 1923.

2508 **Busteed, M.A.** *Northern Ireland: Geographical Aspects of a Crisis.* Oxford: University of Oxford, School of Geography, 1972.

2509 **Caro, Patricia T.** *The Bear and the Bishop: A Geography of the Separatist Movement in the Berner Jura, Switzerland.* Eugene: University of Oregon, Ph.D., 1976.

2510 **Carter, F.W.** *Dubrovnik (Ragusa): A Classic City-State.* New York: Seminar Press, 1972.

2511 **Chamberlin, William Henry.** *The Ukraine; A Submerged Nation.* New York: Macmillan, 1944.

2512 **Cole, Paul M.,** and **Hart, Douglas M.,** eds. *Northern Europe: Security Issues for the 1990's.* Boulder, Colorado: Westview Press, 1986.

2513 **Darby, Phillip.** *Three Forces of Imperialism: British and American Approaches to Asia and Africa, 1870-1970.* New Haven, Connecticut: Yale University Press, 1987.

2514 *Die Gemeinden der Schweiz. Les Communes de la Suisse.* Wabern bei Bern: Eidg. Landestopographie, 1951.

2515 **Doumitt, Donald P.** *Conflict in Northern Ireland: The History, The Problem and The Challenge.* New York: Peter Lang, 1985.

2516 **Dunlop, John B.** *The Rise of Russia and the Fall of the Soviet Empire.* Princeton: Princeton University Press, 1993.

2517 **Dyson, K.H.F.** *The State Tradition in Western Europe: A Study of an Idea and Institution.* Oxford: Martin Robertson, 1980.

2518 **Enders, Michael Jeffery.** *The Impact of National Territorial Size Upon the Utilization and Management of the Environment: A Political Geography of Resource Management and Law-Landscape Relationships in Monaco, Andorra, Menton (France) and San Raneo (Italy).* Worchester, Massachester: Clark University, Ph.D., 1979.

2519 **Finberg, H.P.R.** *The Formation of England 550-1042.* London: Hart-Davis, Macgibbon, 1974.

2520 **Freymond, Jacques.** *The Saar Conflict, 1945-1955.* New York: Praeger, 1960.

2521 **Gerson, L.L.** *Woodrow Wilson and the Rebirth of Poland.* New Haven, Connecticut: Yale University Press, 1953.

2522 **Gregory, James S.** *Russian Land Soviet People. A Geographical Approach to the USSR.* London: George Harrap, 1968.

2523 **Grinius, K.V.** *Lithuania in a Post-war Europe as a Free and Independent State.* New York: Lithuanian Bulletin, 1943.

2524 **Hancock, M. Donald, and Welsh, Helga A.,** eds. *German Unification: Process and Outcomes.* Boulder: Westview Press, 1994.

2525 **Hoffman, George W.** *The Growth and Decline of Austria: A Political and Historical Geography.* Ann Arbor: University of Michigan, Ph.D., 1949.

2526 **Hussey, Gemma.** *Ireland Today: Anatomy of a Changing State.* Dublin: Townhouse, 1993.

2527 **Hutchinson, John.** *The Dynamics of Cultural Nationalism: The Gaelic Revival and the Creation of the Irish Nation State.* London: Allen & Unwin, 1987.

2528 **James, James Alton.** *The First Scientific Exploration of Russian America and the Purchase of Alaska.* (Northwestern University Studies in the Social Sciences, No. 4) Evanston, Illinois: Northwestern University, 1942.

2529 **Jessen, Franz de.** *Manuel historique de la question du Slesvig 1906-1938.* Copenhague: C.A. Reitzel, 1939.

2530 **Jessop, R.** *The Capitalist State.* London: Martin Robertson, 1982.

2531 **Jessop, R.** "The Transformation of the State in Post War Britain." In *The State in Western Europe.* London: Croom Helm, 1980, 23-93.

2532 **Kann, R.A.** *The Habsburg Empire: A Study in Integration and Disintegration.* New York: Praeger, 1957.

2533 **Karp, Regina Cowen,** ed. *Central and Eastern Europe: The Challenge of Transition.* Oxford: Oxford University Press, 1993.

2534 **Kohn, Hans.** *The Future of Austria.* New York: Foreign Policy Association, 1955.

2535 **Laar, Mart.** *War in the Woods: Estonia's Struggle for Survival, 1944-1956.* Washington, D.C.: The Compass Press, 1992.

2536 *Latvia in 1939-1942. Background Bolshevik and Nazi Occupation; Hopes for Future.* Washington, D.C.: Press Bureau of the Latvian Legation, 1942.

2537 *Latvia Under German Occupation, 1941-1943.* Washington, D.C.: Press Bureau of the Latvian Legation, 1943.

2538 **Leff, Carol Skalnik.** *National Conflict in Czechoslovakia: The Making and Remaking of a State, 1918-1987.* Princeton, New Jersey: Princeton University Press, 1988.

2539 **Lovrin, C.D.** *Rumania To-day.* London: Porteous, 1945.

2540 **Machray, Robert.** *East Prussia, Menace to Poland and Peace.* London: Allen & Unwin, 1943.

2541 **Machray, Robert.** *The Eastern Question Revived. Bulgar Claims on Rumania.* London: Allen & Unwin, 1939.

2542 **Madgwick, Peter, and Rose, R.,** eds. *The Territorial Dimension in United Kingdom Politics.* London: Macmillan, 1982.

2543 **Magas, Branka.** *The Destruction of Yugoslavia: Tracking the Break-Up, 1980-92.* London: Verso, 1993.

2544 **Maxwell, Kenneth,** ed. *Portugal in the 1980's: Dilemmas of Democratic Consolidation.* New York: Greenwood Press, 1986.

2545 **Mayo, P.** *The Roots of Identity: Three National Movements in Contemporary European Politics.* London: Allen Lane, 1974.

2546 **McCauley, Martin, and Waldron, Peter.** *The Emergence of the Modern Russian State, 1855-81.* Houndmills: Macmillan, 1988.

2547 **Morgan, K.O.** *Rebirth of a Nation: Wales, 1880-1980.* Oxford: Oxford University Press, 1982.

2548 **Neckermann, Peter.** *The Unification of Germany or the Anatomy of a Peaceful Revolution.* Boulder: East European Monographs, 1991.

2549 **Papanek, Jan.** *Czechoslovakia.* (The World of Tomorrow. Georges Gurvitch, ed.) New York: International Universities Press, 1945.

2550 *Politische Karteder Republik Osterreich.* Wien: Herausgegeben vom Vundesanst fur Eichund Vermissungsweissen, 1965.

2551 **Pringle, D.G.** *One Island, Two Nations: A Political Geographical Analysis of the National Conflict in Ireland.* New York: John Wiley & Sons, 1985.

2552 **Rose, R.** *Understanding the United Kingdom: The Territorial Dimension in Government.* London: Longman, 1982.

2553 **Sanguin, Andre-Louis.** *Les Micro-Etats d'Europe (Andorre, Liechtenstein, Monaco, Saint-Martin); Geographie Politique et Economique* [The Micro-states of Europe (Andorra, Liechtenstein, Monaco, San Marino; Political and Economic Geography]. Belgium: University of Liege, Ph.D., 1973.

2554 **Saucerman, S.** *International Transfers of Territory in Europe.* Washington, D.C.: U.S. Grasing and Printing Office, 1937.

2555 Scase, R., ed. *The State in Western Europe*. London: Croom Helm, 1980.

2556 Schulz, P. *A Viability Concept: Isolated West Berlin as a Case Study*. Urbana: University of Illinois, Ph.D., 1971.

2557 Siegfried, Andre. *La Suisse democratie-temoin*, 4th Rev. ed. Neuchatel La Baconniere: Pierre Beguin, 1969.

2558 Smogorzewski, Casimir. *Lwow and Wilno*. (Free Europe Pamphlet, No. 9) London: Free Europe, 1945.

2559 Stoneman, Elvyn Arthur. *The Partition of Ireland*. Worcester, Massachusetts: Clark University, Ph.D., 1950.

2560 Taracouzio, T.A. *Soviets in the Arctic; An Historical, Economic and Political Study of the Soviet Advance into the Arctic*. New York: Macmillan, 1938.

2561 Vitols, Hugo and Others. *Annexation of the Baltic States*. Stockholm: Baltic Humanitarian Association, 1946.

2562 Wandycz, Piotr S. *The Land of Partitioned Poland, 1795-1918*. Seattle: University of Washington Press, 1974.

2563 Wiskemann, Elizabeth. *Czechs and Germans: A Study of the Struggle in the Historic Provinces of Bohemia and Moravia*. New York: Oxford University Press, 1938.

Journals

2564 Allyn, Emily. "Polish-German Relations in Pomerania and East Prussia." *Bulletin of the Polish Institute of Arts and Sciences in America*, 2, No. 3 (April, 1944), 822-858.

2565 Ancel, Jacques. "Geographie politique de la Prusse Orientale." *La Pologne et la Prusse Orientale*, (1933), 21-43.

2566 Anderson, Albin T. "The Soviets and the Northern Europe." *World Politics*, 19, No. 4 (July, 1967), 646-663.

2567 Andreopoulos, George. "State and Irredentism: Some Reflections on the Case of Greece." *Historical Journal*, 24, No. 4 (December, 1981), 949-959.

2568 Asmus, Ronald D. "A United Germany." *Foreign Affairs* [New York], 69, No. 2 (Spring, 1990).

2569 Austria. Treaties, etc. "State Treaty for the Re-establishment of an Independent and Democratic Austria." *Department of State Bulletin, U.S.*, 32, No. 832 (June 6, 1955), 916-932.

2570 Bachoud, Andree. "Les Territoires de la Nation Espagnole." *Herodote* [Paris], No. 62 (Juillet-Septembre, 1991), 125-135.

2571 Becman, William O. "Terrorism: Community Based or State Supported?" *American-Arab Affairs*, 16 (Spring, 1986), 29-36.

2572 Beneditti, Giancarlo. "Privince d'Italia e Loro Capolvoghi: Centovcnit Anni di Mutamenti Territoriali." *L'Universo*, Anno 62, No. 1 (Gennaio-Febbraio, 1982), 147-192.

2573 Benes, Eduard. "Czechoslovakia Plans for Peace." *Foreign Affairs*, 23, No. 1 (October, 1944), 26-37.

2574 Benes, Eduard. "The Position of the Small Nation in Post-War Europe." *American Journal of Sociology*, 49, No. 5 (March, 1944), 390-396.

2575 Benes, Eduard. "Postwar Czechoslovakia." *Foreign Affairs*, 24, No. 3 (April, 1946), 397-410.

2576 Bilmanis, Alfred. "Latvia as an Independent State." *Journal of Central European Affairs*, 4, No. 1 (April, 1944), 44-60.

2577 Blackman, Tim. "The Politics of Place in Northern Ireland: Perspectives on a Case Study." *International Journal of Urban and Regional Research*, 10, No. 4 (December, 1986), 541-562.

2578 Blacksell, Mark. "Reunification and the Political Geography of the Federal Republic of Germany." *Geography*, 67, Part 4, No. 297 (October, 1982), 310-319.

2579 Boal, F.W. "Two Nations in Ireland." *Antipode*, 11, No. 1 (April, 1980), 38-44.

2580 Brubacker, Rogers. "Nationhood and the National Question in the Soviet Union and Post-Soviet Eurasia: An Institutionalist Account." *Theory and Society* [Dordrecht], 23, No. 1 (February, 1994), 47-78.

2581 Bultin, Robin. "Prologue to an Irish Tragedy." *Geographical Magazine*, 49, No. 2 (November, 1976), 87-92.

2582 Cabot, Jean. "L'Afrique Explosive, Fille du desordre europeen." *Herodote*, 41 (Avril-Juin, 1986), 39-45.

2583 Cakste, Mintauts. "Latvia and the Soviet Union." *Journal of Central European Affairs*, 9, No. 1 (April, 1949), 32-60.

2584 **Camena, D'Almeida P.** "Nouvelle carte politique de la Russie d'Europe." *Annales de Geographie*, 32, No. 175 (15 Janvier, 1923), 75-79.

2585 **Carter, F.W.** "An Analysis of the Medieval Serbian Decumene a Theoretical Approach." *Geografiska Annaler*, 51B (1969), 39-56.

2586 **Carter, Gwendolen M.** "Eire-Its Neutrality and Post-War Prospects." *Foreign Policy Reports*, 20, No. 22 (February 1, 1945), 278-286.

2587 **Catudel, Honore M.** "Steinstucken: The Politics of a Berlin Enclave." *World Affairs*, 134, No. 1 (Summer, 1971), 51-62.

2588 **Chataigneau, Y.** "Le probleme macedonien." *Annales de Geographie*, 32, No. 177 (15 Mai, 1923), 275-278.

2589 **Cochrane, Feargal.** "Any Takers?: The Isolation of Northern Ireland." *Political Studies*, 42, No. 3 (September, 1994), 378-395.

2590 **Clementis, Vladimir.** "The Slovak 'State'; How It Was Born and How It Will Die." *Journal of Central European Affairs*, 4, No. 4 (January, 1945), 341-349.

2591 **Cornea, Victor.** "Bessarabia- and Russo-Rumanian Relations." *Contemporary Review*, 892, No. 4 (April, 1940), 452-458.

2592 **Curtis, L. Perry.** "Moral and Physical Force: The Language of Violence in Irish Nationalism." *Journal of British Studies*, 27, No. 2 (April, 1988), 150-189.

2593 **Dalmay De La Garennie, C.** "La Ruthenie Tchecoslovaque. Russie Subcarpathique." *Annales de Geographie*, 33, No. 185 (15 September, 1924), 443-456.

2594 **Daric, J.** "Le peuplement des nouveaux territoires polonais." *Population*, 3ᵉ Annee, No. 4 (October-Decembre, 1948), 691-712.

2595 **Denangeon, A.** "La Formation de l'Etat Francais." *Acta Geographica*, No. 8 (Octobre-December, 1971), 217-238.

2596 **de Weiss, Elizabeth.** "Dispute for the Burgenland in 1919." *Journal of Central European Affairs*, 3, No. 2 (July, 1943), 147-166.

2597 **DeWilde, John C.** "The Struggle for the Balkans." *Foreign Policy Reports*, 15, No. 19 (December 15, 1939), 230-240.

2598 "The Division of the Spoils in Yugoslavia." *Bulletin of International News*, 18, No. 26 (December 27, 1941), 2008-2010; 19, No. 1 (January 10, 1942), 3-5.

2599 **Djilas, Milovan.** "Yugoslavia and the

Expansionism of the Soviet State." *Foreign Affairs*, 58, No. 4 (Spring, 1980), 852-866.

2600 **Dobell, W.M.** "Division Over Cyprus." *International Journal*, 22, No. 2 (Spring, 1967), 278-292.

2601 **East, W. Gordon.** "The New Frontiers of the Soviet Union." *Foreign Affairs*, 29, No. 4 (July, 1951), 591-607.

2602 **Dumas, Pierre.** "Le partage de la Haute Silesie." *Annales de Geographie*, 31, No. 169 (15 Janvier, 1922), 1-14.

2603 **Edwards, K.C.** "Luxembourg: How Small Can A Nation Be?" *Northern Geography*, (1966), 261-267.

2604 **Eisenmann, L.** "La Nouvelle Hongrie." *Annales de Geographie*, 24, No. 161 (15 Septembre, 1920), 321-333.

2605 **Etzioni, Amitai.** "European Unification: A Strategy of Change." *World Politics*, 16, No. 1 (October, 1963), 32-51.

2606 **Fairhall, David.** "North of Murmansk." *Geogrpahical Magazine*, 49, No. 6 (March, 1977), 347-353.

2607 **Fay, Sidney B.** "The Russo-Polish Dispute." *Current History*, 6, No. 31 (March, 1944), 193-200.

2608 **Field, William O., Jr.** "The International Struggle for Transcaucasia." *American Quarterly on the Soviet Union*, 2, No. 2-3 (July-October, 1939), 21-44.

2609 **Fillip, Karlheinz.** "Facing the Political Map of Germany." *Political Geography Quarterly*, 3, No. 3 (July, 1984), 251-258.

2610 **Fleszar, Mieczyslaw.** "W. Sprawie Badan nad Geografia Polityczna w Polsce." *Przeglad Geograficzny*, 30, No. 1 (1958), 97-110.

2611 **Freeman, T.W.** "The Man-Made Walls of Ulster." *Geographical Magazine*, 46, No. 11 (August, 1974), 594-599.

2612 **Fulbrook, Mary.** "The State and the Transformation of Political Legitimacy in East and West Germany Since 1945." *Comparative Studies in Society and History*, 29, No. 2 (April, 1987), 211-244.

2613 **Genot, Alain, and Lowe, David.** "Belgium: A State Divided." *World Today*, 36, No. 6 (June, 1980), 218-224.

2614 **George, Pierre.** "La renaissance de la Tchecoslovaquie." *Annales de Geographie*, 56, No. 302 (Avril-Juin, 1947), 94-103.

2615 **Giannini, Amedeo.** "Balcanism e problema balcaniu." *L'Universo*, 28, No. 3 (Maggu-Guigor, 1948), 237-255.

2616 **Giannini, Amedeo.** "La Bulgaria e la questione macedone." *L'Universo*, 32, No. 4 (August, 1952), 453-467; 5 (September-October, 1952), 611-624; 6 (November-December, 1952), 767-778.

2617 **Giblin-Delvallet, Beatrice.** "Les Territoires de la Nation a L'heure de la Decentralisation et de L'Europe." *Herodote* [Paris], No. 62 (Juillet-Septembre, 1991), 22-43.

2618 **Glasgow, George.** "The Sudetenland." *Contemporary Review*, 871, No. 7 (July, 1938), 101-112.

2619 **Gorlich, Ernst Josef.** "Die Kroatische Volksgruffe im Burgenland." *Zeitschrift fur Geopolitik*, 34 Jahrg, Heft 9-10 (Sept.-Okt., 1963), 306-307.

2620 **Gorner, Alexander.** "Sudetenkrise und Marsch am Abgrund." *Zeitschrift fur Geopolitik*, 37 Jahrg, Heft 11-12 (Nov.-Dez., 1966), 352-361.

2621 **Graham, Malbone W.** "The Legal Status of the Bukovina and Bessarabia." *American Journal of International Law*, 38, No. 4 (October, 1944), 667-673.

2622 **Gresillon, M.** "Et de L'Amenagement du Territoire (le Politique et le Territoire en France)." *L'Information Geographique* [Paris], 57, No. 5 (1993), 179-183.

2623 **Gribaudi, D.** "Il Problema Della Unificazione Europea Visto da un Geografo." *Congresso Geografico Italiano*, 3 (1957), 506-516.

2624 **Gross, Mirjana.** "On the Integration of the Croatian Nation: A Case Study in Nation Building." *East European Quarterly*, 15, No. 2 (Summer, 1981), 209-225.

2625 **Hadsel, Winifred N.** "The Struggle for Yugoslavia." *Foreign Policy Reports*, 19, No. 24 (March 1, 1944), 314-327.

2626 **Hallsworth, Alan G.** "Some Cross-National Differences in the Perception of the Threat of Nuclear War: The Netherlands, France, West Germany." *Tijdschrift voor economische en sociale goegraphie*, 78, No. 4 (July-Augsut, 1987), 290-296.

2627 **Haumant, Emile.** "La nationalite serbo-croate." *Annales de Geographie*, 13, No. 127 (15 Janvier, 1914), 45-59.

2628 **Held, Colbert Colgate.** "The New Saarland." *Geographical Review*, 41, No. 4 (October. 1951), 590-605.

2629 **Held, Colbert Colgate.** "The Political Geography of the Saarland." *Abstracts of Dissertations and Theses, 1949*. Worcester, Massachusetts: Clark University, Bulletin 192, 21 (1949), 51-55.

2630 **Hechter, M., and Brustein, W.** "Regional Modes of Production ande Pattern of State Formation in Western Europe." *American Journal of Sociology*, 85, No. 1 (March, 1980), 1061-1093.

2631 **Hirschon, Renee B., and Gold, John R.** "Territoriality and the Home Environment in a Greek Urban Community." *Anthropological Quarterly*, 55, No. 1 (January, 1982), 63-73.

2632 **Hoffman, George W.** "The Survival of an Independent Austria." *Geographical Review*, 41, No. 4 (October, 1951), 606-621.

2633 **Hoffman, L.A.** "Germany: Zones of Occupation." *Department of State Bulletin*, 14, No. 354 (April 14, 1946), 599-607.

2634 **Hunter, James N.** "The Extent of the Legal Confines, the State-Ideal and the Zone of Function of France and Germany in the Saarland." *International Studies Quarterly*, 11, No. 3 (September, 1967), 237-243.

2635 **Hustich, I.** "Siebenburgen-problemet; en politiskgeografisk skiss." English Summary: The Transylvanian Question, 90-92. *Terra*, 55, arg, No. 3-4 (1943), 74-93.

2636 **Imnaischwili, N.** "Die Nationalitatfrage in der Sowjetunion." *Zeitschrift fur Geopolitik*, Jahrg 11, Heft 9 (September, 1934), 533-540.

2637 "Independent Malta: Ancient People and New State." *Round Table*, 54, No. 217 (December, 1964), 40-45.

2638 **Jakubowski, Olgierd.** "Nowa granica Polski z Czecho-Slowacja." *Wiadomosci sluzby geograficznej*, Rocznik 12, Zeszyt 4 (October-December, 1938), 409-447.

2639 **Jaszi, Oscar.** "The Choices of Hungary." *Foreign Affairs*, 24, No. 3 (April, 1946), 453-465.

2640 **Joesten, Joachim.** "German Rule in Ostland." *Foreign Affairs*, 22, No. 1 (October, 1943), 143-147.

2641 **Joffe, Josef.** "Once More: The German Question." *Survival*, 32, No. 2 (March/April, 1990), 129-140.

2642 **John, I.G.** "France, Germany and the Saar." *World Affairs*, 4, No. 3 (July, 1950), 277-293.

2643 **Johnson, James H.** "The Political Distinctiveness of Northern Ireland." *Geographical Review*, 52, No. 1 (January, 1962), 78-91.

2644 **Jones, E.** "Problems of Partition and Segregation in Northern Ireland." *Journal of Conflict Resolution*, 4, No. 1 (March, 1960), 96-105.

2645 **Kish, George.** "Fattori Generali dei Compartmenti Elettoriali in Italia." *Nord es Sud; Rivista Mensile Diretta da Francesco Compagna*, 5, No. 38 (June, 1958), 78-87.

2646 **Kolnai, Aurel.** "Austria and the Danubian Nations." *Journal of Central European Affairs*, 3, No. 2 (July, 1943), 167-182; 4 (January, 1944), 441-462.

2647 "Kommunale Gebietsreform in den Landern der Bundesrepublik Deutschland." *Berichte zur Deutscher Landeskunde*, 47 Bd., 1 Heft (Marz, 1973), 3-147.

2648 **Kraner, Johanna.** "Die Sowjetunion und ihre Volker." *Zeitschrift fur Geopolitik*, 24 Jahrg, Heft 4 (April, 1953), 251-253.

2649 **Kucinskas, Linas.** "Lithuania's Independence: The Litmus Test for Democracy in the U.S.S.R. *Lituanus* [Chicago], 37, No. 3 (1991), 5-50.

2650 **Kudryatsev, Vladimir.** "The Soviet State: Continuity and Renewal." *Social Sciences*, 19, No. 3 (1988), 24-37.

2651 **Lambert, John.** "Europe: The Nation-State Dies Hard." *Capital and Class*, 43, No. 2 (1991), 9-23.

2652 **Lendvai, Paul.** "Yugoslavia Without Yugoslavs: The Roots of Crisis." *International Affairs* [Cambridge], 67, No. 2 (April, 1991), 251-261.

2653 **Leslie, Shane.** "Partition and Constitution in Ireland." *United Empire*, 29, No. 3 (March, 1938), 99-106.

2654 **Lotscher, Lienhard; Elsasser, Hans; and Vettiger-Gallusser, Barbara.** "Struktur-und Regionalpolitik in der Schweiz." *Geographische Rundschau*, Jahrg 39, Heft 10 (October, 1987), 563-568.

2655 **Machatschek, Fritz.** "Das deutsche Sudentenland-ein Teil des Deutschen Reiches." *Petermanns geographische Mitteilungen*, 84, Jahrg, 11, Heft (November, 1938), 321-324.

2656 **Marinelli, O.** "The Regions of Mixed Populations in Northern Italy." *Geographical Review*, 7, No. 3 (March, 1919), 129-148.

2657 **Marples, David R.** "Belarus: The Illusion of Stability." *Post-Soviet Affairs* [Silver Spring], 9, No. 3 (July-September, 1993), 253-277.

2658 **Martonne, E. de.** "La carte de la Pologne." *Annales de Geographie*, 38 Annee, No. 213 (15 Mai 1929), 280-284.

2659 **Martonne, E. de.** "Le traite de Saint-Germain et la demembrement de l'Autriche." *Annales de Geographie*, 29 Annee, No. 157 (15 Janvier 1920), 1-11.

2660 **Martonne, E. de.** "L'Etat tchecoslovaque." *Annales de Geographie*, 29 Annee, No. 159 (15 Mai 1929), 161-181.

2661 **Marquis, R.V.** "London's New City within the Old." *Geographical Magazine*, 31, No. 9 (January, 1959), 448-455.

2662 **Melamid, Alexander.** "Partitioning Cyprus: A Class Exercise in Political Geography." *Journal of Geography*, 59, No. 3 (March, 1960), 118-122.

2663 **Melik, Anton.** "Slovenska Kowska." English Summary: Slovene Carinthia, 34-36. *Geografski Vestnik*, 20-21 (1948-49), 3-30.

2664 **Miller, Hunter.** "Russian Opinions on the Cession of Alaska." *American Historical Review*, 48, No. 3 (April, 1943), 521-531.

2665 **Mitchel, N.C., and Douglas, J.N.H.** "Northern Ireland Paradox." *Geographical Magazine*, 51, No. 2 (November, 1978), 113-117.

2666 **Montfort, Henri de.** "L'aspect europeen de la question de Prusse Orientale." *La Pologne et la Prusse Orientale*, (1933), 117-156.

2667 **Moodie, A.E.** "The Cast Iron Curtain." *World Affairs*, 4, No. 3 (July, 1950), 294-305.

2668 **Moodie, A.E.** "States and Boundaries in the Danubian Lands." *Slavonic and East European Review*, 26, No. 67 (April, 1948), 422-437.

2669 **Naimark, Norman M.** "Is It True What They're Saying About East Germany?" *Orbis*, 23, No. 3 (Fall, 1979), 549-577.

2670 **Nowak, Robert.** "Die Zukunft der Slowakei." *Zeitschrift fur Geopolitik*, 15, Jahrg, Heft 10 (Oktober, 1938), 786-791.

2671 **O'Neil, Daniel.** "Enclave Nation-Building: The Irish Experience." *Journal of Baltic Studies*, 17, No. 3 (Fall,1986), 179-193.

2672 **Ozouf-Marignier, Marie-Vic.** "Politique et geographie lors de la creation des departments Francais (1789-1790).' *Herodote*, No. 40 (Janvier-Mrs, 1986), 140-60.

2673 **Palsson, Gisli.** "Territoriality Among Icelandic Fishermen." *Acta Sociologica*, 25, No. 1 (January, 1982), Supplement 5-13.

2674 "The Partition of Central Asia." *Central Asian Review*, 8, No. 4 (December, 1960), 341-351.

2675 **Pluta, Leonard.** "War of the Polish State Against the Polish Nation 1980-1985." *Canadian Review of Studies in Nationalism*, 14, No. 2 (Fall, 1987), 277-295.

2676 **Radcliffe, Cyril John, and Radcliffe, Baron.** "The Problem of Cyprus; ...First Comprehensive Public Statement on Cyprus Since the Publication of the White Paper Containing His Constitutional Proposals for the Island." *United Empire*, 49, No. 1 (January-February, 1958), 15-19+.

2677 **Rogel, Carole.** "Slovenia's Independence: A Reversal of History." *Problems of Communism* [Washington, D.C.], 40, No. 4 (July-August, 1991), 31-40.

2678 **Roucek, Joseph S.** "The Legal Aspects of Sovereignty Over the Dodecanese." *American Journal of International Law*, 38, No. 4 (October, 1944), 701-706.

2679 **Roucek, Joseph S.** "The Eternal Problem of Macedonia." *International Journal*, 2, No. 4 (Autumn, 1947), 297-307.

2680 "The Russian Domination of Sinkiang." *Journal of the Royal Central Asian Society*, 26, Part 4 (October, 1939), 648-653.

2681 **Sanguin, Andre-Louis.** "Le Liechtenstein, Principaux Aspects de la Geographie Politique d'un microetat Alpin." *Revue de Geographie Alpine*, Tome 67, No. 4 (1979), 423-435.

2682 **Savey, Suzanne, and Volle, Jean-Paul.** "Politique de Decentralisation et Amenagement du Territorie en France: Vers Une Autre Division Spatial du Travail?" *Societe Langue docienne de geographie* Bulletin, 106° Annee, 3° Serie, No. 1-2 (Janvier-Juin, 1983), 81-116.

2683 **Schattkowsky, Ralph.** "Separatism in the Eastern Provinces of the German Reich at the End of the First World War." *Journal of Contemporary History* [London], 29, No. 2 (April, 1994), 305-324.

2684 **Scholler, Peter.** "Die spannung Zwischen Zentralismus, Foderalismus und Regionalismus als Grundzug der Politische-geographischen Entwicklung Deutschlands bis zur Gegenwart." *Erdkunde*, Band 41, Heft 2 (Juni, 1987), 77-106.

2685 **Schulz, Eberhard.** "Unfinished Business: The German National Question and the Future of Europe." *International Affairs*, 60, No. 3 (Summer, 1984), 391-402.

2686 **Semjonow, Juri.** "Geographie und politische Expansion Russlands im Fernen Osten. *Geographische Rundschau*, 4 Jahrg, Nr. 8 (August, 1952), 281-285.

2687 **Sereni, Angelo Piero.** "The Status of Croatia Under International Law." *American Political Science Review*, 35, No. 6 (December, 1941), 1144-1151.

2688 **Shute, J.** "Czechoslovakia's Territorial and Population Changes." *Economic Geography*, 24, No. 1 (January, 1948), 35-44.

2689 **Smith, Anthony D.** "National Identity and the Idea of European Unity." *International Affairs* [Cambridge], 68, No. 1 (January, 1992), 55-76.

2690 **Smogorzewski, K.M.** "The Russification of the Baltic States." *World Affairs*, 4, No. 4 (Winter, 1950), 468-481.

2691 "Spitsbergen: Quandary for a Small State." *American Perspective*, 1, No. 2 (May, 1947), 106-111.

2692 "Statement of Norway of Its Paramount Interest in the Island of Jan Mayen in the Arctic Ocean." *U.S. Department of State*, paper relating to the foreign relations of the United States 1926, 2 (1941). Washington, D.C.: U.S. Department of State, (1941), 824-827.

2693 "Sudeten German Claims in Czechoslovakia." *Bulletin of International News*, 15, No. 15 (July 30, 1938), 639-641.

2694 **Taylor, Paul B.** "Germany's Expansion in Eastern Europe." *Foreign Policy Reports*, 15, No. 5 (May 15, 1939), 50-60.

2695 **Taylor, Paul B.** "Partition of Czechoslovakia: The Sudeten Annexation." *Foreign Policy Reports*, 14, No. 17 (November 15, 1938), 198-208.

2696 **Taylor, Paul J.** "The Nation-State in the European Communities: Superficial Realities and Underlying Uncertainties." *International Journal*, 39, No. 3 (Summer, 1984), 577-598.

2697 **Taylor, Paul, and Johnston, R.J.** "The Geography of the British State." In *The Human Geography of Contemporary Britain*, J.R. Short and A.M. Kirby, eds. London: Macmillan, 1984, 23-29.

2698 **Tomasic, Dinko.** "Croatia in European Politics." *Journal of Central European Affairs*, 2, No. 1 (April, 1942), 64-86.

2699 **Translvanus (pseud.)** "Ordeal in Transylvania." *Journal of Central European Affairs*, 1, No. 1 (April, 1941), 18-27.

2700 **Urwin, D.** "Territorial Structures and Political Developments in the United Kingdom." In *The Politics of Territorial Identity*. S. Rokkan and D. Urwin, eds. London: Sage Publications, 1982, 19-73.

2701 **Vaumas, Etienne De.** "La repartition de la population a Chypre et le nouvel Etat chypriote." *Revue de Geographie Alpine*, Tome 47, Fascicule 4 (October, 1959), 457-529.

2702 **Veremis, Thanos.** "From the National State to the Stateless Nation." *European History Quarterly*, 19, No. 2 (April 1989), 135-148.

2703 **Wanklyn, H.G.** "The Middle People: Resettlement in Czechslovakia." *Geographical Journal*, 97, No. 1 (January, 1948), 18-35.

2704 **Weinelt, Herbert.** "Sudetenschlesisches Volkstum um die alte schlesischmahrische Grenze." *Auslardsdeutsche Volksforschung*, 2, Band heft 4 (1938), 449-464.

2705 **Werner, Alfred.** "Is Austria 'Lebensfahig'?" *Journal of Central European Affairs*, 5, No. 2 (July, 1945), 111-118.

2706 **White, A. Silva.** "British Unity." *Scottish Geographical Magazine*, 12, No. 8 (August, 1896), 399-414.

2707 **Whittlesey, Derwent S.** "Trans-Pyrenean Spain: The Val d'Aran." *Scottish Geographical Magazine*, 49, No. 4 (July, 1933), 217-228; idem. "Andorra's Autonomy," *Journal of Modern History*, 6 (1934), 147-155.

2708 **Wilson, Thomas.** "The Ulster Crisis, Reformed Government with a New Border? *Round Table*, 62, No. 245 (January, 1972) 37-54.

2709 **Wiskemann, Elizabeth.** "The 'Drang nach Osten' Continues." *Foreign Affairs*, 17, No. 4 (July, 1939), 764-773.

2710 **Wiskemann, Elizabeth.** "The Saar Moves Towards Germany." *Foreign Affairs*, 34, No. 2 (January, 1956), 287-296.

2711 **Witt, Werner.** "Gebietsreform in Schleswig-Holstein." *Berichte zur deutschen Landeskunde*, 45, Band 1, Heft (Januar 1971), 97-105.

2712 **Xiang, Lanxin.** "Is Germany in the West or in Central Europe? *Orbis* [Philadelphia], 36, No. 3 (Summer, 1992), 411-422.

2713 **Zuber, Maurice P.** "The Nazis in Alsace and Lorraine." *Foreign Affairs*, 21, No. 1 (October, 1942), 168-173.

DEMOGRAPHIC ASPECTS OF A TERRITORY

GENERAL AND THEORY

Books and Journals

2714 **Beaujeu-Garnier, Jacqueline.** *Geography of Population.* London: Longmans, 1966.

2715 **Brass, Paul,** ed. *Ethnic Groups and the State.* London: Croom Helm, 1984.

2716 **Clark, Gordon L.** *Interregional Migration, Social Justice, and National Policy.* Totowa, New Jersey: Rowman and Allanheld, 1983.

2717 **Deutsch, Karl W.** *Politics and Government. How People Decide Their Fate?* New York: John Wiley & Sons, 1975.

2718 **Downs, R.M.** "Geographic Space Perception: Past Approaches and Future Prospects." *Progress in Geography*, 2, No. 2 (1970), 65-108.

2719 **Grasland, Claude.** "Potential de Population, Interaction Spatiale et Frontieres: Des Deux Allemagnes a Punification." *L'Espace Geographique* [Paris], 19-20, No. 3 (1990-1991), 243-254.

2720 **Karmeshu; Jain, V.P.; and Mahajan, A.K.** "A Dynamic Model of Domestic Political Conflict Process." *Journal of Conflict Resolution* [Newbury Park], 34, No. 2 (June, 1990), 252-269.

2721 **Kliot, Nurit,** and **Waterman, Stanley,** eds. *Pluralism and Political Geography: People, Territory, and State.* London: Croom Helm, 1983.

2722 **MacDonald, Barrie.** "Secession in Defense of Identity: The Making of Tavalu." *Pacific Viewpoint*, 16, No. 1 (March, 1975), 26-44.

2723 **Mackinder, H.J.** "Manpower as a Measure of National and Imperial Strength." *National and English Review*, 45 (1905), 136-43.

2724 **Murphy, Alexander B.** "Partitioning as a Response to Cultural Conflict." *Geographical Perspectives*, 13, No. 55 (Spring, 1985), 53-59.

2725 **Peeters, Y.J.D.** "A Documentation of Ethnic Conflict and Nation Building." *Discussion Papers in Geolinguistics-North Staffordshire Polytechnic*, 11 (1987), 11-39.

2726 **Shafer, Boyd C.** "If Only We Knew More About Nationalism." *Canadian Review of Studies in Nationalism*. 7, No. 2 (Fall/Autunmn, 1980), 197-218.

2727 **Simmons, A., et al.** *Social Change and Internal Migration*. Ottawa: IDRC, 1977.

2728 **Smith, Don D.** "Modal Attitude Clusters: A Supplement for the Study of National Character." *Social Forces*, 44, No. 4 (June, 1966), 526-533.

POLITICAL GEOGRAPHY OF REGION

AFRICA

Books and Journals

2729 **Bank, Leslie.** "Between Traders and Trabialistss: Implosion and the Politics of disjuncture in a South African Homeland." *African Affairs* [Oxford], 93, No. 370 (January, 1994), 75-98.

2730 **Berker, Jonathan.** "Political Space and the Quality of Participation in Rural Africa: A Case from Senegal." *Canadian Journal of African Studies*, 21, No. 1 (1987), 1-16.

2731 **Christopher, A.J.** "Partition and Population in South Africa." *Geographical Review*, 72, No. 2 (April, 1982), 127-138.

2732 **Grundy, Kenneth W.** *South Africa: Domestic Crisis and Global Challenge*. Boulder: Westeview Press, 1991.

2733 **Lonsdale, John.** "States and Social Processes in Africa." *African Studies Review*, 24, Nos. 2-3 (June-September, 1981), 139-226.

2734 **Riddell, J. Berry.** "Beyond the Description of Spatial Patterns: The Process of Proletarianization as a Factor in Population Migration in West Africa." *Progress in Human Geography*, 5, No. 3 (September, 1981), 370-392.

2735 **Wakefield, A.J.** "Tanganyika Territory and Native Uplift." *Journal of the Royal African Society*, 39, No. 156 (July, 1940), 231-243.

2736 **Weisfelder, Richard F.** "The Decline of Human Rights in Lesotho: An Evaluation of Domestic and External Determinants." *Issue: A Quarterly Journal of Opinion*, 6 (1976), 22-33.

AMERICAS

Books and Journals

2737 **Allen- Lafayette, Zedreh.** *The Geography of Eugenics Legislation in the United states, 1900-1940*. Syracuse, NY: Master's thesis, Syracuse University, 1994.

2738 **Bamforth, Douglas B.** "Indigenous People, Indigenous Violence: Precontact Warfare on the North American Great Plains." *Man* [London], 29, No. 1 (March, 1994), 95-115.

2739 **Bronson, Leisa,** comp. *Reading List on the Four Freedoms*. Washington, D.C.: The Women's Division, Democratic National Committee, 1943.

2740 **Comeaux, Malcolm Louis.** *Settlement and Folk Occupations of the Atchafalaya Basin*. Baton Rouge: Louisiana State University and Agricultural and Mechanical College, Ph.D., 1969.

2741 **Condrey, Stephen E.** "Organizational and Personnel Impacts on Local Government Consolidation: Athens-Clarke County, Georgia." *Journal of Urban Affairs*, 16, No. 4 (1994), 371-383.

2742 **Dale, Edmund H.** "The Demographic Problem of the British West Indies." *Scottish Geographical Magazine*, 79, No. 1 (1963), 23-31.

2743 "Demarcacion politica; nueva organizacion politica; administrativa del departamento de Loreto." *Boletin de la Sociedad geografica de Lima*, Tomo 60 (Trimestres 3-4, 1943), 259-267.

2744 **Eyre, Lawrence Alan.** *Geographic Aspects of Population Dynamics in Jamaica*. Baltimore: University of Maryland, Ph.D., 1969.

2745 **Hudson, John C.** "North American Origins of Middlewestern Frontier Populations." *Annals of the Association of American Geographers*, 78, No. 3 (September, 1988), 395-413.

2746 **Johnson, Hildegard Binder.** "French Canada and the Ohio Country: A Study in Early Spatial Relationship." *Canadian Geographer*, No. 12 (1958), 1-10.

2747 **Kilgannon, James.** "Ethnic Residential Segregation: The Case of Asian Indians in Chicago." Manhattan: Kansas State University, M.A., 1989.

2748 **Kory, William B.** "Political Significance of Population Homogeneity: A Pittsburgh Example." *Professional Geographer*, 24, No. 2 (May, 1972), 118-122.

2749 **Laatsch, William Garfield.** *Yukon Mining Settlement: An Examination of Three Communities*. Alberta, Edminton Canada: University of Alberta, Ph.D., 1972.

2750 **Levesque, Rene.** *La passion du Quebec*. Montreal: Editions Quebec/Amerique, 1978.

2751 **Lowenthal, David.** "Population Contrasts in the Guianas." *Geographical Review*, 50, No. 1 (January, 1960), 41-58.

2752 **Lumsden, I.**, ed. *Close the 49th Parallel, etc.: The Americanization of Canada.* Toronto: University of Toronto Press, 1970.

2753 **Morehouse, Thomas A.** "Sovereignty, Tribal Government, and the Alaska Native Claims Settlement Act Amendments of 1987." *Polar Record*, 25, No. 154 (July 1989), 197-206.

2754 **Moss, R.** *The Stability of the Caribbean.* London: Institute for the Study of Conflict, 1973.

2755 **Osiel, Mark.** "The Making of Human Rights Policy in Argentina: The Impact of Ideas and Interests on a Legal Conflict." *Journal of Latin American Studies*, 18, No. 1 (May, 1986), 135-178.

2756 **Overton, James.** "Living Patriotism: Songs, Politics and Resources in Newfoundland." *Canadian Review of Studies in Nationalism*, 12, No. 2 (Fall, 1985), 239-259.

2757 **Rousseau, Mark O.**, and **Zariski, Raphael.** *Regionalism and Regional Devolution in Comparative Perspective.* New York: Praeger, 1987.

2758 **Saunders, John**, ed. *Population Growth in Latin America and U.S. National Security.* Boston: Allen & Unwin, 1986.

2759 **Westhues, Kenneth.** "Foreign Gods and Nation-States in the Americas." *Canadian Review of Studies in Nationalism*, 7, No. 2 (Fall, 1980), 351-371.

2760 **Wiarda, Howard J.**, ed. *Politics and Social Change in Latin America: Still a Distinct Tradition?* 3rd rev. and updated ed. Boulder: Westview Press, 1992.

2761 **Wohlenberg, Ernest Harold.** *The Geography of Poverty in the United States: A Spatial Study of the Nation's Poor.* Seattle: University of Washington, Ph.D., 1970.

ASIA

Books and Journals

2762 **Albaum, Melvin.** *An Analysis of Human Fertility Behavior in Spatial Sub-Systems of Turkey.* Columbus: Ohio State University, Ph.D., 1969.

2763 **Amirahmadi, Hooshang.** "The State and Territorial Social Justice in Postrevolutionary Iran." *International Journal of Urban and Regional Research*, 13, No. 1 (March, 1989), 92-120.

2764 "Assimilate or Accommodate? The Case of the Hoa Hao and Vietnam." *Professional Geographer*, 22, No. 6 (November, 1970), 317-320.

2765 **Chickekian, Garo.** "The Armenians Since the Treaty of San Stefano: A Politico-Geographic Study of Population." *Armenian Review*, 22, No. 2-82 (Spring, 1968), 42-56.

2766 **Choueiri, Youssef M.**, ed. *State and Society in Syria and Lebanon.* Exeter: University of Exeter Press, 1993.

2767 **Guilmoto, C.** "Demography and Politics: The Tamils Between Sri Lanka and India." *Population*, 42, No. 2 (1987), 283-303.

2768 **Hardgrave, Robert L., Jr.** "Varieties of Political Behavior Among Nadars of Tamilnad." *Asian Survey*, 6, No. 11 (November, 1966), 614-621.

2769 **Katzenstein, Mary Fainsod.** "Towards Equality? Cause and Consequences of the Political Prominence of Women in India." *Asian Survey*, 18, No. 5 (May, 1978), 473-486.

2770 **Keyes, Charles F.** *Thailand: Buddhist Kingdom as Modern Nation State.* Boulder, Colorado: Westview Press, 1987.

2771 **Kumar, Dharma.** "The Affirmative Action Debate in India." *Asian Survey* [Berkeley], 32, No. 3 (March, 1992), 290-302.

2772 **Lau, Siu-Kai.** "Public Attitudes Toward Political Leadership in Hong Kong." *Asian Survey* [Berkeley], 34, No. 3 (March, 1994), 243-257.

2773 **Noble, Lela Garner.** "Muslim Separatism in the Philippines, 1972-1981: The Making of a Stalemate." *Asian Survey*, 21, No. 11 (November, 1981), 1097-1114.

2774 **Peterson, J.E.** "The Emergence of Nation-States in the Arabian Peninsula." *GeoJournal*, 13, No. 3 (October, 1986), 11-39.

2775 **Pye, Lucian W.** "Reassessing the Cultural Revolution." *China Quarterly*, 108 (Demember, 1986), 597-612.

2776 **Rathjens, Carl.** "Strukturen von Staatsform und Machtausubung in Afghanistan: Zur Politischen Geographie Eines Islamischen Staates." *Geographische Zeitschrift* [Stuttgart], 78, Heft 3 (1990), 186-197.

2777 **Richardson, B.M.** *The Political Culture of Japan.* Berkeley: University of California Press, 1974.

2778 **Roxby, Percy M.** "The Distribution of Population in China: Economic and Political Significance." *Geographical Review*, 15, No. 1 (January, 1925), 1-24.

2779 **Shrestha, Nanda R., and Conway, D.** "Issues in Population Pressure, Land Resettlement and Development: The Case of Nepal." *Studies in Comparative International Development*, 20, No. 1 (Spring, 1985), 55-82.

2780 **Wang, I-Shou.** *Chinese Migration and Population Change in Manchuria, 1900-1940.* Minneapolis: University of Minnesota, Ph.D., 1971.

2781 **Taueber, Irene B.** "Japan's Population: Miracle, Model or Case Study?" *Foreign Affairs*, 40, No. 4 (July, 1962), 595-604.

EUROPE

Books and Journals

2782 **Bendix, John.** "Women and Politics in Germany and Switzerland." *European Journal of Political Research*, 25, No. 4 (June, 1994), 413-438.

2783 **Blouett, B.L.** "The Impact of Armed Conflict on the Rural Settlement Pattern of Malta (AD 1400-1800)." *Transactions of the Institute of British Geographers*, 3, No. 3 (July, 1978), 367-80.

2784 **Budge, I., and Urwin, D.W.** *Scottish Political Behavior: A Case Study in British Homogeneity.* New York: Barnes and Noble, 1966.

2785 **Confino, Michael.** "Russian Customary Law and the Study of Peasant Mentalities." *Russian Review*, 44, No. 1 (January, 1985), 35-43.

2786 **Elsasser, Hans, and Leibundgut, Hans.** "Von der Berggebietpolitik zur Regionalpolitik: Entwicklung und Ansatze der Zeitgemassen Neuorientierung in der Schweiz." *Zietschrift fur Wirtschaftsgeographie*, 31 Jahr, Heft 2 (1987), 65-73.

2787 **Gilbert, Anne.** "L'ideologiespatiale: Conceptualisation, mise en forme et portee pour la geographie." *L'Espace Geographique*, Tome 15, No. 1 (Janvier-Mars, 1986), 57-66.

2788 **Guthier, Steven L.** "The Belorussians: National Identification and Assimilation, 1897-1970." *Soviet Studies*, 29, No. 1 (January, 1977), 37-61.

2789 **Martson, Sallie A.** "Neighborhood and Politics: Irish Ethnicity in Nineteenth Century, Massachusetts." *Annals of the Association of American Geographers*, 78, No. 3 (September, 1988), 414-432.

2790 **Nissel, H.** "Differentiation of Social Space and the Persistence of Electoral Behaviour in Margurg." *Marburger Geographische Schriften*, 100 (1986), 168-185.

2791 **Organski, A.F.K.** "Population and Politics in Europe: Demographic Factors Help Shape the Relative Power of the Communist and Non-communist Blocs." *Science*, 133, No. 3467 (1961), 1803-1807.

2792 **Parrott, A.L.** "The System that Lost Its Way: Social Security Reform in the United Kingdom." *International Labour Reveiw*, 124, No. 5 (1985), 545-558.

2793 **Reis, G., ed.** *Political Action and Soviet Identity.* London: Macmillan, 1985.

2794 **Roof, Michael K., and Leedy, Frederick A.** "Population Redistribution in the Soviet Union." *Geographical Review*, 49, No. 2 (April, 1959), 208-221.

2795 **Seton-Watson, R.W.** "German Versus Slav in the New Europe." *United Empire*, 35, No. 2 (March-April, 1944), 34-39.

2796 **Trehuh, Aaron.** "Social and Economic Rights in the Soviet Union." *Survey*, 29, No. 4 (August, 1987), 6-42.

2797 **Vambery, Rustem.** "The Tragedy of the Magyars: Revisionism and Nazism." *Foreign Affairs*, 20, No. 3 (April, 1942), 477-488.

2798 **Ward, Michael D.** *Unmanageable Revolutionaries: Women and Irish Nationalism.* London: Pluto Press, 1983.

2799 **Whetten, Lawrence L.** "Scope, Nature and Change in Inner-German Relations." *International Affairs*, 57, NO. 1 (Winter, 1980-81), 60-78.

ORGANIZATION OF A TERRITORY

GENERAL AND THEORY

Books

2800 **Advisory Commission Inter-Governmental Relations.** *Multi-State Regionalism.* Washington, D.C.: Department of State, 1978.

2801 **Aunger, E.** *In Search of Political Stability: A Comparative Study of New Brunswick and Northern Ireland.* Montreal: McGill/Queen's University Press, 1981.

2802 **Barth, Frederick.** *Political Leadership Among the Swat Pathans.* (Monograph on Social Anthropology, No. 19) London: University of London, 1959.

2803 **Bayne, E.A.** *Four Ways of Politics: State and Nation in Italy, Somalia, Israel, Iran.* New York: American Universities Field Staff, 1965.

2804 **Bracher, K.D.; Sauer, W.; and Schulz, G.** *Die nationalsozialistische Machtergreifung.* 2nd ed. Koln, Opladen: Westdeutscher Verlag, 1962.

2805 **Buchert, B.J.** *The Tupamaros: Anomalies of Guerrilla War.* Lawrence: University of Kansas, Ph.D., 1979.

2806 **Campbell, A.** *Guerrilla: A Historical Analysis.* Garden City, New York: Doubleday, 1980.

2807 **Carnell, Francis,** comp. *The Politics of the New States.* London: Oxford University Press, 1961.

2808 **Clark, D.** *Colne Valley: Radicalism to Socialism.* London: Longman, 1981.

2809 **Clark, Gordon L.,** and **Dear, M.J.** *State Apparatus: Structures and Language of Legitimacy.* London: Allen & Unwin, 1984.

2810 **Clutterbuck, Richard.** *Guerrilla and Terrorists.* London: Faber and Faber, 1977.

2811 **Duchacek, Ivo D.** *The Territorial Dimensions of Politics Within, Among, and Across Nations.* Boulder, Colorado: Westview Press, 1986.

2812 **Dworkin, R.** *Taking Rights Seriously.* Cambridge, Massachusetts: Harvard University Press, 1978.

2813 **Fox, Annette Baker.** *The Power of Small States.* Chicago, Illinois: University of Chicago Press, 1959.

2814 **Giddens, A.** *The Nation-State and Violence.* Cambridge: Polity Press, 1985.

2815 **Guevara, C.** *Guerrilla Warfare.* London: Penguin, 1969.

2816 **Guillen, A.** *Estratigia de la Guerrilla Urbana.* Translated by D.Hodges as *Philosophy of the Urban Guerrilla.* New York: William Morrow, 1973.

2817 **James, Alan.** "The Equality of Stats: Contemporary Manifestations of an Ancient Doctrine." *Review of International Studies* [Cambridge], 18, No. 4 (October, 1992), 377-391.

2818 **James, Alan.** *Sovereignty Statehood: The Basis of International Society.* London: Allen & Unwin, 1986.

2819 **Kasperson, Roger E.** *The Dodecanese: Diversity and Unity in Island Politics.* Chicago, Illinois: University of Chicago Press, 1966.

2820 **Kazancigil, Ali.** *The State in Global Perspective.* Aldershot: Gower Publishing, 1986.

2821 **Kitson, Brigadier F.** *Low Intensity Operations-Subversions, Insurgency and Peacekeeping.* London: Faber and Faber, 1971.

2822 **Lenin, V.I.** *The Right of Nations to Self Determination.* Moscow: Progress, 1976.

2823 **Lindberg, L.N.,** et al., eds. *Stress and Contradiction in Modern Capitalism: Public Policy and the Theory of the State.* Toronto: Lexington Books, 1975.

2824 **Luttwak, E.** *Coup d'Etat.* New York: Penguin, 1969.

2825 **Madland, Lee Griswold.** *Domains Without Dominion: An Investigation of Areas Lacking Effective Territorial Control by Central Governments.* Los Angeles: University of California, Ph.D., 1970.

2826 **Moss, R.** *Urban Guerrillas: The New Face of Political Violence.* London: Temple-Smith, 1972.

2827 **Mozick, R.** *Anarchy, State, and Utopia.* New York: Basic Books, 1974.

2828 **Nahas, Miridi.** *Hegemonic Constraints and State Autonomy: A Comparative Analysis of Development in 19th Century Egypt, Spain, and Italy (Political Economy International Relations).* Los Angeles: University of California, Ph.D., 1985.

2829 **Pannikar, K.M.** *The States and the Constitutional Settlement.* 9 mimeographed 1. (Indian Paper No. 2) New York: International Secretariat, Institute of Pacific Relations, 1942.

2830 **Phlipponneau, Michel.** *La Gauche et Les Regions.* Paris: Calmann-Levy, 1967.

2831 **Sanford, Terry.** *Storm Over the States.* New York: McGraw-Hill, 1967.

2832 **Sen, A.** *Collective Choice and Social Welfare.* San Francisco: Holden Day, 1970.

2833 **Skocpol, T.** *States and Revolutions: A Comparative Analysis of France, China and Russia.* London: Columbia University Press, 1979.

2834 **Sobel, Lester A.,** ed. *Political Terrorism,* Vol. 2. Washington, D.C.: Fact on File, 1978.

2835 **Stuckmann, Elmar.** *Revolution und Evolution.* Braunschweig: Geogre Westermann Verlag. Zeit & Gesellschaft. Heft 2 (1979).

2836 **Taylor, Ralph B.** *Human Territorial Functioning: An Empirical, Evolutionary Perspective on Individual and Small Group Territorial Cognitions, Behaviors, and Consequences.* Cambridge: Cambridge University Press, 1988.

2837 **Thomas, Caroline**. *New States, Sovereignty and Intervention*. Aldershot: Gower Publishing, 1985.

2838 **Thomas, C.Y.** *The Rise of the Authoritarian State in Peripheral Societies*. New York: Monthly Review Press, 1984.

2839 **Tonsor, Stephen J.** *National Socialism; Conservative Reaction or Nihilist Revolt?* New York: Rinehart, 1959.

2840 **Wilkinson, H.R.** *Maps and Politics*. Liverpool: University of Liverpool Press, 1951.

Journals

2841 **Blomley, Nicholas K.** "Law and the Local State: Enforcement in Action." *Transactions of the Institute of British Geographers*, New Series, 13, No. 2 (1988), 199-210.

2842 **Bradshaw, P.G.** "Conflict as a Spatial Process: The Case of Guerilla Warfare." *Wessex Geographer*, 11 (1970), 17-21.

2843 **Carvalho, Juvenal de.** "Ligeiras Notas Sobre o Acordo de Limites Com o Estado de Sao Paulo." *Anuaro Geografico do Estado do Rio de Janeiro*, 6 (1953), 21-24.

2844 **Clark, Gordon L.** "A Theory of Local Autonomy." *Annals of the Associations of American Geographers*, 74, No. 2 (June, 1984), 195-208.

2845 **Claval, Paul.** "Ideologie Territoriale et Ethnogenese." *International Political Science Review*, 6, No. 2 (April, 1985), 161-170.

2846 **Cordey, Philippe.** "L'echelle geographique comme variable explicative du sens de l'organisation du territoire." *Le Globe*, Tome 124 (1984), 37-51.

2847 **Corson, Mark W., and Minghi, Julian V.** "Reunification of Partioned Nation-State: Theory versus Reality in Vietnam and Germany." *Journal of Geography*, 93, No. 3 (May-June, 1994), 125-131.

2848 **Dahlitz, Julie.** "Coexistence, Reciprocity and the Principle of Marginal Restraint." *Australian Outlook*, 35, No. 1 (April, 1981), 78-87.

2849 **David, Charles M.** "Functional Areas in Political Readjustment." *Economic Geography*, 14, No. 1 (January, 1938), 85-88.

2850 **Dear, M.J., and Clark, G.** "Dimensions of Local State Autonomy." *Environment and Planning*, A13, No. 4 (December, 1981), 1277-1294.

2851 **Faucher, Philippe.** "Crossance et Repression, la Double Logique de l'Etat Dependent: le cas du Bresil." *Canadian Journal of Political Science*, 12, No. 4 (December, 1979), 747-774.

2852 **Fenwick, C.G.** "Freedom of Communication Across National Boundaries." *American Society of International Law*, 44, No. 2 (April, 1950), 363-370.

2853 **Fesler, James W.** "The Reconciliation of Function and Area." *Area and Administration*. Tuscalosa: University of Alabama Press, 1949.

2854 **Frankel, Boris.** "On the State of the State: Marxist Theories of the State After Lenin." *Theory and Society*, 7, Nos. 1-2 (January-March, 1979), 199-242.

2855 **Gamble, A.** "The Free Economy and the Strong State." *Socialist Register*, 16 (1979), 1-25.

2856 **Hanrieder, W.F.** "Dissolving International Politics: Reflections on the Nation-State." *American Political Science Review*, 72, No. 4 (December, 1978), 1276-1287.

2857 **Herzik, Eric B.** "The Legal-Formal Structuring of State Politics: A Cultural Explanation." *Western Political Quarterly*, 38, No. 3 (September, 1985), 413-423.

2858 **Holdegel, Helmut.** "Grenzprobleme de Sudwest-Staates." *Zeitschrift fur Geopolitik*, 30, No. 12 (December, 1959), 9-19.

2859 **Kautsky, John H.** "The Question of Peasant Revolts in Traditional Empires." *Studies in Comparative International Development*, 16, Nos. 3-4, (Fall and Winter, 1981), 3-34.

2860 **Knight, David B.** "Territorial Organization, Self-Determination and the Search for Security." *Operational Geographer*, 5 (1984), 19-22.

2861 **Korinman, Michael.** "L'Allemagne est-elle sure." *Herodote*, No. 40 (Janvier-Mars, 1986), 89-98.

2862 **Mann, Michael.** "The Autonomous Power of the State." *European Journal of Sociology*, 25 (1984), 185-213.

2863 **Mess, Henry A.** "Geography in Relation to National and Local Sentiment." *Sociological Review*, 30, No. 2 (April, 1938), 186-200.

2864 **Morgenthau, H.J.** "The Problem of Sovereignty Considered." *Columbia Law Review*, 48, No. 3 (April, 1948), 341-365.

2865 **Numelin, Ragnar.** "Primitive 'States' and 'Governments'." *Geografisk tidsskrift*, 45, bind (1942), 95-122.

2866 O'Loughlin, John and Van der Wusten, Herman. "Political Geography of Pan-regions." *Geographical Review,* 80, No. 1 (January, 1990), 1-20.

2867 Paleczny, Tadevsz. "Polski ideologie narodowc a panstwo." (Title in English: "Polish National Ideologies and the State.") *Przeglad Polonijny,* Rok 9, Z. 27 (1983), 59-79.

2868 Pearcy, G. Etzel. "Forty Newly Independent States; Some Politico-Geographic Observations." *Department of State Bulletin,* 45, No. 1163 (October 9, 1961), 604-611.

2869 Pearcy, G. Etzel. "Newly Independent States." *Focus,* 15, No. 4 (December, 1964), 1-6.

2870 Perry, Peter. "Towards a Political Geography of Corruption." *New Zealand Geographer,* 41, No. 1 (April, 1985), 2-7.

2871 Philbrick, Allen K. "Principles of Areal Functional Organization in Regional Human Geography." *Economic Geography,* 33, No. 4 (October, 1957), 299-336.

2872 Prescott, J.R.V. "Geography and Secessionist Movements." *Proceedings of the Geographical Society of Rhodesia,* 3 (1970), 50-56.

2873 Rawls, J. "The Basic Liberties and Their Priorities." In *The Tanner Lectures.* S. McMurrin, ed. Cambridge: Cambridge University Press, 1982, 1-87.

2874 Reynolds, David R., and Shelley, Fred M. Justice and Local Democracy." *Political Geography Quarterly,* 4, No. 4 (October, 1985), 267-288.

2875 Richmond, Anthony H. "Ethnic Nationalism Social Science Paradigms." *International Social Science Journal,* 111 (February, 1987), 3-18.

2876 Sanguin, Andre-Louis. "Le Paysage politique: quelques considerations sur un concept resurgent." (Title in English: "The Political Landscape: Some Reflections About a Resurgent Concept.") *L'Espace geographie,* Tome 13, No. 1 (Janvier/Mars, 1984), 23-32.

2877 Sugimura, Oaki. "Current Problems for the Viewpoint of Political Geography - Cases of Current Problems of Nation-States." *Political Geography,* Vol. III. Tokyo: Kokon-Shoin, 1968, 71-89.

2878 Symmons-Symonolewicz, Konstantin. "The Concept of Nationhood: Towards a Theoretical Clarification." *Canadian Review of Studies in Nationalism,* 12, No. 1 (Spring, 1985), 215-222.

2879 Teune, Henry. "Information, Control, and the Governability of Territorial Political Units." *Studies in Comparative International Development,* 14, No. 1 (Spring, 1979), 77-89.

2880 "Three Steps in Democracy." *Eastern Economist,* 47, No. 25 (December 30, 1966), 1162-1228.

2881 Von Vorys, Karl, ed. "New Nations: The Problem of Political Development." *Annals of the Academy of Political and Social Services,* 358 (March, 1965), 1-179.

2882 Williams, C.H. "The Question of National Congruence." In *A World in Crisis?* R.J. Johnston and P.J. Taylor, eds. Oxford: Basil Blackwell, 1986, 196-230.

POLITICAL GEOGRAPHY OF REGIONS

AFRICA

Books and Journals

2883 Abernathy, David B. "Nigeria Creates a New Region." *African Report,* 9, No. 3 (March, 1964), 8-10.

2884 Adejuyigbe, Omolade. "Rationale and Effect of State Creation in Nigeria with Reference to the 19 States." In *Readings in Federalism.* A.B. Akinyemi, et al, eds. Ibadan: University Press, 1979, 190-212.

2885 "Africa: Leaders and Lessons." *International Journal,* 25, No. 3 (Summer, 1970), 445-637).

2886 Aliboni, Roberto. "The Ethiopian Revolution: Stabilization." *Armed Forces and Society,* 7, No. 3 (Spring, 1981), 423-444.

2887 Alperin, Robert J. "The Distribution of Power and the (June, 1979), Zimbabwe Rhodesia Constitution." *Journal of Southern African Affairs,* 5, No. 1 (January, 1980), 41-54.

2888 "Angola: Fragmented Resistance and the Civil War." *Africa Institute Bulletin,* 14, Nos. 1 and 2 (1976), 3-12.

2889 Apter, David E. "The Role of Traditionalism in the Political Modernization of Ghana and Uganda." *World Politics,* 13, No. 1 (October, 1960), 45-68.

2890 Ayoade, J.A.A. "Federalism and Wage Politics in Nigeria." *Journal of Commonwealth and Politics,* 31, No. 3 (November, 1975), 282-289.

2891 Baker, Randall. "Reorientation in Rwanda." *African Affairs,* 69, No. 275 (April, 1970), 141-154.

2892 **Bourdillon, Sir Bernard.** "The Nigerian Constitution." *African Affairs*, 45, No. 179 (April, 1946), 87-96.

2893 **Brett, E. A.** "Rebuilding Organisation Capacity in Uganda Under the National Resistance Movement." *The Journal of Modern African Studies* [Cambridge], 32, No. 1 (March, 1994), 53-80.

2894 **Brown, David J.L.** "Borderline Politics in Ghana: The National Liberation Movement of Western Togoland." *Journal of Modern African Studies*, 18, No. 4 (December, 1980), 575-609.

2895 **Callaghy, Thomas M.** "State-Subject Communication Zaire: Domination and the Concept of Domain Consensus." *Journal of Modern African Studies*, 18, No. 3 (September, 1980), 469-492.

2896 **Clapham, Christopher.** *Transformation and Continuity in Revolutionary Ethiopia.* Cambridge: Cambridge University Press, 1988.

2897 "Constitutional Developments in the Transkei." *International Bulletin*, 2, No. 2 (February, 1964), 54-64.

2898 **Crist, Raymond E.** "Background of Conflict in Egypt." *American Journal of Economics and Sociology*, 11, No. 2 (January, 1952), 113-117.

2899 **Crowder, Michael.** "Whose Dream Was It Anyway? Twenty-Five Years of African Independence." *African Affairs*, 86, No. 342 (January, 1987), 7-24.

2900 **de Blij, Harm J.** *Africa South.* Evanston, Illinois: Northwestern University Press, 1962.

2901 **Decalo, Samuel.** "Chad: The Roots of Centre-Periphery Strife." *African Affairs*, 79, No. 317 (October, 1980), 490-509.

2902 **Deeb, Mary-Jane.** "Inter-Maghribi Relations Since 1969: A Study of the Modalities of Unions and Mergers." *Middle East Journal*, 43, No. 1 (Winter, 1989).

2903 **Doornbos, Martin.** "Some Structural Aspects of Regional Government in Uganda and Ghana." *Journal of Administration Overseas*, 12, No. 2 (April, 1973), 88-99.

2904 **Dudley, B.J.** *Instability and Political Order: Politics and Crisis in Nigeria.* Ibadan: University Press, 1973.

2905 **Gauze, Rene.** *The Politics of Congo-Brazzaville.* Standford: Standford University, Hoover Institution Press, Hoover Institution Publication No. 129, 1973.

2906 **Gillespie, Joan.** *Algeria: Rebellion and Revolution.* New York: Praeger, 1960.

2907 "Gold Coast Independence; Prospects and Problems of the New State of Ghana." *World Today*, 13, No. 2 (February, 1957), 61-73.

2908 **Good, Kenneth.** "Interpreting the Exceptionality of Botswana." *The Journal of Modern African Studies* [Cambridge], 30, No. 1 (March, 1992), 69-95.

2909 **Hadjeres, Sadek.** "Algerie: Quel Etat, Quelle Nation?" *Herodote*, No. 72/73 (Janvier-Juin, 1994), 201-237.

2910 **Hancock, I.R.** "The Uganda Crisis, 1966." *Australian Outlook*, 20, No. 3 (December, 1966), 263-277.

2911 **Hanlon, Joseph.** *Beggar your Neighbours: Apartheid Power in Southern Africa.* London: Catholic Institute of International Relations, 1986.

2912 **Harbeson, John W.** *The Ethiopian Transormation: The Quest for the Post-Imperial State.* Boulder, Colorado: Westview Press, 1988.

2913 **Hodges, Tony.** "Botswana: External Threats and Internal Pressures." *Africa Report*, 22, No. 6 (November-December, 1977), 39-43.

2914 **Ikporukpo, C.O.** "Politics and Regional Policies: The Issue of State Creation in Nigeria." *Political Geography Quarterly*, 5, No. 2 (April, 1986), 127-140.

2915 **Jarmon, Charles.** "Indigenization and Nation Building in Nigeria." *Canadian Review of Studies in Nationalism*, 7, No. 2 (Fall, 1980), 259-273.

2916 **Kastfelt, Niels.** "Rumours of Maitatsine: A Note on Political Culture in Northern Nigeria." *African Affairs*, 88, No. 350 (January, 1989), 83-90.

2917 **Keller, Edmond J.** *Revoultionary Ethiopia: From Empire to People's Republic.* Bloomington: Indiana University Press, 1988.

2918 **Khaketla, B.M.** *Lesotho 1970: An African Coup Under the Microscope.* London: Hurst, 1971.

2919 **Khalid, Mansour.** *The Government They Deserve: The Role of the Elite in Sudan's Political Evolution.* London: Kegan Paul International, 1990.

2920 **Kyle, Keith.** "The Southern Problem in the Sudan." *World Today*, 22, No. 12 (December, 1966), 512-520.

2921 **Lawrence, F.** "Khana and Jonathan: Leadership Strategies in Contemporary Southern Africa." *Journal of Developing Areas*, 15, No. 2 (January, 1981), 173-198.

2922 **Leiden, Carl.** "Egypt: The Drift to the Left." *Middle Eastern Affairs*, 13, No. 10 (December, 1962), 290-299; 14, No. 1 (January, 1963), 2-9.

2923 **Lewis, I.M.** *A Pastoral Democracy: A Study of Pastoralism and Politics Among the Northern Somali of the Horn of Africa*. London: Oxford University Press, 1961.

2924 **MaKinda, Samuel M.** "Sudan: Old Wine in New Bottles." *Orbis*, 31, No. 2 (Summer, 1987), 217-228.

2925 **Mandy, Nigel.** *A City Divided: Johannesburg and Soweto*. New York: St. Martin's Press, 1985.

2926 **Marguerat, Yves.** "L'Etat et l'organisation territoriale du Togo." *Afrique Contemporaine*, 22, No. 145 (1988), 47-54.

2927 **Markakis, John.** *National and Class Conflict in the Horn of Africa*. Cambridge: Cambridge University Press, 1987.

2928 **Marshall, J.** "The State of Ambivalence: Right and Left Options in Ghana." *Review of African Political Economy*, 5 (1976), 49-62.

2929 **McKay, Vernon.** "Nationalism in British West Africa." *Foreign Policy Reports*, 24, No. 1 (March 15, 1948), 1-11.

2930 **Morse, S.J.; Mann, J.W.; and Nel, E.** "National Identity in a 'Multi-Nation' State: A Comparison of Afrikaners and English-Speaking South Africans. *Canadian Review of Studies in Nationalism*, 4, No. 2 (Spring, 1977), 225-246.

2931 **Mosotho, Jeremiah.** "Lesotho Fights to Strengthen Independence." *African Communist*, 76, No. 1 (First Quarter, 1979), 93-98.

2932 **Munoz, Louis J.** "Traditional Participation in a Modern Political System: The Case of Western Nigeria." *Journal of Modern African Studies*, 18, No. 3 (September, 1980), 443-468.

2933 **Nan, Keith.** "The Northern Region of Nigeria: The Geographical Background of Its Political Duality." *Geographical Review*, 43, No. 4 (October, 1953), 451-473.

2934 **Prescott, J.R.V.** "The Geographical Basis of Kenya's Political Problems." *Australian Outlook*, 16, No. 3 (December, 1962), 270-282.

2935 **Rabinow, Paul.** "Governing Morocco: Modernity and Difference." *International Journal of Urban and Regional Research*, 13, No. 1 (March, 1989), 32-46.

2936 **Romdhani, Oussama.** "The Arab Maghreb Union: Toward North African Integration." *American-Arab Affairs*, No. 28 (Spring 1989), 42-48.

2937 **Sada, P.O.** "The Nigerian Twelve-State Political Structure: An Appraisal of Some Aspects of Politico-Geographical Viability." *Nigerian Geographical Journal*, 14, No. 1 (June, 1971), 17-30.

2938 **Saul, John S.** "The State in Post-Colonial Societies: Tanzania." *Socialist Register*, (1974), 349-372.

2939 **Saul, John S.** "The Unsteady State: Uganda, Obote and General Amin." *Review of African Political Economy*, 5 (1976), 12-38.

2940 **Sidaway, James Derrick.** "Mozambique: Destabilization, State, Society and Space." *Political Geography* [Oxford], 11, No. 3 (May, 1992), 239-258.

2941 **Sircar, Parbati, K.** "The Crisis of Nationhood in Nigeria." *International Studies*, 10, No. 3 (January, 1969), 245-269.

2942 **Smith, Michael Joseph.** "Guerilla Warfare in Southern Africa: A Geographical Analysis." Chapel Hill: University of North Carolina, M.A., 1984.

2943 **Sylvester, Christine.** "Simultaneous Revolutions: The Zimbabwean Case." *Journal of African Studies* [Eynsham], 16, No. 3 (September, 1990), 452-475.

2944 **Terrill, W. Andrew.** "The Comoro Islands in South African Regional Strategy." *Africa Today*, 33, Nos. 2 & 3 (March-June, 1986), 59-70.

2945 **Tordoff, William.** *Government and Politics in Africa*. London: Macmillan, 1984.

2946 **Walt, A.J. H. Van der.** "Constitutional Development in the Transkei." *Africa Institute, International Bulletin*, 1, No. 2 (March, 1963), 33-41.

2947 **Weaver, Leon H.** "The Politics of Internal Security in South Africa." *A Current Bibliography on African Affairs*, 11, No. 3 (1978-79), 215-236.

2948 **Weinstein, Brian.** *Gabon: Nation-Building on the Ogooue*. Cambridge: M.I.T. Press, 1966.

2949 **Weisfelder, Richard F.** "The Basotho Nation-State: What Legacy for the Future?" *Journal of Modern African Studies*, 19, No. 2 (June, 1981), 221-256.

2950 **Weisfelder, Richard F.** "Power Struggle in Lesotho." *African Report*, 12, No. 1 (January, 1967), 5-13.

2951 **Wellings, Paul**. "The 'Relative Autonomy' of the Lashotho State: Internal & External Determinants of Lesoho's Political Economy." *Political Geography Quarterly*, 4, No. 3 (July, 1985), 191-218.

2952 **Willmer, John E.** "Political Evolution and the Civil War (in Nigeria)." *Focus*, 21, No. 4 (December, 1970), 7-12.

2953 **Wisenberg, Laurie S., and Nelson, Gary F.** "Sao Tome and Principle: Mini-State with Maxi Problems." *Africa Report*, 21, No. 2 (March-April, 1976), 15-17 and 53.

2954 **Wood, A.** "Rural Development and National Integration: The Experience of Post-Revolution Ethiopia." *Geography*, 66, Part 2, No. 291 (April, 1981), 131-133.

AMERICAS

Books and Journals

2955 **Aschmann, Homer.** "The Immortality of Latin American States." In *Geographic Research on Latin America: Benchmark 1980. Proceedings of the Conference of Latin American Geographers.* Edited by Tom L. Martinson and Gary S. Elbow. Muncie, Indiana: The Conference, Publications Series. 8 (1981), 323-329.

2956 **August, Raymond S.** "The Origins of the Mexican Judicial System." *Revista de Historia de America*, 96 (Julio-Dicembre, 1983), 69-92.

2957 **Barlow, I.M.** "Political Geography and Canada's National Unity Problem." *Journal of Geography*, 79, No. 7 (December, 1980), 259-263.

2958 **Bell, D.** *Marxian Socialism in the United States.* New Jersey: Princeton University Press, 1976.

2959 **Bennet, S., and Earle, C.** "The Geography of Strikes in the United States, 1881-1894." *Journal of Interdisciplinary History*, 13 (Summer, 1982), 63-84.

2960 **Boorstin, Daniel J.** *The Americans: The National Experience.* New York: Random House, 1965.

2961 **Brazil, Constitution of.** *Constitution of the United States of Brazil, with the Constitutional Laws Nos. 1, 2, 3 and 4.* Rio de Janeiro: Departamento de imprensa e propaganda, 1941.

2962 **Cameron, Duncan.** "The Committee of One Hundred and the Quebec Socialiste." *Canadian Forum 42*, 62, No. 719 (June-July, 1982), 22 and 50.

2963 **Carr, Barry.** "Recent Regional Studies of the Mexican Revolution." *Latin American Research Review*, 15, No. 1 (1980), 3-14.

2964 **Cermakian, Jean.** "The Geographic Basis for the Viability of an Independent State of Quebec." *Canadian Geographer*, 18, No. 3 (Fall, 1974), 288-294.

2965 **Cleven, N. Andrew N.** *The Political Organization of Bolivia.* Publication No. 510. Washington, D.C.: Carnegie Institution of Washington, 1940.

2966 **Dahl, R.A.** *Who Governs? Democracy and Power in an American City.* New Haven, Connecticut: Yale University Press, 1961.

2967 **Del Aguila, Juan M.** *Cuba: Dilemmas of a Revolution.* Rev. ed. Boulder, Colorado: Westview Press, 1988.

2968 "Divisao Territorial do Brasil, 1959." *Annuario Geografico du Estado do Rio de Janeiro*, 12 (1959), 153-165.

2969 **Dmytryshyn, Basil.** "The Administrative Apparatus of the Russian-American Company, 1798-1867." *Canadian-American Slavic Studies* [Salt Lake City], 28, No. 1 (Spring, 1994), 1-52.

2970 **Driever, Steven L.** "Insurgency in Gautemala: Centuries-old Conflicts Over Land and Social Inequality Spawn Guerrilla Movements and Hope for Democratic Change." *Focus*, 35, No. 3 (July, 1985), 2-9.

2971 **Falcoff, Mark; Venezuela, Arturo; and Purcell, Susan Kaufman.** *Chili: Prospects for Democracy.* New York: Council on Foreign Relations Press, 1988.

2972 **Fauriol, Georges A., and Loser, Eva.** *Guatemala's Polittical Puzzle.* New Brunswick: Transaction Books, 1988.

2973 **Furtak, Robert K.** "Cuba: Un cuanto de siglo de politica exterior revolucionaria." *Foro interacional*, 25, No. 4 (Abril-Junio, 1985), 343-361.

2974 **Gentilcore, R.L.**, ed. *Geographical Approaches to Canadian Problems.* Toronto: Prentice-Hall, 1971.

2975 **Godard, H.R.** "Approche comparative des mecanismes d'evolution et de consolidation des quarticas populaires a Quito et a Guyaquil (Comparative Study of the Process of Evolution and Consolidation in the Popular Districts of Quito and Guyaquil)." *Bulletin-Institute Francais des Etudes Andines*, 14, Nos. 3-4(1985), 19-41.

2976 **Gonzalez Salinas, Edmundo.** "Los Limites de las Provincias del Rio de la Plata." *Revista Geografica de Chile, Terra Australis*, 17 (1959), 113-130.

2977 **Guerra, Antonio Teixeira, and Guerra, Ignez Amelia L. Feireira.** "Subsidios Para Una Nova Divisao Politica do Brasil." *Revista Brasileira de Geografia*, 22, No. 2 (April-June, 1960), 169-208.

2978 **Hamilton, J. and Pinard C.** "The Quebec Independence Movement." In *National Separatism*. C. Williams, ed. Vancouver: University of British Columbia Press, 1982.

2979 **Hilliker, Grant.** *The Politics of Reform in Peru: The Apusta and Other Mass Parties of Latin America*. Baltimore, Maryland: Johns Hopkins University Press, 1971.

2980 **Johnston, R.J.** "The Management and Autonomy of the Local State: The Role of the Judiciary in the United States." *Environment and Planning*, A, 13, No. 4 (December, 1981b), 1305-1316.

2981 **Jones, Stephen B.** "Geography and Politics in the Hawaiian Islands." *Geographical Review*, 28, No. 2 (April, 1938), 193-213.

2982 **Judd, D.R.** *The Politics of American Cities: Private Power and Public Policy*. Boston: Little Brown, 1979.

2983 **Kantor, Harry.** *The Ideology and Program of the Peruvian Aprista Movement*. Berkeley: University of California Press, 1953.

2984 **Keller, C. Peter.** "Accessibility and Areal Organizational Unit; Geographical Considerations for Dividing Canada's Northwest Territories." *Canadian Geographer*, 30, No. 1 (Spring, 1986), 71-79.

2985 **Larson, G.O.** *The Americanization of Utah for Statehood*. San Marino, California: Huntington Library, 1971.

2986 "Latin America's Nationalistic Revolution." *Annals of the American Academy of Political and Social Science*. 334 (March, 1961), 1-147 (whole issue with various authors).

2987 **Lewis, Gordon K.** *Puerto Rico: Freedom and Power in the Caribbean*. New York: Monthly Review Press, 1963.

2988 **Lowenthal, David.** "Levels of West Indian Government." *Social and Economic Studies*, 11, No. 4 (December, 1962), 363-391.

2989 **Mahnke, Hans-Peter.** "Hauptstadtverlegunen in der USA." *Geographische Rundschau*, Jahrg 24, Heft 9 (September, 1972), 366-371.

2990 **Martz, John D., and Myers, David J., eds.** *Venezuela: The Democratic Experience*. Rev. ed. New York: Praeger, 1986.

2991 **McDonald, Ronald H., and Tamrowski, Nina.** "Technology and Armed Conflict in Central America." *Journal of Inter-American Studies and World Affairs*, 29, No. 1 (Spring, 1987), 93-108.

2992 **Migdail, Carl J.** "Mexico's Failing Political System." *Journal of Inter-American Studies and World Affairs*, 29, No. 3 (Fall, 1987), 107-123.

2993 **Mitchell, E.J.** "Some Econometrics of the Huk Rebellion." *American Political Science Review*, 63, No. 4 (December, 1969), 1159-1171.

2994 **Montaner, Carlos Alberto.** "20 Years After the Cuban Revolution. Translated by Edvar do Zayas-Bazan." *Caribbean Review*, 8, No. 1, (January-March, 1979), 4-10.

2995 **Onuf, Peter S.** "From Colony to Territory: Changing Concepts of Statehood in Revolutionary America." *Political Science Quarterly*, 97, No. 3 (Fall, 1982), 447-459.

2996 **Orvik, Nils.** "Greenland: The Politics of a New Northern Nation." *International Journal*, 39, No. 4 (Autumn, 1984), 932-961.

2997 **Patterson, Samuel C.** "The Political Cultures of the American States." *Journal of Politics*, 30, No. 1 (February, 1968), 187-209.

2998 **Penner, Norman.** "Quebec Explodes a Bombshell: Rene Levesque and the Challenge of Separatism." *Round Table*, 266 (April, 1977), 153-160.

2999 **Remmer, Karen L.** "State in Change in Chile, 1973-1988." *Studies in Comparative Development*, 24, No. 3 (Fall, 1989), 5-29.

3000 **Russell, Philip L.** *El Salvador in Crisis*. Austin: Colorado River Press, 1984.

3001 **Schwartz, Mildred A.** *Politics and Territory: The Sociology of Regional Persistence in Canada*. Montreal and London: McGill-Queen's University Press, 1974.

3002 **Simsarian, James.** "The Acquisition of Legal Title to Terra Nullius." *Political Science Quarterly*, 53, No. 1 (March, 1938), 111-128.

3003 **Strange, I.J.** "Lovely Falkland Islands." *Geographical Magazine*, 40, No. 12 (December, 1968), 1064-1072.

3004 **Thomas, Hugh.** The Origins of the Cuban Revolution." *World Today*, 19, No. 10 (October, 1963), 448-460.

3005 **Will, W. Marvin.** "A Nation Divided: The Quest for Caribbean Integration." *Latin American Research Review* [Albuquerque], 26, No. 2 (1991), 3-37.

3006 **Williams, C.H.**, ed. *National Separatism.* Vancouver: University of British Columbia, 1982.

ASIA

Books

3007 **Afshar, Haleh**, ed. *Iran: A Revolution in Turmoil.* London: Macmillan, 1985.

3008 **Ahmad, Feroz.** *The Making of Modern Turkey.* London: Routledge, 1993.

3009 **Aushai, Berrard.** *Tragedy of Zionism. Revolution & Democracy in the Land of Israel.* New York: Farrar Straus Giroux, 1985.

3010 **Bayat, Mangol.** *Iran's First Revolution: Shi'ism and the Constitutional Revolution of 1905-1909.* New York: Oxford University Press, 1991.

3011 **Bedeski, Robert E.** *The Transformation of South Korea: Reform and Reconstitution in the Sixth Republic Under Roh Tae Woo, 1987-1992.* London: Routledge, 1994.

3012 **Bedford, Ian.** *The Telengana Insurrection: A Study in the Causes and Development of a Communist Insurrection in Rural India, 1946-1951.* Canberra, Australia: Australian National University, Ph.D., 1967.

3013 **Binyan, Liu.** *China's Crisis, China's Hope.* Translated from the Chinese by Howard Goldblatt. Cambridge: Harvard University Press, 1990.

3014 **Callard, Keith B.** *Political Forces in Pakistan: 1947-1959.* New York: Institute of Pacific Relations, 1959.

3015 **Chen, Cheng-Siang.** *The Administrative Divisions and Their Changes in Post-Revolution China.* Hong Kong: The Chinese University of Hong Kong, Graduate School, Geographical Research Center, 1971.

3016 **Chen, Cheng-Siang.** *Tibet Autonomous Region.* Hong Kong: The Chinese University of Hong Kong, Graduate School, Geographical Research Center, Research Report No. 33, 1970.

3017 **Church, Roderick Allan.** *Hill State Politics in Assam.* Durham, North Carolina: Duke University, Master's Thesis, 1968.

3018 **Das, Tapan.** *Pakistan Politics.* Delhi: People's Publishing House, 1969.

3019 **Davis, Uri.** *Israel: An Apartheid State.* London: Zed Books, 1987.

3020 **Dittmer, Lowell.** *China's Continuous Revolution: The Post-Liberation Epoch, 1949-1981.* Berkeley: University of California Press, 1987.

3021 **Duncanson, Dennis J.** *Government and Revolution in Vietnam.* London: Royal Institute of International Affairs, 1968.

3022 **Echikson, William.** *Lighting the Night: Revolution in Eastern Europe.* New York: William Morrow and Company, Inc., 1990.

3023 **Esman, Milton J.** *Administration and Development in Malaysia: Institution Building and Reform in a Plural Society.* Ithaca, New York: Cornell University Press, 1972.

3024 **Esposito, John L.**, ed. *The Iranian Revolution: Its Global Impact.* Miami: Florida International University Press, 1990.

3025 **Ethridge, James M.** *China's Unfinished Revolution: Problems and Prospects Since Mao.* San Francisco: China Books & Periodicals, Inc., 1990.

3026 **Fall, Bernard B.** *The Viet-Minh Regime; Government and Administration in the Democratic Republic of Vietnam.* Rev. and enl. ed. New York: Institute of Pacific Relations, 1956.

3027 **Farhi, Farideh.** *States and Urban-Based Revolution: Iran and Nicaragua.* Urbana: University of Illinois Press, 1990.

3028 **Forouk-Sluglett, Marion, and Slugleh, Peter.** *Iraq Since 1958: From Revolution to Dictatorship.* London: KPI, 1987.

3029 **Gani, H.A.** *Governor in the Indian Constituion; Certain Controversies and Sarkaria Commission.* Delhi: Ajanta, 1990.

3030 **Ghose, Sarkar.** *Socialism and Communism in India.* Bombay: Allied Publishers, 1971.

3031 **Gitisetan, Darinsh.** *Iran, Politics & Government Under the Pahlavis: An Annotated Bibliography.* London: The Scarecrow Press, 1985.

3032 **Goria, Wade R.** *Sovereignty and Leadership in Lebanon, 1943-1976.* London: Ithaca Press, 1985.

3033 **Great Britain.** Department of Foreign Affairs. *Government of India on the Congress Party's Responsibility for the Disturbances in India, 1942-43.* Foreign Office Report. London: Government Printing Office, 1943.

3034 **Haas, Michael**, ed. *Korean Reunification: Alternative Pathways.* New York: Praeger, 1989.

3035 **Hamrin, Carol Lee.** *China and the Challenge of the Future: Changing Political Patterns.* Boulder, Colorado: Westview Press, 1990.

3036 **Harris, George S.** *Turkey: Coping with Crisis.* (Profile: Nations of the Contemporary Middle East) Boulder, Colorado: Westview Press, 1985.

3037 **Henderson, Gregory.** *Korea—The Politics of the Vortex.* Cambridge, Massachusetts: Harvard University Press, 1968.

3038 **Hinnebusch, Raymond A.** *Authoritarian Power and State Formation in Ba'thist Syria: Army, Party, and Peasant.* Boulder, Colorado: Westview Press, 1990.

3039 **Hodgkin, T.** *Vietnam: The Revolutionary Path.* London: Macmillan, 1981.

3040 **Ingram, Edward**, ed. *National and International Politics in the Middle East: Essay in Honour of Elie Kedourie.* London: Frank Cass, 1986.

3041 **Kahin, Audrey R.**, ed. *Regional Dynamics of the Indonesian Revolution: Unity from Diversity.* Honolulu: University of Hawaii Press, 1985.

3042 **Kahin, G. McTurnan**, ed. *Governments and Politics of Southeast Asia.* 2nd ed. Ithaca: Cornell University Press, 1964.

3043 **Khashoggi, Hani Yousef.** *Local Administration in Saudi Arabia.* Claremont, California: Claremont Graduate School, Ph.D., 1979.

3044 **King, Frank H.H.** *The New Malayan Nation: A Study of Communalism and Nationalism.* New York: Institute of Pacific Relations, 1957.

3045 **Kothari, Rajni**, ed. *Politics in India.* Boston: Little Brown, 1970.

3046 **Lane, Kevin P.** *Sovereignty and the Status Quo: The Historical Roots of China's Hong Kong Policy.* Boulder: Westview Press, 1990.

3047 **Leifer, Michael.** *Cambodia—The Search for Security.* New York: Praeger, 1967.

3048 **Leinbach, Thomas Raymond.** *Transportation and Modernization in Malaya.* University Park: Pennsylvania State University, Ph.D., 1971.

3049 **Lieberthal, Kenneth, and Oksenberg, Michel.** *Policy Making in China: Leaders, Structures, and Processes.* Princeton, New Jersey: Princeton University Press, 1988.

3050 **Long, Simon.** *Taiwan: China's Last Frontier.* Houndmills: Macmillan, 1990.

3051 **Mackey, Sandra.** *Lebanon: Death of a Nation.* New York: Congdon & Weed, 1989.

3052 **MacMunn, George F., Sir.** *The Indian States and Princes.* London: Jarrolds, 1936.

3053 **McGurn, William.** *Perfidious Albion: The Abandondment of Hong Kong, 1997.* Washington, D.C.: Ethics and Public Policy Center, 1992.

3054 **Menon, Vapal Pangunni.** *The Story of the Integration of the Indian States.* New York: Macmillan, 1956.

3055 **Moraes, Frank.** *The Revolt in Tibet.* New York: Macmillan, 1960.

3056 **Osborne, Robin.** *Indonesia's Secret War: The Guerilla Struggle in Irian Jaya.* Sydney: Allen & Unwin, 1985.

3057 **Pati, Satyabhama.** *Democratic Movement in India.* New Delhi: Discovery, 1987.

3058 **Peleg, Illan and Seliktar, Ofira**, eds. *The Emergence of a Binational Israel: The Second Republic in the Making.* Boulder, Colorado: Westview Press, 1989.

3059 **Pipes, Daniel.** *Greater Syria: The History of an Ambition.* New York: Oxford University Press, 1990.

3060 **Pradhan, Kumar.** *The Gorkha Conquests: The Process and Consequences of the Unification of Nepal, With Particular Reference to Eastern Nepal.* Calcutta: Oxford University Press, 1991.

3061 **Prizzia, Ross.** *Thailand in Transition: The Role of Oppositional Forces.* Honolulu: University of Hawaii, University of Hawaii Press, 1985.

3062 **Pye, Lucian W.** *Politics, Personality and Nation Building--Burma's Search for Identity.* New Haven, Connecticut: Yale University Press, 1962.

3063 **Sayegh, Fayez A.** *Arab Unity.* New York: Arab Information Center, 1958.

3064 **Seliktar, Ofira.** *New Zionism and Foreign Policy System of Israel.* London: Croom Helm, 1986.

3065 **Sen, D.K.** *The Indian States, Their Status, Rights, and Obligations.* London: Sweet and Maxwell, 1930.

3066 **Sharkansky, Ira.** *Ancient and Modern Israel: An Exploration of Political Parallels.* Albany: State University of New York Press, 1991.

3067 **Sharma, Om Prakash.** *Emerging Pattern of Rural Leadership in India.* Bloomington: Indiana University, Ph.D., 1967.

3068 **Shavit, Y.** *The New Hebrew Nation: A Study in Israeli Heresy and Fantasy.* London: Frank Cass, 1987.

3069 Shepherd, George W. *The Trampled Grass: Tributary States and Self-Reliance in the Indian Ocean Zone of Peace*. New York: Greenwood Press, 1987.

3070 Singh, Katherine Lowe. *Continuity and Change in Pakistan's Internal Politics: The Ayub Years*. Claremont, California: Claremont Graduate School and University Center, Ph.D., 1970.

3071 Tewksbury, Donald G., comp. *Source Materials on Korean Politics and Ideologies*. New York: Institute of Pacific Relations, 1950.

3072 Thomas, S.B. *Government and Administration in Communist China*. Rev. ed. New York: International Secretariat, Institute of Pacific Relations, 1955.

3073 Thompson, Sir Robert. *Defeating Communist Insurgency: The Lessons of Malaya and Vietnam*. New York: Praeger, 1966.

3074 Trullinger, J.B. *Village at War. An Account of Revolution in Vietnam*. New York: Longman, 1980.

3075 Von Vorys, Karl. *Political Development in Pakistan*. Princeton, New Jersey: Princeton University Press, 1965.

3076 Weiner, Myron. *Indian Political Behavior*. Princeton, New Jersey: Princeton University, Ph.D., 1955.

3077 Wilkinson, John C. *The Imamate Traditions of Oman*. Cambridge: Cambridge University Press, 1987.

3078 Wood, John R., ed. *State Politics in Contemporary India: Crisis or Continuity*. Boulder, Colorado: Westview Press, 1984.

3079 Younghusband, Sir Francis Edward. *India and Tibet*. Oxford: Oxford University Press, 1985.

Journals

3080 Adhikari, Sudeepta. "India's National Integration: A Problem in Political Geography. *Geographical Review of India*, Vol. 47, No. 1 (March, 1985), 83-90.

3081 Antoun, Richard T. "The Islamic Court, the Islamic Judge, and the Accommodation of Traditions: A Jordanian Case Study." *International Journal of Middle East Studies*, 12, No. 4 (December, 1980), 455-467.

3082 Barnds, William J. "The Indian Subcontinent: New and Old Political Imperatives." *World Today*, 29, No. 1 (January, 1973), 24-33.

3083 Baum, Richard. "Political Stability in Post-Deng China: Problems and Prospects." *Asian Survey* [Berkeley], 32, No. 6 (June, 1992), 491-505.

3084 Bhatta, Pandit K.A. "Innenpolitische Probleme Indiens." *Zeitschrift fur Geopolitik*, 16 Jahrg, Heft 12 (Dezember, 1939), 837-850.

3085 Blake, Gerald H., and Harris, William Wilson. "Israelis Come to Stay." *Geographical Magazine*, 50, No. 2 (November, 1979), 83-86.

3086 Callard, Keith. "The Political Stability of Pakistan." *Pacific Affairs*, 29, No. 1 (March, 1956), 5-20.

3087 Canfield, Robert L. "Restructuring in Greater Central Asia: Changing Political Configurations." *Asian Survey* [Berkeley], 32, No. 10 (October, 1992), 875-887.

3088 Chau, Phan Thien. "Political Development in the Democratic Republic of Vietnam: The Politics of Survival and Nation-Building through Mass Mobilization." *Montclair Journal of Social Sciences and Humanities*, (1974), 57-78.

3089 Chen, Shih-Tsai. "The Equality of States in Ancient China." *American Journal of International Law*, 35, No. 4 (October, 1941), 641-650.

3090 Chiu, Hungdah. "China's New Legal System." *Current History*, 79, No. 458 (September, 1980), 29-32.

3091 Christensen, Scott R. "Thailand in 1990: Political Tangles." *Asian Survey* [Berkeley], 21, No. 2 (February, 1991), 196-204.

3092 Crane, Nick. "Afghanistan: Rebuilding Begins." *Geographical Magazine*, 61, No. 2 (February, 1989), 10-15.

3093 Das, Taraknath. "India--Past, Present and the Future." *Political Science Quarterly*, 62, No. 2 (June, 1947), 295-304.

3094 Davidson, J.W. "Political Development in Western Samoa." *Pacific Affairs*, 21, No. 2 (June, 1948), 136-149.

3095 Donald, Alan, and Arnold, Thomas. "The Unity of China." *Asian Affairs* [London], 23, Part 3 (October, 1992), 271-280.

3096 Drake, Christine. "National Integration in China and Indonesia." *The Geographical Review* [New York], 82, No. 3 (July, 1992), 295-312.

3097 Dunbar, Charles. "The Unification of Yemen: Process, Politics, and Prospects." *The Middle East Journal* [Bloomington], 46, No. 3 (Summer, 1992), 456-476.

3098 **Duncanson, Dennis J.** "What is Taiwan to China." *Asian Affairs*, 17, Part 3 (October, 1986), 288-297.

3099 **Elwell-Sutton, L.P.** "The Iranian Revolution." *International Journal*, 34, No. 3 (Summer, 1979), 391-407.

3100 **Farlhi, Farideh.** "State Disintegration and Urban-Based Revolutionary Crisis: A Comparative Analysis of Iran and Nicaragua." *Comparative Politicial Studies*, 21, No. 2 (July, 1988), 231-256.

3101 **Finkelstein, David M.** "Vietnam: A Revolution in Crisis." *Asian Survey*, 27, No. 9 (September, 1987), 973-990.

3102 **Finkelstein, Lawrence S.** "Prospects of Self-Government in Malaya." *Far Eastern Survey*, 21, No. 2 (January 30, 1952), 9-17.

3103 **Forster, Keith.** "Repudiation of the Cultural Revolution in China: The Case of Zhejiang." *Pacific Affairs*, 59, No. 1 (Spring, 1986), 5-27.

3104 **Furber, Holden.** "The Unification of India, 1947-1951." *Pacific Affairs*, 24, No. 4 (December, 1951), 352-371.

3105 **Gibbs, David.** "The Peasant as Counter-Revolutionary: The Rural Origins of the Afghan Insurgency." *Studies in Comparative International Development*, 21, No. 1 (Spring, 1986), 36-59.

3106 **Goldmann, Nahum.** "Zionist Ideology and the Reality of Israel." *Foreign Affairs*, 57, No. 1 (Fall, 1978), 70-82.

3107 **Goldstein, Michael.** "Israeli Security Measures in the Occupied Territories: Administrative Detention." *Middle East Journal*, 32, No. 1 (Winter, 1978), 35-44.

3108 **Gong, Gerrit W.** "China and the Dynamics of Unification in Northeast Asia." *The Academy of Political Science, Proceedings* [New York], 38, No. 2 (1991), 95-106.

3109 **Goyal, O.P.,** and **Hahn, Harlan.** "The Nature of Part Competition in Five Indian States." *Asian Survey*, 6, No. 10 (October, 1966), 580-588.

3110 **Gunter, Michael M.** "The Armenian Terrorist Campaign Against Turkey." *Orbis*, 27, No. 2 (Summer, 1983), 447-477.

3111 **Hazelton, Fran,** ed. *Iraq Since the Gulf War: Prospects for Democracy.* London: Zed Books Ltd., 1994.

3112 **Hibbert, R.A.** "The Mongolian People's Republic in the 1960's." *World Today*, 23, No. 3 (March, 1967), 122-130.

3113 **Honey, R.D.,** and **Abukharmeh, S.** "Political Geography in Practice I: Organizing Space for Development and Planning: The Case of Jordan." *Political Geography Quarterly*, 7, No. 3 (July, 1988), 271-287.

3114 **Hong, Kim Byong.** "Korean Reunification." *The Academy of Political Science, Proceedings* [New York], 38, No. 2 (1991), 115-119.

3115 **Hong, Yung Lee.** "Mao's Strategy for Revolutionary Change: A Case Study of the Cultural Revolution." *China Quarterly*, 77, No. 1 (March, 1979), 50-73.

3116 **Hudson, Michael C.** "The Palestinian Factor in the Lebanese Civil War." *Middle East Journal*, 32, No. 3 (Summer, 1978), 261-278.

3117 **Hung, F.** "A New Plan for the Division of Chinese Provinces." *Geo-Quarterly*, 9, No. 4 (October, 1947), 1-12.

3118 "The Independent State of Laos." *World Today*, 13, No. 10 (October, 1957), 432-441.

3119 "India's Revolution by Consent." *World Today*, 11, No. 6 (June, 1955), 254-262.

3120 **Innes, F.M.** "The Political Outlook in Pakistan." *Pacific Affairs*, 26, No. 4 (December, 1953), 303-317.

3121 **Kahin, G. McTurnan.** "The New Indonesian Government...Who are Indonesia's Leaders, and What is Their Program?" *Far Eastern Survey*, 19, No. 20 (November 22, 1950), 209-213.

3122 **Katzenstein, Mary Fainsod.** "Origins of Nativism: The Emergence of Shiv Sena in Bombay." *Asian Survey*, 13, No. 4 (April, 1973), 386-399.

3123 **Khadka, Narayan.** "Crisis in Nepal's Partyless Panchayat System: The Case for More Democracy." *Pacific Affairs*, 59, No. 3 (Fall, 1986), 429-454.

3124 **Kim, C.I. Eugene.** "Emergency, Development, and Human Rights: South Korea." *Asian Survey*, 18, No. 4 (April, 1978), 363-378.

3125 **Leaf, Murray J.** "The Punjab Crisis." *Asian Survey*, 25, No. 5 (May, 1985), 475-498.

3126 **Lesch, Ann,** and **Tessler, Mark A.** "The West Bank and Gaza: Political and Ideological Responses to Occupation." *Muslim World*, 79, Nos. 3-4 (July-October, 1987), 229-249.

3127 **Levi, Werner.** "Government and Politics in Nepal." *Far Eastern Survey*, 21, No. 18 (December 17, 1952), 185-191; 22, No. 1 (January 14, 1953), 5-10.

3128 **Levi, Werner.** "Tibet Under Chinese Communist Rule." *Far Eastern Survey*, 33, No. 1 (January, 1954), 889-894.

3129 **Maddox, William P.** "Singapore: Problem Child." *Foreign Affairs*, 40, No. 4 (December, 1962), 479-489.

3130 **Maniruzzaman, Talukdar.** "National Integration and Political Development in Pakistan." *Asian Survey*, 7, No. 12 (December, 1967), 876-885.

3131 **Maung, Mya.** "The Burma Road from the Union of Burma to Myanmar." *Asian Survey* [Berkeley], 30, No. 6 (June, 1990), 602-624.

3132 **Milivojevic, Marko.** "Soviet Central Asia Cuts Loose." *Geographical Magazine* [London], 62, No. 11 (November, 1990), 30-33.

3133 **Morfit, Michael.** "Pancasila: The Indonesian State Ideology According to the New Order Government." *Asian Survey*, 21, No. 8 (August, 1981), 838-851.

3134 **Mukhopadhyay, Syamal.** "Forms and Functions of Local Urban Government in North Bengal." *Geographical Review of India*, 39, No. 1 (March, 1977), 60-70.

3135 **Noble, Lela Garner.** "Emergency Politics in the Philippines." *Asian Survey*, 18, No. 4 (April, 1978), 350-362.

3136 **Noori, Yahya.** "The Islamic Concept of State." *Hamdard Islamicus*, 3, No. 3 (Autumn, 1980), 71-92.

3137 **O'Harrow, Stephen.** "Nguyen Trai's Binh Ngo Dai Cao of 1428: The Development of a Vietnamese National Identity." *Journal of Southeast Asian Studies*, 10, No. 1 (March, 1979), 159-174.

3138 **Oommen, T.K.** "Political Leadership in Rural India: Image and Reality." *Asian Survey*, 9, No. 7 (July, 1969), 515-521.

3139 **Overholt, William B.** "China and BAritish Hong Kong." *Current History* [Philadelphia], 90, No. 557 (September, 1991), 270-274.

3140 **Overholt, William H.** "Hong Kong and China after 1997: The Real Issues." *The Academy of Political Science, Proceedings* [New York], 38, No. 2 (1991), 30-52.

3141 **Overholt, William H.** "Hong Kong and the Crisis of Sovereignty." *Asian Survey*, 24, No. 4 (April, 1984), 471-484.

3142 **Petrossian, Vahe.** "Dilemmas of the Iranian Revolution." *World Today*, 36, No. 1 (January, 1980), 19-25.

3143 **Puckle, Frederick, Sir.** "The Pakistan Doctrine: Its Origins and Power." *Foreign Affairs*, 24, No. 3 (April, 1946), 526-534.

3144 **Ramazani, R.K.** "Iran's Revolution: Patterns, Problems, and Prospects." *International Affairs*, 56, No. 3 (Summer, 1980), 443-457.

3145 **Riggs, Fred W.** "Tibet in Extremis. Tibetan Claims to Autonomy are Clouded by Old Treaties and by Internal Splits. Meanwhile the Advance of Peking's Troops Agitates New Delhi." *Far Eastern Survey*, 19, No. 21 (December 6, 1950), 224-230.

3146 **Rouleau, Eric.** "Crisis in Jordan." *World Today*, 23, No. 2 (February, 1967), 62-70.

3147 **Rubin, Barnett R.** "Lineages of the State in Afghanistan." *Asian Survey*, 28, No. 11 (November, 1988), 1188-1209.

3148 **Rudolph, Susanne Hoeber.** "Consensus and Conflict in Indian Politics." *World Politics*, 13, No. 3 (April, 1961), 385-399.

3149 **Salem, Elie A.** "Lebanon's Political Maze: The Search for Peace in a Turbulent Land." *Middle East Journal*, 33, No. 4 (Autumn, 1979), 444-463.

3150 **Samuel, Edwin.** "The Government of Israel and Its Problems." *Middle East Journal*, 3, No. 1 (January, 1949), 1-16.

3151 **Sheean, Vincent.** "The People of Ceylon and Their Politics." *Foreign Affairs*, 28, No. 1 (October, 1949), 68-74.

3152 **Singh, Harnam.** "The Indian States: A Study of Their Constitutional Position." *Political Science Quarterly*, 64, No. 1 (March, 1949), 95-106.

3153 **Skilland, W.E.** "The Political Opposition in South Korea." *Asian Affairs*, 9 (Old Series, Vol. 65), Part 1 (February, 1978), 13-22.

3154 **Stone, Jeffrey C.** "Foundations of a Malaysian Nation." *Geographical Magazine*, 42, No. 8 (May, 1970), 552-556.

3155 **Stookey, Robert.** "Social Structure and Politics in the Yemen Arab Republic." *Middle East Journal*, 28, No. 3 (Summer, 1974), 248-260.

3156 **Szyliowicz, Joseph S.** "The Political Dynamics of Rural Turkey." *Middle East Journal*, 16, No. 4 (Autumn, 1962), 430-442.

3157 **Tannenbaum, Michael.** "Politics and the Sword in Syria." *New Leader*, 61, No. 20 (October 9, 1978), 10-12.

3158 Thompson, Laura. "Guam: Study in Military Government." *Far Eastern Survey*, 13, No. 16 (August 9, 1944), 149-154.

3159 Tonkin, Derek. "Whither Vietnam?" *Asian Affairs* [London], 23, Part 3 (October, 1992), 295-303.

3160 Van Der Kroef, Justus M. "Instability in Indonesia." *Far Eastern Survey*, 26, No. 4 (April, 1957), 49-62.

3161 Walker, Richard L. "Taiwan's Development as Free China." *Annals of the American Academy of Political and Social Sciences*, 321 (January, 1959), 122-135.

3162 Weinbaum, M.G. "Legal Elites in Afghan Society." *International Journal of Middle East Studies*, 12, No. 1 (August, 1980), 39-57.

3163 Weiner, Myron. "India's Political Future." *World Politics*, 12, No. 1 (October, 1959), 103-119.

3164 Weiner, Myron. "The Political Demography of Nepal." *Asian Survey*, 13, 6 (June, 1973), 617-630.

3165 Weiner, Myron. "State Politics in India: Report on a Seminar." *Asian Survey*, 1, No. 6 (June, 1961), 35-40.

3166 Wiemer, Reinhard. "The Theories of Nationalism and of Zionism in the First Decade of the State of Israel." *Middle East Journal*, 23, No. 2 (April, 1987), 172-187.

3167 Wilber, Donald N. "Afghanistan, Independent and Encircled." *Foreign Affairs*, 31, No. 3 (April, 1953), 486-494.

3168 Wiley, S.C. "Kashmir." *Canadian Geographical Journal*, 62, No. 1 (January, 1961), 22-31.

AUSTRALIA, OCEANIA AND ANTARCTICA

Books and Journals

3169 Drummond, D.H. *Australia's Changing Constitution; No States or New States.* Sydney: Angus and Robertson, 1943.

3170 Feinberg, R. "The 'Anuta Problem": Local Sovereignty and National Integration in the Solomon Islands." *Man*, 21, No. 3 (1986), 438-452.

3171 Heine, Carl. *Micronesia at the Crossroads: A Reappraisal of the Micronesian Political Dilemma.* Honolulu: University of Hawaii Press, 1974.

3172 Holsman, A.J. "Interstate Interaction Patterns in Australia." *Australian Geographical Studies*, 13, No. 1 (April, 1975), 41-61.

3173 "New States of Australia? A Movement of Decentralization." *Round Table*, 46, No. 184 (September, 1956), 355-361.

3174 Mercer, David. "Patterns of Protest: Native Land Rights and Claims in Australia." *Political Geography Quarterly*, 6, No. 2 (April, 1987), 171-194.

3175 Marcus, George E. "Succession Disputes and the Position of the Nobility in Modern Tonga." *Oceania*, 47, No. 4 (June, 1977)1, 284-299.

3176 Parker, R.S. and Others. *New States for Australia.* Sydney: Australian Institute of Political Science, 1955.

3177 Rumley, Dennis. "Ideology, Regional Policy, and Applied Geography: The Case of the Kimberley, Western Australia." *Australian Journal of Social Issues*, 18, No. 3 (August, 1983), 233-244.

3178 Whebel, C.F.J. "Non-national Separatism: With Special Reference to Australian Cases Past and Present." In *Collected Papers on the Politics of Separation.* W.H. Morris-Jones, ed. London: University of London, Institute of Commonwealth Studies, 1976, 19-29.

EUROPE

Books and Journals

3179 Ahsan, Syed Aziz-al. "Soviet Nation-Building in Central Asia (1917-1979)." *Canadian Review of Studies in Nationalism*, 14, No. 2 (Fall, 1987), 317-329.

3180 Alder, M. "A State Apart (Albania, Politics)." *Geographical Magazine*, 58, No. 3 (March, 1986), 132-137.

3181 Asmus, Ronald. "The GDR and the German Nation: Sole Heir or Socialist Sibling." *International Affairs*, 60, No. 3 (Summer, 1984), 403-418.

3182 Banac, Ivo, ed. *Eastern Europe in Revolution.* Ithaca: Cornell University Press, 1992.

3183 Bertram, Christoph. "The German Question." *Foreign Affairs* [New York], 69, No. 2 (Spring, 1990), 45-62.

3184 **Birch, A.H.** *Political Integration and Disintegration in the British Isles.* London: Allen & Unwin, 1977.

3185 **Biskupski, M. B.** "Re-creating Central Europe: The United States 'Inquiry' into the Future of Poland in 1918." *The International History Review* [Burnaby, BC], 12, No. 2 (May, 1990), 249-279.

3186 **Bond, Andrew R. and others.** "Panels on Patterns of Disintegration in the Former Soviet Union." *Post-Soviet Geography* [Silver Spring], 33, No. 6 (June, 1992), 347-404.

3187 **Bradshaw, Michael J., and Lynn, Nicholas J.** "After the Soviet Union: The Post-Soviet Stats in the World System." *The Professional Geographer,* 46, No. 4 (November, 1994), 439-449.

3188 **Butler, D., and Stokes, D.E.** *Political Change in Britain.* London: Edward Arnold, 1974.

3189 **Calabuig-Odins, Erlends.** "Les Russes de la Baltique: Un Levier Politique Pour la Reconquete?" *Herodote,* No. 72/73 (Janvier-Juin, 1994), 157-169.

3190 **Cankar, Izidor.** "Problems of the New Yugoslavia." *Slavonci and East European Review,* 23, No. 62 (January, 1945), 55-62.

3191 **Carsten, F.L.** *The First Austrian Republic 1918-1938.* Brookfield, Vermont: Gower Publishing, 1986.

3192 "The Central Asian Republics; Their Place in the Soviety System." *World Todlay,* 4, No. 5 (May, 1984), 197-208.

3193 **Churba, Joseph.** *Soviet Breakout: Strategies to Meet It.* Washington, D.C.: Pergamon-Brassey's International Defense Publishers, 1988.

3194 **Clarke, P.F.** *Lancashire and the New Liberalism.* Cambridge: Cambridge University Press, 1971.

3195 **Clarkson, J.D.** *Labor and Nationalism in Ireland.* New York City: Columbia University Press, 1925.

3196 **Coates, David.** *The Context of British Politics.* London: Hutchinson, 1984.

3197 **Colton, Timothy J., and Legvold, Robert,** eds. *After the Soviet Union: Form Empire to Nations.* New York: W. W. Norton & Company, 1992.

3198 **Connely, Alpha Margaret.** *International Law Across the Ages: A Comparison of the Legal Relations of the Greek City-States and of Modern Nation-States.* Montreal: McGill Univ., 1975.

3199 **Cooke, Philip.** "Class Interests, Regional Restructuring and State Formation in Wales." *International Journal of Urban and Regional Research,* 6, No. 2 (June, 1982), 187-204.

3200 **Corson, Mark W., and Minghi, Julian V.** "Reunification of Partitioned Nation-Stats: Theory Versus Reality in Vietnam and Germany." *Journal of Geography* [Indiana, PA], 93, No. 3 (May/June, 1994), 125-131.

3201 **Crawshaw, Steve.** *Goodbye to the USSR: The Collapse of Soviet Power.* London: Bloomsbury, 1992.

3202 **Crepaz, Markus M.L.** "From Semisovereignty to Sovereignty: The Decline of Corporatism and Rise of Parliament in Austria." *Comparative Politics,* 27, No. 1 (October, 1994), 45-65.

3203 **Cullen, Robert.** *Twilight of Empire: Inside the Crumbling Soviet Bloc.* New York: The Atlantic Monthly Press, 1991.

3204 **Czaplinski, Wladyslaw.** "Reunification of Germany--International Legal Issues." *Coexistence* [Dordrecht], 27, No. 4 (December, 1990), 225-232.

3205 **Dawisha, Karen, and Parrott, Bruce.** *Russia and the New States of Eurasia: The Politics of Upheaval.* Cambridge: Cambridge University Press, 1994.

3206 **Demangeon, Albert.** "Les provinces francaises et le probleme d'une reorganisation regionale." *Acta Geographica,* 3, No. 1 (Janvier-Mars, 1972), 43-48.

3207 **Donaldson, Gordon.** *Scotland: The Shaping of a Nation.* New 2nd Rev. Ed. Nairn, Scotland: David St. John Thomas Publisher, 1993.

3208 **Fishlock, Trevor.** *Out of Red Darkness: Reports from the Collapsing soviet Empire.* London: John Murray, 1992.

3209 **Frears, J.R.** "The Decentralization Reforms in France." *Parliamentary Affairs,* 36, No. 1 (Winter, 1983), 56-66.

3210 **Gillette, Philip S.** "The Outlook for Geographic Change in the USSR: Trekking, Chipping, Disintegrating, Fusing." *The Virginia Geographer* [Norfolk], 23, No. 1 (Spring-Summer, 1991), 1-10.

3211 **Goudoever, Albert P. van.** *The Limits of Destalinization in the Soviet Union: Political Rehabilitations in the Soviet Union Since Stalin.* London: Croom Helm, 1986.

3212 **Groenendijk, J.G.** "Reorganisatie Van Het Binenlands Bestuur in Nederland Bezien Vanvit de Relatie Tussen Politieck-Ruimtelijke Structuur en Doelejnder-en Bestuursstructuur." *Geografisch Tijdschrift,* Nievwe Reeks, 15, No. 2 (1981), 131-144.

3213 **Hamilton, Daniel.** "Germany After Unification." *Problems of Communism* [Washington, D.C.], 41, No. 3 (May-June, 1992), 1-18.

3214 **Harris, Chauncy D.** "Unification of Germany in 1990." *The Geographical Review* [New York], 81, No. 2 (April, 1991), 170-182.

3215 **Hauner, Milan.** *What Is Asia to Us?: Russia's Asian Heartland Yeserday and Today.* Boston: Unwin Hyman, 1990.

3216 **Hechter, M.** *International Colonialism: The Celtic Fringe in British National Development, 1536-1966.* London: Routledge and Kegan Paul, 1975.

3217 **Hirschman, Albert O.** "Exit, Voice, and the Fate of the German Democratic Republic: An Essay in Conceptual History." *World Politics* [Baltimore], 45, No. 2 (January, 1993), 173-202.

3218 **Hoffman, Stanley.** "Reflections on the 'German Question.'" *Survival* [London], 32, No. 4 (July/August, 1990), 291-298.

3219 **Holmes, P.** "France: State-sponsored Development in the First NIC?" *Institute of Development Studies Bulletin*, 18, No. 3 (1987), 13-17.

3220 **Hopf, Ted.** "Managing Soviet Disintegration: A Demand for Behavioral Regimes." *International Security* [Cambridge, MA], 17, No. 1 (Summer, 1992, 44-75.

3221 **Hosking, Geoggrey.** *The Awakening of the Soviet Union.* London: Heinemann, 1990.

3222 **Jarvenpaa, Pauli O.** "Finland: An Image of Continuity in Turbulent Europe." *The American Academy of Political and Social Science, Annals* [Newbury Park], 512 (November, 1990), 125-139.

3223 **Jasinska-Kania, Alexsandra.** "National Identity and Image of World Society: The Polish Case." *Images of World Society*, 34, No. 1 (1982), 93-112.

3224 **Johnston, R.J.** "National Power in the European Parliament as Mediated by the Party System." *Environment and Planning*, 9, No. 9 (September, 1977), 1055-1066.

3225 **Karnoouh, Claude.** "National Unity in Central Europe: The State, Peasant Folklore and Mono-Ethnism." *Telos*, 53 (Fall, 1982), 95-105.

3226 **Kavanagh, Dennis.** *Thatcherism and British Politics: The End of Consensus?* 2nd ed. Oxford: Oxford University Press, 1990.

3227 **Kellas, J.G.** *The Scottish Political System.* Cambridge: Cambridge University Press, 1976.

3228 **Knapp, A.F.** "Municipal Communism at Le Harvre." *Etudes Normandes*, 4 (1987), 61-79.

3229 **Kohak, Erazim.** "Ashes, Ashes...Central Europe After Forty Years." *Daedalus* [Cambridge, MA], 121, No. 2 (Spring, 1992), 197-215.

3230 **Kovrig, Bennett.** "Moving Time: The Emancipation of Eastern Europe." *International Journal* [Toronto], 46, No. 2 (Spring, 1991), 242-266.

3231 **Kuran, Timur.** "Now Out of Never: The Element of Surprise in the East European Revolution of 1989." *World Politics* [Baltimore], 44, No. 1 (October, 1991), 7-48.

3232 **Lancaster, Thomas D., and Prevost, Gary,** eds. *Politics and Change in Spain.* New York: Praeger, 1985.

3233 **Lane, David Stuart.** *State and Politics in the USSR.* Oxford: Basil Blackwell, 1985.

3234 **Larrabee, F. Stephen.** "Instability and Change in the Balkans." *Survival* [London], 34, No. 2 (Summer, 1992), 31-49.

3235 **Larrabee, F. Stephen.** "Long Memories and Short Fuses: Change and Instability in the Balkans." *International Security* [Cambridge], 15, No. 3 (Winter, 1990-91), 58-91.

3236 **Lydall, Harold.** *Yugoslavia in Crisis.* Oxford: Clarendon Press, 1989.

3237 **Lewin, Moshe.** "Customary Law and Russian Rural Society in the Post-Reform Era." *Russian Review*, 44, No. 1 (January, 1985), 1-19.

3238 **McElvoy, Anne.** *The Saddled Cow: East Germany's Life and Legacy.* London: Faber and Faber, 1992.

3239 **Merkl, Peter H.,** ed. *The Federal Republic of Germany at Forty.* New York: New York University Press, 1989.

3240 **Mielonen, Mauno.** *Geography of Internal Politics in Finland.* Turku, Finland: Turun Yliopisto, 1969.

3241 **Morawski, Witold.** "Reform Models and Systemic Change in Poland." *Studies in Comparative Communism* [Oxford], 24, No. 3 (September, 1991), 281-294.

3242 **Musil, Jiri.** "Czechoslovakia in the Middle of Transition." *Daedalus* [Cambridge, MA], 121, No. 2 (Spring, 1992).

3243 **Nekrich, Aleksander M.** "Perestroika in History: The First Stage." *Survey*, 30, No. 4 (131) (June, 1989), 22-43.

3244 **Nilseki, Kinya**, ed. *The Soviet Union in Transition*. Boulder, Colorado: Westview Press, 1987.

3245 **Morris, Elizabeth**. "Portugal's Politics Remain Unaltered." *World Today*, 20, No. 1 (January, 1964), 18-25.

3246 **Oleszczuk, Thomas**. "Group Challenges and Ideological Deradicalization in Yugoslavia." *Soviet Studies*, 32, No. 4 (October, 1980), 561-579.

3247 **Oliver, J.H.** "Citizen Demands and the Soviet Political System." *American Political Science Review*, 63, No. 2 (June, 1968), 465-475.

3248 **Olcott, Martha B.**, ed. *The Soviet Multinational State: Reaadings and Documents*. Armonk: M. E. Sharpe, Inc., 1990.

3249 **Parit, P.** "The French Army and la Guerre Revolutionnaire." *Journal of the Royal United Service Institution*, 104 (1959), 59-69.

3250 **Pedreschi, Luigi**. "Le 'Isole Administrative' in Italia." *Revista Geografica Italiona*, 64, No. 2 (June, 1957), 126-144.

3251 **Perrons, D.** "Ireland and the Break-up of Britain." *Antipode*, 12, No. 1 (Summer, 1980), 53-65.

3252 **Petras, James F.** *Latin America: Bankers, Generals, and the Struggle for Social Justice*. Totowa, New Jersey: Rowman & Littlefield, 1986.

3253 **Petry, Ludwig**. "Schlesien im Geschichtsbild der Deutschen." *Schriften des Geographischen Instituts der Universitat Kiel*, Bd. 23 (1964), 78-87.

3254 "Poland and the Polish Nation." *Bulletin of International News*, 18, No. 23 (November 15, 1941), 1859-1870.

3255 **Pond, Elizabeth**. "Germany in the New Europe." *Foreign Affairs* [New York], 71, No. 2 (Spring, 1992), 114-130.

3256 **Rollo, J.M.C.** *The New Eastern Europe: Western Responses*. London: Pinter Publishers, 1990.

3257 **Rotfeld, Adam Daniel**, and **Stutzle, Walther**, eds. *Germany and Europe in Transition*. Oxford: Oxford University Press, 1991

3258 **Sallnow, John**, and **John, Anna**. "Tito's Foundations for Yugoslavia's Future." *Geographical Magazine*, 50, No. 4 (January, 1978), 240-242.

3259 **Sallnow, John**. "What Price Perestroika?" *Geographical Magazine*, 62, 1 (January, 1990), 10-14.

3260 **Salmin, A. M.** "Union after the Union: Problems of Ordering National State Relations in the Former USSR." *Russian Politics and Law* [Armonk], 31, No. 6 (Fall, 1993), 25-63.

3261 **Schlee, Gunther**. "Nomadische Territorialrechte: das Beispiel des kenianisch-althiopischen Grenzlandes." *Die Erde*, Jahr. 120, Heft 2 (1989), 131-138.

3262 **Schwalm, Eberhardt**. "Die Hauptstadt Europas." *Zeitschrift fur Geopolitik*, 24 Jahrg, Heft2 (Februar, 1953), 125-126.

3263 **Sharp, B.** *In Contempt of All Authority: Rural Artisans and Riot in the West of England, 1586-1660*. Berkeley, California: University of California Press, 1980.

3264 **Shevtsov, V.S.** *National Sovereignty and the Soviet State*. Moscow: Progress Publishers, 1974.

3265 **Singleton, F.** "The Roots of Discord in Yugoslavia." *World Today*, 28, No. 4 (April, 1972), 170-180.

3266 **Skilling, H. Gordon**. "The Rumanian National Course." *International Journal*, 21, No. 4 (Autumn, 1966), 470-483.

3267 **Smailes, Peter J.**, and **Kristiansen, Alse**. "Spatial Patterns of Identification with Place and the Norwegian Local Community." *Norsk Geografisk Tidsskrift*, 39, No. 4 (December, 1985), 177-203.

3268 **Solzhenitsyn, Aleksandr**. *Rebuilding Russia: Reflections and Tentative Proposal*. Translated from the Russian and annotated by Alexis Klimoff. New York: Farrar, Straus andGiroux, 1991.

3269 **Stenseth, Dagfinn**. "The New Russia, CIS and the Future." *Security Dialogue* [London], 23, No. 3 (September, 1992).

3270 **Szyndzielorz, Karol J.** "The Drama of Peaceful Change in Poland." *Japan Quarterly*, 37, No. 1 (January-March, 1990), 100-104.

3271 **Taylor, P. J.** "Disunited Kingdom." *Political Geography*, 12, No. 2 (March, 1993), 185-190.

3272 **Thomas, Colin**. "Yugoslavia: The Enduring Dilemmas." *Geography* [Sheffield], 75, Part 3, No. 328 (July, 1990), 265-268.

3273 "The Troubled Outlook in Greece." *World Today*, 4, No. 11 (November, 1948), 461-469.

3274 **Turkey, Mustafa**. "The Balkan Pact and Its Immediate Implications for the Balkan States, 1930-34." *Middle Eastern Studies* [London], 30, No. 1 (January, 1994), 123-144.

3275 **Turner, Henry Ashby, Jr.** *Germany from Partition to Reunification.* Rev. ed. New Haven: Yale University Press, 1992.

3276 **Urban, Michael.** "From Chernenko to Gorbachev: A Repoliticization of Official Soviet Discourse?" *Soviet Union*, 12, No. 2 (1986), 131-161.

3277 **Viitala, Pentti.** "Globaali itschallinto Nakokulma polattisen maantieten teoriaan." *Terra*, 99, No. 4 (1987), 233-240.

3278 **Walker, Christopher J.**, ed. *Armeniea and Karabagh: The Struggle for Unity.* London: Minority Rights Publications, 1991.

3279 **Wallach, H.G.**, and **Francisco, Ronald A.** *United Germany: The Past, Politics, Prospects.* Westport: Greenwood Press, 1992.

3280 **Waller, R.J.** *The Almanac of British Politics.* London: Croom Helm, 1983a.

3281 **Waller, R.J.** *Atlas of British Politics.* London: Croom Helm, 1984.

3282 **Watkins, M.**, ed. *Dene Nation: The Colony Within.* Toronto: University of Toronto Press, 1977.

3283 **Weidenfeld, Werner**, and **Janning, Josef.** "European Integration After the Cold War-- Perspectives of a New Order." *International Social Science Journal* [Oxford], No. 131 (February, 1992), 79-90.

3284 **Wild, Trevor**, and **Jones, Philip N.** "Spatial Impact of German Unification." *The Geographical Journal*, 160, Part 1 (March, 1994), 1-16.

3285 **Wissler, Clark.** "Arctic Geography and Eskimo: A Review of Steensby's Work." *Geographical Review*, 9, No. 2 (February, 1920), 125-138.

3286 **Young, James D.** "Marxism and the Scottish National Question." *Journal of Contemporary History*, 18, No. 1 (January, 1983), 141-163.

3287 **Zudel, Juraj.** "Jozefinska reforma uzemnej organizacie uhorska s osobitnym zretel'om na Slovensko." *Geograficky casopis*, Rocnik 24, Cislo 4 (1972), 313-327.

POWER OF A NATION-STATE

GENERAL AND THEORY

Books and Journals

3288 **Barnett, H.J.** "Energy, Resources, and Growth." In *Resource Scarcity, Economic Growth, and the Environment.* U.S. Congress Joint Economic Committee. Washington, D.C.: U.S. Government Printing Office, 1974, 171-190.

3289 **Bhagwati, J.N.**, and **Desai, P.** *Planning for Industrialization.* New York: Oxford University Press, 1970.

3290 **Brandt, Karl.** "Foodstuffs and Raw Materials as Elements of National Power." In *War in Our Time.* Hans Speier and Alfred Kahler, eds. New York: W.W. Norton, 1939, 105-131.

3291 **Brittan, S.** *Steering the Economy: The Role of the Treasury.* London: Secker and Warburg, 1969.

3292 **Casetti, Emilio**, and **Jones, John Paul III.** "Regional Shifts in the Manufacturing Productivity Response to Output Growth: Sunbelt versus Snowbelt." *Urban Geography*, 4, No. 4 (October-December, 1983), 285-301.

3293 **Cimbala, Stephen Joseph.** "Strategic Vulnerability: A Conceptual Reassessment." *Armed Forces and Society*, 14, No. 2 (Winter, 1988), 191-213.

3294 **Clark, C.** *The Conditions of Economic Progress.* London: Macmillan, 1940.

3295 **Claval, Paul.** *Espace et Pouvoir.* Paris: PUF, 1978.

3296 **Coleman, A.** "Trouble in Utopia: Design Influences in Blocks of Flats." *Geographical Journal*, 150, Part 3 (November, 1984), 351-358.

3297 **Davenport, John Charles.** *The Impact of Economic Sanctions Against South Africa on the Strategic Mineral Position of the United States. The Case of Antimony and Manganese.* New York City: Columbia University, Ph.D., 1982.

3298 **Denoon, D.J.N.** "The Transvaal Labour Crisis, 1901-1906." *Journal of African History*, 7, No. 3 (1967), 481-494.

3299 **Dondo, William Arthur.** *Grain or Dust: A Study of the Soviet New Lands Program 1954-1963.* Minneapolis: University of Minnesota, Ph.D., 1969.

3300 **Easton, David.** "The Environment of a Political System." In *A Framework for Political Analysis.* Englewood Cliffs, New Jersey: Prentice-Hall, 1965, 59-75.

3301 **Engler, Robert.** *The Brotherhood of Oil: Energy Policy and the Public Interest.* Chicago, Illinois: University of Chicago Press, 1977.

3302 **Fox, Irving K.** "Policy Problems in the Field of Water Resources." In *Water Research*, Allen V. Kneese and Stephen C. Smith, eds. Baltimore, Maryland: Resources for the Future, 1966, 271-289.

3303 **Gamble, A.** *The Free Economy and The Strong State.* London: Macmillan, 1988.

3304 **Ginsburg, Norton.** "National Resources and Economic Development." *Annals of the Association of American Geographers*, 47, No. 3 (September, 1957), 197-212.

3305 **Gordon, Lincoln,** and Others. *Eroding Empire: Western Relations with Eastern Europe.* Washington, D.C.: The Brookings Institute, 1987.

3306 **Grayson, J.P.,** ed. *Class, State, Ideology and Change.* Toronto: Holt, Rhinehart & Winston, 1980.

3307 **Greenfield, Liah.** "Nationalism and Class Struggle: Two Forces or One?" *Survey*, 29, No. 3 (126), Autumn, 1985), 153-174.

3308 **Harris, Lillian Craig.** "The State and the Economy: Some Theoretical Problems." *Socialist Register*, 17 (1980), 243-262.

3309 **Hettne, Bjorn.** "Three Worlds of Crisis for the Nation-State." *Development*, Nos. 2-3 (1988), 14-25.

3310 **Hutchins, Wells A.** *Selected Problems in the Law of Water Rights in the West.* Prepared under the supervision of the Solicitor. Miscellaneous Publication No. 418. Washington, D.C.: U.S. Department of Agriculture, 1942.

3311 **Innis, Harold A.** "Political Economy in the Modern State." *Proceedings of the American Philosophical Society*, 87, No. 4 (January 29, 1944), 323-341.

3312 **Johnston, R.J.** "Marxist Political Economy, the State and Political Geography." *Progress in Human Geography*, 8, No. 4 (December, 1984), 473-492.

3313 **Kasperson, Roger E.** "Political Behavior and the Decision-Making Process in the Allocation of Water Resources Between Recreational and Municipal Use." *Natural Resources Journal*, 8, No. 2 (April, 1969).

3314 **Knapp, G.A. van der.** "Labour Market and Spatial Policy." *Tijdschrift voor economische en sociale geografie*, 78, No. 5 (1987), 348-358.

3315 **L'Esperaner, W.L.** *The Structure and Control of a State Economy.* London: Pion, 1981.

3316 **Ley, David,** and Mercer, John. "Locational Conflict and the Politics of Consumption." *Economic Geography*, 56, No. 2 (April, 1980), 89-109.

3317 **Leys, C.** "The 'Overdeveloped' Postcolonial State: A Re-evaluation." *Review of African Political Economy*, 5 (1976), 39-48.

3318 **Macksey, Kenneth.** *Technology in War: The Impact of Science on Weapon Development and Modern Development.* London: Arms and Armour Press, 1986.

3319 **Migdal, Joel S.** *Strong Societies and Weak States: State-Society Relations and State Capabilities in the Third World.* Princeton, New Jersey: Princeton University Press, 1988.

3320 **Mises, Ludwig von.** *Nation, State, and Economy: Contributions to the Politics and History of our Time.* Translated by Leland B. Yeager. The Institute for Humane Studies Series in Economic Theory. New York: New York University Press, 1983.

3321 **Musson, Peter.** "Capitalist Utopias." *Geographical Magazine* [London], 63, No. 8 (August, 1991), 26-28.

3322 **Nicholls, David.** "Prosperous State of Unrest." *Geographical Magazine*, 51, No. 8 (May, 1979), 555-559.

3323 **Platt, Rutherford H.** *The Open Space Decision Process: Spatial Allocation of Costs and Benefits.* Chicago, Illinois: University of Chicago, Department of Geography Research Papers No. 142, 1972.

3324 **Robinson, G.W.S.,** ed. *Economic Consequences of the Size of Nations.* London: Macmillan, 1960.

3325 **Slowe, Peter M.** *Geography and Political Power.* New York: Routledge, 1990.

3326 **Smith, James A.** "Private Players in the Game of Nations." *Washington Quarterly*, 11, No. 3 (Summer, 1988), 17-25.

3327 **Sommerich, Otto C.** "Recent Innovations in Legal and Regulatory Concepts as to the Alien and His Property." *American Journal of International Law*, 37, No. 1 (January, 1943), 58-73.

3328 **Taylor, Peter J.,** and Lijphart, Arend. "Proportional Tenure Versus Proportional Representation: Introducing a New Debate." *European Journal of Political Research.* 13, No. 4 (December, 1985), 387-399.

3329 **Ulman, L.** *The Rise of the National Trade Union.* Cambridge, Massachusetts: Harvard University Press, 1955.

3330 **Woodruff, Douglas.** "Strong Nations or Strong States?" *International Affairs*, 23, No. 1 (January, 1947), 61-71.

POLITICAL GEOGRAPHY OF REGIONS

AFRICA

Books and Journals

3331 **Ashford, Douglas E.** *National Development and Local Reform: Political Participation in Morocco, Tunisia, and Pakistan.* Princeton, New Jersey: Princeton University Press, 1967.

3332 **Azikiwe, Nnamdi.** "Essentials for Nigerian Survival." *Foreign Affairs*, 43, No. 3 (April, 1965), 447-461.

3333 **Barnard, W.S.** "Die Geografie Van'n Revolusionere Oorlog: Swapo In Suidwes-Afrika." *South African Geographer*, 10, No. 2 (September, 1982), 157-174.

3334 **Bassey, Celestine O.** "Retrospects and Prospects of Political Stability in Nigeria." *African Studies Review*, 32, No. 1 (April, 1989), 97-113.

3335 **Bowen, Merle L.** "Beyond Reform: Adjustment and Political Power in Contemporary Mozambique." *The Journal of Modern African Studies* [Cambridge], 30, No. 2 (June, 1992), 255-279.

3336 **Bundy, C.** *The Rise and Fall of the South African Peasantry.* London: Heinemann, 1979.

3337 **Crush, Jonathan S.** "Uneven Labour Migration in Southern Africa: Conceptions and Misconceptions." *South African Geographical Journal*, 66, No. 2 (September, 1984), 115-132.

3338 **Dent, Martin.** "Nigeria after the War." *World Today*, 26, No. 3 (March, 1970), 103-109.

3339 **Eckert, Jerry B.** "The Employment Challenge Facing Lesotho." *Development Studies on Southern Africa*, 5, No. 2 (January, 1983), 248-261.

3340 **Forrest, Joshua.** *Guinea-Bissau: Power, Conflict, and Renewal in a West African Nation.* Boulder: Westview Press, 1992.

3341 **Forrest, T.** "The Political Economy of Civil Rule and the Economic Crisis in Nigeria." *Review of African Political Economy*, 35 (1986), 4-26.

3342 **Government of Lesotho** (GOL). *Kingdom of Lesotho, Third Five-Year Development Plan.* Maserv: Government Printer, 1980.

3343 **Gukiina, Peter M.** *Uganda: A Case Study in African Political Development.* Notre Dame, Indiana: University of Notre Dame Press, 1972.

3344 **Harris, Gordon.** "Political Instability and the Information World in Uganda." *African Research and Documentation*, 37 (1985), 42-46.

3345 **Heinzen, Barbara J.** "The United Fruit Company in the 1950's--Trusteeship in the Cameroons." *African Economic History*, 12 (1983), 141-156.

3346 **Herbst, Jeffrey.** *State Politics in Zimbabwe.* Berkeley: University of California Press, 1990.

3347 **Ihonvbere, Julius O.** "Nigeria as Africa's Great Power: Constraints and Prospects for the 1990s." *International Journal* [Toronto], 46, No. 3 (Summer, 1991), 510-535.

3348 **Jackson, Robert H., and Rosberd, Carl G.** "Why Africa's Weak States Persist: The Empirical and the Juridical in Statehood." *World Politics*, 35, No. 1 (October, 1982), 1-24.

3349 **Lonsdale, J., and Berman, B.** "Coping with Contradictions: The Development of the Colonial State in Kenya, 1895-1914." *Journal of African History*, 20, No. 4 (1979), 487-505.

3350 **Miles, William F.S.** "Self-identity, Ethnic Affinity and National Consciousness: An Example from Rural Hausaland." *Ethnic and Racial Studies*, 9, No. 4 (October, 1986), 427-444.

3351 **Moore, Robert C.** *The Political Reality of Freedom of the Press in Zambia.* Lanham: University Press of America, 1992.

3352 **Murray, L.** *Families Divided: The Impact of Migrant Labour on Lesotho.* London: Cambridge University Press, 1981.

3353 **Sano, H.O.** *The Political Economy of Food in Nigeria 1960-1982.* Research Report No. 65. Uppsala: Scandinavian Institute of African Studies, 1983.

3354 **Schmitz, G.,** ed. *Lesotho: Environment and Management.* Vol. 1. Roma: National University of Lesotho, 1983.

3355 **Southall, Roger J.** *South Africa's Transkei: The Political Econmy of an 'Independent' Bantustan.* London: Heinemann, 1982.

3356 **Tareke, Gubru.** *Ethiopia: Power and Protest-- Peasant Revolts in the Twentieth Century.* Cambridge: Cambridge University Press, 1991.

3357 **Taylor, J.** "Changing Patterns of Labour Supply to the South African Gold Mines." *Tijdschrift voor Economische en Sociale Geografie*, 73, No. 4 (August-September, 1982), 213-220.

3358 **Tripp, Charles**, ed. *Contemporary Egypt: Through Egyptian Eyes. Essays in Honour of Professor P. J. Vatikiotis.* London: Routledge, 1993.

3359 **Turner, Stansfield D.** *Sesotho Farming: The Condition and Prospects of Agriculture in the Lowlands and Foothills of Lesotho.* London, England: University of London, Ph.D., 1978.

3360 **Unger, Sanford J.** *Africa: The People and Politics of an Emerging Continent.* New York: Simon and Schuster, 1985.

3361 **van Deventer, W., and van der Merwe, I.J.** "'N Ruimtelike en sosio-ekonomiese Profiel van Ekonomies Aktiewe Vrove in Kaapstad." *South African Geographer*, 14, No. 1/2 (September, 1986/April, 1987), 65-76.

3362 **Ward, Michael D.** "Economic Independence for Lesotho?" *Journal of Modern African Studies*, 5, No. 3 (November, 1967), 355-368.

3363 **Watts, Michael J.** *Silent Violence: Food, Famine and Peasantry in Northern Nigeria.* Berkeley: University of California Press, 1983.

3364 **Yeebo, Zaya.** *Ghana: The Struggle for Popular Power. Rawlings: Saviour or Demagogue.* London: New Beacon Books, 1991.

3365 **Zartman, William I.** *Morocco: Problems of New Power.* New York: Atherton Press, 1964.

AMERICAS

Books and Journals

3366 **Biechler, Michael Joseph.** *The Coffee Industry of Guatemala: A Geographic Analysis.* Ann Arbor: Michigan State University, Ph.D., 1970.

3367 **Borchert, John R.** "Major Control Points in American Economic Geography." *Annals of the Association of American Geographers.* 68, No. 2 (June, 1978), 214-232.

3368 **Brunn, Stanley D., and Wheeler, J.O.** "Spatial Dimensions of Poverty in the U.S." *Geografiska Annaler*, 53B (January, 1971), 6-15.

3369 **Calvert, Susan and Calvert, Peter.** *Argentina: Political Culture and Instability.* Houndmills: Macmillan, 1989.

3370 **Clarke, C.G.** "Insularity and Identity in the Caribbean." *Geography*, 61, Part 1, No. 270 (January, 1976), 8-16.

3371 **Cusack, David F.** *Revolution and Reaction: The International Dynamics of Conflict and Confrontation in Chile.* Denver, Colorado: University of Denver, Graduate School of International Studies, Monograph Series in World Affairs, Vol. 14, Book 3, 1977.

3372 **Gilmour, James Muckle.** *Structure and Spatial Change in Manufacturing Industry: South Ontario 1850-1890.* Toronto, Ontario, Canada: University of Toronto, Ph.D., 1970.

3373 **Hansen, Roger D.** *The Politics of Mexican Development.* Baltimore, Maryland: Johns Hopkins University Press, 1971.

3374 **Holdsworth, Deryck.** "Dependence, Diversity and the Canadian Identity." *Journal of Geography*, 83, No. 5 (September-October, 1984), 199-204.

3375 **James, Preston E.** "Forces for Unity and Disunity in Brazil." *Journal of Geography*, 38, No. 7 (October, 1939), 260-266.

3376 **Karl, T.** *The Political Economy of Petro-Dollars: Oil and Democracy in Venezuela.* Stanford, California: Stanford University, Ph.D., 1982.

3377 **Kearns, Kevin C.** "Prospects of Sovereignty and Economic Viability for British Honduras." *Professional Geographer*, 21, No. 2 (March, 1969), 97-103.

3378 **Kinzo, Maria D'Alva G.,** ed. *Brazil: The Challenges of the 1990s.* London: The Institute of Latin American Studies, University of London, 1993.

3379 **Large, D.C.** "Cotton in the San Joaquin Valley: A Study of Government in Agriculture." *Geographical Review*, 47, No. 3 (July, 1957), 365-380.

3380 **Lauria, Mickey.** "Toward a Specificaiton of the Local State: State Intervention Strategies in Response to a Manufacturing Plant Closure (Dubuque, Iowa). *Antipode*, 18, No. 1 (1986), 39-63.

3381 **Lloyd, Donald Loftus.** *The Patterns and Problems of Agriculture Within Kent and Northumberland Counties, New Brunswick, Canada, 1961-1968.* Baltimore: University of Maryland, Ph.D., 1971.

3382 **Mack, Andrew.** "The Political Economy of Global Decline: America in 1980's." *Australian Outlook*, 40, No. 1 (April, 1986), 11-20.

3383 **Malloy, James M.** "Democracy, Economic Crisis nad the Problem of Governance: The Case of Bolivia." *Studies in Comparative International Development* [New Brunswick], 26, No. 2 (Summer, 1991, 37-57.

3384 **Morrill, Richard L., and Wohlenberg, Ernest Harold.** *Geography of Poverty in the United States.* New York: McGraw-Hill, 1972.

3385 **Olch, Isaiah**. "A Resume of National Interests in the Caribbean Area." *United States Naval Institute Proceedings*, 66, No. 2 (February, 1940), 165-176.

3386 **Rea, K.J.** *The Political Economy of the Canadian North: An Interpretation of the Course of Development in the Northern Territories of Canada to the Early 1960's*. Toronto: Published in association with the University of Saskatchewan by University of Toronto Press, 1968.

3387 **Schmidt, John D.** "Quebec, A Viable Political State." Washington, D.C.: George Washington University, M.A., 1969.

3388 **Smith, David M.** *Crime Rates as Territorial Indicator: The Case of the United States*. London: University of London, Queen Mary College, Department of Geography, Occasional Paper No. 1, 1974.

3389 **Trouillot, Michel-Rolph.** *Haiti, State Against Nation: The Origins and Legacy of Duvalierism.* New York: Monthly review Press, 1990.

3390 **True, David W.** *State Power Indices: A Case Study of South America*. Athens, OH: Master's thesis, Ohio University, 1993.

3391 **Turner, Frederick C.** "Regional Hegemony and the Case of Brazil." *International Journal* [Toronto], 46, No. 3 (Summer, 1991), 475-509.

3392 **Vidal, Julio.** *Dependency, Regional Inequality and the Role of the State: Puerto Rico, 1950-1982 (Economics, Development Policy, Post-Industrial, International Relations Theory)*. Albany: State University of New York, Ph.D., 1985.

3393 **West, Max I.** "Transportation Networks as Determinants of Effective National Territory--The Case of Bolivia." *Ohio Geographers*, 10 (1982), 31-42.

ASIA

Books and Journals

3394 **Abir, Mordechai.** *Saudi Arabia: Government, Society and the Gulf Crisis*. London: Routledge, 1993.

3395 **Alexander, P.C.** *Industrial Estates in India*. Bombay: Asia Publishing House, 1963.

3396 **Berberoglu, Berch,** ed. *Power and Stability in the Middle East*. London: Zed Books, 1989.

3397 **Bhargava, Pradeep.** *Political Economy of Sri Lanka*. New Delhi: Navrang, 1987.

3398 **Chao, Kuo-Chun.** "The Government and Economy of Manchuria." *Far Eastern Survey*, 22, No. 13 (December, 1953), 169-175; 23, No. 1 (January, 1954), 9-14.

3399 **Cressey, George.** *The Basis of Soviet Strength*. New York: McGraw-Hill, 1945.

3400 **Crossette, Barbara.** *India: Facing the Twenty-First Century*. Bloomington: Indiana University Press, 1993.

3401 **Cutshall, Alden.** "Mineral Resources of the Philippine Islands." *Scientific Monthly*, 44, No. 4 (April, 1942), 295-302.

3402 **Dhar, Panna Lal.** "The Kashmir Problem: Political and Economic Background." *India Quarterly*, 7, No. 2 (April-June, 1951), 142-162.

3403 **Dhar, Panna Lal**, and Lydall, H.F. *Role of Small Scale Industries in India*. Delhi: Asia Publishing House, 1961.

3404 **Drake, Christine.** *National Integration in Indonesia: Patterns and Policies*. Honolulu: University of Hawaii Press, 1989.

3405 **Frankel, Francine R.** *India's Political Economy 1947-1977--The Gradual Revolution*. Oxford: Oxford University Press, 1978.

3406 **Gray, W.A.H.** *Power and Politics in Hyderabad (Andhra Pradesh)*. London, England: University of London School of Oriental and African Studies, Ph.D., 1965.

3407 **Hashim, Ahmed.** "Iraq, the Pariah State." *Current History* [Philadelphia], 91, No. 561 (January, 1992), 11-16.

3408 **Hopwood, Derek; Ishow, Habib; Koszinoski, Thomas,** eds. *Iraq: Power and Society*. Reading: Ithaca Press, 1993.

3409 **Horton, Frank E.; McConnell, Harold;** and **Iirtha, Ranjit.** "Spatial Patterns of Social-Economic Structure in India." *Tijdschrift voor economische en sociale geografie*, 61, No. 2 (March-April, 1970), 101-113.

3410 **Housego, David.** "Iran in the Ascendant, Economic Strengths, Political Weakness." *Round Table*, 28 (October, 1972), 497-507.

3411 **Hudson, M.** *The Precarious Republic: Political Modernization of Lebanon*. New York: Random House, 1968.

3412 **Johnson, W.A.** *Steel Industry of India*. Cambridge, Massachusetts: Harvard University Press, 1966.

3413 **Kamiar, Mohammad.** "Changes in Spatial and Temporal Patterns of Development in Iran." *Political Geography Quarterly*, 7, No. 4 (October, 1988), 323-339.

3414 **Lo, Carlos W.H.** "Deng Xiaoping's Ides on Law: China on the Threshold of a Legal Order." *Asian Survey* [Berkeley], 32, No. 7 (July, 1992), 649-665.

3415 **Mahler, Gregory S.**, ed. *Israel After Begin.* Albany: State University of New York Press, 1990.

3416 **Malenbaum, Wilfred.** "Politics and Indian Business. The Economic Setting." *Asian Survey*, 11, No. 9 (September, 1971), 841-849.

3417 **Maniruzzaman, Talukdar.** "Bangladesh in 1974: Economic Crisis and Political Polarization." *Asian Survey*, 15, No. 2 (February, 1975), 117-128.

3418 **Mathur, Kuldeep.** "The State and the Use of Coercive Power in India." *Asian Survey* [Berkeley], 32, No. 4 (April, 1992), 337-349.

3419 **McGee, T.G.** "Industrial Capital, Labour Force Formation and the Urbanization Process in Malaysia." *International Journal of Urban and Regional Research*, 12, No. 3 (1988), 356-374.

3420 **Mellor, John W., and Talbot, Phillips.** *India: A Rising Middle Power.* Boulder, Colorado: Westview Press, 1979.

3421 **Mirheydar, Dorreh.** *Geographic Factors in the Political Variability in Iran.* Bloomington: Indiana University, Ph.D., 1962.

3422 **Moore, Mick.** *The State & Peasant Politics in Sri Lanka.* Cambridge: Cambridge University Press, 1985.

3423 **Mukerji, A.B.** "Kashmir: A Study in Political Geography. Economic Strength and Weakness." *Geographical Review of India*, 18, No. 1 (March, 1956), 15-29.

3424 **Mukerjee, Radhakamal.** *An Economist Looks at Pakistan.* Bombay: Hind Kitabs, 1944.

3425 **Neher, Clark D.** "Political Succession in Thailand." *Asian Survey* [Berkeley], 32, No. 7 (July, 1992), 585-605.

3426 **Nicholson, Norman L.** "Political Aspects of Indian Food Policy." *Pacific Affairs*, 41, No. 1 (Spring, 1968), 34-50.

3427 **Noorani, A.G.** "India's Quest for a Nuclear Guarantee." *Asian Survey*, 7, No. 7 (July, 1967), 490-502.

3428 **Noman, Omar.** *The Political Economy of Pakistan 1947-85.* London: KPI Limited, 1988.

3429 **O'Ballance, Edgar.** "The Strength of India." *Military Review*, 42, No. 1 (January, 1962), 25-35.

3430 **Owen, Roger.** *State, Power and Politics in the Making of the Modern Middle East.* London: Routledge, 1992.

3431 **Pyle, Kenneth B.** *The Japanese Question: Power and Purpose in a New Era.* Washington, D.C.: The AEI Press, 1992.

3432 **Ra, Jong Yil.** "Political Crisis in Korea, 1952: The Administration, Legislature, Military and Foreign Powers." *Journal of Contemporary History* [London], 27, No. 2 (April, 1992), 301-318.

3433 **Reddy, G.P., and Sudarsen, V.** "The Institution of Captainship: A Traditional Political System of the Nieobar Islands." *Mankind Quarterly*, 27, No. 1 (Fall, 1986), 63-75.

3434 **Regmi, M.C.** *Landownership in Nepal.* Berkeley: University of California Press, 1976.

3435 **Regmi, M.C.** *Land Tenure and Taxation in Nepal* (four vols.). Berkeley: Institute of International Studies, University of California, 1963-1964.

3436 **Reich, Bernard, and Kieval, Gershon R.**, eds. *Israel Faces the Future.* New York: Praeger, 1986.

3437 **Reitsman, H.A.** "Agricultural Transboundary Differences in the Okanagan Region." *Journal of Rural Studies.* 2 (1986), 53-62.

3438 **Salih, Kamal Osman.** "Kuwait: Political Consequences of Modernization, 1750-1986." *Middle Eastern Studies* [London], 27, No. 1 (January, 1991), 46-66.

3439 **Schram, S. R.**, ed. *Foundations and Limits of State Power in China.* London: School of Oriental and African Studies, University of London, 1987.

3440 **Scott, J.C.** *The Moral Economy of the Peasant: Rebellion and Subsistence in Southeast Asia.* New Haven, Connecticut: Yale University Press, 1976.

3441 **Segal, Gerald.** "As China Grows Strong." *International Affairs*, 64, No. 2 (Spring, 1988), 217-231.

3442 **Selya, Roger Mark.** *The Industrialization of Taiwan: A Geographic Analysis.* Minneapolis: University of Minnesota, Ph.D., 1971.

3443 **Shrestha, B.P.** *The Economy of Nepal.* Bombay: Vora, 1967.

3444 **Sulivan, Lawrence R.** "Leadership and Authority in the Chinese Communist Party: Perspectives from the 1950's." *Pacific Affairs*, 59, No. 4 (Winter, 1986-87), 605-633.

3445 **Tanter, Raymond.** *Who's at the Helm?: Lessons of Lebanon.* Boulder: Westview Press, 1990.

3446 **Thrift, N.** "Vietnam: A Geography of a Socialist Siege Economy." *Geography*, 72, No. 4 (1987), 340-344.

3447 **Wallace, Paul.** "India: The Dispersion of Political Power." *Asian Survey*, 8, No. 2 (February, 1968), 87-96.

3448 **Yahr, Charles C.** *Present Economy and Potential Development of the Baluchistan States of Pakistan.* Urbana: University of Illinois, Ph.D., 1956.

3449 **Zaidi, Iqtidar H.** *Land Tenure System: A Problem in Political Geography of Punjab.* New Delhi: Proceedings, International Geographical Congress, 1968.

AUSTRALIA, OCEANIA AND ANTARCTICA

Books and Journals

3450 **Carnegie Endowment.** *The Arctic and Antarctic Regions; With Special Reference to Territorial Claims.* 3 mimeographed 1. Brief Reference List No. 18. Washington, D.C.: Carnegie Endowment for International Peace, 1940.

3451 **Kellow, A.** "Public Project Evaluation on an Australian State: Tasmania's Dam Controversy." *Australian Quarterly*, 55, No. 3 (September, 1983), 263-277.

3452 **Premdas, Ralph R.** "Succession and Political Change: The Case of Papua Besena." *Oceania*, 47, No. 4 (June, 1977), 265-283.

3453 **Sornarajah, M.,** ed. *The Southwest Dam Dispute: The Legal and Political Issues.* Hobart: University of Tasmania, 1983.

3454 **Taplin, R.,** and **Tighe, P.** *The Implications of Uneven Resource Development for Tasmania.* Environmental Studies Occasional Paper No. 14. Hobart: University of Tasmania, 1982.

3455 **Thompson, R.** *Power in Tasmania.* Melbourne: Australian Conservation Foundation, 1981.

EUROPE

Books and Journals

3456 **Bornstein, Stephen; Held, David;** and **Krieger, Joel,** eds. *The State in Capitalist Europe: A Casebook.* Winchester, MA: Allen & Unwin, 1984.

3457 **Brovkin, Vladimir.** "Revolution from Below: Informal Political Associations in Russia, 1988-1989." *Soviet Studies* [Glasgow], 42, No. 2 (April, 1990), 233-257.

3458 **Bryer, R.A.; Brignall, T.J.;** and **Maunders, A.R.** *Accounting for British Steel.* Aldershot: Gower Publishing, 1982.

3459 **Bueno de Mesquita, Bruce.** "Pride of Place: The Origins of German Hegemony." *World Politics* [Baltimore], 43, No. 1 (October, 1990), 28-52.

3460 **Bulpitt, Jim G.** *Territory and Power in the United Kingdom.* Manchester, England: Manchester University Press, 1983.

3461 **Cockerill, A.** "Steel and the State in Great Britain." *annals of Public and Cooperative Economy*, 51, No. 4 (October-December, 1980), 439-457.

3462 **Cox, Kevin R.,** and **Mair, Andrew.** "Locality and Community in the Politics of Local Economic Development." *Annals of the Association of American Geographers*, 78, 2 (June 1988), 307-325.

3463 **CSE State Group.** *Struggle Over the State: Cuts and Restructuring in Contemporary Britain.* London: CSE Books, 1979.

3464 **Davies, R.W.** *Soviet History in the Gorbachev Revolution.* Houndmills: Macmillan, 1989.

3465 **Fourny, M.C.** "Local Politics and Deindustrialisation in the Inner Suburbs of Paris." *Herodote*, 43 (1986), 123-139.

3466 **Frey, B.,** and **Schneider, F.** "A Politico-Economic Model of the United Kingdom." *Economic Journal*, 88, No. 2 (June, 1978), 243-253.

3467 **Hill, Ronald J.** "Glastnost' and Soviet Politics." *Coexistence*, 26, No. 4 (1989), 317-331.

3468 **Holc, Janine P.** "Solidarity and the Polish State: Competing Discursive Strategies on the Road to Power." *East European Politics and Societies* [Berkeley], 6, No. 2 (Spring, 1992), 121-151.

3469 **Horne, Alistair.** *Return to Power; A Report on the New Germany.* New York: Praeger, 1956.

3470 **House, J.W.** *The U.K. Space: Resources, Environment and the Future, 3rd ed.* London: Weidenfeld and Nicolson, 1982.

3471 **Kay, M. A.** "The Yugoslav Government-in-Exile and the Problem of Restoration." *East European Quarterly* [Boulder], 25, No. 1 (Spring, 1991), 1-19.

3472 **Keating, M.,** and **Hainsworth, P.** *Decentralisation and Change in Contemporary France.* London: Gower Publishing, 1986.

3473 **Khasbulatov, Ruslan.** *The Struggle for Russia: Power and Change in the Democratic Revolution.* London: Routledge, 1993.

3474 **MacLaughlin, James G., and Agnew, John A.** "Hegemony and the Regional Question: The Political Geography of Regional Industrial Policy in Northern Ireland, 1945-1972." *Annals of the Association of American Geographers*, 76, No. 2 (June, 1986), 247-261.

3475 **Martin, David.** "Portugal: The Real Structure of Power." *Africa Report*, 20, No. 3 (May-June, 1974), 6-10.

3476 **Nowak, Krzysztof.** "Covert Repressiveness and the Stability of a Political Systlem: Poland and the End of the Seventies." *Social Research*, 55, Nos. 1-2 (Spring/Summer, 1988), 179-208.

3477 **Otto, Archduke of Austria.** "Danubian Reconstruction." *Foreign Affairs*, 20, No. 2 (January, 1942), 243-252.

3478 **Owens, S.** "Environmental Politics in Britain: New Paradigm or Placebo?" *Areas*, 18, No. 3 (March, 1986), 195-201.

3479 **Ruostetsaari, Ilkka.** "The Anatomy of the Finnish Power Elite." *Scandainavian Political Studies* [Oslo], 16, No. 4 (1993), 305-337.

3480 **Shesstani, Kin.** "Synthese economica-politique des Balkans." *Hermes Bulletin de la Faculte de Commerce de l'Universite Laval*, 2, No. 2 (January, 1953), 20-37.

3481 **Wiles, Peter.** "The Soviet Economy Outpaces the West." *Foreign Affairs*, 31, No. 4 (July, 1953), 566-581.

3482 **Wilsford, David.** "Tactical Advantages Versus Administrative Heterogeneity: The Strengths and the Limits of the French State." *Comparative Political Studies* (Newbury Park), 21, No. 1 (April, 1988), 126-168.

3483 **Zuzowski, Robert.** "The Origins of Open Organized Dissent in Today's Poland: KOR and Other Dissident Groups." *East European Quarterly* [Boulder], 25, No. 1 (Spring, 1991), 59-90.

CORE AREAS AND CAPITAL CITIES

GENERAL AND THEORY

Books and Journals

3484 **Adejuyigbe, Omolade.** "Factors in the Location of Administrative Capitals." *Nigerian Geographical Journal*, 15, No. 2 (December, 1972), 127-141.

3485 **Augelli, John P.** "Brasilia: The Emergence of a National Capital." *Journal of Geography*, 62, No. 6 (1963), 241-252.

3486 **Best, Alan C.G.** "Capitals for the Homelands." *Journal of Geography*, 3, No. 10 (April, 1972), 1043-1055.

3487 **Best, Alan C.G.** "Problems and Prospects of a New Capital." *Geographical Review*, 60, No. 1 (January, 1970), 1-14.

3488 **Browning, Clyde E.** "The State Capitals: Meaningful Geographic Analysis V/S Memorization." *Journal of Geography*, 69, No. 1 (January, 1970), 40-44.

3489 **Bueno, Jeronimo Coimbra.** "Interiorizacao do Capital Federal." *Boletin Geografico*, 12, No. 120 (May-June, 1954), 287-297.

3490 **Burghardt, Andrew F.** "The Core Concept in Political Geography: A Definition of Terms." *Canadian Geographer*, 13, No. 4 (Winter, 1969), 349-353.

3491 **Cornish, Vaughan.** *The Great Capitals: An Historical Geography.* London: Methuen, 1923.

3492 **Fabriani, Ferrucio.** "Planejamento geografico e localizacao da nova capital federal." *Engenharia*, 8, No. 90 (1950), 259-266.

3493 **Fisher, Morris, comp.** *Provinces and Provincial Capitals of the World.* New York: Scarecrow Press, 1967.

3494 **Gottmann, Jean.** "The Role of Capital Cities." *Ekisties*, 44, No. 264 (November, 1977), 240-243.

3495 **Hailey, William Malcolm, Baron.** "Capital and Colonies." *Journal of the Royal Society of Arts*, 91, No. 4645 (August 6, 1943), 474-485.

3496 **Halloway, J., and Picciotto, S.** *State and Capital: A Marxist Debate.* London: Edward Arnold, 1978.

3497 **Jefferson, Mark.** "The Law of the Primate City." *Geographical Review*, 29, No. 2 (April, 1939), 226-232.

3498 **Korff, Rudiger.** "Who Has Power in Bangkok? An Approach Towards the Analysis of Straetgic Group and Class Formation in an Asian Primate City." *International Journal of Urban and Regional Research*, 10, No. 3 (September, 1986), 330-350.

3499 **Kazou, Yawata.** "Why and Where to Relocate the Capital." *Japan Quarterly*, 35, No. 2 (April-June, 1988), 127-132.

3500 **Kudriavsten, C.K., and Kubetskaya, L.I.**
"Structural Features of the Formation of New
Capitals and the Restructuring of Old Ones in
Developing Countries. In *Urbanization in
Developing Countries.* Edited by S. Manzoor
Alam and V.V. Pokshishevsky. Hyderabad: India
Osmania University, 1976, 83-111.

3501 **Luz-Neto, Christiano Carneiro Rebeiro da.** "A
Transferencia da capital do pais." *Engenharia
Municipal*, 2, No. 5 (Marco, 1957), 19-21.

3502 **Melo, Mario.** "A evolucao da capital de
Pernambuco." *Revista do Instituto archeologico
historico e geographico pernambucano*,
31, Nos. 147 a 150 (1931), Pub. 1933, 75-85.

3503 **Murphy, Marion F.** "A Capital Idea for Siting
the Seats of Government." *Landscape.* 21, No. 1
(Autumn, 1976), 41-47.

3504 **Parboni, R.** "Capital and the Nation State: A
Reply to Frieden." *New Left Review*, 137
(January-February, 1983), 87-96.

3505 **Peixoto, Joao Batista.** "A mudanca da capital e a
redivisao territorial; dois magnos problemas
geopoliticos, contra os quais nao se tem
argumentos." *A Defesa Nacional*, 494 (Sept.,
1955), 63-71.

3506 **Queiroz, Eunapio.** "Mudanca da Capital do pais:
Parecer da comisssao parlamentar." *Boletim
Geografico*, (Julho, 1949), 333-370.

3507 **Rodrigues, Lysias A.** "A mudanca da capital
federal." *Cultura politica*, 2, No. 20 (Out., 1942),
115-120.

3508 **Saxena, N.P., and Tyagi, R.C.** "Delineation of
the National Capital Region: A Review."
Geographical Observer, 10 (March, 1974), 48-58.

3509 **Spate, O.H.K.** "Factors in the Development of
Capital Cities." *Geographical Review*, 32, No. 4
(October, 1942), 622-631.

3510 **Spate, O.H.K.** "Two Federal Capitals: New
Delhi and Canberra." *Geographical Outlook*, 1,
No. 1 (January, 1956), 1-8.

3511 **Stephenson, Glenn V.** "Two Newly-Created
Capitals: Islamabad and Brasilia." *Town Planning
Review*, 41, No. 4 (October, 1970), 317-332.

3512 **Taylor, John; Lengelle, Jean G.; Andrew,
Caroline,** eds. *Capital Cities: International
Perspectives.* Ottawa: Carleton University Press,
1993.

3513 **Vale, Lawrence J.** "Capitol Complexes: Urban
Design and National Security." *Journal of
Architectural and Planning Research* [Chicago], 10,
No. 4 (Winter, 1993), 273-283.

3514 **Van Der Berg, L.; Drewett, R.; Klaassen, L.H.;
Rossi, A.; and Vijverberg, C.H.T.** *Europe: A
Study of Growth and Decline.* Oxford: Pergamon,
1982.

3515 **Wellhofer, E. Spencer.** "Core and Periphery:
Territorial Dimensions in Politics." *Urban Studies*,
26, No. 3 (June, 1989), 340-355.

3516 **Whebell, C.F.J.** "Core Areas in Intrastate
Political Organization." *Canadian Geographer*,
12, No. 2 (Summer, 1968), 99-112.

POLITICAL GEOGRAPHY OF REGIONS

AFRICA

Books and Journals

3517 **Acquah, Ione.** *Accra, Survey: A Social Survey of
the Capital of Ghana.* London: University of
London Press, 1958.

3518 **Adejuyigbe, Omolade.** "The Case for a New
Federal Capital in Nigeria." *Journal of Modern
African Studies*, 8, No. 2 (July, 1970), 301-306.

3519 **Armstrong, Allen.** "Ivory Coast: Another New
Capital for Africa." *Geography*, 70, Part 1,
No. 306 (January, 1984), 72-74.

3520 **Bening, R.B.** "Locations of Regional and
Provincial Capitals in Northern Ghana,
1897-1960." *Bulletin of Ghana Geographical
Association*, 16 (1974), 54-66.

3521 **Denis, Par Jacques.** "Addis Ababa: Genese
d'une capitale Imperiale." *Revue Belge de
Geographie*, 88, No. 3 (1964), 283-314.

3522 **Christopher, A.J.** "Continuity and Change of
African Capitals." *Geographical Review*, 75,
No. 1 (January, 1985), 44-57.

3523 **Fluchard, Claude.** "Croissance d'une capitale
africaine: Abidjan." *Revue belge de Geographie*,
113° anne Fasc. 42,(1989), 3-12.

3524 **Foran, W. Robert.** "Rise of Nairobi: From
Campsite to City." *Crown Colonist*, 20, No. 220
(1950), 161-165.

3525 **Hamdan, G.** "Capitals of the New Africa."
Economic Geography, 40, No. 3 (July, 1964),
239-253.

3526 **Hoyle, B.S.** "African Socialism and Urban
Development: The Relocation of the Tanzanian
Capital." *Tijdschrift voor Economische en Social
Geografie*, 70, No. 6 (November-December,
1979), 207-216.

3527 **Jensen, Lois.** "Making Human Scale Investments in Tanzania's New Capital." *World Development*, 1, No. 3 (July, 1988), 20-24.

3528 **Kirk-Greene, A.H.M., and Campbell, M.J.** "The Capitals of Northern Nigeria." *Nigeria*, 54 (1957), 243-272.

3529 **Lincoln, David.** "State, Capital and the Reserve Consolidation Issue in South Africa." *Tijdscrift voor Economische en Sociale Geografie*, 73, No. 4 (August-September, 1982), 229-236.

3530 **Lugalla, Joe L.P.** "Is Dodoma, the New Capital City of Tanzania, a Socialist City? *African Urban Quarterly*, 2, No. 2 (May, 1987), 134-148.

3531 **Marguerat, Yves.** "Capitales en Balade: Remarques Historico-Geographiques Sur les Changements de Capitale en Africque Noire." *Les Cahiers d'outre-mer* [Bordeaux], 44e, No. 175 (Juillet-Septembre, 1991), 217-242.

3532 **Matson, A.T.** "Uganda's Old Eastern Province and East Africa's Federal Capital." *Uganda Journal*, 22 (1958), 43.

3533 **Medugbon, Andrew Kayode.** *Kaduna Nigeria: The Vicissitudes of a Capital City, 1917 to 1975.* Los Angeles: University of California, Ph.D., 1976.

3534 "New Nigerian Capital." *Military Engineer*, 69, No. 450 (July-August, 1977), 260-261.

3535 **Nwafor, J.C.** "The Relocation of Nigeria's Federal Capital: A Device for Greater Territorial Integration and National Unity." *GeoJournal*, 4, No. 4 (July, 1980), 359-366.

3536 **Olu Sule, R.A.** "Ethno-Spatial Dimensions of the Abuja Settlement as the New Nigerian Capital City: The Dilemma of Urban Planning Society." *African Urban Quarterly*, 2, No. 2 (May, 1987), 87-95.

3537 **Potts, Deborah.** "Capital Relocation in Africa: The Case of Lilongwe in Malawi." *Geographical Journal*, 151, No. 2 (July, 1985), 182-196.

3538 **Potts, Deborah.** "The Development of Malawi's New Capital at Lilongwe: A Comparison with other New African Capitols." *Comparative Urban Research*, 10, No. 2 (1985), 42-56.

3539 **Simon, David.** *Cities, Capital, and Development: African Cities in the World Economy.* New York: John Wiley and Sons, 1992.

3540 **Vennetier, Pierre.** "Kinshasa, Capitale du Zaire." *Les Cahiers d'Outre-Mer*, 34° Annee, No. 133 (Janvier-Mars, 1981), 70-73.

3541 **Willaims, Geoffrey J.,** ed. *Lusaka and Its Evnirons: A Geographical Study of a Planned Capital City in Tropical Africa.* Lusaka: The Zambia Geographical Association, 1986.

3542 **Wolde-Michael, Akalou.** "The Impermanency of Royal Capitals in Ethiopia." *Yearbook of the Association of Pacific Coast Geographers*, 28 (1966), 147-156.

AMERICAS

Books and Journals

3543 **Agnew, John A.** "Beyond Core and Periphery: The Myth of Regional Political-Economic Restructuring and Sectionalism in Contemporary American Politics." *Political Geography Quarterly*, 71, No. 2 (April, 1988), 127-139.

3544 **Ames, David Lyndle.** *The Utility and Dynamics of Commercial-Industrial Blight: A Case Study of the Core Area of Worcester, Massachusetts.* Worchester, Massachusetts: Clark University, Ph.D., 1969.

3545 **Beardsley, Arthur S.** "Early Efforts to Locate the Capital of Washington Territory." *Pacific Northwest Quarterly*, 32, No. 3 (July, 1941), 239-287.

3546 **Beardsley, Arthur S.** "Latter Attempts to Relocate the Capital of Washington." *Pacific Northwest Quarterly*, 32, No. 4 (October, 1941), 401-447.

3547 **Bernardes, Lysia M.C.** "Les villes capitales d'etat au Bresil: une interpretation." *Cahiers de Geographie de Quebec*, 15 Annee, No. 35 (Septembre, 1971), 171-190.

3548 **Bird, Annie Laurie.** "A Footnote on the Capital Dispute in Idaho." *Pacific Northwest Quarterly*, 36, No. 4 (October, 1945), 341-346.

3549 **Boal, Frederick W.** "One Foot on Each Bank of the Ottawa." *The Canadian Geographer* [Toronto], 37, No. 4 (Winter, 1993), 320-331.

3550 **Bowling, Kenneth R.** *The Creation of Washington, D.C.: The Idea and Location of the American Capital.* Fairfax: George Mason University Press, 1991.

3551 **Carroll, Glenn R., and Meyer, John W.** "Capital Cities in the American Urban System: The Impact of State Expansion." *American Journal of Sociology*, 88, No. 3 (November, 1982), 565-578.

3552 **Castro, Christovam Leite de.** "A Transferencia da capital do Brasil para o Planalto Central." *Revista do instituto Historico e geografico Brasileiro*, 200 (Julho-Set., 1950), 132-133.

3553 Chaffee, Eugene B. "The Political Clash Between North and South Idaho Over the Capital." *Pacific Northwest Quarterly*, 29, No. 3 (July, 1938), 255-267.

3554 Coelho, Djalma Poli. "A localizacao da nov capital do Brasil." *Revista Geografica*, 15, No. 41 (2° Sem., 1954), 1-31.

3555 Cortesao, Jaime. *A Fundacao de Sao Paulo, Capital geografica do Brasil*. Rio de Janeiro: Livros de Portugal, 1955.

3556 Dale, Edmund H. "The West Indies: A Federation in Search of a Capital." *Canadian Geographer*, 5, No. 2 (Summer, 1961), 44-52.

3557 Dalton, John Elmer. *A History of the Location of the State Capital in South Dakota*. Vermillion, South Dakota: South Dakota University, Governmental Research Bureau, Report No. 14, 1945.

3558 Everitt, John C. "Belmopan, Dream and Reality: A Study of the other Planned Capital in Latin America." *Revista Geografica*, 99, No. 1 (Enero-Junio, 1984), 135-144.

3559 Evenson, Norma. *Two Brazilian Capitals: Architecture and Urbanism in Rio de Janeiro and Brasilia*. New Haven, Connecticut: Yale University Press, 1973.

3560 Fifer, J. Valerie. "Unity be Inclusion: Core Area and Federal State and American Independence." *Geographical Journal*, 142, Part 3 (November, 1976), 462-470.

3561 Fifer, J. Valerie. "Washington, D.C.: The Political Geography of a Federal Capital." *Journal of American Studies*, 15, No. 1 (April, 1981), 5-26.

3562 Forster, Paul. "Capital of Dreams." *Geogrphical Magazine*, 58, No. 9 (September, 1986), 462-467.

3563 Fullerton, Douglas. "Wither the Capital Ottawa's Symbolic Role as a Unifying Force in the Nation is Becoming More Important Than Ever." *Canadian Geographic*, 107, No. 6 (December, 1987/January, 1988), 7-19.

3564 Gade, Daniel W. "Spatial Displacement of Latin America Seats of Government: From Sucre to La Paz as the National Capital of Bolivia. *Revista Geografica*, 73, No. 2 (Dezembro, 1970), 43-57.

3565 Garcia Huirolo, Luis. "Las capitales de America." *Revista Geografica Americana*, 13, No. 80 (Mayo, 1940), 327-349.

3566 Greca, Alcides. *Una nueva capital para la nacion Argentina*. Rosario: Cienda, 1950.

3567 Guimaraes, Fabio de Macedo Soares. "Le chocx du site de la nouvelle capitale du Bresil." *Bulletin de l'Associatia de Geographers Francois*, 202-203, No. 3 (May-June, 1949), 85-96.

3568 Gyori, Kenneth A. "State Policy and Urban Development: Brasilia's Satellite City, Ceilandia." University of Texas, Austin, M.A., 1987.

3569 Gyori, Kenneth A. "O Planalto Central e o problema da mudanca do capital do Brasil." *Revista Brasileira de Geografia*, 11, No. 4 (Out.-Dez., 1949), 471-513.

3570 Howes, Helen Claire. "Brasilia, Not Yet a Home for Its People." *Canadian Geographical Journal*, 90, No. 4 (April, 1975), 30-35.

3571 James, Preston E., and Faissol, Speridiao. "The Problem of Brazil's Capital City." *Geographical Review*, 46, No. 3 (July, 1956), 301-317.

3572 Kearns, Kevin C. "Belmopan: Perspective on a New Capital." *Geographical Review*, 63, No. 2 (April, 1973), 147-169.

3573 Kelsey, Vera. *Brazil in Capitals*. New York: Harper & Brothers, 1942.

3574 Kemp, L.W. "The Capitol (?) at Columbia." *The Southwestern Historical Quarterly*, 48, No. 1 (July, 1944), 3-9.

3575 Knight, David B. *A Capital for Canada: Conflict and Compromise in the 19th Century*. Chicago, Illinois: University of Chicago, Department of Geography, Research Series, 1977.

3576 Knight, David B. *Choosing Canada's Capital: Jealousy and Friction in the Nineteenth Century*. Toronto: McClelland and Stewert Limited/Carleton University, Institute of Canadian Studies, 1977.

3577 Lowenthal, David. "The West Indies Chooses a Capital." *Geographical Review*, 48, No. 3 (July, 1958), 336-364.

3578 Martins, Jose Enrico. "Argumentos em favor da mudanca da capital da republica." *Revista Brasileira dos municipos*, 4, No. 16 (Out.-Dez., 1951), 495-504.

3579 McNee, Robert B. "New York Revisited: A Case Study of Former Capital Fatigue." *Transition*, 9, No. 1 (Spring, 1979), 1-7.

3580 Mohaptra, Manindra K., and Mohanty, Sarat Kumari. "Political Culture of a Capital City: A Case Study of Frankfort, Kentucky." *International Review of History and Political Science*, 21, No. 1 (February, 1984), 75-125.

3581 **Moscosocardenas, Alphonso.** "Between the Earth and the Sky; Quito, Capital of Ecuador." *Americas*, 10, No. 5 (May, 1958), 14-19.

3582 **Murphy, Marion Fisher.** *Seven Stars for California. A Story of the Capitals.* Sonoma, California: Sonoma Print Shop, 1979.

3583 **Pearson, Roger W.** "Distance and Dissent: Alaska's Capital Move." *Association of Pacific Coast Geographers Yearbook*, 48 (1986), 89-105.

3584 **Pedroso, Tobajara.** "A Mudanca da capital Federal (Excerpt)." *Kriterion: Revista da Faculdade de Filosofia da Universidade de Minas Gerais*, 6, Nos. 23-24 (Januar-Junho, 1953), 182-205.

3585 **Penna, J.O. de Meira.** "Brazil Builds a New Capital." *Landscape*, 5, No. 3 (Spring, 1956), 17-22.

3586 **Penna, J.O. de Meira.** "A mudanca da capital do Brasil." *Revista Brasileira de geografia*, 17, No. 2 (Abril-Junho, 1955), 153-171.

3587 **Penna, J.O. de Meira.** *Quando mundan as capitais.* Rio de Janeiro: Servico Grafico do IBGE, 1958.

3588 **Platt, Robert S.** "Brazilian Capital and Frontiers." *Journal of Geography*, 53, No. 9 (September, 1954), 369-375 and 54, No. 1 (January, 1955), 5-17.

3589 **Prazeres, Otto.** "A mundanca da capital." *Jornal do Brasil.* 11 (de Agosto, 1958), 3-4.

3590 **Reis, Arthur Cezar Ferreira.** "Mundancas de Capital." *Jornal do Brasil*, 3 (de Novembro, 1958), 1-3.

3591 *Report of the British Caribbean Federal Capital Commission.* London: Great Britain, Colonial Office, 1956.

3592 **Riveiro, Paulo de Assis.** *A margem da transferencia da capital da Uniao.* Rio de Janeiro: Fundacao Brasil Central, 1947.

3593 **Roberts, W. Adolphe.** *Havana, The Portrait of a City.* New York: Coward-McCann, 1953.

3594 **Rodrigues, Jose Honorio.** "O Papel do Rio de Janeiro na unidade nacional." *A Defesa Nacional*, 551 (Junho, 1960), 119-121.

3595 **Santoro, Laura.** "Viedma: una nouva capitale per l'Argentina?" *L'Universo*, 68, No. 4 (Luglio-Agosto, 1988), 396-403.

3596 **Siddall, William R.** "Seattle: Regional Capital of Alaska." *Annals of the Association of American Geographers*, 47, No. 3 (September, 1957), 277-284.

3597 **Simey, T.S.** "A New Capital for the British West Indies." *Town Planning Review*, 28, No. 1 (April, 1957), 63-70.

3598 **Simpich, Frederck.** "Honolulu, Mid-Ocean Capital." *National Geographic Magazine*, 105, No. 5 (May, 1954), 577-624.

3599 **Smith, James Richard.** *Some Changing Features of a Regional Capital: Sioux Falls, South Dakota, 1920-1970.* Lincoln: University of Nebraska, Ph.D., 1971.

3600 **Snyder, D.D.** "Alternate Perspectives on Brasilia." *Economic Geography*, 40, No. 1 (January, 1964), 34-45.

3601 **Sobral, F. Fernando.** "Brasilia, novo eixo da gravitacao nacional." *Revista do instituto Historico e geografico de Minas Gerais*, 5 (1958), 27-53.

3602 "Substituicao dos Marcos Provisorios por Marcos Definitivos na Linha de Juncao dos Estados de Sao Paulo e Rio de Janeiro." *Anuario Geografico do Estado do Rio De Janeiro*, 12 (1959), 80-83.

3603 **Sutherland, Mason.** "Mexico's Booming Capital." *National Geographic Magazine*, 100, No. 6 (June, 1951), 785-824.

3604 **Teixeira de Freitas, M.A.** "A Transferencia da capital." *Revista Brasileira dos municipos*, 4, No. 13 (1951), 59-63.

3605 **Tosta, Octavio.** "Buenos Aires e a luta contra o centrifugismo politico." *A Defesa Nacional*, 551 (Junho, 1960), 131-142.

3606 **Vasconcelos, J.R.** "Brasilia, peca de politica nacionalista." *Revista Brasiliense*, 14 (1957), 171-177.

3607 **Willson, Betty.** "Brasilia, Brazil; Carving a Capital Out of the Wilderness." *Americas*, 10, No. 8 (August, 1958), 2-8.

3608 **Wood, William B.** "Transferring the National Capitol." *Focus*, 36, No. 2 (Summer, 1986), 31-32.

3609 **Wright, Charles L.** and **Turkienicz, Benamy.** "Brasilia and the Ageing of Modernism." *Cities*, 5, No. 4 (November, 1988), 347-364.

3610 **Zagarri, Rosemarie.** "Representaiton and the Removal of State Capitals, 1776-1812." *Journal of American History*, 74, No. 4 (March, 1988), 1239-1256.

ASIA

Books and Journals

3611 **Chan, Steve.** "Cores and Peripherics: Interaction Patterns in Asia." *Comparative Political Studies*, 15, No. 3 (October, 1982), 314-340.

3612 **Chang, Sen-dou.** "Peking: The Growing Metropolis of Communist China." *Geographical Review*, 55, No. 3 (July, 1965), 313-327.

3613 **Chang, Sen-dou.** "Some Aspects of the Urban Geography of the Chinese Hsiem Capital." *Annals of the Association of American Geographers*, 51, No. 1 (March, 1961), 23-45.

3614 **Chapin, Helen B.** "Kyongju, Ancient Capital of Silla." *Asian Horizon*, 1, No. 4 (Winter, 1948), 36-45.

3615 **Fritz, John M.** "Vijayanagara: Authority and Meaning of a South Indian Imperial Capital." *American Anthropologist*, 88, No. 1 (March, 19886), 44-55.

3616 **Ghori, G.K.** "Choice of Capital for New Mysore State: A Plea for Revision." *Deccan Geographer*, 2, No. 1 (January, 1964), 175-177.

3617 **Hitti, Philip K.** *Capital Cities of Arab Islam.* Minneapolis: University of Minnesota Press, 1973.

3618 **Kreutzmann, Hermann.** "Anspruch und Realitat einer Geplanten Hauptstadt: Islamabad in Pakistan." *Erdkunde* [Kleve], 46, Heft 1 (Marz, 1992), 26-39.

3619 **Kureisky, Khalil Ullah.** "Choice of Pak Capital (Karachi): A Politico-Geographical Analysis." *Pakistan Geographical Review*, 5, No. 1 (January, 1950), 13-25.

3620 **Lieberman, Victor B.** "The Transfer of the Burmese Capital from Pegu to Ava." *Royal Asiatic Society of Great Britain and Ireland (London) Journal*, 1 (1980), 64-83.

3621 **London, Bruce.** "Ecological and Political-economic Analysis of Migration to a Primate City: Bangkok, Thailand Ca. 1970." *Urban Affairs Quarterly*, 21, No. 4 (June, 1986), 501-526.

3622 **Murphey, Rhoads.** "New Capitals of Asia." *Economic Development and Cultural Change*, 5, No. 3 (April, 1957), 216-243.

3623 "New Site for the Federal Capital of Pakistan." *Pakistan Geographical Review*, 14, No. 2 (July, 1959), 93-96.

3624 **Ramachandran, J.** "Riyadh: A Brief Note on the Royal Capital of Saudi Arabia and Its Environs." *National Association of Geographers, India*, 4, No. 2 (December, 1984), 76-79.

3625 **Rimmer, Peter J.**, and **Drakakis-Smith, David W.** "La Gestion des capitales de l'Asie du Sud-Est depvis les annees 1960." *L'Espace Geographique*, Tome 11, No. 4 (Octobre/Decembre, 1982), 259-268.

3626 **Rudduck, G.** "Capital of East Pakistan, Dacca." *Pakistan Quarterly*, 7, No. 1 (Spring, 1954), 49-58.

3627 **Schinz, A.** and others. "P'yongyang--Ancient and Modern--The Capital of North Korea." *GeoJournal* [Dordrecht], 22, No. 1 (Spetember, 1990), 21-32.

3628 **Scofield, J.** "Jerusalem, The Divided City." *National Geographic Magazine*, 115, No. 4 (April, 1959), 492-531.

3629 **Singh, Ujagir.** "New Delhi: Its Site and Situation." *National Geographic Journal of India*, 5, Part 3 (September, 1959), 113-120.

3630 **Spate, O.H.K.**, and **Trueblood, L.W.** "Rangoon: A Study in Urban Geography." *Geographical Review*, 32, No. 1 (January, 1942), 56-73.

3631 **Talbot, Phillips.** "Delhi, Capital of a New Dominion." *National Geographic Magazine*, 92, No. 5 (November, 1947), 597-630.

3632 **Traversi, Carlo.** "La Capitale Dell India." *L'Universo*, Anno 49, No. 3 (Maggio-Guigno, 1969), 487-522.

AUSTRALIA, OCEANIA AND ANTARCTICA

Books and Journals

3633 **Bird, James.** "Gateways, Examples from Australia, with Special Reference to Canberra." *Geographical Journal*, 152, No. 1 (March, 1986), 56-64.

3634 **Birtles, Terry G.** "Differing Plans for Canberra." *Globe*, No. 29 (1988), 14-33.

3635 **Holford, William.** "The Future of Canberra." *Town Planning Review*, 29, No. 3 (October, 1958), 139-162.

3636 **Hoppe, E.O.** "Australian Capitals." *Canadian Geographical Journal*, 44, No. 3 (March, 1952), 97-107.

3637 **Keith Bertram.** "Canberra's Changing Scene." *Walkabout*, 19, No. 7 (July, 1953), 10-19.

3638 **Linge, G.J.R.** "Canberra After Fifty Years." *Geographical Review*, 51, No. 4 (October, 1963), 467-486.

3639 **Odeh, Adnan Abu.** "Two Capitals in an Undivided Jerusalem." *Foreign Affairs* [New York], 71, No. 2 (Spring, 1992), 183-188.

3640 **Statham, Pamela,** ed. *The Origins of Australia's Capital Cities.* Cambridge: Cambridge University Press, 1989.

3641 **Stimson, Robert J., and Adrian, Colin.** "Australian Capital City Property Development, Foreign Investment and Investor Attitudes." *Australian Geographical Studies,* 25, No. 1 (April, 1987), 41-60.

3642 **White, H.L.** *Canberra, A Nation's Capital.* Sydney: Angus and Robertson, 1954.

EUROPE

Books and Journals

3643 **Ahnstrom, Leif.** "The Turnaround Trend and the Economically Active Population of Senen Capital Regions in Western Europe." *Norsk Geografisca Tidsskriff,* 40, No. 2 (June, 1986), 55-64.

3644 **Bedford, Richard.** "Bonn or Berlin?: Haupstadt for Reunited Germany." *New Zealand Journal of Geography* [Dunedin], No. 94 (October, 1992), 11-13.

3645 **Carrington, Dorothy.** "The Five Capitals of Corsica." *Geographical Magazine,* 35, No. 1 (January, 1963), 520-531.

3646 **Chapman, Brian.** "Paris." *Great Cities of the World* by William A. Robson, ed. New York: Macmillan, 1957.

3647 **Chiarelli, Giuseppe.** "Rome." *Great Cities of the World*, William A. Robson, ed. New York: Macmillan, 1957.

3648 **Conditt, Georg.** "Vienna: The History of an Urban Landscape." *Landscape,* 5, No. 3 (Spring, 1956), 3-14.

3649 **Conley, Aaron T.** *A New Forward Capital: Berlin and the East German Frontier.* Terre Haute, IN: Master's thesis, Indiana State University, 1993.

3650 **Craig, John Keith.** "Vienna: A Geographical Analysis." *Tydskrif Vir Aardrykskunde - Journal of Geography*, 1, No. 6 (April, 1950), 10-21.

3651 **Hookham, Maurice, and Simon, Roger.** "Moscow." *Great Cities of the World*, William A. Robson, ed. New York: Macmillan, 1957.

3652 **Lampe, John R.** "Urban History in Southeastern Europe: Recent Research on the Capital Cities." *Maryland Historian*, 11, No. 2 (Fall, 1980), 25-38.

3653 **Lappo, G.; Chickishre, A.; and Bekker, A.** *Moscow: Capital of the Soviet Union: A Short Geographical Survey.* Moscow: Progress Publishers, 1976.

3654 **McManis, Douglas R.** "The Core of Italy: The Case for Lombardy-Piedmant." *Professional Geographer*, 19, No. 5 (September, 1967), 251-257.

3655 **Meijide Pardo, Antonio.** *Brasil la gran potentia del siglo XXI.* Santiago de Compostella: Porto y cia, 1955.

3656 **Miller, J.M.** *Lake Europa: A New Capital for a United Europe.* New York: Books International, 1963.

3657 **Palomaki, Mauri.** "On the Possible Future West European Capital." *GeoJournal* [Dordrecht], 24, No. 3 (July, 1991), 257-267.

3658 **Pounds, Norman J.G., and Ball, S.S.** "Core Areas and the Developments of the European States System." *Annals of the Association of American Geographers*, 54, No. 1 (March, 1964), 24-40.

3659 **Sagvari, Agnes,** ed. *The Capitals of Europe: A Guide to the Sources for the History of Their Architecture and Construction.* Munchen: K.G. Saur, 1980.

3660 **Strasburger, Henry K.** *The Core of a Continent; Problems of Central and Eastern Europe.* Philadelphia: The American Academy of Political and Social Science. James-Patten-Rowe Pamphlet Series No. 13, 1943.

3661 **Strassel, Christophe.** "Bonn-Berlin: Une Capitale Pour Quelle Nation?" *Herodote* [Paris], No. 68 (Janvier-Mars, 1993), 138-149.

3662 **Winch, Michel.** "Western Germany's Capital." *Geographical Magazine*, 31, No. 1 (January, 1958), 32-41.

REGIONALISM AND NATIONALISM

GENERAL AND THEORY

Books and Journals

3663 **Anderson, James.** "On Theories of Nationalism and the Size of the States." *Antipode*, 18, No. 2 (September, 1986), 218-232.

3664 Beames, M.R. "The Ribbon Societies: Lower Class Nationalism in Pre-famine Ireland." *Past and Present*, 97 (November, 1982), 128-143.

3665 Bersch, G.K. "The Revival of Nationalism." *Problems of Communism*, 22, No. 6 (November-December, 1973), 1-15.

3666 Blaut, James M. "Nationalism as an Autonomous Force." *Science and Society*, 46, No. 1 (Spring, 1982), 1-23.

3667 Blaut, James M "A Theory of Nationalism." *Antipode*, 18, No. 1 (1986), 5-10.

3668 Boulding, Elise. "The Old and New Transnationalism: An Evolutionary Perspective." *Human Relations* [New York], 44, No. 8 (August, 1991), 789-805.

3669 Brass, Paul R. *Ethnicity and Nationalism: Theory and Comparison*. New Delhi: Sage Publications, 1991.

3670 Breuilly, John. *Nationalism and the State*. 2nd ed. Chicago: The University of Chicago Press, 1994.

3671 Broek, Jan O.M., and Junis, M.A. "Geography and Nationalism." *Geographical Review*, 35, No. 2 (April, 1945), 301-311.

3672 Bugromenko, V.N. "Social Justice and Inter-Nationality Relations: Territorial Aspects." *Soviet Geography* [Silver Spring], 32, No. 8 (October, 1991, 572-575.

3673 Cable, James. "Nationalism: A Durable Cause? *International Relations* [London], 10, No. 3 (May, 1991), 227-236.

3674 Carr, E.H. *Nationalism and After*. London: McMallin, 1945.

3675 Chatelain, Abel. "Le journal, facteur geographique du regionalisme." *Etudes Rhodaniennes*, 4 (1948), 55-59.

3676 Chay, John, and Ross, Thomas E., eds. *Buffer States in World Politics*. Boulder, Colorado: Westview Press, 1986.

3677 Clark, J.C.D. "National Identity, State Formation and Patriotism: The Role of History in the Public Mind." *History Workshop* [London], No. 29 (Spring, 1990), 95-102.

3678 Connor, Walker. "Eco- or Ethno-Nationalism?" *Ethnic and Racial Studies* (Henly-on-Thames), 3, No. 7 (July, 1984), 342-359.

3679 Connor, Walker. *Ethnonationalism: The Quest for Understanding*. Princeton: Princeton University Press, 1994.

3680 Connor, Walker. "The Nation and Its Myth." *International Journal of Comparative Sociology* [Leiden], 33, Nos. 1-2 (January-April, 1992), 48-57.

3681 Connor, Walker. "When Is a Nation? *Ethnic and Racial Studies* [London], 13, No. 1 (January, 1990), 92-103.

3682 Dawn, C. Earnest. "The Formation of Pan-Arab Ideology in the Interwar Years." *International Journal of Middle East Studies*, 20, No. 1 (February, 1988), 67-91.

3683 Deutsch, Karl W. *Nationalism and Social Communication*. New York: John Wiley & Sons, 1953.

3684 Dikshit, R.D. "Idea of a Nationalism: Indian and European." *Indo-Asian Culture*, 15, No. 1 (January, 1966) 15-30.

3685 Diuk, Nadia, and Karatnycky, Adrian. "Nationalism--Part of the Solution." *Orbis* [Philadelphia], 34, No. 4 (Fall, 1990), 531-546.

3686 Douglas, W.A. "A Critique of Recent Trends in the Analysis of Ethnonationalism." *Ethnic and Racial Studies*, 11, No. 2 (April, 1988), 192-206.

3687 Eriksen, Thomas Hylland. "Formal and Informal Nationalism." *Ethnic and Racial Studies* [London], 16, No. 1 (January, 1993), 1-25.

3688 Forcier, P. "La Place, la Nature et le role des Conditions oernussuves dans l'analyse d'un Processus Revolution-naire." *Geoscope*, 9, No. 1 (April, 1978), 57-62.

3689 Gale, Stephen. "A Resolution of the Regionalization Problem and Its Implications for Political Geography and Social Justice." *Geografiska Annaler, Ser. B. Human Geography*, 58 B, No. 1 (January, 1976), 1-16.

3690 Gellner, Ernest. "Nationalism Reconsidered and E. H. Car." *Review of International Studies* [Cambridge], 18, No. 4 (October, 1992), 285-293.

3691 Gellner, E. *Nations and Nationalism*. Oxford: Basil Blackwell, 1983.

3692 Ghosh, Dastidar P. "Regionalism--Hinderance to Nationalism and Rational Thinking." *Parliamentary Studies*, 8, No. 5 (May, 1964), 16-18.

3693 Glatz, Ferenc. "Backwardness, Nationalism, Historiography." *East European Quarterly*, 17, No. 1 (March, 1983), 31-40.

3694 Gottlieb, Gidon. "Nations Without States." *Foreign Affairs* [New York], 73, No. 3 (May/June, 1994), 100-112.

3695 **Gourevitch, P.A.** "The Re-emergence of 'Peripheral Nationalism'." *Comparative Studies in Society and History*, 21, No. 3 (1979), 303-322.

3696 **Green, Leslie.** "Rational Nationalists." *Political Studies*, 30, No. 2 (June, 1982), 236-246.

3697 **Greenfield, Liah, and Chirot, Daniel.** "Nationalism and Aggression." *Theory and Society* [Dordrecht], 23, No. 1 (February, 1994), 79-130.

3698 **Gruffudd, Pyrs.** "Back to the Land: Historiography, Rurality and the Naiton in Interwar Wales." *Institute of British Geographers. Transactions*, 19, No. 1 (1994), 61-77.

3699 **Haas, Ernst B.** "The Challenge of Regionalism." *International Organization*, 12, No. 4 (November, 1958), 440-458.

3700 **Hare, F.K.** "Regionalism: A Development in Political Geography." *Public Affairs*, 10, No. 1 (December, 1946), 34-39.

3701 **Hayes, Carleton, J.H.** *The Historical Evolution of Modern Nationalism.* New York: Macmillan, 1948.

3702 **Hayes, Carleton, J.H.** *Nationalism: A Religion.* New York: Macmillan, 1960.

3703 **Hechter, M.** "Nationalism as group solidarity." *Ethnic and Racial Studies*, 10, No. 4 (October, 1987), 415-426.

3704 **Hennayake, Shanta K.** "Interactive Ethnonationalism: An Alternative Explanation of Minority Ethnonationalism." *Political Geography* [Oxford], 11, No. 6 (November, 1992), 526-549.

3705 **Heske, H.** "Und margen die ganze Welt..." *Erdkundeunterricht im Nationalsocialismus-- Untersuchungen zu seiner theoretischen Konzeption unter besonderer Berucksichtigung der Reichssachgebiete Erdkunde und Geopolitik im Nationalsocialistischen Lebregrbund*, 1988.

3706 **Honey, Rex D.** *Conflicting Problems in the Political Organization of Space: The London Experience.* Minneapolis: University of Minnesota, University Microfilms and Dissertation Abstracts, Ph.D., 1972.

3707 **Horvath, Matyas.** "Patriotism-Internationalism-Globalism." *International Journal on World Peace* [New York], 9, No. 2 (June, 1992), 23-31.

3708 **Hoselitz, Bert F.** "Nationalism, Economic Development, and Democracy." *Annals of the American Academy of Political and Social Sciences*, 305 (May, 1956), 1-11.

3709 **Howe, Paul.** "Neorealism Revisited: The Neorealist Landscape Surveyed Through Nationalist Spectacles." *International Journal* [Toronto], 46, No. 2 (Spring, 1991), 326-351.

3710 **Huo, Y. Paul, and McKinley, William.** "Nation as a Context for Strategy: The Effects of National Characteristics on Business-Level Strategies." *Management International Review* [Wiesbaden], 32, No. 2 (1992), 103-113.

3711 **Hutchinson, John.** "Moral Innovators and the Politics of Regeneration: The Distinctive Role of Cultural Nationalists in Nation-Building." *International Journal ofComparative Sociology* [Leiden], 33, Nos. 1-2 (January-April, 1992), 101-117.

3712 **Jackson, Peter, and Penrose, Jan, eds.** *Constructions of Race, Place and Nation.* Minneapolis: University of Minnesota Press, 1993.

3713 **Jaffrelot, Christophe.** "Nationalisme Hindou, Territoire et Societe." *Herodote* [Paris], No. 71 (Octobre-Decembre, 1993), 93-111.

3714 **Juteau-Lee, Danielle.** "Ethnic Nationalism: Ethnicity and Politics." *Canadian Review of Studies in Nationalism*, 11, No. 2 (Fall, 1984), 189-200.

3715 **Karol, K.S.** "Cuba esta sola: Das Insel-Herzland einer neven latinamerikanischen Hemisphare." *Zeitschrift fur Geopolitik*, 32, No. 2 (Marz-April), 82-85.

3716 **Kauppi, Mark V.** "The Resurgence of Ethno-Nationalism and Perspectives on State-Society Relations." *Canadian Review of Studies in Nationalism*, 11, No. 1 (Spring, 1984), 119-132.

3717 **Kedourie, Elie.** *Nationalism.* London: Hutchinson, 1960.

3718 **Kellas, J.** *The Politics of Nationalism and Ethnicity.* London: Macmillan, 1991.

3719 **Keller, Thomas.** "Les Conceptions de la Nation dans L'Allemagne Nouvelle." *Herodote*, No. 72/73 (Janvier-Juin, 1994), 30-57.

3720 **Kofus, Evangelos.** "National Heritage and National Identity in Nineteenth- and Twentieth-Century Macedonia." *European History Quarterly*, 19, no. 2 (April, 1989), 229-267.

3721 **Kohn, Hans.** *The Idea of Nationalism; A Study in Its Origins and Background.* New York: Macmillan, 1944.

3722 **Kohn, Hans.** *Nationalism: Its Meaning and History.* Princeton, New Jersey: Van Nostrand, 1965, p. 21.

3723 **LeGloannec, Anne-Marie.** "Y a-t-il un Nationalisme Allemand?" *Herodote* [Paris], No. 68 (Janvier-Mars, 1993), 67-73.

3724 **Levin, Michael D.,** ed. *Ethnicity and Aboriginality: Case Studies in Ethnonationalism.* Toronto: University of Toronto Press, 1993.

3725 **Lind, Michael.** "In Defense of Liberal Nationalism." *Foreign Affairs* [New York], 73, No. 3 (May/June, 1994), 87-99.

3726 **Lyon, Judson M.** "The Herder Syndrome: A Comparative Study of Cultural Nationalism." *Ethnic and Racial Studies* [London], 17, No. 2 (April, 1994), 224-237.

3727 **MacLaughlin, James G.** "Nationalism as an Autonomous Social Force: A Critique of Recent Scholarship on Ethnonationalism." *Canadian Review of Studies in Nationalism*, 14, No. 1 (Spring, 1987), 1-18.

3728 **MacLaughlin, James G.** "The Political Geography of 'Nation-Building' and Nationalism in Social Sciences: Structural vs. Dialectical Accounts." *Political Geography Quarterly*, 5, No. 4 (October, 1986), 299-329.

3729 **Massey, Doreen.** "Survey; Regionalism: Some Current Issues." *Capital and Class*, 6 (Autumn, 1978), 106-125.

3730 **Mayail, James.** "Nationalism and International Security after the Cold War." *Survival* [London], 34, No. 1 (Spring, 1992), 19-35.

3731 **McDonogh, Gary W.** "Other People's Nations: Towards an Interactive Model of Nationalist Movements." *Canadian Review of Studies in Nationalism*, 14, No. 2 (Fall, 1987), 297-316.

3732 **McKinley, R.D.,** and **Little, R.** *Global Problems and World Order.* London: Frances Printer, 1986.

3733 **Meadwell, Hudson.** "Cultural and Instrumental Approaches to Ethnic Nationalism." *Ethnic and Racial Studies*, 12, No. 3 (July, 1989), 309-328.

3734 **Meadwell, Hudson.** "Ethnic Nationalism and Collective Choice Theory." *Comparative Political Studies*, 22, No. 2 (July, 1989), 139-154.

3735 **Mendels, Doron.** *The Rise and Fall of Jewish Nationalism.* New York: Doubleday, 1992.

3736 **Mercer, J. A.** "A Comment from the Real North to the Southerner, P. J. Taylor." *Political Geographer*, 12, No. 2 (March, 1993), 169-173.

3737 **Merrill, Gordon C.** "Le regionalisme et le nationalisme." In *Canada, une interpretation Geographique*, Ludger Beauregard, ed. Toronto: Methuen, 1970.

3738 **Meyerson, Martin.** "National Character and Urban Form." *Public Policy*, 12, No. 1 (Fall, 1963), 78-96.

3739 **Michnik, Adam.** "Nationalism." *Social Research* [New York], 58, No. 4 (Winter, 1991), 757-763.

3740 **Mikesell, Marvin W.,** and **Murphy, Alexander B.** "A Framework for Comparative Study of Minority-Group Aspirations." *Annals of the Association of American Geographers*, 81, No. 4 (December, 1991), 581-604.

3741 **Molot, M. Appel,** and **Laux, Jeanne K.** "The Politics of Nationalization." *Canadian Journal of Political Science*, 12, No. 2 (June, 1979), 227-258.

3742 **Orridge, A.W.** "Separatism and Autonomist Nationalisms." In *National Separatism*, C.H. Williams, ed. Vancouver: University of British Columbia Press, 1982, 2, 43-74.

3743 **Padelford, Norman J.** "A Selected Bibliography on Regionalism and Regional Arrangements." *International Organization*, 10, No. 4 (November, 1956), 575-603.

3744 **Pannikar, K.M.** *Regionalism and Security.* New Delhi: Indian Council of World Affairs, 1948.

3745 **Pearson, Chareles Henry.** *National Life and Character.* London and New York: Macmillan, 1893.

3746 **Pfaffenberger, Bryan.** "The Political Construction of Defensive Nationalism: The 1968 Temple-Entry Crisis in Northern Sri Lanka." *Journal of Asian Studies*, 49, No. 1 (February, 1990), 78-96.

3747 **Rawkins, Phillip.** "Nationalist Movements within the Advanced Nationalist State: The Significance of Culture." *Canadian Review of Studies in Nationalism*, 10, No. 2 (Fall, 1983), 221-223.

3748 **Rawkins, Phillip.** "The Role of the State in the Transformation of the Nationalist Movements of the 1960's: Comparing Wales and Quebec." *Ethnic and Racial Studies*, 7, No. 1 (January, 1984), 86-105.

3749 **Reissner, Johannes.** "Mittelasien im Regional-Politischen Kraftefeld." *Geographische Rundschau* [Braunschweig], 46, Heft 4 (April, 1994), 224-228.

3750 **Richmond, Anthony H.** "Ethnic Nationalism and Postindustrialism." *Ethnic and Racial Studies*, 7, No. 1 (January, 1984), 4-18.

3751 **Rosecrance, Richard.** "Regionalism and the Post-Cold War Era." *International Journal* [Toronto], 46, No. 3 (Summer, 1991), 373-393.

3752 **Rosser, M.** *Wissenschaft und Lebensraum. Ostforschung im Nationalsozialismus. Ein Beitrag zur Disziplingeschichte der Geographie.* Hamburg: University of Hamburg. 1988.

3753 **Royal Institute of International Affairs.** *Nationalism.* A report by a study group of members of the Royal Institute of International Affairs. London: Oxford University Press, 1939.

3754 **Schnabel, Fritz.** "Institutionelle und Prozessuale Muster der Politikverflechtung: Das Beispiel regionale wirt schftsforderung." *Raumforschung und Raumordnung,* 34 Jahrg, Heft 5 (Oktober, 1976), 181-187.

3755 **Seers, Dudley.** *The Political Economy of Nationalism.* Oxford: Oxford University Press, 1983.

3756 **Seton-Watson, Hugh.** *Nationalism and Communism: Essays 1946-63 .* London: Methuen, 1964.

3757 **Shafer, Boyd C.** *Faces of Nationalism: New Realities and Old Myths.* New York: Harcourt Brace Jovanovich, 1972.

3758 **Shafer, Boyd C.** *Nationalism: Myth and Reality.* New York: Harcourt Brace, 1955.

3759 **Shafer, Boyd C.** "Webs of Common Interests: Nationalism, Internationalism and Peace." *Historian,* 36, No. 3 (May, 1974), 403-433.

3760 **Sibley, Angus.** "Nationalism: Anarchy and Idolatry." *International Relations,* 8, No. 1 (May, 1984), 81-99.

3761 **Simmons, J.W.,** and **Bourne, L.S.** "Urban/Regional Systems and the State." *Progress in Human Geography,* 6, No. 3 (September, 1982), 431-440.

3762 **Smith, Anthony D.** "The Ethnic Sources of Nationalism." *Survival* [London], 35, No. 1 (Spring, 1993), 48-62.

3763 **Smith, Anthony D.** "Nationalism and Historians." *International Journal of Comparative Sociology* [Leiden], 33, Nos. 1-2 (January-April, 1992), 58-80.

3764 **Smith, Anthony D.** "States and Peoples: Ethnic Nationalism in Multi-Cultural Societies." *Soviet Jewish Affairs* [London], 21, No. 1 (Summer, 1991), 7-21.

3765 **Smith, Anthony D.** *Theories of Nationalism.* London: Duckworth, 1971.

3766 **Smith, Graham E.** "Nationalism, Regionalism and the State." *Government and Policy,* 3 (1985), 3-10.

3767 **Smith, Susan J.** "Social Geography: Patriarchy, Racism, Nationalism." *Progress in Human Geography* [London], 14, No. 2 (June, 1990), 261-271.

3768 **Snyder, Louis L.** "Nationalism and the Flawed Concept of Ethnicity." *Canadian Review of Studies in Nationalism,* 10, No. 2 (Fall, 1983), 253-265.

3769 **Spira, Thomas,** ed. "Annotated Bibliography of Works on Nationalism: A Regional Selection." *Canadian Review of Studies in Nationalism,* 11, No. 1 (Spring, 1984), 149.

3770 **Sulzbach, Walter.** *National Consciousness.* Washington, D.C.: American Council on Public Affairs, 1943.

3771 **Sur, Etienne.** "A Propos de l"Extreme Droite en Allemagne: de la Conception Ethnique de la Nation Allemande." *Herodote* [Paris], No. 68, Fasc. 115 (Janvier-Mars, 1993), 1993.

3772 **Symmons-Symonolewicz, Konstantin.** "Sociology and Typologies of Nationalism." *Canadian Review of Studies in Nationalism,* 9, No. 1 (Spring, 1982), 15-22.

3773 **Tekiner, Roselle.** "Zionism and Racism." *American-Arab Affairs* [Washington, D.C.], No. 33 (Summer, 1990), 35-41.

3774 **Tiryakian, Edward A.,** and **Rogowski, Ronald,** eds. *New Nationalism of the Developed West: Toward Explanation.* Boston: Allen & Unwin, 1985.

3775 **Tournadre, Jean-Francois.** "Extreme Droite, Nationalisme et Probliemes d'Identite Dans l'Ex-RDA." *Herodote* [Paris], No. 68 (Janvier-Mars, 1993), 74-82.

3776 **Urban, Jan.** "Nationalism as a Totalitarian Ideology." *Social Research* [New York], 58, No. 4 (Winter, 1991), 775-779.

3777 **Vilar, P.** "On Nationalism and Nations." *Marxist Perspective,* 5 (1982), 89-97.

3778 **Walby, Sylvia.** "Woman and Nation." *International Journal of Comparative Sociology* [Leiden], 33, Nos. 12- (January-April, 1992), 81-100.

3779 **White, Philip L.** "What is Nationality? *Canadian Review of Studies in Nationalism,* 12, No. 1 (Spring, 1985), 1-23.

3780 **Williams, C.H.** and **Kofman, Eleanor.** *Community Conflict, Partition and Nationalism.* New York: Routledge, 1989.

3781 **Williams, C.H.** "Conceived in Bondage-Called Unto Liberty: Reflections on Nationalism." *Progress in Human Geography*, 9, No. 3 (September, 1985), 331-355.

3782 **Wulf, Jurgen.** "Erfolgskontrollen fur die regionale Wirtschaftspolitik." *Raumforschung und Raumordnung*, 34 Jahrg, Heft 5 (Oktober, 1976), 187-199.

3783 **Zaslavsky, Victor.** "Naitonalism and Democratic Transition in Postcommunity Societies." *Daedalus* [Cambridge, MA], 121, No. 2 (Spring, 1992), 97-121.

3784 **Zelinsky, Wilbur.** "O Say, Can You See? Nationalistic Emblems in the Landscape." *Winterthur Portfolio*, 19, No. 4 (Winter, 1984), 277-286.

3785 **Zimmerman, Michel.** "Aux origines de la Catalogne: Geographie Politique et Affirmation Nationale." *Le Moyen Age*, Tome 89, No. 1 (1983), 5-40.

POLITICAL GEOGRAPHY OF REGIONS

AFRICA

Books and Journals

3786 **Adam, Heribert and Moodley, Kogila.** "Negotiations about What in South Africa." *Journal of Modern African Studies*, 27, No. 3 (September, 1989), 367-381.

3787 **Brett, E.A.** "Rebuilding Organisation Capacity in Uganda Under the National Resistance Movement." *The Journal of Modern African Studies*, 32, No. 1 (March, 1994), 53-80.

3788 **Brummelkamp, J.** "Springvloed van het Afrikaans Nationalisme." *Tidischrift van het Koninklijkk Nederlandsch Aardykskundig Genootschap*, 2, No. 77:1 (January, 1960), 91-116.

3789 **Buchanan, Keith.** "Northern Region of Nigeria: The Geographical Background of Its Political Duality." *Geographical Review*, 43, No. 4 (October, 1953), 451-473.

3790 **Cline, Walter B.** "Nationalism in Morocco." *Middle East Journal*, 1, No. 1 (January, 1947), 18-28.

3791 **Coleman, James S.** *Nigeria: Background to Nationalism.* Los Angeles: University of California Press, 1958.

3792 **Cope, Nicholas.** "The Zulu *Petit Bourgeoisie* and Zulu Naitonalism in the 1920s: Origins of Inkatha." *Journal of Southern African Studies* [Eynsham], 16, No. 3 (September, 1990), 431-451.

3793 **Cornevin, Robert.** "Ibo et Non-Ibo: les chances d'une 'Nation biafraise'." *Revue de Psychologie des Peuples*, 24, No. 2 (2 trimestre, 1969), 157-167.

3794 **Crummey, Donald.** "Society, State and Nationality in the Recent Historiography of Ethiopia." *Journal of African History*, 31, No. 1 (199), 103-119.

3795 **Crush, Jonathan S.** "The Southern African Regional Formation: A Geographical Perspective." *Tidschrift voor Economische en Sociale Geografie*, 73, No. 4 (August-September, 1982), 200-212.

3796 **Decalo, Samuel.** "Regionalism, Political Decay, and Civil Strife in Chad." *Journal of Modern African Studies*, 18, No. 1 (March, 1980), 23-56.

3797 **Divine, Donna Robinson.** "The Rites of Nationalism: One Meaning of Egypt's Struggle for Political Independence." *Canadian Review of Studies in Nationalism*, 8, 1 (Spring, 1981), 37-54.

3798 **Dubow, Saul.** "Afrikaner Nationalism, Apartheid and the Conceptualization of 'Race'. *The Journal of African History* [Cambridge], 33, No. 2 (1992), 209-237.

3799 **DuToit, Andre.** "No Chosen People: The Myth of the Calvinist Origins of Afrikaner Nationalism and Racial Ideology." *American Historical Review*, 88, No. 4 (October, 1983), 920-952.

3800 **Frank, Lawrence P.** "Ideological Competition in Nigeria: Urban Populism Versus Elite Nationalism." *Journal of Modern African Studies*, 17, No. 3 (September, 1979), 433-452.

3801 **Frenay, Patrick.** "Le Cameroun anglophone dans le processus d'integraiton nationale." *Les Cahiers d'Outre Mer*, 10e Annee, No. 159 (Juillet-Septembre, 1987), 217-236.

3802 **Furlong, Patrick J.** "Azikiwe and the National Church of Nigeria and the Cameroons: A Case Study of the Political Use of Religion in African Nationalism." *African Affairs* [Oxford], 91, No. 364 (July, 1992), 433-452.

3803 **Geiger, Susan.** "Women in Nationalist Struggle: TANU Activists in Dar es Salaam." *International Journal of African Historical Studies*, 20, No. 1 (1987), 1-26.

3804 **Ghali, Mirrit Boutros.** "The Egyptian National Conciousness." *Middle East Journal*, 32, No. 1 (Winter, 1978), 59-77.

3805 **Giliomee, Hermann.** "Constructing Afrikaner Nationalism." *Journal of Asian and African Studies*, 18, No. 1-2 (January and April, 1983), 83-98.

3806 **Hahn, Lorna.** *North Africa: Nationalism to Nationhood.* Washington, D.C.: Public Affairs Press, 1960.

3807 **Heaven, Patrick C.L.** "Afrikaner Patriotism Today: The Role of Attitudes and Personality." *Canadian Reviw of Studies in Nationalism*, 11, No. 1 (Spring, 1984), 133-139.

3808 **Heraclides, Alexis.** "Janus or Sisyphus? The Southern Problem of the Sudan." *Journal of Modern African Studies*, 25, No. 2 (June, 1987), 213-231.

3809 **Heywood, Linda M.** "Unita and Ethnic Nationalism in Angola." *Journal of Modern African Studies*, 27, No. 1 (March, 1989), 47-66.

3810 **Iheduru, Okecukwu C.** "The State and Maritime Nationalism in Cote D"Ivoire." *The Journal of Modern African Studies*, 32, No. 2 (June, 1994), 215-245.

3811 **Jenkins, H.L.** "Stratification and Integration in Regional Systems: The Effect of Systematic Status Inconsistency on the Process of Political Integration in Africa from 1965-1980." Worchester, Massachusetts: Clark University, Ph.D., 1984.

3812 **Kapter, John.** "Neo-Nationalism in West Africa." *Wisconsin Geographer*, 2 (Spring, 1986), 67-70.

3813 **Leslie, Winsome J.** *Zaire: Continuity and Political Change in an Oppressive State.* Boulder, CO: Westview Press, 1993.

3814 **Maddox, Gregory,** ed. *African Nationalism and Revolution.* New York: Garland Publishing, Inc., 1993.

3815 **Maren, Otwin.** "Implementing National Unity: Changes in National Consciousness Among Participants in the National Youth Service Corps of Nigeria." *Journal of Ethnic Studies*, 17, No. 2 (Summer, 1989), 23-44.

3816 **Markakis, John.** "The Nationalist Revolution in Eritrea." *Journal of Modern African Studies*, 26, No. 1 (March, 1988), 51-70.

3817 **Matonse, Antonio.** "Mozambique: A Painful Reconcilation." *Africa Today* [Denver], 39, Nos. 1-2 (1992), 29-34.

3818 **Moodey, Kogila.** "The Legitimation Crisis of the South African State." *Journal of Modern African Studies*, 24, No. 2 (June, 1986), 187-201.

3819 **Munger, Edwin S.** *Afrikaner and African Nationalism: South African Parallels and Parameters.* London: Oxford University Press, 1967.

3820 **Mutibwa, Phares.** *Uganda Since Independence: A Story of Unfulfilled Hopes.* London: Hurst & Company, 1992.

3821 "Nationalism in North Africa." *Round Table*, 28, No. 110 (March, 1938), 279-296.

3822 **Nwoke, Chibuzo N.** "Towards Authentic Economic Nationalism in Nigeria." *Africa Today*, 33, No. 4 (1986), 51-69.

3823 **Nyerere, Julius K.** *The Nigeria-Biafra Crisis.* Dar es Salaam: United Republic of Tanzanie, 1969.

3824 **Ogbuagu, Chibuzo S.A.** "The Nigerian Indigenization Policy: Nationalism or Pragmatism?" *African Affairs*, 82, No. 327 (April, 1983), 241-266.

3825 **Patemen, Roy.** "Liberte, Egalite, Fraternite: Aspects of the Eritrean Revolution." *The Journal of Modern African Studies* [Cambridge], 28, No. 3 (September, 1990), 457-472.

3826 **Pereira, Anthony W.** "The Neglected Tragedy: The Return to War in Angola, 1992-3." *The Journal of Modern African Studies* [Cambridge], 32, No. 1 (March 1994), 1-28.

3827 **Perham, Margery.** "Reflections on the Nigerian Civil War." *International Affairs*, 46, No. 2 (April, 1970), 231-246).

3828 **Porter, Philip W.** "Liberia." *Focus*, 12, No. 1 (September, 1961), 1-6.

3829 **Reed, William Cyrus.** "International Politics and National Liberation: ZANU and the Politics of Contested Sovereignty in Zimbabwe." *African Studies Review* [Atlanta], 36, No. 2 (September, 1993), 31-59.

3830 **Rivlin, Benjamin.** "Unity and Nationalism in Libya." *Middle East Journal*, 3, No. 1 (January, 1949), 31-44.

3831 **Ross, Alistair.** "The Capricorn Africa Society and European Reactions to African Nationalism in Tanganiyika, 1949-60." *African Affairs*, 76, No. 305 (October, 1977), 519-535.

3832 **Sapire, Hilary.** "Apartheid's Testing Ground: Urban Native Policy and African Politics in Brakpan, South Africa, 1943-1948." *The Journal of Afarican History* [Cambridge], 35, No. 1 (1994), 99-123.

3833 **Shehim, Kassim.** "Ethiopia, Revolution, and the Question of Nationalities: The Case of the Afar." *Journal of Modern African Studies*, 23, No. 2 (June, 1985), 331-348.

3834 **Shehim, Kassim, and Searing, James.** "Djibouti and the Question of Afar Nationalism." *African Affairs*, 79, No. 315 (April, 1980), 209-226.

3835 **Tou Val, S.** *Somali Nationalism.* Cambridge, Massachusetts: Harvard University Press, 1963.

3836 **Van Zyl Smit, Dirk.** "Adopting and Adapting Criminological Ideas: Criminology and Afrikaner Nationalism in South Africa." *Contemporary Crises*, 13, No. 3 (September, 1989), 227-251.

3837 **Welliver, Timothy K.,** ed. *African Nationalism and Independence.* New York: Garland Publishing, Inc., 1993.

3838 **Woodward, Peter.** "Nationalism and Opposition in Sudan." *African Affairs*, 80, No. 320 (July, 1981), 379-388.

3839 **Young, M. Crawford.** "Natipolism, Ethnicity, and Class in Africa: Retrospective." *Cahiers d'etudes Africanes*, 26(3), No. 103 (1986), 421-495.

3840 **Zaffiro, James J.** "Twin Births: African Nationalism and Government Information Management in the Bechuanaland Protectorate, 1957-1966." *International Journal of African Historical Studies*, 22, No. 1 (1989), 51-77.

AMERICAS

Books and Journals

3841 **Belov, A.L.** "Regional Political Cultures in Geography of Canada." *Vsesoyuznoe Geograficheskoe Obshchestvo* (Leningrad) *Izvestiia*, Tom 115, Vyp. 6 (1983), 518-525.

3842 **Bodnar, John.** *Remaking America: Public Memory, Commemoration, and Patriotism in the Twentieth Century.* Princeton: Princeton University Press, 1992.

3843 **Brenton, Raymond.** "Fron Ethnic to Civic Nationalism: English Canada and Quebec." *Ethnic and Racial Studies*, 11, No. 1 (January, 1988), 85-102.

3844 **Bruman, Henry J.** "Sovereign California: The States Most Plausible Alternative Scenario." *California Geographer*, 26 (1986), 1-43.

3845 **Buchenau, Jurgen.** "Counter-Intervention Against Uncle Sam: Mexico's Support for Nicaraguan Nationalism, 1903-1910." *The Americas* [Washington, DC], L, No. 2 (October, 1993), 207-232.

3846 **Caldwell, Gary.** "Discovering and Developing English-Canadian Nationalism in Quebec." *Canadian Review of Studies in Nationalism*, 11, No. 2 (Fall, 1984), 245-256.

3847 **Cohen, Isaac.** "A New Latin American and Caribbean Nationalism. *American Association of Political and Social Science. Annals* [Newbury Park], 526 (March, 1993), 36-46.

3848 **Cole, Douglas,** ed. "Anglo-Canadian Nationalism and Social Communications." *Canadian Review of Studies in Nationalism.* Special Issue, 7, No. 1 (Spring, 1980).

3849 **Crain, Mary.** "The Social Construction of National Identity in Highland Ecuador." *Anthropological Quarterly* [Washington, D.C.], 63, No. 1 (January, 1990), 43-59.

3850 **Dodds, Klaus-John.** "Geography, Identity and the Creation of the Argentine State." *Bulletin of Latin American Research* [Oxford], 12, No. 3 (September, 1993), 311-331.

3851 **Dorman, Robert L.** *Revolt of the Provinces: The Regionalist Movement in America, 1920-1945.* Chapel Hill: The University of North Carolina Press, 1993.

3852 **Escude, Carlos.** "Argentine Territorial Nationalism." *Journal of Latin American Studies*, 20, Part 1 (May, 1988), 139-165.

3853 **Fenwick, Rudy.** "Social Change and Ethnic Nationalism: An Historical Analysis of the Separatist Movement in Quebec." *Comparative Studies in Society and History*, 23, No. 2 (April, 1981), 196-216.

3854 **Frideres, James S.** "Becoming Canadian: Citizen Acquisition and National Identity." *Canadian Review of Studies in Nationalism*, 14, No. 1 (Spring, 1987), 105-121.

3855 **Gibbins, R.** *Regionalism: Territorial Politics in Canada and the United States.* Toronto: Butterworths, 1982.

3856 **Gorer, Geoffrey.** *The American People: A Study in National Character.* New York: W.W. Norton, 1948.

3857 **Grant, George.** *Lament for a Nation, The Defeat of Canadian Nationalism.* Toronto: McClelland and Stewart, 1965.

3858 **Griffin, Charles C.** "Regionalism's Role in Venezuelan Politics." *Inter-American Quarterly*, 3, No. 4 (October, 1941), 21-35.

3859 **Hahn, Dwight R.** *The Divided World of the Bolivian Andes: A Structural View of Domination and Resistance.* New York: Crane Russak, 1992.

3860 **Handler, Richard.** *Nationalism and the Politics of Culture in Quebec.* Madison: University of Wisconsin Press, 1988.

3861 **Handler, Richard.** "On Sociocultural Discontinuity: Nationalism and Cultural Objectification in Quebec." *Current Anthropology*, 25, No. 1 (February, 1984), 55-71.

3862 **Hart, Keith.** "German Idealism and Jamaican National Culture." *Caribbean Quarterly* [Kingston], 46, Nos. 1 & 2 (June, 1990), 114-125.

3863 **Harvey, Fernand.** "La Question Regionale au Quebec." *Journal of Canadian Studies*, 15, No. 2 (Summer, 1980), 74-87.

3864 **Heusner, Karla.** "Belizean Nationalism: The Emergence of a New Identity." *Belizean Studies*, 15, No. 2 (1987), 3-24.

3865 **Hodges, Donald C.** *Argentina, 1943-1987; The National Revolution and Resistance.* Albuquerque: University of New Mexico Press, 1988.

3866 **Hopkins, Andrew.** "The Nicaraguan Revolution: A Comparative Perspective." *Australian Outlook*, 41, No. 1 (April, 1987), 30-36.

3867 **Kaplan, David H.** "Nationalism at a Micro-Scale: Educational Segretation in Montreal." *Political Geography* [Oxford], 11, No. 3 (May, 1992), 259-282.

3868 **Kaplan, David H.** "Two Nations in Search of a State: Canada's Ambivalent Spatial Identities." *Annals of the Association of American Geographers*, 84, No. 4 (Dcember, 1994), 585-606.

3869 **Knight, David B.** "Regionalisms, Nationalisms, and the Canadian State." *Journal of Geography*, 83, No. 5 (September-October, 1984), 212-220.

3870 **Knight, Franklin W.** *The Caribbean: The Genesis of a Fragmented Nationalism.* 2nd ed. New York: Oxford University Press, 1990.

3871 **Kohn, Hans.** *American Nationalism: An Interpretative Essay.* New York: Crowell-Collier-Macmillan, 1957.

3872 **Kollmorgen, W.** "Political Regionalism in the United States: Fact or Myth." *Social Forces*, 15, No. 1 (October, 1936), 111-122.

3873 **Konard, Victor.** "Recurrent Symbols of Nationalism in Canada." *Canadian Geographer*, 30, No. 2 (Summer, 1986), 175-180.

3874 **Levitt, Joseph.** "English Canadian Nationalists and the Canadian Character 1957-1974." *Canadian Review of Studies in Natinalism*, 12, No. 2 (Fall, 1985), 223-238.

3875 **Magid, Alvin.** *Urban Nationalism: A Study of Political Development in Trinidad.* Gainesville: University of Florida Press, 1988.

3876 **Magosci, Paul Robert.** "Made or Re-Made in America?: Nationality and Identity Formation Among Carpatho-Rusyn Immigrants and Their Descendants." *Coexistence* [Dordrecht], 28, No. 2 (June, 1991), 335-348.

3877 **Mantecon, Carmen Vazquez.** "Espacio KSocial y Crisis Politica: La Sierra Gorda, 1850-1855." *Mexican Studies* [Berkeley], 9, No. 1 (Winter, 1993), 47-70.

3878 **McRoberts, Kenneth.** "The Sources of Neo-nationalism in Quebec." *Ethnic and Racial Studies*, 7, No. 1 (January, 1984), 55-85.

3879 **Meadwell, Hudson.** "The Politics of Nationalism in Quebec." *World Politics* [Baltimore], 45, No. 2 (January, 1993), 203-241.

3880 **Meaney, Neville.** "American Decline and American Nationalism." *Australian Journal of International Affairs* [Canberra], 45, No. 1 (May, 1991), 89-97.

3881 **Metz, Allan.** "Leopoldo Lugones and the Jews: The Contradictions of Argentine Nationalism." *Ethnic and Racial Studies* [London], 15, No. 1 (January, 1992), 36-60.

3882 **Moore, John H.** "The Miskitu National Question in Nicaragua." *Science and Society*, 50, No. 2 (Summer, 1986), 132-147.

3883 **Morris, A.S.** "The Regional Problem in Argentina's Economic Development." *Geography*, 57, No. 4 (November, 1972), 289-306.

3884 **Najera-Ramirez, Olga.** "Engendering Nationalism: Identity, Discourse, and the Mexican Charro." *Anthropological Quarterly* [Washington, DC], 67, No. 1 (January, 1994), 1-14.

3885 **Odum, Howard W., and Moore, Harry Estill.** *American Regionalism: A Cultural-Historical Approach to National Integration.* New York: Holt, Rinehart & Winston, 1966.

3886 **Olwig, Karen Fog.** "Defining the National in the Transnational: Cultural Identity in the Afro-Caribbean Diaspora." *Ethnos* [Stockholm], 58, Nos. 3-4 (1993), 361-376.

3887 **Pang, Evl-Soo.** "From Regionalism to Gaucho Chauvinism in Brazilian Politics: Old and New Views." *Luso Brazilian Review*, 16, No. 1 (Summer, 1979), 104-114.

3888 **Penrose, Jan.** "I. Mon Pays Ce N'est Pas un Pays' Full Stop: The Concept of Nation as a Challenge to the Nationalist Aspirations of the Parti Quebecois." *Political Geography* [Oxford], 13, No. 2 (March, 1994), 161-181.

3889 *Regional Policies in Canada*. Paris: Organisation for Economic Co-operation and Development, 1980.

3890 **Richmond, Douglas W.** "Nationalism and Class Conflict in Mexico, 1910-1920." *Americas*, 43, No. 3 (January, 1987), 279-303.

3891 **Rudolph, James D.** *Peru: The Evolution of a Crisis*. Westport: Praeger Publishers, 1992.

3892 **Sandner, Gerhard.** "Nicaragua: Regionalprobleme und Regionalpolitik." *Geographische Rundschau*, Jahr 35, Heft 10 (Oktober, 1983), 524-533.

3893 **Sharkansky, Ira.** *Regionalism in American Politics*. Indianapolis: Bobbs-Merrill, 1970.

3894 **Simko, Robert A.** *Political Regionalism in New Jersey (1916-1964)*. Bloomington: Indiana University, Ph.D., 1968.

3895 **Slatta, Richard.** "The Gaucho in Argentina's Quest for National Identity." *Canadian Review of Studies in Nationalism*, 12, No. 1 (Spring, 1985), 99-122.

3896 **Spektorowski, Alberto.** "The Ideological Origins of Right and Left Nationalism in Argentina, 1930-43." *Journal of Contemporary History* [London], 29, No. 1 (January, 1994), 155-184.

3897 **Steele, Richard W.** "The War on Intolerance: The Reformation of American Nationalism, 1939-1941." *Journal of American Ethnic History*, 9, No. 1 (Fall, 1989), 9-35.

3898 **Tardanico, Richard.** "Revolutionary Nationalism and State Building in Mexico, 1917-1924." *Politics and Society*, 10, No. 1 (1980), 59-86.

3899 **Todd, Daniel,** and **Simpson, J.** "Aerospace, the State and the Regions: A Canadian Perspective." *Political Geography Quarterly*, 4, No. 2 (April, 1985), 111-130.

3900 **Weaver, R. Kent.** *The Collapse of Canada*. Washington, D.C.: Brooking Institute, 1992.

3901 **Wilk, Richard R.** "Beauty and the Feast: Official and Visceral Naitonalism in Belize." *Ethnos* [Stockholm], 58, Nos. 3-4 (1993), 294-316.

3902 **Zelinsky, Wilbur.** *Nation into State: The Shifting Symbolic Foundations of American Nationalism*. Chapel Hill: University of North Carolina Press, 1988.

3903 **Zelinsky, Wilbur.** "Nationalism in the American Place-Name Cover." *Names*, 31, No. 1 (March, 1983), 1-28.

ASIA

Books and Journals

3904 **AbuKhalil, As'ad.** "A New Arab Ideology?: The Rejuvenation of Arab Nationalism." *The Middle East Journal* [Bloomington], 46, No. 1 (Winter, 1992), 22-36.

3905 **Ahmad, Kazi S.** "Politico-Regional Divisions of India." *Indian Geographical Journal*, 19, No. 3 (July-September, 1944), 97-106.

3906 **Ajami, Fouad.** "Iran: The Impossible Revolution." *Foreign Affairs*, 67, No. 2 (Winter, 1988/89), 135-155.

3907 **Akhavi, Shahrough.** "Elite Facitonalism in the Islamic Republic of Iran." *Middle East Journal*, 41, No. 2 (Spring, 1987), 181-201.

3908 **Alnasrawi, Abbas.** *Arab Nationalism, Oil, and the Political Economy of Dependency*. New York: Greenwood Press, 1991.

3909 **Anderson, Ewan W.** and **Dupree, Nancy Hatch,** eds. *The Cultural Basis of Afghan Nationalism*. London: Pinter Publisher, 1990.

3910 **Antonius, George.** *The Arab Awakening; The Story of the Arab National Movement*. Philadelphia: Lippincott, 1939.

3911 **Baram, Amatzia.** "Territorial Nationalism in the Middle East. *Middle Eastern Studies* [London], 26, No. 4 (October, 1990), 425-448.

3912 **Barnett, A. Doak.** *China's Far West: Four Decades of Change*. Boulder: Westview Press, 1993.

3913 **Barth, T.F.W.** *The Political Organization of Swat Pathans*. Cambridge, England: King's College, University of Cambridge, Ph.D., 1958.

3914 **Bauer, P.T.** "Nationalism and Politics in Malaya." *Foreign Affairs*, 25, No. 3 (April, 1947), 503-517.

3915 **Bjorklund, Ulf.** "Armenia Remembered and Remade: Evolving Issues in a Diaspora." *Ethnos* [Stockholm], 58, Nos. 3-4 (1993), 335-360.

3916 Bowman, Glenn. "Nationalizing the Sacred: Shrines and Shifting Identities in the Israeli-Occupied Territories." *Man* [London], 28, No. 3 (September, 1993), 431-460.

3917 Breasted, James Henry, Jr. *Arab Nationalism in the Near East.* Berkeley: University. Committee on International Relations. Africa, the Near East and the War, 1943.

3918 Brown, David J.L. "From Peripheral Communities to Ethnic Nations: Separatism in Southeast Asia." *Pacific Affairs*, 61, No. 1 (Spring, 1988), 51-77.

3919 Chandra, Bipan. *Indian National Movement: The Long-Term Dynamics.* New Delhi: Vikas Publishing House, 1988.

3920 Chang, Maria Hsia. "China's Future: Regionalism, Federation, or Disintegration." *Studies in Comparative Communism* [Oxford], 25, No. 3 (September, 1992), 211-227.

3921 Corbridge, S. "Industrialisation, Internal Colonialism and Ethnoregionalism: The Jharkhand, India, 1880-1980." *Journal of Historical Geography*, 13, No. 3 (1987), 249-266.

3922 Corbridge, S. "Perversity and Ethnoregionalism in Tribal India: The Politics of Jharkhand." *Political Geography Quarterly*, 6, No. 3 (1987), 225-240.

3923 Cottam, Richard. "Inside Revolutionary Iran. *Middle East Journal*, 43, No. 2 (Spring, 1989), 168-185.

3924 Cottam, Richard. "Nationalism and the Islamic Revolution in Iran." *Canadinan Review of Studies in Nationalism*, 9, No. 2 (Fall, 1982), 263-277.

3925 Dittmer, Lowell, and Kim, Samuel S., eds. *China's Quest for National Identity.* Ithaca: Cornell University Press, 1993.

3926 Dorraj, Manochehr. *From Zarathustra to Khomeini: Populism and Dissent in Iran.* Boulder, Colorado: Lynne Rienner Publishers, 1990.

3927 Drake, Christine. *The Geography of National Integration: A Case Study of Indonesia.* New Brunswick: Rutgers University, The State University of New Jersey, Ph.D., 1977.

3928 Drake, Christine. "Regional Inequalities, National Integration, and Government Policies in Indonesia." *Studies in Comparative International Development*, 15, No. 4 (Winter, 1980), 59-84.

3929 Dryer, June Teufel. "Unrest in Tibet." *Current History*, 88, No. 539 (September, 1989), 281-284.

3930 Elsbree, Willard H. *Japan's Role in Southeast Asian Nationalist Movements.* Cambridge, Massachusetts: Harvard University Press, 1953.

3931 Emerson, Rupert; Mills, L.A.; and Thompson, Virginia. *Government and Nationalism in Southeast Asia.* New York: I.P.R., 1942.

3932 Entessar, Nader. *Kurdish Ethnonationalism.* Boulder: Lynne Rienner Publishers, 1992.

3933 Eriksen, Thomas Hylland. "A Future-Oriented, Non-Ethnic Nationalism? Mauritius as an Exemplary Case." *Ethnos* [Stockholm], 58, Nos. 3-4 (1993), 197-221.

3934 Farmer, B.H. "Social Basis of Nationalism in Ceylon." *Journal of Asian Studies*, 24, No. 3 (May, 1965), 431-440.

3935 Franck, Dorothea Seelye. "Pakhtunistan--Disputed Disposition of a Tribal Land." *Middle East Journal*, 6, No. 1 (Winter, 1952), 49-68.

3936 Fuller, Gary and Pitts, Forrest R. "Youth Cohorts and Political Unrest in South Korea." *Political Geography Quarterly*, 9, No. 1 (January, 1990), 9-22.

3937 Gelvin, James L. "The Social Origins of Popular Nationalism in Syria: Evidence for a New Framework." *International Journal of Middle East Studies*, 26, No. 4 (November, 1994), 645-661.

3938 Ghods, M. Reza. "Iranian Nationalism and Reza Shah." *Middle Eastern Studies* [London], 27, No. 1 (January, 1991), 35-45.

3939 Ginsburg, Norton. "The Political Dimension: Regionalism and Extra-Regional Relations in Southeast Asia." *Focus*, 23, No. 4 (December, 1972), 1-8.

3940 Graham, B. D. *Hindu Nationalism and Indian Politics: The Origins and Development of the Bharatiya Jana Sangh.* Cambridge: Cambridge University Press, 1990.

3941 Haddad, Mahmoud. "The Rise of Arab Nationalism Reconsidered." *International Journal of Middle East Studies* [Cambridge], 26, No. 2 (May, 1994), 201-222.

3942 Hallaj, Mohammad. "Revolt in Occupied Palestine." *American-Arab Affairs*, 24 (Spring, 1988), 40-48.

3943 Han, Sung-Joo. "South Korea in 1988: A Revoultion in the Making." *Asian Survey*, 29, No. 1 (January, 1989), 29-38.

3944 **Hardstone, Peter C.N.** "Nationalism, Integration and New States: The Malaysian Case." *Area*, 9, No. 4 (December, 1977), 293-297.

3945 **Harney, Desmond.** "The Iranian Revoultuion Ten Years On." *Asian Affairs*, 20, Part II (June, 1989), 153-164.

3946 **Harrison, Selig S.** "The Challenge to Indian Nationalism." *Foreign Affairs*, 34, No. 4 (July, 1956), 620-636.

3947 **Hashmi, Zia Hassan.** *The Dynamics of Contemporary Regional Integration: The Growth of Regionalism Among Iran, Pakistan and Turkey.* Los Angeles: University of Southern California, Ph.D., 1970.

3948 **Heehs, Peter.** "Foreign Influences on Bengali Revolutionary Terrorism, 1902-1908." *Modern Asian Studies*, 28, Part 3 (July, 1994), 533-556.

3949 **Hellmann-Rajanayagam, Dagmar.** "Sri Lanka--A Current Perspective." *Asian Affairs* [London], 22, Part 3 (October, 1991), 314-329.

3950 **Hering, Bob.** "Indonesian Nationalism Revisited." *Journal of Southeast Asian Studies*, 18, No. 2 (September, 1987), 294-302.

3951 **Heuze, Gerard.** "Bombay: La Shiv Sena et le Territoire Urbain." *Herodote* [Paris], No. 71 (Octobre-Decembre, 1993), 149-168.

3952 **Holland, William L., ed.** *Asian Nationalism and the West; A Symposium Based on Documents and Reports of the Eleventh Conference, Institute of Pacific Relations.* New York: Macmillan, 1953.

3953 **Hubbell, L. Kenneth.** "The Devolution of Power in Sri Lanka: A Solution to the Separatist Movement?" *Asian Survey*, 27, No. 22 (November, 1987), 1176-1187.

3954 **Hunter, Shireen T.** "Nationalist Movements in Soviet Asia." *Current History* [Philadelphia], 89, No. 549 (October, 1990), 325-328 & 337-339.

3955 "The Implications of Pakhtunistan: Prospects for Pakistani-Afghan Relations." *World Today*, 11, No. 9 (September, 1955), 390-398.

3956 **Jacoby, Eric H.** *Agrarian Unrest in Southeast Asia.* New York: Asia Publishing House, 1961.

3957 **Jansen, Michael.** *Dissonance in Zion.* London: Zed Books, 1987.

3958 **Jennings, W. Ivor, Sir.** *Nationalism and Political Development in Ceylon: The Background of Self-Government.* New York: Institute of Pacific Relations, 1954.

3959 **Jeshurum, Chandran.** *Governments and Rebellions in Southeast Asia.* Brookfield, Vermont: Gower Publishing, 1986.

3960 **Joffe, E.G.H.** "Arab Nationalism and Palestine." *Journal of Peace and Research*, 20, No. 2 (1983), 157-170.

3961 **Kahin, G. McTurnan.** *Nationalism and Revolution in Indonesia.* Ithaca, New York: Cornell University Press, 1952.

3962 **Kearney, Robert N.** "Sinhalese Nationalism and Social Conflict in Ceylon." *Pacific Affairs*, 37, No. 2 (Summer, 1964), 125-136.

3963 **Khalidi, Rashid.** "Arab Nationalism: Hisotical Problems in the Literature." *The American Historical Review* [Washington, D. C.], 96, No. 5 (December, 1991), 1363-1373.

3964 **Khalidi, Rashid and others, eds.** *The Origins of Arab Nationalism.* New York: Columbia University Press, 1991.

3965 **Khashan. Hilal.** "The Revial of Pan-Arabism." *Orbis* [Philadelphia], 35, No. 1 (Winter, 1991), 107-116.

3966 **Khen, Cheah Boon.** "The Erosion of Ideological Hegemony and Royal Power and the Rise of Postwar Malay Nationalism, 1945-46." *Journal of Asian Studies*, 19, No. 1 (March, 1988), 1-26.

3967 **Kitromilides, Paschalis M.** "Greek Irredentism in Asia Minor and Cyprus." *Middle Eastern Studies*, 26, No. 1 (January, 1990), 3-17.

3968 **Koh, B.C.** "North Korea in 1988: The Fortieth Anniversary." *Asian Survey*, 29, No. 1 (January, 1989), 39-45.

3969 **Kohi, Young-Bok.** "The Korean Nationalism and Its Leading Force." *Korea Journal*, 21, No. 2 (February, 1981), 4-11.

3970 **Krawchenko, Bohdan.** *Social Change and National Consciousness in Twentieth Century Ukraine.* Hound Mills, England: Macmillan, 1985.

3971 **Lal, Deepak.** "Nationalism, Socialism and Planning: Influential Ideas in the South." *World Development*, 13, No. 6 (June, 1985), 749-759.

3972 **Lambert, Richard D.** "Factors in Bengali Regionalism in Pakistan." *Far Eastern Survey*, 28, No. 4 (April, 1959), 49-58.

3973 **Lattimore, Owen.** *Nationalism and Revolution in Mongolia.* New York: Oxford Universty Press, 1955.

3974 Lee, Raymond L. M. "The State, Religious Nationalism, and Ethnic Rationaliation in Malaysia." *Ethnic and Racial Studies* [London], 13, No. 4 (October, 1990), 482-502.

3975 Lockman, Zachary. "The Social Roots of Nationalism: Workers and the National Movement in Egypt, 1908-19." *Middle Eastern Studies*, 24, No. 4 (October, 1988), 445-459.

3976 Maksoud, Clovis. "The Implications of the Palestinian Uprising - Where from Here?" *American-Arab Affairs*, 26 (Fall, 1988), 50-55.

3977 Manogaran, Chelvadurai. *Ethnic Conflict and Reconciliation in Sri Lanka.* Honolulu: University of Hawaii Press, 1987.

3978 Marmarstein, Emile. "The Fate of Arabden: A Study in Comparative Nationalism." *International Affairs*, 25, No. 4 (October, 1949), 475-491.

3979 Masliyah, Sadok H. "Zionism in Iraq." *Middle Eastern Studies*, 25, No. 2 (April, 1989), 216-237.

3980 Matthews, Bruce. "Radical Conflict and the Rationalization of Violence in Sri Lanka." *Pacific Affairs*, 59, No. 1 (Spring, 1986), 28-44.

3981 Meyer, Eric. "La crise sri-lankaise: enjeux territoriaux et enjeux symboliques." *Herodote*, 49, (Avril-Juin, 1988), 52-69.

3982 Mishal, Shaul, and Aharoni, Reuben. *Speaking Stones: Communiques from the Intifada Underground.* Syracuse: Syracuse University Press, 1994.

3983 Moten, A. Rashid. "Palestinian Nationalism: Its Growth and Development." *International Studies*, 19, No. 2 (April-June, 1980), 197-219.

3984 Nguyen Thi Tuyet Mai. *The Rubber Tree: Memoir of a Vietnamese Woman Who Was an Anti-French Guerrilla, a Publisher and a Peace Activist.* Edited by Monique Senderowicz. Jefferson: McFarland and Company, Inc., Publishers, 1994.

3985 Nitz, Kiyoko Kurusu. "Independence without Nationalists? The Japanese and Vietnamese Nationalism During the Japanese Period, 1940-45." *Journal of Southeast Asian Studies*, 15, No. 1 (March, 1984), 108-133.

3986 Norbu, Dawa. "The 1959 Tibetan Rebellion: An Interpretation." *China Quarterly*, 77, No. 1 (March, 1979), 74-93.

3987 Norton, Augustus Richard. "Lebanon After Ta'if: Is the Civil War Over?" *The Middle East Journal* [Bloomington], 45, No. 3 (Summer, 1991), 457-473.

3988 Paine, Robert. "Israel: The Making of Self in the 'Pioneering' of the Nation." *Ethnos* [Stockholm], 58, Nos. 3-4 (1993), 222-240.

3989 Pakern, B. *Regionalism in India: With Special Reference to North-East India.* New Delhi: Har Anand Publications, 1993.

3990 Parsons, Anthony. "The Iranian Revolution." *Middle East Review*, 20, No. 3 (Spring, 1988), 3-8.

3991 Portugali, Juval, and Sonis, Michael. "Palestinian National Identity and the Israeli Labor Market: Q-Analysis." *The Professional Geographer* [Washington, D. C.], 43, No. 3 (August, 1991), 265-279.

3992 Qureshi, Khalida Nuzhat. *The Political Geographical Implications of Pukhtoonistan.* Seattle: University of Washington, Master's Thesis, 1965.

3993 Qureshi, Saleem M.M. "Pakistani Nationalism Reconsidered." *Pacific Affairs*, 45, No. 4 (Winter, 1972-1973), 556-572.

3994 Rashid, Ahmed. *The Resurgence of Central Asia: Islam or Nationalism?* London: Zed Books, 1994.

3995 Reid, Donald Malcolm. "Cultural Imperialism and Nationalism: The Struggle to Define nad Control the Heritage of Arab Art in Egypt." *International Journal of Middle East Studies* [Cambridge], 24, No. 1 (February, 1992), 57-76.

3996 Richard, Yann. "The Relevance of 'Nationalism' in Contemporary Iran." *Middle East Review*, 21, No. 4 (Summer, 1989), 27-36.

3997 "The Rise of the Indonesian Republic. Reasons for the Remarkable Strength of Postwar Indonesian Nationalism." *Amerasia*, 11, No. 1 (January, 1947), 16-27.

3998 Rousset, Pierre. "La crise des Phillippines." *Herodote*, No. 52 (1989), 92-114.

3999 Ruether, Rosemalry and Ruether, Herman J. *The Wrath of Jonah: The Crisis of Religious Nationalism in the Israeli-Palestinian Conflict.* San Francisco: Harper & Row, 1989.

4000 Rumer, Boris Z. "The Gathering Storm in Central Asia." *Orbis* [Greenwich, CT], 37, No. 1 (Winter, 1993), 89-105.

4001 Rupen, Robert A. "Mongolian Nationalism." *Royal Central Asian Journal*, 45, No. 2 (April, 1958), 157-178.

4002 Ryang, Sonia. "Historian-Judges of Korean Nationalism." *Ethnic and Racial Studies* [London], 13, No. 4 (October, 1990), 503-526.

4003 **SarDesai, D. R.** *Vietnam: The Struggle for National Identity.* 2nd ed. Boulder: Westview Press, 1992.

4004 **Sayeed, Khalid B.** "Pathan Regionalism." *South Atlantic Quarterly*, 63, No. 4 (Autumn, 1964), 478-507.

4005 **Seigfried, Andre.** "Les Nationalismes asiatiques et l'occident." *Revue francaise de science politique*, 1, No. 1-2 (1951), 9-25.

4006 **Shastri, Amita.** "The Material Bisis for Separatism: The Tamil Eelam Movement in Sri Lanka." *Journal of Asian Studies*, 49, No. 1 (February, 1990), 56-77.

4007 **Siavoshi, Susan.** *Liberal Nationalism in Iran: The Failure of a Movement.* Boulder, Colorado: Westview Press, 1990.

4008 **Sicker, Martin.** *Judaism, Nationalism, and the Land of Israel.* Boulder: Westview Press, 1992.

4009 **Singer, Marshall R.** "New Realities in Sri Lankan Politics." *Asian Survey* [Berkeley], 30, No. 4 (April, 1990), 409-425.

4010 **Sison, Jose Maria.** *The Philippine Revolution: The Leader's View.* New York: Crane Russak, 1989.

4011 **Smith, C.G.** "Arab Nationalism; A Study in Political Geography." *Geography*, 43, No. 202 (November, 1958), 229-242.

4012 **Sopher, David E.** "Indian Regionalism as Viewed by Social Scientists." *Geographical Review*, 58, No. 3 (July, 1968), 489-490.

4013 **Stafford, Charles.** "Good Sons and Virtuous Mothers: Kinship and Chinese Nationalism in Taiwan." *Man* [London], 27, No. 2 (June, 1992), 363-378.

4014 **Stepaniants, Marietta.** "Development of the Concept of Nationalism: The Case of the Muslims in the Indian Subcontinent." *Muslim World*, 69, No. 1 (January, 1979), 28-41.

4015 **Strathern, Andrew.** "Violence nad Political Change in Papua, New Guinea." *Pacific Studies* [Laie], 16, No. 4 (December, 1993), 41-60.

4016 **Talhami, Ghada Hashem.** *Palestine and Egyptian National Identity.* New York: Praeger Publishers, 1992.

4017 **Tillman, Seth.** "Israel and Palestinian Nationalism." *Journal of Palestine Studies*, Issue 33, Vol. 9, No. 1 (Autumn, 1979), 46-66.

4018 **Trivedi, D. N.** "Multipolar Versus Unitary Development: Nation Building and Citizenship: An Indian Case." *Man in India* [Ranchi], 70, No. 1 (March, 1990), 16-25.

4019 **Van Der Kroef, Justus M.** "Society and Culture in Indonesian Nationalism." *American Journal of Sociology*, 58, No. 1 (July, 1952), 11-24.

4020 **Varshney, Ashutosh.** "India, Pakistan, and Kashmir: Antinomies of Nationalism." *Asian Survey* [Berkeley], 31, No. 11 (November, 1991), 997-1019.

4021 **Vaziri, Mostafa.** *Iran as Imagined Nation: The Construction of National Identity.* New York: Paragon House, 1993.

4022 **Verma, Ramesh Kumar.** *Regionalism and Sub-Regionalism in State Politics: Social, Economic, and Political Bases.* New Delhi: Deep and Deep Publications, 1994.

4023 **Weinbaum, Marvin G.** "The Intlernationalization of Domestic Conflict in the Middle East." *Middle East Review*, 20, No. 1 (Fall, 1987), 31-42.

4024 **Wells, Kenneth M.** *New God, New Nation: Protestants and Self-Reconstruction Nationalism in Korea, 1896-1937.* Honolulu: University of Hawaii Press, 1990

4025 **Wignaraja, Ponna,** ed. *The Challenge in South Asia: Development, Democracy and Regional Cooperation.* New Delhi: Sage Publications, 1989.

4026 **Wilson, A Jeyaratnam.** *The Break-Up of Sri Lanak: The Sinhalese-Tamil Conflict.* London: C. Hurst & Company, 1988.

4027 **Woodside, Alexander.** "Nationalism and Poverty in the Breakdown of Sino-Vietnamese Relations." *Pacific Affairs*, 52, No. 3 (Fall, 1979), 381-409.

4028 **Wurfel, David.** *Filipino Politics: Developoment and Decay.* Ithaca, New York: Cornell University Press, 1988.

4029 **Yip, Ka-Che.** "Medicine and Nationalism in the People's Republic of China, 1949-1980." *Canadian Review of Studies in Nationalism*, 10, No. 2 (Fall, 1983), 175-187.

4030 **Yitrim Moksha.** "The Crisis in Burma: Back from the Heart of Darkness?" *Asian Survey*, 29, No. 6 (June, 1989), 543-558.

4031 **Yoshino, Kasaku.** *Cultural Nationalism in Contemporary Japan.* New York: Routledge Japanese Studies, 1995.

4032 **Ziring, Lawrence.** "Public Policy Dilemmas and Pakistan's Nationality Problem: The Legacy of Ziavl-Haq." *Asian Survey*, 28, No. 8 (August, 1988), 795-812.

EUROPE

Books and Journals

4033 Agnew, John A. "'Better Thieves than Reds?'
The Nationalization Thesis and the Possibility of a
Geography of Italian Politics." *Political Geography
Quarterly*, 7, No. 4 (October, 1988), 307-323.

4034 Agnew, John A. "Place and Political Behaviour:
The Geography of Scottish Nationalism." *Political
Geography Quarterly*, 3, No. 3 (July, 1984),
191-206.

4035 Agnew, John A. "Political Regionalism and
Scottish Nationalism in Gaelic Scotland."
Canadian Review of Studies in Nationalism, 8,
No. 1 (Spring, 1981), 115-129.

4036 Alpher, Joseph, ed. *Nationalism and Modernity:
A Mediterranean Perspective*. New York:
Praeger, 1986.

4037 Amersfoort, Hans van, and Knippenberg, Hans,
eds. "States and Nations: The Rebirth of the
'Nationalities Question' in Europe." *Nederlandse
Geografische Studies* [Amsterdam], No. 137
(1991).

4038 Anderson, Christopher; Kaltenthaler, Karl; and
Luthardt, Wolfgang, eds. *The Domestic Politics
of German Unification*. Boulder: Lynne Rienner
Publishers, 1993.

4039 Anderson, Stanley V. *The Nordic Council: A
Study of Scandinavian Regionalism*. Seattle:
University of Washington Press, 1967.

4040 Archer, J.H. "Necessary Ambiguity: Nationalism
and Myths in Ireland." *Eire-Ireland*, 39, No. 2
(Summer, 1984), 23-37.

4041 Armour, Leslie. "Ecnomics and Culture: Lenin's
Troubles with Nationalism." *International Journal
of Social Economics* [Bradford], 20, Nos. 5/6/7
(1993), 84-102.

4042 Armstrong, John A. "Nationalism in the Former
Soviet Empire." *Problems of Communism*
[Washington, D. C.], 41, Nos. 1-2 (January-April,
1992), 121-133.

4043 Armstrong, John A. "Sources of Soviet
Nationality Policy During the Interwar Years."
Soviet Jewish Affairs [London], 21, No. 1
(Summer, 1991), 29-45.

4044 Armstrong, John A. *Ukrainian Nationalism*. 3rd
ed. Englewood: Ukrainian Academic Press, 1990.

4045 Artisien, Patrick F.R. "Albanian Nationalism and
Yugoslav Socialism: The Case of Kosovo."
Co-Existence, 16, No. 2 (October, 1979), 173-189.

4046 Ashauer, Wolfgang and Heller, Wilfried.
"Nationalitat als Faktor der Siedlungsgestaltung?
Eine Fallstudie deutscher Minderheitensiedlungen
in Ungarn 1945-1988." *Geographische Zeitschrift*,
Jahr. 77 Heft 4 (1989), 228-243.

4047 Atwater, Kevin G. "Ethnic Identity in a Divided
Territory: The Geography of Basque
Nationalism." Syracuse, New York: Syracuse
University, M.S., 1988.

4048 Baldwin, Peter. "Social Interpretations of Nazism:
Renewing a Tradition." *Journal of Contemporary
History*, 25, No. 1 (January, 1990), 5-37.

4049 Becker, Seymour. "Contributions to a Nationalist
Ideology: Histories of Russia in the First Half of
the Nineteenth Century." *Russian History*, 13, No.
4 (Winter, 1986), 331-353.

4050 Belknap, Robert L., ed. *Russianness: Studies on
a Nation's Identity: In Honor of Rufus Mathewson,
1918-1978*. Ann Arbor: Ardis, 1990.

4051 Beloff, Nora. "Russia and the Hundred-Headed
Hydra." *Virginia Quarterly Review*, 56, No. 3
(Summer, 1980), 385-395.

4052 Bennett, Robert J. "Regional Movements in
Britain-A Review of Aims and Statements."
Government and Policy, 3 (1985), 75-96.

4053 Berezowski, Stanislaw. "Varsovie. Comme
Chef-Lieu do Region et Capitale d'etat."
Finisterra, 15, No. 29 (1980), 53-78.

4054 Besancon, Alain. "The Nationalities Issue in the
USSR." *Survey* , 30, No. 4 (131) (June, 1989),
113-130.

4055 Betz, Hans-George. "Deutschlandpolitik on the
Margins: On the Evolution of Contemporary New
Right Nationalism in the Federal Republic." *New
German Critique*, No. 44 (Spring/Summer, 1988),
127-157.

4056 Bialer, Seweryn, ed. *Politics, Society, and
Nationality Inside Gorbachev's Russia*. Boulder,
Colorado: Westview Press, 1989.

4057 Biddiss, Michael. "Nationalism and the Moulding
of Modern Europe." *History*, 79, No. 257
(October, 1994), 412-432.

4058 Bilocerkowycz, Jaroslaw. *Soviet Ukranian
Dissent: A Study of Political Alienation*. Boulder,
Colorado: Westview Press, 1988.

4059 Birnbaum, Pierre. "Nationalism: A Comparison
Between France and Germany." *International
Social Science Journal* [Oxford], No. 133 (August,
1992), 375-384.

4060 Bogdanor, Verona. "Ethnic Nationalism in Western Europe." *Political Studies*, 30, No. 2 (June, 1982), 284-291.

4061 Bond, Andrew R. and Others. "Panel on Nationalism in the USSR: Environmental and Territorial Aspects." *Soviet Geography*, 30, No. 6 (June, 1989), 441-509.

4062 Bowden, P.J. "Regional Problems and Policies in the Northeast of England." *Journal of Industrial Economics*, (1965), 20-39.

4063 Boyce, D.G. *Nationalism in Ireland*. Baltimore, Maryland: Johns Hopkins University Press, 1982.

4064 Bremmer, Ian, and Taras, Ray, eds. *Nation and Politics in the Soviet Successor States*. Cambridge: Cambridge University Press, 1993.

4065 Bromlei, Julian Vladimirovich. "Nationality Problems in Conditions of Perestroika.: *Soviet Anthropology & Archaeology*, 28, No. 3 (Winter, 1989/90), 90-40.

4066 Brown, J. F. *Naitonalism, Democracy and Security in the Balkans*. Aldershot: Dartmouth, 1992.

4067 Burg, Steven L. "The European Republics of the Soviet Union." *Current History* [Philadelphia], 89, No. 549 (October, 1990), 321-324, 340-342.

4068 Buschenfeld, Herbert. "Nationalitaten im Bisherigen Jugoslawien." *Die Erde* [Berlin], 123, Heft 3 (1992), 207-220.

4069 Byrnes, Robert. "Kliuchevskii on the Multi-National Russian State." *Russian History*, 13, No. 4 (Winter, 1986), 313-330.

4070 Campbell, John C. "Nationalism and Regionalism in South America." *Foreign Affairs*, 21, No. 1 (October, 1942), 132-148.

4071 Campeanu, Pavel. "National Fervor in Eastern Europe: The Case of Romania." *Social Research* [New York], 58, No. 4 (Winter, 1991), 805-828.

4072 Christensen, Julie. "Tenguz Abuladze's *Rdpentence* and the Georgian Naitonalist Cause." *Slavic Review* [Stanford], 50, No. 1 (Spring, 1991), 163-175.

4073 Cronin, S. *Irish Nationalism*. Dublin: Academy Press, 1980.

4074 Curtin, Nancy J. *The United Irishmen: Popular Politics in Ulster and Dublin, 1791-1798*. Oxford: Clarendon Press, 1994.

4075 Cuvalo, Ante. The Croatian National Movement, 1966-1972. New York: Columbia University Press, 1990.

4076 Dann, Otto and Dinwiddy, John, eds. *Nationalism in the Age of the French Revolution*. London: Hambledon Press, 1988.

4077 Davies, Charlotte Aull. *Welsh Nationalism in the Twentieth Century: The Ethnic Option and the Modern State*. New York: Praeger, 1989.

4078 Deak, Istvan. "Uncovering Eastern Europe's Dark History." *Orbis*, 30, 1 (Winter, 1990), 51-60.

4079 Denber, Rachel, ed. *The Soviet Nationality Reader: The Disintegration in Context*. Boulder: Westview Press, 1992.

4080 Denich, Bette. "Dismembering Yugoslavia: Nationalist Ideologies and the Symbolic Revival of Genocide." *American Ethnologist* [Arlington], 21, No. 2 (May, 1994), 367-390.

4081 Denitch, Bogdan. *Ethnic Nationalism: The Tragic Death of Yugoslavia*. Minneapolis: University of Minnesota Press, 1994.

4082 Diuk, Nadia, and Karatnycky, Adrian. *The Hidden Nations: The People Challenge the Soviet Union*. New York: William Morrow and Company, Inc., 1990.

4083 Dogan, Mattei. "The Decline of Nationalisms Within Western Europe." *Comparative Politics* [New York], 26, No. 3 (April, 1994), 281-305.

4084 Dominion, Leon. *The Frontiers of Language and Nationality in Europe*. Washington, D.C.: American Geographical Society, 1917.

4085 Donneur, Andre. "Un Nationalisme Suisse Romand estil Possible?" *Canadian Review of Studies in Nationalism*, 9, No. 2 (Fall, 1982), 201-224.

4086 Dragnich, Alex N. "The Rise and Fall of Yugoslavia: The Omen of the Upsurge of Serbian Nationalism." *European Quarterly*, 23, No. 2 (Summer, 1989), 183-198.

4087 Duncan, W. Raymond, and Holman, G. Paul, Jr., eds. *Ethnic Nationalism and Regional Conflict: The Former Soviet Union and Yugoslavia*. Boulder: Westview Press, 1994.

4088 Dunlap, John B. *The New Russian Nationalism*. New York: Praeger, 1985.

4089 Dunlap, John B. "The Russian Nationalist Spectrum Today: Trends and Movements." *Canadian Review of Studies in Nationalism*, 2, No. 1 (Spring, 1984), 63-70.

4090 Eagles, Munroe. "The Neglected Regional Dimension in Scottish Ethnic Nationalism." *Canadian Review of Studies in Nationalism*, 12, No. 1 (Spring, 1985), 81-98.

4091 **Eisel, Stephan.** "The Politics of a United Germany." *Daedalus* [Cambridge, MA], 123, No. 1 (Winter, 1994), 149-171.

4092 **Emberhardt, Piotr.** "The Nationalistic Problems of Lithuania." *Czasopismo Geograficzne* [Wroclaw], 63, Zeszyt 1 (1992), 25-49.

4093 **Fairfield, Roy P.** "Cyprus: Revolution and Resolution." *Middle East Journal*, 13, No. 3 (Summer, 1959), 235-248.

4094 **Finlay, Richard J.** *Independent and Free: Scottish Politics and the Origins of the Scottish National Party, 1918-1945.* Edinburgh: John Donald Publishers, 1994.

4095 **Finlay, Richard J.** "National Identity in Crisis: Politicians, Intellectuals and the End of Scotland, 1920-1939." *History* [Oxford], 79, No. 256 (June, 1994), 242-259.

4096 **Fitzpatrick, David.** "The Geography of Irish Nationalism." *Past and Present*, 78 (February, 1978), 113-144.

4097 **Flint, C.** "Back to Front? The Existence and Threat of Extremism in English Nationalism." *Political Geography*, 12, No. 2 (March, 1993), 180-184.

4098 **Friedgut, Theodore H.** "*Perestroyka* and the Nationalities." *Soviet Jewish Affairs* [London], 21, No. 1 (Summer, 1991), 79-89.

4099 **Frykman, Jonas.** "Becoming the Perfect Swede: Modernity, Body Politics, and National Processes in Twentieth-Century Sweden." *Ethnos* [Stockholm], 58, Nos. 3-4 (1993), 259-274.

4100 **Fuller, Bruce and others.** "Nation Building and School Expansion Under the Fragile French State." *Social Forces* [Chapel Hill], 70, No. 4 (June, 1992), 923-936.

4101 **Furtado, Charles F., Jr.** "Nationalism and Foreign Policy in Ukraine." *Political Science Quarterly* [New York], 109, No. 1 (Spring, 1994), 81-104.

4102 **Furtado, Charles F., Jr., and Chandler, Andrea,** eds. *Perestroika in the Soviet Republics: Documents on the National Question.* Boulder: Westview Press, 1992.

4103 **Gallagher, Tom.** "*Vatra Romaneasca* and Resurgent Nationalism in Romania." *Ethnic and Racial Studies* [London], 15, No. 4 (October, 1992), 570-598.

4104 **Gallissot, Rene.** "Pluralisme Culturel en Europe: Identites Nationales et Identite Europeenne. De l'Intellectuel Metis au Metissage Culturel de Masses." *Social Science Information* [London],

31, No. 1 (March, 1992), 117-127.

4105 **Garvin, Tom.** *The Evolution of Irish Nationalism.* Dublin: Gill and Macmillan, 1981.

4106 **Garvin, Tom.** *Nationalist Revolutionaries in Ireland, 1858 to 1928.* Oxford: Oxford University Press, 1987.

4107 **Gastony, Endre B.** *The Ordeal of Naitonalism in Modern Europe, 1798-1945.* Lewiston: The Edwin Mellen Press, 1992.

4108 **Gilbert, E.W.** "Practical Regionalism in England and Wales." *Geographical Journal*, 94, No. 1 (July, 1939), 29-44.

4109 **Gillis, John R.,** ed. *Commemorations: The Politics of National Identity.* Princeton: Princeton University Press, 1994.

4110 **Glaessner, G.J., and Wallace, I.,** eds. *The German Revolution of 1989: Causes and Consequences.* Berg: Oxford, 1992.

4111 **Grasmuck, Sherri.** "Ideology of Ethno-regionalism: The Case of Scotland." *Politics and Society*, 9, No. 4 (1980), 471-494.

4112 **Griffen, Toby D.** "Nationalism and the Emergence of a New Standard Welsh." *Language Problems and Language Planning*, 4, No. 3 (Fall, 1980), 187-194.

4113 **Griffin, Michael and Ward, Susannah.** "Albanians and Serbs--The Conflict Continues." *Geographical Mazagine*, 61, No. 5 (May, 1988), 21-24.

4114 **Griggs, Richard.** *Territory and National Identity: The Catalan Example.* Berkeley: University of California, M.A., 1988.

4115 **Guermond, Y.** "The Impossibilities of Regional Policies and Politics Normandy." *Etudes Normandes*, 4 (1987), 81-90.

4116 **Gruffudd, Pyrs.** "Back to the Land: Historiography, Rurality and the Nations in Interwar Wales." *Institute of British Geographers. Transactions* [London] New Series, 19, No. 1 (1994), 61-77.

4117 **Hachey, Thomas E. and McCaffrey, Lawrence J.,** eds. *Perspectives on Irish Nationalism.* Lexington: University Press of Kentucky, 1989,

4118 **Halbach, Uwe.** "Nationalitatenfrage und Foderation: Die 'Explosion des Ethnischen' in der Sowjetunion." *Osteuropa* [Anstalt], 40, Heft 11 (November, 1990), 1011-1024.

4119 **Hanham, H.J.** *Scottish Nationalism.* Cambridge, Massachusetts: Harvard University Press, 1969.

4120 **Harvie, C.** *Scotland and Nationalism: Scottish Society and Politics, 1707-1976.* 2nd ed. London: Routledge, 1994.

4121 **Hawthorne, Marijean.** "Yugoslavia: Balkan Shatter Belt." *Virginia Geographer*, 21, No. 1 (Spring-Summer, 1989; published 1990), 11-26.

4122 **Heiberg, Marianne.** *The Making of the Basque Nation.* Cambridge: Cambridge University Press, 1989.

4123 **Hellier, Chris.** "Turmoil in the Balkans." *Geographical Magazine*, 61, 10 (October, 1989), 18-21.

4124 **Hoffman, George W.** "The Political-Geographic Bases of the Austrian Nationality problem." *Austrian History Yearbook.* Houston, Texas: Rice University, 3, Part 1 (1967), 121-46.

4125 **Huelshoff, Michael G.; Markovits, Andrei S.; and Reich, Simon,** eds. *From Bundesrepublik to Deutschland: German Politics After Unification.* Ann Arbor: The University of Michigan Press, 1993.

4126 **Irvine, Jill A.** *The Croat Question: Partisan Politics in the Formation of the Yugoslav Socialist State.* Boulder: Westview Press, 1993.

4127 **Jelavich, Charles.** *South Slav Nationalisms-- Textbooks and Ygoslav Union Before 1914.* Columbus: Ohio State University Press, 1990.

4128 **Jenkins, J.R.G.** *Jura Separatism in Switzerland.* Oxford: Oxford University Press, 1986.

4129 **Johnson, Nuala C.** "Building a Nation: An Examination of the Irish Gaeltacht Commission Report of 1926." *Journal of Historical Geography* [London], 19, No. 2 (April, 1993), 157-168.

4130 **Johnson, Nuala C.** "Sculpting Heroic Histories: Celebrating the Centenary of the 1798 Rebellion in Ireland." *Institute of British Geographers. Transactions* [London], 19, No. 1 (1994), 78-93.

4131 **Johnston, Hank.** *Tales of Nationalism: Catalonia, 1939-1979.* New Brunswick: Rutgers University Press, 1991.

4132 **Johnston, R.W.** "The Nationalisation of English Rural Politics: Norfolk South-West, 1945-1970." *Parlimentry Affairs*, 26, No. 1 (Winter, 1972-73), 8-55.

4133 **Jones, Stephen F.** "Glasnost, Perestroika and the Georgian Soviet Socialist Republic." *Armenian Review* [Watertown, MA], 43, Nos. 2-3 (Summer/Autumn, 1990), 127-152.

4134 **Jungst, Peter.** "Deutsche Geographie und Nationalismus--Ein Historisches Thema?" *Geographische Zeitschrift* [Stuttgart], 81, Heft 1-2 (1993), 69-81.

4135 **Kalberer, Jutta K.** *Political Regionalism in France: A Corsican Case Study.* Columbia: Master's thesis, University of South Carolina, 1993.

4136 **Kalyvas, Stathis N.** "Hegemony Breakdown: The Collapse of Nationalization in Britain and France." *Politics & Society*, 22, No. 3 (September, 1994), 316-348.

4137 **Katz, Mark N.** "Anti-Soviet Insurgencies: Growing Trend or Passing Phase?" *Orbis*, 30, No. 2 (Summer, 1986), 365-391.

4138 **Kellog, Fredrick.** "The Structure of Romanism Nationalism." *Canadian Review of Studies in Nationalism*, 11, No. 1 (Spring, 1984), 21-50.

4139 **Keogh, Dermot, and Haltzel, Michael H.,** eds. *Northern Ireland and the Politics of Reconciliation.* Washington, DC: Woodrow Wilson Center Press, 1993.

4140 **Kirk, William.** "Revolt of the Celts." *Geographical Magazine*, 50, No. 11 (August, 1978), 756-762.

4141 **Kofman, Eleanor.** "Regional Autonomy and the Ore and Indivisible French Republic." *Government and Policy*, 3 (1985), 11-25.

4142 **Kofos, Evangelos.** *Nationalism and Communism in Macedonia.* The Saloniki: Institute for Balkan Studies, 1964.

4143 **Kozlov, V.** "The Nationality Questions and Ways to Resolve It." *Soviet Anthropology & Archaeology*, 28, No. 3 (winter, 1989/90), p. 41-68.

4144 **Kurganov, Ivan.** "The Problem of Nationality in Soviet Russia." *Russian Review*, 10, No. 4 (October, 1951), 253-267.

4145 **Lapidus, Gail Warshofsky.** "Ethnonationalism and Political Stability: The Soviet Case." *World Politics*, 36, No. 4 (July, 1984), 555-580.

4146 **Lehtinen, A.** "The Calotte Politics and the Lappish Regionalism." *Terra*, 99, No. 1 (1987), 13-18.

4147 **Lepsius, M. Ranier.** "The Nation and Nationalism in Germany." *Social Research*, 52, No. 1 (Spring, 1985), 43-64.

4148 **Little, David.** *Ukraine: The Legacy of Intolerance.* Washington, kD.C.: United States Institute of Peace Press, 1991.

4149 **Llera Ramo, F.J.** "Territory and Elections in the Spanish Bsque Country." *Espace-Populations-Societes*, 3 (1987), 523-531.

4150 **Llobera, Josep R.** "The Idea of Volkgeist in the Formation of Catalan Nationalist Ideology." *Ethnic and Racial Studies*, 6, No. 3 (July, 1983), 332-350.

4151 **Lofgren, Orvar.** "Materializing the Nation in Sweden and America." *Ethnos* [Stockholm], 58, Nos. 3-4 (1993), 161-196.

4152 **Loyer, Barbara.** "Les Nationalismes Basque et Catalan: Des Representations Geopolitiques Differentes." *Herodote* [Paris], No. 57 (Avril-Jin, 1990), 27-50.

4153 **Loyer, Barbara.** "Nations et Territoires en Espagne: L'Exemple Basque." *Herodote* [Paris], No. 62 (Juillet-Septembre, 1991), 136-149.

4154 **Lubin, Nancy.** "Uzbekistan: The Challenges Ahead." *Middle East Journal*, 43, No. 4 (Autumn, 1989), 619-634.

4155 **Lukaszewski, Jerry,** ed. *The People's Democracies After Prague: Soviet Hegemony, Nationalism, Regional Integration?* Bruges: College d'Europe, 1970.

4156 **MacLaughlin, James G.** *The Political Geography of Unionism and Nationalism in Ulster (1840-1920).* Syracuse, New York: Syracuse University Ph.D., 1987.

4157 **McAllister, I.** and **Mughan, Anthony.** "Values, Protest and Minority Nationalism in Wales." *British Journal of Political Science*, 14, Part 2 (April, 1984), 230-243.

4158 **McCrone, David.** "Explaining Nationalism: The Scottish Experience." *Ethnic and Racial Studies*, 7, No. 1 (January, 1984), 129-137.

4159 **McCrone, David.** "Regionalism and Constitutional Change in Scotland." *Regional Studies* [Abingdon], 27, No. 6 (1993), 507-512.

4160 **McIvor, Peter K.** "Regionalism in Vister: An Historical Perspective." *Irish University Review*, 13, No. 2 (Autumn, 1983), 180-188.

4161 **Miller, W.L.** *The End of British Politics? Scots and English Political Behaviour in the Seventies.* Oxford: Clarendon Press, 1981.

4162 **Moses, Joel C.** "Regionalism in Soviet Politics: Continuity as a Source of Change, 1953-1982." *Soviet Studies)*, 37, No. 2 (April, 1985), 184-211.

4163 **Mosse, George L.** "Friendship and Nationhood: About the Promise and Failure of German Nationalism." *Journal of Contemporary History*, 17, No. 2 (April, 1982), 351-367.

4164 **Motyl, Alexander J.** *Sovietology, Rationality, Nationality: Coming to Grips with Nationalism in the USSR.* New York: Columbia University Pess, 1990.

4165 **Munch, Ronnie.** "The Making of the Troubles in Northern Ireland." *Journal of Contemporary History* [London], 27, No. 2 (April, 1992), 211-229.

4166 **Nagle, Garrett.** "Northern Ireland: Banners, Bombs and Babies." *Geography Review,* 8, No. 1 (Septemer, 1994), 31-35.

4167 **Nairn, Tom.** *The Break-up of Britain: Crisis and Neo-Nationalism.* Atlantic Highlands, New Jersey: Humanities Press, 1977.

4168 **Neal, Fred Warner.** "Yugoslav Approaches to the Nationalities Problem: The Politics of Circumvention." *East European Quarterly*, 18, No. 3 (Fall, 1984), 327-334.

4169 **Nehme, Michel G.** "Saudi Arabia 1950-80: Between Nationalism and Religion." *Middle Eastern Studies*, 30, No. 4 (October, 1994), 930-943.

4170 **Nissman, David B.** *The Soviet Union and Iranian Azerbaijan: The Use of Nationalism for Political Penetration.* Boulder, Colorado: Westview Press, 1987.

4171 **Olcott, Martha B.** "Gorbachev's National Dilemma." *Journal of Internbational Affairs*, 41, No. 2 (Spring, 1989), 399-421.

4172 **Olcott, Martha B,** and **Fierman, William.** "The Challenge of Integration: Soviet Nationality Policy and the Muslim Conscript." *Soviet Union* (Bakersfield), 14, No. 1, 1987, 65-101.

4173 **O'Neill, Shane.** "Pluralist Justice and Its Limits: The Case of Northern Ireland." *Political Studies*, 42, No. 3 (September, 1994), 363-377.

4174 **Otorbayev, K.,** and **Nanayev, K.** "Social Injustice and Inter-nationality Relationships in the USSA." *Soviet Geography* [Silver Spring], 32, No. 8 (October, 1991), 542-544.

4175 **Paddison, R.** "Scotland, the Other and the British State." *Political Geography*, 12, No. 2 (March, 1993), 165-168.

4176 **Paniotto, Vladimir.** "The Ukrainian Movement for *Perestroika*--'Rukh': A Sociological Survey." *Soviet Studies* [Abingdon], 43, No. 1 (1991), 177-181.

4177 **Passchier, N.P., and Amersfoort, J.M.M., van.** "De Sociale Betekenis van de Nederlands se Nationale Grenzen. Twee Onderzockingen in Midden-Limburg en de Aanliggende Dvitse En Belgische Grensgebieden." *Geografisch Tijdschrift Nieuwe Reeks*, 15, 2 (March, 1981), 119-130.

4178 **Passchier, N.P.; Amersfoort, J.M.M.; and Schaik, A., van.** "Etnisch Nationaliseme en Regionale Sociale Structuur: de Poolse Nationale Bewiging in de Pruisische Provincies Posen en Silezie Rond de Eeuwwisseling." *Geografisch Tijdschrift Nieuwe Reeks*, 15, 2 (March 1981), 152-166.

4179 **Patterson, Henry.** "Ireland: A New Phase in the Conflict Between Nationalism and Unionism." *Science and Society* (New York), 53, No. 2 (Summer, 1989), 192-218.

4180 **Payne, S.** "Catalan and Basque Nationalism." *Contemporary History*, 9 (1979), 15-51.

4181 **Pearson, Raymond.** *The Longman Companion to European Nationalism, 1789-1920.* London: Longman, 1994.

4182 **Petro, Nicolai N.** "Rediscovering Russia." *Orbis*, 34, No. 1 (Winter, 1990), 33-49.

4183 **Pettifer, James.** "The New Macedonian Question." *International Affairs* [Cambridge], 68, No. 3 (July, 1992), 475-485.

4184 **Pipes, Richard.** *The Formation of the Soviet Union: Communism and Nationalism, 1917-1923.* Cambridge, Massachusetts: Harvard University Press, 1954.

4185 **Pork, Andrus.** "Global Security and Soviet Nationalities." *Washington Quarterly*, 13, No. 2 (Spring, 1990), 37-47.

4186 **Pringle, D. G.** "An Irish Perspective on the English Question." *Political Geography*, 12, No. 2 (March, 1993), 161-164.

4187 **Ramet, Pedro,** ed. *Religion and Nationalism in Soviet and East European Politics.* Durham, North Carolina: Duke University Press, 1989.

4188 **Ramet, Sabrina P.** *Nationalism and Federalism in Yugoslavia, 1962-1991.* 2nd ed. Bloomington: Indiana University Press, 1992.

4189 **Raymond, Raymond James.** "Irish Nationalism in the Early Twentieth Century: A Reappraisal." *Canadian Review of Studies in Nationalism*, 14, No. 1 (Spring, 1987), 19-30.

4190 "Regionalism in Italy; An Experiment in Decentralization." *World Today*, 5, No. 2 (February, 1949), 81-92.

4191 **Rensenbrink, John.** *Poland Challenges a Divided World.* Baton Rouge: Louisiana State University Press, 1988.

4192 **Rostiere, Stephane.** "Tensions Ethniques en Roumanie: La Transylvanie a la Croisee des Chemins." *Herodote* [Paris], No. 58-59 (Juillet-Decembre, 1990), 284-310.

4193 **Rudolph, Richard L., and Good, David F.,** eds. *Nationalism and Empire: The Habsburg Empire and the Soviet Union.* New York: St. Martin's Press, 1992.

4194 **Rumpf, E.** *Nationalismus und sozialismus in Ireland.* Meisenheim/Glan: Verlag Anton Hain, 1959.

4195 **Rumpf, E., and Hepburn, A.** *Nationalism and Socialism in Twentieth Century Ireland.* New York: Barnes and Noble, 1977.

4196 **Saunders, David B.** "Historians and Concepts of Nationality in Early Nineteenth-Century Russia." *Slavonic and East European Review*, 60, No. 1 (January, 1982), 44-62.

4197 **Schopflin, George.** "Nationalism and National Minorities in East and Central Europe." *Journal of International Affairs* [New York], 45, No. 1 (Summer, 1991), 51-65.

4198 **Schreiber, Thomas.** "La permanence du probleme national en Europe centrale et orientale." *Herodote*, No. 48 (Janvier-Mars, 1988), 69-77.

4199 **Schulze, Hagen.** *The Course of German Nationalism: From Frederick the Great to Bismarck, 1783-1867.* Translated form the German by Sarah Hanbury-Tenison. Cambridge: Cambridge University Press, 1991.

4200 **Sekelj, Laslo.** *Yogoslavia: The Process of Disintegration.* Translated from the Serbo-Croat by Vera Vukelic. Boulder: Social Science Monographs, 1993.

4201 **Sekulic, Dusko; Massey, Garth; and Hodson, Randy.** "Who Were the Yugoslavs? Failed Sources of a Common Identity in the Former Yugoslavia." *American Sociological Review* [Washington, DC], 58, No. 1 (February, 1994), 83-97.

4202 **Senn, Alfred Erich.** *Lithuania Awakening.* Berkeley: University of California Press, 1990.

4203 **Simmonds, G.W.,** ed. *Nationalism in the U.S.S.R. and Eastern Europe in the Era of Brezhnev and Kosygin.* Detroit, Michigan: University of Detroit Press, 1977.

4204 **Simon, Gerhard.** *Nationalism and Policy Toward the Nationalities in the Soviet Union: From Totalitarian Dictatorship to Post-Stalinist Society.* Translated from the German by Karen Forster and Oswald Forster. Boulder: Westview Press, 1991.

4205 **Smith, Graham.** "Gorbachev's Greatest Challenge: Perestroika and the National Question." *Political Geography Quarterly*, 8, No. 1 (January, 1989), 7-20.

4206 **Snyder, Jack.** "Nationalism and the Crisis of the Post-Soviet State." *Survival* [London], 35, No. 1 (Spring, 1993), 5-26.

4207 **Stanley, John.** "Towards a New Nation: The Enlightenment and National Revival in Poland." *Canadian Review of Studies in Nationalism*, 10, No. 1 (Spring, 1983), 83-110.

4208 **Stokes, Gale.** *Nationalism in the Balkans: An Anotated Bibliography.* New York: Garland Publishing. Canadian Review of Studies in Nationalism. Vol. 3, 1984.

4209 **Strauss, E.** *Irish Nationalism and British Democracy.* New York: Columbia University Press, 1951.

4210 **Studlar, Donley T. and McAllister, I.** "Nationalism in Scotland and Wales: A Post-Industrial Phenomenon?" *Ethnic and Racial Studies*, 11, No. 1 (January, 1988), 48-63.

4211 **Swedenburg, Ted.** "The Palestinian Peasant as National Signifier." *Anthropological Quarterly* [Washington, D.C.], 63, No. 1 (January, 1990), 18-30.

4212 **Sweet, J.V.** "The Problem of Nationalities in Soviet Asia." *Ukrainian Quarterly*, 10, No. 3 (Summer, 1954), 229-235.

4213 **Sysyn, Frank.** "The Reemergence of the Ukrainian Nation and Cossack Mythology." *Social Research* [New York], 58, No. 4 (Winter, 1991), 845-864.

4214 **Taras, Ray.** "Official Etiologies of Polish Crisis: Changing Historiographies and Factional Struggles." *Soviet Studies*, 38, No. 1 (January, 1986), 53-68.

4215 **Tauber, Eliezer.** "Syrian and Iraqi Nationalist Attitudes to the Kemalist and Bolshevik Movements." *Middle Eastern Studies*, 30, No. 4 (October, 1994), 896-915.

4216 **Teich, Mikulas, and Porter, Roy,** eds. *The National Question in Europe in Historical Context.* Cambridge: Cambridge University Press, 1993.

4217 **Tilly, Charles.** "States and Nationalism in Europe, 1492-1992." *Theory and Society* [Dordrecht], 23, No. 1 (February, 1994), 131-146.

4218 **Tombs, Robert,** ed. *Nationhood and Nationalism in France: From Boulangism to the Great War, 1889-1918.* London: Harper Collins Academic, 1991.

4219 **Tweraser, Kurt.** "Carl Beurle and the Triumph of German Nationalism in Austria." *German Studies Review*, 4, No. 3 (October, 1981), 403-426.

4220 **Urdze, Andrejs.** "Nationalism and Internationalism: Ideological Background and Concrete Forms of Expression in the Latvian SSR." *Journal of Baltic Studies*, 19, No. 3 (Fall, 1988), 185-196.

4221 **Urla, Jacqueline.** "Cultural Politics in an Age of Statistics: Numbers, Nations, and the Making of Basque Identity." *American Ethnologist* [Arlington], 20, No. 4 (November, 1993), 818-843.

4222 **Urwin, D.** *The Alchemy of Delayed Nationalism in Scotland.* Glasgow: Molendinar Press, 1977.

4223 **Vandermotten, C.** "La Resurgence des Nationalismes en Europe Centre-Orientale et en Union Sovietique." *Revue Belge de Geographie* [Bruxelles], 115, Fascs. 1-3 (1991), 87-101.

4224 **Vichnevski, Anatoli.** "Le Nationalisme Russe: A la Recherche du Totalitarisme Perdu." *Herodote*, No. 72/73 (Janvier-Juin, 1994), 101-118.

4225 **Warburton, T. Rennie.** "The Rise of Nationalism in Switzerland." *Canadian Review of Studies in Nationalism*, 7, No. 2 (Fall, 1980), 274-298.

4226 **Webb, K.** *The Growth of Nationalism in Scotland.* Glasgow: Molendinar Press, 1977.

4227 **Welch, Irene.** "Nationalism and Lithuanian Dissent." *Lituanus*, 29, No. 1 (Spring, 1983), 39-57.

4228 **White, George W.** *The Territorial Component of Nationalism in Southeastern Europe: The Cases of the Hungarians, Romanians, and Serbs.* Eugene: Ph.D. thesis, University of Oregon, 1993.

4229 **Williams, C. H.** "On England's Beleaguered North." *Political Geography*, 12, No. 2 (March, 1993), 174-179.

4230 **Williams, Glyn.** "Economic Development, Social Structure, and Contemporary Nationalism in Wales." *Review*, 5, No. 2 (Fall, 1981), 275-310.

4231 **Zaslavsky, Victor.** "The Soviet World System: Origins, Evolution, Prospects for Reform." *Telds*, 65 (Fall, 1985), 3-22.

4232 **Zulaika, Joseba.** *Basque Violence: Metaphor and
Sacrament.* Reno: University of Nevada Press,
1988.

CHAPTER V

CATEGORIES OF NATION STATES

UNITARY, FEDERAL AND REGIONAL STATES

GENERAL AND THEORY

Books and Journals

4233 **Agnew, John A.** *The Intellectual Devaluation of Place and the Possibility of Strong Democracy.* Syracuse, New York: Center for the Study of Citizenship, Maxwell School, Syracuse University, Occasional Pub. No. 5, 1985.

4234 **Ali, Mohsin.** "Democracy: Prospect and Retrospect." *Pakistan Quarterly,* 9, No. 3 (Winter, 1959), 8-12.

4235 **Almond, Gabriel A., and Verba, S.** The Civic Culture: Political Attitudes and Democracy in Five Nations. Princeton, New Jersey: Princeton University Press, 1963.

4236 **Altman, D.** "Obstacles to Constitutional Change." *Australian Quarterly,* 51, No. 1 (March, 1979), 103-112.

4237 **Amaral Gurgel, J.A.** *Seguranca e Democracia.* Rio de Janeiro: Jose Olympion, 1978.

4238 **Aron, Raymond.** *Democratie et totalitarisme.* Paris: Gillimard, 1965.

4239 **Bailey, Sydney D., ed.** *Parliamentary Government in the Commonwealth.* A symposium. New York: Philosophical Library, 1952.

4240 **Bebler, Anton, and Seroka, Jim, eds.** *Contemporary Political Systems: Classification and Typologies.* Boulder, Colorado: Lynne Rienner Publishers, 1990.

4241 **Brzezinski, Zbigniew.** "The Crisis of Communism: The Paradox of Political Participation." *Washington Quarterly,* 10, No. 1 (Autumn, 1987), 167-174.

4242 **Dahl, R.A.** *Dilemmas of Pluralist Democracy.* New Haven, Connecticut: Yale University Press, 1982.

4243 **Dahl, R.A., and Tufte, E.R.** *Size and Democracy.* Stanford, California: Stanford University Press, 1973.

4244 **Dahrendorf, Ralf.** *New Liberty.* London: Routledge, 1975.

4245 **Earle, V.A., ed.** *Federalism: Infinite Variety in Theory and Practice.* Itasca, Illinois: F.E. Peacock, 1968.

4246 **Elliott, W.E.Y.** *The Rise of Guardian Democracy.* Cambridge, Massachusetts: Harvard University Press, 1974.

4247 **Ely, J.H.** *Democracy and Distrust.* Cambridge, Massachusetts: Harvard University Press, 1980.

4248 **Gilliland, H.B.** "An Approach to the Problem of the Government of Nomadic Peoples." *South African Geographical Journal.* 29, No. 2 (April, 1947), 43-58.

4249 **Glasgow, Arthur Graham.** *Making Democracy and the World Mutually Safe.* Norfolk, Virginia: The Author, 1943.

4250 **Godgil, D.R.** *Some Observations on the Draft Constitution.* Poona: Gokhale Institute of Politics and Economics Publication, No. 19, 1948.

4251 **Gregg, Phillip M., and Banks, Arthur S.** "Grouping Political Systems: Q. Factor Analysis of a Cross. Polity Survey." *American Political Science Review,* 59, No. 3 (September, 1965), 602-614.

4252 **Hailsham, Lord.** *The Dilemma of Democracy.* London: Collins, 1978.

4253 **Hanson, A.H., and Douglas, J.** *India's Democracy.* New York: W.W. Norton, 1972.

4254 **Kolakowski, Leszek.** "Communism as a Cultural Formation." *Survey,* 29, No. 2 (125) (Summer, 1985), 136-148.

4255 **Kudryatsev, Vladimir.** "Reform of the Political System and Social Science." *Social Sciences Quarterly Review,* 21, No. 1 (1990), 8-21.

4256 **Mallory, Walter H., ed.** *Political Handbook of the World. Parliaments, Parties and Press as of January 1, 1945.* New York: Harper & Brothers for Council on Foreign Relations, 1945.

4257 **Maoz, Zeev and Abdolali, Nasrin.** "Regime Types and International Conflict, 1816-1976." *Journal of Conflict Resolutions,* 33, No. 1 (March, 1989), 3-36.

4258 **Meltzner, A., and Richard, S.** "Why Government Grows (and Grows) in a Democracy." *Public Interest,* 52 (1978), 111-118.

4259 **Miliband, R.** *The State in Democratic Society.* London: Weidenfeld and Nicolson, 1969.

4260 **Moore, Barrington.** *Social Origins of Dictatorship and Democracy: Lord and Peasant in the Making of the Modern World.* Boston: Beacon, 1966.

4261 **Nethercoote, J.E.,** ed. *Parliament and Bureaucracy.* Sydney: Hale and Iremonger, 1982.

4262 **Pryor, Frederic L.** "Some Economies of Utopia: The Case of Full Communism." *Survey,* 29, 2 (125) (Summer, 1985), 70-101.

4263 **Revel, Jean-Francois.** *Democracy Against Itself: The Future of the Democratic Impulse.* Translated from the French by Roger Kaplan. New York: The Free Press, 1993.

4264 **Spencer, Arthur.** "Finland Maintains Democracy." *Foreign Affairs,* 31, No. 2 (January, 1953), 301-309.

4265 **Strong, C.F.** *Modern Political Constitutions.* London: Sidgwick and Jackson, 1939.

4266 **Tribe, Lurence A.** "The Puzzling Persistence of Process Based Constitutional Theories." *Yale Law Journal,* 89, No. 6 (May, 1980), 1063-1080.

4267 **Vernes, P.M.** *La Ville, la Fete et la Democratie: Rousseau et les Illusions de la Communaute.* Paris: Payot, 1978.

POLITICAL GEOGRAPHY OF REGIONS

Books and Journals

4268 **Ahmad, Mustaq.** *Government and Politics in Pakistan.* New York: Praeger, 1963.

4269 **Aitkin, D.** *Stability and Change in Australian Politics,* 2nd ed. Canberra: Australian National University Press, 1982.

4270 **Aiyer, S.P.,** and **Srinivasan, R.** *Studies in Indian Democracy.* New Delhi: Allied Publishers, 1965.

4271 **Alford, Robert R.** *Party and Society: The Anglo-American Democracies.* Chicago, Illinois: Rand McNally, 1963.

4272 **Allen, Henry J.** *Venezuela; A Democracy.* New York: Doubleday, 1940.

4273 **Amjad, Mohammed.** *Iran: From Royal Dictatorship to Theocracy.* New York: Greenwood Press, 1989.

4274 **Bahadur, Kalim** and **Uma Singhe,** eds. *Pakistan Transition to Democracy* (Joint Study of Indian and Pakistani Scholars). New Delhi: Patriot, 1989.

4275 **Blair, Harry Wallace.** *Caste, Politics, and Democracy in Bihar State.* Durham, North Carolina: Duke University, Ph.D., 1967.

4276 **Buck, Pearl S.** *Asia and Democracy.* London: Macmillan, 1943.

4277 **Burch, Betty Brand,** and **Cole, Allen B.** *Asian Political Systems: Readings on China, Japan, India and Pakistan.* Princeton, New Jersey: Van Nostrand, 1968.

4278 **Campbell, Robert D.** *Pakistan: Emerging Democracy.* New York: Van Nostrand, 1963.

4279 **Chalapathi Rau, M.** *India Fights to Defend Democracy.* New Delhi: All India Congress Committee, 1962.

4280 **Chi, Wen-Shun.** *Ideological Conflicts in Modern China: Democracy and Authoritarian.* New Brunswick, New Jersey: Transaction Books, 1986.

4281 **Choudhury, G.W.** *Democracy in Pakistan.* Dacca: Green Book House, 1963.

4282 **Choudhury, G.W.** "Democracy on Trial in Pakistan." *Middle East Journal,* 17, No. 3 (Summer, 1963), 1-13.

4283 **Coupland, Reginald, Sir.** *The Indian Problem: Report on the Constitutional Problem in India.* New York: Oxford University Press, 1944.

4284 **Dahl, R.A.** *Democracy in the United States.* Chicago, Illinois: Rand McNally, 1972.

4285 **Das Gupta, Jyotirindra.** "A Season of Caesars: Emergency Regimes and Development Politics in Asia." *Asian Survey,* 18, No. 4 (April, 1978), 315-349.

4286 **Delal Bear, M.** "Between Evolution and Devolution: Mexican Democracy." *The Washington Quarterly,* 11, No. 3 (Summer, 1988), 77-89.

4287 **Dean, Vera Micheles.** *New Patterns of Democracy in India.* Cambridge, Massachusetts: Harvard University Press, 1959.

4288 **Diamond, Larry; Linz, Juan J.;** and **Lipsit, Seymour Martin,** eds. *Democracy in Developing Countries, Vol. 2, Africa.* Boulder, Colorado: Lynne Rienner Publishers, 1988.

4289 **Dovanandan, P.D.,** and **Thomas, M.M.,** eds. *Problems of Indian Democracy.* Bangalore: Christian Institute of the Study of Religion and Society, 1962.

4290 **Drucker, A.; Dunleavy, P.; Gamble, A.; and Peele, G.**, eds. *Development in British Politics*. London: Macmillan, 1984.

4291 **Dunleavy, P., and Husbands, C.T.** *British Democracy at the Crossroads*. London: Allen & Unwin, 1985.

4292 **Edie, Carlene J.** "Jamaican Political Processes: A System in Search of a Paradigm." *Journal of Development Studies*, 20, No. 4 (July, 1984), 248-270.

4293 **Farouk, A.** "Democracy in Pakistan: Ideals and Realities." *Pakistan Quarterly*, 9, No. 3 (Winter, 1959), 2-7.

4294 **Fisher, Marguerite J.** "New Concepts of Democracy in Southern Asia." *Western Political Quarterly*, 15, No. 4 (December, 1962), 625-640.

4295 **Fitzgibbon, Russel H.** "How Democratic is Latin America?" *Inter-American Economic Affairs*, 9, No. 4 (Spring, 1956), 65-77.

4296 **Friedman, Harry J.** "Notes on Pakistan's Basic Democracies." *Asian Survey*, 1, No. 12 (December, 1961), 19-24.

4297 **Heper, Metin, and Evin, Ahmet**, eds. *Politics in the Third Turkish Republic*. Boulder: Westview Pess, 1994.

4298 **Howard, C.** "The Constitutional Crisis of 1975." *Australian Quarterly*, 48, No. 1 (March, 1976), 5-26.

4299 **India Embassy.** Washington, D.C. *India, the World's Largest Democracy*. Washington, D.C.: Embassy of India, Information Services of India, 1967.

4300 "The Indian Dominion and the States." *World Today*, 5, No. 1 (January, 1949), 27-39.

4301 **Khan, Sadath Ali.** "Democracy at the Grass-Roots." *March of India*, 12, No. 8 (August, 1960), 43-47.

4302 **Kumarappa, J.C.** *Swaraj for the Masses*. Bombay: Hind Kitabs, 1948.

4303 **Kunz, Frank A.** "A Liberalization in Africa--Some Preliminary Reflections." *African Affairs* [Oxford], 90, No. 359 (April, 1991), 223-235.

4304 **Mahler, Gregory S.** *New Dimensions of Canadian Federalism: Canada in a Comparatie Perspective*. Rutherford, New Jersey: Fairleigh Dickinson University Press, 1987.

4305 **Malia, Martin.** *The Soviet Tragedy: A History of Socialism in Russia, 1917-1991*. New York: The Free Press, 1994.

4306 **Marquand, Hillary A.** "Grass Roots Democracy in Pakistan." *New Commonwealth*, 38, No. 4 (April, 1960), 212-214.

4307 **Martin, Paul.** "La Nouvelle Constitution de l'Inde Britannique." *L'Asie Francaise*, 38e Annee, No. 360 (Mai, 1938), 142-148, and 39e Annee, No. 366 (Janvier, 1939), 13-17.

4308 **McKahin, George**, ed. *Major Governments of Asia*. Ithaca, New York: Cornell University Press, 1963.

4309 **McMillan, T.; Evans, G.; and Storey, H.** *Australia's Constitution: Time for Change?* Sydney: Allen & Unwin, 1983.

4310 **Meisler, Stanley.** "Spain's New Democracy." *Foreign Affairs*, 56, No. 1 (October, 1977), 190-208.

4311 **Mellema, R.L.** "The Basic Democracies System in Pakistan." *Asian Survey*, 1, No. 8 (August, 1961), 10-15.

4312 **Ministry of Law.** *The Constitution of India*. Nasik: Government of India Press, 1982.

4313 **Morgan, K.O.** "Regional Regeneration in Britain: The Territorial Imperative and the Conservative State." *Political Studies*, 33, No. 4 (December, 1985), 560-577.

4314 **Mortara, Giorgio.** "Os Territorios Federais recem-criados e seus novos limites." *Boletim Geografico*, Ano 2, No. 16 (Julho, 1944), 445-453.

4315 **Munro, David M.** "Problems on the Way to Equador's Democracy." *Geographical Magazine*, 53, No. 12 (September, 1981), 782-786.

4316 **Narain, Iqbal.** "India: Democratic Politics and Political Development in India." *Asian Survey*, 10, No. 2 (February, 1970), 88-99.

4317 "The New Government in Albania." *World Today*, N.s., 2, No. 3 (March, 1946), 122-131.

4318 *The New India; Progress Through Democracy*. New York: Macmillan, 1958.

4319 **Newman, K.J.** "The Background of Basic Democracy." *Pakistan Quarterly*, 10, No. 4 (Spring, 1960), 8-13.

4320 **O'Connor, J.** "The Democratic Movement in the United States." *Kapitalistate*, 7 (1978), 15-26.

4321 **Oxhorn, Philip.** "Understanding Political Change After Authoritarian Rule: The Popular Sectors and Chile's New Democratic Regime." *Journal of Latin American Studies*, 26, Part 3 (October, 1994), 737-759.

4322 **Palmer, Norman D.** *The Indian Political System.* Boston: Houghton Mifflin, 1962.

4323 **Potholm, Christian P.** *Four African Political Systems.* Englewood Cliffs, New Jersey: Prentice-Hall, 1970.

4324 **Purcell, Victor.** *Malaya: Communist or Free?* London: Institute of Pacific Relations, Stanford University Press, 1954.

4325 **Putnam, R.D.** *The Beliefs of Politicians: Ideology, Conflict and Democracy in Britain and Italy.* New Haven, Connecticut: Yale University Press, 1973.

4326 **Quah, Jon S.T.; Chee, Chan Hing; and Meow, Seah Chee,** eds. *Government and Politics of Singapore.* Oxford: Oxford University Press, 1985.

4327 **Race, Jeffrey.** "Thailand in 1974: A New Constitution." *Asian Survey,* 15, No. 2 (February, 1975), 157-165.

4328 **Rath, Kathrine.** "The Process of Democratization in Jordan." *Middle Eastern Studies,* 30, No. 3 (July, 1994), 530-557.

4329 **Ronen, Dov,** ed. *Democracy and Pluralism in Africa.* Boulder, Colorado: Lynne Rienner Publishers, 1986.

4330 **Royal Commission.** *Royal Commission on the Constitution.* London: HMSO, Cmnd 5460, 1973.

4331 **Rushbrook, L.F. Williams.** "Grass Roots Democracy in Pakistan." *Quarterly Review,* 22, No. 630 (October, 1961), 429-436.

4332 **Rweyemamu, A.H.** *Government and Politics in Tanzania: A Bibliography.* Nairobi: The East African Academy, Research Information and Publications Services, 1972.

4333 **Sarkar, N.K.** *The Democracy of Ceylon in the Twentieth Century.* London, England: University of London, Ph.D., 1954.

4334 **Sayeed, Khalid B.** "The Capabilities of Pakistan's Political System." *Asian Survey,* 7, No. 2 (February, 1967), 102-110.

4335 **Sayeed, Khalid B.** "Collapse of Parliamentary Democracy in Pakistan." *Middle East Journal,* 13, No. 4 (Autumn, 1959), 389-406.

4336 **Sayeed, Khalid B.** *Crisis of Democracy in South Asia.* Toronto: Canadian Institute of International Affairs, 1961.

4337 **Sayeed, Khalid B.** "Pakistan: New Challenge to the Political System." *Asian Survey,* 8, No. 2 (February, 1968), 97-104.

4338 **Sayeed, Khalid B.** *The Political System of Pakistan.* Boston: Houghton Mifflin, 1967.

4339 "The Settlement in Cyprus: A Complex and Rigid Constitution." *Round Table,* 49, No. 195 (June, 1959), 256-265.

4340 **Sheeenan, Donald.** *The American Presidency.* Garden City, New York: Doubleday, 1963.

4341 **Shtromas, Alexander.** "The Building of a Multi-National Soviet 'Socialist Federalism:' Success and Failures." *Canadian Review of Studies in Nationalism,* 13, No. 1 (Spring, 1986), 79-97.

4342 **Slater, David.** "Socialism, democracy and the Territorial Imperative for a Comparison of the Cuban and Nicaraguan Experiences." *Antipode,* 18, No. 2 (September, 1986), 155-185.

4343 **Tambiah, Stanley Jeyaraja.** *Sri Lanka: Ethnic Fratricide and the Dismantling of Democracy.* Chicago, Illinois: Univ. of Chicago Press, 1986.

4344 "Towards a New Constitution in Mauritius. A Heterogeneous Population with Varying Interests: States in the Representation of Three Communities." *Crown Colonist,* 15, No. 160 (March, 1945), 197-198.

4345 **Vatujuitus, Michael R.J.** *Indonesian Politics Under Suharto: Order, Development and Pressure for Change.* New York: Routledge Politics in Asia Series, 1994.

4346 **Verba, S., and Nie, N.H.** *Participation in America: Politica Democracy and Social Equality.* New York: Harper & Row, 1972.

4347 **Weiner, Myron.** *Political Change in South Asia.* Calcutta: Ferma K.L. Mukhopadhyay, 1963.

4348 **Wilson, Godfrey.** *The Constitution of Ngonde.* Rhodes Livingstone Papers, No. 3. Livingstone: The Rhodes-Livingston Institute, Paper #3, 1939.

4349 **Zafrulla Khan, Muhammad, Sir.** *Some Aspects of the Constitutional Problems of India in Transition and Final. Indian Paper No. 9.* Quebec: Institute of Pacific Relations, 1942.

UNITARY OR CENTRAL INCLUDING SOCIALISM AND COMMUNISM

GENERAL AND THEORY

Books and Journals

4350 **Bahry, Donna L., and Moses, Joel C.,** eds. *Political Implications of Economic Reform in Communist Systems: Communist Dialectic.* New York: New York University Press, 1990.

4351 Batchelder, Ronald W., and Freudenberger, Herman. "On the Rational Origins of the Modern Centralized State." *Exploration in Economic History*, 20, No. 1 (January, 1983), 1-13.

4352 Becker, Bertha K. "A crise do Estado e a regiao-a estraligia do descentralizacao en questao." *Revista Brasileira de Geografia*, Ano 48, No. 1 (Janearo-Marco, 1986), 43-62.

4353 Beluszky, Pal, and Timar, Judit. "The Changing Political System and Urban Restructuring in Hungary." *Tijdschrift Voor Ecoknomische en Sociale Geografie* [Utrecht], 83, No. 5 (1992), 380-389.

4354 Buchowski, Michal. "The Magic of the King-Priests of Communism." *East European Quarterly* [Boulder], 25, No. 4 (Winter, 1991), 425-436.

4355 Burton, Charles. "China's Post-Mao Transition: The Role of the Party and Ideology in the 'New Period'." *Pacific Affairs*, 60, No. 3 (Fall, 1987), 431-446.

4356 Cothran, Dan A. *Political Stability and Democracy in Mexico: The "Perfect Dictatorship"?* Westport: Praeger Publishers, 1994.

4357 Eisenstadt, S. N. "The Breakdown of Communist Regimes and the Vicissitudes of Modernity." *Daedalus* [Cambridge, MA], 121, No. 2 (Spring, 1992), 21-41.

4358 Fincher, Ruth. "Analysis of the Local Level Capitalist State." *Antipode*, 13, No. 2 (September, 1981), 25-30.

4359 Greenberg, S. *Race and State in Capitalist Development*. Johannesburg: Ravan Press, 1981.

4360 Greffe, X. *La Decentralisation*. Paris: PUF, 1984.

4361 Hudelson, Richard H. *The Rise and Fall of Communism*. Boulder: Westview Press, 1993.

4362 Janos, Andrew C. "Social Scinece, Communism, and the Dynamics of Political Change." *World Politics* [Baltimore], 44, No. 1 (October, 1991), 81-112.

4363 Manuel, Frank E. "A Requiem for Karl Marx." *Daedalus* [Cambridge, MA], 121, No. 2 (Spring, 1992), 1-19.

4364 Milani, Mohsen M. *The Making of Iran's Islamic Revolution: From Monarchy to Islamic Republic*. Boulder, Colorado: Westveiw Press, 1988.

4365 Offe, C. "Structural Problems of the Capitalist State." In *German Political Studies*. K. Van Beyne, ed. London: Sage Publications, 1974, 31-57.

4366 Robison, Richard. "Authoritarian States, Capitol-Owning Classes, and the Politics of Newly Industrializing Countries: The Case of Indonesia." *World Politics*, 14, No. 1 (October, 1988), 52-74.

4367 Rossi-Landi, Ferruccio. *Marxism and Ideology*. Translated from the Italian by Roger Griffin. Oxford: Clarendon Press, 1990.

4368 Roxman, Gilbert, ed. *Dismantling Communism: Common Causes and Regional Variations*. Washington, DC: The Woodrow Wilson Center Press, 1992.

4369 Segal, Gerald, and Phipps, John. "Why Communist Armies Defend Their Parties." *Asian Survey* [Berkeley], 30, No. 10 (October, 1990), 959-976.

4370 Weigel, George. *The Final Revolution: The Resistance Church and the Collapse of Communism*. New York: Oxford University Press, 1992.

4371 Wesson, Robert. "Totalitarian Strengths and Weaknesses." *Survey*, 28, No. 3 (122) (Autumn, 1984), 186-204.

4372 Whittlesey, Derwent S. "The Impress of Effective Central Authority upon the Landscape." *Annals of the Association of American Geographers*, 25, No. 2 (June, 1935), 85-97.

4373 Williams, J. Allen. "Regional Differences in Authoritarianism." *Social Forces*, 45, No. 2 (December, 1966), 273-277.

4374 Wilson, Frank L. "Communism at the Crossroads: Changing Roles in Western Democracies." *Problems of Communism* [Washington, DC], 41, No. 3 (May-June, 1992), 95-106.

4375 Woodward, Peter, and Forsyth, Murray, eds. *Conflict and Peace in the Horn of Africa: Federalism and Its Alternatives*. Aldershot: Dartmouth, 1994.

POLITICAL GEOGRAPHY OF REGIONS

Books and Journals

4376 Aarts, Paul. "Les Limites du Tribalisme Politique: Le Koweit d'Apres-Guerre et le Processus de Democratisation." *Maghreb-Machrek* [Paris], No. 142 (Octobre-Decembre, 1993), 61-79.

4377 Abrams, James and others. *China: From the Long March to Tiananmen Square*. New York: Henry Holt and Company, 1990.

4378 **Adomeit, Hannes; Hohmann, Hans-Hermann; and Wagenlehner, Gunther,** eds. *Die Sowjetunion Unter Gorbatschow: Stand, Probleme und Perspektiven der Perestrojka.* Stuttgart: W. Kohlhammer, 1990.

4379 **Adriano, Fermin D.** "A Critique of the 'Bureaucratic Authoritarian State' Thesis: The Case of the Philippines." *Journal of Contemporary Asia*, 14, No. 4 (1984), 459-484.

4380 **Alexeyeva, Ludmilla.** *Soviet Dissent: Contemporary Movements for National, Religious, and Human Rights.* Middletown, Connecticut: Wesleyan University Press, 1985.

4381 **Al-Tajir, Mahdi Abdalla.** *Bahrain, 1920-1945: Britain, the Shaikh and the Administration.* London: Croom Helm, 1987.

4382 **Arango, E. Ramon.** *Spain: From Repression to Renewal.* Boulder, Colorado: Westview Press, 1985.

4383 **Aslund, Anders.** "Russia's Road from Communism." *Daedalus* [Cambridge, MA], 121, No. 2 (Spring, 1992), 77-95.

4384 **Auch, Eva-Maria.** "Azerbaijan: Take-Off Into Independence." *Geographische Rundschau* [Braunschweig], 46, Heft 4 (April, 1994, 216-223.

4385 **Baloyra, Enrique A., and Morris, James A.,** eds. *Conflict and Change in Cuba.* Albuquerque: University of New Mexico Press, 1993.

4386 **Baradat, Leon P.** *Soviet Political Society.* 3rd ed. Englewood Cliffs: Prentice Hall, 1992.

4387 **Bengelsdorf, Carollee.** *The Problem of Democracy in Cuba: Between Vision and Reality.* New York: Oxford University Press, 1994.

4388 **Berman, B.** "Structure and Process in the Bureaucratic States of Colonial Africa." *Development and Change*, 15, No. 2 (April, 1984), 161-202.

4389 **Best, Alan C.G.** "Angola: Geographic Background of an Insurgent State." *Focus*, 26, No. 5 (May-June, 1976), 1-8.

4390 **Best, Alan C.G.** "Namibia: Political Geography of an Insurgent State." *Focus*, 26, No. 3 (January-February, 1976), 1-7.

4391 **Biberaj, Elez.** "Albania at the Crossroads." *Problems of Communism* [Washington, DC], 40, No. 5 (September-October, 1991), 1-16.

4392 **Bouillon, Hardy.** "The Postcommunist Sociopolitical System of Eastern European States." *International Journal of World Peace* [New York], 9, No. 2 (June, 1992), 15-22.

4393 **Bradley, John F. N.** *Czechoslovakia's Velvet Revolution: A Political Analysis.* Boulder: East European Monographs, 1992.

4394 **Brucan, Silviu.** *The Wasted Generation: Memoirs of the Romanian Journey from Capitalism to Socialism and Back.* Boulder: Westview Press, 1993.

4395 **Brugger, Bill, and Kelly, David.** *Chinese Marxism in the Post-Mao Era.* Stanford: Stanford University Press, 1990.

4396 **Brynen, Rex.** "Economic Crisis and Post-Rentier Democratization in the Arab World: The Case of Jordan." *Canadian Journal of Political Science* [Waterloo], 25, No. 1 (March, 1992), 69-97.

4397 **Burns, John P.** "The Structure of Communist Party Control in Hong Kong." *Asian Survey* [Berkeley], 30, No. 8 (August, 1990), 748-765.

4398 **Busia, K.A.** *The Position of the Chief in the Modern Political System of Ashanti.* A study of the influence of contemporary social changes in Ashanti political institutions. London: Published for the International African Institute by Oxford University Press, 1951.

4399 **Butwell, Richard A.** "Indonesia: How Stable the Soldier-State?" *Current History*, 75, No. 442 (December, 1978), 212-216 and 229.

4400 **Calinescu, Matei, and Tismaneanu, Vladimir.** "The 1989 Revolution and Romania's Future." *Problems of Communism* [Washington, DC], 40, Nos. 1-2 (January-april, 1991), 42-59.

4401 **Canak, William L.** "The Peripheral State Debate: State Capitalist and Bureaucratic-Authoritarian Regimes in Latin America." *Latin American Research Review*, 19, No. 1 (1984), 3-36.

4402 **Carmen, Rolando V. del.** "Philippines 1974: A Holding Pattern-Power Consolidation or Prelude to a Decline." *Asian Survey*, 15, No. 2 (February, 1975), 136-147.

4403 **Cartledge, Bryan.** "The Second Russian Revolution?" *International Relations* [London], 10, No. 1 (May, 1990), 1-11.

4404 **Castaneda, Jorge.** "The Decline of Communism and the Latin American Left." *Problems of Communism* [Washington, DC], 41, Nos. 1-2 (January-April, 1992), 182-192.

4405 **Catterberg, Edgardo.** *Aragentina Confronts Politics: Political Culture and Public Opinion in the Argentine Transition to Democracy.* Boulder: Lynne Rienner Publishers, 1991.

4406 **Caviedes, Cesar N.** *The Southern Core: Realities of the Authoritarian State of South America.* Totowa, New Jersey: Rowman & Allenheld, 1984.

4407 **Chafetz, Glenn R.** "Soviet Ideological Revision and the Collapse of Communism in Eastern Europe." *International Relations* [London], 11, No. 2 (August, 1992), 151-169.

4408 **Chang, King-yuh**, ed. *Mainland China After the Thirteenth Party Congress.* Boulder: Westview Press, 1990.

4409 **Chiesa, Giulietto.** *Transition to Democracy: Political Change in the Soviet Union, 1987-1991.* Hanover: University Press of New England, 1993.

4410 **Chirot, Daniel**,ed. *The Crisis of Leninism and the Decline of the Left: The Revolutions of 1989.* Seattle: University of Washington Press, 1991.

4411 **Chung, Jae Ho.** "The Politics of Prerogatives in Socialism: The Case of Taizidang in China." *Studies in Comparative Communism* [London], 24, No. 1 (March, 1991), 58-76.

4412 **Cliffe, Lionel** and others. *The Transition to Independence in Namibia.* Boulder: Lynne Rienner Publishers, 1994.

4413 **Cobban, Alfred.** "Administrative Centralization in Germany and the New States, 1918-39." *International Affairs*, 20, No. 2 (April, 1944), 249-264.

4414 **Cole, John P.** "The World of Jan Kowalewski: Pauns in Other People's Games." *Scottish Geographical Magazine* [Edinburgh], 106, No. 2 (September, 1990), 66-74.

4415 **Conaghan, Catherine M.**, and **Espinal, Rosario.** "Unlikely transitions to Uncertain Regimes?: Democracy Without Compromise in the Dominican Republic and Ecuador." *Journal of Latin American Studies* [Cambridge], 22, Part 3 (October, 1990), 553-574.

4416 **Danta, Darrick.** "Romania: View From the Front." *Focus* [New York], 41, No. 2 (Summer, 1991), 17-20.

4417 **Darling, Frank R.** "Thailand: Transitional Military Rule?" *Current History*, 75, No. 442 (December, 1978), 208-211 and 227.

4418 **Decalo, Samuel.** "Regionalism, Politics and the Military in Dahomey." *Journal of Developing Areas*, 7, No. 3 (April, 1973), 449-478.

4419 **Diamond, Larry**, ed. *Political Culture and Democracy in Developing Countries.* Boulder: Lynne Rienner Publishers, 1993.

4420 **Dibble, Sandra.** "Paraguay: Plotting a New Course." *National Geographic* [Washington, DC], 182, No. 2 (August, 1992), 88-113.

4421 **Dijilas, Aleksa.** "Communists and Yugoslavia." *Survey*, 28, No. 3 (122) (Autumn, 1984), 24-38.

4422 **Dikshit, R.D.** "A Framework for the Study of the Impress of Effective Central Authority on the Landscape." *Uttad Bharah Bhoogol Patrika*, 9, No. 3 (1973), 111-115.

4423 **Di Leo, Rita.** "The Soviet Union 1985-1990: After Communist Rule the Deluge? *Soviet Studies* [Abingdon], 43, No. 3 (1991), 429-449.

4424 **Dittmer, Lowell.** *China Under Reform.* Boulder: Westview Press, 1994.

4425 **Domanski, Boleshaw.** "Lessons from the Fallen Second World: A View from Within." *Antipode* [Cambridge, MA], 25, No. 1 (January, 1993), 64-68.

4426 **Domes, Jurgen.** "The Reform of Communism: The Case of the People's Republic of China." *International Interactions* [Philadelphia], 17, No. 2 (1991), 145-156.

4427 **Drake, Paul W.**, and **Jaksic, Ivan**, eds. *The Struggle for Democracy in Chile, 1982-1990.* Lincoln: University of Nebraska Press, 1991.

4428 **Dubhashi, P.R.** "Unitary Trends in a Federal System." *Indian Journal of Public Administration*, 6, No. 3 (July-September, 1960), 243-256.

4429 **Dutt, Gargi**, and **Dutt, V. P.** *China After Mao.* New Delhi: Vikas Publishing House Pvt., Ltd., 1991.

4430 **Dwyer, Denis**, ed. *China: The Next Decades.* Harlow: Longman Scientific and Technical, 1994.

4431 **Ebenstein, William.** *The Nazi State.* New York: Farrar & Rinehart, 1943.

4432 **Eberstadt, Nicholas.** "Democraphic Shocks After Communism: Eastern Germany, 1989-93." *Population and Development Review* [New York], 20, No. 1 (March, 1994), 137-152.

4433 **Edie, Carlene J.**, ed. *Democracy in the Caribbean: Myths and Realities.* Westport: Praeger Publishers, 1994.

4434 **Ekiert, Grzegorz.** "Peculiarities of Post-Communist Politics: The Case of Poland." *Studies in Comparative Communism* [Oxford], 25, No. 4 (December, 1992), 341-361.

4435 **Elliot, John E.**, and **Dowlah, Abu F.** "Intellectual Precursors of Perestroika." *International Journal of Social Economics* [Bradford], 18, Nos. 5/6/7 (1991), 175-206.

4436 **Entelis, John P.** "The Crisis of Authoritarianism in North Africa: The Case of Algeria." *Problems of Communism* [Washington, DC], 41, No. 3 (May-June, 1992), 71-81.

4437 **Ferdinand, Peter.** "Russian and Soviet Shadows Over China's Future? *International Affairs* [Cambridge], 68, No. 2 (April, 1992), 279-292.

4438 **Fierman, William, ed.** *Soviet Central Asia: The Failed Transformation.* Boulder: Westview Press, 1991.

4439 **Fischer, Bernd J.** "Resistance in Albania During the Second World War: Partisans, Nationalists and the S.O.E." *East European Quarterly* [Boulder], 25, No. 1 (Spring, 1991), 21-47.

4440 **Frank, Marc.** *Cuba Looks to the Year 2000.* New York: International Publishers, 1993.

4441 **Frankel, Francine R.** "Compulsion and Social Change: Is Authoritarianism the Solution of India's Economic Development Problems." *World Politics*, 30, No. 2 (January, 1978), 215-240.

4442 **Furniss, Norman.** "Northern Ireland as a Case Study of Decentralization in Unitary States." *World Politics*, 27, No. 3 (April, 1975), 387-404.

4443 **Gabriel, Ralph H.** "American Experience with Military Government." *American Historical Review*, 49, No. 4 (July, 1944), 630-643.

4444 **Gargan, Edward A.** *China's Fate: A People's Turbulent Struggle with Reform and Repression 1980-1990.* New York: Doubleday, 1991.

4445 **Getty, J. Arch.** "State and Society Under Stalin: Constitutions and Elections in the 1930s." *Slavic Review* [Stanford], 50, No. 1 (Spring, 1991), 18-35.

4446 **Ghabra, Shafeeq.** "Voluntary Associations in Kuwait: The Foundation of a New System?" *The Middle East Journal* [Washington, DC], 45, No. 2 (Spring, 1991), 199-215.

4447 **Ghods, M. Reza.** "The Iranian Communist Movement Under Reza Shah." *Middle Eastern Studies* [London], 26, No. 4 (October, 1990), 506-513.

4448 **Gill, Graeme F.** "Institutionalisation and Revolution: Rules and the Soviet Political System." *Soviet Studies*, 37, No. 2 (April, 1985), 212-226.

4449 **Glassman, Ronald M.** *China in Transition: Communism, Capitalism, and Democracy.* New York: Praeger Publishers, 1991.

4450 **Goff, James Ferdinand.** *Soviet Mass Communications: A Geography of Political Control.* Urbana: University of Illinois, Ph.D., 1970.

4451 **Goldman, Marshall I.** *What Went Wrong with Perestroika.* New York: W. W. Norton & Company, 1992.

4452 **Gooding, John.** "Perestroika as Revolution from Within: An Interpretation." *The Russian Review* [Columbus], 51, No. 1 (January, 1992), 36-57.

4453 **Gow, James.** "Independent Ukraine: The Politics of Security." *International Relations* [London], 11, No. 3 (December, 1992), 253-267.

4454 **Gradus, Yehuda.** "The Emergence of Regionalism in a Centralized System: The Case of Israel." *Society and Space*, 2 (1984), 87-100.

4455 **Grilli de Cortona, Pietro.** "From Communism to Democracy: Rethinking Regime Change in Hungary and Czechoslovakia." *International Social Science Journal* [Oxford], No. 128 (May, 1991), 315-330.

4456 **Grover, Verinder.** *Trends and Challenges to Indian Political System.* New Delhi: Deep & Deep, 1990.

4457 **Gu, Zhibin.** *China Beyond Deng: Reform in the PRC.* Jefferson, NC: McFarland & Company, Inc., Publishers, 1991.

4458 **Gubman, Boris L.** "Before and After the Abortive Coup in the USSR." *International Social Science Review* [Winfield], 67, No. 1 (Winter, 1992), 3-7.

4459 **Halebsky, Sandor, and Kirk, John M.** *Transformation and Struggle: Cuba Faces the 1990s.* New York: Praeger Publishers, 1990.

4460 **Harris, Marvin.** "Distinguished Lecture: Anthropology and the Theoretical and Paradigmatic Significance of the Collapse of Soviet and East European Communism." *American Anthropologist* [Washington, DC], 94, No. 2 (June, 1992), 295-305.

4461 **Haynes, Jeff.** "Human Rights and Democracy in Ghana: The Record of the Rawlings' Regime." *African Affairs* [Oxford], 90, No. 360 (July, 1991), 407-425.

4462 **Hazard, John N.** "The Federal Organization of the U.S.S.R." *Russian Review*, 3, No. 2 (Spring, 1944), 21-29.

4463 **Henry, Paget.** "Political Accumulation and Authoritarianism in the Caribbean: The Case of Antigua." *Social and Economic Studies* [Kingston], 40, No. 1 (March, 1991), 1-38.

4464 Hershkovitz, L. "Tinanmen Square and the Politics of Place." *Political Geography*, 12, No. 5 (September, 1993), 395-420.

4465 Hertzfeldt, Lothar, ed. *Die Sowjetunion: Zerfall Eines Imperiums.* Frankfurt: Verlag fur Interkulturelle Kommunikation, 1992.

4466 Hibbert, Reginald. *Albania's National Liberation Struggle: The Bitter Victory.* London: Pinter Publishers, 1991.

4467 Hill, Lewis E., and Magas, Istvan. "Requiem for Communism: The Case for Hungary." *International Journal of Social Economics* [Bradford], 20, Nos. 5/6/7 (1993), 35-43.

4468 Hill, Ronald J. "The CPSU: From Monolith to Pluralist?" *Soviet Studies* [Abingdon], 43, No. 2 (1991), 217-235.

4469 Hirst, Paul. "The State, Civil Society and the Collapse of Soviet Communism." *Economy and Society* [London], 20, No. 2 (May, 1991), 217-242.

4470 Honey, P.J. *Communism in North Vietnam.* London: Am Ampersand, 1965.

4471 Hudson, Michael C. "After the Gulf War: Prospects for Democratization in the Arab World. *The Middle East Journal* [Bloomington], 45, No. 3 (Summer, 1991), 407-426.

4472 Hunt, Michael H., and Westad, Odd Arne. "The Chinese Communist Party and International Affairs: A Field Report on New Historical Sources and Old Research Problems." *The China Quarterly* [London], No. 122 (June, 1990), 258-272.

4473 Hutt, Michael, ed. *Nepal in the Nineties: Versions of the Past, Visions of the Future.* Delhi: Oxford University Press, 1994.

4474 India (Republic). Ministry of Home Affairs. *Report on Center-State Relationships.* New Delhi: Publication Division, Government of India Press, 1969.

4475 Joiner, Charles A. "The Vietnam Communist Party Strives to Remain the 'Only Force.'" *Asian Survey* [Berkeley], 30, No. 11 (November, 1990), 1053-1065.

4476 Kaplan, Karel. *Staat und Kirche in der Tschechoslowakei: Die Kommunistische Kirchenpolitik in den Jahren 1948-1952.* Munchen: R. Oldenbourg, 1990.

4477 Karl, Terry Lynn. "Dilemas de la Democratizacion en America Latina." *Foro Internacional* [Mexico, D.F.], 31, No. 3 (Enero-Marzo, 1991), 388-417.

4478 Karsten, Siegfried G. "Justice, Solidarity, Subsidiarity: The Demise of East German Communism." *International Journal of Social Economics* [Bradford], 20, Nos. 5/6/7, 1993.

4479 Katsenelingoigen, Aron J. *The Soviet Union: Empire, Nation, and System.* New Brunswick: Transaction Publishers, 1990.

4480 Kerblay, Basile. *Gorbachev's Russia.* Translated by Rupert Swyer. New York: Pantheon, 1989.

4481 Khagram, Sanjeev. "Democracy and Democratization in Africa: A Plea for Pragmatic Possibilism." *Africa Today* [Denver], 40, No. 4 (1993), 55-72.

4482 Kiernan, Brendan. *The End of Soviet Politics: Elections, Legislatures, and the Demise of the Communist Party.* Boulder: Westview Press, 1993.

4483 King, Dwight Y. "Regime Type and Performance: Authoritarian Rule, Semi-Capitalist Development, and Rule Inequality in Asia." *Comparative Political Studies*, 13, No. 4 (January, 1981), 477-504.

4484 Klehr, Harvey, and Haynes, John Earl. *The American Communist Movement: Storming Heaven Itself.* New York: Twayne Publishers, 1992.

4485 Kozyrev, Andrei. "Russia: A Chance for Survival." *Foreign Affairs* [New York], 71, No. 2 (Spring, 1992), 1-16.

4486 Krasnov, Vladislav. *Russia Beyond Communism: A Chronicle of National Rebirth.* Boulder: Westview Press, 1991.

4487 Kull, Steven. *Burying Lenin: The Revolution in Soviet Ideology and Foreign Policy.* Boulder: Westview Press, 1992.

4488 Lane, Christel. "Legitimacy and Power in the Soviet Union Through Socialist Ritual." *British Journal of Political Science*, 14, Part 2 (April 1984), 207-217.

4489 Lau, Siu-kai. "Social Irrelevance of Politics: Hong Kong Chinese Attitudes Toward Political Leadership." *Pacific Affairs* [Vancouver], 65, No. 2 (Summer, 1992), 225-246.

4490 Lawson, Fred H. *Bahrain: The Modernization of Autocracy.* Boulder, Colorado: Westview Press, 1989.

4491 Lechner, Norberto. "The Search for Lost Community: Challenges to Democracy in Latin America." *International Social Science Journal* [Oxford], No. 129 (August, 1991), 541-553.

4492 **Lee, Robin, and Schlemmer, Lawrence,** eds. *Transition to Democracy: Policy Perspectives 1991.* Cape Town: Oxford University Press, 1991.

4493 **Leighton, Marian.** "A Balance Sheet of Sandisnista Rule in Nicaragua." *Survey,* 29, No. 3 (Autumn, 1985), 73-111.

4494 **Leslie, Winsome J.** *Zaire: Continuity and Political Change in an Oppressive State.* Boulder: Westview Press, 1993.

4495 **Lewis, Paul G.** "Democratization in Eastern Europe." *Coexistence* [Dordrecht], 27, No. 4 (December, 1990), 245-267.

4496 **Linden, Ronald H.** *Communist States and International Change: Romania and Yugoslavia in Comparative Perspective.* Boston: Unwin Hyman, 1987.

4497 **Lizhi, Fang.** *Bringing Down the Great Wall: Writings on Science, Culture, and Democracy in China.* New York: Alfred A. Knopf, 1990.

4498 **Logan, Rayford W.** *The Operation of the Mandate System in Africa, 1919-1927.* Washington, D.C.: The Foundation Publishers, 1942.

4499 **Longley, Kyle.** "Peaceful Costa Rica, the First Battleground: The United States and the Costa Rican Revollution of 1948." *The Americas* [Washington, DC], 50, No. 2 (October, 1993), 149-175.

4500 **Lull, James.** *China Turned On: Television, Reform, and Resistance.* London: Routledge, 1991.

4501 **Macesich, George,** ed. *Yugoslavia in the Age of Democracy: Essays on Economic and Political Reform.* Westport: Praeger Publishers, 1992.

4502 **Maddick, Henry.** "Decentralization in the Sudan." *Journal of Local Administration Overseas,* 1, No. 2 (April, 1962), 75-83.

4503 **Manzo, Kate, and McGowan, Pat.** "Afrikaner Fears and the Politics of Dispair: Understanding Change in South Africa." *International Studies Quarterly* [Oxford], 36, No. 1 (March, 1992), 1-24.

4504 **Martin, Edwin W.** "The Socialist Republic of Burma: How Much Change." *Asian Survey,* 15, No. 2 (February, 1975), 129-135.

4505 **McCord, William.** "A Rebirth of 'Moderation' in China?" *Studies in Comparative International Development* [New Brunswick], 26, No. 1 (Spring, 1991), 29-42.

4506 **McCormick, Barrett L.** *Political Reform in Post-Mao China: Democracy and Bureaucracy in a Lenist State.* Berkeley: University of California Press, 1990.

4507 **McCormick, Barrett L.; Su Shaozhi; and Xiao Xiaoming.** "The 1989 Democracy Movement: A Review of the Prospects for Civil Society in China." *Pacific Affairs* [Vancouver], 65, No. 2 (Summer, 1992), 182-202.

4508 **Mead, Margaret.** *Soviet Attitudes Toward Authority: An Interdisciplinary Approach to Problems of Soviet Character.* New York: William Morrow, 1955.

4509 **Meissner, Boris.** "Die Zweite Phase der Soziopolitischen Reform Gorbatschows. Part 1: Die Sowjetunion vor Dem XXVIII: Parteitag der KPdSU." *Osteuropa* [Anstalt], 40, Heft 11 (November, 1990), 1031-1049.

4510 **Merridale, Catherine, and Ward, Chris,** eds. *Perestroika: The Historical Perspective.* London: Edward Arnold, 1991.

4511 **Mestrovic, Stjepan G.** *Habits of the Balkan Heart: Social Character and the Fall of Communism.* College Station: Texas A&M University Press, 1993.

4512 **Mestrovic, Stjepan G.** *The Road from Paradise: Prospects for Democracy in Eastern Europe.* Lexington: The University Press of Kentucky, 1993.

4513 **Michael, Franz and others.** *China and the Crisis of Marxism-Leninism.* Boulder: Westview Press, 1990.

4514 **Michta, Andrew A., and Prizel, Ilya,** eds. *Postcommunist Eastern Europe: Crisis and Reform.* New York: St. Martin's Press, 1992.

4515 **Mills, Charles W.** "Red Peril to the Green Island: The 'Communist Threat' to Jamaica in Genre Fiction, 1955-1969." *Caribbean Studies* [Rio Piedras], 23, Nos. 1-2 (January-June, 1990), 141-165.

4516 **Moody, Peter R.** "Law and Heaven: The Evolution of Chinese Totalitarianism." *Survey,* 24, No. 1 (106) (Winter, 1979), 116-132.

4517 **Motyl, Alexander J.** *Dilemmas of Independence: Ukraine After Totalitarianism.* New York: Council on Foreign Relations Press, 1993.

4518 **Motyl, Alexander J.,** ed. *The Post-Soviet Nations: Perspectives on the Demise of the USSR.* New York: Columbia University Press, 1992.

4519 "Nepal in Transition, the Gurkha Monarchy in the New Asia." *Round Table,* 41, No. 162 (March, 1951), 127-134.

4520 **Norgaard, Ole.** "The Political Economy of Transition in Post-socialist Systems: The Case of the Baltic States." *Scandinavian Political Studies* [Oslo], 15, No. 1 (1992), 41-60.

4521 **Nugent, David.** "Building the State, Making the Nation: The Bases and Limits of State Centralization in 'Modern' Peru." *American Anthropologist* [Arlington], 96, No. 2 (June, 1994), 333-369.

4522 **Nzouankeu, Jacques-Mariel.** "The African Attitude to Democracy." *International Social Science Journal* [Oxford], 128 (May, 1991), 373-385.

4523 **Offe, Claus.** "Capitalism by Democratic Design?: Democratic Theory Facing the Tripple Transition in East Central Europe." *Social Research* [New York], 58, No. 4 (Winter, 1991), 865-892.

4524 **Ogden, Suzanne** and others, eds. *China's Search for Democracy: The Student and the Mass Movement of 1989.* Armonk: M. E. Sharpe, Inc., 1992.

4525 **Oi, Jean C.** "Communism and Clientelism: Rural Politics in China." *World Politics*, 37, No. 2 (January, 1985), 238-266.

4526 **Omara-Otunnu, Amii.** "The Struggle for Democracy in Uganda." *The Journal of Modern African Studies* [Cambridge], 30, No. 3 (September, 1992), 443-463.

4527 **Opello, Walter C., Jr.** "The Transition to Democracy and the Constitutional Settlement as Causes of Political Instability in Post-Authoritarian Portugal." *Luso-Brazilian Review* [Madison], 27, No. 2 (Winter, 1990), 77-94.

4528 **Oppenheimer, Andres.** *Castro's Final Hour: The Secret Story Behind the Coming Downfall of Communist Cuba.* New York: Simon & Schuster, 1992.

4529 **Owusu, Maxwell.** "Democracy and Africa--A View from the Village." *The Journal of Modern African Studies* [Cambridge], 30, No. 3 (September, 1992), 369-396.

4530 **Pec, Steve S.** "The 1940s Sovietization of Poland: A Historiographic Appraisal." *East European Quarterly* [Boulder], 26, No. 1 (Spring, 1992), 109-122.

4531 **Pereira, Anthony W.** "The Neglected Tragedy: The Return to War in Angola, 1992-3." *The Journal of Modern African Studies*, 32, No. 1 (March, 1994), 1-28.

4532 **Perera, Victor.** *Unfinished Conquest: The Guatemalan Tragedy.* Berkeley: University of California Press, 1993.

4533 **Philby, H. St. J.** "The New Reign in Saudi Arabia." *Foreign Affairs,* 32, No. 2 (January, 1954), 446-458.

4534 **Philip, George.** "Military-Authoritarianism in South America: Brazil, Chile, Uruguay and Argentina." *Political Studies*, 32, No. 1 (March, 1984), 1-20.

4535 **Philip, George,** and Clapham, C., eds. *The Political Dilemmas of Military Regimes.* London: Croom Helm, 1985.

4536 **Pilon, Juliana Geran.** *The Bloody Flag: Post-Communist Nationalism in Eastern Europe: Spotlight on Romania.* New Brunswick: Transaction Publishers, 1992.

4537 **Pipes, Richard.** *Russia Under the Bolshevik Regime.* New York: Alfred A. Knopf, 1993.

4538 **Polian, P.** "Geographical Aspects of 'Perestroika' and 'Derussification.'" *Revue Belge de Geographie* [Bruxelles], 115e, Fascs. 1-3 (1991), 111-115.

4539 **Purcell, Susan Kaufman.** "Collapsing Cuba." *Foreign Affairs* [New York], 71, No. 1 (1992), 130-145.

4540 **Ra'anan, Uri,** ed. *The Soviet Empire: The Challenge of National and Democratic Movements.* Lexington: Lexington Books, 1990.

4541 **Rabkin, Rhods.** "Implications of the Gorbachev Era for Cuban Socialism." *Studies in Comparative Communism* [Guildford], 23, No. 1 (Spring, 1990), 23-46.

4542 **Radu, Michael.** "ANC-Inspired Violence Poses a Threat." *Orbis* [Philadelphia], 35, No. 4 (Fall, 1991), 499-513.

4543 **Rady, Martyn.** *Romania in Turmoil: A Contemporary History.* London: IB Tauris & Co., Ltd., 1992.

4544 **Raillon, Francois.** "Le systeme politique indonesien: quel deviner?" *Herodote*, 52 (1989), 15-39.

4545 **Ram, Haggay.** "Crushing the Opposition: Adversaries of the Islamic Republic of Iran." *The Middle East Journal* [Bloomington], 46, No. 3 (Summer, 1992), 426-439.

4546 **Reisinger, William M.** and others. "Political Values in Russia, Ukraine and Lithuania: Sources and Implications for Democracy." *British Journal of Political Science* [Cambridge], 24, Part 2 (April, 1994), 183-222.

4547 **Remnick, David.** *Lenin's Tomb: The Last Days of the Soviet Empire.* New York: Random House, 1993.

4548 **Riddell, John**, ed. *To See the Dawn: Baku, 1920 - First Congress of the Peoples of the East.* New York: Pathfinder, 1993.

4549 **Rieber, Alfred J.**, and **Rubinstein, Alvin Z.**, eds. *Perestroika at the Crossroads.* Armonk: M. E. Sharpe, Inc., 1991.

4550 **Riordan, James W.** "Life After Communism?: The Cost to Russia and the World of the Failure of an Experiment." *Coexistence* [Dordrecht], 29, No. 3 (September, 1992), 241-256.

4551 **Roca, Sergio G.**, ed. *Socialist Cuba: Past Interpretations and Future Challenges.* Boulder, Colorado: Westview Press, 1988.

4552 **Roeder, Philip G.** "Varieties of Post-Soviet Authoritarian Regimes." *Post-Soviet Affairs* [Silver Spring], 10, No. 1 (January-March, 1994), 61-101.

4553 **Roger, Friedrich A.** "National Autonomy in the Austro-Hungarian Monarchy." *Journal of Central European Affairs*, 1, No. 4 (January, 1942), 417-428.

4554 **Rowley, Gwyn.** "Political Geography of Contemporary Events IV: Local Government or Central Government Agency?--The British Case." *Political Geography Quarterly*, 3, No. 3 (July, 1984), 259-264.

4555 **Rugg, Dean S.** "Communist Legacies in the Albanian Landscape." *The Geographical Review* [New York], 84, No. 1 (January, 1994), 59-73.

4556 **Rutland, Peter.** "The Search for Stability: Ideology, Discipline, and the Cohesion of the Soviet Elite." *Studies in Comparative Communism* [London], 24, No. 1 (March, 1991), 25-57.

4557 **Sagers, Matthew J.** "The Spatial Distribution of Communist Party membership in the U.S.S.R. (1940-75)." *Soviet Geography Review and Translation*, 23, No. 7 (September, 1982), 477-494.

4558 **Salah Tahi, Mohand.** "The Arduous Democratisation Process in Algeria." *The Journal of Modern African Studies* [Cambridge], 30, No. 3 (September, 1992), 397-419.

4559 **Salih, Kamal Osman.** "The Sudan, 1985-9: The Fading Democracy." *The Journal of Modern African Studies* [Cambridge], 28, No. 2 (June, 1990), 199-224.

4560 **Sanders, Alan J. K.** "Mongolia's New Constitution: Blueprint for Democracy." *Asian Survey* [Berkeley], 32, No. 6 (June, 1992), 506-520.

4561 **Sapir, Jacques.** "Les Implications Strategiques de la Dcomposition de l'URSS." *Herodote* [Paris], No. 64 (Janvier-Mars, 1992), 20-29.

4562 **Sawyer, Amos.** *The Emergence of Autocracy in Liberia: Tragedy and Challenge.* San Francisco: Institute for Contemporary Studies Press, 1992.

4563 **Schneider, R.M.** *The Political System of Brazil: Emergence of a 'Modernizing' Authoritarian Regime, 1964-1970.* New York: Columbia University Press, 1971.

4564 **Schopflin, George.** "Conservatism and Hungary's Transition." *Problems of Communism* [Washington, DC], 40, Nos. 1-2 (January-April, 1991), 60-68.

4565 **Schopflin, George.** "Post-Communism: Constructing New Democracies in Central Europe." *International Affairs* [Cambridge], 67, No. 2 (April, 1991), 235-250.

4566 **Schwartz, Herman.** "Constitutional Developments in East Central Europe." *Journal of Ingternational Affairs* [New York], 45, No. 1 (Summre, 1991), 71-89.

4567 **Segal, Gerald.** "China After Tiananmen." *Asian Affairs* [London], New Series, 21, Part 2 (June, 1990), 144-154.

4568 **Seroka, Jim.** "From Authoritarian Rule to Democratic Pluralism: The Transformation of the League of Communism of Yugoslavia." *Coexistence* [Dordrecht], 28, No. 3 (September, 1991), 391-401.

4569 **Seroka, Jim**, and **Pavlovic, Vukasin**, eds. *The Tragedy of Yugoslavia: The Failure of Democratic Transformation.* Armonk: M. E. Sharpe, Inc., 1992.

4570 **Shama, Avraham**, ed. *Perestroika: A Comparative Perspective.* New York: Praeger Publishers, 1992.

4571 **Shevtsova, Lilia.** "The August Coup and the Soviet Collapse." *Survival* [London], 34, No. 1 (Spring, 1992), 5-18.

4572 **Shi, Tianjian.** "The Democratic Movement in China in 1989: Dynamics and Failure." *Asian Survey* [Berkeley], 30, No. 12 (December, 1990), 1186-1205.

4573 **Shlapentokh, Vladimir.** *The Last Years of the Soviet Empire: Snapshots From 1985-1991.* Westport: Praeger Publishers, 1993.

4574 **Shlapentokh, Vladimir.** "The XXVII Congress - A Case Study of the Shaping of a New Party Ideology." *Soviet Studies*, 40, No. 1 (January, 1988), 1-20.

4575 **Shue, Vivienne.** "China: Transition Postponed?" *Problems of Communism* [Washington, DC], 41, Nos. 1-2 (January-April, 1992), 157-168.

4576 **Siisiainen, Martti.** "Social Movements, Voluntary Associations and Cycles of Protest in Finland 1905-91." *Scandinavian Political Studies* [Oslo], 15, No. 1 (1992), 21-40.

4577 **Simms, Peter.** *Trouble in Guyana; An Account of People, Personalities and Politics as They Were in British Guiana.* New York: International Publications Service, 1966.

4578 **Simon, Jeffrey.** "Central Europe: 'Return to Europe' or Descent to Chaos?" *Strategic Review* [Washington, DC], 21, No. 1 (Winter, 1993), 18-25.

4579 **Simonia, Nodari A.** *Socialism in Russia: Theory and Practice.* Westport: Greenwood Press, 1994.

4580 **Singh, Daljit.** *The Politics of Presidential Rule in India.* Claremont, California: Claremont Graduate School and University Center, Ph.D., 1970.

4581 **Singh, S.N.** *Centre-State Relations in India; Major Irritants of Post Sarkaria Review.* New Delhi: H.K., 1990.

4582 **Smart, Christopher.** "Gorbachev's Lenin: The Myth in Service to Perestroika." *Studies in Comparative Communism* [Guildford], 23, No. 1 (Spring, 1990), 5-22.

4583 **Smith, Gordon B.** *Soviet Politics: Struggling with Change.* 2nd ed. New York: St. Martin's, 1992.

4584 **Smith, William C.** *Authoritarianism and the Crisis of the Argentine Political Economy.* Stanford, California: Stanford University Press, 1989.

4585 **Solchanyk, Roman.** "Ukraine, the (Former) Center, Russia, and 'Russia.'" *Studies in Comparative Communism* [Oxford], 25, No. 1 (March, 1992), 31-45.

4586 **Sonn, Tamara.** *Between Qur'an and Crown: The Challenge of Political Legitimacy in the Arab World.* Boulder: Westview Press, 1990.

4587 **Staar, Richard F.,** ed. *Transition to Democracy in Poland.* New York: St. Martin's Press, 1993.

4588 **Staniszkis, Jadwiga.** *The Dynamics of the Breakthrough in Eastern Europe: The Polish Experience.* Translated from the Polish by Chester A. Kisiel. Berkeley: University of California Press, 1991.

4589 **Steele, Jonathan.** *Eternal Russia: Yeltsin, Gorbachev and the Mirage of Democracy.* London: Faber and Faber, 1994.

4590 **Stephenson, Glenn V.** "Cultural Regionalism and the Unitary State Idea in Belgium." *Geographical Review*, 62, No. 4 (October, 1972), 501-523.

4591 **Stewart, Marjorie Helen.** "Kinship and Succession to the Throne of Bussa." *Ethnology* 17, No. 2 (April, 1978), 169-182.

4592 **Stokes, Gale.** "Lessons of the East European Revolutions of 1989." *Problems of Communism* [Washington, DC], 40, No. 5 (September-October, 1991), 17-22.

4593 **Stora, Benjamin.** "Maghreb: L'essor Democratique Fracasse?" *Herodote* [Paris], No. 60-61 (Janvier-Juin, 1991), 195-200.

4594 **Stranahan, Patricia.** "Strange Bedfellows: The Communist Party and Shanghai's Elite in the National Salvation Movement." *The China Quarterly* [London], No. 129 (March, 1992), 26-51.

4595 **Thapa, Bhekh B.** "Nepal in 1991: A Consolidation of Democratic Pluralism." *Asian Survey* [Berkeley], 32, No. 2 (February, 1992), 175-183.

4596 **Tiruneh, Andargachew.** *The Ethiopian Revolution, 1974-1987: A Transformation from an Aritocratic to a Totalitarian Autocracy.* Cambridge: Cambridge University Pess, 1993.

4597 **Titus, David A.** "The Making of the 'Symbol Emperor System' in Postwar Japan." *Modern Asian Studies*, 14, Part 4 (October, 1980), 529-578.

4598 **Tong, Yanqi.** "State, Society, and Political Change in China and Hungary." *Comparative Politics* [New York], 26, No. 3 (April, 1994), 333-353.

4599 **Trudeau, Robert H.** *Guatemalan Politics: The Popular Struggle for Democracy.* Boulder: Lynne Rienner Publishers, 1993.

4600 **Tu, Wei-ming.** "Intellectual Effervescence in China." *Daedalus* [Cambridge, MA], 121, No. 2 (Spring, 1992), 251-292.

4601 **Tzvetkov, Plamen S.** "The Politics of Transition in Bulgaria: Back to the Future?" *Problems of Communism* [Washington, DC], 41, No. 3 (May-June, 1992), 34-57.

4602 **Ule, Otto.** "The Bumpy Road of Czechoslovakia's Velvet Revolution." *Problems of Communism* [Washington, DC], 41, No. 3 (May-June, 1992), 19-33.

4603 **Uwazurike, P. Chudi.** "Confronting Potential Breakdown: The Nigerian Redemocratisation Process in Critical Perspective." *The Journal of Modern African Studies* [Cambridge], 28, No. 1 (March, 1990), 55-77.

4604 **Van Der Kroef, J.** *Communism in South-East Asia.* London: Macmillan, 1981.

4605 **Volten, Peter M. E.** "Security Dimensions of Imperial Collapse." *Problems of Communism* [Washington, DC], 41, Nos. 1-2 (January-April, 1992), 136-147.

4606 **Walder, Andrew G.** "Workers, Managers and the State: The Reform Era and the Political Crisis of 1989." *The China Quarterly* [London], 127 (September, 1991), 467-492.

4607 **Walker, Rachel.** *Six Years that Shook the World: Perestroika--The Impossible Porject.* Manchester: Manchester University Press, 1993.

4608 **Walker, Thomas W.,** ed. *Revolution and Counterrevolution in Nicaragua.* Boulder: Westview Press, 1991.

4609 **Weigle, Marcia A.** "Political Participation and Party Formation in Russia, 1985-1992: Institutionalizing Democracy?" *The Russian Review* [Columbus], 53, No. 2 (April, 1994), 240-270.

4610 **Wendt, Alexander.** "Anarchy Is What States Make of It: The Social Construction of Power Politics." *International Organization* [Cambridge, MA], 46, No. 2 (Spring, 1992), 391-425.

4611 **White, Peter T.** "Cuba at the Crossroads." *National Geographic Magazine* [Washington, DC], 180, No. 2 (August, 1991), 90-121.

4612 **White, Stephen.** *Gorbachev and After.* Cambridge: Cambridge University Press, 1991.

4613 **White, Stephen.** "Rethinking the CPSU." *Soviet Studies* [Abingdon], 43, No. 3 (1991), 405-428.

4614 **Whyte, Martin King.** "Prospects for Democratization in China." *Problems of Communism* [Washington, DC], 41, No. 3 (May-June, 1992), 58-70.

4615 **Wightman, Gordon.** "Membership of the Communist Party of Czechoslovakia in the 1970's: Continuing Divergence from the Soviet Model." *Soviet Studies*, 35, No. 2 (April, 1983), 208-222.

4616 **Williams, Michael.** "Sneevliet and the Birth of Asian Communism." *New Left Review*, 123 (September-October, 1980), 81-91.

4617 **Wilson, Frank L.** *The Failure of West European Communism: Implications for the Future.* New York: Paragon House, 1993.

4618 **Wiseman, John A.** *Democracy in Black Africa: Survival and Revival.* New York: Paragon House Publishers, 1990.

4619 **Yaniv, Avner,** ed. *National Security and Democracy in Israel.* Boulder: Lynne Rienner Publishers, 1993.

4620 **Yoder, Amos.** *Communism in Transition: The End of the Soviet Empires.* London: Taylor & Francis, 1993.

4621 **Young, Crawford.** "Zaire: The Unending Crisis." *Foreign Affairs*, 57, No. 1 (Fall, 1978), 169-185.

4622 **Zang, Xiawei.** "Elite Formation and the Bureaucratic-Technocracy in Post-Mao China." *Studies in Comparative Communism* [London], 24, No. 1 (March, 1991), 114-123.

4623 **Zarrow, Peter.** *Anarchism and Chinese Political Culture.* New York: Columbia University Press, 1990.

4624 **Zeman, Z. A. B.** *The Making and Breaking of Communist Europe.* Oxford: Basil Blackwell, Ltd., 1991.

FEDERAL

GENERAL AND THEORY

Books and Journals

4625 **Acir,** ed. *Significant Features of Fiscal Federalism.* Washington, D.C.: U.S. Advisory Commission on Intergovernmental Relations, 1984.

4626 **Antonova, I.F.,** and **Krysina, E.E.** "British Columbia as a Part of the Canadian Confederation (Social-Geographical Problemsand Tendencies)." *Moskovskii Universitet Vestnik, Seria 5, Geografiia (Moskva)*, 2 (Mart-April, 1986), 71-77.

4627 **Archer, J. Clark.** "Incrementalism and Federal Outlays Among States." *Geographical Perspectives*, 44, No. 2 (Fall, 1979), 5-14.

4628 **Arrendondo, Benjamin.** "Descripcion de los limites del Bistrito Federal." *Revista Mexicana de Geografia*, Tomo 1, Num. 1 (Julio-Septiembre, 1941), 13-32.

4629 **Beloff, Max.** "The Federal Solution in Its Application to Europe, Asia and Africa." *Political Studies*, 1, No. 2 (June, 1953), 114-131.

4630 **Bennett, Robert J.** *The Geography of Public Finance: Welfare under Fiscal Federalism and Local Government Finance.* London: Methuen, 1980.

4631 **Browning, Clyde E.** *The Geography of Federal Outlays: A Introductory and Comparative Inquiry.* Chapel Hill: University of North Carolina, Department of Geography, Studies in Geography No. 4, 1973.

4632 **Brunn, Stanley D., and Hoffman, Wayne L.** "The Geography of Federal Grants-In-Aid to States." *Economic Geography*, 45, No. 3 (July, 1969), 226-238.

4633 **Currie, David P.** *Federalism in the New Nations.* Chicago, Illinois: University of Chicago Press, 1964.

4634 **Dear, M., and Moors, A.** "Structuration Theory in Urban Analysis: 2, Empirical Application." *Environment and Planning*, A18, No. 2 (June, 1986), 351-374.

4635 **Dikshit, R.D.** "Geography and Federalism." *Annals of the Association of American Geographers*, 61, No. 1 (March, 1971), 97-115.

4636 **Dikshit, R.D.** "Military Interpretation of Federal Constitutions: A Critique." *Journal of Politics*, 33, No. 1 (February, 1971), 180-189.

4637 **Dikshit, R.D.** *The Political Geography of Federalism: An Inquiry into Origins and Stability.* New York: John Wiley & Sons, 1975.

4638 **Douglas, W.O.** *Towards a Global Federalism.* New York: New York University Press, 1968.

4639 **Duchacek, Ivo D.** *Comparative Federalism.* New York: Holt, Rinehart & Winston, 1970.

4640 **Frank, T.M., ed.** *Why Federations Fail.* New York: University Press, 1968.

4641 **Fraser, Andrew; Mason, R.H.P.; and Mitchell, Philip.** *Japan's Early Parliament.* New York: Routledge Japanese Studies, 1995.

4642 **Greater Rhodesia.** "An Examination of the Federal Proposals." *Round Table*, 39, No. 155 (June, 1949), 227-233.

4643 **Hicks, U.K., ed.** *Federalism and Economic Growth in Under-developed Countries--A Symposium.* London: Allen & Unwin, 1961.

4644 **Huebsch, Michael.** *An Examination of the Spatial Conditions of Federalism.* Athens: Ohio University Department of Geography, M.A., 1977.

4645 **Kersten, Rikki.** *Democracy in Post War Japan: Maruyama Masao and the Search for Autonomy.*

New York: Routledge Japanese Studies, 1995.

4646 **Laski, Harold.** "The Obsolescence of Federalism." *New Republic*, 98, No. 1274 (May 3, 1939), 367-369.

4647 "Land-Lease Arrangements and United Nations Administrative Agencies. Notes on Organizations. Bibliographical Notes on Federation." *Bulletin of the Commission to Study the Organization of Peace*, 2, No. 8-9 (August-September, 1942), 1-20.

4648 **Lithwick, N.H.** "Is Federalism Good for Regionalism?" *Journal of Canadian Studies*, 15 (1980), 62-73.

4649 **Livingston, William S.** "A Note on the Nature of Federalism." *Political Science Quarterly*, 67, No. 1 (March, 1952), 81-95.

4650 **Lowenthal, David.** "Two Federations." *Social and Economic Studies*, 6, No. 2 (June, 1957), 185-197.

4651 **Lowery, David; Brunn, Stanley D.; and Webster, Gerald.** "From Stable Disparity to Dynamic Equity: The Spatial Distribution of Federal Expenditures, 1971-1983." *Social Sciences Quarterly*, 67, No. 1 (March, 1986), 98-107.

4652 **Macmahon, A.** *Federalism Mature and Emergent.* New York: Doubleday, 1955.

4653 **Madison, J.** *The Federalist.* New York: Modern Library, 1941.

4654 **Marc, A.** "New and Old Federalism: Faithful to the Origins." *Publius*, 9, No. 4 (Fall, 1979), 117-130.

4655 **Marriott, Sir. J.A.R.** *Federalism and the Problem of the Small State.* London: Allen & Unwin, 1943.

4656 **Martin, Roscoe.** *Cities and the Federal System.* New York: Atherton Press, 1965.

4657 **McWhinney, Edward.** *Comparative Federalism. States Rights and National Power.* Toronto: University of Toronto Press, 1962.

4658 **Morton, William Lewis.** *The West and Confederation, 1857-1871.* Ottawa: Canadian Historical Association, 1958.

4659 **Murphy, T.P.** *Science, Geopolitics and Federal Spending.* Lexington, Kentucky: D.C. Heath, 1971.

4660 **Muskin, Selma.** "Federal Grants and Federal Expenditures." *National Tax Journal*, 10, No. 3 (September, 1957), 193-213.

4661 **Oates, W.E.** *Fiscal Federalism.* New York: Harcourt Brace Jovanovich, 1972.

4662 "Rhodesia and Nyasaland; Federation in the Balance." *Round Table; A Quarterly Review of British Commonwealth Affairs*, 52, No. 209 (December, 1962), 89-96.

4663 **Riker, W.** *Federalism: Origin, Operation, Significance.* Boston: Little Brown, 1964.

4664 **Sanguin, Andre-Louis.** "Territorial Aspects of Federalism: A Geography Yet to be Made." *Scottish Geographical Magazine*, 99, No. 2 (September, 1983), 66-76.

4665 **Saywell, John,** ed. "Nationalism and Federalism." *Canadian Annual Review for 1967.* Toronto: University Press, 1968.

4666 **Sigurdson, Richard.** "Preston Manning and the Politics of Postmodernism in Canada." *Canadian Journal of Political Science*, 37, No. 2 (June, 1994), 249-276.

4667 **Spate, O.H.K.** "Geography and Federalism." *Indian Geographical Journal*, 19, No. 1 (January-March, 1944), 24-36.

4668 **Streit, Clarence K.** *Union Now; The Proposal for Inter-Democracy Federal Union.* New York: Harper & Brothers, 1940.

4669 **Tarlton, Charles.** "Symmentry and Asymmetry as Elements of Federalism." *Journal of Politics*, 27, No. 4 (November, 1965), 861-874.

4670 **Thur, L.M.** *Energy Policy and Federalism.* Ottawa: Institute of Public Administration of Canada, 1981.

4671 **Walter, Bob J.** "The Spatial Conditions of Federalism." *Ohio Geographers: Recent Research Themes* (with M. Huebsch), 6 (1978), 51-65.

4672 **Wheare, K.C.** *Federal Government.* London: Oxford University Press, 1946.

POLITICAL GEOGRAPHY OF REGIONS

AFRICA

Books and Journals

4673 "Administration: French Federal Union." *African Transcripts*, 3 (May, 1945), 77-79.

4674 **Awa, Eme O.** *Federal Government in Nigeria.* Berkeley: University of California Press, 1964.

4675 **Banfield, Jane.** "Federation in East Africa." *International Journal*, 18, No. 2 (Spring, 1963), 181-193.

4676 **Bruce, John W.** "The Creation of the Mid-West Region and Its Significance for Nigerian Federalism." In *Columbia Essays in International Affairs*, 3. The Dean's Papers, 1967, Students of Faculty of International Affairs, Columbia University, Edited by Andrew W. Cordier. New York City: Columbia University Press, 1968, 222-249.

4677 "Central Africa in 1962; Can Federation Survive?" *Round Table*, 52, No. 208 (September, 1962), 361-367.

4678 **Church, R.J. Harrison.** "Picking Up the Pieces in a Federated Nigeria." *Geographical Magazine*, 42, No. 6 (March, 1970), 453-454.

4679 **Cowan, L. Gray.** "Federation for Nigeria." *International Journal*, 10, No. 1 (Winter, 1954-55), 51-60.

4680 **de Blij, Harm J.** "Forced Wedding: Federation in the Rhodesias and Nyasaland." In *Africa South* by Harm J. de Blij. Evanston, Illinois: Northwestern University Press, 1962, 292-350.

4681 **Dikshit, R.D.** "Failure of Federalism in Central Africa: A Politico-Geographic Post-Mortem." *Professional Geographer*, 23, No. 3 (August, 1971), 224-248.

4682 **Dikshit, R.D.** "Nigeria from Federation to Civil War: A Study in the Dynanmics of Federalism." *Political Science Review*, 15, No. 1 (March, 1976), 27-40.

4683 **Dugdale, John.** "Can Federation Work in Rhodesia?" *New Commonwealth*, 33, No. 2 (January 21, 1957), 61-62.

4684 "East Africa; Revolution in Zanzibar and Union with Tanganyika." *International Bulletin*, 2, No. 6 (June, 1964), 180-185.

4685 "The Federation Issue in Central Africa." *World Today*, 8, No. 11 (November, 1952), 450-460.

4686 **Foltz, William J.** *From French West Africa to the Mali Federation.* New Haven, Connecticut: Yale University Press, 1965.

4687 **Franklin, H.** *Unholy Wedlock: The Failure of the Central African Federation.* London: Allen & Unwin, 1964.

4688 "The Future of the Central African Federation." *World Today*, 11, No. 12 (December, 1955), 539-548.

4689 **Great Britain Parliament.** *Southern Rhodesia, Northern Rhodesia, and Nyasaland.* Report by the Conference on Federation held in London in January, 1953. Presented to Parliament by the Secretary of State for Commonwealth Relations and the Secretary of State for the Colonies. London: 1953.

4690 **Hance, William A.** "Economic Potentialities of the Central African Federation." *Political Science Quarterly*, 69, No. 1 (March, 1954), 29-44.

4691 **Harbert, A.S.** *Federal Grant-in-Aid: Maximizing Benefits to the States.* New York: Praeger, 1976.

4692 **Hiller, Harry H.** "Dependence and Independence: Emergent Nationalism in Newfoundland." *Ethnic and Racial Studies*, 10, No. 3 (July, 1987), 257-275.

4693 **Hughes, Anthony John.** *East Africa: The Search for Unity: Kenya, Tanganyika, Uganda, and Zanzibar.* Baltimore: Penguin, 1963.

4694 **Ijere, Joseph A.** *Symmetry and Asymmetry in the Delimitation of States in a Federation: A Theoretical Application to Nigeria.* Athens: Ohio University Department of Geography, M.A., 1979.

4695 **Kimble, George H.T.** "The Federation of Rhodesia and Nyasaland." *Focus*, 6, No. 7 (1956), 1-6.

4696 **Kurtz, Donn M.** "Political Integration in Africa: The Mali Federation." *Journal of Modern African Studies*, 8, No. 3 (October, 1970), 405-424.

4697 **Leys, C. and Robson, Peter.** *Federation in East Africa: Opportunities and Problems.* Nairobi: Oxford University Press, 1965.

4698 **Mackintosh, John P.** "Federalism in Nigeria." *Political Studies*, 10, No. 3 (September, 1962), 223-247.

4699 **Mahmud, Sakah.** "The Failed Transition to Civilian Rule in Nigeria: Its Implications for Democracy and Human rights." *Africa Today* [Denver], 40, No. 4 (1993), 87-95.

4700 **Osaghae, Eghosa E.** "The Complexity of Nigeria's Federal Character and the Inadequacies of the Federal Character Principle." *Journal of Ethnic Studies*, 16, No. 3 (Fall, 1988), 1-25.

4701 **Prescott, J.R.V.** "The Geographical Basis of Nigerian Federation." *Nigerian Geographical Journal*, 2, No. 1 (June, 1958), 1-13.

4702 **Rogge, John R.** "The Balkinization of Nigeria's Federal System: A Case in the Political Geography of Africa." *Journal of Geography*, 76, No. 4 (April-May, 1977), 135-140.

4703 **Rubin, Neville.** *Cameroun: An African Federation.* Amsterdam: Hol. Rudolf Muller, 1971.

4704 **Sills, H.D.** "The Break-Up of the Central African Federation: Notes on the Validity of Assurances. *African Affairs*, 73, No. 290 (January, 1974), 50-62.

4705 **Somerville, J.J.B.** "The Central African Federation." *International Affairs*, 39, No. 3 (July, 1963), 386-402.

4706 **Velensky, Roy.** "Toward Federation in Central Africa." *Foreign Affairs*, 31, No. 1 (October, 1952), 142-149.

AMERICAS

Books and Journals

4707 **Archer, J. Clark.** "Federal Spending in New England: 1952-1977." *Proceedings: New England-St. Lawrence Valley Geographical Society*, 8 (1978), 1-10.

4708 **Archibald, Charles H.** "The Failure of the West Indies Federation." *World Today*, 18, No. 6 (June, 1962), 233-242.

4709 "Background to West Indian Federation." *World Today*, 6, No. 6 (June, 1950), 255-264.

4710 **Black, Jan Knippers.** "Brazil's Limited Redemocratization." *Current History* [Philadelphia], 91, No. 562 (February, 1992), 85-89.

4711 **Blood, Sir Hilary.** "Federation in the Caribbean." *Corona*, 8, No. 5 (May, 1956), 166-169.

4712 **Blood, Sir Hilary.** "The West Indian Federation." *Journal of the Royal Society of Arts*, 105, No. 5009 (August 2, 1957), 746-757.

4713 **Boulding, Kenneth E.** "National Images and International Systems." *Journal of Conflict Resolution*, 3, No. 2 (June, 1959), 120-131.

4714 **Burns, Sir Allen.** "Towards a Caribbean Federation." *Foreign Affairs*, 34, No. 1 (October, 1955), 128-140.

4715 **Carroll, William K. and Ratner, R.S.** "Social Democracy, Neo-Conservatism and Hegemonic Crisis in British Columbia." *Critical Sociology*, 16, No. 1 (Spring, 1989), 29-53.

4716 **Clarke, C.G.** "Political Fragmentation in the Caribbean: The Case of Anguilla." *Canadian Geographer*, 15, No. 1 (Spring, 1971), 13-29.

4717 Dale, Edmund H. "The State-Idea, Missing Prop of the West Indies Federation." *Scottish Geographical Magazine*, 78, No. 3 (December, 1962), 166-176.

4718 Elazar, D.J. *American Federalism: A View from the States*. New York: Thomas Y. Crowell, 1972.

4719 "A Federal Plan for the British Caribbean." *Corona*, 2, No. 5 (May, 1950), 175-178.

4720 "Federation in the British West Indies." *World Today*, 13, No. 3 (March, 1957), 109-117.

4721 "Federating the Islands. The Prospects for the West Indies." *Round Table*, 47, No. 187 (June, 1957), 243-250.

4722 Fraser, A.M. "The Nineteenth Century of Negotiations for Confederation of Newfoundland with Canada." *Canadian Historical Association Report of the Annual Meeting*, (1949), 14-21.

4723 "French and English in Canada; A Crisis of Confederation?" *Round Table*, 54, No. 214 (March, 1964), 155-161.

4724 Gallart, Horacio. "Los nuevos territorios federales de Brasil." *Revista Geografica Americana*, 21, Num. 127 (Abril, 1944), 199-207.

4725 Greenridge, C.W.W. "The British Caribbean Federation." *World Affairs*, 4, No. 3 (July, 1950), 321-334.

4726 Havemann, J., Pierce, N., and Stanfield, R. "Federal Spending: The North's Loss is the Sunbelt's Gain." *National Journal*, 8 (1976), 878-891.

4727 Hoffman, George W., ed. *Federation and Regional Development: Case Studies in the Experience in the United States and the Federal Republic of Germany*. Austin: University of Texas Press, 1981.

4728 Holdsworth, Deryck. "Architectural Expressions of the Canadian National State." *Canadian Geographer*, 30, No. 2 (Summer, 1986), 167-171.

4729 Honey, Rex D. *Federally Induced Regional Governance in the United States*. Iowa City: University of Iowa, Institute of Urban and Regional Research, Technical Report 65, 1975.

4730 Johnston, R.J. "Congressional Committees and Department Spending: The Political Influence on the Geography of Federal Expenditure in the United States." *Transactions of the Institute of British Geographers*, New Series, 4, No. 3 (July, 1979), 373-384.

4731 Johnston, R.J. "The Geography of Federal Allocations in the U.S.: Preliminary Tests of Some Tests for Political Geography." *Geoforum*, 8, No. 5-6 (September-December, 1977), 319-326.

4732 Johnston, R.J. *The Geography of Federal Spending in the United States of America*. Chichester, New York: John Wiley & Sons, 1980.

4733 Karnes, Thomas L. *The Failure of the Union: Central America 1824-1960*. Chapel Hill: University of North Carolina Press, 1961.

4734 Kim, In. *Spatial Impact of Federal Outlays on the Metropolitan Areas in the United States*. Chapel Hill: University of North Carolina, Ph.D., 1972.

4735 Knaplund, Paul. "Federation of the West Indies." *Social and Economic Studies*, 6, No. 2 (June, 1957), 99-108.

4736 Lacasse, Jean-Paul. "La notion de conscience territoriale en milieu: Le cas du Quebec." *International Geography*. W. Peter Adams and Frederick M. Helleiner, eds. Montreal: 22nd I.G.U. Congress, 1972.

4737 Legare, Ann. "Towards a Marxist Theory of Canadian Federalism." *Studies in Political Economy*, No. 8 (Summer, 1982), 37-58.

4738 Lewis, Gordon K. "La Federacion Britanica del Caribe: el Tranfando de las Indias Occidentales." *Revista de Ciencias Sociales*, 1, No. 1 (March, 1957), 139-169.

4739 Lopes, Lucas. *Memoria sobre a mudanco do Distrito Federal*. 20 mimeographed 1. Belo Horizonte: Papelaria e tipografia "Brasil," 1946.

4740 Lowenthal, David. *The West Indies Federation: Perspective on a New Nation*. New York City: Columbia University Press, 1961.

4741 MacKenzie, David. *Inside the Atlantic Trianble: Canada and the Entrance of Newfoundland Into Confederation, 1939-1949*. Toronto: University of Toronto Press, 1986.

4742 Mahabir, Dennis J. "The Caribbean Federation." *India Quarterly*, 13, No. 1 (January-March, 1957), 32-40.

4743 Martis, Kenneth C. "Sectionalism and the United States Congress." *Political Geography Quarterly*, 7, No. 2 (April, 1988), 99-109.

4744 Mayo, H.B. "Newfoundland and Confederation in the Eighteen-Sixties." *Canadian Historical Review*, 29, No. 2 (June, 1948), 125-142.

4745 McCowann, Anthony. "British Guiana and Federation." *Corona*, 9, No. 3 (March, 1957), 85-88.

4746 **Merrill, Gordon C.** "The West-Indies--The Newest Federation of Commonwealth." *Canadian Geographical Journal*, 56, No. 2 (February, 1958), 60-69.

4747 **Minghi, Julian V., and Harris, Cole R.** "Diversity, Territorial Organization and Power: Canadian Confederation." In *The Federalist Approach*, John K. Keith, ed. Montreal, Canada: 22nd International Geographical Congress, 1979, 139-142.

4748 **Monmonier, Mark.** "Federal-State Cost-Sharing and the Geography of Cartography in New Hampshire and Vermont." *Proceedings. Pennsylvania Academy of Science*, 57 (1983), 93-98.

4749 **Morton, William Lewis.** "The Geographical Circumstances of Confederation." *Canadian Geographical Journal*, 70, No. 3 (March, 1965), 74-87.

4750 "Newfoundland Looks at Her Future; The Question of Federal Union with Canada." *Round Table*, 38, No. 150 (March, 1948), 551-558.

4751 **Office of Economic Opportunity.** *Federal Outlays in Summary, PB-219 463, National Technical Information Service.* Springfield, Virginia: U.S. Department of Commerce, 1972.

4752 **Orban, E.**, ed. *La Modernisation Politique de Quebec.* Sillery, Quebec: Les Editions de Boreal Express, 1976.

4753 **Ostrom, Vincent.** *The Meaning of American Federalism: Consstituting a Self-governing Society.* San Francisco: Institute for Contemporary Studies, 1991.

4754 **Panitch, L.**, ed. *The Canadian State.* Toronto: University of Toronto Press, 1977.

4755 **Proctor, Jesse Harris.** "Britain's Pro-Federation Policy in the Caribbean; An Inquiry into Motivation." *The Canadian Journal of Economics and Political Science*, 22, No. 3 (August, 1956), 319-331.

4756 **Proctor, Jesse Harris.** "The Development of the Idea of Federation of the British Caribbean Territories." *Caribbean Quarterly*, 5, No. 1 (June, 1957), 5-33.

4757 **Proctor, Jesse Harris.** "The Development of the Idea of Federation of British Caribbean Territories." *Revista de Historia de America*, 39 (Junio, 1955), 61-105.

4758 "Prospects of Federation in the British Caribbean." *Round Table*, 40, No. 159 (June, 1950), 226-232.

4759 "Quadro Sistematico de Divisao Regional das Unidades Federades." *Boletim Geograifco*, 11, No. 116 (September-October, 1953), 531-536.

4760 **Reagan, M.** *The New Federalism.* New York: Oxford University Press, 1972.

4761 **Rosales, Mario.** "Las Nuevas Provincias Argentinas. En Virtud de la Ley 14.408, Sancionada por el Congreso Nacional, el 1S de Julio de 1955, se Suman Cinco Provincias Nuevas al Conjunto Federal Argentino." *Revista Geografia Americana*, 60, No. 235 (July, 1955), 2-5.

4762 **Sage, Walter N.** "British Columbia and Confederation." *British Columbia Quarterly*, 15, No. 1-2 (1951), 71-84.

4763 **Schwartzberg, Joseph E.** "The U.S. Constitution, A Model for Global Government." *Journal of Geography*, 86, No. 6 (November-December, 1987), 246-252.

4764 **Shelley, Fred M.** "Structure, Stability and Section in American Politics." *Political Geography Quarterly*, 7, No. 2 (April, 1988), 153-160.

4765 **Smiley, Donald V., and Watts, Ronald L.** *Interstate Federalism in Canada.* Toronto: University of Toronto Press, 1985.

4766 **Smith, David E.** "Empire, Crown and Canadian Federalism." *Canadian Journal of Political Science* [Ottawa], 24, No. 3 (September, 1991), 451-473.

4767 **Smyth, Steven.** "The Constitutional Context of Aboriginal and Colonial Government in the Yukon Territory." *Polar Record* [Cambridge], 29, No. 169 (April, 1993), 121-126.

4768 "Special Federation Number." University College of the West Indies, Jamaica. Institute of Social and Economic Research. *Social and Economic Studies*, 6, No. 2 (June, 1957), 99-328.

4769 **Springer, Hugh W.** "Federation in the Caribbean: An Attempt that Failed." *International Organization*, 16, No. 4 (Autumn, 1962), 758-775.

4770 **Stellwagon, Marvin A.** *An Analysis of the Spatial Impact of Federal Revenues and Expenditures: 1950 and 1960.* Seattle: University of Washington, Ph.D., 1967.

4771 **Stern, Peter M.; Augelli, John P.; and Lowenthal, David.** "British Caribbean Federation." *Focus*, 7, No. 1 (September, 1956), 1-6.

4772 **Trudeau, P.E.** "Federalism, Nationalism, and Reason." In *The Future of Canadian Federalism.* P.A. Crepeau and C.B. Macpherson, eds. Toronto: University of Toronto Press, 1965, 16-35.

4773 **Tulchin, Joseph S.**, and **Varas, Augusto**, eds. *From Dictatorship to Democracy: Rebuilding Political Consensus in Chile.* Boulder: Lynne Rienner Publishers, 1991.

4774 **Wallace, Elizabeth**. "The West Indies: Improbable Federation?" *Canadian Journal of Economics and Political Science*, 27, No. 4 (November, 1961), 444-459.

4775 **Washington, S. Walter**. "Crisis in the British West Indies." *Foreign Affairs*, 38, No. 4 (July, 1960), 646-656.

4776 **Weinstein, Martin**. *Uruguay: Democracy of the Crossroads.* Boulder, Colorado: Westview Press, 1988.

ASIA

Books and Journals

4777 **Adhikari, Sudeepta**. "Geographical Basis of India's Federal Polity." *Indian Geographical Journal*, 58, No. 2 (1983), 162-171.

4778 **Adhikari, Sudeepta**. "Some Aspects of Indian Federalism: A Study in Political Geography." *Singapore Journal of Tropical Geography*, 7, No. 1 (June, 1986), 1-11.

4779 **Aiyer, S.P.**, and **Mehta, U.** *Essays on Indian Federalism.* New Delhi: Allied Publishers, 1965.

4780 **Almi, Massimo**. "Verso la Federazione dei Sultanati Arabi di Aden." *L'Universo*, 35, No. 2 (March-April, 1955), 263-270.

4781 **Banerjee, D.N.** *Partition or Federation? A Study in Indian Constitutional Problem.* Calcutta: General Printers and Publishers, 1945.

4782 **Baxter, Craig**. "Bangladesh in 1991: A Parliamentary System." *Asian Survey* [Berkeley], 32, No. 2 (February, 1992), 162-167.

4783 **Bernstein, Marverll**. "Israel: Turbulent Democracy at Forty." *Middle East Journal*, 42, No. 2 (Spring, 1988), 193-201.

4784 **Brintan, J.Y.** *Aden and the Federation of South Arabia.* Washington, D.C.: American Society of International Law, 1964.

4785 **Brintan, J.Y.**, comp. *Federations in the Middle East; A Documentary Survey.* Cairo: Egyptian Society of International Law, 1964.

4786 "Britain Faces a New Malaya. What Is Behind Britain's Reversal of Policy on the Malayan Union?" *Amerasia*, 11, No. 1 (January, 1947), 11-14.

4787 **Catley, R.** "Malaysia: The Lost Battle for Merger." *Australian Outlook*, 21, No. 1 (April, 1967), 44-60.

4788 **Chatterji, Amiya**. *The Impact of Planning Upon Federalism in India, 1951-1964.* Cambridge: Cambridge University, Ph.D., 1966.

4789 **Cheng, Tun-jen**, and **Haggard, Stephan**, eds. *Political Change in Taiwan.* Boulder: Lynne Rienner Publishers, 1992.

4790 **Chiang, Meng**. "The New Mongolian Federation." *Foreign Commerce Weekly*, 3, No. 12, (June 21, 1941), 487-489.

4791 **Cobbold, Cameron Fromanteel, Lord**. "Sarawak and North Borneo in Greater Malaysia." *Commonwealth Journal of the Royal Commonwealth Society*, 5, No. 6 (November-December, 1962), 291-297.

4792 "Complications of Union in Malaya." *Round Table*, 36, No. 143 (June, 1946), 238-246.

4793 **De Montmorency, G.F., Sir**. *The Indian States and Indian Federation.* Cambridge: Cambridge University Press, 1942.

4794 **Dodd, Clement**. "The Revival of the Turkish Democracy." *Asian Affairs* [London], 23, Part 3 (October, 1992), 305-314.

4795 **Dubhashi, P.R.** "The Implications and Scope of Democratic Decentralization." *Indian Journal of Public Administration*, 6, No. 4 (October-December, 1960), 369-392.

4796 **Dupree, Louis**. "A Suggested Pakistan-Afghanistan-Iran Federation." *Middle East Journal*, 17, No. 4 (Autumn, 1963), 383-399.

4797 **Emerson, Rupert**. *Malaysia—A Study in Direct and Indirect Rule.* Kuala Lumpur: University of Malaya Press, 1964.

4798 "Federation of Malaysia; United Nations Mission Ascertains Wishes of the People of Sabah and Sarawak." *United Nations Review*, 10, No. 9 (October, 1963), 11-15.

4799 "A Federation Resolved: The Latest Syrian Revolution." *Round Table*, 51, No. 205 (December, 1961), 20-28.

4800 **Finkelstein, Lawrence S.** "The Indonesian Federal Problem." *Pacific Affairs*, 24, No. 3 (September, 1951), 284-295.

4801 **Fisher, Charles A.** "The Geographical Setting of the Proposed Malaysian Federation." *Journal of Tropical Geography*, 17 (May, 1963), 99-115.

4802 **Fisher, Charles A.** "The Malaysian Federation, Indonesia and the Philippines: A Study in Political Geography." *Geographical Journal*, 129, Part 3 (September, 1963), 311-328.

4803 **Franda, Marcus F.** *The Federalizing Process in India: A Study of West Bengal and the Union.* Chicago, Illinois: University of Chicago, Ph.D., 1966.

4804 **Franda, Marcus F.** *West Bengal and Federalizing Process in India.* Princeton, New Jersey: Princeton University Press, 1968.

4805 **Gadgil, D.R.** *The Federal Problem in India.* Publication No. 15. Poona: Gokhale Institute of Politics and Economics, 1947.

4806 **Gadgil, D.R.** *Federating India.* Publication No. 13. Poona: Gokhale Institute of Politics and Economics, 1945.

4807 **Gangal, S.C.** "An Approach to Indian Federalism." *Political Science Quarterly*, 77, No. 2 (June, 1962), 248-253.

4808 **Ginsburg, Norton.** "China's Administrative Boundaries." *Far Eastern Economic Review*, 10, No. 8 (February 22, 1951), 201-222.

4809 **Goodno, James B.** *The Philippines: Land of Broken Promises.* London: Zed Books, Ltd., 1991.

4810 **Gourou, Pierre.** "For a French Indo-Chinese Federation." *Pacific Affairs*, 20, No. 1 (March, 1947), 18-29.

4811 **Great Britain Colonial Office.** *Federation of Malaya; Summary of Revised Constitutional Proposals.* Cmd. 7171. London: Great Britain Colonial Office, 1947.

4812 **Grover, Verinder,** ed. *Federal System, State Autonomy and Centre-State Relations in India (Political System in India-4).* New Delhi: Deep & Deep, 1990.

4813 **Jain, Purnendra C.** "Green Politics and Citizen Power in Japan: The Zushi Movement." *Asian Survey* [Berkeley], 31, No. 6 (June, 1991), 559-575.

4814 **Kamala, S.** "Inter-State Dispute: A Way Out." *Swarajya*, 22, No. 21 (November 18, 1967), 11-12.

4815 **Kochanek, Stanley A.** "The Federation of Indian Chambers of Commerce and Industry and Indian Politics." *Asian Survey*, 11, No. 9 (September, 1971), 866-885.

4816 **Krishnamurti, Y.G.** *Indian States and the Federal Plan.* Bombay: Ratansey Parker, 1939.

4817 **McNamara, Dennis L.** "State and Concentration in Korea's First Republic, 1948-60." *Modern Asian Studies* [Cambridge], 26, Part 4 (October, 1992), 701-718.

4818 **Means, Gordon P.** "Malaysia--A New Federation in Southeast Asia." *Pacific Affairs*, 36, No. 2 (Summer, 1963), 138-159.

4819 **Milne, R.S.** "Malaysia: A New Federation in the Making." *Asian Survey*, 3, No. 2 (February, 1963), 76-82.

4820 **Mitra, Subrata Kumar.** "Crisis and Resilience in Indian Democracy." *International Social Science Journal* [Oxford], No. 129 (August, 1991), 555-570.

4821 **Morkill, A.G.** "The Malayan Union." *Asiatic Review*, 42, No. 150 (April, 1946), 181-187.

4822 **Muni, S. D.** "Patterns of Democracy in South Asia." *International Social Science Journal* [Oxford], No. 128 (May, 1991), 361-372.

4823 **Oh, John C.H.** "The Federation of Malaysia: An Experiment in Nation-Building." *American Journal of Economics and Sociology*, 26, No. 4 (October, 1967), 425-437.

4824 **Osborne, Milton E.** *Singapore and Malaysia.* Ithica: Cornell University, Department of Asian Studies, Southeast Asia Program, 1964.

4825 **Park, Jim.** "Political Change in South Korea: The Challenge of the Conservative Alliance." *Asian Survey* [Berkeley], 30, No. 12 (December, 1990), 1154-1168.

4826 **Purcell, Victor.** "A Malayan Union: The Proposed New Constitution." *Pacific Affairs*, 19, No. 1 (March, 1946), 20-40.

4827 **Rafeek, Y.A.** *Intra-Party Relationships and Federalism: A Comparative Study of the Indian Congress Party and the Australian Political Parties.* Reading: University of Reading, Ph.D., 1967.

4828 **Reza Nasr, Seyyed Vali.** "Democracy and the Crisis of Governability in Pakistan." *Asian Survey* [Berkeley], 32, No. 6 (June, 1992), 521-537.

4829 **Roy, Naresh Chandra.** *Federalism and Linguistic States.* Calcutta: Firma K.L. Mukhopadhyay, 1962.

4830 **Sadka, Emma.** "Singapore and the Federation (of Malaya): Problems of Merger." *Asian Survey*, 1, No. 1 (January, 1962), 17-25.

4831 **Schiller, A. Arthur.** *The Formation of Federal Indonesia 1945-1949.* The Hague: Van Hoeve, 1955.

4832 **Singh, Mahendra Prasad.** "The Crisis of the Indian State: From Quiet Developmentalism to Noisy Democracy." *Asian Survey* [Berkeley], 30, No. 8 (August, 1990), 809-819.

4833 **Singh, Ravindra Pratap.** *Political Geography of Erstwhile Indore State.* Ujjain: Vikram University, Ph.D., 1969.

4834 **Smith, T.E.** "Proposals for Malaysia." *World Today*, 18, No. 5 (May, 1962), 192-200.

4835 **Starner, Frances L.** "Malaysia and the North Borneo Territories." *Asian Survey*, 3, No. 11 (November, 1963), 519-534.

4836 **Sukhwal, B.L.** "The Indian Federation: A Geographical Approach." *Proceedings of the 22nd International Geographical Union Conference* held at Montreal, 1972. Edited by Keith Fraser. Ottawa, Canada: The Canadian Committee for Geography, 1979, 142-145.

4837 **Swami, Manmohan Chand.** "A Geographical Comment on the Federal Structure of Assam." *Geographical Observer*, 5 (March, 1969), 81-88.

4838 **Swidler, Nian Bailey.** *The Political Structure of a Tribal Federation: The Brahui of Baluchistan.* New York: Columbia University, Ph.D., 1969.

4839 **Thompson, W. Scott.** *The Philippines in Crisis: Development and Security in the Aquino Era, 1976-92.* New York: St. Martin's Press, 1992.

4840 **Tummala, Krishna K.** "India's Federalism Under Stress." *Asian Survey* [Berkeley], 32, No. 6 (June, 1992), 538-553.

4841 "United Malaysia: Federation in a Hurry." *Round Table*, 52, No. 208 (September, 1962), 348-354.

4842 **Upadhyaya, Prakash Chandra.** "The Politics of Indian Secularism." *Modern Asian Studies* [Cambridge], 26, Part 4 (October, 1992), 815-857.

4843 **Waseem, Mohammad.** "Pakistan's Lingering Crisis of Dyarchy." *Asian Survey* [Berkeley], 32, No. 7 (July, 1992), 617-634.

AUSTRALIA, OCEANIA AND ANTARCTICA

Books and Journals

4844 **Aldred, J., and Wilkes, J.** *A Fractured Federation? Australia in the 1980's.* Sydney: Allen & Unwin, 1983.

4845 **Blainey, G.** "The Role of Economic Interests in Australian Federation: A Reply to Professor Parker." *Historical Studies of Australia and New Zealand*, 13 (1949), 224-37.

4846 **Canaway, A.P.** *The Failure of Federalism in Australia.* London: Oxford University Press, 1930.

4847 **Connell, John.** "New Caledonia: The Transformation of Anaky Nationalism." *Australian Outlook*, 41, No. 1 (April, 1987), 37-44.

4848 **Finsterbusch, K.** "Federalism's Ideological Dimension and the Australian Labor Party." *Australian Quarterly*, 53, No. 2 (June, 1953), 128-140.

4849 **Greenwood, G.** *The Future of Australian Federalism.* Melbourne: Melbourne University Press, 1946.

4850 **Hughes, Daniel T. and Laughlin, Jr., Stanley K.** "Key Elements in the Evolving Political Culture of the Federated States of Micronesia." *Pacific Studies*, 6, No. 1 (Fall, 1982), 71-84.

4851 **Lane, P.H.** "The Federal Parliament's External Affairs Power: The Tasmanian Dam Case." *Australian Law Journal*, 57, No. 10 (October, 1983), 554-559.

4852 **MacKirdy, K.A.** "Conflict of Loyalties: The Problem of Assimilating the Far West into the Canadian and Australian Federations." *Canadian Historical Review*, 32, No. 4 (December, 1951), 337-355.

4853 **MacKirdy, K.A.** "Geography and Federalism in Australia and Canada." *Australian Geographer*, 6, No. 2 (March, 1953), 38-47.

4854 **Meller, Norman.** "The Micronesian Executive: The Federated States of Micronesia, Kiribati, and the Marshall Islands." *Pacific Studies* [Laie], 14, No. 1 (November, 1990), 55-72.

4855 **Mercer, David.** "Australia's Constitution, Federalism and the 'Tasmanian Dam Case'." *Political Geography Quarterly*, 4, No. 2 (April, 1985), 91-110.

4856 **Overton, John.** "Coups and Constitutions: Drawing a Political Geography of Fiji." *New Zealand Geographer* [Dunedin], 48, No. 2 (October, 1992), 50-58.

4857 **Parker, R.S.** "Australian Federation: The Influence of Economic Interests and Political Pressures." *Historical Studies of Australia and New Zealand*, 4, No. 13 (November, 1949), 1-24.

4858 **Pahence, A., and Scott, J.** *Australian Federalism: Future Tense.* Melbourne: Oxford University Press, 1983.

4859 **Peachment, A.,** and **Reid, G.S.** *New Federalism in Australia: Rhetoric or Reality?* Australian Political Studies Association, Monograph 18. Adelaide: Flinders University, 1977.

4860 **Richardson, J.E.** *Patterns of Australian Federalism.* Research Monograph 1. Canberra: Centre for Research on Federal Financial Relations, Australian National University, 1973.

4861 **Robinson, K.W.** "Sixty Years of Federation in Australia." *Geographical Review,* 51, No. 1 (January, 1961), 1-20.

4862 **Rose, A.J.** "The Border Between Queensland and New South Wales; A Study of Political Geography in a Federal Union." *Australian Geographer,* 6, No. 4 (January, 1955), 3-18.

4863 **Rumley, Dennis.** "The Political Geography of Australian Federal-State Relations." *Geoforum,* 19, No. 3 (1988), 367-379.

4864 **Sawer, Geoffrey.** *Australian Federalism in the Courts.* Melbourne: Melbourne University Press, 1967.

4865 **Sawer, Geoffrey.** "The Dynamics of Australian Federalism; The Resilience of the Regions." *Round Table,* 62, No. 248 (October, 1972), 441-450.

4866 **Sawer, Geoffrey.** *Federalism, An Australian Jubilee Study.* Melbourne: F.W. Cheshire for the Australian Naitonal University, 1952.

4867 **Solomon, R.J.** "The Geography of Political Affiliation in a Federal-State System: Tasmania 1913-1966." *Australian Geographical Studies,* 7, No. 1 (April, 1969), 28-40.

4868 **Wilcox, M.** "The 'Dam Case'--Implication for the Future." *Habitat,* 11 (1983), 32-34.

EUROPE

Books and Journals

4869 **Bermeo, Nancy.** "Democracy in Europe." *Daedalus* [Cambridge, MA], 123, No. 2 (Spring, 1994), 159-178.

4870 **Brecht, Arnold.** *Federalism and Regionalism in Germany. The Division of Prussia.* Institute of World Affairs, Monograph series. London: Oxford University Press, 1945.

4871 **Burgess, M.,** ed. *Federalism and Federation in Western Europe.* London: Croom Helm, 1986.

4872 **Dubrulle, Marc.** "Belgium-Federalisation or Breakdown." *Ecologist,* 13, No. 1 (1983), 22-26.

4873 **Ferfila, Bogomil.** "Yugoslavia: Confederation or Disintegration?" *Problems of Communism* [Washington, DC], 40, No. 4 (July-August, 1991), 18-30.

4874 **Fierlbeck, Katherine.** "Redefining Responsibility: The Politics of Citizenship in the United Kingdom." *Canadian Journal of Political Science* [Ottawa], 24, No. 3 (September, 1991), 575-593.

4875 **Fishman, Robert M.** *Working-Class Organization and the Return to Democracy in Spain.* Ithaca: Cornell University Press, 1990.

4876 **Geshkoff, Theodore I.** *Balkan Union; A Road to Peace in Southeastern Europe.* New York: Columbia University Press, 1940.

4877 **Golay, J.F.** *The Founding of the Federal Republic of Germany.* Chicago, Illinois: University of Chicago Press, 1958.

4878 **Goldfarb, Jeffrey C.** *After the Fall: The Pursuit of Democracy in Central Europe.* New York: BasicBooks, 1992.

4879 **Grazynski, M.** "The Oder-Neisse Line--A Frontier of Central Eastern European Federation and a Guarantee of Lasting Peace." *Eastern Quarterly,* 5, No. 1/2 (January-April, 1952), 2-14.

4880 **Gross, Feliks.** *Crossroads of Two Continents; A Democratic Federation of East-Central Europe.* New York City: Columbia University Press, 1945.

4881 **Hertz, Frederick.** "Danubian Union." *Contemporary Review,* 891, No. 3 (March, 1940), 284-290.

4882 **Houseman, Gerald L.** "Devolution, Federalism, Regionalism, and the Possible Breakup of the United Kingdom." *Indiana Academy of the Social Sciences Proceedings 1976,* 11, 3rd series (1976), 147-157.

4883 **Jovanovic, P.S.** "La Republique Federative Populaire de Yugoslavie." *Bulletin de la Societe de Geographie de Belgrade,* Tome 27 (1947), 5-17. In Serbian with French summary, 17-20.

4884 **Kearns, Adrian J.** "Active Citizenship and Urban Governance." *Institute of British Geographers. Transactions* [London], New Series, 17, No. 1 (1992), 20-34.

4885 **Kendle, John.** *Ireland and the Federal Solution: The Debate over the United Kingdom Constitution, 1870-1921.* Kingston: McGill-Queen's University Press, 1989.

4886 **Kirchheimer, Otto.** "The Decline of Intra-State Federalism in Western Europe." *World Politics,* 3, No. 3 (April, 1951), 281-298.

4887 **Kolinsky, Eva, ed.** *The Federal Republic of Germany: The End of an Era.* New York: Berg Publishers Limited, 1991.

4888 **Odlozilik, Otakar.** "A Czech Plan for a Danubian Federation-1848." *Journal of Central European Affairs*, 1, No. 3 (October, 1941), 253-274.

4889 **Opello, Walter C.** *Portugal: From Monarchy to Pluralist Democracy.* Boulder: Westview Press, 1991.

4890 **Peyronnet, Georges.** "La psychologie des peuples au service de la construction de la Federation Europeenne." *Revue de Psychologie des Peuples*, 7 Annee, No. 3 (1952), 231-327.

4891 **Phillips, Peggy Anne.** *Republican France: Divided Loyalties.* Westport: Greenwood Press, 1993.

4892 **Pickles, Dorothy.** *French Politics; The First Years of the Fourth Republic.* London: Royal Institute of International Affairs, 1953.

4893 **Ramet, Pedro.** *Nationalism and Federalism in Yugoslavia, 1963-1983.* Bloomington: Indiana University Press, 1984.

4894 "Reflexions sur une federlisation de l'Europe Danubienne." *Politique Etrangere*, 17, No. 6 (January, 1953), 499-505.

4895 **Scholler, Peter.** "The Tension Between Centralism, Federalism, and Regionalism as a Characteristic of Germany's Politico-Geographical Development up to the Present." *Erdkunde*, 41, No. 2 (1987), 77-106.

4896 **Stavrianos, L.S.** *Balkan Federation; A History of the Movement Toward Balkan Unity in Modern Times.* Northampton, Massachusetts: Smith College, Studies in History, Vol. 27, Nos. 1-4, 1944.

4897 **Szacki, Jerzy.** "Polish Democracy: Dreams and Reality." *Social Research* [New York], 58, No. 4 (Winter, 1991), 711-755.

4898 **U.S. Department of State,** "The Bonn Constitution: Basic Law for the Federal Republic of Germany." *European and British Commonwealth Series*, 8, Publication 3526. Washington, D.C.: U.S. Department of State, 1949.

4899 **Valkenier, Elizabeth K.** "Eastern European Federation: A Study in the Conflicting National Aims and Plans of the Exile Groups." *Journal of Central European Affairs*, 14, No. 4 (January, 1955), 354-370.

4900 **Vinding, M., and Larson, L. Hansen.** *The Federal State of South-Slesviy.* Kobenhan,

Fr. Bagges: Kgl. Hofboglryski, 1948.

CHAPTER VI

POLITICAL GEOGRAPHY OF ADMINISTRATIVE AREAS: LOCAL SYSTEMS, INTERNAL REGIONS AND STRUCTURES

GENERAL AND THEORY

Books

4901 **Adams, J.G.V.** *Transport Planning: Vision and Practice.* London: Routledge, 1981.

4902 **Alderfer, H.F.** *Local Government in Developing Countries.* New York: McGraw-Hill, 1964.

4903 **Baker, Gordon E.** *Rural Versus Urban Political Power.* New York: Doubleday, 1955.

4904 **Barlow, I.M.** *Metropolitan Government.* London: Routledge, 1991.

4905 **Barry, David, and Steiker, Gene.** *The Concept of Justice in Regional Planning: Some Policy Implications.* Philadelphia, Pennsylvania: Regional Science Research Institute, 1973.

4906 **Berger, R.** *Government and Judiciary.* Cambridge, Massachusetts: Harvard University Press, 1977.

4907 **Bergman, Edward Fisher.** *Metropolitan Political Geography Achieving Area-Wide Systems.* Seattle: University of Washington, Ph.D., 1971.

4908 **Blowers, A.T.** *The Limits of Power: The Politics of Local Planning Policy.* Oxford: Pergamon, 1980.

4909 **Bookchin, Murray.** *Urbanization Without Cities: The Rise and Decline of Citizenship.* Montreal: Black Rose Books, 1992.

4910 **Books, J.W., and Prysby, C.L.** *Political Behaviour and the Local Context.* New York: Praeger, 1991.

4911 **Borgatta, Edgar F.** *L'interazione sociale-ricerca e teoria.* Trieste: Lint, 1972.

4912 *Brighton on the Rocks: Monetarism and the Local State.* Brighton, Sussex: Queenspark Rates Book Group, Queenspark New Series, 1983.

4913 **Campbell, Alan K., ed.** *The States and the Urban Crisis.* Englewood Cliffs, New Jersey: Prentice-Hall, 1970.

4914 **Carney, J.; Hudson, Ray; and Lewis, Jim.** *Regions in Crisis: New Perspectives in European Regional Theory.* New York: St. Martin's Press, 1980.

4915 **Castells, M.** *City, Class and Power.* London: Macmillan, 1978.

4916 **Castells, M.** *La Question urbane.* Paris: Maspero, 1972.

4917 **Castells, M.** *The Urban Question.* London: Arnold, 1977.

4918 **Castells, M, and Godard, F.** *Monopolville.* Paris: Mouton, 1974.

4919 **Chapman, Shirley.** *State and Local Government.* Chicago: Rand McNally, 1969.

4920 **Choper, J.** *Judicial Review and the National Political Process.* Chicago, Illinois: University of Chicago Press, 1980.

4921 **Clark, T.N., and Ferguson, L.C.** *City Money: Political Processes, Fiscal Strain and Retrenchment.* New York City: Columbia University Press, 1983.

4922 **Cowart, Susan.** *Impacts of the Spatial Organization of Service Supply in Bureaucratic Production.* Iowa City: University of Iowa, Ph.D., 1983.

4923 **Cox, K.R.** *Conflict, Power and Politics in the City: A Geographic View.* New York: McGraw-Hill, 1973.

4924 **Cox, K.R., and Johnston, R.J.** *Conflict, Politics and the Urban Scene: Case Studies in Urban Political Geography.* London: Longman, 1982.

4925 **Dear, M.J., and Scott, A.J., eds.** *Urban and Urban Planning in Capitalist Society.* London: Methuen, 1981.

4926 **Dickens, P.; Duncan, S.S.; Goodwin, M., and Gray, F.** *Housing, States and Localities.* London: Methuen, 1985.

4927 **Dickinson, Robert E.** *City Region and Regionalism.* New York: Oxford University Press, 1947.

4928 **Duncan, Otis Dudley.** *Metropolis and Region.* Baltimore, Maryland: Johns Hopkins University Press, 1960.

4929 **Duncan, S.S., and Goodwin, M.** *The Local State and Restructuring Social Relations: Theory and Practice: Working Paper 24, Urban and Regional Studies.* Brighton: University of Sussex, 1980.

4930 **Duncan, S.S., and Goodwin, M.** *The Local State and Uneven Development.* Oxford: Polity Press, 1988.

4931 **Dunleavy, P.** *Urban Political Analysis.* London: Macmillan, 1980.

4932 **Elliot, Jeffrey M., and Ali, Sheikh Rustum.** *The State and Local Government Political Dictionary.* Santa Barbara, California: ABC-Clio, 1988.

4933 **Fenno, R.F.** *The Power of the Purse.* Boston: Little Brown, 1968.

4934 **Fesler, James W.** *Area and Administration.* Birmingham: University of Alabama Press, 1949.

4935 **Flowerdew, R.T.N.,** ed. *Institutions and Geographical Patterns.* London: Croom Helm, 1982.

4936 **Freeman, T.W.** *Geography and Regional Administration.* London: Hutchinson, 1968.

4937 **Geisler, Charles C., and Popper, Frank J.** *Land Reform, American Style.* Totowa, New Jersey: Rowman and Littlefield, 1984.

4938 **Geisler, Charles C., and Popper, Frank J.** *Geography and Regional Planning.* London: Hutchinson, 1968.

4939 **Gottmann, J.,** ed. *Centre and Periphery. Spatial Variation in Politics.* London: Sage Focus Editions 19, 1980.

4940 **Griffith, J.A.G.** *The Politics of the Judiciary.* London: Fontana, 1977.

4941 **Hanson, G.H.** "The Geographic Factor and Its Influence in Utah Administrative Units." *Yearbook of the Association of Pacific Coast Geographers,* (1937), 3-8.

4942 **Harris, G. Montague.** *Comparative Local Government.* London: Hutchinson, 1948.

4943 **Harvey, David W.** *Consciousness and the Urban Experience.* Oxford: Blackwell, 1985c.

4944 **Harvey, David W.** *The Urbanization of Capital.* Oxford: Blackwell, 1985b.

4945 **Hillery, George.** *Communal Organizations. A Study of Local Societies.* Chicago, Illinois: University of Chicago Press, 1968.

4946 **Holmes, James Macdonald.** *The Geographical Basis of Planning.* Sydney: Angus and Robertson, 1944.

4947 **Isard, Walter.** *Location and Space Economy.* New York: John Wiley & Sons, 1956.

4948 **Johnston, R.J.** *City and Society.* London: Penguin, 1980.

4949 **Lipietz, A.** *Le Capital et son Espace.* Paris: Maspero, 1977.

4950 **Lipman, V.D.** *Local Government Areas 1834-1945.* Oxford: Blackwell, 1949.

4951 **Maass, Arthur,** ed. *Area and Power: A Theory of Local Government.* Glencoe, Illinois: The Free Press, 1959.

4952 **Massam, Bryan H.** *Location and Space in Social Administration.* London: Edward Arnold, 1975.

4953 **Massam, Bryan H.** *The Spatial Structure of Administrative Systems.* Washington, D.C.: Association of American Geographers, 1972.

4954 **Moseley, M.** *Accessibility: The Rural Challenge.* London: Methuen, 1979.

4955 **Moskowitz, D.H.** *Exclusionary Zoning Legislation.* Cambridge, Massachusetts: Ballinger, 1977.

4956 **Newman, O.** *Defensible Space.* New York: Architectural Press, 1974.

4957 **Newton, K.** *Second City Politics.* Oxford: Clarendon Press, 1976.

4958 **O'Connor, J.** *The Fiscal Crisis of the State.* New York: St. Martin's Press, 1973.

4959 **Pahl, R.E.** *Whose City?* Harmondsworth: Penguin, 1975.

4960 **Pettit, P.** *Judging Justice: An Introduction to Contemporary Political Philosophy.* London: Routledge, 1980.

4961 **Pred, A.** *Advanced City Systems.* London: Hutchinson, 1977.

4962 **Rawls, J.** *A Theory of Justice.* Cambridge, Massachusetts: Harvard University Press, 1971.

4963 **Saunders, P.** *Urban Politics.* London: Penguin, 1980.

4964 **Saunders, P.** *Urban Politics: A Sociological Interpretation.* London: Heinemann, 1979.

4965 **Sayer, A.** *Theory and Empirical Research in Urban and Regional Political Economy: A Sympathetic Critique.* Brighton: University of Sussex: Urban and Regional Studies Unit, Working Paper 14, 1979.

4966 **Scott, E. Keith, Jr.; Fetter, Theodore, J.; and Crites, Laura L.** *Rural Courts: The Effects of Space and Distance on the Administration of Justice.* Denver, Colorado: National Center for State Courts, Publication No. R0032, July, 1977.

4967 **Sharkansky, Ira.** *The Routines of Politics.* New York: Van Norstrand Rheinhold, 1970a.

4968 **Simon, Herbert A.** *Administrative Behavior,* 2nd ed. New York: The Free Press, 1957.

4969 **Steiner, G.Y.** *The State of Welfare.* Washington, D.C.: The Brookings Institute, 1971.

4970 **Street, H.** *Governmental Liability: A Comparative Study.* Cambridge: Cambridge University Press, 1953.

4971 **Tabb, William K. and Sawers, Larry, eds.** *Marxism and Metropolis: New Perspectives in Urban Political Economy.* New York: Oxford University Press, 1984.

4972 *Theories of Planning and Spatial Development.* London: P. Cooke, Hutchinson, 1983.

4973 **Winkle, Kenneth J.** *The Politics of Community.* New York: Cambridge University Press, 1988.

4974 **Wolff, R.P.** *Understanding Rawls: A Reconstruction and Critique of A Theory of Justice.* Princeton, New Jersey: Princeton University Press, 1977.

Journals

4975 **Ackerman, Edward A.** "Public Policy Issues for the Political Geographer." *Annals of the Association of American Geographers.* 52, No. 3 (September, 1962), 292-298.

4976 **Amaral, Ilidio do.** "The Geographical Factor in the Formation of Modern States." *Fnisterra,* 21, No. 41 (1986), 57-76.

4977 **Archer, J. Clark.** "Public Choice Paradigms in Political Geography." In *Political Studies from Spatial Perspectives,* A.D. Burnett and P.J. Taylor, eds. Chichester: John Wiley & Sons, 1981, 73-90.

4978 **Balas, Antonio; Pieres, Cristina; and Garcia, Teresa.** "Delimitacao de Actuacoes na Perspectiva da Desconcentracao e Descentralizacao Administrativas." *Sociedade de Geografia de Lisboa, Boletim,* Serie 100ᵃ, Nos. 1-12

(Janiero-Dezembro, 1982), 18-55.

4979 **Baraletti, Fabrizio.** "Le Anomalie Amministrative Della Toscana." *Revista Geografica Italiana,* Annata 90, Fasc. 2 (Guigno, 1983), 273-290.

4980 **Bataillon Claude.** "Organisation Administrative et Regionalisation en pays Sons-developpe." *L'Espace Geographique,* Tome 3, No. 1 (1974), 5-11.

4981 **Beneditti, Giancarlo.** "La Riforma delle Suddivision: Amministrativo-Territoriali in Gran Bretagna." *L'Universo,* Anno 59, No. 6 (Novembre-Dicembre, 1979), 1117-1136.

4982 **Bennett, Robert J.** "A Bureaucratic Model of Local Government Tax and Expenditure Decisions." *Applied Economics,* 16 (1984), 257-268.

4983 **Bennett, Robert J.** "A Model of Local Authority Fiscal Behavior." *Public Finance,* 38, No. 2 (1983), 317-321.

4984 **Berry, Brian J.L.** "A Method for Deriving Multi-Factor Uniform Regions." *Przeglad Geogriczny,* 33, No. 2 (February, 1961), 263-79.

4985 **Berry, David.** "The Geographic Distribution of Governmental Powers: The Case of Regulation." *Professional Geographer,* 39, No. 4 (November, 1987), 428-437.

4986 **Blacksell, Mark, and Others.** "Legal Services in Rural Areas." *Progress in Human Geography,* 12, No. 1 (March, 1988), 47-65.

4987 **Blomley, Nicholas K.** "Mobility, Empowerment and the Rights Revolution." *Political Geography,* 13, No. 5 (September, 1994), 407-422.

4988 **Blowers, Andrew T.** "Master of Fate or Victim of Circumstance? The Exercise of Corporate Power in Environmental Policy-making." *Policy and Politics,* 11, No. 4 (October, 1983), 393-415.

4989 **Bodely, Martin.** "Central-Local Government Relations: Theory and Practice." *Political Geography Quarterly,* 2, No. 2 (April, 1983), 119-138.

4990 **Bohland, James R., and Gist, J.** "The Spatial Consequences of Bureaucratic Decisionmaking." *Environment and Planning,* A. 15, No. 4 (December, 1983), 1489-1500.

4991 **Bradford, Calvin P., and Rubinowitz, Leonard P.** "The Urban-Suburban Investment-Disinvestment Process: Consequences for Older Neighborhood." *Annals of the Academy of Political and Social Sciences,* 422, No. 4 (November, 1975), 77-88.

4992 **Brewer, Michael F.** "Local Government Assessment: Its Impact on Land and Water Use." *Land Economics*, 37, No. 3 (August, 1961), 207-217.

4993 **Brodsky, Harold.** "Residential Land and Improvement Valves in Central City." *Land Economics*, 46, No. 3 (August, 1970), 229-249.

4994 **Bruyelle, Pierre.** "1968-1975-1982-les evolutions urbaines et rurales departmentales." *L'information geographique*, 50, No. 3 (Mai-Juin, 1986), 89-95.

4995 **Castells, M.** "Local Government, Urban Crisis and Political Change." *Political Power and Social Theory*, 2 (1981), 1-19.

4996 **Clark, G. L.** "'Real Regulation': The Administrative State" *Environment and Planning A* [London], 24, No. 5 (May, 1992), 615-627.

4997 **Clark, Gordon L.** "Rights, Property and Community." *Economic Geography*, 58, No. 2 (April, 1982), 120-138.

4998 **Claval, Paul.** "Center-Periphery and Space: Models of Political Geography." In *Centre and Periphery: Spatial Variation in Politics*, J. Gottmann, ed. Beverly Hills, California: Sage Publications, 1980, 63-71.

4999 **Connor, Walker F.** "Myths of Hemispheric, Continental Regional and State Unity." *Political Science Quarterly*, 84, No. 4 (December, 1969), 555-567 and 570-582.

5000 **Cooke, Philip.** "Recent Theories of Political Regionalism: A Critique and an Alternative Proposal." *International Journal of Urban and Regional Research*, 8, No. 4 (December, 1984), 549-572.

5001 **Cox, K.R.** "Residential Mobility, Neighbourhood Activism and Neighbourhood Problems." *Political Geography Quarterly*, 2, No. 2 (April, 1983), 99-117.

5002 **Cox, K.R.** "Review Essay: The Division of Labor, the State and Local Politics." *Political Geography*, 12, No. 4 (July, 1993), 382-385.

5003 **Cox, K.R.** "Review Essay: Space and the Urban Question." *Political Geography Quarterly*, 3, No. 1 (January, 1983), 77-84.

5004 **Cox, K.R., and Jonas, A.E.G.** "Urban Development, Collective Consumption and the Politics of Metropolitan Fragmentation." *Political Geography*, 12, No. 1 (January, 1993), 8-37.

5005 **Deutsch, Karl W.** "On Social Communication and the Metropolis." *Daedalus*, 90, No. 1 (Winter, 1961), 99-110.

5006 **Dikshit, R.D.** "Government as a Geographical Aspect: A Framework for Study." *Uttar Bharat Bhugol Patrika*, 9, Nos. 3-4 (September-December, 1973), 111-117.

5007 **Divay, Gerard.** "La Dimension Spatiale dans les Reformes Institutionnelles Locales." *L'Espace Geographique*, Tome 10, No. 2 (Avril/Juin, 1981), 107-111.

5008 **Douglas, J.N.H.** "Political Geography and Administrative Areas: A Method of Assessing the Effectiveness of Local Government Areas." *Essays in Political Geography*, Charles A. Fisher, ed. London: Methuen, 1968, 13-26.

5009 **Dube, S.C.** "Bureaucracy and Nation Building in Transitional Societies." *International Social Science Journal*, 16, No. 2 (Spring, 1964), 229-236.

5010 **Duncan, S.S., and Goodwin, M.** "The Local State and Restructuring Social Relations: Theory and Practice." *International Journal of Urban and Regional Research*, 6, 2 (June, 1982), 157-186.

5011 **Elin, Stephen L.** "Comparative Urban Politics and Inter-Organisational Behaviour." *Policy and Politics*, 2, No. 4 (June, 1974), 289-308.

5012 **Fisher, G.W.** "The Determinants of State and Local Government Expenditures: A Preliminary Analysis." *National Tax Journal*, 14, No. 4 (December, 1961), 349-355.

5013 **Foster, K.A.** "Exploring the Links Between Political Structure and Metropolitan Growth." *Political Geography*, 12, No. 6 (November, 1993), 523-547.

5014 **Gilbert, E.W.** "The Boundaries of Local Government Areas." *Geographical Journal*, 111, No. 4-6 (April-June, 1948), 172-206.

5015 **Goodsell, Charles T.** "An Empirical Test of 'Legalism' in Administration." *The Journal of Developing Areas*, 10, No. 4 (July, 1976), 485-494.

5016 **Griffith, J.A.G.** "A New Shape for Local Government." *New Society*, 160 (1965), 7-9.

5017 **Guimaraes, Fabio de Macedo Soares.** "A proposito do problema da delimitacao das unidades politicas." *Revista Brasileira de Geografia*, Ano 5, No. 4 (Outubro-Dezembro, 1943), 638-645.

5018 **Haile, Getatchew.** "The Unity and Territorial Integrity of Ethiopia." *The Journal of Modern African Studies*, 24, No. 3 (September, 1986), 465-487.

5019 **Hajdu, Zoltan.** "Administrative Geogrpahy and Reforms of the Administrative Areas in Hungary." *Political Geography Quarterly*, 6, No. 3 (July, 1987), 269-278.

5020 **Haqqi, S.A.H., and Sharma, A.P.** "Urban Politics: A Study of 'Influentials' and 'Participants'." In *Urbanization in Developing Countries*, S. Manzoor Alam and V.V. Pokshishevsky, eds. Hyderabad, India: Osmania University, 1976, 219-235.

5021 **Hays, S.P.** "The Politics of Reform in Municipal Government in the Progressive Era." *Pacific Northwest Quarterly*, 55, No. 2 (April, 1964), 157-169.

5022 **Herson, Lawrence J.R.** "The Lost World of Municipal Government." *American Political Science Review*, 51 (June, 1957), 330-345.

5023 **Hirsch, Werner Z.** "Local versus Area Wide Urban Government Services." *National Tax Journal*, 17, No. 4 (December, 1964), 331-339.

5024 **Hoch, Irving.** "Income and City Size." *Urban Studies*, 9, No. 3 (October, 1972), 299-328.

5025 **Hoggart, Keith.** "Geography, Political Control and Local Government Policy Outputs." *Progress in Human Geography*, 10, No. 1 (March, 1986), 1-23.

5026 **Honey, Rex D.** "Metropolitan Governance: Transformation of Political Space." In *Urban Policymaking and Metropolitan Dynamics*, John S. Adams, ed. New York: Ballinger, 1976, 425-462.

5027 **Horn, D.L.; Hampton, C.R., and Vandenberg, A.J.** "Practical Application of District Compactness." *Political Geography*, 12, No. 2 (March, 1993), 103-120

5028 **Irvine, W.P.** "Assessing Regional Effects in Data Analysis." *Canadian Journal of Political Science*, 4, No. 1 (March, 1971), 21-24.

5029 **Jacob, Philip E., and Teune, Henry.** "The Integrative Process: Guidelines for Analysis of Political Community." In *Integration of Political Communities*, Philip E. Jacob and J.V. Toscano, eds. Philadelphia: Lippincott, 1964, 1-45.

5030 **Janelle, D.G., and Millward, H.A.** "Locational Conflict Patterns and Urban Ecological Structure." *Tijdschrift voor Economische en Sociale Geografie*, 67, No. 2 (March-April, 1976), 102-113.

5031 **Johnston, R.J.** "The Neighbourhood Effect Revisited: Spatial Science or Political Culture?" *Environment and Planning D: Society and Space*, 4, No. 1 (March, 1986), 41-45.

5032 **Johnston, R.J., and Taylor, P.J.** "Political Geography: A Politics of Places within Places." *Parliamentary Affairs*, 39, No. 2 (April, 1986), 135-149.

5033 **King, Russell.** "Corporatism and the Local Economy." In *The Political Economy of Corporatism*, W. Grant, ed. London: Macmillan, 1985, 202-228.

5034 **Knight, David B.** "Impress of Authority and Ideology on Landscape: A Review of Some Unanswered Questions." *Tijdschrift voor Economische en Sociale Geographie*, 62, No. 6 (November-December, 1971), 383-387.

5035 **Krishan, Gopal.** "Administrative Geography." *Transactions of the Institute of Indian Geographers*, 5, No. 2 (July, 1983), 101-108.

5036 **Lake, Robert W.** "Negotiating Local Autonomy." *Political Geography*, 13, No. 5 (September, 1994), 423-442.

5037 **Lauria, Mickey.** "The Internal Transformation of Community Controlled Implementation Organizations." *Administration and Society*, 17 (1986), 387-410.

5038 **Lea, A.C.** "Welfare Theory, Public Goods, and Public Facility Location." *Geographical Analysis*, 11, No. 3 (July, 1979), 217-239.

5039 **Leitner, Helga.** "Cities in Pursuit of Economic Growth: The Local State as Entrepreneur." *Political Geography Quarterly*, 9, No. 2 (April, 1990), 146-170.

5040 **Massam, Bryan H.** "A Test of a Model of Administrative Areas." *Geographical Analysis*, 3, No. 4 (1971), 402-406.

5041 **Massam, Bryan H., and Goodrich, M.F.** "Temporal Trends in the Spatial Organization of a Service Agency." *Canadian Geographer*, 15, No. 3 (Fall, 1971), 193-206.

5042 **McCrone, G.** "Next Steps in Regional Planning." *Journal of Industrial Economics*, (1965), 115-130.

5043 **Meyer, William H., and Brown, Michael.** "Locational Conflict in Nineteenth-Century City." *Political Geography Quarterly*, 8, No. 2 (April, 1989), 107-122.

5044 **Mollenkopf, J.H.** "The City as a Growth Machine: Towards a Political Economy of Place." *American Journal of Sociology*, 82, No. 2 (September, 1976), 309-332.

5045 **Molotch, Harvey, and Logan, John.** "Review Essay: The Space for Urban Action: Urban Fortunes; A Rejoinder." *Political Geography Quarterly*, 9, No. 1 (January, 1990), 85-92.

5046 **Moran, W.** "Rural Space as Intellectual Property." *Political Geography*, 12, No. 3 (May, 1993), 263-277.

5047 **Norcen, A.** "Confini politici, limiti e termini amministrativi." *L'Universo*, 39, No. 3 (May-June, 1959), 547-556.

5048 **Nye, J.S.** "Patterns and Catalysts in Regional Integration." *International Organization*, 19, No. 4 (Autumn, 1965), 870-884.

5049 **Ojo, O.J.B.** "Federalism and State Administration an Introduction." *Quarterly Journal of Administration*, 10, No. 2 (January, 1976), 105-124.

5050 **Olson, M., Jr.** "The Principle of Fiscal Equivalence: The Division of Responsibilities Among Different Levels of Government." *American Economic Review*, 59, No. 3 (June, 1969), 479-487.

5051 **Ostrem, C.; Tiebout, C.M.; and Warren, R.** "The Organization of Government in Metropolitan Areas: A Theoretical Inquiry." *American Political Science Review*, 55, No. 3 (September, 1961), 831-842.

5052 **Peake, H.J.E.** "Geographical Aspects of Administrative Areas." *Geography*, 15, No. 7 (July, 1930), 531-546.

5053 **Preston, Richard E.** "Christaller's Research on the Geography of Administrative Areas." *Progress in Human Geography* [London], 16, No. 4 (1992), 523-539.

5054 **Putnam, R.D.** "Political Attitudes and the Local Community." *American Political Science Review*, 60, No. 3 (July, 1966), 640-654.

5055 **Raffestin, Claude, and Lawrence, Roderick.** "Comment: Human Ecology and Environmental Policies: Prospects for Politics and Planning." *Political Geography Quarterly*, 9, No. 2 (April, 1990), 103-107.

5056 **Rawls, J.** "Fairness to Goodness." *Philosophical Review*, 84, No. 4 (October, 1975), 536-554.

5057 **Rawls, J.** "Justice as Fairness." *Philosophical Review*, 67, No. 2 (April, 1958), 164-194.

5058 **Rhodes, R.A.W.** "Regional Policy and a 'Europe of Regions': A Critical Assessment." *Regional Studies*, 8, No. 2 (August, 1974), 105-114.

5059 **Richards, P.G.** "Local Government Reform: Smaller Towns and the Countryside." *Urban Studies*, 2, No. 2 (November, 1965), 147-162.

5060 **Riggs, Fred W.** "Public Administration: A Neglected Factor in Economic Development." *Annals of the American Academy of Political and Social Science*, 305 (May, 1956), 70-80.

5061 **Robertson, J.B., and Edberg, S.C.** "Technical Considerations in Extracting and Regulating Springwater for Public Consumption." *Environmental Geology* [Berlin], 22, No. 1 (September, 1993), 52-59.

5062 **Rodriguez Arias, Julio C.** "The Theory and Practice of Geoadministration." *Ekistics*, 44, No. 262 (September, 1977), 172-177.

5063 **Russett, Bruce M.** "El problema de la identificacion de regiones." *Ciencias politicas y sociales*, 10, No. 38 (Octubre-Diciembre de, 1964), 619-639.

5064 **Samuelson, P.** "The Pure Theory of Public Expenditure." *Review of Economics and Statistics*, 26, No. 3 (July, 1954), 387-389.

5065 **Schulz, Peter.** "The Viability of Area Units: A Definition and Model." In 22nd *I.G.U. Congress Proceedings*, J. Keith Fraser, ed. Montreal: Canadian Committee for Geography, 1978, 511-512.

5066 **Scott, Allen.** "Location Process, Urbanization and Territorial Development: An Exploratory Essay." *Environment and Planning*, A17, No. 3 (August, 1985), 479-501.

5067 **Staeheli, Lynn A.** "Empowering Political Struggle: Spaces and Scales of Resistance." *Political Geography*, 13, No. 5 (September, 1994), 387-391.

5068 **Stark, Oded.** "Research on Rural-to-Urban Migration in LDCs." *World Development*, 10, No. 1 (January, 1982), 63-70.

5069 **Taylor, E.G.R.** "Discussion on the Geographical Aspects of Regional Planning." *Geographical Journal*, 99, No. 1 (January, 1942), 61-81.

5070 **Tiebout, C.** "A Pure Theory of Local Expenditure." *Journal of Political Economy*, 64, No. 5 (October, 1956), 416-424.

5071 **Ullman, Edward L.** "Regional Development and the Geography of Concentration." *Papers and Proceedings of Regional Science Association*, 4 (1958), 179-198.

5072 **Urry, J.** "Localities, Regions and Social Class." *International Journal of Urban and Regional Research*, 5, No. 4 (December, 1981), 455-471.

5073 **Van Amersfoort, J.M.M., and Van der Wusten, H.** "Politicke Geografie: Inleiding van een Themanummer." *Geografisch Tijdschrift*, Nieuwe Reek, 15, Nr. 2 (March, 1981), 105-107.

5074 **Walker, R.A., and Greenberg, D.A.**
"Post-Industrialism and Political Reform in the
City: A Critique." *Antipode*, 14, No. 1 (April,
1983), 17-32.

5075 **Westfall, John Edward.** "Estimating Minor Civil
Division Boundaries through the Manuscript
Census Schedules: A Methodological Note."
Historical Geography Newsletter, 3, No. 1 (Spring,
1973), 3-6.

5076 **White, Gilbert F.** "Geography and Public
Policy." *Professional Geographer*, 23, No. 2
(May, 1972), 101-104.

5077 **Williams, P.** "Restructuring Urban
Managerialism: Towards a Political Economy of
Urban Allocation." *Environment and Planning*,
A 14, No. 1 (March, 1982), 95-106.

5078 **Williams, W.W.** "Internal Colonialism,
Coreperiphery Contrasts and Devolution: An
Integrative Comment." *Area*, 9, No. 4 (December,
1977), 272-278.

5079 **Williamson, J.G.** "Regional Inequality and the
Process of National Development." *Economic
Development and Cultural Change*, 13, No. 2
(April, 1965), 44.

5080 **Wilson, Thomas.** "Papers on Regional
Development." *Journal of Industrial Economics*,
(1965), 8-14.

5081 **Wirth, Louis.** "Localism, Regionalism and
Centralization." *American Journal of Sociology*,
42, No. 4, (Janury, 1937), 496-509.

5082 **Wolpert, J.** "Regressive Siting of Public
Facilities." *Natural Resources Journal*, 16, No. 1
(January, 1976), 103-115.

POLITICAL GEOGRAPHY OF REGIONS

AFRICA

Books and Journals

5083 **Algerie, Nord.** *Limited Administratives*. Decret
du 20 Mai 1957. Algiers: Service
Cartographique, 1957.

5084 **Baker, Christopher.** "Tax Collection in Malawi:
An Administrative History, 1891-1972."
International Journal of African Historical Studies,
8, No. 1 (1975), 40-62.

5085 **Barnett, Michael N., and Levy, Jack S.**
"Domestic Sources of Alliances and Alignments:
The Case of Egypt, 1962-73." *International
Organization* [Stanford], 45, No. 3 (Summer,
1991), 369-395.

5086 **Bayart, Jean-Francois.** *The State in Africa: The
Politics of the Belly.* London: Longman, 1993.

5087 **Brasseur, G.** "La region dans les limites
administratives des etats de l'Ofrique de l"Quest."
Bulletin de l"institut Fondamental d'Afrique Noire.
Ser. B. Sciences Humaines, Tome 30, No. 3
(Juillet, 1968), 861-867.

5088 **Brierly, T.G.** "The Evolution of Local
Administration in French-Speaking West Africa."
Journal of Local Administration Overseas, 5, No. 1
(January, 1966), 56-71.

5089 **Brown, Nathan J.** *Peasant Politics in Modern
Egypt: The Struggle Against the State.* New
Haven: Yale University Press, 1990.

5090 **Cabot, Jean.** "Delimitation de l'espace et
developpment: reflexion sur les decoupages
administratifs successifs de l'Algerie." *Recherches
Geographiques a Strasbourg*, Numero 22-23
(1983), 189-196.

5091 **Cachalia, Y.** "The Ghetto Act." *Africa South*, 2,
No. 1 (October-December, 1957), 39-44.

5092 **Clarke, John I.** "Economic and Political Changes
in the Sahara." *Geography*, 46, No. 211, Part 2
(April, 1961), 102-119.

5093 **Creecy, B.** "Urbanization in the Homelands." In
Debate on Housing (DSG/SARS, eds.).
Johannesburg: Southern African Research
Services, 1983, 46-56.

5094 **Diop, Momar Coumba, and Diouf, Mamadou.**
"Enjeux et Contraintes Politiques de la Gestion
Municipale au Senegal." *Canadian Journal of
African Studies* [Toronto], 26, No. 1 (1992), 1-23.

5095 **Drummond, James.** "Reincorporating the
Bantustans into South Africa: The Question of
Bophuthatswana." *Geography* [Sheffield], 76, Part
4, No. 333 (October, 1991), 369-373.

5096 **Dugard, J.** "Some Realism about the Judicial
Process and Positivism--A Reply." *South African
Law Journal*, 98 (1981), 372-387.

5097 **Essien, Victor.** "Sources of Law in Ghana."
Journal of Black Studies [Thousand Oaks, CA], 24,
No. 3 (March, 1994), 246-262.

5098 **Fombad, Charles Manga.** "The Scope for
Uniform National Laws in Cameroon." *The
Journal of Modern African Studies* [Cambridge],
29, No. 3 (September, 1991), 443-456.

5099 **Jeeves, A.** *Migrant Labour in South Africa's
Mining Economy.* Montreal: McGill-Queen's
Press, 1985.

5100 Johnson, Ladd Linn. *Luanda, Angola: The Development of Internal Forms and Functional Patterns*. Los Angeles: University of California, Ph.D., 1970.

5101 Kagermeier, Andreas. "Marokko: Dezentralisierung und Verwaltung." *Geographische Rundschau*, Jahr. 42, Heft 2 (February, 1990), 76-80.

5102 Kees van Donge, Jan. "The Arbitrary State in the Uluguru Mountains: Legal Arenas and Land Disputes in Tanzania." *The Journal of Modern African Studies* [Cambridge], 31, No. 3 (September, 1993), 431-448.

5103 Kirk-Greene, A.H.M., ed. *The Principles of Native Administration in Nigeria; Selected Documents, 1900-1947*. London: Oxford University Press, 1965.

5104 Knight, David B. "Botswana at the Development Threshold." *Focus* (American Geographical Society), 26, No. 2 (November-December, 1975), 9-13.

5105 Lucas, John. "The State, Civil Society and Regional Elites: A Study of Three Associations in Kano, Nigeria." *African Affairs* [Oxford], 93, No. 370 (January, 1994), 21-38.

5106 Luchaire, Francois. "The Political and Administrative System of the Territories of the Comores." *Journal of Local Administration Overseas*, 4, No. 2 (April, 1965), 88-98.

5107 Mabin, A.S. "Some Aspects of the Spatial Structure of the South African Administrative System." *The South African Geographical Journal*, 54, No. 2 (September, 1972), 124-132.

5108 Mabogunje, Akin L. "Urbanization and Regional Inequalities in Nigeria." In *International Geographical Union, Commission on Regional Aspects of Development, Vol. 1, Methodology and Case Studies*, Richard S. Thoman, ed. Brazil: Victoria, April 12-15, 1947.

5109 Mallows, E.W.N. "Planning Problems of the Witwatersrand." *South African Geographical Journal*, 43, No. 1 (April, 1961), 41-48.

5110 McCarthy, J.J., and Smith, D.P. *South African City: Theory in Analysis and Planning*. Cape Town: Juta, 1984.

5111 Nwankwo, G. Onyekwere. "Management Problems of the Proliferation of Local Government in Nigeria." *Public Administration and Development*), 4, No. 1 (January-March, 1984), 63-76.

5112 Ominde, S.H., and Odingo, R.S. "Demographic Aspects of Regional Inequalities in Kenya." In

International Geographical Union Commission on Regional Aspects of Development, Proceedings, Vol. 1; Methodology and Case Studies. Brazil: Victoria, April 12-15, 1971.

5113 Peiress, J.B. "The Implosion of Transkei and Ciskei." *African Affairs* [Oxford], 91, No. 364 (July, 1992), 365-387.

5114 Perham, Margery. *Native Administration in Nigeria*. London: Oxford University Press, 1937.

5115 Picard, Louis A. "Attitudes and Development: The District Administration in Tanzania." *The African Studies Review*, 23, No. 3 (December, 1980), 49-67.

5116 Picard, Louis A. "Development Administration and Political Control: The District Administration in Lesotho." *Rural Africana*, 18 (Winter, 1984), 27-44.

5117 Pirie, Gordon. "Urban Bus Boycott in Alexandra Township 1957." *African Studies*, 42, No. 1 (1983), 67-77.

5118 Prescott, J.R.V. "Les regions politiques des Camerouns anglofrancais." *Annales de Geographie*, 68, No. 367 (Mai-Juin, 1959), 263.

5119 *Republique de Senegal. Carte Administrative*. Paris: Institut Geographique National, 3rd edition, 1966.

5120 Robertazzi, Chiara. "Evoluzione del Sistema di Administrazione Fiduciaria e Republica del Camerren." *L'Universo*, 39, No. 5 (September-October, 1959), 963-974.

5121 Ross, Stanley D. "The Rule of Law and Lawyers in Kenya." *The Journal of Modern African Studies* [Cambridge], 30, No. 3 (September, 1992), 421-442.

5122 Seethal, Cecil. *Civic Organizations and the Local State in South Africa (1979-1993)*. Iowa City: Ph.D. Dissertation, University of Iowa, 1993.

5123 Seethal, Cecil. "Restructuring the Local State in South Africa: Regional Services Councils and Crisis Resolution." *Political Geography Quarterly* [Oxford], 10, No. 1 (January, 1991), 8-25.

5124 Sidaway, James D. "Contested Terrain: Transformation and Continuity of the Territorial Organisation in Post-Independence Mozambique." *Tijdschrift Voor Economische en Sociale Geografie* [Amsterdam], 82, No. 5 (1991), 367-376.

5125 Southall, Roger J. "Trade Unions and the Internal Working Class in Lesotho." *South African Labour Bulletin*, 10, No. 3 (December, 1984), 85-113.

5126 **Stamp, Patricia.** "Local Government in Kenya: Ideology and Political Practice, 1895-1974." *The African Studies Review*, 29, No. 4 (December, 1986), 17-42.

5127 **Stone, Jeffrey.** "Guide to the Administrative Boundaries of Northern Rhodesia." *University of Aberdeen, Department of Geography. O'Dell Memorial Monograph*, 7 (1979), complete issue.

5128 **Thomas, Ian D.** *A Survey of Administrative Boundary Changes in Tanganyika/Tanzania, 1957 to 1967 for Use in Intercensal Comparisons.* Dar es Salaam, University College, Bureau of Resource Assessment and Land Use Planning, 1967.

5129 **Todes, A., and Watson, Vincent.** "Local Government Reform in South Africa: An Interpertation of Aspects of the State's Current Proposals." *The South African Geographical Journal*, 67, No. 2 (September, 1985), 201-211.

5130 **U.S. Department of State.** *Africa: Civil Divisions.* Washington, D.C.: Office of the Geographer, 1969.

5131 **Voges, E.M.** *Accessibility, Transport and the Spatial Structure of South African Cities: An Historic Perspective.* Pretoria: National Institute for Transport and Road Research, CSIR, 1983.

5132 **Wellings, P.A.** "Making a Fast Buck: Capital Leakage and the Public Accounts of Lesotho." *African Affairs*, 82, No. 329 (October, 1983), 495-507.

5133 **Williams, David.** "How Deep is the Split in West Africa?" *Foreign Affairs*, 40, No. 1 (October, 1961), 118-127.

AMERICAS

Books

5134 **Acir.** *Central City--Suburban Fiscal Disparity and Distress 1977.* Report M119. Washington, DC: U.S. Advisory Commission on Intergovernmental Relations, 1980.

5135 **Agnew, John A.** *Public Policy and the Spatial Form of the City: The Case of Public Housing Location.* Columbus: Ohio State University, 1976.

5136 **Alcaly, R.E., and Mermelstein, D.,** eds. *The Fiscal Crisis of American Cities.* New York: Vintage Books, 1977.

5137 **Anderson, Eileen.** *Municipal Fragmentation, Annexation, and Race: A Case Study of the Impact of Annexation on the Racial Balance of Columbus, Ohio.* Columbus: Master's thesis, Ohio State University, 1993.

5138 **Anderson, W.** *The Units of Government in the United States.* Chicago: Public Administration Service, 1934.

5139 **Anderson, W, and Weidner, E.W.** *State and Local Government in the United States.* New York: Holt, Rinehart & Winston, 1951.

5140 **Barlow, I.M.** *Metropolitan Political Fragmentation, Municipal Expenditures, and Public Service Provision in the Montreal Area: A Study in Urban Political Geography.* Montreal: Department of Geography, McGill University, Ph.D., 1978.

5141 **Batey, William L.** *The Location Requirements and Spatial Organization of Federal Services: The Case of Edmonton.* Alberta, Edmonton, Canada: Department of Geography, University of Alberta, M.A., 1976.

5142 **Berger, B.M.** *Working-Class Suburb: A Study of Auto Workers in Suburbia.* Berkeley: University of California, 1960.

5143 **Berry, Brian J.L.** *Organization and Counterorganization.* Beverly Hills, California: Sage Publications, 1960.

5144 **Bosworth, Karl A.** *Tennessee Valley County; Rural Government in the Hill Country of Alabama.* University, Alabama: University of Alabama, Bureau of Public Administration, 1941.

5145 **Brandt, Donald Paul.** *Urbanization and Open Space: Local Park-Residential Patterns in the Expansion of Urban Functions into Rural Areas--with Particular Attention to Monroe County, Indiana.* Bloomington: Indiana University, Ph.D., 1969.

5146 **Brown, Robert Harold.** *Political Areal Functional Organization: With Special Reference to St. Cloud, Minnesota.* Chicago: University of Chicago, Department of Geography, Research Paper No. 51, 1957.

5147 **Burns, N.** *Making Politics Permanent: The Formation of American Local Government.* Ann Arbor: University of Michigan, Unpublished Manuscript, 1992.

5148 **Canada.** Department of Resources and Development. Northern Administration and Lands Branch. *Administration of the Northwest Territories.* Ottawa: Department of Resource and Development, 1953.

5149 **Castells, M.** *The City and the Grass Roots.* London: Arnold, 1983.

5150 **Cleaves, Peter S.** *Developmental Processes in Chilean Local Government*. Berkeley, California: University of California, Institute of International Studies, 1969.

5151 **Clark, Gordon L.** *Judges and the Cities: Interpreting Local Autonomy*. Chicago: University of Chicago Press, 1985.

5152 **Corbitt, David L.** *The Formation of North Carolina Counties, 1663-1943*. Raleigh: North Carolina Department of Archives and History, 1950.

5153 **Costa Rica.** *Division territorial administrativa de la Republica de Costa Rica*. San Jose: Direccion General de Estadistica, 1949.

5154 **Cox, Kevin R.** *Local Interests and Political Processes in American Cities*. Riverside, California: University of California, Riverside Working Paper in Public Policy, 1976.

5155 **Cox, Kevin R.**, ed. *Urbanization Processes and Conflict in Market Societies*. Chicago: Maarouta Press, 1977.

5156 **Cox, Kevin R.**, and **Agnew, John A.** *The Location of Public Housing: Towards a Comparative Analysis*. Columbus, Ohio: Ohio State University, Department of Geography, Discussion Paper No. 45, 1974.

5157 **Cox, Kevin R.**, and **Dear, Michael.** *Juridictional Organization and Urban Welfare*. Columbus: Ohio State University, Department of Geography, Discussion Paper No. 47, 1975.

5158 **Czernaik, Robert Jack.** *Municipal Annexation and the Politial Geographic Growth of the Central City with Special Reference to Denver, Colorado*. Boulder: University of Colorado, Ph.D., 1979.

5159 **Dale, Edmund H.** *The Role of Successive Town and City Councils in the Evolution of Edmonton, Alberta from 1892 to 1966*. Alberta, Canada: University of Alberta, Ph.D., 1969.

5160 *Division Politico-territorial de la Republica de Honduras*. Tegucigalpa, Honduras: Direccion General de Censos y Esladistica Nacional, 1951.

5161 **Domhoff, G.W.** *Who Rules America Now?* Englewood Cliffs, New Jersey: Prentice-Hall, 1983.

5162 **Dominican Republic.** *Division Territorial de la Republica Dominican. Provincias, Municipios, Secciones, Parajes*. Cuidad Triyillo, Direccion General du Estadistica y Censos, 1961.

5163 **Dykstra, T.L.** *The Political Geography of Lloydminister*. Alberta, Edmonton, Canada: University of Alberta, M.A., 1970.

5164 **Fainstein, N.**, and **Fainstein, S.S.** "Restructuring the American City: A Comparative Perspective. In *urban Policy under Capitalism*. Beverly Hills, California: Sage Publications, 1982, 161-190.

5165 **Ford, Larry Royden.** *The Skyscraper: Urban Symbolism and City Structure*. Eugene: University of Oregon, Ph.D., 1970.

5166 *Geographic Townships in the Province of Ontario*. Toronto: Department of Lands and Forests, Division of Surveys, 1959.

5167 **Glasgow, Jon Arthur.** *Changes in the Governmental Geography of the Urbanized Areas of the United States, 1950 to 1960*. Worcester, Massachusetts: Clark University, Ph.D., 1971.

5168 **Greenberg, Edward S.** *Serving the Few: Corporate Capitalism and the Bias of Government Policy*. New York: John Wiley & Sons, 1974.

5169 **Halverson, F. Douglas**, comp. *County Histories of the United States Giving Present Name, Date Formed, Parent County, and County Seat*. Assisted by Eva H. Halverson. Salt Lake City, Utah: F. Douglas Halverson, 1943.

5170 **Harvey, David W.** *Society, the City and the Space-Economy of Urbanism*. Washington, D.C.: Association of American Geographers Commission on College Geography, Resource Paper No. 18, 1972.

5171 **Hensman, C.R.** *Rich Against Poor*. Harmonds, Middlesex: Penguin, 1971.

5172 **Hoffmann, Phillip P.** *School District Reorganization in Cortland County, New York, 1930-1970: A Geographical Analysis*. Syracuse, New York: Syracuse University, M.A., 1976.

5173 **Hoffmann, Phillip P.** *School District Reorganization in Upstate New York: Case Studies from Homer and Truxton*. Syracuse, New York: Syracuse University Department of Geography Discussion Paper Series, No. 29, March 1977.

5174 **Holloway, Thomas H.** *Policing Rio de Janeiro: Repression and Resistance in a 19th-Century City*. Stanford: Stanford University Press, 1993.

5175 **House, J.W.** *United States Public Policy: A Geographical View*. Oxford: Clarendon Press, 1983.

5176 **Johnston, R.J.** *Residential Segregation, the State and Constitutional Conflicts in American Urban System*. London: Academic Press, 1984.

5177 **Jones, B.**, and **Bachelor, L.W.** *The Sustaining Hand: Community Leadership and Corporate Power*. Lawrence: University of Kansas Press, 1986.

5178 **Kostbade, J. Trenton.** *Geography and Politics in Missouri*. Ann Arbor: University of Michigan, Ph.D., 1957.

5179 **Langum, Resni B.** *Regional Compacts and Low-Level Radioactive Waste Management*. Chicago: University of Illinois, M.A., 1985.

5180 **Lee, Yuk.** *Two Stochastic Models of the Geometric Patterns of Urban Settlements*. Columbus: Ohio State University, Ph.D., 1970.

5181 **Liversedge, David.** *Urban Political Fragmentation in the United States: An Analysis of Its Characteristics*. Akron, Ohio: University of Akron, M.A., 1985.

5182 **Logan, Roderick M.** *The Geography of Intermunicipal Relation: A Case Study in the Grimby Area, Ontario*. Hamilton, Ontario, Canada: McMaster University, Ph.D., 1973.

5183 **Low, Murray McIntosh.** "The Elimination of Geography from Politics: Ideological Uneven Development and Direct Democracy in Progressive Ohio." Columbus: Ohio State University, M.S., 1988.

5184 **Macdonald, Austin F.** *American City Government and Administration*. New York: Thomas Y. Crowell, 1942.

5185 **Mair, Andrew.** *The Geographical Politics of Homelessness*. Columbus: Ohio State University, Department of Geography, Unpublished Paper, 1985.

5186 **Marionneaux, Ronald Lee.** *Monroe, Louisiana: Areal Expansion of the Corporate City*. Bloomington: Indiana University, Ph.D., 1970.

5187 **McBeath, Gerald A.,** and **Morehouse, Thomas A.** *Alaska Politics and Government*. London: University of Nebraska Press, 1994.

5188 **McCutcheon, Henry Richard.** *Town Formation in Eastern Massachusetts, 1630-1802: A Case Study in Political Areal Organization*. Worchester, Massachusetts: Clark University, Ph.D., 1970.

5189 **McGibbon, M.J.** *Citizen Protest in the Urban Planning Process: A Case Study of the North Saskatchewan River Valley Area Redevelopment Plan*. Alberta, Ontario, Canada: University of Alberta, M.A., 1984.

5190 **Mexico.** Direccion General de Estadistica. *Division Municipal de la entidades federativos Diciembre de 1964*. Mexico: Division Municipal, 1965.

5191 **Miles, Edward J.** *Political Regionalism in New York State*. Syracuse, New York: Syracuse University, Ph.D., 1958.

5192 *Montgomery County; A Governmental Picture*. 8th ed. Norristown, Pennsylvania: Commissioners of Montgomery County, 1962.

5193 **Morner, Magnus.** *Region and State in Latin America's Past*. Baltimore: The Johns Hopkins Press, 1993.

5194 **Nelson, Richard R.** *The Moon and the Ghetto: An Essay on Public Policy Analysis*. New York: W.W. Norton, 1977.

5195 **Norris, Robert E.** *A Diagrammatic Analysis of Urban Political Dominance*. Tempe: Arizona State University, Geography Department, M.A., 1965.

5196 **Parsons, Stanley B.** *The Populist Concept: Rural Versus Urban Power on a Great Plains Frontier*. Westport, Connecticut: Greenwood Press, 1973.

5197 **Patton, H. Milton,** et al. *The West in the 1970's: Profile of a Region in Change*. Lexington, Kentucky: The Council of State Governments, 1978.

5198 **Penniman, C.** *State Income Taxation*. Baltimore, Maryland: Johns Hopkins University Press, 1980.

5199 **Penzkofer, Mary Elizabeth.** *The Evolution of the Gull Lake Community, 1900-1975*. Kalamazoo: Western Michigan University, M.A., 1975.

5200 **Pollak, Gerald Harris.** *Municipal Annexation: A Study in the Political Geography of Columbia, South Carolina*. Columbia: University of South Carolina, M.S., 1978.

5201 **Pratt, G.** *An Appraisal of the Incorporation Thesis-Housing Tenure and Political Values in Urban Canada*. Vancouver, British Columbia, Canada: University of British Columbia, Ph.D., 1984.

5202 *Province de Quebec. Regions et Sous-regions administratives*. Ministere de l'Industrie et du Commerce, Division du Desoin, Bureau de Recherches Economiques, Quebec, 1967.

5203 **Republica Argentina.** *Division Politica*. Buenos Aires: Instituto Geografico Militar, 1958.

5204 **Robson, Brian T.** *Urban Analysis*. Cambridge, Massachusetts: Harvard University Press, 1969.

5205 **Robson, W.A.** *Local Government in Crisis*. London: Allen & Unwin, 1966.

5206 **Rosenthal, Joyce Ruth.** *The Use of Standardized Zoning Data in Planning. Case Study: Orange County*. Fullerton: California State University, M.A., 1973.

5207 **Sacko, Seymour; Harris, Robert; and Carroll, John J.** *The State and Local Government: The Role of State Aid.* Albany, New York: Department of Audit and Control, 1963.

5208 **Salmore, Barbara G., and Salmore, Stephen A.** *New Jersey Politics nad Government: Suburban Politics Comes of Age.* Lincoln: University of Nebraska Press, 1993.

5209 **Senykoff, Ronald Sergei.** *Rural-Urban Fringe Delineation by Instrumented Interpretation of Imagery from High-Altitude and Orbital Remote Sensors: An Experimental Application of TV Scanning Waveform Analysis and Color-Infrared Imagery Interpretation for Extracting Geographic Patterns.* Boca Raton: Florida Atlantic University, M.A., 1975.

5210 **Sayer, Wallace S, and Kaufman, Herbert.** *Governing New York City.* New York: Russell Sage Foundation, 1960.

5211 **Sigueira, Ioao G.** *Divisao territorial do Brasil. Cartogramas dos estados e territorios. Os antigos e novos municipios e districtos brasileiros de acordo com as alteracoes efetuadas para os quinquenios 1944-48-1949-53.* Dados do Instituto Brasileiro de Geografia e Estatistica. Belo Horizonte: Editora Minas Gerais, S.A., 1949.

5212 **Smith, William C.; Acuna, Carlos H.; and Gamarra, Eduardo A., eds.** *Democracy, Markets, and Structural Reform in Latin America.* New Brunswick, Transaction Publishers, 1994.

5213 **Spring, John Walton.** *The Sunset-Bolsa Chica Area: An Analysis of the Impact of Urbanization upon a Politically Fragmented Coastal Zone.* Fullerton: California State University, M.A., 1975.

5214 **Stenberg, Carl W.** *American Intergovernmental Relations: A Selected Bibliography.* Monticello, Illinois: Council of Planning Librarians, 1971.

5215 **Stetzer, Donald Foster.** *Special Districts in Cook County: Towards a Geography of Local Government.* Chicago, Illinois: University of Chicago, Department of Geography Research Papers No. 169, 1975.

5216 **Sublett, Michael D.** *Preserving the Territorial Integrity of Champaign County, Illinois: 1855-1867.* Normal: Illinois State University, Department of Geography-Geology, 1980.

5217 **Taylor, Robert G.** *A Comparison of the Civil and Congressional Townships in Indiana.* Bloomington: Indiana University, M.A., 1953.

5218 *The Small City and Regional Community.* Stevens Point, Wisconsin: Proceedings of the First Conference on the Small City and Regional Community, March 30-31, 1978.

5219 **U.S. Bureau of Census.** *Congressional District Atlas (Districts of 90th Congress).* Washington, D.C.: U.S. Government Printing Office, 1966.

5220 **U.S. Conference of Mayors.** *Homelessness in America's Cities: Ten Case Studies.* Washington, D.C.: U.S. Conference of Mayors, 1984.

5221 **U.S. Department of State.** *Congressional District Atlas of the United States.* Washington, D.C.: Bureau of the Census, 1960.

5222 **U.S. Department of State.** *South America: Civil Divisions.* Washington, D.C.: Office of the Geographer, 1968.

5223 **U.S. Library of Congress.** Division of Documents. Bibliography of official publications and the administrative systems in Latin American countries. Washington, D.C., 1938. "Reprinted from Proceedings of the First Convention of the Inter-American Bibliographical and Library Association." New York: Wilson, 1938.

5224 **Walker, Pamela.** *Public Policy, Neighborhood Opposition, and the Geography of Community Residences for the Mentally Retarded: A Case Study of Onondaga County, New York.* Syracuse, New York: Syracuse University, M.A., 1984.

5225 **Walter, Richard J.** *Politics and Urban Growth in Buenos Aires, 1910-1942.* Cambridge: Cambridge University Press, 1993.

5226 **Webster, Gerald R.** *The Spatial Reorganization of the Local State: The Case of County Boundaries in Kentucky.* Lexington: University of Kentucky, Ph.D., 1984.

5227 **Westfall, John Edward.** *The Geographical Estimated of Classical Population Numbers.* Washington, D.C.: George Washington University, Ph.D., 1969.

5228 **Whalley, Diane.** *Approaches to Locational Conflicts Analysis: An Application to Housing Rehabilitation in Minneapolis.* Iowa City: University of Iowa, Ph.D., 1983.

5229 **White, Anthony G.** *A Selected Bibliography: City-County Consolidation in the United States.* Monticello, Illinois: Council of the Planning Libraries, 1972.

5230 **Wood, Robert.** *1400 Governments: The Political Economy of the New York Metropolitan Region.* Cambridge, Massachusetts: Harvard University Press, 1961.

5231 **Zink, H.** *Government of Cities in the United States.* New York: Macmillan, 1939.

Journals

5232 **Alexander, John W.** "Rockford, Illinois: A Medium-Sized Manufacturing City." *Annals of the Association of American Geographers*, 42, No. 1 (March, 1952), 1-23.

5233 **Alonso, William.** "Urban and Regional Imbalances in Economic Development." *Economic Development and Cultural Change*, 17, No. 1 (October, 1968), 1-14.

5234 **Andrade, Thompson Almeida.** "Regional Inequalities in Brazil." In *International Geographical Union, Commission on Regional Aspects of Development. Proceedings, Vol. I, Methodology and Case Studies* held in Victoria, Brazil, April 12-15, 1971. Edited by Richard S. Thoman. Montreal: Auister Typsetting and Graphics, 1974, 337-359.

5235 **Antonoff, Nicolas.** "La Bulgarie et les Detriots." *Politique Etrangere*, 17, No. 5 (November, 1952), 361-378.

5236 **Arija Rivares, Emilio.** "Acerca de una variacion de limites entre las Provincias de Burgos y Santander." *Estudios Geograficos*, 26, No. 101 (Noviembre, 1965), 439-506.

5237 **Baer, W.** "Regional Inequality and Economic Growth in Brazil." *Economic Development and Cultural Change*, 12 (1964), 268-285.

5238 **Bartels, L.A.; Nicoll, W.R.; and Van Duijn, J.J.** "Estimating the Impact of Regional Policy." *Regional Science and Urban Economics*, 12 (1982), 3-41.

5239 **Bennett, J.O.,** et al. "Forseeable Effects of Nuclear Detonations on a Local Environment: Boulder County, Colorado." *Environmental Conservation*, 11 (1984), 155-65.

5240 **Berry, Brian J.L.** "Relationships Between Regional Economic Development and the Urban System-The case of Chile." *Tijdschrift voor Economische en Sociale Geografie*, 60, Nr. 5 (Sept.-Okt., 1969), 283-307.

5241 **Binkley, Clark S., and Tabors, Richard D.** "A Louisiana Case Study. Towards a Single System of Substate Regions." *Growth and Change*, 11, No. 1 (January, 1980), 20-28.

5242 **Blomley, Nicholas K.** "Editorial: Making Space for Law." *Urban Geography* [Silver Spring], 14, No. 1 (January-February, 1993), 3-6.

5243 **Borchert, John R.** "American Metropolitan Evolution." *Geographical Review*, 57 (1967), 301-332.

5244 **Brand, Jack, and McCrone, Donald.** "The SNP: From Protest to Nationalism." *New Society*, 20, No. 11 (November, 1975), 416-418.

5245 **Britt, Robert D.** "The Appalachian Regional Development Program." *Growth and Change*, 2 (1971), 3-13.

5246 **Brown, Marilyn A.** "Case Studies and a Dialogue on the Role of Geographic Analysis in Public Policy." *University of Illinois (Urbana) Occasional Publications*, 12 (June, 1979), 1-51.

5247 **Bryant, C.R.** "La Villeregional nord-americaine: le cas de Toronto." *Annales de Geographie*, 527 (1986a), 69-85.

5248 **Burghardt, Andrew F.** "The Proposal Regional Government for the Hamilton Area: An Analysis of City and Suburban Positions." *Communication au XXIIe Congres International de Geographie* (Section VII). Montreal, I.G.U. Congress, 1972, 501-503.

5249 **Burghardt, Andrew F., and Massam, Bryan H.** "The Administrative Subdivisions of Southern Ontario: An Attempt at Evaluation." *The Canadian Geographer*, (1968), 34-36.

5250 **Callard, Keith B.** "The Present System of Local Government in Canada: Some Problems of Status, Area, Population, and Resources. *The Canadian Journal of Economics and Political Science*, 17, No. 2 (May, 1951), 204-217.

5251 **Carlyle, W.** "The Changing Geogrpahy of Administrative Units for Rural Schooling and Local Government on the Canadian Prairies." *Prairie Forum*, 12, No. 1 (1987), 5-35.

5252 **Cavalcanti, Temistoctes.** "Divisao do Estado da Guanabara em Municipios." *Boletim Geografico*, 21, No. 172 (Janeiro-Fevereiro, 1963), 44-49.

5253 **Cermakian, Jean.** "L'amenagement de l'espace rural au Quebec." *Bulletin de la Societe Neuchateloise de Geographie*, 28 (1984), 55-65.

5254 **Cermakian, Jean.** "The Geographic Basis for the Viaility on an Independent State of Quebec." *The Canadian Geographer*, 18 (1974), 288-294.

5255 **Childs, James B.** "Bibliography of Official Publications and the Administrative System in Latin American Countries." *Inter-American Bibliographical and Library Association*, proceedings of the first convention, Washington, D.C., 1938. (1938), 131-172.

5256 **Clark, Gordon L.** "Adjudicating Jurisdictional Disputes in Chicago and Toronto: Legal Formalism and Urban Structure." *Urban Geography*, 7 (1986), 63-80.

5257 **Clarke, Collin G.** "Political Fragmentation in the Caribbean: The Case of Anguilla." *The Canadian Geographer*, 15, No. 1 (Spring, 1971), 13-29.

5258 **Cooper, Sherwin H.** "The Census County Division: A Major Revision of the Minor Civil Division." *Professional Geographer*, 15, No. 4 (July, 1963), 4-8.

5259 **Cox, Kevin R., and Nartowicz, F.** "Jurisdictional Fragmentation in the American Metropolis: Alternative Perspectives. *International Journal of Urban and Regional Research*, 4 (1980), 196-209.

5260 **Daniel, Warren J.** "Etymology and Genealogy of Pennsylvania Counties." *Pennsylvania Department of Internal Affairs Monthly Bulletin*, 11, No. 10 (September, 1943), 3-9; 12, No. 2 (January, 1944), 19-31; No. 3 (February, 1944), 27-31; No. 4 (March, 1944), 27-31; No. 5 (April, 1944), 23-32.

5261 **Desmeules, Jean.** "Nomenclatures des Divisions Administratives de la Trovince de Quebec." *Review Canadienne de Geographie*, 15, Nos. 1-2-3-4 (1961), 63-71.

5262 **Dickenson, J.P.** "The Spread of Development in Brazil at the Level of States: Some Observations." In *International Geographical Union, Commission on Regional Aspects of Development, Vol. 2, Spatial Aspects of the Development Process*, held in London, Ontario, Canada, August 2-7, 1972. Edited by Frederick M. Helleiner and Walter Stohr. Montreal: Allister Typesetting and Graphics, 1974, 377-389.

5263 **Dingemans, Dennis and Munn, Andrew.** "Acquisition-Based Assessment and Property Tax Inequalities after California's 1978 Proposition Thirteen." *Growth and Change*, 20, No. 1 (Winter, 1989), 55-66.

5264 **Divisao Territorial do Brasil.** "1. Numero de Municipios, Segundo as Unidades da Federacao. 2. Relacao dos Municipios, Segundo as Unidades do Federacao. 3. Municipios Relacionades na Ordem Alfabetica." *Revista Brasileira de Geografia*, 19, No. 1 (January-March, 1957), 95-115.

5265 "Divisao Territorial do Brasil; quadro Municipal em 30-VI 1962." *Anuario Geografico do Estado de Rio de Janeiro*, 15 (1962/1963), 24-40.

5266 "Divisao territorial do Estado do Rio de Janeiro (administrativa e judiciaria)." *Anuario Geografico do Estado do Rio de Janeiro*, 5, 1952 (1953), 159-165.

5267 "Divisao Territorial e Administrativa do Estado do Rio de Janeiro." *Anuario Geografico do Estado do Rio de Janeiro*, 8, Pub. 1956 (1955), 199-282.

5268 "Division Politica del Peru, 1821-1962." *Anuario Geografico del Peru*, No. 1 (1962), 93-153.

5269 **Dorion, Henri.** "Las divisiones geografico-administrativas como cuadro de una geografia voluntaria: el ejemplo del Estado de Quebec." Mexico: *Communication au Congres Regional de l'Union Geographique Internationale*, 1966.

5270 **Duncan, S.S., and Goodwin, M.** "The Local State and Local Economic Policy: Why the Fuss?" *Policy and Politics*, 13, No. 3 (July, 1985), 227-253.

5271 **Dunleavy, P.** "The Political Implications of Sectoral Cleavages and the Growth of State Employment, Part I and II." *Political Studies*, 28, No. 3 (September, 1980), 364-383 and No. 4 (December, 1980), 527-549.

5272 **Dwyre, Diana** and others. "Disorganized Politics and the Have-Nots: Politics and Taxes in New York and California." *Polity*, 27, No. 1 (Fal, 1994), 25-47.

5273 **Dye, Thomas R.** "Urban Political Integration: Conditions Associated with Annexation in American Cities." *Midwest Journal of Political Science*, 8, No. 4 (November, 1964), 430-446.

5274 "En pro de una division geografico-administrativa de Espana." *Estudios Geograficos*, Ano 2, Num. 3 (Mayo, 19410, 330-322.

5275 **Figueiredo, Jose de Lima.** "Nova divisao territorial do Brasil." *Revista Brasileira de Geografia*, Ano 2, No. 2 (Abril, 1940), 250-255.

5276 **Fincher, Ruth.** "The State Apparatus and the Commodification of Quebec's Housing Cooperatives." *Political Geography Quarterly*, 3, No. 2 (April, 1984), 127-143.

5277 "Formation of Counties and Changes in Their Boundaries by Years." Florida, Commissioner of Agriculture. *The Seventh Census of the State of Florida, 1945*, (1946), 5-6.

5278 **Forrest, S.; Hay, A.M.; and Johnston, R.J.** "In What Ways are the Suburbs Different? A Note." *Politics*, 19, No. 1 (May, 1984), 97-101.

5279 **Fowler, Phillip Moseley.** *A Theoretical Construct for City Rank Size Relationships*. Iowa City: University of Iowa, Ph.D., 1969.

5280 **Fried, C.** "Liberalism, Community, and the Objectivity of Values. *Harvard Law Review*, 96, No. 4 (February, 1983), 960-968.

5281 Gerston, Larry N., and Haas, Peter J. "Political Support for Regional Government in the 1990s: Growing in the Suburbs?" *Urban Affairs Quarterly* [Thousand Oaks], 29, No. 1 (September, 1993), 154-163.

5282 Goodchild, M.F., and Massam, Bryan H. "Some Least-Cost Models of Spatial Administrative Systems in Southern Ontario." *Human Geography. Geografiska Annaler*, Ser. B. 51B, No. 2 (1969), 86-94.

5283 Grande, J.C. Pedro. "Proposicao de uma nova divisao politica do Brasil." *Revista Brasileira de Geografia*, Ano 27, N. 4 (Outubro-Dezembro, 1965), 625-640.

5284 Grunbaum, W.F., and Wenner, L.M. "Comparing Environmental Litigation in State and Federal Court." *Publius*, 10, No. 3 (Summer, 1980), 129-142.

5285 Hall, Kermit L. "The Legal Culture of the Great Plains." *Great Plains Quarterly* [Lincoln], 12, No. 2 (Spring, 1992), 86-98.

5286 Hamelin, Louis-Edmond. "Developpement politique et finances publiques dans les Territoires Nordiques du Canada." In *The Arctic Circle: Aspects of the North from the Circumpolar Nations*, William C. Wonders, ed. Don Mills, Ontario: Longman Canada, 1976, 42-66.

5287 Hamelin, Louis-Edmond. "L'implantation Politique du Quebec dans sis Territoires Nordiques." *Revue de Geographie de Montreal*, 28, No. 4 (1974), 313-321.

5288 Hamelin, Louis-Edmond. "Manifestations amerindiennes de caractere politique dans les Territoires-du-Nord-Ouest." In *Les facettes de l'identite amerindienne*, M.A. Tremblay, ed. Quebec: Presses de l'Universite Laval, 1976, 81-106.

5289 Handelman, Howard. "The Political Mobilization of Urban Squatter Settlements: Santiago's Recent Experience and its Implications for Urban Research." *Latin American Research Review*, 10, No. 2 (Summer, 1975), 35-72.

5290 Hanson, G.H. "The Geographic Factor and its Influence in Utah Administrative Units." In *Yearbook of the Association of Pacific Coast Geographers*, Seattle: University of Washington, 1937, 3-8.

5291 Hare, F.K. "Regionalism and Administration: North American Experiments." *Canadian Journal of Economic and Political Sciences*, 15, No. 3 (August, 1949), 344-352.

5292 Henripin, Jacques. "Les Divisions de Recensement au Canada de 1871 a 1951: Methode Permettant d'en Uniformiser Les Territories." *L'Actualite Economique*, 30, No. 4 (January-March, 1955), 633-659.

5293 Hill, R.C. "State Capitalism and the Urban Fiscal Crisis in the United States." *International Journal of Urban and Regional Research*, 1, No. 1 (March, 1977), 76-100.

5294 Hindell, K. "Canada's Arctic Claim." *Geographical Magazine*, 58, No. 1 (1986), 16-20.

5295 Hoggart, Keith. "Geography and Local Administration: A Bibliography." *Monticello, Illinois, Vance Bibliographies. Public Administration Series: Bibliography*, Monticello, Illinois: Council of Planning Libraries, Exchange Bibliography P-530, 1980.

5296 Hope, M., and Young, J. "From Back Wards to Back Alleys: Deinstitutionalization and the Homeless. *Urban and Social Change Review*, 17, No. 2 (Summer, 1984), 7-11.

5297 Illinois. Secretary of State. *Counties of Illinois: Their Origin and Evolution*. Comp. and pub. by Edward J. Hughes. Springfield: Edward J. Hughes, 1941.

5298 Johnston, R.J. "The Political Element in Suburbia: A Key Influence in the Urban Geography of the United States." *Geography*, 66, Part 4, No. 293 (November, 1981), 286-296.

5299 Kasperson, Roger E. "Toward a Geography of Urban Politics: Chicago, A Case Study." *Economic Geography*, 41, No. 2 (April, 1965), 95-107.

5300 Kaufman, N.K. "Homelessness: A Comprehensive Approach." *Urban and Social Change Review*, 17, No. 1 (Winter, 1984), 21-26.

5301 Kirby, Andrew. "Law and Disorder: Morton Grove and the Community Control of Handguns." *Urban Geography* [Silver Spring], 11, No. 5 (September-October, 1990), 474-487.

5302 Knapp, Gunnar, and Morehouse, Thomas A. "Alaska's North Slope Borough Revisited." *Polar Record* [Cambridge], 27, No. 163 (October, 1991), 303-312.

5303 Knight, David B. "Canada in Crisis: The Power of Regionalisms." In *Tension Areas of the World*. D.G. Bennett, ed. Champaign, Illinois: Park Press, 1982, p. 254-79.

5304 Koschnik, Albrecht. "Political Conflict and Public Contest: Rituals of National Celebration in Philadelphia, 1788-1815." *The Pennsylvania Magazine of History and Biography* [Philadelphia], 118, No. 3 (July, 1994), 209-248.

5305 **Langlois, C.** "The State of Local Government in Greater Montreal." *Canadian Geographer*, 8, No. 3 (1964), 160-162.

5306 **Lazarus-Black, Mindie.** "Why Women Take Men to Magistrate's Court: Caribbean Kinship Ideology and Law." *Ethnology* [Pittsburgh], 30, No. 2 (April, 1991), 119-133.

5307 **Lewis-Beck, M., and Rice, T.** "Government Growth in the United States." *Journal of Politics*, 47, No. 1 (February, 1985), 2-30.

5308 **Ley, David, and Mills, Charles W.** "Gentrification and Reform Politics in Montreal." *Cashiers de Geografie du Quebec*, 30, No. 81 (1986), 419-427.

5309 "Limites Municipais e divisas interdistritais em que se baseia o Quadro Territorial Administrativo do Estado de Minas Gerais..." *Bolletim Geografico de Minas Gerais*, 1, No. 2 (Dezembro, 1958), 9-255; 2, No. 3 (1959), 7-98.

5310 **Lowery, David, and Berry, W.** "The Growth of Government in the United States: An Empirical Assessment of Competing Explanations." *American Journal of Political Science*, 37, No. 4 (November,1983), 665-694.

5311 **Lowi, Theodore J.** "American Business, Public Policy Case Studies and Political Theory." *World Politics*, 16, No. 4 (July, 1964), 677-715.

5312 **Lutz, James M.** "The Spatial and Temporal Diffusion of Selecting Licensing Laws in the United States." *Political Geography Quarterly*, 2, No. 2 (April, 1986), 141-159.

5313 **Maia Forte, Jose Matoso.** "Estado do Rio-de-Janeiro. A novo divisao territorial administrativa e judiciaria." *Revista da Sociedade de Geografia do Rio de Janeiro*, Tomo 45 (1938), 105-112.

5314 **Mair, Andrew.** "Locating Shelters for the Homeless." *Area*, 16, No. 4 (December, 1984), 338-340.

5315 **Marando, Vincent C.** "Inter-Local Cooperation in Metropolitan Areas: Detroit." *Urban Affairs Quarterly*, 4, No. 2 (December, 1968), 185-200.

5316 **Martis, Kenneth C.** *The Historical Atlas of United States Congressional Districts, 1789-1983*. Vol. 1. West Drayton, Middx: Collier Macmillan, Stockley Close, 1983.

5317 **Massam, Bryan H.** *An Approach to the Analysis of Spatial Administrative Patterns: Ontario Hydro-Electric Power Commission*. Hamilton, Ontario, Canada: McMaster University, Ph.D., 1969.

5318 **Massam, Bryan H.** "Evolution of Local Government Units (Toronto)." *Communication au XXIIᵉ Congres International de Geographie* (Section VII). Montreal, I.G.U. Congress, 1972, 505-506.

5319 **Massam, Bryan H., and Burghardt, Andrew.** "The Administrative Subdivisions of Southern Ontario: An Attempt at Evaluation." *Canadian Geographer*, 12, No. 3 (1968), 125-134.

5320 **Maynier, Andre.** "Departments et communes de France sont-ils trop Petits?" In *Melanges de geographie: Physique, humaine, economique, appliquee, offerts a M. Omer Tulippe*. Tome 2. Geographie economique, geographie appliquee, regionalisation et theorie. Glembloux, Editions J. Duculox, 1967, 442-451.

5321 **Miller, Byron.** "Political Empowerment, Local-Central State Relations, and Geographically Shifting Political Opportunity Structures: Strategies of the Cambridge, Massachusetts Peace Movement." *Political Geography*, 13, No. 5 (September, 1994), 393-406.

5322 **Moises, Jose A., and Slotcke, Verena.** "Urban Transport and Popular Violence: The Case of Brazil." *Past and Present*, 86 (February, 1980), 174-191.

5323 **Morrill, Robert W.** *A Political Geography of Educational Systems*. Worcester, Massachusetts: Clark University, Ph.D., 1973.

5324 **Morrill, Robert W.** "School Districts for Millersburg" and "Metro-Space." *Geography in an Urban Age*. Revised edition of Political Geography, Unit 4 of the High School Geography Project of the Association of American Geographers. New York: Macmillan, 1979.

5325 **Muir, Richard.** "Political Geography: Dead Duck or Phoenix?" *Area*, 8, No. 3 (September, 1976), 195-200.

5326 **Murphy, Raymond E.** "Town Structure and Urban Concepts in New England." *Professional Geographer*, 16, No. 2 (March, 1964), 1-6.

5327 **Nelson, C.A., and Wolch, Jennifer.** "Intrametropolitan Planning for Community Based Residential Care." *Socio-Economic Planning Sciences*, 19, No. 3 (1985), 205-212.

5328 **Nelson, H.J.** "The Vernon Area of California. A Study of the Political Factor in Urban Geography." *Annals of the Association of American Geographers*, 42, No. 2 (June, 1952), 177-191.

5329 **Newton, Kenneth.** "American Urban Politics: Social Class, Political Structures and Public Goods in American Urban Politics." *Urban Affairs Quarterly*, 11, No. 2 (December, 1975), 241-264.

5330 **Osborne, R.H.** "New Counties for Old in the East Midlands: An Outline Scheme for the Reform of Local Government Areas." *The East Midland Geographer*, 4, Part 4, No. 28 (December, 1967), 207-223.

5331 **Prado, Jr., Caio.** "O factor geografico na formacio e no desenvolvimento de cidale de Sao Paulo." *Geografica*, 1, No. 3 (1935), 239-262.

5332 **Pritchett, Herman C.** "Equal Protection and the Urban Minority." *American Political Science Review*, 18, No. 4 (December, 1964), 869-875.

5333 **Proudfoot, M.J.** "Chicago's Political Structure." *Geographical Review*, 47, No. 1 (January, 1957), 107-117.

5334 "Quadro Sistematico do Divisio Regional das Unidades Federades, Brazil." *Boletim Geografico*, 11, No. 116 (Septembre-October, 1953), 531-536.

5335 **Quintino dos Santos, Benedito.** "Limites e divisao territorial do Estado." *Revista do Instituto historico e geografico de Minas Gerais*, 1 (1943-1944, Publ. 1945), 128-150.

5336 **Reichman, Shalom, and Hasson, Shlomo.** "Exploratory Survey of the Geographic Classification of the 1975/76 State Budget." *City and Region*, 1, Nos. 1 and 2 (1976), 63-66.

5337 **Ricketson, Oliver G., Jr.** "Municipal Organization of an Indian Township in Guatemala." *The Geographical Review*, 29, No. 4 (October, 1939), 643-647.

5338 **Romney, Paul.** "The Nature and Scope of Provincial Autonomy: Oliver Mowat, the Quebec Resolutions and the Construction of the *British North America Act*. *Canadian Journal of Political Science* [Waterloo], 25, No. 1 (March, 1992), 3-28.

5339 **Salinas, Patricia Wilson, and Garza, Jose M.** "Prospects for Political Decentralization: Peru in the 1980's." *International Journal of Urban and Regional Research*, 9, No. 3 (September, 1985), 330-340.

5340 **Salisbury, Howard Graves III, and Worthington, Wayne.** *The USAIDS Handbook on Urban Terrorism.* The United States Army Intelligence Center and School, Fort Huachuca, Arizona. Washington, D.C.: U.S. Government Printing Office 1978-783-183-1602-9-1.

5341 **Schrieke, J.J.** "The Administrative System of the Netherlands Indies." *Bulletin of the Colonial Institute of Amsterdam*, 2, No. 3 (May, 1939), 165-182; No. 4 (August, 1939), 245-266.

5342 **Seligmann, Linda J.** "The Burden of Visions Amidst Reform: Peasant Relations to Law in the Peruvian Andes." *American Ethnologist* [Arlington], 20, No. 1 (February, 1993), 25-51.

5343 **Sexton, Patricia Cayo.** "The Life of the Homeless." *Dissent*, 30, No. 1 (Winter, 1983), 79-84.

5344 **Shelley, Fred M.** "Local Control and Financing of Education: A Perspective from the American State Judiciary." *Political Geography*, 13, No. 4 (July, 1994), 361-376.

5345 **Smyth, Steven.** "The Quest for Provincial Status in Yukon Territory." *Polar Record* [Cambridge], 28, No. 164 (January, 1992), 33-36.

5346 **Soares Guimaraes, Fabio de Macedo.** "A proposito do problema da delimitacao de unidades politicas." *Revista brasileira de geografia*, Ano 5, No. 4 (Outubro-Dezembro, 1943), 638-645.

5347 **Steinberg, Philip E.** "Territorial Formation on the Margin: Urban Anti-Planning in Brooklyn." *Political Geography*, 13, No. 5 (Spetember, 1994), 461-476.

5348 **Stoner, Madeline R.** "The Plight of Homeless Women." *Social Service Review*, 57, No. 4 (December, 1983), 565-581.

5349 **Strathman, James and Honey, Rex D.** "Jurisdictional Consequences of Optimizing Public Good." *Annals of Regional Science*, 12, No. 2 (July, 1978) 32-40.

5350 **Tobler, W.** "Depicting Federal Fiscal Transfers." *Professional Geographer*, 33, No. 4 (November, 1981), 419-422.

5351 **Vance, James E., Jr.** "Areal Political Structure and Its Influence on Urban Patterns." In *Yearbook of the Association of Pacific Coast Geographers*, Seattle: University of Washington, 22 (1960), 40-49.

5352 **Vollmar, Rainer.** "Grundriss der regionalen Enwichlungspolitik in den USA: Gesellschaftliche Einflusse, historische Entwicklung, Theoretische Ansatre und neuere gestezliche Grundlagen." *Raumforschung und Raumordnung*, 34 Jahrg, Heft 5 (Oktober, 1976), 200-206.

5353 **Webster, G.R., and Samson, S.A.** "On Defining the Alabama Black Belt: Historical Changes and Variations." *Southeastern Geographer*, 32 (1992), 163-172.

5354 **Westcoat, James L., Jr.** "Water Law, Urbanization, and Urbanism in the American West: The 'Place of Use' Reconsidered." *Urban Geography* [Silver Spring], 14, No. 5 (September-October, 1993), 414-420.

5355 **White, Max R.** "Town and City Consolidation in
      Connecticut." *The American Political Science
      Review*, 36, No. 3 (June, 1942), 492-502.

5356 **Wolch, Jennifer**, and **Gabriel, S.A.**
      "Development and Decline of Service-Dependent
      Population Ghettos. *Urban Geography*. 5, No. 2
      (April-June, 1984), 111-129.

ASIA

Books

5357 *Atlas of the Administrative Subdivisions of Japan.*
      Tokyo: Nitchi Shuppan (Nippon Map Co.), 1953.

5358 **Bedeski, Robert E.** *The Transformation of South
      Korea: Reform and Reconstitution in the Sixth
      Republic Under Roh Tae Woo, 1987-1992.*
      London: Routledge, 1994.

5359 **Bhatt, G.D.** *Municipal Administration in Uttar
      Pradesh; Case Study with Particular Reference to
      Pithoragarh District.* New Delhi: EBL, 1989.

5360 **Chander, N. Jose**, ed. *Dynamics of State Politics:
      Kerala.* New Delhi: Sterling Publishers, 1986.

5361 **Collins, Charles, Sir.** *Public Administration in
      Ceylon.* London: Royal Institute of International
      Affairs, 1951.

5362 **Collins, Charles, Sir** *Public Administration in
      Hong Kong.* Published in cooperation with the
      International Secretariat Institute of Pacific
      Relations. London: Royal Institute of
      International Affairs, 1952.

5363 *District Boundary Changes and Population Growth
      for Pakistan, 1881-1961.* Dacca: Dacca
      University, 1969.

5364 **Drysdale, Alasdair Duncan.** *Center and
      Periphery in Syria: A Political Geography Study.*
      Ann Arbor: University of Michigan, Ph.D., 1977.

5365 **Gananathan, V.S.** *Effects of the Division of India
      on the Distribution, Orientation and Function of the
      Major Political Centers.* Syracuse, New York:
      Syracuse University, M.A., 1948.

5366 **Gandhi, Mohandas Karamchand.** *The Indian
      States' Problem.* Ahmedabad: Navajivan Press,
      1941.

5367 **Gudoshnikov, Leonid Moiseevich.** *Local Organs
      of State Power and State Administration of the
      Chinese People's Republic.* Moscow: Academy of
      Sciences of the U.S.S.R. A. IA. Vyshinskii
      Institute of Law, 1959.

5368 **Guzman, Raul P. de** and **Reforma, Mila A.**, eds.
      Government and Politics of the Philippines.

                Singapore: Oxford University Press, 1988.

5369 **Henriot, Christian.** *Shanghai, 1927-1937:
      Municipal Power, Locality, and Modernization.*
      Translated from the French by Noel Castelino.
      Berkely: University of California Press, 1993.

5370 **Hyma, Balasubramanyam I.** *The Rural-Urban
      Fringe of a Growing Metropolis: Madras, and
      Indian Example.* Pittsburgh: University of
      Pittsburgh, Ph.D., 1971.

5371 **India.** Government of Bombay. *The Provinces of
      Bombay, Showing the Divisions of Collectorates,
      Talukas and Principal Native States.* Poona:
      Government Photozinco Office, 1947.

5372 **India.** Ministry of Home Affairs. *The Jawaharlal
      Nehru, Sadar Vallabhbhai Patel and Pattabhi
      Sitaramayya Committee Report.* Delhi:
      Publication Division, Government of India Press,
      1949.

5373 **India (Republic).** Ministry of Home Affairs.
      Report of the States Reorganization Commission.
      S. Fazl Ali, Chairman. New Delhi: Publication
      Division, Government of India Press, 1956.

5374 **India (Republic).** Ministry of Home Affairs.
      White Paper on Indian States. New Delhi:
      Publication Division, Government of India Press,
      1950.

5375 **India.** Ministry of Home Affairs. *White Paper on
      Indian States.* Delhi: Publication Division,
      Government of India Press, 1984.

5376 **India.** Survey of India. *Survey of India, Map of
      India (Showing Provinces and Districts*, 4th ed.
      Calcutta: Survey of India, 1936.

5377 **Ismael, Tareq Y.**, and **Ismael, Jacqueline S.**
      *Politics and Government in the Middle East and
      North Africa.* Miami: Florida International
      Univesity Press, 1991.

5378 *Israeli Administrative Divisions.* Tel-Aviv: Survey
      Department, 1953.

5379 *Jammer and Kashmir: Administrative Divisions,
      Map No. 189.* New York: United Nations,
      Cartographie Section, 1949.

5380 **Johan, Klasnor.** *The Emergence of the Modern
      Malay Administrative Elite.* Oxford: Oxford
      University Press, 1984.

5381 **Jones, S.W.** *Public Administration in Malaya.*
      London: Royal Institute of International Affairs,
      1953.

5382 **Karasov, Deborah.** "Ideology and the Politics of
      Landscape in Israeli Planning." Minneapolis:
      University of Minnesota, Ph.D., 1988.

5383 **Lavalle, Eduard Marcus.** *The Politics of Decentralization: Perspectives on the Relevance of Statutory Village Councils as an Inducement to Political and Social Change in India.* Durham, North Carolina: Duke University, M.A., 1970.

5384 **Mukerji, Krishna Prasada** and **Ramaswamy, Suhasini.** *Reorganization of Indian States.* Bombay: Popular Book Depot, 1955.

5385 **Oldenburg, Philip K.** *Indian Urban Politics, with Particular Reference to the Nagpur Corporation.* Chicago, Illinois: University of Chicago, M.A., 1968.

5386 **Osborn, James.** *Area, Development Policy and the Middle City in Malaysia.* Chicago: Department of Geography, University of Chicago Research Series, No. 153, 1974.

5387 **Pannikar, K.M.** *Indian States.* (Oxford Pamphlets on Indian Affairs, No. 4), 2nd ed. Bombay: Humphrey Milford, Oxford University Press, 1943.

5388 **Rajamannar, P.V.** *Report of the Centre-State Relations Enquiry Committee.* Madras: Government of Tamil Nadu, 1971.

5389 **Reeve, W.D.** *Public Administration in Siam.* London: Royal Institute of International Affair, 1951.

5390 *Report of the States Reorganization Commission.* New Delhi: Publication Division, Government of India, 1951.

5391 **Santhanam K.** *Union State Relations in India.* New York: Asia Publishing House, 1960.

5392 **Sastry, K.R.R.** *Indian States.* Allahabad: Kitabistan, 1941.

5393 **Shahani, S.J.** *A Comparative Study of Traditional Political Organization of Kerala and Punjab.* London: School of Oriental and African Studies, University of London, Ph.D., 1965.

5394 **Shepperdson, M.J.** *Political Conflict in Selected Villages of India, Pakistan and Ceylon.* London: School of Oriental and African Studies, University of London, M.A., 1967.

5395 **Singh, Amarjit.** *The Reorganization of States in India: A Case Study of the Punjab.* Claremont, California: Claremont Graduate School and University Center, Ph.D., 1967.

5396 *South Asia. Administrative Divisions. Syracuse Outline Series, SA 101,* ed. J.A. Fonda. Syracuse, New York: Syracuse University, Department of Geography, 1967.

5397 **Steiner, K.** *Local Government in Japan.*

Stanford, California: Stanford University Press, 1965.

5398 **Tepper, Elliot L.** *Changing Patterns of Administration in Rural East Pakistan.* East Lansing: Asian Studies Center, Michigan State University, Asian Study Center, 1966.

5399 **Tirtha, Ranjit.** *Geographical Reorganization of Indian States, 1947-1960.* Chapel Hill: University of North Carolina, Ph.D., 1961.

5400 **U.S. Department of State.** The Geographer. *Asia: Civil Divisions.* Washington, D.C.: U.S. Department of State, 1968.

5401 **U.S. Department of State.** *Administrative Subdivisions of Japan; with Appendix of 47 Prefectural Maps.* (Japanese Gazetter, Publication No. 2749) (Far Eastern Series, No. 19) Washington, D.C.: U.S. Department of State, 1946.

5402 **Whitney, J.B.R.** *China: Area, Administration and Nation-Building.* Chicago: University of Chicago, Department of Geography, Research Paper 123, 1970.

5403 **Zaidi, Iqtidar H.** *Administrative Areas of West Pakistan: A Geographic Evaluation.* Syracuse, New York: Syracuse University, Ph.D., 1961.

Journals

5404 **Adhikari, Sudeepta.** "India's National Integration: A Problem in Political Geography." *Geographical Review of India,* 47, No. 1 (March, 1985), 83-90.

5405 **Ahmad, Kazi S.** "Regional Balance in Pakistan." *Pakistan Geographical Review,* 9, No. 2 (July, 1954), 1-15.

5406 **Ahmad, Kazi S.** "Politico-Regional Plan." *Pakistan Geographical Review,* 4, No. 2 (July, 1949), 18-25.

5407 **Alexander, William.** "Government in the Villages of Modern India." *Journal of Administration Overseas,* 7, No. 1 (January, 1968), 303-310.

5408 **Arora, Satish Kumar.** "The Reorganization of Indian States." *Far Eastern Survey,* 25, No. 2 (February, 1956), 27-30.

5409 **Ata, Rashida.** "Provincial Administration Commission Report." *Pakistan Geographical Review,* 15, No. 2 (June, 1960), 51-53.

5410 **Breton, R.J.L.** "Reorganisation de la carte politique de l'Inde." *Information Geographique,* 36, No. 3 (1972), 127-130.

5411 **Borton, Hugh**. "The Administration and Structure of Japanese Government." *Department of State Bulletin*, 2, No. 287 (December 24, 1944), 817-833.

5412 **Borton, Hugh**. "Korea: Internal Political Structure." *The Department of State Bulletin*, 2, No. 281 (November 12, 1944), 578-583.

5413 **Brown, Michael P.** "The Possibility of Local Autonomy." *Urban Geography* [Silver Spring], 13, No. 3 (May-June, 1992), 257-279.

5414 **Burns, Creighton**. "Goa Since Liberation." *Reporter*, 26, No. 6 (March 15, 1962), 28-30.

5415 **Canfield, Robert L.** "Afghanistan: The Trajectory of Internal Alignments." *The Middle East Journal*, 43, No. 4 (Autumn, 1989), 635-648.

5416 **Cleary, Mark, and Shaw, Brian**. "Limbang: A Lost Province of Oil-Rich Brunei Daussalam." *Geography* [Sheffield], 77, Part 2, No. 335 (April, 1992), 178-181.

5417 **Cooke, Philip**. "Radical Regions." In *Political Action and Social Identity*, G. Rees, et al, eds. London: Macmillan, 1985.

5418 **Dastur, Aloo J.** "Reorganization of States." *Gujarat Research Society, Bombay, Journal*, 24, No. 2 (April, 1962), 18-23.

5419 **Deshpande, C.D.** "India Reorganized; A Geographical Evaluation." *The Indian Geographer*, 1, No. 2; and 2, No. 2 (August, 1957), 164-169.

5420 **Douglas, Henry H.** "A New Map for China." *Asia and the Americas*, 46, No. 7 (July, 1946), 304-306.

5421 **Easterlin, Richard A.** "Israel's Development: Past Accomplishments and Future Problems." *Quarterly Journal of Economics*, 75, No. 1 (February, 1961), 63-86.

5422 **Farid-Chen, Ahmad**. "Pakistan Pod Inostrannym Jarmom--Prismo UZ Karaci." In *Mezdunarodnaja Zizn, No. 10*. Moscow: Universitat, 1959, 103-111.

5423 **Fifield, Russell H.** "New States in the Indian Realm." *The American Journal of International Law*, 46, No. 3 (July, 1952), 450-463.

5424 **Glassner, Martin Ira**. "Drawing Boundaries of Planning Regions: A Political Geographer's Contribution." *ITCC* (International Technical Cooperation Centre) *Review*, July, 1972. Reprinted in Hebrew in *Environmental Planning*, July-December, 1972.

5425 **Gokhle, B.G.** "Nagaland--India's Sixteenth State." *Asian Survey*, 1, No. 5 (May, 1961), 36-40.

5426 **Gradus, Yehuda**. "The Role of Politics in Regional Inequity: The Israeli Case." *Annals of the Association of American Geographers*, 73, No. 3 (September, 1983), 388-403.

5427 **Huque, M. Azizula, Sir**. "Rural Self-Governing Bodies in India." *Journal of the Royal Society of Arts*, 91, No. 4631 (January 22, 1943), 94-105.

5428 "India: Redrawing the Map." *Round Table*, 44, No. 181 (December, 1955), 70-73.

5429 **Kalita, B.C.** "Administrative Units of North East India: A Geographical Note." *The Journal of North East India Geographical Society*, 12, Nos. 1 and 2 (1980), 53-56.

5430 **Kant, Surya**. "Evolution of Administrative Areas in British India with Special Reference to the Punjab." *Geographical Review of India*, 51, No. 1 (March, 1989), 18-26.

5431 **Kant, Surya and Dubey, K.N.** "Spatial Structure of Administrative Units and the Development Process: A Case Study of Uttar Pradesh." *The National Geographical Journal of India*, 30, Part 1 (March, 1984), 31-39.

5432 **Krishan, Gopal**. "Administrative Geography." *Transactions of the Institute of Indian Geograpny*, 5, No. 2 (July, 1983), 101-108.

5433 **Landron, Andre**. "Divisions Administratives de la Cochinchine." *Bulletin de la Societe des Etudes Indochinoises*, Tome 20 (Annee, 1945), 15-35.

5434 **Lehrer, A.** "The Administered Areas: To Whom Do They Belong?" *Jerusalem Post*, (January 29, 1971), 1-3.

5435 **Liebesny, Herbert J.** "Administration and Legal Development in Arabia." *The Middle East Journal*, 9, No. 4 (Autumn, 1955), 385-396; 10, No. 1 (Summer, 1956), 33-42.

5436 "Maps of Yunnan Province in Southern China: Administrative Divisions and Nationalities; Cultivation Zones; Industries; Mineral Resources." [Various Scales] *Geographische Rundschau*, 38 Jahrg, 3 Heft (1986), 114-123.

5437 **McColl, Robert W.** "Development of Supra-Provincial Administrative Regions in Communist China 1949-1960." *Pacific Viewpoint*, 4, No. 1 (March, 1963), 53-64.

5438 **Mendelsohn, Oliver**. "The Pathology of the Indian Legal System." *Modern Asian Studies*, 15, Part 4 (October, 1981), 823-863.

5439 **Nandy, Ashis**. "The Political Culture of the Indian State." *Daedalus*, 18, No. 4 (Fall, 1989), 1-26.

5440 **Narasimhacharya Rao, Bahadur K.N.** "How a Talluk Map is Compiled and Described." *The Journal of the Madras Geographical Association*, 15, No. 4 (October-December, 1940), 369-370.

5441 **Pannikar, K.M.** "Indian States Reorganization." *Asian Review*, 52, No. 192 (October, 1956), 247-258.

5442 **Prakasa Rao, V.L.S.** "Rational Grouping of the Districts of the Madras State." *The Indian Geographical Journal*, 28, Nos. 1 and 2 (January-June, 1953), 33-43.

5443 **Prakasa Rao, V.L.S.** "Regional Planning Units and Re-Arrangement of Administrative Boundaries." *Calcutta Geographical Review*, 11, No. 1 (March, 1949), 16-25.

5444 **Prakasa Rao, V.L.S., et al.** "Regional Disparities in India." In *International Geographical Union, Commission on Regional Aspects of Development, Proceedings, Vol. I: Methodology and Case Studies*, held in Victoria, Brazil, April 12-15, 1971. Edited by Richard S. Thoman. Montreal: Allister Typesetting and Graphics, 1974, 623-691.

5445 **Rasheed, K.B. Sajjadur.** "An Examination of the Shapes of the Administrative Districts of Bangla Desh." *Geografiska Annulu, Ser. B. Human Geography*, 54B, No. 2 (April, 1972), 104-108.

5446 **Rice, Stanley.** "Administration in Baroda." *The Asiatic Review*, 37, No. 131 (July, 1941), 557-565.

5447 **Riggs, Fred W.** "Chinese Administration in Formosa." *Far Eastern Survey*, 20, No. 21 (December, 1951), 209-215.

5448 **Rood, Steven.** "Issues on Creating an Autonomous Region for the Cordillera, Northern Philippines." *Ethnic and Racial Studies* [London], 14, No. 4 (October, 1991), 516-544.

5449 **Rubinoff, Arthur G.** "Goa's Attainment of Statehood." *Asian Survey* [Berkeley], 32, No. 5 (May, 1992), 471-487.

5450 **Rushbrook, L.F. Williams.** "Inside Kashmir." *International Affairs*, 33, No. 1 (January, 1957), 26-35.

5451 **Sabratnam, Lakshmanan.** "The Boundaries of the State and the State of Ethnic Boundaries: Sinhala-Tamil Relations in Sri Lankan History." *Ethnic and Racial Studies*, 10, No. 3 (July, 1987), 291-316.

5452 **Sajjadur, Rasheed K.B.** "The Spatial Efficiency of Administrative Units in Bangladesh." *Geografisea Annaler, Series B. Human Geography*, 68B, No. 1 (1986), 21-28.

5453 **Shrivastava, V.K.** "Sidhi; A District Headquarters in Transition (In Madhya Pradesh)." *Geographical Thought*, 3, No. 1 (June, 1967), 50-55.

5454 **Siddiqui, Nafis Ahmad.** "Block Headquarters: A New Dimension of Settlement Function." *Geographical Outlook*, 8 (1971-72), 57-62.

5455 **Spate, O.H.K.** "A Year of Change: Territorial Reorganization in the Indian Union." *The Geographical Journal*, 111, Nos. 4-6 (April to June, 1948), 288-292.

5456 **Srivastava, R.P.** "The Uttar-Pradesh Boundary in India: A Case of Intra-National Boundary Problem." *National Geographer*, 7 (1972), 49-57.

5457 **Stanley, Bruce.** "Raising the Flag over Jerusalem; The Search for a Palestinian Government." *American-Arab Affairs*, No. 26 (Fall, 1988), 9-27.

5458 **Sternstein, Larry.** "The Growth of the Population of the World's Pre-Eminent 'Primate City': Bangkok at its Bicentenary." *Journal of Southeast Asian Studies*, 15, No. 1 (March, 1984), 43-68.

5459 **Stevens, Georgiana G.** "Reform and Power Politics in Iran." *Foreign Policy Reports*, 26, No. 19 (February 15, 1951), 214-223.

5460 **Sundram, K.V.** "The Boundaries of Local Government Areas in India." *The Indian Geographical Journal*, 43, Nos. 1-4 (January-December, 1968), 34-39.

5461 **Thomas, S.B.** "Government and Administration in China Today." *Pacific Affairs*, 23, No. 3 (September, 1950), 248-270.

5462 **Tiwari, R.C.** "The Changing Political Map of Assam." *National Geographer*, 9 (1974), 67-73.

5463 **Verma, R.V.** "The Territorial Evolution of Oudh." *The Geographical Viewpoint*, 2, No. 1 (April, 1971), 37-42.

5464 **Wake, William H., III.** "States Reorganization in India: A Centrifugal or Centripetal Force for the Future." *The California Geographer*, 4 (1963), 35-47.

5465 **Wiber, M. G.** "Levels of Property Rights, Levels of Law: A Case Study from the Northern Philippines." *Man* [London], 26, No. 3 (September, 1991), 469-492.

5466 **Windmiller, Marshall.** "The Politics of States Reorganization in India: The Case of Bombay." *Far Eastern Survey*, 25, No. 9 (September, 1956), 129-143.

5467 **Wirsing, Robert G.** "Association 'Micro-Arenas' in Indian Urban Politics." *Asian Survey*, 13, No. 4 (April, 1973), 408-420.

5468 **Wong, J. Y.** "The Rule of Law in Hong Kong: Past, Present and Prospects for the Future." *Australian Journal of International Affairs* [Canberra], 46, No. 1 (May, 1992), 81-92.

5469 **Yonekura, J.** "Historical Development of the Political-Administrative Divisions of Japan." *Abstract of Papers*, Rio de Janeiro, 18th International Geographical Congress, 1956.

5470 **Zaidi, Iqtidar H.** "Farmers' Perception and Management of Pest Hazard: A Pilot Study of a Punjabi Village in Lower Indus Region." *Insect Science and Its Application*, 5 (1984), 187-201.

5471 **Zorn, Jean G.** "*Graun Bilong Mipela*: Local Land Courts and the Changing Customary Law of Papua New Guinea." *Pacific Studies* [Laie], 15, No. 2 (June, 1992), 1-38.

AUSTRALIA, OCEANIA AND ANTARCTICA

Books and Journals

5472 **Atchison, J.F.** "The Counties of New South Wales." *Australian Surveyor*, 30, No. 1 (March, 1980), 32-43.

5473 **Bobek, H.** "The Formation of Regional Inequalities in Development: The Case of Australia." In *International Geographical Union, Commission on Regional Aspects of Development, Proceedings, Vol. 1, Methodology and Case Studies*, held in Victoria, Brazil, April 12-15, 1971. Edited by Richard S. Thoman. Montreal: Allister Typesetting and Graphics, 1974, 779-794.

5474 **Holmes, J.M.** "Regional Boundaries in the Murray Valley." *Australian Geographer*, 4, No. 3 (March, 1944), 197-203.

5475 **Holmes, J.M.** "Regional Planning in Australia." *Geographical Journal*, 112, No. 1-3 (July to September, 1948), 78-82.

5476 **Jeans, D.N.** "Territorial Divisions and the Locations of Towns in New South Wales, 1826-1842." *Australian Geographer*, 10, No. 4 (September, 1967), 243-255.

5477 **Logan, W.S.** "The Evolution and Significance of Local Government Boundaries in South-Western Victoria." *Australian Geographical Studies*, 4, No. 2 (October, 1966), 154-170.

5478 **Marsh, I.** "Politics, Policymaking and Pressure Groups: Some Suggestions for Reform of the Australian Political System." *Australian Journal of Public Administration*, 42 (1963), 433-458.

5479 **Patton, H. Milton.** *The Pacific Basin: Toward a Regional Future*. Georgetown, Kentucky: State Research Associates, January, 1980.

5480 **Premdas, Ralph R.,** and **Steeves, Jeffrey.** "Ethnic Politics nad Inequalityin Figi: Understanding the New Constitution." *Societe des Oceanistes. Journal* [Paris], 96, No. 1 (1993), 63-75.

5481 **Saffu, Yaw.** "Changing Civil-Military Relations in Fiji." *Australian Journal of International Affairs* [Canberra], 44, No. 2 (August, 1990), 159-170.

5482 **Sant, M.E.C.,** and **Oatley, J.** "Incrementalism as the Route to a Blueprint? Changes in the Geography of Local Government in New South Wales, 1974-1981." *Australian Geographer*, 15, No. 6 (November, 1983), 391-402.

5483 **Scott, R.,** ed. *Interest Groups and Public Policy. Case Studies from the Australian State.* Melbourne: Macmillan, 1980.

5484 **Walmsley, D.J.** "Australian Local Government in the 1970's." *Australian Geographical Studies*, 22, No. 1 (April, 1984), 88-99.

EUROPE

Books

5485 **Bennett, R.J.,** and **Krebs, G.** *Local Authority Finance in German Cities: Analysis of the Budget in Relation to Spatial Structure of Committees.* London: London School of Economics, Working Paper 'Local Business Tax' Project, 1986.

5486 **Bennett, R.J.,** and **Krebs, G.** *Local Taxes in German Cities: Analysis of the Spatial Structure and Development of Tax Yields, Tax Base and Tax Rates.* London: London School of Economics, Working Paper 'Local Business Tax' Project, 1986.

5487 **Bennett, R.J.; Krebs, G.;** and **Zimmermann, H.** *Local Business Taxes in Britain and Germany: The Policy Debate.* London and Bonn: Anglo-German Foundation, 1986.

5488 **Boddy, M.; Lovering, J.;** and **Bassett, Keith.** *Sunbelt City? A Study of Economic Change in Britain's M4 Growth Corridor.* Oxford: Clarendon Press, 1986.

5489 **Bond, Andrew R.** *Inter-Republic Variations in Belorussian and Ukrainian Russianization, 1959-1970.* Madison: University of Wisconsin, M.A., 1979.

5490 **Brette, Armand.** *Les limites et les divisions territoriales de la France en 1789.* Paris: E. Cornely et Cie, 1907.

5491 **Daunton, M.,** ed. *Councillors and Tenants: Local Authority Housing in English Cities.* Leicester: Leicester University Press, 1984.

5492 **Demarchi, Franco.** *L'associazionismo in provincia di Gorizia.* Gorizia: Institute of International Sociology, 1970.

5493 **Duclaud-Williams, R.** *The Politics of Housing in Britain and France.* London: Heinemann, 1982.

5494 **Goddard, J.B., and Champion, A.G.** *The Urban and Regional Transformation of Britain.* London: Methuen, 1983.

5495 **Grauhan, R.R.,** ed. *Lokale Politikforschung.* Two Volumes. Frankfurt: Campus, 1975.

5496 *German Territorial Organization.* Special Report of the Military Governor, U.S. Zone. Prepared by Civil Administration Division, November 1, 1946.

5497 **Great Britain Government.** *Paying for Local Government,* Cmnd 9714. London: Her Majesty's Stationery Office, 1986.

5498 **Gremion, P.** *Le Pouvoir peripherique: Bureaucratie et Notables dans le Systeme politique francais.* Paris: Le Seuil, 1976.

5499 **Goodway, D.** *London Chartism 1838-1848.* Cambridge: Cambridge University Press, 1982.

5500 **Gyford, J.** *Local Politics in Britain.* London: Croom Helm, 1976.

5501 **Hall, P., and Hay, D.** *Growth Centres in the European Urban System.* London: Heinemann, 1980.

5502 **Hansen, Jens Christian.** *Administrative grenser og tettstedsvekst.* Bergen: Universitetsforlaget, 1970.

5503 **Jacobs, B.O.** *Black Politics and Urban Crisis in Britain.* Cambridge: Cambridge University Press, 1986.

5504 **Jenkins, Peter.** *Mrs. Thatcher's Revolution: The Ending of the Socialist Era.* Cambridge, Massachusetts: Harvard University Press, 1988.

5505 **Joyce, P.** *Work, Society and Politics.* Brighton: Harvester Press, 1980.

5506 **Kalk, E.,** ed. *Regional Planning and Regional Government in Europe.* The Hague: International Union of Local Authorities, 1971.

5507 **Kirby, Andrew, and Pinch, Stephen,** eds. *Public Provision and Urban Politics: Papers from IBG Annual Conference, January, 1982.* Geography Paper No. 80, Department of Geography, University of Reading, 1982.

5508 **Lennert, James W.** *A Second Partition of Ireland?* Chicago, Illinois: University of Chicago, M.A., 1983.

5509 **Little, D. Richard.** *Governing the Soviet Union.* New York: Longman, 1989.

5510 *Local Government Boundary Commission for England, Report No. 1.* London: Her Majesty's Stationery Office, 1972.

5511 **Matthews, Mervyn.** *The Passport Society: Controlling Movement in Russia and the USSR.* Boulder: Westview Press, 1993.

5512 **Maud Report.** *Committee on the Management of Local Government.* London: Her Majesty's Stationery Office, 1967.

5513 **Mawson, J.** *Local Authority Economic Policies in West Yorkshire 1974-77.* Occasional Papers, Centre for Urban and Regional Studies, University of Birmingham, 1983.

5514 **Menz, Yves, and Wright, Vincent,** eds. *Centre-Periphery Relations in Western Europe.* London: Allen & Unwin, 1985.

5515 **Mirot, Albert.** *Les divisions religieuses et administratives de la France.* 2nd ed. Paris: Picard, 1950.

5516 **Murgatroyd, L., and Others,** eds. *Localities, Class and Gender.* London: Pion, 1985.

5517 **Newton, K., and Sharpe, L.J.** *Does Politics Matter?* Oxford: Clarendon Press, 1984.

5518 **Nogee, Joseph L.,** ed. *Soviet Politics: Russia After Brezhnev.* New York: Praeger, 1985.

5519 **Offord, J.** *The Fiscal Implications of Differential Population Change for Local Authorities in England and Wales.* Cambridge: Cambridge University Department of Geography, Ph.D., 1986.

5520 **Otok, Stanislaw.** *Rola podziatu administracyjnego w rozmieszczeniu sit uytworczych* (The Role of the Administrative Division in the Distribution of Productive Forces) Workpaper, Warsaw, 1967.

5521 **Pisano, Vittorfranco S.** *The dynamics of Subversion and Violence in Contemporary Italy.* Stanford, California: Hoover Institution Press, 1987.

5522 **Pliatzky, L.** *Getting and Spending: Public Expenditure, Employment and Inflation.* Oxford: Blackwell, 1982.

5523 **Plowden Report.** *Control of Public Expenditure.* London: Her Majesty's Stationery Office, Cmnd, 1432, 1961.

5524 **Poulsen, Thomas M.** *The Provinces of Russia: Changing Patterns in the Regional Allocation of Authority, 1708-1962.* Madison: University of Wisconsin, Ph.D, 1962.

5525 *Republica Populara Romina. Harta Politico-Administrativa.* Bucharest: Intocmita de Clement Vlad. Institutul de Geologie si Geografie al Academiei RPR., 1963.

5526 **Rota, Maria Pia.** *I limiti amministrativi della liguria: osservazioni geografische.* Genova: Universita di Genova, Facolta di Magistero, Publicatzioni dell'Istituto di Scienze Geografische, 26, 1975.

5527 **Rowntree, Lester Bradford.** *To Save A City: Urban Preservation in Salzburg, Austria.* Eugene: University of Oregon, Ph.D., 1971.

5528 **Russian Embassy.** Washington, D.C. *The Sixteen Soviet Republics.* Washington, D.C.: Information Bulletin, Embassy of the U.S.S.R., 1945.

5529 **Savage, M.** *The Dynamics of Working Class Politics: The Labour Movement 1890-1940.* Cambridge: Cambridge University Press, 1987.

5530 **Schapiro, L.** *The Government and Politics of the Soviet Union.* London: Hutchinson, 1979.

5531 **Smallwood, Frank.** *Greater London, The Politics of Metropolitan Reform.* Indianapolis: Bobbs-Merrill, 1965.

5532 **Smith, Gordon B.** *Soviet Politics: Continuity and Contradiction.* New York: St. Martin's Press, 1988.

5533 **Smith, P.J.** *Urban Site Selection in the Fourth Basin.* Edinburg: Faculty of Social Sciences, University of Edinburg, Ph.D., 1964.

5534 **Terrero, Jose.** *Divisiones Territoriales: Geografia de Espana.* Barcelona: Editorial Ramon Sopena, 1966.

5535 **U.S. Department of State.** The Geographer. *U.S.S.R.: Civil Divisions.* Washington, D.C.: Department of State, 1967.

5536 **U.S. Office of Strategic Services.** Research and Analysis Branch. *A Guide to the Changes in Administrative Divisions of the USSR, including Area and Population Figures.* (R & A No. 1163) Washington, D.C.: U.S. Office of Strategic Services, 1943.

5537 **Zink, H.** *Dictionnaire national des communes de France.* Paris: Albin Michel, 1973.

5538 **Zink, H.** *Areas and Status of Local Authorities in England and Wales.* London: Her Majesty's Stationery Office, 1956.

Journals

5539 **Aiken, M., and Depre, R.** "Policy and Politics in Belgian Cities." *Policy and Politics,* 8 (1980),
73-106.

5540 **Axford, Nicholas, and Pinch, Stephen.** "Growth Coalitions and Local Economic Development Strategy in Southern England: A Case Study of the Hampshire Development Association." *Political Geography,* 13, No. 4 (July, 1994), 344-360.

5541 **Bassett, K., and Hoare, T.** "Bristol and the Saga of Royal Portbury: A Case Study in Local Politics and Municipal Enterprise." *Political Geography Quarterly,* 3, No. 3 (July, 1984), 223-250.

5542 **Batowski, Henryk.** "Podzial Administracyjno Terytorialny ZSRR." *Przeglad Geograficznez,* Rok 24, Nr. 4 (1952), 25-42.

5543 **Bennett, Robert J.** "Alternative Local Government Taxes in Britain." *Regional Studies,* 17 (1983), 478-481.

5544 **Bennett, Robert J.** "The Finance of Cities in West Germany." *Progress in Planning,* 21 (1984), 1-62.

5545 **Bernier, Lynne Louise.** "Decentralizing the French State: Implications for Policy." *Journal of Urban Affairs* [Greenwich], 13, No. 1 (1991), 21-32.

5546 **Bialer, Seweryn.** "The Passing of the Soviet Order?" *Survival,* 32, No. 2 (March/April, 1990), 107-120.

5547 **Blazek, M. Zmeny.** "V administrativnism cleneni rumunska a Polska." *Sborninik Ceskoslovenska Spolecnosti Zemepisne,* Svazek 81, Cislo 4 (1976), 296-299.

5548 **Breslauer, George W.** "Provincial Parity Leaders' Demand Articulation and the Nature of Conter-Periphery Relations in the U.S.S.R." *Slavic Review,* 45, No. 4 (Winter, 1986), 650-672.

5549 **Bugayev, V.K.** "Improving the Administrative-Territorial Division of the USSR." *Soviet Geography* [Silver Spring], 32, No. 8 (October, 1991), 545-550.

5550 **Burenko, S.F.** "Novoe administratcino-ekonomicheskoe raronirovanie Narodnoi respubliki Rumynii." (The New Administrative-Economic Regioning of the People's Republic of Romania) *Bulletin of the All-Union Geographical Society,* 82, No. 6 (November-December, 1950), 623-625.

5551 **Burenko, S.F.** "Novoe Administrativno-Territorial'noe Delenie Albanskoi Narodnoi Respubliki." (The New Administrative-Territorial Division of the Albanian People's Republic) *Izvestiia Vsesoiuznogo Geograficheskogo Obschestva.* (Bulletin of the All-Union Geographical Society) 84, No. 1 (January-February, 1952), 53-58.

5552 **Burenko, S.F.** "Novoe Administrativno-Territorial-noi Delenie Narodno-Demokraticheskoi Respubliki Pol'shi." *Izuestica Vsesouiznogo Geograficheskogo Obschestva*, 85, No. 4 (July-August, 1953), 413-422.

5553 **Buschenfeld, Herbert.** "The New States of the Former Yugoslavia." *Geographische Rundschau* [Braunschweig], 46, Heft 3 (Marz, 1994), 148-154.

5554 **Busteed, M.A.** "The Belfast Region: Local Government in Need of Change." *Public Affairs*, 1, No. 3 (1968), 12-13.

5555 **Busteed, M.A., and Mason, Hugh.** "Local Government Reform in Northern Ireland." *Irish Geography*, 6, No. 3 (1971), 315-323.

5556 **Carney, J.G., and Hudson, R.** "Capital, Politics and Ideology: The North East of England, 1870-1946." *Antipode*, 10, No. 2 (August, 1978), 64-78.

5557 **Carroue, Laurent.** "Berlin Reunifiee: Une Nouvelle Metropole a Vocation Internationale en Europe Centrale." *Annales de Geographie* [Paris], 102e, No. 570 (Mars-Avril, 1993), 113-129.

5558 **Christensen, N.O.** "Some Features of the History of the Greenland Administration." *The Arctic Circular*, 7, No. 1 (January, 1954), 1-8.

5559 **Crewe, Ivor.** "The Politics of 'Affluent' and 'Traditional' Workers in Britain: An Aggregate Analysis." *British Journal of Political Science*, 3, Part 1 (January, 1973), 29-52.

5560 **Cucu, Vasile S.** "Imbunatatirea Impartirii Administrative Economice a Teritoriului Republicu Populare Romine." *Probleme de Geografie*, 8 (1961), 265-284.

5561 **Cucu, Vasile S.** "Organizarea administrativ-teriroriala a R.S. Romania. Retrospectiva ultimilor 20 de ani." *Revista Ocrotirea Mediului Inconjurator, Natura, Terra; Subtitul Terra*, Anul. 20, Nr. 1 (Januarie-Martie, 1988), 3-9.

5562 **Douglas, J.N.H.** *A Method of Analysing the Effectiveness of Local Government Areas in Great Britain*. Sheffield: Paper delivered to the International Geographical Union's Symposium on Political Geography, at Sheffield, 1964.

5563 **Edwards, K.C.** "The New Towns of Britain." *Geography*, 49, No. 3 (July, 1964), 272-285.

5564 **Evenden, L.J.** "The Spatial Hierarchical Principle in the Evolution of Modern Local Governments in Scotland." *The Canadian Geographer*, 29, No. 2 (Summer, 1985), 123-136.

5565 **Fawcett, C.B.** "Natural Divisions of England." *Geographical Journal*, 49, No. 2 (February, 1917), 124-141.

5566 **Fenelon, Paul.** "Structure geographique et frontieres des departements francais." *Abstract of Papers*. Rio de Janeiro: 18th International Geographical Congress, 1956.

5567 **Foster, J.** "How Imperial London Preserved its Slums." *International Journal of Urban and Regional Research*, 3, No. 1 (March, 1979), 93-114.

5568 **Friedland, Roger; Piven, F.F.; and Alford, R.** "Personal Conflict, Urban Structure and the Fiscal Crisis." *International Journal of Urban and Regional Research*, 1, No. 3 (October, 1977), 447-471.

5569 **Friedgut, Theodore H.** "Citizens and Soviets: Can Ivan Ivanovich Fight City Hall?" *Comparative Politics*, 10, No. 4 (July, 1978), 461-477.

5570 **Garrahan, P.** "Housing, the Class Milieu, and Middle Class Conservatism." *British Journal of Political Science*, 7, No. 1 (January, 1977), 126-127.

5571 **Goddard, J.B., and Smith, I.J.** "Changes in Corporate Control in the British Urban System." *Environment and Planning*, A 10, No. 9 (September, 1978), 1073-1084.

5572 **Groenendijk, Jan.** "Regionalisering Van Bestuur: Drie Soorten Provincies Op Komst." *Geographie*, 3, Nu. 5 (Oktober, 1994), 8-14.

5573 **Guseyn-Zade, S.M.** "Models of Region Size in a Hierarchial Administrative-Territorial System." *Soviet Geography: Review & Translation*, 23, No. 8 (October, 1982), 599-607.

5574 **Haimson, Leopold H.** "Three Generations of the Soviet Intelligentsia." *Foreign Affairs*, 37, No. 2 (January, 1959), 235-246.

5575 **Hamnett, C.** "The Post Ware Restructuring of the British Housing and Labour Market: A Critical Comment on Thorns." *Environment and Planning*, A16, No. 2 (February, 1984), 147-162.

5576 **Harrop, M.** "The Urban Basis of Political Alignment: A Comment." *British Journal of Political Science*, 10, Part 3 (July, 1980), 388-402.

5577 **Helin, Ronald A.** "The Volatile Administrative Map of Rumania." *Annals of the Association of American Geographers*, 57, No. 3 (September, 1967), 481-502.

5578 **Hirsch, Abraham M. and Kooy, A.** "Industry and Employment in East London." *South African Labour Bulletin*, 7, Nos. 4 and 5 (February, 1982), 50-64.

5579 **Hoare, A.G.** "Dividing the Pork Barrel: Britain's Enterprise Zone Experience." *Political Geography Quarterly*, 4, No. 1 (January, 1985), 29-46.

5580 **Ivanicka, Koloman.** "Geograficke aspekty uzemno-administrativneho clenenia slovenska." *Sbornik Ceskoslovenske Spolecnosti Zemepisne*, Svazek 75, Cislo 4 (1970), 301-313.

5581 **James, J.R.; House, J.W.; and Hall, P.** "Local Government Reform in England: A Symposium." *Geographical Journal*, 136, Part I (March, 1970), 1-23.

5582 **Jasny, Naum.** "Improving Soviet Planning: Thirty-Five Years of Mediocrity." *International Affairs*, 37, No. 4 (October, 1961), 465-476.

5583 **Johnson, R.W.** "The Nationalisation of English Rural Politics: South West Norfolk 1945-1970." *Parliamentary Affairs*, 26, No. 1 (Winter, 1972-1973), 8-55.

5584 **Johnston, R.J.** "Human Geography as a Generalizing Social Science: Transatlantic Contrasts in Local Government." *Geographic Journal*, 150, Part 3 (November, 1984), 335-341.

5585 **Johnston, R.J.** "A Place for Space (or a Space for Place) in British Psephology." *Environment and Planning*, A 18, No. 5 (May, 1986), 573-598.

5586 **Kemeny, J.; Karn, V.; and Williams, P.** "Polarization in the Inner Birmingham Housing Market: First Interim Report of the Inner City Housing Ownership Project." CURS *Working Paper 81*, University of Birmingham, 1981.

5587 **King, Desmond S.** "Political Centralization and State Interests in Britain: The 1986 Abolition of the GLC and MCCs." *Comparative Political Studies* (Newbury Park), 21, No. 4 (January, 1989), 467-494.

5588 **Kirby, Andrew.** "Voluntarism and State Funding of Housing: Political Explanations and Geographic Outcomes in Britain." *Tijdschrift voor Economische en Sociale Geografie*, 76, Nr. 1 (Jan.-Feb., 1985), 53-62.

5589 **Kirk, William.** "Political Factors int he Delineation of Local Government Areas in the United Kingdom, 1966-1973." *Giessener Geographische Shriften*, Heft 35 (1975), 11-16.

5590 **Koulov, Boian.** "Tendencies in the Administrative Territorial Development of Bulgaria (1878-1990)." *Tijdschrift Voor Economische en Sociale Geografie* [Utrecht], 83, No. 5 (1992), 390-401.

5591 **Lampert, Nick.** "Law and Order in the USSR: The Case of Economic and Official Crime." *Soviet Studies*, 36, No. 3 (July, 1984), 366-385.

5592 **Lang, Nicholas R.** "The Dialectics of Decentralization: Economic Reform and Regional Inequities in Yugoslavia." *World Politics*, 27, No. 3 (april, 1975), 309-335.

5593 **Langbein, Otto.** "Les nouvelles division administratives de l'Autriche." *Annales de Geographie*, 48e Annee, No. 274 (Juillet 15, 1939), 401-403.

5594 **Limouzin, P.** "Contraintes financieres et developpement communal en Alsace [Tight Budget and Local Development in Alsace]." *Recheaches Geographiques a Strasbourg*, 24 (1986), 41-43.

5595 **Lindberg, Dennis; McCrone, D; and Dennis, Jack.** "Support for Nation and Government Among English Children." *British Journal of Political Science*, 1, Part 1 (January, 1971), 25-48.

5596 **MacLennan, M.C.** "Regional Planning in France." *Journal of Industrial Economics*, (1965), 62-75.

5597 **Makoev, X.X.** "Democratic Berlin: New Geography of a Socialist City." *Vestnik-Leningradskogo Universiteta, Seriya Geologiya; Geografia*, 3 (1986), 123-127.

5598 **Mather, Jean.** "The Justices of the Peace and the Reform of the Law in England." *Virginia Social Science Journal*, 14, No. 1 (April, 1979), 27-33.

5599 **Mellor, Roy.** "Trouble with the Regions: Planning Problems in Russia." *Scottish Geographical Magazine*, 75, No. 1 (April, 1959), 44-47.

5600 **Melon, Amando.** "El mapa perfectual de Espana (1810)." *Estudios Geograficos*, Ano 13, Num. 46 (February, 1952), 5-72.

5601 **Meriaudeau, Robert.** "Impots locaux et iniquite territoriale: le cas de la taxe fonciere non batie." *Revue de Geographie Alpine*, Tome 75, No. 1 (1987), 5-22.

5602 **Morrison, John A.** "The Evolution of the Territorial-Administrative System of the USSR." Excerpt: *The American Quarterly on the Soviet Union*, 1, No. 3 (October, 1938), 25-46.

5603 **Munchow, Sabine.** "Strukturprobleme sudfrankreichs." *Geographische Rundschau*, Jahr 32, Heft 10 (Oktober, 1980), 453-460.

5604 **Nicholson, R.J., and Topham, W.** "The Determinants of Investment in Housing by Local Authorities: An Econometric Approach." *Journal of Royal Statistical Society*, A 134, Part 2 (1971), 272-303.

5605 **Ogborn, M.J.** "Local Power and State Regulation in Nineteenth Century Britain." *Transactions of the Institute of British Geographers*, 17, No. 2 (1992), 215-226.

5606 **Ogborn, M.** "Ordering the City; Surveillance, Public Space and the Reform of Urban Policing in England, 1835-56." *Political Geography*, 12, No. 6 (November, 1993), 505-521.

5607 **Pierre, Jon.** "Organized Capital and Local Politics: Local Business Organizations, Public-Private Committees, and Local Government in Sweden." *Urban Affairs Quarterly* [Newbury Park], 28, No. 2 (December, 1992), 236-257.

5608 **Pinch, Philip.** "Ordinary Places?: The Social Relations of the Local State in Two 'M4-Corridor' Towns." *Political Geography* [Oxford], 11, No. 5 (September, 1992), 485-500.

5609 **Poulsen, Thomas M.** "Administrative and Economic Regionalization of Bulgaria: The Territorial Reform of 1959." In *Bulgaria Past and Present*, Thomas Butler, ed. Columbus, Ohio: American Association for the Advancement of Slavic Studies, 1976, 187-201.

5610 **Poulsen, Thomas M.** "Administration and Regional Structure in East-Central and Southeast Europe." In *Eastern Europe: Essays in Geographical Problems*, George W. Hoffman, ed. New York: Praeger, 1970, 225-257.

5611 **Rantala, O.** "Political Regions of Finland." *Scandinavian Political Studies*, 2 (1967), 117-140.

5612 **Racz, Barnabas.** "The Parliamentary Infrastructure and Political Reforms in Hungary." *Soviet Studies*, 41, No. 1 (January, 1989), 39-66.

5613 **Reece, J.** "Internal Colonialism: The Case of Brittany." *Ethnic Racial Studies*, 2, No. 3 (July, 1979), 275-292.

5614 **Roberts, Brian.** "Administrative Divisions of the Soviet Arctic and Sub-Artic." *The Polar Record*, 4, No. 31 (January, pub. October, 1946), 320-323.

5615 **Rochefort, Michel.** "La localisation du pouvoir de commandement economique dans une capitale: les sieges sociaux des entreprises dans Paris et la region parisienne." *Revue de Geographie Alpine*, 60, No. 2 (1972), 225-244.

5616 **Ross, Dennis.** "Coalition Maintenance in the Soviet Union." *World Politics*, 32, No. 2 (January, 1980), 258-280.

5617 **Roubitschek, Walter.** "Die Administrative Gliederung der Rumanischen Volksrepublik." *Petermanns Geographische Mitteilungen*, 107, Jahrg 1 (Quartalsheft, 1963), 45-48.

5618 **Santos Velasco, Juan A.** "City and State in Pre-Roman spain: The Example of Ilici." *Antiquity* [Oxford], 68, No. 259 (June, 1994), 289-299.

5619 **Schultz, Lothar.** "The Relationship of the Union to the Republics in Soviet Constitutional Law." *Journal of Baltic Studies*, 19, No. 3 (Fall, 1988), 215-218.

5620 **Sevoka, Jim.** "Prognosis for Political Stability in Yugoslavia in the Post-Tito Era." *East European Quarterly*, 22, No. 2 (June, 1988), 173-190.

5621 **Sewel, John.** "Reorganized Scottish Local Government: A Review." *Scottish Geographical Magazine*, 103, No. 1 (April, 1987), 5-11.

5622 **Shabad, Theodore.** "The Administrative-Territorial Patterns of the Soviet Union." *The Changing World*, W.G. East and A.E. Moodie, eds. New York: World Book, 1956.

5623 **Shabad, Theodore.** "Political-Administrative Divisions of the U.S.S.R., 1945." *The Geographical Review*, 36, No. 2 (April, 1946), 303-311.

5624 **Sharpe, L.J.** "The Role and Function of Local Government in Modern Britain." In *Report of the Committee of Inquiry into Local Government Finance*, Appendix 6. London: Her Majesty's Stationery Office, 1976, 203-220.

5625 **Smith, P.J.** "Rural Interests in the Physical Expansion of Edinburg." In *The Geographer and the Public Environment*, J.V. Minghi, ed. Vancouver: Tantulus Research, B.C. Geographical Series No. 7, 1966, 55-67.

5626 **Smith, S.J.** "Police Accountability and Local Democracy (UK)." *Area*, 18, No. 2 (1986), 99-107.

5627 **Smith, Timothy B.** "In Defense of Privilege: The City of London and the Challenge of Municipal Reform, 1875-1890." *Journal of Social History* [Pittsburgh], 27, No. 1 (Fall, 1993), 59-83.

5628 **Smyth, Howard McGraw.** "Evolution of Local Government in Italy." *The Department of State Bulletin*, 2, No. 277 (October 15, 1944), 404-428.

5629 **Steins, Gerhard.** "Auf dem wege zu einer regionalistischen Raumorganisation? Uber Dezentralisierung-stendenzen in der Bundesrepublik Deutschland unter raumlichen Aspekten." *Geographische Rundschen*, Jahr 39, Heft 10 (October, 1987), 548-553.

5630 **Stern, Jessica Eve.** "Moscow Meltdown: Can Russia Survive?" *International Security* [Cambridge, MA], 18, No. 4 (Spring, 1994), 40-65.

5631 **Syrett, Stephen.** "Local Power and Economic Policy: Local Authority Economic Initiatives in Portugal." *Reigonal Studies* [Abingdon], 28, No. 1 (1994), 53-67.

5632 **Taubert, Heinrich.** "Die Okonomische-Administrativen Rayons der Sowjet-Union." *Petermanns Geographische Mitteilungen*, 102, No. 1 (March, 1958), 75-78.

5633 **Taylor, P.J.** "The Meaning of the North: England's 'Foreign Country' Within?" *Political Geography*, 12, No. 2 (March, 1993), 136-155.

5634 **Thomas, J.G.** "Local Government Areas in Wales." *Geography*, 37, No. 175, Part 1 (January, 1952), 9-19.

5635 **Thomas, Richard; Robson, Brian; and Nutter, Richard.** "Planning the Work of County Courts: A Location-Allocation Anlaysis of the Northern Circuit." *Institute of British Geographers. Transactions* [London], 16, No. 1 (1991), 38-54.

5636 **Thornburgh, Richard.** "The Soviet Union and the Rule of Law." *Foreign Affairs* [New York], 69, No. 2 (Spring, 1990), 13-27.

5637 **Vooys, A.C. de.** "De Regionale Differentierung in de Politieke Gezindte op het Platteland der drie Noordelijke Provincien 1933-1963." *Tijdschrift van het koninklijk Nederlandsch Aardrijkskundig Genootschap*, 2 Ser. 82, No. 3 (Juli, 1965), 245-260.

5638 **Warde, Alan.** "Spatial Change, Politics and the Division of Labour." In *Social Relations and Spatial Structures*, D. Gregory and J. Urry, eds. London: Macmillan, 1985, 190-212.

5639 **Webb, John.** "Krasnodar: A Case Study of the Rural Factor in Russian Politics." *Journal of Contemporary History* [London], 29, No. 2 (April, 1994), 229-260.

5640 **Weeks, Theodore R.** "Nationality and Municipality: Reforming City Government in the Kingdom of Poland, 1904-1915." *Russian History* [Salt Lake City], 21, No. 1 (Spring, 1994), 23-47.

5641 **Winn, S., and McAuley, A.** "Conflicts in Civil Defence (Britain)." *Contemporary Issues in Geography & Education*, 2, No. 3 (1987), 51-57.

5642 **Wise, Charles R., and Amna, Erik.** "'New Managerialism' in Swedish Local Government." *Scandinavian Political Studies* [Oslo], 16, No. 4 (1993), 339-358.

5643 **Wise, M.J.** "The Impact of a Channel Tunnel on the Planning of S.E. England." *Geographical Journal*, 131, No. 2 (June, 1965), 167-185.

CHAPTER VII

POLITICS OF MANAGING RESOURCES OF A NATION-STATE: DEVELOPMENT OF RESOURCES, NATIONAL SELF-SUFFICIENCY AND STOCKPILING

GENERAL AND THEORETICAL

Books and Journals

5644 **Barnett, Harald J.** "The Changing Relation of Natural Resources to National Security." *Economic Geography*, 34, No. 3 (July, 1958), 189-201.

5645 **Bidwell, Percy W.** "Raw Materials and National Policy." *Foreign Affairs*, 37, No. 1 (October, 1958), 144-155.

5646 **Bodman, Andrew R.** "Measuring Political Change." *Environment and Planning A*, 14, No. 1 (January, 1982), 33-48.

5647 **British Steel Corporation.** *The Road to Viability.* London: Her Majesty's Stationery Office, Cmnd 7149, 1978.

5648 **Bryant, R.W.G.** *Land, Private Property, Public Control.* Montreal: Harvest House, 1972.

5649 **Butt, N.A., and Atkinson, T.** "Shortfalls in Minerals Investment." *Resources Policy*, 8 (1982), 261-276.

5650 **Clark, Gordon L.** "A Question of Integrity: The National Labor Relations Board, Collective Bargaining and the Relocation of Work." *Political Geography Quarterly*, 7, No. 3 (July, 1988), 209-229.

5651 **Clawson, Marion.** "Economic and Social Conflicts in Land Use Planning." *Natural Resources Journal*, 15, No. 3 (July, 1975), 473-489.

5652 **Cloud, P.E.** "Realities of Mineral Distribution." *Texas Quarterly*, 11 (1968), 103-126.

5653 **Coates, B.E.; Johnston, R.J.; and Knox, P.L.** *Geography and Inequality.* Oxford: Oxford University Press, 1977.

5654 **Collins, L., and Walker, Leslie W.**, eds. *Location Dynamics of Manufacturing.* New York: John Wiley & Sons, 1975.

5655 **Cooper, R.N.** "Natural Resources and National Security." *Resources Policy*, 1 (1975), 192-203.

5656 **Crenson, M.A.** *The Un-Politics of Air Pollution: A Study of Non-decisionmaking in the Cities.* Baltimore, Maryland: John Hopkins University Press, 1971.

5657 **Crowson, P.C.F.** "Investment and Future Mineral Production." *Resources Policy*, 8 (1982), 3-12.

5658 **Cutright, Phillips.** "National Political Development: Measurement and Analysis." *American Sociological Review*, 28, No. 2 (April, 1963), 253-264.

5659 **Fisher, Allan G.B.** *Economic Self-sufficiency.* New York: Oxford University Press, 1939.

5660 **Flynn, R.** "Co-optation and Strategic Planning in the Local State." In *Capital and Politics*, R. King, ed. London: Routledge, 1983, 85-106.

5661 **Goldsmith, M., and Villadsen, S.**, eds. *Urban Political Theory and the Management of Fiscal Stress.* Brookfield: Gower Publishing, 1986.

5662 **Govett, G.J.S., and Govett, M.H.** "The Concept and Measurement of Mineral Reserves and Resources." *Resources Policy*, 1 (1974), 46-55.

5663 **Gregory, R.** in **P.J. Smith**, ed. *The Politics of Physical Resources.* Harmondsworth: Penguin, 1975.

5664 **Grotewold, A.** "Nations as Economic Regions." *GeoJournal*, 15, No. 1 (1987), 91-96.

5665 **Hall, G.H.** "The Myth and Reality of Multiple-Use." *Natural Resources Journal*, 3, No. 2 (April, 1963), 287.

5666 **Ham, C.** *Policy-making in the National Health Service.* London: Macmillan, 1981.

5667 **Henning, D.H.** "The Politics of National Resources Administration." *Annals of Regional Science*, 2, No. 2 (December, 1968), 239-248.

5668 **Holmes, H.N.** *Strategic Materials and National Strength.* New York: Macmillan, 1942.

5669 **Hunter, Floyd.** *From Community Power Structure.* Garden City, New Jersey: Doubleday, 1963.

5670 **Huddle, F.P.** "The Evolving National Policy for Materials." *Science*, 191, No. 4228 (February 20, 1976), 654-659.

5671 Illich, I. *Energy and Equity.* London: Calder and Boyars, 1974.

5672 Johnston, K. "Judicial Adjudication and the Spatial Structure of Production: Two Decisions by the National Labor Relations Board." *Environment and Planning, A*, 18, No. 1 (January, 1986), 27-40.

5673 Johnston, R.J., and Rossiter, D.J. "An Approach to the Definition of Planning Regions." *Applied Geography*, 1 (1981), 55-70.

5674 Jumper, S.R.; Bell, T.L.; and Ralston, B.A. *Economic Growth and Disparities.* Englewood Cliffs, New Jersey: Prentice-Hall, 1980.

5675 Kasperson, Roger E. "Political Behaviour and the Decision-Making Process in the Allocation of Water Resources between Recreational and Municipal Use." *National Resources Journal*, 9, No. 1 (January, 1969), 176-211.

5676 Koropeckyj, I.S. "Equalisation of Regional Development in Socialist Countries: An Empirical Study." *Economic Development and Cultural Change*, 21, No. 1 (October, 1972), 68-86.

5677 Kuklinski, J.H.; Metlay, D.S.; and Kay, W.D. "Citizen Knowledge and Choices on the Complex Issue of Nuclear Energy." *American Journal of Political Science*, 26, No. 4 (November, 1982), 615-642.

5678 Lane, J.E. and Ersson, S. "Unpacking the Political Development Concept." *Political Geography Quarterly*, 8, No. 2 (April, 1989), 123-143.

5679 Linge, G.J.R., and Rimmer, Peter J., eds. *Government Influence on Location of Economic Activity.* Canberra: Australian National University, 1971.

5680 Lowe, P., and Goyder, J. *Environmental Groups in Politics.* London: Allen & Unwin, 1983.

5681 Mayer, T. "Reflections on 'The End of History.'" *Political Geography*, 12, No. 3 (May, 1993), 79-83.

5682 McLafferty, Sara L. "Constraints on Distributional Equity in the Location of Public Services." *Political Geography Quarterly*, 3, No. 1 (January, 1984), 33-47.

5683 McMichael, P. "World Food System Restructuring Under a GATT Regime." *Political Geography*, 12, No. 3 (May, 1993), 198-214.

5684 McMichael, P. "World Food System Restructuring Under a GATT Regime." *Political Geography*, 12, No. 2 (March, 1992), 198-214.

5685 McMichael, P., and Myhre, D. "Global Regulations vs. the Nation-State: Agro-Food Systems and the New Politics of Capital." *Capital and Class*, 43, No. 2 (1991), 83-105.

5686 McQueen, J. *The Franklin-Not Just a River.* Ringwood: Penguin, 1983.

5687 Mercer, D.C., and Peterson, J.A. "Battle for a Wild River." *The Geographical Magazine*, 55, No. 3 (March, 1983), 122-128.

5688 Mitias, Michael H. "The Possibility of World Economy." *Coexistence* [Dordrecht], 27, No. 3 (September, 1990), 199-214.

5689 Momayezi, Nasser. "Economic Correlates of Political Violence: The Case of Iran." *The Middle East Journal*, 40, No. 1 (Winter, 1986), 68-81.

5690 Musgrave, R.A. *The Theory of Public Finance.* New York: McGraw-Hill, 1959.

5691 Nellor, David C.L. "Sovereignty and Natural Resource Taxation in Developing Countries." *Economic Development and Cultural Change*, 35, No. 2 (January, 1987), 367-392.

5692 O'Riordan, T. *Perspectives on Resource Management.* London: Pion, 1971.

5693 Orridge, A.W. "Uneven Development and Nationalism." *Political Studies*, 29, No. 2 (June, 1981), 181-190.

5694 Orridge, A.W. and Williams, C.H. "Autonomist Nationalism: A Theoretical Framework for Spatial Variations in its Genesis and Development." *Political Geography Quarterly*, 1, No. 1 (January, 1982), 19-39.

5695 Pahl, R.E. "Socio-Political Factors in Resource Allocation." In *Social Problems and the City*, D.T. Herbert and D.M. Smith, eds. Oxford: Oxford University Press, 1979, 33-46.

5696 Papageorgiou, G.J. "Fundamental Problems of Theoretical Planning." *Environment and Planning*, A9, No. 12 (December, 1977), 1329-1356.

5697 Pitelis, Chrisos. "Beyond the Nation-State?: The Transnational Firm and the Nation-State." *Capital and Class*, 43, No. 2 (1991), 131-152.

5698 Price, K.A., ed. *Regional Conflict and National Policy.* Baltimore, Maryland: Johns Hopkins University Press, 1982.

5699 Rempel, H., and Lobdell, R.A. "The Role of Urban-to-Rural Remittances in Rural Development." *Journal of Development Studies*, 14, No. 3 (April, 1978), 324-341.

5700 **Russett, Bruce M.** "Inequality and Instability: The Relation of Land to Tenure to Politics." *World Politics*, 16, No. 3 (April, 1964), 442-454.

5701 **Seninger, S.F.** "Labor Turnover and Employment Impacts in Regional Labor Markets." *Environment & Planning A*, 20, No. 1 (January, 1988), 41-53.

5702 **Smith, Neil.** "Deindustrialization and Regionalization: Class Alliance and Class Struggle." *Papers. Regional Science Association*, 54 (1984), 113-128.

5703 **Smith, Neil.** "Gentrification and Uneven Development." *Economic Geography*, 58, No. 2 (April, 1982), 139-155.

5704 **Spengle, J.J.** "Economic Development: Political Pre-conditions and Political Consequences." *Journal of Politics*, 22, No. 3 (August, 1960), 387-416.

5705 **Stahl, Rudolf.** "Power Supply, Today and Tomorrow." *Universitas*, 1, No. 3 (1957), 247-254.

5706 **Stamp, L. Dudley.** "The Exploitation of Minerals in Relation to National and World Planning." *Nature*, 150, No. 3805 (October 3, 1942), 395-396.

5707 **Van Dusen, Peter.** *The Spatial Organization of Watershed Systems.* Ann Arbor: University of Michigan, Ph.D., 1971.

5708 **Walker, R.A.** "Two Sources of Even Development Under Advanced Capitalism: Spatial Differentiation and Capital Mobility." *Review of Radical Political Economy*, 10, No. 3 (Fall, 1978), 28-37.

5709 **Warren, A.,** and **Goldsmith, F.B.,** eds. *Conservation in Practice.* London: John Wiley & Sons, 1974.

5710 **Wengert, Norman.** "Resource Development and the Public Interest: A Challenge for Research." *Natural Resources Journal*, 1, No. 4 (November, 1961), 207-223.

5711 **Whitelegg, John.** "Transport Policy, Fiscal Discrimination and the Role of the State." *Political Geography Quarterly*, 3, No. 4 (October, 1984), 313-329.

5712 **Wilson, A.G.** *Transport, Location, and Spatial Systems: Planning with Spatial Interaction Models and Related Approaches.* Leeds: University of Leeds, School of Geography. Working Paper, No. 347, 1983.

5713 **Wilson, David.** "Toward a Revised Urban Managerialism: Local Managers and Community Development Block Grants." *Political Geography Quarterly*, 8, No. 1 (January, 1989), 21-41.

5714 **Wood, Colin James Barry.** *The Diffusion of Innovations Requiring Community Decisions: A Geographical Analysis.* Hamilton, Ontario: McMaster University, Ph.D., 1971.

5715 **Zaidi, Iqtidar H.** "Political and Administrative Problems in Watershed Management: A Geographical Framework for Analysis." *Proceedings. The First West Pakistan Watershed Management Conference*, Islamabad: Ministry of Water and Power, 1968, 494-502.

POLITICAL GEOGRAPHY OF REGIONS

AFRICA

Books and Journals

5716 **Arvidson, Richard.** *Rhodesian Irrigation: A Study in the Politics of Resource Development.* Baltimore, Maryland: Johns Hopkins University, Ph.D., 1971.

5717 **Asadi, Fawsi Abdul-Majid.** *Socio-Economic and Political Institutional Factors Influencing the Land Use Pattern in Egypt.* Ann Arbor: University of Michigan, Ph.D., 1971.

5718 **Ashford, Douglas E.** *National Development and Local Reform: Political Participation in Morocco, Tunisia and Pakistan.* Princeton, New Jersey: Princeton University Press, 1967.

5719 **Bardill, J.** "Review of G. Winai-Strom (1978), 'Development and Dependence in Lesotho'." (Uppsala: Scandinavian Institute of African Studies) *South African Labour Bulletin*, 6, No. 4 (November, 1980), 79-90.

5720 **Brown, Robert Wylie.** *A Spatial View of Oil Development in the Desert: Libya in the First Decade, 1955-1965.* New York City: Columbia University, Ph.D., 1970.

5721 **Brook, Richard C.** "Politics, the Cocoa Crisis, and Administration in Cote d'Lvoire." *The Journal of Modern African Studies* [Cambridge], 26, No. 4 (December, 1990), 649-669.

5722 **Dodoo, Robert, Jr.** *Resource Perception and Its Developmental Determinants in Ashanti, Ghana: A Study in Cultural-Resource Geography.* Los Angeles: University of California, Ph.D., 1970.

5723 **El Arifi, Salih Abdalla.** *Regional Economic Development in the Sudan: A Geographic Analysis of the Emergent Regional Patterns.* Los Angeles: University of California, Ph.D., 1971.

5724 **El-Shakhs, Salah, and Obudho, Robert A.**, eds. *Urbanization, National Development, and Regional Planning in Africa.* New York: Praeger, 1974.

5725 **Fair, T.J.D.** "A Regional Approach to Economic Development in Kenya." *South African Geographical Journal*, 45, No. 1 (April, 1963), 55-77.

5726 **Good, Kenneth.** "Corruption and Mismanagement in Botswana: A Best-Case Example?" *The Journal of Modern African Studies*, 32, No. 3 (September, 1994), 499-521.

5727 **Mijere, Nsolo.** "The State and Development: A Study of the Dominance of the Political Class in Zambia." *Africa Today*, 35, No. 2 (1988), 21-36.

5728 **Nobe, K.C., and Seckler, D.W.** *An Economic and Policy Analysis of Soil-Water Problems and Conservation Programs in the Kingdom of Lesotho.* Maserv: Lesotho Agricultural Services Project Research Report No. 3, 1979.

5729 **Ottaway, Marina**, ed. *The Political Economy of Ethiopia.* New York: Praeger Publishers, 1990.

5730 **Prescott, J.R.V.** *Resources, Policy and Development in West and North Central Africa.* Newcastle: House, 1966.

5731 **Reitsma, Henk, and De Haan, Leo.** "Northern Togo and the World Economy." *Political Geography* [Oxford], 11, No. 5 (September, 1992), 474-484.

5732 **Senftleben, Wolfgang.** "Swaziland's Proposed Land Deal with South Africa-The Case of Ingwavuma and Kangwane." *Philippine Geographical Journal*, 28, Nos. 1 and 2 (January-June, 1984), 50-58.

5733 **Sterkenberg, J.** "Agricultural Commercialisation in Africa South of the Sahara: The Case of Lesotho and Swaziland." *Development and Change*, 11, No. 4 (October, 1980), 573-606.

5734 **Stone, Jeffrey.** "Economic Development and Political Change in Malaui." *The Journal of Tropical Geography*, 27 (December, 1968), 59-65.

5735 **Sutcliffe, Michael.** "The Crisis in South Africa: Material Conditions and the Reformist Reform." *Geoform*, 17, No. 2 (1986), 141-159.

5736 **Wallman, Sandra.** "Conditions of Non-Development: The Case of Lesotho." *Journal of Development Studies*, 8, No. 2 (January, 1972), 251-261.

AMERICAS

Books

5737 **Alao, Nurudeen Oladapo.** *Some Problems in Axiomatic Theory of Location and Regional Economic Growth.* Evanston, Illinois: Northwestern University, Ph.D., 1970.

5738 **Arev, David Gordon.** *The Role of Drought in the Augmentation of Municipal Water Supplies in Massachusetts.* Worchester, Massachusetts: Clark University, Ph.D., 1969.

5739 **Ashley, Joseph Milton, Jr.** *Selected Alternatives to Current Water and Related Resource Utilization, Humboldt River Basin, Nevada.* Boulder: University of Colorado, Ph.D., 1971.

5740 **Baker, Marvin Wesley, Jr.** *Land Use Transition in Mexican Cities: A Study in Comparative Urban Geography.* Syracuse, New York: Syracuse University, Ph.D., 1970.

5741 **Barnett, Russell K.** *Does Location Matter? A Quantitative Analysis of Opposition to the Shoreham Nuclear Power Plant.* New York City: Columbia University, M.A., 1984.

5742 **Barrett, Elinore Magee.** *Land Tenure and Settlement in the Tepalcatepec Lowland, Michoacan, Mexico.* Berkeley: University of California, Ph.D., 1970.

5743 **Bland, Warren Roger.** *The Changing Locational Pattern of Manufacturing in Southern Ontario from 1881 to 1932.* Bloomington: Indiana University, Ph.D., 1970.

5744 **Burgess, Lawrence Charles Norman.** *The Application of Airphoto Interpretation to Watershed Planning and Development with Special Reference to Flood Susceptibility and Frequency Determinations.* Ithaca, New York: Cornell University, Ph.D., 1970.

5745 **Cameron, Eugene N.**, ed. *The Mineral Position of the United States.* Madison: University of Wisconsin Press, 1973.

5746 **Cannon, James Bernard.** *An Analysis of Manufacturing as an Instrument of Public Policy in Regional Economic Development: Canadian Area Development Agency Program 1963-1968.* Seattle: University of Washington, Ph.D., 1969.

5747 **Carlos, Manuel L.** *Politics and Development in Rural Mexico: A Study of Socio-Economic Modernization.* New York: Praeger, 1974.

5748 **Chang, Stephen Sin-Tak.** *The Role of Water Resources in the West Rice Agricultural System of the Sacramento Valley.* Los Angeles: University of California, Ph.D., 1971.

5749 **Charbonneau, Randall J.**, ed. *Regional and State Water Resources Planning Symposium, Proceedings.* Washington, D.C.: American Water Resources Association, 1984.

5750 **Clay, James William.** *Water-Related Problems and Their Effects on the Spatial Arrangement of Agriculture Production in the Mexicali-San Luis Valley of Northwest Mexico.* Chapel Hill: University of North Carolina, Ph.D., 1969.

5751 **Cooley, Richard A.** *Politics and Conservation: The Decline of the Alaska Salmon.* New York: Harper & Row, 1963.

5752 **Curti, G. Philip.** "The Colorado River: Its Utilization by Southern California." *Geography,* 42, No. 2 (July, 1957), 230-238.

5753 **Cutter, Susan L.; Renwick, H.L.; and Renwick, W.H.** *Exploitations, Preservation, Conservation: A Geographic Perspective on Natural Resources Use.* Totowa, New Jersey: Roman and Allenheld, 1985.

5754 **Dagodag, William Tim.** *Public Policy and the Housing Patterns of Urban Mexican-Americans in Selected Cities of the Central Valley.* Eugene: University of Oregon, Ph.D., 1972.

5755 **Dewhurst, J. Frederic** and Associates. *America's Needs and Resources: A New Survey.* New York: Twentieth Century Fund, 1955.

5756 **Duncan, Kristin Louise.** *Water Supply, Use, and Management in the Santa Margarita Watershed, California.* Long Beach: California State University, Master's Thesis, 1973.

5757 **Dunigan, Clyde James.** *Information Dissemination and Regional Development through Urban Linkages in the Laguna Region of Mexico.* Knoxville: University of Tennessee, Ph.D., 1969.

5758 **Dyreson, Delmar A.** *Settlement Pattern Changes and Self-Organizing Systems in the Central Rio Grande Watershed of New Mexico, A.D. 1350-1968.* Denver, Colorado: University of Denver, Ph.D., 1971.

5759 **Evans, Kathleen.** *Regional Administrative Centralization of Water Management Authority in the United States: Ideal or Impossibility.* Seattle: University of Washington, M.A., 1987.

5760 **Finer, Herman.** *The TVA: Lessons for International Application.* Montreal: International Labor Organization, 1944.

5761 **Foggin, Peter Michael.** *An Inductive Model of Changes in the Intra-Urban Land Value Surface: The Impact of Transportation, Land Use and Socio-Economic Factors in Central Montreal.* Montreal, Province of Quebec: McGill University,

Ph.D., 1970.

5762 **Fuhr, Stanley Dean.** *The Economic Health of the North Central Region.* Long Beach: California State University, Master's Thesis, 1973.

5763 **Glickman, N.J.** *The Urban Impacts of Federal Policies.* Baltimore, Maryland: Johns Hopkins University Press, 1980.

5764 **Greenberg, Michael Richard.** *The Implications of Urbanization for Public Water Supply Systems in the New York Metropolitan Region.* New York City: Columbia University, Ph.D., 1969.

5765 **Grima, Angelo Paul.** *Residential Water Demand: Alternative Choices for Management.* Toronto, Ontario, Canada: University of Toronto, Ph.D., 1970.

5766 **Hamburg, James Fredric.** *The Influence of Railroads upon the Processes and Patterns of Settlement in South Dakota.* Chapel Hill: University of North Carolina, Ph.D., 1969.

5767 **Hays, S.P.** *Beauty, Health and Permanance: Environmental Politics in the United States, 1955-1985.* Cambridge: Cambridge University Press, 1987.

5768 **Hodgins, Larry Edwin.** *Morphology of the South Saskatchewan River Valley, Outlook to Saskatoon.* Montreal, Province of Quebec: McGill University, Ph.D., 1970.

5769 **Hordon, Robert Marshall.** *A Graph-Theoretical Analysis of the Water Transfer Networks of the New York Metropolitan Region.* New York City: Columbia University, Ph.D., 1970.

5770 **House, J.W.** *Frontier on the Rio Grande: A Political Geography of Development and Social Deprivation.* Oxford: Clarendon Press, 1982.

5771 **Jacob, Gerald R.** *Conflict, Location and Politics, Siting a Nuclear Waste Repository.* Boulder: University of Colorado, Ph.D., 1988.

5772 **Johnson, James.** *Renovated Waste Water: An Alternative Source of Municipal Water Supply in the United States.* Chicago, Illinois: University of Chicago, Ph.D., 1971.

5773 **Kelly, Charles Robert.** *The Canadian River Municipal Water Authority Project in West Texas: A Geographic Analysis.* Norman: University of Oklahoma, Ph.D., 1971.

5774 **Kesler, Stephen E.** *Our Finite Mineral Resources.* New York: McGraw-Hill, 1976.

5775 **Khalaf, Jassim M.** *The Water Resources of the Lower Colorado River Basin.* Chicago, Illinois: University of Chicago Press, 1951.

5776 **Kirkby, Anne Veronica Tennant.** *The Use of Land and Water Resources in the Past and Present Valley of Oaxaca, Mexico.* Baltimore, Maryland: Johns Hopkins University, Ph.D., 1971.

5777 **Kohler, Fred Eric.** *A Linear Programming Approach to Water Supply Alternatives.* Columbus: Ohio State University, Ph.D., 1971.

5778 **Kuhn, R.G.** *Geography, Energy, and Environmental Attitudes: An Investigation of Policy Scenarios and Public Preferences.* Edmonton, Alberta, Canada: University of Alberta, Ph.D., 1988.

5779 **Kureth, Elwood John Clark.** *The Geographic, Historic and Political Factors Influencing the Development of Canada's Chemical Valley.* Ann Arbor: University of Michigan, Ph.D., 1971.

5780 **Labovitz, I.** *Federal Revenues and Expenditures in the Seneral States.* Washington, D.C.: Library of Congress, Legislative Reference Service, 1962.

5781 **Lasris, Roy H., ed.** *Florida Water Resources Law: A Bibliography.* Washington, D.C.: U.S. Department of the Interior, Office of the Water Research and Technology, Water Resources Scientific Center, 1977.

5782 **Leuchtenburg, W.E.** *Flood Control Politics.* Cambridge, Massachusetts: Harvard University Press, 1953.

5783 **Lupton, Austin Albert.** *An Analysis of Some Factors Affecting the Areal Variability of Farm Size in Alberta.* Edmonton, Alberta, Canada: University of Alberta, Ph.D., 1970.

5784 **MacIver, Ian.** *Urban Water Supply Alternatives: Perception and Choice in the Grand Basin, Ontario.* Chicago, Illinois: University of Chicago, Ph.D., 1970.

5785 **Majumdar, Shajamal A., and Millar, Willard, eds.** *Hazardous and Toxic Wastes: Technology Management, and Health Effects.* Easton, Pennsylvania: Pennsylvania Academy of Science, 1984.

5786 **Mann, Dean E.** *The Politics of Water in Arizona.* Tucson: University of Arizona Press, 1963.

5787 **Manni, Ann.** *Assessing the Political and Institutional Arrangements for the British Columbia Coastal Sand and Gravel Industry.* Victoria, British Columbia, Canada: University of Victoria, Ph.D., 1984.

5788 **Marchioni, Michael Peter.** *Economic Development and Settlement Patterns in the Flood Plain of the Upper Ohio Valley with Special Reference Given to Flood Damage Reach II (Pt. Pleasant, West Virginia to Marietta, Ohio).* Cincinnati, Ohio: University of Cincinnati, Ph.D., 1971.

5789 **McCabe, James O.** *The San Juan Water Boundary Question.* Toronto, Ontario, Canada: University of Toronto Press, 1964.

5790 **McGuire, Michael Edwin.** *An Approximation of Michigan's Spatial Waters Needs.* East Lansing: Michigan State University, Ph.D., 1970.

5791 **McNeil, Lois.** *Changes in Small Scale Agriculture: The Role of Governments, Westmoreland Parish, Jamaica, 1962-1970.* Montreal, Ontario, Canada: McGill University, Ph.D., 1984.

5792 **Moultrie, William Anthony.** *Computer Simulation of Erosional Patterns in a Natural Watershed: A Study of Drainage Basin Development.* Iowa City: University of Iowa, Ph.D., 1971.

5793 **Muckelston, Keith Way.** *The Problem of Implementing the Federal Water Project Recreation Act in Oregon.* Seattle: University of Washington, Ph.D., 1970.

5794 **Murauskas, G. Thomas.** *Nuclear Waste Repository Siting and Locational Conflict Analysis: A Contextual Approach.* Norman: University of Oklahoma, Ph.D., 1989.

5795 **Mushkin, S.** *Illustrative Estimates of Federal Expenditures and Revenues by States.* Washington, D.C.: U.S. Department of Health, Education and Welfare, 1956.

5796 **Nelson, Charles Edward.** *Southwest Montana Ski Area Resources Development and Use Patterns.* Lincoln: University of Nebraska, Ph.D., 1971.

5797 **Newton, Thomas.** *Redistribution and the Fiscal Disparities Act: An Analysis of Regional Tax Base Sharing.* Iowa City: University of Iowa, Ph.D., 1983.

5798 **Nietschmann, Bernard Quinn.** *Between Land and Water: The Subsistence Ecology of the Miskito Indians, Eastern Nicaragua.* Madison: University of Wisconsin, Ph.D., 1970.

5799 **Pagenhart, Thomas Harsha.** *Water Use in the Yuba and Bear River Basin, California.* Berkeley: University of California, Ph.D., 1969.

5800 **Pearson, Roger William.** *Resource Management Strategies and Regional Viability: A Study of the Great Slave Lake Region, Canada.* Urbana: University of Illinois, Ph.D., 1970.

5801 **Perloff, H.S.; Dunn, E.S., Jr.; Lampard, E.E.; and Muth, R.F.** *Regions, Resources and Economic Growth.* Lincoln: University of Nebraska Press, 1960.

5802 **Philip, George.** *Oil and Politics in Latin America: Nationalist Movements and State Companies.* London: Cambridge University Press, Cambridge Latin American Studies, Vol. 4, 1982.

5803 **Pouliot, Marcel G.** *Transport, Politique et Geographie: Aspects du Transport Aerien Regional au Canada.* Montreal, Province of Quebec: McGill University, Ph.D., 1985.

5804 **Quinn, Frank James.** *Area-of-Origin Protectionism in Western Waters.* Seattle: University of Washington, Ph.D., 1970.

5805 **Rae, J.** *The American Automobile Industry.* Boston: Twayne, 1984.

5806 **Schwind, Paul J.** *Migration and Regional Development in the United States, 1950-1960.* Chicago, Illinois: University of Chicago, Ph.D., 1971.

5807 **Senger, Leslie Walter.** *Irrigated Agricultural Developments on the Southern 'West Side' of the San Joaquin Valley with Special Reference to Major Oil Company Holdings.* Los Angeles: University of California, Ph.D., 1972.

5808 **Shannon, F.A.** *The Farmers' Last Frontier 1860-1897.* New York: Farrar and Rinehart, 1945.

5809 **Shaw, R.P.** *Land Tenure and Rural Exodus.* Gainesville, Florida: University of Florida Books, 1976.

5810 **Slakey, Stephen Louis.** *The Acorn Redevelopment Project, Oakland, California.* Fullerton: California State University, M.A., 1974.

5811 **Smith, Bruce Wayne.** *Locational Analysis of Thermal Power Plants in the Eastern United States.* Urbana: University of Illinois, Ph.D., 1970.

5812 **Sternlieb, G.,** and **Hughes, J.W.,** eds. *Revitalizing the Northwest: Prelude to an Agenda.* New Jersey: Rutgers University Center for Urban Policy Research, 1978.

5813 **U.S. Bureau of Mines.** *Report Upon Certain Deficient Strategic Minerals by the Staffs of the Geological Survey and the Bureau of Mines.* Washington, D.C.: U.S. Bureau of Mines, 1939.

5814 **United States Department of Commerce.** *Federal Activities Affecting Location of Economic Development,* 2 volumes. Washington, D.C.: United States Department of Commerce, 1970.

5815 **U.S. Works Progress Administration.** *Marketing Laws Survey. Comparative Charts of State Statutes Illustrating Barriers to Trade Between States.* Prepared by members of Survey staff under direction of Charlotte A. Hankin. Washington, D.C.: U.S. Works Progress Administration, 1939.

5816 *Water Resources Data for California, 1977. Vol. 3, Southern Central Valley Basins and the Great Basin from Walker River to Tuckee River.* Menlo Park, California: U.S. Geological Survey, Water Resources Division, USGS Water Data Report CA-77-3, 1978.

Journals

5817 **Allred, Charles E.; Atkins, Samuel W.;** and **Bohanan, L.P.** "Chapter 33: County Government. Chapter 34: Municipal Government." In *Human and Physical Resources of Tennessee.* Rural Research Series Monography No. 86. Knoxville, Tennessee: College of Agriculture (1938), 524-555.

5818 **Bassett, Keith.** "Labour in the Sunbelt: The Politics of Local Economic Development Startegy in an "M4-Corrlidor Town". *Political Geography Quarterly,* 9, No. 1 (January, 1990), 67-84.

5819 **Beard, Daniel P.** "Implications of Recent Environmental Legislation on the Supply and Demand of Energy Resources." *Geographical Review,* 65, No. 2 (April, 1975), 229-244.

5820 **Beard, Daniel P.** "The National Environmental Policy Act in the Courts and Congress, 1970-1972." *Professional Geographer,* 25, No. 4 (November, 1973), 377-381.

5821 **Beard, Daniel P.** "The President's Water Policy." In *1979 Technical Proceedings Conference.* Silver Spring, Maryland: The Irrigation Association (1979), 1-8.

5822 **Blankstein, C.S.,** and **Zuvekas, C.** "Agrarian Reform in Ecuador: An Evaluation of Past Efforts and the Development of a New Approach." *Economic Development and Cultural Change,* 22, No. 1 (October, 1973), 73-94.

5823 **Bolton, Roger E.** "Impacts of Defense Spending on Urban Areas." *Glickman,* (1980), 151-174.

5824 **Burke, M.** "Land Reform and Its Effects Upon Production and Productivity in the Lake Titicaca Region." *Economic Development and Cultural Change,* 18, No. 3 (April, 1970), 410-450.

5825 **Cuzan, Alfred G.** "Resource Mobilization and Political Opportunity in the Nicaraguan Revolution: The Praxis." *The American Journal of Economics and Sociology* [New York], 50, No. 1 (January, 1991), 71-83.

5826 de Nevers, N. "Tar Sands and Oil Shales."
Scientific American, 214, No. 2 (February, 1966),
21-9.

5827 Fielding, G.J. "The Los Angeles Milkshed: A
Study of the Political Factor in Agriculture."
Geographical Review, 54, No. 1 (January, 1964),
1-12.

5828 Hansen, N.H. "The New International Division of
Labor and Manufacturing Decentralization in the
United States. *Review of Regional Studies*, 9
(1979), 1-11.

5829 Hall, Robert Burnett. "American Raw-Material
Deficiencies and Regional Dependence." *The
Geographical Review*, 30, No. 2 (April, 1940),
177-186.

5830 Haynes, Kingsley E.; Bal Kumar, K.C.; and
Briggs, Ronald. "Regional Patterns in the Spatial
Diffusion of Public Policy Innovations in the U.S.,
1870-1970." *Political Geography Quarterly*,
2, No. 4 (October, 1983), 289-307.

5831 Honey, Rex D. "Conflict in the Location of
Salutary Public Facilities." In *Urbanization
Processes and Conflict in Market Societies*, Kevin
R. Cox, ed., co-authored with David R. Reynolds.
Chicago, Illinois: Maarouga Press, 1978, 144-160.

5832 Ironside, R.G. "The Territorial States of the
Canadian National Park." *The Rocky Mountain
Social Science Journal*, 7, No. 1 (April, 1970),
69-75.

5833 Lauria, Mickey. "The Transformation of Local
Politics: Manufacturing Plant Closurs and
Governing Coalition Fragmentation." *Political
Geography*, 13, No. 6 (November, 1994), 515-539.

5834 Metz, W.C. "Cooling Ponds, Lakes and
Reservoir-A Positive Factor in Power Plant Siting."
Aware, (April, 1977), 5-9.

5835 Mitchell, Bruce. "The Natural Resources
Development Debate in Canada." *Geoforum*, 12,
No. 3 (1981), 227-236.

5836 Mitchell, Bruce. "Value Conflicts and Water
Supply Decisions." In *University of Victoria.
Department of Geography. Western Geographical
Series.* Vol. 8. *Priorities in Water Management*,
Francis M. Teversedge, ed. Victoria, British
Columbia, Canada: University of Victoria, 1974,
37-59.

5837 Moriarty, B.M. "Hierarchies of Cities and the
Spatial Filtering of Industrial Development."
Papers of the Regional Science Association, 53
(1983), 59-82.

5838 Muckelston, Keith Way; Maresh, T.J.; and
Mukerji, D. "Legislative Voting on

Environmental Bills in Oregon." In *Yearbook of
the Association of Pacific Coast Geographers*, 38
(1976), 77-86.

5839 Murauskas, G. Thomas, and Shelley, Fred M.
"Local Political Responses to Nuclear Waste
Disposal." *Cities*, 3 (1986), 157-162.

5840 Mushkin, S. "Distribution of Federal
Expenditures Among the States." *Review of
Economics and Statistics*, 39, No. 4 (September,
1957), 435-450.

5841 Norris, R.S.; Cochran, T.B.; and Arkin, William
M. "History of the Nuclear Stockpile." *Bulletin
of the Atomic Scientists*, 41, No. 7 (August, 1985),
106-109.

5842 Norton, R.D., and Rees, J. "The Product Cycle
and the Spatial Decentralization of American
Manufacturing." *Regional Studies*, 13, No.
2 (August, 1979), 141-151.

5843 Olson, Ralph E. "Management of Water in
Oklahoma." *Proceedings of the Oklahoma
Academy of Science*, 51 (1971), 136-139.

5844 Peet, J.R. "Relations of Production and the
Relocation of United States Manufacturing Industry
Since 1960." *Economic Geography*, 59, No. 2
(April, 1983), 112-143.

5845 Philip, George. "Mexican Oil and Gas: The
Politics of a New Resource." *International Affairs*,
56, No. 3 (Summer, 1980), 474-483.

5846 Quinn, Frank James. "Water Transfers: Must
the American West be Won Again?" *Geographical
Review*, 58, No. 1 (January, 1968), 108-132.

5847 Raushenbush, Stephen, ed. "The Future of Our
Natural Resources." *Annals of the American
Academy of Political and Social Science*,
281 (May, 1952), 1-202.

5848 Richards, J. Howard. "Provincialism,
Regionalism and Federalism as Seen in Joint
Resource Development Programmes." *Canadian
Geographer*, 9, No. 4 (1965), 205-215.

5849 Shelley, Fred M. "Groundwater Supply Depletion
in West Texas: The Farmer's Perspective." *Texas
Business Review*, 57 (1983), 279-283.

5850 Shelley, Fred M., and Wijeyawickrema, C.
"Local Opposition to the Transfer of Water
Supplies: An Oklahoma Case Study." *Water
Resource Bulletin*, 20 (1984), 721-727.

5851 Smith, C.G. "Public Participation in Policy
Making: The State of the Art in Canada."
Geoforum, 15 (1984), 253-259.

5852 **Sukhwal, B.L.** "Water Scarcity in Southwestern United States and Alternatives of Its Proper Utilization as well as Political and Legal Implications." *Geojournal*, 15, No. 3 (July, 1987), 1-10.

5853 **Templer, Otis W.** "Legal Constraints on Water Resource Management in Texas." *The Environmental Professional*, 5 (1983), 72-83.

5854 **Templer, Otis W.** "Texas Ground Water Law: Changing a Venerable Legal Doctrine. *Papers and Proceedings of Applied Geography Conferences* [Denton], 15 (1992), 1-9.

5855 **Vogel, D.** "The Power of Business in America: A Reappraisal." *British Journal of Political Science*, 13, Part 1 (January, 1983), 18-43.

5856 **Wolfe, Roy I.** "Transportation and Politics: The Example of Canada." *Annals of the Association of American Geographers*, 62, No. 2 (June, 1962), 176-190.

ASIA

Books and Journals

5857 **Ackerman, Edward A.** *Japan's Natural Resources and Their Relation to Japan's Economic Future.* Chicago, Illinois: University of Chicago, 1953.

5858 **Bhat, L.S.,** and Others, eds. *Regional Inequities in India; Inter-State and Intra-State.* New Delhi: SSRD, 1982.

5859 **Bhat, L.S.,** and Others, eds. *Regional Planning in India.* Calcutta: Statistical Publishing Society, 1972.

5860 **Burrowes, Robert D.** *The Yemen Arab Republic: The Politics of Development, 1962-1986.* Boulder, Colorado: Westview Press, 1987.

5861 **Chaturvedi, B.N.** "The Godavari Krishna Water Dispute: A Geographical Appraisal." *Deccan Geographer*, 5, Nos. 1 and 2 (January-December, 1967), 30-58.

5862 **Fernea, R.A.** "Land Reform and Ecology in Post-revolutionary Iraq." *Economic Development and Cultural Change*, 17, No. 3 (April, 1969), 356-381.

5863 **Gadgil, D.R.** *Planning and economic Policy in India.* Poona: Gokhale Institute of Politics and Economics, 1972.

5864 **Government of India.** *Report on the Machinery for Planning.* New Delhi: Administrative Reforms Commission, 1968.

5865 **Government of Madhya Pradesh.** *New Iron and Steel Plant.* Nagpur: Government of Madhya Pradesh Press, 1953.

5866 **Gradus, Yehuda,** and Krakover, S. "The Effect of Government Policy on the Spatial Structure of Manufacturing in Israel." *Journal of Developing Areas*, 11, No. 3 (April, 1977), 393-409.

5867 **Guha, A.K.** *Location of New Steel Plants and Its Economic Aspects.* Alipore: West Bengal Government, 1954.

5868 **Hafner, James Allan.** *The Impact of Road Development in the Central Plain of Thailand.* Ann Arbor: University of Michigan, Ph.D., 1970.

5869 **Hasson, Shlomo.** "Social Differentiation Among Public Housing Projects in Israel." *Geografiska Annaler*, B, 65 (January, 1984), 95-103.

5870 **Hazari, R.K.** *Industrial Planning and Licensing Policy.* New Delhi: Planning Commission, Government of India, 1967.

5871 **Kim, Hyun Kil.** *Land Use Policy in Korea: With Special Reference to the Oriental Development Company.* Seattle: University of Washington, Ph.D., 1971.

5872 **Kirk, William.** "Cores and Peripheries-The Problems of Regional Inequality in the Development of Southern Asia." *Geography*, 66, No. 3 (July, 1981), 188-201.

5873 **LaPorte, Robert, Jr.** "Intergovernmental Change in India: Politics and Administration of the Damodar Valley Scheme." *Asian Survey*, 8, No. 9 (September, 1968), 748-760.

5874 **Lefeber, L.,** and Chaudhuri, Manoranjan. *Regional Development Experiences and Prospects in South and Southeast Asia.* Paris: Mouton, 1971.

5875 **Lieber, Robert J.** "Oil and Power After the Gulf War." *International Security* [Cambridge, MA], 17, No. 1 (Summer, 1992), 155-176.

5876 **Ma, Laurence Jun-Chao.** *Commercial Development and Urban Change in Sun China.* Ann Arbor: University of Michigan, Ph.D., 1971.

5877 **Mohanty, H.B.** *Location of Steel Plant in Orissa.* Bhubaneswar: Industries Department, Government of Orissa, 1957.

5878 **Moore, R.H.** "Resistance to Japanese Rice Policy: A Case Study of the Hachirogata Model Farm Project." *Political Geography*, 12, No. 3 (May, 1993), 278-296.

5879 **National Committee on the Development of Backward Areas.** *Report on Industrial Dispersal*, B. Sivaraman, Chairman. New Dehli: Planning Commission, 1980.

5880 **Oshiro, Kenji Kenneth.** *Dairy Policies and the Development of Dairying in Tohoko, Japan.* Seattle: University of Washington, Ph.D., 1972.

5881 **Planning Commission.** *Draft Sixth Five-Year Plan.* New Delhi: Government of India, 1978.

5882 **Prakasa Rao, V.L.S.** *Regional Planning.* Calcutta: Dorchester Printing Works, 1974.

5883 **Raymond, Wayne, and Mulliner, K.,** eds. *Southeast Asia: An Emerging Center of World Influence.* Athens, Ohio: Ohio University, Center for International Studies, Southeast Asia Program, 1977.

5884 **Renaud, B.M.** "Conflicts Between National Growth and Regional Income Equality in a Rapidly Growing Economy: The Case of Korea." *Economic Development and Cultural Change*, 21, No. 4 (July, 1972), 429-445.

5885 **Roy, M.N.** *People's Plan for Economic Development.* Delhi: Ajanta Publications, 1944 (1981 reprint).

5886 **Roy, Subroto, and James, William E.,** eds. *Foundations of India's Political Economy: Towards an Agenda for the 1990s.* New Delhi: Sage Publications, 1992.

5887 **Rudra, A.** *Indian Plan Models.* Bombay: Allied Publishers, 1975.

5888 **Sahawneh, Fouzi Eid.** *Irrigation and Irrigated Agriculture in Jordan: An Economic Geographic Appraisal.* East Lansing: Michigan State University, Ph.D., 1970.

5889 **Seth, Vijay K.** *Spatial Dimensions of the Process of Industrialisation in India.* New Delhi: Delhi School of Economics, Ph.D., 1983.

5890 **Seth, Vijay K.** "State and Spatial Aspects of Industrialization in Post-Independence India." *Political Geography Quarterly*, 5, No. 4 (October, 1986), 331-348.

5891 **Sherman, Betty Jane.** *Political Parties and Political Development: An Exploratory Study of Legislators' Perceptions in the Indian States of Punjab and Haryana.* Minneapolis: University of Minnesota, Ph.D., 1970.

5892 **Shyamala, Kammana Manakkadan.** *The Politics of Decision-Making for Economic Development: The Case of the Location of Heavy Industries in India.* Syracuse, New York: Syracuse University, Ph.D., 1969.

5893 **Starr, Joyce R., and Stoll, David C.,** eds. *The Policy of Scarcity: Water in the Middle East,* Boulder, Colorado: Westview Press, 1988.

5894 **Sukhwal, B.L.** *India: Economic Resource Base and Contemporary Political Patterns.* New Delhi and New York: Sterling Publishers, New Delhi, and APT Books, New York, 1986.

5895 **Sukhwal, B.L.** "Problems, Probable Solutions and Prospects of Canal Water Supply on the Ecosystem of the Rejasthan Canal Command Area, India." *Resource Management in Drylands; Stuttgartu Geographische Studien*, Band 105. Stuttgart: Geographische Institut der Universitat, Stuttgart, 1985, 115-124.

5896 **Sukhwal, B.L.** "River Water Management and Disputes in India." *The National Geographer*, 14, No. 2 (December, 1979), 1-9.

5897 **Tabors, Richard Dean.** *Space, Planning, and Economic Development: A Case Study of Regional Planning in East Pakistan.* Syracuse, New York: Syracuse University, Ph.D., 1971.

5898 **Upreti, B.C.** *Politics of Himalayan River Waters: An Analysis of the River Water Issues of Nepal, India, and Bangladesh.* Jaipur: Nirala Publications, 1993.

5899 **Vander Velde, Edward Jay, Jr.** *The Distribution of Irrigation Benefits: A Study in Haryana, India.* Ann Arbor: University of Michigan, Ph.D., 1971.

5900 **Weiner, Myron.** *Politics of Scarcity: Public Pressure and Political Responses in India.* Chicago, Illinois: University of Chicago Press, 1962.

5901 **Yeung, Yue-Man.** *National Development Policy and Urban Transformation in Singapore: A Study of Public Housing and the Marketing System.* Chicago, Illinois: University of Chicago, Ph.D., 1972.

AUSTRALIA, OCEANIA AND ANTARCTICA

Books and Journals

5902 **Crabb, P.** "Hydro Power on the Periphery: A Comparison of Newfoundland, Tasmania and the South Island." *Alternatives*, 10 (1982), 12-20.

5903 **Gilpin, A.** *The Australian Environment. Twelve Controversial Issues.* Melbourne: Sun Books, 1980.

5904 **Linge, G.J.R.** "Governments and the Location of Secondary Industry in Australia." *Economic Geography*, 43, No. 1 (January, 1967), 43-63.

5905 **Prescott, J.R.V.** *The Reciprocal Relations Between Geography and National Policy.* Melbourne, Australian and New Zealand Association for the Advancement of Science, 1967.

5906 **Stevenson, G.** *Mineral Resources and Australian Federalism.* Research Monograph No. 17. Canberra: Centre for Research on Federal Financial Relations, Australian National University, 1976.

5907 **Van Steenkiste, Richard John.** *The Pass Lander: A Political Geographical Analysis of Western Austria.* Austin: University of Texas, Ph.D., 1971.

5908 **Wilvert, Calvin.** *The Changing Location of the Australian Dairying Industry.* Berkeley: University of California, Ph.D., 1972.

EUROPE

Books and Journals

5909 **Allen, D.** *Hospital Planning: The 1962 Hospital Plan for England and Wales.* London: Pitman Medical, 1979.

5910 **Bassett, Keith.** "Economic Restructuring, Spatial Coalitions, and Local Economic Development Strategies: A Case Study of Bristol." *Political Geography Quarterly*, 5, No. 4 (October, 1986), S163-S178.

5911 **Bennett, Robert J.** *Central Grants to Local Government: The Political and Economic Impact of the Rate Support Grant in England and Wales.* Cambridge: Cambridge University Press, 1982.

5912 **Bowen, P.** *Social Control in Industrial Organization: A Strategic and Occupational Study of British Steelmaking.* London: Routledge, 1976.

5913 **British-North American Committee.** *Mineral Development in the Eighties: Prospects and Problems.* London: BNAC, 1976.

5914 **Broggio, Celine.** "Les Enjeux d'une Politique Montagne Pour l'Europe." *Revue de Geographie Alpine* [Grenoble], 80, No. 4 (1992), 26-39.

5915 **Burghardt, Andrew F.** *Development Regions in the Soviet Union, Eastern Europe, and Canada.* New York: Praeger, 1975.

5916 **Bush, K.** "Environmental Problems in the USSR." *Problems of Communism*, 21, No. 4 (July-August, 1972), 27-31.

5917 **Christie, Robert Charles.** *A Geographical Analysis of the Industrial Development of the Socialist Republic of Macedonia.* Philadelphia: Pennsylvania State University, Ph.D., 1971.

5918 **Cooke, Philip.** *Theories of Planning and Spatial Development.* London: Hutchinson, 1983.

5919 **Dando, William Arthur.** *A Study of the Soviet New Lands Program.* Minneapolis: University of Minnesota, Ph.D., 1970.

5920 **Dear, M.J.** "Planning for Mental Health Care: A Reconsideration of Public Facility Location Theory." *International Regional Science Review*, 3 (1978), 93-112.

5921 **DHSS.** *Sharing Resources for Health in England: The Report of the Resource Allocation Working Party.* London: Her Majesty's Stationery Office, 1976.

5922 **Dienes, Leslie.** *Locational Factors and Locational developments in the Soviet Chemical Industry.* Chicago, Illinois: University of Chicago, Ph.D., 1969.

5923 **Elder, A.T.** "How Many Hospital Beds?" *British Medical Journal*, 1 (1957), 753.

5924 **Fothergill, S., and Gudgin, G.** *Unequal Growth, Urban and Regional Employment Change in the U.K.* London: Heinemann Educational Books, 1982.

5925 **Friedland, Roger.** *Power and Crisis in the City: Corporations, Unions and Urban Policy.* London: Macmillan, 1982.

5926 **Galbraith, J.K.** *Economics and the Public Purpose.* London: Andre Deutsch, 1974.

5927 **Gibson, James R.** "Russia on the Pacific: The Role of the Amur." *Canadian Geographer*, 12, No. 1 (Spring, 1968), 15-27.

5928 **Greenberg, Arthur Henry.** *The Migration of Farmers from the West to the East of Ireland: A Study of Government-Sponsored Agricultural Settlement.* Eugene: University of Oregon, Ph.D., 1972.

5929 **Gregory, R.G.** *The Miners and British Politics, 1906-1914.* Oxford: Oxford University Press, 1968.

5930 **Haegen, H. Vander.** "La Nouvelle Subdivision Administrative en Belgique a la Suite des Recentes Lois linguistiques." *Bulletin de la Societe Belage d'Etudes Geographiques*, 33, No. 1 (1964), 175-185.

5931 **Hoggart, Keith.** "Political Parties and Local Authority Capital Investment in English Cities." *Political Geography Quarterly*, 3, No. 1 (January, 1984), 5-32.

5932 **House of Commons.** *The Financial and Economic Obligations of the Nationalised Industries.* London: Her Majesty's Stationery Office, Cmnd 1337, 1961.

5933 **Hovinen, Gary Robert.** *Land Tenure and Residential Development in Greater Stockholm.* Minneapolis: University of Minnesota, Ph.D., 1971.

5934 **Macgregor, M.** *Synopsis of the Mineral Resources of Scotland.* (Great Britain Memoirs of the Geological Survey. Special reports on the mineral resources of Great Britain, Vol. 33.) Edinburgh: Her Majesty's Stationery Office, 1940.

5935 **Malefakis, E.E.** *Agrarian Reform and Peasant Revolution in Spain: Origins of the Civil War.* New Haven, Connecticut: Yale University Press, 1970.

5936 **Mandel, David.** *Perestroika and the Soviet People: Rebirth of the Labour Movement.* Montreal: Black Rose Books, 1991.

5937 **Massey, D.** "Industrial Restructuring as Class Restructuring: Production Decentralisation and Local Uniqueness." *Regional Studies*, 17, No. 2 (April, 1983), 73-90.

5938 **Massey, D.** *Spatial Divisions of Labour: Social Structures and the Geography of Production.* London: Macmillan, 1984.

5939 **McEachern, D.** *A Class Against Itself: Power and the Nationalisation of the British Steel Industry.* Cambridge: CUP, 1980.

5940 **McEachern, D.** "Party Government and the Class Interest of Capital: Conflict Over the Steel Industry, 1945-70." *Capital & Class*, 8 (Summer, 1979), 125-143.

5941 **Micklewright, Malcolm Algernon.** *The Geography of Development in Northern Ireland.* Seattle: University of Washington, Ph.D., 1970.

5942 **Mohan, J.** "State Policies and the Development of the Hospital Services of Northeast England, 1948-1982." *Political Geography Quarterly*, 3, No. 4 (October, 1984), 275-295.

5943 **Nove, Alec.** "Soviet Agriculture Marks Time." *Foreign Affairs*, 40, No. 4 (July, 1962), 576-594.

5944 **Ovenden, K.** *The Politics of Steel.* London: Macmillan, 1978.

5945 **Pounds, Norman J.G.** "Planning in the Upper Silesian Industrial Region." *Journal of Central European Affairs*, 18, No. 4 (January, 1959), 409-422.

5946 **Pryde, Philip Rust.** *Natural Resource Management and Conservation in the Soviet Union.* Seattle: University of Washington, Ph.D., 1969.

5947 **Ross, E.W.** *The Nationalisation of Steel: One Step Forward, Two Steps Back?* London: Macgibbon and Kee, 1965.

5948 **Rossiter, D.J.** *The Miners' Sphere of Influence.* Sheffield: University of Sheffield, Ph.D., 1980.

5949 **Sadler, D.** "Works Closure at British Steel and the Nature of the State." *Political Geography Quarterly*, 3, No. 4 (October, 1984), 297-311.

5950 **Saunders, P.** "The Relevance of Weberian Sociology for Political Analysis." *Geographical Papers*, No. 80. Reading: Department of Geography, University of Reading, 1982.

5951 **Scott, James William.** *The Metalliferous Mining and Smelting Industries of the British Isles, 1540-1640.* Bloomington: Indiana University, Ph.D., 1971.

5952 **Shimkin, Demitri B.** *Minerals: A Key to Soviet Power.* Cambridge, Massachusetts: Harvard University Press, 1953.

5953 **Stern, Jonathon P.** "Soviet Energy Prospects in the 1980's." *The World Today*, 36, No. 5 (May, 1980), 185-195.

5954 **Taaffe, Robert N.** "Transportation and Regional Specialization: The Example of Soviet Central Asia." *Annals of the Association of American Geographers*, 52, No. 1 (March, 1962), 80-98.

5955 **Teitz, M.B.** "Toward a Theory of Urban Public Facility Location." *Papers and Proceedings of the Regional Science Association*, 31 (1968), 35-44.

5956 **Tem, Aubrey.** "The Economic Basis of Autonomy in the Val D'Aosta, Italy." *Journal of Geography*, 57, No. 1 (January, 1958), 5-12.

5957 **Thorns, D.** "Industrial Restructuring and Change in the Labour and Property Markets in Britain." *Environment and Planning A*, 14, No. 6 (June, 1982), 745-764.

CHAPTER VIII

CIVILIZATIONS AND CULTURES: RACES AND TRIBES; PEOPLES AND ETHNIC GROUPS; AND LANGUAGES AND RELIGIONS

GENERAL AND THEORY

Books

5958 **Ackerman, B.** *Social Justice in the Liberal State.* New Haven, Connecticut: Yale University Press, 1980.

5959 **Ardrey, Robert.** *The Social Contract.* New York: Delta Books, 1970.

5960 **Arrow, K.J.** *Social Choice and Individual Values,* 2nd ed. New York: John Wiley & Sons, 1963.

5961 **Balan, J.,** ed. *Why People Move.* Paris: The UNESCO Press, 1981.

5962 **Balindier, Georges.** *Anthropolotie Politique.* Paris: Presses Universitaires de France, 1967.

5963 **Banfield, Edward C.** *The Moral Basis of a Backward Society.* Glencoe: The Free Press, 1958.

5964 **Bell, C.,** and **Newby, H.** *Social Areas in Cities.* Chichester: John Wiley & Sons, 1976.

5965 **Benedict, Ruth.** *Patterns of Culture.* New York: Penguin-Mentor Books, 1946.

5966 **Borgatta, Edgar F.** *L'Internazione Sociale.* Trieste: Instituto di Sociologia Internazionale di Gorizia, 1973.

5967 **Bourciez, Edward E.J.** *Elements de linguistique romane.* Paris: C. Klincksick, 1923.

5968 **Bowles, C.** *Ideas, People and Peace.* New York: Harper and Brothers, 1958.

5969 **Breton, R.J.L.** *Geographie des Langues.* Paris: PUF, 1976.

5970 *Britanica World Language Dictionary.* Chicago, Illinois: Encyclopaedia Britanica, 1981.

5971 **Buffelan, Jean-Paul.** *Introduction a la Sociologie Politique.* Paris: Masson, 1969.

5972 **Castro, Eugenio de.** *Ensaios de geografia Linguistica.* Sao Paulo: Companhia Editora Nacional, 1941.

5973 **Chamberlain, James Franklin.** *Geography and Society.* Philadelphia: Lippencott, 1938.

5974 **Charpin, F.** *Pratique religieuse et formation d'une grande ville.* Marseille: Éditions du Centurion, 1964.

5975 **Clarke, C.; Ley, David;** and **Peach, Cheri,** eds. *Geography and Ethnic Pluralism.* Boston: Allen & Unwin, 1984.

5976 **Coulborn, R.** *The Origin of Civilized Societies.* Princeton, New Jersey: Princeton University Press, 1959.

5977 **Dauzat, Albert.** *La geographie linguistique.* Paris: Flammarion, 1922.

5978 **Deffontaines, Pierre.** *Geographie et Religions.* Paris: Gallimard NRF, 1948.

5979 **Dekar, Paul Richard.** *Crossing Ritual Frontiers: Christianity and the Transformation of Bulu Society, 1892-1925.* Chicago, Illinois: University of Chicago, Ph.D., 1978.

5980 **Demangeon, Albert.** *NouVeau de Geographic Humaine.* Paris: Armand Colin, 1969.

5981 **Demolins, Edmond.** *Les grandes routes des peuples.* Paris: Firmin Didot, 1901.

5982 **Deniker, J.** *Les Races et les Peuples de la Terre.* Paris: Schleicher, 1900.

5983 **Dicken, Samuel N.,** and **Pitts, Forrest R.** *Introduction to Cultural Geography.* Toronto: Xerox College Publishing, 1970.

5984 **Dogan, Mattel,** and **Rokkan, S.,** eds. *Quantitative Ecological Analysis in the Social Sciences.* Cambridge: Massachusetts Institute of Technology Press, 1969.

5985 **Dollard, Jerome Robert.** *Ethics and International Relations in the Realist School of International Relations and the Teachings of Vatican II and Pope Paul VI: A Critical Comparison.* Washington, D.C.: Catholic University of America, Ph.D., 1975.

5986 **DuBois, W.E. Burghardt.** *Color and Democracy: Colonies and Peace.* New York: Harcourt Brace and Company, 1945.

5987 **Edwards, J.,** ed. *Liguistic Minorities, Policies and Pluralism.* London: Academic Press, 1984.

5988 Enloe, Cynthia. *Ethnic Soldiers: State Security in Divided Societies*. Athens: University of Georgia Press, 1980.

5989 Foster, J. *Class Struggle in the Industrial Revolution*. London: Methuen, 1974.

5990 Giddens, A. *Central Problems in Social Theory*. London: Macmillan, 1979.

5991 Goldstein, Julius. *Rasse und Politik*. Leipig: Oldenburg Verlag, 1925.

5992 Gordon, D.L. *The French Language and National Identity*. The Hague: Mouton, 1978.

5993 Grant, R.M., and Others, eds. *Ethno-Nationalism: Multinational Corporations and the Modern State*. Denver, Colorado: University of Denver Press, 1979.

5994 Gregory, J.W. *Race as a Political Factor*. London: Watts, 1931.

5995 Gross, Feliks. *Ethnics in a Borderland: An Inquiry into the Nature of Ethnicity and Reduction of Ethnic Tensions in a One-Time Genocide Area*. Westport, Connecticut: Greenwood Press, Contribution to Sociology, No. 32, 1978.

5996 Hall, Raymond L., ed. *Ethnic Autonomy: The Comparative Dynamics, the Americas, Europe and the Developing World*. New York: Pergamon Press, 1979.

5997 Harvey, David E. *Social Justice and the City*. London: Edward Arnold, 1973.

5998 Hedstrom, John. *A Conceptual Study of Ethnic Conflict*. Chicago, Illinois: University of Chicago, Department of Geography, M.A., 1979.

5999 Herbertson, A.J., and Herbertson, F.D. *Man and His Work*. London: Adam Black, 1902.

6000 Highet, Gilbert. *The Migration of Ideas*. New York: Oxford University Press, 1954.

6001 Hodgkin, Thomas. *A Landscape with Figures: Political Geography with Human Conflict*. London: Butterworth, 1983.

6002 Hoffman, S. *Duties Beyond Borders: On the Limits and Possibilities of Ethical International Politics*. Syracuse, New York: Syracuse University Press, 1981.

6003 Huntington, Ellsworth. *Mainsprings of Civilisation*. New York: John Wiley & Sons, 1945.

6004 Imbright, Gastone. *Lineamenti di Geografia Religiosa*. Rome: Editrice Studium, 1961.

6005 Jackson, Peter. *Race and Racism: Essays in Social Geography*. London: Allen & Unwin, 1987.

6006 Jackson, Peter, and Smith, S.J. *Social Interaction and Ethnic Segregation*. London: Academic Press, 1981.

6007 Jones, G.S. *Languages of Class*. Cambridge: Cambridge University Press, 1983.

6008 Jung, Carl. *Man and His Symbols*. Garden City, New Jersey: Doubleday, 1964.

6009 Kephart, C. *Races of Mankind: Their Origin and Migration; All Recognized Ancient Tribes and Nations Identified and Their Migrations Traced*. New York: Philosophical Library, 1960.

6010 Kirchhoff, Alfred. *Mensch und Erde*. Leipzig: B.G. Teubner, 1901.

6011 Kraemer, Hendrick. *World Cultures and World Religions: The Coming Dialogue*. Philadelphia: Westminster Press, 1960.

6012 Kuhn, Arthur, and Wolpe, A., eds. *Feminism and Materialism*. London: Routledge, 1978.

6013 Kurdi, Abdulrahman Abdulkadia. *The Islamic State: A Study Based on the Islamic Holy Constitutions*. London: Mansell, 1984.

6014 Laponce, J.A. *Languages and Their Territories*. Toronto: University of Toronto Press, 1987.

6015 Laponce, J.A. *Les Etats Multilingues: Problemes et Solutions*. Quebec: Presses de l'Universite Lauel, 1975.

6016 Lefebvre, Andre. *Les Races et les Langues*. Paris: Alcan, 1893.

6017 Le Fur, Lorris. *Races, Nationalites, Etats*. Paris: Alcan, 1922.

6018 Lenski, Gerhard. *The Religious Factor: A Sociological Study of Religion's Impact on Politics, Economics and Family Life*. New York: Doubleday, 1961.

6019 Leopold, W.F. *Speech Development of a Bilingual Child: A Linguistic Record*. 4 Vols. Evanston, Illinois: Northwestern University Press, 1939-1949.

6020 Lepage, R.B. *The National Language Question*. New York: Oxford University Press, 1964.

6021 Levin, Michael D., ed. *Ethnicity and Aboriginality: Case Studies in Ethnonationalism*. Toronto: University of Toronto Press, 1993.

6022 **Leyburn, James G.** *Frontier Folkways.* New Haven, Connecticut: Yale University Press, 1935.

6023 **Mackey, Sandra.** "The Ecology of Language Shift." In *Langues en Contact eten Conflit.* Brussels: CRP, 1980.

6024 **Marks, S., and Rathbone, R.,** eds. *Industrialisation and Social Change in South Africa.* London: Longman, 1982.

6025 **Mason, Philip.** *An Essay on Racial Tension.* London: Royal Institute of International Affairs, 1954.

6026 **Massialas, Byron G., and Zevin, Jack.** *Cultural Exchange.* Chicago: Rand McNally, 1970.

6027 **Meillet, A., and Cohen, M.** *Les Langues du Monde.* Paris: Centre National de la Recherche Scientifique, 1952.

6028 **Milne, Robert Stephen.** *Politics in Ethnically Bipolar States: Guyana, Malaysia, Fiji.* Vancouver: University of British Columbia Press, 1981.

6029 **Mingione, E.** *Social Conflict and the City.* Oxford: Blackwell, 1981.

6030 **Nelde, P.H.,** ed. *Plurilingues, Theory, Methods and Models of Contact Linguistics.* Bonn: Ferd Dummler Verlag, 1983.

6031 **O'Bryan, K.** *Attitudes and Behavior of Members of Non-Official Language Groups.* Downsview, Ontario: York University, Institute of Behavioural Analysis, 1973.

6032 **Palley, Claire.** *Constitutional Law and Minorities.* Report No. 36. London: Minority Rights Group, 1978.

6033 **Peach, Cheri; Robinson, V.; and Smith, S.,** eds. *Ethnic Segregation in Cities.* London: Croom Helm, 1981.

6034 **Rabushka, A., and Shepsle, K.A.** *Politics in Plural Societies.* Columbus: Merrill, 1972.

6035 *Racial Exclusionism and the City: The Urban Support of the National Front.* London: Allen & Unwin, 1983.

6036 **Radcliffe-Brown, A.R.** *Structure and Function in Primitive Society.* Glencoe, Illinois: The Free Press, 1952.

6037 **Rapoport, Amos.** *House Form and Culture.* Englewood Cliffs, New Jersey: Prentice-Hall, 1969.

6038 **Rex, J., and Moore, R.** *Race, Community and Conflict.* London: Oxford University Press, 1967.

6039 **Richardson, Benjamin F.** *Atlas of Cultural Features.* Northbrook: Hubbard, 1972.

6040 **Rudolph, Joseph R., Jr., and Thompson, Robert J.** eds. *Ethnoterritorial Politics, Policy and the Western World.* Boulder, Colorado: Lynne Rienner Publishers, 1989.

6041 **Runciman, W.** *Relative Deprivation and Social Justice.* London: Routledge, 1966.

6042 **Russell, A.G.** *Colour, Race and Empire.* London: V. Gollancz, 1944.

6043 **Samuels, Leynard,** ed. *Humanistic Geography: Prospects and Problems.* Chicago: Maarouta, 1978.

6044 **Sayer, A.** *Method in Social Science: A Realist Approach.* London: Hutchinson, 1984.

6045 **Scantling, Frederick Holland.** *Factors and Processes in the Establishment of Cultural Boundaries: A Study of Discrete Boundaries on the Landscape.* Los Angeles: University of California, Ph.D., 1970.

6046 **Schurtz, Heinrich.** *Volkerkunde.* Wein: Deuticke, 1903.

6047 **Schurtz, Heinrich.** *Urges chichte der Kultur.* Leipzig: Bibiographisches Institut, 1900.

6048 **Siegfried, Andre, and Latreille, A.** *Les forces religieuses et la vie politique.* Paris: Armand Colin, 1969.

6049 **Slater, Robert L.** *World Religions and World Community.* New York City: Columbia University Press, 1963.

6050 **Slvert, K.H.** *Expectant Peoples: Nationalism and Development.* New York: Random House, 1963.

6051 **Smith, Anthony D.** *The Ethnic Revival.* Cambridge: Cambridge University Press, 1982.

6052 **Smith, D.,** ed. *Living Under Apartheid.* London: Allen & Unwin, 1982.

6053 **Sopher, David E.** *Geography of Religions.* Englewood Cliffs, New Jersey: Prentice-Hall, 1967.

6054 **Stoddard, Lothrop.** *The New World of Islam.* New York: Charles Scribner's Sons, 1921.

6055 **Thomas, F.** *The Environmental Basis of Society.* New York: Century, 1925.

6056 **Varagnac, Andre.** *Civilisations traditionnelles et genres de vie.* Paris: Albin Michel, 1948.

6057 **Vendryes, Joseph.** *Le langage: Introduction linguistique a l'histoire.* Paris: Renaissance du Livre, 1921.

6058 **Vogler, Carolyn M.** *The National State: The Neglected Dimension of Class.* Aldershot, England: Gower Publishing, 1985.

6059 **Wagner, Philip L.** *Environments and Peoples.* Englewood Cliffs, New Jersey: Prentice-Hall, 1972.

6060 **Wagner, Philip L., and Mikesell, Marvin W.,** eds. *Readings in Cultural Geography.* Chicago, Illinois: University of Chicago Press, 1971.

6061 **Waldron, J.,** ed. *Theories of Rights.* Oxford: Oxford University Press, 1984.

6062 **Walzer, M.** *Spheres of Justice: A Defense of Pluralism and Equality.* New York: Basic Books.

6063 **Weinrech, U.** *Languages in Contact.* The Hague: Mouton, 1968.

6064 **Whitreck, R.H., and Thomas, O.J.** *The Geographic Factor: Its Role in Life and Civilization.* New York: Century, 1932.

6065 **Williams, B.** *Ethics and the Limits of Philosophy.* Cambridge, Massachusetts: Harvard University Press, 1985.

6066 **Williams, C.H.,** ed. *Language in Geographic Context.* Philadelphia, Pennsylvania: Multilingual Matters, 1988.

6067 **Wolf, Eric R.,** ed. *Religious Regimes and State-Formation: Perspectives from European Ethnology.* Albany: State University of New York Press, 1991.

6068 **Wright, E.O.** *Classes.* London: Verso, 1985.

Journals

6069 **Agnew, John A.** "Sociologizing the Geographical Imagination: Spatial Concepts in the World-System Perspective." *Political Geography Quarterly*, 1, No. 2 (April, 1982), 159-166.

6070 **Allardt, Erik.** "Implications of the Ethnic Revival in Modern Industrial Society." *Commentations Scientiarum Socialium*, 12 (1979), whole issue.

6071 **Ayubi, Nazih.** "State Islam and Communal Plurality." *The American Academy of Political and Social Science. Annals* [Newbury Park], 524 (November, 1992), 79-91.

6072 **Boisard, Marcel A.** "On the Probable Influence of Islam on Western Public and International Law." *International Journal of Middle Eastern Studies*),

11, No. 4 (July, 1980), 429-450.

6073 **Bottiglioni, G.** "Linguistic Geography: Its Achievements, Methods and Orientations." *World*, 10 (1954), 375.

6074 **Breton, R.J.L.** "Les criteres de determination des ethnies." *Revue de Psychologie des Peuples*, 1 (1968), 44-61.

6075 **Bunge, William W.** "Comment: Racial Continents." *Political Geography Quarterly*, 9, No. 1 (January, 1990), 5-8.

6076 **Butterworth, Charles E.** "Political Islam: The Origins." *The American Academy of Political and Social Science. Annals* [Newbury Park], 524 (November, 1992), 26-37.

6077 **Carroll, Terrance G.** "Secularization and States of Modernity." *World Politics*, 36, No. 3 (April, 1984), 362-382.

6078 **Clark, Gordon L.** "Making Moral Landscapes: John Rawl's Original Position." *Political Geography Quarterly*, 5, No. 4 Supplement (October, 1986), S147-S162.

6079 **Clark, Gordon L.** "Who's to Blame for Racial Segregation?" *Urban Geography*, 4 (1984), 193-209.

6080 **Clifford, E.H.M.** "Recording Native Place Names." *Geographical Journal*, 109, No. 1-3 (January-March, 1947), 99-102.

6081 **Coleman, James S.** "Inequality, Sociology, and Moral Philosophy." *American Journal of Sociology*, 80, No. 3 (November, 1974), 739-764.

6082 **Connor, Walker F.** "The Politics of Ethnonationalism." *Journal of International Affairs*, 27, No. 1 (Spring, 1973), 1-21.

6083 **Credner, W.** "Kultbauden in der brinterindischen Landschaft." *Erdkunde*, Band 1-2 (Mai, 1947), 48-61.

6084 **Davis, Charles.** "Social Mistrust as a Determinant of Political Cynicism in a Traditional Society: A Empirical Examination." *The Journal of Developing Areas*, 11, No. 1 (October, 1976), 91-102.

6085 **Delgado de Carvalho, Carlos.** "Geografia das linguas." *Boletin Geografico*, 1 (1943), 45-62.

6086 **Deffontaines, Pierre.** "Le facteur Spirituel et religieux en geographie humaine." In *La Pensee Geographique Francaise Contemporaine*. Saint-Brieuc: Presses Universitaires de Bretagne, 1972.

6087 **Demangeon, Albert.** "La geographie des langues." *Annales de Geographie*, 38 (October-December, 1929), 427.

6088 **Dorion, Henri.** "Races, Nations, Peuples...Une Terminologie a Preciser." *Cahiers de Geographie de Quebec*, 18 (1965), 243-251.

6089 **Douglas, N.** "Amorphous People's Will Not Succeed: A Lesson for 'the North.'" *Political Geography*, 12, No. 2 (March, 1993), 156-160.

6090 **Dressler, W., and Wodak-Leodolter, R.** "Language Death." *International Journal of the Sociology of Language*, 12 (1977), 5-144.

6091 **Drysdale, Alasdair Duncan, and Watts, Michael J.** "Modernization and Social Protest Movement." *Antipode*, 9, No. 1 (April, 1977), 40-56.

6092 **Ferguson, Charles A.** "Diglossia." *World*, 15 (1949), 325-340.

6093 **Fickeler, Paul.** "Grundfagen der religions geographie." *Erdkunde*, Band 1 (Dezember, 1947), 121-144.

6094 **Fields, Karen E.** "Christian Missionaries as Anticolonial Militants." *Theory and Society*, 11, No. 1 (January, 1982), 95-108.

6095 **Fincher, Ruth.** "Identifying Class Struggle Outside Commodity Production." *Society and Space*, 2 (1984), 309-327.

6096 **Fisher, Otto.** "Landscape as Symbol." *Landscape*, 4, No. 3 (Spring, 1955), 24-33.

6097 **Fishman, J.A.** "Bilingualism with and without Diglossia: Diglossia with and without Bilingualism." *Journal of Social Issues*, 23, No. 2 (April, 1967), 29-38.

6098 **Fleure, H.J.** "The Geographical Distribution of the Major Religions." *Bulletin de la Societe Royale de Geographie d'Egypte*, 24 (1951), 1-18.

6099 **Fosdick, Dorothy.** "Ethical Standards and Political Strategies." *Political Science Quarterly*, 52, No. 2 (June, 1942), 214-228.

6100 **Geyl, Pieter.** "Toynbee's System of Civilizations." *Journal of the History of Ideas*, 9, No. 1 (January-March, 1948), 93-124.

6101 **Goodwin-Gill, G.S.** "International Law and the Detention of Refugees and Asylum Seekers." *Internation Migration Review*, 20, No. 2 (1986), 193-219.

6102 **Gourou, Pierre.** "Civilisations et malchance geographique." *Annales Economies Societes Civilisations*, 4, No. 4 (Octobre-Decembre, 1949), 445-446.

6103 **Hall, Thomas D.** "Peripheries, Regions of Refuge, and Nonstate Societies: Toward a Theory of Reactive Social Change." *Social Science Quarterly*, 64, No. 3 (September, 1983), 582-597.

6104 **Hechter, M., and Levi, M.** "The Comparative Analysis of Ethnoregional Movements." *Ethnic and Racial Studies*, 2, No. 3 (July, 1979), 206-274.

6105 **Huntington, Ellsworth.** "Season of Birth and the Distribution of Civilization." *Annals of the Association of American Geographers*, 27, No. 2 (June, 1937), 109-110.

6106 **Isaac, Erich.** "The Act and the Convenant: The Impact of Religion on the Landscape." *Landscape*, 11, No. 2 (Winter, 1962), 12-17.

6107 **Isaac, Erich.** "Religion, Landscape and Space." *Landscape*, 9, No. 2 (Winter, 1959), 14-17.

6108 **Isard, Walter.** "Social System Framework and Casual History 2: Behavior Under Stress and Cognition." *Conflict Management and Peace Science*, 6, No. 2 (Spring, 1983), 59-93.

6109 **Isard, Walter.** "Social System Framework and Casual History 3: Interdependent Multi-Role Behavior and Operationality." *Conflict Management and Peace Science*, 7, No. 1 (Fall, 1984), 87-110.

6110 **Johnson, G.** "Human Rights Concepts and Policy Choices in India and the United States." *Policy Studies Journal*, 15, No. 1 (1986), 58-70.

6111 **Karawan, Ibrahim.** "Monarchs, Mullas, and Marshals: Islamic Regimes?" *The American Academy of Political and Social Science. Annals* [Newbury Park], 524 (November, 1992), 103-119.

6112 **Laponce, J.A.** "La Distribution Geographique des Groupes Linguistiques et les Solutions Personnelles aux Problemes de l'Etat Bilinque." *Revue Internationale de Science Politique*, 4 (1980), 478-494.

6113 **Le Bras, Gabriel.** "La Geographie Religieuse." *Annales d'Histoire Sociale*, (1945), 87-112.

6114 **Lowry, M.** "Racial Segregation: A Geographical Adaptation and Analysis." *Journal of Geography*, 71, No. 1 (January, 1972), 28-40.

6115 **Martin, Lisa L.** "Interests, Power, and Multiculturalism." *International Organization* [Cambridge, MA], 46, No. 4 (Autumn, 1992), 765-792.

6116 **Mayall, James, and Simpson, Mark.** "Ethnicity Is Not Enough: Reflections on Protracted Secessionism in the Third World." *International Journal of Comparative Sociology* [Leiden], 33, Nos. 1-2 (January-April, 1992), 5-25.

6117 **Melanoer, G.** "Responsibility for Examining an Asylum Request." *International Migration Review*, 20, No. 2 (1986), 220-229.

6118 **Murphy, Alexander B.** "Territorial Policies in Multiethnic States." *The Geographical Review*, 79, No. 4 (October, 1989), 410-421.

6119 **Offe, C., and Wiesenthal, H.** "Two Logics of Collective Action: Theoretical Notes on Social Class and Organisational Form." *Political Power and Social Theory*, 1 (1980), 67 and 115.

6120 **Ornstein, Jacob.** "Patterns of Language Planning in the New States." *World Politics*, 17, No. 1 (October, 1964), 40-49.

6121 **Plongeron, Bernard.** "Religion et Nationalisme aux Etas-Unis au Cours de L'Independance." *Annals Historiques de la Revolution Francaise*, 249, No. 3 (Juillet-Septembre, 1982), 416-439.

6122 **Reinicke, John.** "Trade Jargons and Creole Dialects as Marginal Languages." *Social Forces*, 17, No. 1 (October, 1938), 107-118.

6123 **Reynolds, David R.** "The Geography of Social Choice." In *Political Studies from Spatial Perspectives*. Chichester: John Wiley & Sons, 1981, 91-110.

6124 **Simnett, W.E.** "Colour Question and the Colonies. Various Aspects of a Problem Which Lies at the Root of Colonial Policy." *The Crown Colonist*, 11, No. 118 (September, 1941), 397-396.

6125 **Smith, Anthony D.** "Towards a Theory of Ethnic Separatism." *Ethnic and Racial Studies*, 2 (1979), 21-37.

6126 **Sorre, Max.** "La notion de genre de vie et sa vsleur actuelle." *Annales de Geographie*, 57, No. 306 (Avril-Juin, 1948), 97-108 and 57, No. 307 (Juillet-Septembre, 1948), 193-204.

6127 **Staeheli, Lynn A., and Cope, Meghan S.** "Empowering Women's Citizenship." *Political Geography*, 13, No. 5 (September, 1994), 443-460.

6128 **Stanley, Manfred.** Church Adaptation to Social Change." *Journal for the Scientific Study of Religion*, 2 (1962), 64-73.

6129 **Taylor, Peter J.** "Editorial Comments: Children and Politics." *Political Geography Quarterly*, 8, No. 1 (January, 1989), 5-6.

6130 **Terrero, Jose.** "Idiomas y dialectos." In *Geografia de Espana*. Barcelona: Editorial Ramon Sopena, 1966.

6131 **Thrift, N.J.** "On the Determination of Social Action in Space and Time." *Environment and Planning A: Society and Space*, 1, No. 1 (March, 1983), 23-58.

6132 **Veness, A. R.** "Neither Homed or Homeless: Contested Definitions nad the Personal Worlds of the Poor." *Political Geography*, 12, No. 4 (July, 1993), 319-340.

6133 **Vidal de la Blache, Paul.** "Les genres de vie dans la geographie humaine." *Annales de Geographie*, 20, 109 (January, 1911), 193-212 and 20, No. 1 (Mai, 1911), 289-367.

6134 **Vielle, Paul.** "The State of the Periphery and Its Heritage." *Economy and Society*, 17, No. 1 (February, 1988), 52-89.

6135 **Vierkandt, A.** "Die Kulterformen und ihre Geographische Verbreitung." *Geographisch Zeitschrift*, 3, No. 3 (Oktober, 1897), 256-279 and 3, No. 4 (Dezembre, 1897), 315-367.

6136 **Wagner, Philip L.** "Remarks on the Geography of Language." *Geographical Review*, 48, No. 1 (January, 1958), 86-97.

6137 **Ward, R. De Courcy.** "Primitive Civilization and the Tropics." *Journal of Geography*, 6, No. 6 (January, 1908), 224-226.

6138 **Williams, C.H.** "Ethnic Resurgence in the Periphery." *Area*, 11 (1979), 279-283.

6139 **Williams, C.H.** "Ideology and the Interpretation of Minority Cultures." *Political Geography Quarterly*, 3, No. 2 (April, 1984).

6140 **Williams, C.H.** "Language Planning and Minority Group Rights." *Cambria*, 9 (1982), 61-74.

6141 **Williams, C.H.** "More Than Tongue Can Tell." In *Linguistic Minorities, Policies and Pluralism*, J. Edwards, ed. London: Academic Press, 1987.

6142 **Williams, C.H.** "Social Mobilization and Nationalism in Multicultural Societies." *Ethnic and Racial Studies*, 5, No. 3 (July, 1982), 349-365.

6143 **Williams, C.H, and Smith, Anthony D.** "National Construction of Social Space." *Progress in Human Geography*, 7, No. 4 (December, 1983), 502-518.

6144 **Williams, G.** "Review of E. Allardt's Implications of Ethnic Revival in Modern Industrial Society." *Journal of Multilingual and Multicultural Development*, 1 (1980), 363-370.

6145 **Williams, J. Paul.** "The Nature of Religion." *Journal for the Scientific Study of Religion*, 2 (1962), 3-14.

POLITICAL GEOGRAPHY OF REGIONS

AFRICA

Books

6146 **Bing, John Howard.** *Tribe and Elections in Uganda.* Seattle: Washington University, Ph.D., 1974.

6147 **Boles, Elizabeth.** *The West and South Africa: Myths, Interests and Policy Options.* London: Croom Helm for the Atlantic Institute for International Affairs, 1988.

6148 **Brookes, E.H., and Macaulay, J.B.** *Civil Liberty in South Africa.* Capetown: Oxford University Press, 1958.

6149 **Carter, G.M.** *The Politics of Inequality: South Africa Since 1948.* New York: Praeger, 1958.

6150 **Davies, William J.** *Patterns of Non-White Population Distribution in Port Elizabeth with to the Application of Group Areas Act.* Port Elizabeth: University of Port Elizabeth, Institute for Planning Research, Special Publication No. 1, Series B, 1971.

6151 **Davis, John W.** *Libyan Politics: Tribe and Revolution. An Account of the Zuwaya and Their Government.* London: I.B. Tauris, 1987.

6152 **Deng, Francis Mading.** *Tradition and Modernization: A Challenge for Law among the Dinka of the Sudan.* 2nd ed. New Haven, Connecticut: Yale University Press, 1987.

6153 **Dison, L.R., and Mohammed, I.** *Group Areas and Their Development.* Durban: Butterworth, 1962.

6154 **Dugard, John.** *Human Rights and the South African Legal Order.* Princeton, New Jersey: Princeton University Press, 1978.

6155 **Evenden, L.J., and Cunningham, F.F.** *Cultural Discord in the Modern World: Geographical Themes.* Vancouver: Tantalus, 1974.

6156 **Fanon, F.** *Black Skins, White Masks.* London: Penguin, 1967.

6157 **Feghali, Michel.** *Varia. En bonne partie sur: La France, 'Le Liban' et la Syrie. Discourse-a llocutions. Articles: litte aires, politiques, historiques, linguistiques, ethnologiques 1908-1938.* Recueillis et publies par Mgr. Pierre Hobeika. Hommage a Monsigneur Michel Feghali pour ses travaux scientifiques et son devouement patriotique. Jounieh, Liban: Imp. Des Missionaires Libanais, 1938.

6158 **Gordon, D.L., ed.** *A Survey of Rare Relations in South Africa 1988.* Johannesburg: South African Institute of Race Relations, 1989.

6159 **Gutkind, Peter C.W., ed.** *The Passing of Tribal Man in Africa.* Leiden, Netherlands: E.J. Brill, NV, 1970.

6160 **Hogben, S.J.** *The Muhammedan Emirates of Northern Nigeria.* London: Oxford University Press, 1920.

6161 **Horrell, M.** *The Group Areas Act-Its Effect on Human Beings.* Johannesburg: South African Institute of Race Relations, 1956.

6162 **Horrell, M.** *Group Areas: The Emerging Pattern with Illustrative Examples from the Transvaal.* Johannesburg: South African Institute of Race Relations, 1966.

6163 **Horrell, M.** *A Survey of Race Relations in South Africa 1976.* Johannesburg: South African Institute of Race Relations, 1977.

6164 **Horton, Alan W.** *The Social Dimension of Sudanese Politics: Some Tribal and Elite Pressures on the Sudan's Political Structure.* New York: American University Field Staff, 1964.

6165 **Huxley, Elspeth, and Perham, Margery.** *Race and Politics in Kenya.* London: Faber and Faber, 1956.

6166 **Ingham, Kenneth.** *Politics in Modern Africa: The Uneven Tribal Dimension.* London: Routledge, 1990.

6167 **Joffe, George, ed.** *North Africa: Nation, State, and Religion.* London: Routledge, 1993.

6168 **Joosub, H.E.** *Bitterness Towards Indians.* Pretoria: Indian Commercial Association, 1958.

6169 **Kuper, L.; Watts, H.D.; and Davies, R.J.** *Durban: A Study in Racial Ecology.* London: Jonathan Cape, 1958.

6170 **Kuper, L.; Watts, H.D.; Davies, R.J.; and Smith, M.G., eds.** *Pluralism in Africa.* Berkeley: University of California Press, 1969.

6171 **Langenhore, Fernand Van.** *Consciences tribales et nationales en Afrique noire.* The Hague: Martinus Nijheff, 1960.

6172 **Lemon, A.** *Apartheid: A Geography of Separation.* Farnborough: Saxon House, 1976.

6173 **Lewis, I.M.** *Peoples of the Horn of Africa.*
London: International African Institute, 1955.

6174 **Lodge, T.** *Black Politics in South Africa Since
1945.* Johannesburg: Raven Press, 1983.

6175 **Lonsdale, John,** ed. *South Africa in Question.*
Cambridge: University of Cambridge, African
Studies Centre, 1988.

6176 **Maasdorp, G.N., and Pillay, P.N.** *Urban
Relocation and Racial Segregation: The Case of
Indian South Africans.* Durban: University of
Natal, Department of Economics, Research
Monograph, 1977.

6177 **Marais, J.S.** *The Cape Coloured People,
1652-1937.* London: Longman, 1939.

6178 **McCuen, Gary E.** *The Apartheid Reader.*
Hudson, Wisconsin: Gary E. McCuen
Publications, 1986.

6179 **Mkhondo, Rich.** *Reporting South Africa.*
London: James Currey, 1993.

6180 **Munson, Henry, Jr.** *Religion and Power in
Morocco.* New Haven: Yale University Press,
1993.

6181 **Neres, P.** *French-Speaking West Africa.* London:
Oxford University Press, 1962.

6182 **Okpu, U.** *Ethnic Minority Problems in Nigerian
Politics, 1960-65.* Almquist: Uppsala, 1977.

6183 **Ottaway, David.** *Chained Together: Mandela, de
Klerk, and the Struggle to Remake South Africa.*
New York: Times Books, 1993.

6184 *Outcast Cape Town.* Minneapolis: University of
Minnesota Press, 1981.

6185 **Pachai, B.** *The International Aspects of the South
African Indian Question 1860-1971.* Cape Town:
Struik, 1971.

6186 **Palmer, Robin.** *Land and Racial Domination in
Rhodesia.* Berkeley: University of California
Press, Perspective on Southern Africa, 24, 1977.

6187 **Randall, P.** *Survey of Race Relations in South
Africa.* Johannesburg: South African Institute of
Race Relations.

6188 **Reed, Daniel.** *Beloved Country: South Africa's
Silent Wars.* London: BBC Books, 1994.

6189 **Rothchild, Donald S., and Chatan, Naomi,** eds.
*The Precarious Balance: State and Society in
Africa.* Boulder, Colorado: Westview Press,
1988.

6190 **Rousseau, F.P.** *Handbook on the Group Areas*

Act. Cape Town: Juta, 1960.

6191 **Saari, Eleanore Marie.** *Non-Economic Factors
and Systems of Cities. The Impact of Islamic
Culture on Egypt's Urban Settlement Pattern.*
Minneapolis: University of Minnesota, 1971.

6192 **Sachs, A.** *Justice in South Africa.* London:
Heinemann, 1973.

6193 **Smith, David M.,** ed. *Living Under Apartheid:
Aspects of Urbanization and Social Change in
South Africa.* London: Allen & Unwin, 1982.

6194 **Smith, David M.,** ed. *Separation in South Africa:
People and Policies.* London: University of
London, Queen Mary College, Department of
Geography, Occasional Papers, No. 6, 1976.

6195 **Soggot, David.** *Namibia: The Violent Heritage.*
London: Rex Collings, 1986.

6196 **Stultz, Newell M.** *Transkei's Half Loaf: Race
Seperatism in South Africa.* New Haven,
Connecticut: Yale University Press, 1979.

6197 **Talbot, Lee Merriam.** *The Ecology of Masailand
(East Africa).* Los Angeles: University of
California, Ph.D., 1963.

6198 **United Nations.** *Apartheid in South Africa, 2.*
New York: Office of Public Information. 1965.

6199 **Ward, B.E.** *The Social Organization of the
Ewe-Speaking People.* London: University of
London, M.A., 1949.

6200 **Western, John.** *Outcase Cape Town.*
Minneapolis: University of Minnesota Press, 1981.

6201 **Williams, G.** *Rural Inequalities in Nigeria.*
Geneva: ILO, 1980.

Journals

6202 **Adejuyigbe, Omolade.** "Social Factors in the
Development of the Political Map." In *A
Geography of Nigerian Development,* J.S.
Oguntoyinbo et al, eds. Ibadan: Heinemann,
1978, 175-192.

6203 **Bassett, Thomas J.** "The Political Ecology of
Peasant-Herder Conflicts in the Northern Ivory
Coast." *Annals of the Association of American
Geographers,* 78, No. 3 (September, 1988),
453-472.

6204 **Beavon, K.S.O.** "Black Townships in South
Africa: Terra Incognita for Urban Geographers."
South Africa Geographical Journal, 64,
No. 1 (April, 1982), 3-20.

6205 Best, Alan C.G. "The Republic of South Africa: White Supremacy." *Focus*, 25, No. 6 (March-April, 1975), 1-13.

6206 Booth, Douglas, and Biyela, Mlandu. "Exploring the Spatial Dimensions of Black Resistance and Political Violence in South Africa: The Case of Durban." *Urban Geography*, 9, No. 6 (November-December, 1988), 629-653.

6207 Brookes, E.H. "Racial Separation in South Africa: Anomalies and Injustices of the Group Areas Act." *African World*, (June, 1952), 9-10.

6208 Brookfield, Harold C. "Some Geographic Implications of the Apartheid and Partnership of Policies of Southern Africa." *Transactions of the Institute of British Geographers*, 23 (1957), 225-247.

6209 Brookfield, Harold C., and Tatham, M.A. "The Distribution of Racial Groups in Durban." *Geographical Review*, 47, No. 1 (January, 1957), 44-65.

6210 Buchanan, Keith, and Hurwitz, N. "The 'Colored' Community in the Union of South Africa." *The Geographical Review*, 40, No. 3 (July, 1950), 397-414.

6211 "Burundi: Political and Ethnic Powder Keg." *Africa Report*, 15, No. 8 (November, 1970), 18-20.

6212 Champion, A.M. "The Reconditioning of Native Reserves in Africa." *Journal of the Royal African Society*, 38, No. 153 (October, 1939), 442-464.

6213 Coleman, James S. "Political Systems in Multiracial Africa: Race Tensions Pose Threat to Stability." *Africa Special Report*, 3, No. 6 (June, 1958), 3-6.

6214 Cowley, C. "'Occupy' in Terms of the Group Areas Act." *South African Law Journal*, 77 (1960), 425-427.

6215 Crush, Jonathan S., and Wellings, P.A. "The Southern Africa Pleasure Periphery, 1966-87." *Journal of Modern African Studies*, 21, No. 4 (December, 1983), 673-698.

6216 Dubow, Saul. "Afrikaner Nationalism, Apartheid and the Conceptualization of 'Race.'" *The Journal of African History* [Cambridge], 33, No. 2 (1992), 209-237.

6217 Duder, C.J.D., and Youe, C.P. "Paice's Place: Race and Politics in Nanyuki District, Kenya, in the 1920s." *African Affairs* [Oxford], 93, No. 371 (April, 1994), 253-278.

6218 Evans-Pritchard, E.E. "The Political Structure of the Nandi-Speaking Peoples of Kenya." *Africa*, 13, No. 3 (July, 1940), 250-267.

6219 Fields, Karen. "Political Contingencies of Witchcraft in Colonial Central Africa: Culture and the State in Marxist Theory." *Canadian Journal of African Studies*, 16, No. 3 (1982), 567-594.

6220 Frankel, Philip. "The Politics of Passes: Control and Change in South Africa." *The Journal of Modern African Studies*, 17, No. 2 (June, 1979), 199-217.

6221 Furlong, Patrick J. "Azikiwe and the National Church of Nigeria and the Cameroons: A Case Study of the Political Use of Religion in African Nationalism." *African Affairs* [Oxford], 91, No. 364 (July, 1992), 433-452.

6222 Griffiths, I.L. "South Africa Divided." *The Geographical Magazine*, 52, No. 2 (November, 1978), 92-98.

6223 Gunn, L.H. "Group Areas Act in Relation to Race Zoning." *Public Health*, 15 (1951), 258-266.

6224 Gunn, L.H. "Rhodesia: Prospects for White Resistance." *Africa Report*, 22, No. 5 (September-October, 1977), 9-14.

6225 Herisson, Charles-Daniel. "Problemes raciaux en Afrique de Sud." *L'Actualite Economique*, 15e Annee, 1, No. 7 (October, 1939), 427-436.

6226 Howe, Russell Warren. "War in Southern Africa." *Foreign Affairs*, 48, No. 1 (October, 1969), 150-165.

6227 Huff, D.C., and Lutz, J.M. "The Contagion of Political Unrest in Independent Black Africa." *Economic Geography*, 50, No. 4 (October, 1974), 353-367.

6228 Hunter, J.M. "The Clans of Nangodi." *Africa*, 38 (1968), 377-412.

6229 Hyden, Goran, and Williams, Donald C. "A Community Model of African Politics: Illustrations from Nigeria and Tanzania." *Comparative Studies in Society and History* [Cambridge], 36, No. 1 (January, 1994), 68-96.

6230 Jackson, Robert H., and Rosberg, Carl G. "Popular Legitimacy in African Multi-Ethnic States." *The Journal of Modern African Studies*, 22, No. 2 (June, 1984), 177-198.

6231 Joffee, H. "The State in Post-Colonial Societies: An Overview of the Works of Alavi, Saul, Shivji, Mandani and Leys." *Africa Perspectives*, 7 (1978), 27-37.

6232 Johnson, H. Binder. "The Locations of Christian Missions in Africa." *Geographical Review*, 57, No. 2 (April, 1967), 168-202.

6233 **Knight, David B.** "Racism and Reaction: The Development of a Batswana 'raison d'etre' for the Country." In *Cultural Discord in the Modern World: Geographical Themes*, L.J. Evenden and F.F. Cunningham, eds. Vancouver: Tantalus, 1974, 111-26.

6234 **Kubiak, T.J.** "Rhodesia (Zimbabwe): White Minority Rule in a Black State." *Focus*, 27, No. 2 (November-December, 1976), 1-8.

6235 **Kuper, L.** "Race Zoning in Cloud Cucko Land." *Africa South*. 2, No. 1 (October-December, 1957), 33-38.

6236 **Magubare, Bernard.** "The Mounting Class and National Struggles in South Africa." *Review*, 8, No. 2 (Fall, 1984), 197-231.

6237 **Martin, Abel.** "Berber und Arabei." *Zeitschrift fur Geopolitik.* Jahrggang, 24, Heft 11 (November, 1953), 609-614.

6238 **Mayotte, Judy.** "Civil War in Sudan: The Paradox of Human Rights and National Sovereignty." *Journal of International Affairs* [New York City], 47, No. 2 (Winter, 1994), 497-524.

6239 **Merrett, Christopher.** "The Significance of the Political Boundary in the Apartheid State, with Particular Reference to Transkei." *The South African Geographical Journal*, 66, No. 1 (April, 1984), 79-93.

6240 **Millner, M.A.** "Apartheid and the South African Courts." *Current Legal Problems*, 14 (April, 1961), 280-306.

6241 **Mittelman, James H.** "Cutting the Weak Link in the Apartheid Chain: Namibia." *Africa Today,* 35, No. 2 (1988), 51-56.

6242 **Nel, A.** "Geographical Aspects of Apartheid in South Africa." *Tijdschrift Voor Economische en Sociale Geografie*, 53, Jaarg, 10 (October, 1962), 215-217.

6243 **Nel, A.** "Nie-blanke kolle in Paarl: Die probleme van interpretaise en begrensing in die stedelike geografie." *South African Geographical Journal*, 36, No. 1 (April, 1954), 24-30.

6244 **Okoh, N.** "Bilingualism and Divergant Thinking Among Nigerian and Welsh School Children." *Journal of Social Psychology*, 110, Second Half (April, 1980), 163-170.

6245 **Oliver, J.J., and Booysen, J.J.** "Some Impacts of Black Commuting on Pretoria." *South African Geographical Journal*, 65, No. 2 (September, 1983), 124-134.

6246 **Parker, M.** "Race Relations and Political

Development in Kenya." *African Affairs*, 50, No. 198 (January, 1951), 41-52.

6247 **Patten, J.W.** "Alternatives to Apartheid in South Africa." *Foreign Affairs*, 30, No. 2 (January, 1952), 310-326.

6248 **Perham, Margery.** "White Minorities in Africa." *Foreign Affairs*, 37, No. 4 (July, 1959), 637-648.

6249 **Pirie, Gordon.** "Ethno-Linguistic Zoning in South Africa: Black Townships." *Area*, 16, No. 4 (December, 1984), 291-298.

6250 **Pirie, Gordon.** "Race Zoning in South Africa-Board, Court, Parliament, Public." *Political Geography Quarterly*, 3, No. 3 (July, 1984), 207-221.

6251 **Potts, Deborah.** "The Geography of Apartheid: The Relationship Between Space and Ideology in South Africa." *Contemporary Issues in Geography and Education*, 2, No. 1 (Spring, 1985), 2-7.

6252 **Ranger, Terence.** "White Presence and Power in Africa." *The Journal of African History*, 20, No. 4 (December, 1979), 463-469.

6253 **Roberts, Margaret.** "The Ending of Apatheid: Shifting Inequalities in South Africa." *Geography* [Sheffield], 79, Part 1, No. 342 (January, 1994), 53-76.

6254 **Rogerson, C.M.** "Apartheid, Decentralization and Spatial Industrial Change." In *Living Under Apartheid: Aspects of Urbanization and Social Change in South Africa*, D.M. Smith, ed. New York: Allen & Unwin, 1982, 47-63.

6255 **Ryan, Patrick J.** "Islam and Politics in West Africa: Minority and Majority Models." *The Muslim World*, 77, No. 1 (January, 1987), 1-15.

6256 **Sabbagh, M. Ernest.** "Some Geographical Characteristics of a Plural Society: Apartheid in South Africa." *Geographical Review*, 58, No. 1 (January, 1968), 1-28.

6257 **Sanda, A.O.** "Ethnic Interests and Political Fragmentation in Nigeria: 1950-1976." *Nigerian Behavioural Sciences Journal*, 2, Nos. 1 and 2 (1979), 53-68.

6258 **Schwartz, Walter.** "Tribialism and Politics in Nigeria." *The World Today*, 22, No. 11 (November, 1966), 460-467.

6259 **Scott, P.** "Cape Town: A Multi-Racial City." *Geographical Journal*, 121, No. 2 (June, 1955), 149-157.

6260 **Sisk, Timothy D.** "White Politics in South Africa: Polarization Under Pressure." *Africa Today,* 36, No. 1 (1989), 29-39.

6261 **Smith, David M.** "Conflict in South African Cities." *Geography*, 27, Part 2, No. 315 (April, 1987), 153-158.

6262 **Sundiata, Ibrahim K.** "The Roots of African Despotism: The Question of Political Culture." *The African Studies Review*, 31, No. 1 (April, 1988), 9-32.

6263 **Tripp, Aili Mari.** "Gender, Political Participation and the Transformation of Associational Life in Uganda and Tanzania." *African Studies Review* [Atlanta], 37, No. 1 (April, 1994), 107-131.

6264 **Watt, W.M.** "The Political Relevance of Islam in East Africa." *International Affairs*, 42, No. 1 (January, 1966), 35-44.

6265 **Wellings, Rand McCarthy J.J.** "Whither Southern African Human Geography?" *Area*, 15, No. 4 (December, 1983), 337-345.

6266 **Wollheim, O.D.** "The Suicide of Group Areas." *Africa South*, 4, No. 3 (April-June, 1960), 57-62.

AMERICAS

Books

6267 **Adjei-Barwuah, Barfour.** *Socio-Economic Regions in the Louisville Ghetto.* Bloomington: Indiana University, Ph.D., 1972.

6268 **Allen, Harold B.** *The Linguistic Atlas of the Upper Midwest.* Minneapolis: University of Minnesota Press, 1973.

6269 **Allen, James Paul.** *Catholics in Maine: A Social Geography.* Syracuse, New York: Syracuse University, Ph.D., 1970.

6270 **America's Watch Committee.** *Peru Under Fire: Human Rights Since the Return to Democracy.* New Haven: Yale University Press, 1992.

6271 **Bahadur Singh, I.J.,** ed. *Indians in the Caribbeans.* New Delhi: Sterling, 1987.

6272 **Ballas, Donald Joseph.** *A Cultural Geography of Todd Country, South Dakota, and the Rosebud Sioux Indian Reservation.* Lincoln: University of Nebraska, Ph.D., 1970.

6273 **Brown, Donald Andrew.** *Socio-Cultural Patterning on the Lower Great Lakes Frontiers of New France.* Toronto, Ontario, Canada: University of Toronto, Ph.D., 1985.

6274 **Brown, William Henry, Jr.** *Class Aspects of Residential Development and Choice in the Oakland Black Community.* Berkeley: University of California, Ph.D., 1970.

6275 **Cartwright, D.G.** *Language Zones in Canada.* Ottawa: Bilingual Districts Advisory Board, 1976.

6276 **Castelli, Joseph Roy.** *Basques in the Western United States: A Functional Approach to Determination of Cultural Presence in the Geographic Landscape.* Boulder: University of Colorado, Ph.D., 1970.

6277 **Coppock, Henry Aaron.** *Interactions Between Russians and Native Americans in Alaska, 1741-1840.* East Lansing: Michigan State University, Ph.D., 1970.

6278 **Darden, Joe Turner.** *The Spatial Dynamics of Residential Segregation of Afro-Americans in Pittsburgh.* Pittsburg, Pennsylvania: University of Pittsburgh, Ph.D., 1972.

6279 **Deskins, Donald Richard.** *Residential Mobility of Negro Occupational Groups in Detroit 1837-1965.* Ann Arbor: University of Michigan, Ph.D., 1971.

6280 **Despres, L.A.** *Cultural Pluralism and Nationalist Politics in British Guiana.* Chicago: Rand McNally, 1967.

6281 **Detro, Randall Augustus.** *Generic Terms in the Place Names of Louisiana, An Index to the Cultural Landscape.* Baton Rouge: Louisiana State University and Agricultural and Mechanical College, Ph.D., 1970.

6282 **Elazar, Daniel J.** *The American Mosaic: The Impact of Space, Time, and Culture on American Politics.* Boulder: Westview Press, 1994.

6283 **England, R.E.** *The Planning and Development Process in Indian Reserve Communities.* Waterloo, Ontario, Canada: University of Waterloo, Ph.D., 1970.

6284 **Fimian, Charles.** *The Effects of Religion on Abortion Policy: A Study of Voting Behaviour in the U.S. Congress, 1976-1980 (Constituency; United States).* Tempe: Arizona State University, Ph.D., 1983.

6285 **Gaustad, Edwin S.** *Historical Atlas of Religion in America.* New York: Harper & Row, 1962.

6286 **Genovese, E.D.** *From Rebellion to Revolution: Afro-American Slave Revolts in the Making of the New World.* New York: Vintage, 1981.

6287 **Graff, Henry F.,** and **Krout, John A.** *The Adventure of the American People.* Chicago: Rand McNally, 1968

6288 **Hallowell, A.I.** *The Blacklash of the Frontier: The Impact of the Indian on American Culture.* Washington, D.C.: Annual Report of the Smithsonian Institution for the year ended June 30, 1959, 447-472.

6289 **Hamelin, Louis-Edmond** and **Colette**. *Quelques materiaux de sociologie religieuse canadienne*. Montreal: Bibliotheque Generale et Canadienne de Sociologie Religieuse, 1956.

6290 **Harris, Keith Donald**. *An Analysis of Inter-Ethnic Variations in Commercial Land-Use in Los Angeles*. Los Angeles: University of California, Ph.D., 1969.

6291 **Hauk, Mary Ursula**. *Changing Patterns of Catholic Population in Eastern United States (1790-1950)*. Worcester, Massachusetts: Clark University, Ph.D., 1958.

6292 **Heydenreich, Titus**, ed. *Chile: Geschichte, Wirtschaftr und Kultur der Gegenwart*. Frankfurt am Main: Vervuert Verlag, 1990.

6293 **Hodson, Dean R.** *The Origin of Non-Morman Settlements in Utah: 1847-1896*. East Lansing: Michigan State University, Ph.D., 1971.

6294 **Hopple, Lee Charles**. *Spatial Development and Internal Spatial Organization of the Southeastern Pennsylvania Plain Dutch Community*. University Park: Pennsylvania State University, Ph.D., 1971.

6295 **House, J.W.** *Frontier on the Rio Grande: A Political Geography of Development and Social Deprivation*. Oxford: Clarendon Press, 1982.

6296 **Innis, Donald K.** *The Human Ecology of Jamaica*. Berkeley: University of California, Ph.D., 1958.

6297 **Johnson, Hugh Grayson**. *The American Schools in the Republic of Turkey, 1923-1933: A Case Study of Missionary Problems in International Relations*. Washington, D.C.: American University, Ph.D., 1975.

6298 **Joy, R.** *Canada's Official Language Minorities*. Montreal: C.D. Howe Institute, 1971.

6299 **Kaplan, Amy**, and **Pease, Donald E.**, eds. *Cultures of United States Imperialism*. Durham: Duke University Press, 1993.

6300 **King, William M.** *Blacks, Crime, and Criminal Justice: An Introductory Bibliography*. Monticello, Illinois: Council of Planning Librarians, Exchange Bibliography No. 570, 1974.

6301 **Knuth, Clarence Paul Edward**. *Early Immigration and Current Residential Patterns of Negroes in Southwestern Michigan*. Ann Arbor: University of Michigan, Ph.D., 1969.

6302 **Kuntz, Leonard Irvin**. *The Changing Pattern of the Distribution of the Jewish Population of Pittsburgh from Earliest Settlement to 1963*. Baton Rouge: Louisiana State University and Agricultural and Mechanical College, Ph.D., 1970.

6303 **Kwiat, Joseph J.**, and **Turpie, Mary S.** *Stadies in American Culture: Dominant Ideas and Images*. Minneapolis: University of Minnesota Press, 1960.

6304 **Lambert, Jacques**. *Latin America: Social Structure and Political Institutions*. Tr. by Helen Katel. Berkeley: University of California Press, 1967.

6305 **Levine, Daniel H.**, ed. *Constructing Culture and Power in Latin America*. Ann Arbor: University of Michigan Press, 1993.

6306 **Lewis, Lawrence Thomas**. *Some Migration Models: Their Applicability to Negro Urban Migration*. Worchester, Massachusetts: Clark University, Ph.D., 1971.

6307 **Lieberson, S.** *Language and Ethnic Relations in Canada*. New York: John Wiley & Sons, 1970.

6308 **Lowry, Nelson**. *The Mormon Village*. Salt Lake City: University of Utah Press, 1952.

6309 **Marsden, Michael Thomas**. *A Selected Annotated Edition of Henry Rowe School-Craft's 'Personal Memoirs of a Residence of Thirty Years with the Indian Tribes on the American Frontiers'."* Bowling Green, Ohio: Bowling Green State University, Ph.D., 1972.

6310 **McGlynn, Edward James**. *The Effects of Ethnicity on Presidential Voting*. Ithaca, New York: Cornell University, Ph.D., 1974.

6311 **Mencken, H.L.** *The American Language: An Inquiry into the Development of English in the United States*. New York: Knopf, 1936.

6312 **Messenger, Lewis Clement, Jr.** *Excavations at Guarabuqui, El Cajon, Honduras: Frontiers, Culture Areas, and the Southern Mesoamerican Periphery*. Minneapolis: University of Minnesota, Ph.D., 1984.

6313 **Meyer, David Ralph**. *Spatial Variations of Black Households in Cities*. Chicago, Illinois: University of Chicago, Ph.D., 1971.

6314 **Meyer, Douglas Kermit**. *The Changing Negro Residential Patterns in Lansing, Michigan, 1850-1969*. East Lansing: Michigan State University, Ph.D., 1970.

6315 **Myers, Sarah Kerr**. *Language Shift Among Migrants to Lima, Peru*. Chicago, Illinois: University of Chicago, Ph.D., 1972.

6316 **Minshall, Charles William**. *A Model of Residential Site Selection: The Jewish Population of Columbus, Ohio*. Columbus: Ohio State University, Ph.D., 1971.

6317 **Nardone, Richard Morton.** *Church Elections in Theory and Practice: A Study of Canonical Legislation in the Fourth-Century and Fifth-Century.* Toronto, Ontario, Canada: University of St. Michael's College, Ph.D., 1972.

6318 **Petersen, Albert Jepmond, Jr.** *German-Russian Catholic Colonization in Western Kansas: A Settlement Geography.* Baton Rouge: Louisiana State University and Agricultural and Mechanical College, Ph.D., 1970.

6319 **Radcliffe, Sarah A., and Westwood, Sallie,** eds. *Viva Women and Popular Protest in Latin America.* London: Routledge, 1993.

6320 **Raimundo, Jacques.** *A lingua portuguesa no Brasil: Expansao, penetracao, unidade e estado atual.* Rio de Janeiro: Departamento de Imprensa Nacional, 1941.

6321 **Rauch, Dolores.** *The Changing Status of Urban Catholic Parochial Schools: An Explanatory Model Illustrating Demand for Catholic Elementary Education in Milwaukee County.* Milwaukee: University of Wisconsin, Ph.D., 1971.

6322 **Rehder, John Burkhardt.** *Sugar Plantation Settlements of Southern Louisiana: A Cultural Geography.* Baton Rouge: Louisiana State University and Agricultural and Mechanical College, Ph.D., 1971.

6323 **Sante, Molefi, and Mattson, Mark.** *The Historical and Cultural Atlas of the African Americans.* New York: Macmillan, 1990.

6324 **Sherman, C.B.** *The Jew Within American Society.* Detroit, Michigan: Wayne State University Press, 1961.

6325 **Siegfried, Andre.** *Le Canada, les deux races. Problemes politiques contemporains.* Paris: Armand Colin, 1906.

6326 **Siegfried, Andre.** *The Race Question in Canada.* Toronto: McLelland and Stewart, 1966.

6327 **Sklare, Marshall.** *The Jews: Social Patterns of an American Group.* New York: The Free Press of Glencoe, 1958.

6328 **Smith, David M.** *The Geography of Social Well-Being in the United States.* New York: McGraw-Hill, 1973.

6329 **Smith, Peter Craig.** *Negro Hamlets and Gentlemen Farms: A Dichotomous Rural Settlement Pattern in Kentucky's Bwegrass Region.* Lexington: University of Kentucky, Ph.D., 1972.

6330 **Swan, Michael.** *British Guiana: Land of the Six Peoples.* London: Her Majesty's Stationery Office, 1957.

6331 **Tatum, Charles Edward.** *The Christian Methodist Episcopal Church, with Emphasis on Negroes in Texas, 1870-1970: A Study in Historical-Cultural Geography.* East Lansing: Michigan State University, Ph.D., 1971.

6332 **Thompson, Bryan.** *Settlement Ties as Determinants of Immigrant Settlement in Urban Areas: A Case Study of the Growth of an Italian Neighborhood in Worcester, Massachusetts, 1875-1922.* Worchester, Massachusetts: Clark University, Ph.D., 1971.

6333 **Thompson, J.E.S.** *The Rise and Fall of Maya Civilization.* Norman: University of Oklahoma Press, 1954.

6334 **Tweedie, Stephen William.** *The Geography of Religious Group in Ohio, Pennsylvania, and New York: Persistence and Change, 1890-1965.* Syracuse, New York: Syracuse University, Ph.D., 1969.

6335 **Vaillant, G.C.** *The Aztecs of Mexico.* New York: Doubleday, 1950.

6336 **Villeneuve, Paul Yvon.** *The Spatial Adjustment of Ethnic Minorities in the Urban Environment.* Seattle: University of Washington, Ph.D., 1971.

6337 **Wagner, Melinda Bollar.** *Metaphysics in Midwestern America: Spiritual Frontiers Fellowship.* Ann Arbor: University of Michigan, Ph.D., 1977.

6338 **Ware, Caroline F.** *The Cultural Approach to History.* New York City: Columbia University Press, 1940.

6339 **Wilhelm, Eugene Joseph Jr.** *Folk Geography of the Blue Ridge Mountains.* College Station: Texas A & M University, Ph.D., 1971.

6340 **Wright, Don W.** *The Utes: A Study in Political Geography from Aboriginal Times to Reservations.* Provo, Utah: Brigham Young University, M.A., 1983.

6341 **Zelinsky, Wilbur.** *The Cultural Geography of the United States.* Englewood Cliffs, New Jersey: Prentice-Hall, 1973.

Journals

6342 **Allen, Tip H. Jr.** "Mississippi Nationalism in the Desegregation Crisis of September 1962." *Canadian Review of Studies in Nationalism,* 14, No. 1 (Spring, 1987), 49-63.

6343 **Anderson, Leslie.** "Alternative Action in Costa Rica: Peasants as Positive Participants." *Journal of Latin American Studies,* 22, Part 1 (February, 1990), 89-113.

6344 **Augelli, John P.** "The Rimland-Mainland Concept of Culture Areas in Middle America." *Annals of the Association of American Geographers*, 52, No. 2 (June, 1962), 119-129.

6345 **Augelli, John P, and Taylor, Harry W.** "Race and Population Patterns in Trinidad." *Annals of the Association of American Geographers*, 50 (June, 1960), 123-138.

6346 **Blakeslee, George H.** "Hawaii: Racial Problem and Naval Base." *Foreign Affairs*, 17, No. 1 (October, 1938), 90-99.

6347 **Brainerd, G.W.** "The Maya Civilization." *Masterkey*, 27, No. 3 (1953), 83-96 and 27, No. 4 (1953), 128-133.

6348 **Cartwright, D.G.** "Language Policy and the Political Organization of Territory: A Canadian Dilemma." *The Canadian Geographer* (Toronto), 25, No. 3 (Fall, 1981), 205-224.

6349 **Cartwright, D.G., and Williams, C.H.** "Bilingual Districts as an Instrument in Canadian Language Policy." *Transactions of the Institute of British Geographers*, 17, No. 4 (1982), 474-493.

6350 **Chouinard, Vera.** "Review Essay, Making Sense of Social Movements: The Canadian Experience." *Political Geography Quarterly*, 9, No. 2 (April, 1990), 197-202.

6351 **Collin-Delavaud, Claude.** "Perou, la Desagregation?" *Herodote* [Paris], No. 57 (Avril-Juin, 1990), 121-159.

6352 **Cozzetto, Don.** "Financing Aboriginal Government: The Case of Canada's Eastern Arctic." *American Indian Culture and Research Journal* [Los Angeles], 16, No. 1 (1992), 87-109.

6353 **Davis, Diane E.** "Failed Democratic Reform in Contemporary Mexico: From Social Movements to the State and Back Again." *Journal of Latin American Studies* [Cambridge], 26, Part 2 (May, 1994), 375-408.

6354 **Fester, Gustav.** "Sudamerikanishe Volks-und Rassenfragen." *Zeitschrift fur Geopolitik*, 16, No. 8-9 (August-September, 1939), 588-595.

6355 **Galloway, J.H.** "Human Geography in Brazil During the 1970's: Debates and Research." *Luso-Brazilian Review*, 19, No. 1 (Summer, 1982), 1-21.

6356 **Gammage, Judie K.** "Pressure Group Techniques: The Texas Equal Rights Amendment." *Great Plains Journal*, 16, No. 1 (Fall, 1976), 45-65.

6357 **Gillin, John.** "National and Regional Cultural Values in the United States." *Social Forces*, 34, No. 2 (December, 1955), 107-113.

6358 **Harris, Richard.** "A Political Chameleon: Class Segregation in Kingston, Ontario, 1961-1976." *Annals of the Association of American Geographers*, 74, No. 3 (September, 1984), 454-476.

6359 **Hart, John Fraser.** "The Changing Distribution of the American Negro." *Annals of the Association of American Geographers*, 50, No. 3 (September, 1960), 242-266.

6360 **Hartshorne, Richard.** "Racial Maps of the United States." *Geographical Review*, 28, No. 2, (April, 1938), 276-288.

6361 **Hofmeister, Burkhard.** "Indianerreservationen in den U.S.A. Territoriale Entwicklung und Wirtschaftliche Eignung." *Geographische Rundschau Braunschweig*, 28, No. 12 (December, 1976), 507-578.

6362 **Huntington, Ellsworth.** "The Relation of Health to Racial Capacity: The Example of Mexico." *Geographical Review*, 11, No. 2 (April, 1921), 243-264.

6363 **Hymes, Dell.** "Pidginization and Creolization of Languages: Their Social Contexts." *Social Science Research Council Items*, 22, No. 2 (June, 1968), 13-18.

6364 **Jackson, Peter.** "Race, Ethnicity and Politics in Chicago." *The Bloomsbury Geographer*, 12 (1984), 34-38.

6365 **Justus, Joyce Bennett.** "Language and National Integration: The Jamaican Case." *Ethnology*, 17, No. 1 (January, 1978), 39-51.

6366 **Kaplan, David H.** "Population and Politics in a Plural Society: The Changing Geography of Canada's Linguistic Groups." *Annals of the Association of American Geographers*, 84, No. 1 (March, 1994), 48-67.

6367 **Keiser, Richard A.** "Explaining African-American Political Empowerment: Windy City Politics from 1900 to 1983." *Urban Affairs Quarterly* [Thousand Oaks], 29, No. 1 (September, 1993), 84-116.

6368 **Laponce, J.A.** "The City Center as Conflictual Space in the Bilingual City: The Case of Montreal." In *Center and Periphery*, J. Gottman, ed. Beverly Hills, California: Sage Publications, 1980, 149-162.

6369 **Laponce, J.A.** "The French Language in Canada: Tensions Between Geography and Politics." *Political Geography Quarterly*, 3, No. 2 (April, 1984), 91-104.

6370 **Lazerwitz, Bernard.** "A Comparison of Major United States Religious Groups." *Journal of the American Statistical Association*, 56, No. 295 (September, 1961), 568-579.

6371 **Lowenthal, David.** "Population Contrasts in the Guianas." *Geographical Review*, 50, No. 1 (January, 1960), 41-58.

6372 **Marable, M.** "Black Power in Chicago: An Historical Overview of Class Stratification and Electoral Politics in a Black Urban Community." *Review of Radical Political Economics*, 17, No. 3 (1985), 157-182.

6373 **Masland, John W.** "Missionary Influence Upon American Far Eastern Policy." *The Pacific Historical Review*, 10, No. 3 (September, 1941), 279-296.

6374 **McGuire, Thomas R.** "Operations on the Concept of Sovereignty: A Case Study of Indian Decision-Making." *Urban Anthropology and Studies of Cultural Systems and World Economic Development*, 17, No. 1 (Spring, 1988), 75-86.

6375 **Meinig, Donald W.** "The Mormon Culture Region: Strategies and Patterns in the Geography of the American West 1847-1964." *Annals of the Association of American Geographers*, 55, No. 2 (June, 1965), 191-220.

6376 **Monroy, Douglas.** "Like Swallows at the Old Mission: Mexicans and the Racial Politics of Growth in Los Angeles in the Interwar Period." *The Western Historical Quarterly*, 14, No. 4 (October, 1983), 435-458.

6377 **Moore, John II.** "The Muskoke National Question in Oklahoma." *Science & Society*, 52, No. 2 (Summer, 1988), 163-190.

6378 **Morisett, Jean.** "The Aboriginal Nation: The Northern Challenge and the Construction of Canadian Unity." *Canadian Review of Studies in Nationalism*, 7, No. 2 (Autumn, 1980), 237-249.

6379 **Munro, K.** "Official Bilingualism in Alberta." *Prarie Forum*, 12, No. 1 (1987), 37-47.

6380 **Munroe, Trevor.** "The Impact of the Church on the Political Culture of the Caribbean: The Case of Jamaica." *Caribbean Quarterly* [Kingston], 37, No. 1 (March, 1991), 83-97.

6381 **Nostrand, Richard L.** "The Hispanic-American Borderland: Delimitation of an American Culture Region." *Annals of the Association of American Geographers*, 60, No. 4 (December, 1970), 638-661.

6382 **Pearlman, K.** "The Closing Door: The Supreme Court and Residential Segregation." *Journal, American Institute of Planners*, 44, No. 2 (March, 1976), 160-169.

6383 **Russell, John C.** "Racial Groups in the New Mexico Legislature." *The Annals of the American Academy of Political and Social Science*, 195 (January, 1938), 62-71.

6384 **Ryan, C.** "The French-Canadian Dilemma." *Foreign Affairs*, 43, No. 3 (April, 1965), 462-474.

6385 **Schmieder, Oscar.** "The Brazilian Culture Hearth." *University of California Publications in Geography*, 3 (1928), 159-198.

6386 **Shelley, Fred M.** "Geography, Territory, and Ethnicity: Current Perspectives from Political Geography." *Urban Geography* [Columbia, MD], 15, No. 2 (March, 1994), 189-200.

6387 **Stomp, Roger W.** "Toward a Geography of American Civil Religion." *Journal of Cultural Geography*, 5, No. 2 (Spring/Summer, 1985), 87-95.

6388 **Sumler, D.E.** "Subcultural Persistence and Political Clevage in the Third French Republic." *Comparative Studies in Society and History*, 19, No. 4 (1977), 431-453.

6389 **Taylor, Donald M., and Sigal, Ronald J.** "Defining 'Quebecois': The Role of Ethnic Heritage, Language, and Political Orientation." *Etudes Ethniques au Canada*, 14, No. 2 (1982), 59-70.

6390 **Troll, Carol.** "Die geographischen Grundlagen der Andinen Kulturen und des inkareiches." *Ibero-Amerikanishes Archiv*, 5, No. 5 (1931), 1-37.

6391 **Termer, von Franz.** "Die Ethnischen Grundlagen der Politischen Geographie von Mittelamerika." *Zeitschrift due Gesellschaft fur Erdkunde zu Berlin*, 34 (September, 1943), 148-171.

6392 **Valencia, Richard R.** "The School Closure Issue and the Chicano Community." *Urban Review*, 12, No. 1 (Spring, 1980), 5-21.

6393 **Willems, Emilio.** "Protestantism as a Factor in Culture Change in Brazil." *Economic Development and Culture Change*, 3, No. 4 (July, 1955), 321-333.

6394 **Zelinsky, Wilbur.** "An Approach to the Religious Geography of the United States. *Annals of the Association of American Geographers*, 51, No. 1 (March, 1961), 139-144.

ASIA

Books

6395 **Almong, Shmuel.** *Zionism and History: The Rise of a New Jewish Consciousness.* Translated from Hebrew by Ina Freedman. New York: St. Martin's Press, 1987.

6396 **Al Rasheed, Madawi.** *Politics in an KArabian Oasis: The Rashidi Tribal Dynasty.* London: I. B. Tauris & Co., 1991.

6397 **American Zionist Emergency Council.** *The Jewish Case; The Place of Palestine in the Solution of the Jewish Question.* New York: American Zionist Emergency Council, 1945.

6398 **Arjomand, Said Amir.** *The Turban for the Crown: The Islamic Revolution in Iran.* New York: Oxford University Press, 1988.

6399 **Atiyah, E.** *The Arabs.* London: Penguin, 1955.

6400 **Banu, Zenab.** *Politics of Communalism: A Politico-Historical Analysis of Communal Riots in Post-Independence India with Special Reference to the Gujarat and Rajasthan Riots.* Bombay: Popular, 1989.

6401 **Banuazizi, Ali, and Weiner, Myron, eds.** *The State, Religion, and Ethnic Politics: Afghanistan, Iran, and Pakistan.* Syracuse, New York: Syracuse University Press, 1986.

6402 **Bhalla, G.S., and Others.** *India: Nation-State and Communalism (To Honor Dr. Nandlal Gupta).* New Delhi: Patriot, 1989.

6403 **Bhardwaj, Surinder Mohan.** *Hindu Palaces of Pilgrimage in India: A Study in Cultural Geography.* Minneapolis: University of Minnesota, Ph.D., 1970.

6404 **Blum, Yehuda Z.** *For Zion's Sake.* New York: Cornwall Books, 1987.

6405 **Brown, David.** *The State and Ethnic Politics in Southeast Asia.* London: Routledge Politics in Asia Series, 1994.

6406 **Caraudy, R.** *The Case of Israel: A Study of Political Zionism.* Shorouk International, 1983.

6407 **Chatterji, Suniti K.** *Languages and the Linguistic Problem.* London: Oxford University Press, 1943.

6408 **Cohen, Raymond.** *Culture and Conflict in Egyptian-Israeli Relations: A Dialogue of the Deaf.* Bloomington: Indiana University Press, 1990.

6409 **Debysingh, Molly.** *Poultry and Cultural Distributions in India.* Syracuse, New York: Syracuse University, Ph.D., 1970.

6410 **Doeppers, Daniel Frederick.** *Ethnicity and Class in the Structure of Philippine Cities.* Syracuse, New York: Syracuse University, Ph.D., 1972.

6411 **Fredholm, Michael.** *Burma: Ethnicity and Insurgency.* Westport: Praeger Publishers, 1993.

6412 **Gandhi, Mohandas Karamchand.** *Linguistic Provinces.* Ahmedabad: Navajivan, 1945.

6413 **Hardgrave, Robert L., Jr.** *The Dravidian Movement.* Bombay: Bopular Prakashan, 1965.

6414 **Heyworth-Dunne, James.** *Pakistan, the Birth of a New Muslim State.* Cairo: Renaissance Bookshop, 1952.

6415 **Holtom, D.C.** *Modern Japan and Shinto Nationalism: A Study of Present-Day Trends in Japanese Religions.* Chicago, Illinois: University of Chicago Press, 1947.

6416 **Horowitz, Dan, and Lissak, M.** *The Origins of the Israeli Polity-The Political System of the Jewish Community in Palestine Under the Mandate.* Tel-Aviv: Am-ved, 1977.

6417 **Hunter, Guy.** *South-East Asia: Race, Culture and Nation.* London: Institute of Race Relations, 1966.

6418 **Johnson, Edward William, II.** *Comparative Approaches to the Study of the Hindu Communal Political Parties in Contemporary India: Some Limitations in the Applicability of (1) Systems Analysis and (2) Political Modernization and Development Theory.* New York City: New York University, Ph.D., 1970.

6419 **Kang, T.D., ed.** *Nationalism and the Crises of Ethnic Minorities in Asia.* Westport, Connecticut: Greenwood Press, 1979.

6420 **Khan, Mohammed H.** *Muslims in India After 1947: A Study in Political Geography.* Worcester, Massachusetts: Clark University, Ph.D., 1957.

6421 **Kimmerling, Baruch.** *Zionism and Territory: The Socio-Territorial Dimensions of Zionist Politics.* Berkely: University of California Institute of International Studies, Research Series No. 51, 1983.

6422 **Kinnane, Derk.** *The Kurds and Kurdistan.* London: Oxford University Press, 1964.

6423 **Lauterpacht, E.** *Jerusalem and the Holy Places.* London: Anglo-Israel Association, 1968.

6424 **Li, Peter; Mark, Steven; and Li, Marjorie H.,** eds. *Culture and Politics in China: An Anatomy of Tiananmen Square.* New Brunswick: Transaction Publishers, 1991.

6425 **Little, David.** *Sri Lanka: The Invention of Enmity.* Washington, D.C.: United States Institute of Peace Press, 1994.

6426 **Manogaran, Chelvadurai.** *Ethnic Conflict and Reconciliation in Sri Lanka.* Honolulu: University of Hawaii Press, 1987.

6427 **Manogaran, Chelvadurai, and Burger, Bryan Pfaffen,** eds. *Sri Lankan Tamils: Ethnicity and Identity.* Boulder, Colorado: Westsview Press, 1994.

6428 **Menashri, David,** ed. *The Iranian Revolution and the Muslim World.* Boulder: Westview Press, 1990.

6429 **Miller, J.** *Linguistic Regionalism in the Philippines: Past and Prospect.* Syracuse, New York: Syracuse University, Department of Geography, Discussion Paper Series, No. 52, 1979.

6430 **Morris, James.** *Islam Inflamed; A Middle East Picture.* New York: Pantheon, 1957.

6431 **Nisan, Mordechai.** *Toward a New Israel: The Jewish State and the Arab Question.* New York: AMS Press, 1992.

6432 **Nooruzzaman, A.H.M.** *Rise of the Muslim Middle Class as a Political Factor in India and Pakistan, 1858-1947.* London: School of Oriental and African Studies, University of London, Ph.D., 1965.

6433 **Oren, Stephen A.** *Religious Groups as Political Organizations: A Comparative Analysis of Three Indian States.* New York City: Columbia University, Ph.D., 1969.

6434 **Pakistan Embassy.** *Map of Jammu and Kashmir State and Gilgit Agency (Showing) Percentage of Muslim Population by District.* Washington, D.C.: Pakistan Embassy, 1963.

6435 **Parfitt, Tudar.** *The Jews in Palestine, 1880-1882.* Woodbridge, England: The Boydell Press, 1987.

6436 **Parvathamma, C.** *Politics and Religion in a Mysore Village.* Manchester: University of Manchester, Ph.D., 1962.

6437 **Petrov, V.P.** *Mongolia: A Profile. The People, History, Language, Religion, Literature.* New York: Praeger, 1970.

6438 **Phadnis, Urmila.** *Ethnicity and Nation-Building in South Asia.* New Delhi: Sage Publications, 1990.

6439 **Richter, William L.** *The Politics of Language in India.* Chicago, Illinois: University of Chicago, Ph.D., 1968.

6440 **Tapper, Richard,** ed. *The Conflict of Tribe and State in Iran and Afghanistan.* London: Croom Helm, 1983.

6441 **West, Richard.** *Thailand, the Last Domino: Cultural and Political Travels.* London: Michael Joseph, 1991.

6442 **Wheeler, Geoffrey.** *Racial Problems in Soviet Muslim Asia.* London: Oxford University Press, 1962.

6443 **Zaidi, Iqtidar H.** *Muslims in the Philippines: A Study of Their Attitude and Their Effect on Philippine Politics.* Manila: University of the Philippines, M.A., 1956.

Journals

6444 **Ahmed, Akbar S.** "Tribes and States in Central and South Asia." *Asian Affairs*, 11 (Old Series Vol. 67), Part 2 (June, 1980), 152-168.

6445 **Ahmed, A.U.D.** "A Geographer's Approach Towards the Problem of National Language of Pakistan." *Pakistan Geographical Review*, 10, No. 1 (January, 1955), 17-24.

6446 **Al-Yassini, Ayman.** "Islamic Revival and National Development in the Arab World." *Journal of Asian and African Studies*, 21, Nos. 1-2 (January/April, 1986), 104-121.

6447 **Amani, K.Z.** "A Geographical View of Hindi as the Official Language of India." *The National Geographical Journal of India*, 27, Pts. 2 and 3 (June-September, 1971), 120-126.

6448 **Arnold, Anthony.** "The Stony Path to Afghan Socialism: Problems of Sovietization in an Alpine Moslim Society." *Orbis*, 29, No. 1 (Spring, 1985), 40-57.

6449 **Ashkenazi, Touvia.** "Kurdistan for the Kurds?" *Asia and the Americas*, 46, No. 4 (April, 1946), 164-167.

6450 **Barthakur, M.** "Socio-Political Uprising in the North East--A Diagnostic Appraisal." *The Journal of North East India Geographical Society,* 12, Nos. 1 and 2 (1980), 1-7.

6451 **Beals, Alan R.** "Cleavage and Internal Conflict: An Example from India." *Journal of Conflict Resolution*, 5, No. 1 (March, 1961), 27-34.

6452 **Beckingham, C.F.** "The Cypriot Turks." *Royal Central Asian Journal*, 43, Part II (April, 1956), 126-130.

6453 **Brothwick, Bruce M.** "Religion and Politics in Israel and Egypt." *The Middle East Journal*, 33, No. 2 (Spring, 1979), 145-163.

6454 **Brown, Norman.** "The Santity of the Cow in Hinduism" *Bulletin of the Institute of Traditional Cultures*, 28 (1957), 29-41.

6455 **Brush, John E.** "The Distribution of Religious Communities in India." *Annals of the Association of American Geographers*, 39, No. 2 (June, 1949), 81-98.

6456 **Carde, O.** "Pathans at the Crossroads." *Eastern World*, 15, No. 12 (December, 1961), 12-13.

6457 **Chowdhury, Ila Pal.** "What I Saw in the Border Areas of West Bengal." *Modern Review*, 118, No. 8 (August, 1965), 143-145.

6458 **Cohen, Saul B.** "The City in the Zionist Ideology." *The Jerusalem Quarterly*, 4 (1977), 126-44.

6459 **Das Gupta, A.K.** "The Language Problem." *Man in India*, 48, No. 1 (January-March, 1968), 18-28.

6460 **Drysdale, Alasdair Duncan.** "Ethnicity in the Syrian Officer Corps: A Conceptualization." *Civilizations*, 29 (1979), 359-374.

6461 **Drysdale, Alasdair Duncan.** "The Syrian Political Elite, 1966-1976: A Spatial and Social Analysis." *Middle Eastern Studies*, 17 (1981), 3-30.

6462 **Duffy, Terence.** "Toward a Culture of Human Rights in Cambodia." *Human Rights Quarterly* [Baltimore], 16, No. 1 (February, 1994), 82-104.

6463 **Elphinston, W.G.** "The Future of the Bedouin of Northern Arabia." *International Affairs*, 21, No. 3 (July, 1945), 370-375.

6464 **Elphinston, W.G.** "The Kurdish Question." *International Affairs*, 22, No. 1 (January, 1946), 91-103.

6465 **Falah, Ghazi.** "Israeli 'Judaization' Policy in Gaililee and its Impact on Local Arab Urbanization." *Political Geography Quarterly*, 8, No. 3 (July, 1989), 229-253.

6466 **Federspiel, Howard M.** "Muslim Intellectuals and Indonesia's National Development." *Asian Survey* [Berkeley], 31, No. 3 (March, 1991), 232-246.

6467 **Freiherr Von Eickstedt, Egon.** "Der Motor der Ostasiatischen Volkerdynamik." *Zeitschrift fur Geopolitik*, Jahrgang 24, Heft 1 (January, 1953), 1-69.

6468 **Freiherr Von Eickstedt, Egon.** "Der Zusammenschluss der Volker Chinas." *Zeitschrift fur Geopolitik*, Jahrgang 24, Heft 10 (October, 1953), 530-536.

6469 **Giannini, Amedeo.** "Il Curdistan e la questione curda." *L'Universo*, Anno 30, N. 6 (Novembre-Dicembre, 1950), 791-798.

6470 **Goyal, O.P.** "Caste and Politics--A Conceptual Framework." *Asian Survey*, 5, No. 10 (October, 1965), 522-525.

6471 **Gupta, Sisir K.** "Moslems in Indian Politics, 1947-60." *Indian Quarterly*, 18, No. 4 (October, 1962), 355-381.

6472 **Hamdani, Abbas.** "Islam and Politics: Egypt, Algeria, and Tunisia." *DOMES: Digest of Middle East Studies*, 3, No. 3 (Summer, 1994), 36-46.

6473 **Hardgrave, Robert L., Jr.** "The Riots of Tamilnad: Problems Prospects of India's Language Crisis." *Asian Survey*, 5, No. 8 (August, 1965), 399-407.

6474 **Hensel, Howard M.** "Soviet Policy Toward the Kurdish Question, 1970-75. *Soviet Union*, 6, No. 1 (1979), 61-80.

6475 **Humphreys, R. Stephen.** "Islam and Political Values in Saudi Arabia, Egypt and Syria." *The Middle East Journal*, 33, No. 1 (Winter, 1979), 1-19.

6476 **Huntington, Ellsworth.** "The Arabian Desert and Human Character." *Journal of Geography*, 10, No. 5 (January, 1912), 169-175.

6477 **Inbar, Efraim.** "War in Jewish Tadition." *The Jerusalem Journal of International Relations*, 9, No. 2 (June, 1987), 83-99.

6478 **Islam, Nasir.** "Islam and National Identity: The Case of Pakistan and Bangladesh." *International Journal of Middle East Studies*, 13, No. 1 (February, 1981), 55-72.

6479 **Kendall, Stephen H.** "The Barangay as Community in the Philippines." *Ekistics*, 41, No. 242 (January, 1976), 15-19.

6480 **Kennedy, Charles H.** "Islamization and Legal Reform in Pakistan, 1979-1989." *Pacific Affairs* [Vancouver], 63, No. 1 (Spring, 1990), 62-77.

6481 **Khan, Rashid Amhad.** "Religion, Race and Arab Nationalism." *International Journal*, 34, No. 3 (Summer, 1979), 353-368.

6482 **Klatt, W.** "Caste, Class and Communism in Kerala." *Asian Affairs*, 59, Pt. 3 (October, 1972), 275-287.

6483 **Kodikara, Shelton U.** "The Continuing Crisis in Sri Lanka: The JVP, the Indian Troops, and Tamil Politics." *Asian Survey*, 29, No. 7 (July, 1989), 716-724.

6484 **Lambert, Richard D.** "Religion, Economics, and Violence in Bengal." *Middle East Journal*, 4, No. 4 (Autumn, 1950), 307-328.

6485 **Latukefu, Sione.** "Noble Traditions and Christian Principles as National Ideology in Papua New Guinea: Do Their Philosophies Compliment or Contradict Each Other." *Pacific Studies*, 11, No. 2 (March, 1988), 83-96.

6486 **Lautensach, Hermann.** "Religion und Landschaft in Korea." *Nippon Zeitschrift fur Japanolgie*, 7 (1942), 204-219.

6487 **Lee, Yong Leng.** "Race, Language, and National Cohesion in Southeast Asia." *Journal of Southeast Asian Studies*, 11, No. 1 (March, 1980), 122-138.

6488 **Liebesny, Herbert J.** "Judicial Systems in the Near and Middle East: Evolutionary Development and Islamic Revival." *The Middle East Journal*, 37, No. 2 (Spring, 1983), 202-217.

6489 **Maillart, Ella.** "Nepal, Meering-Place of Religions." *Geographical Magazine*, 29, No. 6 (October, 1956), 273-288.

6490 **Mandelbaum, David G.** "Hindu-Moslem Conflict in India." *The Middle East Journal*, 1, No. 4 (October, 1947), 369-385.

6491 **Marx, Emanuel.** "Anthropological Studies in a Centralized State: Max Gluckman and the Bernstein Israel Research Project." *The Jewish Journal of Sociology*, 17, No. 2 (December, 1975), 131-150.

6492 **Mattiesen, Heinz.** "'Livland' und 'Kurland'. Der Kampf um eine baltendeutsche Stattsbildung im 16. und 17. Jahrhundert." *Jonsburg*, Jahrg, 3, Heft 1-2 (1939), 114-138.

6493 **Meir, Avinoam.** "Nomads and the State: The Spatial Dynamics of Centrifugal and Centripetal Forces Among the Israeli Negev Bedouin." *Political Geography Quarterly*, 7, No. 3 (July, 1988), 251-27.

6494 **Moghadam, Val.** "Women, Work, and Ideology in the Islamic Republic." *International Journal of Middle East Studies*, 20, No. 2 (May, 1988), 221-243.

6495 **Mukonoweshuro, Eliphas G.** "Containing Political Instability in a Poly-ethnic Society: The Case of Mauritius." *Ethnic and Racial Studies* [London], 14, No. 2 (April, 1991), 199-224.

6496 **Neville, Warwick.** "Singapore: Ethnic Diversity and Its Implications." *Annals of the Association of American Geographers*, 56, No. 2 (June, 1966), 236-253.

6497 **Nikitine, B.** "Probleme kurde." *Politique Etrangere*, 11° annee, No. 3 (Juillet, 1946), 251-262.

6498 **Noble, Allen G., and Efrat, Elisha.** "Geography of the Intifada." *Geographical Review* [New York], 80, No. 3 (July, 1990), 288-307.

6499 "Pakistan and the Tribes: The Legacy of the North-West Frontier." *Round Table*, 38, No. 156 (September, 1949), 329-336.

6500 **Parvin, Manoucher, and Sommer, Maurie.** "Dar Al-Islam: The Evolution of Muslim Territoriality and Its Implications for Conflict Resolution in the Middle East." *International Journal of Middle East Studies*, 11, No. 1 (February, 1980), 1-21.

6501 **Patterson, George N.** "The Naga Problem." *Royal Central Asian Journal*, 50, Pt. 1 (January, 1963), 30-40.

6502 **Pearl, David.** "Bangladesh: Islamic Laws in a Secular State." *The South Asian Review*, 8, No. 1 (October, 1974), 33-41.

6503 **Planbol, Xavier de.** "Geography, Politics, and Nomadism in Anatolia." *International Social Science Journal*, 11, No. 4 (1959), 525-553.

6504 **Rocher, Ludo.** "Les Problemes Linquistiques de l'Inde Contemporaine." *Revue de l'Universite de Bruxelles*, 9 Annee, No. 1 (Octobre-Decembre, 1956), 72-88.

6505 **Roosevelt, Archie, Jr.** "The Kurdish Republic of Mahabad." *The Middle East Journal*, 1, No. 3 (July, 1947), 247-269.

6506 **Roxby, Percy M.** "The Terrain of Early Chinese Civilization." *Geography*, 23, No. 122, Part 4 (December, 1938), 225-236.

6507 **Rudolph, Lloyd I., and Rudolph, Susanne Hoeber.** "The Political Role of India's Caste Associations." *Pacific Affairs*, 33, No. 1 (March, 1960), 5-22.

6508 **Salamone, S.D.** "The Dialectics of Turkish National Identity: Ethnic Boundary Maintenance and State Ideology." *East European Quarterly*, 23, No. 1 (Spring, 1989), 33-61, and 23, No. 2 (Summer, 1989), 225-248.

6509 **Samual, Geoffrey.** "Tibet as a Stateless Society and Some Islamic Parallels." *The Journal of Asian Studies*, 141, No. 2 (February, 1982), 215-229.

6510 Sayeed, Khalid B. "Religion and Nation Building in Pakistan." *Middle East Journal*, 17, No. 3 (Summer, 1963), 279-291.

6511 Scigliano, Robert. "Vietnam: Politics and Religion." *Asian Survey*, 4, No. 1 (January, 1964), 666-673.

6512 Shah, Pradeep J. "Caste and Political Process." *Asian Survey*, 6, No. 9 (September, 1966), 516-522.

6513 Sheen, Vincent. "The People of Ceylon and Their Politics." *Foreign Affairs*, 28, No. 1 (October, 1949), 68-74.

6514 Shiloah, Z. "The Notion of 'Transfer' in Zionist Thinking and Policy." *Native*, 1 (1988), 20-25.

6515 Sivan, Emmanuel. "Sunni Radicalism in the Middle East and the Iranian Revolution." *International Journal of Middle EasT Studies*, 21, No. 1 (February, 1989), 1-30.

6516 Sneath, David. "The Impact of the Cultural Revolution in China on the Mongolians of Inner Mongolia." *Modern Asian Studies* [Cambridge], 28, Part 2 (May, 1994), 409-430.

6517 Suhrke, Astri. "Loyalties and Separatists: The Muslim in Southern Thailand." *Asian Survey*, 17, No. 3 (March, 1977), 237-250.

6518 Symonds, Richard. "State-Making in Pakistan. Is Islam a 'Third Force?' Religion Still Dominates Pakistan. Politics but Other Issues are Emerging as Pakistanis Hammer Out Structure of Their New State." *Far Eastery Survey*, 19, No. 5 (March 8, 1950), 45-50.

6519 Thomson, Curtis N. "Political Identity Among Chinese in Thailand." *The Geographical Review*, 83, No. 4 (October, 1993), 397-409.

6520 Van Willigen, John, and Channa, V. C. "Law, Custom, and Crimes Against Women: The Problem of Dowry Death in India." *Human Organization* [Oklahoma City], 50, No. 4 (Winter, 1991), 369-377.

6521 Walt van Praag, Michael C. van. "Earnest Negotiations: The Only Anser to Growing Unrest in Tibet." *International Relations*, 9, No. 5 (May, 1989), 377-392.

6522 Watson, Vincent C. "Communal Politics in India and United States." *Political Science Review*, 5, No. 29 (October, 1966), 209-229.

6523 Westermann, William Linn. "Kurdish Independence and Russian Expansion." *Foreign Affairs*, 24, No. 4 (July, 1946), 675-686.

6524 Weryho, Jan A. "The Persian Language and Shia

as Nationalist Symbols: A Historical Survey." *Canadian Review of Studies in Nationalism*, 13, No. 1 (Spring, 1986), 49-55.

6525 Wilson, A. Jeyaratnam. "Cultural and Language Rights in the Multi-National Society." *Tamil Culture*, 7, No. 1 (January, 1958), 22-32.

AUSTRALIA, OCEANIA AND ANTARCTICA

Books and Journals

6526 Barrau, J., ed. *Plants and the Migrations of Pacific Peoples*. Honolulu: Bishop Museum Press, 1963.

6527 Carter, G.F. "Movement of People and Ideas Across the Pacific." In *Plants and the Migrations of Pacific Peoples*, J. Barrau, ed. Honolulu: Bishop Museum Press, 1963.

6528 Castigiano, L. *Il Mondo Anglosassone*. Milan: A.P.E., 1960.

6529 Chidell, Fleetwood. *Australia-White or Yellow*. London: Heineman, 1926.

6530 Cleaves, Peter. "Tribal and State-Like Political Formations in New Zealand Maori Society 1750-1900." *The Polynesian Society (Avckland) Journal*, 92, No. 1 (March, 1983), 51-92.

6531 Eisenstadt, S.N. "Religious Organizations and Political Process in Centralized Empires." *Journal of Asian Studies*, 21, No. 3 (May, 1962), 271-294.

6532 Ekblaw, W. Elmer. *The Polar Eskimo: Their Land and Use*. Worcester, Massachusetts: Clark University, Ph.D., 1926.

6533 Hall, Robert A. "Pidgin Languages." *Scientific American*, 200, No. 2 (1959), 124-134.

6534 Halligan, J.R. "Administration of Native Races." *Oceania*, 9, No. 3 (March, 1939), 276-285.

6535 Langhans, M. "Karte der Selbstbestimmungsrechtes der Volker." *Petermann's Mitteilungen*, 72, No. 1 (March, 1929), 1-9.

6536 Lawson, Stephanie. "The Myth of Cultural Homogenity and Its Implications for Chiefly Power and Politics in Fiji." *Comparative Studies in Society and History* [Cambridge, Eng.], 32, No. 4 (October, 1990), 795-821.

6537 **Mercer, D.** "Terra Nullius, Aboriginal Sovereignty and Land Rights in Australia: The Debate Continues." *Political Geography,* 12, No. 4 (July, 1993), 299-318.

6538 **Monk, Janice Jones.** *Socio-Economic Characteristics of Six Aboriginal Communities in Australia: A Comparative Ecological Study.* Urbana: University of Illinois, Ph.D., 1972.

6539 **Premdas, Ralph R.** "Fiji Under a New Political Order: Ethnicity and Indigenous Rights." *Asian Survey* [Berkeley], 31, No. 6 (June, 1991), 540-558.

6540 **Raby, Stewart.** "Aboriginal Territorial Aspirations in Political Geography." *Proceedings of the International Geographical Union Regional Conference.* Palmerston North: New Zealand Geographical Society, 1974, 169-74.

6541 **Sawer, Marian,** and **Simms, Marian.** *A Woman's Place: Women and Politics in Australia.* St. Leonards, Australia: Allen & Unwin, 1993.

6542 **Wilson, Lynn B.** *Speaking to Power: Gender and Politics in the Western Pacific.* New York: Routledge, International Studies of Women and Place, 1995.

6543 **Wright, T.** *New Deal for the Aborigines.* Sidney: Modern Publishers, 1939.

EUROPE

Books

6544 **Battisti, C.** *Il Censimento del 1961 e il bilionuismo nell' Alto Adige.* Firenze: Francolini, 1962.

6545 **Bell, G.** *The Protestants of Ulster.* London: Pluto Press, 1976.

6546 **Boulard, Fernand.** *An Introduction to Religious Sociology.* London: Darton Longman Todd, 1960.

6547 **Chapman, Murray Thomas.** *Population Movement in Tribal Society: The Case of Duidui and Pichahila, British Solomon Islands.* Seattle: University of Washington, Ph.D., 1970.

6548 **Cholvy, Gerard.** *Geographie religieuse de l'Herault contemporain.* Paris: Presses Universitaires de France, 1968.

6549 **Colakovic, Branko Mita.** *Yugoslav Migrations to America.* Minneapolis: University of Minnesota, Ph.D., 1970.

6550 **Clementis, Vladimir.** *The Czechoslovak Magyar Relationship.* (No. 1) First published in print, 1943, in Slovak, under the title "Medzi nami a Madarmi." London: The Central European Observer, 1943.

6551 **Collingwood, R.G.,** and **Myres, J.N.L.** *Roman Britain and the English Settlements.* Oxford: Clarendon Press, 1937.

6552 **Cornish, Vaughan.** *Borderlands of Language in Europe and Their Relation to the Historic Frontiers of Christendom.* London: Sifton Praed, 1936.

6553 **Falch, Jean.** *Consribution a l'etude du statut des langues en Europe.* Quebec: Presses de l'Universite Laval, 1973.

6554 **Farrell, M.** *Arming the Protestants: Royal Ulster Constabulary.* London: Pluto Press, 1984.

6555 **Farrell, M.** *Northern Ireland: The Orange State.* London: Pluto Press, 1978.

6556 **Ford, G.,** ed. *Fascist Europe: The Rise of Racism and Xenophobia.* London: Pluto Press, 1992.

6557 **Froese, Walter.** *The Early Norbertines on the Religious Frontiers of Northeastern Germany.* Chicago, Illinois: University of Chicago, Ph.D., 1978.

6558 **Fulton, John.** *The Tragedy of Belief: Division, Politics, and Religion in Ireland.* Oxford: Clarendon Press, 1991.

6559 **Goldschmidt, V.** *Anthropologie et Politique: Les Principes du Systeme de Rousseau.* Paris: Vrin, 1974.

6560 **Guaraldo, Alberto.** *Note sulla tipoligia ed evoluzione della migrazioni pastorali.* Trieste: Lint, 1973.

6561 **Haugen, E.,** ed. *Minority Language Today.* Edinburgh: Edinburgh University Press, 1980.

6562 **Hechter, H.** *Internal Colonialism: The Celtic Fringe in British National Development, 1576-1966.* Berkeley: University of California Press, 1975.

6563 **Hondius, Fritz W.** *The Yugoslav Community of Nations.* The Hague: Mouton, 1969.

6564 **Husbands, C.T.** *Racial Exclusionism and the City: The Urban Support of the National Front.* London: Allen & Unwin, 1983.

6565 **Le Bras, Gabriel.** *Introduction a l'histoire de la pratique religieuse en France.* Paris: Presses Universitaires de France, 1945.

6566 **Lefebvre, Andre.** *Germains et Slaves, Origines et Croyances.* Paris: Schleicher, 1903.

6567 **Lorimer, F.** *The Population of the Soviet Union.* Geneve: League of Nations, 1946.

6568 **Mannion, John Joseph.** *Irish Imprints on the Landscape of Eastern Canada in the Nineteenth Century: A Study of Cultural Transfer and Adoptation.* Toronto, Ontario, Canada: University of Toronto, Ph.D., 1971.

6569 **Miller, D.W.** *Church, State and Nation in Ireland, 1898-1921.* Dublin: Richview Press, 1972.

6570 **Murgatroyd, L.; Savage, M.; Shapiro, D.; Urry, J.; Walby, S.; and Warde, Allen.** *Localities, Class and Gender.* London: Pion, 1985.

6571 **Murphy, Alexander B.** *The Regional Dynamics of Language Differentiation in Belgium: A Study in Cultural-Political Geography.* Chicago, Illinois: University of Chicago, University Research Paper #227, 1988.

6572 **Nielsen, Niels C.** *Revolutions in Eastern Europe: The Religious Roots.* Maryknoll: Orbis Books, 1991.

6573 **O'Connor, Raymond G.** *The Irish: Portrait of a People.* New York: Putnam, 1971.

6574 **Pittard, Eugene.** *Les Peuples des Balkans.* Paris: Editions Leroux, 1920.

6575 **Poulton, Hugh.** *The Balkans: Minorities and States in Conflict.* London: Minority Rights Publications, 1991.

6576 *The Question of 200,000 Yugoslavs in Austria: The Slovene Carinthia and the Brugenland Croats.* Beograd: Government of the Federative People's Republic of Yugoslavia, 1947.

6577 **Rees, G., and Rees, T.L.** *Poverty and Social Inequality in Wales.* London: Croom Helm, 1980.

6578 **Romer, E.** *Statistics of Languages of the Provinces Being Under the Polish Civil Administration of the Eastern Land.* Lwiw-Warsaw: Geographical Works, 1919.

6579 **Rose, R.** *Studies in British Politics.* London: Macmillan, 1976.

6580 **Rundle, Stanley.** *Language as a Social and Political Factor in Europe.* London: Faber and Faber, 1946.

6581 **Rywkin, Michael.** *Moscow's Muslim Challenge: Soviet Central Asia.* Rev. ed. Armonk: M. E. Sharpe, Inc., 1990.

6582 **Savage, M.** *Ethnic Divisions in the Labour Market and Working Class Politics.* Paper at Conference on "Segregation in the Labour Market," Lancaster,

July, 1985.

6583 **Simmonds, G.W., ed.** *Nationalism in the USSR and Eastern Europe in the Era of Brezhnev and Kosygin.* Detroit, Michigan: University of Detroit Press, 1977.

6584 **Slezkine, Yuri.** *Arctic Mirrors: Russia and the Small Peoples of the North.* Ithaca: Cornell University Press, 1994.

6585 **Smith, D.** *Conflict and Compromise: Class Formation in English Society 1830-1914.* London: Routledge, 1982.

6586 **Stephens, Michael D.** *Linguistic Minorities in Western Europe.* Llandysul Dyfed, Wales: Gomer Press, 1976.

6587 **Union of Slovenian Parishes of America.** *Shall Slovenia Be Sovietized?* A rebuttal to Louis Adamic, gathered and translated from the pages of the Slovenian Daily, "Ameriska Domovina." Cleveland, Ohio: Union of Slovenian Parishes of America, 1944.

6588 **Weigend, Guido G.** *The Cultural Pattern of South Tyrol.* Chicago, Illinois: University of Chicago, Ph.D., 1949.

6589 **Wilser, Ludwig.** *Die Germanen.* Leipzig: Thuringische Verlag Anstalt, 1903.

6590 **Zipf, G.K.** *Human Behavior and the Principle of Least Effort: An Introduction to Human Ecology.* New York: Hafner, 1965.

6591 **Zwitter, Fran.** *To Destroy Nazism or to Reward It? An Aspect of the Question of Slovene Carinthia.* Belgrad: Yugoslav Institute for International Affairs, 1947.

Journals

6592 **Ancel, Jacques.** "La montagne et l'unite de la civilisation balkanique." *Annales de Geographie,* 36 Annee, No. 199 (Janvier 15, 1927), 74-76.

6593 **Arrighi, J.M.** "The Clan: Its Reneweal and Permanency." In *Peoples Mediterraneeens, Mediterranean Peoples,* 38-39 (1987), 49-55.

6594 **Banton, M.** "The Beginning and the End of the Racial Issue in British Politics." *Policy & Politics,* 15, No. 1(1987), 39-47.

6595 **Battisti, C.** "Nazionalita e lingua, con particolare riguardo all' Alto Adige." *Archivi Alto Adige,* 56 (1962), 1-25.

6596 **Bennigsen, Alexandre.** "Several Nations or One People? Ethnic Consciousness Among Soviet Central Asian Muslims." *Survey,* 24, No. 3 (108) (Summer, 1979), 51-64.

6597 **Berger, Kurt Martin.** "Der Vatikan und der Osten." *Zeitschrift fur Geopolitik*, Jahrgang 39, Heft 1 (Januar, 1968), 45-47.

6598 **Breton, Roland.** "L'Ukraine, Sixieme Grand d'Europe?: Analyse de sa Structure Ethnolonguistique." *Herodote* [Paris], No. 58-59 (Juillet-Decembre, 1990), 210-232.

6599 **Buxell, Gunner.** "DieVolker der Sowjetnnion." *Zeitschrift fur Geopolitik*, Jahrgang, 24, Heft 9 (September,1953), 502-503.

6600 **Carbouet, Michel.** "Apercu sur differents exemples d'espares' culturels transfrontaliers en Europe du Nend (Scandinavie et Findlande). *Revue Geographique de l'est*, 27, No. 1-2 (1987), 53-70.

6601 **Celerier, J.** "Islam et Geographie." *Hesperis*, 39, N° 3 and 4 Trimestres (1952), 331-371.

6602 **Cerami, Charles A.** "Belgium: Do Two Halves Make One Whole?" *The Atlantic Community Quarterly*, 18, No. 3 (Fall, 1980), 338-345.

6603 **Chickekian, Garo.** "Ethnic Conflict in Cyprus: A Political Geographical Perspective." *Zambian Geographical Journal*, 29-30 (1975), 75-109.

6604 **Chickekian, Garo.** "Recent Trends in the Distribution and Ethnic Homogeneity of the Armenians in the U.S.S.R.: A Brief Statistical Survey." *The Armenian Review*, 26, No. 3-111 (Autumn, 1975), 325-331.

6605 **Chipman, John.** "Managing the Politics of Parochialism." *Survival* [London], 35, No. 1 (Spring, 1993), 143-170.

6606 **Christopher, A.J.** "'Divide and Rule': The Impress of British Segregation Policies." *Area*, 20, (1988a), 233-240.

6607 **Clem, Ralph S.** "Russians and Others: Ethnic Tensions in the Soviet Union." *Focus*, 31, No. 1 (September-October, 1980), 1-16.

6608 **Dami, Aldo.** "Une nouvelle carte linguistique de la Suisse." *Geographica Helvetica*, 4 (1949), 199-205.

6609 **Dauzat, Albert.** "Le deplacement des frontieres linguistiques du francais de 1806 a nos jours." *La Nature*, (1927), 529-536.

6610 **Delaruelle, Etienne.** "Contribution a l'etude de la geographie religieuse du Sud-Quest." *Revue geographique des Pyrenees et du Sud-Ouest*, (1943), 48-78.

6611 **Di Palma, Giuseppe.** "Legitimation from the Top to Civil Society: Politico-Cultural Change in Eastern Europe." *World Politics* [Baltimore], 44, No. 1 (October, 1991), 49-80.

6612 **Dogan, M.** "Political Cleavage and Social Stratification in France and Italy." In *Party Systems and Voter Alignments*, S.M. Lipset and S. Rokkan, eds. New York: The Free Press, 1967, 129-95.

6613 "Ethnic Lithuania and the Curzon Line." Excerpt: *Lithuanian Legation, Washington, D.C. Current News on the Lithuanian Situation*, 3, No. 7 (July, 1944), 2-5.

6614 **Fulbrook, Mary.** "Aspects of Society and Identity in the New Germany." *Daedalus* [Cambridge, MA], 123, No. 1 (Winter, 1994), 211-234.

6615 **Goguel, Francois.** "Religion et politique en France." *Revue Fracaise des Science Politiques*, 16 (1966), 1174-1180.

6616 **Goulbourne, Harry.** "New Issues in Black British Politics." *Social Science Information* [London], 31, No. 2 (June, 1992), 355-373.

6617 **Hautamaki, Lauri; Sirila, Seppo; and Sippola, Matti.** "Communal Reform and Spheres of Influence at the Town Level in Finnish-Speaking Southern Ostrobothnia." *Fennia*, 97, No. 9 (September, 1968), 1-48.

6618 **Hildebrandt, Walter.** "Die Volker Jugoslawiens." *Zeitschrift fur Geopolitik*, Jahrgang 24, Heft 2 (February, 1953), 127-128.

6619 **Huggett, Frank E.** "Communal Problems in Belgium." *The World Today*, 22, No. 10 (October, 1966), 446-452.

6620 **Jankuhn, Frithiof.** "Politische-geographische Betrachtungen uber Lappland." *Zeitschrift fur Erdkunde*, 6, Jahrg, Heft 8 (April 18, 1938), 322-326.

6621 **Joo, Rudolf.** "Slovenes in Hungary and Hungarians in Slovenia: Ethnic and State Identity." *Ethnic and Racial Studies* [London], 14, No. 1 (January, 1991), 100-106.

6622 **Kelley, J., McAllister, I., and Mughan, Anthony.** "The Decline of Class Revisited: England, 1964-79." *American Political Science Review*, 79, No. 2 (June, 1985), 400-420.

6623 **Khleif, Bud B.** "Ethinicity and Language in Understanding the New Nationalism: The North Atlantic Region." *International Journal of Comparative Sociology*, 23, No. 1-2 (March-June, 1982), 114-121.

6624 **Klemencic, Vladimir, and Gosar, Anton.** "Grenzuberschreitende Raumwirksame Leithilder dargestellt an Beispielen de Grenzraume Sloweniens in Jugoslawien." *Revue Geographique de l'est*, 27, No. 1-2 (1987), 27-38.

6625 **Klienetz, Alvin.** "Ethnonationalism and Decolonization in Greenland and Northern Eurasia." *Canadian Review of Studies in Nationalism*, 14, No. 2 (Fall, 1987), 247-260.

6626 **Koenig, Samuel.** "Geographic and Ethnic Characteristics of Galicia." *Journal of Central European Affairs*, 1, No. 1 (April, 1941), 55-65.

6627 **Kovacs, Zoltan.** "Ethnic Tensions in Eastern Europe." *Geography Review* [Oxford], 4, No. 4 (March, 1991), 37-41.

6628 **Lagerspetz, Mikko.** "Social Problems in Estonian Mass Media, 1975-1991." *Acta Sociologica* [Oslo], 36, No. 4 (1993), 357-369.

6629 **Laitin, David D.; Sole, Carlotta; and Kalyvas, Stathis N.** "Language and the Construction of States: The Case of Catalonia in Spain." *Politics and Society* [Thousand Oaks], 22, No. 1 (March, 1994), 5-29.

6630 **Landsman, G.** "Ganienkeh: Symbol and Politics in an Indian/White Conflict." *American Anthropologist*, 87, No. 4 (1985), 826-839.

6631 **Larkin, E.** "Church, State and Nation in Modern Ireland." *American Historical Review*, 80, No. 5 (December, 1975), 1244-1276.

6632 **Laver, M.** "Ireland: Politics With Some Social Bases: An Interpretation Based on Aggregate Data." *Economic & Social Review*, 17, No. 2 (1986), 107-131.

6633 **Laver, M.** "Ireland: Politics With Some Social Bases: An Interpretaion Based on Survey Data." *Economic & Social Review*, 17, No. 3 (1986), 193-213.

6634 **Le Bras, Gabriel.** "Caractere sociologique des cartes religieuses de la Fance." *Lumen Vitae*, (1948), 633-644.

6635 **Lencek, Rado L.** "The Enlightenment's Interest in Languages and the National Revival of the South Slavs." *Canadian Review of Studies in Nationalism*, 10, No. 1 (Spring, 1983), 111-134.

6636 **Letiner, H.** "The State and the Foreign Worker Problem: A Case Study of the Federal Republic of Germany, Switzerland, and Austsria." *Environment & Planning C: Government & Policy*, 4, No. 2 (1986), 199-219.

6637 **Loizos, Peter.** "Intercommunal Killing in Cyprus." *Man*, 23, No. 4 (December, 1988), 639-653.

6638 **Pallis, A.A.** "Racial Migrations in the Balkans During the Years 1912-1924." *Geographical Journal*, 66, No. 4 (October, 1925), 315-331.

6639 **Pattanayak, D.P., and Bayer, J.M.** "Laponce's 'The French Language in Canada: Tensions Between Geography and Politics'-A Rejoinder." *Political Geography Quarterly*, 6, No. 3 (1987), 261-263.

6640 **Pillard, J.P.** "Current Trends and Developments Patterns and Forms of Immigrant Participation and Representation at the Local and National Levels in Western (Continental) Europe." *International Migration*, 24, No. 2 (1986), 501-513.

6641 **Pion-Berlin, David.** "To Prosecute or to Pardon?: Human Rights Decisions in the Latin American Southern Cone." *Human Rights Quarterly* [Baltimore], 16, No. 1 (February, 1994), 105-130.

6642 **Prety, J.W.** "The Land of the Two Proud Peoples: The Walloons and Felmings of Belgium." *Geographical Perspectives*, 57 (1986), 40-46.

6643 **Ricketts, Peter.** "Geography and International Law: The Case of the 1984 Gulf of Maine Boundary Dispute." *Canadian Geographer*, 30, No. 3 (1986), 194-205.

6644 **Schuttel, L.** "Die Makedonische Frage." *Zeitschrift fur Geopolitik*, Jahrgang 12, Heft 3 (Marz, 1935), 179-182.

6645 **Sieger, Robert.** "Grundlinien einer geographie des Duetschtums." *Zeitschrift fur Geopolitik*, Jahrg 4, Heft 7 (Juli, 1927), 630-641.

6646 **Smith, Graham E.** "Ethnic Nationalism in the Soviet Union: Territory, Cleavages and Control." *Government and Policy*, 3 (1985), 49-74.

6647 **Sperber, Jonathan.** "Roman Catholic Religious Identity in Rhineland-Westphalia, 1800-70: Quantitative Examples and Some Political Implications." *Social History*, 7, No. 3 (October, 1982), 305-318.

6648 **Sugden, J., and Bairner, A.** "Northern Ireland: The Politics of Leisure in a Divided Society." *Leisure Studies*, 5, No. 3 (1986), 341-352.

6649 **Van Boeschoten, Riki.** "The Peasant and the Party: Peasant Options and Folk' Communism in a Greek Village." *The Journal of Peasant Studies* [London], 20, No. 4 (July, 1993), 612-639.

6650 **Van Wettere-Verhasselt, Yola.** "La singnification linguistique de la frontiere belgo-neerlandaise." *Revue Belge de Geographie*, N° 1 (1961), 83-89.

6651 **Van Wettere-Verhasselt, Yola.** "Aspecten van menselijke aardrijkskunde langsheen de Belgisch-Nederlandse grens." *Geografisch Tijaschrift*, N.R. Dell 3, Nr. 5 (December, 1969), 409-418.

6652 **Vermeil, Edmond.** "Religion and Politics in Alsace." *Foreign Affairs*, 10, No. 2 (January, 1932), 250-263.

6653 **Williams, C.H.** "Ethnic Separatism in Western Europe." *Tijdschrift voor Economische en Sociale Geographie*, 71, Nr. 3 (May-June, 1980), 142-58.

6654 **Williams, C.H.** "The Spatial Analysis of Welsh Culture." *Etudes Celtiques XIX*, (1982), 283-322.

6655 **Willis, Richard H.** "Finnish Images of the Northern Land and People." *Acta Sociologica*, Fasc. 7, No. 2 (1964), 73-88.

6656 **Wood, Richard E.** "Selected Recent Studies in Linguistic Nationalism in the German Languages." *Canadian Review of Studies in Nationalism*, 8, No. 1 (Spring, 1981), 55-84.

6657 **Wright, Herbert.** "The Status of the Vatican City." *The American Journal of International Law*, 38, No. 3 (July, 1944), 452-457.

CHAPTER IX

FRONTIERS, BOUNDARIES, LANDLOCKED STATES AND BUFFER ZONES

GENERAL AND THEORY

BOUNDARY CONCEPTS AND THEORIES

Books and Journals

6658 Anderson, Eric. *Distant Neighbors: Political Boundaries and the Flow of News.* Minneapolis: Ph.D. Dissertation, University of Minnesota, 1993.

6659 Beard, William. "Technology and Political Boundaries." *American Political Science Review*, 25, No. 3 (August, 1931), 557-572.

6660 Boggs, S. Whittemore. *International Boundaries: A Study of Boundary Functions and Problems.* New York City: Columbia University Press, 1940.

6661 Bouchez, Leo J. "The Fixing of Boundaries in International Boundary Rivers." *International and Comparative Law Quarterly*, 12, No. 4 (October, 1963), 789-817.

6662 Bowell, Geoffrey. *Boundaries.* London: Methuen, 1958.

6663 Brown, Curtis M.; Robillard, Walter G.; and Wilson, Donald A. *Boundary Control and Legal Principles.* New York: John Wiley & Sons, 1986.

6664 Brown, Curtis M.; Robillard, Walter G.; and Wilson, Donald A. *Evidence and Procedures for Boundary Location.* 2nd Edition. New York: John Wiley & Sons, 1981.

6665 Brown, Peter G. *Boundaries: National Autonomy and Its Limits.* Totowa, New Jersey: Rowman and Little Field, 1981.

6666 Buffington, Robert. "Prohibition in the Borderlands: National Government-Border Community Relations." *Pacific Historical Review* [Berkeley], 63, No. 1 (February, 1994), 19-38.

6667 Calderwood, H.B. "Borderlines of National and International Jurisdiction." *American Society of International Law Proceedings*, (April 28-29, 1944), 40-60.

6668 Clark, William A.V. "Geography in Court: Expertise in Adversarial Settings." *Institute of British Geographers. Transactions* [London], 16, No. 1 (1991), 5-20.

6669 Coelho, Djalma Poli. "Geografor, cartografor e demarcadores." *Anuario*, 4 (1951), 35-47.

6670 Cox, Kevin R. "Locational Effects of Boundaries." In *Fundamentals of Human Geography: A Reader*, Peter Haggett, et al, eds. New York: Harper & Row, 1978, Chapter 22.

6671 Cumpston, J.H.L. "The Story of the Boundaries." *Walkabout*, 17, No. 4 (April, 1951), 18-20.

6672 Finch, John. *The Natural Boundaries of Empires.* London: Longman, 1844.

6673 Fisher, Eric. "On Boundaries." *World Politics*, 1, No. 2 (January, 1949), 196-222.

6674 Fraser, Marian Botsford. *Walking the Line.* San Francisco: Sierra Club Books, 1990.

6675 Goggin, Daniel T., comp. *Preliminary Inventory of the Records Relating to International Boundaries.* Washington, D.C.: National Archives and Records Service, The National Archives, 1968.

6676 Gupte, Pranay. *The Silent Crisis: Despair, Development and Hope in a World without Borders.* New Delhi: Vikas, 1990.

6677 Hartshorne, Richard. "Suggestions on the Terminology of Political Boundaries." *Mitteilungen des Vereins der Geographen an der Universitat Leipzig*, No. 14-15 (1936), 180-192.

6678 Hartshorne, Richard. "Suggestions the Terminology of Political Boundaries." *Annals of the Association of American Geographers*, 26, No. 1 (March, 1936), 56-57.

6679 Holdich, Thomas H. "Political Boundaries." *Scottish Geographical Magazine*, 32, No. 11 (November, 1916), 497-507.

6680 Holdich, Thomas H. "Geographical Problems in Boundary Marking." *Geographical Journal*, 47, No. 6 (June, 1916), 421-440.

6681 Holt, A.H. "Everlasting Boundaries." *Bulletin of the American Congress on Surveying and Mapping*, 4, No. 1 (January, 1944), 36-40.

6682 Holt, A.H. "Trends in Boundary Surveying." *Civil Engineering*, 9, No. 6 (June, 1939), 359-362.

6683 **Hudson, Manley O.** *International Tribunals, Past and Future.* Washington: Carnegie Endowment for International Peace and The Brookings Institute, 1944.

6684 **Hyde, C.C.** "Boundary River." *British Year Book of International Law*, 18 (1937), 4-5.

6685 **Hyde, C.C.** "Notes on Rivers as Boundaries." *American Journal of International Law*, 6, No. 4 (October, 1912), 901-909.

6686 **Iraq and Iran.** "Boundary Treaty, and Protocol." Signed at Teheran, July 4th, 1937." *League of Nations. Treaty Series*, 190, Nos. 4401-4430 (1938), 241-258.

6687 **Johnson, Douglas Wilson.** "The Role of Political Boundaries." *Geographical Review*, 4, No. 2 (April, 1917), 208-213.

6688 **Jones, Stephen B.** "Boundary Concepts in the Setting of Place and Time." *Annals of the Association of American Geographers*, 49, No. 3 (September, 1959), 241-255.

6689 **Jones, Stephen B.** "The Description of International Boundaries." *Annals of the Association of American Geographers*, 33, No. 2 (June, 1943), 99-117.

6690 **Kishimato, H.**, ed. *Geography and Boundary.* Berne: Kumoerly and Frey, 1980.

6691 **Kitchin, Joseph A.** "The International Law of State Boundaries and Suits Between Member States of Federations." *Papers of the Michigan Academy of Science, Arts, and Letters*, 27 (1941) (1942), 625-638.

6692 **Kristof, Ladis K.D.** "The Nature of Frontiers and Boundaries." *Annals of the Association of American Geographers*, 49, No. 3 (September, 1959), 269-282.

6693 **Kuhn, Delia, and Kuhn, Ferdinand.** *Borderlands.* New York: Knopf, 1962.

6694 **Kupper, V.I.** "The Contribution of German Geographers to Local Boundary Reforms." *Area* (Institute of British Geographers), 5, No. 3 (September, 1973), 172-176.

6695 **Kuseielwicz, Eugene.** "New Light on the Carzon Line." *Polish Review*, 1, No. 2-3 (Spring and Summer, 1956), 82-88.

6696 **Lemon, Donald P.** "Boundaries." *Association of Canadian Map Libraries and Archives. Bulletin* [Ottawa], 77 (December, 1990), 7-12.

6697 **Limpo-Serra, Manuel P.B.** "A Zona Economica Exclusiva Historia e Aspectos Juridicos." *Sociedade de Geografiade Lisboa Boletim*, Serie

99, Nos. 7-9 and 10-12 (Julho-Setembro and Outubro-Dezembro, 1981), 209-226.

6698 **Malcomson, Scott L.** *Borderlands: Nation and Empire.* Boston: Faber and Faber, 1994.

6699 **Malloy, W.M.** *Treaties, Conventions, International Acts, Protocols and Agreements Between the United States of America and Other Powers, 1776-1909.* Washington, D.C.: U.S. Department of State, 1910.

6700 **Martin, R.J.** "Some Comments on Correction Techniques for Boundary Effects and Missing Value Techniques." *Geographical Analysis*, 19, No. 3 (July, 1987), 273-282.

6701 **Martin-Chauffier, Jean.** *Trieste. Liberation de la Venetie Julienne. Conferences de Londres et de Paris. Le probleme de l'internationalisation.* Centre d'etudes de politique etrangere, Section d'information, Publication No. 18. Paris: P. Hartman, 1947.

6702 **McMahon, A. Henry.** "International Boundaries." *Journal of the Royal Society of Arts*, 84, No. 4330 (November 15, 1935), 2-16.

6703 **Melamid, Alexander.** "Political Boundaries and Nomadic Grazing." *Geographical Review*, 2 (1965), 287-290.

6704 **Minghi, Julian V.** "Boundary Studies in Political Geography." *Annals of the Association of American Geographers*, 53, No. 3 (September, 1963), 407-428.

6705 **Munger, Edwin S.** "Boundaries and African Nationalism." *California Geographer*, 4 (1963), 1-7.

6706 **Murawski, Klaus Eberhard.** "Die Entstehung der Zovengrenze." *Zeitschrift fur Geopolitik*, 27 Jahrgang, Heft 12 (Dezember, 1956), 29-32.

6707 **Murzaev, E.M.** "Where Should One Draw the Geographical Boundary Between Europe and Asia?" *Soviet Geography; Review and Translation*, 5, No. 1 (January, 1964), 15-25.

6708 **Norcen, Antonio.** "Political Boundaries, Frontiers, and Administrative Limits." *L'Universo*, 39, No. 3 (May-June, 1959), 547-556.

6709 **Pattan, R.S.** "Relation of the Tide to Property Boundaries." *U.S. Coast & Geodetic Survey, Field Engineers Bulletin*, 13, No. 4 (December, 1939), 44-57.

6710 **Pearcy, G. Etzel.** *Boundary Concepts and Definitions.* Washington, D.C.: U.S. Department of State, 1961.

6711 **Pearcy, G. Etzel.** "Boundary Functions." *Journal of Geography*, 64, No. 8 (November, 1965), 346-349.

6712 **Pearcy, G. Etzel.** "Boundary Types." *Journal of Geography*, 54, No. 7 (October, 1965), 300-303.

6713 **Pearcy, G. Etzel.** "Dynamic Aspects of Boundaries." *Journal of Geography*, 64, No. 9 (December, 1965), 388-394.

6714 **Pearcy, G. Etzel.** "The International Boundary Pattern." *Special Libraries Association. Geography and Map Division. Bulletin.* 89, No. 3 (September, 1972), 2-15.

6715 **Pearcy, G. Etzel.** *Pattern of International Boundaries with Measurement Tables.* Fullerton, California: Plycon Press, 1972.

6716 **Penck, Albrecht.** *Uber Politische Grenzen-Rede.* Berlin: Buchdruckerei und Verlaganstalt, 1917.

6717 **Prescott, J.R.V.** "Maps and Boundary Disputes." *Globe*, 12 (1980), 1-9.

6718 **Prescott, J.R.V.** *The Geography of Frontiers and Boundaries.* Chicago: Aldine Publishing, 1965.

6719 **Prescott, J.R.V.** *Political Frontiers and Boundaries.* London: Allen & Unwin, 1987.

6720 **Queensland.** *Committee on Regional Boundaries. Regions Agreed Upon by the Committee.* Brisbane: Queensland Bureau of Industry, 1947.

6721 **Reed, Rose Romaine.** *The Effects of a Political Boundary Running Through a Metropolitan Area: A Case Study of the Establishment and Functioning of the Jantzen Beach Shopping Center.* Portland, Oregon: Portland State University, Department of Geography, 1977.

6722 **Reynolds, David R., and McNulty, Michael L.** "On the Analysis of Political Boundaries as Barriers: A Perpetual Approach." *East Lake Geographer*, 4 (December, 1968), 21-38.

6723 **Rose, Stephen.** "Historical Origin of Boundaries." *Military Engineer*, 38, No. 251 (September, 1946), 378-380.

6724 **Rumley, Dennis, and Minghi, Julian V., eds.** *The Geography of Border Landscapes.* London: Routledge, 1991.

6725 **Rykiel, Zbigniew.** "Region Przygraniczny Jako Przemiot Badan Geograficznych." *Przeglad KGeograficzny* [Warszawa], 62 (Zeszyt 3-4, 1990), 263-273.

6726 **Sanders, William.** "Treaties, Conventions, International Acts, Protocols, and Agreements." *Handbook of Latin American Studies, 1940, 6* (1941), 327-338.

6727 **Semple, Ellen Churchill.** "Geographical Boundaries." *Bulletin of American Geographical Society*, 39 (1907), 385-397 and 449-463.

6728 **Sharma, Surya Prakash.** *International Boundary Disputes and International law.* Bombay: N.M. Tripathi Private, 1976.

6729 **Skiffington, Kerry K.** "Noblesse Oblige: A Strategy for Local Boundary Making." *Ethnology* [Pittsburgh], 30, No. 3 (July, 1991), 265-277.

6730 **Solch, Johann.** *Natural Boundaries.* Innsbruck: Innsbruck University Press, 1924.

6731 **Stacey, C.P.** *The Undefended Border: The Myth and the Reality.* Ottawa: Canadian Historical Association, 1953.

6732 **Staten, George L.** "The Use and Misuse of Maps in a Boundary Dispute." *Special Libraries Association. Geography and Map Division Bulletin*, 93, No. 3 (September, 1973), 18-22.

6733 **Strassoldo, Raimondo.** "The Study of Boundaries: A Systems-Oriented, Multi-Disciplinary, Bibliographical Essay." *Jerusalem Journal of International Relations*, 2, No. 3 (Spring, 1977), 81-107.

6734 **Strassoldo, Raimondo, ed.** *Boundaries and Regions.* Trieste: Lint, 1973.

6735 **Tullock, Gordon.** "Territorial Boundaries: An Economic View." *American Naturalist*, 121, No. 3 (March, 1983), 440-442.

6736 **U.S. Department of State.** Office of the Geographer. *Boundary Concepts and Definitions.* Washington, D.C.: U.S. Department of State, 1961.

6737 **U.S. Department of State.** *International Boundaries and Disclaimers.* Washington, D.C.: U.S. Department of State, 1967.

6738 **U.S. Department of State.** *Straight Baselines: Svalbard.* Washington, D.C.: U.S. Department of State, 1972.

6739 **Visher, Stephen S.** "Influences Locating International Boundaries." *Journal of Geography*, 37, No. 8 (November, 1938), 301-308.

6740 **Visher, Stephen S.** "What Sort of International Boundary is Best?" *Journal of Geography*, 31, No. 7 (October, 1932), 288-296.

6741 **Visher, Stephen S.** "Where Should the International Boundaries Be?" Reprint from *Social Science*, 14, No. 1 (January, 1939), 55-58.

6742 **Wagner, Wolfgang E.** *The Genesis of the Oder-Neisse Line; A Study in the Diplomatic Negotiations During World War II.* Stuttgart: Brentano-Verlag, 1957.

6743 **Waller, R.J.** "The 1983 Boundary Commission: Policies and Effects." *Electoral Studies*, 2 (1983), 195-206.

6744 **Weissberg, Guenter.** "Maps as Evidence in International Boundary Disputes: A Reappraisal. *American Journal of International Law*, 57, No. 4 (October, 1963), 781-803.

6745 **Winterbotham, H. St. J.** "The Demarcation of International Boundaries." In *Empire Conference of Survey Officers, 1928, Report of Proceedings.* Colonial No. 41. London: Her Majesty's Stationery Office, 1929.

6746 **Zartman, William I.** "Boundaries and Nations." *Focus*, 29, No. 4 (March-April, 1979), 2-3 and 6-7.

POLITICAL GEOGRAPHY OF REGIONS

AFRICA

Books and Journals

6747 **Anene, J.C.** *The International Boundaries of Nigeria, 1885-1960: The Framework of an Emergent African Nation.* New York: Humanities Press, 1970.

6748 **Attuoni, Pietro.** "I Confini Della Somalia e le Low Vicende." *Bollettino Della Societa Geografica Italiana*, 8, No. 6 (March-April, 1953), 96-125.

6749 **Bening, R.B.** "Indigenous Concepts of Boundaries and Significance of Administrative Stations and Boundaries in Northern Ghana." *Bulletin of the Ghana Geographical Association*, 15 (1973), 7-20.

6750 **Best, Judy, and Zinyama, L.M.** "The Evolution of the National Boundary of Zimbabwe." *Journal of Historical Geography*, 11, No. 4 (October, 1985), 419-432.

6751 **Bono, Salvatore.** "State Boundaries in Independent Africa." *A Current Bibliography on African Affairs*, 2, No. 11 (November, 1969), 5-12 and 2, No. 12 (December, 1969), 5-12.

6752 **Bright, R.G.T.** "The Uganda-Congo Boundary Commission." *Geographical Journal*, 32, No. 5 (November, 1908), 488-493.

6753 **Gershoni, Yekutiel.** "The Drawing of Liberian Boundaries in the Nineteenth Century: Treaties with African Chiefs Versus Effective Occupation."

International Journal of African Historical Studies, 20, No. 2 (1987), 293-307.

6754 **Gore-Browne, Sir Stewart.** "The Anglo-Belgian Boundary Commission, 1911-14." *Northern Rhodesia Journal*, 5, No. 4 (1964), 315-329.

6755 **Great Britain.** Secretary of State for the Colonies. *Kenya: Report of the Regional Boundaries Commission.* London: Her Majesty's Stationery Office, 1962.

6756 **Kibulya, H.M., and Langlands, B.W.** *The Political Geography of the Uganda-Congo Boundary.* Kampala: Occasional Paper No. 6, Department of Geography, Makerere University College, 1967.

6757 **Marcus, H.G.** "A History of the Negotiations Concerning the Border Between Ethiopia and British East Africa, 1897-1914." In *Boston University Papers on Africa*, Vol. 2, Boston: Boston University Press, 1966.

6758 **McEwen, A.C.** *International Boundaries of East Africa.* Oxford: Clarendon Press, 1971.

6759 **Moss, David.** "Bandits and Boundaries in Sardalas." *Man*, 14, No. 3 (September, 1979), 477-496.

6760 **Reyner, A.S.** *Current Boundary Problems in Africa.* Pittsburgh, Pennsylvania: Duquesne University Press, 1964.

6761 **Reyner, A.S.** "The Republic of the Congo: Development of Its International Boundaries." *DuQuesne Review*, 6, No. 2 (Spring, 1961), 88-95.

6762 **Smith, G.E.** *Report on the Anglo-German Boundary Commission from Victoria Nyanza to Kilimanjaro and Lake Jipe.* Confidential No. 8932, F.O. 367/10. London: Her Majesty's Office, 1906.

6763 **Thom, Derrick James.** *The Niger-Nigeria Borderlands: A Politico-Geographical Analysis of Boundary Influence Upon the Hausa.* East Lansing: Michigan State University, Ph.D., 1970.

6764 **Thomas, H.B.** "Evolution of Uganda's Boundaries." *Atlas of Uganda.* Entebbe: Government Press, 1962.

6765 **Thornton, Robert.** "Modelling of Spatial Relations in a Boundary-Making Ritual of the Iraqw of Tanzania." *Man* (London), 17, No. 3 (September, 1982), 528-545.

6766 **Touval, Saadia.** *The Boundary Politics of Independent Africa.* Cambridge, Massachusetts: Harvard University Press, 1972.

6767 **Touval, Saadia.** "Treaties, Borders, and the Partition of Africa." *Journal of African History*, 7, No. 2 (June, 1966), 279-292.

6768 **Widstrand, Carl Gosta,** ed. *African Boundary Problems*. Uppsala: Scandinavian Institute of African Studies, 1969.

6769 **Yadlin, Rivka.** "The Egyptian Opposition and the Boundaries of National Concensus." *Middle East Review*, 21, No. 4 (Summer, 1989), 18-26.

6770 **Zartman, I.W.** "The Politics of Boundaries in North and West Africa." *Journal of Modern African Studies*, 3, No. 2 (August, 1965), 155-173.

AMERICAS

Books and Journals

6771 *The Affair of Boundaries Between Venezuela and British Guiana: The Outcome of a Colonial Epoch*. Caracas: Impuso en Venezuela por Cromotip, 1967.

6772 **Aramburu Menchaca, Andres A.** "Peru-Ecuador Boundary Question." *West Coast Leader*, 24, No. 1328 (July 27, 1937), 5-7.

6773 "Argentine and Chilean Territorial Claims in the Antarctic." *Polar Record*, 4, No. 32 (July, 1946), 412-418.

6774 **Bandy, William R.** "In Search of the North Boundary of Wyoming; A Study of the Field Notes of the Original Survey and an Account of Recent Retracements." *Civil Engineering*, 10, No. 4 (April, 1940), 215-218.

6775 **Bayliff, William H.** *Boundary Monuments on the Maryland-Pennsylvania and the Maryland-Delaware Boundaries*. Annapolis, Maryland: Board of Natural Resources, 1951.

6776 **Birge, John R.** "Redistricting to Maximize the Preservation of Political Boundaries." *Social Science Research*, 12, No. 3 (September, 1983), 205-214.

6777 **Boggs, S. Whittemore.** "The Map of Latin America by Treaty." *Proceedings of the American Philosophical Society*, 79, No. 3 (September 30, 1938), 399-410.

6778 **Boggs, S. Whittemore.** "Problems of Water-Boundary Definition." *Geographical Review*, 27, No. 3 (July, 1937), 445-456.

6779 **Braden, Spruille.** "A Resume of the Role Played by Arbitration in the Chaco Dispute." Excerpt: *Arbitration Journal*, 2, No. 4 (October, 1938), 387-395.

6780 **Bridger, Clyde A.** "The Counties of Idaho." *Pacific Northwest Quarterly*, 31, No. 2 (April, 1940), 187-206.

6781 **Briggs, John Ely.** "County Evolution in 1839. (Iowa)." *Palimpsest*, 20, No. 3 (March, 1939), 161-174.

6782 **Brightman, George F.** "The Boundaries of Utah." *Economic Geography*, 16, No. 1 (January, 1940), 87-95.

6783 **Brown, Lenard E.** *Survey of the United States-Mexico Boundary, 1849-1855. Background Study*. Washington, D.C.: U.S. National Park Service, Division of History, Office of Archeology and Historical Preservation, 1969.

6784 **Canyes, Manuel.** "Registration of Treaties in the Pan American Union." *Bulletin of the Pan American Union*, 76, No. 9 (September, 1942), 524-530.

6785 **Carpenter, W.C.** "The Red River Boundary Dispute (Oklahoma-Texas)." *American Journal of International Law*, 19, No. 3 (July, 1925), 517-529.

6786 **Castilhos Goicocheia, Luiz Filipe de.** "O mapa da Linha Verde e a questao acreana." *Revista do Instituto Historico e Geografico de Sao Paulo*, 40 (1942), 209-225.

6787 **Chamorro, Diego Manuel.** *La controversia territorial entre Nicaragua y Honduras; analisis del Manifiesto de la Sociedad de abogados de Honduras a los pueblos del continente y a sus entidade juridicas*. Managua, Nicaragua: Los Talleres Nacionales, 1938.

6788 **Chester, Peter.** "Governor Peter Chester's Observations on the Boundaries of British West Florida, About 1775," ed. by James A. Padgett. *Louisiana Historical Quarterly*, 26, No. 1 (January, 1943), 5-11.

6789 **Classen, H. George.** *Thrust and Counterthrust: The Genesis of the Canada-United States Boundary*. Toronto, Ontario: Longmans Canada, 1965.

6790 "Demarcacion territorial. Informes de la Comision de la Sociedad geografica de Lima." *Boletin de la Sociedad Geografica de Lima*, Tomo 40, Trimestre 4 (1923), 279-296.

6791 **Deutsch, Herman J.** "A Contemporary Report on the 49th Boundary Survey." *Pacific Northwest Quarterly*, 53, No. 1 (January, 1962), 17-33.

6792 **Deutsch, Herman J.** "The Evolution of the International Boundary in the Inland Empire of the Pacific Northwest." *Pacific Northwest Quarterly*, 51, No. 2 (April, 1960), 63-79.

6793 **Fifer, J. Valerie.** "Bolivia's Boundary with Brazil: A Century of Evolution." *Geographical Journal*, 132, Pt. 3 (September, 1966), 360-372.

6794 **Ganong, William F.** "A Monograph on the Evolution of the Boundaries of New Brunswick." *Transactions Royal Society of Canada*, 7, Section 2 (1901), 139-449.

6795 **Gerhard, Peter.** "A Method of Reconstructing Pre-Columbian Political Boundaries in Central Mexico." *Journal de la Societe des Americanistes*, Tome 59 (1970), 27-41.

6796 **Goetzmann, W.H.** "The United States-Mexican Boundary Survey, 1848-1853." *Southwestern Historical Quarterly*, 62, No. 2 (October, 1958), 164-190.

6797 **Green, Lewis.** *The Boundary Hunters: Surveying the 141st Meridian and the Alaska Panhandle.* Vancouver: University of British Columbia Press, 1982.

6798 **Griswold, Erwin H.** "Hunting Boundaries with Car and Camera in the Northeastern United States." *Geographical Review*, 29, No. 3 (July, 1939), 353-382.

6799 **Hale, Richard W.** "The Forgotten Maine Boundary Commission." *Proceedings of the Massachusetts Historical Society, Boston*, 71 (October, 1953-May, 1957) (1959), 147-153.

6800 **Ireland, Willard E.** "The Evolution of the Boundaries of British Columbia." *British Columbia Historical Quarterly*, 3 (1939), 263-282.

6801 **James, Preston E.** *The Changing World.* New York: World Book, 1956.

6802 **Jones, Stephen B.** "Intra-State Boundaries in Oregon." *Commonwealdh Review*, 16, No. 3 (July, 1934), 105-126.

6803 **King, L.N.** "The Work of the Jubuland Boundary Commission." *Geographical Journal*, 72, No. 4 (October, 1928), 420-435.

6804 **Mackay, J. Ross.** "The Interactance Hypothesis and Boundaries in Canada: A Preliminary Study." *Canadian Geographer*, 11, No. 2 (Spring, 1958), 1-8.

6805 **Marchant, Alexander.** *Boundaries of the Latin American Republics; An Annotated List of Documents, 1493-1943.* (Tentative version.) U.S. Department of State, Inter-American Series, 24. Publication 2082. Washington, D.C.: U.S. Department of State, 1944.

6806 **McFarlane, Susan E.** *The Ontario-Mnaitoba Boundary and Regional Identity: Crytallization at the Edges.* Kingston, Ontario: Master's Thesis, Queens University, 1994.

6807 **Melvin, M.E.** "Story of the Oklahoma Boundaries." *Chronicles of Oklahoma*, 22, No. 4 (Winter, 1944-45), 382-391.

6808 **Miller, Hunter.** *Treaties and Other Acts of the United States of America.* 5 (1931). Washington, D.C.: Government Printing Press (several volumes), 1931.

6809 **Minghi, Julian V.** *Some Aspects of the Impact of an International Boundary on Spatial Patterns: An Analysis of the Pacific Coast Lowland Region of the Canada-United States Boundary.* Seattle: University of Washington, Ph.D., 1962.

6810 **Minghi, Julian V.** "Television Preferences and Nationality in a Boundary Region." *Sociological Inquiry*, 33, No. 2 (Spring, 1963), 165-179.

6811 **Minghi, Julian V.** *The Diplomatic History of the Canadian Boundary, 1749-1763.* New Haven, Connecticut: Yale University Press, 1940.

6812 **Minghi, Julian V.** "The Forty-Ninth Degree of North Latitude as an International Boundary, 1719; The Origin of an Idea." *Canadian Historical Review*, 38, No. 3 (September, 1957), 183-201.

6813 **Nicholson, Norman L.** *A Dissertation on Canadian Boundaries.* Ottawa, Ontario, Canada: University of Ottawa, Ph.D., 1951.

6814 **Parsons, John E.** *West on the 49th Parallel; Red River to the Rockies, 1872-1876.* New York: William Morrow, 1963.

6815 *The Question of the Boundaries Between Peru and Ecuador.* Reply of the Peruvian Delegation to the Ecuadorian Document of August 9. Baltimore: Reese Press, 1937.

6816 **Rabinowitz, Alan,** ed. *Directory of Special Districts Based on Information Compiled for the U.S. Census of Governments, 1962.* Boston: Urban Survey Corporation, 1964.

6817 **Reitsman, Hendrik J.** "Crop and Livestock Production in the Vicinity of the United States-Canada Border." *Professional Geographer*, 23, No. 3 (July, 1971), 216-233.

6818 **Sanders, William, and Canyes, Manuel.** "Registration of Treaties in the Pan American Union." *Bulletin of the Pan American Union*, 75, No. 11 (November, 1941), 630-641.

6819 **Savelle, Max.** *The Diplomatic History of the Canadian Boundary,1749-1763.* New Haven, Connecticut: Yale University Press, 1940.

6820 **Savelle, Max.** "The Forty-Ninth Degree of North Latitude as an International Boundary, 1719; The Origin of an Idea." *Canadian Historical Review*, 38, No. 3 (September, 1957), 183-201.

6821 **Sipe, F. Henry.** "Retracement of Old Boundary Lines in West Virginia: Past, Present, and Future." *Surveying and Mapping*, 49, No. 3 (September, 1989), 123-127.

6822 **Smirnov, Mark.** "Bureau of Land Management Cadastral Survey." *Surveying and Land Information Systems* [Bethesda], 51, No. 4 (December, 1991), 197.

6823 **Snyder, John P.** *The Story of New Jersey's Civil Boundaries*. Trenton: Bureau of Geology and Topography, 1969.

6824 **Talbott, Robert D.** *A History of the Chilean Boundaries*. Ames: Iowa State University Press, 1974.

6825 **Timm, Charles A.** *The International Boundary Commission United States and Mexico*. The University of Texas Publications, No. 4134. Austin: University of Texas, 1941.

6826 **Timm, Charles A.** "Some Observations on the Nature and Work of the International Boundary Commission, United States and Mexico." *Southwestern Social Science Quarterly*, 15, No. 4 (March, 1934-1935), 271-297.

6827 *United States-Canada Boundary Treaty Centennial, 1846-1946. One Hundred Years of Peace*. Issued in cooperation with the Department of Trade and Industry, British Columbia. Tacoma, Washington, D.C.: Department of Conservation and Development, 1946.

6828 **U.S. Department of State.** *Boundaries of the Latin American Republics; An Annotated List of Documents, 1493-1825*. Tentative Version. Prepared in the Office of the Geographer, Department of State. Publication 1835. Washington, D.C.: U.S. Department of State, 1942.

6829 **U.S. Department of State.** *Boundary: Solution of the Problem of Chamiyal*. Washington, D.C.: U.S. Department of State, 1964.

6830 **Van Zandt, Franklin K.** *Boundaries of the United States and the Several States*. Geological Survey Bulletin 1212. Washington, D.C.: U.S. Government Printing Office, 1966.

ASIA

Books and Journals

6831 **Abu-Dawood, A.S.** *Political Boundaries of Saudi Arabia: Their Evolution and Functions*. Lexington: University of Kentucky, Ph.D., 1984.

6832 **Ahmad, Nafis.** "The Evolution of the Boundaries of East Pakistan." *Oriental Geographer*, 2, No. 2 (July, 1958), 97-106.

6833 **Armstrong, Hamilton Fish.** "Thoughts Along the China Border: Will Neutrality be Enough." *Foreign Affairs*, 38, No. 2 (January, 1960), 238-260.

6834 **Bar-Gal, Y.** "Boundaries as a Topic in Geographic Education: The Case of Israel." *Political Geography*, 12, No. 6 (November, 1993), 421-435.

6835 **Bar-Gal, Y.** "Perception of Borders in a Changing Territory: The Case of Israel." *Journal of Geography*, 78, No. 7 (December, 1979), 273-276.

6836 **Bar-Yaacov, N.** *The Israel-Syrian Armistice—Problems of Implementation, 1949-1966*. Jerusalem: Magnes Press, 1967.

6837 **Bhat, Budhi Prasad.** "The Himalayan Border." *The Himalayan Border: Selected Readings*. New Delhi: Foreign Affairs Report, No. 13, Publication Division, Government of India, 1963.

6838 **Bhattacharya, S.S.** *Evolution of Boundaries of U.P. from 1775-1955*. Aligarh: Aligarh Muslim University, Ph.D., 1970.

6839 **Blum, Yehuda Z.** *Secure Boundaries and Middle East Peace*. Jerusalem: Hebrew University of Jerusalem Faculty of Law, 1971.

6840 "The Borderlands of Soviet Central Asia: India and Pakistan." *Central Asian Review*, 5, No. 2 (February, 1957), 163-207.

6841 *Boundary Treaty Between the People's Republic of China and the People's Republic of Mangolia*. Hong Kong: Government Printing Office: 1963.

6842 **Burr, Malcolm.** "A Note on the History of the Turko-Caucasian Border." *Asiatic Review*, 43, No. 156 (October, 1947), 351-356.

6843 **Chakravarti, Prithwis Chandra.** "Evolution of India's Northern Borders." *India Quarterly*, 24, No. 1 (January-March, 1968), 6-16.

6844 **Cukwurah, A.Oye.** *The Settlement of Boundary Disputes in International Law*. Manchester: Manchester University Press, 1967.

6845 **Dayan, Moshe.** "Israel's Border and Security Problems." *Foreign Affairs*, 33, No. 2 (January, 1955), 250-267.

6846 **Dobell, W.M.** "Ramifications of the China-Pakistan Border Treaty." *Pacific Affairs*, 37, No. 3 (Fall, 1964), 283-285.

6847 **Haupert, John S.** "Some Aspects of the Boundaries and Frontiers of Israel." *California Council of Geography Teachers Bulletin*, 4, No. 3 (1956-57) (June 15, 1957), 2-6.

6848 **Haupert, John S.** "Some Aspects of the Boundaries and Frontiers of Israel." *Journal of Geography*, 56, No. 8 (November, 1957), 385-390.

6849 **Jones, Garth N.** "Sukarno's Early Views Upon the Territorial Boundaries of Indonesia." *Australian Outlook*, 18, No. 1 (April, 1964), 30-39.

6850 **Lauterpacht, E.** "River Boundaries: Legal Aspects of the Shatt-Al-Arab Frontier." *International and Comparative Law Quarterly*, 9, No. 2 (April, 1960), 208-236.

6851 **Lee, C.S.** "An Account of the International Boundaries of North Sinkiang." *China Institute of Geography, Pehpei, Szechuan, Geography*, 4, Nos. 1-2 (July, 1944), 37-48.

6852 **Murty, T.S.** *India-China Boundary-India's Options*. New Delhi: ABC Publications, 1987.

6853 **Nijim, Basheer K.** "Elusive Boundaries of Peace in the Holy Land." *Intellect*, 106 (December, 1977), 202-205.

6854 **Rahul, Ram.** "The Politics of China's Other Boundaries." Excerpt from *Indian and Foreign Review*, 1, No. 9 (February 15, 1964), 16-18.

6855 **Rao, K. Krisna.** "The Sino-Indian Boundary Question and International Law." *International and Comparative Law Quarterly*, 11, No. 2 (1962), 375-415.

6856 **Schofield, Richard N.** *Evolution of the Shatt al-'Arab Boundary Dispute*. Cambridgeshire, England: Middle East and North African Studies Press, 1986.

6857 **Smith, S.G.** "The Boundaries and Population Problems of Israel." *Geography*, 37, No. 177 (July, 1952), 152-165.

6858 **Solomon, Robert L.** *Boundary Concepts and Practices in Southeast Asia*. Santa Monica, California: Rand Corporation, 1969.

6859 **Solomon, Robert L.** "Boundary Concepts and Practices in Southeast Asia." *World Politics*, 23, No. 1 (October, 1970), 1-23.

6860 **Stephens, Michael D.** *A Political Geography of China's Boundaries*. Edinburgh: University of Edinburgh, Ph.D., 1966.

6861 **Toomre, J.** *An Analysis of the Principal Factors Affecting India's Policy Toward Her Himalayan Border*. Manchester: University of Manchester, Master's Thesis, 1960.

6862 **Waldron, Arthur.** *The Great Wall of China: From History to Myth*. Cambridge: Cambridge University Press, 1990.

6863 **Williamson, N.** "The Lohit-Brahmaputra Between Assam and Southeastern Tibet." *Geographical Journal*, 34, No. 4 (October, 1909), 363-383.

AUSTRALIA, OCEANIA AND ANTARCTICA

Books and Journals

6864 **Connell, H.B.** "External Affairs Power and the Domestic Implementation of Treaties." *Australian Foreign Affairs Record*, 54 (1983), 492-499.

6865 **Harris, S., ed.** *Australia's Antartic Policy Options*. Canberra: Australian National University, Center for Resource and Environmental Studies, Monograph 11, 1984.

6866 **Logan, W.S.** *The Evolution and Significance of Selected Intra-National Boundaries in Southwest Victoria*. Melbourne, Australia: University of Melbourne, B.A. dissertation, 1963.

6867 **Prescott, J.R.V.** "Actual and Potential Political Boundaries in the Antarctic Region." *Globe*, 21 (1984), 12-26.

6868 **Prescott, J.R.V.** "Boundaries in Antarctica." In *Australia's Antarcitc Policy Options*, S. Harris, ed. Canberra: Australian National University, Centre for Resource and Environmental Studies Monography 11, 1984, 83-112.

6869 **Van der Veur, Paul,** comp. *Documents and Correspondence on New Guinea's Boundaries*. Canberra: A.N.V. Press; The Hague: Martinus Nijhoff, 1966.

6870 **Van der Veur, Paul.** "The Irian Boundary Slumber, 1905-1962." *Australian Outlook*, 19, No. 1 (April, 1965), 73-96.

6871 **Van der Veur, Paul.** "New Guinea Annexations and the Origin of the Irian Boundary." *Australian Outlook*, 18, No. 3 (December, 1964), 313-339.

6872 **Van der Veur, Paul.** *Search for New Guinea's Boundaries from Torres Straight to the Pacific*. The Hague: Martinus Nijhoff, 1966.

6873 Winton, W.A. "History of the Surveys of the Eastern Boundaries of the Province of South Australia." *Royal Geographical Society of Australasia, South Australian Branch. Proceedings*, 55 (December, 1954), 1-11.

EUROPE

Books and Journals

6874 Albano-Muller, A. *Die Deutschland-Artikel in der Satzung der Vereinten Nationen.* Stuttgarz: Kohlhammer, 1967.

6875 Arciszewski, Franciszek. "Some Remarks About the Strategic Significance of the New and Old Soviet-Polish Border." *Polish Review*, 1, Nos. 2 and 3 (Spring-Summer, 1956), 89-96.

6876 Block, Mathilde de. *Sudtbrol.* Groningen: J.B. Wolters, 1954.

6877 Boundary Commission for England. *Third Periodical Report, Vol. 2.* London: Her Majesty's Stationery Office, Cmnd 8797II, 1983.

6878 Boundary Commission for Scotland. *Third Periodical Report, Vol. 2.* London: Her Majesty's Stationery Office, Cmnd 8794II, 1983.

6879 Boundary Commission for Wales. *Third Periodical Report.* London: Her Majesty's Stationery Office, Cmnd 8798, 1983.

6880 Capps, Edward. *Greece, Albania and Northern Epirus.* Chicago: Argonaut, 1963.

6881 Cree, D. "The Yugoslav-Hungarian Boundary Commission." *Geographical Journal*, 65, No. 2 (1925), 89-112.

6882 "The Future of the Saar." *World Today*, 9, No. 5 (May, 1953), 193-201.

6883 Gilfillan, S. "European Political Boundaries." *Political Science Quarterly*, 39, No. 3 (September, 1924), 458-484.

6884 Grundy-Warr, Carl, ed. *Eurasia.* London: Routledge, 1994.

6885 Hartshorne, Richard. "A Survey of the Boundary Problems of Europe." In *Geographic Aspects of International Relations*, C.C. Colby, ed. Chicago, Illinois: University of Chicago Press, 1938, 163-217.

6886 Hasson, Shlomo, and Razin, Eran. "What is Hidden Behind a Municipal Boundary Conflict." *Political Geography Quarterly*, 9, No. 3 (July, 1990), 267-283.

6887 Hiscocks, Richard. "Progress East of the Oder-Neisse." *World Today*, 16, No. 11 (November, 1960), 491-500.

6888 Hoffman, George W. "Boundary Problems in Europe." *Annals of the Association of American Geographers*, 44, No. 1 (March, 1954), 102-107.

6889 Holdich, Thomas H. *Boundaries in Europe and the Near East.* London: Macmillan, 1918.

6890 Holdich, Thomas H. "Political Boundaries." *Scottish Geographical Magazine*, 32 (1916), 497.

6891 Holdich, Thomas H. *Political Frontiers and Boundary Making.* London: Macmillan, 1916.

6892 House, J.W. "A Local Perspective on Boundaries and the Frontier Zone: Two Examples from the European Economic Community." In *Essays in Political Geography*, Charles A. Fisher, ed. London: Methuen, 1968, 327-344.

6893 Jack, Ernest. *Report on the Work of the British Section of the Anglo-German-Belgian Boundary Commission.* London: Her Majesty's Stationery Office, 1911.

6894 Lloyd, Trevor. *The Norwegian-Soviet Boundary; A Study in Political Geography.* Hanover, New Hampshire: Dartmouth College Department of Geography, 1954.

6895 "The Macedonian Question; A Note on the Historical Background." *Bulletin of International News*, 22, No. 12 (June 9, 1945), 509-515.

6896 Minghi, Julian V. "Boundary Studies and National Prejudices: The Case of the South Tyrol." *Professional Geographer*, 15, No. 1 (January, 1963), 4-8.

6897 Pakstas, Kazys. "National and State Boundaries (of Lithuania)." *Lituanus; Lithuanian Collegiate Quarterly*, 5, No. 3 (September, 1959), 67-72.

6898 Patten, Simon N. "Unnatural Boundaries of European States." *Survey*, 34, No. 1 (April 3, 1915), 24-27.

6899 Paul, Barbara Dotts, comp. *The Polish-German Borderlands: An Annotated Bibliography.* Westport: Greenwood Press, 1994.

6900 Rahul, Ram. "China-USSR Boundary Question: Historical Perspective." Excerpt: *Indian and Foreign Review*, 6, No. 18 (July, 1969), 17-19.

6901 Schiffrer, Carlo. *Venezie Guilia; Study of a Map of the Italo-Yugoslav National Borders.* Roma: Stabilimenti Tipografici C. Colombo, 1946.

6902 Semenon, I.V., and Sisko, P.K. "Complex Boundary of Arctic." *Izvestiya Vsesoyuznogo Geograficheskogo Obschestva* (Bulletin of the All-Union Geographical Society), Tom 105, No. 4 (July-August, 1973), 313-319.

6903 Weigend, Guido G. "Effects of Boundary Changes in the South Tyrol." *Geographical Review*, 40, No. 3 (July, 1950), 364-375.

6904 Winterbotham, H.S.L. "The International Boundaries of Europe." *Empire Survey Review*, 8, No. 58 (October, 1945), 133-137.

6905 Woosley, Lester H. "The Polish Boundary Question." *American Journal of International Law*, 38, No. 3 (July, 1944), 441-448.

BOUNDARY CLASSIFICATION AND DELINEATION

GENERAL AND THEORY

Books and Journals

6906 Biger, Gideon. "Physical Geography and Law: The Case of International River Boundaries." *GeoJournal*, 17, No. 3 (October, 1988), 341-347.

6907 Boggs, S. Whittemore. "Boundary Functions and the Principles of Boundary-Making." *U.S. Dept. of State. Press Releases*, Weekly Issue No. 118, Publication No. 268 (January 2, 1932), 3-10.

6908 Boulmois, P.K. "International Boundary Delimitation." *Rohal Engineers Journal*, 43 (1929), 425-438.

6909 Brigham, Albert Perry. "Principles in the Determination of Boundaries." *Geographical Review*, 7, No. 2 (April, 1919), 201-219.

6910 Classen, H. George. "Keepers of the Boundary." *Canadian Geographical Journal*, 65, No. 4 (October, 1962), 122-129.

6911 Clifford, E.H.M. "Boundary Commissions." *Royal Engineers Journal*, 51, No. 4 (December, 1937), 363-374.

6912 Dawson, Samuel Edward. "Line of Demarcation of Pope Alexander VI in AD 1493." *Transactions Royal Society of Canada*, 5, Section 2 (1899), 467-546.

6913 Essed, F.E. "De Bepaling van de Grenslihn tyssen twee Groungebieden in greensrivieren de evenredigheidslign," (La ligne proportionnelle comme frontiere entre deux pays separes par une riviere). *Tigdschrift Koninkrijk Nederlanden Aardrijkunde*, 82, No. 4 (1965), 348-358.

6914 Gallois, L. *La ligne de partage des eaux et le trace des frontieres.* Belgrade: Drzavna Stamparija Kraljevine Srba, 1924.

6915 Garner, J.W. "The Doctrine of the Thalweg (Notes)." *British Year Book of International Law*, 16 (1935), 177.

6916 Garner, J.W. "The Doctrine of the Thalweg as a Rule of International Law." *American Journal of International Law*, 29, No. 2 (April, 1935), 309-310.

6917 Holdich, Thomas H. "Geographical Problems in Boundary Making." *Geographical Journal,* 47, No. 6 (June, 1916), 421-440.

6918 Holdich, Thomas H. "Use of Practical Geography Illustrated by Recent Frontier Operations." *Geographical Journal*, 13, No. 5 (May, 1899), 465-480.

6919 Jones, Stephen B. *Boundary-Making; A Handbook for Statesmen, Treaty Editors and Boundary Commissioners.* Monograph Series, No. 8. Washington, D.C.: Carnegie Endowment for International Peace, Div. of International Law, 1945.

6920 Longley, Paul A., and Batty, Michael. "On the Fractal Measurement of Geographical Boundaries." *Geographical Analysis*, 21, No. 1 (January, 1989), 47-67.

6921 Morrison, Peter A., and Clark, William A. V. *The Demographer's Role in the Local Boundary-Drawing Process.* Santa Monica: RAND, April 1991.

6922 Pietkiewicz, Stanislaw. "O granicy panstwowej i jej przeprawdzaniu." *Przeglad Geograficzny*, Tome 20 (1946), 9-53.

6923 Potter, Pitman B. "Stephen B. Jones: Boundary-Making." *American Journal of International Law*, 34, No. 4 (October, 1945), 859.

6924 Prescott, Victor. "Surveyors and International Boundaries." *The Globe* [Sydney], No. 38 (1993), 17-26.

POLITICAL GEOGRAPHY OF REGIONS

AFRICA

Books and Journals

6925 Belgium, Great Britain and Northern Ireland. "Treaty Regarding the Boundary Between Tanganyika and Ruwanda-Uurndi, Signed in London, November 22, 1934. *League of Nations, Treaty Series*, 190, Nos. 4401-4430 (1938), 103-107.

6926 **Bennett, George.** "The Eastern Boundary of Uganda in 1902." *Uganda Journal*, 23, No. 1 (March, 1959), 69-72.

6927 **Bentwich, Norman.** *Ethiopia, Eritrea & Somaliland.* London: V. Gollancz, 1947.

6928 **Clifford, E.H.M.** "The British Smolaliland-Ethiopia Boundary." *Geographical Journal*, 87, No. 4 (April, 1936), 289-337.

6929 **Collins, Robert O.** "Sudan-Uganda Boundary Rectification and the Sudanese Occupational of Madial, 1914." *Uganda Journal*, 26, No. 2 (September, 1962), 140-153.

6930 **Delme-Radcliffe, C.** "Extracts from Lt.-Col. Delme-Radcliffe's Typescript Diary Report on the Delimitation of the Anglo-German Boundary, Uganda, 1902-1904." *Uganda Journal*, 11, No. 1 (March, 1947), 1-11.

6931 **Demhardt, Imre Josef.** "Namibia's Orange River Boundary—Origin and Reemerged Effects of an Inattentive Colonial Boundary Delimitation." *GeoJournal* [Dordrecht], 22, No. 3 (November, 1990), 355-362.

6932 **Detzner, V.H.** "Die Nigerische Grenze von Kamerun zwischen Yola und dem Cross-Fluss." *Mitteilungen aus den deutschen Schutzgebeiten*, 26, Band 4 (1913), 317-338.

6933 "Extracts from Lt. Col. C. Delme-Radcliffe's Typescript Diary Report on the Anglo-German Boundary, Uganda, 1902-1904." *Uganda Journal*, 2, No. 1 (March, 1947), 9-29.

6934 **Federal Republic of Nigeria.** *First Report of the Boundary Adjustment Commission.* Lagos: Federal Ministry of Information, 1976.

6935 **Foulkes, C.H.** "The Anglo-French Boundary Commission, Niger to Lake Chad." *Royal Engineers Journal*, 73, No. 4 (December, 1959), 429-437.

6936 **Great Britain.** "Exchange of Notes between the Government of the United Kingdom of Great Britain and Northern Ireland and the Government of the Portuguese Republic Accepting the Report of the Nyasalaid-Mozambique Boundary Commission of the 27th of August, 1956." London: Secretary of State for Foreign Affairs, 1965.

6937 **Great Britain.** Parliament. *Exchange of Notes Constituting an Agreement between the Government of the United Kingdom and the Government of Ethiopia, Amending the Description of the Kenya/Ethiopia Boundary.* Addis Ababa, 29th September, 1947. London: Great Britain Parliament, 1948.

6938 **Great Britain.** Treaties, etc. *Agreement between the Government of the United Kingdom and the Belgian Government Regarding the Water Rights on the Boundary between Tanganyika and Ruanda-Urundi, London, November 22, 1934.* Ratifications exchanged in London on May 19, 1938. Treaty Series No. 42 (1938). London: Great Britain Parliament, 1938.

6939 **Griffiths, I.L.** "The Scramble for Africa: Inherited Political Boundaries." *Geographical Journal*, 152, No. 2 (1986), 204-216.

6940 **Hamilton, David Napier.** *Ethiopia's Frontiers: The Boundary Agreements and Their Demarcation, 1896-1956.* Oxford: University of Oxford, Ph.D., 1974.

6941 **Hatchell, G.W.** "The Boundary Between Tanganyika and Kenya." *Tanganyika Notes and Records*, No. 43 (June, 1956), 41.

6942 **Herbst, Jeffrey.** "The Creation and Maintenance of National Boundaries in Africa." *International Organization*, 43, No. 4 (Autumn, 1989), 673-692.

6943 **Killott, G.S.** "The Anglo-French Niger-Chad Boundary Commission." *Geographical Journal*, 24, No. 5 (November, 1904), 505-524.

6944 **King, L.N.** *Report on the Work of the Jubaland Boundary Commission, 1925-1928* (typescript). A copy of this report is held as Catalogue No. DT 436. London: Commonwealth Relations Office Library, Great Smith Street, 1928.

6945 **Laws, J.B.** "A Minor Adjustment in the Boundary between Tanganykia Territory and Ruanda." *Geographical Review*, 80, No. 2 (April, 1932), 244-247.

6946 **Lawuyi, Olatunde Bayo.** "Ogun: Diffusion Across Boundaries and Identity Constructions." *African Studies Review*, 31, No. 2 (September, 1988), 127-139.

6947 **Leverson, J.J.** "Geographical Results of the Anglo-Portuguese Delimitation Commission in South East Africa, 1892." *Geographical Journal*, 2, No. 6 (December, 1893), 505-510.

6948 **Martonne, E. de.** "La delimitation du Cameroun." *La Geographie*, Tome 72, No. 2 (Aout-Septembre, 1939), 115-119.

6949 **Mayall, James.** "The Malawi-Tanzania Boundary Dispute." *Journal of Modern African Studies*, 11, No. 4 (December, 1973), 611-628.

6950 **Nugent, W.V.** "The Geographical Results of the Nigeria-Kamerun Boundary Demarcation Commission." *Geographical Journal*, 43, No. 6 (June, 1914), 630-651.

6951 **Peake, E.R.L.** "Northern Rhodesia-Belgian Congo Boundary." *Geographical Journal*, 83, No. 3 (March, 1934), 263-280.

6952 **Prescott, J.R.V.** "The Evolution of the Anglo-French Inter-Cameroons Boundary." *Nigerian Geographical Journal*, 5, No. 2 (December, 1962), 103-120.

6953 **Prescott, J.R.V.** "The Evolution of Nigeria's Boundaries." *Nigerian Geographical Journal*, 2, No. 2 (March, 1959), 80-104.

6954 **Prescott, J.R.V.** *The Evolution of Nigeria's International and Regional Boundaries: 1861-1971*. Vancouver: Tartalus Research Limited, 1971.

6955 **Prescott, J.R.V.** "Geographical Problems Associated with the Delimitation and Demarcation of the Nigeria-Kamerun Boundary, 1885-1916." Ibadan, University College, Department of Geography. *Research Notes*, 12 (February, 1959), 1-14.

6956 **Ravenstein, E.G.** "The Anglo-French Boundaries in Africa." *Geographical Journal*, 12, No. 1 (July, 1898), 73-75.

6957 **Reyner, Anthony S.** *The Length and Status of International Boundaries in Africa*. Photocopy: African Boundary Problems, C.G. Widstrand, ed. Uppsala: Scandinavian Institute of African Studies, 1969.

6958 **Rouire, Dr.** "La delimitation de la Republique de Liberia." *Annales de Geographie,* (Octobre-Decembre), 489-498.

6959 **Shaw, W.B.K.** "International Boundaries of Libya." *Geographical Journal*, 85, No. 1 (January, 1935), 50-53.

6960 **Smith, C.S.** "The Anglo-German Boundary in East Equatorial Africa. Proceedings of the British Commission, 1892." *Geographical Journal*, 4, No. 5 (November, 1894), 424-436.

6961 **U.S. Department of State.** "Steps Taken Toward Completing the Delimitation of the Franco-Liberian Boundary." *Papers relating to the foreign relations of the United States, 1926 2 (1941)*. Washington, D.C.: U.S. Department of State, 1941, 600-604.

AMERICAS

Books and Journals

6962 **Andrew, Bunyan H.** "Some Queries Concerning the Texas-Louisiana Sabine Boundary." *Southwestern Historical Quarterly*, 53, No. 1 (July, 1949), 1-18.

6963 **Argentina Ministry for Foreign Affairs and Worship.** *Complementary Treaty on Definitive Boundaries Signed Between the Republics of Argentina and Paraguay on the Pilcomayo River*. Buenos Aires: Department of Information for Abroad, Argentine News, 75 (June, 1945), 2-3+.

6964 *Atlas-Report of the Commission Appointed to Delimit the Boundary Between the Province of Saskatchewan and the Northwest Territories*. Ottawa, Ontario, Canada: Office of the Surveyor General, 1963.

6965 **Avery, William P.** "Origins and Consequences of the Border Dispute Between Equador and Peru." *Inter-American Economic Affairs*, 38, No. 1 (Summer, 1984), 65-77.

6966 **Baldwin, J.R.** "The Ashburton-Webster Boundary Settlement." *Canadian Historical Association*. Report of the annual meeting, 1938, with historical papers, (1938), 121-133.

6967 **Beatty, F.W.** "Ontario-Manitoba Boundary." *Annuary Report of the Association of Ontario Land Survey*, (1949), 138-139.

6968 **Bateman, Alfredo D.** "Division territorial de Colombia." *Boletin de la Sociedad Geografica de Colombia*, 6, Num. 5 (Noviembre de 1940), 324-326.

6969 **Bertrand, A.** "Methods of Survey Employed by the Chilean Boundary Commission in the Cordillers of the Andes." *Geographical Journal*, 16, No. 4 (October, 1990), 329.

6970 **Billman, Christine W.** "Jack Craig and the Alaska Boundary Survey." *Beaver*, Outfit 302, No. 2 (Autumn, 1971), 44-49.

6971 **Bonetti, E.** "L'Honduras Britannico e le rivendicazioni territoriali del Guatemala." *Geopolitica*, Anno 2, Num. 8-9 (Agosto-Settembre, 1940), 374-376.

6972 **Brazil.** Ministerio das relacoes exteriores. *Limites Brasil-Colombia*. Rio de Janeiro: Ministerio das relacoes exteriores, 1937.

6973 **Briggs, Vernon M.** *The Mexico-United States Border: Public Policy and Chicano Economic Welfare*. Austin: University of Texas, Bureau of Business Research, Center for the Study of Human Resources, Studies in Human Resource Development, No. 2, 1974.

6974 **Brooks, Philip Collidge.** *Diplomacy and the Borderlands: The Adams-Onis Treaty of 1819*. Vol. 24. Berkeley: University of California Publications in History, 1939.

6975 **Brown, P.M.** "Costa Rica-Nicaragua." *American Journal of International Law*, 11, No. 1 (January, 1917), 156-160.

6976 **Campbell, A.J.** *British Columbia Boundary Survey.* Victoria: Report of the Deputy Minister of Lands for 1948, 1949.

6977 **Canada-United States, International Boundary Commission.** *Joint Report upon the Survey and Demarcation of the Boundary, from the Gulf of Georgia to the Northernmost Point of Lake of the Woods.* Washington, D.C.: Government Printing Office, 1937.

6978 **Cebreros, Francisco.** "Breve Resena del Proceso de Nuestra demarcacion territorial." *Boletin de la Sociedad Geografica de Lima,* 80, No. 1 (Enero-Abril, 1963), 41-49.

6979 "The Chaco Boundary Award." *Bulletin of the Pan American Union,* 72, No. 11 (November, 1938), 620-622.

6980 **Clark, J. Stanley.** "The Northern Boundary of Oklahoma." *Chronicles of Oklahoma,* 15, No. 3 (September, 1937), 271-290.

6981 **Cushing, S.W.** "The Boundaries of the New England States." *Annals of the Association of American Geographers,* 10, No. 1 (March, 1920), 17-40.

6982 **da Fonseca Hermes, J.S.** "Demarcacao da linha divisoria entre o Brasil e a Colombia." *Revista do Sociedad de Geografia do Rio de Janeiro,* Tomo 48 (1941), 37-44.

6983 **Davidson, G.** *The Alaska Boundary.* San Francisco: Alaska Packers Associd, 1903.

6984 **Davis, John W.** "The Unguarded Boundary (Canada-United States Boundary)." *Geographical Review,* 12, No. 4 (October, 1922), 585-601.

6985 **Delafield, Joseph.** *The Unfortified Boundary: A Diary of the First Survey of the Canadian Boundary Line from St. Regis to the Lake of the Woods.* From the original manuscript, Robert McElroy and Thomas Riggs, eds. New York: Private Printing, 1943.

6986 "Demarcacaode limites entre o Brasil e a Colombia." *Revista da Sociedade de Geografia do Rio de Janerio,* Tomo 44 (1937), 89-98.

6987 "Descripcion Sintetica de las fronteras del Peru." *Anuario Geografico del Peru,* Num. 1 (1962), 7-11.

6988 **Douglas, Jesse S.** "The Clackamas-Clark County Boundary, 1850." *Oregon Historical Quarterly,* 39, No. 2 (June, 1938), 147-151.

6989 **Dunbar, M.J.** "Notes on the Delimitation of the Arctic and Subarctic Zones." (N.p., 1947). Reprinted from *Canadian Field-Natura-List,* 61, No. 1 (January-February, 1947), 12-14.

6990 **Edwards, H.A.** "Boundary Survey Between Brazil and Bolivia." *Geographical Journal,* No. 2 (February, 1914), 206-207.

6991 **Edwards, H.A.** "Frontier Work on Bolivia-Brazil Boundary, 1911-1912." *Geographical Journal,* 42, No. 2 (August, 1913), 113-128.

6992 **Fawcett, Lois M.** "Marking Minnesota's Western Boundary." *Minnesota History,* 19, No. 4 (December, 1938), 424-426.

6993 **Foster, Austin T.** "The Blazed Trail of Vermont's Northern Boundary." *Vermont Quarterly,* 17, No. 1 (January, 1949), 3-8.

6994 **Gardner, Gerard.** "La frontiere Canada-Labrador." *Revue Trimestrielle Canadienne,* 24° annee, No. 95 (Septembre, 1938), 272-289.

6995 **Gavito, Sanchez.** "Sanchez Gavito on a Border Dispute Settled; OAS Peace Committee Aids Honduras, Nicaragua." *Americas,* 14, No. 1 (January, 1962), 10-12.

6996 **Great Britain Foreign Office.** *Award of Her Majesty Queen Elizabeth II for the Arbitration of a Controversy between the Argentine Republic and the Republic of Chile Concerning Certain Parts of the Boundary between Their Territories.* London: Her Majesty's Stationery Office, 1966.

6997 **Great Britain. Parliament.** *Exchange of Notes between His Majesty's Government in the United Kingdom and the Government of Brazil, Approving the General Report of the Special Commissioners Appointed to Demarcate the Boundary-Line Between British Guiana and Brazil (with General Report) Rio de Janairo, 15th March, 1940.* Treaty Series, No. 51, Cmd. 6965. London: Great Britain Parliament, 1946.

6998 **Great Britain. Treaties, etc.** *Treaty between His Majesty in Respect of the United Kingdom and the President of the United States of Venezuela Concerning the Status of the Island of Patos, Caracas, February 26, 1942.* Treaty Series, No. 11 (1942), Cmd. 6401. London: Great Britain Parliament, 1942.

6999 **Gregory, Gladys.** "The Chamizal Settlement; A View from El Paso." *Southwestern Studies Texas Western College,* 1, No. 2 (Summer, 1963), entire issue.

7000 **Guatemala and Salvador.** "Treaty for the Delimitation of the Boundary between the Two Countries with Annexes. Signed at Guatemala, April 9th, 1938." *League of Nations. Treaty Series,* 189, Nos. 4732-4400 (1938), 275-311.

7001 **Hackett, Charles Wilson.** "Tratado de Pichardo sobre los limites de Luisiana y Tejas; su olvido y su significado." *Boletin de la Sociedad Mexicana de Geografia y Estadistica*, Tomo 59, Nums. 5-6 (Septiembre-Diciembre, 1944), 455-471.

7002 **Harris, C. Alexander.** "The Labrador Boundary." *Contemporary Review*, 131 (April, 1927), 415-421.

7003 **Hincks, Sir Francis.** *The Northerly and Westerly Boundaries of the Province of Ontario, and the Award Relating Thereto, as Discussed and Explained by. . .* Toronto: C.B. Robinson, 1881.

7004 **Hill, James E.** "Nevada South of 37° North: An Unprecedented Political Blunder." *Yearbook of the Association of Pacific Coast Geographers*, 35 (1973), 61-74.

7005 **Holdich, Thomas H.** "The Alaska Boundary." *Geographical Journal*, 22, No. 6 (December, 1903), 674-676.

7006 **Holdich, Thomas H.** "The Geographical Results of the Peru-Bolivia Boundary Commission." 47, No. 2 (February, 1916), 95-116.

7007 **Holmes, Jack D.L.** "The Southern Boundary Commission, the Chattahoochee River, and the Florida Seminoles, 1799." *Florida Historical Quarterly*, 44, No. 4 (April, 1966), 312-341.

7008 **Honduras.** Ministerio de relaciones exteriores. *Limites entre Honduras y Nicaragua. Incidente suscitado por Nicaragua.* 2a ed. Tegucigalpa: Publicaciones de la Secretaria de relaciones exteriores de Honduras, 1938.

7009 **Honduras.** Ministerio de la relaciones exteriores. *Limites entre Honduras y Nicaragua. Replica al alegato de Nicaragua presentada a Su Majestad Catolica el Rey de Espana en calidad de arbitro por los representantes de la Repca. de Honduras.* 2a ed. Tegucigalpa: Publicackones de la Secretaria de rr..ee., 1938.

7010 **Hubbard, William O., and Johnson, Joe.** *Kentucky's Ohio River Boundary from the Big Sandy to the Great Miami.* Frankfort, Kentucky: Kentucky Legislative Research Commission, 1969.

7011 **International Boundary Commission (U.S. and Canada).** *Joint Report upon the Survey and Demarcation of the Boundary between the United States and Canada from the Gulf of Georgia to the Northwesternmost Point of Lake of the Woods.* Washington, D.C.: Government Printing Office, 1937.

7012 **International Boundary Commission (U.S. and Canada).** *Joint Report upon the Survey and Demarcation of the Boundary between Canada and the United States from Jongass Passage to Mount St. Elias; In Accordance with the Convention of January 24, 1903.* Ottawa: Queen's Printer, E. Cloutier, 1952.

7013 **Jones, Stephen B.** "The Cordilleran Section of the Canada-United States Borderland." *Geographical Journal*, 89, No. 5 (May, 1937), 439-450.

7014 **Jones, Stephen B.** "The Forty-Ninth Parallel in the Great Plains: The Historical Geography of a Boundary." *Journal of Geography*, 31, No. 9 (December, 1932), 357-368.

7015 **Jones, Wilbur Deverex.** "Lord Ashburton and the Maine Boundary Negotiations." *Mississippi Valley Historical Review*, 40, No. 3 (December, 1953), 447-490.

7016 **King, Shirley.** "The Ontario-Quebec Boundary." *Annuary Report of the Association of Ontario Land Survey*, (1934), 143-155.

7017 **Kleber, Louis C.** "The Mason-Dixon Line." *History Today*, 18, No. 2 (February, 1968), 117-123.

7018 **Klotz, O.** "The History of the Forty-Ninth Parallel Survey West of the Rocky Mountains." *Geographical Review*, 3, No. 3 (July, 1917), 382.

7019 **LaForest, G.V.** "The Delimitation of National Territory: Re Dominion Coal Company and County of Cape Breton." *Canadian Yearbook of International Law*, 2 (1964), 233-244.

7020 **Lamb, W.A., and Hoover, O.H.** "International Forecasting and Apportionment of Waters by United States and Canada in St. Mary and Milk River Drainage Basins (Montana, U.S.A.-Alberta and Saskatchewan, Canada)." *Union internationale de geodesie et de geophysique. Association internationale d'hydrologie scientifique. Bulletin*, No. 23 (1938), 169-193.

7021 **Lambert, A.F.** "Maintaining the Canada-United States Boundary." *Cartographer*, 2, No. 2 (October, 1965), 67-71.

7022 **Lambert, A.F.** "The United States-Canada Boundary." *Surveying and Mapping*, 28, No. 1 (March, 1968), 31-39.

7023 **Landrum, Francis S.** "A Major Monument: Oregon-California Boundary." *Oregon Historical Quarterly*, 72, No. 1 (March, 1971), 723-740.

7024 **Lass, William E.** "How the Forty-Ninth Parallel Became the International Boundary." *Minnesota History*, 44, No. 6 (Summer, 1975), 209-219.

7025 **Lass, William E.** *Minnesota's Boundary with Canada: Its Evolution Since 1783.* St. Paul: Minnesota Historical Society Press, 1980.

7026 **Lass, William E.** "Minnesota's Separation from Wisconsin: Boundary Making on the Upper Mississippi Frontier." *Minnesota History* (St. Paul), 50, no. 8 (Winter, 1987), 309-320.

7027 **Lates, R.V.N.** *The Changing Functions of the Vermont-Quebec Segment of the U.S.-Canadian Boundary.* Montpelier: University of Vermont, Master's Thesis, 1971.

7028 **Lefevre, Vlademar.** "Limites do Estado de Sao Paulo." *O.I.G.G.* Revista do Instituto Geografica e Geologico, Sao Paulo, 8, Nos. 1-4 (January-December, 1950), 340-416.

7029 **Lynden, A.J.H. van.** "Op zoek naar Suriname's zuidgrens. De grensbepaling tusschen suriname en Brazilie. 1935-1938." *Tijdschrift van het Koninklijk Nederlandsch aardrijkskundig genootschap,* 2, reeks, dl. 56, No. 6 (November, 1939), 793-805.

7030 **Mayo, Lawrence Shaw.** "The Forty-Fifth Parallel or Detail of the Unguarded Boundary." *Geographical Review,* 13, No. 2 (April, 1923), 255-265.

7031 **McEwen, A.C.** "The International Boundary Commission, Canada-United States." *Canadian Surveyor,* 40, No. 3 (1986), 277-290.

7032 **Meade, B.K.** "Delaware-Maryland North-South Boundary Resurvey of 1961-62." *Survey and Mapping,* 34, No. 1 (March, 1964), 33-36.

7033 **Melbourne, W.H.** "Exploration and Survey on the Bolivia-Peru Border." *Geographical Journal,* 126, No. 3 (September, 1960), 455-458.

7034 **Merrett, Christopher D.** "Changing Border Function of the Canada-United States Boundary: 1947-1977." *New England-St. Lawrence Valley Geographical Society. Proceedings,* 17, (1987), 60-68.

7035 **Merrett, Christopher D.** "The Canada-United States Boundary: The Spatial Variation of Its Functions." Burlington: University of Vermont, M.A., 1988.

7036 **Meserve, Peter.** "Boundary Water Along the Forty-Ninth Parallel: State and Provincial Legislative Innovations." University of Washington, Seattle, Ph.D., 1989.

7037 **Miller, Hunter, ed.** "Northwest Water Boundary." *Report of the Experts Summoned by the German Emperor as Arbitrator Under Articles 34-42 of the Treaty of Washington of May 8, 1871, Preliminary to His Award Dated October 21, 1872.* Ed., with a translation by University of Washington Publications in the Social Sciences, Vol. 13, No. 1. Seattle: University of Washington, 1942.

7038 **Mills, David.** *A Report on the Boundaries of Ontario.* Toronto: Hunter Ross, 1873.

7039 **Minghi, Julian V.** "The Evolution of a Border Region: The Pacific Coast Section of the Canada-United States Boundary." *Scottish Geographical Magazine,* 80, No. 1 (April, 1964), 37-52.

7040 **Morrill, Richard L.** "Redistricting, Region, and Representation." *Political Geography Quarterly* (Guildford), 6, No. 3 (July, 1987), 241-260.

7041 **Nelson, L.D.M.** "The Arbitration of Boundary Disputes in Latin America." *Netherlands International Law Review,* 20, No. 3 (1973), 267-294.

7042 **Nesham, E.W.** "The Alaska Boundary Demarcation." *Geographical Journal,* 69, No. 1 (January, 1927), 49.

7043 **Nicholson, Norman L.** "Boundary Adjustments in the Gulf of Saint Lawrence Region." *Newfoundland Quarterly,* 53 (1954), 13-17.

7044 **Nicholson, Norman L.** *The Boundaries of Canada, Its Provinces and Territories.* Ottawa: Geographical Branch, Mines and Technical Surveys, 1964.

7045 **Nicholson, Norman L.** *The Boundaries of the Canadian Confederation.* Ottawa: Macmillan, 1979.

7046 **Paulin, C.O.** "The Early Choice of the 49th Parallel as a Boundary Line." *Canadian Historical Review,* 4, No. 2 (June, 1923), 127-131.

7047 **Peru.** Comision del Estatuto y Redemarcacion Territorial. *Cuadro de la Demarcacion Politica del Peru.* Lima: Comision del Estatuto y Redemarcacion Territorial, 1947.

7048 **Pessoa, Epitacio.** "Demarcacao das divisas do Estado de Sao Paulo com o do Parana." *O.I.G.G. Revista do Instituto Geografico e Geologico,* 18, Ano 23 (Janeiro-Marco, 1966), 119-131.

7049 **Peters, F.H.** "The Longest Surveyed Straight Line." Boundary line between Alberta and Saskatchewan. *Empire Survey Review,* 5, No. 33 (July, 1939), 130-133.

7050 **Pichardo, Jose, Antonio, Father.** *Pichardo's Treatise on the Limits of Louisiana and Texas; An Argumentative Historical Treatise with Reference to the Verification of the True Limits of the Provinces of Louisiana and Texas...to Disprove the Claim of the United States that Texas was included int he Louisiana Purchase of 1803.* 3v. Published from a transcript of the original manuscript in the Mexican Archives; translated into English by Charles Wilson Hackett, Chairmion Clair Shelby, and Mary Ruth Splawn, and edited by Charles Wilson Hackett. Austin: University of Texas Press, 1931-1941.

7051 **Pierce, J.W.** "The Ontario-Manitoba Boundary." *Canadian Surveyor.* Special Edition, proceedings of 31st annual meeting of the Canadian Institute of Surveying, (1938), 46-54.

7052 **Porter, Eugene O.** "Boundary and Jurisdictional Problems of the Kentucky-Ohio Border." *Ohio State Archaeological and Historical Quarterly,* 55, No. 2 (April-June, 1946), 155-164.

7053 *The Question of the Boundaries between Peru and Ecuador. Statement of the Peruvian Delegation to the Washington Conference Concerning the Scope of the Boundary Negotiations with Ecuador, in Accordance with the Protocol of the 21st of June, 1924, within the historical-Juridical Process of the Controversy.* Baltimore, Maryland: Reese Press, 1937.

7054 *The Question of the Boundaries between Peru and Equador. A Historical Outline Covering the Period Since 1910.* Baltimore, Maryland: Reese Press, 1936.

7055 **Reid, R.L.** "The Indian Stream Territory; An Episode of the North-East Boundary Dispute." *Transactions of the Royal Society of Canada.* 3d series. 34, Section 2 (1940), 143-171.

7056 **Revel-Movroz, Jean.** "Permeabilite de la Frontiere Mexique-Etas-Unis: La Mobilite des Consommateurs, des Travailleurs et des Entreprises." *Association de Geographes Francais (Paris) Bulletin,* 57ᵉ Annee, No. 470-471 (Mai-Juin, 1980), 227-234.

7057 **Riccardo, Riccardo.** "La delimitazione del confine tra l'Ecuador e il Peru." *Bollettino della Reale Societa Geografica Italiana,* Serie 7, 8, Fasc. 2 (Marzo-Aprile, 1943), 65-77.

7058 **Riggs, Thomas.** "Running the Alaska Boundary." *Beaver,* Outfit 276 (September, 1945), 40-43.

7059 **Rister, Carl Coke,** and **Lovelace, Bryan W.** "A Diary Account of a Creek Boundary Survey, 1850." *Chronicles of Oklahoma,* 27, No. 3 (Autumn, 1949), 268-302.

7060 **Rosenvall, L.A.** "Interstate Boundaries and Settlement Patterns: The Example of Utah." In

University of British Columbia. Department of Geography. B.C. Geographical Series, No. 17. Occasional Papers in Geography. Malaspina Papers: Studies in Human and Physical Geography, ed. by Roger Leigh. Vancouver: University of British Columnia, 1973, 35-50.

7061 **Saskatchewan-Northwest Territories Boundary Commission.** *Report of the Commissioners Appointed to Direct the Survey and Demarcation of the Boundary between the Province of Saskatchewan and the Northwest Territories.* Ottawa: Government Printing Press, 1963.

7062 "Settlement of the Ecuador-Peru Boundary Dispute." *Bulletin of the Pan American Union,* 76, No. 5 (May, 1942), 241-244.

7063 "Settlement of Peru-Ecuador Boundlary Dispute." *Department of State Bulletin,* 6, No. 140 (February, 1942), 194-196.

7064 "The Signing of the Bolivian-Paraguayan Peace Treaty." *Bulletin of the Pan American Union,* 72, No. 9 (September, 1938), 497-502.

7065 **Swisher, J.A.** "Seven New Counties." *Palimpsest,* 19, No. 1 (January, 1938), 22-30.

7066 **Talbott, Robert D.** "The Chilean Boundary in the Strait of Magellan." *Hispanic American Historical Review,* 47, No. 4 (November, 1964), 519-531.

7067 **Teran Gomez, Luis.** *Los partidos politicos y su accion democratica.* La Paz: Editorial 'La Paz', 1942.

7068 "Texto del protocolo de paz, amistad y limites suscrito por el Peru y el Ecuador el 29 de enero de 1942." *Boletin de la Sociedad Geografica de Lima,* Tomo 59, Trim. 3 (1942), 238-241.

7069 **Thomas, Benjamin E.** "Demarcation of the Boundaries of Idaho." *Pacific Northwest Quarterly,* 40, No. 1 (January, 1949), 24-34.

7070 **Thomas, Benjamin E.** "The California-Nevada Boundary." *Annals of the Association of American Geographers,* 42, No. 1 (March, 1952), 51-68.

7071 **Thomson, Don W.** "The 49th Parallel." *Geographical Journal,* 134, Part 2 (June, 1968), 209-215.

7072 **Thorndale, William.** "Reconstructing Historical U.S. County Boundaries." *Western Association of Map Libraries. Information Bulletin,* 18, No. 2 (March, 1987), 159-164.

7073 **Tikekar, S.R.** "The Durand Line; A Survey." *India Quarterly,* 6, No. 4 (October-December, 1950), 326-331.

7074 **Tompkins, Stuart R.** "Drawing the Alaskan Boundary." *Canadian Historical Review*, 26, No. 1 (March, 1945), 1-24.

7075 **Ullman, Edward L.** "The Eastern Rhode Island-Massachusetts Boundary Zone." *Geographical Review*, 29, No. 2 (April, 1939), 291-302.

7076 **Ullman, Edward L.** *The Historical Geography of the Eastern Boundary of Rhode Island.* Washington, D.C.: State College Research Studies No. 4, 1936.

7077 **U.S. Congress**, 76th, 1st Session. Senate. *Joint Resolution Giving the Consent of the Congress to an Agreement between the States of Iowa and Missouri Establishing a Boundary between Said States.* (S.J. Res. 181). Washington, D.C.: U.S. Congress, 76th, 1st Session, 1939.

7078 **U.S. Congress**, 92nd, 1st Session. Senate. *Treaty with Mexico Resolving Boundary Differences. Message from the President, signed at Mexico City on November 23, 1970.* Washington, D.C.: 1971.

7079 **U.S. Congress**, 88th, 1st Session. Senate. *Convention with Mexico for Solution of the Problem of the Chamizal.* Washington, D.C.: U.S. Congress, 88th Session, 1963.

7080 **U.S. Department of State.** *Emergency Regulation of Level of the Rainy lake and of Other Boundary Waters in the Rainy Lake Watershed. Convention between the United States of America and Canada. Signed at Ottawa, September 15, 1938. Proclaimed by the President of the United States October 18, 1940.* Treaty Series No. 961. Washington, D.C.: U.S. Department of State, 1940.

7081 **U.S. Department of State.** *Peace, Friendship, and Boundaries between Peru and Ecuador. Protocol between Peru and Ecuador (Signed also by Representatives of the United States of America, Argentina, Brazil, and Chile). Signed at Rio de Janeiro January 29, 1942.* Executive Agreement Series 288. Washington, D.C.: U.S. Department of State, 1943.

7082 **U.S. Department of State.** *Resume of the Historical-Juridicial Proceedings of the Boundary Question Between Peru and Equador.* Washington, D.C.: Office of the Geographer, Department of State, 1937.

7083 **U.S. Department of State.** *Settlement of the Chamizal Boundary Dispute.* Washington, D.C.: Department of State, 1963.

7084 **Van Zandt, Franklin K.** *Boundaries of the United States and the Several States.* Washington, D.C.: U.S. Geological Survey, Professional Paper No. 909, 1976.

7085 **Varela, L.V.** *La Republique Argentine et le Chili: Histoire de la demarcaction de leurs frontieres (depuis 1843 jusqu'a 1899).* 2 vols. Buenos Aires: Government Press, 1899.

7086 **Vevier, Charles.** "American Continentalism: An Idea of Expansion, 1845-1910." *American Historical Review*, 65, No. 2 (January, 1960), 323-335.

7087 **Visher, Stephen S.** "Indiana's Boundaries and Size." *Proceedings of the Indiana Academy of Science*, 64 (1954; pub. 1955), 214-216.

7088 **Waugh, B.W.** "The Completion Survey of the Saskatchewan-Alberta Boundary." *Photogrammetric Engineering*, 5, No. 1 (January-March, 1939), 10-17.

7089 **Waugh, B.W.** "Completing the World's Longest Surveyed Straight Line." *Canadian Geographical Journal*, 21, No. 2 (August, 1940), 75-87.

7090 **Waugh, B.W.** "Saskatchewan-Alberta Boundary." *Canadian Surveyor*, 6, No. 7 (January, 1939), 20-23.

7091 **Webster, Gerald R.** "The Spatial Reorganization of County Boundaries in Kentucky." *Southeastern Geographer*, 24, No. 1 (May, 1984), 14-29.

7092 **Werne, Joseph Richard.** "Partisan Politics and the Mexican Boundary Survey, 1848-1853." *Southwestern Historical Quarterly* (Austin), 90, No. 4 (April, 1987), 329-346.

7093 **Wilson, Ben Hur.** "The Southern Boundary. (Iowa)." *Palimpsest*, 19, No. 10 (October, 1938), 413-424.

7094 **Woolsey, L.H.** "The Tacna-Arica Settlement." *American Journal of International Law*, 23, No. 3 (July, 1929), 605-610.

ASIA

Books and Journals

7095 **Aberbach, Moses.** "The Boundaries of Israel." *Midstream*, 30, No. 5 (May, 1984), 13-18.

7096 "Agreement for the Delimitation of Boundaries Between Jordan and Saudi Arabia." *Middle East Journal*, 22, No. 3 (Summer, 1968), 346-349.

7097 **Al-Baham, H.M.** "A Note on the Kuwait-Saudi Arabia Neutral Zone Agreement of July 7, 1965." *International & Comparative Law Quarterly*, 17, No. 4 (October, 1968), 730-735.

7098 **Ali, Arshad.** "The Punjab Boundary Commission's Award." *Punjab Geographical Review*, 3, Nos. 1 and 2 (1948), 32-38.

7099 **Ali, M.** "Eastern and Southern Boundaries of Afghanistan Until 1876 A.D." *Geographical Review of Afghanistan*, 8, No. 1 (August, 1969), 27-28.

7100 **Allen, W.E.D.** "New Political Boundaries in the Caucasus." *Geographical Journal*, 69, No. 5 (November, 1927), 430.

7101 **Anand, R.P.** "The Kutch Award." *India Quarterly*, 24, No. 3 (July-September, 1968), 183-212.

7102 **Bancroft, A.D.** "Modern Techniques Applied to a Boundary Survey in the Mountains of Southern Iran." *Chartered Surveyor*, May, 1962.

7103 **Bebler, Ales.** "The Indo-Pakistani Western Boundary: Dissenting Opinion of Judges Ales Bebler." *India Quarterly*, 24, No. 2 (April-June, 1968), 77-139; 24, No. 3 (July-September, 1968), 239-269.

7104 **Bhattacharya, S.S.** "The McMahon Line." *Modern Review*, 117, No. 2 (February, 1965), 140-145.

7105 "China's North and Norhtwest Boundaries." *Contemporary China*, 5, (1961, 1962), 33-56.

7106 **Chopra, Surendra.** "Sino-Pakistan Boundary Agreement." *Journal of African and Asian Studies*, 1, No. 2 (Spring, 1968), 220-237.

7107 **Crone, Gerald R.** "Notes on Survey Work with the Indo-Afghan Boundary Commission, Arandu, July, 1932." *Geographical Journal*, 82, No. 4 (October, 1933), 354.

7108 **Crone, Gerald R.** "The Turkish-Iranian Boundary." *Geographical Journal*, 91, No. 1 (January, 1938), 57-59 and 92, No. 2 (August, 1938), 149-150.

7109 **Day, Winifred M.** "Relative Permanence of Former Boundaries in India." *Scottish Geographical Magazine*, 65, No. 3 (December, 1949), 113-122.

7110 *District Boundary Changes and Population Growth for Pakistan, 1881-1961.* Dacca: Dacca University, Bangladesh Geographical Society, 1971.

7111 **Dzurek, Daniel J.** "Deciphering the North Korean-Soviet (Russian) Maritime Boundary Agreements." *Ocean Development and International Law* [Washington, DC], 23, No. 1 (January-March, 1992), 31-54.

7112 **G.R.C.** "The Turkish-Iranian Boundary. *Geographical Journal*, 91, No. 1 (January, 1938), 57-59.

7113 **Ghatate, N.M.** "The Sino-Burmese Border Settlement." *India Quarterly*, 24, No. 1 (January-March, 1968), 17-49.

7114 **Great Britain.** *Exchanges of Notes Between His Majesty's Government in the United Kingdom and the Government of Burma, and the National Government of the Republic of China, Concerning the Burma-Yunnan Boundary.* London: Her Majesty's Government, 1956.

7115 **Great Britain.** Foreign Office. *London and Kingdom of Saudi Arabia; Treaty Collection, 1922-1975.* Jeddah: Ministry of Foreign Affairs, 1976.

7116 **Great Britain.** Treaties, etc. *Treaty between His Majesty in Respect of the United Kingdom and India and His Excellency the President of the National Government of the Republic of China for the Relinquishment of Extraterritorial Rights in China and the Regulation of Related Matters. Chungking, January 11, 1943.* Treaty Series No. 2, 1943. London: Great Britain Parliament, 1943.

7117 **Greenip, W.E.** "Jordan-Saudi Border Demarcation." *Viewpoints*, 6, No. 1 (1966), 24.

7118 **Grey, Arthur L.** "The Thirty-Eighth Parallel." *Foreign Affairs*, 29, No. 3 (April, 1951), 482-487.

7119 **Hay, H.R.** "Demarcation of the Indo-Afghan Boundary in the Vicinity of Arandu." *Geographical Journal*, (October, 1933), 351-354.

7120 **Holdich, Thomas H.** "The Perso-Baluch Boundary." *Geographical Journal*, 9, No. 4 (April, 1897), 416-422.

7121 **India (Republic).** Ministry of Home Affairs. *Punjab Boundary Commission Report* by J.C. Shah and Others. New Delhi: Publication Division, Government of India Press, 1966.

7122 **India.** Survey of India. *Map Showing Approximate Boundaries of Orissa.* 2nd ed. Calcutta: Survey of India, 1937.

7123 **Jackson, W.A. Douglas.** *Russo-Chinese Borderland.* Princeton, New Jersey: Van Nostrand, 1962.

7124 **Johri, Sitaram.** *Our Borderlands.* Lucknow: Himalaya Publications, 1964.

7125 "Kashmir and Jammu: The Lines of Settlement." *Round Table*, 36, No. 159 (June, 1950), 215-219.

7126 **Khan, Farzana**. "The Rann of Kutch Award." *Pakistan Horizon*, 21, No. 2 (Second Quarter, 1968), 123-133.

7127 **King, Russell**. "North from the Attila Line." *Geographical Magazine* (London), 52, No. 2 (November, 1979), 117-124.

7128 **Kingdom of Saudi Arabia**. *Arbitration for the Settlement of the Territorial Dispute Between Muscat and Abu Dhabi on One Side and Saudi Arabia on the Other: Memorial of the Government of Saudi Arabia*. Cairo: al Maaref Press, 1955.

7129 "The Kutch Award: Extract from the Opinion of the Chairman of the Tribunal." *Foreign Affairs, Reports*, 17, No. 1 (March, 1968), 27-41.

7130 **Lamb, Alastair**. "The Indo-Tibetan Border." *Australian Journal of Politics and History*, 6, No. 1 (May, 1960), 28-40.

7131 **Lamb, Alastair**. *The McMahon Line; A Study in the Relations Between India, China and Tibet, 1904 to 1914*. 2 Vols. London: Routledge, 1966.

7132 **Lamb, Alastair**. "The Sino-Indian and Sino-Russian Borders: Some Comparisons and Contrasts." In *Studies in the Social History of China and South-East Asia*, Jerome Ch'en and Nicholas Tailing, eds. Cambridge University Press, 1970, 135-152.

7133 **Lamb, Alastair**. "The Sino-Pakistani Boundary Agreement of March 2, 1963." *Australian Outlook*, 18, No. 3 (December, 1964), 299-312.

7134 **Lloyd, H.I.** "The Geography of the Mosul Boundary." *Geographical Journal*, 68, No. 2 (August, 1926), 104-117.

7135 **Maung, Maung**. "The Burma-China Settlement." *Asian Survey*, 1, No. 1 (March, 1961), 38-43.

7136 **McCune, Shannon**. "Physical Bases for Korean Boundaries." *Far Eastern Quarterly*, 5, No. 3 (May, 1946), 272-288.

7137 **McCune, Shannon**. "The Thirty-Eighth Parallel in Korea." *World Politics*, 1, No. 2 (January, 1949), 223-232.

7138 **McMahon, A. Henry**. "The Southern Borderlands of Afghanistan." *Geographical Journal*, 9, No. 4 (April, 1897), 393-415.

7139 **Mehta, Swarnjit**. "A Framework for the Study of District Boundaries." *Indian Geographical Journal*, 58, No. 1 (1983), 74-76.

7140 **Murti, B.S.N.** "The Kutch Award: A Preliminary Study." *Indian Journal of International Law*, 8, No. 1 (January, 1968), 51-56.

7141 **Narayana Rao, Gondker**. *The India-China Border: A Reappraisal*. New York: Asia Publishing House, 1968.

7142 *Pakistan-China Boundary Agreement*. Karachi: Saifee, 1963.

7143 **Plotkin, Nathan**. *The McMahon Line*. Manhattan: Kansas State University, Master's Thesis, 1964.

7144 **Reichman, Shalom**, Seminar Director. *Factors in the Delimination of Israel's Eastern Boundary*. Jerusalem: The Hebrew University of Jerusalem. Leonard Davis Institute for International Relations. Policy Oriented Publications, No. 5, April, 1982.

7145 **Reyner, Anthony S.** "Sudan-United Arab Republic Boundary: A Factual Background." *Middle East Journal*, 17, No. 3 (Summer, 1963), 313-316.

7146 **Ryder, C.H.D.** "The Demarcation of the Turco-Persian Boundary in 1913-1914." *Geographical Journal*, 66, No. 3 (September, 1925), 227-242.

7147 **Saxena, K.C.** "The Kutch Award in Perspective." *Socialist Congressmen*, 7, No. 23 (March 7, 1968), 18-19.

7148 **Simla, India**. *Tripartite Conference, 1913-1914. The Boundary Question between China and Tibet; A Valuable Record of the Tripartite Conference between China, Britain and Tibet held in India, 1913-1914*. Peking: Government of China Press, 1940.

7149 **Singh, Bhawani**. "Sino-Pak Border Pact in Retrospect." *Political Science Review*, 3, No. 2 (May, 1964), 143-158.

7150 **Singh, Biswanath**. "Kutch-Award: A Study in Indo-Pakistan Relations." *Indian Journal of Political Science*, 29, No. 2 (April-June, 1968), 155-162.

7151 **Sharma, Surya Prakash**. *Delimitation of Land and See Boundaries Between Neighbouring Countries*. New Delhi: Lancer, 1989.

7152 **Sondhi, M.L.** "Implications of the Kutch Award." *Shakti*, 5, No. 3 (March, 1968), 9-11.

7153 **Spate, O.H.K.** "The Boundary Award in the Punjab." *Asiatic Review*, 44, No. 157 (January, 1948), 1-15.

7154 **Stephens, Michael D.** "Laos and the Sino-Loatian Boundary." *Asian Review*, 3, No. 1 (April, 1966), 39-44.

7155 **Stephens, Michael D.** "The Sino-Burmese Border Agreement." *Asian Review*, 59, No. 217 (January, 1963), 46-58.

7156 **Sugimura, Oaki.** "The Chino-Mongolian Border Zone in Inner Mongolia-Kansu Area." *New Geography/The Shin-Chiri*, 7, No. 2 (December, 1958), 124-142.

7157 **Sugimura, Oaki.** "The Cino-Mongolian Border Zone in Inner Mongolia-Kansu Area--One Method of Determining the Area of a Border Region." *New Geography* (Shin-Chiri). *Annals of the Japanese Association of Professional Geographers*, 7, No. 2 (1958), 124-142.

7158 **Sugimura, Oaki.** "Spatial Concept of Manchu-Korean Border Region, Part 2." *New Geography*, 9, No. 4 (1961), 1-21 and 10, No. 1 (1962), 16-25.

7159 **Waldron, Arthur N.** "The Problem of the Great Wall of China." *Harvard Journal of Asiatic Studies*, 43, No. 2 (December, 1983), 643-663.

7160 **Wetter, J. Gillis.** "The Rann of Kutch Arbitration." *American Journal of International Law*, 65, No. 2 (April, 1971), 346-357.

7161 **Yerasimos, Stephane.** "Comment furent tracees les frontieres actuelles au Proche-Orient. Des c rayons, des gommes, des cartes, des ratures." *Herodote*, 41 (Avril-Juin, 1986), 123-161.

AUSTRALIA, OCEANIA AND ANTARCTICA

Books and Journals

7162 **Aitchison, J.F.** "The Counties of New South Wales." *Australian Surveyor*, 30, No. 1 (March, 1980), 32-43.

7163 **Forbes, V. L.** "Australia's International Obligation to Maritime Boundary Determination." *Cartography* [Canberra], 20, No. 2 (December, 1991), 19-28.

7164 **Logan, W.S.** "The Changing Landscape Significance of the Victoria-South Australia Boundary." *Annals of the Association of American Geographers*, 58, No. 1 (March, 1968), 128-154.

7165 **Ogier, J.C.H.** "The Question of the Original Official Boundary between the States of New South Wales and Victoria." *Victorian Geographical Journal*, 20 (1902), 71-84.

7166 **Ogier, J.C.H.** "The Victorian State Boundary." *Victorian Geographical Journal*, 23 (1905), 78-106.

EUROPE

Books and Journals

7167 **Arciszewski, Franciszek.** "Some Remarks about the Strategical Significance of the New and Old Soviet Polish Border." *Polish Review*, 1, No. 2-3 (Spring-Summer, 1956), 89-96.

7168 **Bluhm, Georg.** *Die Oder-Neisse-Linie in der Deutschen Aussenpolitik*. Breisgau: Verlag Rombach Freiburg, 1963.

7169 **Boswell, A. Bruce.** *The Eastern Boundaries of Poland*. Birkenhead, England: Polish Publications Committee, 1944.

7170 *The Boundaries of Poland. Part 1, Western Frontiers*. Birkenhead, England: Polish Publications Committee, 1944.

7171 **Campbell, John C.** "The European Territorial Settlement." *Foreign Affairs*, 26, No. 1 (October, 1947), 196-218.

7172 **Cant, Garth.** "Waitangi: Treaty and Tribunal." *New Zealand Journal of Geography*, 89 (April, 1990), 7-12.

7173 **Columb Gilfillan, S.** "European Political Boundaries." *Political Science Quarterly*, 39, No. 4 (December, 1924), 458-484.

7174 **Cornwall, J.H.M.** "The Russo-Turkish Boundary and Territory of Nakhchivan." *Geographical Journal*, 61, No. 6 (June, 1923), 445450.

7175 **Cramer, Noel.** "De Maasgrens als socio-goegrafische determinant." *Societe Belge d'Etudes Geographiques Bulletin*, Tome 57, No. 2 (1983), 169-184.

7176 **Daveau, Suzanne.** "Declin des Rapports Fronlaliers Avec la France aux Limites du Canton de Neuchatel." *Bulletin de la Societe Neuchateboise de Geographie*, 52:1, No. 11 (1956-1959), 305-313.

7177 **Dodge, Stanely D.** "The Finnish-Russian Boundary North of 68 Degrees." *Geographical Journal*, 72, No. 3 (September, 1928), 297-298.

7178 **Erich, R.** "La question des zones demilitarisees." *Recueil des Cours*. Hague Academy, 26 (1929-I), 591.

7179 **Fox, Sir Cyril.** *The Boundary Line of Cymru*. The Sir John Rhys Memorial Lecture, British Academy, 1940. "From the Proceedings of the British Academy, Volume 26." London: H. Milford, 1941.

7180 "Franco-Italian Border Change." *American Perspective*, 1, No. 1 (April, 1947), 35-40.

7181 **Gidel, Gilbert.** "A Propos de Bases Juridiques des Pretentions des Etats Riverains sur le Plateau Continental: les Doctrines du 'Droit Inherent'." *Zeitschrift fur auslandisches offentliches Recht und Volkerrecht*, 19 (1958), 81-101.

7182 **Giles, F.L.** "Boundary Work in the Balkans." *Geographical Journal*, 75, No. 3 (March, 1930), 300-312.

7183 **Great Britain.** Treaties, etc. *Agreement Regarding the Extension to the Sudetenland of the Anglo-German Transfer Agreement of July 1, 1938 and the Supplementary Agreement of August 13, 1938, London, June 16, 1939.* Treaty Series, No. 30 (1939), Cmd. 6047. London: Great Britain Parliament, 1939.

7184 **Greer, Deon Carr.** *The Russo-Finnish Border Change of 1940-1944 and Its Effect Upon Finland.* Bloomington: Indiana University, Ph.D., 1969.

7185 **Griffiths, M.** "What's in a Line? Some Causes and Effects of the Oder-Neisse Boundary." *Swansea Geographer*, 2 (Spring, 1964), 85-99.

7186 **Hartshorne, Richard.** "The Franco-German Boundary of 1871." *World Politics*, 2, No. 2 (January, 1950), 209-250.

7187 **Hartshorne, Richard.** "Geographic and Political Boundaries in Upper Silesia." *Annals of the Association of American Geographers*, 23, No. 4 (December, 1933), 195-228.

7188 **Helin, Ronald A.** *Economic-Geographic Reorientation in Western Finnish Karelia: A Result of the Finno-Soviet Boundary Demarcations in 1940 and 1944,* s.l., University of California, 1961.

7189 **Hinks, Arthur R.** "The Belgium-German Boundary Demarcation." *Geographical Journal*, 57, No. 1 (January, 1921), 43-51.

7190 **Hinks, Arthur R.** "The Boundaries of Czecho-Slovakia." *Geographical Journal*, 54, No. 3 (September, 1919), 185-188.

7191 **Hinks, Arthur R.** "Boundary Delimitations in the Treaty of Versailles." *Geographical Journal*, 54, No. 1 (July, 1919), 103-113.

7192 **Hinks, Arthur R.** "The Progress of Boundary Delimitation in Europe." *Geographical Journal*, 54, No. 6 (December, 1919), 363-367.

7193 **House, J.W.** "The Franco-Italian Boundary in the Alpes Maritimes." *Transactions and Papers of the Institute of British Geographers*, 26 (1959), 107-131.

7194 **Johnston, R. J.** and others. "The Changing Interpretation of Ambiguous Rules: The Boundary Commission for England." *Urban Geography* [Silver Spring], 14, No. 6 (November-December, 1993), 507-516.

7195 **Justice for Bulgaria Committee.** *Bulgaria Claims Western Thrace.* 6 pts. Sofia: 1946.

7196 **Kaeckenbeeck, Georges.** *The International Experiment of Upper Silesia; A Study in the Working of the Upper Silesian Settlement, 1922-1937.* London: Oxford University Press, 1942.

7197 **Kielczewska-Zaleska, M., and Grodek, A.** *Odra-Nisa Najlepsze Granica Polski* (The Odra and the Nysa-Poland's Best Boundary). Poznan, Polish Academy of Sciences, 1946.

7198 **Kirkien, L.** *Poland and the Curzon Line.* 2nd ed. Duns, Scotland: Caldra House, 1945.

7199 **Kuehnelt-Leddihn, Erik R.V.** "The Southern Boundaries of Austria." *Journal of Central European Affairs*, 5, No. 3 (October, 1945), 243-259.

7200 **Kunz, Josef L.** "Italo-Austrian Agreement on the Austrian Tyrol." *American Journal of International Law*, 41, No. 2 (April, 1947), 439-445.

7201 **Lloyd, Trevor.** "The Norwegian-Soviet Boundary; A Study in Political Geography." *Norsk Geografisk Tidsskrift*, 15, Nos. 5-6 (April-May, 1956), 187-242.

7202 **Lloyd, Trevor.** "The Norwegian-Soviet Boundary in Lapland." *International Geographical Congress Proceedings*, (1957), 533-538.

7203 **Marchesi, Arnaldo.** "Definizione del confine Italo-Svizzero e Notizie sui Lavori Compierti Dalle Commission di Determinazione e di Manutenzione della Frontiera Stressa." *L'Universo*, 40, No. 2 (March-April, 1960), 279-300.

7204 **Martonne, E. de.** "La frontiere franco-espagnole au Maroc en 1936." *L'Afrique Francaise*, 48ᵉ annee, No. 2 (Fevrier, 1938), 77-84, cont.

7205 **Minghi, Julian V.** "Railways and Borderlands: The Rebirth of the Franco-Italian Line Through the Alpes Maritimes." *Tijdschrift voor Economische en Sociale Geografie*, 75, No. 5 (Sept.-Okt., 1984), 322-328.

7206 **Moodie, A.E.** "The Italo-Yugoslav Boundary." *Geographical Journal*, 101, No. 2 (February, 1943), 49-63. Discussion: 63-65.

7207 **Moodie, A.E.** *The Italo-Yugoslav Boundary; A Study in Political Geography.* London: G. Philip & Son, 1945.

7208 **Norcen, Antonio.** "Su Zlcune Rettifiche del Confine Italo-Svizzero." *Bolletino della Societa Geografica Italiana*, 11, Nos. 9-10 (September-October, 1958), 445-450.

7209 "Nova fronteira entre Minas Gerais e Espirito Santo: demarcadas definitivamente os Novos limites." *Boletim Mineiro de Geografia*, 6, No. 10-11 (Julho, 1965), 75-76.

7210 **Pegna, Mario Lopes.** "La Divisione Territoriale dell 'antica Etruria." *Rivista Geografica Italiana*, 67, No. 2 (June, 1960), 318-323.

7211 **Platt, Robert S.** *A Geographical Study of the Dutch-German Border.* Munster-Westfalen: Selbstverlag de Geographischen Komission, 1958.

7212 **Polin, Anatoli K.** "History of the Borders of the Republic of Karelia." *Terra* [Helsinki], 105, No. 4 (1993), 264-269.

7213 **Pounds, Norman J.G.** "The Western Boundary of Poland." *Journal of Geography*, 62, No. 8 (November, 1963), 377-378.

7214 **Rhode, Gotthold.** "La Ligne Oder-Neisse et la Politique Europeenne." *Politique Etrangere*, 25 Annee, No. 5 (1960), 451-475.

7215 **Rupnik, Jacques.** "Europe's New Frontiers: Remapping Europe." *Daedalus* [Cambridge, MA], 123, No. 3 (Summer, 1994), 91-114.

7216 **Sadowski, George.** "Poland's Western Boundaries; Safeguard of Peace." Excerpt: *Slavic American*, 1, No. 1 (Fall, 1947), 5+.

7217 **Sahlins, Peter.** *Boundaries: The making of France and Spain in the Pyrenees.* Berkeley: University of California Press, 1989.

7218 **Schlier, O.** "Berlins Verflechtungen mit der Umwelt fruher und heute." *Geographische Rundschau*, 11, Heft 4 (April, 1959), 125-51.

7219 "The Settlement between Hungary and Czechoslovakia." *The Bulletin of International News*, 15, No. 23 (November 19, 1938), 1062-1065.

7220 **Slawinski, Zygmunt.** "Poland's Western Frontier on the Odra-Western Nysa Line and the Interests of the Central European Federation. *Eastern Quarterly*, 4, No. 4 (October, 1951), 15-26.

7221 **Smogorzewski, Casimir.** *About the Curzon Line and Other Lines.* (Free Europe Pamphlet, No. 7) London: Free Europe, 1945.

7222 "The South Tirol and Its Future." *World Today.* N.s., 1, No. 6 (December, 1945), 270-280.

7223 "Tension in the South Tyrol: A Settlement in Dispute." *World Today*, 14, No. 1 (January, 1958), 26-37.

7224 **Withers, Charles W.J.** "The Scottish Highlands Outlined: Cartographic Evidence for the Position of the Highland-Lowland Boundary." *Scottish Geographical Magazine* (Edinburgh), 98, No. 3 (December, 1982), 143-157.

7225 **Yokoyama, Shoichi.** "The Saarland and Sarrlbrucken Stadt." *Bulletin of the Faculty of Law and Literature*, 5 (1973), 219-270. Tokyo: Ehime University, 1973.

7226 **U.S. Department of State**, Office of the Geographer, Washington, D.C., *Boundary Studies.*

Africa

7227 *Algeria-Libya Boundary*, 1961.

7228 *Algeria-Mali Boundary*, 1970.

7229 *Algeria-Mauritania Boundary*, 1969.

7230 *Algeria-Niger Boundary*, 1970.

7231 *Algeria-Spanish Sahara Boundary*, 1968.

7232 *Angola-Congo Boundary*, 1970.

7233 *Angola-Namibia Boundary*, 1972.

7234 *Angola-Zambia Boundary*, 1972.

7235 *Bostwana-South Africa Boundary*, 1972.

7236 *Burundi-Rwanda Boundary*, 1966.

7237 *Burundi-Tanzania Boundary*, 1966.

7238 *Burundi-Zaire Boundary*, 1965.

7239 *Cameroon-Central African Republic Boundary*, 1970.

7240 *Cameroon-Chad Boundary*, 1970.

7241 *Cameroon-Congo Boundary*, 1971.

7242 *Cameroon-Nigeria Boundary*, 1969.

7243 *Central African Republic-Chad Boundary*, 1968.

7244 *Central African Republic-Sudan Boundary*, 1962.

7245 *Central African Republic-Zaire Boundary*, 1971.

7246 *Chad-Libya Boundary*, 1961.

7247 *Chad-Niger Boundary*, 1966.

7248 *Chad-Nigeria Boundary*, 1969.

7249 *Chad-Sudan Boundary*, 1962.

7250 *Dahomey-Niger Boundary*, 1973.

7251 *Dahomey-Nigeria Boundary*, 1969.

7252 *Dahomey-Togo Boundary*, 1972.

7253 *Dahomey-Upper Volta Boundary*, 1970.

7254 *French Territory of Afars and Issas-Somalia Boundary*, 1968.

7255 *Ghana-Ivory Coast Boundary*, 1973.

7256 "Ghana-Togo Boundary." *International Boundary Study No. 126*, 1972.

7257 "Guinea-Liberia Boundary." *International Boundary Study No. 131*, 1972.

7258 *Guinea-Senegal Boundary*, 1970.

7259 "Guinea-Sierra Leone Boundary." *International Boundary Study No. 136*, 1973.

7260 "Ivory Coast-Liberia Boundary." *International Boundary Study No. 132*, 1973.

7261 "Kenya-Somalia Boundary." *International Boundary Study No. 134*, 1973.

7262 *Kenya-Tanzania Boundary*, 1966.

7263 "Kenya-Uganda Boundary." *International Boundary Study No. 139*, 1973.

7264 "Lesotho-South Africa Boundary." *International Boundary Study No. 143*, 1974.

7265 "Liberia-Sierra Leone Boundary." *International Boundary Study No. 129*, 1972.

7266 *Libya-Egypt Boundary*, 1966.

7267 *Libya-Niger Boundary*, 1961.

7268 *Libya-Sudan Boundary*, 1961.

7269 *Libya-Tunisia Boundary*, 1972.

7270 *Libya-United Arab Republic Boundary*, 1966.

7271 *Malawi-Mozambique Boundary*, 1971.

7272 *Malawi-Tanzania Boundary*, 1964.

7273 *Mali-Mauritania Boundary*, 1963.

7274 "Mali-Niger Boundary." *International Boundary*

Study No. 150, 1975.

7275 *Mauritania-Senegal Boundary*, 1967.

7276 "Mauritania-Spanish Sahara Boundary." *International Boundary Study No. 149*, 1975.

7277 *Morocco-Spanish Sahara Boundary*, 1961.

7278 *Mozambique-Rhodesia Boundary*, 1971.

7279 "Mozambique-South Africa Boundary." *International Boundary Study No. 133*, 1973.

7280 *Mozambique-Swaziland Boundary*, 1973.

7281 *Mozambique-Tanzania Boundary*, 1964.

7282 *Mozambique-Zambia Boundary*, 1971.

7283 *Namibia-Zambia Boundary*, 1972.

7284 *Niger-Nigeria Boundary*, 1969.

7285 *Northern Rodesia-Southern Rodesia Boundary*, 1964. Office of Research in Economics and Science. Bureau of Intelligence and Research.

7286 *Rwanda-Tanzania Boundary*, 1966.

7287 *Rwanda-Uganda Boundary*, 1965.

7288 *South Africa-Namibia Boundary*, 1972.

7289 *South Africa-Southern Rhodesia Boundary*, 1971.

7290 *South Africa-Swaziland Boundary*, 1973.

7291 *Sudan-Egypt Boundary*, 1962.

7292 *Sudan-Uganda Boundary*, 1970.

7293 *Tanzania-Uganda Boundary*, 1965.

7294 *Tanzania-Zambia Boundary*, 1965.

7295 "Togo-Upper Volta Boundary." *International Boundary Study No. 128*, 1972.

7296 *Zaire-Rwanda Boundary*, 1965.

7297 *Zaire-Sudan Boundary*, 1970.

7298 *Zaire-Tanzania Boundary*, 1965.

7299 *Zaire-Uganda Boundary*, 1970.

7300 *Zambia-Rhodesia Boundary*, 1964.

Americas

7301 *Argentina-Chile Boundary (Palena Sector)*, 1970.

7302 *Argentina-Uruguay Boundary, 1966.*

7303 *Bolivia-Chile Boundary, 1966.*

7304 *British Guiana-Venezuela Boundary, 1963.*

7305 *British Honduras-Guatemala Boundary, 1961.*

7306 *Chile-Peru Boundary, 1966.*

7307 *Colombia-Panama Boundary, 1966.*

7308 *Dominican Republic-Haiti Boundary, 1961.*

7309 *El Salvador-Guatemala Boundary, 1968.*

7310 *Guyana-Venezuela Boundary, 1963.*

7311 *Honduras-Nicaragua Boundary, 1964.*

7312 *United States-Russia Convention Line, 1965.*
     Asia

7313 *Afghanistan-China Boundary, 1969.*

7314 *Afghanistan-Iran Boundary, 1961.*

7315 *Afghanistan-USSR Boundary, 1963.*

7316 *Burma-China Boundary, 1964.*

7317 *Burma-India Boundary, 1968.*

7318 *Burma-Laos Boundary, 1964.*

7319 *Burma-Thailand Boundary, 1966.*

7320 *Cambodia-Laos Boundary, 1964.*

7321 *Cambodia-Thailand Boundary, 1966.*

7322 *China-Hong Kong Boundary, 1962.*

7323 *China-Korea Boundary, 1962.*

7324 *China-Laos Boundary, 1964.*

7325 *China-Nepal Boundary, 1965.*

7326 *China-Pakistan Boundary, 1968.*

7327 *China-USSR Boundary, 1966.*

7328 *China-Vietnam Boundary, 1964.*

7329 *India-Pakistan Boundary (Rann of Kutch), 1968.*

7330 *Indonesia-Malaysia Boundary, 1965.*

7331 *Iran-Turkey Boundary, 1964.*

7332 *Iran-USSR Boundary, 1963.*

7333 *Iraq-Jordan Boundary, 1970.*

7334 *Iraq-Saudi Arabia Boundary, 1971.*

7335 *Iraq-Syria Boundary, 1970.*

7336 *Iraq-Turkey Boundary, 1964.*

7337 *Israel-Egypt Armistice Line, 1965.*

7338 *Israel-Lebanon Armistice Line, 1967.*

7339 *Jordan-Saudi Arabia Boundary, 1965.*

7340 *Jordan-Syria Boundary, 1969.*

7341 *Korea Military Demarcation Line, 1963.*

7342 *Korea-USSR Boundary, 1965.*

7343 *Kuwait-Saudi Arabia Boundary, 1970.*

7344 *Laos-Thailand Boundary, 1962.*

7345 *Laos-Vietnam Boundary, 1966.*

7346 *Malaysia-Thailand Boundary, 1965.*

7347 *Turkey-USSR Boundary, 1964.*

7348 *Vietnam Demarcation Line, 1962.*

Europe

7349 *Albania-Greece Boundary, 1971.*

7350 *Albania-Yugoslavia Boundary, 1971.*

7351 *Austria-Italy Boundary, 1966.*

7352 *Belgium-Germany Boundary, 1961.*

7353 *Bulgaria-Greece Boundary, 1965.*

7354 *Bulgaria-Rumania Boundary, 1965.*

7355 *Bulgaria-Turkey Boundary, 1965.*

7356 *Bulgaria-Yugoslavia Boundary, 1972.*

7357 *Czechoslovakia-Hungary Boundary, 1966.*

7358 *Czechoslovakia-USSR Boundary, 1967.*

7359 *Denmark-Germany Boundary, 1968.*

7360 *Findland-USSR Boundary, 1967.*

7361 *France-Italy Boundary, 1961.*

7362 *France-Switzerland Boundary, 1961.*

7363 *Germany-Netherlands Boundary, 1964.*

7364 *Greece-Turkey Boundary, 1964.*

7365 *Greece-Yugoslavia Boundary*, 1968.

7366 *Hungary-Rumania Boundary*, 1965.

7367 *Hungary-USSR Boundary*, 1967.

7368 *Italy-Switzerland Boundary*, 1961.

7369 *Norway-USSR Boundary*, 1963.

7370 *Rumania-USSR Boundary*, 1964.

BOUNDARY PROBLEMS IN THE CONTEMPORARY WORLD

GENERAL AND THEORY

Books and Journals

7371 **Berkowitz, Leonard.** "Simple Views of Aggression: An Essay Review." *American Scientist*, 57, No. 4 (October, 1959), 372-373.

7372 **Bhattacharjee, Tarun Kumar.** *Enticing Frontiers*. New Delhi: Omsons Publications, 1992.

7373 **Bishop, W.W. Jr.** "Case Concerning Sovereignty over Certain Frontier Lands, 1959." *American Journal of International Law*, 53, No. 4 (October, 1959), 937.

7374 **Brasnett, J.** "The Karasuk Problem." *Uganda Journal*, 22 (1958), 113-122.

7375 **Burghardt, Andrew F.** "The Bases of Territorial Claims." *Geographical Review*, 63, No. 2 (April, 1973), 225-245.

7376 **Cheng, Bin.** *General Principles of Law as Applied by International Courts and Tribunals*. London: London Institute of World Affairs, 1953.

7377 **Crook, John H.** "The Nature and Function of Territorial Aggression." In *Man and Aggression*, M.F.A. Montagu, ed. New York: Oxford University Press, 1968.

7378 **Dennis, W.C.** "Compromise: The Great Defect of Arbitration." *Columbia Law Review*, 11, No. 6 (June, 1911), 493-513.

7379 **Falabrino, Ghan Luigi.** "Le Possibili Soluzioni del Problema del Territorio Libero di Trieste." *L'Universo*, 34, No. 2 (March-April, 1954)^R, 7253-268; and 34, No. 2 (May-June, 1954), 397-410.

7380 **Fawcett, J.E.S.** "Intervention in International Law: A Survey of Some Recent Cases." *Hague Recueil*, 103 (1961), 343-421.

7381 **Fifield, Russell H.** "The Postwar World Map: New States and Boundary Changes." *American Political Science Review*, 42, No. 3 (June, 1948), 533-541.

7382 **Hall, Arthur R.** "Boundary Problems in Cartography." *Surveying and Mapping*, 12, No. 2 (April-June, 1952), 138-141.

7383 **Hutchison, Bruce.** *The Struggle for the Border*. New York: Longmans Green, 1955.

7384 **Hyde, C.C.** "Maps as Evidence in International Boundary Disputes." *American Journal of International Law*, 27, No. 2 (April, 1933), 311-316.

7385 **Kapil, Ravi L.** "Political Boundaries and Territorial Instability." *International Review of History and Political Science*, 5, No. 3 (August, 1968), 46-78.

7386 **Lorenz, Konrad.** *On Aggression*. New York: Harcourt Brace and World, 1966.

7387 **Laurd, Eva.** *International Regulation of Frontier Disputes*. New York: Praeger, 1970.

7388 **McNair, Lord.** *The Law of Treaties*. Oxford: Clarendon Press, 1961.

7389 **Menon, P.K.** "Settlement of International Boundary Disputes." *Revue de Droit International de Sciences Diplomatiques et Politiques*, 57 (1979), 139-152.

7390 **Miller, H.** "The Hague Codification Conference." *American Journal of International Law*, 24, No. 4 (October, 1930), 674-693.

7391 **Minghi, Julian V.** "Boundary Studies and National Prejudice." *Professional Geographer*, 15, No. 1 (January, 1963), 4-8.

7392 **Moodie, A.E.** "Some New Boundary Problems in the Julian March." *Transactions and Papers, Institute of British Geographers*, 16 (1950), 81-93.

7393 **Moore, J.G.** *International Adjudications*. New York: Modern Series, 1929.

7394 **Nystuen, John D.** *Boundary Shapes and Boundary Problems*. Chicago, Illinois: 4th North American Peach Research Conference, 1966.

7395 **O'Connell, D.P.** "International Law and Boundaries Disputes." *American Society of International Law Proceedings*, (April 28-30, 1960), 77-95.

7396 **Petras, Elizabeth.** "The Role of National Boundaries in a Cross-National Labour Market." *International Journal of Urban and Regional Research*, 4, No. 2 (June, 1980), 157-195.

7397 **Ralston, J.H.** *The Law and Procedure of International Tribunals.* Stanford, California: Stanford University Press, 1926.

7398 **Sandifer, D.V.** *Evidence before International Tribunals.* Chicago: Foundation Press, 1939.

7399 **Simpson, J.L., and Fox, Hazel.** *International Arbitration: Law and Procedure.* London: Stevenson *or* Institute of International Studies, 1959.

7400 **Singer, D.** "International Conflict: Three Levels of Analysis." *World Politics*, 12 (1960), 453-461.

7401 **Sinnhuber, K.A.** "The Representation of Disputed Political Boundaries in General Atlases." *Cartographic Journal*, 1, No. 2 (December, 1964), 20-28.

7402 **Sohn, L.B.** "Exclusion of Political Disputes from Judicial Settlement." *American Journal of International Law*, 38, No. 4 (October, 1944), 694-700.

7403 **Strassoldo, Raimondo.** *Boundaries and Regions: Explorations in the Growth and Peace Potential of the Peripheries.* Trieste: Lint, 1973.

7404 **Stuyt, A.M.** *Survey of International Arbitrations 1794-1938.* The Hague: Martinus Nijhoff, 1939.

7405 **Wright, Quincy.** "The Nature of Conflict." *Western Political Quarterly*, 4, No. 2 (July, 1951), 193-209.

POLITICAL GEOGRAPHY OF REGIONS

AFRICA

Books and Journals

7406 **Adejuyigbe, Omolade.** *Boundary Problems in Western Nigeria: A Geographical Analysis.* Ile-Ife: University of Ife Press, 1975.

7407 **Adejuyigbe, Omolade.** "Ife-Ijesa Boundary Problem." *Nigerian Geographical Journal*, 13, No. 1 (June, 1970), 23-38.

7408 **Africa Research.** "The Ethiopia-Somali Republic Boundary Dispute." *Africa Report*, 12, No. 4 (April, 1967), 42-45.

7409 **Austin, Dennis.** "The Uncertain Frontier: Ghana-Togo." *Journal of Modern African Studies*, 1, No. 2 (June, 1963), 139-146.

7410 **Boyd, Jr., J. Barron.** "African Boundary Conflict: An Empirical Study." *African Studies Review*, 22, No. 3 (December, 1979), 1-14.

7411 **Brasnett, J.** "The Karasuk Problem." *Uganda Journal*, 22 (1958), 113-122.

7412 **Brown, David J.L.** "The Ethiopia-Somaliland Frontier Dispute." *International and Comparative Law Quarterly*, 5, No. 2 (April, 1956), 245-264.

7413 **Brown, David J.L.** "Recent Developments in the Ethiopia-Somaliland Frontier Dispute." *International and Comparative Law Quarterly*, 10, No. 1 (January, 1961), 167-178.

7414 **Cumming, Duncan Cameron Sir.** "The Disposal of Eritrea." *Middle East Journal*, 7, No. 1 (Winter, 1953), 18-32.

7415 **Cumming, Duncan Cameron Sir.** "The U.S. Disposal of Eritrea." *African Affairs*, 52, No. 207 (April, 1953), 127-136.

7416 **Dean, Vera Micheles.** "Italy's African Claims Against France." *Foreign Policy Reports*, 15, No. 6 (June, 1939), 62-67.

7417 **Deasy, George F.** "Spanish Territorial Boundary Changes in Northwest Africa." *Geographical Review*, 32, No. 2 (April, 1942), 303-306.

7418 **Denyer-Green, B.** "Libya and Tunisia go to Court over Boundary." *Land & Minerals Surveying*, 4, No.3 (1986), 146-148, 150.

7419 **Drummond, James.** "The Demise of Territorial Apartheid: Re-Incorporating the Bantustans in a 'New' South Africa." *Tijdschrift Voor Economische en Sociale Geografie* [Amsterdam], 82, No. 5 (1991), 338-344.

7420 **Drysdale, John.** *The Somali Dispute.* New York: Praeger, 1964.

7421 **Friedman, R.A.** "Italy's Claim to Jibuti." *Contemporary Review*, 881 (May, 1939), 573-577.

7422 **Friters, Gerard M.** "Italy's Claims to Tunis." *Contemporary Review*, 878 (February, 1939), 186-192.

7423 **Gascon, Alain.** "L'Ethiopie, Autres Balkans: L'Ethiopie Fantome." *Herodote* [Paris], No. 62 (Juillet-Septembre, 1991), 161-173.

7424 **Goldblatt, I.** *The Mandated Territory of South West Africa in Relation to the United Nations.* Capetown: C. Struik, 1961.

7425 **Hill, Christopher R.** "The Botswana-Zambia Boundary Question; A Note of Warning. *Round Table*, 63, No. 252 (October, 1973), 535-541.

7426 **Huntingford, C.W.B.** *The Galla of Ethiopia: The Kingdom of Kafa and Janjero.* London: International African Institute, 1955.

7427 "Italo-Abyssinian Dispute." *Documents on International Affairs*, 1935, 2 (1937), 1-567.

7428 **Jaenen, C.J.** "The Somali Problem." *African Affairs*, 56, No. 223 (April, 1957), 147-157.

7429 **Kapil, R.L.** "On the Conflict Potential of Inherited Boundaries in Africa." *World Politics*, 18, No. 4 (July, 1966), 656-673.

7430 **Kelly, J.B.** "The Buraimi Oasis Dispute." *International Affairs*, 32, No. 3 (July, 1956), 318-326.

7431 **Kyerematen, A.A.Y.** *Inter-State Boundary Litigation in Ashanti.* Cambridge: University of Cambridge, African Study Center, African Social Research Documents, 4 (1975).

7432 **Lewis, I.M.** "Recent Developments in the Somali Dispute." *African Affairs*, 66, No. 263 (April, 1967), 104-112.

7433 **Melamid, Alexander.** "The Background of the Kenya-Somalia Boundary Conflict." *Scope: A Journal of the Social Sciences*, 1, No. 1 (December, 1964), 1-7.

7434 **Melamid, Alexander.** "The Buraimi Oasis Dispute." *Middle Eastern Affairs*, 7, No. 2 (February, 1956), 56-63.

7435 **Miriam, Mesfin Wolde.** *The Background of the Ethio-Somalia Boundary Dispute.* Addis Ababa: Berhanena Selam Printing Press, 1964.

7436 **Prescott, J.R.V.** "Africa's Major Boundary Problems." *Australian Geographer*, 9, No. 1 (March, 1963), 3-12.

7437 **Prescott, J.R.V.** "Nigeria's Boundary Problems." *Geographical Review*, 49, No. 4 (October, 1959), 485-505.

7438 **Rasmussen, Susan.** "Disputed boundaries: Tuareg Discourse on Class and Ethnicity." *Ethnology* [Pittsburgh], 31, No. 4 (October, 1991), 351-365.

AMERICAS

Books and Journals

7439 **Augelli, John P.** "The Nationalization of Frontiers: The Dominican Borderlands under Trujillo." *Annals of the Association of American Geographers*, 57, No. 1 (March, 1967), 166.

7440 **Beech, Geraldine.** "Sources of the History of Canadian Cartography in the Public Record Office, London: The Alaskan Boundary." *Association of Canadian Map Libraries Bulletin*, 58-59 (March-June, 1986), 18-26.

7441 **Begg, Alexander.** *Statement of Facts Regarding the Alaska Boundary Question.* Victoria: King's Printer, 1902.

7442 **Beriault, Yvon.** *Les problemes politiques du Nord canadien. Le Canada et le Groenland. A qui appartient l'archipel arctique?* Ottawa: Universite d'Ottawa, 1942.

7443 **Betts, Dianne C.,** and **Slottje, Daniel J.** *Crisis on the Rio Grande: Poverty, Unemployment, and Economic Development on the Texas-Mexican Border.* Boulder: Westview Press, 1994.

7444 **Bianchi, William J.** *Belize; The Controversy Between Guatemala and Great Britain Over the Territory of British Honduras in Central America.* New York: Las Americas Publishing, 1959.

7445 **Billington, Monroe.** "The Red River Boundary Controversy." *Southwestern History Quarterly*, 62, No. 3 (January, 1959), 356-363.

7446 **Bloomfield, L.M.** *The British Honduras-Guatemala Dispute.* Toronto: Carswell, 1953.

7447 **Bloomfield, L.M.,** and **Fitzgerald, Gerald F.** *Boundary Waters Problems of Canada and the United States.* Toronto: Carswell, 1958.

7448 **Boundary Disputes.** "An American Boundary Dispute: Decision of the Supreme Court of the United States with Respect to the Texas-Oklahoma Boundary." *Geographical Review*, 13, No. 2 (April, 1923), 161-189.

7449 **Boundary Disputes.** "Boundary Dispute Between Ecuador and Peru: Friendly Offices of Argentina, Brazil, and the United States." *U.S. Department of State Bulletin*, 4, No. 99 (May 17, 1941), 596-598.

7450 **Boundary Disputes.** "Bolivia and Paraguay." *U.S. Department of State. Papers relating to the foreign relations of the United States 1926, 1 (1941).* Washington, D.C.: U.S. Department of State, 1941, 531-534.

7451 **Boundary Disputes.** "Columbia and Peru." *U.S. Department of State. Papers relating to the foreign relations of the United States 1926, 1 (1941).* Washington, D.C.: U.S. Department of State, 1941, 534-539.

7452 **Boundary Disputes.** "Costa Rica and Panama." *U.S. Department of State. Papers relating to the foreign relations of the United States 1926, 1 (1941).* Washington, D.C.: U.S. Department of State, 1941, 539-543.

7453 **Boundary Disputes.** "Dominican Republic and Haiti." *U.S. Department of State.* Papers relating to the foreign relations of the United States 1926, 1 (1941). Washington, D.C.: U.S. Department of State, 1941, 543-547.

7454 **Bowman, Isaiah.** "An American Boundary Dispute: Decision of the Supreme Court of the United States with Respect to the Texas-Oklahoma Boundary." *Geographical Review,* 13, No. 2 (April, 1923), 161-189.

7455 **Braveboy-Wagner, Jacqueline Anne.** *The Venezuela-Guyana Border Dispute: Britain's Colonial Legacy in Latin America.* Boulder, Colorado: Westview Press, 1984.

7456 **Carpenter, W.C.** "The Red River Boundary Dispute." *American Journal of International Law,* 19 (1925), 517-529.

7457 **Chapman, Brian.** "The Claims of Texas to Greer County." *Southwestern History Quarterly,* 53 (1949), 401-424.

7458 **Child, Clifton J.** "The Venezuela-British Guiana Boundary Arbitration of 1899." *American Journal of International Law,* 44, No. 3 (July, 1950), 682-693.

7459 **Clergern, W.N.** "New Light on the Belize Dispute." *American Journal of International Law,* 52, No. 2 (April, 1958), 280-297.

7460 **Comeaux, Malcolm Louis.** "Attempts to Establish and Change Western Boundary." *Annals of the Association of American Geographers,* 72, No. 2 (June, 1982), 254-271.

7461 **Cope, Thomas D., and Robinson, H.W.** "When the Maryland-Pennsylvania Boundary Survey Changed from a Political and Legal Struggle into a Scientific and Technological Project." *Proceedings of the American Philosophical Society,* 98, No. 6 (December, 1954), 432-441.

7462 **Dagenais, Pierre.** "Petits conflits d'une grande frontiere." *Revue Canadienne de Geographie,* 2, No. 1 (Mars, 1948), 3-8.

7463 **Delachaux, Henri S.** "La question des limites chilo-argentines." *Annales de Geographie,* 7, No. 33 (May, 1898), 239-262.

7464 **Dennis, W.C.** "The Venezuela-British Guiana Boundary Arbitration." *American Journal of International Law,* 44, No. 3 (July, 1950), 720-727.

7465 **Dennis, W.C.** *Tacna and Arica.* New Haven, Connecticut: Yale University Press, 1931.

7466 **DeVorsey, Jr., Louis.** *The Georgia-South Carolina Boundary: A Problem in Historical Geography.* Athens: University of Georgia Press, 1982.

7467 **Dillman, C. Dariel.** "Recent Developments in Mexico's National Border Program." *Professional Geographer,* 22, No. 5 (September, 1970), 243-247.

7468 **Dykstra, T.L., and Tronside, R.G.** "The Effects of the Division of the City of Lloyminster by the Alberta-Saskatchewan Inter-Provincial Boundary." *Cahiers de Geographie de Quebec,* 16, No. 38 (Septembre, 1972), 263-283.

7469 **Eichen, Marc Alan.** *Wishes, Dreams and Lies: Congressional Redistricting After the 1970 Decennial Census in Ohio, Massachusetts and New York.* Worchester, Massachusetts: Clark University, Ph.D., 1976.

7470 **Fauchille, P.** "Le conflit de limites entre la Colombie et le Venezuela." *Revue de Droit International Public,* 27, New Series 2 (1920), 181-216.

7471 **Fenwick, C.G.** "The Arms Embargo Against Bolivia and Paraguay." *American Journal of International Law,* 28, No. 3 (July, 1934), 534-538.

7472 **Fenwick, C.G.** "The Honduras-Nicaragua Boundary Dispute." *American Journal of International Law,* 51, No. 4 (October, 1957), 761-765.

7473 **Fester, Gustav.** "Das Chaco Problem." *Zeitschrift fur Geopolitik,* Jahrgang 9, Heft 1 (Nov., 1932), 664-669; Jahrgang 10, Heft 3 (Marz, 1933), 136-141 and Jahrgang 11, Heft 2 (Feb., 1934), 111-114.

7474 **Fisher, F.C.** "Arbitration of the Guatemalan-Honduran Boundary Dispute." *American Journal of International Law,* 27, No. 3 (July, 1933), 403-427.

7475 **Fitte, E.J.** *La disputa con Gran Bretana por las islas del Atlantico Sur.* Buenos Aires: Emece Edit., 1968.

7476 **Gallois, L.** "Le territoire conteste entre le Venezuela et la Guyane anglaise." *Annales de Geographie,* 6, No. 28 (Juillet, 1897), 369-372.

7477 **Gandia, Enrique de.** "Los limites de la Republica Argentina." *Revista Geografica Americana,* 13, No. 81 (Junio, 1940), 361-368.

7478 **Gardner, Gerard.** "La frontiere Canada-Labrador." *Revue Trimestrielle Canadienne,* 24 (1938), 1-18.

7479 **Gibson, F.W.** "The Alaskan Boundary Dispute." *Canadian Historical Association, Report of the Annual Meeting, Kingston*, (1945), 25-41.

7480 **Gibson, Hope.** "The Boundary Dispute between Chile and Argentina." *Scottish Geographical Magazine*, 18, No. 2 (February, 1902), 87-90.

7481 **Gill, William H.** "A Ghost Boundary that Won't Stay 'Laid'." *Military Engineer*, 34, No. 196 (February, 1942), 113-114.

7482 **Gillin, John,** and **Silvert, K.H.** "Ambiguities in Guatemala." *Foreign Affairs*, 34, No. 3 (April, 1956), 469-482.

7483 **Gough, Barry M.** "British Policy in the San Juan Boundary Dispute, 1854-72." *Pacific Northwest Quarterly*, 62, No. 2 (April, 1971), 59-68.

7484 **Greve, Ernesto.** "Diego Barros Arana en la Cuistion de Limites Entre Chile y la Republica Argentina." *Anales de la Universidad de Chile*, 116, Nos. 109-110 (1-2 Trimestre, 1958), 283-306.

7485 **Grubb, W.B.** "The Paraguayan Chaco and Its Possible Future." *Geographical Journal*, 54, No. 3 (September, 1919), 157-178.

7486 **Guatemala.** Ministry of Foreign Affairs.. *Controversy between Guatemala and Great Britain Relative to the Convention of 1859 on Territorial Matters. Belize Question.* Guatemala: Ministry of Foreign Affairs, 1938.

7487 **Gudymar, Genevieve.** *Nicaragua-Honduras.* Paris; Annuaire francais de droit international, 1960.

7488 **Harper, William A.** "The Alaska Boundary Question: The Seattle Commercial Interest and the Joint High Commission of 1898-99." *Journal of the West*, 10, No. 2 (April, 1971), 253-272.

7489 **Hill, James E.** "El Chamizal: A Century-Old Boundary Dispute." *Geographical Review*, 55, No. 4 (October, 1965), 300-312.

7490 **Humphreys, R.A.** "The Anglo-Guatemalan Dispute." *International Affairs*, 24, No. 3 (July, 1948), 387-404.

7491 **Hyde, C.C.** "Looking Towards the Arbitration of the Dispute Over the Chaco Boreal." *American Journal of International Law*, 28, No. 4 (October, 1934), 718-723.

7492 **Ireland, Gordon.** *Boundaries, Possessions, and Conflicts in Central and North America and the Caribbean.* Cambridge, Massachusetts: Harvard University Press, 1941.

7493 **Ireland, Gordon.** *Boundaries, Possessions and Conflicts in Latin America.* Cambridge,

Massachusetts: Harvard University Press, 1938.

7494 **Jessup, Philip C.** "The Palmas Island Arbitration." *American Journal of International Law*, 22, No. 4 (October, 1928), 746-752.

7495 **Johnson, Wayne Earl.** *The Honduras-Nicaragua Boundary Dispute, 1957-1963: The Peaceful Settlement of an International Conflict.* Ann Arbor: University of Michigan Microfilms, 1966.

7496 **Kanter, Helmuth.** "Die neue Grenze Zwischen Bolivien und Paraguay, ein geopolitisches Problem." *Zeitschrift fur Geopolitik*, 12, No. 10 (Oct., 1935), 608-613.

7497 **Kunz, Josef L.** "Guatemala versus Great Britain: In Re Belice." *American Journal of International Law*, 40, No. 2 (April, 1946), 383-390.

7498 **Lapalme, Lise A.** "The Problem of the Quebec-Labrador Boundary." *Geoscope*, 10, No. 1 (April, 1979), 91-98.

7499 **Lawrence, Henry.** "Waterway Problems on the Canadian Boundary." *Foreign Affairs*, 4, No. 3 (April, 1926), 556-574. (Special Supplement).

7500 **Le Duc, Thomas.** "The Maine Frontier and the Northeastern Boundary Controversy." *American Historical Review*, 53, No. 1 (October, 1947), 30-41.

7501 **Lindgren, David Treadwell.** *The Interruptive-Effect of the Maine-New Brunswick Boundary: A Study in Political Geography.* Boston, Massachusetts: Boston University Graduate School, Ph.D., 1970.

7502 **Lippincott, J.B.** "Southwestern Border Water Problems." *Journal of the American Water Works Association*, 31, No. 1 (January, 1939), 1-28.

7503 **Mahler, Susan.** "Vermont: Land of Debatable Boundaries." *Vermont History*, 34, No. 4 (October, 1966), 241-245.

7504 **Maier, Georg.** "The Boundary Dispute between Ecuador and Peru." *American Journal of International Law*, 63, No. 1 (January, 1969), 28-46.

7505 **Markham, C.R.** "Putumayu and the Question of Boundaries between Peru and Colombia." *Geographical Journal*, 41, No. 2 (February, 1913), 145-147.

7506 **Martin, Lawrence W.** "The Michigan-Wisconsin Boundary Case in the Supreme Court of the United States." *Annals of the Association of American Geographers*, 20, No. 3 (September, 1930), 105-163.

7507 **Martin, Lawrence W.** "The Second Wisconsin-Michigan Boundary Case in the Supreme Court of the United States, 1930-1936." *Annals of the Association of American Geographers*, 28, No. 2 (June, 1938), 77-126.

7508 **Martinez, Oscar J.** *Border People: Life and Society in the U.S.-Mexico Borderlands.* Tucson: The University of Arizona Press, 1994.

7509 **Martis, Kenneth C.** *United States International Land Border Crossings, San Ysidro, California.* San Diego, California: San Diego State University Department of Geography, Master's Thesis.

7510 **McCarty, Virgil L.** "Boundary Controversy; The Brownington-Johnson Land Problem." *Vermont Quarterly*, 15, No. 3 (July, 1947), 157-176.

7511 **McGrath, Patrick.** "The Labrador Boundary Decision." *Geographical Review*, 17, No. 4 (October, 1927), 632-660.

7512 **Mendoza, Jaime.** *La Tesis Andinista, Bolivia y el Paraguay.* Secre: Imp. Bolivar, 1933.

7513 **Menon, P.K.** "The Anglo-Guatemalen Territorial Dispute Over the Colony of Belize (British Honduras)." *Journal of Latin American Studies* (Cambridge), 2, Part 2 (November, 1979), 343-371.

7514 **Methol Ferre, Alberto.** *El Uruguay Como Problema en la Cuenca del Plata entre Argentina y Brasil.* Montevideo: Ed. Dialogo, 1967.

7515 **Mills, David.** *The Canadian View of the Alaskan Boundary Dispute.* Ottawa: Government Printing Bureau, 1899.

7516 **Moore, J.G.** *History and Digest of the International Arbitrations to which the United States has been a Party.* Washington, D.C.: Government Printing Office, 1898.

7517 **Moulin, H.A.** *Le litige chilo-argentin et la delimitation politique des frontieres naturelles.* Paris: Rousseau, 1902.

7518 **Panzarini, R.N.** "Los intereses argentinos en el Antartico, las isles Malvinas y demas territorios insulares." *Boletin Centro Navel*, 86, No. 677 (1968), 419-432.

7519 **Patterson, Todd C.** *The New Jersey Eastern Boundary Dispute with New York: A Political Geographic Analysis.* Columbia: Master's Thesis, University of South Carolina, 1993.

7520 **Penlington, Norman.** *The Alaska Boundary Dispute: A Critical Re-Appraisal.* Toronto: McGraw-Hill, 1972.

7521 **Platt, Robert S.** "Conflicting Territorial Claims in the Upper Amazon." In *Geographic Aspects of International Relations*, Charles C. Colby, ed. Freeport: Books for Libraries Press, 1969.

7522 **Raymond, Allen R.** "Benning Wenworth's Claims in the New Hampshire-New York Border Controversy: A Case of Twenty-twenty Hindsight?" *Vermont History*, 43, No. 1 (Winter, 1975), 20-32.

7523 **Reeves, Jesse S.** "Vermont versus New Hampshire." *American Journal of International Law*, 27, No. 3 (July, 1933), 506-508.

7524 **Robertson, Ian E.** "The Dutch Linguistic Legacy and the Guyana/Venezuela Border Question." *Boletin de Estudios Latinoamericanos y del Caribe* (Amsterdam), No. 34 (Junio de 1983), 75-97.

7525 **Rout, Leslie B.** *Which Way Out? A Study of the Guyana-Venezuela Boundary Dispute.* East Lansing: Michigan State University, Latin American Studies Center, 1971.

7526 **Rowland, Donald W.** "Latin-American Boundary Controversies." (California. University. University at Los Angeles. Institute of Political Geography.) *Global Politics*, Russell H. Fitzgibbon, ed. Summer, 1942. Berkeley: University of California Press, 1944, 43-56.

7527 **Sapper, Karl.** "Eine moderne Grenzsaumfrage, betrifft den Grenzatreit Zwischen Guatemala und Honduras." *Zeitschrift fur Geopolitik*, Jahrgang 5, Heft 11 (Nov., 1928), 955-968.

7528 **Schoenrich, Otto.** "The Venezuela-British Guiana Boundary Dispute." *American Journal of International Law*, 43, No. 3 (July, 1949), 523-530.

7529 **Scott, J.B.** "Swiss Decision in the Boundary Dispute between Colombia and Venezuela." *American Journal of International Law*, 16 (1922), 428-431.

7530 **Settle, T.S.** "District of Columbia-Virginia Boundary Act Settling Century-Old Conflict." *Planning and Civic Comment*, 2d quarter (April-June, 1946), 10-11.

7531 **Skaggs, Marvin Lucian.** *North Carolina Boundary Disputes Involving Her Southern Line.* (The James Sprunt studies in history and political science. Published under the direction of the Departments of History and Political Science of the University of North Carolina, Vol. 25, No. 1.) Chapel Hill: University of North Carolina Press, 1941.

7532 **Sloan, Jennie A.** "Anglo-American Relations and the Venezuelan Boundary Dispute." *Hispanic American Historical Review*, 18, No. 4 (November, 1938), 486-506.

7533 **Sobol, John.** "Life Along the Line." *Canadian Geogrphaic* [Vanier], 112, No. 1 (January-February, 1992), 47-56.

7534 **Sousa Brasil, Temistocles Pais de.** "Demarcacao dos limites entre o Brasil e a Colombia-psicologia e embiente." *Revista da Sociedad de geografia do Rio de Janeiro*, Tomo 45 (1938), 3-13.

7535 **Steffen, von Hans.** *Grenzprobleme und Forschungrecht im Patagonien. Erinnerungsblaatter aus der Zeit des chilenische-argentinische Grenz Konfliktes.* Suttgart: Strecker Schroder, 1929.

7536 **Steffen, von Hans.** "Tacna und Arica, ein sudamerikawischen Dreilander Grenzgebiet." *Zeitschrift der Gesellschaft fur Erdkunde*, Nr. 5/6 (1925), 191-209.

7537 **Thomas, Benjamin E.** "Boundaries and Internal Problems of Idaho." *Geographical Review*, 39, No. 1 (January, 1949), 99-109.

7538 **Toppin, H.S.** "The Diplomatic History of the Peru-Bolivia Boundary." *Geographical Journal*, 47, No. 2 (February, 1916), 81-116.

7539 **Tudela, Francisco.** *The Controversy between Peru and Ecuador.* Lima: Torres Aguirre, 1941.

7540 **Venezuela.** *Report on the Boundary Question with British Guiana Submitted to the National Government by the Venezuelan Experts.* Caracas: Ministerio de Relaciones Exteriores, 1967.

7541 **Vidal de la Blache, Paul.** "Le conteste franco-bresilien." *Annales de Geographie*, 10, No. 49 (Janvier, 1901), 68-70.

7542 **Waddell, D.A.G.** "Developments in the Belize Question (1946-1960)." *American Journal of International Law*, 55, No. 2 (April, 1961), 459-469.

7543 **Waldock, C.H.M.** "Disputed Sovereignty in the Falkland Island Dependencies." *British Year Book of International Law*, 25 (1948), 311-353.

7544 **Weeks, John R., and Ham-Chande, Roberto,** eds. *Demographic Dynamics of the U.S.-Mexico Border.* El Paso: Texas Western Press, 1992.

7545 **Winter, Carl George.** "A Note on the Passamaquoddy Boundary Affair." *Canadian Historical Review*, 34, No. 2 (July, 1951), 193-209.

7546 **Woolsey, L.H.** "The Bolivia-Paraguay Dispute (1928)." *American Journal of International Law*, 23, No. 1 (January, 1929), 110-112.

7547 **Woolsey, L.H.** "The Bolivia-Paraguay Dispute (1929)." *American Journal of International Law*,

24, No. 1 (January, 1930), 122-124 and No. 3 (July, 1930), 573-577.

7548 **Woolsey, L.H.** "The Chaco Dispute (1931)." *American Journal of International Law*, 26, No. 4 (October, 1932), 796-801.

7549 **Woolsey, L.H.** "The Leticia Dispute between Colombia and Peru (1932)." *American Journal of International Law*, 27, No. 2 (April, 1933), 317-324 and No. 3 (July, 1933), 525-527.

7550 **Woolsey, L.H.** "The Chaco Dispute (1933)." *American Journal of International Law*, 28, No. 4 (October, 1934), 724-729.

7551 **Woolsey, L.H.** "The Leticia Dispute between Colombia and Peru (1934)." *American Journal of International Law*, 29, No. 1 (January, 1935), 94-99.

7552 **Woolsey, L.H.** "The Ecuador-Peru Boundary Controversy." *American Journal of International Law*, 31, No. 1 (January, 1937), 97-100.

7553 **Woolsey, L.H.** "The Settlement of the Chaco Dispute." *American Journal of International Law*, 33, No. 1 (January, 1939), 126-129.

7554 **Wright, L.A.** "A Study of the Conflict between the Republics of Peru and Ecuador." *Geographical Journal*, 98, No. 5-6 (November-December, 1941), 253-272.

ASIA

Books

7555 **Abu-Dawood, A.S., and Karan, Pradyumna P.** *International Boundaries of Saudi Arabia.* New Delhi: Galaxy Publications, 1990.

7556 **Albert, Donald P.** "Migration Across International Boundaries: A Case Study of Refugees in Thailand." Boone, North Carolina: Appalachian State University, M.A., 1989.

7557 **Bettati, Mario.** *Le conflit sinp-sovietique.* Paris: Armand Colin, 1971.

7558 **Birdwood, Christopher Bromhead, 2nd Baron.** *Two Nations and Kashmir.* London: R. Hale, 1956.

7559 **Brawer, Michael.** *Israel's Boundaries--Past, Present and Future: A Study in Political Geography.* Tel Aviv: Yevneh Publishers, 1988.

7560 **Brecher, Michael.** *The Struggler for Kasmir.* New York: Oxford University Press, 1953.

7561 **Brown, Jessica S., and Kinnel, Susan K.**, Project Coordinators. *Sino-Soviet Conflict: A Historical Bibliography.* ABC-Clio Research Guides, Vol. 13. Santa Barbara: ABC-Clio Information Services, 1985.

7562 **Cantril, Albert Hadley.** *The Indian Perception of the Sino-Indian Border Clash: An Inquiry in Political Psychology.* Princeton, New Jersey: Institute for International Social Research, 1963.

7563 **Chang, Pao-Min.** *The Sino-Vietnamese Territorial Dispute.* New York: Praeger, 1986.

7564 **China.** *The Sino-Indian Boundary Question.* Peking: Government Press, 1962.

7565 **China Ministry of External Affairs.** *Report of the Officials of the Governments of India and the People's Republic of China on the Boundary Question.* New Delhi: Government Printing Press, 1961.

7566 *The Chinese Agression; Some Facts About the India-China Border; Colombo Proposals.* Vol. 1. Calcutta: Ganges Printing, 1963.

7567 **Chopra, Pran.** *On an Indian Border.* New York: Asia Publishing House, 1964.

7568 **Doolin, Dennis D.** *Territorial Claims in the Sino-Soviet Conflict: Documents and Analysis.* Stanford, California: Stanford University, Hoover Institution on War, Revolution and Peace, 1965.

7569 **Drake, Charles.** *China's Boundary Problems.* Chicago: Northeastern Illinois State College, Master's Thesis, 1972.

7570 **Fisher, Margaret W.; Rose, Leo E; and Huttenback, Robert A.** *Himalayan Battleground; Sino-Indian Rivalry in Ladakh.* New York: Praeger, 1963.

7571 **Ghose, Kalobaran.** *Chinese Invasion of India.* Calcutta: Banachhaya Ghore, 1963.

7572 **Haupert, John S.** *Political Geography of the Israeli-Syrian Boundary Dispute, 1949-1967.* Association of American Geographers, New York-New Jersey Division. West Point, New York: Proceedings of the 8th Annual Meeting, October 13-14, 1967, April, 1968, 104-116.

7573 **Hudson, G.F.** *The Aksai Chin.* In *St. Anthony's College Far Eastern Affairs, No. 3, St. Anthony's Papers, No. 14.* London: Oxford University Press, 1963.

7574 **India.** Department of Foreign Affairs. *Tripartite Conferences 1913-14. The Boundary Question between China and Tibet; a Valuable Record of the Tripartite Conference between China, Britain and Tibet Held in India, 1913-14.* Simla: Government Printing Office, 1940.

7575 **India (Republic).** Ministry of External Affairs. *China's Foreign Ministry's Reply Memorandum to India on Sino-Indian Boundary Question.* Current Background, No. 703. New Delhi: Publication Division, Government of India Press, 1963.

7576 **India (Republic).** Ministry of External Affairs. *Chinese Aggression in Maps with an Introduction and Explanatory Notes.* New Delhi: Publication Division, Government of India Press, 1962.

7577 **India (Republic).** Ministry of External Affairs. *Concluding Chapter of the Report of the Indian Officials on Boundary Question.* New Delhi: Publication Div., Government of India Press, 1961.

7578 **India (Republic).** Ministry of External Affairs. *Facts About Kutch-Sind Boundary in Maps.* New Delhi: Publication Division, Government of India Press, 1965.

7579 **India (Republic).** Ministry of External Affairs. *India-China Border Problem.* New Delhi: Publication Division, Government of India Press, 1962.

7580 **India (Republic).** Ministry of External Affairs. *Indian Communists Condemn Chinese Aggression.* New Delhi: Publication Division, Government of India Press, 1962.

7581 **India (Republic).** Ministry of External Affairs. *Notes, Memoranda and Letters Exchanged between the Governments of India and China. White Paper No. 1-9.* New Delhi: Publication Division, Government of India Press, 1963.

7582 **India (Republic).** Ministry of External Affairs. *The Sino-Indian Dispute: Questions and Answers.* New Delhi: Publication Division, Government of India Press, 1963.

7583 **India (Republic).** Ministry of External Affairs. *Report of the Officials of the Government of India and the People's Republic of China on the Boundary Question.* New Delhi: Publication Division, Government of India Press, 1961.

7584 **India (Republic).** Ministry of External Affairs. *Report on the Boundary Dispute between U.P. and Bihar. Vol. 1.* New Delhi: Publication Division, Government of India Press, 1964.

7585 **India (Republic).** Ministry of External Affairs. *Report on the Indian Officials on the Boundary Question.* New Delhi: Publication Division, Government of India Press, 1961.

7586 **India (Republic).** Ministry of External Affairs. *The Sino-Indian Border Dispute. Current Notes on International Affairs.* New Delhi: Publication Division, Government of India Press, 1963.

7587 **India (Republic).** Ministry of Home Affairs. *Report of the Commission on Maharastra--Mysore--Kerala Boundary Disputes.* New Delhi: Publication Division, Government of India Press, 1967.

7588 *The India-China Boundary Question: A Legal Study with a Brief Historical Introduction.* New Delhi: Indian Society of International Law, 1963.

7589 **Jackson, W.A. Douglas.** *The Russo-Chinese Borderlands: Zone of Peaceful Contact or Potential Conflict?* Princeton, New Jersey: Van Nostrand, 1968.

7590 **Japan.** Ministry of Foreign Affairs. Public Information Bureau. *Northern Territorial Issue: Japan's Position on Unsettled Question between Japan and Soviet Union.* Tokyo: Ministry of Foreign Affairs, 1968.

7591 **Krishna Rao, K.** *International Law Aspects of the Sino-Indian Boundary; All India Radio Talks.* New Delhi: Indian Society of International Law, 1963.

7592 **Krishna Rao, K.** *The Preah Vihear Case and the Sino-Indian Boundary Question.* New Delhi: Indian Society of International Law, 1963.

7593 **Krishna Rao, K.** *The Sino-Indian Boundary Question and International Law.* New Delhi: Indian Society of International Law, 1963.

7594 *The Kutch-Sind Border Question: A Collection of Documents with Comments.* New Delhi: Indian Society of International Law, 1965.

7595 **Lamb, Alastair.** *The China-India Border: The Origins of the Disputed Boundaries.* London: Oxford University Press, 1964.

7596 **League of Nations.** *Question of the Frontier between Turkey and Iraq; Report Submitted to the Council by the Commission Instituted by the Council Resolution of September 30th, 1924.* Geneve: League of Nations, 1925.

7597 **Leifer, Michael.** *The Philippine Claim to Sabah.* Zug, Switzerland: Inter Documentation, 1968.

7598 **Lee, Yong Leng.** *The Razor's Edge: Boundaries and Boundary Disputes in Southeast Asia.* Singapore: Institute of Southeast Asian Studies. Research Notes and Discussions. Paper No. 15, 1980.

7599 **Mehra, Parshotam.** *An Agreed Frontier: Ladakh and India's Northeasternmost Borders, 1846-1947.* Delhi: Oxford University Press, 1992.

7600 **Merani, Pritam T.** *India's Territorial Disputes: A Legal Analysis.* Baltimore, Maryland: Johns Hopkins University, Ph.D., 1966.

7601 **Meyer, Milton Walter.** *India-Pakistan and the Border Lands.* Totowa, New Jersey: Littlefield Adams, 1968.

7602 **Osborn, George Knox III.** *Sino-Indian Border Conflicts: Historical Background and Recent Developments.* Stanford, California: Stanford University, Ph.D., 1963.

7603 **Pakistan.** Embassy. Information Division. *Dispute-Rann of Kutch; Background Report.* Washington, D.C.: Embassy of Pakistan, 1965.

7604 **Rao, Gondker Narayana.** *The India-China Border: A Reappraisal.* New York: Asia Publishing House, 1968.

7605 *The Sino-Indian Boundary: Texts of Treaties, Agreements and Certain Exchange of Notes Relating to the Sino-Indian Boundary.* New Delhi: Indian Society of International Law, 1962.

7606 *The Sino-Indian Boundary Question, Part I.* Peking: Foreign Languages Press, 1962.

7607 *The Sino-Indian Boundary Question Part II.* Peking: Foreign Languages Press, 1965.

7608 *Sino-Indian Border Conflict, A Symposium.* Jaipur: Rajasthan University, Department of Political Science, 1963.

7609 **Srivastava, Harisankar Prasad.** *The India-China Boundary: A Study in Political Geography.* Gainesville: University of Florida, Ph.D., 1961.

7610 **Tapia, Augusto.** "Causas Geologicas y consecuencias politicas de los cambios de Cause del Pilcomayo en Formosa." *Anales de la Sociedad Argentine de Estudios Geogradicos,* 4 (1935), 245-262.

7611 **U.S. Department of State.** *Vietnam Demarcation Line.* Washington, D.C.: Office of the Geographer, 1962.

Journals

7612 **Ahmad, Nafis.** "The Indo-Pakistan Boundary Disputes Tribunal, 1949-1950." *Geographical Review,* 43, No. 3 (July, 1953), 329-337.

7613 **Ahmad, Nafis.** "The Revolution of the Boundaries of East Pakistan." *Oriental Geography,* 2, No. 2 (1958), 97-106.

7614 **Ahmad, Syed Ijaz.** "The Rann of Kutch." *Pakistan Review,* 13, No. 7 (July, 1965), 33-35.

7615 **Ahmed, S.H.** "Chronology of the Sino-Indian Border Dispute." *International Studies,* 5, Nos 1-2 (July-October, 1963), 212-220.

7616 **Alexander, Lewis M.** "The Arab-Israeli Boundary Problem." *World Politics*, 6, No. 3 (April, 1954), 322-337.

7617 **Armstrong, Hamilton Fish.** "Where India Faces China (Nepal)." *Foreign Affairs*, 37, No. 4 (July, 1959), 617-625.

7618 **Arora, R.S.** "The Sino-Indian Border Dispute: A Legal Approach." *Public Law*, (Spring, 1963), 172-200.

7619 "The Azarbaijan Problem." *World Today*, N.s. 2, No. 2 (February, 1946), 45-48.

7620 **Bajpai, S.C.** "Barahoti; On Sino-Indian Border: An Historical Appraisal." *Parliamentary Studies*, 8, No. 5 (May, 1964), 12-14.

7621 **Barton, William P., Sir.** "Pakistan's Claim to Kashmir." *Foreign Affairs*, 28, No. 2 (January, 1950), 299-308.

7622 **Bernheim, Roger.** "Peking's Agression in the Himalayas." *Swiss Review of World Affairs*, 12 (December, 1962), 3-5.

7623 **Blake, G. H.** "International Boundaries and Territorial Stability in the Middle East: An Assessment." *GeoJournal* [Dordrecht], 28, No. 3 (November, 1992), 365-373.

7624 **Brod, Raymond.** "A Bibliography of the Sino-Soviet Border Dispute." *Special Libraries Association. Geography and Map Division. Bulletin*, 77, No. 11 (September, 1969), 10-16.

7625 **Caroe, Olaf, Sir.** "The India-Tibet-China Triangle." *Asian Review*, 58, No. 205 (January, 1960), 3-13.

7626 **Caroe, Olaf, Sir.** "The Sino-Indian Question." *Journal of the Royal Central Asian Society*, 50, Parts 3 and 4 (July-October, 1963), 238-251.

7627 **Chang, Pao-Min.** "The Sino-Vietnamese Territorial Dispute." *Asian Pacific Community*, 8 (Spring, 1980), 130-165.

7628 **Chaudhri, Mohammed Ahsen.** "The Indo-China Struggle." *Pakistan Horizon*, 7, No. 3 (September, 1954), 127-138.

7629 **Chen Yi.** "Chen Yi on the Sino-Indian Boundary Question." *Peking Review*, 12 (March 22, 1963), 10-14.

7630 **Connell, John.** "The India-China Frontier Dispute." *Royal Central Asian Journal*, 47, Parts 3 and 4 (July-October, 1960), 270-285.

7631 **Das Choudhury, J; and Bhattacharyya, N.N.** "Geopolitical Significance of McMahon Line." *Journal of North East India Geographical Society*, 15, Nos. 1 and 2; 16, Nos. 1 and 2 (1984), 55-58.

7632 **Eckelan, W.F. van.** "Simla Convention and McMahon Line." *Royal Central Asian Journal*, 54, Part 2 (June, 1967), 179-184.

7633 **Egerton, R.A.D.** "The Indonesian Dispute." *Australian Outlook*, 3, No. 2 (June, 1949), 117-127.

7634 **Elkin, Jerrold F., and Fredericks, Brian.** "Sino-Indian Border Talks: The View from New Delhi." *Asian Survey*, 23, No. 10 (October, 1983), 1128-1139.

7635 **Eyre, John D.** "Japanese-Soviet Territorial Issues in the Southern Kurile Islands." *Professional Geographer*, 20, No. 1 (January, 1968), 11-15.

7636 **Field, Alvin R.** "Das Problem der Grenze Zwischen Birma and China." *Zeitschrift fur Geopolitik*, 30, No. 11 (November, 1959), 7-39.

7637 **Fisher, Margaret W., and Rose, Leo E.** "Ladakh and the Sino-Indian Border Crisis." *Asian Survey*, 2, No. 8 (October, 1962), 27-37.

7638 **Fitzgerald, C.P.** "Tension on the Sino-Soviet Border." *Foreign Affairs*, 45, No. 4 (July, 1967), 683-693.

7639 **Freeberne, Michael.** "Conflict on Sino-Soviet Frontiers." *Geographical Magazine*, 42, No. 3 (December, 1969), 167-172.

7640 **Freeberne, Michael.** "Minority Unrest and Sino-Soviet Rivalry in Sinkiang, China's Northwestern Frontier Bastion, 1949-1965." In *Essays in Political Geography*, Charles A. Fisher, ed. London: Methuen, 1968, 177-209.

7641 **Gallicchio, Marc.** "The Kuriles Controversy: U.S. Diplomacy in the Soviet-Japan Border dispute, 1941-1956." *Pacific Historical Review* [Los Angeles], 60, No. 1 (February, 1991), 69-101.

7642 **Garver, John W.** "The Sino-Soviet Territorial Dispute in the Pamir Mountains Region." *China Quarterly*, 85, No. 1 (March, 1981), 107-118.

7643 **Gopalachari, K.** "India-China Boundary." *Africa Quarterly*, 2, No. 4 (October, 1962), 201-211.

7644 **Gopalachari, K.** "The India-China Boundary Question." *International Studies*, 5, Nos. 1-2 (July-October, 1963), 33-42.

7645 **Grundy-Warr, Carl E.R.** "Coexistent Borderlands and Intra-State Conflicts in Mainland Southeast Asia." *Singapore Journal of Tropical Geography* [Singapore], 14, No. 1 (June, 1993), 42-57.

7646 **Gupta, Sisir K.** "The India-China Border: Review Article." *Foreign Affairs Reports*, 13, No. 5 (May, 1964), 70-72.

7647 **Harper, Norman.** "Sino-Indian Border Dispute, 3. India and the Border Conflict with China." *Australia's Neighbours*, Nos. 133-134 (November-December, 1962), 5-8.

7648 **Haupert, John S.** "Jerusalem: Aspects of Reunification and Integration." *Professional Geographer*, 23, No. 4 (October, 1971), 312-318.

7649 **Haupert, John S.** "Political Geography of the Israeli-Syrian Boundary Dispute, 1949-1967." *Professional Geographer*, 21, No. 3 (May, 1969), 163-171.

7650 **Hay, Sir Rupert.** "The Persian Gulf States and Their Boundary Problems." *Geographical Journal*, 120, No. 4 (December, 1954), 433-445.

7651 **Huck, Arthur.** "Sino-Indian Border Dispute, 2. The Chinese Arguments." *Australia's Neighbours*, Nos. 133-134 (November-December, 1962), 4-5.

7652 **Husain, K.Z.** "On the North Western Boundary of the Oriental Region." *Asiatic Society of Pakistan Journal*, 11, No. 3 (December, 1966), 103-111.

7653 **Huttenback, Robert A.** "A Historical Note on the Sino-Indian Dispute Over the Aksai Chin." *China Quarterly*, 18 (April-June, 1964), 201-207.

7654 **Inlow, E. Burke.** "The McMahon Line; The Disputed Boundary of the Eastern Sector of the Sino-Indian Border." *Journal of Geography*, 63, No. 6 (September, 1964), 261-274.

7655 **Jacob, Lucy, and Others.** " A Selected Bibliography (on Sino-Indian Border Conflict)." *Political Science Review*, 2, No. 1 (March, 1963), 1-42.

7656 **Jangam, R.T.** "An Analysis of Sino-Indian Correspondence of Border Disputes." *United Asia*, 15, No. 1 (January, 1963), 18-21.

7657 **Jones, P.H.M.** "China on the Himalayas." *Far Eastern Economic Review*, 36 (June 14, 1962), 565-567.

7658 **Jones, P.H.M.** "Passes and Impasses: A Study of the Sino-Indian Border Dispute." *Far Eastern Economic Review*, 39 (February 28, 1963), 443-458.

7659 **Kao, Teh.** "A Chinese View of the 'McMahon Line'." *Eastern World*, 17, No. 2 (February, 1963), 13-14.

7660 **Karan, Pradyumna Prasad.** "The India-China Boundary Dispute." *Journal of Geography*, 59, No. 1 (January, 1960), 16-21.

7661 **Karan, Pradyumna Prasad.** "Indo-Pakistan Boundaries: Their Fixation, Functions and Problems." *Indian Geographical Journal*, 28, No. 1-2 (January-June, 1953), 19-23.

7662 **Karan, Pradyumna Prasad.** "The Sino-Soviet Border Dispute." *Journal of Geography*, 63, No. 5 (May, 1964), 216-222.

7663 **Khan, Farzana.** "The Rann of Kutch Dispute." *Pakistan Horizon*, 18, No. 4 (Fourth Quarter, 1965), 374-384.

7664 **Klinghoffer, H.** "The Territorial Integrity of the Land of Israel in the Light of Security Council Resolution 242." *Haderekh*, 3, No. 2 (February, 1971), 7.

7665 **Krishna Rao, K.** "The Sino-Indian Boundary Question: A Study of Some Related Legal Issues." *Indian Journal of International Law*, 3, No. 2 (April, 1963), 151-189.

7666 **Krishna Rao, K.** "The Sino-Indian Boundary Question and International Law." *International and Comparative Law Quarterly*, 11, No. 2 (April, 1962), 375-415.

7667 "The Latest Map of Occupied Areas in China." *China Journal*, 30, No. 5 (May, 1939), 252-253.

7668 **Leighton, Marian Kirsch.** "Perspective on the Vietnam-Cambodia Border Conflict." *Asian Survey*, 18, No. 5 (May, 1978), 448-457.

7669 **Levy, Roger.** "Les Confrontations Territoriales Sino-Russis, Particulierement dans la region de l'Ili, au Sinkiang." *Politique Etrangere*, 31 Annee, No. 2 (1966), 157-172.

7670 **Lord, Robert Howard.** "The Russo-Polish Boundary Problem." *Proceedings of the Massachusetts Historical Society*, 68 (October, 1944-May, 1947) (1952), 407-423.

7671 **Maung, Maung.** "The Burma-China Border." *India Quarterly*, 16, No. 4 (October-December, 1960), 358-364.

7672 **McPeak, Merrill A.** "Israel: Borders and Security." *Foreign Affairs*, 54, No. 3 (April, 1976), 426-443.

7673 **Meadows, Martin.** "The Philippines Claim to North Borneo." *Political Science Quarterly*, 77, No. 3 (September, 1962), 321-335.

7674 **Melamid, Alexander.** "The Shatt Al-'Arab Boundary Dispute." *Middle East Journal*, 22, No. 3 (Summer, 1968), 351-357.

7675 **Merani, Pritam T.** "The India-China Border Dispute." *Journal of Public Law*, 13, No. 1 (1964), 162-188.

7676 **Misra, S.D.** "The Sino-Indian Dispute; A Geographical Analysis." *Indian Geographical Journal*, 34, Nos. 3 and 4 (July-September and October-December, 1959), 59-64.

7677 **Mussio, Giovanni.** "Le Questioni Himalayane dell India." *L'Universo*, Anno 32, No. 5 (Septembre-Ottobre, 1952), 717-730.

7678 **Nigam, R.K.** "Indo-China Frontier Along the Himalayas, Its Geographical Implications." *Geographical Knowledge*, 3, Nos. 1 and 2 (1970), 36-40.

7679 **Njoroge, Lawrence M.** "The Japan-Soviet Union Territorial Dispute." *Asian Survey*, 25, No. 5 (May, 1985), 499-511.

7680 **Om, Hari.** "A Selected Bibliography on Sino-Indian Border Dispute." *Indian Affairs, Record*, 9, No. 1 (January, 1963), 38-42.

7681 **Pandey, D.C.**, and **Pandey, R.K.** "International Boundaries with Special Reference to Kumaon and Its Neighborhood." *Geographical Outlook*, 15 (1979-1980).

7682 **Patil, R.K.** "The India-China Border Dispute—The Western Sector." *India Quarterly*, 20, No. 2 (April-June, 1964), 156-179.

7683 **Petkovic, R.** "Conflict in the Himalayas." *Review of International Affairs*, 13, No. 304 (December 5, 1962), 11-13.

7684 **Phadnis, Urmila.** "Ceylon and the Sino-Indian Border Conflict: An Appraisal." *United Asia*, 15, No. 11 (November, 1963), 745-752.

7685 **Pitts, Forrest R.** "The Logic of the Seventeenth Parallel as a Boundary in Indochina." *Yearbook of the Association of Pacific Coast Geographers*, 18 (1956), 42-56.

7686 **Prabhakar, Purushottam.** "Sino-Indian Border Dispute." *Parliamentary Studies*, 8, No. 12 (December, 1964), 11-14.

7687 **Prabhakar, Purushottam.** "The Sino-Indian Border Dispute: A Survey of Research and Source Material." *International Studies*, 7, No. 1 (July, 1965), 120-127.

7688 **Prescott, J.R.V.** "Sino-Indian Border Dispute, 1. The Borderland." *Australia's Neighbours*, Nos. 133 and 134 (November-December, 1962), 1-4.

7689 **Pringsheim, Klaus H.** "China, India, and Their Himalayan Border, 1961-1963." *Asian Survey*, 3, No. 10 (October, 1963), 474-495.

7690 **Rahul, Ram.** "The Himalayan Border." *Foreign Affairs Reports*, 13, No. 2 (February, 1964), 15-18.

7691 **Rana, R.P.** "The Sino-Indian Border Conflict and India's Foreign Policy." *Journal of Maharaja Sayajirao University of Baroda*, 12, No. 3 (July, 1963), 37-45.

7692 **Rao, K. Krisna.** "The Sino-Indian Boundary Question and International Law." *International and Comparative Law Quarterly*, 11, No. 2 (April, 1962), 375-415.

7693 **Rawlings, E.H.** "The India-China Border." *Asian Review*, 58, No. 213 (January, 1962), 21-26.

7694 **Raza, Moonis.** "Extent and Boundaries of Suba Awadh, 1550-1605; A Study in Historical Geography." *Geographer*, 12 (January, 1965), 21-27.

7695 **Rees, David.** "Japan's Northern Territories." *Asia Pacific Community* (Tokyo), 7 (Winter, 1980), 13-42.

7696 **Romagnano, Paulo Torella Di.** "La Contraversia Cino-Indian Per le Frontiere." *Storia e Politica*, Anno 6, Fascicolo 1 (January-March, 1967), 121-148.

7697 **Rose, Leo E.** "Conflict in the Himalayas." *Military Review*, 43, No. 2 (February, 1963), 3-15.

7698 **Rubin, Alfred P.** "The Sino-Indian Border Disputes." *International and Comparative Law Quarterly*, 9, No. 1 (January, 1960), 96-125.

7699 **Sahwell, A.S.** "The Buraimi Dispute, the British Armed Aggression." *Islamic Review*, 44, No. 2 (April, 1956), 13-17.

7700 **Saraf, D.N.** "Legal Aspects of the Sino-Indian Boundary Dispute." *Patna University Journal*, 19, No. 1 (January, 1964), 36-67.

7701 **Satyapalan, C.N.** "The Sino-Indian Border Conflict." *Orbis*, 13, No. 2 (Summer, 1964), 374-390.

7702 "Saudi Arabia and South Yemen's Border Clash: Its Background and Implications." *Arab World*, (March, 1973), 11-12.

7703 **Sen, D.K.** "China, Tibet and India." *India Quarterly*, 7, No. 2 (April-June, 1951), 112-132.

7704 **Sharma, Surya Prakash.** "The India-China Border Dispute: An Indian Perspective." *American Journal of International Law*, 59, No. 1 (January, 1965), 16-47.

7705 **Sharan, Sarojini.** "The Sino-Indian Border Dispute Under International Law." *Patna University Journal*, 18, No. 3 (July, 1963), 184-185.

7706 **Singh, Biswanath.** "The Legality of the McMahon Line: An Indian Perspective." *Orbis*, 11, No. 1 (Spring, 1967), 271-284.

7707 **Singh, Govind Saran.** "The Chinese Claim: A Glacier in India." *Deccan Geographer*, 2, No. 2 (January, 1964), 171-174.

7708 "Some Aspects of the Rann Kutch Dispute." *Pakistan Horizon*, 19, No. 1 (First Quarter, 1966), 53-67.

7709 **Srivastava, R.P.** "Inter-State Tensions and Boundary Persistence: The Indian Scene." *National Geographer*, 23, No. 2 (December, 1988), 119-123.

7710 **Srivastava, R.P.** "The Uttar Pradesh-Bihar Boundary in India: A Case of an International Boundary Problem." *National Geographer*, 8 (1972), 49-57.

7711 **Steiner, H. Arthur.** "Chinese Policy in the Sino-Indian Border Dispute." *Current Scene*, 1, No. 17 (November 7, 1961), 1-9.

7712 **Sugimura, Oaki.** "Geographical Setting in the Rendering of 'Packutu San' and 'Changpai Shan' in China-Korean Border Region." *Political Geography*, 2 (1963), 31-54.

7713 "Survey of India-China Border Issue." *United Asia*, 14, No. 11 (November, 1962), 618-621.

7714 **Tayyab, Ali.** "A Note on the Political Geography of the India-China (Tibet) Border." *Canadian Geographer*, 16, No. 3 (July, 1960), 22-26.

7715 **Tewari, B.C.,** and **Phadnis, Urmila.** "The India-China Border Area Disputes; A Selected Bibliography." *India Quarterly*, 16, No. 2 (April-June, 1960), 155-169.

7716 **Tregonning, K.G.** "The Claim for North Borneo by the Philippines." *Australian Outlook*, 16, No. 3 (December, 1962), 283-291.

7717 **Vertzberger, Yaacov Y.I.** "India's Border Conflict with China: A Perceptual Analysis." *Journal of Contemporary History*, 17, No. 4 (October, 1982), 607-631.

7718 **Wittam, Daphne E.** "The Sino-Burmese Boundary Treaty." *Pacific Affairs*, 34, No. 2 (Summer, 1961), 174-183.

7719 **Winslow, Charles H.** "An Empirical Road to a Normative Barrier: A Study of Palestinian Taxi Drivers Crossing a One Lane Bridge in South Lebanon." *Middle East Journal*, 34, No. 1 (Winter, 1980), 25-41.

7720 **Womack, Brantly.** "Sino-Vietnamese Border Trade: The Edge of Normalization." *Asian Survey* [Berkeley], 34, No. 6 (June, 1994), 495-512.

7721 **Wright, Quincy.** "The Mosul Dispute." *American Journal of International Law*, 20, No. 3 (July, 1926), 453-464.

AUSTRALIA, OCEANIA AND ANTARCTICA

Books and Journals

7722 **Habicht, M.** *Post-Ware Treaties for the Pacific Settlement of International Disputes.* Cambridge, Massachusetts: Harvard University Press, 1931.

7723 **Hanessian, John.** "Antarctica: Current National Interests and Legal Realities." *Proceedings of American Society of International Law*, 52 (1958), 145-164.

7724 **Hunter, Christie E.W.** *The Antarctic Problem: An Historical and Political Study.* London: Allen & Unwin, 1951.

7725 **Logan, W.A.** *The Evolution and Significance of Select International Boundaries in South-Western Victoria.* Melbourne: Univ. of Melbourne, 1963.

7726 **Van der Veur, Paul.** "Australian New Guinea's Borders and Shelves; Inequities and Idiosyncrasies." *Australian Outlook*, 18, No. 1 (April, 1964), 17-19.

EUROPE

Books and Journals

7727 **Alexander, Lewis M.** "Recent Changes in the Benelux-German Boundary." *Geographical Review*, 43, No. 1 (January, 1953), 69-76.

7728 **Beeley, B.W.** "The Greek-Turkish Boundary: Conflict at Interface." *Institute of British Geographers, Transactions*, New Series, 3, No. 3 (1978), 351-366.

7729 **Bicik, Ivan,** and **Stepanek, Vit.** "Post-War Changes of the Land-Use Structure in Bohemia and Moravia, Case Study Sudetenland." *GeoJournal* [Dordrecht], 32, No. 3 (March, 1994), 253-259.

7730 **Brown, Neville.** "Cyprus. A Study in Unresolved Conflict." *World Today*, 23, No. 9 (September, 1967), 396-405.

7731 **Brunet, Roger.** "Sas et finisterre: models de la Slovaquie orientale." *L'Espace Geographique*, 17, No. 2 (Avril/Juin, 1988), 150-157.

7732 "The Bulgarian Claim to Southern Dobruja."
Bulletin of International News, 17, No. 4 (February
24, 1940), 211-213.

7733 **Cornish, Vaughan.** *Borderlands of Language in
Europe and Their Relation to the Historic Frontiers
of Christendom.* London: Sifton Praed, 1936.

7734 **Dacier, Michael.** "Le Probleme de la Sarre."
Ecrits de Paris, No. 115 (May, 1954), 1-8.

7735 **Dehmel, R.** "Die Demarkationslinie in
Ostpreussen." *Zeitschrift fur Geopolitik*, 24,
No. 10 (Oktober, 1953), 634+.

7736 **Deroubaix, Jean-Claude.** "Les frontieres France-
Belgique et Wallonie-Flandre: se marquent-elles
dans la repartition par age des populations? *Revue
Belge de Geographie*, 113 Annee, Fasc. 43 (1989),
119-138.

7737 **Dima, Nicholas.** *Bessarabia and Bukovina:
Soviet-Romanian Territorial Dispute.* Boulder:
East European Monographs, No. 108, 1982.

7738 **Dobell, W.M.** "Division Over Cyprus."
International Affairs, 22, No. 2 (April, 1967),
278-292.

7739 **Douglas, J.N.H.** "The Irreconcilable Border."
Geographical Magazine, 49, No. 3 (December,
1976), 172-178.

7740 **Frei, Otto.** "The Barrier Across Berlin and Its
Consequences." *World Today*, 17,
No. 11 (November, 1961), 459-470.

7741 **Garloch, Lorene A.** "Alsace-Lorraine: A Border
Problem." *Journal of Geography*, 45, No. 7
(October, 1946), 268-279.

7742 **Gervais, Andre.** *L'affaire du lac Lanoux.* Paris:
Annuaire francais de droit international, 1960.

7743 **Hilton, T.E.** "Finish Boundary Problems: The
Latest Phase-A Study in Political Geography."
Bulletin of the Ghana Geographical Association,
11, No. 2 (July, 1966), 5-19.

7744 **Hinks, Arthur R.** "The New Boundaries of
Bulgaria." *Geographical Journal*, 55, No. 2
(February, 1920), 127-138.

7745 **Hinks, Arthur R.** "The Slesvig Plebiscite and the
Danish-German Boundary." *Geographical Journal*,
56, No. 6 (December, 1920), 484-491.

7746 **Hoffman, George W.** "South Tyrol: Borderland
Rights and World Politics." *Journal of Central
European Affairs*, 7, No. 3 (October, 1947),
285-308.

7747 **Kiss, George.** "Italian Boundary Problems: A
Review." *Geographical Review*, 37, No. 1

(January, 1947), 137-141.

7748 **Kovacs, Zoltan.** "Border Changes and Their
Effect on the Structure of Hungarian Society."
Political Geography Quarterly, 8, No. 1 (January,
1989), 79-86.

7749 **Kruszewski, Z. Anthony.** *The Oder-Neisse
Boundary and Poland's Modernization: The
Socioeconomic and Political Impact.* New York:
Praeger, 1972.

7750 **Lorenzen, S.** "Deutschlands Grenze Gegen
Danemark." *Zeitschrift fur Geopolitik*,
Jahrgang 23, Heft 8 (August, 1952), 463-470.

7751 **Mackray, Robert.** *The Problem of Upper Silesia.*
London: Allen & Unwin, 1945.

7752 **Meyer, Peggy Falkenheim.** "Moscow's Releations
with Tokyo: Domestic Obstacles to a Territorial
Agreement." *Asian Survey* [Berkeley], 33, No. 10
(October, 1993), 953-967.

7753 **Newbigin, Marion.** *Geographical Aspects of the
Balkan Problems in Their Relation to The Great
European War.* New York: Putnam, 1915.

7754 **Ogilvie, Alan.** *Some Aspects of Boundary
Settlement at the Peace Conference.* London:
Society for Promoting Christian Knowledge, 1922.

7755 **Paasi, Anssi.** "The Changing Geography of
Boundaries: The Finnish-Russian Border as an
Example." *Terra* [Helsinki], 105, No. 4 (1993),
253-263.

7756 **Pollock, James K.** "Germany's Post-War
Boundaries--A Suggestion." *Journal of Central
European Affairs*, 4, No. 4 (January, 1945),
349-356.

7757 **Posselt, von A.** "Die Annektion von Dollart,
Bourtanger Veen und Neder-Bentheim."
*Mitteilungen der Geographischen Gesellschaft Zu
Wien*, Band 98, Heft 7-12 (July-Dec., 1946),
145-149.

7758 **Randall, Richard B.** *The Political Geography of
the Klagenfurt Plebiscite Area.* Worchester,
Massachusetts: Clark University, Ph.D., 1955.

7759 **Raup, Philip M.** "The Agricultural Significance
of German Boundary Problems." *Lands
Economics*, 26, No. 2 (May, 1950), 101-114.

7760 **Reymond, Jacques.** *The Saar Conflict,
1945-1955.* New York: Praeger, 1960.

7761 **Ritter Gert,** and **Hajdu, Joseph.** "The East-West
German Boundary." *Geographical Review*, 79,
No. 3 (July, 1989), 326-344.

7762 **Russell, Frank M.** *The Saar, Battleground and Pawn*. Stanford, California: Stanford University Press, 1951.

7763 "The Saar as an International Problem." *World Today*, 8, No. 7 (July, 1952), 299-307.

7764 **Seifrid, Thomas.** "Getting Across: Border-Consciousness in Soviet and Emigre Literature." *Slavic and East Euorpean Journal* [Tucson], 38, No. 2 (Summer, 1994), 245-260.

7765 **Sigalos, Louis.** *The Greek Claims on Northern Epirus*. Chicago: Argonaut, 1963.

7766 *The Sino-Soviet Dispute*. Kessing's Research Report 3. New York: Charles Scribner's Sons, 1969.

7767 **Sleurink, H.** "De aanpassing van de Belgische Provincie-, arrondissementsen gemeentegrenzen aan de Nederlands-Franse Taalgrens." *Geografisch Tijdschrift*, 17, No. 2 (Mei, 1964), 62-69.

7768 **Solch, Johann.** "The Brenner Region." *Sociological Review*, 19, No. 4 (October, 1927), 318-334.

7769 **Szaz, Zoltan Michael.** *Germany's Eastern Frontiers: The Problem of the Oder-Neisse Line*. Chicago: H. Regnery, 1960.

7770 **Toynbee, Arnold J.** "The Franco-Turkish Dispute Over the Sanjaq of Alexanderatta, 1936-1397." *Survey of International Affairs*, (1937), 767-783.

7771 **Uhlig, H.** "Revier uber Grenzen: das Aachen-Limburg-Kempen Kohlenfeld." *Berichte zur Deutsche Landerkunde*, 23 (1959), 255-278.

7772 **Van Valkenburg, Samuel.** *European Jigsaw; An Atlas of Boundary Problems*. New York: Foreign Policy Association, Headline Series, No. 53, 1945.

7773 **Volacic, M.** "The Curzon Line and Territorial Changes in Eastern Europe." *Bielorussian Review*, 2 (1956), 37-72.

7774 **Weigend, Guido G.** "Effects of Boundary Changes in the South Tyrol." *Geographical Review*, 40, No. 3 (July, 1950), 364-375.

7775 **Whyte, John H.** "How is the Boundary Maintained Between Two Commities in Northern Ireland." *Ethnic and Racial Studies*, 9, No. 2 (April, 1986), 219-234.

7776 **Wilkinson, H.R.** "Jugoslav Kosmet." *Transactions and Papers*, No. 21. *Institute of British Geographers*, (1955), 171-193.

7777 **Wright, Herbert.** "Poland and the Crimea Conference." *American Journal of International Law*, 39, No. 2 (April, 1939), 300-308.

7778 **Xydis, S.G.** *Cyprus: Conflicts and Conciliation 1954-1958*. Columbus: Ohio State University Press, 1967.

7779 **Zorgbibe, Charles.** *La Question de Berlin*. Paris: Armand Colin, 1970.

FRONTIERS

GENERAL AND THEORY

Books and Journals

7780 **Adami, C.V.** *National Frontiers in Relation to International Law*, T.T. Behrens (tr.), ed. London: Oxford University Press, 1927.

7781 **Ahnlund, Nils.** "The Historical Frontiers off the Northern Nations." *Le Noro*, 5, No. 4 (1942), 243-255.

7782 **Ancel, Jacques.** *Geographie des Frontieres*. Paris: Gillimard NRF, 1938.

7783 **Ancel, Jacques.** "Ajustement des frontieres; reflexions d'un geographe." *Le Monde Slave*, 15e annee, Tome II (Mai, 1938), 186-201.

7784 **Ancel, Jacques.** "L'evolution de la notion de frontiere." *Bulletin des Sciences Historiques*, 5, No. 20 (1933), 538-554.

7785 **Ancel, Jacques.** "Les frontieres, etude de geographie politique." *Academie de Deroit International, Recueil des Cours*, 55 (1936), 207-210.

7786 **Ancel, Jacques.** "Une theorie francaise sur la geographie des frontieres." *Revue des Affaires Etrangeres*, 2 (1931), 279-289.

7787 **Barragelata, H. David.** *Frontieres, contribution a l'histoire du droit international americain*. Paris: Ollendorf, 1911.

7788 **Bhattacharjee, Tarun Kumar.** *Alluring Frontiers*. New Delhi: Omsons, 1987.

7789 **Broek, Jan O.M.** *The Problem of Natural Frontiers*. Berkeley: University of California Press, 1940.

7790 **Bussagli, Mario.** "Osservazione Sulla Frontiera." *De Homine*, No. 24/24 (1968), 111-122.

7791 **Curzon of Keddleston, Lord.** *Frontiers*. Oxford: Clarendon Press, 1908.

7792 **Dannenbaum, M.** *Mathematisch-Politische Grenzen*. Stalluponen: Klutke, 1932.

7793 **Dunbar, George.** *Frontiers.* London: Nicholson and Watson, 1932.

7794 **Fawcett, CB.** *Frontiers: A Study in Political Geography.* Oxford: Clarendon Press, 1918.

7795 **Foucher, Michael.** "Les geographes et les frontieres." *Herodotes*, 2°-3° Trimestres, Nos. 33-34 (Avril-Septembre, 1984), 117-130.

7796 **Fowler, John Richard.** *New Frontiers in the Clinical Practice of Dreikusian Theory.* Tallahassee: Florida State University, Ph.D., 1974.

7797 "A Frontier Problem: A Suggested Solution." *Journal of the Royal Central Asian Society*, 32, Part 1 (January, 1945), 80-84.

7798 **Garcia, Castellanos, Telasco.** *Geologia de Fronteras; Bases Geologicas Para la Determinacion Limites Internacionales.* Cordoba: Direccion General de Publicidad de la Universidad Nacional de Cordoba, Republica Argentina, 1954.

7799 **Garg, Pulin Krishna.** *Berkeley: The New Frontiers of Modern Society (A Study in Social Crisis and Identity).* Berkeley: University of California, Ph.D., 1969.

7800 **Gallois, L.** "La paix de Versailles: les nouvelles frontieres de l'Allemagne." *Annales de Geographie*, 28, No. 145 (October-Dezember, 1919), 241-248.

7801 **George, Pierre.** "De la frontiere a la region. A propos de quelques ouvrages recents." *Annales de Geographie*, 75, No. 412 (November-December, 1966), 704-706.

7802 **Gial Vung, Shillong.** "Frontiers of Freedom." *Far Eastern Economic Review*, 61, No. 33 (August 15, 1968), 316-318.

7803 **Gubert, Renzo.** *La situazione confinaria.* Trieste: Lint, 1972.

7804 **Guichonnet, P., and Raffestin, C.** *Geographie des frontieres* (Geography of Frontiers). Paris: Presses Universitaires de Paris, 1974.

7805 **Hall, Duncan.** "The International Frontier." *American Journal of International Law*, 42, No. 1 (January, 1948), 42-65.

7806 **Hall, Duncan.** "Zones of the International Frontier." *Geographical Review*, 38, No. 4 (September, 1948), 615-625.

7807 **Hills, E.H.** "The Geography of International Frontiers." *Geographical Journal*, 28, No. 2 (August, 1906), 145-155.

7808 **Kosinski, L.** "Problemes de peuplement des regions frontieres tcheques." *Dokumentacja Geograficzna*, 5 (1961), 26-81.

7809 **Lapradelle, Paul Geoffre de.** *La frontiere: etude de droit international.* Paris: Les Editions Internationales, 1928.

7810 **Mikesell, Marvin W.** "Comparative Studies in Frontier History." *Annals of the Association of American Geographers*, 50 (March, 1960), 62-74.

7811 **Murty, T.S.** *Frontier: A Changing Concept.* New Delhi, India: Palit and Palit, 1978.

7812 **Peattie, Roderick.** *Look to the Frontiers; A Geography for the Peace Table.* New York: Harper & Brothers, 1944.

7813 **Quaremme, J.** "Les frontaliers." *Revue du Travail*, 60 (1959), 251-282.

7814 **Rose, W.J.** "The Sociology of Frontiers." *Sociological Review*, 27, No. 1 (January, 1935), 201-219.

7815 **Sastri, V.V., and Mithal, R.S.** "New Frontiers of Study by Indian Geo-Scientists." *National Geographical Journal of India*, 24, Parts 3 and 4 (September-December, 1978), 42-48.

7816 **Sidaritsch, M.** "Grossenklassen der Grenzgliederung." *Zeitschrift fur Geopolitik*, 3 Jahrgang, Heft 7 (July, 1926), 552-566.

7817 **Sieger, Robert.** "Naturlische Grenzen." *Petermans Mitteilungen*, 71 Jahrg, 1-2 Heft, No. 430 (1925), 57-59.

7818 **Souza, Jr. Antonio de.** *Fronteiras Flutuantes.* Rio de Janeiro: Grafica Laemert, 1954.

7819 **Spykman, N.J.** "Frontiers, Security, and International Organization." *Geographic Review*, 32, No. 3 (July, 1942), 436-447.

7820 **Trotter, J.K.** "The Science of Frontier Delimitation." *Minutes of Proceedings of the Royal Artillery Institution*, 24 (1897), 207-30.

7821 **Turner, F.J.** *Frontier and Section.* Englewood Cliffs, New Jersey: Prentice-Hall, 1961.

7822 **Vallaux, Camille.** "Nouveaux aspects du probleme des frontieres." *Scientia*, 36, No. 10 (October, 1924), 323-331.

7823 **Weinstein, Brian.** "Language Strategists Redefining Political Frontiers on the Basis of Linguistic Choices." *World Politics*, 31, No. 3 (April, 1979), 345-364.

7824 **Woodman, Dorothy.** *Himalayan Frontiers: A Political Review of British, Chinese, Indian and Russian Rivalries.* New York: Praeger, 1969.

7825 **Wright, L.B.**, and **Fowler, E.W.** *The Moving Frontier.* New York: Delacorte Press, 1972.

7826 **Wyman, W.D.**, and **Kroeber, C.B.** *The Frontier in Perspective.* Madison: University of Wisconsin Press, 1957.

POLITICAL GEOGRAPHY OF REGIONS

AFRICA

Books and Journals

7827 **Alluaud, Charles.** "La frontiere anglo-allemande dans l'afrique Orientale." *Annales de Geographie,* 25, No. 133 (January, 1916), 206-217.

7828 **Asiwaju, A.I.** "The Concept of Frontier in the Setting of States in Pre-Colonial Africa." *Presence Africaine,* 3° et 4° Trimestres, No. 127-128 (29 Novembre-3 Decembre, 1983), 43-49.

7829 **Barber, James.** *Imperial Frontier.* Nairobi: East African Publishing House, 1968.

7830 **Barber, James.** "The Moving Frontier of British Imperailism in Northern Uganda 1898-1919." *Uganda Journal,* 29 (1965), 1-27.

7831 **Bernard, Augustin.** *Les Confins Algero-Marocains.* Paris: Emile Larose, 1911.

7832 **Boulmois, P.K.** "On Western Frontier of Sudan." *Geographical Journal,* 63, No. 6 (June, 1924), 465-479.

7833 **Butter, A.E.** *Report by Mr. A.E. Butter on the Survey of the Proposed Frontier between British East Africa and Abyssinia.* Africa No. 13 (1904), Cd. 2312. London: Her Majesty's Stationery Office, 1904.

7834 **Carrington, C.E.** "Frontiers in Africa." *International Affairs,* 36, No. 4 (October, 1960), 424-439.

7835 **Close, C.F.** "The Western Frontier of the Sudan." *Geographical Journal,* 66, No. 4 (October, 1925), 349-352.

7836 **Cox, R.E.** "Notes on the Anglo-Liberian Frontier." *Geographical Journal,* 24, No. 4 (October, 1904), 427-429.

7837 **Freshfield, D.W.** "Ruwenzori and the Frontier of Uganda." *Geographical Journal,* 28, No. 5 (November, 1906), 481-486.

7838 **Gallais, Jean.** "Poles d'Etats et Frontieres en Afrique Contemporaine." *Les Cahiers d'Outre-mer,* 35° Annee, No. 138 (Avril-Juin, 1982), 103-122.

7839 **Glickman, Harvey.** "Frontiers of Liberal and Non-Liberal Democracy in Tropical Africa." *Journal of Asian and African Studies,* 23, Nos. 3-4 (July and October, 1988), 234-254.

7840 **Great Britain.** Treaties, etc. *Agreement between the Government of the United Kingdom of Great Britain and Northern Ireland and the Government of Portugal Regarding the Nyasaland-Mozambique Frontier, Lisbon, November 18, 1954.* London: Great Britain Parliament, 1958.

7841 **Great Britain.** Treaties, etc. *Exchange of Notes between His Majesty's Government in the United Kingdom and the Portuguese Government Regarding the Delimitation of the Southern Rhodesia-Portuguese East Africa Frontier, London, October 29, 1940.* Treaty Series No. 13, Cmd. 6280. London: Great Britain Parliament, 1941.

7842 **Gwynn, C.W.** "The Frontiers of Abyssinia." *Journal of the Royal African Society,* 36 (1937), 150-161.

7843 **Hickey, Dennis Charles.** *Ethiopia and Great Britain: Political Conflict in the Southern Borderlands, 1916-1935 (Africa; Frontiers).* Evanston, Illinois: Northwestern University, Ph.D., 1984.

7844 **Jentgen, P.** *Les Frontieres du Congo Belge.* Institut Royal Colonial Belge, *Memoires.* Brussels: Tome 25, 1952.

7845 **Jentgen, P.** *Les Frontieres du Ruanda-Urundi et le Regime International de Tutelle.* Bruxelles: Institut Royal Colonial Belge, 1957.

7846 **Lewis, L.M.** "The Problem of the Northern Frontier District of Kenya." *Race,* 5, No. 1 (July, 1963), 48-60.

7847 **Maximy, Rene de,** and **Brugaillere, Marie-Christine.** "Un voi-homme d'affaires, des geographes et le trace des frontieres de l'Etat independant du Congo (Zaire)." *Herodote,* 41 (Avril-Juin, 1986), 46-74.

7848 **Pourtier, Roland.** Konsequenzen Einer Grenzziehung im Franzosischen Kolonialafrika: Das Beispiel der Region Ober-Ogowe, Gabun." *Geographische Rundschau* [Braunschweig], 46, Heft 1 (Januar, 1994), 35-41.

7849 **Saint-Yves, G.** "A travers l'Erythree italienne: les confins de l'Abyssinie et du Soudan." *Annales de Geographie,* 11, No. 55 (Janvier, 1902), 153-168.

7850 **Sanford, K.S.** "Libyan Frontiers." *Geographical Journal,* 96, No. 6 (December, 1940), 377-388.

7851 **Sanford, K.S.** "Western Frontiers of Libya." *Geographical Journal*, 99, No. 1 (January, 1942), 29-40.

7852 **Scott, John.** *Africa, World's Last Frontier.* New York: Foreign Policy Association, 1959.

7853 **Sevrin, R.** "Les echanges de population a la frontiere entre la France et la Tournaisis." *Annales de Geographie*, 58, No. 311 (Juillet-September, 1949), 237-244.

7854 **Smith, G.E.** "From the Victoria Nyanza to Kilimanjaro." *Geographical Journal*, 29, No. 3 (March, 1907), 249-273.

7855 **Stewart, C.C.** "Frontier Disputes and Problems of Legitimation: Sokoto-Masina Relations, 1817-1837." *Journal of African History*, 17, No. 4 (1976), 497-514.

7856 **Trout, Frank E.** *Morocco's Saharan Frontiers.* Geneva: Droz, 1969.

7857 **Touval, Saadia.** "Africa's Frontiers." *International Affairs*, 42, No. 4 (October, 1966), 641-654.

7858 **Vidal de la Blache, Paul.** "La zone frontiere de l'Algerie et du Maroc d'apers de nouveaux documents." *Annales de Geographie*, 6, No. 28 (Juillet, 1897), 357-363.

7859 **Yakemtchouk, Romain.** *Les Frontieres Africaines.* Paris: Pedone, 1970.

7860 **Zartman, L. William.** "A Disputed Frontier is Settled." *African Report*, 8, No. 8 (August, 1963), 13-14.

AMERICAS

Books

7861 **Abernethy, Thomas P.** *Three Virginia Frontiers.* Baton Rouge: Louisiana State University Press, 1940.

7862 **Accioly, Hildebrando.** *Limites do Brasil. A fronteira com o Paraguay.* Sao Paulo: Companhia Editora Nacional, 1938. (Brasiliana; bibliotheca pedagogica brasileira. Serie 5.a, Vol. 131.)

7863 **Alvarado, Rafael.** *Demarcacion de Fronteras.* Quito, Ecuador: Talleres graficos de educacion, 1942.

7864 **Billington, R.A.** *Westward Expansion.* 2nd ed. New York: Macmillan, 1960.

7865 **Bowen, William Adrian.** *Migration and Settlement on a Far Western Frontier: Oregon to 1850.* Berkeley: University of California, Ph.D., 1972.

7866 **Brunnschweiler, Dieter.** *The Llanos Frontier of Columbia,* East Lansing: Michigan State University, Latin American Studies Center, 1972.

7867 **Colley, Charles Clifford.** *Robert Humphrey Forbes of Arizona: The Frontiers of Arid Lands Agriculture.* Tempe: Arizona State University, Ph.D., 1975.

7868 **Colombia.** Oficina de longitudes y fronteras. *Limites de la Republica de Colombia.* 2nd ed. Bogota: Ministerio de relaciones exteriores, 1944.

7869 Comision mixta de limites de la frontera entre Guatemala y El Salvador. *Informe de la Comision mixta de limites relativo al trazo de la frontera entre Guatemala y El Salvador, y rendido a los respectivos goviernos por los delegados, Florencio Santiso (de Guatemala) e Jacinto Castellanos (de El Salvador) el 31 de Octubre de 1940.* Guatemala: Tipografia Nacional, 1942.

7870 **de Macedo Soares, Jose Carlos.** *Froneiras do Brasil no Regime Colonial.* (Comemoracao do primeiro centenario da fundacao do Instituto historico e geografico brasileiro. Primeiro congresso de historia nacional. Tese 17.) Rio de Janeiro: J. Olimpio, 1939.

7871 **Dorion, Henri.** *La frontiere Quebec-Terreneuve: contribution a l'etude systematique des frontieres.* Quebec: Presses de l'Universite Laval, 1963.

7872 **Findlay, John Moorman.** *A Fast People: Frontiers of Gambling and Society from Jamestown to Las Vegas.* Berkely: University of California, Ph.D., 1982.

7873 **France.** *Mission de Delimitation de la Frontiere Guyane Francaise-Bresil, Frontiere Sird, 1956-1957.* Paris: Institut Geographique National, 1959.

7874 **Guatemala.** Ministray for Foreign Affairs. *Continuation of the White Book. Controversy between Guatemala and Great Britain on Territorial Matters. The Question of British Honduras. VIII. Bordering Territories of the Captaincies General of Guatemala and Yucatan During the Colonial Period.* Guatemala: Ministry for Foreign Affairs, 1943, 389-424.

7875 **Herbert, Katherine Clara.** *American Frontiers in Literature: The Evolution of a Curriculum.* Pittsburgh, Pennsylvania: Carnegia-Mellon University, 1972.

7876 **Herzog, Lawrence A.** *Where North Meets South: Cities, Space, and Politics on the U.S.-Mexico Border.* Austin: University of Texas at Austin. Center for Mexican American Studies, 1990.

7877 *La Frontera de la Republica Dominicana, Con Haiti*. Ciudad Triyillo, R.D.: Editorial La Nacion, 1946.

7878 **Lagos Carmona, Guillermo.** *Las Fronteras de Chile*. Santiago de Chile: Empresa Editora Zig-Zag, 1966.

7879 **Macdonald, R. St. J.,** ed. *The Artic Frontier.* Toronto: University of Toronto Press, 1966.

7880 **McInnis, Edgar W.** *The Unguarded Frontier; A History of American-Canadian Relations.* Garden City, New York: Doubleday Doran, 1942.

7881 **Meller, Patricio.** *Production Functions and Efficiency Frontiers for Industrial Establishments of Different Sizes: The Chilean Case, Year 1967.* Berkeley: University of California, Ph.D., 1975.

7882 **Murdoch, Richard K.** *The Georgia-Florida Frontiers, 1793-1796, Spanish Reaction to French Intrigue and American Designs.* Berkeley: University of California Press, 1951.

7883 **Pahlke, Loren Gail.** *On Two Frontiers: White Social Structure in the Alaskan Bush (Yukon River, Eagle, Alaska, Network Analysis).* New Haven, Connecticut: Yale University, Ph.D., 1985.

7884 **Pellerin, Michel,** and **Tremblay, Yves.** *La frontiere Canada-Etats Unis: le troncon quebecois Coaticook-Lac Frontiere.* Chicoutimi: Universite du Quebec, 1974.

7885 **St. John, Ronald Bruce.** *Peruvian Foreign Policy, 1919-1939: The Delimitation of Frontiers.* Denver: University of Denver, Ph.D., 1970.

7886 **Soucy, Claude.** *Le segment du 45ᵉ parallele de la frontiere Quebec-Etats-Unis.* Bordeaux: Universite de Bordeau, These de maitrise es lettres, 1970.

7887 **Stacey, C.P.** *The Undefended Border; The Myth and The Reality.* Ottawa: Canadian Historical Association, 1953.

7888 **Stanley, George F.G.,** ed. *Mapping the Frontier: Charles Wilson's Dieary of the Survey of the 49th Parallel, 1858-1862, While the Secretary of the British Boundary Commission.* Seattle: University of Washington Press, 1970.

7889 **Steffen, Jerome O.** *Comparative Frontiers: A Proposal for Studying the American West.* Norman: University of Oklahoma Press, 1980.

7890 **Treckel, Paula Ann.** *English Women on Seventeenth Century American Frontiers.* Syracuse, New York: Syracuse University, Ph.D., 1978.

7891 **Turner, F.J.** *The Frontier in American History,* 3rd Impression. New York: Holt, Rinehart & Winston, 1953.

7892 **Webb, Melody Rae.** *Yukon Frontiers: The Westward Movement to the North Country.* Albuquerque: University of New Mexico, Ph.D., 1983.

7893 **Weisman, Alan.** *La Frontera: United States Border with Mexico.* Tuscon: The University of Arizona Press, 1991.

7894 **Wilkinson, Nancy Lee.** *Perpetual Frontiers of the Central Coast: The Lompoc and Santa Maria Valleys, Santa Barbara County, California.* Eugene: University of Oregon, Ph.D., 1983.

Journals

7895 **Augelli, John P.** "Costa Rica's Frontier Legacy." *Geographical Review,* 77, No. 1 (January, 1987), 1-16.

7896 **Becker, Bertha K.** "Present-day Signification of Frontier: A Geopolitical Interpretation Based on Brazilian Amazonia." *Cahiers-Orstom, Serie Sciences Humaines,* 22, Nos. 3-4 (1986), 297-317.

7897 **Blanc, Andre.** "Le Probleme des regions frontieres: le cas de Tachov." *Revue Geographique de l'Est,* 3, No. 2 (Avril-Juin, 1963), 155-165.

7898 **Butland, Gilbert J.** "Frontiers of Settlement in South America." *Revista Geografica,* 65, No. 2 (Dezembro de, 1966), 93-108.

7899 **Coelho, Djalma Poli.** "A foz do Rio Apa Como Elemento da Fronteira Entre o Brasil e o Paraguai-Revisao e Conservacao das Fronteiras." *Congresso Brasileiro de Geografia,* 2, No. 10 (Oct., 1952), 573-587.

7900 **Correa, Virgilio.** "Frontera Meridional: frustracoes de tentativas demarcatorias." *Instituto Historico e Geografico Brasileiro,* 2 (1966), 145-256.

7901 **da Fonseca Hermes, J.S.** "Congresso brasileiro de geograficas das fronteiras do Brasil." *Congresso Brasileiro de Geografia, 9ᵉ, Florianopolis, 1940,* Anais, 2 (1942), 165-198.

7902 **de Macedo Soares, Jose Carlos.** "Fronteiras do Brasil no regime colonial." *Instituto historico e geografico brasileiro, Terceiro congresso de historia nacional,* Anais, 9 vol. (Outubro, 1938), (1944), 3-237.

7903 **Dixon, G.G.** "The British Guiana and Venezuela Boundary Frontier." *Geographcial Journal,* 7, No. 1 (January, 1896), 99-101.

7904 **Dorion, Henri.** "La Representation cartographique des frontieres litigieuses. Le cas du Labrador." *Cahiers de Geographie de Quebec*, 9, No. 17 (Octobre, 1964-Mars, 1965), 77-87.

7905 **Edwards, H.A.** "Further Frontier Work on the Bolivia-Brazil Northern Boundary." *Geographical Journal*, 45, No. 5 (May, 1915), 384-405.

7906 **Eyzaguirre, Jaime.** "La Frontera Historica Chileno-Argentina; Notas a Proposito de un Libro." *Anales de la Universidad de Chile*, 120, No. 1 (1962), 155-174.

7907 **Ferreira Reis, Artur Cesar.** "As cabeceiras do Orenoco e a fronteira brasileiro-venezuelana." *Revista Brasileira de Geografia*, Ano 6, No. 2 (Abril-Junho, 1944), 245-257.

7908 **Gallois, L.** "La frontiere argentino-chilienne." *Annales de Geographie*, 12, No. 61 (Janvier, 1903), 47-53.

7909 **Herzog, Lawrence A.** "International Boundary Cities: The Debate on Transfrontier Planning in Two Border Regions." *Natural Resources Journal* [Albuquerque], 31, No. 3 (Summer, 1991), 587-608.

7910 **Herzog, Lawrence A.** "The Transfrontier Organization of Space Along the U.S.-Mexico Border." *Geoforum* [Oxford], 22, No. 3 (1991), 255-269.

7911 **Innis, H.A.** "Canadian Frontiers of Settlement; A Review." *Geographical Review*, 25, No. 1 (January, 1935), 92-106.

7912 **Latorre y Setien, G.** "Intervencion tutelar de Espana en los problemas de limites de Hispano-America. Indeterminacion de fronteras." *Boletin del Centro de Estudios Americanos*, 7, No. 38-39 (1920), 1-9.

7913 **Latorre y Setien, G.** "Las fronteras naturales y historicas. Agrupacion ideal de los estados de Hispano America." *Boletin del Centro de Estudios Americanos*, 8, No. 40-41 (1921), 1-37.

7914 **Laverde Goubert, Luis.** "Bibliografia sobre, fronteras de Colombia." *Boletin Bibliografico de la Sociedad Geografica de Colombia*, Nos. 1-8 (1963-1968), 33-45.

7915 **Mariaca Pando, Oscar.** "La frontera occidental de Bolivia." *Boletin de la Sociedad Geografica de la Paz*, Ano 56, No. 70 (Diciembre, 1949), 29-33.

7916 **Mitchell, Robert Davis.** "The Shenandoah Valley Frontier." *Annals of the Association of American Geographers*, 62 (September, 1972), 461-486.

7917 **Morales Padion, F.** "La Frontera peruano-ecuatoriana." *Estudios Americanos*, 2, No. 2 (Septembre, 1950), 455-466.

7918 **Reis, Arthur Cezar Ferreira.** "Limites e Demarcacoes na Amazonia Brasileira, a Frontiera com os Colonias Espanlolas o Tratado de S. Ildefonso." *Revista do Instituto Historica e Geografico Brasileiro*, 244, No. 3 (July-September, 1959), 3-103.

7919 **Richards, J. Howard.** "Changing Canadian Frontiers." *Canadian Geographer*, 5, No. 4 (Winter, 1961), 23-29.

7920 **Rodrigues Pereira, Renato Barbosa.** "O Barao do Rio Branco e o tracado das fronteiras do Brasil." *Revista Brasileira de Geografia*, Ano 7, No. 2 (Abril-Junho, 1945), 187-241.

7921 **Rodrigues Pereira, Renato Barbosa.** "Fronteira com a Colombia." *Boletim Geografico*, Ano 4, No. 48 (Marco, 1947), 1636-1641; No. 49 (Abril, 1947), 48-66.

7922 **Rodrigues Pereira, Renato Barbosa.** "Fronteira com o Peru." *Boletim Geografico*, Ano 5, No. 50 (Maio, 1947), 161-165.

7923 **Roma Machado, Carlos.** "Fronteira do Uruguai com o Brasil." *Boletim da Sociedade de Geografia de Lisboa*, 56a serie, Nos. 1-2 (Janeiro-Fevereiro, 1938), 31-42.

7924 **Rushworth, W.D.** "Defining a Frontier in the Andes." *Geographical Magazine*, 40, No. 11 (March, 1968), 972-980.

7925 **Rushworth, W.D, and Smith, W.P.** "Mapping and Demarcation for the Argentine-Chile Frontier Case." *Photogrammetric Record*, 6, No. 32 (October, 1968), 150-167.

7926 **Sampognaro, Virgilio.** "Descripcion geografica de la frontera Uruguay-Brasil." *Revista del Instituto Historico y Geografico del Uruguay*, Tomo 7 (1930), 19-37.

7927 **Sanguin, Andre-Louis.** "La frontiere Quebec-Maine: quelques aspects limologiques et socio-economiques." *Cahiers de Geographie de Quebec*. N° special sur les frontieres internationales, 18, No. 43 (Avril, 1974), 158-185.

7928 **Sequera de Sergnini, I., and Others.** "La Ocupacion de los espacios Fronteriros como medio para reafirmar la Soberania Territorial. Caso: espacios colindantes con la Guayana Esequiba [The Occupation of Frontier Zones as a Means of Reaffirming Territorial Sovereignty. The Case of the Lands Bordering Guayana Esequiba.]." *Revista Geografica*, 102 (1985), 159-162.

7929 Silva, Moacir M.F. "Geografia das fronteiras no Brasil. (Alguns aspectos.)" *Revista Brasileira de Geografia*, Ano 4, No. 4 (Outubro-Dezembro, 1942), 748-770.

7930 Smith, H. Carington. "On the Frontier of British Guiana and Brazil." *Geographical Journal*, 92, No. 1 (July, 1938), 40-54.

7931 Stacey, C.P. "The Myth of the Unguarded Frontier, 1815-1871." *American Historical Review*, 56, No. 1 (October, 1950), 1-18.

7932 Starr, Harvey, and Most, B.A. "A Return Journey: Richardson, Frontiers,' and Wars in the 1946-1965 Era." *Journal of Conflict Resolution*, 22, No. 3 (September, 1978), 441-467.

7933 Thery, Herve. "Frontieres Pionnieres et Frontieres Politique en Amazonie." *Association de Geographes Francais Bulletin*, 57° Annee, No. 470-471 (Mai-Juin, 1980), 213-217.

7934 Toynbee, Arnold J. "The Dispute Between Bolivian and Paraguay in the Chaco Boreal, 1934-1937." *Survey of International Affairs*, 1937, 837-872.

7935 Ulloa, Bolivar. "La Geografia del Peru y sus Fronteras." *Boletin de la Sociedad Geographica de Lima*, 73 (3rd Trimester, 1956), 19-27.

7936 Vogeler, Ingolf. "The Dependency Model Applied to the Mexican Tropical Frontier Region." *Journal of Tropical Geography*, 43, No. 2 (December, 1976), 63-68.

7937 Watson, J.W. "The Influence of the Frontier on Niagara Settlements." *Geographical Review*, 38, No. 1 (January, 1948), 113-119.

7938 Williams, John Hoyt. "The Undrawn Line: Three Centuries of Strife on the araguayan-Mato Grosso Frontier." *Luso-Brazilian Review*, 17, No. 1 (Summer, 1980), 17-40.

ASIA

Books

7939 Adami, C.V. *National Frontiers in Relation to International Law*, T.T. Behrens (tr.), ed. London: Oxford University Press, 1927.

7940 Alder, G.J. *British India's Northern Frontier, 1865-95. A Study in Imperial Policy*. London: Longmans, Green, 1963.

7941 Barton, William P., Sir. *India's North-West Frontier*. London: J. Murray, 1939.

7942 Davies, C.C. *The Problem of the Northwest Frontier, 1890-1908*. Cambridge: University Press, 1932.

7943 Edmonds, Richard Louis. *Northern Frontiers of Qing China and Tokugawa, Japan: A Comparative Study of Frontier Policy*. Chicago, Illinois: University of Chicago, Ph.D., 1983.

7944 Elwin, Verrier. *India's North-East Frontier in the Nineteenth Century*. Bombay: Oxford University Press, 1959.

7945 Finnie, David H. *Shifting Lines in the Sand: Kuwait's Elusive Frontier with Iraq*. Cambridge: Harvard University Press, 1992.

7946 Frischwasser-Ra'anan, H.F. *The Frontiers of a Nation-A Re-Examination of the Forces which Created the Palestine Mandate and Determined Its Territorial Shape*. London: Batchworth Press, 1955.

7947 Government of India. *Atlas of the Northern Frontiers of India*. New Delhi: Government of India, 1960.

7948 Great Britain Foreign Office. *United Kingdom Memorial: Arbitration Concerning Buraimi and the Common Frontier Between Abu Dhabi and Saudi Arabie*. London: Her Majesty's Stationery Office, 1955.

7949 Great Britain. Treaties, etc. *Agreement between Palestine and Syria and the Lebanon Amending the Agreement of February 2, 1926, Regarding Frontier Question, November 3, 1938*. Treaty Series No. 34 (1939) Cmd. 6065. London: Great Britain Parliament, 1939.

7950 Harrison, John A. *Japan's Northern Frontier; A Preliminary Study in Colonization and Expansion with Special Reference to the Relations of Japan and Russia*. Gainsville: Universtiy of Florida Press, 1953.

7951 Hof, Frederic C. *Galilee Divided: The Israel-Lebanon Frontier, 1916-1984*. Boulder, Colorado: Westview Press, 1985.

7952 Jaffe, Philip. *New Frontiers in Asia; A Challenge to the West*. New York: Alfred A. Knopf, 1945.

7953 Kapur, A.D. *The Problem of the North West Frontier of India*. Lahori: University of Punjab, Ph.D., 1945.

7954 Karamat, Saida K. *The Western Frontier of West Pakistan, A Study in Political Geography*. Ann Arbor: University of Michigan, Ph.D., 1958.

7955 Kelly, J.B. *Eastern Arabian Frontiers*. New York: Praeger, 1964.

7956 **Lal, B.B.; Gupta, S.P.; and Asthana, Shasi**, eds. *Frontiers of the Indus Civilization.* New Delhi: Books and Books for Indian Archaeological Society and Indian History and culture Society, 1984.

7957 **Lamb, Alastair.** *Asian Frontiers: Studies in a Continuing Problem.* New York: Praeger, 1968.

7958 **Lattimore, Owen.** *Frontiers Russo-Chioines.* Washington, DC: American Geographical Society, Research Series No. 21, 1940.

7959 **Lattimore, Owen.** *Inland Frontiers between China, Russia, and Japan.* Abstract of Address. 4 mimeographed 1. Adress, June 14, 1940. Charlottesville, Virginia: Institute of Public Affairs, University of Virginia, 1940.

7960 **Lattimore, Owen.** *Inner Asian Frontiers of China.* Boston, Massachusetts: Beacon Press, 1962.

7961 **Lattimore, Owen.** *Pivot of Asia: Sinkiang and the Inner Asian Frontiers of China and Russia.* With the Assistance of Chang Chih-yi. Boston: Little Brown, 1950.

7962 **Leifer, Walter.** *Weltprobleme am Himalaya.* Wurzburg: Marienburg-Verlag, 1959.

7963 **Lohia, Ram Manohar.** *India, China and Northern Frontiers.* Hyderabad: Navahind, 1963.

7964 **Michael, Franz.** *The Origin of Manchu Rule in China; Frontier and Bureaucracy as Interacting Forces in the Chinese Empire.* Baltimore, Maryland: Johns Hopkins University Press, 1942.

7965 **Moseley, George V.H.** *The Consolidation of the South China Frontier.* Berkeley: University of California Press, 1973.

7966 **Norins, Martin R.** *Gateway to Asia: Sinkiang, Frontier of the Chinese Far West.* New York: John Day Company, 1944.

7967 **Ramsson, Robert Eric.** *Closing Frontiers, Farmland Tenancy, and Their Relation: A Case Study of Thailand, 1937-1973.* Urbana: University of Illinois, Ph.D., 1977.

7968 **Reid, Sir R.** *History of the Frontier Areas Bordering on Assam from 1883-1941.* Shillong: Government Press, 1942.

7969 **Rizvi, Syed Mohammad Mujtaba.** *Frontier Problems in Pakistan's Foreign Policy.* London: London School of Economics, University of London, Ph.D., 1969.

7970 **Rose, Leo E., and Fisher, Margaret W.** *The North-East Frontier Agency of India.* Berkeley: University of California, Institute of International Studies, 1967.

7971 **Rustomji, Nari.** *Enchanted Frontiers; Sikkim, Bhutan and India's North-Eastern Borderlands.* London: Oxford University Press, 1971.

7972 **Singhvi, Ramesh.** *India's Northern Frontier and China.* Bombay: Contemporary Publishers, 1962.

7973 **Spain, James W.** *Pakistan's North-West Frontier: Political Problems of a Borderland.* New York: Columbia University, Ph.D., 1959.

7974 **Sugimura, Oaki.** *The Collection of Geographical Treaties Celebrating Professor Kanichi Uchida.* Vol. 1. Tokyo: Teikoku-Shoin, 1952.

7975 **Sugimura, Oaki.** *The Shifting Farmer's Belt in Treatises Celeberating Professor Keiji Tanaka's Sixty-first Birthday.* Tokyo: Meguro-Shoten, 1950.

7976 **Watson, Francis.** *The Frontiers of China; A Historical Guide.* New York: Praeger, 1966.

7977 **Wilkinson, John C.** *Arabia's Frontiers: The Story of Britain's Boundary Drawing in the Desert.* London: I. B. Tauris & Co., Ltd., 1991.

7978 **Wilson, Woodrow.** *The Frontier between Armenia and Turkey as Decided by President Woodrow Wilson, November 22, 1920.* New York: Armenian National Committee, 1945.

7979 **Yeh, Te-Bien.** *The Frontiers of China: A Study of the Bandary Policy of the People's Republic of China.* Carbondale: Southern Illinois University, Ph.D., 1977.

Journals

7980 **Ahmed, Nasim.** "China's Himalayan Frontiers II: Pakistan's Attitude." *International Affairs,* 38, No. 4 (October, 1962), 478-484.

7981 **Ahmad, Zahiruddin.** "The Ancient Frontier of Ladakh." *World Today,* 16, No. 7 (July, 1960), 313-318.

7982 **Ballis, William.** "Soviet Russia's Asiatic Frontier Technique: Tana Tuva." *Pacific Affairs,* 14, No. 1 (March, 1941), 91-96.

7983 **Barton, William P., Sir.** "India's North-West Frontier." *Geographical Magazine,* 15, No. 3 (July, 1942), 97-105.

7984 **Barton, William P., Sir.** "The Northwest Frontier." *Fortnightly,* 172 (August, 1949), 105-111.

7985 **Basu, B.K.** "India's Frontier Problems in the 19th and 20th Centuries with Tibet and China: Historical Background." *Quarterly Review of Historical Studies,* 5, No. 1 (1965-66), 30-36.

7986 Basu, N. "Evolution of National Frontiers in Bengal." *Geographical Review of India*, 6, No. 3 (September, 1944), 1-6.

7987 Beecroft, Eric. "British Policy on India's Northwest Frontier." *Amerasia*, 4, No. 1 (March, 1940), 30-37.

7988 "Between Delhi and Peking: The Disputed Himalayan Frontier." *Round Table*, 53, No. 209 (1962), 31-39.

7989 Birch, Brian P. "Pattern and Process in Frontier Farm Settlement." *National Geographical Journal of India*, 21, Parts 3 and 4 (September-December, 1975), 166-171.

7990 "The Borderlands of Soviet Central Asia: India and Pakistan, Part 2--Pakistan." *Central Asian Review*, 5, No. 2 (April, 1957), 163-207.

7991 Bowerman, J.F. "The Frontier Areas of Burma." *Journal of the Royal Societ of Arts*, 95, No. 4732 (December 6, 1946), 44-55.

7992 Brissenden, Rosemary. "India and the Northern Frontier." *Australian Outlook*, 14, No. 1 (April, 1960), 15-29.

7993 Bunker, D.G. "The South-West Borderlands of the Rub and Khali." *Geographical Journal*, 119, No. 3 (November, 1953), 421-430.

7994 "The Burma-China Frontier Disptue." *World Today*, 13, No. 2 (February, 1957), 86-92.

7995 Bush, C.W.F. "The North-West Frontier: Pakistan's Inherited Problem." *Geographical Magazine*, 22, No. 3 (July, 1949), 85-92.

7996 Caroe, Olaf, Sir. "The Geography and Ethnics of India's Northern Frontiers." *Geographical Journal*, 126, Part 3 (September, 1960), 298-309.

7997 Caroe, Olaf, Sir. "India and Pakistan: Attitude to One Another's Frontier Problems." *Royal Central Asian Journal*, 51, Part 2 (April, 1964), 112-119.

7998 Caroe, Olaf, Sir. "The Northwest Frontier." *United Empire*, 40 (1949), 161-165.

7999 Caroe, Olaf, Sir. "The Northwest Frontier: Old and New." *Journal of the Royal Central Asian Society*, 48, No. 3/4 (July-December, 1961), 289-298.

8000 Caroe, Olaf, Sir. "The North West Frontier (Punjab) Re-Visited." *Asian Review*, 52, No. 191 (July, 1956), 201-215.

8001 Caroe, Olaf, Sir. "The Sino-Indian Frontier Dispute." *Asian Review*, 52, No. 218 (April, 1963), 67-81.

8002 "Chinese Frontier Guards Complete Withdrawal Along Sino-Indian Border." *Peking Review*, No. 10/11 (March 15, 1963), 71-73.

8003 Cobb, E.H. "The Frontier State of Dir, Swat, and Chitral." *Journal of the Royal Central Asian Society*, 38, No. 2 (April, 1951), 170-176.

8004 Cola Alberich, Julio. "La Cuestion del Himalaya: La India y Su Pleito Fronterizo con la Republkca Popular China." *Revista de Politica International*, 65, No. 1 (January-February, 1963), 63-75.

8005 Dudos, Louis-Jean. "La Question des Frontieres d'Israel." *Revue Francais de Science Politique*, 33, No. 5 (Octobre, 1983), 847 and 865.

8006 Dumont, H. "La Frontiere Entre la China et le Pakistan." *Politique Entrangere*, 27 Annee, No. 3 (1962), 252-272.

8007 Feer, Mark C. "India's Himalayan Frontier." *Far Eastern Survey*, 22, No. 11 (October, 1953), 137-141.

8008 Furer-Haimendorf, C. Von. "Through the Unexplored Mountains of the Assam-Burma Border." *Geographical Journal*, 91, No. 3 (March, 1938), 201-219.

8009 Haldipeir, R.N. "NEFA (North East Frontier Agency; An Introduction." *Bulletin of Tibetology*, 3, No. 2 (July, 1966), 73-84.

8010 "Historical Variations of China's Frontiers." *Pacific Affairs*, 18, No. 4 (December, 1945), 346-354.

8011 Holdich, Thomas H. "The Geography of the North West Frontier of India." *Geographical Journal*, 17, No. 5 (May, 1901), 461-477.

8012 Hudson, G.F. "The Frontier of China and Assam: Background to Fighting." *China Quarterly*, 12, No. 4 (October-December, 1962), 203-206.

8013 Husain, Sohail. "Strategy for the North-West Frontier." *Geographical Magazine*, 51, No. 12 (September, 1979), 816-821.

8014 James, E. Renouard. "The Russo-Turkish Frontier Commission in Asia Minor, 1857." *Royal Engineers Journal*, 55, No. 2 (June, 1941), 234-244.

8015 Johnstone, W.C. "Strategic Frontiers of India and Pakistan." *Foreign Policy Bulletin*, 34, No. 8 (January 1, 1955), 61-63.

8016 Karan, Pradyumna Prasad. "The Fringes and Frontiers of India and Pakistan." *Geographer*, 4, No. 1 (May, 1951), 6-14.

8017 Kaulback, R. "Zayed and the Eastern Tibet Border Country." *Royal Central Asian Journal*, 21, Part III (July, 1934) 435-444.

8018 Kerr, George H. "Formosa: Island Frontier." *Far Eastern Survey*, 14, No. 7 (April 11, 1945), 80-85.

8019 Kirk, William. "The Inner Asian Frontier of India." *Institute of British Geographers*; Transactions and Papers, 31 (Dec., 1962), 131-168.

8020 Kirk, William. "The Sino-Indian Frontier Dispute: A Geographical Review." *Scottish Geographical Magazine*, 76, No. 1 (April, 1960), 3-13.

8021 Kozicki, Richard J. "The Sino-Burmese Frontier Problem." *Far Eastern Survey*, 26, No. 3 (March, 1957), 33-38.

8022 Kureisky, Khalil Ullah. "THe Natural Frontier of Pakistan." *Pakistan Geographical Review*, 7, No. 1 (January, 1952), 35-52.

8023 Lamb, Alastair. "Studying the Frontiers of the British Indian Empire." *Royal Central Asian Journal*, 53, Part 3 (October, 1966), 245-254.

8024 Lattimore, Owen. "Frontieres Russo-Chinoises." *Politique Entrangere*, 23, Annee No. 4 (1958), 365-375.

8025 Lattimore, Owen. "Origins of the Great Wall of China." *Geographical Review*, 27, No. 4 (September, 1937), 529-549.

8026 Lattimore, Owen. "The Outer Mongolian Horizon." *Foreign Affairs*, 24, No. 4 (July, 1946), 648-660.

8027 League of Nations. "Great Britain and Northern Ireland and Thailand. Exchange of notes regarding the rectification of the frontier between Burma and Thailand in the sections where it is formed by the Riers Meh Sai and Meh Rauk. Bangkok, October 1st and December 10th, 1940." *Geneva: League of Nations, Treaty Series*, 203, Nos. 4746-4783 (1940-1941), 433-443.

8028 Monroe, Elizabeth. "The Arab-Israel Frontier." *International Affairs*, 29, No. 4 (October, 1953), 439-448.

8029 Neher-Bernheim, Renee. "Frontieres du Sinai: un siede de diplomahe au Moyen-Orient 1840-1948." *Politique Etrangere*, 36 Anne, No. 2 (1971), 146-164.

8030 Norins, Martin R. "Tribal Boundaries of the Burma-Yunnan Frontier." *Pacific Affairs*, 12, No. 1 (March, 1939), 67-79.

8031 "North-East Frontier of India." *India Quarterly*, 15, No. 4 (October-December, 1959), 393-395.

8032 Patterson, George N. "Problems of the Himalayan Frontier." *Royal United Service Institution Journal*, 108 (May, 1963), 95-106.

8033 Philby, H. St. J. "The Trouble in Arabia: Iraq and Najd Frontier." *Contemporary Review*, 41, No. 3 (July, 1928), 705-708.

8034 Qureshi, Saleem M.M. "Pakhtunistan: The Frontier Dispute between Afghanistan and India." *Pacific Affairs*, 39, Nos. 1 and 2 (Spring-Summer, 1966), 99-114.

8035 Rahul, Ram. "The Himalaya Frontier in the Nineteenth Century." *Quarterly Review of Historical Studies*, 4, No. 3 (1964-1965), 138-151.

8036 Reilly, Bernard, and Morgan, J.C. "South Arabian Frontiers." *Corona*, 10, No. 3 (March, 1958), 88-91.

8037 Rose, A.J. "Chinese Frontiers of India." *Geographical Journal*, 39, No. 3 (March, 1912), 193-223.

8038 Ryder, C.H.D. "Exploration and Survey with the Tibet Frontier Commission, and from Gyangtse to Simla via Gertok." *Geographical Journal*, 26, No. 4 (October, 1905), 369-395.

8039 Schweinfurth, Ulrich. "The Himalayas-Divider of Landscape, Region of Withdraval and Zone of Political Tension." *Geographische Zeitschrift*, 53 (Oktober, 1965), 241-260.

8040 Shelrankar, K.S., and Ahmed, Nasim. "China's Himalayan Frontiers." *International Affairs*, 38, No. 4 (October, 1962), 472-484.

8041 Shiva Rao, B. "That Stormy Indian Frontier." *Asia*, 39, No. 3 (March, 1939), 131-136.

8042 Siddiqi, Mohamed Ismail. "The Himalayan Frontier." *Pakistan Geographical Review*, 18, No. 1 (January, 1963), 33-42.

8043 Spain, James W. "Pakistan's North West Frontier." *Middle East Journal*, 8, No. 1 (Winter, 1954), 27-40.

8044 Spain, James W. "The Pathan Borderlands." *Middle East Journal*, 15, No. 2 (Spring, 1961), 165-177.

8045 "A Survey of China's Frontiers with the Soviet, from a Correspondent." *Royal Central Asian Journal*, 52, Parts 3-4 (July-October, 1965), 281-286.

8046 Thomas, Benjamin E. "The South-Eastern Borderlands of Rub al Khali." *Geographical Journal*, 73, No. 3 (November, 1929), 193-215.

8047 **Todd, Herbert.** "The Sinkiang-Hunza Frontier." *Journal of the Royal Central Asian Society*, 38, Part 1 (January, 1951), 73-81.

8048 **Toynbee, Arnold J.** "The Controversies Over the Frontier Between Ira (Persia) on the One Side and Turkey and Iraq on the Other; and the Four-Power Middle Eastern Pact of the 8th July, 1937." *Survey of International Affairs*, (1937), 793-803.

8049 **Toynbee, Arnold J.** "Impressions of Afghanistan and Pakistan's Northwest Frontier in Relation to the Communist World." *International Affairs*, 37, No. 2 (April, 1961), 161-169.

8050 **Varma, S.P.** "Sino-Indian Frontiers: A Study in Origins." *Political Science Review*, 3, No. 4 (October, 1964), 12-29.

8051 **Ward, F. Kingdon.** "Explorations on the Burma-Tibet Frontier." *Geographical Journal*, 80, No. 6 (December, 1932), 465-483.

8052 **Ward, F. Kingdon.** "Glacial Phenomenon on the Yun-nan Tibet Frontier." *Geographical Journal*, 48, No. 1 (July, 1916), 55-62.

8053 **Ward, F. Kingdon.** "The Hydrography of the Yun-nan Tibet Frontier." *Geographical Journal*, 52, No. 4 (Otober, 1918), 288-299.

8054 **Yang, R.** "Sinkiang Under the Administration of Governor Yang Tseng-hsin, 1911-1928." *Central Asiatic Journal*, 6 (1961), 270-316.

8055 **Yerasimos, Stephane.** "Frontieres d Arabie." *Herodote* [Paris], Nos. 58-59 (Juillet-Decembre, 1990), 59-103.

AUSTRALIA, OCEANIA AND ANTARCTICA

Books and Journals

8056 **Greenway, John.** *Australia: The Last Frontier.* New York: Dodd, Mead, 1973.

8057 **Gunther, John.** "Our Pacific Frontier." *Foreign Affairs*, 18, No. 4 (July, 1940), 583-600.

8058 **Pelzer, Karl J.** "Micronesia: A Changing Frontier." *World Politics*, 2, No. 2 (January, 1950), 251-266.

8059 **Rose, A.J.** "The Border Zone Between Queensland and New South Wales." *Australian Geographer*, 6 (1955), 3-18.

8060 **Taylor, Griffith.** "Frontiers of Settlement in Australia." *Geographical Review*, 16, No. 1 (January, 1926), 1-25.

EUROPE

Books

8061 **Albissin, Nelly Girard d'.** *Genese de la frontiere Franco-Belge: les variations des limites septenticonales de la France de 1659 a 1789.* Paris: A & J Picard, 1970.

8062 **Bracewell, Catherine Wendy.** *The Uskoks of Senj: Banditry and Piracy in the Sixteente-Century Adriatic (Social, Dalamatia, Yugoslavia, Frontiers).* Stanford, California: Stanford University, Ph.D., 1986.

8063 **Buratti, Luigi.** *La frontiera italiana-introduzione e testi.* Gorizia: Institute of International Sociology, 1971.

8064 **Cherubim, C.** *Flusse als Grenzen von Staaten und Nationen in Mitteleuropa.* Halle: Kaemerer, 1897.

8065 **Cooter, William Sidney.** *Preindustrial Frontiers and Interaction Spheres: Aspects of the Human Ecology of Roman Frontiers Regions in Northwest Europe.* Norman: University of Oklahoma, Ph.D., 1976.

8066 **Daveau, Suzanne.** *Les regions frontalieres de la montagne jurassienne.* Lyon: Institut d'Etudes Rhodaniennes, 1959.

8067 **Dion, Roger.** *Les Frontieres de la France.* Paris: Hachette, 1947.

8068 **Dixon, M. Vibart.** *The True Facts About the Disputed Frontiers of Europe.* London: Burke Publishing, 1945.

8069 **Gayre, G.R.** *Teuton and Slav on the Polish Frontier; A Diagnosis of the Racial Basis of the Germano-Polish Borderlands with Suggestions for the Settlement of German and Slav Claims.* London: Eyre and Spottiswoode, 1944.

8070 **Gerhard, Peter.** *The North Frontier of New Spain.* Rev. ed. Norman: University of Oklahoma Press, 1993.

8071 **Gerhard, Peter.** *The southeast Frontier of New Spain.* Rev. ed. Norman: University of Oklahoma Press, 1993.

8072 **Girard D'Albissin, Nelly.** *Genese de la frontiere franco-belge.* Paris: A. et J. Picard, 1970.

8073 **Gravier, Gaston.** *Les frontieres historiques de la Serbie.* Paris: Armand Colin, 1919.

8074 **Great Britain.** *Agreement between the Government of the United Kingdom and Northern Ireland and the Government of Portugal Regarding the Nyasoland-Mozambique Frontier. Lisbon, November 18, 1954.* London: Secretary of State for Foreign Affairs, 1962.

8075 **Hanson, William S., and Maxwell, Gordon S.** *Rome's North West Frontier: The Antoine Wall.* Edinburgh: Edinburgh University Press, 1983.

8076 **Heslinga, M.W.** *The Irish Border as a Cultural Divide: A Contribution to the Study of Regionalism in the British Isles.* New York: Humanities Press, 1963.

8077 **Kadlubowski, John Felix.** *The Experts and Poland's Frontiers at the Paris Peace Conference.* College Park: University of Maryland, Ph.D., 1977.

8078 **Lavallee, E.M.** *Les frontieres de la France.* Paris: J. Hetzel, 1864.

8079 **Lederer, Ivo J.** *Yugoslavia at the Paris Peace Conference; A Study in Frontiermaking.* London: Yale University Press, 1963.

8080 **Lentacker, F.** *La frontiere franco-belge Etude geographique des effects 'une frontiere internationale sur la vie des relations.* Lille: University of Lille, Doctoral Thesis, 1974.

8081 **Lyde, Lionel William.** *Some Frontiers of Tomorrow: An Aspiration for Europe.* London: A. and C. Black, 1915.

8082 **McNeill, William H.** *Europe's Steppe Frontier.* Chicago, Illinois: University of Chicago Press, 1964.

8083 **Platt, Robert S., and Bucking-Spitta, P.** *A Geographical Study of the Dutch-German Border.* Munster-Westfalen: Selbstverlag der Geographischen Kommission, 1958.

8084 **Raffestin, Claude.** *Travail et frontiere: le cas franco-genevois.* Thonon, Geneve: Universite Department de Geographie, 1971.

8085 **Ronai, Andras.** *Biographie des frontieres politiques du centre-est europeen.* Budapest: Edition de l'Institute des Sciences Politiques de la Societe Renoroise de Statisque, 1936.

8086 **Sambri, Claudio.** *Una frontiera aperta. Indagini su i valichi italo-jugoslavi.* Gorizia: Institute of International Sociology, 1970.

8087 **Schlesser, Norman Dennis.** *Frontiers, Politics, and Power in Eastern France 1152-1369.* Iowa City: University of Iowa, Ph.D., 1981.

8088 **Tardy, Roger.** *Le Pays de Gex, terre frontaliere.* Lyon: Institut d'Etudes Rhodaniennes, 1970.

8089 **Tulippe, Omer.** *Le mouvement des frontailiers belges vers la France.* Liege: Societe Geographique de Liege, 1968.

8090 **Valussi, Giorgio.** *Il confine nordorientale d'Italia.* Trieste: Lint, 1972.

8091 **Wanklyn, H.G.** *The Eastern Marchlands of Europe.* London, G.Philip & Son, 1941.

8092 **Winiewicz, J.M.** *The Polish-German Frontier.* London: W. Hodge, 1945.

8093 **Wiskemann, Elizabeth.** *Germany's Eastern Neighbours; Problems Relating to the Oder-Neisse Line and the Czech Frontier Regions.* London: Oxford University Press, 1956.

Journals

8094 **Albrecht-Carrie, Rene.** "A Note on the Brenner Frontier." *Journal of Central European Affairs*, 1, No. 3 (October, 1941), 339-344.

8095 **Albrecht-Carrie, Rene.** "The Northeastern Frontier of Italy. *Journal of Central European Affairs*, 5, No. 3 (October, 1945), 229-242.

8096 **Bonazzi, Roger.** "Un probleme urbain frontalier: L'influence de Geneve sur le departement de la Haute Savoie." *Revue de Geographie Alpine*, 60, No. 2 (April, 1972), 359-386.

8097 **Cahnman, Werner J.** "Frontiers between East and West in Europe." *Geographical Review*, 39, No. 4 (October, 1949), 605-624.

8098 **Carbouret, U.** "The Demarcation of Land Frontiers in Northern Scandinavia and Finland." *Norosis*, 33, No. 130 (1986) 137-150.

8099 **Church, R.J. Harrison.** "New Franco-Italian Frontier." *Geographical Journal*, 111 (1948), No. 1-3 (January-March, 1948), 143-146; and No. 4-6 (April-June, 1948), 293-294.

8100 **Czyzewski, Julian.** "Pryzczynek do analizy kartometrycznej granic politycznych Polski." *Przegad Geograficzny*, 22, 1948/49, (1950), 59-81.

8101 **Dickinson, Robert E.** "Germany's Frontiers." *World Affairs*. N.S., 1, No. 3 (July, 1947), 262-277.

8102 **Dresler, Adolf.** "Der Polnisch-Sowjetische Grenzstreit." *Zeitschrift fur Geopolitik*, 20 Jahrgang, Heft 6 (Juni,1943), 204-208.

8103 **East, W. Gordon.** "The New Frontiers of the Soviet Union." *Foreign Affairs*, 29, No. 4 (July, 1951), 591-607.

8104 Ferro, Gaetano. "Le Frontiere del Portogallo e la sua Suddivisione Regionale." *Revista Geografica Italiana*, 71, Fasc 2 (Guigno, 1964), 101-119.

8105 Freshfield, D.W. "The Southern Frontiers of Austria." *Geographical Journal*, 46, No. 4 (October, 1915), 414-435.

8106 Genicot, L. "Ligne et Zone: La frontiere des principautes mediavales (Academia Royale de Belgique), *Bulletin de al Classe des Lettres et des Sciences Morales et Politiques*, 5 Serie, Tome 56) 1970, 29-42.

8107 Goblet, Y.M. "La frontiere de l'Ulster." *Annales de Geographie*, 31, No. 173 (Septembre, 1922), 402-416.

8108 Haataja, Kyosti. "Questions juridiques surgies lors de la revision de la frontiere finlandaise entre le golfe de Bothnie et l'Ocean Glacial." *Fennia*, 49 (1929), 1-46.

8109 Hare, F.K. "The Labrador Frontier." *Geographical Review*, 42, No. 3 (July, 1952), 405-424.

8110 Haushofer, Karl. "Das Wissen von der Grenze un die Grenzen des deutschen Volkes." *Deutsche Rundschau*, 50 (1924), 237.

8111 Kosinski, L. "Les problemes demographiques dans les territoires occidentaux de la Pologne et les regions frontieres de la Tchecoslovaquie." *Annales de Geographie*, 71, No. 382 (Janvier-Fevrier, 1962), 79-98.

8112 League of Nations. Germany and Switzerland. "Convention Regarding the Modification of the Frontier Line Between the Canton of Thurgau and the District of the Town of Constance. Signed at Berne, September 21st, 1938." *League of Nations, Treaty Series*, 196 (1939), 365-370.

8113 League of Nations. "Germany-Poland: Convention Relating to the Mines of Upper-Silesia, Oppeln, June 23, 1922." *League of Nations, Treaty Series*, 22 (1924), 25-61.

8114 League of Nations. Germany and Belgium. "Treaty Regarding and Exchange of Territories at the German-Belgian Frontier, with Annex. Signed at Aix-la-Chapelle, May 10th, 1935." *League of Nations, Treaty Series*, 182 , Nos. 4201-4224 (1937-1938), 323-333. Germany and Belgium. "Additional Agreement to the Agreement of November 7th, 1929, Concerning the Frontier Between the Two Countries, with Annex and Final Protocol. Signed at Aix-la-Chapelle, May 10th, 1935." (ibid, 335-361).

8115 Lentacker, Firmin. "Les frontaliers dans la region du Nord." *Revue Politique et Parlementaire*, 61, No. 690 (Mai, 1959), 467-479.

8116 Lyde, Lionel William. "Types of Political Frontiers in Europe." *Geographical Journal*, 45, No. 2 (February, 1915), 126-145.

8117 Malchus, Viktor Freihur Von. "Methode et pratique de la cooperation internationale des regions frontalieres europeennes. In *Boundaries and Regions*, Raimondo Strassoldo, ed. Trieste, Lint, 1973.

8118 Mead, W.R. "Finnish Karelia: An International Borderland." *Geographical Journal*, 118, Part 1 (March, 1952), 40-57.

8119 Mosely, Philip E. "The Occupation of Germany: New Light on How the Zones Were Drawn." *Foreign Affairs*, 28, No. 4 (1950), 580-604.

8120 Naciri, Mohamed. "Les villes mediterraneennes du Maroc: entre frontieres et peripheries." *Herodote*, 45 (Avril-Juin, 1987), 121-144,

8121 Plande, R. "La formation politique de la frontiere des Pyrenees." *Revue geographique des Pyrenees et du sud-ouest*, Tome 9 (Fasc. 3, 1938), 221-242.

8122 Platt, Robert S. "The Saarland, An International Borderland." *Erdkunde*, Band 15, No. 1 (1961), 54-68.

8123 Plowman, J.P. "The German-Polish Frontier Dispute." *Journal of the Durham University Geographical Society*, 9 (1967), 20-25.

8124 "The Polish-German Frontier: Polish Claims and Diplomatic History." *American Perspective*, 1, No. 4 (September, 1947), 211-235.

8125 Pounds, Norman J.G. "The Origin of the Idea of Natural Frontiers in France." *Annals of the Association of American Geographers*, 41, No. 2 (June, 1951), 146-157.

8126 Prochazka, Theodore. "The Delimitation of Czechoslovak-German Frontiers After Munich." *Journal of Central European Affairs*, 21, No. 2 (July, 1961), 200-218.

8127 Renner, George T. "Poland's New Frontiers." Excerpt: *American Magazine*, 140, No. 1 (July, 1945), 34-36 and 103-104.

8128 Rimbert, Sylvie J. "Frontieres et influences urbaines dans le Dreilanderecke." *Regio Basiliensis*, Jahrg 7 (1959), 37-57.

8129 Rochefort, Michel. "Le role perturbateur des frontieres sur le reseau des petites villes en Alsace." *Bulletin de l'Association des Geographes Francais*, 255-256 (Janvier 7, 1956), 10-20.

8130 Ronai, Andras. "Les nouvelles frontieres de la Hongrie. *Bulletin international de la Societe hongroise de geographie*, Tome 67, No. 1 (1939), 27-38.

8131 Rousseau, Charles. "Les frontieres de la France." *Revue Generale de Droit International*, Public, 58 (1954), 23.

8132 Salvemini, Gaetano. "The Frontiers of Italy." *Foreign Affairs*, 23, No. 1 (October, 194), 57-65.

8133 Salvemini, Gaetano. "The Italo-Jugoslav Frontier." *Foreign Affairs*, 24, No. 2 (January, 1946), 341-346.

8134 Sanguin, Andre-Louis. "La Border France-Italienne des Alpes-Masitimes ou les Consequences de la Modification d'une Frontiere Internationale." *Mediterranee*, 24, No. 1 (1983), 17-25.

8135 Schiffrer, Carlo. "La formazione ed i caratteri attuali del confine nord-orientale d'Italia." *Geografia nel Scuole*, 13 (1968), 34-41.

8136 Skendi, Stevro. "The Origin of the Idea of Natural Frontiers in France." *Annals of the Association of American Geographers*, 41 (1951), 146-58.

8137 Skubiszewski, Krysztof. "Poland's Western Frontier and the 1970 Treaties." *American Journal of International Law*, 67, No. 1 (January, 1973), 23-43.

8138 "'Slovene Carinthia'; The Austro-Yugoslav Frontier Question." *World Today*, 3, No. 9 (September, 1947), 389-397.

8139 Teal, John J., Jr. "Europe's Northernmost Frontier." *Foreign Affairs*, 29, No. 2 (January, 1951), 263-275.

8140 Toraldo di Francia, Orazio. "Italia e Jugoslavia di fronte alla Venezie Giulia." *Quaderni Geografici d'Attualita*, Serie 1ª: I Confini d'Italia, Il Confine orientale d'Italia, 7 (1946), 143-161.

8141 Unstead, J.F. "The Belt of Political Change in Europe." *Scottish Geographical Magazine*, 39, No. 3 (July, 1923), 183-192.

8142 Van Wettere-Verhasselt, Yola. "Les frontieres du Nord et de lest de la Belgique; etude de geographie humaine." *Revue Belge de Geographie*, 89, Nos. 1-3 (Supplement, 1965), 1-402.

8143 Vidal de la Blache, Paul. "La frontiere de la Sarre." *Annales de Geographie*, 28, No. 154 (1Juillet, 1919), 249-267.

8144 von Kuehnelt-Leddih, Erik R. "The Problem of Frontiers in Postwar Euorpe." *Thought; Fordham University Quarterly*, 20, No. 76 (March, 1945), 55-84.

8145 Ward, Michael. "The Northern Greek Frontier." *Geographical Magazine*, 21, No. 9 (January, 1949), 329-335.

8146 Wilkinson, H.R. "Yugoslav Kosmet: The Evolution of a Frontier Province and Its Landscape." *Transactions and Papers of the Institute of British Geographers*, 21 (1955), 171-193.

BUFFER ZONES AND TERRITORIES

GENERAL, THEORY AND REGIONS

Books and Journals

8147 Allan, Nigel J.R. "Afghanistan: The End of a Buffer State." *Focus*, 36, No. 3 (Fall, 1986), 3-9.

8148 Barton, Thomas Frank. "Siam: Buffer State or Gradual Piecemeal Consumption?" *Journal of Geography*, 63, No. 7 (October, 1964), 302-313.

8149 Boesch, Hans. "Neutrales Land-in Nordarabien." *Geographica Helvetica*, 18, No. 2 (1963), 209-211.

8150 Bouhabib, Abdallah. "Lebanon: A Fuse Instead of a Buffer: How Did Every Single Problem in the Middle East End Up In My Country?" *American-Arab Affairs*, 19 (Winter, 1986-87, 13-16.

8151 Brintan, J.Y. "The Saudi-Kuwait Neutral Zone." *International Law Quarterly*, 16, No. 3 (July, 1967), 820-823.

8152 Brown, Peter G., and Shue, H. *The Border That Joins*. Totowa, New Jersey: Rowman and Littlefield, 1983.

8153 "Buffer States; Their Historic Service to Peace." *Round Table*. 45, No. 180 (September, 1955), 334-345.

8154 Cahnman, Werner J. "Frontier between East and West in Europe." *Geographical Review*, 39, No. 4 (October, 1949), 605-624.

8155 Church, R.J. Harrison. "Problems and Development of the Dry Zone of West Africa." *Geographical Journal*, 127, No. 3 (April, 1961), 187-204.

8156 Donald, Robert. *The Polish Corridor and the Consequences*, London: Thornton Butterworth, 1929.

8157 Evans, Richard. "Afghanistan: Another Lebanon?" *Geographical Magazine*, 60, No. 4 (April, 1988), 2-10.

8158 **Freeman, T.W., and Macdonald, Mary M.** "The Arctic Corridor of Finland." *Scottish Geographical Magazine*, 54, No. 4 (December, 1938), 219-230.

8159 **Gear, Mary Barnes.** "Role of Buffer States in International Relations." *Journal of Geography*, 40, No. 3 (March, 1941), 81-89.

8160 **Haggard, J. Villasana.** "The Neutral Ground between Louisiana and Texas, 1806-1821." *Louisiana Historical Quarterly*. 28, No. 4 (October, 1945), 1001-1128.

8161 **Haggard, M.T.** "Mongolia: The Uneasy Buffer." *Asian Survey*, 5, No. 1 (January, 1965), 18-24.

8162 **Hardwick, Walter G.** "Changing Corridors to Alaska." *Journal of Geography*, 61, No. 1 (January, 1962), 49-57.

8163 **Hartshorne, Richard.** "The Polish Corridor." *Journal of Geography*, 36, No. 5 (May, 1937), 161-176.

8164 **Hensel, Paul R., and Diehl, Paul F.** "Testing Empirical Propositions About shatterbelts, 1945-76." *Political Geography* [Oxford], 13, No. 1 (January, 1994), 33-51.

8165 **Hunter, John M., and de Blij, Harm J.** "Concept as a Teaching Device: The Example of Buffer Zones in Africa." *Journal of Geography*, 71, No. 9 (December, 1972), 549-562.

8166 **Kelly, J.B.** "Sovereignty and Jurisdiction in Eastern Arabia." *International Affairs*, 34, No. 1 (January, 1958), 16-24.

8167 **Levi, Werner.** "Bhutan and Sikkim: Two Buffer States." *World Today*, 15, No. 12 (December, 1959), 492-500.

8168 **McPhail, I.R., and Woolmington, E.R.** "Changing Functions of the State Border as a Northern New South Wales." *Australian Geographical Studies*, 4, No. 2 (October, 1966), 129-153.

8169 **Mojumdar, K.K.** "Hunza: Axis or Buffer." *Geographical Observer*, 6 (March, 1970), 42-47.

8170 **Partem, Michael Greenfield.** "The Buffer System in International Relations." *Journal of Conflict Resolution*, 27, No. 1 (March, 1983), 3-26.

8171 **Petrovic, Rude.** "Yugoslav Free Zone in Thessaloniki: Historical Account, Functions and Discontinuances of Work." *Glasnik Srpskog Geografskog Drushtva-Bulletin de la Societe Serbe de Geographie*, Tome 56, No. 2 (1976), 27-47 (with English Summary 44-47).

8172 **Philby, H. St. J.** "Jauf and the North Arabian Desert." *Geographical Journal*, 62, No. 2 (July, 1923), 251-259.

8173 **Rahul, Ram.** *Magnolia Between China and the USSR.* New Delhi: MRML, 1989

8174 **Reis, Arthur Cezar Ferreira.** "Neutralidade e boa Vizenhanca no Inicia das Relacoes Entre Brasileiros e Venezuelanos." Documentaria, *Revista do Instituto Historico e Geografico Brasileiro*, 235, No. 2 (April-June, 1957), 3-84.

8175 **Rose, Leo E.** "The Himalayan Border States: 'Buffers' in Transition." *Asian Survey*, 3, No. 2 (February, 1963), 116-121.

8176 **Salisbury, Howard Graves III.** "The Israeli-Syrian Demilitarized Zone: An Examination of Unresolved Conflict." *Journal of Geography*, 71, No. 2 (February, 1972), 109-116.

8177 **Smogorzewski, Casimir.** *Poland, Germany and The Corridor*, London: Williams and Norgate, 1930.

8178 **Toye, Hugh.** *Laos-Buffer State or Battleground*, London: Oxford University Press, 1968.

8179 **Umiastowski, R.** *Granice polityczne, naturalne i obronne w czasie pokoju i wojny* (Political Boundaries, Natural and Defensive, in Time of Peace and War), Cracow: 1925.

8180 **Vonkries, Wilhem.** *Deutschland und der Korridor*, Berlin: Volkand Reich Verlag, 1933.

8181 **Ydit, Meir.** *Internationalized Territories from the "Free City of Cracow" to the "Free City of Berlin".* Leyden: A.W. Sythoff, 1961.

ENCLAVES AND EXCLAVES

GENERAL, THEORY AND REGIONS

Books and Journals

8182 "Aerien aux Territoires Enclaves." [Chronicle of International Events, South Africa and Great Britain, Conflicting Views of the Two States on the Subject of Basutoland, Problem of Aerial Access to Enclave Territories.] *Revue Generale de Droit International Public*, 70 (1966), 131-137.

8183 **Banerji, R.N.** "Indo-Pakistani Enclaves." *India Quarterly*, 25, No. 3 (July-September, 1969), 254-257.

8184 **Barnard, W.S.** "The Political Geography of an Exclave: Walvis Bay." *South-African Geographer*, 15, No. 1/2 (September 1987/April 1988), 85-99.

8185 **Berger, Kurt Martin.** "Eine Freie Stade West Berlin." *Zeitschrift fur Geopolitik*, Jahrgang 31, Heft 3 (Marz, 1960), 1-7.

8186 **Bolli, M.** "Die Enklave Busingen." *Geographica Helvetica*, 9 (1954), 225.

8187 **Catudel, Honore M.** "The Enclave Problem in Political Geography." *Indian Geographical Journal*, 47, Nos. 3 and 4 (July-December, 1972), 11-18.

8188 **Charpentier, Jean.** "Le Probleme des Enclaves." [The Problem of Enclaves], in Societe Francais pour le Droit International, *La Frontiere; Colloque de Politiers*, 1980, 41-56; discussion p. 57-73.

8189 **Collins, Robert O.** "The Transfer of the Lado Enclave to the Anglo-Egyptians Sudan, 1910." *Zaire*, 14 , Nos. 2 and 3 (1960), 193-210.

8190 **Elkins, T.H., with Hoffmeister, B.** *Berlin: The Spatial Structure of a Divided City.* London: Methuen, 1988.

8191 **Farran, C.D.** "International Enclaves and the Question of State Servitude." *International and Comparative Law Quarterly.* 4, No. 2 (April, 1955), 294-307.

8192 **Frenz, Frank E.** *International Enclaes and Rights of Passage.* Geneva and Paris: E. Droz and Minard, 1961.

8193 **Garst, John D.** "Enclaves Freckle the Face of Europe." *National Geographic School Bulletin*, 44, No. 27 (April 25, 1966), 422-423.

8194 **Jaquay, Barbara G.** "The Town of Parker: An Anglo Enclave on the Colorado River Indian Reservation." Tempe: Arizona State University, Master's Thesis, 1988.

8195 **Karan, Pradyumna Prasad.** "The India-Pakistan Enclave Problem." *Professional Geographer*, 18, No. 1 (January, 1966), 23-25.

8196 **Lauer, Ph.** "Une enquete au sujet de la frontiere francaise dans le Val d'Arran, sous Philippe-le-Bel." *Bulletin de la Section de Geographie du Comite des Travaux historiques et scientifiques*, 35 (1920), 17-38.

8197 **Maryland, University, Bureau of Business and Economic Research.** *Where East is West; European Enclaves in Asia*, College Park, Maryland: University of Maryland, 1954.

8198 **Melamid, Alexander.** "Enclaves in Territorial Waters." *Professional Geographer*, 17, No. 1 (January, 1965), 19.

8199 **Merritt, Richard L.** "Infrastructural Changes in Berlin." *Annals of the Association of American Geographers*, 63, No. 1 (March, 1973), 58-70.

8200 **Merritt, Richard L.** "West Berlin: Center or Periphery?" In *Comparing Nations*, Richard L. Merritt and Stein Rokkan, eds, New Haven, Connecticut: Yale University Press, 1966, 321-336.

8201 **Minghi, Julian V.** "Point Roberts, Washington-The Problem of an American Exclave." *Association of Pacific Coast Geographers.* 24, No. 1 (March, 1962), 29-34.

8202 **Pedreschi, Luigi.** "L'exclave italiano in terra Svizzera di Campione d'Italia." *Rivista Geografica Italiana*, Annata 64 , Fasc. 1 (Januaro, 1958), 23-40.

8203 **Ramm, Francois.** "Enclavement-desenclavement." *Etudes et Statistiques BEAC*, 35 (1976), 619-630.

8204 **Raton, Pierre.** *Les Enclaves*, Paris: Annuaire Francais de Droit International, 1958.

8205 **Robinson, G.W.S.** "Ceuta and Melilla: Spain's Plazas de Soberania." *Geography*, 43, No. 202, Part 4 (November, 1958), 266-269.

8206 **Robinson, G.W.S.** "Exclaves." *Annals of the Association of American Geographers*, 49, No. 3 (September, 1959), 283-295.

8207 **Robinson, G.W.S.** "West Berlin: The Geography of an Exclave." *Geographical Review*, 43, No. 4 (October, 1953), 540-557.

8208 **Rumley, Dennis, and Minghi, Julian V.** "Integration and System Stress in an International Enclave: Point Roberts, Washington." In *Peoples of the Living Land: Geography of Cultural Diversity in BC*, J. Minghi, ed, Vancouver: Tantalus, 1972, 213-224.

8209 **Sanguin, Andre-Louis.** "Varrous, Glacis, Corridors, Poches et Enclaves: Une Curieuse Geographie des frontieres." *Protee*, 1, No. 2 (1971), 27-48.

8210 **Scholler, Peter.** "Stadtgeographische Probleme des Geneilten Berlin." *Erdkunde*, Band 7 (1953), 1-11.

8211 **Schroeder, Klaus.** "Der Stadtverkehr als Kriterium der Strukturwandlungen Berlins." *Erdkunde*, Band 14 (1960), 29-35.

8212 **Siedentop, Irmfried.** "Geographie der Enklaven und Exklaven." *Zeitschrift fur Wirtschaftsgeographie, Angewandte-und Sozial-Geographie*, 12, Heft 1 (1968), 12-14.

8213 **Singh, Govind Saran.** "British Enclaves and the Reorganization of the Maharastra State." *Deccan Geographer*, 2, No. 2 (January, 1964), 146-153.

8214 **Stigand, C.H.** *Equatoria: The Lado Enclave.* London: Constable, 1923.

8215 **Van Zandt, Howard F.** "Geographical Enclaves in Japan." *Asiatic Society of Japan Bulletin*, Special Issue (June, 1969), 21-27.

8216 **Whiteford, Gary Thomas.** *The Municipal Enclaves of Oklahoma City: An Analysis of Their Functional Relationship to Oklahoma City.* Norman: University of Oklahoma, Ph.D., 1972.

8217 **Yuill, R.S.** *A Simulation Study of Barrier Effects in Spatial Diffusion Problems.* Ann Arbor: Michigan Inter-University Community of Mathematical Geographers, 1966.

8218 **Zimm, Alfred.** "Zur Dynamik der Territorialstruktur der DDR–Haupstadt Berlin und ihres Umlandes." *Petermanns Geographische Mitteilungen,*125 Jahr, Heft 3 (September,1981), 157-165.

LANDLOCKED STATES AND ACCESS TO SEA

GENERAL AND THEORY

Books

8219 **Bahadur, Prakash.** *Free Access to the Sea of Land-Locked Countries in International Law and Practice.* Ithaca, New York: Cornell Law School, LL.M. Thesis, 1959.

8220 **Bish and Partners Ltd.** McCreary-Koretsky Engineers. *Harbour of Africa.* The Hague: Martinus Nighoff, 1963.

8221 **Bowen, Robert E.** *The Geographically Disadvantaged States and the Law of the Sea: A Study in Coalition Formation, 1967-1975.* Los Angeles: University of Southern California, Ph.D., 1983.

8222 **Caflisch, Lucius C.** *Rights, Claims and Interests of Land-Locked States and the New Law of the Sea.* Paper read to a regional meeting of the American Society of International Law, Boston, February, 1975.

8223 **Cukwurah, A. Oye.** *The Participation of Land-Locked Developing Countries in the New International Economic Order.* Paper read to the biennial meeting of the International Law Association, Manila, August, 1978.

8224 **Daibagya, Bhubaneshwor Prasad.** *Access to the Sea for the Land-Locked States: A Policy-Oriented Study.* Seminar paper for Professor Myres S. McDougal, New Haven, Connecticut: Yale Law School, September, 1966.

8225 *The Most Seriously Affected, the Land-Locked, and the Island Developing Countries.* New York: UNDP, Development Issue Paper for the 1980's No. 15, 1981.

8226 **Fischer, Wolfgang E.** *The Problems in Land-Locked States: Some Basic Thoughts.* Economic Development Research Paper No. 117. Kampala: Makerere Economic Research Institute, February 3, 1967.

8227 **Fried, John H.E.** *Comments on Part X ('Right of Access of Land-Locked States to and from the Sea and Freedom of Transit') of the Informal Composite Negotiating Text of the Third U.N. Conference on the Law of the Sea.* Paper prepared for the Land-Locked States Committee of the American Branch of the International Law Association, January, 1978.

8228 **Friedheim, Robert L., et al.** *The Landlocked and Shelf-Locked States in the Law of the Sea Negotiations.* Arlington, Virginia: Center for Naval Analyses, January 31, 1974.

8229 **Gabryelska, Barbara.** *Wolny Dostep do Morza Panstw Srodladowych.* [Free Access to the Sea of Land-Locked Countries]. Wroclow, Poland: University of Wroclaw, Doctoral Dissertation, 1969.

8230 **Gautam, Lakshan Kumar.** *Trade and Welfare Consequences of Land-Lockedness: Theory and Empiricial Evidence from Developing Countries.* Canberra: Australian National University, Master's Thesis, 1978.

8231 **Gelineau, Louis.** *Le Desenclavement; ou Acces au Marche Mondial ou National" [Reducing the Effects of Enclosure; or Access to the World or National Market].* Paris: Ministere de la Cooperation, Direction du Developpement Economique, May, 1980. Prepared for the French delegation to the VII Franco-African Conference, Nice, May 8-10, 1980.

8232 **Gilas, Janusz.** *Tranzyt przez Porty Morskie w Swietle Prawa Miedzynarodowego* [Transit through Sea Ports in the Light of International Law]. Gdansk: Wydawnictwo Morski, 1969.

8233 **Gilas, Janusz.** *Tranzyt w Prawie Miedzynarodowym* [Transit in International Law]. Torun: Wydawnictwa Uniwersytetu Mikolaja Kopernika, 1967.

8234 **Glassner, Martin Ira.** *Access to the Sea for Developing Land-Locked States.* The Hague: Martinus Nijhoff, 1970.

8235 **Glassner, Martin Ira, ed.** *Bibliography on Land-Locked States.* 3rd rev. and enl. ed. Dordrecht: Martinus Nijhoff Publishers, 1991.

8236 **Glassner, Martin Ira.** *Bibliography on Land-Locked States,* rev. ed. Boston, Massachusetts: Martinus Nijhoff, 1986.

8237 **Glassner, Martin Ira.** *Problems of Developing Land-Locked Countries.* ESCAP/UNCTAD/UNDP Workshop on Special Measures in Favour of Least Developed Land-Locked Countries, Bangkok, August 7-13, 1979.

8238 **Golitsyn, Vladimir Vladimirovich.** *Vnutrikontinental'nye Gosudarstva i Mezhdunarodno Morsko Pravo* [Land-Locked States and the International Law of the Sea]. Moscow: Izdatel'stvo Mezhdunarodno Otnosheniya, 1978.

8239 **Gumpel, Werner.** *Die Seehafen- und Schiffahrtspolitik des COMECON* [The Seaport and Navigation Policy of COMECON]. Berlin: Duncker and Humblot, 1963.

8240 **Hafner, Gerhard.** *Acces a la Mer: Aspects Economiques et Juridiques. Problemes des Pays Industrialises et des Pays en Voie de Developpement et sans Littoral* {Access to the Sea: Economic and Juridicial Aspects. Problems of Industrialized and Developing Land-Locked Countries]. Paper read at a meeting in Algiers, October, 1983.

8241 **Hafner, Gerhard.** *Die Gruppe der Binnen- und Geographischebenachteiligten Staaten auf der Dritten Seerechtskonferenz der Vereinten Nationen* [The Group of Land-Locked and Geographically Disadvantaged States at the Third United Nations Conference of the Law of the Sea]. New York: UNCLOW, 1976.

8242 **Haquani, Zalmai.** *"Les Pays sans Littoral aux Nations Unies* [The Land-Locked Countries at the United Nations]. Nice: Faculte de Droit et des Sciences Economiques, Universite de Nice, DES Thesis, October, 1972.

8243 **Kallu-Kalumiya, Charles.** *Landlocked States and the Concept of Exclusive Zone: Their Rights and Duties.* Cambridge, Massachusetts: Harvard Law School, LL.M. Thesis, 1976.

8244 **Knypl, Zenon.** *Dostep Panstw o Niekorzystnym Polozeniu Geograficznym do Stret Ekonomicznych Panstw Nadbrzeznych* [Access of the Geographically Disadvantaged States to the Exclusive Economic Zone of the Coastal States]. Materialy Instytutu Morskiego Nr. 853. Gdansk-Slupsk-Szeczin: Wydawnictwo Instytutu Morskiego, 1981.

8245 **Kopal, Vladimir.** *Problemy Nove Kodifikace Mezinarodniho Prava Morskeho se Zvastnim Zretelem na Prava a Zajmy Vnitrozemskych Statu* [Problsms of the New Codification of the Law of the Sea with Special Reference to Rights and Interests of Land-Locked States]. Prague: Academia, 1983.

8246 **Kwiatkowska-Czechowska, Barbara.** *Status Prawny Morskiej Strefy Ekonomicznej* [Legal Status of the Maritime Economic Zone]. Warsaw: Polish Institute of International Affairs, Ph.D., 1979.

8247 **Little, George T.** *Water Boundaries of Land-Locked States.* Paper read to the annual meeting of The New England Political Science Association, Lowell, Massachusetts, April, 1983.

8248 **Milic, Milenko.** *Access of the Land-Locked States to and from the Sea.* Workpaper of the World Peace Through Law Center Delivered at the Law of the Sea Conference, Geneva, 1977. Completed January 31, 1981.

8249 **Milic, Milenko.** *Land-Locked States.* Workpaper of the World Peach Through Law Center for the 1977 New York Session of the Third United Nations Conference on the Law of the Sea. Originally "Working Paper on Land-Locked States" prepared for the biennial meeting of the International Law Association, Madrid, August, 1976.

8250 **Milic, Milenko.** *Les Etats Prives de Littoral Maritime* [The Land-Locked States]. Report presented to the biennial meeting of the International Law Association, Belgrade, August, 1980.

8251 **Moufflet, Raphele.** *Les Etats en Developpement Geographiquement Desavantages et le Droit de la Merr* [The Developing Geographically Disadvantaged States and the Law of the Sea]. Memoire D.E.A., Institut du Droit de la Paix et du Developpement, Universite de Nice, February, 1977.

8252 *Multilateral Agreements Providing for Freedom of Transit in General: Background Paper Reviewing International Agreements Containing Provisions Relevant to the Question of the Transit Trade of Land-Locked States.* Geneva: ECE/UNCTAD Reference Unit in the United Nations Library, Palais des Nations.

8253 **Nezam, Zia.** *Les Etats sans Littoral Maritime* [The Land-Locked Countries]. Nice: Institut du Droit de la Paix et du Developpement de l'Universite de Nice, Doctoral Dissertation in Law, May, 1977.

8254 **Nordquist, Myron H., and Park, Choon-ho.** *Reports of the United States Delegation to the Third United Nations Conference on the Law of the Sea.* Honolulu: Law of the Sea Institute, University of Hawaii, Occasional Paper No. 33, 1983.

8255 **Ochan, Ralph W.** *Marine Policy and Developing Landlocked States: The Search for a New Equity in the Law of the Sea.* Dalhousie University, LL.M. Thesis, 1977.

8256 **Paraguay**. *Marina Mercante Nacional; Consideraciones sobre su Organizacion* [National Merchant Marine; Considerations on its Organization]. Contains the following articles: "Contribucion al Estudio de la Marine Mercante Nacional" by Jose Bozzano; "Marine Mercante Paraguaya" by Miguel Cardona; "Flota Mercante del Estado; Funcion Especifica de la Misma como Institucion Nacional" by Jose Munoz Chavez; and "Marine Mercante Nacional' by Humberto Infante Rivarola. Asuncion: Imprenta Naval, 1947. (Articles are reprinted from various issues of *Boletin Naval* [Asuncion] 1945-1947.)

8257 **Pechota, Vratislav**. *Free Access to the Sea of Land-Locked Countries*. Working paper prepared for the biennial meeting of the International Law Association, Madrid, August, 1976.

8258 **Report of the ESCAP/UNCTAD/UNDP**. *Workshop on Special Measures in Favour of Least Developed Land-Locked Countries*. Bangkok: August 7-13, 1979.

8259 **Report of the ESCAP/UNCTAD/UNDP**. *Workshop on Special Measures in Favour of Least Developed Land-Locked Countries*. Bangkok: July 20-27, 1981.

8260 **Report of the ESCAP/UNCTAD/UNDP**. *Workshop on Special Measures in Favour of Least Developed Land-Locked Countries*. Kathmandu: November 22-27, 1982.

8261 **Report of the ESCAP/UNCTAD/UNDP**. *Workshop on Special Measures in Favour of Least Developed Land-Locked Countries*. Bangkok: November 7-12, 1983.

8262 **Reza, Abu**. *Problems of Land-Locked Countries*. UNCTAD/ESCAP Project RAS/72/077. Regional Transport Course, BIDS/EDI-IBRD/ESCAP. Dacca, March 7, 1981.

8263 **Schroder, Dieter**. *Der Freie Zugang der Binnenstaaten zum Meer; Die Internationalen Ubereinkommen mit einer Einfuhrung* [Free Access of Land-Locked States to the Sea; The International Confention with an Introduction]. Frankfurt am Main: Alfred Metzner Verlag, 1966.

8264 **Shearer, Ivan A**. *Land-Locked States in International Law--An Overview*. Working paper prepared for the biennial meeting of the International Law Association, Madrid, August, 1976.

8265 **Sherzo, M.R**. "Les Etats Enclaves et le Libre Acces a la Mer." Warsaw: Universitat, 1964.

8266 **Sinjela, Andrew Mpazi**. *Land-Locked States and the Contemporary Ocean Regime*. New Haven, Connecticut: Yale Law School, J.S.D. Dissertation, 1978.

8267 **Sinjela, Andrew Mpazi**. *Land-Locked States and the UNCLOS Regime*. Dobbs Ferry, New York: Oceana Publications, 1983.

8268 **Spiropulos, Jean** [Spyropoulos, Ioannes]. *Das Recht der Binnenstaaten auf Beteiligung an der Meeresschiffahrt* [The Right of Land-Locked States to Participation in Maritime Commerce]. Leipzig: Rossberg'sche Verlagsbuchhandlung, 1923.

8269 **Stoddard, Robert H**. *To be Land-Locked and Poverty-Locked*. Paper read to the National Conference on Culture Change, Ecology and Development in Nepal: Multidisciplinary Approaches, Sponsored by the Nepal Studies Association in conjunction with the Association for Asian Studies, Chicago, April, 1978.

8270 **Tabibi, Abdul Hakim**. *Hoquq al-doval va monasabat-i an ba mamelek-i mohafez bekhoskeh* [International Law and Its Relation to Land-Locked Countries]. Kabul: Matba'eh-yi doulati, 1958.

8271 **Tabibi, Abdul Hakim**. *The Right of Free Access to the Sea*. Kabul: Afghan Book Publishing House, 1966.

8272 **Tabibi, Abdul Hakim**. *The Right of Transit of Land-Locked Countries*. Kabul: Afghan Book Publishing House, 1970.

8273 **Trade Promotion Centre (TPC)**. *Land-Locked Aspects of Development*, 2nd ed. Kathmandu: TPC, 1976.

8274 **Upadhya, Devendra Raj**. *Transit Trade of Land-Locked States*. Occasional Paper No. 53. The Hague: Institute of Social Studies, August, 1975.

8275 **Zekrya, Sultan Hamid**. *Les Etats sans Littoral et la Liberte des Mers* [Land-Locked States and Freedom of the Seas]. Paris, France: University of Paris: Doctoral Thesis in Law, 1959.

Journals

8276 **Alexander, Lewis M**. "The 'Disadvantaged' States and the Law of the Sea." *Marine Policy*, 5, No. 3 (July, 1981), 185-193.

8277 **Alexander, Lewis M., and Hodgson, Robert D**. "The Role of the Geographically--Disadvantaged States in the Law of the Sea." *San Diego Law Review*, 13, No. 3 (March, 1976), 558-582.

8278 "An Action Programme for Land-Locked LDC's." *Afro-Asian Economic Review*, 14, No. 154-155 (July-August, 1972), 5-8.

8279 **Anchordoqui, Enrique**. "Las Zonas Francas Industriales y el Comercio Exterior" [Industrial and Foreign Trade Free Zones]. *Integracion Latinoamericana*, 2, No. 17 (September, 1977), 3-17.

8280 **Arancibia Herrera, Mario.** "Commentarios a un Estatuto de los Paises sin Litoral" [Commentaries on a Statute for the Land-Locked Countries]. *Arquivos do Ministerio da Justica*, 32, No. 134 (April-June, 1975), 34-38.

8281 **Arnold, Guy.** "Changing the Communications Map." *Africa Report*, 20, No. 4 (July-August, 1975), 37-41.

8282 **Becher, Ernst.** "An Action Programme for Land-Locked LDCs." *Intereconomics*, 5 (May, 1972), 145-148. Also in *Afro-Asian Economic Review*, 14, No. 154-155 (July-August, 1972), 5-8.

8283 **Belhassen, Souhayr.** "De la Piete a l'Autoroute" [From Track to Superhighway]. *Jeune Afrique*, 19 Annee, No. 962 (June 13, 1979), 47, 49, 51.

8284 **Boas, Frank.** "Landlocked Countries and the Law of the Sea." *American Bar Association Section of International and Comparative Law Bulletin*, 4, No. 6 (December, 1959), 22-27.

8285 **Borges Fortes, Betty Y.B.** "Primeiro Encontro da Comissao Internacional de Juristas para Estudo do 'Status' Juridico dos Paises sem Litoral Maritimo—Exposicao de Motivos" [First Meeting of the International Commission of Jurists to Study the Juridical 'Status' of the Land-Locked Countries—Explantion and Reasons]. *Arquivos do Ministerio da Justica*, 32, No. 134 (April-June, 1975), 1-5.

8286 **Brankovic, Branko.** "Land-Locked Countries—Positions and Demands." *Review of International Affairs*, 26, No. 598 (March 5, 1975), 12-14.

8287 **Cabanius, Philippe, and Pusar, Alfred B.** "Economic Appraisal of the Required Transport Infrasturcture for Land-Locked Countries and External Financing Constraints." Chapter 1 in Institution of Civil Engineers, *Highway Investment in Developing Countries*. London: Thomas Telford, 1983, 5-7.

8288 **Cabello Sarubbi, Oscar J.** "La Participacion de los Estados sin Litoral en la Tercera Conferencia de las Naciones Unidas sobre el Derecho del Mar" [The Participation of the Land-Locked States in the Third United Nations Conference on the Law of the Sea]. *Estudios Paraguayos*, 6, No. 1 (September, 1978), 63-84.

8289 **Caflisch, Lucius C.** "The Access of Land-Locked States to the Sea." *Revue Iranienne des Relations Internationales*, 5-6 (Winter, 1975-76), 53-76.

8290 **Caflisch, Lucius C.** "La Convention des Nations Unies sur le Droit de la Mer Adoptee le 30 Avril 1982" [The United Nations Convention on the Law of the Sea Adopted on 30 April 1982]. *Annuaire Suisse de Droit International*, 39 (1983), 39-104.

8291 **Caflisch, Lucius C.** "The Fishing Rights of Land-Locked and Geographically Disadvantaged States in the Exclusive Economic Zone." In *La Zona Economica Esclusiva*, Benedetto Conforti, ed. Studi e Documenti sul Diritto Internazionale del Mare No. 11. Milan: Giuffre, 1983, 31-48.

8292 **Caflisch, Lucius C.** "Land-Locked and Geographically Disadvantaged States and the New Law of the Sea." *Thesaurus Acroasium*, 7 (1977), 345-404.

8293 **Caflisch, Lucius C.** "Land-Locked States and Their Access to and from the Sea." *British Yearbook of International Law*, 49 (1978), 71-100.

8294 **Caflisch, Lucius C.** "What is a Geographically Disadvantaged State?" *Ocean Development and International Law*, 18, No. 6 (1987), 641-663.

8295 **Carillo Salcedo, Juan Antonio.** "Los Estados sin Litoral y en Situacion Geografica Desventajosa, Ante la Revision del Derecho del Mar" [The Land-Locked and Geographically Disadvantaged States, in View of the Revision of the Law of the Sea]. Chapter 4 in *La Actual Revision del Derecho del Mar; Una Perspectiva Espanola*. Volume 1, Part 1. Madrid: Instituto de Estudios Politicos, Centro de Documentacion, 1974, 155-199.

8296 **Chauhan, Balbir R.** "The Position of Land-Locked States in International Law." *Law Review*, 18, No. 2 (October, 1966), 422-440.

8297 **Childs, Patrick.** "The Interests of Land-Locked States in Law of the Seas." *San Diego Law Review*, 9, No. 3 (May, 1972), 701-734. Excerpted in *Development Digest*, Vol. 11, No. 2 (April, 1973), 31-38.

8298 **Cipolatti, Elio Carlos.** "La Copnvencion de Transporte Internacional de Mercancias (TIR): Consideraciones Acerca de la Adhesion de los Paises del Cono Sur" [The Convention on International Transport of Goods (TIR): Considerations About the Accession of the Countries of the Southern Cone]. *Intergracion Latinoamericana*, 5, No. 47 (June, 1980), 94-98.

8299 "Co-operation Between Land-Locked and Transit Countries." *Transport Newsletter*. (Published semi-annually by the United Nations Department of International Economic and Social Affairs, Office for Programme Planning and Coordination.), 2, No. 2 (December, 1979), 18-20.

8300 **Dahmani, M.** "Access of Landlocked and Geographically-disadvantaged States to the Fisheries Resource of the Economic Exclusion Zone (EEZ) Under the New Convention on the Law of the Sea." *Maritime Policy and Management*, 10, No. 4 (October–December, 1983), 265–273.

8301 **Delupis, Ingrid.** "Land–Locked States and the Law of the Sea." *Scandinavian Studies in Law*, 19 (1975), 103–120. Reprinted in *Acta Universitatis Stockholmiensis: Studia Juridica Stockholmiensia*, 49 (1975), 103–120.

8302 **Delupis, Ingrid.** "Passage over Land." Chapter 4 in her *International Law and the Independent State*. New York: Crane, Russak, 1974, p. 59–78.

8303 **Dobry, Ana Maria.** "El Estatuto de los Paises sin Litoral Maritimo a Luz de la Integracion" [The Statute of the Land–Locked Countries in the Light of Integration]. *Arquivos do Ministerio da Justica*, 32, No. 134 (April–June, 1975), 39–45.

8304 **Dubey, M.** "International Law Relating to the Transit Trade of Land–Locked Countries." *Indian Year Book of International Affairs*, 14 (1967), 22–44.

8305 **Dubinina, V.** "New International Railway Transit Tariff of the CMEA Member Countries." *Foreign Trade*, 8, No. 1 (1978), 21–28.

8306 **Dudzinski, Jerzy, and Nakonieczna-Kisiel, Halina.** "Brak Dostepu do Morza Jako Bariera Wzrostu" [No Access to the Sea Seen as a Factor Limiting Economic Growth]. *Sprawy Miedzyarodowe*, No. 37, Zeszyt 2 (Luty, 1984), 113–124.

8307 **East, W. Gordon.** "The Geography of Land–Locked States." *Transactions and Papers of the Institute of British Geographers*, 8 (1960), 1–22.

8308 **Ferguson, Susan.** "UNCLOS III: Last Chance for Land–Locked States?" *San Diego Law Review*, 14, No. 3 (April, 1977), 637–655.

8309 **Franck, Thomas M., et al.** "The New Poor: Land–Locked, Shelf–Locked and Other Geographically Disadvantaged States." *New York University Journal of International Law and Politics*, 7, No. 1 (Spring, 1974), 33–57.

8310 **Freeman, Dillon Smith.** "Special Problems of Landlocked Countries Relating to the Exploration and Exploitation of the Sea Beyond the Limites of National Jurisdiction." In Universtiy of North Carolina School of Law, *Attitudes Regarding a Law of the Sea Convention to Establish an International Seabed Regime*. University of North Carolina Sea Grant Publication; National Technical Information Service No. COM-72-10824 (April,

1972), 106–115.

8311 **Fried, John H.E.** "The New Convention on Transit Trade of Land-Locked States, and the Development of Law under United Nations Auspices." *Journal of the Tribhuvan University Department of Political Science*, (1966), 16–29.

8312 **Fried, John H.E.** "The 1965 Convention on Transit Trade of Land-Locked States." *Indian Journal of International Law*, 6, No. 1 (January - March, 1966), 9–30.

8313 **Friedheim, Robert L.** "The 'Satisfied' and 'Dissatisfied' States Negotiate International Law: A Case Study." *World Politics*, 18, No. 1 (October, 1965), 20–41.

8314 **Gabreyelska-Straburzynska, Barbara.** "Panstwa Srodladowe a Nowe Prawo Morza" [The Land-Locked States and the New Law of the Sea]. *Przeglad Stosunkow Miedzynarodowych*, 2–3 (1981), 129–138.

8315 **Gabreyelska-Straburzynska, Barbara.** "Problem Udostpnienia Portow Morskich Panstwom Srodladowym' [The Problem of Rendering Seaports Accessible to Land-Locked States]. *Zeszyty Naukowe Wydzialu Prawa y Administraciji Universytetu Gdanskiego, Prawo*, 1 (1972), 49–59.

8316 **Gabreyelska-Straburzynska, Barbara.** "Problem Wolnego Dostepu do Morza Panstw Srodladowych w Nauce przed Konferencja Genewska 1958R." [The Quesiton of Free Access of Land-Locked States to the Sea in the Legal Writings before the Geneva Conference of 1958]. *Acta Universitatis Wratislaviensis*, 32, No. 125 (1970), 55–61.

8317 "Genfer Seerechskonferenz mit Vorbesprechung der Binnenlander' [Geneva Law of the Sea Conference with Preliminary Discussion of the Land-Locked Countries]. *Strom und See*, 53, No. 2 (February, 1958), 47.

8318 **Ghaussy, Saadollah.** "Land-locked and Geographically Disadvantaged States vis-a-vis Deepsea Mining." In *The Deep Seabed and Its Mineral Resources*, Proceedings of the Third International Ocean Symposium, 15–17 November, 1978, Tokyo. Tokyo: Ocean Association of Japan, March, 1969, 115–117.

8319 **Gilas, Janusz.** "Developing Land-Locked States and the Resources of the Seabed." *San Diego Law Review*, 11, No. 3 (May, 1974), 633–655.

8320 **Gilas, Janusz.** "Final Report of the Committee on Landlocked States." *Proceedings and Committee Reports of the American Branch of the Internatinal Law Association 1983-84*, 75–147.

8321 Gilas, Janusz. "International Law Regarding Land-Locked States." *Nepal Review*, 11, No. 8 (June, 1972), 388-393.

8322 Gilas, Janusz. "Kodifikacja Uprawnien Panstw Srodladowych w Zakresie Dostepu do Morza i Wolnosci Tranzytu" [The Codification of the Rights of Land-Locked States in Respect of Access to the Sea and Freedom of Transit] in Polska Akademia Nauk, Komitet Badan Morza, *Wspolczesne Tendencie w Prawie Morza*. Wroclaw, Polska Akademia, 1981, 87-110. (Summary in English)

8323 Gilas, Janusz. "Land-Locked Nations and Development." *International Development Review*, 19, No. 2 (September, 1977), 19-23.

8324 Gilas, Janusz. "The Land-Locked States at the Third United Nations Conference on the Law of the Sea." In *Proceedings of the Committee on Marine Geography of the Association of American Geographers*, 1978, 119-122.

8325 Gilas, Janusz. "Special Problems of Land-locked and Geographically Disadvantaged States." *Proceedings of the Symposium on Marine Regionalism*, Galilee, Rhode Island, 25-26 October, 1979, 22-28; discussion 29-32. (Sponsored by the Marine Affairs Program, University of Rhode Island.)

8326 Gilas, Janusz. "The Status of Developing Land-Locked States Since 1965." *Lawyer of the Americas*, 5, No. 3 (October, 1973), 480-498.

8327 Gilas, Janusz. "Transit Rights for Land-Locked States and the Special Case of Nepal." *World Affairs*, 140, No. 4 (Spring, 1978), 304-314.

8328 Gilas, Janusz. "Zagadnienie Tranzytu w Zwiazku z Dostepem Panstw Srodladowoych do Morza" [The Problems of Transit in Connection with Access to the Sea for Land-Locked States]. *Ruch Prawniczy, Ekonomiczny i Socjologiczny*, 28, No. 3 (1966), 1-19.

8329 Glaser, Edwin, and Duculescu, Victor. "Cu Privire la Regimul de Drept International al Tranzitului Statelor Anclavate" [A Look at the Regime of International Law on Transit of Land-Locked States]. *Revista Romana de Studii Internationale*, 7, No. 3 (1973), 149-169.

8330 Golitsyn, Vladimir Vladimirovich. "O Pravakh Vnutrikontinental'ny;kh Gosudarstv v Otnosheniyi'zhivykh Resursov Ekonomicheskh Zon" [The Rights of Land-Locked States to the Living Resources of Economic Zones]. In *Mezhdunarodno-pravovyye Problemy Mirovogo Okeana na Sovremennom Etape*, S.V. Prigradova, ed. Moscow: Transport, 1976, 72-78.

8331 Gilas, Janusz. "Ponyatne Svobodye Tranzyta v Mezhdunarodnom Prave" [The Concept of Freedom of Transit in International Law]. In *Mezhdunarodnye Otnosheniya v Usloviyah Razrydki Napryzhennosti* [International Relations and Conditions During Detente]. (Proceedings of a Conference) Moscow: 1975, 71-79.

8332 Gilas, Janusz. "Pravo Vnutrikontinental'nuikh Gosudarstu na Svobodnuii Dostup k Moru i ot Morya" [The Right of Free Access to and from the Sea of Land-Locked States]. *Aktual'nye Problemy Sovremennogo Mezhdunarodnogo Prava*, 5 (1976), 114-131.

8333 Gilas, Janusz. "Stanovleniye i Razvitiye Prava Dostiyupa k Moryu Vnutrikontinental'nuikh Gosudarstu" [Emergence and Development of the Right of Access to the Sea of Land-Locked States]. *Materialy po Morskomu Prava i Mezhdunardomu Tergovomu* (Moscow), 7 (1975), 38-46.

8334 Gilas, Janusz. "Svobodnui Zonyi Vnutrikontinental'nyye Gosudarstu" [Free Zones of Land-Locked States]. *Morskoe Pravo i Praktika*, 64 , No. 305 (1975), 49-54.

8335 Gilas, Janusz. "Vnutrikontinental'nyye Gosudarstva i Voproos o Predelakh Yurisdiktsii Pribnezhnykh Gosudarstu' [Land-Locked States and the Question of Limites of Coastal States' Jurisdiction]. *Materialy po Morskomu Prava i Mezhdunardomu Tergovomu* (Moscow), 8 (1975), 19-24.

8336 Goncalves Mariano, Alfredo. "Notas acerca da Mediterraneidade—Um Enfoque Tridimensional' [Notes about Land-Lockedness—A Tridimensional Focus]. *Arquivos do Ministerio da Jujstica*, 32, No. 134 (April-June, 1975), 52-58.

8337 Govindaraj, V.C. "Geographically Disadvantaged States and the Law of the Sea." In *Law of the Sea; Caracas and Beyond*, Ram Prakash Anand, ed. The Hague: Martinus Nijhoff, 1980, 253-262.

8338 Govindaraj, V.C. "Land-Locked States and their Right of Access to the Sea." *Indian Journal of International Law*, 14, No. 2 (April, 1974), 190-216.

8339 Govindaraj, V.C. "Land-Locked States—Their Right to the Resources of the Sea-bed and the Ocean Floor." *Indian Journal of International Law*, 14, No. 3-4 (July-December, 1974), 409-424.

8340 Guillerez, Bernard. "Dix Ans de FIDES" [Ten Years of FIDES (Fonds d'Investissement pour le Developpement Economique et Social des Territoires d'Outre-mer)]. *Perspectives d'Outre-mer*, 35 (September, 1960), 8-39.

8341 Hafner, Gerhard. "The 'Land-Locked' Viewpoint." *Marine Policy*, 5, No. 3 (July, 1981), 281-282.

8342 Haquani, Zalmai. "La Participacion des Pays sans Littoral a l'Exploitation des Ressources de la Zone Economique Exclusive' [Participation of Land-Locked Countries in the Exploitation of the Resources of the Exclusive Economic Zone]. In *La Gestion des Ressources por l'Humanite: Le Droit de la Mer/The Management of Humanity's Resources: The Law of the Sea*. The Hague: Martinus Nijhoff, 1982, 257–279.

8343 Hassan, Tariq. "Third Law of the Sea Conference; Fishing Rights of Land-Locked States." *Lawyer of the Americas*, 8, No. 3 (October, 1976), 686–742.

8344 Hilling, David. "Routes to the Sea for Land-Locked States." *Geographical Magazine*, 44, No. 4 (January, 1972), 257–264.

8345 Ibler, Vladimir. "The Land- and Shelf-Locked States and the Development of the Law of the Sea." *Annales d'Etudese Internationales/Annals of International Studies*, 4 (1973), 55–65.

8346 Illanes Fernandez, Javier. "Paises sin Litoral" [Land-Locked Countries]. In *El Derecho del Mar y sus Problemas Actuales*. Buenos Aires: Editorial Universitaria de Buenos Aires, 1974, 139–150.

8347 Iturriza, Jorge E. "Acciones de Apoyo a los Paises Mediterraneos de Menor Desarrollo Relativo" [Actions of Assistance tot he Relatively Less Developed Land-Locked Countries]. *Intergracion Latinoamericana*, 6, No. 59 (July, 1981), 77–83.

8348 Jayakumar, S. "The Issue of the Rights of Landlocked and Geographically Disadvantaged States in the Living Resources of the Economic Zone." *Virginia Journal of International Law*, 18, No. 1 (Fall, 1977), 69–115.

8349 Johnston, Douglas M. "The New Equity in the Law of the Sea." *International Journal*, 31, No. 1 (Winter, 1975–76), 79–99.

8350 Kappeler, Dietrich. "La Convention Relative au Commerce de Transit des Etats sans Littoral de 8 Juillet 1965" [The Convention on Transit Trade of Land-Locked States of 8 July 1965]. *Annuaire Francais de Droit International*, 13 (1967), 673––685.

8351 Kawakami, Sohichiroh. "Freedom of Transit of Land-Locked States." *Kaiyoho no Kenkyu*, 1, No. 1 (March, 1974), 185–199.

8352 Kawakami, Sohichiroh. "Issue of the Right of Landlocked States in the Living Resources in the Economic Zone." *Hogaku Shimpo; Chuo Law Review*, 87, No. 5–6 (August, 1980), 1–42.

8353 Kawakami, Sohichiroh. "Land-Locked States." *Ho to Chitsujyo*, 6, No. 4–5 (September, 1976), 23–28.

8354 Kawakami, Sohichiroh. "Land-Locked States. *Kaiyoho no Kenkyu*, 8, No. 3 (August, 1976), 105–111.

8355 Kawakami, Sohichiroh. "Land-Locked States and the Exclusive Economic Zone." *Kayomondai*, 1 (1975), 36–50.

8356 Kawakami, Sohichiroh. "Land-Locked States and the Ocean." *Kaiyoho no Kenkyu*, 2, No. 4 (October, 1975), 116–125.

8357 Kawakami, Sohichiroh. "Land-Locked States' Fishing Rights within the Exclusive Economic Zone." *Ho to Chitsujyo*, 10, No. 1 (January, 1980), 19–26.

8358 Kawakami, Sohichiroh. "The Problems of Free Access to the Sea of Land-Locked States." *Hogaku Shimpo; The Chuo Law Review*, 82, Nos. 1–3 (March, 1975), 1–37.

8359 Kawakami, Sohichiroh. "Right of Access of Land-Locked States to and from the Sea and Freedom of Transit." *Ocean Age*, 14, No. 3 (March, 1982), 29–33.

8360 Klimenko, B.M. "Pravo Vnutrikontinental'nykh Stran Na Dostup k Moryu" [The Right of Access to the Sea of Land-Locked Countries]. In *Sovremennoye Mezhdunarodnoye Morskoye Pravo; Rezhim Vod i dna Mirovogo Okeana*, M.I. Lazaryev, ed. Moscow: Publishing House Science, 1974, 46–56.

8361 Klimenko, B.M. "Prohod Cherez Suxoputnou Territoriu Gosudarstva" [Transit through Land Territory of a State]. Chapter 1 in his *Pravo Prohoda Cherez Inestrannou Territoriu* [Right of Transit through Foreign Territory]. Moscow: Publishing House International Relations, 1967, 7–47.

8362 Konate, Yaya. "Are Landlocked Countries Condemned?" *Ceres*, 6, No. 5 (September–October, 1973), 48–50.

8363 Kopal, Vladimir. "K Boji o Uznani a Plne Uplatneni Prava Vnitrozemskych Statu na Svabodny Pristup k Mori' [On the Fight for Recognition and Full Implementation of the Right of Land-Locked States to Free Access to the Sea]. *Acta Universitatis Carolinae Iuridica l*, 20 (1975), 37–51.

8364 Kopal, Vladimir. "K Navrhu Nove Umluvy o Morskem Pravu' [The New Informal Draft Convention on the Law of the Sea]. *Pravnik*, 115, No. 4 (1976), 306–318.

8365 **Kopal, Vladimir.** "Pravo Vnitrozemskych Statu na Pristup k Mori a do Oblasti Morskeho dna' [The Right of Land-Locked States to Access to the Sea and to the Seabed Area]. *Pravnik*, 113, No. 5 (1974), 396-415.

8366 **Kopal, Vladimir.** "Vyvoj Pravni Upravy Pristupu Vnitrozemskych Statu k Mori" [The Development of the Legal Regulation Concerning the Access of Land-Locked Countries to the Sea]. *Pravnik*, 113, No. 4 (1974), 268-299.

8367 **Kopal, Vladimir.** "Zakladni Rysy a Problemy Nove Kodifikace Mezinarodniho Prava Morskeho z Hlediska Prav a Zajmu Vnitrozemskych a Zemepisne Znevyhodnenych Stat" [Main Features and Problems of the New Codification of the Law of the Sea, with Particular Reference to the Rights and Interests of Land-Locked and Geographically Disadvantaged States]. *Pravnik*, 120, No. 3 (1981), 217-233.

8368 **Kramarov, E.** "Problems in the Transit Trade of Land-Locked Developing Countries." *Foreign Trade*, 1 (1971), 48-50.

8369 **Kwiatkowska-Czechowska, Barbara.** "Tranzyt Panstw Srodladowych Przez Obce Terytoria w Swietle Konwencji Nowojorskiej z 1965 Roku" [Transit of Land-Locked States through Foreign Territories in the Light of the New York Convention of 1965]. *Technika i Gospodarka Morska*, 4 (1971), 164-166.

8370 **Lackman, Conway Lee.** "Problems of Access for Land-Locked Nations." *National Development/Modern Government*, 17, No. 9 (November-December, 1976), 74-82.

8371 "Land-Lockeds and GD's Protest." *Neptune* (published by NGO's at UNCLOS III), 6 (May 7, 1975), 1, 12.

8372 **Latimer, Paul.** "The Law of the Sea: Problems Arising in the Analysis of the Rights of Land-Locked States." *International Relations*, 5, No. 6 (November, 1977), 180-197.

8373 **Linarres Fleytas, Antonio.** "Los Principios y Normas Generales que Regulan el Ejercicio de los Derechos de Transito de las Naciones Carentes de Litoral" [The Principles and General Norms that Regulate the Exercise of the Transit Rights of the Nations Lacking Seacoasts]. In *Estudios de Derecho Internacional Maritimo (Homenaje al Profesor Jose Luis de Azcarraga)*. Madrid: Sindicato Nacional de la Marina Mercante, 1968, 105-117.

8374 **Makil, R.** "Transit Rights of Land-Locked Countries; An Appraisal of International Conventions." *Journal of World Trade Law*, 4, No. 1 (January-February, 1970), 35-51.

8375 **Makil, Balram.** "Land-Locked Countries and Their Rights of Transit." *Nyayadoot*, 8, No. 22 (April-May, 1977), 1-16.

8376 **Mazilu, Dumitru.** "Statele fara Litoral si Dezavanttajate Geografic" [Land-Locked and Geographically Disadvantaged States]. Chapter 5 in his *Dreptul Mariii; Tendinte si Orientari Contemporane*. Bucharest: Editura Acaademici Republicii Socialiste Romania, 1980, 89-98. Summary in English, 263-265.

8377 **McKinnell, Robert T.** "Land-Locked Countries; A Test for UNCTAD III?" *Journal of World Trade Law*, 6, No. 2 (March-April, 1972), 227-236.

8378 **McKinnell, Robert T.** "Land-Locked Countries and the United Nations Conference on Trade and Development (UNCTAD)." In Zdenek Cervenka, *Land-Locked Countries of Africa*. Uppsala: The Scandinavian Institute of African Studies, 1973, 300-315.

8379 **Medeiros Querejazu, Gustavo.** "Los Paises sin Litoral en la Conferencia de Caracas" [The Land-Locked Countries at the Caracas Conference]. In *Derecho del Mar; Una Vision Latino-americana* by Jorge A. Vargas and Edmundo Vargas Carreno. Mexico: Editorial Jus, 1976, 119-144.

8380 **Meira Matos, Aderbal.** "Paises sem Litoral" [Land-Locked Countries]. *Arquivos do Ministerio da Justica*, 32, No. 134 (April-June, 1975), 46-51.

8381 **Menzel, Eberhard.** "Der Festlandsockel der Bunderepublik Deutschland und das Urteil des Internationalen Gerichtshofs vom 20.Februar 1969." *Jahrbuch fur Internationales Recht*, 14 (1969), 13-100.

8382 **Miaja de la Meula, Adolfo.** "El Derecho al Comercio Maritimo de los Estados sin Litoral" [The Right to Maritime Commerce of Land-Locked States]. In *Estudios de Derecho Internacional Maritimo (Homenaje al Profesor Jose Luis de Azcarraga)*. Madrid: Sindicato Nacional de la Marina Mercante, 1968, 119-141.

8383 **Milic, Milenko.** "Access of Land-Locked States to and from the Sea." *Case Western Reserve Journal of International Law*, 13, No. 3 (Summer, 1981), 501-516.

8384 **Milic, Milenko.** "Pristup Moru Neobalnih Drzava" [Access to the Sea by Land-Locked Countries]. *Pomorskog Zbornika*, 24, No. 1 (January, 1963), 321-358.

8385 **Mirvahabi, Farin.** "The Rights of the Landlocked and Geographically Disadvantaged States in Exploitation of Marine Fisheries." *Netherlands International Law Review*, 26, No. 2 (1979), 130–162.

8386 **Monnier, Jean.** "Desenclavement et Transit dans le Droit International des Transports" [Reducing the Effects of Enclosure through Transit in the International Law of Transport]. In Societe Francaise pour le Droit International, *Aspecats Actuels du Droit International des Transports*. Paris: Editions A. Pedone, 1981, 70–82.

8387 **Morinigo, Victor.** "El Problema de los Paises sin Litoral" [The Problem of the Land-Locked Countries]. In *Integracion Latinoamericana*. Asuncion: Asociacion Nacional Republicana (Partido Colorado), 1965.

8388 **Moya Dominguez, Maria Teresa.** "Estatuto de los Paises sin Litoral Maritimo" [Statute of the Land-Locked Countries]. *Arquivos do Ministerio da Justica*, 32, No. 134 (April–June, 1975), 22–33.

8389 **Naghmi, Shafqat Hussain.** "Exclusive Economic Zone and the Land-Locked States." *Pakistan Horizon*, 33, Nos. 1 and 2 (1st and 2nd Quarters, 1980), 37–48.

8390 **Okolie, Charles Chukwuma.** "The Need for Multilateral Transfer of Resources and Technolgoy to Landlocked Developing Countries." Chapter 10 in his *Legal Aspects of the International Transfer of Technology to Developing Countries*. New York: Praeger, 1975, 164–179.

8391 **Paat, Edgardo.** "Land-Locked and Geographically Disadvantaged States." *Philippine Seas* (published by the Secretariat to the Cabinet Committee on the Law of the Sea, Manila), 1, No. 1 (1982), 23–27.

8392 **Palazzoli,Claude.** "De Quelques Developpements Recents du Droit des Gens en Matiere d'Acces a la Mer des Pays Depourvus de Littoral" [On Some Recent Developments of the Law of Nations on the Subject of Access to the Sea of Land-Locked Countries]. *Revue Generale de Droit International Public*, 70, No. 3 (July-September, 1966), 667–735.

8393 **Pearcy, G. Etzel.** "Geographical Aspects of the Law of the Sea." *Annals of the Association of American Geographers*, 49, No. 1 (March, 1959), 1–23.

8394 **Pechota, Vratislav.** "Konference Vnitrozemskych Statu o Uprave Jejich Prava na Pristup k Mori" [The Conference of Land-Locked States on the Codification of Their Rights Regarding Free Access to the Sea]. *Casopis pro Mezinarodni Pravo*, 2, No. 4 (1958), 297–302.

8395 **Pechota, Vratislav.** "Pravni rezim morskeho dna se Zvalastnim Zretelem na Prava Vnitrozemskych Statu" [The Legal Regime of the Seabed with a Particular Emphasis on Ensuring the Rights of Land-Locked States]. *Casopis pro Mezinarodni Pravo*, 3, No. 2 (1969), 188–200.

8396 **Pounds, Norman J.G.** "A Free and Secure Access to the Sea." *Annals of the Association of American Geographers*, 49, No. 3 (September, 1959), 256–268.

8397 **Prandler, Arpad.** "Promotion of the Interests of Land-Locked States in the New Law of the Sea.' In *Questions of International Law*, Vol. 2, Gyorgy Haraszti, ed. Budapest: Publishing House of the Hungarian Academy of Sciences, 1980; and Alphen aan den Rijn: Sijthoff and Noordhoff, 1981, 147–169.

8398 **Pulvenis, Jean-Francois.** "La Notion d'Etat Geographiquement Desavaantage et le Nouveau droit de la Mer" [The Notion of the Geographically Disadvantaged State and the New Law of the Sea]. *Annuaire Francais de Droit International*, 22 (1976), 678–719.

8399 **Pusar, Alfred B.** "Technical Co-operation Activities in Transit-Transport for Developing Land-Locked Countries." Paper read at the 9th International Road Federation World Meeting, Stockholm, June, 1981. *Road Planning and Prioriting*, 3–TS2, 299–311.

8400 **Reintanz, Gerhard.** "Konvention uber den Transithandel der Binnenstaaten von 1965" [The Convention on the Transit Trade of Land-Locked States of 1965]. *Seeverkehr*, 5, No. 12 (December, 1965), 727–728.

8401 **Reitsman, Hendrik-Jan A.** "Boundaries as Barriers—The Predicament of Land-Locked Countries." In *Pluralism and Political Geography; People, Territory and State*, Nurit Kliot and Stanley Waterman, eds. (Papers given at the Seminar on Contemporary Trends in Political Geography, University of Haifa, Israel, January, 1982). New York: St. Martin's Press, 1983, 259–269.

8402 **Rubin, Alfred P.** "Report of the Committee on Land-locked States." *Proceedings and Committee Reports of the American Branch of the International Law Association*, 1977–78, 89–91. Dissent by John H.E. Fried, 91.

8403 **Sambrailo, Branko.** "Continental Countries Demand Sea Outlet." *Review of International Affairs* (Belgrade), 9, No. 193 (April 16, 1958), 7–8. The German version of this article appears in *Internationale Politik*, 9, No. 193 (April 16, 1958) 7–8.

8404 Sambrailo, Branko. "Land–Locked Countries and Free Access to the Sea." *Annuaire de l'Association des Auditeurs et Anciens Auditeurs de l'Academie de Droit International de la Haye*, 29, No. 1 (1959), 28–37.

8405 Saveliev, A.A. "O Svobodnom Dostupe k Morya Gosudarstu, ne Imeyashih Morskogo Poberezhiya" [Free Access to the Sea of States without Seacoast]. In *Ocherki Mezhdunarodnog Morskogo Prava* [Essays on the International Law of the Sea], by Vladimir M. Koretsky and Grigory Tunkin. Moscow: Juridicheskaya Literatura, 1962, 291–303.

8406 Schweisfurth, Hans–Theodor. "Exklaven– und Binnenstaaten-transitrechte" [Transit Rights of Exclaves and Land–Locked States]. *Internationales Recht und Diplomatie*, 1, No. 1 (1970), 53–62.

8407 Shearer, Ivan A. "Land–Locked States" and "Committee on Land-Locked States." In International Law Association *Report of the 57th Conference Held at Madrid* (1976), 541–563.

8408 Shearer, Ivan A. "Second Progress Report of the Committee [on Land-locked States]." Followed by commentaries made during the working session. Internatinal Law Association, *Report of the Fifty-Eighth Conference held at Manila, 1978*, 450–460.

8409 Shearer, Ivan A. "Third Progess Report of the Committee; The Concept of Equity in Relation to Land-locked States." Followed by commentaries made during the working session. Internatinal Law Association, *Report of the Fifty-Ninth Conference held at Belgrade, 1980*, 312–326.

8410 Sibert, Marcel. "Les Etats sans Littoral et la Liberte des Mers" [Land-Locked States and the Freedom of the Seas]. In *Traite de Droit International Public; Le Droit de la Paix*. 1 (1951), 660–665.

8411 Simonnet, Maurice–Rene. "Libre Acces a la Mer des Etats sans Littoral" [Free Access to the Sea of Land-Locked States]. In *La Convention sur la Haute Mer*. Paris: Librairie Generale de Droit et de Jurisprudence, 1966, 38–48.

8412 Sinjela, Andrew Mpazi. "Freedom of Transit and the Right of Access for Land-Locked States: The Evolution of Principle and Law." *Georgia Journal of International and Comparative Law*, 12, Issue 1 (1982), 31–52.

8413 Straburzynska, Barbara. "Problem Tranzytu przez Terytoria Panstw Nadbrzeznych w Swietle III Konferencji Prawa Morza" [The Problem of Transit through Coastal State Territory in Light of the Third Conference on the Law of the Sea]. *Aktualne Problemy Miedzynarodowego Prawa Morza*, 1 (1975), 127–142.

8414 Sukijasovic, Miodrag. "Konferencija UN o Trazitnoj Trgovini Zemalja bez Morske Obale" [UN Conference on Transit Trade of Land-Locked Countries]. *Medunarodno Pravo*, (1965), 1087–1117.

8415 Symonides, Janusz. "Geographically Disadvantaged States and the New Law of the Sea." *Polish Yearbook of International Law*, 8 (1976), 55–73.

8416 Symonides, Janusz. "Prawo Tranzytu Krajo bez Dostepu do Morza" [Transit Rights of Land-Locked States]. In *Actualne Problemy Prawa Morza* (Gdansk) 1976, 271–273.

8417 Tabibi, Abdul Hakim. "The Right of Free Access to and from the Sea for Land-Lockedd States, as well as Their Right to Exploitation of Living and Non-living Resources of the Sea." *Osterreichische Zeitschrift fur Offentliches Recht und Volkerrecht*, 29, No. 1–2 (1978), 75–79.

8418 Tabibi, Abdul Hakim. "The Right of Free Access to and from the Sea for Land-Locked States." In Asian-African Legal Consultataive Committee, *Essays on International Law*. New Delhi: Secretariat of the Committee, 1976, 97–100.

8419 Tabibi, Abdul Hakim. "The Right of Free Access to the Sea for Countries without Sea-Coast." *Casopis pro Mezinarodni Pravo*, 5, No. 4 (1961), 310–321.

8420 Tabibi, Abdul Hakim. "The Right of Land-Locked Countries to Free Access to the Sea." *Osterreichische Zeitschrift fur Offentliches Recht*, 23 (1972), 117–146.

8421 Tabibi, Abdul Hakim. "The Voice of Land–Locked Countries: 117 Nations Sign Law of Sea Treaty." *Firmest Bond*, 9, No. 1 (Spring, 1983), 18–25.

8422 Tabibi, Abdul Hakim. "Working Paper on Right of Transit for Land-locked Countries." Asian-African Legal Consultative Committee, *Report of the 13th Session Held in Lagos from January 18 to 25, 1972*. New Delhi, 1973, 203–262.

8423 Tarski, Ignacy; Teichmanowa E.; and Patryn, Emil. "Tranzyt Miedzynarodowy" [International Transit]. In *Transport i Spedycja w Handlu Zagranicznym*. Warsaw: Panstwowe Wydawnictwo Ekonomiczne, 1968, 133–143.

8424 Thierry, Hubert. "Les Etats Prives de Littoral Maritime" [The States without Seacoast]. *Revue Generale de Droit International Public*, 62, No. 4 (October-December, 1958), 610–617.

8425 "The Transit Transport Problems of Land-Locked Developing Countries." *Transport Newsletter*, 4, No. 1 (March, 1982), whole number. Published semi-annually by the United Nations Department of International Economic and Social Affairs, Office for Programme Planning and Coordination.

8426 Upadhyaya, **Lakshman Kumar**. "A Review of Doctrinal Foundation of the Right of Free Access to the Sea for Land-Locked Countries." *Nepal Law Review*, 3, No. 2 (October, 1979), 25–36.

8427 **Valladao (Valadao), Haroldo**. "'Status' dos Paises sem Litoral Maritimo" ["Status" of the Land-Locked Countries]. *Arquivos do Ministerio de Justica*, 32, No. 134 (April-June, 1975), 6–10. A slightly longer version of this paper appears in *Revista da Faculdade de Direito*, 70 (1975), 245–251. Another slight variation appears in *Scientia Iuridica*, 25, No. 138–139 (January-April, 1976), 30–34.

8428 **Venkatesan, S.** "UNCTAD and the Least Developed and Land-Locked Countries." *Foreign Trade Review*, 7, No. 3 (October-December, 1972), 280–289.

8429 **Vieira, Manuel A.** "Status Juridico de los Paises sin Litoral Maritimo" [Juridical Status of Countries without a Seacoast]. *Arquivos do Ministerio da Justica* 32, No. 134 (April-June, 1975), 11–21.

8430 **Vigarie, Andre.** "Les Rivages du Point du Jour" [The Seacoasts at Dawning]. In *Ports de Commerce et Vie Littorale*. Paris: Hachette, 1979, 331–348.

8431 **Villacres Moscoso, Jorge W.** "El Nuevo Derecho Economico Internacional Debe Otorgar un Tratamiento Mas Favorable a los Estados Enclaustrados" [The New International Economic Order Ought to Grant More Favorable Treatment to the Enclosed States]. *Revista de Derecho Internacional y Ciencias Diplomaticas*, 22–24, Nos. 43–45 (1973–76), 131–142.

8432 **Villacres Moscoso, Jorge W.** "El Reconocimiento de los Derechos de los Estados sin Litoral en la Convencion Internacional sobre el Mar" [Recognition of the Land-Locked States in the International Convention on the Sea]. *Revista de la Universidad de Guayaqui*, 83–1 (51) (January-March, 1983), 275–281.

8433 **Villacres Moscoso, Jorge W.** "Los Estados Enclaustrados." *Comparative Juridical Review*, 17 (1980), 151–168; and "Landlocked States." *Comparative Juridical Review*, 18 (1980), 169–184.

8434 **Wani, Ibrahim J.** "An Evaluation of the Convention on the Law of the Sea from the Perspective of the Land-Locked States." *Virginia Journal of International Law*, 22, No. 4 (Summer, 1982), 627–665.

8435 **Weisberg, Robert I.** "Developments in the Ocean Rights of Land-Locked Nations." In *Current Aspects of Sea Law*, Seymour W. Wurfel, ed. Chapel Hill: University of North Carolina Sea Grant Publication UNC-SG-74-03, March 1974, 18–27.

8436 **Winterbach, Peter.** "The Great Dust Road." *Horizon*, 7, No. 12 (December, 1965), 10–15.

8437 **Wolf, Karl.** "The Biggest Poker Game Ever Played." *Ceres*, 9, No. 6 (November-December, 1976), 27–29.

8438 **Zourek, Jaroslav.** "Kodifikace Pravidel Tykajicich se Pravniho Rezimu More" [The Codification of Rules Regarding the Legal Regime of the Sea]. *Casopis pro Mezinarodni Pravo*, 2, No. 4 (1958), 261–283.

POLITICAL GEOGRAPHY OF REGIONS

AFRICA

Books

8439 *Appraisal of a Third Highway Project; Central African Empire.* Report No. 1246–CA (August 21, 1978). Restricted. Bengui: Central African Republic, 1978.

8440 **Arnold, Guy.** *Sanctions Against Rhodesia 1965 to 1972.* London: The Africa Bureau, May, 1972.

8441 **Arnold, Guy,** and **Weiss, Ruth.** *Strategic Highways of Africa.* London: Julian Friedmann, Publishers, 1977.

8442 **Bailey, Martin.** *Freedom Railway: China and the Tanzania-Zambia Link.* London: Rex Collings, 1976.

8443 **Ballance, Frank C.** *Zambia and the East African Community.* Syracuse University, The Program of Eastern African Studies, Eastern African Studies I, July, 1971.

8444 **Belgium.** *Mission d'Etude des Nouvelles Liaisons de Surface Internationales dans la Sous-Region D'Afrique Centrale,* Brussels: Office de la Cooperation au Developpement,1966.

8445 **Bertlin and Partners.** Consulting Engineers for the IBRD and the East African Harbours Corporation. *Dar es Salaam Port Development Study.* Surrey, England: Redhill, 1975.

8446 **Bertlin and Partners.** Consulting Engineers for the United Republic of Tanzania, Tanzania harbours Authority. *Reaview of Dar es Salaam Port Development Studies.* Surrey, England: Redhill, 1979.

8447 **Bertlin and Partners.** For the Commonwealth Fund for Technical Cooperation and the Government of Botswana. *Prefeasibility Study on Trans-Kalahari Transport Route.* Surrey, England: Redhill, November, 1979.

8448 **Best, Alan C.G.** *The Swaziland Railway; A Study in Politico–Economic Geography.* East Lansing: African Studies Center, Michigan State University, 1966.

8449 **Bocker, Hans–Jurgen.** *Air Transport Potential and Problems of Developing Countries with Special Reference to the Republic of Botswana.* Doctor of Commerce Dissertation, University of South Africa (Pretoria), 1978.

8450 **Bureau Central d'Etudes pour les Equipements d'Outre–mer (BCEOM) for the Government of the Central African Republic.** *4eme Project Routier; Analyse Prospective des Options en Matiere de Couloirs de Transport vers la Mer* [Fourth Highway Project; Prospective Analysis of the Options Regarding Transport Cororidors to the Sea]. Bangui: Central African Republic, March, 1983.

8451 **Burgess, Julian.** *Interdependence in Southern Africa; Trade and Transport Links to South, Central and East Africa.* EIU Special Report 32. London: Economist Intelligence Unit, July, 1976.

8452 **Cabanius, Philippe.** *Diagnostic sur la Situation des Transports en Transit de la Haute–Volta, du Mali et du Niger.* Upper Volta: Government, 1980.

8453 **CANAC Consultants Ltd.** For Canadian International Development Agency (CIDA). *Report on a Railroad Study Plan for Botswana.* Montreal: Canadian IDA, August, 1975.

8454 **Canadian National Railways.** International Consulting Division for Canadian International Development Agency (CIDA). *Botswana Rail Transportation.* Montreal: Canadian IDA, 1970.

8455 **CATRAM** for the Government of Benin, Commission ad hoc Chargee du Suivi de l'Extension du Port de Cotonou. *Etude du Transit International des Marchandises au Benin.* Paris: Rapport Provisoire, October, 1983–March, 1984.

8456 **Cervenka, Zdenek,** ed. *Land-Locked Countries of Africa.* Uppsala: The Scandinavian Institute of African Studies, 1973.

8457 **Church, R.J. Harrison.** *The Evolution of Railways in French and British West Africa.* Paper read to the 16th International Geographical Congress, Lisbon, 1949. Published in Volume 4 of the *Proceedings* of the Congress, Lisbon: Centro Tip. Colonial, 1952, 95–114.

8458 **Croxton, Anthony H.** *Railways of Zimbabwe; The Story of the Beira, Mashonaland and Rhodesia Railways.* Newton Abbott, Devon and Noroth Pomfret, Vermont: David and Charles, 1982.

8459 **Cukwurah, A. Oye.** *The Importance of Nigeria as a Transit State.* Madrid: Working paper prepared for the biennial meeting of the International Law Association, August, 1976.

8460 **Cukwurah, A. Oye.** *Nigeria's Transit Relations with Land-Locked Chad and Niger.* Lagos: Paper read at the National Conference on Nigeria's Internatiotnal Boundaries organized by the Nigerian Institute of International Affairs, April, 1982.

8461 **Curran, James C.** *Communist China in Black Africa: The Tanzam Railay 1965-1970.* Carlisle Barracks, Pennsylvania: U.S. Army War Railway College, April 26, 1971.

8462 **Cutler, Walter L.** *The Tazara Railroad Project: Progress and Prospects.* Washington, D.C.: Department of State, 16th Session, Senior Seminar in Foreign Policy, 1973–74. Research Paper FAR 19868.

8463 **Dale, Richard.** *Botswana and Its Southern Neighbor: The Patterns of Linkage and the Options in Statecraft.* Papers in International Studies, African Series No. 6. Athens: Ohio University Center for International Studies, Africa Program, 1970.

8464 **Darnault, Paul.** *Avant-Projet du Chemin de Fer Douala-Tchad* [Preliminary Study of the Douala-Chad Railroad]. Rapport d'ensemble. Paris: Societe d'Etudes du Chemin de Fer Douala-Tchad, 1969.

8465 **Day, John R.** *Railways of South Africa.* London: Arthur Barker Ltd.; New York: Fernhill; Toronto: McClelland, 1963.

8466 **Dembele, Issaga.** *Relations Economiques des Pays sans Access Cotier avec les Pays de la Cote.* Ibadan: IDEP/ET/CS/2497/27, Seminar on Regionalization of Development Planning, 1973.

8467 **Department of Technical Cooperation for Development.** *Amenagement d'une Partie de la Riviere Oubangui. Rapport de Mission en Republique Centrafricaine, en Republique Populaire du Congo et en Republique du Zaire du 18 Octobre au 28 Novembre 1982.* [Planning of a Section of the Ubangi River]. Quoc-Lan Nguyen. Project RAF/82/054, December, 1982. Restricted.

8468 **Dialli, Mamadou Hamma.** *Probleme de Transport et Communication, Haute Volta.* Ibadan: IDEP/ET/CS/2497/22, Seminar on Regionalization of Development Planning, April 16-May 4, 1973.

8469 **Diarra, Adama Moussa.** *Transport et Developpement Economique du Mali: Les Niveaux d'Enclavement: National, Regional, Local.* Paris: Dissertation in Geography, 3e Cycle, Paris I, 1977.

8470 **Diarra, Fatoumata Agnes.** *Rapport du Seminaire sur les Strategies de Development Applicables aux Pays sans Access Cotier.* Ibadan: IDEP/ET/CS/2497/32, Seminar on Regionalization of Development Planning, April 16-May 4, 1973.

8471 *Dry Ports; Lesotho.* Blantyre, November, 1983. UNCTAD/LDC/70. February 29, 1984.

8472 *Dry Ports Pre-feasibility Study for Zambia* by Ronobir Roy. Blantyre, August, 1983. UNCTAD/LDC/68. March 1, 1984.

8473 *Dry Ports Report: Malawi.* Blantyre, September, 1983. UNCTAD/LDC/63. December 1, 1983.

8474 *Dry Ports Report: Swaziland.* Blantyre, November, 1983. UNCTAD/LDC/71. March 1, 1984.

8475 **East African Railways and Harbours.** *Report on an Engineering Survey of a Rail Link between the East African and Rhodesian Railway Systems.* Nairobi: East African Railways and Harbours, June, 1952.

8476 **Evaluation Technologies,** Inc. for USAID. *A Sahel Transportation Survey; A Regional Profile,* by Thomas Philippi. Contract AID-otr-C-1553. Arlington, Virginia, April, 1979.

8477 **Festinger, Georges.** *Les Relations Commercialesentre la Cote d'Ivoire, le Dahomey, la Haute Volta, le Niger, le Nigeria, le Tongo, et le Ghana.* Ibadan: IDEP/ET/CS/2479/3, Seminar on Regionalization of Development Planning, June, 1973.

8478 *First Interim Technical Report Covering Malawi, Mozambique, Zambia, Zimbabwe.* Blantyre: February 28, 1981.

8479 **Fischer, Wolfgang.** *Die Entwicklungsbedingungen Ugandas; Ein Beispiel fur die Probleme Afrikanischer Binnenstaaten* [Conditions of Development in Uganda; An Example for the Problems of African Land-Locked States]. Munich: Weltforum Verlag, 1969.

8480 **Gautier, Olivier.** *Etude sur l'Amenagement du Fleuve Niger* [Study of the Development of the Niger River]. Paris: Secretariat d'Etat aux Affaires Etrangeres, April, 1967.

8481 **Gelineau, Louis.** *Note Methodologique Relative a l'Amelioration du Syteme International de Transport au Sahel* [Methodological Note Relative to the Improvement of the International Transport System in the Sahel]. S.1. Club des amis du sahal, September 30, 1976.

8482 **Glab, John Edward.** *Transportation's Role in Development of Southern Africa.* Washington, D.C.: American University, Ph.D., 1970.

8483 **Gyamfi-Fenteng, Lord Justice.** *Inter-West African Linkages: A Spatio-Temporal Study of the Patterns and Implications of Inter-West African Commodity Flows, 1961-1970.* Kent, Ohio: Kent State University, Ph.D., 1974.

8484 **Haefele, Edwin T., and Steinberg, Eleanor B.** *Government Controls on Transport; An African Case.* Washington, D.C.: The Brookings Institute, 1965.

8485 **Hall, Richard, and Peyman, Hugh.** *The Great Uhuru Railway: China's Showpiece in Africa.* London: Gollancz, 1976.

8486 **Harrison, Eugene.** *Reorientation of Transportation Patterns from Zambia after the Rhodesian Declaration of Independence.* New York City: Columbia University, Ph.D., 1972.

8487 **Hartland-Thunberg, Penelope.** *Botswana: An African Growth Economy.* Boulder, Colorado: Westview Press, 1978.

8488 **Hazlewood, Arthur.** *Rail and Road in East Africa: Transport Co-ordination in Under-developed Countries.* Oxford: Basil Blackwell, 1964.

8489 **Heraty, Margaret and Poutet, Jacques.** *Le Traffic Import-Export du Burundi; le Transport Aerien Solution Possible dans le Cadre des Mesures pour le Desenclavement du Pays* [Import-Export Traffic of Burundi; Air Transport Possible Solution within the Framework of Measures for the Reduction of the Land-lockedness of the Country]. Paris: Ministry of Foreign Affairs, 1979.

8490 **Higgott, Richard A.** *Colonial Origins and Environmental Influences on the Foreign Relations of a West African Land-Locked State: The Case of Niger.* Logan, Utah: Brigham Young University, Ph.D., 1979.

8491 **Hill, M.F.** *Permanent Way: The Story of the Kenya and Uganda Railway.* Nairobi: East African Railways and Harbours, 1950.

8492 **Hoyle, Brian Stewart.** *Seaports and Development; The Experience of Kenya and Tanzania.* New York: Gordon and Breach, 1983.

8493 **Hoyle, Brian Stewart.** *The Seaports of East Africa; A Geographical Study.* Nairobi: East African Publishing House, 1967.

8494 **Hoyle, Brian Stewart, and Hilling, David,** eds. *Seaports and Development in Tropical Africa.* London: Macmillan, 1970.

8495 **Hromic, Muhammed.** *Transport Planning Advisor Zambia: Project Findings and Recommendations.* New York: UNDP, Project ZAM/72/023/A/01/01, 1976.

8496 **Jardim, Jorge.** *Rodesia--O Escandalo das Sancoes.* Lisbon, 1978. Also publishe d in English version titled *Sanctions Double-cross; Oil to Rhodesia.* Lisbon, 1978. Reprinted in English, Bulwayo Books of Rhodesia, 1979.

8497 **Jeske, Joachim.** *Verkehrsgeographische Strukturwandlungen im Sudlichen Afrika 1975-1980* [Structural Changes in the Transport Geography of Southern Africa 1975-1980]. Hamburg: Institut fur Afrika-Kunde, 1981.

8498 **Katzenellenbogen, Simon E.** *Railways and the Copper Mines of Katanga.* Oxford: Oxford University Press, 1973.

8499 **King, James Wilhelmsen.** *Nile Transport in Uganda.* Evanston, Illinois: Northwestern University, Ph.D., 1964.

8500 **Kline, Hibberd V.B., Jr.** *Southern Interior Africa and the Sea.* Paper read to the annual meeting of the Association of American Geographers, Cleveland, March-April, 1953.

8501 Knappen-Tippets-Abbett Engineering Co. *Alternative Port and Rail Facilities in Mozambique and Southern Rhodesia--A Report to the Government of Portugal and the Government of Southern Rhodesia.* New York: Knappen-Tippets-Abbett Engineering Co., January, 1952.

8502 **Kobe, Susumu.** *Transport Problems in West Africa.* Paris: OECD Development Centre, 1967.

8503 **Lamacz, Tadeusz.** *Handel Wewnatrzafrykanski* [Intra-African Trade]. Warsaw: African Institute of Warsaw University, 1976.

8504 *L'Autorite de Developpement Integre de la Region du Liptako-Gourma; Ses Structures, Ses Objectifs* [The Integrated Development Authority of the Liptako-Gourma Region; Its Structure, Its Objectives]. Ouagadougou: Government of Burkina, January, 1979.

8505 *Le Developpement du Fret Aerien au Rwanda dans le Cadre des Mesures pour le Descenclavement du Pays* [Development of Air Freight of Rwanda within the Framework of Measures for the Reduction of the Land-Lockedness of the Country] by Jaacques Poutet and Robert Desbiens, August, 1979.

8506 **Lotz, W.P.N.** *Geskiedkundige Ontwikkeling van Internasionale Spoorvervoer in Suider-Afrika* [Historical Development of International Railroads in Southern Africa]. Pretoria: Communications of the Africa Institute No. 25, 1974.

8507 **Louis Berger International.** For Comite de la Liaison Transsaharienne. *Transsharan Road Project Description; Mali Report.* Paris: Louis Berger International, April, 1978.

8508 **Louis Berger International.** For Comite de la Liaison Transsaharienne. *Transsaharan Road Project Description; Niger Report.* Paris: Louis Berger International, April, 1978.

8509 **Louis Berger International.** For USAID. *Central African Transport; Chad, Cameroons, CAR, Gabon, Congo and Northeastern Nigeria.* Paris: Louis Berger International, 1972.

8510 **Louis Berger International.** For USAID. *Coastal Transport Links for Zambia. An Examination of Route Options through Northern Mozamabique and Associated Project Development* by Philip W. Moeller. Contract AID/afr-C-1953. Washington, D.C.: USAID, January, 1980.

8511 **Louis Berger International.** For USAID. *Economic and Technical Feasibility Study, Bukombe-Isaka Road Link, Tanzania.* Contract AID/OTR-C-1788, Work Order No. 3. Washington, D.C.: USAID, April, 1981.

8512 **Louis Berger International.** For USAID. *Malawi; Commercial Transport Project* by Philip W. Moeller. Washington, D.C.: USAID, (612-0218), 1984.

8513 **Louis Berger International,** and USAID Sahel Development Project International for the Transport and Infrastructure Working Group of the Club des Amis du Sahel. *Inventory of Data on the Transport Infrastructure of the Sahel* by Peter Cook. Washington, D.C.: USAID, January, 1977.

8514 **Louis Berger International.** For USAID. *Southern Africa Regional Transportation Strategy Paper.* Washington, D.C.: USAID, February 20, 1985.

8515 **Louis Berger International.** For USAID. *Southern Africa Transportation Program Planning Study* by Rogers S. Cannel and William R. Thomas, 3rd. Contract No. AID/2fr-C-1132. Washington, D.C.: USAID, September, 1976.

8516 **Louis Berger International.** For USAID. *Transport Corridors in Southern AFrica. Considerations Relative to Regional Rail Linkage, Containerization, Logistics/Handling and Unitary Commodity Analysis* by Philip W. Moeller. Contract OTR-C-1788. Washington, D.C.: USAID, February, 1982.

8517 **Louis Berger International.** For USAID. *Transport Sector Assessment, Malawi* by Philip W. Moeller. Washington, D.C.: USAID,September, 1983.

8518 **Louis Berger International.** For USAID. *Transportation and Telecommunications in the Southern Africa Regions: An Assistance Strategy* by Philip W. Moeller. Contract AID/afr-C-1132. Washington, D.C.: USAID, November, 1978.

8519 **Louis Berger International.** For The World Bank. *Chad Transport Sector Memorandum* by Harold Kurzman. New York: World Bank, September, 1976.

8520 **Lyon Associates, Inc.** (Maryland, USA) for USAID. *Economic and Preliminary Engineering Design Studies for the Fada N'Gourma-Niamey Highway Link in the Republics of Upper Volta and Niger.* Contract No. REDSO/WA-C-74-5. Maryland: Lyon Associates, 1974.

8521 **Maasdorp, Gavin Grant.** *Transport and Development in Small Peripheral Countries: A Case Study of Swaziland.* Durban: University of Natal, Ph.D., 1974.

8522 **Maasdorp, Gavin Grant.** *Transport Policies and Economic Development in Southern Africa; A Comparative Study in Eight Countries.* Durban: Economic Research Unit, University of Natal, 1984.

8523 **Maasdorp, Gavin Grant,** et al., for the Government of the Kingdom of Swaziland. *Transportation in Swaziland.* Durban: Department of Economics, University of Natal, 1971.

8524 **Makalou, Oumar.** *Les Relations Economiques des Pays sans Access Cotier avec l'Economie Mondiale.* Ibadan: IDEP/ET/CS/2497/20, Seminar on Regionalization of Development Planning, 1973.

8525 **Mali, Ministere du Plan.** *Strategies de Development pour les Pays de l'Interieur.* Ibadan: IDEP/ET/CS/2497/5. Seminar on Regionalization of Development Planning, 1973.

8526 **Mayer, Norman J.,** and **Braida, Richard** L., for USAID and CILSS. *Air Transport Alternatives vs. Surface Transport in the Sahel.* Washington, D.C., USAID, April 1, 1983.

8527 **Mazou-Liamidi, Moussibaou.** *Les Problemes de Developpement des Services Postaux dans les Pays sans Littoral d'Afrique.* Paris: Dissertation in Development Economics, 3e Cycle, Paris X, 1976.

8528 **McKinnell, Robert T.** *Economic Claustrophobia: The Development Problems of Land-Locked States, with Particular Reference to Zambia, Malawi, Rhodesia, Botswana, Lesotho and Swaziland.* Ottawa: Carleton University, 1968.

8529 **Michell, Earl L.,** for United States Department of State. *The Lobito Route; A Survey of the Capacity of the Rail Route between Zambia and the Port Lobito.* Washington, D.C.: U.S. Department of State, February, 1966.

8530 **Mihalya, Louis J.** *Geographic Factors and Socio-Economic Projections of the New Line-of-Rail in Zambia.* Seattle: Paper read to the Annual Meeting of the Association of American Geographers, October, 1974.

8531 **Mkinga, J.O.** *Prospects and Problems of Transit Ports: A Study of the Port of Dar-es-Salaam.* Cardiff: Dissertation for Diploma in Port and Shipping Administration, University of Wales Institute of Science Technology, April, 1981.

8532 **Moeller, Philip W.,** for USAID. *Field Report: An Assessment of Transport Infrastructure Relative to Zambian Coastal Linkage.* Contract AID-611-002-T; Project 698-0135. Lusaka: AID, March, 1980.

8533 **Mtshali, Benedict Vulindela.** *Zambia's Foreign Policy; The Dilemmas of a New State.* New York City: New York University, Ph.D., 1973.

8534 **Munger, Edwin S.** *Geography of Ocean Outlets for the Belgian Congo.* Elizabethville: Institute of Current World Affairs, 1952.

8535 **Mutukwa, Kasuka Simwinji.** *Politics of the Tanzania-Zambia Railway Project: A Study of Tanzania-China-Zambia Relations.* Washington, D.C.: University Press of America, 1979.

8536 **Nock, O.S.** *Railways of Southern Africa.* London: Adam and Charles Black, 1971.

8537 **Norconsult, A.S.,** and **Electrowatt, S.A.** *Amenagement du Basin de la Riviere Kagera; Phase II; Burundi-Rwanda-Republique de la Tanzanie* [Planning of the Kagera River Basin]. Vol. 8, *Transports.* United Nations Development Programme, Project RAF/71/147. April, 1976. Restricted.

8538 **Ntsaba, Seeng C.** *Transit Rights of Land-Locked States in International Law; A Case Study of Lesotho.* Lesotho: National University of Lesotho, LL.B. Dissertation, 1984.

8539 **O'Connor, Anthony M.** *Railways and Development in Uganda.* Nairobi: Oxford University Press, 1965.

8540 *Operational Assistance on the Zambia to Dar es Salaam Transit Corridor; Final Report.* January, 1981. UNCTAD/LDC/TA/1. 1981.

8541 *Organization of Zambia Transit Authority.* Lusaka: Addendum to Report No. 4B. April, 1980.

8542 **Pacific Consultants for USAID.** *Transportation and Telecommunications in the Southern Africa Region* by Allen LeBel and Philip W. Moeller. Annex B to AID Report to the Congress on Development Needs and Opportunities for Cooperation in Southern Africa. Contract afr–C–1424. Washington, D.C.: U.S. Aid, March, 1979.

8543 **Pallier, Ginette.** *Les Problemes de Developpement dans les Pays Interieurs de l'Afrique Occidentale; Contribution a l'Etude du Phenomene d'Enclavement* [The Problems of Development in the Interior Countries of West Africa; Contribution to the Study of the Phenomenon of Land-Lockedness]. Bordeaux: University of Bordeau XXX, Doctoral Dissertation in Geography, November, 1982.

8544 *Partners in Progress: Opening of Swaziland's Railway and Iron Ore Mine.* Johannesburg: Anglo-American Corporation, 1964.

8545 **Peterec, Richard J.** *Dakar and West African Economic Development.* New York: Columbia University Press, 1967.

8546 **Peterec, Richard J.** *The Port of Abidjan: An Important Factor in the Development of the Ivory Coast.* New York: Division of Economic Geography, Columbia University, Technical Report Cu 24–63 Nonr 266 (29) Geography, 1963.

8547 **Pinckney, Annette** for African-American Scholar's Council, Inc., and USAID. *Zimbabwe; Survey of the Transport-Communications Sector.* Subcontract AID/afr–C–1254. Ann Arbor: Center for Research on Economic Development, University of Michigan Occasional Paper No. 12, January, 1977.

8548 **Pirie, Gordon H.** *Aspects of the Political-Economy of Railways in Southern Africa.* Johannesburg: Department of Geography and Environmental Studies, University of the Witwatersrand, Environmental Studies Occasional Paper No. 24, 1982.

8549 *A Preliminary Assessment of the Problems and Potential of the Transit Corridors in East-Central Africa by Simon Thomas:* The Central Transit Corridor (*The Lake Victoria Corridor*). UNCTAD/LDC/17. March, 1981; *La Voie du Transit du Nord (Rwanda)* [The Northern Transit Corridor (Rwanda)]. UNCTAD/LDC/22. March, 1981; *La Voie du Transit du Nord* (Le Burundi) [The Northern Transit Corridor (Burundi)]. UNCTAD/LDC/23. March, 1981; *Potentiel Economique du Chemin de Chemin de Fer pour le Burundi* [Economic Potential of Railroads for Burundi]. UNCTAD/LDC/24. March, 1981; *Potentiel Economique du Chemin de Fer pour le Rwanda* [Economic Potential of Railroads for Rwanda]. UNCTAD/LDC/25. March, 1981; *Couts d'Entretien des Routes* [Costs of Highway Maintenance]. UNCTAD/LDC/26. March, 1981; *Documents et Formalites Trafic Zaire-Burundi-Rwanda* [Documents and Formalities: Zaire-Burundi-Rwanda Traffic]. UNCTAD/LDC/28. March, 1981; *Transit Routes for the Province of Kivu (Zaire).* UNCTAD/LDC/29. March, 1981; *Air Transport for Burundi.* UNCTAD/LDC/30. March, 1981; *Recommendations Regarding Axle Load Limites and Estimates of the Costs of and Appropriate Charges for the Passage of Heavy Goods Vehicles Through Kenya, Uganda, Rwanda and Burundi* by J.D. Dent. October, 1983. UNCTAD/LDC/64. Blantyre: December, 1983.

8550 **Prinsloo, Daan S.** *Revolutions and Railways in Southern Africa.* Pretoria: Foreign Affairs Association Study Report No. 9, March, 1978.

8551 *Recommendations on Improving Regulations and Procedures Controlling Road Transit in Kenya, Uganda, Rwanda and Burundi* by Peter J. Boyes. October, 1983. Blantyre: UNCTAD/LDC/65. December 5, 1983.

8552 **Reichman, Shalom.** *Air Transport in West Africa; A Geographical Approach, Vol. II.* Paris: ITA Special Series Publication, 1964. Liverpool: University of Liverpool, Ph.D., 1963/64.

8553 **Rembe, Nasila S.** *Africa and the Law of the Sea.* Alphen aan den Rijn: Sijthoff & Noordhoff, 1980. Passim.

8554 *A Report on the International Transportation Bottlenecks Affecting Rwanda and Burundi.* Report No. 3224–EAF. December, 1980. Restricted.

8555 *Resume du Rapport de la Societe NEDECO* [Summary of the Report of the NEDECO Company (on transport on the River Niger]. Niamey: NEDEO, December 14, 1971.

8556 *The Rhodesia-Zambia Border Closure January-February, 1973.* London: International Defence and Aid Fund, Special Report No. 1, May, 1973.

8557 *Role of Rail in Northern Corridor Transit Traffic* by Peter J. Boyes. October, 1983. Blantyre: UNCTAD/LDC/66. December, 1983.

8558 Sautter, Gilles. *Le Chemin de Fer Bangui-Tchad dans son Contexte Economique Regional* [The Bangui-Tchad Railroad in its Regional Economic Context]. Institute de Geographie Appliquee de l'Universite de Strasbourg; Bangui: Societe Civile d'Etudes du Chemin de Fer de Bangui au Tchad, 1958.

8559 *Second Interim Technical Report.* UNCTAD/LDC/Misc.3. October, 1981.

8560 Sedes (Paris) for Republic of Niger. *Etude de synthese sur les Tranasports au Niger* [Synthesis Study of the Transport of Niger]. Tome I, Rapport, by J. Delorme and Ph. Trocme. Paris: Sedes, July, 1967.

8561 *Selected Working Papers Presented at the Conference on the Special Problems of Land-Locked and Least Developed Countries in Africa Held at the University of Zambia, Lusaka: University of Zambia, 1977.*

8562 SEMA Marketing, Etudes Economiques, Finance (Paris) for Club du Sahel. *A Trans-Sahelian Railway and the Development of the Sahel.* Paris: SEMA Marketing, November, 1977.

8563 Sendler, Gerhard. *Angola und Seine Seehafen* [Angola and Its Seaports]. Hamburg: Deutsches Institut fur Afrika-Forschung, Hamburger Beitrage zur Afrika-Kunde, Vol. 7, 1967.

8564 Shaffer, N. Manfred. *The Competitive Position of the Port of Durban.* Evanston, Illinois: Department of Geography, Northwestern University, 1965.

8565 Shamuyarira, Nathan M. *Self-Reliance and Internal Mobilization of Land-Locked Economies.* No 25.

8566 *Shipping Study.* Report No. 3A. March, 1980.

8567 Sidibe, Mory. *Probleme de Transport et de Communications dans les Pays sans Access Cotier. Ibadan: IDEP/ET/CS/2497/4, Seminar onRegionalization of Development Planning, 1973.*

8568 Simwinga, George K. *The Backwash of Landlockedness: The Zambian Case.* No. 26. Lusaka: University of Zambia, 1973.

8569 *Social and Labour Aspects of Road and Rail Transport in African Land-Locked Countries.* Geneva: International Labour Office, 1984.

8570 *A Special Paper on Some Economic Consequences of Being Land-Locked; Unavoidable Additional Costs to Malawi of Interruptions During 1982 to Her Traditional Transit Routes.* Blantyre, August, 1983. UNCTAD/LDC/72. February 29, 1984.

8571 Stanford Research Institute for the Republics of Zambia and Tanzania and USAID. *Tanzania-Zambia Highway Study.* Contract AID/afr-364. Menlo Park, California: Stanford Research Institute, June, 1966.

8572 Stanford Research Institute for USAID. *Middle Africa Transportation Study (MATS).* Contract AID/afr-503. SRI Project 6594. Menlo Park, California: Stanford Research Institute, July, 1969.

8573 Stuckey, Barbara. *Moyens de Transport et Developpment Africain: les pays sans Access Cotier.* Ibadan: IDEP/ET/CS/2497/3, Seminar on Regionalization of Development Planning, 1973.

8574 Surveys and Research Corporation for the Government of Nysaland and USAID. *National Transportation Plan for Nyasaland.* Contract AID/afe-114. Washington, D.C.: USAID, June, 1964.

8575 Surveys and Research Corporation for the Government of Nysaland and USAID. *Nyasaland Transportation Planning Survey, Draft Report.* Contract AID-afe-114. Washington, D.C.: USAID, December, 1963.

8576 Symonides, Janusz. *Tranzyt w Swietle Prava Miedzynarodowego* [Transit in the Light of International Law]. Poland: University of Torun, 1970.

8577 Tanzania-Zambia. *Zambia-Dar es Salaam Corridor.* UNDP/UNCTAD Project RAF/77/017. Satellite "A".

8578 *Taxation of Trucks in Transit Through the Northern Corridors* by Peter J. Boyes. October, 1983. UNCTAD/LDC/67. February 1, 1984.

8579 Thom, Derrick. *Niger's Landlocked Position: The Problem of Groundnut Evacuation.* Laramie, Wyoming: Paper read at the annual Rocky Mountain Social Science Meeting, April, 1973.

8580 Thomas, Benjamin E. *Transportation and Physical Geography in West Africa.* Los Angeles: Department of Geography, University of California, 1960.

8581 Tostensen, Arne. *Dependence and Collective Self-Reliance in Southern Africa; The Case of the Southern African Development Conference (SADCC0).* Uppsala: The Scandinavian Institute of African Studies, 1982.

8582 *Transit Corridors Analysis: Country Reports—Malawi.* Blantyre: August, 1983. UNCTAD/LDC/61. December 1, 1983.

8583 *Transit Corridors Analysis: Country Reports—Zimbabwe.* Blantyre: Department of Transportation, May, 1983.

8584 *Transit Transport in the Land-Locked Southern African Sub-Region: Draft Report by the Preparatory Assistance Mission.* UNCTAD/ECDC/22. Geneva: UNCTAD, December, 1978.

8585 *Transport and Communications.* Mbabane, Swaziland: Prepared by Southern Africa Transport and Communications Commission for the SADCC Conference, January 31 - February 1, 1985.

8586 Trzakala, T. *Rozwoj transportu w Zambii* [Transport Development in Zambia]. Warsaw: Warsaw University, Master's Thesis, 1975.

8587 Tschakert, Harald. *Verkehrsstrome, Infrastruktur und Kooperation in der Konfliktregion Sudliches Afrika* [Traffic Flow, Infrastructure and Cooperation int he Southern African Conflict Region]. Hamburg: Institut fur Afrika-Kunde, 1977.

8588 UNDP. For the Government of Zambia. *Port Operations and Freight Forwarding. Zambia. Project Findings and Recommendations.* Project ZAM-73-006/1. New York: UNDP, 1975. Restricted.

8589 UNCTAD/LDC/81. *First Inventory of Port Facilities and Administrative Procedures Available to Land-Locked Countries of West and Central Africa in the Countries of Transit.* Summary Report. By Ministerial Conference of West and Central African States, Special Technical Commission for the Study of the Problems of Land-Locked Countries. Geneva: UNCTAD, May, 1981.

8590 United Nations Economic Commission for Africa. African Institute for Economic Development and Planning [IDEP] (Dakar). *Seminaire sur les Strategies de Developpement Applicables aux Pays d'afrique de l'Ouest sans Acces Cotier* [Seminar on the Development Strategies Applicable to the West African Land-Locked Countries], Bamako: Government of Mali, March 5-30, 1973.

8591 United Nations Economic Commission for Africa. *Prospects for the Development of Surface Transport in the Lake Chad Conventional Basin Area* by Ousmane Gueye. New York: UNECF, June, 1977.

8592 United States. Department of State. Agency for International Development. *An Analysis of PL 480 Food Transport and Distribution in Uganda* by Charles A. Hedges. Washington, D.C.: U.S. Department of State, August, 1981.

8593 Universite de Burundi, Faculte des Sciences Economiques et Administratives. *Colloque sur l'Enclavement* du 4 au 12 Apr. 1981. Papers given at this colloquium on land-lockedness:

"L'Approvisionnment du Burundi en Fer a Beton" by Vital Bankuwungka; "L'Approvisionnement du Burundi en Farine de Froment" by Biroli Bineza; "Les Problemes Associes au Transport via DSM–KGM et leurs Solutions Immediates" [The Problems Associated with Transport via Dar–es–Salaam–Kigoma and Their Immediate Solutions] by Louis Hagorinkebe; "Les Importations du Burundi 1969–1979; Evolution Quantitative et Fonctions de Demande" by J. Hunkeler; "L'Approvisionnement du Burundi en Sel" aby Damase Masambiro and Jean Ndenzako; "L'Approvisionnement du Burundi en Pieces de Rechange pour Vehicules" by Titien Muberangabo. Bujumbura: Universite de Burundi, 1981.

8594 University of Arizona, Arid Lands Natural Resources Committee for USAID. *Rapport Final du Project de Planification de Ressources Naturelles pour le Departement de Zinder* (Niger). Appendice 6: Evaluation des Effets Produits par le Bitumage de la Route Trans-Saharienne sur l'Economie de la Region de Zinder [Evaluation of the Effects Produced by the Paving of the Trans-Saharan Highway on the Economy of the Zinder Region] by Mamadou Jibir Abdoua. Contract AID/afr-6-1447. Tuscon: University of Arizona, April, 1979.

8595 UN/OTC–UNDP for the Government of Zambia. *Economic/Statistical Adviser to Contingency Planning Secretariat, Final Report.* Lusaka: Government of Zambia, August, 1978. Restricted.

8596 URS Research Company for USAID. *Botswana-Zambia Transportation Survey.* Project No. 786. San Mateo, California: URS Research, July, 1970.

8597 van Dongen, Irene S. *The British East African Transport Complex.* Chicago: University of Chicago Department of Geography Research Paper No. 38. December, 1954.

8598 Wilbur Smith and Associates for USAID. *The Entente States; Highway Feasibility Study.* Task 1, Upper Volta-Niger, Fada N'Gourma to Niamey. Washington, D.C.: USAID, December, 1970.

8599 Wilbur Smith and Associates for USAID. *The Entente States; Highway Reconnaissance Study.* Task 2, Dahomey-Upper Volta, Dassa Zoume to Fada N'Gourma. Wasington, D.C.: USAID, December, 1970.

8600 Wiese, Bernd. *Seaports and Port Cities of Southern Africa.* Wiesbaden: Franz Steiner Verlag, 1981.

Journals

8601 "Abidjan-Niger: New Track Could Win More Traffic." *International Railway Journal*, 16, No. 10 (October, 1976), 21-27.

8602 **Adams, John,** and **Belcher, William.** "Prospects for Economic Development in Botswana: The Impact of Changes in the Southern Africa Region." Paper read to the Atlantic Economic Association, Washington, D.C., October, 1978.

8603 **Alexandre, Pierre.** "The Land-Locked Countries of Afrique Occidentale Francaise (AOF): Mali, Upper Volta and Niger." In *Land-Locked Countries of Africa*, Zdenek Cervenka, ed. Uppsala: The Scandinavian Institute of African Studies, 1973, 137-145.

8604 **Amissah, Austin N.E.** "Air Transport in Africa and Its Importance for African Land-Locked Countries." In *Land-Locked Countries of Africa*, Zdenek Cervenka, ed. Uppsala: The Scandinavian Institute of African Studies, 1973, 63-78.

8605 **Anglin, Douglas G.** "Confrontation in Southern Africa: Zambia and Portugal." *International Journal*, 25, No. 3 (Summer, 1970), 497-517.

8606 **Anglin, Douglas G.** "The Politics of Transit Routes in Land-Locked Southern Africa." In *Land-Locked Countries of Africa*, Zdenek Cervenka, ed. Uppsala: The Scandinavian Institute of African Studies, 1973, 98-133.

8607 **Anglin, Douglas G.** "Zambian Disengagement from Southern Africa and Integration with East Africa, 1964-1972: A Transaction Analysis." In *Cooperation and Conflict in Southern Africa: Papers on a Regional Subsystem* by Timothy M. Shaw. Washington, D.C.: University Press of America, 1977, 228-289.

8608 **Anglin, Douglas G,** and **Shaw, Timothy M.** "Disengagement and Integration, 1964-1974: A Transaction Analysis." In *Zambia's Foreign Policy; Studies in Diplomacy and Dependence.* Boulder, Colorado: Westview Press, 1979, 169-233.

8609 **Arnold, Guy.** "Growing Demands of a Land-Locked Country; Swaziland." *African Business*, (December, 1978), 56.

8610 **Ashton, Chris.** "Rail Routes to Mocambique." *Commerce*, 30, No. 4 (June, 1980), 16-17.

8611 **Bailey, Martin.** "Freedom Railroad." *Monthly Review*, 27, No. 11 (April, 1976), 34-44.

8612 **Bayon, J.** "L'Abidjan-Niger" [The Abidjan-Niger (Railway)]. *Industries et Travaux d'Outremer*, 7, No. 71 (October, 1959), 699-710.

8613 **Bayon, J.** "Le Chemin de Fer Abidjan-Niger" [The Abidjan-Niger Railroad]. *Revue Encyclopedique de l'Afrique*, 1 (January, 1960), 26-33.

8614 **Belisario, Joao.** "El Ferrocarril de Benguela" [The Benguela Railway]. *Cuadernos del Tercer Mundo*, 3, No. 30 (June, 1979), 87-89.

8615 **Bernard, Georges.** "Le Chemin de Fer de Bangui au Tchad" [The Railroad from Bangui to Chad]. *Perspectives d'Outr-mer*, 35, No. 3 (September, 1960), 184-210.

8616 **Best, Alan C.G.,** and **de Blij, Harm J.** "On the Tightrope; Land-Locked Zambia and Malawi." In *African Survey.* New York: John Wiley & Sons, 1977, 279-292.

8617 **Bordenave, Jean.** "La Regie Abidjan-Niger Hier et Aujourd'hui" [The Abidjan-Niger Railway Yesterday and Today]. *La Vie du Rail Outre-Mer*, 168 (March, 1968), 12-17, and 169 (April, 1968).

8618 **Bostock, R.M.** "The Transport Sector." In *Constraints on the Economic Development of Zambia*, Charles Elliott, ed. Nairobi: Oxford University Press, 1971, 323-376.

8619 "Botswana Railways Taking Shape." *Africa*, 84, No. 8 (August, 1978), 116.

8620 **Bottelier, P.C.C.** "China en het Zambia-Tanzania Spoorwegproject" [China and the Zambia-Tanzania Railway Project], *Internationale Spectator*, 2, No. 4 (December 8, 1967), 1764-1782.

8621 **Botting, Douglas.** "Triumph of the Benguela Railway." *Geographical Magazine*, 40, No. 4 (August, 1967), 255-268.

8622 **Bowman, Larry W.** "The Politics of Dependency and Racism in Rhodesia." In *Land-Locked Countries of Africa*, Zdenek Cervenka, ed. Uppsala: The Scandinavian Institute of African Studies, 1973, 182-187.

8623 **Bradenburg, Frank.** "Transport Systems and Their External Ramifications." In *Portuguese Africa; A Handbook*, David M. Abshire and Michael A. Samuels, eds. New York: Praeger, 1969, 332-344.

8624 **Breitengross, Jens Peter.** "Kooperation in Zentralafrika, Aussenhandel und Verkehr im Raum Zaire-Kongo-Zentralafrikanische Republik (ZAR)" [Cooperation in Central Africa, Foreign Trade and Transport in the Area of Zaire-Congo-Central African Republic (CAR)]. In *Kooperation in Afrika*, Goswin Baumhogger, ed. Hamburg: Institut fur Afrika-Kunde, 1976, 143-192.

8625 **Brookfield, Harold C.** "New Railroad and Port Developments in East and Central Africa." *Economic Geography*, 31, No. 1 (January, 1955), 60-70.

8626 **Byrne, Raymond.** "Central Africa's Lifeline." *African Market*, (August, 1950), 26-29, 31.

8627 **Cabezas, Miguel.** "Zambia Begins to Clear the Transport Backlog." *African Business*, 5 , No. 1 (January, 1979), 16-17.

8628 "Central African Headache; Finding Outlets to the Sea." *Bulletin of the Africa Institute*, 4, No. 7 (July, 1966), 138-144.

8629 **Cervenka, Zdenek.** "The Limitations Imposed on African Land-Locked Countries." In *Land-Locked Countries of Africa*. Uppsala: The Scandinavian Institute of African Studies, 1973, 17-33.

8630 **Cervenka, Zdenek.** "The Need for a Continental Approach to the Problems of African Land-Locked States." In *Land-Locked Countries of Africa*. Uppsala: The Scandinavian Institute of African Studies, 1973, 316-328.

8631 **Cervenka, Zdenek.** "The Right of Access to the Sea of African Land-Locked Countries." *Verfassung und Recht in Ubersee*, 6, No. 3 (Third Quarter, 1973), 299-310.

8632 **Cervenka, Zdenek.** "Swaziland's Links with the Outside World." In *Land-Locked Countries of Africa*. Uppsala: The Scandinavian Institute of African Studies, 1973, 263-270.

8633 **Champaud, Jacques.** "La Navigation Fluviale dans le Moyen Niger" [River Navigation on the Middle Niger]. *Les Cahiers d'Outre-mer*, 14, No. 55 (July-September, 1961), 255-292.

8634 **Charles, J.L.** "Zambia's Rail Situation." *Canadian Geographical Journal*, 75, No. 6 (June, 1967), 206-217.

8635 **Charlet, M.** "Le Benin-Niger" [The Benin-Niger (Railway)]. *Industries et Travaux d'Outremer*, 7, No. 71 (October, 1959), 689-697.

8636 **Church, R.J. Harrison.** "The Transport Pattern of British West Africa." In *Geographical Essays on British Tropical Lands*, Robert Walton Steel and Charles Alford Fisher, eds. London: George Philip & Sons, 1956, 53-76.

8637 **Church, R.J. Harrison.** "Trans-Saharan Railway Projects." In *London Essays in Geography*, L. Dudley Stamp and S.W. Woolridge, eds. Cambridge, Massachusetts: Harvard University Press, 1951, 135-150.

8638 **Clark, W. Marshall.** "African Development Curbed by Transport Disabilities." *Optima*, 2, No. 2 (June, 1952), 1-4.

8639 **Clark, W. Marshall.** "Transport in Southern, Central and East Africa." *Journal of the South African Institution of Mechanical Engineers*, 1, No. 3 (September, 1951), 31-48.

8640 **Clarke, John I.** "The Trans-Cameroon Railway."

Geography, 51, No. 1 (January, 1966), 55-58.

8641 **Cliffe, Lionel.** "The Implications of the Tanzam Railway for the Liberation and Development of South Eastern Africa." In *Land-Locked Countries of Africa*, Zdenek Cervenka, ed. Uppsala: The Scandinavian Institute of African Studies, 1973, 293-299.

8642 **Clute, Robert E.** "The International Rights of African Land-locked Countries." *Journal of African Studies*, 6, No. 3 (Fall, 1979), 165-170.

8643 **Coetzee, David.** "New Attention Focused on Tanzania's Small Ports." *African Development*, 10, No. 12 (December, 1976), 1365.

8644 **Connell, John.** "Africa's Brave New Railway." *Geographical Magazine*, 43, No. 10 (July, 1971), 721-726.

8645 "Co-ordinated Railway Development in Southern Africa." *Railway Engineering*, 16, No. 3 (May-June, 1972), 1, 5-13.

8646 **Costantini, Zaira.** "La Tanzania-Zambia Railroad." *Notiziario di Geografia Economica*, 1, No. 3 (September, 1970), 40-43.

8647 **Coursin, Leon.** "Dakar: Port Atlantique." *Les Cahiers d'Outre Mer*, 1, No. 3 (July-September, 1948), 275-285.

8648 "Cout des Transports Resultant de l'Enclavement du Burundi" [Cost of Transport Resulting from the Land-Lockedness of Burundi]. *Bulletin Trimestriel*, 49 (June, 1974), 5-16.

8649 **Crouzet, Etienne.** "La Transversale du Sahel" [The Sahel Transversal (highway)]. *Industries et Travaux d'Outremer*, 25, No. 283 (June, 1977), 432-434.

8650 **Dale, Edmund H.** "Some Geographical Aspects of African Land-Locked States." *Annals of the Association of American Geographers*. 58, No. 3 (September, 1968), 485-505. Commentaries on this article by Robert H. Schmidt, Jr. and Ladd L. Johnson and a rejoinder by Dale appear in *Annals of the Association of American Geographers*, 59, No. 4 (December, 1969), 820-822.

8651 **Dale, Richard.** "Botswana." In *Southern Africa in Perspective; Essays in Regional Politics*, Christian P. Potholm and Richard Dale, eds. New York: The Free Press, 1972, 110-124.

8652 **Dale, Richard.** *Botswana and Rhodesia: An Analysis of a Dyadic Relationship, 1966-1975*. Paper read to the annual meeting of the Western Association of Africanists, Denver, May, 1975.

8653 **Darnault, Paul.** "Le Chemin de Fer du Doualal-Tchad" [The Douala-Chad Railway]. *Industries et Travaux 'Outremer*, 7, No. 1 (October, 1959), 735-740.

8654 **Davenport, G.A.** "The Rhodesias Must Have a New Rail Artery to Sea." *Commerce*, 2, No. 7 (July, 1951), 18-21, 61.

8655 **David, Luis.** "Porto da Beira: Uma Alavanca para o Desenvolvimento" [Port of Beira: A Lever for Expansion]. *Tempo*, 495 (April 6, 1980), 6-17.

8656 **Delarue, Philippe.** "Les Ports Africains; Port Etienne (Nouadhibou), Cotonou" [African Ports; Port Etienne (Nouadhibou), Contonou]. *Afrique Contemporaine*, 8, No. 46 (November-December, 1969), 2-8.

8657 **Delarue, Philippe.** "Les Ports de l'Afrique Noirre; Dakar, Abidjan" [Ports of Black Africa; Dakar, Abidjan]. *Afrique Contemporaine*, 8, No. 43 (May-June, 1969), 2-9.

8658 **Derrick, Jonathan.** "The Transamerounais; By Rail from Chad to the Sea." *New Africa*, 13, No. 5/6 (May–June, 1971), 7-8.

8659 **Diagne, Adama.** "UAC [African Union of Railways] Forges Trans-Africa Links." *Railway Gazette International*, 134, No. 7 (July, 1978), 471-474.

8660 **Diallo, Sory Seride.** "La Transafricaine; De Lagos a Mombasa" [The Transafrican (Highway): From Lagos to Mombasa]. *Jeune Afrique*, 962 (June 13, 1979), 51, 53, 55.

8661 **Diallo, Sory Seride.** "Un Reseau Ferre qui Reste Embryonnaire" [An Iron Network that Remains Embryonic]. *Jeune Afrique*, 962 (June 13, 1979), 58-59.

8662 **Diguimbaye, Georges,** and **Langue, Robert,** eds. "Les Infrastructures de Liaisons" [The Infrastructure of Connections]. In *l'Essor du Tchad*. Paris: Presses Universitaires de France, 1969, 254-298.

8663 **Doganis, Rigas S.** "Zambia's Outlet to the Sea." *Journal of Transport Economics and Policy*, 1, No. 1 (January, 1967), 46-51.

8664 **Due, John F.** "The Problems of Rail Transport in Tropical Africa." *Journal of Developing Areas*, 13, No. 4 (July, 1979), 375-393.

8665 **Durant, A.E.** "Rhodesia Railways: Serving a Land-Locked Country." *Railways Southern Africa*, (February, 1978), 17-21.

8666 **Durant, A.E.** "Swaziland Railway." *Railways Southern Africa*, (October, 1977), 20-21.

8667 "EAC's Overall Progress Shows in Harbour Development Boom." *African Development*, 11, No. 2 (February, 1974), P.E.A. 43.

8668 **East, W. Gordon.** "Some Geographical Aspects of African Landlocked States." *Annals of the Association of American Geographers*, 58, No. 4 (December, 1968), 485-505.

8669 **Erlham, Brian.** "The Vital Link for Trading; Transport." *Industrial Review*, (October, 1984), 54-57.

8670 **Ethiopia.** "Franco-Ethiopian Railway from Djibouti to Addis Ababa." *Bulletin of the International Union of Railways*, 31, No. 4 (April, 1960), 108-110.

8671 **Everwyn, Gerhard.** "Das Nacala-Eisenbahnverbindungsprojekt" [The Nacala Rail Link Project]. *Schienen der Welt*, 1, No. 9 (September, 1970), 649-652.

8672 **Everwyn, Gerhard.** "Malawi-Mozambique; The Grand Rail Strategy." *African Development*, 7, No. 4 and 5 (April-May, 1970), 10-11.

8673 **Everwyn, Gerhard.** "The Nacala Rail Link Project of Malawi." *New Africa*, 11, No. 11/12 (November-December, 1969), 6-7.

8674 **Farah, Nuruddin.** "I Negus, Menghistu e la Via del Mare" [The Negus, Menghistu and the Way to the Sea]. *Politica Internazionale*, 4, No. 4 (April, 1978), 18-25.

8675 **Fauvet, Paul.** "Beira: A Port for Independent Africa." *AIM Information Bulletin* (Maputo), 59, No. 5 (May, 1981), 38-42.

8676 **Fischer, Eric.** *Landlocked Countries of Africa.* Paper read to the annual meeting of the Association of American Geographers, Denver, September, 1963.

8677 **Forson, Robert.** "Great Implications of Proposed Walvis Bay-Rhodesia Rail Link." *Commercial Opinion*, 34, No. 402 (July, 1956), 21 and 41.

8678 **Galvao, Lopes.** "A Rede Ferro-viaria das Rodesias e as suas Ligacoes com o Mar" [The Railroad Network of the Rhodesias and Their Links with the Sea]. *Boletim Geral das Colonias*, 23, No. 268 (October, 1947), 3-24.

8679 **Garreau, Gerard.** "Afrique: "Vers un Axe Lourd Transahelien?" [Africa: Toward a Trans-Sahelian Heavy-Duty Axis?]. *Actual Developement*, 24, No. 3 (May-June, 1978), 43-44.

8680 **Garson, Noel George.** "The Swaziland Question and a Road to the Sea 1887-1895." *Archives Year Book for South Africa History*, 20, No. 2 (1957), 263-434.

8681 Gladden, E.N. "The East African Common Services Organization." *Parliamentary Affairs*, 16, No. 4 (Autumn, 1963), 428-439.

8682 Gomer, Hilaire. "Ports and Harbours" (African). *African Business*, 34, No. 6 (June, 1981), 78-89.

8683 Gourou, Pierre. "Le Partage de l'Afrique et ses Effets Geographiques" [The Partition of Africa and Its Geographical Effects]. In *Exchanges et Communications. Melanges Offerts a Claude Levi-Strauss a l'Occasion de son 60e Anniversaire, Reunis par Jean Pouillon et Pierre Maranda*. The Hague and Paris: Mouton, 1970, Vol. 1, 462-468.

8684 Graham, James D. "The Tanzam Railway: Consolidating the People's Development and Building the Internal Economy." *Africa Today*, 21, No. 3 (Summer, 1974), 27-42.

8685 Green, Reginald Herbold. "Economic Co-ordination, Liberation and Development: Botswana-Namibia Perspectives." In *Papers on the Economy of Botswana*, Charles Harvey, ed. London: Heinemann, 1981, 178-195.

8686 Griffiths, I.L. "Strategy for Zambia." *Geographical Magazine*, 42, No. 1 (October, 1969), 3-8.

8687 Griffiths, I.L. "The Tazama Oil Pipeline." *Geography*, 54, No. 2 (April, 1969), 214-217.

8688 Griffiths, I.L. "Transport and Communications in the Relationship of a Land-Locked State: Zambia." In *Transport in Africa*. Edinburgh: Proceedings of a seminar held in Centre of African Studies, University of Edinburgh, Oct. 31-Nov. 1, 1969, 95-109 (discussion, 119-131).

8689 Griffiths, I.L. "Zambian Links with East Africa." *East African Geographical Review*, 6 (April, 1968), 87-89.

8690 Grull, J. "Sambia-Tansania; Eine Ostafrikanische Transitbahn" [Zambia-Tanzania; An East African Transit Route]. *Mitteilungen der Osterreichischen Geographischen Gesellschaft*, 108, No. 1 (1966), 199-201.

8691 Grundy, Kenneth W. "Economic and Transport Relationships." In *Confrontation and Accommodation in Southern Africa*. Berkeley: University of California Press, 1973, 28-82.

8692 Hall, Richard. "Zambia and Rhodesia: Links and Fetters." *Africa Report*, 11, No. 1 (January, 1966), 8-12.

8693 Hance, William A., and van Dongen, Irene S. "Beira, Mozambique Gateway to Central Africa." *Annals of the Association of American Geographers*, 47, No. 4 (December, 1957), 307-335.

8694 Hance, William A., and van Dongen, Irene S. "Dar es Salaam, the Port and Its Tributary Area." *Annals of the Association of American Geographers*, 48, No. 4 (December, 1958), 419-435.

8695 Hance, William A., and van Dongen, Irene S. "Lourenco Marques in Delagoa Bay." *Economic Geography*, 33, No. 3 (July, 1957), 238-256.

8696 Hance, William A., and van Dongen, Irene S. "Matadi, Focus of Belgian African Transport." *Annals of the Association of American Geographers*, 48, No. 1 (March, 1958), 41-72.

8697 Hance, William A., and van Dongen, Irene S. "The Port of Lobito and the Benguela Railway." *Geographical Review*, 66, No. 4 (October, 1956), 460-487.

8698 "Hardpacked and Fast." *Agenda*, 2, No. 7 (September, 1979), 14-17.

8699 Harkema, Roelof C. "The Ports and Access Routes of Land-Locked Zambia." *Geografisch Tijdschrift*, 6, No. 3 (May, 1972), 223-231.

8700 Harkema, Roelof C. "Zambia's Changing Pattern of External Trade." *Journal of Geography*. 71, No. 1 (January, 1972), 19-27.

8701 Harrison, Charles. "East African Rail: The Three-way Split." *African Development*, 11, No. 12 (December, 1974), K9, K11.

8702 Hawkins, R.T.R. "Transport in Relation to Exports." *Rhodesian Journal of Economics*. 6, No. 4 (December, 1972), 49-57.

8703 Henderson, Robert D'A. "Relations of Neighborliness—Malawi and Portugal, 1964-74." *Journal of Modern African Studies*, 15, No. 3 (September, 1977), 425-455.

8704 Hermans, H.C.L. "Botswana's Options for Independent Exence." In *Land-Locked Countries of Africa*, Zdenek Cervenka, ed. Uppsala: The Scandinavian Institute of African Studies, 1973, 197-211.

8705 Hetzel, Wolfgang. "Seehafenplatze und -Wege der Binnenstaaten Tschad und Zentralafrinkanische Republik" [Seaport Sites and Routes of the Land-locked Countries Chad and Central African Republic]." In *Raumliche und Zeitliche Bewegungen*, Gerhard Braun, ed. Wurtzburg: Universitat Wurtzburg, Wurtzburger Geographische Arbeiten Heft 37, 1972, 371-400.

8706 Hetzel, Wolfgang. "Zum Problem der Binenlage der Republik Niger" [The Problem of the Land-Lockedness of the Niger Republic]. *Erdkunde*, 24, No. 1 (March, 1970), 1-14.

8707 Higgott, Richard A. "Niger." Chapter 7 in *The Political Economy of African Foreign Policy*, Timothy M. Shaw and Olajide Aluko, eds. New York: St. Martin's Press, 1984, 165-189.

8708 Higgott, Richard A. "Structural Dependence and Decolonisation in a West African Land-Locked State: Niger." *Review of African Political Economy*, 17, No. 1 (January-April, 1980), 43-58.

8709 Hill, Alistair. "Benefits of Transport Network Hit by Dependence on Kenya" and "Burundi Route Also Suggested for Trans African Highway." *African Development*, 9, No. 6 (June, 1972), U.14-U.17.

8710 Hilling, David. "Chad-Sea Road." *Geographical Magazine*. 41, No. 5 (May, 1969), 628.

8711 Hilling, David. "Cotonou--Dahomey's New Deep water Port." *Bulletin of the Ghana Geographical Association*, 11, No. 1 (January, 1966), 64-69.

8712 Hilling, David. "Politics and Transportation: The Problems of West Africa's Land-Locked States." In *Essays in Political Geography*, Charles Alford Fisher, ed. London: Methuen, 1968, p. 252-269.

8713 Hilling, David. "Ports and Economic Development in Equatorial Africa." *Bulletin of the Ghana Geographical Association*, 8, No. 1 (January, 1963), 32-37.

8714 Hilling, David. West Africa's Land-Locked States--Some Problems of Transport and Access." In *Drought in Africa*, David Dalby and R.J. Harrison Church, eds. London: Centre for African Studies, University of London, 1973, 112-116.

8715 "Hinterlands of the East African Ports" and "Notes on East African Ports." *Africa Institute Bulletin*, 13, No. 7-8 (September-October, 1975), 275-290.

8716 "History of a Road; Beira to Salisbury." *African Roads and Transport*. 16, No. 6 (November-December, 1958), 11, 13, 15.

8717 Hofmeier, Rolf. "Die Politische Okonomie von Verkehrsvorhaben in Afrika" [The Political Economy of Transport Planning in Africa]. *Afrika Spectrum*, 14, No. 1 (1979), 4-17.

8718 Hofmeier, Rolf. "Die Transafrikastrassen--Stand der Planung und Realisierung" [The Trans-African Highways--Status of the Plans and Realization]. *Afrika Spectrum*, 14, No. 1 (1979), 31-51.

8719 Hoyle, Brian Stewart. "African Politics and Port Expansion at Dar es Salaam." *Geographical Review*, 68, No. 1 (January, 1978), 31-50.

8720 Hoyle, Brian Stewart. "The Emergence of Major Seaports in a Developing Economy: The Case of East Africa." In *Seaports and Development in Tropical Africa*, Brian Steweart Hoyle and David Hilling, eds. London: Macmillan, 1970, 225-245.

8721 Hoyle, Brian Stewart. "Expansion of Facilities at East African Seaports." *East African Geographical Review*, 5 (April, 1967), 59-61.

8722 Hoyle, Brian Stewart. "The Maritime Facade of South-Eastern Africa: Port Traffic through Mozambique 1964-74." *Annuaire des Pays de l'Ocean Indien*, 4 (1977), 209-225.

8723 Hoyle, Brian Stewart. "Port Developments in East Africa, 1965-1975." *Annuaire des Pays de l'Ocean Indien*, 3 (1976), 175-196.

8724 Hoyle, Brian Stewart. "The Proposed Tanzania-Zambia Railway." *East African Geographical Review*, 3 (April, 1965), 51-52.

8725 Hoyle, Brian Stewart. "Recent Changes in the Pattern of East African Railways." *Tijdschrift voor Economische en Sociale Geografie*, 4, No. 11 (November, 1963), 237-242.

8726 Hoyle, Brian Stewart. "Transport and Economic Growth in Developing Countries: The Case of East Africa." In *Transport and Development*, Brian Stewart Hoyle, ed. London: Macmillan, 1973, 50-62.

8727 Hoyle, Brian Stewart. "Transport and Economic Growth in Developing Countries: The Case of East Africa." In *Geographical Essays in Honour of K.C. Edwards*, R.H. Osborne, et al, eds. Nottingham: Department of Geography, University of Nottingham, 1970, 187-196.

8728 Hveem, Helge. "Relationship of Underdevelopment of African Land-Locked Countries with the General Problem of Economic Development." In *Land-Locked Countries of Africa*, Zdenek Cervenka, ed. Uppsala: The Scandinavian Institute of African Studies, 1973, 278-287.

8729 "Implementada a Cooperacao no Dominio dos Transportes, Telecomunicaoes e Energia" [Cooperation Implemented in the Field of Transport, Telecommunications and Energy]. *Tempo*, 507 (June 29, 1980), 47-51.

8730 "The Invisible Barriers: and "Africa's Railway Network." *Africa*, 80, No. 4 (April, 1978), 71-76.

8731 Janin, Bernard. "Le Nouveau Port de Cotonou" [The New Port of Cotonou]. *Revue de Geographie Alpine*, 52, No. 4 (1964), 701-712.

8732 **Jatzold, Ralph.** "Tanzania–Zambia; Gelande– und Wirtzschaftsprobleme in Zusammenhang mit dem Bau der Neuen Tanzania–Zambia Eisenbahn' [Tansania–Zambia; Topographic and Economic Problems in Connection with the Construction of a New Tanzania–Zambia Railroad]. *Internationales Afrikaforum*, 11, No. 6 (June, 1975), 343–345.

8733 **Jeske, Joachim.** "Neue Hafen und Eisenbahnen im Sudlichen Afrika" [New Ports and Railroads in Southern Africa]. In *Natur– und Wirtschafts Geographische Forschungen in Africa*, H. Hagedorn and H.G. Wagner, eds. Wurzburg: Wurzburger Geographische Arbeiten No. 49, Instituts fur Geographie der Univeristat Wurzburg, 1979, 287–313.

8734 **Jeske, Joachim.** "The Role of Southern Africa's Physical Infrastrucutre in the Establishment of Trade Relations." In *Proceedings of the Seminar on Botswana's External Trade in the Light of the Lome Convention*. Gaberone: Documentation Unit, University College of Botswana, December, 1978, 89–110.

8735 **Jeske, Joachim.** "Zimbabwes Eingliederung in den Regionalen Wirtschaftsverbund des Sudlichen Afrika" [Zimbabwe's Integration into the Economic Union of Southern Africa]. *Afrika Spectrum*, 16, No. 3 (1981), 267–296.

8736 **Johnson, Ladd Linn.** "African Landlocked States: Inconsistencies and Inaccuracies of Prose." *Annals of the Association of American Geographers*, 59, No. 4 (December, 1969), 820–822.

8737 **Jorgensen, A.A.** "Rail Transport in Southern Africa." *Africa Insight*, 13, No. 1 (1983), 29–42.

8738 **Josse, Paul.** "Le Dakar–Niger" [The Dakar–Niger (Railway)]. *Industries et Travaux d'Outremer*, 7, No. 71 (October, 1959), 681-688.

8739 **Juzeau, A.** "Le Chemin de Fer de Bangui au Tchad" [The Railraod from Bangui to Chad]. *Industries et Travaux d'Outremer*, 7, No. 71 (October, 1959), 741–746.

8740 **Kane–Berman, John.** "Re–routing Rail Traffic; The Plan to Bypass SA." *Tradelink*, 1, No. 1 (March, 1981), 12–17.

8741 **Katzenellenbogen, Simon E.** "The Miner's Frontier, Transport and General Economic Development." In *Colonialism in Africa 1870–1960*, Peter Duignan and L.H. Gann, eds. Vol. 4, Cambridge: Cambridge University Press, 1975, 360–426.

8742 **Katzenellenbogen, Simon E.** "Zambia and Rhodesia: Prisoners of the Past; A Note on the History of Railway Politics in Central Africa." *African Affairs*, 73, No. 290 (January, 1974), 63–66.

8743 **Kauffmann, Jean.** "La Quatrieme Conference Routiere Africaine" [The Fourth African Highway Conference]. *Industries et Travaux d'Outre Mer*, 28, No. 317 (April, 1980), 211–226.

8744 "Keeping Zambia's Trade Routes Open." *Enterprise*, 2 (1975), 37 and 39.

8745 **King, James Wilhelmsen.** "Nile Transport in Uganda." *East African Geographical Review*, 4 (April, 1966), 25–36.

8746 **Kotowski, Klemens.** "Zambia Orientiert sich nach Tanzania" [Zambia Orients Toward Tanzania]. *Afrika Heute*, 7, No. 2 (April, 1968), April 15, 1968), 97–103.

8747 **Kotsokoane, J.R.L.** "Lesotho and Her Neighbours." *African Affairs*, 68, No. 271 (April, 1969), 135–138.

8748 **Kowet, Donald.** "Lesotho and the Customs Union with the Republic of South Africa." In *Land–Locked Countries of Africa*, Zdenek Cervenka, ed. Uppsala: The Scandinavian Institute of African Studies, 1973, 250–257.

8749 **Labasse, Jean.** "Le 'Dakar–Niger' et sa Zone d'Action" [The 'Dakar-niger' and Its Zone of Activity]. *Revue de Geographie de Lyon*, 29, No. 3 (1954), 183–204.

8750 **Laight, J.C.** "Transportation Problems in Southern Africa." *Transport and Communications Review*, 6, No. 2 (April–June, 1953), 12–23.

8751 "La Maitrise des Couts des Transports Devient une Necessite Imperieuse" [Mastery of transport Costs Becomes an Urgent Necessity]. *Afrique Transport* (Paris), 6 (September 15, 1978), 31.

8752 "La Navigation Fluviale en Republique Centrafricaine" [River Navigation int he Central African Republic]. *Revue de la Navigaiton Fluviale Europeenne*, 46, No. 22 (December 25, 1974), 732–736.

8753 **Land, Thomas.** "Back Door to Zambia." *Atlas*, 10, No. 6 (December, 1965), 376–377.

8754 **Land, Thomas.** "China's African Railway." *Contemporary Review*, 213, No. 1230 (July, 1968), 24–27.

8755 "La Route Transsaharienne devrait Etre Terminee en 1980" [The Transsaharan Highway Should be Completed in 1980]. *Europe Outremer*, 54, No. 568 (April–May, 1977), 15–18.

8756 **Laurent, Jean.** All of the following articles appear in *Perspectives d'Outremer*. 35 (September, 1960), on pages indicated: "La Voie Federale" [The Federal Way], 114–116; "Le Chemin de Fer Congo-Ocean" [The Congo–Ocean Railroad], 117–133; "Le Port de Pointe-Noire" [The Port of Pointe–Noire], 134–147; "Le Port de Libreville" [The Port of Librevi 148–150; "Traffic et Travaux Portuaires a Port–Gentil" [Traffic and Port Works at Port-Gentil], 151–153; "Le Port de Brazzaville" [The Port of Brazzaville], 154–157; "Le Port de Bangui" [The Port of Bangui], 159–160; "L'Equipement Routier" [The Highway Facilities], 161–171; "L'Infrastructure Aerienne" [The Aviation Infrastructure], 172–183.

8757 **Lavrencic, Karl.** "Transport Crisis for Totally Landlocked Economies; Burundi-Rwanda." *African Business*, 19, No. 3 (March, 1980), 25 and 27.

8758 **Leech, John.** "Why Zambia Turned North." *African Development*. 7, No. 10 (October, 1970), Z.13–15.

8759 **Legum, Colin.** "The Problems of the Land-Locked Countries of Southern Africa in the Confrontation between Independent Africa and South Africa, Rhodesia and Portugal." In *Land-Locked Countries of Africa*, Zdenek · Cervenka, ed. Uppsala: The Scandinavian Institute of African Studies, 1973, 165–181.

8760 "Le Rattachement de la RCA aux Voies Ferrees du Cameroun ou du Gabon" [Reconnection of the Central African Republic to Railraods of Cameroun or of Gabon]. *Bulletin de l'Afrique Noire*, 877 (July 20, 1976), 17113.

8761 "Le Reseau Routier Trans–West–African" [The Trans–West African Highway Network]. *Industries et Travaux d'Outremer*, 22, No. 249 (August, 1974), 712–714.

8762 "Le Transport du Minerai de Manganese entre Tambao et Abidjan par Wagons Mineraliers de 40 m³ d'un Type Entierement Nouveau" [The Transport of Manganese Ore between Tambao and Abidjan by Ore Wagons of 40 m³ of an Entirely New Type]. *Industries et Travaux d'Outremer*, 23, No. 261 (August, 1975), 638–639.

8763 "Les Chemins de Fer Africains et Malagaches" [African and Malagache Railroads]. *Industries et Travaux d'Outremer*, 18, No. 205, Special Number (December, 1970), complete issue.

8764 "Les Chemins de Fer en Afrique Noire Francophone" [Railroads in Francophone Black Africa]. *Europe Outremer*. 57, No. 590 (March, 1979), 22–30.

8765 "Les Grands Projets Ferroviaires en Afrique et les Orientations de la Technique Ferroviaire." Special Number of *Industries et Travaux d'Outre Mer*, Vol. 15, No. 163 (June, 1967). Included are the following articles: "Et le Transsaharien?" by G. Bernard, 506–509; "Les Projets de Liaison Ferroviare Ouagadougou–Tambao et Anoumoda–Oume–Daloa" by J. Bordenave, 520–524; "Le Projet d'Extension du Reseau de l'O.C.D.N. de Parakou a Dosso" by J. Houdet, 525–528; "La Ligne Trans–Africaine Nigeria–Soudan a Travers le Tchad," 529; "Le Desenclavement de l'Afrique Centrale et la Liaison Doula–Victoria" by Henri Hamel, 530-533; "les Projets d'Extension des Chemins de Fer du Mozambique," 545–546; "Le Projet de Creation d'une Liaison Ferroviaire entre le Republique Sud–africaine et la Rhodesie," 550–551; "L'Extension des Chemins de Fer du Malawi," 552–554; "Le Reseau de l''East African Railways and Harbours' et ses Projets d'Extension," 555–557.

8766 "Les Ports de l'Afrique Noire Francophone: de Nouvelles Extensions pour un Traffic Croissant" [Ports of Francophone Black Africa: New Extensions for a Growing Traffic]. *Europe Outremer*, 57, No. 599 (December, 1979), 29–43.

8767 "Les Ports du Mozambique" [The Ports of Mozambique]. *Industries et Travaux d'Outre-mer*, 21, No. 233 (April, 1973), 351–355.

8768 "Les Voies de Desserte du Tchad" [The connecting Routes of Chad]. *L'A.E.F Economique et Financiere*, 3, No. 1 (January, 1958), pages unnumbered.

8769 **Leys, Roger and Tostensen, Arne.** "Regional Co-operation in Southern Africa: The Southern African Development Co-ordination Conference." *Review of African Political Economy*, 23, No. 1 (January-April, 1982), 52–71.

8770 **Libya, Government Representative.** "Problems Facing Libya as a Transit Country." Paper readat the Fifth African Highway Conference, Libreville, June, 1983, and published in the booklet *Pays Enclaves et de Transit/Land-Locked and Transit Countries*. Washington, D.C.: International Road Federation, 1983, 27-31.

8771 **Liebenow, J. Gus.** "SADCC: Challenging the 'South African Connection'." In Washington, D.C.: *Universities Field Staff International (UFSI) Reports*, African Series, 1982/No. 13 [JGL-1-'82].

8772 **Limbio, Florence.** "Le Reseau Routier Centrafricain" [The Central African Highway Network]. *Etudes et Statistiques BEAC*, 111, No. 2 (April, 1984), 90–107.

8773 **Liniger-Goumaz, Max.** "Transsaharien et Transafricain: Essai Bibliographique." *Geneve-Afrique*, 7, No. 1 (Januar, 1968), 70–85.

8774 **Lipets, Yu. G.** "Problems of Transport Services for Central and South African Mining Industry Basins." In *Ekonomicheskiye Svyazi i Transport* [Economic Communications and Transport]. No. 61 in Series Voprosy Geografii—Sbornik Shest 'desyat Pervyy. Moscow: State Publishing House of Geographic Literature, 1963, 201-221, U.S. Department of Commerce, Joint Publications Research Service No. 20236; also available from National Technical Information Service, Springfield, Virginia.

8775 **Long, A.** "Internal Transport Developments in East Africa." *Geography*, 50, No. 1 (January, 1965), 78-82.

8776 **Lousber, J.G.H.** "Transport Cooperation in Southern Africa." *ISSUP Strategic Review*, (November, 1982), 2-10.

8777 **Lousber, J.G.H.** "Transport Diplomacy, with Special Reference to Southern Africa." *Afrikaans in Politikon*, 6 (December, 1979), 137-153.

8778 **Louis Berger International and Ingecot (Abidjian) for CILSS and Club du Sahel, Transport and Infrastructure Working Group.** *Road Maintenance Diagnostic Study for the Sahel.* Vol. 1 *Synthesis*, July, 1977; Vol. 4 *Haute Volta*, March, 1978; Vol. 5 *Mali*, March, 1978; Vol. 7 *Niger*, September, 1978, complete issue.

8779 **Lugan, Bernard.** "Commerce de Traite et Projets de Desenclavement du Rwanda sous le Regime Allemand" [The Slave Trade and Projects to Reduce the Land-Lockedness of Rwanda Under the German Regime]. *Etudes Rwandaises*, 10, No. 1 (January, 1977), 23-42.

8780 **Lugan, Bernard.** "Le Commerce de Traite au Rwanda sous le Regime Allemand (1896-1916)" [Slave Trade of Rwanda under the German Regime (1896-1916)]. *Canadian Journal of African Studies*, 11, No. 2 (1977), 235-268.

8781 **MacGregor-Hutcheson, A.** "New Developments in Malawi's Rail and Lake Services." *Society of Malawi Journal*, 22, No. 1 (January, 1969), 32-45.

8782 **Makoni, Tonderai.** "The Economic Appraisal of the Tanzania-Zambia Railway." *African Review*, 2, No. 4 (March, 1972), 599-616.

8783 **Malan, Theo.** "The Lesotho-Transkei Border Closure: Fact or Fallacy?" *Bulletin of the Africa Institute of South Africa*, 15, No. 1-2 (1977), 36-39.

8784 **Malan, Theo.** "SADCC [Southern African Development Coordination Commission] and the Ports of Mozambique." *Africa Institute of South Africa Bulletin*, 21, No. 16 (1981), 121-126.

8785 "Mali Plans New Outlet to the Atlantic." *International Railway Journal*, 16, No. 10 (October, 1976), 37-38.

8786 **Manning, Robert.** "Oil for Smith: Following the Paperchase into Rhodesia." *African Development*, 10, No. 10 (October, 1976), 976, 977, 979.

8787 **Maro, Paul S.** "The Tanzania-Zambia Railway." *Journal of the Geographical Association of Tanzania*, 9 (December, 1973), 63-80.

8788 **Martin, David.** "The Tanzam Rail Link Means a New, Vital Freedom for East Africa." *African Development*, 4, No. 11 (November, 1970), 10-11.

8789 **Mascarenhas, Adolfo C.** "The Port of Dar es Salaam." *Tanzania Notes and Records*, 71 (1970); Volume titled "Dar es Salaam; City, Port and Region," J.E.G. Sutton, 71 (1970), 81-118.

8790 **Mbanga, Trish.** "Beira Port—Vital Step Forward." *Commerce*, 34, No. 1 (January, 1984), 11, 13.

8791 **Mihalya, Louis J.** "Some Socio-Economic Projections of the New Line-of-Rail in the Geography of Zambia." In East African Universities Social Science Council, *Eighth Annual Conference December 19-23rd, 1972, Nairobi*, 3, Paper No. 48, (1972) 421-443.

8792 "Mozambique, Zambia, Zaire e Zimbabwe Assinam Acordo no Dominio dos Transportes" [Mozambique, Zambia, Zaire and Zimbabwe Sign Accord int he Field of Transport]. *Tempo*, 507 (June 29, 1980), 44-46.

8793 **Ndongko, Wilfred A.** "Le Transcamerounais: Intensifier les Echanges et Desenclaver le Nord" [The Transcameroonian: To Intensify Trade and to Reduce the Isolation of the North]. *Actuel Developpement*, 10, No. 6 (November-December, 1975), 15-18.

8794 **Nendigui, Jean.** "Les Problemes des Transports au Tchad" [The Transport Problems of Chad]. *Etudes et Statistiques* (Bulletin Mensuel, Banque Centrale des Etats de l'Afrique Equatoriale et du Cameroun), 182 (March, 1973), 151-166.

8795 **Nobilo, Mario.** "Problems of the Landlocked African Countries." *Review of International Affairs*, 34, No. 798-799 (July 5-20, 1983), 33-36.

8796 "Nouvelle Liaison Ferroviaire entre le Rhodesie et l'Afrique du Sud" [New Rail Link between Rhodesia and South Africa]. *Industries et Travaux d'Outre-mer*, 23, No. 257 (April, 1975), 336-337.

8797 **Nsekela, Amon J.** "Transport and Communications." In his *Southern Africa Toward Economic Liberation*. London: Rex Collings, 1981, 71–91.

8798 **O'Connor, Anthony M.** "New Railway Construction and the Pattern of Economic Development in East Africa." *Transactions of the Institute of British Geographers*, 36 (June, 1965), 21–30.

8799 **Odier, Lionel.** "Routes de Transit et Desenclavement" [Transit Routes and Reducing the Effects of Enclosure]. Paper read at the Fifth African Highway Conference, Libreville, June, 1983, and published in the booklet *Pays Enclaves et de Transit/Land–Locked and Transit Countries* by the International Road Federation, Washington, D.C., 1983, 15–26.

8800 **Ogundana, Babafemi.** "Seaport Development—Multi-National Co-operation in West Africa." *Journal of Modern African Studies*, 12, No. 3 (September, 1974), 395–407.

8801 **Okoth, Pius George.** "Railways Chaos—Another Nail in East Africa's Coffin." *African Development*, 9, No. 5 (May, 1975), 17–19.

8802 "Opening the Railways Link-up; Angola-Zaire-Zambia." *Africa*, 88, No. 12 (December, 1978), 35–36.

8803 **Ostrander, F. Taylor.** "Zambia in the Aftermath of Rhodesia UDI: Logistical and Economic Problems." *African Forum*, 2, No. 3 (Winter, 1967), 50–65.

8804 **Owens, W.H.** "New Links in Central African Transport." *New Commonwealth*. 38, No. 6 (June, 1960), 367–370.

8805 **Pankhurst, Richard.** "Ethiopia's Access to the Sea" and "The Ports and Foreign Trade." Chapters in his *An Introduction to the Economic History of Ethiopia from Early Times to 1800*. London: Lalibela House, distributed by Sidgwick and Jackson, 1961, 322–355.

8806 **Pankhurst, Richard.** "The Franco-Ethiopian Railway and Its History." *Ethiopia Observer*, 6, No. 4 (1963), 342–379.

8807 **Parenteau, Ch.** "L'Oeuvre et l'Avenir de l'Organiszation Commune Dahomey-Niger des "Chemin de Fer et des Transports (O.C.D.N.)" [The Work and the Future of the Dahomey-Niger Common Organization of Railraods and Transprot]. *Europe-France Outremer*, 426–427 (July–August, 1965), 55–59.

8808 **Parsons, Q.N.** "Economics of the Zambia-Botswana Highway." *Enterprise*, 3 (1974), 56–59.

8809 **Payne, Richard J.** "Deep Sea–bed Mining: Implications for Zaire and Zambia." *Review of African Political Economy*, 12, No. 2 (May–August, 1978), 98–105.

8810 **Payne, Richard J.** "Southern Africa and the Law of the Sea: Economic Political Implications." *Journal of Southern African Affairs*, 4, No. 2 (April, 1979), 175–186.

8811 **Pechota, Vratislav.** "The Right of Access to the Sea." In *Land–Locked Countries of Africa*, Zdenek Cervenka, ed. Uppsala: The Scandinavian Institute of African Studies, 1973, 37–43.

8812 **Pederson, Ole Karup and Leys, Roger.** "A Theoretical Approach to the Problem of African Land–Locked States." In *Land–Locked Countries of Africa*, Zdenek Cervenka, ed. Uppsala: The Scandinavian Institute of African Studies, 1973, 288–292.

8813 **Perry, John W.B.** "The Growth of the Transport Network of Malawi." *Society of Malawi Journal*, 22, No. 2 (July, 1969), 23–37.

8814 **Perry, John W.B.** "Malawi's New Outlet to the Sea." *Geography*, 56, No. 2 (April, 1971), 138–140.

8815 **Peterec, Richard J.** "The Port of Dakar: A Case Study of the Effect of Independence Upon a Former Colonial Port." *Pennsylvania Geographer*, 4, No. 2 (March, 1966), 12–16.

8816 **Pirie, Gordon H.** "The Decivilizing Rails: Railways and Underdevelopment in Southern Africa." *Tijdschrift voor Economische en Sociale Geografie*, 73, No. 4 (August, 1982), 221–228.

8817 **Polhemus, James H.** *The Impact of Zimbabwean Independence on Regional International Relations: Towards Congruence between Economics and Politics in the Southern African Subsystem*. Paper read to the Annual Meeting of the International Studies Association, Cincinnati, March, 1982.

8818 **Pollock, Norman Charles.** "Communications in Africa with Special Reference to the Land–Locked States and Their Transport Problems: and "Case Studies of the Transport Problems of LandLocked Countries." In *Studies in Emerging Africa*. Totowa, New Jersey: Rowman and Littlefield, 1971, 125–149 and 150–169.

8819 **Pollock, Norman Charles.** "Some Geographical Aspects of East African Transport." *Bulletin of the Africa Institute*, 7, No. 4 (May, 1969), 125–133.

8820 **Pollock, Norman Hall, Jr.** "Transportation: The Heart of the Problem." In *Nyasaland and Northern Rhodesia: Corridor to the North*. Pittsburgh: Duquesne University Press, 1971, 361–394.

8821 "Pour Desenclaver et Fertiliser le Sahel; Conseil de l'Entente" [To Reduce the Effects of Land–Lockedness and Enrich the Sahel; Council of the Entente]. *Remarques Arabo–Africaines*, 20, No. 517 (March, 1978), 19.

8822 **Prescott, J.R.V.** "Resources, Policies and Development in West and North Central Africa." In *Northern Geographical Essays in Honour of G.H.J. Daysh*, Johon William House, ed. Newcastle Upon Tyne: Oriel Press, 1966, 292–307.

8823 "Pres de 95% des Echanges avec l'Exterieur s'Effectuent par la Voie Fluviale" [Nearly 95% of Foreign Trade Carried Out by River]. *Europe Outremer*, 51, No. 527 (December, 1973), 41–43.

8824 **Protat, P.** "L'Equipement du Dakar–Niger" [The Equipment of the Dakar–Niger (Railway)]. *Industries et Travaux d'Outremer*, 8, No. 82 (September, 1960), 591–595.

8825 **Puri, Shamlal.** "From the Benguela to the Tan–Zam Railway." *African Development*, 10, No. 10 (October, 1976), 1021 and 1023.

8826 **Rake, Alan.** "Benguela: Africa's Lifeline Reopens." *African Business*, No. 9 (September, 1978), 9.

8827 **Rake, Alan.** "Central Africa's Transport Tangle." *African Business*, 26, No. 10 (October, 1980), 15–16.

8828 **Rake, Alan.** "Railways Race for the Copper Trade." *African Development*, 8, No. 8 (August, 1971), 9, 11, 13.

8829 **Rake, Alan.** "Why Zimbabwe Cut Zambia's Transport Links." *African Business*, 17, No. 1 (January, 1980), 11–12.

8830 **Rake, Alan.** Zambia's Intractable Transport Problems." *African Development*, 9, No. 11 (November, 1975), Z.27 and Z.29.

8831 **Ramaer, R.** "Verkeersnetwerken in Ontwikkelingslanden: het Voorbeeld van de East African Railways" [Transport Networks in Developing Countries: The Example of the East African Railways]. *Geografisch Tijdschrift*, 12, No. 2 (March, 1978), 81–96.

8832 **Rathbone, R.D.** "A Southern Trans–Bechauna Road." *African Roads and Transport*, 15, No. 5 (September–October, 1957), 3–5.

8833 **Reitsman, Hendrik–Jan A.** "Africa's Land–Locked Countries: A Study of Dependency Relations." *Tijdschrift voor Economische en Sociale Geografie*, 71, No. 3 (June, 1980), 130–141.

8834 **Reitsman, Hendrik–Jan A.** "De Binnenstaten van Africa" [The Land–Locked States of Africa]. In *Een Wereld van Staten*, J.M.M. van Amersfoort, et al., eds. Alphen aan den Rijn: Samson Uitgeverij, 1981, 199–208.

8835 **Reitsman, Hendrik–Jan A.** "Malawi's Problem of Allegiance." *Tijdschrift voor Economische en Sociale Geografie*, 65, No. 6 (December, 1974), 421–429.

8836 **Rettman, Rosalyn J.** "The Tanzam Rail Link: China's 'Loss–Leader' in Africa." *World Affairs*, 136, No. 3 (Winter, 1973–74), 232–258.

8837 **Robie, David.** "Africa's Highway Takes Shape—Bureaucrats, Mud and All." *African Development*, 11, No. 4 (April, 1974), 11–13.

8838 **Robins, Sir Reginald E.** "The Development of the Transport System of East Africa." *Uganda Journal*, 14, No. 2 (September, 1950), 129–138.

8839 **Roskam, K.L.** "De Weg Tussen Botswana en Zambia" [The Road between Botswana and Zambia]. *Kroniek van Afrika*, 2, No. 1 (Mai, 1970), 106–107.

8840 **Rubin, Alfred P.** "Land–Locked African Countries and Rights of Access to the Sea." In *Land–Locked Countries of Africa*, Zdenek Cervenka, ed. Uppsala: The Scandinavian Institute of African Studies, 1973, 44–62.

8841 **Rule, M.L.** "The Report of the Beit Bridge Rail Link Commission 1967." *Rhodesian Journal of Economics*, 1, No. 1 (August, 1967), 61–68.

8842 "The Rwandese Equation." *Africa*, 80, No. 4 (April, 1978), 52 and 57.

8843 **Sabourin, Louis.** "Problems and Prospects of the Seven Land–Locked Countries of French–speaking Africa: Central African Republic, Chad, Mali, Niger, Upper Volta, Rwanda and Burundi." In *Land–Locked Countries of Africa*, Zdenek Cervenka, ed. Uppsala: The Scandinavian Institute of African Studies, 1973, 146–157.

8844 "SADCC Transport" (Suite of short articles by various correspondents). *African Business*, 49, No. 9 (September, 1982), 14–17.

8845 **Sautter, Gilles.** *Isolement Geographique et Cout des Transports: l'Example du Tchad* [Geographic Isolation and Cost of Transport: The Example of Chad]. Paper read to the 19th International Geographical Congress, Stockholm, 1960. Abstract appears in the *Proceedings* of the Congress, 255.

8846 Sautter, Gilles. "Les Liaisons entre le Tchad et la Mer: Essai d'Analyse Geographique d'une Situation de Concurrence dans le Domaine des Transports" [The Links between Chad and the Sea: An Attempt at Geographical Analysis of a Competitive Situation in the Sphere of Transport]. *Bulletin de l'Association de Geographes Francais*, 286-287 (November–December, 1959), 9–17.

8847 Schmidt, Robert H. "Some Comments on Geographical Aspects of African Landlocked States." *Annals of the Association of American Geographers*, 59, No. 4 December, (1969), 820.

8848 Schreiber, Marc. "Vers un Nouveau Regime International du Fleuve Niger" [Toward a New International Regime of the River Niger]. *Annuaire Francais de Droit International*, 9 (1963), 866–889.

8849 Seck, Assane. "The Changing Role of the Port of Dakar." In *Seaports and Development in Tropical Africa*, Brian Stewart Hoyle and David Hilling, eds. London: Macmillan, 1970, 41–56.

8850 Secretariat General. "Etudes sur les Transports Routiers et Ferroviaires dans les Pays de l'OCAM" [Studies on Highway and Rail Transport in the OCAM Countries]. Organisation Commune Africaine Malagache et Maurichienne (OCAM). *Etudes et Statistiques OCAM*, New Series No. 2 (1971), whole number.

8851 Secretariat General. "Les Transports Maritimes et Fluviaux dans les Pays de l'OCAM" [Maritime and River Transport in the OCAM Countries]. *Etudes et Statistiques OCAM*. New Series No. 3 (May, 1972), whole number.

8852 Secretariat General de l'U.D.E.A.C. "Etude sur le Transit des Marchandises en U.D.E.A.C. (1967)" [Study on the Transit of Goods in U.D.E.A.C. (1967)]. Union Douanier et Economique de l'Afrique Centrale (UDEAC). *Etudes Statistiques No. 10*, Supplement au *Bulletin des Statistiques Generales de l'U.D.E.A.C.*, June, 1969.

8853 Segal, Aaron. "Tanzania–Zambia Rail Prospect." *Venture*, 17, No. 6 (June, 1965), 12–18.

8854 Segal, Aaron. "The Tanganyika–Zambia Railway Project." *Africa Report*, 9, No. 10 (November, 1964), 9–10.

8855 Sendler, Gerhard. "Zur Problematik der Seehafen Mocambique's" [On the Problem of Mozambique's Seaports]. In *Studien zur Allegemeinen und Regionalen Geographie*, G.[unther] Gruber, et al, eds. Frankfurter Wirtshafts- und Sozialgeographische Schriften, No. 26. Selbstverlag des Seminars fur Wirtshaftsgeographie der Johann Wolfgang Goethe – Universitat Frankfurt/Main, 1977, 435-463.

8856 Shaffer, N. Manfred. "Transit Traffic and the Ports of Portuguese Africa." Paper read at the annual meeting of the Association of Pacific Coast Geographers, 1971.

8857 Shaw, Timothy M. "The International Sub–system of Southern Africa: Introduction." In *Land-Locked Countries of Africa*, Zdenek Cervenka, ed. Uppsala: The Scandinavian Institute of African Studies, 1973, 161–164.

8858 Sircar, Parbati K. "The Great Uhuru (Freedom) Railway: China's Link to Africa." *China Report*, 14, No. 2 (March–April, 1978), 15-24.

8859 "Situation des Projets Ferroviares de Desenclavement de la RCA" [Status of Rail Projects to Reduce the Effects of Land-Lockedness of the CAR]. *Bulletin de l'Afrique Noir*, 19, No. 877 (July 21, 1976), 17–113.

8860 Sklar, Richard L. "Zambia's Response to the Rhodesian Unilateral Declaration of Independence." Chapter 9 in *Politics in Zambia*, William Tordoff, ed. Manchester University Press, 1974, 320-362.

8861 Smit, P. "Botswana Railway Line." *Bulletin of the Africa Institute*, 8, No. 7 (August, 1970), 272–280.

8862 Somerville, Keith. "Great Uhuru Railway or Great White Elephant?" *African Business*, 58, No. 6 (June, 1983), 10–11.

8863 Soudan, Francois. "Le Drame du Benguela" [The Drama of the Benguela]. *Jeune Afrique*, 19 Annee, No. 962 (June 13, 1979), 61, 63.

8864 "Southern Africa Transport and Communications Commission: Summary of the Progress Made in the Field of Transport and Communications Since the Lusaka Summit." *SADEX*, 3, No. 5 (September–October, 1981), 8–10.

8865 Strack, Harry Robert. "Communications and Transportation." Chapter 5 in his *Sanctions: The Case of Rhodesia*. Syracuse, New York: Syracuse University Press, 1978, 167–189, notes on 267-269.

8866 Stuckey, Barbara. "Moyens de Transport et Developpement Africain: Les Pays sans Acces Cotier" [Means of Transport and African Development: The Land-Locked Countries]. *Espaces et Societes*, 10-11 (October, 1973 – February, 1974), 119-126.

8867 "Swaziland: National Shipping Line." *Africa Research Bulletin*; Economic, Financial and Technical Series, 15, No. 1 (February, 1978), 4587.

8868 "Swaziland: [Shipping] Line Starts Service." *Africa Research Bulletin*; Economic, Financial and Technical Series. 15, No. 4 (May, 1978), 46–92.

8869 Szentes, Tamas. "The Economic Problems of Land-Locked Countries." In *Land-Locked Countries of Africa*, Zdenek Cervenka, ed. Uppsala: The Scandinavian Institute of African Studies, 1973, 273–277.

8870 Tandon, Yashpal. "Transit Problems of Uganda Within the East African Community." In *Land-Locked Countries of Africa*, Zdenek Cervenka, ed. Uppsala: The Scandinavian Institute of African Studies, 1973, 79–97.

8871 "The Tanzam Railway." *Afro-Asian Economic Review*, 13, No. 138-139 (March–April, 1971), 24–26.

8872 "Tanzam Railway—Breakthrough for Red China." *Bulletin of the Africa Institute of South Africa*, 10, No. 6 (July, 1972) 237–241.

8873 "Tanzania: Rwanda Links." *Africa Confidential*, 18, No. 16 (August 5, 1977), 3–4.

8874 Tarski, Ignacy. "Wezlowe Zagadnienia Tranzytu Ladowomorskiego" [Key Problems of Land-Sea Transit Shipments]. *Handel Zagraniczny*, 16, Nr. 8 (Dec. 1961), 342–348.

8875 "Tazama Pipeline." *Standard Bank Review*, (October, 1968), 2–4.

8876 "Tazama Pipelines Undergoes a Major Expansion." *Enterprise*, (2nd Quarter, 1972), 22–23.

8877 Thahane, T.T. "Lesotho, an Island Country: The Problems of Being Land-Locked." *African Review*, 4, No. 2 (1974), 279–290.

8878 Thahane, T.T. "Lesotho, the Realities of Land-lockedness." In *Land-locked Countries of Africa*. Zdenek Cervenka, ed. Uppsala: The Scandinavian Institute of African Studies, 1973, 239–249.

8879 Thomas, Benjamin E. "Railways and Ports in french West Africa." *Economic Geography*, 33, No. 1 (January, 1957), 1–15.

8880 Thomas, Benjamin E. *Trade Routes of Algeria and the Sahara*. University of California Publications in Geography, 8, No. 3 (1957), 165–288.

8881 Thomas, C.J. "Economic Interaction between South Africa and Other States in Southern Africa." *South African Yearbook of International Law*, 3 (1977), 1–32.

8882 Thriscutt, H.S., and O'Sullivan, K.P. "Two Studies of the Transafrican Highway." *Proceedings of the Institution of Civil Engineers*, 58, Part 1 (August, 1975), 335–360.

8883 Tilbury, Michael. "The International Law of Non-aerial Transit Trade: The Case of Zimbabwe." *Zimbabwe Law Journal*, 20, No. 1 (April, 1980), 4–33 and 20, No. 2 (October, 1980), 125–161.

8884 "Transport." Suite of articles including the following: "Transport Planning; Which Way to Go?" by A.M.H. Muyovwe, 9–15; "Zambia's Mines Break the Transport Bottleneck" [copper airlift] by N. Mwanyungwi, 17, 19, 21; "Zambia Railways; Out of the Past into the Future," 23, 25, 27; and "Tanzama Pipeline; Fuel Artery," 39. *Enterprise*, 2 (1977).

8885 "Transport and Communications in United Nations Trust Territories; III. Ruanda-Urundi." *Transport and Communications Review*, 2, No. 2 (April–June, 1949), 45–51.

8886 "Un Pays de Transit [Dahomey]; Les Travaux d'Infrastructure" [A Transit Country; The Infrastructure Works]. *Europe-France Outremer*, 50, No. 515 (December, 1972), 40–41.

8887 Vail, Leroy. "Railway Development and Colonial Underdevelopment: The Nyasaland Case." In *The Roots of Rural Poverty in Central and Southern Africa*, Robin Palmer and Neil Parsons, eds. Berkeley and Los Angeles: University of California Press, 1977, 365–395.

8888 van Dongen, Irene S. "Mombasa in the Land and Sea Exchanges of East Africa." *Erdkunde*, 17, No. 1–2 (June, 1963), 16–38.

8889 van Dongen, Irene S. "Nacala; Newest Mozambique Gateway to Interior Africa." *Tijdschrift voor Economische en Sociale Geografie*, 48, No. 3 (March, 1957), 65–73.

8890 van Dongen, Irene S., and Hance, William A. "Port Development and Rail Lines in Portuguese West Africa." *Proceedings of the 18th International Geographical Congress*, Rio de Janeiro, 1956. Rio de Janeiro: Brazilian National Committee of the International Geographical Union, 1966, 380–387.

8891 Varian, H.F. "The Geography of the Benguella Railway." *Geographical Journal*, 78, No. 6 (December, 1931), 497–523.

8892 Vellas, Pierre. "Les Transports Fluviaux et le Developpement Economique de l'Afrique" [River Transport and Economic Development of Africa]. *Canadian Journal of Development Studies*, 3, No. 1 (1982), 161–166.

8893 **Vennetier, Pierre.** "La Navigation Interieure en Afrique Noire; le Reseau Francais Congo–Oubangui" [Inland Navigation in Black Africa; The French Congo–Oubangui Network]. *Les Cahiers d'Outre-Mer*, 12, No. 48 (October–December, 1959), 321–348.

8894 **Vennetier, Pierre.** "Problems of Port Development in Gabon and Congo Brazzaville." In *Seaports and Development in Tropical Africa*, Brian Stewart Hoyle and David Hilling, eds. London: Macmillan, 1970, 183–201.

8895 **Viall, John D.** "The Transit of Persons to and from Lesotho." *Comparative and International Law Journal of Southern Africa*, , No. 1 (March, 1968), 1–21; 1, No. 2 (July, 1968), 187–208 and 1, No. 3 (November, 1968), 363–389.

8896 **Vigarie, Andre.** "Ports et Vie Portuaire de l'Afrique de l'Ouest" [Ports and Port Life of West Africa]. *Annuaire de Droit Maritime et Aerien*, 3 (1976), 69–82.

8897 **Voss, Joachim.** "Die Guinea–mali Bahn—ein Afrikanisches Politikum" [The Guinea–Mali Road—An African Political Matter]. *Afrika Spectrum*, 1 (May, 1970), 46–50.

8898 **Wasserman, Ursula.** "Economic Sanctions—The Rhodesian Experience." *Journal of World Trade Law*, 9, No. 5 (SeptemberOctober, 1975), 590–593.

8899 **Watts, Ronald L.** "Benguela Railway: Hangover from the Past but Lifeline Now." *African Development*, 9, No. 11 (November, 1975), 111.

8900 **Weenink, W.H.** "Het Tanzanie Zambia Spoorwegproject; Transportproblemen Langs een Front" [The Tanzania–Zambia Railway Project; Problems of Transport along a Front]. *Internationale Spectator*, 25, No. 22 (December, 1971), 2101–2125.

8901 **Weiss, Ruth.** "Imports put Strain on Zambia's Lifelines." *African Development*, 10, No. 10 (October, 1973), Z23, Z25.

8902 **Weiss, Ruth.** "Southern Africa Gets Together [SATCC]." *African Business*, 26, No. 10 (October, 1980), 16–17.

8903 **Welensky, Sir Roy.** "Railway, Road and Air Plans for Central Africa." *New Commonwealth*, 29, No. 2 (January 24, 1955), 65–68.

8904 **Wells, F.B.** "Transport in the Rhodesian Copperbelt." *Geography*, 42, No. 2 (April, 1957), 93–95.

8905 **Westebbe, Richard.** "The Critical Role of Transport." In *Chad: Development Potential and Constraints*, New York: IBRD, 1974, 42–48.

8906 **Whittington, G.** "Some Effects on Zambia of Rhodesian Independence." *Tijdschrift voor Economische en Sociale Geografie*, 58, No. 2 (April, 1967), 103–106.

8907 **White, H.P.** "The Ports of West Africa; Some Geographical Considerations." *Tijdschrift voor Economische en Sociale Geografie*, 50, No. 1 (January, 1959), 1–8.

8908 **Whittington, G.** "The Swaziland Railway." *Tijdschrift voor Economische en Sociale Geografie*, 57, No. 3 (March-April, 1966), 68–73.

8909 **Yu, George T.** "Chinese Aid to Africa: The Tanzania-Zambia Railway." In *Chinese and Soviet Aid to Africa*, Warren Weinstein, ed. New York: Praeger, 1975, 29–55.

8910 **Yu, George T.** "Working on the Railroad: China and the Tanzania-Zambia Railway." *Asian Survey*, 11, No. 11 (November, 1971), 1101–1117.

8911 *Zambia and the World; Essays on Problems Relating to Zambia's Foreign Policy*. Articles collected for the occasion of the Non-aligned Summit Conference held in Lusaka, September, 1970. Lusaka: University of Zambia School of Humanities and Social sciences, 1970. Contains the following articles: "Zambia's Foreign Policy," by B.V. Mtshali, 1-9 (Reprinted from *Current History*, Vol. 58, No. 343 (March, 1970); "Confrontation in Southern Africa; Zambia and Portugal," by Douglas G. Anglin, 10-22 (Reprinted from *International Journal*, Vol. 25, No. 3 (Summer, 1970), 497-517; "Zambia-Botswana Road Link: Some Border Problems," by James Craig, 23-29; and "South Africa's Drive to the North: A Study of the Economic Consequences for African States," by Robert Molteno, 30-54.

8912 "Zambia; Lifelines to the Sea." *The Courier; ACP-EC*, No. 56 (July-August, 1979), 106-107.

8913 "Zambia-Tanzania Crisis." *Bulletin of the Africa Institute of South Africa*, 12, No. 5 (1974), 200-203.

8914 "Zentralafrikas Handel auf Portugals Eisenbahnen" [Central Africa's Trade on Portugal's Railroads]. *Verkehr in Afrika*, 8 (1969), 24-35.

AMERICAS

Books

8915 **Abecia Baldivieso, Valentin.** *Laqs Relaciones Internacionales en la Historia de Bolivia* [International Relations in Bolivian History]. 2 vols. La Paz: Editorial Los Amigos del Libro, 1979.

8916 **ALAF (Associacion Latinoamericana de Ferrocarriles).** Comision Estudios Economicos. *Analisis Operativo y Perspectivas del Ferrocarril Internacional Arica-La Paz* [Operational Analysis and Prospects of the Arica-La Paz International Railway]. Santiago: ALAF, April, 1970.

8917 **ALAF (Associacion Latinoamericana de Ferrocarriles).** Grupo Zonal Chile-Bolivia. *Estudio de la Operacion de la Via Arica a Bolivia* [Study of the Operation of the Arica-Bolivia Route]. La Paz: Association Latinoamericana de Ferrocarriles, February, 1968.

8918 **Aramayo Avila, Cesareo.** *Ferrocarriles Bolivianos; Pasado, Presente, Futuro* [Bolivian Railroads; Past, Present, Future]. La Paz: Imprenta Nacional, 1959.

8919 **Avila, Federico.** *Bolivia en el Concierto del Plata* [Bolivia in the La Plata Agreement]. Mexico City: Editorial Cultura, 1941.

8920 **Bejarano, Ramon Cesar.** *El Paraguay en Busca del mar* [Paraguay in Searach of the Sea]. Asuncion: Casa Editorial Toledo, 1965.

8921 **Bejarano, Ramon Cesar.** *Vias y Medios de Communicaciones del Paraguay (1811-1961)* [Paraguay's Communications Routes and Means (1811-1961)]. Asuncion: Editorial Toledo, 1963.

8922 **Bocchio Rejas, Luis Orlando.** *Los Tacnenos y el Corredor para Bolivia* [The Residents of Tacna and the Cororidor for Bolivia]. Lima: Pueblo Libre, 1978.

8923 **Bolivia, Administracion Autonoma de Almacenes Aduaneros.** *Ayuda Memoria sobre Facilidades para el Transito de Carga Boliviana por el Puerto de Buenos Aires* [Aide Memoire on Facilities for the Transit of Bolivian Cargo through the Port of Buenos Aires]. La Paz: Bolivia, Administracion Autonoma de Almacenes Aduaneros, 1979.

8924 Bolivia, Ministerio de Relaciones Exteriores y Culto and BID-INTAL. *El Transporte en la Cuenca del Plata; Analisis Critico* [Transport in the Plata Basin; Critical Analysis]. La Paz: BID-INTAL, 1975.

8925 **Botelho Gosalvez, Raul.** *El Litoral Boliviano: Perspectiva Historica y Geopolitica* [The Bolivian Coast; Historical and Geopolitical Perspective]. Buenos Aires: El Cid Editor, 1980.

8926 **Cantero Ojeda, Carlos.** *Impacto de la Funcion Corredor de Transporte en el Puerto de Antofagasta* [Impact of the Transport Corroidor Function on the Port of Antofagasta]. Antofagasta, Chile: Universidad del Norte, Departamento de Geosciencias, Master's Thesis, 1982.

8927 **Cardona, G.; Ortiz, Miguel; and Ramon**

Recalde. For Institute of Inter-American Affairs, Technical Cooperation Administration, U.S. Department of State. *The Role of River Transport in Paraguayan International Trade.* Asuncion: U.S. Department of State, June, 1952.

8928 **CEPAL.** Division de Comercio Internacional y Desarrollo. *Paraguay: Los Fletes de Comercio Exterior y la Economia Nacional* [Paraguay: Foreign Commerce Cargoes and the National Economy], by Tomas Sepulveda Whittle. Asuncion: CEPAL, October 31, 1980.

8929 **CEPAL.** Division de Comercio Internacional y Desarrollo. *Paraguay: Viabilidad del Transporte Multimodal Internacional* [Paraguay: Viability of International Multimodal Transport], by Tomas Sepulveda Whittle. Asuncion: CEPAL, November 14, 1980.

8930 **Chile.** *Facilidades de Libre Transito que Chile Otorga a Bolivia* [Free Transit Facilities which Chile Grants to Bolivia]. Santiago: Ministerio de Relaciones Exteriores, 1963 and 1978.

8931 **Chile.** *History of the Chilean-Bolivian Negotiations 1975-1978.* Santiago: Ministry of Foreign Affairs, 1978.

8932 **Chile.** Programa de Cooperacion Tecnica Chile-California, Proyecto Transportes. *Programa de Inversiones en el Puerto de Arica y en el Ferrocarril Arica-La Paz* [Program of Investments in the Port of Arica and in the Arica-La Paz Railroad]. Santiago: Ministry of Foreign Affairs, August, 1966.

8933 **Comite Departmental de Obras Publicas, Santa Cruz de la Sierra, Bolivia.** *El Transporte del Comercio Exterior de Santa Cruz, Bolivia* [Transport of the Foreign Trade Goods of Santa Cruz, Bolivia], Santa Cruz, Bolivia: Comite Departmental de Obras Publicas, 1981.

8934 *Costo de Transporte y Comercio Subregional Andino* [Transport Cost and Andean Subregional Trade]. Santa Cruz, Bolivia: Comite Departmental de Obras Publicas, August, 1981.

8935 **Daniel, Mann, Johnson and Mendenhall; Stanford Research Institute; and Alan M. Voorhees and Associates for the Government of Bolivia, the World Bank and UNDP/Special Fund.** *Bolivia Transport Survey.* La Paz: Government of Bolivia, May, 1968.

8936 **De Soto, Anthony Essex.** *Bolivia's Right to an Access to the Sea.* Pasadena, California: Jensen Publishing, 1962.

8937 **Diaz Albonico, Rodrigo.** *La Respuesta Chilena a Bolivia y el Derecho Internacional* [The Chilean Reply to Bolivia and International Lawa]. Santiago: Instituto de Estudios Internacionales, Universidad de Chile. Serie de Publicaciones Especiales No. 23, 1977.

8938 **Di Natale, Remo.** *Bolivia, Chile, Peru y el Mar* [Bolivia, Chile, Peru and the Sea]. Valencia, Venezuela: Universidad de Carabobo, Publicaciones de la Facultad de Derecho, Studia 3, 1978.

8939 *El Transporte en la Cuenca del Plata* [Transport in the Plata Basin]. Washington, D.C.: Secretaria Ejecutiva para Asuntos Economicos y Sociales, Departamento de Desarrollo Regional. February, 1984.

8940 *El Transporte Fluvial en la Cuenca del Plata* [River Transport in the Plata Basin]. Asuncion: Government of Paraguay, January, 1984.

8941 **Escobari Cusicanqui, Jorge.** *El Derecho al Mar* [The Right to the Sea]. 2nd ed. La Paz: Escobari, 1979.

8942 **Escobari Cusicanqui, Jorge.** *Historia Diplomatica de Bolivia; (Politica Internacional)* [Diplomatic History of Bolivia; (International Policy)]. 3rd ed. La Paz: Universidad Boliviana, 1978.

8943 **Espinosa Moraga, Oscar.** *Bolivia y el Mar 1810-1964* [Bolivia and the Sea 1810-1964]. Santiago: Editorial Nascimento, 1965.

8944 *Estudio de Transportes en la Region Amazonica y en el Alto Paraguay. Primera Parte* [Study of Transport in the Amazon Region and on the Upper Paraguay. Part One]. Convenio ATN/SF-2084-RE. November, 1983.

8945 **Eyzaguirre, Jaime.** *Bolivia—An Isolated Country?* Santiago: Empresa Editora Zig-Zag, 1965.

8946 **Fifer, J. Valerie.** *Bolivia: Land, Location, and Politics Since 1825.* Cambridge: Cambridge University Press, 1972.

8947 **Fournier, Cynthia Ann.** *Access to the Sea for Bolivia.* New Haven, Connecticut: Southern Connecticut State College, M.S., 1979.

8948 **Frontaura Argandona, Manuel.** *El Litoral de Bolivia* [The Coast of Bolivia]. La Paz: Honorable Municipalidad de La Paz, 1968.

8949 **Galindo Quiroga, Eudoro.** *Litoral Andino* [Andean Coast]. Cochabamba: Los Amigos del Libro, 1977.

8950 **Garcia Rendon, Godofredo.** *La Problematica Juridico-Internacional de las Relaciones entre Bolivia, Chile y Peru* [The Juridical-International Problem of the Relations Among Bolivia, Chile and Peru]. La Paz: Editorial Letras, 1964.

8951 **Glassner, Martin Ira.** *Bolivia and an Access to the Sea.* Fullerton: California State University, Master's Thesis, 1964.

8952 **Gonzalez, Luis J.** *Paraguay: Prisionero Geopolitico* [Paraguay: Geopolitical Prisoner]. Buenos Aires: Ediciones Nogal, 1947.

8953 **Guevara Arze, Walter.** *Radiografia de la Negociacion con Chile* [X-ray Picture of the Negotiations (Over a Corridor to the Sea) with Chile]. Cochabamba: Editorial Universo, 1978.

8954 **Gutierrez Gutierrez, Mario R.** *Alegato Historico de los Derechos de Bolivia al Pacifico* [Historical Assertion of the Rights of Bolivia to the Pacific]. La Paz: Government of Bolivia, 1962.

8955 **Gutierrez Gutierrez, Mario R.** *El Jefe de Falange Socialista Boliviana Enfoca la Cuestion Maritima Boliviana* [The Chief of the Falange Socialists Boliviana Focuses on Bolivia's Maritime Question]. La Paz: Government of Bolivia, 1973.

8956 **Haine, Edgar A.** *Railways Across the Andes.* Boulder, Colorado: Pruett, 1981.

8957 **Holland, E. James.** *Bolivian Relations with Chile and Peru: Hopes and Realities.* Paper read at the Conference on Modern Day Bolivia: Legacy of the Past and Prospects for the Future. Tempe: The Center for Latin American Studies, Arizona State University, March 15-17, 1978.

8958 **Infante Caffi, Maria Teresa.** *El Acceso de Bolivia al Mar: Una Vision Prospectiva* [The Access of Bolivia to the Sea: A Prospective Vision]. Seville, Spain: Paper produced for the project on "Solution Pacifica de Controversias en Iberoamerica," sponsored by the Instituto Universitario Iberoamericano de Estudios Internacionales, Universidad de Seville, 1984.

8959 **Informe Final.** Estudios Sobre Transportes en el Area URUPABOL [Final Report. Studies on Transport in the URUPABOL Area], by Daniel E. Batalla. Project ATN/SF-1438-RE. Lima: Inter American Develop Bank (BTD), 1976.

8960 **Instituto de Investigaciones Historicas y Culturales de La Paz.** *Mesa Redonda sobre el Problema del Litoral Boliviano* [Round Table on the Problem of the Bolivian Coast]. La Paz: Honorable Municipalidad, 1966.

8961 **Iturriza, Jorge E.** *Acciones de Apoyo a Los Paises de Menor Desarrollo Relativo Mediterraneos* [Actions in Support of the Relatively Less Developed Land-Locked Countries]. La Paz: Universidad, March, 1981.

8962 **Jordan Sandoval, Santiago.** *Bolivia y el Equilibrio del Cono Sudamericano* [Bolivia and the Equilibrium of the South American Cone]. Cochabamba: Editorial Los Amigos del Libro, 1979.

8963 **Krieg, William L.** *Bolivia: En Route to the Sea?* Washington, D.C.: Department of State External Research Program, Research Paper FAR 27708, October, 1977.

8964 **Krieg, William L.** *Legacy of the War of the Pacific.* Washington, D.C.: Department of State External Research Program, Research Paper FAR 20565, October, 1974.

8965 *La Compensacion en el Transporte Internacional-- Esquema Conceptual y Metodologico* [Compensation in International (Transit) Transport- -Conceptual and Methodological Scheme]. La Paz: Government of Bolivia, May, 1981.

8966 *La Eficiencia del Transporte Fluvial en la Cuenca del Plata* [The Efficiency of River Transport in the Plata Basin]. Ascunsion: Government of Paraguay, November, 1981.

8967 **Lang, Gerhard.** *Boliviens Streben nach Freiem Zugang zum Meer* [Bolivia's Aspirations for a Free Access to the Sea]. Hamburg: Hamburger Gesellschaft fur Volkerrecht und Auswartige Politik, 1966.

8968 **Lindman, Bertram H.** For the Institute of Inter- American Affairs, Technical Cooperation Administration, U.S. Department of State. *The Transportation Problem of Paraguay.* Asuncion: Institute of Inter-American Affairs, 1952.

8969 *Los Derechos de Bolivia al Mar; Antologia de Juicios Eminentes* [The Rights of Bolivia to the Sea; Anthology of Eminent Opinions]. La Paz: Editorial America Latina, 1962.

8970 **Meneses, Romulo.** *El imperativo geografico en la mediterraneidad de Bolivia.* La Paz, Ed.: Renacimiento, 1943.

8971 **Merryman, John H.,** and **Ackerman, Edgar D.** *International Law, Development and the Transit Trade of Land-Locked States: The Case of Bolivia.* Hamburg: Alfred Metzner Verlag, 1969.

8972 *Modalidades, Repercusion y Alternativas de una Zona Franca para Paraguay en Territorio Uruguayo* [Modalities, Repercussions and Alternatives of a Free Zone for Paraguay in Uruguayan Territory]. CEP/Repartido 1944, February 14, 1980. Restricted.

8973 **Monróy Cardenas, Arturo.** *Historia Aduanera de Bolivia y Tratados Comerciales con los Paises Vecinos 1825-1958* [Customs History of Bolivia and Commercial Treaties with Neighboring Countries 1825-1958]. La Paz: Publicidad Nueva Bolivia, 1959.

8974 **Morzone, Luis Antonio.** *La Mediterraneidad Boliviana ante el Derecho Internaciona; Posicion Argentina* [Bolivian Land-Lockedness in the Light of International Law; Argentine Position]. Buenos Aires: Ediciones Depalma, 1979.

8975 **Moya Quiroga, Victor.** *Internacionalizacion de Arica; Documentos para la Historiografia de una Salida al Mar* [Internationalization of Arica; Documents for the Historiography of an Outlet to the Sea]. La Paz: Editorial El Siglo, 1977.

8976 **Nielsen Reyes, Federico.** *Del Lauca al Mar!* [From the Lauca to the Sea!]. La Paz: Government of Bolivia, 1963.

8977 **Organization of American States.** Economic Conference of the Organization of American States, Buenos Aires, 1957. *Transportation and Economic Growth: The La Plata River System.* Document 11, July, 1957.

8978 **Organization of American States.** *Informe sobre el Problema Maritimo de bolivia* [Report on the Maritime Problem of Bolivia]. Presented by the Delegation of Bolivia. OEA/Ser.P. AG/doc.1145. October 26, 1979.

8979 **Organization of American States, BID, CEPAL, and Paraguay,** Technical Planning Secretariat. *Estudio sobre el Transporte Fluvial en el Paraguay* [Study of River Transport on the Paraguay]. Asuncion: Technical Planning Secretariat, June, 1964.

8980 **Organization of American States and CEPAL.** *Flujos de Comercio Exterior de los Paises sin Litoral* [Foreign Trade Flows of Land-Locked Countries], by Thomas Sepulveda Whittle. Prepared for the X Reunion Ordinaria de la Comision Especial de Consulta y Negociacion (CECON), Washington, D.C.: CECON, October 6-8, 1980.

8981 **Organization of American States, CEPAL, and General Secretariat.** *Textos de Documentos sobre el Uso Comercial de Rios y Lagos Internacionales* [Texts of Documents on the Commercial Use of International Rivers and Lakes]. OEA/Ser.I.VI.1.CIJ-97. November, 1968.

8982 **Organization of American States, CEPAL, General Secretariat, Paraguay,** and Ministry of Industry and Commerce. *Paraguay: Fletres de Exportacion* [Paraguay: Export Cargoes], by Thomas Sepulveda Whittle, Asuncion, December, 1976.

8983 **Organization of American States, CEPAL, General Secretariat, Paraguay**, Ministry of Industry and Commerce, Permanent Council. *Acta de la Sesion Extraordinaria Celebrada el 14 de Febrero de 1979* [Final Act of the Extraordinary Session Held 14 February 1979]. OEA/Ser.g. CP/ACTA 368/79, February 14, 1979.

8984 **Paraguay.** *Facilitacion de Procedimientos de Comercio Exterior, Transportes y Transito; Recomendaciones Preliminares* [Facilitation of Procedures of Foreign Trade, Transport and Transit; Preliminary Recommendations], by Johannes Moe and Jose Maria Rubiato. UNDP/UNCTAD Project INT/77/023. January, 1980.

8985 **Paraguay.** *Estudios sobre el Transporte Fluvial en el Paraguay* [Studies of River Transport in Paraguay]. Washington, UP/Ser. H/V.11, January, 1963.

8986 **Paraguay**, Ministerio de Relaciones Exteriores. *Libre Navegacion de los Rios Paraguay, Parana y de la Plata* [Free Navigation of the Rivers Paraguay, Parana and de la Plata]. Asuncion, 1970.

8987 **Paraguay**, Secretaria Technica de Plantificacion, Presidencia de la Republica. *Estudio sobre el Transporte Fluvial en el Paraguay* [Study of River Transport in Paraguay]. Asuncion, June, 1964.

8988 **Paraguay**, Secretaria Tecnica de Planificacion, Presidencia de la Republica. *Sintesis del Estudio sobre el Transporte en el Paraguay* [Synthesis of the Study on Transport in Paraguay]. Asuncion, July, 1964.

8989 *Plan Andino de Accion Conjunta para Coadyuvar en la Solucion de los Problemas de Transporte Derivados de la Mediterraneidad Boliviana* [Andean Plan of Joint Action to Contribute to the Solution of the Transport Problems Deriving from Bolivia's Land-Lockedness]. JUN/dt 158, February 23, 1981.

8990 **Ponce Caballaro, Jaime.** *Geopolitica Chilena y mar Boliviano* [Chilean Geopolitics and the Bolivian Sea]. La Paz: Ponce Caballero, November, 1976.

8991 *Posibilidades de Utilizacion de Zonas y Depositos Francos en Territorio Uruguayo por Parte del Paraguay* [Possibilities of Utilization of Free Zones and Warehouses in Uruguayan Territory by Paraguay]. CEP/Repartido 1873, December 29, 1978. Restricted.

8992 **Prudencio, Roberto Romecin.** *El Problema martimo de Bolivia.* La Paz: Editorial U.M.S.A., 1951.

8993 *Puertos Regionales en America Latina; Caso de Estudio: Puerto de Antofagasta* [Regional Ports in Latin America; Case Study: The Port of Antofagasta]. Antofagsta: Government of Chile, April, 1982.

8994 *Puertos Regionales en America Latina; Caso de Estudio: Puerto de Paranagua* [Regional Ports in Latin America; Case Study: The Port of Paranagual]. June, 1982.

8995 *Puertos Regionales en America Latina* [Regional Ports in Latin America]. June, 1982.

8996 **Rios Gallardo, Conrado.** *Chile y Bolivia Definen Sus Fronteras 1842-1904* [Chile and Bolivia Define Their Boundaries 1842-1904]. Santiago: Editorial Andres Belle, 1963.

8997 **Saavedra Weise, Agustin.** *Documentos sobre la Mediterraneidad Boliviana* [Documents on Bolivian Land-Lockedness]. Buenos Aires: Ediciones Depalma, 1979.

8998 **Sepulveda Whittle, Tomas B.** *Paraguay: Necesidades Navieras y Portuarias en el Periodo 1978-1985* [Paraguay: Shipping and Port Needs in the Period 1978-1985]. Montevideo: Latin America, Freed Trade Association (ALALC), April, 1978.

8999 **Sepulveda Whittle, Tomas B.** *Transporte y Comercio Exterior del Paraguay* [Transport and Foreign Trade of Paraguay]. Montevideo: Produced for ALALC and INTAL, 1967.

9000 **Sir William Halcrow and Partners.** *Mejoramiento de la Navegacion del Rio Paraguay* [Improvement of Navigation of the River Paraguay]. New York: UNDP Project Arg. 75/012-Par.75/006. October, 1980. Restricted.

9001 **UNDP for the Governments of Argentina and Paraguay.** *Estudio de la Navegacion del Rio Paraguay al Sur de Asuncion* [Study of the Navigation of the Paraguay River to the South of Asuncion]. Project RLA-65-235/1. New York: UNDP, 1974. Restricted.

9002 **Valencia Vega, Alipio.** *Geopolitica del Litoral Boliviano* [Geopolitics of the Bolivian Coast]. La Paz: Libreria Editorial Juventud, 1974.

9003 **Vargas Valenzuela, Jose.** *Tradicion Naval del Pueblo de Bolivia* [Naval Tradition of the Bolivian People]. La Paz and Cochabamaba: Editorial Los Amiagos del Libro, 1974.

9004 **Vidaurre P., Juan Jose.** *Puerto Para Bolivia; Antecedentes Diplomaticos; Bases de Negociacion* [Port for Bolivia: Diplomatic Antecedents; Bases for Negotiation]. La Paz: Editorial Universo, 1950.

9005 **Villacres Moscoso, Jorge W.** *Bolivia y Paraguay: Acceso hacia el Mar.* Madrid: Publicaciones de la Real Sociedada Geografica, Serie B, Numero 405, 1959.

9006 **Virreira Paccieri, Alberto.** *Puerto Propio y Soberano para Bolivia* [Suitable and Sovereign Port for Bolivia]. La Paz: Vice-Presidencia de la Nacion, Departamento de Relaciones Publicas, 1966.

9007 **Wilbur Smith and Associates for Republic of Bolivia, IBRD and UNDP.** *Bolivia National Transport Study.* La Paz: IBRD, July, 1981.

Journals

9008 "Acuerdos Peru-Bolivianos sobre el Ferrocarril Puno-Guaqui y el Aprovechamiento Comun de las Aguas del Lago Titicaca" [Peru-Bolivia Agreements on the Puno-Guaqui Railroad and the Common Utilization of the Waters of Lake Titicaca]. *Revista Peruana de Derecho Internacional,* 15, No. 47-48 (January-December, 1955), 76-99.

9009 **Anglarill, Nilda Beatriz,** and **La Madrid, Monica Vilgre.** "Le Salida al Mar de Bolivia" [Bolivia's Outlet to the Sea]. *Revista Argentina de Relaciones Internacionales,* 3, No. 8 (May-August,1977), 19-36.

9010 **Baptista Gumucio, Mariano.** "Geopolitica de Bolivia; Mediterraneidad y Destino" [Geopolitics of Bolivia; Land-Lockedness and Destiny]. *Geopolitica ,* 9, No. 26 (1983), 5-18.

9011 **Baryshev, Alexander.** "Seeking Access to the Ocean." *New Times,* 12 (March, 1979), 22-23.

9012 **Blanchard, W.O.** "Foreign Trade Routes of Bolivia." *The Journal of Geography,* 22, No. 9 (Abril-Agosto, 1983), 341-345.

9013 **Boscovich, Nicolas.** "El Proyecto Bermejo y la Salida de Bolivia al Mar" (The Bermejo Project and Bolivia's Outlet to the Sea). Chapter 7 in his *Geostrategia de la Cuenca del Planta.* Buenos Aires: El cit Editor, 1979, 157-172.

9014 **Boscovich, Nicolas.** "Geopolitica y Geoestrategia en la Cuenca del Platta" [Geopolitics and Geostrategy in the Plata Basin]. *Geopolitica* 9, No. 27 (Diciembre, 1983), 19–24.

9015 **Boscovich, Nicolas.** "Un Proyecto Regional Argentino y la Natural Salida de Bolivia al Mar" [An Argentine Regional Project and Bolivia's Natural Outlet to the Sea]. *Estrategia,* 6, No. 30 (September-October, 1974), 28-43.

9016 **Bowman, Isaiah.** "Trade Routes in the Economic Geography of Bolivia." *Bulletin of the American Geographical Society,* 42, Nos. 1,2,3 (January, February, March, 1910), 22-37, 90-104, 180-192.

9017 **Brown, Robert T.** "The Future of the International Railways of South America. A Historical Approach." *CEPAL Review,* 8 (August, 1979), 7-38.

9018 **Bustamante, Jose de C.** "A Criacao de um Sistema Integrado de Transportes na Bacia do Prata" [Creation of an Integrated Transport System in the Plata Basin]. *Revista Brasileira de Politica Internacional,* 12, No. 45-46 (March-June, 1969), 44-50.

9019 **Cabrera, Ramon A.** "Ampliacion de los Puertos de Asuncion y Villeta" [Expansion of the Ports of Asuncion and Villeta]. *Navegacion y Puertos,* 5 (June, 1984), 9-12.

9020 **Canamero Galvez, Carlos.** "El Puerto do Matarani" [The Port of Matarani]. *El Ingeniero Civil,* 11 (1981), 20-35.

9021 "Carta de Porto Alegre" [Charter of Porto Alegre (Brazil)]. (18 April 1975) *Arquivos do Ministerio da Justica,* 32, No. 134 (April-June, 1975), 71-75.

9022 **Castillo, P.** "Bolivia: La Salida al Mar" [Bolivia: Outlet to the Sea]. *Analisis de Realidades,* 1 (March 19, 1977), complete issue.

9023 **Costas E., Humberto.** "A Confraternidade Americana e a Clausura Geopolitica da Bolivia" [American Brotherhood and the Geopolitical Enclosure of Bolivia]. *A Defesa Nacional,* 26, No. 537 (April, 1959), 133-139.

9024 "Cuestiones Fluviales con Paraguay y Uruguay" [River Disputes with Paraguay and Uruguay]. *Revista de Derecho Internacional y Coiencias Diplomaticas,* 13, No. 25-26 (January-February, 1964), 107-111.

9025 **de Castro, Therezinha.** "Problemas Bolivianos" [Bolivian Problems]. *Atlas de Relacoes Internacionais,* No. 5 (Caderno Especial da *Revista Brasileira de Geografia,* 30, No. 1 (January-March, 1968), 2-9.

9026 **Diaz Albonico, Rodrigo,** et al. "Les Negociations entre le Chile et la Bolivie Relatives a un Acces Souverain a la Mer" [The Negotiations between Chile and Bolivia Regarding a Sovereign Access to the Sea]. *Annuaire Francais de Droit International,* 23 (1977), 343-356.

9027 **Echeverria, Gloria; Infante, Maria Teresa;** and **Sanchez G., Walter.** "Chile y Bolivia: Conflicto y Negociacion en la Subregion" [Chile and Bolivia: Conflict and Negotiation in the Subregion]. In *Las Relaciones entre los Paises de America Latina,* Walter Sanchez G., ed. Santiago: Editorial Universitaria, 1980,153-183.

9028 "El Trafico Internacional de Contenedores entre Montevideo y Asuncion ya es una Realidad" [International Container Traffic between Montevideo and Asuncion is Now a Reality]. *Revista ALAF*, 9, No. 30 (January-April, 1984), 2-4.

9029 Fernandez Cendoya, Andres. "Bolivia-Chile: Epilogo de un Siglo de Malas Relaciones" [Bolivia-Chile: Epilogue of a Century of Bad Relations]. *Estrategia*, 8, Nos. 37-38 (November, 1975 - February, 1976), 36-50.

9030 Fernandez Cendoya, Andres. "Una Nueva Guerra del Pacifico?" [A New War of the Pacific?]. *Estrategia*, 6, No. 27 (March-April, 1974), 30-40.

9031 Fifer, J. Valerie. "Arica: A Desert Frontier in Transition." *Geographical Journal*, 130, No. 4 (December, 1964), 507-518.

9032 Garcia-Calderon K., Manuel. "La Consulta de Chile al Peru sobre una Salida al Mar para Bolivia" [The Chilean Consultation with Peru about an Outlet to the Sea for Bolivia]. *Revista del Foro*, 63, No. 1 (January-March, 1976), 99-114.

9033 Glassner, Martin Ira. "Bolivia's Access to the Sea." *National Geographic Society Research Reports*, 21 (1980–1983), 193-196.

9034 Glassner, Martin. "The Transit Problems of Land-locked States: The Cases of Bolivia and Paraguay." In *Ocean Yearbook 4*, Elizabeth Mann Borgese and Norton Ginsburg, eds. Chicago: University of Chicago Press, 1983, 366–389.

9035 Gordon, Dennis R. "The Question of the Pacific: Current Perspectives on a Long-Standing Dispute." *World Affairs*, 141, No. 4 (Spring, 1979), 321-335.

9036 Greno Velasco, Jose Enrique. "Bolivia y su Retorno al Mar" [Bolivia and her Return to the Sea]. *Revista de Politica Internacional*, 150, No. 2 (March-April, 1977), 199-230.

9037 Guachalla, Luis Fernando. "Bolivia-Chile; La Negociacion Maritima 1975-1978" [Bolivia-Chile; The Maritime Negotiations 1975-1978]. *Cuadernos de "Hoy"*, 1, No. 5 (February, 1982), complete issue.

9038 Hayman-Joyce, J.G. "River Ports." *Dock and Harbour Authority*, 59 (January, 1979), 274-277, 284.

9039 Hebe Gaveglio, Silvia. "Bolivia. Perdida de su Acceso al Rio Paraguay. La Guerra del Chaco (1932-38)" [Bolivia. Loss of Her Access to the Paraguay River. The Chaco War (1932-38)]. *Estrategia*, 66, II Parte (September-October, 1980), 84-125.

9040 Hebe Gaveglio, Silvia. "La Mediterraneidad de Bolivia (1534-1879)" [The Land-Lockedness of Bolivia (1534-1879)]. *Revista de Politica Internacional*, 164, No. 4 (July-August, 1979), 67-105.

9041 Hernandez, Santiago. "La Mediterraneidad de Bolivia" [The Land-Lockedness of Bolivia]. *Cuadernos del Tercer Mundo*, 1, No. 10 (February, 1977), 30-34.

9042 Jerez Ramierz, Luis. "Bolivia: Reivindicacion y Litoral" [Bolivia: Recovery and Seacoast]. In *Chile: La Vecindad Dificil*. Rotterdam: Instituto para el Nuevo Chile, 1981, 88-161, notes on 296-306.

9043 Kain, Ronald Stuart. "Bolivia's Claustrophobia." *Foreign Affairs*, 16, No. 4 (July, 1938), 704-713.

9044 Kempff Bacigalupo, Rolando. "Un Paliativo al Problema de la Mediterraneidad de Bolivia a traves del Sistema Hidrogorafico de la Cuenca del Plata" [A Paliative for the Problem of Bolivia's Land-Lockedness by means of the Hydrographic System of the Plata Basin]. *Revista Argentina de Relaciones Internacionales*, 4, No. 10 (January-April, 1978), 77-81. Also in *Revista de Politica Internacional*, 58 (July-August, 1978), 197-201.

9045 Kuehnelt-Leddihn, Erik R.V. "The Petsamo Region." *Geographical Review*, 34, No. 3 (July, 1944), 405-417.

9046 "La Aspiracion Portuaria Boliviana" [The Port Aspiration of Bolivia]. (Collection of documents on Peru-Bolivia Relations.) *Revista Peruana de Derecho Internacional*, 11, No. 36-37 (January-August, 1951), 21-228.

9047 "La Salida al Mar de Bolivia; Neuvos Aportes: POR, MIR Disidente, PCB m-1, Mineros Bolivianos" [Bolivia's Outlet to the Sea; New Contributions (from various parties and other groups)]. *S.E.U.L.*, 8, No. 67 (March, 1976), whole volume. (Brussels: Servicio Europeo de Universitarios Latinoamericanos), 1976.

9048 "La Salida al Mar de Bolivia; Polemica entre: el MIR Chileno y el ELN Boliviano" [Bolivia's Outlet to the Sea; Polemics Between (two political parties)]. *S.E.U.L.*, 7, No. 63 (November, 1975), whole volume. (Brussels: Seravicio Europeo de Universitarios Latinoamericanos), 1975

9049 "Le Projet de Chemin de Fer Parakou-Niamey." *Europe Outremer*, 57, No. 597 (October, 1979), 51-52.

9050 Lofstrom, William. "Cobija, Bolivia's First Outlet to the Sea." *Americas*, 31, No. 2 (October, 1974), 185-205.

9051 **Lopez Escobar, Mario.** "La Mediterraneidad del Paraguay]. *Arquivos do Ministerio da Justica* 32, No. 134 (April-June, 1975), 59-70.

9052 **Maffucci, Mario.** "Una Questione Sudamericana: lo Sbocco al Mare della Bolivia" [A South American Question: Bolivia's Outlet to the Sea]. *Civitas*, 28, No. 2 (February, 1977), 53-68.

9053 **Meneses, Romulo.** *El Imperativo Geografico en la Mediterraneidad de Bolivia* [The Geographical Imperative in the Land-Lockedness of Bolivia]. La Paz: Editorial Renacimiento, 1943. Reprinted in his *Tres Ensayos sobre Geopolitica Indoamericana*. Lima: Ediciones Continente, 1963, 65-129.

9054 **Menon, P.K.** "The Plate River Basin—Some Legal Aspects of Navigation Development." *International Lawyer*, 5, No. 4 (October, 1971), 667-689.

9055 **Morelli Pando, Jorge.** "Facilidades de Transito Otorgadas a Bolivia por el Peru y Chile, a traves de su Historia Republicana" [Transit Facilities Granted to Bolivia by Peru and Chile through its Republican History]. *Revista Peruana de Derecho Internacional*, 17, No. 51 (January-June, 1957), 82-118.

9056 **Nohlen, Dieter, and Fernandez B., Mario.** "Cooperacion y Conflicto ena Cuenca del Plata" [Cooperation and Conflict in the Plata Basin]. *Estudios Internacionales*, 14, No. 55 (July-September, 1981), 412-443.

9057 **O'Connor d'Arlach, Octavio.** "Una Ruta Fluvial para el Sud de Bolivia y la Navegacion del Rio Bermejo" [A River Route for the South of Bolivia and the Navigation of the Bermejo River]. *Revista de la Sociedad Geografica y de Historia "Tarija"*, 5 (March 15, 1946), 5-9.

9058 **Pincus, Joseph.** "Transportation and Telecommunications." In *The Economy of Paraguay*. New York: Praeger, 1968, 199-233.

9059 **Ponce Paz, Jorge.** "Bolivia antes un Dilema geografico." *Universidad*, 8, No. 20 (Junio, 1958), 10-14.

9060 **Prieto, Justo.** "El Problema del Paraguay Mediterraneo" [The Problem of Land-Locked Paraguay]. *Pan America*, 1, No. 11 (December, 1946), 29-45.

9061 **Prudencio, Roberto Romecin.** "Nuestro Problema Maritimo" [Our Maritime Problem]. *Kollasuyo*, 88 (First Semester, 1975), 5-37.

9062 **Pugayeva, S.M.** "Bolivia i More" [Bolivia and the Sea]. *America Latina*, 10, No. 5 (September-October, 1978), 168-175.

9063 **Puig, Juan Carlos.** "El Conflicto Fluvial con el Paraguay y el Tratado de Navegacion de 1967" [The Fluvial Conflict with Paraguay and the Treaty of Navigation of 1967]. *Revista de Derecho Internacional y Ciencias Diplomaticas*, 15-16, Nos. 29-32 (1966-1967), 119-133.

9064 **Reyno Gutierrez, Manuel.** "Algunos Antecedentes Historicos sobre la Contraposicion Peruana para Otorgar una Salida al Pacifico a Bolivia" [Some Historical Antecedents for the Peruvian Counterproposal on Granting Bolivia an Outlet to the Pacific]. *Revista Chilena de Historia y Geografia*, Nr. 144 (1976), 7-20.

9065 **Riviere D'Arc, Helene.** "Economie Frontaliere et 'Poles de Developpement'; El Mutum et Itaipu" [Frontier Economy and "Poles of Development"; El Mutun and Itaipu]. *Cahiers des Ameriques Latines*, 18 (2nd half 1978), 25-31.

9066 "The Road to the Sea Continues to be Full of Obstructions." *Commercio Exterior de Mexico*, 23, No. 3 (March, 1977), 88-94.

9067 **Rojas, Rafael Armando.** "El Sesquicentenario de Bolivia y el Mar" [The Sesquicentenary of Bolivia and the Sea]. *Boletin de la Academia Nacional de la Historia*, 58, No. 231 (July-September, 1975), 453-460.

9068 **Romero A.G., Gonzalo.** "Derechos Seculares de Bolivia sobre la Costa del Pacifico" [Century-long Rights of Bolivia on the Pacific Coast]. *Kollasuyo*, 88 (First Semester 1975), 38-75.

9069 **Rowe, D. Trevor.** "Railways of Bolivia." *Railway Magazine*, 118, No. 850 (February, 1972), 68-70.

9070 **St. John, Ronald Bruce.** "Hacia el Mar: Bolivia's Quest for a Pacific Port." - *Inter-American Economic Affairs*, 31, No. 3 (Winter, 1977), 41-73.

9071 **Sanchez G., Walter, and Echeverria, Gloria.** "Cronologia Politica de las Negociaciones Chileno-Boliviana (1975-1978)" [Political Chronology of the Chilean-Bolivian Negotiations (1975-1978)]. In *150 Anos de Politica Exterior Chilena*, Walter Sanchez G. and Teresa Pereira L., eds. Santiago: Editorial Universitaria, 1979, 318-351.

9072 **Seleme, Susana.** "Bolivia's Outlet to the Sea: An Imperialist Way Out." *Tricontinental*, 49-50 (May-August, 1976), 36–53.

9073 **Shumavon, Douglas H.** "Bolivia: Salida al Mar." In *Latin American Foreign Policies: Global and Regional Dimensions*, Elizabeth G. Ferris and Jennie K. Lincoln, eds. Boulder, Colorado: Westview Press, 1981, 179-190.

9074 **Vargas Hidalgo, Rafael.** "La Funcion de los Transportes y las Telecomunicaciones en la Integracion de los Paises Andinos" [The Function of Transport and Telecommunications in the Integration of the Andean Contries]. *Mundo Nuevo*, 3, No. 7-8 (January-June, 1980), 132-148.

9075 **Vasquez, Alfonso.** "Bolivia y su Salida hacia el Pacifico" [Bolivia and her Outlet toward the Pacific]. *Geopolitica*, 7, No. 23 (December, 1981), 56-58.

9076 **Verissimo, Ignacio Jose.** "Bolivia, Pais do Atlantico" [Bolivia, Atlantic Country]. *A Defesa Nacionala*, 532-533 (November-December, 1958), 115-118.

9077 **Vieira, Flavio.** "Estradas Transcontinentais Interoceanicas na America Meridional" [Transcontinental Interoceanic Routes in South America]. *Revista Geografica*, 5-8, Nos. 13-24 (1949), 35-56.

9078 **Villacres Moscoso, Jorge W.** "La Posicion del Ecuador con Relacion a los Estados sin Litoral" [Ecuador's Position in Relation to the Land-Locked States]. In *La Defensa del Mar Territorial Ecuatoriano y sus Recursos* (Separado de Vol. 7, No. 7 of the *Revista de la Escuela de Diplomacia de la Universidad de Guayaquil*). Guayaquil: Departamento de Publicaciones de la Universidad de Guayaquil, 1979, 90-95.

9079 **Volmuller, J.** "Transport in Bolivia." *Transport and Communications Review*, 7, No. 2 (April-June, 1954), 14-27.

9080 **Whately, Luis Alberto.** "Brasil-Bolivia: Interligacao dos Sistemas Ferroviarios" [Brazil-Bolivia: Interconnection of the Rail Systems]. *Revista Brasileira de Politica Internacional*, 1, No. 3 (September, 1958), 113-120.

ASIA

Books

9081 **Ackermann, Ernst.** International Trade Centre UNCTAD/GATT. *Identification of the Special Problems of the Three Asian Land-Locked Contries, Afghanistan, Laos and Nepal, in the Field of the Expansion of Exports.* ITC/TPAS/17. April, 1970. Restricted.

9082 **Ackermann, Ernst.** *Transit Cost Analysis-Nepal.* Kathmandu: UNCTAD/TAC/Rerp. 1 (December 1, 1971).

9083 **Almeen, Ali.** *Land-locked States and Internatinal Law, with Special Reference to the Role of Nepal.* New Delhi: SAP, 1989.

9084 **Centre for Economic Development and Administration (CEDA).** *Trade and Transit: Nepal's Problem with Her Southern Neighbour.* CEDA Study Series, Occasional paper No. 1. Kathmandu: CEDA, Tribhuvan University Campus, 1971.

9085 **Comtec in collaboration with Alpina and Macchi for the United Nations and the Government of Nepal.** *Road Feasibility Study for the Kathmandu-Birganj Corridor. Report.* Kathmandu: Government of Nepal, March, 1974. Restricted.

9086 **Delpaix, J.M.,** and **Kaphley, K.P.** *Prospects of Inland Waterway Transportation in Bangladesh for Nepal Transit Traffic.* UNDP/UNCTGAD Project RAS/81/114. Kathmandu: UNDP, January 31, 1982.

9087 **Ditmar, W.P.** *A River Transportation Study in Nepal.* Bangkok: ESCAP/UNCTAD Project RAS/72/077, June, 1976.

9088 *An Engineering Reconnaissance Report on Highways, Airfields, River Crossings, Water Transportation and External Routes of Supply for the Royal Kingdom of Laos.* Washington, D.C.: Transportation Consultants, Inc., June, 1957.

9089 **ESCAP.** *Report of the Joint Roving Team of Railway Experts, Nepal.* Report of the Technical Mission to Nepal for an Intermodal Study of Rail, Road, Ropeway Transportation from Indian Border at Raxaul to Kathmandu. Kathmandu: ESCAP, April 11 to 25, 1976.

9090 **Gallagher, John S., Jr.** *Facilities for Cross Border Movement of Import and Export at Raxaul-Birganj.* Kathmandu: UNDP and Nepal Ministry of Transport, 1973.

9091 **Gallagher, John S., Jr.** "Transit Problems of the Land-Locked Islamic Countries." Kabul: Report to the Islamic Conference. December 15, 1976.

9092 **Gallagher, John S., Jr.,** and **Wasniewska-Kacperska, Teresa,** eds. *Transport and Communications Nepal: Project Findings and Recommendations.* Kathmandu: Project NEP/68/001/, 1977.

9093 **Glassner, Martin Ira.** *Transit Problems of Three Asian Land-Locked Countries: Afghanistan, Nepal and Laos.* Occasional Papers/Reprints Series in Contemporary Asian Studies No. 4-1983 (57). Baltimore: University of Maryland School of Law, August, 1983.

9094 **Hecker, Helmuth.** *Sikkum und Bhutan--Die Verfassungsgeschichtliche Entwicklung der Indischen Himalaya-Protektorate* [Sikkim and Bhutan - The Historical Constitutional Development of the Indian Himalayan Protectorates]. Frankfurt am Main: Alfred Metzner Verlag, 1970.

9095 **Heraty, Margaret.** *Report on the Transit Transport Situation in Afghanistan, Nepal and Lao PDR in 1983.* UNDP/UNCTAD Project RAS/81/114. UNCTAD/LDC/56. Geneva: UNCTAD, August, 1983.

9096 **Imus, Merla E.** *Nepal Freight Transshipment Study.* Calgery: Trimac Consulting Services, Ltd., December, 1975.

9097 **Jacquemond, J.B.** "Etude des Mesures Propres a Ameliorer les Transports pour le Commerce Exterieur et Assurer le Desenclavement de l'Afghanistan" [Study of Measures Suitable for Improving Transport for Foreign Commerce and Assure Ending the Geographic Isolation of Afghanistan]. Kabul: Afghanistan, Ministry of Commerce, June 30, 1971.

9098 **Kaphley, K.P.,** and **Shakya, M.R.** *Transit Cargo Congestion and the Need for More Transshipment Facilities.* UNCTAD/ESCAP Project RAS/72/077. Kathmandu, February 26, 1981.

9099 **Koebig and Koebig, Inc.** *Report on Transportation Facilities of Afghanistan and Pakistan.* Los Angeles: Koebig and Koebig, Inc., October, 1957.

9100 **Koosuwan, Thongchai.** *Analysis of Transportation of Intransit Goods to Laos.* Bangkok: Thammasat University, Master's Thesis, 1971.

9101 **Lehmann, Josef A.** *Transit Procedures from and to Bangladesh Ports; Bangladesh-Nepal.* Bangkok: UNCTAD/FALPRO, May, 1976.

9102 **Louis Berger Inc.** and **Daniel, Mann, Johnson and Mendenhall** for **SEATAC.** *Development of the Ports of Sattahip and Da Nang and of Route 9.* Contract AID/SA/IR-197 (Regional). Bangkok: SEATAC, December, 1972 and March, 1973.

9103 **Malwan, M.K.,** and **Pokhrel, G.P.** *Present Conditions of Nepal Ropeway Operations and Need for Ropeway and Railway Service Coordination.* UNCTAD/ESCAP Project RAS/72/077. Kathmandu: UNCTAD, October 20,1980.

9104 **Ministry of Commerce.** *Implication of High Transit Taxes on Afghan International Road Transport Operation* (Overland Transit to Europe). UNCTAD/ESCAP Project RAS/72/077. Kabul: Ministry of Commerce, January 27, 1980.

9105 **Nedlson, J.C.** *Transport in Relation to Economic Development of Afghanistan: Transit Routes, Facilities, Rates, Costs and Transit Agreements.* Papers, Department of Economics, Pullman: Washington State University, 1964.

9106 **Pandey, B.R.** *Mukdahan Trans-shipment Point for Laotian Freight Traffic;.* ESCAP/UNCTAD/UNDP Project Lao/RAS/72/077. Bangkok: UNCTAD, February, 1980.

9107 **Pandey, B.R.** *Overall Difficulties of Laotian Freight Traffic via Thailand.* ESCAP/UNCTAD/UNDP Project Lao/RAS/72/077. Bangkok: UNCTAD, October, 1979.

9108 **Pandey, B.R.** *Preliminary Study on Trucking Costs and Operations from Bangkok to Thanaleng for Laos Traffic-in-Transit.* UNCTAD/ESAP Project Lao/RAS/72/077. Bangkok: UNCTAD, March, 1981.

9109 **Pandey, B.R.** *Statistical Report—Intransit to Laos via Nongkhai Trans-shipment Point.* ESCAP/UNCTAD/UNDP Project Lao/RAS/72/077. Bangkok: UNCTAD, March, 1980.

9110 *Performance Evaluation of the Ports Sherkhan, Hairatan and Turghundi* (Transfer Points on the Transit Route through Soviet Union.) UNCTAD/ESCAP Project AFG/RAS/72/077. Kabul: Ministry of Commerce, January 5, 1980.

9111 **Pradhan, Gajendra Mani.** *Transit of Land-Locked States with Special Reference to Nepal.* Kathmandu: Tribhuvan University, Ph.D., 1980.

9112 **Rana, Madhukar Shumshere.** *Laos-Thailand Transit Operations and Costs.* UNCTAD/ESCAP Project Lao/RAS/72/077. Vientiane: UNCTAD, July-December, 1980.

9113 *Report of the ESCAP/UNCTAD Seminar on Special Problems of Shipping and Receiving Goods in Afghanistan.* Kabul, June 2-7, 1979. Among the papers presented at this seminar were the following: "Role of Iran Transit Route in the Economic Development of Afghanistan" by Shanta L. Shrestha; "Pakistan Transit Route" by G.L. Citrakar; "Transit Route via USSR" by S. Garin; "Role of Air Transport in Afghanistan" by A.A. Hamid.

9114 *Report on the Operation of Ports in Afghanistan; Sherkhan Bandar, Hairatan Bandar and Turghundi Port* (Transfer Points on the Transit Route through Soviet Union). ESCAP/UNCTAD Project RAS/72/077. Kabul: Ministry of Commerce, December 16, 1978.

9115 **Reza, Abu.** *Transit Transport Problems Faced by Afghanistan.* UNCTAD/ESCAP Project AFG/RAS/72/077. Kabul: UNCTAD, February 16, 1980.

9116 **Robinson, Ross.** *The Port of Karachi; An Examination of Transit Procedures.* ESCAP/UNCTAD Project RAS/72/077. Bangkok: UNCTAD, September, 1976.

9117 **Shakya, M.R.** *Documentation and Procedures Governing Nepal's Trade with Third Countries.* UNCTAD/ESCAP Project RAS/72/077. Kathmandu: UNCTAD, January 23, 1981.

9118 **Sharma, Shanti Ram.** *Transit Transport of Goatskin Exports.* UNDP/UNCTAD Project NEP/82/002. Kathmandu: UNCTAD, October, 1983.

9119 **Singh, Upendra Kumar.** *Report on Afghanistan's Frontier Formalities.* Kabul: Asian Highway Transport Technical Bureau for Bureau of Technical Assistance Operations, 1967.

9120 *Status of Recommendations to Improve the Flow of Nepal's Third Country Exports and Imports (Revised).* UNCTAD/ESCAP Project RAS/72/077. Kathmandu: UNCTAD, September 20, 1981.

9121 **Stonier, Charles E.** *Notes on the Indian Railway Network Serving Nepal Border Points and Possible Extensions into Nepal.* UNCTAD/ESCAP Project RAS/72/077. Kathmandu: UNCTAD, May, 1980.

9122 **Stonier, Charles E.** *Proposal for Bangladesh Transit Routes; Study and Investment Requirements.* UNCTAD/ESCAP Project RAS/72/077. Dakha: UNCTAD, February 27, 1981.

9123 **Stojkovic, Ivan.** *Les Problemes du Transport et du Transit au Laos* [Problems of Transport and Transit of Laos]. Viangchan: Bureau of Technical Assistance, Department of Economic and Social Affairs, 1962.

9124 *Summary Report on Transit Conditions Affecting Nepal's Third Country Trade.* UNDP/UNCTAD Project RAS/81/114. Kathmandu: UNCTAD, July, 1982.

9125 **Tabibi, Abdul Hakim.** *Free Access to the Sea for Countries without Sea Coast; The Position of Afghanistan on this Question.* Geneva: Afghan Delegation to UNCLOS I. April, 1958.

9126 **Thapa, Laxman,** and **Sharma, Harihar.** *Transit Transport of Pulses.* UNDP/UNCTAD Project NEP/82/002. Kathmandu: UNCTAD, January, 1983.

9127 **Thomas, Simon.** *The Afghanistan-Pakistan Transit System; A Preliminary Review.* ESCAP/UNCTAD Project RAS/72/077. Bangkok: UNCTAD, September, 1976.

9128 **Thomas, Simon.** *Air Freight for Nepal and Afghanistan; A Preliminary Volume and Cost Analysis.* ESCAP/UNCTAD Project RAS/72/077. Bangkok: UNCTAD, September, 1976.

9129 **Thomas, Simon.** *Nepal-India Transit Study.* ESCAP/UNCTAD Project RAS/72/077. Bangkok: UNCTAD, May, 1976.

9130 **UNDP/ICAO Project RAS/79/134.** *Air Freight Study for Least Developed Countries; Afghanistan, Bangladesh, Maldives, Nepal.* New York: UNCTAD, June, 1981.

9131 **UNDP.** *Transport and Communications Nepal; Project Findings and Recommendations* by John S. Gallagher, Jr. and Teresa Wasniewska-Kacperska. Project NEP/68/001. 1977.

9132 *Workshop on Nepal Transit Transport Operations and Documentation; Final Report on Proceedings.* UNCTAD/ESCAP Project RAS/72/077. Kathmandu: UNCTAD, February, 1980.

Journals

9133 **Amin, Hamidullah,** and **Schilz, Gordon B.** "Transportation." In *A Geography of Afghanistan.* Omaha: Center for Afghanistan Studies, University of Nebraska, 1976, 133-147.

9134 **Barton, Thomas Frank.** "Outlets to the Sea for Land-Locked Laos." *Journal of Geography*, 59, No. 5 (May, 1960), 206-220.

9135 **Drysdale, Alasdair Duncan.** "Political Conflict and Jordanian Access to the Sea." *Geographical Review*, 77, No. 1 (January,1987), 86-102.

9136 **Dupree, Louis.** "The Indian Merchants in Kabul; the Economic Impact of the Afghan-Pakistan Border Dispute." *American Universities Field Staff Reports*, South Asia Series, 6, No. 3 (February, 1962).

9137 **Dupree, Louis.** "'Pushtunistan': The Problem and Its Larger Implications." *American Universities Field Staff (AUFS) Reports*, South Asia Series. Part I: "The Complex Interrelationships of Regional Disputes." 5, No. 2 (November, 1961); Part II: "The Effects of the Afghan-Pakistan Border Closure." 5, No. 3 (November, 1961); Part III: "The Big Gamble Continues." 5, No. 4 (December, 1961).

9138 **Franck, Peter G.** "Problems of Economic Development in Afghanistan." *Middle East Journal*, 3, No. 3 (July, 1949), 293–314 and 3, No. 4 (October, 1949), 421-440.

9139 **Ghaussy, A. Ghanie.** "Landerstudie: Das Verkehrssystem Afghanistans" [Country Study: The Afghan Transport System]. In *Verkehrsprobleme in Entwicklungslandern*, H. Attar, et al., eds. Bern and Stuttgart: Verlag Paul Haupt, 1971, 71-112.

9140 **Glassner, Martin Ira.** "Transit Problems of Land-Locked States and the Special Case of Nepal." *Foreign Affairs Journal*, 2, No. 2 (May-August, 1976), 61-72.

9141 **Govindaraj, V.C.** "The 1971 Treaty of Trade and Transit between Nepal and India." *Indian Journal of International Law*, 12, No. 2 (April, 1972), 247-251.

9142 **Hardstone, Peter C.N.** "Laos: The Transportation Difficulties of a Third World Landlocked State." In *Geography and the Third Worlds*, Ismail Ahmad and Jamaluddin Md. Jahi, eds. Bangi, Selangor, Malaysia: Penerbit Universiti Kebangsaan Malaysia, 1982, 112-118.

9143 **Hardstone, Peter C.N.** "Laos: The Transportation Problems of an Indochinese Landlocked State." *Philippine Geographical Journal*, 22, No. 3 (July-September, 1978), 151-160.

9144 **Hasan, Zubeida.** "The Foreign Policy of Afghanistan." *Pakistan Horizon*, 17, No. 1 (First Quarter, 1964), 48-57.

9145 **Hasan, Khursid.** "Pakistan-Afghanistan Relations." *Asian Survey*, 2, No. 9 (September, 1962), 14-19.

9146 **Hussain, Ijaz.** "Pakistan's Attitude towards the Question of Free Access to the Sea of Landlocked States." *Archiv des Volkerrechts*, 22, No. 4 (1984), 475-503.

9147 **Jayaraman, T.K., and Shrestha, Omkar Lal.** "Some Trade Problems of Landlocked Nepal." *Asian Survey*, 16, No. 12 (December, 1976), 1113-1123.

9148 **Jha, Shree Krishna.** "Stresses and Strains 1969-1971." In *Uneasy Partners: India and Nepal in the Post-Colonial Era*. New Delhi: Manas Publications, 1975, 264-293.

9149 **Karan, Pradyumna Prasad.** "Sikkim and Bhutan: A Geographical Appraisal." *Journal of Geography*, 60, No. 2 (February, 1961), 58–66.

9150 **Kukhtin, V.G.** "Problema Tanzita v Ekonomike i Politike Afganistana" [The Problem of Transit in the Economics and Politics of Afghanistan]. In *Voprosy Ekonomiki Afganistana*, Akademija Nauk SSR, Institut Nardov Azii, ed. Moscow: Izdatelstvo Vostochnoi Literatury (IVL), 1963, 3-56.

9151 "Land-locked Afghanistan" (Editorial). *Eastern World*, 16, No. 7 (July, 1962), 9-10.

9152 **Lee, Yong Leng.** "Land-Locked States." In *Southeast Asia and the Law of the Sea*. Singapore: Singapore University Press, 1980, 45-48.

9153 **Major, I.** "Tensions in Transportation and the Development Level of Transport in Some Socialist Countries." *Acta Oeconomica*, 30, No. 2 (1983), 221-240.

9154 **Michel, Aloys A.** "Foreign Trade and Foreign Policy in Afghanistan." *Middle Eastern Affairs*, 12, No. 1 (January, 1961), 7-15.

9155 **Montagno, George L.** "The Pak-Afghan Detente." *Asian Survey*, 3, No. 12 (December, 1963), 616-624.

9156 **Nagpal, Subhash C.** "Indo-Nepalese Treaty of Trade and Transit (1971)." *Journal of World Trade Law*, 6, No. 5 (September-October, 1972), 593-603.

9157 *Nepal; Recent Developments and Selected Issues in Trade Promotion.* Report No. 4663-NEP, October 14, 1983. Restricted. "Transport and Transit of External Trade," 66-74.

9158 **Ramazani, Rouhollah K.** "Afghanistan and the U.S.S.R." *Middle East Journal*, 13, No. 2 (Spring, 1958), 144-152.

9159 **Rana, Bhola Bikram.** "Nepal-India Treaty on Trade and Transit." *Foreign Affairs Journal*, 2, No. 2 (May-August, 1976), 73-77.

9160 "Rights and Interests of Landlocked States." Asian-African Legal Consultative Committee. *Report of the Fifteenth Sessions, Held in Tokyo, January 7-14, 1974*, 48-52.

9161 **Sarup, Amrit.** "Transit Trade of Land-Locked Nepal." *International and Comparative Law Quarterly*, 21, No. 2 (April, 1972), 287-306.

9162 **Shireff, David.** "Afghanistan: Landlocked Exporters Aim for New Markets." *Middle East Economic Digest*, 21, No. 21 (May 27, 1977), 12, 14, 16.

9163 **Shrestha, Omkar Lal.** "An Epitaph on Indo-Nepal Trade Treaty of 1971." *Vashuda* (Kathtmandu), 16, No. 2 (April-May, 1977), 3-7. Reprinted in *Public Opinion Trends Analyses and News Service--POT*, Nepal series (New Delhi), 2, No. 118 (July 11, 1977), 559-563.

9164 **Shrestha, Sita.** "Problems of Land-Locked States." Chapter 6 in her *Nepal and the United Nations*. New Delhi: Sindhu Publications, 1974, 156-202.

9165 **Tahir-Kheli, Shirin.** "Pakhtoonistan and its International Implications." *World Affairs*, 137, No. 3 (Winter, 1974-75), 233-245.

9166 **Upadhaya, Shailendra Kumar.** "Law of the Sea and Nepal." *Foreign Affairs Journal*, 2, No. 2 (May-August, 1976), 78-84.

9167 **Upadhyaya, Lakshman Kumar.** "Reflections on the Problems and Prospects of Land-Locked Countries." *Nepal Law Review*, 1, No. 3 (October-December, 1977), 49-53.

9168 **Zhinkin, V.** "Transit Traffic Across Soviet Territory." *Foreign Trade* (Moscow), 2, No. 1 (1972), 48-49.

EUROPE

Books

9169 **ab Egg, Andre.** *Die Volokswirtschaftliche Bedeutung des Hafens von Genua fur Die Schweiz* [The Political-Economic Importance of the Port of Genoa for Switzerland]. Bern: A. Francke Ag. Verlag, 1949.

9170 **Bachman, Hans R.** *Schweizer Schiffahrt auf den Meeren* [Swiss Navigation on the Seas]. Zurich: Orell Fussli Verlag, 1966.

9171 *Depositos y Zonas Portuarias para los Paises Mediterraneos de la ALALC (Port Warehouses and Free Zones for the Land-locked Countries of ALALC).* CEP/Repartido 1861, october 27, 1978.

9172 **Eberlin, Ph.** *Rapport de Mer; Navires et Marins au Service de la Suisse et de la Croix-Rouge Pendant la Guerre de 1939-1945* [Connection to the Sea; Ships and Seamen in the Service of Switzerland and the Red Cross during the War of 1939-1945]. Berne: Office Central Federale des Imprimese et du Materiel, 1970.

9173 **Erhard, Alfred.** *Die Schweizerische Seesechiffahrt.* Basal, Switzerland: University of Basel, Dissertation, 1948.

9174 **Erhard, Alfred.** *Zur Entwicklung der Schweizerischen Seeschiffahrt 1848-1941* [On the Development of Swiss Navigation 1848-1941]. Siegen i.W. Vorlander, 1950.

9175 **Hafner, Gerhard.** *The Land-locked Profile of Austria.* New York: Working Paper for the Land-locked States Committee of the International Law Association, 1977.

9176 **Haller, Hans Rudolf.** *Seeschiffahrt unter Schweizerflagge.* Dissertation, University of Zurich, Zurich, Switzerland, 1967.

9177 **Haller, Hans Rudolf.** *Seeschiffahrt unter Schweizerflagge* [Navigation under the Swiss Flag]. Baden: Baden-Verlag, 1968.

9178 **Hayoz, Franz.** *Die Ausubung der Staatsgewalt uber Schweizerische Schiffe auf Hoher See* [The Exercise of State Power over Swiss Vessels on the High Seas]. Fairburg, Switzerland: University of Freiburg, LL.D. Dissertation, 1948.

9179 **Kaliny, Stanislawa.** *Situacja Prawna Tranzytu w Polsce* [The Legal Status of Transit in Poland]. Torun, Poland: Mikolaja Kopernika University, Instytut Nauk Prawno-Ustrojowych, Doctoral Dissertation, February, 1982.

9180 **Kaufmann, Konrad.** *Die Schweizerische Schiffahrt* [Swiss Navigation]. Zurich: Institut fur Orts-, Regional- und Landesplanung an der ETH, September, 1966.

9181 **Kielbinski, Miroslav.** *Rola Polskiej Zeglugi w Obsludze Tranzytu Czechoslowackiego.* Sopot, Poland: Wyzsza Szkola Ekonomiczna, Master's Thesis, 1960.

9182 **Kuligowski, Joachim.** *Die Seehafen des Osterreichischen Aussenhandels* [The Seaports of Austrian Foreign Trade]. Vienna: Verlag Ferdinand Berger, Horn, Niederosterrich, 1957.

9183 **Matter, Ulrich.** *Die Schweizer Hochseeflotte auf dem Internationalen Frachtmarkt* [The Swiss High Seas Fleet in the International Cargo Market]. Zurich, Switzerland: University of Zurich, Juris Druck & Verlag, Dissertation, 1975.

9184 **Mianecki, Pawel.** *Der Seewartige Transitverkehr uber Polen* [Waterborne Transit Traffic Across Poland]. Gottingen: Vandenhoeck and Ruprecht, 1966.

9185 **Nef, Urs Ch.** *Das Recht zum Abbau Mineralischer Rohstoffe vom Meeresgrund und Meeresuntergrund unter Besonderer Berucksichtigung der Stellung der Schweiz* [The Right to Mine Mineral Raw Materials from the Seabed and Subsoil with Special Considerations for the Position of Switzerland]. Zurich: Schulthess Polygraphischer Verlag, 1975.

9186 **Ocioszynski, Tadeusz.** *Zagadienie Tranzytowe w Polskich Portach Morskich.* Sopot, Poland: 1948.

9187 **Patryn, Emil.** *Tranzyt a Gospodarka Narodowa* [Transit and the National Economy]. Warsaw: Panstwowe Wydawnictwo Ekonomiczne, 1967.

9188 **Pichler, Franz.** *Die Donaukommission und die Donaustaaten: Kooperation und Integration* [The Danube Commission and the Danube States: Cooperation and Integration]. Thesis No. 242, University of Geneva, University Institute of Graduate International Studies, 1973. Vienna: Wilhelm Braumuller, 1973.

9189 **Starczewska, Maria.** *Potentialities for Polish-Czechoslovak Cooperation in Transportation.* New York: Columbia University, Ph.D., 1971.

9190 **Stoll, Christian Th.** *Daas Recht Polens auf Freien und Sicheren Zugang zum Meer uber Danzig* [The Polish Right to a Free and Secure Access to the Sea via Danzig]. Frankfurt am Main: Alfred Metzner Verlag, 1966.

Journals

9191 **Boesch, Hans.** "Basle, Switzerland: A Port Terminal." *Economic Geography*, 12, No. 3 (July, 1936), 259-264.

9192 **Breitenmoser, Albin.** "Die Schweizerische Rheinschiffahrt nach Zahl und Bedeutung" [Swiss Rhine Traffic According to Number and Importance]. *Schweizerische Zeitschrift fur Verkehrswirtschaft*, 34, No. 1 (March, 1979),30-36.

9193 **Caflisch, Lucius C.,** ed. "Pratique Suisse en Matiere de Droit International Public 1974" [Swiss Practice in the Field of Public International Law 1974]. *Annuaire Suisse de Droit International*, 31 (1975), 243-257.

9194 "Der Scheizerische Transitverkehr" [Swiss Transit Transport]. Suite of articles including the following: "Redaktionelle Anmerkung," p. 2; "Die Schweizerische Transitpolitik und ihre Europaische Funktion" by F. Hegner, p. 3-12; "Der Gutertransport im Transit aus der Sicht der Strasse" by H. Fischer, p. 13-21; "Transit-route Brenner" by H. Lamprecht, p. 22-30; and "Que Representent pour la Suisse les Nouvelles Lignes de Transport Transeuropeenes?" by Paul Keller, p. 31–32. *Schweizerische Zeitschrift fur Verkehrswirtschaft/Revue Suisse d'Economie des Transports*, 35, No. 3 (September, 1980).

9195 **Fichelle, Alfred.** "Les Debouches Maritimes de la Tchecoslovaquie" [The Maritime Outlets of Czechoslovakia]. *Annales de Geographie*, 30, No. 166 (July 15,1921), 241-248.

9196 **Gabryelska, Barbara.** "Prawo Wolnego Dostepu do Morza w Swietle Praktyki Polsko-Czechoslowackiej" [The Right of Free Access to the Sea in the Light of Polish-Czechoslovak Practice]. *Technika i Gospodarka Morska*, 11 (1967), 494-497.

9197 **Gronowski, Franciszek.** "Zegulga Srodladowa w Obsludze Potrzeb Transportowych dolnej Odry Oraz Zespolu Portowego Szczecin-Swinoujscie" [Inland Water Transportation in Service of Transportation of the Lower Oder and of the Harbor Complex of Szczecin-Swinoujscie]. *Przeglad Zachodnio Pomorski*, 11 (1967), 5-27.

9198 **Hafner, Gerhard.** "Osterreich und die Gestaltung des Internationalen Seerechts" [Austria and the Formulation of the International Law of the Sea]. *Die Vereinten Nationen und Osterreich*, 29, No. 6 (1980), 49-52.

9199 **Hauser, Julius.** "Ceskoslovenska Dopravna Sustava v Socialistickej Ekonomickej Integracii" [Czechoslovak Transport System in Socialist Economic Integration]. *Ekonomicky Casopis*, 30, No. 8 (1982), 747-758.

9200 **Januszkiewicz, Wlodzimierez.** "The Role of the Transit of Goods in the Polish Economy." *Studies on International Relations*, 2 (1973), 137-152.

9201 **Kappeler, Dietrich.** "Die Schweiz und das Ubereinkommen uber den Transithandel der Binnenlander vom 8 Juli 1965" [Switzerland and the Convention on Transit Trade of Land-Locked States of 8 July 1965]. *Annuaire Suisse de Droit International*, 23 (1966), 55-62.

9202 **Kotowski, A.** "Porty Polskie w Obsludze Tranzytu Czechoslowackiego" [Polish Ports in Czechoslovak Transit Service]. *Morski Przeglad Gospdarczy*, 3, No. 5 (May, 1948), 6-9.

9203 **Kudrnka, Jiri.** "Rozwoj Sieci Drogowej w CSRS" [Development of the Road System in Czechoslovakia]. *Miedzynarodowy Rocznik Transportu*,1969, 233-247.

9204 "Le Role de la Pologne dans le Trafic de Transit de l'Est Europeen" [The Role of Poland in the Transit Traffic of Eastern Europe]. *Bulletin des Transports Internationaux par Chemins de Fer*, 56, No. 10 (October, 1948), 385-386.

9205 **Lesiak, Jerzy.** "Wolnosc Tranzytu i Rozwoj Przewozow Tranzytowych przez Polske" [Freedom of Transit and Development of Transit Transport through Poland]. *Technika i Gospodarka Morska*, 17, No. 1 (November, 1967), 483-485.

9206 **Lettke, Kazimierz.** "Perspektywy Rozwojowe Tranzytu Czechoslowackiego" [Prospects of Raising the Volume of Czechoslovak Transit Trade]. *Technika i Gospodarka Morska*, 13, No. 6 (June, 1963), 165-167.

9207 **Matwikow, Bohdan.** "Ekonomiczne Aspekty Tranzytu Towarow Czechoslowackich przez Porty Polskie i RFN" [Economic Aspects of Czechoslovak Goods Traffic through Polish and West German Ports]. *Transport a Handel Zagraniczny*, 26, No. 10-12 (1981), 28-35.

9208 **Merenne, Emile.** "Le Benelux dans l'Espace Rhenan; l'Example des Transports." *Revue Geographique de l'Est*, 23, No. 2 (April-June, 1983), 231-245.

9209 **Mianecki, Pawel.** "O Konkurencyjnosc Portow w Dziedzinie Tranzytu" [On Port Competition in Transit Activities]. *Handel Zagraniczny*, 2, Nr. 10 (Oct., 1956), 20-23.

9210 **Muller, Walter.** "Grundsatze der Schweizerischen Rheinschiffahrtspolitik" [Principles of the Swiss Rhine Traffic Policy]. *Strom und See*, 74, No. 4 (June, 1979), 106–112.

9211 **Ortiz de Guinea, Federico**. "Suiza y la Ley del Mar" [Switzerland and the Law of the Sea]. *Revista de Derecho Internacional y Ciencias Diplomaticas*, 7, No. 14 (July-December, 1958), 27-59.

9212 "Osterreichs Seehafenbilanz 1966" [Austrian Seaport Statement 1966]. *Verkehr*, 23, No. 31 (August 5, 1967), 1101-1107.

9213 "Osterreichische Seehafenbilanz 1983" [Austrian Seaport Statement 1983]. *Verkehr*, 40, No. 31 (1984), 1033-1077.

9214 **Prusa, Petr**. "Transport and Czechoslovakia's Foreign Trade." *Czechoslovak Foreign Trade*, 7 (June, 1967), 7-8.

9215 **Riley, Raymond Charles**, and **Ashworth, G.J.** "Transport in Benelux," Chapter 5 and "The Ports of Benelux," Chapter 6, in their *Benelux: An Economic Geography of Belgium, The Netherlands and Luxembourg*. New York: Holmes and Meir Publishers, 1975, 153-167 and 168-194.

9216 **Ritter, Jean**. "Le Port Rhenan de Bale, 'Port Maritime' de la Suisse" [The Rhine Port of Basle, 'Maritime Port' of Switzerland]. *Revue Geographique de l'Est*, 1, No. 2 (April-June, 1961), 103-131.

9217 **Sanguin, Andre-Louis**. "L'Andorre, Micro-Etat Pyrennean: Quelques Aspects de Geographie Politique" [Andorra as a Pryennean Microstate: On Some Problems of Political Geography]. *Revue Geographique des Pyrenees et du Sud Ouest*, 49, No. 4 (October, 1978), 455-474.

9218 **Sermet, Jean**. "L'Economie des Communications dans la Geographie de l'Andorre" [The Communications Economy in the Geography of Andorra]. In *Les Problemes Actuels des Vallees d'Andorre*, Anne-Marie Magnou, ed. Paris: Pedone, 1970, 33-85.

9219 **Thoman, Richard S.** "The Free Port: An Outmoded Trade and Transport Device in Northern Europe?" Paper read to the annual meeting of the Association of American Geographers, Memphis, April, 1955. Abstract appears in *Annals of the Association of American Geographers*, 45, No. 3 (September, 1955), 298-300.

9220 **Vancleef, Eugene**. "Finland-Bridge to the Atlantic." *Journal of Geography*, 48, No. 3 (1949), 99-105.

9221 "Verkehrspolitik" [Transport Policy]. In *Jahrbuch der Osterreichischen Wirtschaft 1983*. Vienna: Bundeswirtschaftskammer, 1983, 83-94.

9222 **Waldner, Kurt**. "Die Schweizerische Rheinschiffahrt im Jahre 1979" [Swiss Rhine Traffic in the Year 1979]. *Strom und See*, 75, No. 1 (January-February, 1980), 6-23.

9223 **Walther, H.** "The International Statute of the Rhine and the Central Commission for the Navigation of the Rhine." *Transport and Communications Review*, 2, No. 4 (October-December, 1949), 8-24.

9224 **Weigend, Guido G.** "The Problems of Hinterland and Foreland as Illustrated by the Port of Hamburg." *Economic Geography*, 32, No. 1 (January, 1956), 1-16.

9225 **Zlabek, Karel**. "Equalization of the Land-Locked and Coastal Countries in the World Economy." *Research Reports in Social Science*, 10, No. 1 (February, 1967), 1-33.

CHAPTER X

ELECTORAL GEOGRAPHY, VOTING PATTERNS AND VOTING BEHAVIOR

GENERAL AND THEORY

Books

9226 **Alexander, Yonah,** and **Friedlander, Robert A.,** eds. *Self-determination: National, Regional, and Global Dimensions.* Boulder, Colorado: Westview Press, 1980.

9227 **Amatot, John Dennis.** *Elections Under International Auspices, 1948-1970.* Baltimore, Maryland: Johns Hopkins University, Ph.D., 1972.

9228 **Aranson, Peter Howard.** *A Theory of the Calculus of Voting for Alternative Three-Contestant Election Systems.* Rochester, New York: University of Rochester, Ph.D., 1972.

9229 **Archer, J. Clark** and **Reynolds, David R.** *An Inquiry into the Spatial Basis of Electoral Geography: Discussion Paper Series No. 11.* Iowa City: University of Iowa, Department of Geography, January, 1969.

9230 **Auardt, E.,** and **Rokkan, S.,** eds. *Mass Politics.* New York: The Free Press, 1970.

9231 **Berelson, Bernard R.,** et al. *Voting.* Chicago, Illinois: University of Chicago Press, 1954.

9232 **Blondel, J.** *Political Parties.* London: Wildwood House, 1978.

9233 **Blondel, J.** *Voters, Parties and Leaders.* Harmondsworth: Penguin, 1965.

9234 **Bogdanor, Verona.** *The People and the Party System.* Cambridge: Cambridge University Press, 1981.

9235 **Brady, Henry Eugene.** *Choice Theoretic Approaches to Voting Behaviour.* Cambridge: Massachusetts Institute of Technology, Ph.D., 1980.

9236 **Broh, Charles Anthony.** *Issue Attitudes, Conceptualization, and: Toward a Theory of Issue Voting.* Madison: University of Wisconsin, Ph.D., 1972.

9237 **Buchheit, Lee C.** *Secession: The Legitimacy of Self-determination.* New Haven, Connecticut: Yale University Press, 1978.

9238 **Butler, D.E.** *Governing Without a Majority.* London: Macmillan, 1983.

9239 **Campbell, A.,** et al. *The Voter Decides.* Evanston, Illinois: Row Peterson, 1954.

9240 **Campbell, Donald Edward.** *Voting and Social Choice.* Princeton, New Jersey: Princeton University, Ph.D., 1972.

9241 **Chadwick, Thomas Timothy.** *Electoral Patterns in Coal Mining Areas: An Examination of National Elections in Great Britain and the United States, 1924-1970.* Charlottesville: University of Virginia, Ph.D., 1979.

9242 **Cobban, Alfred.** *The Nation State and National Self-determination.* 2nd ed. London: Collins, 1969.

9243 **Cox, Kevin R.** *The Spatial Evolution of National Voting Response Surfaces: Theory and Measurement.* Discussion Paper No. 9. Columbus, Ohio: Ohio State University, Department of Geography, 1969.

9244 **Dalton, Russell J.** *Citizen Politics in Western Democracies: Public Opinion and Political Parties in the United States, Great Britain, West Germany and France.* Chatham, N.J.: Chatham House, 1988.

9245 **Dalton, Russell J.,** and **Others,** eds. *Electoral Change in Advanced Industrial Democracies: Realignment or Dealignment?* Princeton, New Jersey: Princeton University Press, 1984.

9246 **Daudt, H.** *Floating Voters and the Floating Vote.* Leiden: H.F. Stenfert Kroese, 1961.

9247 **Denzau, Arthur Thomas.** *Majority Voting and General Economic Equilibrium: A Synthesis.* Seattle: University of Washington, Ph.D., 1973.

9248 **Duverger, M.** *Political Parties.* New York: John Wiley & Sons, 1961.

9249 **Enelow, James M.,** and **Hinich, Melvin J.,** eds. *Advances in the Spatial Theory of Voting.* Cambridge: Cambridge University Press, 1990.

9250 **Fishel, J.,** ed. *Parties and Elections in an Anti-Party Age.* Bloomington: Indiana University Press, 1978.

9251 **Franklin, Mark N.; Mackie, Thomas T.;** and **Valen, Henry,** eds. *Electoral Change: Responses to Evolving Social and Attitudinal Structures in Western Countries.* Cambridge: Cambridge University Press, 1992.

9252 **George, Pierre; Moraze, Ch.; MacCallum, R.B.; and Le Bras, G.** *Etudes de Sociologie Electorale*. Paris: Armand Colin, 1947.

9253 **Gibson, George Charles.** *Congressional Voting on Defense Policy: An Examination of Voting Dimensions, Determinants and Change*. Columbus: Ohio State University, Ph.D., 1975.

9254 **Gillespie, John Vincent.** *Formal Models of Voting in Mass Publics: Toward a Theory of Political Elections*. Minneapolis: University of Minnesota, Ph.D., 1969.

9255 **Goguel, Francois.** *Nouvelles Etudes de Sociologie Electorale*. Paris: Armand Colin, 1954.

9256 **Goguel, Francois.** *Initiation aux recherches de geographie electrale*. Paris: C.D.U., 1969.

9257 **Goldman, Robert Michael,** ed. *Transnational Parties: Organizing the World's Precincts*. Lanham, Maryland: University Press, 1983.

9258 **Goodey, Brian R.** *The Geography of Elections: An Introductory Bibliography*. Grand Forks: University of North Dakota Press, 1968.

9259 **Greenfield, Arnold Lee.** *Two Theories of Legislative Voting Behavior: A Theoretical and Empirical Assessment*. East Lansing: Michigan State University, Ph.D., 1980.

9260 **Grofman, B.; Handley, L.; and Niemi, R. G.** *Minority Representation and the Quest for Voting Equality*. New York: Cambridge University Press, 1992.

9261 **Grofman, B., and Lijphart, A.,** eds. *The Political Consequences of Electoral Laws*. Beverly Hills, California: Sage Publications, 1983b.

9262 **Gudgin, G., and Taylor, P.J.** *Seats, Votes and Spatial Organisation of Elections*. London: Pion, 1979.

9263 **Handelman, John Robert.** *The Saliency of Issues and Voting Patterns in the United Nations General Assembly*. Syracuse, New York: Syracuse University, Ph.D., 1974.

9264 **Happy, John Raymond.** *Voting Behavior and the Policy-Making Process*. Rochester, New York: University of Rochester, Ph.D., 1972.

9265 **Havard, William C., and Beth, Loren P.** *The Politics of Misrepresentation*. Baton Rouge: Louisiana State University Press, 1962.

9266 **Heller, M.J.,** ed. *The Logic of Multiparty Systems*. Munich: Springer–Verlag, 1986.

9267 **Herstein, John Arthur, Jr.** *A Process Analysis of Voting*. Pittsburgh, Pennsylvania: Carnegie-

Mellon University, Ph.D., 1979.

9268 **Hilliard, Michael Ross.** *Weighted Voting: Theory and Applications*. Ithaca, New York: Cornell University, Ph.D., 1983.

9269 **Hiummelweit, H.; Humphreys, P.; Jaegar, M.; and Katz, M.** *How Voters Decide: A Longitudinal Study of Political Attitudes and Voting Over Fifteen Years*. New York: Academic Press, 1981.

9270 **Hover, Robert William.** *Some Multivariate Problems of a Spatial Model of Voting Under Majority Rule*. Blacksburg: Virginia Polytechnic Institute and State University, Ph.D., 1977.

9271 **Huntington, Samuel P.** *The Third Wave: Democratization in the Late Twentieth Century*. Norman: University of Oklahoma Press, 1991.

9272 **Hyun, Min Chong.** *The Social Bases of Politics in Western Democracies: Voting Behavior in the United States, Great Britain, West Germany, and the Netherlands*. Washington, D.C.: George Washington University, Ph.D., 1980.

9273 **Janda, Kenneth.** *Political Parties: A Cross-National Survey*. New York: The Free Press, 1980.

9274 **Johnston, R.J.** *Political Electoral and Spatial Systems*. Oxford, England: Oxford University Press, 1973.

9275 **Johnston, R.J.** *Political, Electoral and Spatial Systems: An Essay in Political Geography*. Oxford: Clarendon Press, 1979.

9276 **Johnston, R.J.; Shelley, Fred M.; and Taylor, Peter J.,** eds. *Developments in Electoral Geography*. London: Routledge, 1990.

9277 **Johnston, R.J.; Shelley, Fred M.; and Taylor, P.J.** *Development in Electoral Geography*. New York: Rutledge, 1990.

9278 **Joyce, Ralph Charles.** *Sophisticated Voting for Three-Candidates Contests Under the Plurality Rule*. Rochester, New York: University of Rochester, Ph.D., 1977.

9279 **Knight, David B., and Davies, Maureen.** *Self-Determination: An Introductory Annotated Bibliography*. New York: Garland Publishing, 1987.

9280 **La Pollambara, J., and Weiner, M.,** eds. *Political Parties and Political Development*. Princeton, New Jersey: Princeton University Press, 1966.

9281 **Lee, Calvin B.T.** *One Man, One Vote*. New York: Charles Scribner's Sons, 1967.

9282 **Lee, William Charles.** *An Analysis of Economic Development and Ideology as Variables Determining Afro-Asian Voting Support for the United States in the United Nations General Assembly in the 1960's.* Hattiesburg: University of Southern Mississippi, Ph.D., 1973.

9283 **Linehan, William Joseph.** *Electoral Systems and Citizen Participation: A Decision-Theoretic Analysis of the Effects of Electoral Systems on Participation in Elections.* Bloomington: Indiana University, Ph.D., 1979.

9284 **Lipset, Seymour M.,** and **Rokkan, S.,** eds. *Party Systems and Voter Alignments.* New York: The Free Press, 1967.

9285 **Lovenduski, J.,** and **Hills, J.** *The Politics of the Second Electorate: Women and Public Participation.* London: Routledge, 1981.

9286 **Mackelprang, Alonzo J.** *Voting Behavior: A Test of the Stability of a Causal Model.* Iowa City: University of Iowa, Ph.D., 1972.

9287 **Maisel, L.,** and **Cooper, J.,** eds. *Political Parties: Development and Decay.* Beverly Hills, California: Sage Publications, 1978.

9288 **Marks, John Spencer.** *Split Ticket Voting in 1964: Explanations from Four Theoretical Perspectives.* Syracuse, New York: Syracuse University, Ph.D., 1975.

9289 **Michels, R.** *Political Parties.* Translated by Eden and Cedar Paul. Glencoe, Illinois: The Free Press, 1949.

9290 **Milbrath, L.W.** *Political Participation.* Chicago, Illinois: Rand McNally, 1965.

9291 **Miller, W.** *Electoral Dynamics.* London: Macmillan, 1977.

9292 **Milner, A.J.,** ed. *Comparative Political Parties.* New York: Thomas Y. Crowell, 1969.

9293 **Morrill, Richard L.** *Political Redistricting and Geographic Theory.* Seattle: University of Washington, Department of Geography, 1981.

9294 **Mukundan, Rangaswamy.** *Equilibrium Points in Game Theory and Voting.* West Lafayette, Indiana: Purdue University, Ph.D., 1973.

9295 **Mulligan, Jean E.** *Voting for and Ratings of Political Candidates as a Function of Type and Amount of Advertising and Machiavellianism of Subjects.* Hempstead, New York: Hofstra University, Ph.D., 1983.

9296 **Park, Han-Shik.** *Voting Participation and Socio-Economic Status in the United States and Korea: A Comparative Study.* Minneapolis: University of Minnesota, Ph.D., 1971.

9297 **Parks, Oral Eugene.** *An Analysis of Net Deviation Voting.* East Lansing: Michigan State University, Ph.D., 1972.

9298 **Rae, D.W.** *The Political Consequences of Electoral Laws.* 2nd ed. New Haven, Connecticut: Yale University Press, 1971.

9299 **Rokkan, S.** *Citizens, Elections, Parties.* New York: McKay, 1969.

9300 **Rose, R.** *Governing without Consensus.* London: Faber, 1971.

9301 **Rose, R.,** and **McAllister, I.** *Voters Begin to Choose.* London: Sage Publications, 1986.

9302 **Rule, Wilma,** and **Zimmerman, Joseph F.,** eds. *Electoral Systems in Comparative Perspective: Their Impact on Women and Minorities.* Westport: Greenwood Press, 1994.

9303 **Satterthwaite, Mark Allen.** *Existence of a Strategy Proof Voting Procedure: A Topic in Social Choice Theory.* Madison: University of Wisconsin, Ph.D., 1973.

9304 **Shapiro, M.** *The Politics of Representation.* Madison: University of Wisconsin Press, 1988.

9305 **Sharpe, L.J.,** ed. *Voting in Cities.* London: Macmillan, 1967.

9306 **Strom, Kaare.** *Minority Government and Majority Rule.* Cambridge: Cambridge University Press, 1990.

9307 **Sweet, David C.,** ed. *Models of Urban Structure.* Lexington, MA: D.C. Heath, 1972.

9308 **Taylor, P.J.,** and **Johnston, R.J.** *Geography of Elections.* London, United Kingdom: Penguin, 1979.

9309 **Traugott, Michael Wolfe.** *An Economic Model of Voting Behavior.* Ann Arbor: University of Michigan, Ph.D., 1974.

9310 **Unger, Bruce Michael.** *The General Assembly and Its Main Committees: A Study in Voting Alignments.* New Orleans: Tulane University of Louisiana, Ph.D., 1973.

9311 **Van Wingen, John Richard.** *The Voting Decision: A Derivation of Campaign Strategy from a Mathematical Model of Ambivalenced.* Columbia: University of Missouri, Ph.D., 1975.

9312 **Wambaugh, Sarah.** *Plebiscites Since the World War, with a Collection of Official Documents.* Washington, D.C.: Carnegie Endowment for International Peace, 1933.

9313 **Warde, Alan.** *Space, Class and Voting.*
Unpublished Paper, Lancashire: University of
Lancaster, 1985.

9314 **Wolfinger, R.E., and Rosenstone, S.J.** *Who
Votes.* New Haven, Connecticut: Yale University
Press, 1980.

9315 **Zechman, Martin Jay.** *Dynamic Models of Voting
Behavior and Spatial Models of Party Competition:
Beyond the Assumption of Perfect Spatial Mobility.*
Rochester, New York: University of Rochester,
Ph.D., 1977.

Journals

9316 **Adams, Bruce.** "Model State Reapportionment
Process: The Continuing Quest for 'Fair and
Effective' Representation." *Harvard Journal on
Legislation*, 14, No. 4 (June, 1977), 825-904.

9317 **Ahmad, Hamiduddin.** "Election Data Analysis as
a Pool of Research in Political Geography."
Pakistan Geographical Review, 21, No. 21
(January, 1966), 34-40.

9318 **Amersfoort, Hans van, and Van der Wusten,
Herman.** "Democratic Stability and Ethnic
Parties." *Ethnic and Racial Studies*, 4, No. 4
(October, 1981), 476-485.

9319 **Ametistov, Ernest.** "Reform of the Political
System and Democracy" *Social Sciences*, 20, No.
2 (1989), 107-119.

9320 **Banzhaf, John F.** "One Man,? Votes:
Mathematical Analysis of Voting Power and
Effecting Representation." *George Washington
Law Review*, 36, No. 4 (May, 1968), 808-823.

9321 **Barton, D.M.** "Constitutional Choice and Simple
Majority Rule: Comment." *Journal of Political
Economy*, 81, No. 2, Part 1 (March-April, 1973),
471-479.

9322 **Bennett, W.L., and Haltom, W.** "Issues, Voter
Choice, and Critical Elections." *Social Science
History*, 4, No. 4 (Fall, 1980), 379-418.

9323 **Berry, B.J.L., and Dye, Thomas R.** "The
Discriminatory Effects of At-Large Elections."
Florida State University Law Review, 7, No. 1
(Winter, 1979), 85-122.

9324 **Blais, Andre.** "The Debate Over Electoral
Systems." *International Political Science Review*,
12, No. 3 (July, 1991), 239-260.

9325 **Brownill, Sue, and Halford, Susan.**
"Understanding Women's Involvement in Local
Politics: How Useful is a Formal/Informal
Dichotomy?" *Political Geography Quarterly*, 9,
No. 4 (October, 1990), 396-414.

9326 **Burklin, Wilhelm P.** "Was Leistet die
Wahlgeographie" [Results in Election Geography].
Geographische Rundschau, Jahr. 32, Heft 9
(September, 1980), 396-403.

9327 **Chappell, H.W.** "Presidential Popularity and
Microeconomic Performance: Are Voters Really
So Naive." *Review of Economics and Statistics*, 65
(August, 1983), 385-392.

9328 **Chatelain, Abel.** "La geographie du journal."
Annales Economies, Societes, Civilisations, 10,
No. 4 (Octobre-Decembre, 1955), 554-558.

9329 **Chrisholm, Michael; Devereux, Bernard; and
Versey, Roy.** "The Myth of NonPartisan
Cartography: The Tale Continued." *Urban
Studies*, 18, No. 2 (June, 1981), 213-218.

9330 **Connor, Walker F.** "Self-Determination: The
New Phase." *World Politics*, 20, No. 1 (October,
1967), 30–53.

9331 **Conway, M.M., and Wcykoff, M.L.** "The
Kelley-Mirer Rule and Prediction of Voter Choice
in the 1974 Elections." *Journal of Politics*, 42,
No. 4 (November, 1980), 1146-1152.

9332 **Craig, W.J.** "Reapportionment and the
Computer." *Law and Computer Technology*, 6,
No. 2 (March-April, 1973), 50-56.

9333 **Darcy, R., and Mackerras, Malcolm.** "Rotation
of Ballots: Minimizing the Number of Rotations."
Electoral Studies, 12, No. 1 (March, 1993), 77-82.

9334 **Davies, R.B., and Crouchley, Robert.** "Control
for Omitted Variables in the Analysis of Panel and
Other Longitudinal Data." *Geographical Analysis*,
17, No. 1 (January, 1985), 1-15.

9335 **Dikshit, R.D.** "On the Place of Electoral Studies
in Political Geography." *Transactions of the
Institute of British Geographers*, 2, No. 2 (1980),
23–28.

9336 **Dikshit, S.K., and Giri, H.H.** "Concept and
Purpose of Electoral Geography." *Transactions*, 6,
No. 1 (January, 1984), 86-88.

9337 **Dikshit, S.K., and Giri, H.H.** "A Review of
Research in Electoral Geography." *Geographical
Review of India*, 47, No. 4 (June, 1985), 13–21.

9338 **Dobson, D., and St. Angelo, D.** "Party
Identification and the Floating Vote: Some
Dynamics." *American Political Science Review*,
69, No. 2 (June, 1975), 481-490.

9339 **Dorling, Daniel.** "Bringing Elections Back to
Life." *Geographical*, 66, No. 12 (December,
1994), 20-21.

9340 **Emerson, Rupert.** "Self-determination." *American Journal of International Law*, 65, No. 3 (July, 1971), 459-475.

9341 **Esposito, John L., and Piscatori, James P.** "Democratization and Islam." *The Middle East Journal* [Bloomington], 45, No. 3 (Summer, 1991), 427-440.

9342 "Final Regulations for the First Elections in the Sanjak of Alexandretta." League of Nations. *Official Journal*, 19th year, 7 (July, 1938), 622-635.

9343 **Fincher, Ruth.** "The Inconsistency of Electicism." *Environment and Planning*, A, 15, No. 5 (May, 1983), 607-622.

9344 **Foladare, I.S.** "The Effect of Neighbourhood on Voting Behavior." *Political Science Quarterly*, 16, No. 2 (June, 1968), 266-272.

9345 **Gant, R.L., and Edwards, J.A.** "Electoral Registers as a Resource for Geographical Inquiry." *Geography*, 62, Part 1, No. 274 (January, 1977), 17-24.

9346 **Gilbert, Christopher P.** "Religion, Neighborhood Environments and Partisan Behavior: A Contextual Analysis." *Political Geography Quarterly* [Oxford], 10, No. 2 (April, 1991), 110-131.

9347 **Glenn, N.D., and Grimes, M.** "Ageing, Voting and Political Interest." *American Sociological Review*, 33 (1968), 563-575.

9348 **Goldberg, A.L.** "The Statistics of Malapportionment." *Yale Law Journal*, 72, No. 1 (January, 1962), 90-101.

9349 **Grofman, B.; Lijphart, A.; McKay, R.; and Scarrow, H.** "Symposium on Reapportionment." *Policy Studies Journal*, 9, No. 6, Special Issue No. 3 (Spring, 1981), 819-948.

9350 **Gross, D.A., and Sigelman, L.** "Comparing Party Systems: A Multidimensional Approach." *Comparative Politics*, 7 (1984), 463-479.

9351 **Gross, Leo.** "Voting in the Security Council: Abstention in the Post-1965 Amendment Phase and Its Impact on Article 25 of the Charter." *American Journal of International Law*, 62, No. 2 (April, 1968), 315-334.

9352 **Gudgin, G,, and Taylor, Peter J.** "Electoral Bias and the Distribution of Party Votes." *Institute of British Geographers Transations*, 63 (November, 1974), 53-74.

9353 **Guillorel, Herve, and Levy, Jacques.** "Space and Electoral System." *Political Geography* [Oxford], 11, No. 2 (March, 1992), 205-224.

9354 **Hahn, Harlan, and Kemper, F.J.** "Sozialokonomische Struktur und Wahlveshalten am Beispiel der Bundestagswahlem von 1980 und 1983 in Essen [Socio-economic Structure and Voting Behavior. The Example of the National Elections 1980 and 1983 in Essen]. *Arbeitem zur Rheinsischen Landeskunde*, 53 (1985), 1-60.

9355 **Hampton, W.** "The Electoral Response to a Multi-Vote Ballot." *Political Studies*, 16, No. 2 (July, 1968), 266-272.

9356 **Hill, K.Q., and Harley, P.A.** "Nonvoters in Voters' Clothing: The Impact of Voting Behavior Mes-reporting on Voting Behavior Research." *Social Science Quarterly*, 65, No. 1 (March, 1984), 199-206.

9357 **Hodge, David C., and Staeheli, Lynn A.** "Social Relations and Geographical Patterns of Urban Electoral Behavior." *Urbana Geography* [Silver Spring], 13, No. 4 (July-August, 1992), 307-333.

9358 **Huckfeldt, R.R.** "Political Participation and the Neighbourhood Social Context." *American Journal of Political Science*, 23, No. 3 (August, 1979), 579-592.

9359 **Husbands, Christopher T.** "The Support for the *Front National*: Analyses and Findings." *Ethnic and Racial Studies* [London], 14, No. 3 (July, 1991), 382-416.

9360 **Jacob, H.** "The Consequences of Malapportionment: A Note of Caution." *Social Forces*, 43, No. 2 (December, 1964), 254-261.

9361 **Janda, Kenneth, and Gillies, Robin.** "How Well Does 'Region' Explain Political Party Characteristics." *Political Geography Quarterly*, 2, No. 3 (July, 1983), 179-203.

9362 **Johnson, R.J., and Pattie, C.J.** "Evaluating the Use of Entropy-Maximising Procedures in the Study of Voting Patterns: 1. Sampling and Measurement Error in the Flow-of-the-Vote Matrix and the Robustness of Estimates." *Environment and Planning A* [London], 23, No. 3 (March, 1991), 411-420.

9363 **Johnston, R.J.** "Realignment, Vollatiltiy, and Electoral Geography." *Studies in Comparative International Development*, 22, No. 3 (Fall, 1987), 3-25.

9364 **Johnston, R.J.** "The Definition of Voting Regions in Multi-Party Contests." *European Journal of Political Research*, 10, No. 3 (September, 1982), 293-304.

9365 **Johnston, R.J.** "Environment, Elections and Expenditures: Analyses of Where Governments Spend." *Regional Studies*, 11, No. 6 (December, 1977), 383-394.

9366 **Johnston, R.J.** "Electoral Geography and Political Geography." *Australian Geographical Studies*, 18, No. 1 (April, 1980), 37-50.

9367 **Johnston, R.J.** "The Geography of Electoral Change: An Illustration of an Estimating Procedure." *Geografiska Annaler (Stockholm) Series B: Human Geography*, 64B, No. 1 (January, 1982), 51-60.

9368 **Johnston, R.J.** "On Contagion and Voting." *Politics*, 11 (1976), 102-103.

9369 **Johnston, R.J.** "Places and Votes: The Role of Location in the Creation of Political Attitudes." *Urban Geography*, 7, No. 2 (March-April, 1986), 103-117.

9370 **Johnston, R.J.** "Political Geography of Contemporary Events II: A Reapportionment Revolution that Failed." *Political Geography Quarterly*, 2, No. 4 (October, 1983), 309-317.

9371 **Johnston, R.J.** "The Political Geography of Electoral Geography." In *Agendas for Political Geography*. London: Croom Helm, 1984.

9372 **Johnston, R.J.** "Population Distributions and Electoral Power: Preliminary Investigations of Class Bias." *Regional Studies*. 11, No. 5 (October, 1977), 309-321.

9373 **Johnston, R.J.**, and **Hay, A.M.** "On the Parameters of Uniform Swing in Single-Member Constituency Electoral Systems." *Environment and Planning*, A14, No. 1 (January, 1982), 61-74.

9374 **Johnston, R.J.**, and **Hay, A.M.** "Voter Transition Probability Estimates: An Entropy-Maximising Approach." *European Journal of Political Research*, 11, No. 4 (March, 1983), 93-98.

9375 **Johnston, R.J.; Hay, A.M.;** and **Rumley, Dennis.** "Entropy Maximizing Methods for Estimating Voting Data: A Critical Test." *Area*, 15, No. 1 (March, 1983), 35-41.

9376 **Johnston, R.J.; Hay, A.M.;** and **Rumley, Dennis.** "On Testing for Structural Effects in Electoral Geography, Using Entropy-Maximising Methods to Estimate Voting Patterns." *Environment & Planning A*, 16, No. 2 (February, 1984), 233-240.

9377 **Johnston, R.J. Openshaw, S.; Rhind, D.W.;** and **Rossiter, D.J.** "Spatial Scientists and Representative Democracy: The Role of Information Processing Technology in the Design of Parliamentary and Other Constituencies." *Government and Policy*, 2 (1984), 57-66.

9378 **Jones, F.L.** "Individual Versus Contextual Effects on Voting Behaviour." *Politics*, 16, No. 1 (May, 1981), 63-71.

9379 **Jones, John Paul III.** "A Spatially Varying Parameter Model of AFDC Participation: Empirical Analysis Using the Expansion Method." *Professional Geographer*, 36, No. 4 (November, 1984), 455-461.

9380 **Kasperson, Roger E.** "On Suburbia and Voting Behaviour. *Annals of the Association of American Geographers*, 59, No. 2 (June, 1969), 405-411.

9381 **Kaufman, W.C.,** and **Greer, S.** "Voting in a Metropolitan Community: An Application of Social Area Analysis." *Social Forces*, 38, No. 3 (March, 1960), 196-204.

9382 **Kayden, X.** "The Political Campaign as an Organization." *Public Policy*, 21, No. 2 (Spring, 1973), 263-290.

9383 **Kendall, M.G.,** and **Stuart, A.** "The Law of Cubic Proportions in Election Results. *British Journal of Sociology*, 1, No. 1 (March, 1950), 183-97.

9384 **Kenny, Christopher B.** "Partisanship and Political Discussion." *Political Geography Quarterly* [Oxford], 10, No. 2 (April, 1991), 97-109.

9385 **Key, V.O., Jr.** "Secular Realignment and the Party System." *Journal of Politics*, 21, No. 2 (May, 1959), 198-210.

9386 **Key, V.O., Jr.** "A Theory of Critical Elections." *Journal of Politics*, 17, No. 1 (February, 1955), 3-18.

9387 **Klimasewski, Ted.** "Analysis of Spatial Voting Patterns: An Approach to Political Socialization." *Journal of Geography*, 73, No. 3 (March, 1973), 26-32.

9388 **Klimasewski, Ted.** "Geographical Perspectives on Self-determination." In *Political Geography: Recent Advances and Future Directions*, P.J. Taylor and J.W. House, eds. London: Croom Helm, 1984, 168-190.

9389 **Kolosov, V.A.** "Political Geography in the Service of the Bourgeois State Using Political-Geographic Differences in the Organization of Elections as a Weapon in the Political Struggle)." *Soviet Geography*, 26, No. 2 (February, 1985), 91-97.

9390 **Kramer, David C.** "Those People Across the Water Just Don't Know Our Problems: An Analysis of Friends and Neighbors Voting in a Geographically-Split Legislative District." *Political Geography Quarterly*, 9, No. 2 (April, 1990), 189-196.

9391 **Lijphart, Arend.** "Majority Rule in Theory and Practice: The Tenacity of a Flawed Paradigm." *International Social Science Journal* [Oxford], No. 129 (August, 1991), 483-493.

9392 **McBurnett, Michael.** "The Instability of Partisanship Due to Context." *Political Geography Quarterly* [Oxford], 10, No. 2 (April, 1991), 132-148.

9393 **Migranyan, Adnranit.** "Democratisation Proceses in Socialist Society." *Social Sciences*, 20, No. 1 (1989), 105-120

9394 **Milder, D.N.** "Definitions and Measures of the Degree of Macro-Level Party Competition in Multiparty Systems." *Comparative Political Studies*, 6, No. 4 (January, 1974), 431-456.

9395 **Miller, Arthur H., and Wlezien, Christopher.** "The Social Group Dynamics of Partisan Evaluations." *Electoral Studies*, 12, No. 1 (March, 1993), 5-22.

9396 **Molinar, Juan.** "Counting the Number of Parties: An Alternative Index." *American Political Science Review*, 85, No. 4 (December, 1991), 1383-1391.

9397 **Morrill, Richard.** "Gerrymandering." *Focus* [New York], 41, No. 3 (Fall, 1991), 23-27.

9398 **Morrill, Richard L.** "Ideal and Reality in Reapportionment." *Annals of the Association of American Geographers*, 63, No. 4 (December, 1973), 463-477.

9399 **Morton, Rebecca B.** "Groups in Rational Turnout Models." *American Journal of Political Science*, 35, No. 3 (August, 1991), 758-776.

9400 **Nagel, Stuart S.** "Simplified Bipartisan Computer Redistricting." *Stanford Law Review*, 17, No. 5 (May, 1965), 863-899.

9401 **Nathanson, C.** "The Social Construction of the Social Threat: A Study of the Politics of Representation." *Alternatives*, 13, No. 4 (December, 1988), 443-483.

9402 **Nawaz, M.K.** "The Meaning and Range of the Principle of Self-determination." *Duke Law Journal*, 82, No. 1 (Winter, 1965), 82-101.

9403 **Nelson, Daniel N.** "On Political Participation in Communist Systems." *East European Quarterly*, 14, No. 1 (Spring, 1980), 109-116.

9404 **Neumann, Sigmund.** "Toward a Comparative Study of Political Parties." In *Comparative Political Parties*, A.J. Milner, ed. New York: Thomas Y. Crowell, 1969, 29-47.

9405 **Niemi, R.G.; Grofman, B.; Carlucci, C.; and Hofeller, T.** "Measuring Compactness and the Role of Compactness in a Test for Partisan and Racial Gerrymandering." *Journal of Politics*, 52 (1990), 1155-1181.

9406 **Norcliff, G.B.** "Discretionary Aspects of Scientific Districting." *Area*, 9, No. 4 (December, 1977), 240-246.

9407 **Patjin, C.L.** "A Formula for Weighted Voting." In *Symbolae Verzijl*. The Hague: Martinus Nijhoff, 1958, 255-264.

9408 **Prescott, J.R.V.** "The Function and Methods of Electoral Geography." *Annals of the Association of American Geographers*, 49, No. 3 (September, 1959), 296-304.

9409 **Redcliff, B.** "Solving a Puzzle: Aggregate Analysis and Economic Voting Revisited." *Journal of Politics*, 50, No. 2 (May, 1988), 446-455.

9410 **Reynolds, David R.** "A Spatial Model for Analysing Voting Behavior." *Acta Sociologica*, Fasc. 12, No. 3 (1969), 122-131.

9411 **Reynolds, David R., and Shelley, Fred M.** "Applications of Procedural Justice to Electoral Systems." *European Journal of Political Research*, 3, No. 4 (December, 1985), 401-408.

9412 **Rokkan, S., and Campbell, A.** "Citizen Participation in Political Life: Norway and the United States of America." *International Social Science Journal*, 12, No. 1 (1960), 69-99.

9413 **Rose, R.** "From Simple Determinism to Interactive Models of Voting." *Comparative Political Studies*, 15, No. 2 (July, 1982), 145-169.

9414 **Rossiter, D.J., and Johnston, R.J.** "Program GROUP: The Identification of all Possible Solutions to a Constituency-Delimitation Problem." *Environment and Planning A*, 13, No. 2 (February, 1981), 231-238.

9415 **Rowley, Gwyn.** "Electoral Behavior and Electoral Behaviour: A Note on Certain Recent Developments in Electoral Geography." *Professional Geographer*, 21, No. 6 (November, 1969), 398-400.

9416 **Rumley, Dennis.** "The Geography of Political Participation." *Australian Geographer*, 16, No. 4 (November, 1965), 279-285.

9417 **Rumley, Dennis.** "Spatial Structural Effects in Voting Behaviour: Description and Explanation." *Tijdschrift voor Economische en Sociale Geografie*, 72, Nr. 4 (July-August, 1981), 214-223.

9418 **Rumley, Dennis.** "Whither Electoral Geography?" *Annals of the Association of American Geographers*, 65, No. 2 (June, 1975), 342-343.

9419 **Salisbury, B.R.** "Evaluative Voting Behavior: An Experimental Examination." *Western Political Quarterly*, 36, No. 1 (March, 1983), 88-97.

9420 Sanguin, Andre-Louis. "Attitudes politico-electorales et perception des affaires internationales chez les etudiants en Sciences Humaines." *Protee*, 2, No. 2 (1972), 79-89.

9421 Shelley, Fred M. "Spatial Effects on Voting Power in Representative Democracies." *Environment and Planning*, A16, No. 3 (March, 1984), 401-405.

9422 Sigelman, L., and Gross, Donald A. "How Well Does 'Region' Explain Party System Characteristics?" *Political Geography Quarterly*, 4, No. 2 (April, 1985), 131-139.

9423 Singh, C.P. "Geography and Electoral Studies." *Transactions*, 3, No. 1 (January, 1981), 81-87.

9424 Sinha, S.K. "Measuring Party Competition-A New Approach." *Geographical Review of India*, 47, No. 4 (December, 1985), 1-6.

9425 Staar, Richard F. "Checklist of Communist Parties in 1989. *Problems of Communism*, 39, No. 2 (March-April, 1990), 75-84.

9426 Sztompka, Piotr. "The Intangibles and Imponderables of the Transition to Democracy." *Studies in Comparative Communism* [Oxford], 24, No. 3 (September, 1991), 295-311.

9427 "Tacna-Arica Arbitration: Termination of the Plebiscite." *U.S. Department of State*. Papers relating to the foreign relations of the United States 1926, 1 (1941). Washington, D.C.: U.S. Department of State, 1941, 260-486.

9428 Takagi, Akihiko. "Recent Trends in Electoral Geography." *Human Geography*, 38, No. 1 (February, 1986), 26-40.

9429 Taylor, A.H. "The Place of Geography in Election Study." *Southampton Research Series in Geography*, 7 (October, 1972), 3-31.

9430 Taylor, Peter J. "Accumulation, Legitimation and the Electoral Geographies within Liberal Democracy." In *Political Geography Recent Advances and Future Directions*. P.J. Taylor and J.W. House, eds. Beckenham, United Kingdom: Croom Helm, (1984), 117-132.

9431 Taylor, Peter J. "All Organization is Bias: The Political Geography of Electoral Reform." *Geographical Journal*, 151, No. 3 (November, 1985), 339-346.

9432 Taylor, Peter J. "A New Shape Measures for Evaluating Electoral District Patterns." *American Political Science Review*, 67, No. 4 (December, 1973), 947-950.

9433 Taylor, Peter J. "Some Implications of the Spatial Organization of Elections." *Institute of British Geographers Transaction*, 60 (November, 1973), 121-136.

9434 Taylor, Peter J, and Gudgin, G. "A Fresh Look at the Parliamentary Boundary Commission." *Parliamentary Affairs*, 28, No. 4 (Autumn, 1975), 405-415.

9435 Taylor, Peter J, and Gudgin, G. "The Myth of Non-partisan Cartography." *Urban Studies*, 13, No. 1 (February, 1976), 13-25.

9436 Thalmann, Nadia, and Others. "ELECT/An Interactive Graphical System for the Automatic Generation of Electoral Maps." *Cartographica*, 19, No. 1 (Spring, 1982), 28-40.

9437 Tibbits, Clark. "Majority Votes and the Business Cycle." *American Journal of Sociology*, 36, No. 3 (November, 1931), 596-606.

9438 Tufte, E.R. "The Relationship between Seats and Votes in Two-Party Systems." *American Political Science Review*, 67, No. 2 (June, 1973), 540-554.

9439 Varynen, R. "Analysis of Party Systems by Concentration, Fractionalization, and Entropy Measures." *Scandinavian Political Studies*, 7 (1972), 137-155.

9440 Waldman, L.K. "Measures of Party Systems' Properties: The Number and Sizes of Parties." *Political Methodology*, 3, No. 2 (February, 1976), 199-214.

9441 Walker, R.E. "One Man, One Vote: In Pursuit of an Elusive Ideal." *Hastings Constitutional Law Quarterly*, 3, No. 2 (Spring, 1976), 453-484.

9442 Warf, Barney. "Power, Politics, and Locality." *Urban Geography* [Silver Spring], 12, No. 6 (November-December, 1991), 563-569.

9443 Waterhouse, D. "Estimation of Voting Behavior from Aggregated Data: A Test." *Journal of Social History*, 16, No. 3 (Spring, 1983), 35-53.

9444 Weatherford, M. Stephen. "Economic Voting and the Symbolic Politics Argument: A Reinterpretation and Synthesis." *American Political Science Review*, 77, No. 1 (March, 1983), 158-174.

9445 Weatherford, M. Stephen. "Interpersonal Networks and Political Behavior." *American Journal of Political Science*, 26, No. 1 (February, 1982), 117-143.

9446 Weaver, James B., and Hess, Sidney W. "A Procedure for Nonpartisan Districting: Development of Computer Techniques." *Yale Law Journal*, 73, No. 2 (December, 1963), 288-308.

9447 **Wildgen, J.K.** "The Matrix Formulation of Gerrymanders: The Political Interpretation of Eigenfunctions of Connectivity Matrices." *Environment and Planning B: Planning and Design* [London], 17, No. 3 (1990), 269-276.

9448 **Woolstencroft, Robert Peter.** "Electoral Geography: Retrospect and Prospect." *International Political Science Review*, 1, No. 4 (October, 1980), 540-561.

9449 **Zartman, I. William.** "Democracy and Islam: The Cultural Dialectic." *The American Academy of Political and Social Science. Annals* [Newbury Park], 524 (November, 1992), 181-191.

POLITICAL GEOGRAPHY OF REGIONS

AFRICA

Books and Journals

9450 **Abate, Yohannis.** *Foreign Aid, UN Voting Behavior, and Alliances: The Case of Africa, The U.S., and the U.S.S.R.* East Lansing: Michigan State University, Ph.D., 1976.

9451 **Agbaje, Adigun.** "Freedom of the Press and Party Politics in Nigeria: Precepts, Retrospect and Prospects." *African Affair*, 89, No. 355 (April, 1990), 205-226.

9452 **Akinola, Anthony A.** "Critique of Nigeria's Proposed Two-Party System." *Journal of Modern African Studies*, 27, No. 1 (March, 1989), 109-123.

9453 **Beaujeu-Garnier, Jacqueline.** "Essai de geographie electorale guineenne." *Cahiers d'Outre-Mer*, N°. 44, 11ᵐᵉ Annee (Octobre-Decembre, 1958), 309-333.

9454 **Bjornlund, Eric; Bratton, Michael; and Gibson, Clark.** "Observing Multiparty Elections in Africa: Lessons from Zambia." *African Affairs* [Oxford], 91, No. 364 (July, 1992), 405-431.

9455 **Christopher, A.J.** "Parliamentary Delimitation in South Africa, 1910-1980." *Political Geography Quarterly*, 2, No. 3 (July, 1983), 205-217.

9456 **Crais, Clifton C.** "Representation and the Politics of Identity in South Africa: An Eastern Cape Example." *The International Journal of African Historical Studies* [Boston], 25, No. 1 (1992), 99-126.

9457 **Denoeux, Guilain.** "Tunisie: Les Elections Presidentielles et Legislatives, 20 Mars 1994." *Maghreb-Machrek*, No. 145 (Juillet-Septembre, 1994), 49-72.

9458 **Diamond, Larry.** *Class, Ethnicity and Democracy in Nigeria: The Failure of the First Republic.* Houndmills: Macmillan, 1988.

9459 **Du Toit, Brian.** "The Far Right in Current South African Politics." *The Journal of Modern Afarican Studies* [Cambridge], 29, No. 4 (December, 1991), 627-667.

9460 **Ellingson, Lloyd.** "The Emergence of Political Parties in Eritrea, 1941-1950." *Journal of African History*, 18, No. 2 (1977), 261-281.

9461 **Gastrow, Shelagh.** *Who's Who in South African Politics. No. 3.* Johannesburg: Ravan Press, 1990.

9462 **Guyer, Jane I.** "Representation Without Taxation: An Essay on Democracy in Rural Nigeria, 1952-1990." *African Studies Review* [Atlanta], 35, No. 1 (April, 1992), 41-79.

9463 **Hargreaves, Alex G.** "The Political Mobilization of the North African Immigrant Community in France." *Ethnic and Racial Studies* [London], 14, No. 3 (July, 1991), 350-367.

9464 **Heard, K.A.** *General Elections in South Africa, 1943-1970.* London: Oxford University Press, 1974.

9465 **Hirschmann, David.** "Women and Political Participation in Africa: Broadening the Scope of Research." *World Development* [Oxford], 19, No. 12 (December, 1991), 1679-1694.

9466 **Hodgkin, Thomas.** *African Political Parties.* London: Penguin, 1961.

9467 **Hynning, Clifford J.** "The Future of South West Africa: A Plebiscite?" *American Journal of International Law*, 65, No. 4 (September, 1971), 144-148.

9468 **Jeffries, Richard.** "The Ghanaian Elections of 1979." *African Affairs*, 79, No. 316 (July, 1980), 397-414.

9469 **Johnston, Alexander.** "South Africa: The Election and the Emerging Party System." *International Affairs*, 70, No. 4 (October, 1994), 721-736.

9470 **Jones, A.H.** "The Spatial Dimensions of Rational Integration in Uganda and the Relevance to this of Uganda's New Electoral System." In Makerere University, Department of Geography, Occasional Paper No. 20. *Graph Theory Approaches to Regional Development in Uganda*, K.J. Tinkler, ed. Kampala: Department of Geography, 1971, 39-47.

9471 **Keller, Edmond J.** "Eritrean Self-Determination Revisited." *Africa Today* [Denver], 38, No. 2 (1991), 7-13.

9472 **Knill, Greg.** "State, Structure, and Strategy: South Africa's Municipal Elections." *Antipode*, 22, No. 1 (April, 1990), 73-84.

9473 **Lever, Henry.** "The Jewish Voter in South Africa." *Ethnic and Racial Studies*, 2, No. 4 (October, 1979), 428-440.

9474 **Malekane, Khoto.** "Lesotho: The Role of the Communist Party." *African Communist*, 83 (4th Quarter, 1980), 67-69.

9475 **Mortimer, Robert.** "Islam and Multiparty Politics in Algeria." *The Middle East Journal* [Bloomington], 45, No. 4 (Autumn, 1991), 575-593.

9476 **Nixon, Charles R.** "Self-determination: The Nigeria-Biafra Case." *World Politics*, 24, No. 4 (July, 1972), 473-497.

9477 **Ododa-Kidi, Harold OtieNo.** *A Comparative Analysis of the Impact of Level of Development and Foreign Aid on United Nations Voting Patterns of African States (1960-1972).* Atlanta, Georgia: Emory University, Ph.D., 1978.

9478 **Okpu, Ugbana.** "Nigerian Political Parties and the 'Federal Character'." *Journal of Ethnic Studies*, 12, No. 1 (Spring, 1984), 107-122.

9479 **Osci-Kwane, Peter,** and **Taylor, Peter J.** "A Politics of Failure: The Political Geography of Ghanaian Elections, 1954-1979." *Annals of the Association of American Geographers*, 74, No. 4 (December, 1984), 574-589.

9480 **Polhemus, James H.** "Botswana Votes: Parties and Elections in an African Democracy." *Journal of Modern African Studies*, 21, No. 3 (September, 1984), 189-212.

9481 **Rich, Tony.** "Legacies of the Past? The Results of the 1980 Elections in Midlands Province, Zimbabwe." *Africa*, 52, No. 3 (March, 1982), 42-55.

9482 **Shaw, William H.** "Towards the One-Party State IN Zimbabwe: A Study in African Political Thought." *Journal of Modern African Studies*, 24, No. 3 (September, 1986), 373-394.

9483 "Self-determination in Algeria; Issues for the Referendum." *The Round Table*, 50, No. 197 (December, 1959), 32-40.

9484 **Sylvester, Christine.** "Unities and Disunities in Zimbabwe's 1990 Election." *The Journal of Modern African Studies* [Cambridge], 28, No. 3 (September, 1990), 375-400.

9485 **Sylvester, Christine.** "Zimbabwe's 1985 Elections: A Search for National Mythology." *Journal of Modern African Studies*, 24, No. 2 (June, 1986), 229-25.

9486 **Tevera, D.S.** "Voting Patterns in Zimbabwe's Elections of 1980 and 1985." *Geography*, 74, Part 2 (April, 1989), 162-165.

9487 **Uwazurike, P. Chudi.** "Confronting Potential Breakdown: The Nigerian Redemocratisation Process in Critical Perspective." *Journal of Modern African Studies*, 28, No. 1 (March, 1990), 55-77.

9488 **Van Donge, Jan Kees,** and **Liviga, Athumani J.** "The 1985 Tanzanian Parliamentary Elections: A Conservative Election." *African Affairs*, 88, No. 350 (January, 1989), 47-62.

9489 **Villalon, Leonardo A.** "Democratizing a (quasi) Democracy: The Senegalese Elections of 1993." *African Affairs* [Oxford], 93, No. 371 (April, 1994), 163-193.

9490 **Williams, C.H.** "National Self-determination: The Case of Nigeria/Biafra." *Swansea Geographer*, 11 (1973), 78-84.

9491 **Williams, G.J.** "Regional Contrasts and Electoral Geography in Sierra Leone." *Swansea Geographer*, 8 (August, 1970), 37-48.

9492 **Wiseman, John A.** *Democracy in Black Africa: Survival and Revival.* New York: Paragon House, 1990.

9493 **Zolberlg, A.** *One-Party Government in the Ivory Coast.* Princeton, New Jersey: Princeton University Press, 1969.

AMERICAS

Books

9494 **Abney, Francic Glenn.** *The Mississippi Voter: A Study of Voting Behavior in a One-Party, Multifactional System.* New Orleans: Tulane University of Louisiana, Ph.D., 1969.

9495 **Abramowitz, Alan Ira.** *An Assessment of Party and Incumbent Accountability in Midterm Congressional Elections.* Stanford, California: Stanford University, Ph.D., 1976.

9496 **Ahmad, Hamiduddin.** *Kansas Gubernatorial Elections: A Study Political Geography.* Lawrence: University of Kansas, Ph.D., 1963.

9497 **Aldrich, John Herbert.** *Voting in Two U.S. Presidential Elections: An Analysis Based on the Spatial Model of Electoral Competition.* Rochester, New York: University of Rochester, Ph.D., 1975.

9498 **Allen, David.** *David Duke and National Republicans in Louisiana.* Ypsilanti: Master's Thesis, Eastern Michigan University, 1992.

9499 **Allen, David R.** *Democratic Party Strength in Manhattan: A Study of the Effect of the Reform-Regular Split in the Democratic Party in New York County on the Strength of the Democratic Party in General Elections from 1953 to 1968.* New York City: Columbia University, Ph.D., 1975.

9500 **Alpert, Eugene Jay.** *Risk and Uncertainty in Political Choice: Candidates' Policy Positions in Congressional Elections.* East Lansing: Michigan State University, Ph.D., 1977.

9501 **Altschuler, Bruce Elliot.** *Political Polling and Presidential Elections.* New York City: City University of New York, Ph.D., 1980.

9502 **Anderson, Melvin J.** *Factors Affecting the Vote of Community College Faculty Members in Collective Bargaining Elections.* Denver, Colorado: University of Denver, Ph.D., 1984.

9503 **Angus, Edward Luverne.** *The 1966 Memphis Charter Referendum: A Comparative Case Study of Local Voting Behavior.* University Park: Pennsylvania State University, Ph.D., 1970.

9504 **Arcelus, Francisco Javier.** *Effects of Aggregate Economic Variables on Congressional Elections.* Pittsburgh, Pennsylvania: Carnegie-Mellon University, Ph.D., 1976.

9505 **Archer, J. Clark; Shelley, Fred M.; and White, Allen R.** *American Electoral Mosaic.* Washington, D.C.: Association of American Geographers, Resource Paper in Geography, 1987.

9506 **Archer, J. Clark; Shelley, Fred M.; White, Allen R.; and Taylor, Peter J.** *Section and Party: A Political Geography of American Presidential Elections. From Andrew Jackson to Ronald Reagan.* Chichester and New York: Research Studies Press, John Wiley & Sons, 1981.

9507 **Archer, Keith Allan.** *Canadian Unions and the NDP: The Failure of Collective Action* (Voting, Behavior). Durham, North Carolina: Duke University, Ph.D., 1985.

9508 **Arnold, James.** *Section and Party in Tennessee: An Electoral Geography of Tennessee Presidential Elections, 1868-1984.* Norman: University of Oklahoma, M.A., 1985.

9509 **Arseneau, Robert Baldwin.** *The Relationship between the Vote in Presidential and Congressional Elections, 1952-1980.* Berkeley: University of California, Ph.D., 1985.

9510 **Asakura, Koki Theodore.** *Election Primary Turnout Differences: The Application of Voting Histories as a Way to Study Voter Turnout.* Los Angeles: University of Southern California, Ph.D., 1978.

9511 **Ayres, Robert Lewis.** *Some System-Level Implications of Elections in the Communes and Provinces of Chile, 1957-1967.* Chapel Hill: University of North Carolina, Ph.D., 1970.

9512 **Bainbridge, William Lee.** *An Analysis of the Relationship between Selected Economic, Social, Demographic and Election Variables and Voter Behavior in Ohio City School District Property Tax Elections.* Columbus: Ohio State University, Ph.D., 1979.

9513 **Baker, Gordon E.** *The Politics of Reapportionment in Washington State.* New York: Holt, Rinehart & Winston, 1960.

9514 **Baker, Samuel Thomas.** *Codasyl COBOL Committee Voting Patterns and the Acceptance of Proposed Changes to the COBOL Language.* Murfreesboro: Middle Tennessee State University, Master's Thesis, 1982.

9515 **Barbara, Daniel.** *Mutual Exclusion in Distributed Systems (Databases, Voting, Partitions).* Princeton, New Jersey: Princeton University, Ph.D., 1985.

9516 **Basehart, Hubert Harry.** *Constituency and Legislative Voting Behavior: An Exploratory Analysis of the Effects of Issues, Competition, Roles, and the Legislator's Image of His District.* Knoxville: University of Tennessee, Ph.D., 1972.

9517 **Batz, Roger William.** *An Analysis of the Voting Behavior in the 1972 Presidential Election of Caucasian Residents in Ecologically-Distinct Living Areas in Baton Rouge, Louisiana.* Baton Rouge: Louisiana State University and Agricultural and Mechanical College, Ph.D., 1974.

9518 **Baughman, Rowland Groves.** *Industrial and Exclusive Unions' Success in White Collar Representation Elections: An Evaluation of the 1969-1973 Period.* Washington, D.C.: George Washington University, D.B.A., 1975.

9519 **Baum, Dale.** *The Political World of Massachusetts Radicalism: Voting Behavior and Ideology in the Civil War Party System, 1954-1872.* Minneapolis: University of Minnesota, Ph.D., 1978.

9520 **Bayes, John Robert.** *Elections, Parties and Responsive Public Policy: The Case of the American County.* Los Angeles: University of California Press, 1974.

9521 **Bell, Lillian Smith.** *The Role and Performance of Black and Metro Newspapers in Relation to Political Campaigns in Selected, Racially-Mixed Congressional Elections: 1960-1970.* Evanston, Illinois: Northwestern University, Ph.D., 1973.

9522 **Berelson, Bernard R.; Lazarsfeld, Paul F.;** and **McPhee, William N.** *Voting: A Study of Opinion Formation in a Presidential Campaign.* Chicago, Illinois: University of Chicago Press, 1954.

9523 **Berg, John A.** *A Study of the Relationship between Demographic Variables and Voting Behavior in Gubernatorial, School Board, School Bond, and State Superintendent Elections.* Madison: University of Wisconsin, Ph.D., 1974.

9524 **Berner, William Sherman.** *The Influence of Pre-Voting Activity on the Outcome of Selected Library Bond Referendums.* Urbana: University of Illinois, Ph.D., 1970.

9525 **Bian, Teshale Engliz.** *Uncontested Elections in the Sixth Class Cities of the Jefferson County.* Louisville, Kentucky: University of Louisville, Master's Thesis, 1975.

9526 **Bicker, William Elmer.** *The Assembly Party: Change and Consistency in Legislative Voting Behavior in the Indiana House, 1923-1963.* Bloomington: Indiana University, Ph.D., 1969.

9527 **Bidinger, Jerome R.** *The Ecological Basis of Costa Rican Voting Patterns: 1958-1966.* Washington, D.C.: Georgetown University, Ph.D., 1973.

9528 **Biegeleisen, Joseph Alan.** *Rational Voting in Three Atlanta Local Option Sales Tax Referenda (Georgia).* Atlanta: Georgia State University, Ph.D., 1983.

9529 **Bierly, Robert Foust.** *District of Columbia Teachers' Needs and the Effect of Those Needs on the April, 1967, Voting for a Single Negotiation Agent.* Washington, D.C.: George Washington University, Ph.D., 1969.

9530 **Black, Jerome Harold.** *Second-Choice Voting in Canadian Federal Elections: A Test of the Multicandidate Calculus of Voting.* Rochester, New York: University of Rochester, Ph.D., 1976.

9531 **Blackburn, William Herman.** *A Study of Participative Management as Related to Voter Behavior in School Tax Elections.* St. Louis, Missouri: Saint Louis University, 1979.

9532 **Blake, Donald Edward.** *Regionalism in Canadian Voting Behaviour, 1908-1968.* New Haven, Connecticut: Yale University, Ph.D., 1972.

9533 **Blake, Donald Edward.** *Two Political Worlds: Parties and Voting in British Columbia.*

Vancouver: University of British Columbia Press, 1985.

9534 **Blank, Robert Henry.** *Voting Turnout in the Border States: Political System and Environmental Influence on the Presidential Vote.* Baltimore: University of Maryland, Ph.D., 1971.

9535 **Blossom, William C., III.** *North Carolina Congressional Districts 1789-1960.* Chapel Hill: Unpublished Study for the Institute of Government, University of North Carolina at Chapel Hill, 1966.

9536 **Boddy, M.,** and **Fudge, C.,** eds. *Local Socialism? Labour Councils and New Left Alternatives.* London: Macmillan, 1984.

9537 **Bohmer, David Alan.** *Voting Behavior During the First American Party System: Maryland, 1796-1816.* Ann Arbor: University of Michigan, Ph.D., 1974.

9538 **Bonar, Clyde Albert.** *Voting Turnout in Presidential Elections: A Casual Model.* Washington, D.C.: George Washington University, Ph.D., 1980.

9539 **Bone, H.A.** *Impact of Reapportionment on the 13 Western States.* Salt Lake City: University of Utah Press, 1970.

9540 **Bone, H.A.,** and **Morill, R.** *Reapportionment Politics: The History of Redistricting in the 50 States.* Beverly Hills: Sage Publications, 1981.

9541 **Books, John William.** *Status Inconsistency, Cross-Pressures, and Voting: The 1968 American Presidential Election as a Test Case.* East Lansing: Michigan State University, Ph.D., 1972.

9542 **Booth, John A.,** and **Selligson, Mitchell A.,** eds. *Elections and Democracy in Central America.* Chapel Hill: University of North Carolina Press, 1989.

9543 **Boozer, Raymond L.** *A Study of the Voting Publics in Grand Rapids, Michigan, to Provide the Basis for Planning and Conducting Future Public School Operating Millage Elections in that District.* East Lansing: Michigan State University, Ph.D., 1969.

9544 **Born, Richard Jules.** *The Influence of State Party Delegations on Roll Call Voting in the United States House of Representatives.* Stanford, California: Stanford University, Ph.D., 1973.

9545 **Bowen, Bruce David.** *The Paradox of Voting: A Theoretical and Empirical Examination.* Lexington: University of Kentucky, Ph.D., 1969.

9546 **Bowley, Christopher.** *An Analysis of Voting Patterns on Environmental Legislation in the United States House of Representatives During the 1980's.* Tallahassee, FL: Master's thesis, Florida State University, 1993.

9547 **Boyd, Steven Ray.** *The Constitution in State Politics: From the Calling of the Constitutional Convention to the Calling of the First Federal Elections.* Madison: University of Wisconsin, Ph.D., 1974.

9548 **Boyd, Thomas Alan.** *Voter Choice in Congressional Elections: A Casual Analysis.* Columbus: Ohio State University, Ph.D., 1983.

9549 **Boyd, William J.D.** *Patterns of Apportionment.* New York: National Municipal League, 1962.

9550 **Boyle, Lorraine Coller.** *A Study of Variables Related to Successful and Unsuccessful Minnesota Public School Referenda Elections in 1981 and in 1982.* Minneapolis: University of Minnesota, Ph.D., 1984.

9551 **Brady, David William.** *A Congressional Response to a Stress Situation: Party Voting in the McKinley Era.* Iowa City: University of Iowa, Ph.D., 1970.

9552 **Brandt, Linda Susan.** *The Politics of Non-partisanship: The 1973 New York City School Board Elections.* Boulder: University of Colorado, Ph.D., 1979.

9553 **Brown, Carol Ann.** *Does a Representative Change His Voting Behavior Once He is No Longer Seeking Re-election to the House of Representatives?* Fullerton: California State University, Master's Thesis, 1977.

9554 **Brown, Dennis Edward.** *The San Francisco Press in Two Presidential Elections: A Study of the Effects of Newspaper Concentration on Diversity in Editorial-Page Comment.* Columbia: University of Missouri, Ph.D., 1970.

9555 **Brown, Ronald Miles.** *The Dissent Voting Patterns of Selected Public University Governing Boards.* Ann Arbor: University of Michigan, Ph.D., 1971.

9556 **Browne, Gregory Michael.** *American Ideologies and Senatorial Voting Records.* East Lansing: Michigan State University, M.A., 1984.

9557 **Brunk, G.G.** *Locational Models of Congressional Voting.* Iowa City: University of Iowa, Ph.D., 1981.

9558 **Brye, David Laffrans.** *Wisconsin Voting Patterns in the Twentieth-Century, 1900 to 1950.* Cambridge, Massachusetts: Harvard University, Ph.D., 1973.

9559 **Buehler, Marilyn H.** *Political Efficacy, Political Discontent, and Voting Turnout Among Mexican-Americans in Michigan.* Notre Dame, Indiana: University of Notre Dame, Ph.D., 1975.

9560 **Burger, Paul R.** *Who Is the Unaligned Voter? Spatial Variations Among Kansas' Third-Party Votes in American Presidential Elections.* Manhattan: Master's thesis, Kansas State University, 1994.

9561 **Burroughs, Julia Ewing.** *Senior Citizen Attitudes and Opinions about Voting and Nonvoting in Partisan and Non-partisan School Elections.* Madison: University of Wisconsin, Ph.D., 1982.

9562 **Burroughs, Wayne Ashmore.** *A Study of White Females' Voting Behavior Toward Black Female Corroborators in a Modified Leaderless Group Discussion.* Knoxville: University of Tennessee, Ph.D., 1969.

9563 **Burton, John Henry.** *A Computer Assisted Analysis of Elections and Roll Call Votes in the California Assembly.* Claremont, California: Claremont Graduate School, Ph.D., 1982.

9564 **Cade, Robert Burr.** *Mass media Influences on the Candidate Choice, Time of Vote Decision, and Ticket-Splitting Voting Behavior of Jasper County, Mississippi, Voters in the 1975 General Election.* Hattiesburg: University of Southern Mississippi, Ph.D., 1977.

9565 **Cama, Vincent Joseph.** *Family Background, Social Location, Personal Political Factors and Voting Behavior: The 1976 Presidential Election of Syracuse.* Syracuse, New York: Syracuse University, Ph.D., 1981.

9566 **Camp, Roderic Ai.** *Politics in Mexico.* New York: Oxford University Press, 1993.

9567 **Campbell, Angus,** et al. *The American Voter.* New York: John Wiley & Sons, 1960.

9568 **Campbell, Ballard Crooker, Jr.** *Political Parties, Cultural Groups and Contested Issues: Voting in the Illinois, Iowa and Wisconsin House of Representatives 1886-1895.* Madison: University of Wisconsin, Ph.D., 1970.

9569 **Campbell, James David.** *Electoral Participation and the Quest for Equality: Black Politics in Alabama Since the Voting Rights Act of 1965.* Austin: University of Texas, Ph.D., 1976.

9570 **Campbell, James Edward.** *A Casual Analysis of Voting Behavior in Presidential Primary Elections.* Syracuse, New York: Syracuse University, Ph.D., 1980.

9571 **Campbell, Julia Dyanne.** *Level of Educational Attainment, Parental Status, Age, and Sex as they Relate to Voting Patterns in Seven Iowa School Bond Elections in 1977.* Iowa City: University of Iowa, Ph.D., 1978.

9572 **Cantrall, William Randolph, II.** *The Impact of Issues and Voting on Changing Attitudes Toward Political Institutions in the 1972 Election.* Urbana: University of Illinois, Ph.D., 1975.

9573 **Carroll, Susan Jane.** *Women as Candidates: Campaigns and Elections in American Politics.* Bloomington: Indiana University, Ph.D., 1980.

9574 **Casper, Dale E.** *Voting Patterns in the United States: Recent Writings, 1980-1984.* Monticello, Illinois: Vance Bibliographies, P 1716, 1985.

9575 **Caviedes, Cesar N.** *Elections in Chile.* Boulder, Colorado: Lynne Rienner Publishers, 1991.

9576 **Caviedes, Cesar N.** *Elections in Chile: The Road Toward Redemocratization.* Boulder, CO: Lynne Rienner Publishers, 1991.

9577 **Chou, Feng-Zse.** *Nationalization of State Politics: A Case Study (Connecticut, Elections).* Syracuse, New York: Syracuse University, Ph.D., 1985.

9578 **Cimbala, Stephen Joseph.** *Senate Voting and Foreign Policy: Symbols and Issues.* Madison: University of Wisconsin, Ph.D., 1969.

9579 **Clark, Jimmy Ed.** *An Analysis of the Relationship between Selected Social Characteristics and Voting Patterns in a Community College Operational Millage Election.* Detroit, Michigan: Wayne State University, Ph.D., 1972.

9580 **Clark, H.,** ed. *The National Election Studies; Machine-Readable Data Deposited at York.* Vancouver: University and other data banks, 1974, 1979, and 1980.

9581 **Clarke, H.D., Jenson, J.; Leduc, L.,** and **Pammett, Jon H.** *Political Choice in Canada.* Toronto: McGraw-Hill, 1980.

9582 **Cohen, Roger Stephen.** *An Examination of the Relationships between Voting Patterns in School Elections and Selected Social Variables of Community Members in Elementary School Districts in Cook, Dupage, Lake, McHenry, and Will Counties, Illinois (Supervision, Boards, Referendum, Decision-Making).* Chicago, Illinois: Loyola University, Ph.D., 1985.

9583 **Cohen, Sylvan H.** *Voting Behavior in School Referenda: An Investigation of Attitudes and Other Determinants by Q Technique and Survey Research.* Kent, Ohio: Kent State University, Ph.D., 1971.

9584 **Cole, Roland Jay.** *Campaign Spending in the United States Senate Elections.* Cambridge, Massachusetts: Harvard University, Ph.D., 1975.

9585 **Coleman, Kenneth Mac.** *Public Opinion and Elections in a One Party System: The Case of Mexico.* Chapel Hill: University of North Carolina, Ph.D., 1970.

9586 **Collie, Mary Melissa Pratka.** *Party Voting and Policy Content Perspectives of Alignments in the Post-New Deal House of Representatives.* Houston, Texas: Rice University, Ph.D., 1984.

9587 **Comer, John Charles.** *Political Orientations and Voting Behavior: A Study of Independents and Party Identifiers.* Columbus: Ohio State University, Ph.D., 1971.

9588 **Commons, J.R.; Saposs, D.J.; Summer, H.L.; Mittelman, E.B.; Hoagland, H.E.; Andrews, John B.;** and **Perlman, S.** *Congressional Quarterly's Guide to U.S. Elections.* Washington, D.C.: Congressional Quarterly, 1975.

9589 *Congressional District Atlas of the United States.* Washington, D.C.: U.S. Department of Commerce, Bureau of the Census, 1960.

9590 *Congressional Districts for the 90th Congress.* Washington, D.C.: U.S. Department of Commerce, Bureau of the Census, Geography Division, 1966.

9591 *Congressional Districts in the 1970's.* Washington, D.C.: Congressional Quarterly, 1974.

9592 **Copeland, Gary Wayne.** *The Effects of Congressional Campaign Expenditures on Voting Behavior: A Behavioral and Policy Analysis.* Iowa City: University of Iowa, Ph.D., 1979.

9593 **Copren, William George.** *The Political History of Sierra County, California, 1849-1861: Local Elections and Non-Local Issues.* Reno: University of Nevada, Master's Thesis, 1975.

9594 **Courtney, John C.,** ed. *Voting in Canada.* Scarborough: Prentice-Hall, 1933.

9595 **Cover, Albert David.** *The Advantage of Incumbency in Congressional Elections.* New Haven, Connecticut: Yale University, Ph.D., 1976.

9596 **Cox, Kevin R.,** and **McCarthy, J.J.** *Neighborhood Activism: Contexts, Interests and Communication.* Columbus, Ohio: Ohio State University, Research Report No. 10, Center for Real Estate Education and Research, 1980.

9597   **Craig, Robert Emmet.** *Voting Behavior in a Presidential Primary: The New Hampshire Democratic Presidential Primary of 1968.* Chapel Hill: University of North Carolina, Ph.D., 1971.

9598   **Craven, Eugene Charles.** *Discriminating Factors Among Legislator Voting-Groups Within the Wisconsin State Legislature, 1945-1967.* Madison: University of Wisconsin, Ph.D., 1969.

9599   **Crawford, Joseph Charles.** *The Relative Effect of Selected Budgeted Dissemination Media on Voter Reaction to School Bond Elections in Selected Cities.* Grand Forks: University of North Dakota, Ph.D., 1972.

9600   **Crisler, Robert M.** *The Little Dixie Region of Missouri.* Evanston, Illinois: Northwestern University Press, 1949.

9601   **Criswell, Larry Wayne.** *The Episodic Nature of Local School District Elections.* Riverside: University of California, Ph.D., 1979.

9602   **Crook, Leo Vincent.** *An Analysis of Union Representation Elections in Mississippi, 1968-1972.* Mississippi State: Mississippi State University, D.B.A. Dissertation, 1978.

9603   **Crumplin, William.** "Electoral Redistribution: The Case of the Preliminary Report of the Fisher Commission for British Columbia, Canada." British Columbia: University of Victoria, M.A., 1989.

9604   **Daniels, Richard Steven.** *Undimensionality in Congressional Voting: A Longitudinal Study of Interest Group Ratings, 1959-1978.* Eugene: University of Oregon, Ph.D., 1981.

9605   **Darby, Charles Edgar.** *The Relationship between Selected Personal Characteristics of Texas State Teachers Association Professional Members and Their Voting Behavior on School and Partisan Issues.* College Station: Texas A & M University, Ph.D., 1970.

9606   **David, P.T.,** and **Eisenberg, R.** *Devaluation of the Urban and Suburban Vote.* Bureau of Public Administration, University of Virginia, Charlottesville, 1961.

9607   **Davidson, David.** *Computer Simulation Models for Evaluating Potential Tax Savings of Federal Revenue Code Sections 6166, 6166A, and 2032A When Elections are Mutually Exclusive.* Greeley: University of Northern Colorado, Ph.D., 1982.

9608   **Davis, Marilyn Ann.** *Political Participation in Georgia's Fifth Congressional District: An Analysis of Racial and Socioeconomic Voting Patterns, 1946 to 1978.* Atlanta: Atlanta University, Ph.D., 1979.

9609   **Davison, Donald Lambert.** *The Political Consequences of the Voting Rights Act of 1965 (South, Participation, Black, Policy, Mobilization).* St. Louis, Missouri: Washington University, Ph.D., 1985.

9610   **De Grazia, Alfred.** *Apportionment and Representative Government.* Washington,D.C.: American Enterprise Institute for Public Policy Research, 1963.

9611   **Denham, William Alfred, III.** *Systemic Patterns, Contextual Variables and Radical Voting: The U.S. Midwest and the Province of Ontario, 1968 and 1972.* DeKalb: Northern Illinois University, Ph.D., 1980.

9612   **De Voursney, Robert Merle.** *Issues and Electoral Instability: A Test of Alternative Explanations for Voting Defection in the 1968 American Presidential Election.* Chapel Hill: University of Northern Carolina, Ph.D., 1977.

9613   **Diba, Behzad Tabatabai.** *Essays on Economic Equilibria. Part 1: Majority Voting Equilibria in the Public Sector. Part 2: Rational Asset Price Bubbles: Theory and Evidence.* Providence, Rhode Island: Brown University, Ph.D., 1984.

9614   **Dickens, William Theodore.** *Union Representation Elections: Campaign and Vote.* Cambridge: Massachusetts Institute of Technology, Ph.D., 1981.

9615   **Dietz, Karen Dulura Rowlett.** *An Attitudinal Approach to Voting Behavior.* Austin: University of Texas, Ph.D., 1976.

9616   **Diffenbaugh, Donald Louis.** *The Influence of Political and Socio-Economic Variables on Roll Call Votes: A Study of Voting Behavior in the United States House of Representatives.* Washington, D.C.: George Washington University, Ph.D., 1973.

9617   **Dixon, R.G.** *Representation and Redistricting Issues.* Lexington, Massachusetts: Lexington Books, 1982.

9618   **Dodd, Thomas J.** *Managing Democracy in Central America: A Case Study. United States Election Supervision in Nicaragua, 1927-1933.* New Brunswick: Transaction Publishers, 1992.

9619   **Dreier, John A.** *The Politics of Isolationism: A Quantitative Study of Congressional Foreign Policy Voting, 1937-1941.* Lexington: University of Kentucky, Ph.D., 1977.

9620   **Dubois, Philip Leon.** *Judicial Elections in the States: Patterns and Consequences.* Madison: University of Wisconsin, Ph.D., 1978.

9621 **Duffy, Charles Anthony.** *Teacher Involvement in School Board Elections: A Description and Evaluation of a Political Education Program by the California Teachers Association.* San Diego, CA: United States International Univ., Ph.D., 1979.

9622 **Dunham, Patricia Marie.** *Voting Behavior and Ideology in the House of Representatives: The Impact of Socialization.* Oxford, Ohio: Miami University, Ph.D., 1983.

9623 **Dunlap, Riley Eugene.** *Legislative Voting on Environmental Issues: An Analysis of the Impact of Party Membership.* Eugene: University of Oregon, Ph.D., 1973.

9624 **Dunn, Richard Byam.** *Voter Registration and Turnout in School Board Elections: Theoretical Bases.* Stanford, California: Stanford University, Ph.D., 1981.

9625 **Duvall, Wallace L.** *Impact of Labor Union Representation Elections on Wages and Selected Employer-Employee Relations in Nonprofit Hospitals in Texas.* Denton: North Texas State University, Ph.D., 1981.

9626 **Edend, Edward N.** *Reform vs. Status Quo: Presidential Elections of 1912 and 1924.* Fayetteville: Master's thesis, University of Arkansas, 1993.

9627 **Eisele, Frederick Robert.** *Age and Political Change: A Cohort Analysis of Voting Among Careerists in the United States Senate, 1947-1970.* New York City: New York University, Ph.D., 1972.

9628 **Eli, Jack Clemeth.** *A Study of Political Attitudes and Voting Behavior in the 1970 Tennessee Gubernatorial Election.* Carbondale: Southern Illinois University, Ph.D., 1971.

9629 **Elkins, D.,** and **Simeon, R.** *Small Worlds: Provinces and Parties in Canadian Political Life.* Toronto: Methuen, 1980.

9630 **Elliott, Robert Herman.** *A Survey of County Party Organization and County Voting Patterns in a Southern State.* Houston, Texas: University of Houston, Ph.D., 1975.

9631 **Epstein, Lavrily Keir.** *Components of Presidential Voting in Selected American Cities, 1872-1968.* Seattle: University of Washington, Ph.D., 1974.

9632 **Erickson, Richard Edward.** *The Presidential Election of 1896 in Pennsylvania: An Analysis of Party Development and Voting Behavior.* Philadephia, Pennsylvania: Temple University, Ph.D., 1981.

9633 **Erikson, Robert Stanley.** *A Multivariate Analysis of Congressional Elections.* Urbana: University of Illinois, Ph.D., 1969.

9634 **Esterly, Robert Elden.** *A Longitudinal Analysis of Legislative Roll Call Voting: Patterns of Stability and Change in the New Mexico House of Representatives, 1961-1969.* Tucson: University of Arizona, Ph.D., 1971.

9635 **Eubank, Robert Broocke.** *Incumbency, Partisan, and Saliency Effects in Congressional Elections from 1956-1978.* Houston, Texas: Rice University, Ph.D., 1981.

9636 **Fagin, Vernon Allen.** *Franklin D. Roosevelt, Liberalism in the Democratic Party, and the 1938 Congressional Elections: The Urge to Purge.* Los Angeles: University of California, Ph.D., 1979.

9637 **Falk, Marvin William.** *The Reichstag Elections of 1912: A Statistical Study.* Iowa City: University of Iowa, Ph.D., 1976.

9638 **Ferber, Paul H.** *Voting Behavior in a State Election: The 1977 Virginia Governor's Race (Politics, Parties).* Washington, D.C.: George Washington University, Ph.D., 1986.

9639 **Fernandez, Julio A.** *Belize: Case Study for Democracy in Central America.* Aldershot: Avebury, 1989.

9640 **Ferro, Lisa.** *Territory vs. Ideology: Congressional Voting on Below-Cost Timber Sales.* Knoxville: Master's thesis, University of Tennessee, 1994.

9641 **Fiorina, M.P.** *Retrospective Voting in American National Elections.* New Haven, Connecticut: Yale University Press, 1981.

9642 **Fisk, Larry John.** *Controversy on the Prairies: Issues in the General Provincial Elections of Manitoba 1870-1969.* Edmonton, Alberta, Canada: University of Alberta, Ph.D., 1975.

9643 **Flannery, Vernon P.** *Money and Votes: A Study of Councilmanic Elections in Southwestern Ohio.* Oxford, Ohio: Miami University, Ph.D., 1977.

9644 **Flavin, Michael John.** *Measuring Gains and Losses of Democrats and Republicans in Congressional Elections.* Tucson: University of Arizona, Ph.D., 1977.

9645 **Fleitas, Daniel William.** *The Underdog Effect: An Experimental Study of Voting Behavior in a Minimal Information Election.* Tallahassee: Florida State University, Ph.D., 1970.

9646 **Flint, Kenneth Douglas.** *Political Exchange and Guatemalan Voting Patterns: The Presidential Elections of 1966 and 1970.* Long Beach: California State University, Master's Thesis, 1974.

9647 **Flood, Lawrence Garis.** *Voting in Primary Elections: The Case of Hillsborough, North Carolina.* Chapel Hill: University of North Carolina, Ph.D., 1970.

9648 **Forman, Brenda.** *American Politics--1793-1809: A Case Study in the Theory of Critical Elections.* New York City: City University of New York, Ph.D., 1970.

9649 **Forman, L.A.** *Congressmen and Their Constituencies.* Chicago, Illinois: Rand McNally, 1963.

9650 **Fournier, P.** *Quebec and the Parti Quebecois.* San Francisco: Synthesis, 1978.

9651 **Fraser, Jeannette Lynn.** *The Effects of Voting Systems on Voter Participation: Punch Card Voting Systems in Ohio (Machines, Election Administration, Overvoting, Equipment, Ballot Form).* Columbus: Ohio State University, Ph.D., 1985.

9652 **Frazier, Thomas Patrick.** *Consultants, Unions, and NLRB Elections (Logit Models).* Washington, D.C.: American University, Ph.D., 1984.

9653 **Freedman, Stanley Richard.** *American Presidential Elections: Issues and Voter Motivation.* Tallahassee: Florida State University, Ph.D., 1975.

9654 **Friedman, Gordon David.** *Issues, Partisanship, and Political Subcultures: A Study of Voting in Statewide Referenda in New Jersey, 1944-1966.* Chapel Hill: University of North Carolina, Ph.D., 1971.

9655 **Friedman, Sally.** *Alternative Models of Issue Voting in the 1978 Congressional Elections.* Ann Arbor: University of Michigan, Ph.D., 1983.

9656 **Frisbie, Douglas William.** *Status Voting and Status Polarization: The Influence of Class Consciousness, True and False Class Identification, Social Mobility and Status Inconsistency.* Minneapolis: University of Minnesota, Ph.D., 1970.

9657 **Frizzell, Alan; Pammett, Jon H.; and Westell, Anthony.** *The Canadian General Election of 1988.* Ottawa: Carleton University Press, 1989.

9658 **Gagne, Wallace Donald George.** *Class Voting in Canada.* Rochester, New York: University of Rochester, Ph.D., 1970.

9659 **Garrison, Glenn David.** *An Analysis of Media, Social, and Political Influences on Time of Voting Decision in Presidential Elections, 1952-1976.* Denton: North Texas State University, Ph.D., 1981.

9660 **Gates, John Boatner.** *The American Supreme Court, Critical Elections, and the Invalidation of State and Federal Policies, 1837-1964: Supreme Court Policymaking During Periods of major Change in the Political Party System (Judicial Review, Realignment).* Baltimore: University of Maryland, Ph.D., 1985.

9661 **Gayk, William Franklyn.** *An Analysis of Voting Patterns on Propositions 13, 4, and 9.* Riverside: University of California, Ph.D., 1982.

9662 **Gaziano, Joseph Lawrence.** *The Role of Professional Media Consultants in Political Advertising Campaigns for Statewide Candidates in the 1972 and 1973 General Elections.* DeKalb: Northern Illinois University, Ph.D., 1975.

9663 "Gerrymandering." *Encyclopedia of Southern History.* Baton Rouge: Louisiana State University Press, 1976.

9664 **Gildea, John A.** *A Theory of Federal Open Market Committee Voting Behavior (Federal Reserve, Public Choice).* Durham, North Carolina: Duke University, Ph.D., 1985.

9665 **Gilliam, Franklin D., II.** *An Examination of Voter Turnout for the 1978 Congressional Elections.* Iowa City: University of Iowa, Ph.D., 1983.

9666 **Ginsberg, Benjamin.** *Critical Elections and American Public Policy.* Chicago, Illinois: University of Chicago, Ph.D., 1973.

9667 **Goldman, Robert Michael.** *A Free Ballot and a Fair Count: The Department of Justice and the Enforcement of Voting Rights in the South, 1877-1893.* East Lansing: Michigan State University, Ph.D., 1976.

9668 **Goldstein, Joel Harris.** *The Effects of the Adoption of Woman Suffrage: Sex Differences in Voting Behavior--Illinois 1914-1921.* Chicago, Illinois: University of Chicago, Ph.D., 1973.

9669 **Gopian, James David.** *Issue-Voting in Presidential Primary Elections: A Comparative State Analysis of the 1976 Presidential Primaries.* Bloomington: Indiana University, Ph.D., 1980.

9670 **Goudinoff, Peter Alexis.** *Party, Constituency, and Issue Salience in Congressional Voting.* Columbus: Ohio State University, Ph.D., 1969.

9671 **Grande, John W.** "Impact of the Geographic Concentration of the Elderly on Voting in West Virginia." Morgantown, West Virginia: West Virginia University, Morgantown, M.A., 1988.

9672 **Grayson, John Paul.** *Neighborhood and Voting: The Social Basis of Conservative Support in Broadview.* Toronto, Ontario, Canada: University of Toronto, Ph.D., 1972.

9673 **Green, Justin James.** *An Experiment in Voting Behavior.* Lexington: University of Kentucky, Ph.D., 1970.

9674 **Grofman, B.; Lijphart, A.; Mckay, R.; and Scarrow, H.** *Representation and Redistricting Issues.* Lexington, Massachusetts: Lexington Books, 1982.

9675 **Grogan, Fred Leroy.** *Institutional Change in Congress: The Impact of Elections.* Columbia: University of Missouri, Ph.D., 1979.

9676 **Hacker, A.** *Congressional Districting*, rev. ed. Washington, D.C.: The Brookings Institute, 1964.

9677 **Hadley, David Jeffery.** *Role Orientations and Roll-Call Voting: A Computer Simulation Analysis of the Indiana House of Representatives.* Bloomington: Indiana University, Ph.D., 1974.

9678 **Hais, Michael David.** *Change and Stability of the American Party Voting Coalitions 1952-1968: Description and Explanation.* Baltimore: University of Maryland, Ph.D., 1973.

9679 **Hall, Eugene C.** "The City of Gainesville, Florida, 1987, Reapportionment for Single Member Districts: An Empirical Analysis." Gainesville: University of Florida, M.A., 1989.

9680 **Hall, John Stuart.** *An Analysis of Voter Behavior in School Financial Elections.* Eugene: University of Oregon, Ph.D., 1973.

9681 **Hall, William Keeny.** *The "Divisive" Primary in State Legislative Elections.* Lawrence: University of Kansas, Ph.D., 1969.

9682 **Halpin, Stanislaus Anthony, Jr.** *The Anti-Gerrymander: The Impact of Section 5 of the Voting Rights Act of 1965 Upon Louisiana Parish Redistricting.* Washington, D.C.: George Washington University, Ph.D., 1978.

9683 **Hamilton, Howard D.** *Legislative Apportionment.* New York: Harper & Row, 1964.

9684 **Hamilton, Howard D.** *Reapportioning Legislatures: A Consideration of Criteria and Computers.* Columbus, Ohio: Charles Merrill Books, 1966.

9685 **Hannah, Susan Blackmore.** *An Evaluation of Judicial Elections in Michigan, 1948-1968.* East Lansing: Michigan State University, Ph.D., 1972.

9686 **Hardy, L.; Helsop, A.; and Anderson, S.,** eds. *Reapportionment Politics: The History of Redistricting in the 50 States.* Beverly Hills: Sage Publications, 1981.

9687 **Haring, L. Lloyd.** *An Analysis of Spatial Aspects of Voting Behavior in Tennessee.* Iowa City: University of Iowa, Ph.D., 1959.

9688 **Harlow, Caroline Wolf.** *A Longitudinal Analysis of the Stability of Voting Blocs in the United States House of Representatives During the Eisenhower Years, 1955-1958.* Minneapolis: University of Minnesota, Ph.D., 1969.

9689 **Harmatuck, Donald John.** *An Analysis of Bus Transportation Referenda Voting in Madison, Wisconsin.* Madison: University of Wisconsin, Ph.D., 1973.

9690 **Harris, Lillian Craig.** *Is There a Republican Majority? Political Trends 1952-1956.* New York: Harper and Brothers, 1954.

9691 **Harrison, Edward Lindsay, Jr.** *The Influence of the Interaction of Supervisory style and Employee Locus-of-Control on Voting Behavior in Union Representation Elections.* Denton: North Texas State University, Ph.D., 1975.

9692 **Hartzenbuehler, Ronald L.** *Foreign Policy Voting in the United States Congress, 1808-1812.* Kent, Ohio: Kent State University, Ph.D., 1972.

9693 **Hegstad, Patsy Adams.** *Citizenship, Voting, and Immigrants; A Comparative Study of the Naturalization Propensity and Voter Registration of Nordics in Seattle and Ballard, Washington, 1892-1900.* Seattle: University of Washington, Ph.D., 1982.

9694 **Heighberger, Neil P.** *Congress and Postwar National Security Policy: A Study of Roll-Call Voting in the House of Representatives.* Cincinnati, Ohio: University of Cincinnati, Ph.D., 1971.

9695 **Helinger, Daniel C.** *Venezuela: Tarnished Democracy.* Boulder: Westview Press, 1991.

9696 **Helwig, Raymond Clark.** *Common Stock Price Premiums for Voting Control.* East Lansing: Michigan State University, Ph.D., 1973.

9697 **Henry, Charles P.** *Culture and African American Politics.* Bloomington: Indiana University Press, 1990.

9698 **Henstock, Thomas Frank.** *Factors Related to Voting Preference in Four Public School Bond Referendums in Western New York.* Buffalo: State University of New York, Ph.D., 1971.

9699 **Heppen, John J.** *The Political Geography of the 1991 Louisiana Gubernatorial Elections: David Duke Versus Edwin Edwards.* Baton Rouge, LA: Master's thesis, Louisiana State University, 1994.

9700 **Hetrick, Virginia R.** *Factors Influencing Voting Behavior in Support of Rapid Transit in Seattle and Atlanta.* Seattle: University of Washington, Ph.D., 1974.

9701 **Hillard, Jan William.** *Understanding Urban Voting: An Analysis of Cincinnati Council Elections from 1969 through 1977 (Ohio).* Cincinnati, Ohio: University of Cincinnati, Ph.D., 1984.

9702 **Hilty, James Walter.** *Voting Alignments in the United States Senate, 1933-1944.* Columbia: University of Missouri, Ph.D., 1973.

9703 **Hirsch, Robert Oliver.** *The Influence of Channel, Source, and Message Variables on Voting Behavior in the 1972 Illinois Primary Election.* Carbondale: Southern Illinois University, Ph.D., 1972.

9704 **Hoadley, John Frank.** *The Development of American Political Parties: A Spatial Analysis of Congressional Voting, 1789-1803.* Chapel Hill: University of North Carolina, Ph.D., 1979.

9705 **Hoffman, Marvin Kenneth.** *Behavioral and Attitudinal Correlates of Ideological Consistency and Inconsistency: The Impact of Political Belief System Structure on Party Voting and Opinion Patterning.* Athens: University of Georgia, Ph.D., 1972.

9706 **Hoffman, Wayne L.** *A Comparative Analysis of Two Urban Nonpartisan Referendums: A Factor Analysis Solution.* Gainesville: University of Florida, Ph.D., 1970.

9707 **Hubbard, Duke Byron.** *School Board Member Recruitment, Political Ideology and Voting Behavior: Methodology for Testing Pluralist and Elitist Assumptions.* Claremont, California: Claremont Graduate School, Ph.D., 1970.

9708 **Hudson, Margaret Duff.** *Collective Bargaining for CSUC: Some Determinants of Voting Behavior.* Carson: California State University--Dominguez Hills, Ph.D., 1981.

9709 **Hudson, Tim William.** *Mississippi's 1975 Gubernatorial Race in Hattiesburg-Petal: An Electoral Geography.* Hattiesburg: University of Southern Mississippi, Master's Thesis, 1977.

9710 **Humphrey, Craig Reed.** *Voting Patterns in City-County Consolidation Referenda: Case Studies of Memphis and Nashville, Tennessee.* Providence, Rhode Island: Brown University, Ph.D., 1971.

9711 **Hwang, Su-Ik.** *Constitutional Choice and the Individual Calculus of Voting.* Bloomington: Indiana University, Ph.D., 1985.

9712 **Hynson, Lawrence McKee, Jr.** *Status Inconsistency, Massification and the George Wallace Support in the 1968 Presidential Elections.* Knoxville: University of Tennessee, Ph.D., 1972.

9713 **Imai, Haruo.** *Voting, Bargaining, and Factor Income Distribution.* Stanford, California: Stanford University, Ph.D., 1979.

9714 **Ingalls, Gerald Lynn.** *Spatial Change in Postwar Southern Republican Voting Responses.* East Lansing: Michigan State University, Ph.D., 1973.

9715 **Irwin, William Joseph, Jr.** *The CEDA in the 1933 Cortes Election.* New York City: Columbia University, Ph.D., 1975.

9716 **Isreal, Michael Louis.** *The Lost Cause Candidate: The Myth of Competition in Uncompetitive American Congressional Elections.* New Brunswick: Rutgers University--The State University of New Jersey, Ph.D., 1974.

9717 **Jackson, Alan.** *Boundary Effects on Voting in Oklahoma.* Stillwater: Oklahoma State University, Geography Department, Master's Thesis, 1979.

9718 **Jackson, Jesse Jefferson.** *Republicans and Florida Elections and Election Cases, 1877-1891.* Tallahassee: Florida State University, Tallahassee, Ph.D., 1974.

9719 **Jackson, John Edgar.** *A Statistical Model of United States' Voting Behavior.* Cambridge, Massachusetts: Harvard University, Ph.D., 1969.

9720 **Jacobson, G.C.** *Money in Congressional Elections.* New Haven, Connecticut: Yale University Press, 1980.

9721 **Jennings, John Kelley.** *The Regulators and the Regulated: A Study of Broadcasters' Perceptions of Federal Communications Commission Members and FCC Voting Behavior.* Stanford, California: Stanford University, Ph.D., 1975.

9722 **Jewell, Malcolm E.** *The Politics of Reapportionment.* New York: Atherton Press, 1962.

9723 **Johnson, Linda Louise.** *The Determinants of Congressional Real Estate Voting Patterns.* Athens: University of Georgia, Ph.D., 1983.

9724 **Johnston, Robert Elbert.** *Constituency Characteristics and Congressional Voting Behavior on Aid-for-Education Legislation.* Berkeley: University of California, Ph.D., 1971.

9725 **Jones, Ruth Schuessler.** *The Electorate Parties and Policy in United States Presidential Elections, 1952-1964.* Washington, D.C.: Georgetown University, Ph.D., 1969.

9726 **Ju, Sung Whan.** *An Econometric Model of Congressmen's Voting Behavior with Sample Selectivity.* Albany: State University of New York, Ph.D., 1984.

9727 **Jucewicz, Joseph.** *Voting and Abstention in Presidential Elections: A Simulation Model of Individual Vote Choice.* Baltimore, Maryland: John Hopkins University, Ph.D., 1986.

9728 **Kaiser, Diane Sue.** *A Critique of Empirical Voting Behavior as a Form of Explanation.* Madison: University of Wisconsin, Ph.D., 1984.

9729 **Kalt, Morse Frederick.** *The Impact of Membership Change on Roll Call Voting in the U.S. House of Representatives.* Chapel Hill: University of North Carolina, Ph.D., 1980.

9730 **Karrenberg, Jo Ann Kennedy.** *Illinois: An Examination of the Voting Behavior of Its 102 Counties.* Long Beach: California State University, Master's Thesis, 1981.

9731 **Kazee, Thomas Allen.** *Congressional Elections and the Rerun Phenomenon: A Study of Candidate Recruitment and Incumbency Advantage.* Columbus: Ohio State University, Ph.D., 1978.

9732 **Keeter, Charles Scott.** *Television, Newspapers, and the Bases of Choice in American Presidential Elections.* Chapel Hill: University of North Carolina, Ph.D., 1979.

9733 **Keith, Nelson W., and Keith, Novella Z.** *The Social Origins of Democratic Socialism in Jamaica.* Philadelphia: Temple University Press, 1992.

9734 **Kelly, P.L.** *The Consistency of Voting by the Latin American States in the United Nations General Assembly.* Lincoln: University of Nebraska, Ph.D., 1971.

9735 **Kelley, Richard Charles.** *Independent Voting and Its Implications for the Rational Voter Model: A Microanalytic Behavioral Approach.* Seattle: University of Washington, Ph.D., 1983.

9736 **Kennedy, Shirley Graves.** *Political Money and the Candidacy of Women (Public Policy, Campaign Finance, Congress, Federal Elections, United States).* Claremont, California: Claremont Graduate School, Ph.D., 1986.

9737 **Key, V.O., Jr.** *Southern Politics.* New York: Alfred A. Knopf, 1949.

9738 **Kharasch, Shari B.** *Political Attitudes and Voting Turnout in a Politically Important Population.* Baltimore: University of Maryland, Ph.D., 1974.

9739 **Killait, Berthold Richard.** *A Quasi-Market and Policy Model for Local School Finance Based Upon California School Tax Elections in 1971-72.* Santa

Barbara: University of California, Ph.D., 1974.

9740 **King, James Dale.** *Millage and Bond Elections in the Pennfield School District: An Analysis of Three Ballot Proposals.* Kalamazoo: Western Michigan University, Ph.D., 1977.

9741 **King, Gary.** *Do President's Make a Difference? (Political Parties, Elections, United States Congress).* Madison: University of Wisconsin, Ph.D., 1984.

9742 **Kitchens, James Travis.** *An Experimental Study of Campaign Issues and Candidates' Personality Traits as Influencing Variables on Voting Behavior.* Gainesville: University of Florida, Ph.D., 1974.

9743 **Klein, Frederick Allen.** *A Cross-Sectional and Diachronic Analysis of Split and Straight Ticket Voting.* Milwaukee: University of Wisconsin, Ph.D., 1975.

9744 **Knight, Kathleen Mary.** *The Use and Understanding of Ideological Terms: Comparisons between Elected Partisan Activists and the Voting Public.* Los Angeles: University of California, Ph.D., 1980.

9745 **Koempel, Wayne F.** *The Effects of Distance on Voter Turnout in Selected Precincts in Richard County, South Carolina.* Columbia: University of South Carolina, M.A., 1975.

9746 **Koenig, David J.** *Latent Ideological Components of Legislative Voting; A Guttman Scale Analysis of Roll Call Votes in the House of Representatives, 1955-1962.* Chapel Hill: University of North Carolina, Ph.D., 1973.

9747 **Kokkeler, Larry Anthony.** *Communication Variables, Candidate Image and Voting Behavior: A Study of Influence in the 1972 Presidential and Gubernatorial Elections.* Carbondale: Southern Illinois University, Ph.D., 1973.

9748 **Kornberg, Harvey Richard.** *Charles Evans Hughes and the Supreme Court: A Study in Judicial Philosophy and Voting Behavior.* Providence, Rhode Island: Brown University, Ph.D., 1972.

9749 **Kostroski, Warren Lee.** *Elections and Senatorial Accountability: 1920-1970.* St. Louis, Missouri: Washington University, Ph.D., 1976.

9750 **Kram, Sanford Edward.** *Correlates of Legislative Voting in the United States House of Representatives, 1967-1968.* Riverside: University of California, Ph.D., 1973.

9751 **Krassa, Michael Andrew.** *Contextually Conditional Political Interactions: Party Activity and Mass Behavior Response (Elections, Mass Behavior, Turnout, Contacting).* St. Louis, Missouri: Washington University, Ph.D., 1985.

9752 **Krosnick, Jon Alexander.** *Policy Voting in American Presidential Elections: An Application of Psychological Theory to American Politics.* Ann Arbor: University of Michigan, Ph.D., 1986.

9753 **Kurtz, Karl Theodore.** *Elections and the House of Representatives, 1882-1968.* St. Louis, Missouri: Washington University, Ph.D., 1972.

9754 **Lacy, Donald Pat.** *Voting Patterns on School Bond Referenda in Mercer County, West Virginia: A Test of Selected Hypotheses.* Knoxville: University of Tennessee, Ph.D., 1976.

9755 **Laine, Charles Russell.** *Selecting Sets of Alternatives: A Comparison of Voting Schemes.* Davis: University of California, Ph.D., 1980.

9756 **Lambert, R., et al.** *The 1984 Canadian National Election Study.* Vancouver: Machine readable data deposited with University of British Columbia and other Canadian data banks. 1986.

9757 **Lamis, Alexander P.** *The Two-Party South.* Expanded edition. New York: Oxford University Press, 1988.

9758 **Larsen, James E.** *Reapportionment and the Courts.* Tuscaloosa: Bureau of Public Administration, University of Alabama Press, 1962.

9759 **Larson, William Kemp.** *A Comparison Study of Ohio Community and Non-Community School District Voting Records from 1960 through 1974.* Bowling Green, Ohio: Bowling Green State University, Ph.D., 1975.

9760 **Latus, Margaret Ann.** *The Operations of Ideological Political Action Committees: Thirteen Liberal and Conservative Pacs in the 1982 Election (Public Interest).* Princeton, New Jersey: Princeton University, Ph.D., 1984.

9761 **Lawrence, David Gilbert.** *Issue-Voting and Demand Failure in American Presidential Elections: 1952-1968.* Chicago, Illinois: University of Chicago, Ph.D., 1975.

9762 **Lawson, Steven Fred.** *"Give Us the Ballot": The Expansion of Black Voting Rights in the South, 1944-1969.* New York City: Columbia University, Ph.D., 1974.

9763 **Lazarsfeld, Paul F., et al.** *The People's Choice: How the Voter Makes up His Mind in a Presidential Campaign.* New York: Dwell, Sloan & Pearce, 1944.

9764 **Leeds, Patricia Giles.** *The Conditions for Issue Voting: A Comparison of Presidential and Congressional Elections.* Madison: University of Wisconsin, Ph.D., 1977.

9765 **Leib, Jonathan I.** "The Theoretical and Practical Value of Popular Methods of Measuring Political Fairness and Partisan Gerrymandering in Congressional Redistricting Plans." Syracuse, New York: Syracuse University, M.A., 1987.

9766 **Lenchner, Paul.** *Senate Voting Patterns and American Politics, 1949-1965.* Ithaca, New York: Cornell University, Ph.D., 1973.

9767 **Leroy, Frederick E.** *A Geographic Analysis of Non-Voting Among Massachusetts Registered Voters in the 1960 Presidential Election.* Athens: Ohio University, Department of Geography, M.A., 1973.

9768 **Lewis, Evelyn.** *The Jewish Vote: Fact or Fiction. Trends in Jewish Voting Behavior.* Muncie, Indiana: Ball State University, Ph.D., 1976.

9769 **Lilie, Stuart Allen.** *Apathy about Apathy: A Critical Analysis of Contemporary Evaluations of Non-Voting.* Baltimore, Maryland: Johns Hopkins University, Ph.D., 1970.

9770 **Litchfield, F.H.** *Voting Behavior in a Metropolitan Area.* Ann Arbor: University of Michigan Press, 1941.

9771 **Little, Jill Ann.** *A Study to Determine What Factors are Associated with Regular, Occasional and Nonparticipation of Voter Households in School Budget Elections.* Syracuse, New York: Syracuse University, Ph.D., 1979.

9772 **Lombard, Rudolph Joseph.** *Achieving 'Maximum Feasible Participation' of the Poor in Anti-Poverty Elections.* Syracuse, New York: Syracuse University, Ph.D., 1970.

9773 **Macaluso, Theodore Francis.** *Parameters of Responsible Voting: Issues and the American Electorate, 1952-1968.* Baltimore, Maryland: John Hopkins University, Ph.D., 1975.

9774 **Magleby, David Blyth.** *Direct Legislation: Voting on Ballot Propositions in the United States.* Berkeley: University of California, Ph.D., 1980.

9775 **Maher, Frederick Joseph.** *Vermont Elections.* New York City: Columbia University, Ph.D., 1969.

9776 **Majete, Clayton Aaron.** *Locus of Control and Voting Behavior Across Socio-Economic Groups.* New York City: New York University, Ph.D., 1984.

9777 **Malsberger, John William.** *The Emergence of a Moderate Coalition: Senate Voting, 1938-1952.* Philadelphia, Pennsylvania: Temple University, Ph.D., 1980.

9778 **Manheim, Jarol Bruce.** *The Effect of Campaign Techniques on Voting Patterns in a Congressional Election.* Evanston, Illinois: Northwestern University, Ph.D., 1971.

9779 **Mann, Thomas Edward.** *Candidate Saliency and Congressional Elections.* Ann Arbor: University of Michigan, Ph.D., 1977.

9780 **Marash, Elizabeth Redfield.** *Geographical Isolation and Social Conservation in Pennsylvania Small Towns.* University Park: Pennsylvania State University, Ph.D., 1971.

9781 **Marc, Kathryn Taschler.** *Analysis of the Effect of Community Education on Voting Behavior in School Financial Elections in New Jersey.* Ann Arbor: University of Michigan, Ph.D., 1977.

9782 **Marcus, Robert Simon.** *Federal Spending and Congressional Voting: A Study of the House of Representatives.* Albany: State University of New York, Ph.D., 1975.

9783 **Marsick, Nicholas Marsh.** *A Survey of the Voting Attitudes of Eighteen to Twenty-Year-Old Voters in Portage County, Ohio Toward Increased School Taxers in 1974.* Kent, Ohio: Kent State University, Ph.D., 1975.

9784 **Martin, Glenn Richards.** *Conservatism and Liberalism in the American Congress: A Selected Study of Congressional Voting Ratings, 1947-1972.* Muncie, Indiana: Ball State University, Ph.D., 1973.

9785 **Martin, Jeanne Louise.** *Exchange Theory and Legislative Behavior: A Computer Simulation of Roll-Call Voting in the United States Senate.* East Lansing: Michigan State University, Ph.D., 1971.

9786 **Martin, Joseph Lee.** *The Voting Behavior of Blacks as a Function of Socio-Economic Status and Expectancy for Reinforcement.* Ann Arbor: University of Michigan, Ph.D., 1973.

9787 **Martinez, Michael David.** *Issue Voting, Projection, and Persuasion: Who Does What?* Ann Arbor: University of Michigan, Ph.D., 1985.

9788 **Martis, Kenneth C.** *The History of Natural Resources Roll Call Voting in the United States House of Representatives: An Analysis of the Spatial Aspects of Legislative Voting Behavior.* Ann Arbor: University of Michigan, Ph.D., 1976.

9789 **Martis, Kenneth C.** *The Historical Atlas of Political Parties in the United States Congress, 1789 to 1989.* New York: Macmillan, 1988.

9790 **Matloff, Norman Saul.** *Equilibrium Behavior in an Infinite Voting Model.* Los Angeles: University of California, Ph.D., 1975.

9791 **McCabe, Don Franklin.** *Voting in Idaho, 1960-1966: A Precinct Analysis of Social and Economic Characteristics.* Moscow: University of Idaho, Ph.D., 1972.

9792 **McCallister, Paul Eugene.** *Missouri Voters, 1840-1856: An Analysis of Ante-Bellum Voting Behavior and Political Parties.* Columbia: University of Missouri, Ph.D., 1976.

9793 **McCarthy, John Lockhart.** *Reconstruction Legislation and Voting Alignments in the House of Representatives, 1863-1869.* New Haven, Connecticut: Yale University, Ph.D., 1970.

9794 **McCleneghan, Jack Sean.** *The Effects of Media Interaction and Other Campaign Variables in Mayoral Elections in Twenty-Three Texas Metro Areas.* Austin: University of Texas, Ph.D., 1979.

9795 **McConachie, Michael Paul.** *Presidential Campaigning for Congressional Candidates and Midterm Elections, 1962-1982 (Political Parties, Seat Loss, Off-Year).* Columbia: University of Missouri, Ph.D., 1985.

9796 **McCue, Kenneth Frank.** *The Structure of Individual Decisions in American Elections: The Influence of Relevant Alternatives.* Pasadena: California Institute of Technology, Ph.D., 1984.

9797 **McKay, Douglas.** *Social-Class Voting: A Geographical Analysis of the 1968 and 1972 Presidential Elections in Columbia, South Carolina.* Columbia: University of South Carolina, M.A., 1976.

9798 **McKay, Robert B.** *Reapportionment.* New York: The Twentieth Century Fund, 1965.

9799 **McKenzie, Robert M.** *Identification and Analysis of Factors Affecting School Bond Elections in Kansas School Districts During 1966-1967.* Lawrence: University of Kansas, Ph.D., 1969.

9800 **McMullan, John Calvin.** *Factors Affecting the Results of School Bond Elections as Reported by the School Districts of Missouri, which Held Bond Elections between July 1, 1960 and June 30, 1967.* Oxford: University of Mississippi, Ph.D., 1969.

9801 **McPhee, William N., and Glaser, W.A., eds.** *The Public Opinion and Congressional Elections.* Glencoe: The Free Press, 1962.

9802 **Mebane, Walter Richard, Jr.** *Understanding Popular Political Understanding through Survey Analysis (American, Voting, Methodology, Conversation, Phenomenology).* New Haven, Connecticut: Yale University, Ph.D., 1985.

9803 **Meisel, J.** *The Canadian General Election of 1957.* Toronto: University of Toronto Press, 1962.

9804 **Meisel, J.** *Papers on the 1962 Election.* Toronto: University of Toronto Press, 1965.

9805 **Menendez-Carrion, Amparo.** *The 1952-1978 Presidential Elections and Guayaquil's 'Suburbio': A Micro-Analysis of Voting Behavior in a Context of Social Control (Ecuador, Clientelism, Political Behavior, Urban).* Baltimore, Maryland: Johns Hopkins University, Ph.D., 1985.

9806 **Merrin, Mary Beth.** *The Issues in Issue Voting: An Analysis of the 1972 Election.* Washington, D.C.: George Washington University, Ph.D., 1976.

9807 **Meulemans, Williams Charles.** *The Presidential Majority: Presidential Campaigning in Congressional Elections.* Moscow: University of Idaho, Ph.D., 1970.

9808 **Meyer, C. Kenneth.** *A Longitudinal Analysis of State Question Voting Patterns in Oklahoma: 1907-1972.* Norman: University of Oklahoma, Ph.D., 1979.

9809 **Miles, Afton Olson.** *Morman Voting Behavior and Political Attitudes.* New York City: New York University, Ph.D., 1978.

9810 **Miller, Anthony John.** *Functionalism and Foreign Policy: An Analysis of Canadian Voting Behaviour in the General Assembly of the United Nations, 1946-1966.* Montreal, Quebec, Canada: McGill University, Ph.D., 1971.

9811 **Miller, Arthur Herbert.** *The Impact of Committees on the Structure of Issues and Voting Coalitions: The United States House of Representatives 1955-1962.* Ann Arbor: University of Michigan, Ph.D., 1971.

9812 **Miller, Harold J., Jr.** *A Review of Southern Congressional Voting on Foreign Aid, 1953-1960.* Washington, D.C.: American University, M.I.S., 1971.

9813 **Miller, Nicholas Rowsell.** *The Structure of Collective Decisions: Committees, Elections, and Parties.* Berkeley: University of California, Ph.D., 1973.

9814 **Miller, Penny M, and Jewell, Malcolm E.** *Political Parties and Primaries in Kentucky.* Lexington: The University Press of Kentucky, 1990.

9815 **Mittrick, Robert.** *A History of Negro Voting in Pennsylvania During the Nineteenth Century (Reconstruction, Fifteenth Amendment, Motives, Results, Philadelphia Politics, Republican,* Democratic Party).* New Brunswick: Rutgers University–The State University of New Jersey, Ph.D., 1985.

9816 **Moen, Allen Walter.** *Superintendent Turnover As Predicted by School Board Incumbent Defeat in Pennsylvania's Partisan Elections.* University Park: Pennsylvania State University, Ph.D., 1971.

9817 **Monell, Joel Chrisite.** *School Tax Elections: A Longitudinal Comparative Case Study of Twelve Districts in California.* Stanford, California: Stanford University, Ph.D., 1979.

9818 **Monroe, Allen Lathem.** *A Study of Supportive and Non-Supportive Voter Response within a Spatial Context to the Creation of a Joint Vocational School in Ohio.* Columbus: Ohio State University, Ph.D., 1970.

9819 **Montgomery, B. Ruth.** *The Determinants of Voting Intentions and Votes in a Union Representation Election (Clerical Workers, Fishbein Model, Theory of Reasoned Action).* Ann Arbor: University of Michigan, Ph.D., 1985.

9820 **Montjoy, Robert Sabin.** *Election Laws, Voting Decisions, and Political Linkage: An Empirically-Based Computer Simulation.* Bloomington: Indiana University, Ph.D., 1977.

9821 **Moore, Thomas Clifford.** *The Impact of Management Opposition to Unions on Certification Elections, Decertification Elections and State-Employee Bargaining Laws.* Athens: University of Georgia, 1984.

9822 **Morrill, Robert W.; Wright, Robert; and Smilnak, Roberta.** *Politics, Politics, School Redistricting.* Provo, Utah: Stem Publications, 1974.

9823 **Morton, Rebecca Bradford.** *Interest Groups and Majority Voting.* New Orleans: Tulane University of Louisiana Press, 1984.

9824 **Moskowitz, Jay Henry.** *Electorate Behavior in School Property Tax Millage Elections and Its Relationship to the School Finance Reform Movement.* Syracuse, New York: Syracuse University, Ph.D., 1975.

9825 **Moss, R.** *Voting Propensities of Government Employees in Virginia.* Blacksburg: Virginia Polytechnic Institute and State University, Ph.D., 1976.

9826 **Moyer, Henry Wayne, Jr.** *Congressional Voting on Defense in World War II and Vietnam: Toward a General Ideological Explanation.* New Haven, Connecticut: Yale University, Ph.D., 1976.

9827 **Muise, Delphin Andrew.** *Elections and Constituencies: Federal Politics in Nova Scotia, 1867-1878.* London, Ontario, Canada: University of Western Ontario, Ph.D., 1971.

9828 **Mulcahy, Patrick Herbert.** *Urban Social and Spatial Structure: A Case Study of Los Angeles Voting Patterns, 1960-1968.* Los Angeles: University of California, Ph.D., 1971.

9829 **Munck, Ronaldo.** *Latin America: The Transition to Democracy.* London: Zed Books.

9830 **Murphy, William Thomas, Jr.** *Youth and Politics: A Study of Student Involvement in the 1970 Congressional Elections.* Princeton, New Jersey: Princeton University, Ph.D., 1974.

9831 **Nesbitt, Frederick H.** *The Impact of a Labor Endorsement on the Voting Behavior of Rank-and-File Members: A Case Study of the 1974 General Election in Pennsylvania.* Morgantown: West Virginia University, Ph.D., 1975.

9832 **Newcomer, Owen Eugene.** *Partisan and Nonpartisan Elections: A Reevaluation.* Los Angeles: University of Southern California, Ph.D., 1980.

9833 **Newman, Bruce Ira.** *The Prediction and Explanation of Actual Voting Behavior in a Presidential Primary Election.* Urbana: University of Illinois, Ph.D., 1981.

9834 **Nie, N.H.; Verba, S.; and Petrocik, J.R.** *Changing American Voter,* enlarged ed. Cambridge, Massachusetts: Harvard University Press, 1979.

9835 **No, Kyu Hyung.** *The Incumbency Effect and Congressional Voting Decisions (Election).* Stony Brook: State University of New York, Ph.D., 1985.

9836 **Nunes, Ralph Da Costa.** *Patterns of Congressional Change: Critical Realignment, Policy Clusters, and Party Voting in the House of Representatives.* New York City: Columbia University, Ph.D., 1978.

9837 **O'Connor, Patrick Franklin.** *Voting Structure in a One-Party Legislature: The Arkansas House of Representatives Over Five Sessions.* Bloomington: Indiana University, Ph.D., 1973.

9838 **Onwumere, Sampson Onuigbo.** *The Libertarian Party of America and Presidential Elections: An Analysis of a New Political Party Struggling to Capture Political Power and Authority.* Washington, D.C.: Howard University, Ph.D., 1982.

9839 **Oppenheim, Karen.** *Voting in Recent American Presidential Elections.* Chicago, Illinois: University of Chicago, Ph.D., 1970.

9840 **Orr, Douglas Milton, Jr.** *Congressional Redistricting: The North Carolina Experience.* Chapel Hill: University of North Carolina, Department of Geography, Studies in Geography, No. 2, 1970.

9841 **Orr, Douglas Milton, Jr.** "Gerrymandering." *Encyclopedia of Southern History.* Shreveport: Louisiana State University Press, 1976.

9842 **O'Rourke, T.B.** *Reapportionment.* Washington, D.C.: American Enterprise Institute, 1972.

9843 **Osterling, Jorge P.** *Democracy in Columbia: Clientelist Politics and Guerrilla Warfare.* New Brunswick, New Jersey: Transaction Publishers, 1989.

9844 **Overhuls, Timothy Ray.** *Voting Turnout in the Twenty-Five Cities of Orange County.* Long Beach: California State University, Ph.D., 1973.

9845 **Palaich, Robert Michael.** *The Emergence and Development of Federal Education Policy: A Dimensional Analysis of Congressional Roll Call Voting, 1909-1968.* New York City: Columbia University, Ph.D., 1981.

9846 **Papayanopoulos, Lycourgus.** *Convexity and Other Properties of Weighted Voting Reapportionment.* New York City: Columbia University, Eng. Sc.D., 1981.

9847 **Parker, A.C.** *Empire Stalemate: Voting Behavior in New York State, 1860-1892.* Seattle: University of Washington, Ph.D., 1975.

9848 **Parker, Frank R.** *Black Votes Count: Political Empowerment in Mississippi After 1965.* Chapel Hill: The University of North Carolina Press, 1990.

9849 **Parks, Charles Douglas.** *A Study of Voting Behavior, Political Issue Preference and Human Values of Missouri Education Association Members.* Kansas City: University of Missouri, Ph.D., 1983.

9850 **Parks, Georgia M. Thomas.** *The Relationships between Self-Concept, Political Activity, and Voting Regularity of the Urban and Rural Poor.* Washington, D.C.: Howard University School of Social Work, Ph.D., 1983.

9851 **Parsons, Stanley B.; Beach, William W.; and Dubin, Michael J.** *United States Congressional Districts and Data, 1843-1883.* New York: Greenwood Press, 1986.

9852 Parsons, Stanley B.; Dubin, Michael J.; and Parsons, Karen Tooms. *United States Congressional Districts, 1883-1913.* New York: Greenwood Press, 1990.

9853 Pastor, Robert A., ed. *Democracy in the Americas: Stopping the Pendulum.* New York: Holmes & Meier, 1989.

9854 Patsy, William Paul. *Factors Affecting School Bond Elections in School Districts in Florida During 1960-1970.* Charlottesville: University of Virginia, Ph.D., 1973.

9855 Patterson, Graeme Hazlewood. *Studies in Elections and Public Opinion in Upper Canada.* Toronto, Ontario, Canada: University of Toronto, Ph.D., 1969.

9856 Pearson, Robert W. *Congress and Elections: An Empirical Assessment of the Electoral Accountability Theory.* Chicago, Illinois: University of Chicago, Ph.D., 1980.

9857 Peffley, Mark Alan. *Economic Conditions and Electoral Behavior (Voting Behavior, Public Opinion, Political Responsibility).* Minneapolis: University of Minnesota, Ph.D., 1984.

9858 Pernacciaro, Samuel John. *A Dimensional Analysis of Roll Call Voting in the Senate of the 91st Congress.* Carbondale: Southern Illinois University, Ph.D., 1975.

9859 Perrin, Alan Francis. *The Relationship between Socioeconomic Characteristics, Town Characteristics and Voting Behavior on a School Finance Referendum.* Storrs: University of Connecticut, Ph.D., 1981.

9860 Peters, Donald C. *The Democratic System in the Eastern Caribbean.* New York: Greenwood Press, 1992.

9861 Petersen, Roger Dewey. *The Reaction to a Heterogeneous Society: A Behavioral and Quantitative Analysis of Northern Voting Behavior 1845-1870, Pennsylvania A Test Case.* Pittsburgh, Pennsylvania: University of Pittsburgh, Ph.D., 1970.

9862 Petras, James, and Leiva, Fernando Ignacio. *Democracy and Poverty in Chile: The Limits to Electoral Politics.* Boulder: Westview Press, 1994.

9863 Petras, James, and Morley, Morris. *Latin America in the Time of Cholera: Electoral Politics, Market Economics, and Permanent Crisis.* New York: Routledge, 1992.

9864 Phillips, Harry Charles John. *Challenges to the Voting System in Canada, 1874-1974.* London, Ontario, Canada: University of Western Ontario, Ph.D., 1976.

9865 Phillips, Kevin P. *The Emerging Republican Majority.* New Rochelle, New York: Arlington House, 1970.

9866 Pierce, John Charles. *Ideology, Attitudes, and Voting Behavior of the American Electorate: 1956, 1960, 1964.* Minneapolis: University of Minnesota, Ph.D., 1969.

9867 Plumb, Elizabeth Walker. *Presidential Election Campaign Influence: Re-examination of a Thesis (Voters, Voting, 1984).* Pullman: Washington State University, Ph.D., 1984.

9868 Polich, Jon Michael. *Dimensionality, Attitudes, and Voting: Models of Structure and Linkage.* Cambridge, Massachusetts: Harvard University, Ph.D., 1976.

9869 Pollard, Walker Aylett. *Effects of Economic Conditions on Elections: A Study Controlling for Political Variables.* Blacksburg: Virginia Polytechnic Institute and State University, Ph.D., 1978.

9870 Pollock, James K., and Eldersveld, Samuel J. *Michigan Politics in Transition; an Areal Study of Voting Trends in the Last Decade.* University of Michigan. Michigan Governmental Studies, No. 10. Ann Arbor: University of Michigan Press, 1942.

9871 Pollock, Stephen M., and Others. *Algocithmic Approaches to Political Redistricting; A Report of the Activities of a Seminar.* Ann Arbor: University of Michigan, College of Engineering, Department of Industrial Engineering, 1972.

9872 Polsby, N., ed. *Reapportionment in the 1970's.* Berkeley: University of California Press, 1971.

9873 Powers, Kathleen Jay. *Factors that Explain Faculty Voting in the Higher Education Union Representation Elections (Public Sector, Instrumentality, Intention, Authorization Cards).* Gainesville: University of Florida, Ph.D., 1986.

9874 Price, Pam. *Electoral Targeting for Female Candidates.* M.A., University of North Carolina-Charlotte, 1983.

9875 Pritchard, Anita Christensen. *Presidential-Congressional Relations: Presidential Influence on Congressional Voting Behavior.* Columbus: Ohio State University, Ph.D., 1978.

9876 Prysby, Charles Lee. *Social Mobilization, Economic Development, and Left Voting: Chile, 1958-1964.* East Lansing: Michigan State University, Ph.D., 1973.

9877 **Przybylski, James Thaddeus.** *Twentieth-Century Elections in Illinois: Patterns of Partisan Change.* Urbana: University of Illinois, Ph.D., 1974.

9878 **Qualls, James Harold.** *Voting and the Economy in the Fifth Party-System.* Baltimore, Maryland: Johns Hopkins University, Ph.D., 1980.

9879 **Ra, Jong Oh.** *Labor Union Voting Behavior in America, 1952-1964.* Urbana: University of Illinois, Ph.D., 1972.

9880 *Reapportionment: Law and Technology.* Washington, D.C.: National Conference of State Legislatures, 1980.

9881 *Representation and Apportionment.* Washington, D.C.: Congressional Quarterly Service, 1966.

9882 **Riley, Robert Tarrant.** *Racial Voting Models: A Study of Carl Stoke's Reelection.* Cambridge, Massachusetts: Harvard University, Ph.D., 1975.

9883 **Robbins, James H.** *Voting Behavior in Massachusetts, 1800-1820: A Case Study.* Evanston, Illinois: Northwestern University, Ph.D., 1970.

9884 **Robinson, Edgar E.** *The Presidential Vote, 1896-1932.* New York: Octagon Books, 1970.

9885 **Robinson, Edgar E.** *They Voted for Roosevelt: The Presidential Vote 1932-1944.* Stanford, California: Stanford University Press, 1947.

9886 **Rosales, Jean Kufrin.** *The Effect of Local Economic Conditions on National Elections (Voting, Congressional, Presidential).* Austin: University of Texas, Ph.D., 1985.

9887 **Rose, Joseph Barker.** *An Analysis of Organizational Union Representation Elections Conducted Under the National Labor Relations Act.* Buffalo: State University of New York, Ph.D., 1971.

9888 **Rose, Winfield Harrison.** *Referendum Voting and the Politics of Health Care in Durham County, North Carolina.* Durham, North Carolina: Duke University, Ph.D., 1973.

9889 **Rosenstone, Steven Jay.** *Forecasting Presidential Elections.* Berkeley: University of California, Ph.D., 1979.

9890 **Ross, Ruth Aura.** *A Comparison of the Effect of Certain Demographic Characteristics Upon Conservative Voting Behavior in California and the United States: 1968.* Los Angeles: University of Southern California, Ph.D., 1971.

9891 **Rothschild, Michael Lindsay.** *The Effects of Political Advertising on the Voting Behavior of a Low Involvement Electorate.* Stanford, California:

Stanford University, Ph.D., 1975.

9892 **Rozett, John Michael.** *The Social Bases of Party Conflict in the Age of Jackson: Individual Voting Behavior in Greene County, Illinois, 1838-1848.* Ann Arbor: University of Michigan, Ph.D., 1974.

9893 **Rufolo, Anthony Michael.** *Tie-In Sales and Local Public Goods: A General Equilibrium Analysis of "Voting with Your Feet."* Los Angeles: University of California, Ph.D., 1975.

9894 **Rule, Wilma,** and **Zimmerman, Joseph F.,** eds. *United States Electoral Systems: Their Impact on Women and Minorities.* New York: Greenwood Press, 1992.

9895 **Russell, Charles G.** *A Multi-Variate Descriptive Field Study of Media and Non-Media Influences on Voting Behavior in the 1970 Texas Gubernatorial Election.* Carbondale: Southern Illinois University, Ph.D., 1971.

9896 **Rystrom, Kenneth Fred, Jr.** *Measuring the Apparent Impact of Newspaper Endorsements in Statewide Elections in California, 1970-1980.* Los Angeles: University of Southern California, Ph.D., 1984.

9897 **St. Dizier, Byron.** *The Effect of Newspaper Endorsements and Party Identification on Voting Behavior: A Controlled Laboratory Experiment.* Knoxville: University of Tennessee, Ph.D., 1984.

9898 **Sanders, John L.** *Materials on Congressional Districts in North Carolina.* Chapel Hill: Institute of Government, University of North Carolina, 1967.

9899 **Sanders, John L.** *Maps of North Carolina Congressional Districts, 1789-1960 and of State Senatorial Districts and Apportionment of State Representatives, 1776-1960.* Chapel Hill: Institute of Government, University of North Carolina, 1961.

9900 **Sanders, John L.** Report of the Joint Select Committee of the House of Representatives and the Senate on Congressional Redistricting. *Documents Pertaining to Legislative Representation in North Carolina.* Chapel Hill: Institute of Government, University of North Carolina, 1966.

9901 **Sanders, Thomas G.** *Chile-The Elections and After.* Hanover, New Hampshire, New York: American Universities Field Staff Report, Vol. 17, No. 10, 1970.

9902 **Sanders, Thomas G.** *The Process of Partnership in Chile.* Hanover, New Hampshire, New York: American Universities Field Staff Report, Vol. 20, No. 1, 1973.

9903 **Santi, Lawrence Lee.** *Voter Turnout in Presidential Elections, 1964-1976.* Tucson: University of Arizona, Ph.D., 1981.

9904 **Sawyer, Thomas R.** *Voting on City-County Consolidation: A Systems Approach to the Study of the 1982 Louisville-Jefferson County Merger Referendum.* Louisville, Kentucky: University of Louisville, Ph.D., 1983.

9905 **Saxton, Judith Elaine.** *The Interaction of Political Alienation and Information in a Local Millage Election Campaign: A Case Study (Michigan, Media Use, Voting Behavior).* East Lansing: Michigan State University, Ph.D., 1984.

9906 **Scammon, Richard M., and McGillivray, Alice V.** *American Votes 19: A Handbook of Contemporary American Election Statistics.* Washington, DC: Congressional Quarterly, 1991.

9907 **Scharfenberger, Gilbert Earl.** *Massachusetts Elects a Governor and a United States Senator: A Comparative Analysis of the 1978 Elections.* Cambridge: Massachusetts Institute of Technology, Ph.D., 1983.

9908 **Scheele, Raymond Harold.** *Voting in Primary Elections.* Columbia: University of Missouri, Ph.D., 1972.

9909 **Schellenberg, James A.** *Conflict Between Communities: American County Seat Wars.* New York: Paragon House, 1987.

9910 **Schildhaus, Salomon.** *Leverage Politics: American Group Attitudes, Voting, and Public Policy, 1952-1972.* Syracuse, New York: Syracuse University, Ph.D., 1975.

9911 **Schmeckebier, Laurence F.** *Congressional Reapportionment.* Washington, D.C.: The Brookings Institute, 1941.

9912 **Schubert, Glendon.** *Reapportionment.* New York: Charles Scribner's Sons, 1965.

9913 **Schmitt, Carl M.** *Voting Behavior in Western Democracies: A Cross National Study of Factors Influencing Voter Turnout and Partisanship in the United States.* New York City: New York University, Ph.D., 1976.

9914 **Schomisch, Thomas Paul.** *The Effect of Personal Communication Networks on Member Voting in a Merger of Agricultural Cooperatives.* Madison: University of Wisconsin, Ph.D., 1983.

9915 **Schwartz, Alan Jerry.** *An Analysis of Selected Television Political Debates Produced in a New York by WCBS-TV and Transmitted Locally During the Elections of 1962 and 1966.* New York City: New York University, Ph.D., 1970.

9916 **Segur, Winthrop Hubbard, Jr.** *Representation Elections for Farm Workers: Voting Power Under Alternative Rules of Eligibility.* Davis: University of California, Ph.D., 1980.

9917 **Senior, Clarence.** *Self-Determination for Puerto Rico.* New York: Post War World Council, 1946.

9918 **Shaffer, Stephen Daryl.** *Voting Behavior in Congressional Gubernatorial, and Presidential Elections: A Comparative Analysis.* Columbus: Ohio State University, Ph.D., 1978.

9919 **Shaffer, William Ross.** *Computer Simulation of Voting Behavior.* Syracuse, New York: Syracuse University, Ph.D., 1969.

9920 *The Shameful Blight: The Survival of Racial Discrimination in Voting in the South.* Washington, D.C.: Washington Research Project, 1972.

9921 **Shaw, James Kevin.** *The Impact of Politics on United States Senate Voting on Impeachment.* Reno: University of Nevada, Ph.D., 1980.

9922 **Sheingold, Carl Alexander.** *New Parties and New Voting: A Social Structural Analysis of the Wallace Vote in 1968.* Cambridge, Massachusetts: Harvard University, Ph.D., 1972.

9923 **Shelley, Walter Lumley.** *Political Profiles of the Nixon, Humphrey, and Wallace Voters in the Texas Panhandle, 1968: A Study in Voting Behavior.* Lubbock: Texas Tech University, Ph.D., 1972.

9924 **Shepard, William Bruce.** *Political Preferences, Participation, and Local Policy-making: A Study of Referendum Voting Behavior in American Cities.* Riverside: University of California, Ph.D., 1972.

9925 **Sherman, Joel D.** *A Comparative Study of Referendum Voting Behavior in Oregon, Ohio and Switzerland.* New York City: Columbia University, Ph.D., 1977.

9926 **Shortridge, Ray Myles.** *Voting Patterns in the American Midwest, 1840-1872.* Ann Arbor: University of Michigan, Ph.D., 1974.

9927 **Sipher, Roger Earl.** *Popular Voting Behavior in New York, 1890-1896: A Case Study of Two Counties.* Syracuse, New York: Syracuse University, Ph.D., 1971.

9928 **Slutsky, Steven Myles.** *Majority Voting and the Allocation of Public Goods.* New Haven, Connecticut: Yale University, Ph.D., 1975.

9929 **Smart, John Carson III.** *Personality and Voting Behavior: A Study of Voting and Non-Voting College Students.* Lexington: University of Kentucky, Ph.D., 1971.

9930 **Smith, James George.** *Presidential Elections and Racial Discrimination: Campaign Promises, Presidential Performance, and Democratic Accountability, 1960–1980.* Bloomington: University of Indiana, Ph.D., 1981.

9931 **Smith, Jeffrey Alan.** *Trust as a Political Variable in American Presidential Elections.* Austin: University of Texas, Ph.D., 1978.

9932 **Smith, Wayne Sanford.** *The Argentine Elections of 1973: Demilitarization and the Struggle for Consensus.* Washington, D.C.: George Washington University, Ph.D., 1980.

9933 **Snider, Gregory Alan.** *Non–Partisanship in American Elections: Independents, Swing Voters, and Ticket Splitters.* Iowa City: University of Iowa, Ph.D., 1974.

9934 **Snow, Peter G., and Manzetti, Luigi.** *Political Forces in Argentina.* 3rd ed. Westport: Praeger Publishers, 1993.

9935 **Sola–Pool, I. De; Abelson, R.P.; and Popkin, S.** *Candidates, Issues and Strategies: A Computer Simulation of the 1960 Presidential Election.* Cambridge: Massachusetts Institute of Technology Press, 1964.

9936 **Stampen, Jacob Ola.** *Voting Behavior in the Wisconsin State Legislature: 1945–1967.* Madison: University of Wisconsin, Ph.D., 1969.

9937 *State Politics and Redistricting,* Parts I and II. Washington, D.C.: Congressional Quarterly, 1982.

9938 **Stegmaier, Mark Joseph.** *The U.S. Senate in the Sectional Crisis, 1846-1861: A Roll–Call Voting Analysis.* Santa Barbara: University of California, Ph.D., 975.

9939 **Stengel, Daniel B.** *Strategic Behavior in Single Issue Collective Choice Settings: An Experimental Analysis with Application to Millage Issue Elections.* East Lansing: Michigan State University, Ph.D., 1984.

9940 **Stepan, Alfred,** ed. *Democratizing Brazil: Problems of Transition and Consolidation.* New York: Oxford University Press, 1989.

9941 **Stevens, Susan F.** *Congressional Elections of 1930: Politics of Avoidance.* Buffalo: State University of New York, Ph.D., 1980.

9942 **Stewart, David Michael.** *Supreme Court Appointments During the Harding and Coolidge Administrations: Influence, Critics and Voting.* Detroit, Michigan: Wayne State University, Ph.D., 1974.

9943 **Stewart, Patricia Shannon.** *Voter Turnout in Issue Referenda Compared to Candidate Elections.* Louisville, Kentucky: University of Louisville, Ph.D., 1983.

9944 **Strand, Joyce Troutman.** *The Role of Parties and Elections in Authoritarian Brazil, 1964 to 1974.* Washington, D.C.: George Washington University, Ph.D., 1977.

9945 **Surette, Raymond Bernard.** *Uncertainty and Organizational Reaction: The Special Case of Sheriff Elections and Arrests.* Tallahassee: Florida State University, Ph.D., 1979.

9946 **Swansbrough, Robert H., and Brodsky, David M.,** eds. *The South's New Politics: Realignment and Dealignment.* Columbia: University of South Carolina Press, 1988.

9947 **Swindel, Steven Hendricks.** *The Use of Mass Media and Decision Making Processes in the 1980 Presidential Election: Application of the Accumulated Information Model (Political Communication, Proximity Voting Model).* Knoxville: University of Tennessee, Ph.D., 1985.

9948 **Tacker, Barry Milton.** *Fiscal Constraints, Tax Limitations and Property Tax Rollback Elections: Effects on Taxing and Budgeting Practices in Texas Public Schools.* Austin: University of Texas, Ph.D., 1985.

9949 **Tetzlaff, Jonathan Craig.** *A Comparison of Voting Patterns in the Senate Foreign Relations Committee and the House Foreign Affairs Committee—94th and 95th Congress.* Washington, D.C.: American University, Ph.D., 1980.

9950 **Thomas, David Allen.** *A Qualitative Content Analysis of Richard M. Nixon's Treatment of Selected Issues in His Presidential Campaign Oratory in the 1960 and 1968 Elections.* East Lansing: Michigan State University, Ph.D., 1973.

9951 **Thomas, Martin.** *Senatorial Voting Behavior and the Temporal Proximity of Elections.* Tallahassee: Florida State University, Ph.D., 1981.

9952 **Thornton, James William.** *A Study to Determine the Effects of Collective Bargaining Elections on Faculty Participation in Institutional Governance in Roman Catholic Related Four-Year Institutions of Higher Education.* Eugene: University of Oregon, Ph.D., 1981.

9953 **Thorsted, Richard Rudolph.** *Predicting School Board Members Defeat: Demographic and Political Variables that Influence School Board Elections.* Riverside: University of California, Ph.D., 1974.

9954 **Torma, John J.** "Participatory Democracy: The Theory, the Practice, and a Model for Missoula." Missoula: University of Montana, M.A., 1989.

9955 **Towle, Jerry.** *The Areal Base of Southern Democratic Strength, 1920-1960.* Carbondale: Southern Illinois University, Ph.D., 1965.

9956 **Trudeau, Robert Harvey.** *Costa Rican Voting: Its Socio-Economic Correlates.* Chapel Hill: University of North Carolina, Ph.D., 1971.

9957 **Turner, Norma Lee.** *Analysis of Attitudes of Oklahomans of Voting Age Toward Sex Education, Teen Contraception, and Abortion.* Oklahoma City: University of Oklahoma Health Sciences Center, Ph.D., 1981.

9958 **Unekis, Joseph Keith.** *Illuminating Wilson's Dim Dungeons of Silence: An Analysis of House Committee Roll Call Voting, 1971-1974.* Bloomington: University of Indiana, Ph.D., 1977.

9959 **Vandenbosch, Susanne Elaine.** *The 1968 Seattle Forward Thrust Election: An Analysis of Voting on an Ad Hoc Effort to Solve Metropolitan Problems without Metropolitan Government.* Seattle: University of Washington, Ph.D., 1974.

9960 **Van Duzer, Edward F.** *An Analysis of the Differences in Republican Presidential Vote in Cities and Their Suburbs.* Iowa City: University of Iowa, Ph.D., 1962.

9961 **Vega-Palacin, Manuel.** *Elections, Parties and Congress: Brazil: 1945-1964.* Austin: University of Texas, Ph.D., 1981.

9962 **Voyles, James Everett.** *An Analysis of Voting Patterns in Mobile, Alabama, 1948-1970.* Denton: North Texas State University, Ph.D., 1973.

9963 **Wagner, Dale Earl.** *Public Financing of Federal Elections: Enactment and Recision of the 1966 Long Act.* Baltimore: University of Maryland, Ph.D., 1975.

9964 **Wahlstrom, Gregory.** *An Electoral Geographic Study of Fresno County, California.* Fresno: California State University, Master's Thesis, 1973.

9965 **Walker, Dennis Lyle.** *A Comparative Analysis of the Factors Influencing Party Voting Cohesion in Democratic Legislatures.* Pullman: Washington State University, Ph.D., 1971.

9966 **Wall, Diane Eve.** *Bases of Electoral Competition in Michigan Appellate Court Elections, 1948-1982.* East Lansing: Michigan State University, Ph.D., 1983.

9967 **Wando, Joyce S.** *Economic Conditions and Political Behavior for Presidential Elections: A Study of the Relationship between Employment and Voter Turnout in the Black Community.* Washington, D.C.: Howard University, Ph.D., 1985.

9968 **Waters, Anita M.** *Symbols, Social Class and Politics: Rastafari and Reggae in Jamaican Elections 1967-1980.* New York City: Columbia University, Ph.D., 1984.

9969 **Watts, Lynda L.** *A Bayesian Model of Voting in Two-Candidate Elections.* Rochester, New York: University of Rochester, Ph.D., 1974.

9970 **Weiss, William Walton.** *A Visual Analysis of the Coverage Given the 1984 Presidential Campaign by CBS Television on the CBS Evening News with Dan Rather (Journalism, Semeiotics, Elections).* Madison: University of Wisconsin, Ph.D., 1985.

9971 **Weurding, Jerome Louis.** *A Study of the Relationships between Voting and Patterns of Senior Citizens and Selected Demographic, School Exposure, and Opinion Variables (Michigan).* Ann Arbor: University of Michigan, Ph.D., 1983.

9972 **Whitby, Kenny J.** *Competition in Congressional Elections.* Iowa City: University of Iowa, Ph.D., 1983.

9973 **White, Debra Margaret.** *An Empirical Inquiry into the Effect of Direct and Indirect Voting Structures on the Efficient Provision of Public Goods.* Stillwater: Oklahoma State University, Ph.D., 1980.

9974 **White, Larry.** *Southern Congressional Politics: Change and Continuity Since the 1965 Voting Rights Act.* New Haven, Connecticut: Yale University, Ph.D., 1978.

9975 **White, Samuel L.** *Legislative and Court-Ordered Reapportionment and Minority Voting Strength: The Mississippi Experience.* Washington, D.C.: Howard University, Ph.D., 1980.

9976 **Whitney, Frederick Corwin.** *Field Study, Analysis and Prediction of Voting Behavior in a Suburban Community of High Socio-Economic Status.* San Diego, California: United States International University, Ph.D., 1971.

9977 **Wiebe, Russell Gordon.** *Teacher Involvement in School Board Elections.* Eugene: University of Oregon, Ph.D., 1981.

9978 **Wiener, Donald Edward.** *Heterogeneity, Electoral Competitiveness and Congressional Voting Behavior.* Boca Raton: Florida Atlantic University, Ph.D., 1975.

9979 **Wilkinson, Thomas Charles.** *The Voting Behaviors of Educator Board Members and Non Educator Board Members on Issues in Public Education.* Pittsburgh, Pennsylvania: University of Pittsburgh, Ph.D., 1976.

9980 **Willett, Lynn Howe.** *Factors Related to Student Involvement in Student Government Elections.* Iowa City: University of Iowa, Ph.D., 1970.

9981 **Williams, Robert Hoyt.** *Governor Hiram W. Johnson and the California Elections of 1916.* Fullerton: California State University, Master's Thesis, 1977.

9982 **Wissel, Peter A.** *Foreign Policy Decisionmaking: An Analytic Approach to Collective Decisions without Voting.* Rochester, New York: University of Rochester, Ph.D., 1973.

9983 **Wolfe, Gerald William.** *The Kansas–Nebraska Bill and Congressional Voting Behavior in the Thirty–Third Congress.* Iowa City: University of Iowa, Ph.D., 1969.

9984 **Wolfe, Jacqueline S.** *Political Information Channels in At–Large Municipal Electoral System (City of Guelph, 1972 and 1974.* Hamilton, Ontario, Canada: McMaster University, Ph.D., 1975.

9985 **Wolfle, Lee Morrill.** *Radical Third–Party Voting Among Coal Miners, 1896–1940.* Ann Arbor: University of Michigan, Ph.D., 1976.

9986 **Wolfson, Richard Martin.** *The Nonpartisan Perspective on Municipal Voting: The Cases of Minneapolis and Los Angeles.* Minneapolis: University of Minnesota, Ph.D., 1972.

9987 **Woolstencroft, Robert Peter.** *National, Regional, Provincial, and Constituency Effects in Canadian Voting Behavior, 1953–1965.* Edmonton, Alberta, Canada: University of Alberta, Ph.D., 1977.

9988 **Worner, Roger Blair.** *The Effects of Teacher Representation Elections on the Power Sources of Majority and Minority Teacher Organizations in Middle–Sized School Districts.* New York City: New York University, Ph.D., 1970.

9989 **Wright, Gerald Clement, Jr.** *Candidate Choice in State and National Elections.* Chapel Hill: University of North Carolina, Ph.D., 1973.

9990 **Wright, Larry Lee.** *Attitudinal and Behavioral Congruence of Coalition Voting Deviations.* Tallahassee: Florida State University, Ph.D., 1980.

9991 **Wright, Robert Crunn.** *Urban Political Geography: A Black Perspective of Black Political Behavior in the 1961, 1965, 1969 Mayoral Elections of Detroit, Michigan.* Worchester, Massachusetts: Clark University, Ph.D., 1972.

9992 **Wyckoff, Mikel L.** *Belief System Constraint and Policy Voting: A Test of the Unidimensional Consistency Model.* Baltimore: University of Maryland, Ph.D., 1982.

9993 **Wyman, Roger Edwards.** *Voting Behavior in the Progressive Era: Wisconsin as a Case Study.* Madison: University of Wisconsin, Ph.D., 1970.

9994 **Yatrakis, Kathryn B.** *Electoral Demands and Political Benefits: Minority as Majority. A Case Study of Two Mayoral Elections in Newark, New Jersey: 1970, 1974.* New York City: Columbia University, Ph.D., 1981.

9995 **Zoetewey, James Marvin.** *A Statistical Study of the Voting Behavior of the Counties of Colorado in Presidential and Gubernatorial Elections, 1904–1964.* Boulder: University of Colorado, Ph.D., 1971.

Journals

9996 **Abney, F. Glen, and Hill, Larry B.** "Natural Disasters as a Political Variable: The Effects of a Hurricane on an Urban Election." *American Political Science Review*, 60, No. 4 (December, 1966), 974–981.

9997 **Abney, F. Glen; Hill, Larry B.; and Hutcheson, J.D.** "Race, Representation, and Trust: Changes in Attitudes (in Atlanta) after the Election of a Black Mayor." *Public Opinion Quarterly*, 45, No. 1 (Spring, 1981), 91–101.

9998 **Abramowitz, Alan Ira.** "A Comparison of Voting for U.S. Senator and Representative in 1978." *American Political Science Review*, 74, No. 3 (September, 1980), 633–640.

9999 **Alonso, Paula.** "Politics and Elections in Buenos Aires, 1890-1898: The Performance of the Radical Party." *Journal of Latin American Studies* [Cambridge], 25, Part 2 (October, 1993), 465-487.

10000 **Andersch, Ulrich.** "Rolle und Funkitonen von Koalitionen im Amerikanischen Regierungssystem. Eine Fallstudie: Die *National Low Income Housing Coalition. American Studien*, Jahr 33, Heft 1 (1988), 105-122.

10001 **Anderson, G.M.** "Voting Behavior and the Ethnic-Religious Variable: A Study of the Election in Hamilton, Ontario." *Canadian Journal of Economic and Political Science*, 32, No. 1 (February, 1966), 27–37.

10002 **Anderson, Robert W.** "Political Parties and the Politics of Status: The Study of Political Organization in Puerto Rico." *Caribbean Studies*, 21, Nos. 1-2 (Enero-Junio, 1988), 1-43.

10003 **Anderson, T.** "Eighteenth Century Suffrage: The Case of Maryland." *Maryland Historical Magazine*, 76, No. 2 (June, 1981), 141-158.

10004 **Angell, Alan, and Pollack, Benny.** "The Chilean Elections of 1989 and the Politics of the Transition to Democracy." *Bulletin of Latin American Research* [Oxford], 9, No. 1 (1990), 1-23.

10005 **Archer, J. Clark.** "Congressional–Incumbent Reelection Success and Federal Outlays Distribution: A Test of the Electoral Connection Hypothesis." *Environment and Planning*, A12, No. 3 (March, 1980), 263–277.

10006 **Archer, J. Clark.** "Macrogeographical Versus Microgeographical Cleavages in American Presidential Elections, 1940–1984." *Political Geography Quarterly*, 7, No. 2 (April, 1988), 111–125.

10007 **Archer, J. Clark.** "Political Geography of Contemporary Events. VI: Some Geographical Aspects of the American Presidential Election of 1984." *Political Geography Quarterly*, 4, No. 2 (April, 1985), 159–172.

10008 **Archer, J. Clark; Shelley, Fred M.; Taylor, Peter J.; and White, Allen R.** "The Geography of U.S. Presidential Elections." *Scientific American*, 259, No. 1 (July, 1988), 44–51.

10009 **Archer, J. Clark; Murauskas, G. Thomas; Shelley, Fred M.; Taylor, Peter J.; and White, Ellen R.** "Counties, States, Sections and Parties in the 1984 Presidential Election." *Professional Geographer*, 37, No. 3 (August, 1985), 279–287.

10010 **Archer, J. Clark, and Johnson, Marquis.** "Inflation, Unemployment and Canadian Federal Voting Behavior." *Canadian Journal of Political Science*,, 22, No. 3 (September, 1988, 569–584.

10011 **Argersinger, P.H.** "To Disfranchise the People: The Iowa Ballot Law and Elections of 1897." *Mid America*, 63, No. 1 (January, 1981), 18-35.

10012 **Arrington, T.S., and Brenner, S.** "The Advantages of a Plurality Election of the President." *Presidential Studies Quarterly*, 10, No. 3 (Summer, 1980), 476–482.

10013 **Arrington, T.S.; Brenner, S.; and Ingalls, Gerald.** "Effects of Campaign Spending on Local Elections" The Charlotte Case." *American Political Quarterly*, 12, No. 1 (January, 1984), 117–127.

10014 **Arrington, T.S.; Brenner, S.; and Ingalls, Gerald.** "Race and Campaign Finance in Charlotte, North Carolina." *Western Political Quarterly*, 37, No. 4 (December, 1984), 578-583.

10015 **Backstrom, C.** "The Practice and Effect of Redistricting." *Political Geography Quarterly*, 1, No. 4 (October, 1982), 351–359.

10016 **Backstrom, C.; Robbins, L.; and Eller, S.** "Issues in Gerrymandering: An Exploratory Measure of Partisan Gerrymandering Applied to Minnesota." *Minnesota Law Review*, 62, No. 6 (July, 1978), 1121–1159.

10017 **Bailey, John, and Gomez, Leopoldo.** "The PRI and Political Liberalization." *Journal of International Affairs* [New York], 43, No. 2 (Winter, 1990), 291-312.

10018 **Barnes, B.M.** "The Congressional Elections of 1882 on the Eastern Shore of Virginia." *Virginia Magazine of History and Biography*, 89, No. 4 (October, 1981), 467–486.

10019 **Barraza, Leticia, and Bizberg, Ilan.** "El Partido Accion Nacional y el Regimen Politico Mexicano." *Foro Internacional* [Mexico, DF], 31, No. 3 (Enero-Marzo, 1991), 418-445.

10020 **Baum, Dale.** "Irish Vote and Party Politics in Massachusetts, 1860-1876." *Civil War History*, 26, No. 2 (June, 1980), 117–141.

10021 **Bean, Wilf.** "Ruling Canada's North: Democracy in a Frozen State." *Community Development Journal* (Oxford), 24, No. 1 (January, 1989), 19–28.

10022 **Bent, Devin.** "Partisan Elections and Public Policy: Response to Black Demands in Large Cities." *Journal of Black Studies*, 12, No. 3 (March, 1982), 291–314.

10023 **Berman, David R.** "Environment, Culture, and Radical Third Parties: Electoral Support for the Socialists in Arizona and Nevada, 1912-1916." *Social Science Journal*, 27, No. 2 (1990), 147–158.

10024 **Bilzin, M.D.** "Reapportionment on the Substate Level of Government: Equal Representation or Equal Vote." *Boston University Law Review*, 50, No. 3 (Summer, 1970), 231–270.

10025 **Blackford, M.G.** "Civic Groups, Political Action and City Planning in Seattle." *Pacific Historical Review*, 49, No. 4 (November, 1980), 557-580.

10026 **Bledsoe, Timothy.** "A Research Note on the Impact of District/at Large Elections on Black Political Efficacy." *Urban Affairs Quarterly*, 22, No. 1 (September, 1986), 166–174.

10027 **Bledsoe, Timothy, and Welch, Susan.** "Patterns of Political Party Activity Among U.S. Cities." *Urban Affairs Quarterly*, 23, No. 2 (December, 1987), 249–269.

10028 **Blossner, J.K.** "Politics and Voting in the Mennonite Church in America, 1860–1940." *Pennsylvania Mennonite Heritage*, 3 (October, 1980), 12–15.

10029 **Born, Richard Jules.** "The Influence of House Primary Election Divisiveness on General Election Margins, 1962–1976." *Journal of Politics*, 43, No. 3 (August, 1981), 640–661.

10030 **Born, Richard Jules.** "Reassessing the Decline of Presidential Coattails; U.S. House Elections from 1952–1980." *Journal of Politics*, 46, No. 1 (February, 1984), 60–79.

10031 **Boyd, R.W.** "Voter Turnout." *America Political Quarterly*, 9, No. 2 (April, 1981), 131–256.

10032 **Brink, Gregory G.; Ramesh, Subha; and Adams, Johns.** "Contagion-based Voting in Birmingham, Alabama." *Political Geography Quarterly*, 7, No. 1 (January, 1988), 39–47.

10033 **Brams, Steven J., and Davis, M.D.** "The 3/2's Rule in Presidential Campaigning." *American Political Science Review*, 68, No. 1 (March, 1974), 113-134.

10034 **Broh, Charles Anthony.** "Horse–Race Journalism Reporting the Polls in the 1976 Election." *Public Opinion Quarterly*, 44, No. 4 (Winter, 1980), 514-529.

10035 **Brown, Canter, Jr.** "Carpetbagger Intrigues, Black Leadership, and a Southern Loyalist Triumph: Florida's Gubernatorial Election of 1872." *The Florida Historical Quarterly* [Tampa], 72, No. 3 (January, 1994), 275-301.

10036 **Brown, Robert Harold.** "Political Party Preferences in the Rocky Mountain Region." *Great Plains–Rocky Mountain Geographical Journal*, 6, No. 2 (1977), 154–161.

10037 **Bruce, John M.; Clark, John A.; and Kessel, John H.** "Advocacy Politics in Presidential Parties." *American Political Science Review,* 85, No. 4 (December, 1991), 1089-1105.

10038 **Brunk, Gregory G.** "Congressional Rationality and Spatial Voting." *Public Choice*, 45, No. 1 (1985), 3–17.

10039 **Brunk, Gregory G.** "On Estimating Distance–Determined Voting Functions." *Political Geography Quarterly*, 4, No. 1 (January, 1985), 55–65.

10040 **Brunk, Gregory G.** "Turn Over and Voting Stability in the Senate." *American Political Quarterly*, 10, No. 3 (July, 1982), 363–373.

10041 **Brunn, Stanley D.; Hoffman, Wayne L.; and Romsa, Gerald H.** "The Youngstown School Levies: A Geographical Analysis in Voting Behavior." Reprint: *Urban Education*, 5, No. 1 (April, 1970), 20-52.

10042 **Brunn, Stanley D.; Hoffman, Wayne L.;**

Romsa, Gerald H.; and Ingalls, Gerald L. "The Emergence of Republicanism in the Urban South." *Southeastern Geographer*, 12, No. 2 (November, 1972), 133–144.

10043 **Bryan, F.M., and Hand, S.B.** "A Perspective on the 1980 Election in New England." *State Government*, 54, No. 1 (Winter, 1981), 28–33.

10044 **Budgor, J.,** et al. "The 1896 Election and Congressional Modernization." *Social Science History*, 5, No. 1 (Winter, 1981), 28-33.

10045 **Bullock, C.S.** "Congressional Voting and the Mobilization of a Black Electorate in the South." *Journal of Politics*, 43, No. 3 (August, 1981), 662–682.

10046 **Bullock, C.S.** "The Inexact Science of Congressional Redistricting." *Political Studies*, 15, No. 3 (Summer, 1982), 431–438.

10047 **Bullock, C.S.** "Redistricting and Congressional Stability, 1962–1972." *Journal of Politics*, 37, No. 2 (May, 1975), 569–575.

10048 **Bunge, William.** "Gerrymandering, Geography, and Grouping." *Geographical Review*, 56, No. 2 (April, 1966), 256–63.

10049 **Buren, Brenda A., and McHugh, Kevin E.** "Residence Histories and Electoral Success in the Arizona Legislature." *Social Science Journal* [Greenwich], 29, No. 1 (1992), 107-118.

10050 **Bushman, Donald O., and Stanley, William R.** "State Senate Reapportionment in the Southeast." *Annals of the Association of American Geographers*, 61, No. 4 (December, 1971), 654–670.

10051 **Button, James and Rosenbaum, Walter.** "Gray Power, Gray Peril, or Gray Myth? The Political Impact of the Aging in Local Sunbelt Politics. *Social Science Quarterly*, 71, No. 1 (March, 1990), 25-38.

10052 **Cairns, A.C.** "The Electoral System and the Party System in Canada, 1921-1965." *Canadian Journal of Political Science*, 1, No. 1 (March, 1968), 55-80.

10053 **Cameron, James M., and Norcliff, G.B.** "The Canadian Constitution and the Political Muskeg of One Person, One Vote." *Operational Geographer*, 8 (1985), 30–34.

10054 **Cameron, James M.; Norcliff, G.B.; and Norcliffe, G.B.** "Science and Politics in Electoral Districting: The Ward System in the Town of Vaughan, Ontario." *Ontario Geography*, No. 24 (1984), 63-80.

10055 **Cavanagh, T.E.** "Changes in American Voter Turnout, 1964–1976." *Political Science Quarterly*, 96, No. 1 (Spring, 1981), 53–65.

10056 **Centeno, Miguel Angel, and Maxfield, Sylvia.** "The Marriage of Finance and Order: Changes in the Mexican Political Elite." *Journal of Latin American Studies* [Cambridge], 24, Part 1 (February, 1992), 57–85.

10057 **Chabat, Jorge.** "Mexico's Foreign Policy in 1990: Electoral Sovereignty and Integration with the United States." *Journal of Interamerican Studies and World Affairs* [Coral Gables], 33, No. 4 (Winter, 1991), 1–25.

10058 **Chapin, F. Stuart.** "The Variability of the Popular Vote at Presidential Elections." *American Journal of Sociology*, 18, No. 2 (September, 1912), 222–240.

10059 **Claggett, W., et al.** "Nationalization of the American Electorate." *American Political Science Review*, 78, No. 1 (March, 1984), 77–91.

10060 **Clark, C., and Walter, B. Oliver, eds.** "A Symposium on Politics in the West: The 1980 Election." *Social Science Journal*, 18, No. 3 (October, 1981), 1–157.

10061 **Clark, Cal, and Clark, Janet.** "Wyoming Political Surprises in the Late 1980s: Deviating Elections in a Conservative Republican State." *Great Plains Quarterly* [Lincoln], 11, No. 3 (Summer, 1991), 181–197.

10062 **Clark, Gordon L.** "The Context of Federal Regulation: Propaganda in U.S. Union Elections." *Institute of British Geographers, Transactions*, new series, 14, No. 1 (1989), 59–73.

10063 **Clark, Gordon L., and Johnston, K.** "The Geography of U.S. Union Elections 1: The Crisis of U.S. Unions and a Critical Review of the Literature." *Environment & Planning A*, 19, No. 1 (March, 1987), 33–57.

10064 **Clark, Gordon L., and Johnston, K.** "The Geography of U.S. Union Elections 2: Performance of the United Auto Workers Union and the International Brotherhood of Electrical Workers Union, 1970–82. *Environment and Planning A*, 19, No. 2 (February, 1987), 153–172.

10065 **Clark, Gordon L., and Johnston, K.** "The Geography of U.S. Union Elections 3: The Context and Structure of Union Electoral Performance (The International Brotherhood of Electrical Workers Union and the United Auto Workers Union, 1970–82." *Environment and Planning A*, 19, No. 3 (March, 1987), 289–311.

10066 **Clarke, Harold D., and Kronberg, Allan.** "Support for the Canadian Federal Progressive Conservative Party Since 1988: The Impact of Economic Evaluations and Economic Issues." *Canadian Journal of Political Science* [Waterloo], 25, No. 1 (March, 1992), 29–53.

10067 **Clotfelter, Charles T., and Vavricheck, Bruce.** "Campaign Resource Allocation and the Regional Impact of Electoral College Reform." *Journal of Regional Science*, 20, No. 3 (August, 1980), 311–329.

10068 **Cohen, R.** "Despite Map Maker's Best Efforts, Redistricting Won't Help Either Party." *National Journal*, 14 (1982), 752–756.

10069 **Colantoni, C.C.; Levesque, T.J.; and Ordeshook, P.C.** "Campaign Resource Allocations Under the Electoral College." *American Political Science Reviews*, 69, No. 1 (March, 1975), 141–154.

10070 **Collie, Mary Melissa Pratka.** "Incumbency, Electoral Safety, and Turnover in the House of Representatives, 1952–1976." *American Political Science Review*, 75, No. 1 (March, 1981), 119–131.

10071 **Collins, William P.** "Race as a Factor in Nonpartisan Elections." *Western Political Quarterly*, 33, No. 3 (September, 1980), 330–335.

10072 "Congressional Apportionment: The Unproductive Search for Standards and Remedies." *Michigan Law Review*, 63, No. 2 (December, 1964), 374–380.

10073 **Congressional Quarterly.** "CQ Census Analysis: Congressional Districts of the United States." *Congressional Quarterly Weekly Report*, 22 (1964), 1783–1894.

10074 **Converse, Philip E.; Clausen, Aage R.; and Miller, Warren E.** "Electoral Myth and Reality: The 1964 Election." *American Political Science Review*, 59, No. 2 (June, 1965), 321–336.

10075 **Conway, M.M., and Wyckoff, Mikel L.** "Voter Choice in the 1974 Congressional Elections." *American Politics Quarterly*, 8, No. 1 (January, 1980), 3–13.

10076 **Corbitt, David L.** "Congressional Districts of North Carolina 1789-1934." *North Carolina Historical Review*, 173, No. 2 (April, 1935), 173–174.

10077 **Cornacchia, Eugene J.**, and **Nelson, Dale C.**
"Historical Differences in the Political
Experiences of American Blacks and White
Ethnics: Revisiting an Unresolved Controversy."
Ethnic and Racial Studies [London], 15, No. 1
(January, 1992), 102-124.

10078 **Cox, Kevin R.** "The Spatial Components of
Urban Voting Response Surfaces." *Economic
Geography*, 47, No. 1 (January, 1971), 27-35.

10079 **Cox, Kevin R.**, and **McCarthy, J.J.**
"Neighborhood Activism in the American City:
Behavioral Relationships and Evaluation." *Urban
Geography*, 1, No. 1 (January-March, 1980),
22-38.

10080 **Courtney, John C.** "Parliament and
Representation: The Unfinished Agenda of
Electoral Redistributions." *Canadian Journal of
Political Science*, 21, No. 4 (December, 1988),
675-690.

10081 **Crisler, Robert M.** "Republican Areas in
Missouri." *Missouri Historical Review*, 42
(1948), 299-310.

10082 **David, O.S.**, et al. "Self-Interest vs. Symbolic
Politics in Policy Attitudes and Presidential
Voting." *American Political Science Review*, 74,
No. 3 (September, 1980), 670-684.

10083 **Davis, Diane E.** "Divided Over Democracy:
The Embeddedness of State and Class Conflicts in
Contemporary Mexico." *Politics & Society*, 17,
No. 3 (September, 1989), 247-280.

10084 **Davis, M.H.** "Voting Intentions and the 1980
Carter-Reagan Debate." *Journal of Applied
Social Psychology*, 12, No. 6 (November-
December, 1982), 481-492.

10085 **Dawsey, III, Cyrus B.** "An Alogrithm for
Developing Gerrymandered School Zone
Boundaries." *Southeastern Geographer*, 3, No. 1
(May, 1983), 26-34.

10086 **Day, Frederick A.**, and **Weeks, Gregory A.**
"The 1984 Helms-Hunt Senate Race: A Spatial
Postmortem of Emerging Republican Strength in
the South." *Social Science Quarterly*, 69, No. 4
(December, 1988), 942-960.

10087 **Dean, Vera K.** "Geographic Aspects of the
Newfoundland Referendum." *Annals of the
Association of American Geographers*, 39, No. 1
(March, 1949), 70.

10088 **DeMaio, G.**, and **Muzzio, D.** "The 1980
Elections and Approval Voting." *Presidential
Studies Quarterly*, 11, No. 3 (Summer, 1981),
364-373.

10089 **Dettaven-Smith, L.**, and **Gatlin, D.** "The

Florida Voter, A Regional Analysis." *Florida
Geographer*, 19, No. 1 (1985), 23-27.

10090 "The Discreet Common Sense of the American
Voter." *Economist*, 289, No. 7315 (November
12, 1983), 19-20.

10091 **Dix, Robert H.** "Democratization and the
Institutionalization of Latin American Political
Parties." *Comparative Political Studies*, 24, No.
4 (January, 1992), 488-511.

10092 **Dix, Robert H.** "Incumbency and Electoral
Turnover in Latin America." *Journal of
Interamerican Studies and World Affairs*, 26, No.
4 (November, 1984), 435-448.

10093 **Dixon, R.G.** "The Warren Court for the Holy
Grail of 'One Man, One Vote'." In *Supreme
Court Review 1969*. Chicago: University of
Chicago Press, 1969.

10094 **Doutrich, P.E.** "A Pivotal Decision: The 1824
Gubernatorial Election in Kentucky." *Filson Club
Historical Quarterly*, 56, No. 1 (January, 1982),
14-29.

10095 **Downing, Bruce**, and **Others.** "The Decline of
Party Voting: A Geographical Analysis of the
1978 Massachusetts Election." *Professional
Geographer* (Washington, D.C.), 32, No. 4
(November, 1980), 454-461.

10096 **Dryer, E.** "Media Use and Electoral Choice:
Some Consequences of Information Exposure."
Public Opinion Quarterly, 35, No. 4 (Winter,
1971), 544-553.

10097 **Duncan, P.** "House Vote: A Major Midterm
Setback for the Republicans." *Congressional
Quarterly Weekly Report*, 39 (1982), 2780-2788.

10098 **Dutt, Ashok K.; Kendrick, Frank J.;** and **Nash,
Thomas.** "Areal Variation in the 1976
Presidential Vote: A Case Study of Akron."
Ohio Journal of Sciences, 79, No. 3 (May, 1979),
120-125.

10099 **Eamon, Thomas F.**, and **Elliott, David.**
"Modernization Versus Traditionalism in North
Carolina Senate Races: Hidden Hope for the
Democrats? *Social Science Quarterly* [Austin],
75, No. 2 (June, 1994), 354-364.

10100 **Edwards, J.M.** "The Gerrymander and "One
Man, One Vote." *New York University Law
Review*, 46, No. 5 (November, 1971), 479-499.

10101 **Ellner, Steve.** "The Deepening of Democracy in
a Crisis Setting: Political Reform and the
Electoral Process in Venezuela." *Journal of
Interamerican Studies and World Affairs* [Miami],
35, No. 4 (Winter, 1993-94), 1-42.

10102 **Engstrom, Richard L.** "The Hale Boggs Gerrymander: Congressional Redistricting, 1969." *Louisiana History*, 21, No. 1 (Winter, 1980), 59–66.

10103 **Engstrom, Richard L., and McDonald, M.** "The Election of Blacks to City Councils: Clarifying the Impact of Electoral Arrangements on the Seats/Population Relationships." *American Political Science Review*, 75, No. 2 (June, 1981), 344–354.

10104 **Engstrom, Richard L., and Wildgen, J.K.** "Pruning Thorns from the Thicket: An Empirical Test of the Existence of Racial Gerrymandering." *Legislative Studies Quarterly*, 2, No. 4 (November, 1977), 465–479.

10105 **Epstein, Lavrily Keir, and Stram, G.** "Election Night Projections and West Coast Turnout." *American Politics Quarterly*, 9, No. 4 (October, 1981), 479–491.

10106 **Falcoff, Mark.** "The Democratic Prospect in Latin America." *Washington Quarterly*, 13, No. 2 (Spring, 1990), 183-192.

10107 **Fishman, Joshua A.** "Yiddish and Voting Rights in New York, 1915 and 1921." *Language Problems and Language Planning* [Amsterdam], 18, No. 1 (Spring, 1994), 1-18.

10108 **Flaherty, Mark S., and Crumplin, William W.** "Compactness and Electoral Boundary Adjustment: An Assessment of Alternative Measures." *The Canadian Geographer* [Toronto], 36, No. 2 (Summer, 1992), 159-171.

10109 **Foladare, I.S.** "The Effect of Neighbourhood on Voting Behaviour." *Political Science Quarterly*, 83, No. 4 (December, 1968), 516–529.

10110 **Fonstad, Todd A., and Jones, David.** "Spatial Voting Patterns in the 1988 Wisconsin Presidential Election." *Wisconsin Geographer*, 5 (1989), 1–15.

10111 **Forrest, Edward.** "Electronic Reapportionment Mapping." *Data Processing Magazine*, 7, No. 7 (July, 1965), 52–54.

10112 **Fraga, Luis Ricardo.** "Domination Through Democratic Means: Nonpartisan Slating Groups in City Electoral Politics." *Urban Affairs Quarterly*, 23, No. 4 (June, 1988), 528–555.

10113 **Garand, J.C., and Gross, D.A.** "Changes in the Vote Margins for Congressional Candidates: A Specification of Historical Trends." *American Political Science Review*, 78, No. 1 (March, 1984), 17-30.

10114 **Geer, John G.** "New Deal Issues and the American Electorate, 1952-1988." *Political Behavior*, 14, No. 1 (March, 1992), 45-65.

10115 **Gidengil, Elisabeth.** "Class and Region in Canadian Voting: A Dependency Interpretation." *Canadian Journal of Political Science*, 22, No. 3 (September, 1989), 563-587.

10116 **Gilhodes, Pierre.** "Les Elections Colombiennes de 1978." *Problemes d'Amerique Latiene*, Nos. 4 523 - 4 524 (Juillet, 1979), 63–88.

10117 **Gitelson, A.R., and Richard, P.B.** "Ticket-Splitting: Aggregate Measures vs. Actual Ballots." *Western Political Quarterly*, 36, No. 3 (September, 1983), 410-419.

10118 **Glanz, O.** "The Negro Voter in the Northern Industrial Cities." *Western Political Quarterly*, 13, No. 4 (December, 1960), 999–1010.

10119 **Goodin, R.E.** "Voting Through the Looking Glass." *American Political Science Review*, 77, No. 2 (June, 1983) 420-434.

10120 **Gosnell, Harold F.** "The Negro Vote in Northern Cities." *National Municipal Review*, 30, No. 5, total number 299 (May, 1941), 264–267.

10121 **Gosnell, Harold F., and Gill, Norman N.** "An Analysis of the Presidential Vote in Chicago." *American Political Science Review*, 29, No. 4 (December, 1935), 967-984.

10122 **Gow, D.J., and Eubank, Robert Broocke.** "THe Pro-Incumbent Bias in the 1982 National Election Study." *American Journal of Political Science*, 28, No. 1 (February, 1984), 224-230.

10123 **Greenberg, Michael R., and Amer, Samy.** "Self-Interest and Direct Legislation: Public Support of a Hazardous Waste Bond Issue in New Jersey." *Political Geography Quarterly*, 8, No. 1 (January, 1989), 67–78.

10124 **Grofman, B.** "Reformers, Politicians, and the Courts: A Preliminary Look at Redistricting." *Political Geography Quarterly*, 1, No. 4 (October, 1982), 303-316.

10125 **Grofman, B., and Scarrow, H.A.** "The Riddle of Apportionment: Equality of What?" *National Civic Review*, 70, No. 5 (May, 1981), 242-254.

10126 **Gross, D.A., and Garand, J.C.** "The Vanwhuy Marginals, 1824-1980." *Journal of Politics*, 46, No. 1 (February, 1984), 224-237.

10127 **Guest, Avery M.; David, C.; and Stacheli, Lynn.** "Industrial Affiliation and Community Culture: Voting in Seattle." *Political Geography Quarterly*, 7, No. 1 (January, 1988), 47-73.

10128 **Hackey, Robert B.** "Competing Explanations of Voter Turnout Among American Blacks." *Social Science Quarterly* [Austin], 73, No. 1 (March, 1992), 70-89.

10129 **Hallowell, A.I.** "Women on the Threshold: An Analysis of Rural Women in Local Politics, Vermont (1921-1941)." *Rural Scoiology*, 52, No. 4 (1987), 510-521.

10130 **Halpin, S.A., Jr., and Engstrom, Richard L.** "Racial Gerrymandering and Southern State Legislative Redistricting: Attorney General Determinations Under the Voting Rights Act." *Journal of Public Law*, 22, No. 1 (1973), 37-66.

10131 **Hamelin, Jean; Letarte, Jacques; and Hamelin, Marcel.** "Les Elections Provinciales dans le Quebec." *Cahiers de Geographie de Quebec*, 4, No. 7 (October, 1959 - March, 1960), 5-207.

10132 **Hamilton, Howard D.** "Congressional Redistricting: A Land-Mark Decision of the Supreme Court." *Social Education*, 29, No. 1 (January, 1965), 23-26.

10133 **Hamm, K.E., et al.** "Impacts of Districtly Change or Voting Cohesion and Representation." *Journal of Politics*, 43, No. 2 (May, 1981), 544-555.

10134 **Happy, J.R.** "The Effect of Economic and Fiscal Performance on Incumbency Voting: The Canadian Case." *British Journal of Political Science*, 22, No. 1 (January, 1992), 117-130.

10135 **Hatcher, Richard G.** "The Black Role in Urban Politics." *Current History*, 57, No. 339 (November, 1969), 287-289 and 306-307.

10136 **Hendricks, Wanda A.** "'Vote for the Advantage of Ourselves and Our Race': The Election of the First Black Alderman in Chicago." *Illinois Historical Journal*, 87, No. 3 (Autumn, 1994), 171-184.

10137 **Hewitt, W.E.** "Religion and the Consolation of Democracy in Brazil: The Role of the Comunidades Eclesiasis de Base (CEBs)." *Sociological Analysis*, 51, No. 2 (Summer, 1990), 139-152.

10138 **Hinckley, B.** "The American Voter in Congressional Elections (1978)." *American Political Science Review*, 74, No. 3 (September, 1980), 641-650.

10139 **Howell, S.E.** "Local Election Campaigns: The Effects of Office Level on Campaign Style." *Journal of Politics*, 42, No. 4 (November, 1980), 1135-1145.

10140 **Hurt, R.D.** "The Populist Judiciary: Election Reform and Contested Offices." *Kansas History*, 4, No. 2 (Summer, 1981), 130-141.

10141 **Ingalls, Gerald L.** "Jesse Helms and Electoral Change in Southern Politics." *Southeastern Geographer*, 30, No. 1 (May, 1990), 68-73.

10142 **Ingalls, Gerald L.** Jesse Helms and Electoral Change in Southern Politics." *Southeastern Geographer*, 30, No. 1 (May, 1990), 68-73.

10143 **Ingalls, Gerald L., and Brunn, Stanley D.** "Electoral change in the American South, 1948-1976: The Influence of Population Size." *Southeastern Geographer*, 19, No. 2 (November, 1979), 80-90.

10144 **Israel, Jerold.** "Nonpopulation Factors Relevant to an Acceptable Standard of Apportionment." *Notre Dame Law,* 38, No. 5 (August, 1963), 499-517.

10145 **Jackman, R.W.** "Political Parties, Voting and National Integration: The Canadian Case." *Comparative Politics*, 4, No. 4 (July, 1972), 511-536.

10146 **Jacobson, G.C.** "Money in the 1980 and 1982 Congressional Elections." In *Money and Politics in the United States*, M.J. Malbin, ed. Washington, D.C.: American Enterprise Institute, 1984, 38-69.

10147 **Jacobson, G.C., et al.** "The 1978 U.S. Congressional Elections." *Legislative Studies Quarterly*, 6, No. 2 (May, 1981), 183-200.

10148 **Jacques, Wayne, and others.** "Some Aspects of Major Newspaper Coverage of the 1992 Presidential Debates." *American Behavioral Scientist* [Thousand Oaks], 37, No. 2 (November/December, 1993), 252-256.

10149 **Jenkins, M.A., and Shepherd, J.W.** "Decentralizing High School Administration in Detroit: An Evaluation of Alternative Strategies of Political Control." *Economic Geography*, 48, No. 1 (January, 1972), 95-106.

10150 **Jensen, Richard.** "The Cities Reelect Roosevelt: Ethnicity, Religion and Class in 1940." *Ethnicity*, 8, No. 2 (June, 1981), 189-195.

10151 **Jentz, J.B.** "The Antislavery Constituency in Jacksonian New York City.;" *Civil War History*, 27, No. 2 (June, 1981), 101-122.

10152 **Johnston, R.J.** "The Changing Geography of Voting in the United States, 1946-1980." *Transactions, Institute of British Geographers*, 7, No. 2 (1982), 187-204.

10153 **Johnston, R.J.** "From Nixon to Carter: Estimates of the Geography of Voting Change, 1972-76." *Journal of Geography*), 82, No. 6 (November-December, 1983), 261-264.

10154 **Johnston, R.J.** "Local Effects in Voting at a Local Election." *Annals of the Association of American Geographers*, 64, No. 2 (September, 1974), 418-429.

10155 **Johnston, R.J., and Hay, A.M.** "The Geography of Ticket-Splitting: A Preliminary Study of the 1976 Elections Using Entropy-Maximizing Methods." *Professional Geographer*, 36, No. 2 (May, 1984), 201-206.

10156 **Johnston, Richard.** "Political Generations and Electoral Change in Canada." *British Journal of Political Science*, 22, No. 1 (January, 1992), 93-115.

10157 **Just, A.E.** "Urban School Board Elections: Changes in the Political Environment Between 1950 and 1980." *Education and Urban Society*, 12, No. 4 (August, 1980), 421-435.

10158 **Jones, Mark P.** "The Political Consequences of Electoral Laws in Latin America and the Caribbean." *Electoral Studies*, 12, No. 1 (March, 1993), 59-75.

10159 **Jones, Mark P.** "Presidential election Laws and Multipartism in Latin America." *Political Research Quarterly* [Salt Lake City], 47, No. 1 (March, 1994), 41-57.

10160 **Kaiser, Henry F.** "An Objective Method for Establishing Legislative Districts." *Midwest Journal of Political Science*, 10, No. 2 (May, 1966), 200-213.

10161 **Kapstein, Ethan B.** "America's Arms-Trade Monopoly: Lagging Sales Will Starve Lesser Suppliers." *Foreign Affairs* [New York], 73, No. 3 (May/June, 1994), 13-19.

10162 **Kerber, Stephen.** "The Initiative and Referendum in Florida, 1911-1912." *The Florida Historical Quarterly* [Tampa], 72, No. 3 (January, 1994), 302-315.

10163 **Kerstein, Robert.** "Growth Politics in Tampa and Hillsborough County: Strains in the Privatistic Regimes." *Journal of Urban Affairs* [Greenwich], 13, No. 1 (1991), 55-75.

10164 **Kiewiet, D.R.** "Policy-Oriented Voting in Response to Economic Issues." *American Political Science Review*, 75, No. 2 (June, 1981), 448-459.

10165 **King, James Dale.** "Comparing Local and Presidential Elections." *American Politics Quarterly*, 9, No. 3 (July, 1981), 227-290.

10166 **Kleppner, P.** "Search for the Indiana Voter: A Review Essay." *Indiana Magazine of History*, 76, No. 4 (December, 1980), 346-366.

10167 **Kleppner, P., and Baker, S.C.** "The Impact of Voter Registration Requirements on Electoral Turnout, 1900-1916." *Journal of Political and Military Sociology*, 8, No. 3 (Fall, 1980), 205-226.

10168 **Knight, B.B.** "The States and Reapportionment: One Man, One Vote Revisited." *State Government*, 49, No. 3 (Summer, 1976), 155-160.

10169 **Koeniger, A.C.** "The Politics of Independence: Carter Glass and the Elections of 1936." *South Atlantic Quarterly*, 80, No. 1 (Winter, 1981), 95-106.

10170 **Kuklinski, J.H., and West, D.M.** "Economic Expectations and Voting Behavior in United States House and Senate Elections (1978)." *American Political Science Review*, 75, No. 2 (June, 1981), 436-447.

10171 **Ladd, E.C.** "The Brittle Mandate: Electoral Dealignment and the 1980 Presidential Election." *Political Studies Quarterly*, 96, No. 1 (Spring, 1981), 1-25.

10172 **LaPonce, J.A.** "Assessing the Neighbour Effect on the Vote of Francophone Minorities in Canada." *Political Geography Quarterly*, 6, No. 1 (January, 1987), 77-86.

10173 **LaPonce, J.A.** "Left or Centre? The Canadian Jewish Electorate, 1953-1983." *Canadian Journal of Political Science*, 21, No. 4 (December, 1988), 691-714.

10174 **LaPonce, J.A.** "Post-Dicting Electoral Cleavages in Canadian Federal Elections." *Canadian Journal of Political Science*, 5, No. 2 (June, 1972), 270-286.

10175 **Lehne, Richard.** "Representation in Congress: A Projection for 1972." *National Civic Review*, 60, No. 7 (July, 1971), 372-376.

10176 **Levy, M.R.** "Methodology and Performance of Election Day Polls." *Public Opinion Quarterly*, 47, No. 1 (Spring, 1983), 54-67.

10177 **Lewis, P.C.** "Impact of Negro Migrations on the Electoral Geography of Flint, Michigan, 1932-1962: A Cartographic Analysis." *Annals of the Association of American Geographers*, 55, No. 1 (March, 1965), 1-25.

10178 **Lichtman, A.J.** "Political Realignment and Ethnocultural Voting in Late Nineteenth Century America." *Journal of Social History*, 16, No. 3 (Spring, 1983), 55-82.

10179 **Lipset, Seymour M.** "Marx, Engels, and America's Political Parties." *Wilson Quarterly*, 2, No. 1 (Winter, 1978), 90-104.

10180 **Loaeza, Soledad.** "Derecha y Democracia en el Cambio Politico Mexicano: 1982-1988." *Foro Internacional* [Mexico, DF], 30, Num. 4 (Abril-Junio, 1990), 631-658.

10181 **Lovink, J.A.A.** "Is Canadian Politics Too Competitive?" *Canadian Journal of Political Science*, 6, No. 3 (September, 1973), 341–379.

10182 **Luttbeg, N.R.** "Differential Voting Turnout Decline in the American States 1960-1982." *Social Science Quarterly*, 65, No. 1 (March, 1984), 60–73.

10183 **MacDonald, Stuart Elaine; Listhaug, Ola; and Rabinowitz.** "Issues and Party Support in Multiparty Systems." *American Political Science Review*, 85, No. 4 (December, 1991), 1107-1131.

10184 **Mainwaring, Scott.** "Political Parties and Democratization in Brazil and the Southern Cone." *Comparative Politics*, 21, No. 1 (October, 1988), 91–120.

10185 **Maisel, L.S.** "Congressional Elections in 1978: The Road to Nomination, the Road to Election." *American Politics Quarterly*, 9, No. 1 (January, 1981), 23-47.

10186 **Mann, Thomas Edward, and Wolfinger, R.E.** "Candidates and Parties in Congressional Elections (1978)." *American Political Science Review*, 74, No. 3 (September, 1980), 617-632.

10187 **Maram, Sheldon.** "Juscelino Kubitschek and the 1960 Presidential Election." *Journal of Latin American Studies* [Cambridge], 24, Part 1 (February, 1992), 123-145.

10188 **Marston, Sallie A., and Saint-Germain, Michelle.** "Urban Restructuring and the Emergence of New Political Groupings: Women and Neighborhood Activism in Tucson, Arizona." *Geoforum* [Oxford], 22, No. 2 (1991), 223-236.

10189 **Martz, John D.** "Electoral Campaigning and Latin American Democratization: The Grandcolombian Experience." *Journal of Interamerican Studies and World Affairs*, 32, No. 1 (Spring, 1990), 17-43.

10190 **Martz, John D.** "Party Elites and Leadership in Colombia and Venezuela." *Journal of Latin American Studies* [Cambridge], 24, Part 1 (February, 1992), 87-121.

10191 **Martz, Mary Jeanne Reid.** "Studying Latin American Political Parties: Dimensions Past and Present." *Journal of Latin American Studies*, 12, Part 1 (May, 1980), 139-167.

10192 **Mayhew, D.** "Congressional Representation: Theory and Practice in Drawing the Districts. In *Reapportionment in the 1970s*, N. Polsby, ed.

Berkeley, California: University of California Press, 1971, 349-385.

10193 **McAdams, J.C., and Johannes, J.R.** "1980 House Elections: Reexamining Some Theories in a Republican Year." *Journal of Politics*, 45, No. 1 (February, 1983), 143-162.

10194 **McClintock, Cynthia.** "The Prospects for Democratic Consolidation in a 'Least Likely' Case: Peru." *Comparative Politics*, 21, No. 2 (January, 1989), 127–148.

10195 **McCormick, Peter.** "Is the Liberal Party Declining? Liberals, Conservatives and Provincial Politics 1867-1980." *Journal of Canadian Studies*, 18, No. 4 (Winter, 1983–1984), 88–107.

10196 **McCoy, D.R.** "Senator George S. McGill and the Election of 1938." *Kansas History*, 4, No. 1 (Spring, 1981), 2-19.

10197 **McDonnell, R.A.** "The Direction of the Wallace Vote in 1972 and 1976." *Presidential Studies Quarterly*, 11, No. 3 (Summer, 1981), 374-383.

10198 **McGuire, James W.** "Union Political Tactics and Democratic Consolidation in Alfonsin's Argentina, 1983-1989." *Latin American Research Review* [Albuquerque], 27, No. 2 (1992), 37-74.

10199 **McKay, Robert B.** "The Federal Analogy and State Apportionment Standards." *Notre Dame Lawyer*, 38, No. 5 (August, 1963), 487-498.

10200 **McPhail, I.R.** "The Vote for Mayor of Los Angeles in 1969." *Annals of the Association of American Geographers*, 61, No. 4 (December, 1971), 744–758.

10201 **Meerse, D.E.** "The 1857 Kansas Territorial Delegate Election Contest." *Kansas History*, 4, No. 2 (Summer, 1981), 96-113.

10202 **Merom, Gil.** "Democracy, Dependency, and Destabilization: The Shaking of Allende's Regime." *Political Science Quarterly*, 105, No. 1 (Spring 1990), 75-95.

10203 **Meyers, Dee Dee.** "New Technology and the 1992 Clinton Presidential Campaign." *American Behavioral Scientist* [Thousand Oaks], 37, No. 2 (November/December, 1993), 181-187.

10204 **Miller, Warren E.** "The Puzzle Transformed: Explaining Declining Turnout." *Political Behavior*, 14, No. 1 (March, 1992), 1-43.

10205 **Mintz, Eric.** "Election Campaign Tours in Canada." *Political Geography Quarterly*, 4, No. 1 (January, 1985), 47-54.

10206 **Miscamble, Wilson D.** "Harry S. Truman, the Berlin Blockade and the 1984 Election." *Presidential Studies Quarterly*, 10, No. 3 (Summer, 1980), 306–316.

10207 **Misse, F.B.** "Franklin Roosevelt and the Polish Vote in 1944." *Midwest Quarterly*, 21 (Spring, 1980), 317–332.

10208 **Moises, Jose Alvaro.** "Elections, Political Parties and Political Culture in Brazil: Changes and Continuities." *Journal of Latin American Studies* [Cambridge], 25, Part 2 (October, 1993), 575–611.

10209 **Molloy, Ivan.** "The Empire Strikes Back: The Sandinista Defeat in Context." *Australian Journal of International Affairs* [Canberra], 46, No. 1 (May, 1992), 109–126.

10210 **Morrill, Richard L.** "On Criteria for Redistricting." *Washington Law Review*, 48 (1973), 847-856.

10211 **Morrill, Richard L.** "Redistricting Revisited." *Annals of the Association of American Geographers*, 66, No. 4 (December, 1976), 548-556.

10212 **Morrill, Richard L.** "Redistricting Standards and Strategies After 20 Years." *Political Geography Quarterly*, 1, No. 4 (October, 1982), 361–369.

10213 **Morrissey, M., and Johnston, R.J.** "The Sources of Electoral Bias in Jamaican Election Results, 1967-1980." *Caribbean Geographer*, 1, No. 3 (May, 1984), 176–185.

10214 **Muckelston, Keith Way; Marsh, T.J.; and Mukerji, D.** "Legislative Voting on Environmental Bills in Oregon." In *Yearbook of the Association of Pacific Coast Geographers,* 38 (1976), 77-86.

10215 **Murauskas, G.Thomas; Archer, J. Clark; and Shelley, Fred M.** "Metropolitan, Non-Metropolitan and Sectional Variations in Voting Behavior in Recent Presidential Elections." *Western Political Quarterly*, 41, No. 1 (April, 1988), 63–84.

10216 **Nagler, Jonathan.** "The Effect of Registration Laws and Education on U.S. Voter Turnout." *American Political Science Review,* 85, No. 4 (December, 1991), 1393-1405.

10217 **Navarro, Zander.** "Democracy, Citizenship and Representation: Rural Social Movements in Southern Brazil, 1978-1990." *Bulletin in Latin American Research* [Oxford], 13, No. 2 (May, 1994), 129-154.

10218 **Nichols, Glenn A.** "Voting in Pre-1964 Brazil: The Need for Reassessment." *Luso-Brazilian Review*, 17, No. 1 (Summer, 1980), 63-78.

10219 **Nicholson, Richard L.** "Redistricting Cities: The Case of Buffalo, New York." *Ontario Geography*, 20, No. 20 (1982), 65-82.

10220 **Niemi, R., and Deegan, J., Jr.** "A Theory of Political Districting." *American Political Science Review*, 72, No. 4 (December, 1978), 1304-1323.

10221 **Niemi, Richard G.; Craig, Stephen G.; and Mattei, Franco.** "Measuring Internal Political Efficacy in the 1988 National Election Study." *American Political Science Review,* 85, No. 4 (December, 1991), 1407-1413.

10222 **Nodyne, K.R.** "Ohio County and the Election of 1860: A Preliminary Study." *Journal of West Virginia History Association*, 4, No. 1 (Spring, 1980), 15-23.

10223 **Noragon, J.** "Congressional Redistricting and Population Composition, 1964–1970." *Midwest Journal of Political Science*, 16, No. 2 (May, 1972), 295–302.

10224 **Noragon, J.** "Redistricting, Political Outcomes, and Gerrymandering in the 1960's. *Annals of the New York Academy of Sciences*, 219 (1973), 314-333.

10225 **Oder, B.N.** "Andrew Johnson and the 1866 Illinois Election." *Journal of the Illinois Historical Society*, 73, No. 3 (Autumn, 1980), 189-200.

10226 **Ogburn, William Fielding, and Talbot, N.S.** "A Measurement of Factors in the Presidential Election of 1928." *Social Forces*, 8, No. 2 (December, 1929), 175-183.

10227 **Ogburn, William Fielding; Talbot, N.S.; and Jaffe, Abe J.** "Independent Voting in Presidential Elections." *American Journal of Sociology*, 42, No. 2 (September, 1936), 186-201.

10228 **O'Hare, William.** "City Size, Racial Composition, and Election of Black Mayors Inside and Outside the South." *Journal of Urban Affairs* [Greenwich], 12, No. 3 (1990), 307-313.

10229 **Olson, John Kevin, and Beck, Ann C.** "Religion and Political Realignment in the Rocky Mountain States." *Journal for the Scientific Study of Religion* [West Lafayette], 29, No. 2 (June, 1990), 198-209.

10230 **O'Loughlin, John.** "The Election of Black Mayors, 1977." *Annals of the Association of American Geographers*, 70, No. 3 (September, 1980), 353-370.

10231 **O'Loughlin, John.** "The Identification and Evaluation of Racial Gerrymandering." *Annals of the Association of American Geographers*, 72, No. 2 (June, 1982), 165-184.

10232 **O'Loughlin, John.** "Malapportionment and Gerrymandering in the Ghetto." in *Urban Policymaking and Metropolitan Dynamics: A Comparative Geographical Analysis*, J.S. Adams, ed. Cambridge, Massachusetts: Ballinger, 1976, 539-565.

10233 **O'Loughlin, John., and Berg, Dale A.** "The Election of Black Mayors, 1969 and 1973." *Annals of the Association of American Geographers*, 67, No. 2 (June, 1977), 223-238.

10234 **Orr, Douglas M.** "The Persistence of the Gerrymander in North Carolina Congressional Redistricting." *Southeastern Geographer*, 9, No. 2 (November, 1969), 39-54.

10235 **Owen, Guillermo, and Grofman, B.** "Optimal Partisan Gerrymandering." *Political Geography Quarterly*, 7, No. 1 (January, 1988), 5-22.

10236 **Pammett, Jon H.** "Class Voting and Class Consciousness in Canada." *Canadian Review of Sociology & Anthropology*, 24, No. 2 (1987), 269-290.

10237 **Park, James W.** "Regionalism as a Factor in Columbia's 1875 Election." *Americas*, 42, No. 4 (April, 1986), 453-472.

10238 **Parker, A.C.** "Beating the Spread: Analyzing American Election Outcomes (Sample from New York State 1860-92)." *Journal of American History*, 67, No. 1 (June, 1980), 61-87.

10239 **Paul, Peter.** "Mapping the Referendum." *Association of Canadian Map Libraries and Archives* [Ottawa], No. 86 (March, 1993), 22-27.

10240 **Peet, R.** "Reading Fukuyama; Politics at the End of History." *Political Geography*, 12, No. 1 (January, 1993), 64-68.

10241 **Peritore, N. Patrick.** "Brazilian Communist Opinion: A Q-Methodology Study of Ten Parties." *Journal of Developing Areas*, 23, No. 1 (October, 1988), 105-136.

10242 **Peters, J.G., and Welch, Susan.** "The Effects of Corruption of Voting Behavior in Congressional Elections (1968-1978)." *American Political Science Review*, 76, No. 3 (September,1980), 697-708.

10243 **Petrocik, J.R.** "Voting in a Machine City, Chicago 1975." *Ethnicity*, 8, No. 3 (September, 1981), 320-340.

10244 **Phelps, Glenn A.** "Mr. Gerry Goes to Arizona: Electoral Geography and Voting Rights in Navajo Country." *American Indian Culture and Research Journal* [Los Angeles], 15, No. 2 (1991), 63-92.

10245 **Piott, Steven.** "Giving Voters a Voice: The Struggle for Initiative and Referendum in Missouri." *Gateway Heritage* [St. Louis], 14, No. 4 (Spring, 1994), 20-35.

10246 **Plotnick, Robert D., and Winters, Richard F.** "Party, Political Liberalism, and Redistribution: An Application to the American States." *American Politics Quaterly* [Newbury Park], 18, No. 4 (October, 1990), 430-458.

10247 **Posada-Carbo, Eduardo.** "Elections and Civil Wars in Nineteenth-Century Colombia: The 1875 Presidential Campaign." *Journal of Latin American Studies*, 26, Part 3 (October, 1994), 621-649.

10248 **Power, Timothy J.** "Political Landscapes, Politicial Parties, and Authoritarianism in Brazil and Chile." *International Journal of Comparative Sociology*, 29, Nos. 3-4 (September-December, 1988), 251-263.

10249 **Pritchard, Anita.** "Changes in Electoral Structures and the Success of Women Candidates: The Case of Florida." *Social Science Quarterly* [Austin], 73, No. 1 (March, 1992), 62-70.

10250 **Rable, G.C.** "Southern Interests and the Election of 1876: A Reappraisal." *Civil War History*, 26, No. 4 (December, 1980), 347-361.

10251 **Ragsdale, L., et al.** "Congressional Elections." *American Politics Quarterly*, 8, No. 4 (October, 1980), 375-512.

10252 **Redard, Thomas E.** "The Election of 1844 in Louisiana: A New Look at the Ethno-Cultural Approach." *Louisiana History*, 22, No. 4 (Fall, 1981), 419-433.

10253 **Riehle, T.** "Regan is Leading in Almost Every State." *National Journal*, 16, No. 40 (October 6, 1855), 1882.

10254 **Rodriguez, Victoria E., and Ward, Peter M.** "Opposition Politics, Power and Public Administration in Urban Mexico." *Bulletin of Latin American Research* [Oxford], 10, No. 1 (1991), 23-36.

10255 **Roeck, Ernest C., Jr.** "Measuring Compactness as a Requirement of Legislative Apportionment." *Midwest Journal of Political Science*, 5, No. 1 (February, 1961), 70-74.

10256 **Roett, Riordan and Tollefson, Scott D.** "The Year of Elections in Brazil." *Current History*, 89, No. 543 (January, 1990), 25-29.

10257 **Roettger, W.B., and Winebrenner, H.** "Voting Behavior of American Political Scientists: The 1980 Presidential Election." *Western Political Quarterly*, 36, No. 1 (March, 1983), 134–148.

10258 **Rogers, George W.** "Party Politics or Protest Politics: Current Political Trends in Alaska." *Polar Record*, 14, No. 91 (January, 1969), 445-458.

10259 **Rogers, W.W.** "Alabama and the Presidential Election of 1836." *Alabama Review*, 35, No. 2 (April, 1982), 111-126.

10260 **Rogin, M.** "Politics, Emotion and the Wallace Vote." *British Journal of Sociology*, 20, No. 1 (March, 1969), 27-49.

10261 **Rosdil, Donald L.** "The Context of Radical Populism in US Cities: A Comparative Analysis." *Journal of Urban Affairs* [Greenwich], 13, No. 1 (1991), 77-96.

10262 **Rosenzweig, A., and Wildgen, J.K.** "A Statistical Analysis of the 1977 Mayor's Race in New Orleans." *Louisiana Business Survey*, 9 (April, 1978), 4-8.

10263 **Rumage, K.W.** "Some Spatial Characteristics of the Republican and Democratic Presidential Vote in Iowa, 1900-1956." *Iowa Business Digest*, 31, No. 2 (February, 1960), 17-22.

10264 **Rumley, Dennis, and Minghi, Julian V.** "The Vancouver Civic Elections of 1970 and 1972: A Comparative Analysis." In *The Kootenay Collection of Research Studies in Geography*, B.M. Barr, ed. Vancouver: Tantalus, 1974, 35-49.

10265 **Rumley, Dennis, and Minghi, Julian V.** "A Geographic Framework for the Study of the Stability and Change of Urban Electoral Patterns." *Tijdschrift voor Economische en Sociale Geographie*, 68, Nr. 3 (May-June, 1977), 177-182.

10266 **Rumley, Dennis, and Minghi, Julian V.** "Toward a Geography of Campaigning: Some Evidence from a Provincial Election in Vancouver, B.C." *Canadian Geographer*, 22, No. 2 (Summer, 1978), 145-162.

10267 **Rumley, Dennis; Minghi, Julian V.; and Swain, Harry.** "The Vancouver Civic Election of 1970." In *Contemporary Geography: Western Viewpoints*, R. Leigh, ed. Vancouver: Tantalus, 1971, 97-114.

10268 **Ryan, T.G.** "Farm Prices and the Farm Vote in 1948." *Agricultural History*, 54, No. 3 (July, 1980), 387-401.

10269 **Sarasohn, D.** "The Election of 1916: Realigning the Rockies." *Western Historical Quarterly*, 11 (July, 1980), 285-305.

10270 **Sauer, Carl.** "Geography and the Gerrymander." *American Political Science Review*, 12, No. 3 (September, 1918), 403-426.

10271 **Scarrow, H.A.** "Communication of Election Appeals in Canada." *Journalism Quarterly*, 36, No. 2 (Spring, 1959), 219-220.

10272 **Schoolmaster, F.A.** "West Texas Versus East Texas: A Geographical Analysis of Voting Patterns for Water-Related Constitutional Amendments." *Water Resources Bulletin*, 20 (1984), 151-162.

10273 **Schoyer, George.** "The Coverage of Political Patterns and Eletions in Some Selected State Atlases of the United States." *Special Libraries Association (New York) Geography and Map Division Bulletin*, 117 (September, 1979), 2-7.

10274 **Schreiber, E.M.** "Class Awareness and Class Voting in Canada: A Reconsideration of the Ogmundson Thesis." *Canadian Review of Sociology and Anthropology*, 17, No. 1 (1980), 37-44.

10275 **Schubert, G., and Press, C.** "Measuring Malapportionment." *American Political Science Review*, 58, No. 2 (June, 1964), 302-327.

10276 **Schwab, L.** "The Impact of Equal-Population Redistricting on the House of Representatives: A District, State and Regional Analysis." *Capital Studies*, 4 (1976), 67-84.

10277 **Schwartzberg, Joseph E.** "Reapportionment, Gerrymanders and the Notion of Compactness." *Minnesota Law Review*, 50, No. 3 (January, 1966), 443-452.

10278 **Scranton, Margaret E.** "Consolidation After Imposition: Panama's 1992 Referendum." *Journal of Interamerican Studies and World Affairs* Coral Gables], 35, No. 3 (Fall, 1993), 65-102.

10279 **Seligson, Mitchell A.** "Trust, Efficacy, and Modes of Political Participation: A Study of Costa Rican Peasants." *British Journal of Political Science*, 10, Part 1 (January, 1980), 75-98.

10280 **Shafer, B.** "Dealignment Affirmed or Explosion Deferred? The American Mid-Term Elections of 1986." *Electoral Studies*, 6, No. 1 (1987), 47-51.

10281 **Shaffer, S.D.** "Policy Differences between Voters and Non-Voters in American Elections." *Western Political Quarterly*, 35, No. 4 (December, 1982), 496-510.

10282 **Sheffield, Jr., James, F.,** and **Handley, Charles D.** "Racial Voting in a Biracial City: A Reexamination of Some Hypotheses." *American Politics Quarterly*, 12, No. 4 (October, 1984), 449–464.

10283 **Shelley, Fred M.,** and **Archer, J. Clark.** "The Electoral Mosaic of a Border Region." *Geographical Perspectives*, 54 (Fall, 1984), 7-20.

10284 **Shelley, Fred M.,** and **Archer, J. Clark.** "Sectionalism and Presidential Politics: Voting Patterns in Illinois, Indiana, and Ohio." *Journal of Interdisciplinary History*, 20, No. 2 (Autumn, 1989), 227-255.

10285 **Shelley, Fred M.,** and **Archer, J. Clark.** "Some Geographical Aspects of the American Presidential Election of 1992." *Political Geography* [Oxford], 13, No. 2 (March, 1994), 137-159.

10286 **Shelley, Fred M.; Archer, J. Clark;** and **Muraauskas, G. Thomas.** "The Geography of Recent Presidential Elections in Southwest." *Arkansas Journal of Geography*, 2 (1986), 1-11.

10287 **Shelley, Fred M.; Archer, J. Clark;** and **White, Ellen R.** "Rednecks and Quiche Eaters: A Cartographic Analysis of Recent Third-Party Electoral Campaigns." *Journal of Geography*, 83, No. 1 (January -February, 1984), 7-12.

10288 **Sigel, R.S.** "Race and Religion as Factors in the Kennedy Victory in Detroit, 1960." *Journal of Negro Education*, 31, No. 4 (Fall, 1962), 436–442.

10289 **Sigelman, L.,** and **Sigelman, C.K.** "Sexism, Racism, and Ageism in Voting Behavior: An Experimental Analysis." *Social Psychology Quarterly*, 45, No. 4 (December, 1982), 263-269.

10290 **Sigelman, L.; Sigelman, C.K.;** and **Yough, S.N.** "Left-Right Polarization in National Party Systems: A Cross-national Analysis." *Comparative Political Studies*, 11 (1978), 355-380.

10291 **Sigelman, Lee.** "If You Prick Us, Do We Not Bleed? If You tickle Us, Do We Not Laugh? Jews and Pocketbook Voting." *Journal of Politics,* 53, No. 4 (November, 1991), 977-992.

10292 **Silva, Ruth C.** "Reapportionment and Redistricting; the Court Decisions that Reinforce the Concept of "One Man, One Vote" are Now Operating to Change Two Aspects of the U.S. Political Structure: Apportionment of Elective Offices and the Form of Election Districts." *Scientific American*, 213, No. 5 (November, 1965), 20-27.

10293 **Smith, William C.** "State, Market and

Neoliberalism in Post-Transition Argentina: The Menem Experiment." *Journal of Interamerican Studies and World Affairs* [Coral Gables], 33, No. 4 (Winter, 1991), 45-82.

10294 **Sonenshein, Raphael J.** "Can Black Candidates Win Statewide Elections?" *Political Science Quarterly* [New York], 105, No. 2 (Summer, 1990), 219-241.

10295 **Stanley, George F.G.** "The 1867 Election in California." *Pacific Historian*, 24, No. 4 (Winter, 1980), 443-455.

10296 **Stanley, Harold W.** "Southern Republicans in Congress: Have They Fallen and They Can't Get Up?" *Social Science Quarterly* [Austin], 73, No. 1 (March, 1992), 136-140.

10297 **Stern, N.B.** "Los Angeles Jewish Voters During Grant's First Presidential Race." *Western States Jewish History Quarterly*, 13, No. 1 (January, 1981), 179-185.

10298 **Stone, Carl.** "The Changing Caribbean-Regional Voting in Jamaica: Trends, Causes and Implications." *Caribbean Geography*, 2, No. 2 (October, 1986), 122–133.

10299 **Stone, W.J.** "Electoral Change and Policy Representation in Congress: Domestic Welfare Issues from 1956 to 1972." *British Journal of Political Science*, 12, Part 1 (January, 1982), 95-115.

10300 **Strum, H.** "Property Qualifications and Voting Behavior in New York, 1870–1816." *Journal of the Early Republic*, 1, No. 4 (Winter, 1981), 347-371.

10301 **Swanson, Stoakley W.** "Wisconsin's Congressional Elections: A Process in Need of Repair." In *Wisconsin and Its Region*. La Crosse, Wisconsin: La Crosse University of Wisconsin System, 1988, 29-40.ol., p. 29-40.

10302 **Swauger, John.** "Measuring Regional Agreement in Senate Voting, 1977." *Professional Geographer*, 32, No. 4 (November, 1980), 446-453.

10303 **Swauger, John.** "Regionalism in the 1976 Presidential Election." *Geographical Review*, 70, No. 2 (April, 1980), 157–166.

10304 "Symposium on Legislative Reapportionment." *Law and Contemporary Problems*, 17, No. 2 (Spring, 1952), 253-469 (complete issue, multiple authors).

10305 **Tatalovich, R.** "Friends and Neighbors Voting: Mississippi, 1943-73." *Journal of Politics*, 37, No. 3 (August, 1975), 807-815.

10306 **Taylor, P.J.**, and **Gudgin, G.** "The Statistical Basis of Decision-making in Electoral Districts. *Environment and Planning*, A8, No. 1 (January, 1976), 43-58.

10307 **Tedin, K.L.**, and **R.W. Murray.** "Dynamics of Candidate Choice in a State Election." *Journal of Politics*, 43, No. 2 (May, 1981), 435-455.

10308 **Terchek, R.J.** "Political Participation and Political Structures: The Voting Rights Act of 1965." *Phylon*, 41, No. 1 (Spring, 1980), 25-35.

10309 **Thielemann, Gregory S.** "Party Development in the South: The Case for Southern Exceptionalism." *Social Science Quarterly* [Austin], 73, No. 1 (March, 1992), 141-143.

10310 **Thielemann, Gregory S.** "The Rise and Stall of Southern Republicans in Congress." *Social Science Quarterly* [Austin], 73, No. 1 (March, 1992), 123-135.

10311 **Tremblay, Manon.** "Quand Les Femmes Se Distinguent: Feminisme et Representation Politique au Quebec." *Canadian Journal of Political Science* [Waterloo], 25, No. 1 (March, 1992), 55-68.

10312 **Trindale, Helgio.** "Presidential Elections and Political Transition in Latin America." *International Social Science Journal* [Oxford], No. 128 (May, 1991), 301-314.

10313 **Tucker, Harvey J.** "State Legislative Appointment: Legal Principles in Empirical Perspective." *Political Geography Quarterly*, 4, No. 1 (January, 1985), 19-28.

10314 **Tuckel, P.**, and **Tejera, F.** "Changing Patterns in American Voting Behavior, 1914-1980." *Public Opinion Quarterly*, 47 (Summer, 1983), 230-246.

10315 **Tyler, Gus.** "Court versus Legislature: The Socio-Politics of Malapportionment." *Laws and Contemporary Problems*, 27, No. 3 (Summer, 1962), 390-407.

10316 **Van Wingen, John R.** "Localism, Factional Fluidity, and Factionalism: Louisiana and Mississippi Gubernatorial Contests." *Social Science History*, 8, No. 1 (Winter, 1984), 3-4.

10317 **Valenzuela, Arturo** and **Constable, Pamela.** "The Chilean Plebiscite: Defeat of a Dictator." *Current History,* 88, No. 536 (March, 1989), 129-132.

10318 **Vickery, William.** "On the Prevention of Gerrymandering." *Political Science Quarterly*, 76, No. 1 (March, 1961), 105-10.

10319 **Wade, Larry L.** "The Influence of Sections and Periods on Economic Voting in American Presidential Elections, 1828-1984." *Political Geography Quarterly*, 8, No. 3 (July, 1989), 271-288.

10320 **Waisbord, Silvio R.** "Television and Election Campaigns in Contemporary Argentina." *Journal of Communication* [New York], 44, No. 2 (Spring, 1994), 125-135.

10321 **Waldrep, C.H.** "Who Were Kentucky's Whig Voters? A Note on Voting in Eddyville Precinct in August 1850." *Register of the Kentucky Historical Society*, 79, No. 3 (Autumn, 1981), 326-332.

10322 **Walter, Richard J.** "Politics, Parties, and Elections in Argentina's Province of Buenos Aires, 1912-42." *Hispanic American Historical Review*, 64, No. 4 (November, 1984), 707-735.

10323 **Ward, J.C.** "The Election of 1880 and Its Impact on Atlanta." *Atlanta Historical Journal*, 25, No. 1 (Spring, 1981), 5-15.

10324 **Warntz, William.** "A Methodological Consideration of Some Geographic Aspects of the Newfoundland Referendum on Confederation with Canada, 1948." *Canadian Geographer*, No. 6 (1955), 39-49.

10325 **Wattier, M.J.** "Ideological Voting in 1980 Republican Presidential Primaries." *Journal of Politics*, 45, No. 4 (November, 1983), 1016-1026.

10326 **Webster, G.R.** "Congressional Redistricting and African-American Representation in the 1990s: An Example from Alabama." *Political Geography,* 12, No. 6 (November, 1993), 549-564.

10327 **Webster, Gerald R.** "Demise of the Solid South." *The Geographical Review* [New York], 82, No. 1 (January, 1992), 43-55.

10328 **Webster, Gerald R.** "Factors in Growth of Republican Voting in the Miam-Dade County SMSA." *Southeastern Geographer*, 27, No. 1 (May, 1987), 1-17.

10329 **Webster, Gerald R.** "Geography of a Senate Confirmation Vote." *The Geographical Review* [New York], 82, No. 2 (April, 1992), 154-165.

10330 **Webster, Gerald R.** "Partisanship in American Presidential Senatorial and Gubernatorial Elections in Ten Western States." *Political Geography Quarterly*, 8, No. 2 (April, 1989), 161-179.

10331 **Webster, Gerald R.** "Presidential Voting in the West." *Social Science Journal*, 25, No. 2 (1988), 211-232.

10332 **Webster, Gerald R.** "Size of Place and Voting in Presidential Elections in the Interior West (USA)." *Geographical Perspectives*, 58–59 (1987), 78–92.

10333 **Webster, Gerald R., and Webster, Roberta Haven.** "Ethnic Bloc Voting in Miami." *Florida Geographer*, 20 (October, 1986), 37–42.

10334 **Webster, Gerald R., and Webster, Roberta Haven.** "Ethnicity and Voting in the Miami-Dade County SMSA." *Urban Geography*, 8, No. 1 (January-February, 1987), 14–30.

10335 **Weiner, P.H.** "Boundary Changes and the Power of the Vote." *University of Detroit Journal of Urban Law*, 54, Symposium Issue (1977), 959–1023.

10336 **Welch, W.P.** "The Effectiveness of Expenditures in State Legislative Races." *American Politics Quarterly*, 4, No. 3 (July, 1976), 333–356.

10337 **Wells, D.** "Con Affirmative Gerrymandering." *Policy Studies Journal*, 9, No. 6, Special Issue No. 3 (Spring, 1980-1981), 863–874.

10338 **Whitehead, Laurence.** "Miners as Voters: The Electoral Process in Bolivia's Mining Camps." *Journal of Latin American Studies*, 13, Part 2 (November, 1981), 313-346.

10339 **Wildgen, J.K., and Engstrom, Richard L.** "Spatial Distribution of Partisan Support and the Seats/Votes Relationship." *Legislative Studies Quarterly*, 5, No. 3 (August, 1980), 423-435.

10340 **Will, W. Marvin.** "From Authoritarianism to Political Democracy in Grenada: Questions for U.S. Policy." *Studies in Comparative International Development* [New Brunswick], 26, No. 3 (Fall, 1991), 29-57.

10341 **Williams, J.C.** "Economics and Politics: Voting Behavior in Kansas During the Populist Decade." *Explorations in Economic History*, 18, No. 3 (July, 1981), 233-256.

10342 **Williams, Rt. Hon. Eric.** "Proportional Representation in Trinidad and Tobago." *Round Table*, 250, No. 2 (April, 1973), 233-245.

10343 **Wilson, R. Jeremy.** "Geography, Politics, and Culture: Electoral Insularity in British Columbia." *Canadian Journal of Political Science*, 13, No. 4 (December, 1980), 751-774.

10344 **Wineberry, John J.** "Formation of the West Virginia-Virginia Boundary." *Southeastern Geographer*, 17, No. 1 (November, 1977), 108-124.

10345 **Winearls, Joan.** "Federal Electoral Maps of Canada, 1867-1970." *Canadian Cartographer*, 9, No. 1 (June, 1972), 1-24.

10346 **Wright, John K.** "Voting Habits of the United States." *Geographical Review*, 22, No. 4 (October, 1932), 666-672.

10347 **Young, H.P.** "The Allocation of Funds in Lobbying and Campaigning." *Behavioral Science*, 23, No. 1 (January, 1978), 21-31.

10348 **Zagorski, Paul W.** "Civil-Military Relations and Argentine Democracy: The Armed Forces Under the Menem Government." *Armed Forces & Society* [New Brunswick], 20, No. 3 (Spring, 1994), 423-437.

ASIA

Books

10349 **Abe, Marion K.** *An Analysis of the Relative Effects of District Characteristics on Voting in India.* New York City: Columbia University, Ph.D., 1976.

10350 **Ahmad, Muzaffar.** *The Communist Party of India and Its Formation Abroad.* Calcutta: National Book Agency, 1962.

10351 **Ahn, Byong Man.** *Congressional Elections in Korea, 1954-1971: An Analysis of Crucial and Normal Elections.* Gainesville: University of Florida, Ph.D., 1974.

10352 **Ahn, Kenneth Kunil.** *Mobilization and Participation in Elections: A Study of Korean Voting Behavior.* Athens: University of Georgia, Ph.D., 1975.

10353 **Ando, Hirofumi.** *Elections in the Philippines: Mass-Elite Interaction through the Electoral Process, 1946-1969.* Ann Arbor: University of Michigan, Ph.D., 1971.

10354 **Avishai, Bernard.** *A New Israel: Democracy in Crisis.* New York: Ticknor & Fields. 1990.

10355 **Azini, Fakhreddin.** *Iran: The Crisis of Democracy.* New York: St. Martin's Press, 1989.

10356 **Barnett, M.R.,** ed. *Electoral Politics in the Indian States.* Delhi: Manohar Publishers, 1975.

10357 **Baxter, Craig.** *The Jana Sangh: A Biography of an Indian Political Party.* Philadelphia: University of Pennsylvania, Ph.D., 1967.

10358 **Begam, N.** *Political Parties and the Labour Movement in India in the 1920's.* London, England: University of London, School of Oriental and African Studies, Master's Thesis, 1966.

10359 **Bhagat, K.P.** *The Kerala Mid-Term Election of 1960; The Communist Party Conquest of New Positions.* Bombay: Popular Book Depot, 1962.

10360 **Brass, Paul.** *Functional Politics in an Indian State: The Congress Party in Uttar Pradesh.* Berkeley: University of California Press, 1965.

10361 **Burstein, Paul.** *Social Structure and Politics in Isreal: Voting in the 1969 Israeli Election.* Cambridge, Massachusetts: Harvard University, Ph.D., 1974.

10362 **Chalothorn, Supannee.** *Greater Bangkok: An Analysis in Electoral Geography, 1957-1976.* Milwaukee: University of Wisconsin, Ph.D., 1982.

10363 **Chandidas, R.,** and Others, eds. *India Votes: A Source Book on Indian Elections.* New York: Humanities Press, 1967.

10364 **Choe, Sunki.** *Urbanization and Voting Participation in Korea (1963-1978): An Urban-Rural Comparison.* Morgantown: Morgantown: West Virginia University, Ph.D., 1983.

10365 **Curry, James Allan.** *The Determinants of Philippine Political Competition in Presidential and Off-Year Elections, 1946-1971.* Lawrence: University of Kansas, Ph.D., 1974.

10366 **Davey, Hampton Thomason, Jr.** *The Transformation of an Ideological Movement into an Aggressive Party: A Case Study of Bharatiya Jana Sangh.* Los Angeles: University of California, Ph.D., 1969.

10367 **Dikshit, S.K.** *Electoral Geography of India.* Varanasi: VIshwavidhalaya Prakashau, 1993.

10368 **Duley, Margot Iris.** *The Parliamentary Supporters of the Indian National Congress, 1866-1909.* Durham, North Caroline: Duke University, Master's Thesis, 1968.

10369 **Elliott, Carolyn Margaret.** *Participation in an Expanding Polity: A Study of Andhra Pradesh, India.* Cambridge, Massachusetts: Harvard University, Ph.D., 1968.

10370 **Fisher, Margaret W.,** and **Bondurant, Joan V.** *The Indian Experience with Democratic Elections.* Berkeley: University of California Press, 1956.

10371 **Gibney, Frank.** *Korea's Quiet Revolution: From Garrison State to Democracy.* New York: Walker and Company, 1992.

10372 **Gould, Harold A.,** and **Ganguly, Sumit,** eds. *India Votes: Alliance Politics and Minority Governments in the Ninth and Tenth General Elections.* Boulder: Westview Press, 1993.

10373 **Grover, Verinder,** ed. *Party System and Political Parties in India (Political System in India-5).* New Delhi: Deep & Deep, 1990.

10374 **Grover, Verinder,** ed. *Politics of Influence, Violence and Presser Groups (Political System in India-8),* New Delhi: Deep & Deep, 1990.

10375 **Hahn, Joon-Woo.** *The Development of Electoral Politics in Japan: A Study of General Elections, 1890-1976.* Cincinnati, Ohio: University of Cincinnati, Ph.D., 1978.

10376 **Hartman, H.** *Political Parties in India.* New Delhi: Meenakshi Prakashan, 1980.

10377 **Hartman, H.** *Die Struktur des Indischen Parteiensystems.* Koln: Koln Universitat, Dissertationssiche, 1962.

10378 **Haynes, Rodney.** *Political Participation by Ethnic Minorities in East Asia, 1950-1970.* Vancouver, British Columbia, Canada: University of British Columbia, Master's Thesis, 1976.

10379 **Held, Colbert Colgate.** *Middle East Patterns: Places, Peoples and Politics.* Boulder, Colorado: Westview Press, 1989.

10380 **Hepre, Metin,** and **Landau, Jacob M.,** eds. *Political Parties and Democracy in Turkey.* London: I. B. Tauris & Co., Ltd., 1991.

10381 **Higa, Mikio.** *Politics and Parties in Postwar Okinawa.* Vancouver: University of British Columbia, Publications Centre, 1963.

10382 **Houghton, Nigel.** *An Electoral Geographic Analysis of Areas of Competition of Indian Political Parties.* Minneapolis: University of Minnesota, M.A., 1968.

10383 **Hrebener, Ronald.** *The Japanese Party System: From One-Party Rule to Coalition Government.* Boulder, Colorado: Westview Press, 1986.

10384 **India (Republic).** Election Commission. *Bye-election Brochure: House of the Peoples and Legislative Assemblies (31-3-1967 to 31-12-1969), Council of States and Legislative Councils (1-3-1964 to 31-12-1968): An Analysis.* New Delhi: Publication Division, Government of India Press, 1971.

10385 **India (Republic).** Election Commissioner. *Delimitation of Parliamentary and Assembly Constituencies Order, 1966.* New Delhi: Publication Division, Government of India Press, 1967.

10386 **India (Republic).** Election Commissioner. *Fourth General Elections: An Analysis.* New Delhi: Publication Division, Government of India Press, 1967.

10387 **India (Republic).** Election Commissioner. *Report on the First General Elections in India, 1951–52.* 2 Vols. New Delhi: Publication Division, Government of India Press, 1955.

10388 **India (Republic).** Election Commissioner. *Report on the Fourth General Elections in India, 1967.* 2 Vols. New Delhi: Publication Division, Government of India Press, 1968.

10389 **India (Republic).** Election Commissioner. *Report on the Midterm General Elections in India, 1968–69.* 2 Vols. New Delhi: Publication Division, Government of India Press, 1970

10390 **India (Republic).** Election Commissioner. *Report on the Second General Elections in India, 1962.* 2 Vols. New Delhi: Publication Division, Government of India Press, 1959.

10391 **India (Republic).** Election Commissioner. *Report on the Third General Elections in India.* 2 Vols. New Delhi: Publication Division, Government of India Press, 1963. Vol. 2, 1966.

10392 **India (Republic).** Ministry of Home Affairs. *Report of the Committee on Defections.* New Delhi: Publication Division, Government of India Press, 1969.

10393 **India (Republic).** Ministry of Scientific Research and Cultural Affairs. *India; Parliamentary Constituencies* by S.P. Chaterjee. New Delhi: Publication Division, Government of India Press, 1962.

10394 **Ishida, Takeshi, and Krauss, Ellis S.,** eds. *Democracy in Japan.* Pittsburgh, Pennsylvania: University of Pittsburgh Press, 1989.

10395 **Islamic Republic of Pakistan.** Department of Films and Publications. *General Elections in Pakistan: An Outline.* Karachi: Pakistan Government Printing Press, 1970.

10396 **Islamic Republic of Pakistan.** Election Commission. *Pakistan General Elections, 1962.* Karachi: Pakistan Government Printing Press, 1963.

10397 **Islamic Republic of Pakistan.** Election Commission. *Presidential Election Results, 1965.* Rawalpini: Pakistan Government Printing Press, 1965.

10398 **Islamic Republic of Pakistan.** Election Commission. *Report on General Elections in Pakistan, 1964-1965.* Rawalpindi: Pakistan Government Printing Press, 1967.

10399 **Jayanntha, Dilesh.** *Electoral Allegiance in Sri Lanka.* Cambridge: Cambridge University Press, 1992.

10400 **Jeans, Roger B.,** eds. *Roads Not Taken: The Struggle of Opposition Parties in Twentieth-Century China.* Boulder: Westview Press, 1992.

10401 **Jhangiani, Motilal A.** *Jana Sangh and Swatantra: A Profile of the Rightist Parties in India.* Bombay: Mankatalas, 1967.

10402 **Kashyap, Subhash C.** *The Politics of Defection; A Study of State Politics in India.* Delhi: National Publishing House for the Institute of Constitutional and Parliamentary Studies, 1969.

10403 **Kaur, Jitinder.** *Punjab Crisis: The Political Perceptions of Rural Voters.* New Delhi: Ajanta, 1989.

10404 **Kies, Naomi Eleanor.** *Constituency Support and the Israeli Party System: An Analysis of Elections in Jerusalem, 1959-1965.* Cambridge: Massachusetts Institute of Technology, Ph.D., 1970.

10405 **Kothari, Rajni,** ed. *Party System and Election Studies.* New Delhi: Allied Publishers, 1967.

10406 **Kumar, K.N.** *Political Parties in India: Their Ideology and Organisation.* New Delhi: Mittal, 1990.

10407 **Lehman-Wilzig, Sam N.** *Wildfire: Grassroots Revolts in Israel in the Post-Socialist Era.* Albany: State University of New York Press, 1992.

10408 **MacDonald, Donald Stone.** *Korea and the Ballot: The International Dimension in Korean Political Development as Seen in Elections.* Washington, D.C.: George Washington University, Ph.D., 1978.

10409 **Medding, Peter Y.** *The Founding of Israeli Democracy, 1948-1967.* New York: Oxford University Press, 1990.

10410 **Misquitta, L.P.** *Pressure groups and Democracy in India.* New Delhi: Sterling Publishers Private Limited, 1991.

10411 **Misra, B.B.** *The Congress Party and Government: Policy and Performance.* New Delhi: Concept Publishers, 1988.

10412 **Misra, Surya Narayan.** *Party Politics and Electoral Choice in an Indian State, Orissa.* Delhi: Ajanta, 1989.

10413 **Moody, Peter R., Jr.** *Political Change on Taiwan: A Study of Ruling Party Adaptability.* New York: Praeger, 1992.

10414 **Mozier, Jeanne M.** *Kerla and the Communist Party: Election Analysis.* New York City: Columbia University, Master's Thesis, 1968.

10415 **Nair, M.B.** *Politics of Bangladesh (A Study of Awami League: 1949-1958).* New Delhi: NBC, 1990.

10416 **Nuna, Sheel C.** *Spatial Fragmentation of Political Behavior in India: A Geographical Perspective on Parliamentary Elections.* New Delhi: Concept Publishers, 1988.

10417 *The October 1990 Elections in Pakistan.* London: National Democratic Institute for International Affairs, 1991.

10418 **Palmer, Norman D.** *Elections and Political Development: The South Asian Experience.* Durham, North Carolina: Duke University Press, 1975.

10419 **Pandey, Sumana.** *Women in Politics.* Jaipur: Rawat, 1990.

10420 **Pattabhiram, M.,** ed. *General Election in India, 1967.* Bombay: Allied Publishers, 1967.

10421 **Peiris, H.A.** *Political Parties in Sri Lanka Sinu Independence: A Bibliography.* New Delhi: Navrang, 1988.

10422 **Popkin, S.L.,** ed. *1962 General Elections in India.* New Delhi: Allied Publishers, 1962.

10423 **Popkin, S.L.,** ed. *National Politics and 1957 Elections in India.* Delhi: Metropolitan, 1957.

10424 **Poullada, Leon B.** *Contemporary Political Parties in the Punjab.* Philadelphia: University of Pennsylvania, M.A., 1954.

10425 **Sadasivan, S.N.** *Party and Democracy in India.* New Delhi: Tata McGraw-Hill, 1977.

10426 **Saxena, P.K.** *The Scheduled Caste Voter.* New Delhi: Radha, 1990.

10427 **Sen Gupta, Prasanta.** *The Congress Party in West Bengal: A Study of Factionalism.* Calcutta: Minerva, 1988.

10428 **Shukla, B.D.** *A History of the Indian Liberal Party.* Allahabad: Indian Press, 1960.

10429 **Singh, H.K.** *The Rise and Growth of the Praja Socialist Party of India.* Oxford: St. Anthony's College, University of Oxford, Bachelor's Thesis, 1958.

10430 **Singh, Ravindra Pratap.** *Electoral Politics in Manipur (India): A Spatio-temporal Study.* New Delhi: Concept Publishing, 1981.

10431 **Singh, S.** *Nihal: Countdown to Elections.* New Delhi: Allied, 1989.

10432 **Sinha, R.P.** *Indian Democracy and Opposition Parties.* New Delhi: Classical, 1989.

10433 **Sirsikar, V.M.** *Political Behavior in India; A Case Study of the 1962 General Elections.* Bombay: Manaktalas, 1965.

10434 **Sisson, John Richard.** *The Congress Party System in Rajasthan: Political Institutionalization in a Traditional Society.* Berkeley: University of California, Ph.D., 1967.

10435 **Steinbach, Udo.** "Turkei: der lange weg zur Demokratic." *Geographisehe Rundschau,* Jahr 4, Heft 4 (April, 1989), 202-205.

10436 **Smith, Charles B., Jr.** *The Burmese Communist Party in the 1980's.* Brookfield, Vermont: Gower Publishing, 1985.

10437 **Suwannarat, Gary S. Merritt.** *A Quantitative Analysis of Socio-Economic Distributional, and Political Effects on Voting Turnout in Thailand, 1976-1979.* DeKalb: Northern Illinois University, Ph.D., 1983.

10438 **Tetsuya, Kataoka,** ed. *Creating Single-Party Democracy: Japan's Postwar Political System.* Stanford: Hoover Institution Press, 1992.

10439 **Wang, John Kuo-Chang.** *United Nations Voting on Chinese Representation: An Analysis of General Assembly Roll-Calls, 1950-1971.* Norman: University of Oklahoma, Ph.D., 1977.

10440 **Weerawardana, I.D.S.** *Ceylon General Elections, 1956.* Colombo: M.D. Gunasena, 1960.

10441 **Weiner, Myron.** *Party Politics in India. The Development of a Multi-Party System.* Princeton, New Jersey: Princeton University Press, 1957.

10442 **Weiner, Myron,** and **Kothari, Rajni,** eds. *Indian Voting Behaviour: Studies of the 1962 General Elections.* Calcutta: Firma K.L. Mukhopadhayay, 1965.

10443 **Weisberg, Walter Leonard.** *Coalition Politics in the Indian States: the Case Study of the Fourth General Elections (1967) in Bihar, Tamilnadu, and West Bengal.* Austin: University of Texas, Ph.D., 1972.

10444 **Yanagihashi, Minoru.** *Electoral Politics in Contemporary Japan: Candidates in Different Levels and Types of Elections in Hyogo Prefecture.* Ann Arbor: University of Michigan, Ph.D., 1975.

10445 **Yishai, Yael.** *Land of Paradoxes: Interests Politics in Israel.* Albany: State University of New York Press, 1991.

10446 **Youn, Jung-Suk.** *Recruitment of Political Leadership in Postwar Japan, 1958-1972: An Empirical Study of the Impact of the Political Environment on the Selection of Party Candidates in General Elections.* Ann Arbor: University of Michigan, Ph.D., 1977.

10447 **Zohar, D.M.** *Political Parties in Isreal: The Evolution of Israeli Democracy.* New York: Praeger, 1974.

Journals

10448 **Ahmad, Bashiruddin.** "Caste and Electoral Politics." *Asian Survey,* 10, No. 11 (November, 1970), 979-992.

10449 **Ahmad, Hamid-Ud-Din.** "Election Data Analysis as a Tool of Research in Political Geography." *Pakistan Geographical Review,* 20, No. 2 (July, 1966), 160-161.

10450 **Allen, Philip M.** "Self-Determination in the Western Indian Ocean." *International Conciliation,* 560 (November, 1966), 1–74.

10451 **Al-Muhahid, Sharif.** "The Assembly Elections in Pakistan." *Asian Survey,* 5, No. 11 (November, 1965), 538-552.

10452 **Al-Muhahid, Sharif.** "Pakistan's First Presidential Elections." *Asian Survey,* 5, No. 6 (July, 1965), 280-294.

10453 **Amani, K.Z.** "Elections in Haryana (India)--A Study in Electoral Geography." *Geographer,* 17 (January, 1970), 27-40.

10454 **Amani, K.Z.** "Electoral Geography and Indian Elections." *Geographical Review of India,* 35, No. 4 (December, 1973), 353-363.

10455 **Amani, K.Z.** "Voting Patterns in Indian Elections: Uttar Pradesh, A Case Study." *Geographical Review of India,* 34, No. 2 (June, 1972), 123-133.

10456 **Andersen, Walter K.** "Election 1989 in India: The Dawn of Coalition Politics?" *Asian Survey* [Berkeley], 30, No. 6 (June, 1990), 527-540.

10457 **Andersen, Walter K.** "India's 1991 Election: The Uncertain Verdict." *Asian Survey* [Berkeley], 31, No. 10 (October, 1991), 976-989.

10458 **Aquino, Belinda A.** "Democracy in the Philippines." *Current History,* 88, No. 537 (April, 1989), 181-184.

10459 **Arian, Asher; Shamir, Michal; and Ventura, Raphael.** "Public Opinion and Political Change; Israel and the Intifada." *Comparative Politics,* 24, No. 3 (April, 1992), 317-334.

10460 **Baerwald, Hans H.** "Japan's House of Councillors Election." *Asian Survey,* 29, No. 9 (September, 1989), 833-841.

10461 **Baerwald, Hans H.** "Japan's 39th House of Representatives Election." *Asian Survey* [Berkeley], 30, No. 6 (June, 1990), 541-559.

10462 **Bawa, Noorjahan.** "The Elections in Madras." *Indian Political Science Review, Special Issue: Indian Elections, 1967,* 1, Nos. 3 and 4 (April-October, 1967), 204-224.

10463 **Baxter, Craig, and Rahman, Syedur.** "Bangladesh Votes--1991: Building Democratic Institutions." *Asian Survey* [Berkeley], 31, No. 8 (August, 1991), 683-693.

10464 **Billet, Bret L.** "South Korea at the Crossroads: An Evolving Democracy or Authoritarianism Revisited?" *Middle Eastern Studies,* 26, No. 2 (April, 1990), 300-311.

10465 **Bosco, Joseph.** "Taiwan Factions: Guanxi, Patronage, and the State in Local Politics." *Ethnology* [Pittsburgh], 31, No. 2 (April, 1992), 157-183.

10466 **Brady, David, and Mo, Jongryn.** "Electoral Systems and Institutional Choice: A Case Study of the 1988 Korean Elections." *Comparative Political Studies,* 24, No. 4 (January, 1992), 405-429.

10467 **Brass, Paul.** "Ethnic Cleavages in the Punjabi Party System, 1957-1972." In *Electoral Politics in the Indian States,* M.R. Barnett, ed. Delhi: Manohar, 1975, 107-127.

10468 **Brown, Nathan.** "Peasants and Notables in Egyptian Politics." *Middle Eastern Studies,* 26, No. 2 (April, 1990), 145-160.

10469 **Chai, Trong R.** "The Communist Party of China: The Process of Institutionalization." *Asian Survey* (London), 11 (Old Series 67), Part 1 (February, 1980), 43-54.

10470 **Cheng, Joseph Y.S.** "The Democracy Movement in Hong Kong." *International Affairs,* 65, No. 3 (Summer, 1989), 443-462.

10471 **Cheng, Peter P.** "Japanese Interest Group Politics: An Institutional Framework." *Asian Survey,* 30, No. 3 (March, 1990), 251-265.

10472 **Chhibber, Pradeep K.; Misra, Subhash; and Sisson, Richard.** "Order and the Indian Electorate: For Whom Does the Shiva Dance?" *Asian Survey* [Berkeley], 32, No. 7 (July, 1992), 606-616.

10473 **Christensen, Raymond V.** "Electoral Reform in Japan: How It Was Enacted and Changes It May Bring." *Asian Survey* [Berkeley], 34, No. 7 (July, 1994), 589-605.

10474 **Dikshit, R.D., and Sharma, J.C.** "The 1980 Assembly Elections in Punjab: An Enquiry into Bases of Political Party Support. *Annab, National Association of Geographers, India,* 2, No. 1 (June-December, 1982), 36-48.

10475 **Dikshit, R.D., and Sharma, J.C.** "Electoral Performance of the Congress Party in Punjab (1952-1977): An Ecological Analysis." *Transactions, Institute of Indian Geographers,* 4 (1982), 1-15.

10476 **Dikshit, R.D., and Sharma, J.C.** "A Solution to the Unit of Analysis Problem in the Electoral Geography of India." *National Geographical Journal of India,* 27, Parts 1 and 2 (March-June, 1981), 14-20.

10477 **Dikshit, R.D., and Sharma, J.C.** "Trends and Patterns in Voter Turnout in Punjab (1967-1980): An Ecological Analysis."" *National Geographic Journal of India,* 29, Parts 1 and 2 (March-June, 1983), 18-29.

10478 **Dikshit, S.K.** "Patterns of Party Performance in Haryana 1982 Vidhan Sabha Elections." *National Geographer,*22, No. 1 (June, 1988), 75-83.

10479 **Dikshit, S.K.** "Regional Variation in Electoral Participation of Malwa." *Geographical Review of India,* 54, No. 3 (September, 1992), 22-287.

10480 **Dikshit, S.K.** "Spatial Analysis of Electoral Participation in Haryana." *Geographical Review of India,* 50, No. 2 (June, 1988), 1-7.

10481 **Dikshit, S.K., and Giri, H.H.** "A Review of Research in Electoral Geography." *Geographical Review of India,* 47, No. 4 (June, 1985), 13-21.

10482 **Domes, Jurgen.** "Taiwan in 1991: Searching for Political Consensus." *Asian Survye* [Berkeley], 32, No. 1 (January, 1992), 42-49.

10483 **Donnelly, Michael W.** "No Great Reversal in Japan: Elections for the House of Representatives in 1990." *Pacific Affairs* [Vancouver], 63, No. 3 (Fall, 1990), 303-320.

10484 **Dreyer, June Teufel.** "Taiwan in 1989: Democratization and Economic Growth." *Asian Survey,* 30, No. 1 (January, 1990), 52-58.

10485 **Fickett, Lewis P., Jr.** "The Major Socialist Parties of India in the 1967 Election." *Asian Survey,* 8, No. 6 (June, 1968), 489-498.

10486 **Freedman, Robert O.** "Religion, Politics, and the Israeli Elections of 1988." *Middle East Journal,* 43, No. 3 (Summer, 1989), 406-422.

10487 **Fretty, Ralph E.** "Ceylon: Election--Oriented Politics." *Asian Survey,* , No. 2 (February, 1969), 99-103.

10488 **Gaige, Fred, and Scholz, John.** "The 1991 Parliamentary Elections in Nepal: Political Freedom and Stability." *Asian Survey* [Berkeley], 31, No. 11 (November, 1991), 1040-1060.

10489 **Ghabra, Shafeeq.** "Kuwait: Elections and Issues of Democratization in a Middle Eastern State." *Digestof Middle East Studies* [Milwaukee], 2, No. 1 (Winter, 1993), 1-27.

10490 **Giri, H.H., and Dikshit, S.K.** "Changing Spatial Pattern of the Parliamentary Constituencies in India from 1951-1976." *Geoglraphical Review of India,* 45, No. 2 (June, 1983), 83-95.

10491 **Gordon, Joel.** "Political Opposition in Egypt." *Current History,* 89, No. 544 (February, 1990), 65-68.

10492 **Gray, Hugh.** "The 1962 General Election in a Rural District of Andhra." *Asian Survey,* 2, No. 2 (September, 1962), 25-35.

10493 **Hadar, Leon T.** "The 1992 Electoral Earthquake and the Fall of the 'Second Israeli Republic.'" *The Middle East Journal* [Bloomington], 46, No. 4 (Autumn, 1992), 594-616.

10494 **Hale, William.** "The Role of the Electoral System in Turkish Politics." *International Journal of Middle East Studies,* 11, No. 3 (May, 1980), 401-417.

10495 **Hall, Andrew.** "India After the Elections." *Asian Affairs* [London], 21, Part 3 (October, 1990), 312-323.

10496 **Harik, Iliya.** "Voting Participation and Political Integration in Lebanon 1943-1974." *Middle Eastern Studies,* 16, No. 1 (January, 1980), 27-48.

10497 **Hauser, Walter.** "Violence, Agrarian Radicalism and Electoral Politics: Reflections on the Indian People's Front." *The Journal of Peasant Studies* [London], 21, No. 1 (October, 1993), 85-126.

10498 **Hazama, Yasushi.** "The Politics of Amendment in the Turkish Legislature." *The Developing Economies* [Tokyo], 30, No. 3 (September, 1992), 284-298.

10499 **Heginbotham, Stanley J.** "The 1971 Revolution in Indian Voting Behavior." *Asian Survey*, 11, No. 12 (December, 1971), 1133-1152.

10500 **Huxley, Tim.** "Singapore's Politics in the 1980s and 90s." *Asian Affairs* [London], 23, Part 3 (October, 1992), 282-294.

10501 **Indorf, Hans M.** "Malaysia at the Polls." *Current History*, 75, No. 442 (December, 1978), 217-220 and 229.

10502 **Ishibashi, Michihiro, and Reed, Steven R.** "Second-Generation Diet Members and Democracy in Japan: Hereditary Seats." *Asian Survey* [Berkeley], 32, No. 4 (April, 1992), 366-379.

10503 **Izmirlian, Harry, Jr.** "Dynamics of Political Support in a Punjab Village." *Asian Survey*, 6, No. 3 (March, 1966), 125-133.

10504 **Jennings, W. Ivor, Sir.** "The Ceylon General Election in 1947." *University of Ceylon Review*, 6, No. 3 (July, 1948), 133-195.

10505 **Johnston, Scott D.** "Reflections on Israeli Electoral Politics." *International Social Science Review*, 57, No. 1 (Winter, 1982), 3-12.

10506 **Joseph, Ralph.** "Pakistan's First General Elections." *Eastern World*, 19, No. 2 (February, 1965), 9-10.

10507 **Juanico, Meliton B.** "Problematical Scenarios on the Mindanao Autonomy Plebiscite." *Philippine Geographical Journal*, 33, No. 3 (July-September, 1989), 97-102.

10508 **Kalaycioglu, Ersin.** "Elections and Party Preferences in Turkey: Changes and Continuities in the 1990s." *Comparative Political Studies*, 27, No. 3 (October, 1994), 402-424.

10509 **Kalita, B.C., and Das, M.M.** "Voting Patterns in Assam: A Study in Political Geography." *Journal of North East India Geographical Society*, 11, Nos. 1 and 2 (1979), 58-69.

10510 **Kashyap, Subhash C.** "The Politics of Defection: An Enquiry into the Changing Contours of the Political Power Structure in State Politics in India." *Asian Survey*, 10, No. 3 (March, 1970), 195-208.

10511 **Kihl, Young Whan.** "South Korea in 1989: Slow Progress Toward Democracy." *Asian Survey*, 30, No. 1 (January, 1990), 67-73.

10512 **Kim, Hong Nack.** "The 1988 Parliamentary Elections in South Korea." *Asian Survey*, 29, No. 5 (May, 1989), 480-485.

10513 **King, Dwight Y., and Rasjid, M. Ryaas.** "The GOLDKAR Landslide in the 1987 Indonesian Elections; The Case of Aceh." *Asian Survey*, 28, No. 9 (September, 1988), 916-925.

10514 **Kohli, Atul.** "The NTR Phenomenon in Andhra Pradesh." *Asian Survey*, 28, No. 10 (October, 1988), 991-1017.

10515 **Kothari, Rajni.** "India: The Congress System on Trial." *Asian Survey*, No. 2 (February, 1967), 83-86.

10516 **Lipovsky, Igor.** "The Legal Socialist Parties of Turkey, 1960-80." *Middle Eastern Studies* [London], 27, No. 1 (January, 1991), 94-111.

10517 **Long, Simon.** "Taiwan's National Assembly Elections." *The China Quarterly* [London], No. 129 (March, 1992), 216-228.

10518 **Madsen, Douglas.** "Solid Congress Support in 1967: A Statistical Inquiry." *Asian Survey*, 10, No. 11 (November, 1970), 1004-1014.

10519 **Malik, Yogendra K., and Singh, V.B.** "Bharatiya Janata Party: An Alternative to the Congress(I)? *Asian Survey* [Berkeley], 32, No. 4 (April, 1992), 318-336.

10520 **Maniruzzaman, Talukdar.** "The Fall of the Military Dictator: 1991 Elections and the Prospect of Civilian Rule in Bangladesh." *Pacific Affairs* [Vancouver], 65, No. 2 (Summer, 1992), 203-224.

10521 **Manor, James.** "How and Why Liberal and Representative Politics Emerged in India." *Political Studies*, 38, No. 1 (March, 1990), 20-38.

10522 **Marcus, Jonathan.** "Israel's General Election: Realignment or Upheaval?" *International Affairs* [Cambridge], 68, No. 4 (October, 1992), 693-705.

10523 **Mayer, Adrian C.** "Rural Leaders and the Indian General Election." *Asian Survey*, 1, No. 8 (October, 1960), 23-29.

10524 **McGee, T.G.** "The Malayan Elections of 1959: A Study in Electoral Geography." *Journal of Tropical Geography*, 16, No. 2 (October, 1962), 70-99.

10525 **McGee, T.G.** "The Malayan Parliamentary Elections 1964." *Pacific Viewpoint*, 6, No. 1 (May, 1965), 96-101.

10526 **Mehta, Swarnjit.** "A Framework for the Study of District Boundaries." *Indian Geographical Journal*, 58, No. 1 (June, 1983), 74-76.

10527 **Mehta, Swarnjit.** "Voting Behavior of Tribals of Himachal Pradesh." *Deccan Geographer,* 19 and 20, Nos. 3 and 1 (October, 1982-June, 1983), 294.

10528 **Mir, Ali Mohammed,** and **Husainn, Majid.** "The Assembly Election in Jammu and Kashmir: A Study in Spatial Structure of Voting Behaviour in 1983." *National Geographical Journal of India,* 30, Part 1 (March, 1984), 53-62.

10529 **Morris-Jones, W.H.** "India Elects for Change and Stability." *Asian Survey,* 11, No. 8 (August, 1971), 719-741.

10530 **Morris-Jones, W.H.,** and **Das Gupta, B.** "India's Political Areas: Interim Report on an Ecological Electoral Investigation." *Asian Survey,* 9, No. 6 (June, 1969), 399-424.

10531 **Murashimi, Eiji.** "Local Elections and Leadership in Thailand: A Case Study of Nakhon Sawan Province." *Developing Economies,* 25, No. 4 (December, 1987), 363-385.

10532 **Naamani, Israel.** "The Kurdish Drive for Self-determination." *Middle East Journal,* 20, No. 3 (Summer, 1966), 279-295.

10533 **Narain, Iqbal,** and **Sharma, Mohan Lal.** "Election Politics in India: Notes Towards an Empirical Theory." *Asian Survey,* 9, No. 3 (March, 1969), 202-220.

10534 **Narain, Iqbal,** and **Sharma, Mohan Lal.** "The Fifth State Assembly Elections in India." *Asian Survey,* 13, No. 3 (March, 1973), 318-335.

10535 **Nathan, S.K.S.** "The DMK and the Politics of Tamilnad." *Economic and Political Weekly,* 2, No. 48 (December 9, 1967), 2133-2140.

10536 **Ockey, James.** "Political Parties, Factions, and Corruption in Thailand." *Modern Asian Studies* [Cambridge], 28, Part 2 (May, 1994), 251-277.

10537 **Osman, Sabihah.** "Sabah State Elections: Implications for Malaysian Unity." *Asian Survey* [Berkeley], 32, No. 4 (April, 1992), 380-391.

10538 **Ozbudun, Ergun.** "The Turkish Party System: Institutionalization, Polarization, and Fragmentation." *Middle Eastern Studies,* 17, No. 2 (April, 1981), 228-240.

10539 **Pal, Subimal.** "The Leftist Alliance in West Bengal." *Indian Political Science Review, Special Issue: Indian Elections, 1967,* 1, Nos. 3 and 4 (April-October, 1967), 169-190.

10540 **Palmer, Norman D.** "India's Fourth General Elections." *Asian Survey,* 7, No. 5 (May, 1967), 275-291.

10541 **Park, Chan Wook.** Legislators and Their Consttituents in South Korea: The Patterns of District Representation." *Asian Survey,* 28, No. 10 (October, 1988), 1049-1065.

10542 **Parker, Barbara.** "Beyond the Vote: Responses to Centralization Among Nepal's Marpha Thakali." *Human Organization* [Oklahoma City], 50, No. 4 (Winter, 1991), 349-357.

10543 **Patterson, Dennis.** "Electoral Influence and Economic Policy: Political Origins of Financial Aid to Small Business in Japan." *Comparative Political Studies,* 27, No. 3 (October, 1994), 425-447.

10544 **Peretz, Don,** and **Smooha, Sammy.** "Israel's Eleventh Knesset Election." *Middle East Journal,* 39, No. 1 (Winter, 1985), 86-103.

10545 **Peretz, Don,** and **Smooha, Sammy.** "Israel's Tenth Knesset Elections--Ethnic Upsurgence and Decline of Ideology." *Middle East Journal,* 35, No. 4 (Autumn, 1981), 506-526.

10546 **Peretz, Don,** and **Smooha, Sammy.** "Israel's Twelfth Knesset Election: An All-Loser Geme." *Middle East Journal,* 43, No. 3 (Summer, 1989), 388-405.

10547 "Political Parties in Pakistan." *Eastern World,* 6, No. 10 (October, 1952), 12-13.

10548 **Prasad, Nageshwar.** "Oligarachy in Indian Parties at the Local Level." *Asian Survey,* 19, No. 9 (September, 1979), 896-909.

10549 **Quraishi, Zahee Masood.** "Electoral Strategy of a Minority Pressure Group: The Muslim Majlis-E-Mushawarat." *Asian Survey,* 8, No. 12 (December, 1968), 976-987.

10550 **Qureshi, Saleem M.M.** "Party Politics in the Second Republic of Pakistan." *Middle East Journal,* 20, No. 4 (Autumn, 1966), 456-472.

10551 **Ramanathan, Kalimuthu K.** "The Sabah State Elections of April, 1985." *Asian Survey,* 26, No. 7 (July, 1986), 815-837.

10552 **Rashiduzzaman, M.** "The Awami League in the Political Development of Pakistan." *Asian Survey,* 10, No. 7 (July, 1970), 574-587.

10553 **Ray Chaudhury, N.C.B.** "India's Third General Election." *Political Quarterly,* 33, No. 3 (July, 1962), 294-305.

10554 **Rood, Steven.** "Perspectives on the Electoral Behaviour of Baguio City (Philippines) Voters in a Transition Era." *Journal of Southeast Asian Studies* [Singapore], 22, No. 1 (March, 1991), 86-108.

10555 **Roy, Ramashray.** "Dynamics of One-Party Dominance in an Indian State." *Asian Survey*, 8, No. 7 (July, 1968), 553-575.

10556 **Roy, Ramashray.** "Intra-Party Conflict in the Bihar Congress." *Asian Survey*, 6, No. 12 (December, 1966), 706-715.

10557 **Rudolph, Lloyd I.** "Continuities and Change in Electoral Behavior: The 1971 Parliamentary Election in India." *Asian Survey*, 11, No. 12 (December, 1971), 1119-1132.

10558 **Rudolph, Susanne Hoeber.** "The Writ from Delhi: The Indian Government's Capabilities AFter the 1971 Election." *Asian Survey*, 11, No. 10 (October, 1971), 958-969.

10559 **Sayeed, Khalid B.** "1965: An Epoch-Making Year in Pakistan--General Elections and War with India." *Asian Survey*, 6, No. 2 (February, 1966), 76-85.

10560 Self-determination and Settlement of the Arab-israeli Conflict." *American Journal of International Law*, 65, No. 4 (September, 1971), 31-70.

10561 **Senftleban, W.** "Principles and Problems of Delimitation of Electoral Districts." *Geographical Research, Institute of Geography.* Teipeh: National Taiwan Normal University, 3 (1977), 57-104.

10562 **Sharma, K.C.** "The Indian Context and Geographical Study of Voting Behavior." *Indian Geographical Studies Bulletin, Patna,* No. 19 (September, 1982).

10563 **Shin, Doh Chul; Chey, Myung; and Kim, Kwang-Woong.** "Cultural Origins of Public Support for Democracy in Korea: An Empirical Test of the Douglas-Wildavsky Theory of Culture." *Comparative Political Studies,* 22, No. 2 (July, 1989), 217-238.

10564 **Singh, C.P.** "Indian Electoral Geography." *National Association of Geographers, India,* 1, No. 2 (December, 1981), 105-108.

10565 **Singh, Hari, and Narayanan, Suresh.** "Changing Dimensions in Malaysian Politics: The Johore Baru By-Election." *Asian Survey,* 29, No. 5 (May, 1989), 514-529.

10566 **Singh, Mahendra Prasad.** "The Dilemma of the New Indian Party System: To Govern or Not to Govern? *Asian Survey* [Berkeley], 32, No. 4 (April, 1992), 303-317.

10567 **Sirsikar, V.M.** "The Study of Voting Behaviour in India: Limitations and Problems." *Political Science Review*, 2, No. 1 (March, 1963), 54-59.

10568 **Sisson, John. Richard.** "India in 1989: A Year of Elections in a Culture of Change." *Asian Survey,* 30, No. 2 (February, 1990), 111-125.

10569 **Sisson, John. Richard.** "Institutionalization and Style in Rajasthan Politics." *Asian Survey*, 6, No. 11 (November, 1966), 605-613.

10570 **Sisson, John. Richard.** "Peasant Movement and Political Mobilization: The Jats of Rajasthan." *Asian Survey*, 9, No. 12 (December, 1969), 946-963.

10571 **Sisson, John Richard,** and **Vanderbok, William.** "Mapping the Indian Electorate: Trends in Party Support in Seven National Elections." *Asian Survey*, 23, No. 10 (October, 1983), 1140-1158.

10572 **Smith, Thomas B.** "Referendum Politics in Asia." *Asian Survey*, 26, No. 7 (July, 1986), 793-814.

10573 **Sprinzak, Ehud.** "The Emergence of the Israeli Radical Right." *Comparative Politics*, 21, No. 2 (January, 1989), 171-192.

10574 **Takagi, Akihiko.** "The Distribution and Its Change of Voting Returns in the Elections to the House of Councilors in Aichi Prefecture." *Geographical Review of Japan*, 56, No. 6 (June, 1983), 420-439.

10575 **Thaper, Romesh.** "Election Analysis: A Symposium on the Trends Revealed by the Results of the Third General Election." *Seminar*, 34 (June, 1962), 10-55.

10576 "The Third General Election: An Analysis of Results." *United Asia.* 14 (April, 1962), 209-232.

10577 **Upadhyaya, Prakash Chandra.** "The Politics of Indian Secularism." *Modern Asian Studies* [Cambridge], 26, Part 4 (October, 1992), 815-857.

10578 **Waller, Harold M.** "The 1988 Israeli Election: Proportional Representation with a Vengeance." *Middle East Review*, 21, No. 4 (Summer, 1989), 9-17.

10579 **Waseem, Mohammad.** "Pakistan's Lingering Crisis of Dyarchy." *Asian Survey* [Berkeley], 32, No. 7 (July, 1992), 617-634.

10580 **Waterman, Stanley.** "The Dilemma of Electoral Districting for Israel. *Tijdschrift Voor Economische en Sociale Geografie*, 71, Nr. 2 (Jan.-Febr., 1980), 88-97.

10581 **Waterman, Stanley.** "Electoral Reform in Israel: A Geographer's View." *Ben Gurion University of the Negev* (Beer-Sheva, Israel), *Department of Geography, Geographical Research Forum*. No. 3, Occasional Papers, (May, 1981) 16–24.

10582 **Waterman, Stanley.** "The Non-Jewish Vote in Israel in 1992." *Political Geography,* 13, No. 6 (November, 1994), 540-558.

10583 **Waterman, Stanley, and Zefadia, Eliahu.** "Political Geography in Practice II: Israeli Electoral Reforms in Action." *Political Geography* [Oxford], 11, No. 6 (November, 1992), 563-578.

10584 **Weerawardana, I.D.S.** "The General Elections in Ceylon, 1952." *Ceylon Historical Journal*, 2, Nos. 1 and 2 (July-October, 1952), 111-178.

10585 **Weiner, Myron.** "The 1971 Election and the Indian Party System." *Asian Survey*, 11, No. 12 (December, 1971), 1153-1166.

10586 **Weiner, Myron.** "India's Third General Election." *Asian Survey*, 2, No. 5 (May, 1962), 3-19.

10587 **Wiebe, Paul.** "Elections in Peddur: Democracy at Work in an Indian Town." *Human Organization*, 28, No. 2 (Summer, 1969), 140–147.

10588 **Wright, Jr., Theodore P.** "Muslims and the 1977 Indian Elections: A Watershed?" *Asian Survey*, 17, No. 12 (December, 1977), 1207-1220.

10589 **Wurfel, David.** "The Phillippines' Precarious Democracy: Coping with Foreign and Domestic Pressures Under Aquino." *International Journal*, 44, No. 3 (Summer, 1989), 676-697.

10590 **Yiftachel, Oren.** "The Concept of 'Ethnic Democracy' and Its Applicability to the Case of Israel." *Ethnic and Racial Studies* [London], 15, No. 1 (January, 1992), 125-136.

10591 **Zinkin, Maurice.** "The Indian Elections." *Asian Review*, 58 (July, 1962), 141-151.

AUSTRALIA, OCEANIA AND ANTARCTICA

Books and Journals

10592 **Bay, S.K.N.** "Self-Determination and teh Crisis in New Caledonia: The Search for a Legitimate Self." *Asian Survey*, 28 (August, 1988), 863–880.

10593 **Burdess, Neil.** "Variations in Municipal Electorate Size in New South Wales." *Australian Geographer*, 14, No. 5 (May, 1980), 278-285.

10594 **Campbell, I.C.** "The Emergence of Parliamentary Politics in Tonga." *Pacific Studies* [Laie], 15, No. 1 (March, 1992), 77-97.

10595 **Clark, Alan.** "Formal Conflict: On Recent Elections in New Caledonia." *Pacific Studies*, 6, No. 2 (Spring, 1983), 1-10.

10596 **Claspy, Everett M.** *An Atlas of Political Parties in Australia and the United States*, Sydney, Now South Wales: U.S. Office of War Information, 1944.

10597 **Duncan, C.J.** "Ethnicity, Election and Emergency: The 1987 Fiji General Election in the Context of Contemporary Political Geography." *Political Geography Quarterly* [Oxford], 10, No. 3 (July, 1991), 221-239.

10598 **Duncan, C.J., and Epps, W.R.** "The Demise of 'Countrymindedness': New Players or Changing Values in Australian Rural Politics." *Political Geography* [Oxford], 11, No. 5 (September, 1992), 430-448.

10599 **Forrest, James.** "The Geography of Campaign Funding, Campaign Spending and Voting at the New South Wales Legislative Assembly Elections of 1984." *Australian Geographer* [Gladesville], 23, No. 1 (May, 1992), 66-76.

10600 **Forrest, James.** "Social Status, Urbanisation and the Ethnic Dimension of Voting Behavior in Australia." *Ethnic and Racial Studies*, 11, No. 4 (November, 1988), 489-505.

10601 **Gale, Fay.** "The Participation of Australian Aboriginal Women in a Changing Political Environment." *Political Geography Quarterly*, 9, No. 4 (October, 1990), 381-395.

10602 **Gow, Neil.** "The Introduction of Compulsory Voting in the Australian Commonwealth." *Politics*, 6, No. 2 (November, 1971), 201–210.

10603 **Hamilton, B.M.,** ed. *The Firm Hands: The Western Australia State Election of 1977.* Nedlands: Department of Politics, Western Ausstralian University, 1979.

10604 **Hughes, Colin A.** "Changes in Queensland Electoral Boundaries." *Queensland Geographical Journal* [Fortitude Valley], 4th series, 7 (1992), 25-44.

10605 **Jaensch, D., and Loveday, P.,** eds. *Election in the Northern Territory, 1974–1977.* Darwin: ANV., 1979.

10606 **Johnston, R.J.** "Changing Voter Preferences, Uniform Electoral Swing, and the Geography of Voting in New Zealand, 1972-1975." *New Zealand Geographer*, 37, No. 1 (April, 1981), 13-18.

10607 **Johnston, R.J.**, ed. *People, Places and Votes: Essays on the Electoral Geography of Australia and New Zealand.* Armidale, Now South Wales: University of New England, 1977.

10608 **Johnston, R.J.**, and **Forest, J.** "Spatial-Structural Effects and the Geography of Voting in Australia, 1977." *Australian Geographer [North Ryde, Now South Wales]*, 16, No. 4 (November, 1985), 286-290.

10609 **Johnston, R.J.**, and **Honey, Rex.** "Political Geography of Contemporary Events X: The 1987 General Election in New Zealand: The Demise of Electoral Cleavages?" *Political Geography Quarterly*, 7, No. 4 (October, 1988), 363-369.

10610 **Johnston, R.J.**, and **Hughes, Colin A.** "Constituency Delimitation and the Unintentional Gerrymander in Brisbane." *Australian Geographical Studies*, 16, No. 2 (October, 1978), 99-110.

10611 **Kelley, J.**, and **McAllister, I.** "Class and Party in Australia, with British and United States Comparisons." *British Journal of Sociology*, 36 (1985b), 383-420.

10612 **Kemp, D.** *Society and Electoral Behaviour in Australia.* Brisbane: University of Queensland Press, 1978.

10613 **Lal, Brij V.** "Before the Storm: An Analysis of the Fiji General Election of 1987. *Pacific Studies*, 12, No. 1 (November, 1988), 71-96.

10614 **Lawson, Stephanie.** "Constitutional Change in Fiji: The Apparatus of Justification." *Ethnic and Racial Studies* [London], 15, No. 1 (January, 1992), 61-84.

10615 **McAllister, I.** "Compulsory Voting, Turnout and Party Advantage in Australia." *Politics*, 21 (1986), 89-93.

10616 **McAllister, I.** "Social Context, Turnout, and the Vote: Australian and British Comparisons." *Political Geography Quarterly*, 6, No. 1 (January, 1987), 17-30.

10617 **McAllister, I.**, and **Kelley, J.** "Contextual Characteristics of Australian Federal Electorates." *Australia and New Zealand Journal of Sociology*, 19 (1983), 113-135.

10618 **McAllister, Ian**, and **Makkai, Toni.** "Institutions, Society or Protest? Explaining Invalid Votes in Australian Elections." *Electoral Studies*, 12, No. 1 (March, 1993), 23-40.

10619 **McCallum, Wayne.** "European Loyalist and Polynesian Political Dissent in New Caledonia: The Other Challenge to RPCR Orthodoxy." *Pacific Studies* [Laie], 15, No. 3 (September, 1992), 25-58.

10620 **Perry, Peter J.** "Les Causes Geographiques du Partage Politiques des iles Somoa." *Les Cashiers d'Outre-Mer*, 38e, Annee. No. 149 (Janvier-Mars, 1985), 53-63.

10621 **Premdas, Ralph.** "General Rabuka and the Fiji Elections of 1992." *Asian Survey* [Berkeley], 33, No. 10 (October, 1993), 997-1009.

10622 **Reid, G.S.**, ed. *The 1974 Western Australian State Election.* Nedlands: Department of Politics, Western Australian University, 1976.

10623 **Roth, Herbert.** "Distribution of New Zealand Radicalism: 1890-1917." *New Zealand Geographer*, 15, No. 1 (April, 1959), 76-83.

10624 **Rumley, Dennis.** "The Evaluation of Electoral Redistribution: The Case of Western Australia." *Australian Geographical Studies*, 23, No. 1 (April, 1985), 105-114.

10625 **Rumley, Dennis.** "The Geography of Campaigning: the Case of the 1977 WA State Election." In *In Firm Hands: The WA State Election of 1977*, B.M. Hamilton, ed. Nedlands: Department of Politics, University of Western Australia, 1979, 98-104.

10626 **Rumley, Dennis.** "Ideology, Regional Policy and Applied Geography: The Case of the Kimberley, Western Australia." *Australian Journal of Social Issues*, 18, No. 4 (November, 1983), 233-244.

10627 **Rumley, Dennis.** "The 1974 Election in Darwin: A Survey of Three Electorates." In *Election in the Northern Territory 1974-1977*, D. Jaensch and P. Loveday, eds. Darwin: ANV, 1979, 97-111.

10628 **Rumley, Dennis.** "The 1974 WA State Election: A Survey Analysis of Three Electorates in Metropolitan Perth." In *The 1974 WA State Election*, G.S. Reid, ed. Nedlands: Department of Politics, University of Western Australia, 1976, 188-208.

10629 **Rumley, Dennis.** "Social and Political Attitudes." In *Election in the Northern Territory 1974-1977*, D. Jaensch and P. Loveday, eds. Darwin: ANV, 1979, 6-20.

10630 **Rumley, Dennis.** "Some Aspects of the Geography of Political Participation in Western Australia." *Environment and Planning*, A18, No. 6 (June, 1980), 671-684.

10631 **Rumley, Dennis.** "Some Determinants of Voting Behaviour in Metropolitan Perth 1974-1977." In *In Firm Hands: The WA State Election of 1977*, B.M. Hamilton, ed. Nedlands: Department of Politics, UWA, 1979, 136-160.

10632 **Rumley, Dennis**, and **Hirst, M.** "Preliminary Mapping of the State Electoral Results in Metropolitan Perth." In *The 1974 WA State Election*, G.S. Reid, ed. Nedlands: Department of Politics, UWA, 1976, 209-220.

10633 **Ward, Brian J.** "The Use of Electoral Rolls in the Study of Internal Migration." *Australian Geographical Studies*, 13, No. 1 (April, 1975), 94-107.

10634 **Ward, Ian.** "'Media Intrusion' and the Changing Nature of the Established Parties in Australia and Canada." *Canadian Journal of Political Science* [Ottawa], 26, No. 3 (September, 1993), 477-506.

EUROPE

Books

10635 **Allardt, Erik;** and **Littunen, Yrjo**, eds. *Cleavages, Ideologies and Party Systems.* Helsinki: Westermarck Society, 1964.

10636 **Babkina, M.A.,** ed. *New Political Parties and Movements in the Soviet Union.* Commack, NY: Nova Science Publishers, Inc., 1991.

10637 **Benaryoun, C.** *Practiques, Options et Representations in Mileiu Juif Dans la France Contemporaine.* Toulouse: Universite de Toulouse, These 3c Cycle, 1983.

10638 **Bealey, F.; Blondel, J.;** and **McCann, L.** *Constituency Politics: A Study of Newcastle Under Lyme.* London: Faber, 1965.

10639 **Bealey, F.; Blondel, J.; McCann, L.;** and **Pelling, H.** *Labour and Politics 1900-1906: A History of the Labour Representation Committee.* London: Macmillan, 1958.

10640 **Biesinger, Joseph Anton.** *The Presidential Elections in Bavaria in 1925 and 1932 in Relation to the Reich.* New Brunswick: Rutgers University, The State University of New Jersey, Ph.D., 1972.

10641 **Bochel, J.M.,** and **Denver, D.T.** *The Scottish Local Government Elections in 1974.* Edinburgh: Scottish Academic Press, 1975.

10642 **Bochel, J.M.,** and **Denver, D.T.** *The Scottish Regional Elections 1982.* Dundee: University of Dundee, Department of Political Science, 1982.

10643 **Bochel, J.M.; Denver, D.T.;** and **McHardy, B.J.** *The Scottish Regional Elections 1978.* Dundee: University of Dundee, Department of Political Science, 1978.

10644 **Bogdanor, Verona.** *Multi-Party Politics and the Constitution.* Cambridge: Cambridge University Press, 1983.

10645 **Bozoki, Andras; Korosenyi, Andras;** and **Schopflin, George,** eds. *Post-Communist Transition: Emerging Pluralism in Hungary.* London: Pinter Publishers, 1992.

10646 **Brantley, Susan Ann Kay.** *Voting Stability and Party Identification in the United States and West Germany.* Iowa City: University of Iowa, Ph.D., 1974.

10647 **Bristol District Labour Party.** *A Social Strategy for the Labour Party in Bristol.* Bristol: Bristol District Labour Party, 1983.

10648 **Brookshire, Jerry Hardman.** *British Labour Recovering: Labour between the General Elections of 1931 and 1935.* Nashville, Tennessee: Vanderbilt University, Ph.D., 1970.

10649 **Bulpitt, Jim G.** *Party Politics in English Local Government.* London: Longmans, 1967.

10650 **Busteed, M.A.** *Voting Behaviour in the Republic of Ireland: A Geographical Perspective.* Oxford: Clarendon Press, 1990.

10651 **Butler, D.E.** *Coalitions in British Politics.* London: Macmillan, 1978.

10652 **Butler, D.E.** *The British Electoral System Since 1918.* Oxford: Clarendon Press, 1963.

10653 **Butler, D.E.** *The British General Elections of 1955.* London: Macmillan, 1955.

10654 **Butler, D.E.,** and **Kavanagh, D.** *The British General Elections of 1983.* London: Macmillan, 1984.

10655 **Butler, D.E.,** and **King, Anthony,** eds. *The British General Elections of 1966.* London: Macmillan, 1966.

10656 **Butler, D.E.,** and **Stokes, D.E.** *Political Change in Great Britain, the Evolution of Electoral Choice*, 2nd ed. London: Macmillan, 1974.

10657 **Campbell, Bruce Alan.** *French Elections and Voter Stability: A Model of Voting Behavior for the French National Electorate.* Ann Arbor: University of Michigan, Ph.D., 1971.

10658 **Carstairs, A.M.** *A Short History of Electoral Systems in Western Europe.* London: Allen & Unwin, 1980.

10659 **Childers, Thomas C., Jr.** *The Social Bases of Electoral Politics in Urban Germany 1919-1933: A Sociological Analysis of Voting Behavior in the Weimar Republic.* Cambridge, Massachusetts: Harvard University, Ph.D., 1976.

10660 **Ciporen, Marvin.** *A Social Analysis of the French Socialist Vote in the 1914 Legislative Elections in Sceaux.* Chicago, Illinois: University of Chicago, Ph.D., 1983.

10661 **Coats, Richard Morris.** *Voter Participation in Nineteenth Century British Parliamentary Elections.* Blacksburg: Virginia Polytechnic Institute and State University, Ph.D., 1984.

10662 **Cook, C.** *The Age of Alignment.* London: Macmillan, 1976.

10663 **Cox, Kevin R.** *Regional Anomalies in the Voting Behavior of the Population of England and Wales, 1921-1951.* Urbana: University of Illinois, Ph.D., 1966.

10664 **Craig, F.W.S.** *Britain Votes: 3.* Chichester: Parliamentary Research Services, 1984.

10665 **Craig, F.W.S.** *British Electoral Facts, 1832-1980.* Chichester: Political Reference Publications, 1981.

10666 **Craig, F.W.S.** *British Parliamentary Election Statistics, 1918-1970.* Chichester: Political Reference Publications, 1971.

10667 **Craig, F.W.S.** *Minor Parties at British Parliamentary Elections.* London: Macmillan, 1975.

10668 **Crewe, I., and Fox, Annette Baker.** *British Parliamentary Constituencies: A Statistical Compendium.* London: Faber, 1984.

10669 **Crewe, Ivor; Norris, Pippa; Denver, David; and Broughton, David,** eds. *British Elections and Parties Yearbook, 1991.* London: Harvester Wheatsheaf, 1992.

10670 **Denver, David, and Hands, Gordon,** eds. *Issues and Controversies in British Electoral Behaviour.* London: Harvester Wheatsheaf, 1992.

10671 **Dimitras, Panayote Elias.** *Social-Classes and Voting Behavior in France: The Political Economy of Class Voting in the Fifth Republic.* Cambridge, Massachusetts: Harvard University, Ph.D., 1979.

10672 **Fitzmaurice, John.** *The Politics of Belgium: Crisis and Compromise in a Plural Society.* 2nd ed. London: C. Hurst & Company, 1988.

10673 **Friend, Julius W.** *Seven Years in France: Francois Mitterrand and the Unintended Revolution: 1981-1988.* Boulder, Colorado: Westview Press, 1989.

10674 **Goguel, Francois,** ed. *Nouvelles Etudes de Sociologie Electorale.* Paris: Armand Colin, 1954.

10675 **Goguel, Francois.** *Geographie des elections francaises de 1870 a 1951.* Paris: Armand Colin, 1951.

10676 **Gottmann, Jean.** *La Campagne Presidentielle de 1952 aux Etats Unis.* Paris: Presses Universitaires de France, 1953.

10677 **Guth, Gloria Jean Anne.** *Croakers, Tackers, and Other Citizens: Norwich Voters in the Early Eighteenth Century (Volumes I and II) (England, Elections, Poll Books, Party, Politics).* Stanford, California: Stanford University, Ph.D., 1985.

10678 **Gyford, J., and James, M.** *National Parties and Local Politics.* London: Allen & Unwin, 1983.

10679 **Hanley, D.** *Keeping Left? Ceres and the French Socialist Party. A Contribution to the Study of Fractionalism in Political Parties.* Manchester: Manchester University Press, 1986.

10680 **Heath, A.; Jowell, R.; and Curtice, J.** *How Britain Votes.* Oxford: Pergamon, 1985.

10681 **Heberle, H.** *From Democracy to Nazism. A Regional Case Study on Political Parties in Germany.* Baton Rouge: Louisiana State University Press, 1945.

10682 **Hirsch, Helmut.** *The Saar Plebiscite.* Reprinted from: *South Atlantic Quarterly,* 45, No. 1 (January, 1946). Chicago, Illinois: University of Chicago Press, 1946.

10683 **Hollander, Rose Marie T.** *The European Parliament and the 1979 Elections.* Fullerton: California State University, Master's Thesis, 1981.

10684 **Houghton Committee.** *Report of the Committee on Financial Aid to Political Parties.* London: Her Majesty's Stationery Office, Cmnd 6601, 1976.

10685 **Houska, Joseph John, Jr.** *The Organizational Connection: Elites, Masses, and Elections in Austria and the Netherlands.* New Haven, Connecticut: Yale University, Ph.D., 1979.

10686 **Hudson, Ray.** *Wrecking a Region: State Politics, Party Politics, and Regional Change in North East England.* London: Rion Limited, 1989.

10687 **Hudson, Robert Bowman, III.** *Public Policy Formation in France: Application of a Policy Typology to Roll Call Voting in the National Assembly of the Fourth Republic.* Chapel Hill: University of North Carolina, Ph.D., 1972.

10688 **Istituto Studie Ricerche Cattaneo.** *Il comportamento elettorale in Italia.* Bologna: Mulino, 1968.

10689 **Johnston, R.J.** *The Geography of English Politics: The 1983 General Election.* London: Croom Helm, 1985.

10690 **Johnston, R.J.; Patlie, C.J.; and Allsopp, J.G.** *A Nation Building: The Electoral Map of Great Britain, 1979-1987.* New York: John Wiley & Sons, 1988.

10691 **King, Anthony, and others.** *Britain at the Polls, 1992.* Chatham, NJ: Chatham House Publishers, Inc., 1993.

10692 **Kinnear, Michael.** *The British Voter: An Atlas and Survey Since 1885.* London: Batsford Academic and Education, 1981.

10693 **Kolinsky, Eva,** ed. *The Greens in West Germany: Organisation and Policy Making.* Oxford: Berg Publishers, 1989.

10694 **La Ponce, J.A.** *The Government of the Fifth Republic: French Political Parties and the Constitution.* Berkeley: University of California Press, 1961.

10695 **Leaney, Joseph Robert.** *The Influence of St. Bernard on Episcopal Elections in France.* Bronx, New York: Fordham University, Ph.D., 1973.

10696 **Leltore, G.; Bruni, G.G.; and Gueli, I.** *La elezione amminitrative nelle citta gemelle di Rome e Parigi.* Roma: Centro Studi Sociologici, 1966.

10697 **Lewis, P.W., and Skipworth, G.E.** *Some Geographical and Statistical Aspects of the Distribution of Votes in Recent General Elections.* Hull: University of Hull, Department of Geography, 1966.

10698 **Limberes, Nickolas Michael.** *Greek Political Attitudes and Voting Behavior: A Statistical Analysis of Socio-Demographic and Ecological Relationships.* Tallahassee: Florida State University, Ph.D., 1984.

10699 **Longhurst, Brian; Martin, A.; Savage, M.; and Warde, Alan.** *Class, Consumption and Voting.* Lancaster Regionalism Group Working Paper, 1987.

10700 **Mair, Peter,** ed. *The West European Party System.* Oxford: Oxford University Press, 1990.

10701 **McAllister, I., and Rose, R.** *The Nationwide Competition for Votes.* London: Francis Pinter, 1984.

10702 **McLeod, William Reynolds.** *Parliamentary Elections in the Home Counties, 1713-1715: A Comparative Study.* Baltimore: University of Maryland, Ph.D., 1970.

10703 **Merkl, P.H.,** ed. *Western European Party Systems.* New York: The Free Press, 1980.

10704 **Meynaud, J.** *Les partis politiques en Italie.* Paris: Presses Universitaires de France, 1965.

10705 **Miles, William Franklin Scherer.** *Paradox in Paradise: Martinique and the 1981 French National Elections (France Overseas Department, Colonies, Caribbean).* Medford, Massachusetts: Tufts University, Fletcher School of Law and Diplomacy, Ph.D., 1983.

10706 **Olivesi, Antoine, and Roncayolo, Marcel.** *Geographie electorale des Bouches du Rhone sous la IVe Republique.* Paris: Armand Colin, 1961.

10707 **Parliamentary Research Services.** *The BBC/ITN Guide to the New Parliamentary Constituencies.* Chichester: Parliamentary Research Services, 1983.

10708 **Pasquino, Gianfranco, and McCarthy, Patrick,** eds. *The End of Post-War Politics in Italy: The Landmark 1992 Elections.* Boulder: Westview Press, 1993.

10709 **Pelling, H.** *Social Geography of British Elections, 1885-1910.* London: Macmillan, 1967.

10710 **Penniman, H.R.,** ed. *Britain at the Polls, 1979.* Washington, D.C.: American Enterprise Institute, 1981.

10711 **Pinto-Duschinsky, M.** *British Political Finance 1830-1980.* Washington, D.C.: American Enterprise Institute, 1981.

10712 **Pulzer, P.G.J.** *Political Representation and Elections in Britain.* London: Allen & Unwin, 1975.

10713 **Rohe, Karl,** ed. *Elections, Parties and Political Traditions: Social Foundations of German Parties and Party Systems, 1867-1987.* New York: Berg Publishers, 1990.

10714 **Sabaliunas, Leonas.** *Lithuanian Social Democracy in Perspective, 1893-1914.* Durham: Duke University Press, 1990.

10715 **Sarlvik, B., and Crewe, I.** *Decade of Dealignment: The Conservative Victory of 1979 and Trends in the 1970's.* Cambridge: Cambridge University Press, 1983.

10716 **Sen, Subrata Kumar.** *The Calculus of Voting: Empirical Studies for France.* Pittsburgh, Pennsylvania: Carnegie-Mellon University, Ph.D., 1974.

10717 **Sharpe, L.J.,** ed. *Voting in Cities.* London: Macmillan, 1967.

10718 **Shriver, David Perry.** *The Problem of Corruption in British Parliamentary Elections, 1750-1860.* Cleveland, Ohio: Case Western Reserve University, Ph.D., 1974.

10719 **Siegfried, Andre.** *Geographie electorale de l'Ardeche.* Paris: Armand Colin, 1947.

10720 **Siegfried, Andre.** *Geographie electorale de l'Ardeche sous la III° Republique.* Paris: Armand Colin, 1949.

10721 **Siegfried, Andre.** *Tableau des partis en France.* Paris: Grasset, 1930.

10722 **Siegfried, Andre.** *Tableau politique de la France de l'Ouest sous la Troisieme Republique.* Paris: Armand Colin, 1913.

10723 **Smith, Donald Robert.** *The French Elections of 1824 and 1827: A Quantitative Analysis.* Iowa City: University of Iowa, Ph.D., 1978.

10724 **Smith, J.** *Commonsense Thought and Working-Class Consciousness: Some Aspects of the Glasgow and Liverpool Labour Movement in the Early Years of the Twentieth Century.* Edinburgh, Scotland: University of Edinburgh, Ph.D., 1980.

10725 **Spreafico, A., and La Pollambara, J.** *Elezioni e comportamento politico in Italia.* Milano: Comunita, 1963.

10726 **Stokes, Gale.** *Politics as Development: The Emergence of Political Parties in Nineteenth-Century Serbia.* Durham: Duke University Press, 1990.

10727 **Sweeney, Jane Patricia.** *The First European Elections: A Critique of Neo-Functionalist Integration Theory.* New York City: New School for Social Research, Ph.D., 1980.

10728 **Szajkowski, Bogdan,** ed. *New Political Parties of Eastern Europe and the Soviet Union.* Harlow: Longman Current Affairs, 1991.

10729 **Tangney, Michael J.** "The Electoral Geography of Ireland: Case Studies of West Limerick and East Limerick, 1982-1987." Columbia: University of South Carolina, M.A., 1988.

10730 **Taylor, O.R.** *The Fourth Republic of France, Constitution and Political Parties.* London: Royal Institute of International Affairs, 1951.

10731 **Taylor, Patricia.** *French Voting Behavior in 1962; The Role of the Electorate in the Consolidation of the Fifth Republic.* Storrs: University of Connecticut, Ph.D., 1970.

10732 **Tor, S. Ahman Funnar Schalin.** *Geteilte Welt. Weltlpolitischer Atlas.* Translated from Swedish by Robert L. Hatt. Bern: Kummerly & Frey, Geographischu Verlag, 1964.

10733 **Unger, A.L.** *The Totalitarian Party.* Cambridge: Cambridge University Press, 1974.

10734 **Vinogradoff, Eugene Dmitri.** *The Russian Peasantry and the Elections to the Fourth Duma: Estate Political Consciousness and Class Political Consciousness.* New York City: Columbia University, Ph.D., 1974.

10735 **Wambaugh, Sarah.** *The Doctrine of Self-determination.* New York: Oxford University Press, 1919.

10736 **Wambaugh, Sarah.** *A Monography on Plebiscite.* New York: Oxford University Press, 1920.

10737 **Wambaugh, Sarah.** *The Saar Plebiscite, with a Collection of Official Documents.* Cambridge, Massachusetts: Harvard University Press, 1940.

10738 **Ward, Cedric Charles.** *Disputed Elections to the House of Commons, 1604-1641.* Lincoln: University of Nebraska, Ph.D., 1974.

10739 **Wells, Harold Stanley.** *An Ecological Analysis of Communist Voting in France and Britain.* Stanford, California: Stanford University, Ph.D., 1975.

10740 **Wernette, Dee Richard.** *Political Violence and German Elections: 1930 and July, 1932.* Ann Arbor: University of Michigan, Ph.D., 1974.

10741 **Wiarda, Howard J.** *The Transition to Democracy in Spain and Portugal.* Washington, D.C.: American Enterprise Institute for Public Policy Research (AEI Studies, No. 482), 1989.

10742 **Wiste, Richard Allen.** *Dimensional Analysis of Multi-Party Roll Call Voting: Parliamentary Precursors of the 1966 Finnish Popular Front.* Los Angeles: University of California, Ph.D., 1970.

Journals

10743 **Agnew, John A.** "Models of Spatial Variation in Political Expression: The Case of the Scottish National Party." *International Political Science Review,* 6, No. 2 (April, 1985), 171-196.

10744 **Alexander, Alan.** "Scottish Nationalism: Agenda Building, Electoral Process, and Political Culture." *Canadian Review of Studies in Nationalism,* 7, No. 2 (Fall, 1980), 372-385.

10745 **Allum, P.A.** "Comportamento elettorale e ceti sociali a Napoli." *Nord e Sud,* 10, No. 45 (106) (Settembre, 1963), 78-101.

10746 **Alt, J.E.; Sarlvik, B.; and Crewe, I.** "Angels in Plastic: The Liberal Surge in 1974." *Political Studies*, 25, No. 3 (September, 1977), 343-368.

10747 **Ante, Ulrich.** "Wahlen als Gegenstand der Geographie: Geographische Ansatzezur Wahlanalyse Unter Bezugnahne Auf die Bundestagswahl 1980." *Geographische Zeitschrift*, Jahr. 70, Heft 2, Quartal 2 (June, 1982), 106-126.

10748 **Arambourou, Robert.** "Reflexions sur la geographie electorale: a propos d'une etude de l'arrondissement de le Reole (Gironde)." *Revue de Science Politique*, 2 (1952), 521-542.

10749 **Bakvis, Herman.** "Electoral Stability and Electoral Change: The Case of Dutch Catholics." *Canadian Journal of Political Science*, 14, No. 3 (September, 1981), 519-555.

10750 **Barany, Zoltan D.** "Political Participation and the Notion of Reform: Electoral Practices and the Hungarian National Assembly." *East Central Europe*, 16, Nos. 1 and 2 (1989), 107-121.

10751 **Baudelle, Guy, and Matykowski, Roman.** "Naissance D'une Democratie: Les Premieres Elections Libres en Pologne (1989-1991)." *L'Information Geographique* [Paris], 58, No. 2 (1994), 72-81.

10752 **Beaujeu-Garnier, Jacqueline.** "Essai de Geographie Electorale Guineenne." *Les Cahiers d'Outre-Mer*, 11, No. 44 (October-December, 1958), 309-333.

10753 **Bennett, Robert J.** "Demographic and Budgetary Influence on the Geography of the Poll Tax: Alarm or False Alarm? *Institute of British Geographers, Transactions* New Series, 14, No. 4 (1989), 400-417.

10754 **Berezkin, A.V. and Others.** "The Geography of the 1989 Elections of People's Deputies of the USSR (Preliminary Results)." *Soviet Geography*, 30, No. 8 (October, 1989), 607-634.

10755 **Bernard, Marie-Claire, and Carriere, Pierre.** "The 1986 General Election and Le Den's Party in Languedoc-Roussillon." *Espace-Populations Societes*, 87, No. 3 (1987), 497-509.

10756 **Bernard, Marie-Claire, and Carriere, Pierre.** "Mobilite demographique et compartement electoral: le front national en Languedoc-Roussilion aux Europeennes de 1984. Societe Languedocrenne de *Geographie Bullegin*, Annee 109, Fasc. 1 (Janvier-Mars, 1986), 81-99.

10757 **Bibes, G.** "Left-Wing Vote and Society in Southern Italy." *Espace-Populations-Societes*, 87, No. 3 (1987), 487-496.

10758 **Biel, H.S.** "Suburbia and Voting Behaviour in the London Metropolitan Area: An Alternative Explanation." *Tijdschrift voor Economische en Sociale Geografie*, 63, Nr. 1 (Jan.-Febr., 1972), 39-42.

10759 **Billelt, H.** "L'expression politique en Gresivaudan et son interpretation geographique." *Revue de Geographie Alpine*, 46, No. 1 (1958), 97-128.

10760 **Bodman, Andrew R.** "Regional Trends in Electoral Support in Britain, 1950-1983." *Professional Geographer*, 37, No. 3 (August, 1985), 288-295.

10761 **Bonatt, Edward.** "International Law and the Plebiscites in Eastern Poland, 1939." *Journal of Central European Affairs*, 5, No. 4 (January, 1946), 378-393.

10762 **Bose, Gerhard.** "Raumliche Aspekte des Wahlerverhaltens in Einer Grobstadt der Ehemaligen DDR Nach der Politischen Wende--Eine Politische-Geographische Analyse der Wahlen 1990 in Jena." *Petermanns Geographische Mitteilungen* [Gotha], 136, Nos. 2-3 (1992), 121-138.

10763 **Boyer, Jean-Claude.** "Les Pays-Bas en 1989: Retour a la 'Grande Coalition.'" *Notes et Etudes Documentaires* [Paris], No. 4912-13 (1990), 103-117.

10764 **Brand, Jack.** "National Conciousness and Voting in Scotland." *Ethnic and Racial Studies*, 10, No. 3 (July, 1987), 334-348.

10765 **Brand, Jack.** "Political Parties and the Referendum on National Sovereignty: The 1979 Scottish Referendum on Devolution." *Canadian Review of Studies in Nationalism*, 13, No. 1 (Spring, 1986), 31-47.

10766 **Brennan, Paul.** "L'Irlande in 1989: Un Gouvernement de Coalition." *Notes et Etues Documentaires* [Paris], No. 4912-13 (1990), 127-135.

10767 **Brustein, William.** "A Mode of Production Explanation of the Origins of French Political Regionalism: The 1849 Election." *Journal of Political & Military Sociology*, 12, No. 2 (Fall, 1984), 277-294.

10768 **Bruszt, Laszlo, and Stark, David.** "Remaking the Political Field in Hungary: From Politics of Confrontation to the Politics of Competition." *Journal of International Affairs* [New York], 45, No. 1 (Summer, 1991), 201-245.

10769 **Buleon, P.** "The 1986 Elections in Lower Normandy." *Etudes Normandes*, 4 (1987), 35-48.

10770 **Burghardt, Andrew F.** "The Bases of Support for Political Parties in Burgenland." *Annals of the Association of American Geographers*, 54, No. 3 (September, 1964), 372-390.

10771 **Burghardt, Andrew F.** "Regions of Political Party Support in Burgenland." *Canadian Geographer*, 7, No. 2 (1963), 91-98.

10772 **Busteed, M.A.** "Irish Labour in the 1969 Election." *Political Studies*, 18, No. 3 (September, 1970), 373-379.

10773 **Capeechi, V., and Galli, G.** "Determinants of Voting Behaviour in Italy; a Linear Casual Model of Analysis." In *Quantitative Ecological Analysis in the Social Sciences*, M. Dogan and S. Rokkan, eds. Cambridge, Massachusetts: Massachusetts Institute of Technology Press, 1969, 235-284.

10774 **Catsiapis, Jean.** "La Grece en 1989: La Cascade des Elections et des Gouvernements." *Notes et Etudes Documentaires* [Paris], No. 4912-13 (1990), 195-207.

10775 "Causes and Consequences of the Plebiscite in the Saar." *World Today*, 11, No. 12 (December, 1955), 530-539.

10776 **Cauvin, C., and Reymond, H.** "Les Elections Presidentielles. Deuxiene Tour 1987 (The Second Round of the French Presidential Elections of 1981)." *Information Geographique*, 49, No. 4 (1985), 154-155.

10777 **Chadjipadelis, Theodore, and Zafiropoulos, Costas.** "Electoral Changes in Greece 1981-90: Geogrpahical Patterns and the Uniformity of the Vote." *Political Geography*, 13, No. 6 (November, 1994), 492-514.

10778 **Chatelain, Abel.** "Les donnees actuelles de la geographie des journaux lyonnais." *Etudes Rhodaniennes*, 5 (1949), 189-200.

10779 **Chatelain, Abel.** "Geographie sociologique de la presse et regions francaises." *Revue de Geographie de Lyon*, 32 (1957), 127-134.

10780 **Chevallier, M.** "Problemes de la Geographie elecotrale Francaise (Problems of the Geography of French Elections)." *Revue Geographique de l'Est*, 25, No. 1 (1985), 93-118.

10781 **Clem, Ralph S., and Craumer, Peter R.** "The Geography of the April 25 (1993) Russian Referendum." *Post-Soviet Geography* [Silver Spring], 34, No. 8 (October, 1993), 481-496.

10782 **Cole, Matthew.** "The Role of the Deposit in British Parliamentary Elections." *Parliamentary Affairs*, 45, No. 1 (January, 1992), 77-91.

10783 **Cook, Elizabeth Adell, and Wilcox, Clyde.** "Feminism and the Gender Gap--A Second Look." *Journal of Politics*, 53, No. 4 (November, 1991), 1111-1122.

10784 **Cox, Kevin R.** "Suburbia and Voting Behaviour in the London Metropolitan Area." *Annals of the Association of American Geographers*, 58, No. 1 (March, 1968), 111-127.

10785 **Crampton, Peter.** "Spatial Polarisation of Political Representation in Great Britain 1945-1979." *Geography*, 69, Part 1, No. 302 (January, 1984), 28-37.

10786 **Crewe, I., and Payne, C.** "Another Game with Nature: An Ecological Regression Model of the British Two-Party Vote Ratio in 1970." *British Journal of Political Science*, 6, No. 1 (1976), 43-81.

10787 **Crewe, I.; Payne, C.; Sarlvik, B.; and Alt, J.E.** "Partisan Realignment in Britain 1964-1974." *British Journal of Political Science*, 7, No. 2 (April, 1977), 129-190.

10788 **Criddle, Byron.** "Electoral Systems in France." *Parliamentary Affairs*, 45, No. 1 (January, 1992), 108-116.

10789 **Curtice, J., and Steed, M.** "An Analysis of the Voting." In *The British General Election of 1983*, D. Butler and D. Kavanagh, eds. London: Macmillan, 1984, 333-373.

10790 **Curtice, J., and Steed, M.** "Electoral Choice and the Production of Government: The Changing Operation of the Electoral System in the United Kingdom Since 1955. *British Journal of Political Science*, 12, No. 3 (July, 1982), 249-298.

10791 **Davies, R.B., and Crouchley, Robert.** "The Determinants of Party Loyalty: A Disaggregate Analysis of Panel Data from the 1974 and 1979 General Elections in England." *Political Geography Quarterly*, 4, No. 4 (October, 1985), 307-320.

10792 **Day, Frederick A., and Jones, Alice L.** "Portrait of Modern Texas Politics: The Regional Geography of the 1990 Governor's Race." *The Social Science Journal*, 31, No. 2 (1994), 99-110.

10793 **Dijkink, Gertjan, and Van der Wusten, Herman.** "Green Politics in Europe: The Issues and the Voters." *Political Geography* [Oxford], 11, No. 1 (January, 1992), 7-11.

10794 **Doumenge, Jean-Pierre.** "L'enracinement des Mouvements Politiques en Nouvelle-Caledonie: Faits et Perspective." *Acta Geographica* [Paris], No. 98 (Juin, 1994), 20-42.

10795 **Dunbabin, J.P.D.** "British Elections in the Nineteenth and Twentieth Centuries, A Regional Approach." *English Historical Review*, 95, No. 375 (April, 1980), 241-267.

10796 **Dunleavy, P.** "The Urban Basis of Political Alignment." *British Journal of Political Science*, 9, Part 4 October, (1979), 403-443.

10797 **Dyson, Simon.** "Polls Apart?: The 1990 Nicaraguan and 1992 British General Elections." *The Political Quarterly*, 65, No. 4 (October-November, 1994), 425-431.

10798 **Elklit, Jorgen.** "Simpler Than Its Reputation: The Electoral System in Denmark Since 1920." *Electoral Studies*, 12, No. 1 (March, 1993), 41-57.

10799 **Feldblum, Miriam.** "Paradoxes of Ethnic Politics: The Case of Franco-Maghrebis in France." *Ethnic and Racial Studies* [London], 16, No. 1 (January, 1993), 52-74.

10800 **Fischer, O.** "Les Determinants du comportement geoelectoral en Alsace (Voting Behavior in Alsace, 1981)." *Recherches Geographiques a Strasbourg*, 24 (1986), 91-110.

10801 **Fitton, M.** "Neighbourhood and Voting: A Sociometric Explanation." *British Journal of Political Science*, 3, Part 4 (October, 1973), 445-472.

10802 **Fletcher, P.** "The Results Analysed." In *Voting in Cities*, L.J. Sharpe, ed. London: Macmillan, 1967, 290-321.

10803 **Forster, Keith.** "The Silent Vote in Finish Politics." *International Journal*, 19, No. 2 (Spring, 1964), 341-352.

10804 **Franklin, M.N.** "Demographic and Political Components in the Decline of British Class Voting 1964-1979." *Electoral Studies*, 1 (1983), 195-220.

10805 **Franklin, M.N.** "How the Decline of Class Voting Opened the Way to Radical Change in British Politics." *British Journal of Political Science*, 14, No. 4 (October, 1984), 483-508.

10806 **Franklin, M.N., and Mucghan, A.** "The Decline of Class Voting in Britain: Problems of Analysis and Interpretation." *American Political Science Review*, 72, No. 2 (June, 1978), 523-534.

10807 **Fremont, A.** "Re-reading Siegfried on Electoral Behaviour in Normandy." *Etudes Normandes*, 4 (1987), 9-16.

10808 **Gallagher, Michael.** "Candidate Selection in Ireland: The Impact of Localism and the Electoral System." *British Journal of Political Science*, 10, Part 4 (October, 1980), 489-503.

10809 **Gasper, J.** "Le Vote Rural an Portugal (The Rural Vote in Portugal)." *Espace-Populations-Societies*, 3 (1987), 533-539.

10810 **Geremek, Bronislaw.** "Postcommunism and Democracy in Poland." *Washington Quarterly*, 13, No. 3 (Summer, 1990), 125-131.

10811 **Gillmor, Desmond A.** "The 1973 General Election in the Republic of Ireland." *Irish Geography*, 7 (1974), 97-106.

10812 **Girod, Roger.** "Geography of the Swiss Party System." In *Cleavages, Ideologies and Party Systems*, Erik Allardt and Yrjo Littunen, eds. Helsinki: Westermarck Society, *Transactions*, 10 (1964), 132-161.

10813 **Glassberg, A.** "Linkage Between Urban Policy Output and Voting Behaviour." *British Journal of Political Science*, 3, Part 3 (July, 1973), 341-361.

10814 **Goguel, Francois.** "Geographie du referendum et des elections de mai-juin 1946." *Esprit*,14 , No. 124 (1st Juillet, 1946), 27-54.

10815 **Goguel, Francois.** "Geographie des elections sociales de 1950-1951." *Revue Francaise de Science Politique*, 3 (1953), 246-271.

10816 **Goguel, Francois.** "Geographie du referendum du 8 janvier 1961." *Revue Francaise de Science Politique*, 11 (1961), 5-28.

10817 **Goguel, Francois.** "Les elections francaises du 2 janvier 1956." *Revue Francaise de Science Politique*, 6 (1956), 5-17.

10818 **Golde, Gunter.** "Voting Patterns, Social Context, and Religious Affiliation in Southwest Germany." *Comparative Studies in Society and History*, 24, No. 2 (January, 1982), 25-56.

10819 **Grange, Jean.** "Les Deformations de la Representation des Collectives Territoriales et de la Population au Senat." *Revue Francaise de Science Politique*, 40, Nu. 1 (Fevrier, 1990), 5-45.

10820 **Greene, A.E.** "Changing Electoral Practices in England, 1885-1984." *Journal of Historical Geography*, 11, No. 3 (July, 1985), 297-311.

10821 **Grimble, I.** "Caithness and Sutherland." In *The British General Election of 1966*, D.E. Butler and A. King, eds. London: Macmillan, 1966, 227-232.

10822 **Guichonnet, Paul.** "La geographie et le temperament politique dans les montagnes de la Haute Savoi." *Revue de Geographie Alpine*, 31, No. 1 (1943), 39-85.

10823 Halford, Susan. "Spatial Divisions and Women's Initiatives in British Local Government." *Geoforum*, 20, No. 2 (1989), 161–174.

10824 Heineberg, Heinz. "Die Einmaligkeit Von Vier Wahlen in Den Neuen Deutschen Bundeslandern 1990–Grundlage Fur Vergleichende Geographische Wahlanalysen?" *Die Erde* [Berlin], 122, Heft 1 (1991), 55-73.

10825 Hepple, Leslie W. "Destroying Local Leviathans and Designing Landscapes of Liberty?" Public Choice Theory and the Poll Tax." *Institute of British Geographers*, Transactions, New Series, 14, No. 4 (1989), 387-399.

10826 Herbert, G. "Party Voting Contagion in City Regions." *Politics*, 10, No. 1 (May, 1975), 58-68.

10827 Herin, Robert. "Elections and Electorates in Spain. Electoral Behaviour and Regional Societies in Spain." *Espace-Populations-Societes*, 87, No. 3 (1987), 453–464.

10828 Herin, Robert, and Bertrand, Jean-Rene. "Deux Etudes de Geographie Electorale en Espagne (Galice et Sud-Est)." *Revue Geograpique des Pyrenees et du Sud-Ouest*, Tome 53, Faasc. 4 (1982), 355-402.

10829 Hibbing, John R., and Patterson, Samuel C. "A Democratic Legislature in the Making: The Historic Hungarian Elections of 1990." *Comparative Political Studies*, 24, No. 4 (January, 1992), 430-454.

10830 Hoppen, K. Theodore. "Grammars of Electoral Violence in Nineteenth-Century England and Ireland." *The English Historical Review*, 59, No. 432 (June, 1994), 597-620.

10831 Hough, Jerry F. "The Russian Election of 1993: Public Attitudes Toward Economic Reform and Democratization." *Post-Soviet Affairs* [Silver Spring], 10, No. 1 (January-March, 1994), 1-37.

10832 Hugonnies, Simone. "Temperaments Politiques et Geographie Electorale de deux Grandes Vallees Intra-Alpines des Alpes du Nord: Maurienne et Tarentaise." *Revue de Geographie Alpine*, 42, No. 1 (1954), 45-80.

10833 Jaensch, D. "The Scottish Vote 1974: A Realigning Party System?" *Political Studies*, 24, No. 3 (September, 1976), 306-319.

10834 Johnson, Nuala C. "An Analysis of the 'Friends and Neighbors' Effect in an Irish Urban Constituency." *Irish Geography*, 22, Part 2 (1989), 93-105.

10835 Johnston, R.J. "Campaign Spending and Voting in England: Analyses of the Efficacy of Political Advertising." *Environment and Planning C: Government and Policy*, 1, No. 1 (January, 1983), 117-126.

10836 Johnston, R.J. "Class and the Geography of Voting in England: Towards Measurement and Understanding." *Institute of British Geographers. Transactions*, New Series, 10, No. 2 (1985), 245-255.

10837 Johnston, R.J. "Class Locations. Consumption Locations, and the Geography of Voting in England." *Social Science Research*, 12, No. 3 (September, 1983), 215-235.

10838 Johnston, R.J. "Cracking the Mold: The Changing Geographical Pattern of Voting in England, 1979-1983." *Area*, 16, No. 2 (June, 1984), 101-108.

10839 Johnston, R.J. "The Current Redistribution of Parliamentary Seats: Eight Greater London Boroughs." *Area*, 12 (1980), 223-228.

10840 Johnston, R.J. "Embourgeoisement, The Property-Owning Democracy and Ecological Models of Voting in England." *British Journal Political Science*, 11, Part 4 (October, 1981), 499-503.

10841 Johnston, R.J. "Embourgeoisement and Voting: England, 1974." *Area*, 13, No. 4 (December, 1981), 345-351.

10842 Johnston, R.J. "The Electoral Geography of an Election Campaign: Scotland in October, 1974." *Scottish Geographical Magazine*, 93, No. 2 (September, 1977), 98-108.

10843 Johnston, R.J. "The Feedback Component of the Pork Barrel: Tests Using the Results of the 1983 General Election in Britain." *Environment and Planning*, A15, No. 12 (December, 1983), 1691-1696.

10844 Johnston, R.J. "The Geography of the Working Class and the Geography of the Labour Vote in England, 1983: A Prefatory Note to a Research Agenda." *Political Geography Quarterly*, 6, No. 1 (January, 1987), 7–16.

10845 Johnston, R.J. "Information Flows and Votes: An Analysis of Local Campaign Spending in England, 1983." *Geoforum*, 17, No. 1 (1986), 69-79.

10846 Johnston, R.J. "Information Provision and Individual Behavior: A Case Study of Voting at an English General Election." *Geographical Analysis*, 18, No. 2 (April, 1986), 129-141.

10847 **Johnston, R.J.** "The Neighbourhood Effect Revisited." *Environment and Planning D: Society and Space*, 4 , No. 4 (December, 1986), 41–55.

10848 **Johnston, R.J.** "The Neighbourhood Effect Won't Go Away: Observations on the Electoral Geography of England in the Light of Dunleavy's Critique." *Geoforum*, 14, No. 2 (1983), 161-168.

10849 **Johnston, R.J.** "Parliamentary Seat Redistribution: More Opinions on the Theme." *Area*, 8, No. 1 (March, 1976), 30-34.

10850 **Johnston, R.J.** "Party Strength, Incumbency and Campaign Spending as Influences in Voting in Four English General Elections." *Tijdschrift voor Economische en Sociale Geografie*, 76, Nr. 2 (March-April, 1985), 82-87.

10851 **Johnston, R.J.** "People's Places and Parliaments: A Geographical Perspective on Electoral Reform in Great Britain." *Geographical Journal*, 151, Part 3 (November, 1985), 327-348.

10852 **Johnston, R.J.** "Political Geography of Contemporary Events XIII: Redistricting in England Revisited." *Political Geography* [Oxford], 11, No. 6 (November, 1992), 579-587.

10853 **Johnston, R.J.** "Redistricting by Neutral Commissions and Its Electoral Impact: The UK Case." *Annals of the Association of American Geographers*, 72 (1982e).

10854 **Johnston, R.J.** "Regional Variations in British Voting Trends 1966-1979: Tests of an Ecological Model." *Regional Studies*, 15 (1981), 23-31.

10855 **Johnston, R.J.** "Regional Variations in the 1979 Election: Results for England." *Area*, (1979), 294-297.

10856 **Johnston, R.J.** "Research Policy and Review 9. A Space for Place (Or a Place for Space) in British Psssephology: A Review of Recent Writings with Especial Reference to the General Election of 1983." *Environment & Planning A*, 18, No. 5 (May, 1986), 573-598.

10857 **Johnston, R.J.** "The Rural Milieu and Voting in Britain." *Journal of Rural Studies*, 3, No. 2 (1987), 95–103.

10858 **Johnston, R.J.** "Shape and Definition of Parliamentary Constituencies." *Urban Studies*, 18 (1981), 219-223.

10859 **Johnston, R.J.** "A Space for Place (or A Place for Space) in British Psephology." *Environment and Planning A*, 18 (1986a), 573–598.

10860 **Johnston, R.J., and Hunt, A.J.** "Voting Power in the E.E.C.'s Council of Ministers: An Essay on Method in Political Geography." *Geoforum*, 8, No. 1 (1977), 1-9.

10861 **Johnston, R.J.; O'Neill, A.B.; and Taylor, P.J.** "The Changing Electoral Geography of the Netherlands: 1946-1981." *Tijdschrift voor Economische en Sociale Geografie*, 74, No. 3 (1983), 185-195.

10862 **Johnston, R.J., and Pattie, C.J.** "Changing Voter Allegiances in Great Britain, 1979-1987: An Exploration of Regional Patterns." *Regional Studies*, 22, No. 3 (June, 1988), 179–192.

10863 **Johnston, R.J., and Pattie, C.J.** "Class, Attitudes, and Retrospective Voting: Exploring the Regional Variations in the 1983 General Election in Great Britain." *Environment and Planning A* [London], 22, No. 7 (July, 1990), 893-908.

10864 **Johnston, R.J., and Pattie, C.J.** "Class Dealignment and the Regional Polarization of Voting Patterns in Great Britain, 1964-1987." *Political Geography* [Oxford], 11, No. 1 (January, 1992), 73-86.

10865 **Johnston, R.J., and Pattie, C.J.** "A Dividing Nation? An Initial Exploration of the Changing Electoral Geography of Great Britain, 1979-1987." *Environment and Planning A*, 19, No. 8 (August, 1987), 1001–1003.

10866 **Johnston, R.J., and Pattie, C.J.** "Familing Background, Ascribed Characteristics, Political Attitudes and Regional Variations in Voting Within England, 1983: A Further Contribution." *Political Geography Quarterly*, 6, No. 4 (October, 1987), 347–349.

10867 **Johnston, R.J., and Pattie, C.J.** "A Growing North-South Divide in British Voting Patterns, 1979-1987." *Geoforum*, 20, No. 1 (1989), 93–106.

10868 **Johnston, R.J., and Pattie, C.J.** "Is the Seesaw Tipping Back? The End of Thatcherism and Changing Voting Patterns in Great Britain, 1979-92." *Environment and Planning A* [London], 24, No. 10 (October, 1992), 1491-1505.

10869 **Johnston, R.J., and Pattie, C.J.** "People, Attitudes, Mileux and Votes: An Exploration of Voting at the 1983 Brigish General Election." *Institute of British Geographers Transactions*, 13, No. 3 (1988), 303-323.

10870 **Johnston, R.J., and Pattie, C. J.** "The Regional Impact of Thatcherism: Attitudes and Votes in Great Britain in the 1980s." *Regional Studies* [Cambridge], 24, No. 6 (December, 1990), 479-493.

10871 Johnston, R.J.; Pattie, C.J., and Johnston, L.C. "Great Britain's Changing Electoral Geography: The Flow-of-the-Vote and Spatial Polarisation." *Tijdschrift Economische en Social Geografie* [Amsterdam], 81, No. 3 (1990), 189-206.

10872 Johnston, R.J., and Rossiter, D.J. "Constituency Building, Political Representation and Electoral Bias in Urban England." In *Geography and the Urban Environment*, Vol. 5, D.T. Herbert and R.J. Johnston, eds. Chichester: John Wiley & Sons, 1982, p. 113-155.

10873 Johnston, R.J., and Taylor, P.J. "The Baby's Gone: On Regional Polarization in British Elections." *Professional Geographer*, 39, No. 1 (February, 1987), 62-64.

10874 Kaufman, Stuart J. "Organiational Politics and Change in Soviet Military Policy." *World Politics* [Baltimore], 46, No. 3 (April, 1994), 355-382.

10875 Kelley, J., and McAllister, I. "Social Context and Electoral Behaviour in Britain." *American Journal of Political Science*, 29 (1985), 565-586.

10876 Keruel, Anne. "Referendum sur Maastricht, Legislatives 1993: La Dimension Bretonne." *Herodote* [Paris], No. 69/70 (Avril-Septembre, 1993), 104-128.

10877 Knowles, Richard D. "Malapportionment in Norway's Parliamentary Elections Since 1921." *Norsk Geografisk Tidsskrift*, 35, No. 3 (1981), 147-159.

10878 Kopstein, Jeffrey, and Richter, Karl-Otto. "Communist Social Structure and Post-Communist Elections: Voting for Reunification in East Germany." *Studies in Comparative Communism* [Oxford], 25, No. 4 (December, 1992), 363-380.

10879 Kovacs, Zoltan. "Az 1990, Evi Parlamenti Valasztasok Politikai Foldrajzi Tapasztalatai." *Foldrajzi Ertesito* [Budapest], 40, Fuzet 1-2 (1991), 55-80.

10880 Krehbiel, Edward. "Geographic Influences in British Elections." *Geographical Review*, 6, No. 2 (July, 1916), 419-432.

10881 Laux, H.D., and Simms, A. "Parliamentary Elections in West Germany: The Geography of Political Choice." *Area*, 5, No. 3 (September, 1973), 166-171.

10882 Laver, M. "Measuring Patterns of Party Support in Ireland." *Economic & Social Review*, 18, No. 2 (1987), 95-100.

10883 Laver, Michael, and Shepsle, Kenneth A. "Government Coalitions and Intraparty Politics." *British Journal of Political Science*, 20, No. 4 (October, 1990), 489-507.

10884 Leruez, Jacque. "Le Royaume-Uni en 1989: Mme. Thatcher Face a Une Crise de Confiance." *Notes et Etudes Documentaires* [Paris], No. 4912-13 (1009), 15-36.

10885 Lewis-Beck, Michael S. and Lockerbie, Brad. "Economics, Votes, Protests: Western European Cases." *Comparative Political Studies*, 22, No. 2 (July, 1989), 155-177.

10886 Lijphart, A. "Religous vs. Linguistic vs. Class Voting: The Crucial Experiment of Comparing Belgium, Canada, South Africa and Switzerland." *American Political Science Review*, 73, No. 2 (June, 1979), 442-458.

10887 Linz, Juan J., and Stepan, Alfred. "Political Identities and Electoral Sequences: Spain, the Soviet Union, and Yugoslavia." *Daedalus* [Cambridge, MA], 121, No. 2 (Spring, 1992), 123-139.

10888 Lodge, Juliet. "Toward a Directly Elected European Parliament." *Australian Outlook*, 32, No. 3 (December, 1978), 345-356.

10889 Lutz, James M. "Diffusion of Nationalist Voting in Scotland and Wales." *Political Geograph Quarterly*, 9, No. 3 (July, 1990), 249-266.

10890 Mamadough, V.D.; and VanderWusten, H.H. "The Influence of the Change of Electoral System on Political Representation: The Case of France in 1985." *Political Geography Quarterly*, 8, No. 2 (April, 1989), 145-159.

10891 Mariot, Peter. "Die Wahlen in Den Slowakischen Nationalrat in Den Jahren 1990 und 1992." *Geographische Zeitschrift* [Stuttgart], 81, Heft 1-2 (1993), 82-97.

10892 Martis, Kenneth C., and others. "The Geography of the 1990 Hungarian Parliamentary Elections." *Political Geography* [Oxford], 11, No. 3 (May, 1992), 283-305.

10893 Masseport, Jean. "Le comportement politique du massif du Diois, essaid'interpretation geographique." *Revue de Geographie Alpine*, 48, No. 1 (1960), 5-167.

10894 Mathieu, Daniel, and Robert, Andrew. "Le paysage politique de la Franche-Comte et son evolution a travers les resultats des trois elections presidentielles de 1965, 1974 et 1981." *Revue Geographieque de l'Est*, tome 22, No. 3-4 (Juillet-Decembre, 1982), 257-279.

10895 McAllister, I. "Campaign Activity and Electoral Outcomes in Britain." *Public Opinion Quarterly*, 49, No. 3 (Fall, 1985), 300-309.

10896 **McDonough, Peter; Barnes, Samuel H.; Lopez Pina, Antonio.** "The Nature of Political Support and Legitimacy in Spain." *Comparative Political Studies*, 27, No. 3 (October, 1994), 349-380.

10897 **Melamed, Assia.** "Les Elections Legislatives de Mars 1993 en Seine-Saint-Denis." *Herodote* [Paris], 69/70 (Avril-Septembre, 1993), 53-88.

10898 **Mercer, John, and Agnew, John.** "Small Worlds and Local Heroes: The 1987 General Election in Scotland." *Scottish Geographical Magazine*, 104, No. 3 (December, 1988), 138–145.

10899 **Miller, Arthur H., and Wlezien, Christopher.** "The Social group Dynamics of Partisan Evaluations." *Electoral Studies*, 12, No. 1 (March, 1993), 5-22.

10900 **Miller, W.L.** "Class, Region and Strata at the British General Election of 1979." *Parliamentary Affairs*, 32, No. 4 (Autumn, 1979), 376-382.

10901 **Miller, W.L.** "There Was No Alternative: The British General Election of 1983." *Parliamentary Affairs*, 37, No. 4 (Autumn, 1984), 364-384.

10902 **Miller, W.L.** "Variations in Electoral Behaviour in the United Kingdom." In *The Territorial Dimension in United Kingdom Politics*, P. Madgwick and R. Rose, eds. London: Macmillan, 1982, 224–250.

10903 **Miller, W.L.; Sarlvik, B.; Crewe, I.; and Alt, J.E.** "The Connection between SNP Voting and the demand for Scottish Self-Government." *European Journal of Political Research*, 5, No. 1 (March, 1977), 88-102.

10904 **Moderne, Franck.** "L'Espagne en 1989: Consolidation ou Sursis Pour le Gouvernement de F. Gonzalez?" *Notes et Etudes Documentaires* [Paris], 4912-13 (1990), 163-182.

10905 **Molini Fernandez, Fernando.** "La Presion Fiscal en EE.UU: Un Factor de Localization." *Estudios Geograficos*, 49, No. 192 (Julio-Septiembre, 1988), 341-356.

10906 **Mughan, Anthony, and McAllister, Ian.** "The Mobilization of the Ethnic Vote: A Thesis with Some Scottish and Welsh Evidence." *Ethnic and Racial Studies*, 4, No. 2 (April, 1981), 189-204.

10907 **Muller, Heribert, and Nissel, Heinz.** "Wahlgeographie und Sozialraumanzalyse-das Beispeil Wien." *Erkunde*, Band 37, Heft 3 (September, 1983), 165-175.

10908 **Newman, Saul.** "The Rise and Decline of the Scottish National Party: Ethnic Politics in a Post-Industrial Environment." *Ethnic nad Racial Studies* [London], 15, No. 1 (January, 1992), 1-35.

10909 **Nooij, A.T.J.** "Political Radicalism Among Dutch Farmers." *Sociologia Ruralis*, 9 (1969), 43-61.

10910 **O'Loughlin, John; Flint, Colin; and Anselin, Luc.** "The Geography of the Nazi Vote: Context, Confession and Class in the Reichstag Election of 1930." *Annals of the Association of American Geographers*, 84, No. 3 (September, 1994), 351-380.

10911 **Osborne, Robert D.** "Northern Ireland: Representation at Westminster and the Boundary Commission." *Irish Geography*, 9 (1976), 115-120.

10912 **Paddison, Ronan.** Spatial Bias and Redistricting in Proportional Representation Systems: A Case Study of the Republic of Ireland. *Tijdschrift voor Economische en Social Geografie*, 67, 4 (July-Aug., 1976), 230–240.

10913 **Pailhe, Joel.** "Les Elections de 1979 Aux Conseils de Prud'Hommes de la Gironde: Contribution a l'etude de la Population Active Salariee" [A Contribution to the Study of the Salariat in Gironde (SW France): An Analysis of the Results of the 1979 Elections to the Conseils de prud'hommes.] *Revue Geographique des Pyrenees et du Sud-Ouest*, Tome 51, Fasc. 2 (Avril, 1980), 111-135.

10914 **Parker, A.J.** "Breaking the Mould?" The Irish General Election of February 1987." *Irish Geography*, 20, Part 1 (1978), 50–53.

10915 **Parker, A.J.** "Geography and the Irish Electoral System. The Presidential Adress of 1984-85." *Irish Geography*, 199, Part 1 (1986), 1-14.

10916 **Partch, Richard D.** "The Transformation of the West German Party System: Patterns of Electoral Change and Consistency." *German Studies Review*, 3, No. 1 (February, 1980), 85-120.

10917 **Parysek, Jerzy J.; Adamczak, Zbigniew; and Grobelny, Ryszard.** "Geografia Polskich Wyborow Prezydenckich 1990 r." *Przeglad Geograficzny* [Warsawa], 63, Zeszyt 3-4 (1991), 245-270.

10918 **Parysek, Jerzy J.; Adamczak, Zbigniew; and Grobelny, Ryszard.** "Regional Differences in the Results of the 1990 Presidential Election in Poland as the First Approximation to a Political Map of the Country." *Environment and Planning A* [London], 23, No. 9 (September, 1991), 1315-1329.

10919 **Pascal, Pierre.** "Deconpage des circonscriptions et Resultats electoraux en france Metropolitaine" [The Impact of the Distribution of Constituencies on Election Results in Metropolitan France]. *Bulletin de l'Association de Geographes Francais,* 56ᵉ, No. 458 (Janvier, 1979), 31-39.

10920 **Pattie, C.J.** "Angels in Carbon? The Mining Vote in the East Midlands." *The East Midland Geographer* [Nottingham], 15, Part 2 (1992), 30-35.

10921 **Pattie, C.J., and Johnston, R.J.** "Embellishment and Delail? The Changing Relationship Between Voting, Class Attitudes, and Core-Periphery Division of Great Britain, 1979-1987." *Institute of British Geographers,* Transactions, New Series, 15, No. 2 (1990), 205-226.

10922 **Peak, L.J.** "Review Essay: How Sarlvik and Crewe Fail to Explain the Conservative Victory of 197 and Electoral Trends in the 1970s." *Political Geography Quarterly,* 3, No. 2 (April, 1984), 161-167.

10923 **Pickles, A.R.; Davies, R.B.; and Crouchley, Robert.** "Individual and Geographical Variation in Longitudinal Voting Data for England 1964-1970." *Environment and Planning A* , 16, No. 9 (September, 1984), 1237-1247.

10924 **Pinto-Duschinsky, M.** "Financing the British General Election of 1979." In *Britain at the Polls, 1979,* H.R. Penniman, ed. Washington, D.C.: American Enterprise Institute, 1981, 210-242.

10925 **Pinto-Duschinsky, M.** "Trends in British Political Funding: 1979-1983." *Parliamentary Affairs,* 38, No. 3 (Summer, 1985), 328-347.

10926 **Piveteau, Jean-Luc.** "A propos de deux referendums en Suisse: quelques reflexions sur l'organisation des espaces mentaux." *Espace Geogaphique,* 1, No. 3 (1972), 177-182.

10927 **Pringle, D.G.** "Further Checks in the Mould? The 1992 Irish General Election." *Irish Geography* [Dublin], 25, No. 2 (1992), 177-181.

10928 **Pringle, Dennis.** "The 1990 Presidential Election." *Irish Geography* [Dublin], 23, No. 2 (1990), 136-141.

10929 **Quellien, J.** "Politics and Elections in Calvados, Normandy, during the Third Republic." *Etudes Nomandes,* 4 (1987), 17-34.

10930 **Racine, Jean-Bernard.** "Langues et Identites Territoriales en Suisse: Les Lecons Geographiques d'un Vote Historique ou la Suisse a L'Heure du Rideau de Rosti." *Annales de Geographie* [Paris], 103e, No. 576 (Mars-Avril, 1994), 152-169.

10931 **Racz, Barnabas.** "Political Participation and Developed Socialism: The Hungarian Elections of 1985." *Soviet Studies,* 39, No. 1 (1987), 40-62.

10932 **Racz, Barnabas.** "Political Pluralisation in Hungary: The 1990 Elections." *Soviet Studies* [Glasgow], 43, No. 1 (1991), 107-136.

10933 **Rae, D./w.** "A Note on the Fractionalization of Some European Party Systems." *Comparative Political Studies,* 1, No. 3 (October, 1968), 413-418.

10934 **Rey, H., and Roy, J.** "Thoughts on the Electoral Evolution of a Department in the Suburbs of Paris; Seine-Saint-Denis." *Herodote,* 43, No. 1 (January-March, 1986), 6-38.

10935 **Roberts, Michael C., and Rumage, Kennard W.** "The Spatial Variations in Urban Left-Wing voting in England and Wales in 1951." *Annals of the Association of American Geographers,* 55, No. 1 (March, 1965), 161-178.

10936 **Roeder, Philip G.** "Electoral Avoidance in the Soviet Union." *Soviet Studies,* 41, No. 3 (July, 1989), 462-483.

10937 **Rokkan, S., and Vallen, H.** "The Mobilisation of the Periphery: Data on Turnout, Party Membership and Candidate Recruitment in Norway. *Acta Sociologica,* Fasc. 1 and 2 (1962), 111-158.

10938 **Rokkan, S., and Vallen, H.** "Regional Contrasts in Norweigan Politics." In *Mass Politics,* E. Allardt and S. Rokkan, eds. New York: Free Press, 1970, 190-250.

10939 **Rokkan, S., and Vallen, H.** "Regional Contrasts in Norweigan Politics." In *Cleavages, Ideologies and Party Systems,* Erik Allardt and Yrjo Littunen, eds. Helsinki: Westermarck Society, *Transactions,* 10 (964), 162-238.

10940 **Rollet, J.** "Regional Elections in Upper Normandy." *Etudes Normandes,* 4 (1987), 49-59.

10941 **Rossiter, D.J.; Johnston, R.J.; and Pattie, C.J.** "Redistricting London: The Issues and Likely Political Effects." *Environment and Planning A* [London], 24, No. 9 (September, 1992), 1221-1230.

10942 **Rusciano, Frank Louis.** "Rethinking the Gender Gap: The Case of West German Elections, 1949-1987." *Comparative Politics,* 24, No. 3 (April, 1992), 335-357.

10943 **Saceamea, Jean.** "Geographie electorale de la France." *L'Information Geographique,* 49, No. 3 (1985), 95-108.

10944 **Savage, M.** "Understanding Political Alignments in Contemporary Britain: Do Localities Matter?" *Political Geography Quarterly*, 6, No. 1 (January, 1987), 53-76.

10945 **Schlesinger, Mildred.** "Legislative Governing Coalitions in Parliamentary Democracies: The Case of French Third Republic." *Comparative Political Studies*, 22, No. 1 (April, 1989), 33-65.

10946 **Sendra, JoaQuin Bosque.** "Modelos Ecologicos del Comportancioto Elecotral en Espana, 1977-1979." *Estudios Geograficos*, 43, No. 166 (Febrero, 1982), 33-59.

10947 **Seroka, Jim.** "THe Interdependence of Institutional Revitalisation and Intra-party Reform in Yugoslavia." *Soviet Studies*, 40, No. 1 (January, 1988), 84-99.

10948 **Sevrin, Robert.** "Un essai d'utilisation geographiques des listes electorales en Belgique." *Annales de Geographie*, 62, No. 332 (July-August, 1953), 293.

10949 **Studlar, Donley T., and Welch, Susan.** "Does District Magnitude Matter? Women Candidates in London Local Elections." *Western Political Quarterly*, 44, No. 2 (June, 1991), 457-466.

10950 **Sulek, Antoni.** "The Polish United Worker's Party: From Mobilisation to Non-Representation." *Soviet Studies* [Glasgow], 42, No. 3 (July, 1990), 499-511.

10951 **Szulkin, Ryszard.** "The 1990 Presidential Election in Poland." *Scandinavian Political Studies* [Oslo], 16, No. 4 (1993), 359-381.

10952 **Taagepera, Rein.** "A Note on the March 1989 Elections in Esotnia." *Soviet Studies* [Glasgow], 42, No. 2 (April, 1990), 329-339.

10953 **Tate, C.N.** "Individual and Contextual Variables in British Voting Behaviour: An Exploratory Note." *American Political Science Review*, 68, No. 4 (Decmeber, 1974), 1656-1662.

10954 **Taylor, A.H.** "Chronological Electoral Geography-The Example of the Liberal Party in South-West England from 1918." *Wessex Geographer*, 9 (1968), 24-32.

10955 **Taylor, P.J.** "The Changing Geography of Representation in Britain." *Area*, 11, No. 4 (December, 1979), 289-294.

10956 **Thomas, G.H.** "The Changing Pattern of Parliamentary Representation in Wales, 1945-1966." *Swansea Geographer*, 6 (1968), 45-49.

10957 **Togeby, Lise.** "The Nature of Declining Party Memership in Denmark: Causes and Consequences." *Scandinavian Political Studies* [Oslo], 15, No. 1 (1992), 1-19.

10958 **Tremblay, Manon.** "Political Party, Political Philosophy and Feminism: A Case Study of the Female and Male Candidates in the 1989 Quebec General Election." *Canadian Journal of Political Science* [Ottawa], 26, No. 3 (September, 1993), 507-522.

10959 **Tuckel, P.; Maisel, Richard; and Schlichting, Kurt.** "Unaffiliated Voters." *Social Science Journal*, 25, No. 4 (1988), 421-436.

10960 **Unger, Aryeh L.** "The Travails of Intra-Party Democracy in the Soviet Union: The Elections to the 19th Conference of the CPSU." *Soviet Studies* [Abingdon], 43, No. 2 (1991), 329-354.

10961 **Upton, G.J.G.** "A Memory Model for Voting Transitions in British Elections." *Journal of the Royal Statistical Society, Series A*, A140, Part 1 (1977), 86-94.

10962 **Upton, G.J.G., and Stray, S.J.** "The Effect of the Environment on Party Identification (UK)." *Environment and Planning A*, 18, No. 1 (October, 1986), 1391-1400.

10963 **Urban, Michael.** "December 1993 as a Replication of Late-Soviet Electoral Practices." *Post-Soviet Affairs*, 10, No. 2 (April-June, 1994), 127-158.

10964 **Valenta, Jiri, and Cunningham, John.** "How Moscow Votes in U.S. Presidential Elections." *Orbis*, 33, No. 1 (Winter, 1989), 3-20.

10965 **Valles I Sanchis, Ismael.** "Eleccions al Crongres dels Diputats, Parlament de Catalunya, Corts Valencianes i Parlament Balear (1977-1991)." *Cuadernos de Geografia* [Valencia], No. 50 (1991), 263-278.

10966 **Vanlaer, Jean.** "Geographie des elections europeennes de juin 1984 (en Belgigue et dans la Communaute)." *Revue Belge de Geographie*, 108e Anne, No. 1, Fasc. 27 (1984), 3-56.

10967 **Vanlaer, Jean.** "Les familles politiques europeennes lors des dernieves election s legislatives (European Political Famileis at the Time of the Last Parliamentary Elections)." *Espace-Populations-Societes*, 3 (1987), 545-556.

10968 **Vanlaer, Jean.** "Les Premieres Elections Libres en Europe de L'Est; Systemes de Partis et Clivages Regionaux." *Revue Belge de Geographie* [Bruxelles], 115e, Fascs. 1-3 (1991), 141-158.

10969 **Vanlaer, Jean.** "Opposition centre-peripherie et vote d'extreme droite en Europe (Care-Periphery Opposition and Extreme Right Vote in Europe)." *Espace-Populations-Societes*, 87, No. 3 (1987), 475-486.

10970 **Wallon-Leduc, C.M.** "Electors and Electorates in France." *Espace-Populations-Societes*, 3 (1987), 540–544.

10971 **Warde, Alan; Savage, M.; Longhurst, Brian; and Martin, Ann.** "Class Consumption and Voting: An Ecological Analysis of Wards and Towns in the 1980 Local Elections in England." *Political Geography Quarterly*, 7, No. 4 (October, 1988), 339–353.

10972 **White, Stephen.** "'Democratisation' in the USSR." *Soviet Studies,* 42, No. 1 (January, 1990), 3-24.

10973 **White, Stephen.** "The Soviet Elections of 1989: From Acclamation to Limited Choice." *Coexistence* [Dordrecht], 28, No. 4 (December, 1991), 513-539.

10974 **Whitefield, Stephen, and Evans, Geoffrey.** "The Russian Election of 1993: Public Opinion and the Transition Experience." *Post-Soviet Affairs* [Silver Spring], 10, No. 1 (January-March, 1994), 38-60.

10975 **Wightman, Gordon.** "Notes on Recent Elections: The Czechoslovak Parliamentary Elections of 1992." *Electoral Studies,* 12, No. 1 (March, 1993), 83-86.

10976 **Williams, Allan.** "Polls Apart in Portugal." *Geographical Magazine,* 56, No. 12 (December, 1984), 645-649.

10977 **Zaslavsky, Victor, and Brym, Robert J.** "The Functions of Elections in the U.S.S.R." *Soviet Studies* (University of Glasgow), 30, No. 3 (July, 1978), 362-371.

10978 **Zoubov, Andrefl, and Kolossov, Vladimir.** "Que Cherchent Les Russes? Traduit par Charle Urjewicz." *Herodote,* No. 72/73 (Janvier-Juin, 1994), 135-156.

10979 **Zubeck, Voytek.** "Poland's Party Self-Destructs." *Orbis,* 34, No. 2 (Spring, 1990), 179-193.

CHAPTER XI

GEOGRAPHY OF INTERNATIONAL RELATIONS

GENERAL AND THEORY

Books

10980 **Abu-Sulayman, Abdul-Hamid Ahmad.** *The Islamic Theory of International Relations: Its Relevance, Past and Present.* Philadelphia: University of Pennsylvania, Ph.D., 1973.

10981 **Anderson, Howard R.,** ed. *Approaches to an Understanding of World Affairs.* Washington, D.C.: National Council for the Social Studies, 1954.

10982 **Armstrong, Tony.** *Breaking the Ice: Repprochement Between East and West Germany, the United States and China, and Israel and Egypt.* Washington, DC: United States Institute of Peace Press, 1993.

10983 **Baxter, Richard Meredith.** *The Theory of International Relations of Walt Whitman Rostow.* Washington, D.C.: American University, Master's Thesis, 1971.

10984 **Beitz, Charles Richard.** *Political Theory and International Relations.* Princeton, New Jersey: Princeton University, Ph.D., 1978.

10985 **Bentwich, Norman.** *International Law.* ("Looking Forward" Pamphlets, No. 2.) London: Royal Institute of International Affairs, 1945.

10986 **Blaikie, Peter Rutherford.** *National Interests and Contractarian Consideration of Justice in International Relations.* Edmonton, Alberta, Canada: University of Alberta, Ph.D., 1977.

10987 **Bobrow, Davis B.** *International Relations: New Approaches.* New York: Foreign Policy Association, 1972.

10988 **Bollens, John C.** *Communities and Government in a Changing World.* Chicago, Illinois: Rand McNally, 1966.

10989 **Bowett, D.W.** *The Law of International Institutions.* London: Stevens, 1970.

10990 **Bowman, Isaiah.** *The Pioneer Fringe.* New York: American Geographical Society, 1931.

10991 **Bradshaw, P.G.** *Geography and International Relations: An Attempt at Synthesis.* United Kingdom: University of Southampton, Ph.D., 1971.

10992 **Bravo, Julio Faundez.** *A Critique of Contemporary Legal and Political Theories of International Relations.* Cambridge, Massachusetts: Harvard University, S.J.D., 1972.

10993 **Brierly, J.L.** *The Law of Nations.* Oxford: Sir Humphrey Waldock, 1963.

10994 **Briggs, H.W.** *The Law of Nations.* New York: Appleton-Century-Crofts, 1952.

10995 **Brook, David,** ed. *Search for Peace: A Reader in International Relations.* New York: Dodd, Mead, 1970.

10996 **Buchanan, W., Cantril, H.,** et al. *How Nations See Each Other: A Study in Public Opinion.* Urbana: University of Illinois Press, 1953.

10997 **Butterfield, H.** *International Conflict in the Twentieth Century.* London: Routledge, 1960.

10998 **Buzan, Barry.** *People, States, and Fear: The National Security Problem in International Relations.* Brighton: Wheatsheaf Books, 1983.

10999 **Cantori, Louis J.,** and **Spiegel, Steven L.** *The International Politics of Regions: A Comparative Approach.* Englewood Cliffs, New Jersey: Prentice-Hall, 1970.

11000 **Carnegie Endowment for International Peace.** *Current Research in International Affairs; A Selected Bibliography of Work in Progress by Private Research Agencies in Australia, Canada, India, Pakistan, Union of South Africa, United Kingdom and the United States.* Introduction by Frederick S. Sunn. New York: Carnegie Endowment for International Peace, 1952.

11001 **Chu, Ebenezer Johnson.** *The Nature and Scope of International Amateur Sports Participation by Selected Countries and the Implications for International Relations.* New York City: New York University, Ph.D., 1976.

11002 **Cioffi-ReVilla, Claudio.** *Formal International Relations Theory: An Inventory, Review, and Integration.* Buffalo: State University of New York, Ph.D., 1979.

11003 **Cohen, Raymond.** *Negotiating Across Cultures: Communication Obstacles in International Diplomacy.* Washington, DC: United States Institute of Peace Press, 1991.

11004 **Cohen, Robert.** *The Color of Man.* New York: Random House, 1968.

11005 **Colby, Charles C.,** ed. *Geographic Aspects of International Relations.* Chicago, Illinois: University of Chicago Press, 1938.

11006 **Colliard, C.A.** *Institutions Internationales.* Paris: Delloz, 1967.

11007 **Corbett, P.E.** *Law in Diplomacy.* Princeton, New Jersey: Princeton University Press, 1959.

11008 **Crowley, Desmond W.** *The Background on Current Affairs.* London: Macmillan, 1958.

11009 *Current Notes on International Affairs.* Canberra: Department of External Affairs, 1958.

11010 **Dalby, Simon.** *Creating the Second Cold War: The Discourse of Politics.* London: Pinter Publishers, 1990.

11011 **Dallin, David J.** *The Big Three: The United States, Britain, Russia.* New Haven, Connecticut: Yale University Press, 1945.

11012 **de Madariaga, Salvador.** *Theory and Practice in International Relations.* Philadelphia: University of Pennsylvania Press, 1937.

11013 **de Rivera, Joseph.** *The Psychological Dimensions of Foreign Policy.* Columbus, Ohio: Charles Merrill, 1968.

11014 **Deutsch, Karl W.** *The Analysis of International Relations.* Englewood Cliffs, New Jersey: Prentice-Hall, 1968.

11015 **Dewitt, David Brian.** *Adaptive Systems: A Contribution to Theory and Method in International Relations.* Stanford, California: Stanford University, Ph.D., 1977.

11016 **Dougherty, John Edson.** *Mexico and Guatemala, 1856-1872: A Case Study in Extra-Legal International Relations.* Los Angeles: University of California, Ph.D., 1969.

11017 **Dougherty, John Edson,** and **Pfaltzgraff, R.L.** *Contending Theories of International Relations. A Comprehensive Survey,* 2nd ed. New York: Harper & Row, 1981.

11018 **Drucker, Peter F.** *Landmarks of Tomorrow.* New York: Harper & Row, 1959.

11019 **Duroselle, Jean-Baptiste,** and **Renouvin, Pierre.** *La communaute internationale, face aux jeunes Etats.* Paris: Armand Colin, 1964.

11020 **Ewing, Ethel E.** *Our Widening World.* Chicago, Illinois: Rand McNally, 1967.

11021 **Factor, Regis Anthony.** *A Comparison of the Basic Assumptions Underlying Three Contemporary Views of International Relations: The Views of: Hans J. Morgenthau, Morton A. Kaplan and Pope John XXIII.* Notre Dame, Indiana: University of Notre Dame, Ph.D., 1974.

11022 **Farrell, John C.,** and **Smith, Asa P.** *Image and Reality in World Politics.* New York City: Columbia University Press, 1967.

11023 **Finnegan, Richard Brendan.** *International Relations: Profile of a Discipline.* Tallahassee: Florida State University, Ph.D., 1971.

11024 **Fowler, William Warner.** *The Semantics of International Relations Data: Mapping the Structure of Complex Social Systems.* Los Angeles: University of Southern California, Ph.D., 1980.

11025 **Friedmann, Wolfgang.** *An Introduction to World Politics.* London: Macmillan, 1965.

11026 **Frolick, David Alfred.** *The Law and Practice of Collective Security in Contemporary International Relations.* Washington, D.C.: American University, Ph.D., 1971.

11027 **Gardner Feldman, Lily Elizabeth.** *The Special Relationship: West Germany and Israel as a Case in International Relations Theory.* Cambridge, Massachusetts: Massachusetts Institute of Technology, 1977.

11028 **George, Alexander L.** *Forceful Persuasion: Coercive Diplomacy as to War.* Washington, DC: United States Institute of Peace Press, 1992.

11029 **George, Pierre.** *Panorama du monde actuel.* Paris: Presses Universitaires de France, Collection Magellan, 1968.

11030 **Gilmozzi, Marcello.** *Dieci anni di vita internazionale, della cronaca alla sintesi.* Gorizia: Institute of International Sociology, 1971.

11031 **Goblet, Y.M.** *Le crepuscule des traites.* Paris: Berger-Levrault, 1934.

11032 **Goodrich, Leland M.,** and **Carroll, Marie J.,** eds. *Documents on American Foreign Relations.* Boston: World Peace Foundation, 1945.

11033 **Grabendorff, Wolf,** and **Roet, Riordan,** eds. *Latin America, Western Europe and the U.S.: Reevaluating the Atlantic Triangle.* New York: Praeger, 1985.

11034 **Grundy, Milton.** *Tax Havens, A World Survey.* Vaduz: Etablissement General des Instituts Financiers, 1969.

11035 **Hall, W.E.** *A Treatise on International Law*, 8th ed., A.P. Higgins, ed. Clarendon Press, 1924.

11036 **Hansen, Niles M.**, ed. *Public Policy and Regional Economic Development: The Experience of Nine Western Countries.* Cambridge, Massachusetts: Ballinger, 1974.

11037 **Hart, Jeffrey Allen.** *Graph Theoretical Models of International Relations.* Berkeley: University of California, Ph.D., 1975.

11038 **Hartman, F.H.** *The Relations of Nations.* New York: Macmillan, 1957.

11039 **Henderson, James L.** *World Questions: A Study Guide.* London: Methuen, 1970.

11040 **Herz, John.** *Political Realism and Political Idealism.* Chicago, Illinois: University of Chicago Press, 1951.

11041 **Higgins, Rosalyn.** *The Development of International Law through the Political Organs of the United Nations.* London: Oxford University Press, 1963.

11042 **Hill, N.** *Claims to Territory in International Law and Relations.* London: Oxford University Press, 1945.

11043 **Hoopes, Roy.** *Getting with Politics.* New York: Delacorte Press, 1968.

11044 **Horrabin, J.F.** *An Atlas of Current Affairs.* London: Victor Gollancz, 1934.

11045 **Horrabin, J.F.** *The Opening-Up of the World.* London: Methuen, 1936.

11046 **Hybel, Alex Roberto.** *Balance of Power and Interaction Theory: A Cross-Sectional and Time-Series Comparison of Theories of International Relations.* Washington, D.C.: American University, Master's Thesis, 1976.

11047 **Jacobs, John Boyd, Jr.** *The Reciprocal Relationships Among Political Process, Technological Change and Political-Spatial Organization: An Analysis Using Communication Satellites, Jet Aircraft in Civil Aviation and Cable Television as Examples of Technological Change.* Worcester, Massachusetts: Clark University, Ph.D., 1971.

11048 **Jenks, C.W.** *The Prospects of International Adjudication.* London: New York: Oceana Publications, 1964.

11049 **Jennings, R.Y.** *The Acquisition of Territory in International Law.* Manchester: Manchester University Press, 1963.

11050 **Kalgutkar, Anjali.** *Biodiversity and the Debate on Genetic Imperialism.* Amherst, MA: Master's thesis, University of Massachusetts, 1994.

11051 **Kanin, David Benjamin.** *The Role of Sport in International Relations.* Medford, Massachusetts: Tufts University, Fletcher School of Law and Diplomacy, Ph.D., 1976.

11052 **Kaplan, Morton A.** *System and Process in International Politics.* New York: John Wiley & Sons, 1964.

11053 **Keohane, R.O.**, and **Nye, J.S.** *Transnational Relations and World Politics.* Cambridge, Massachusetts: Harvard University Press, 1972.

11054 **Laabi, Abdelhai.** *Les Modeles de la Politique Etrangere et du Systeme International Face Aux Relations Nord-Sud: Evaluation et Proposition d'un Nouveau Modele d'Interdependance.* Montreal, Province of Quebec, Canada: University de Montreal, Ph.D., 1979.

11055 **Lambert, Wallace E.**, and **Klineberg, Otto.** *Children's Views of Foreign Peoples: A Cross-National Study.* New York: Appleton-Century Crofts, 1967.

11056 **Langer, W.** *The Diplomacy of Imperialism*, 2nd ed., New York: Alfred A. Knopf, 1960.

11057 **Larus, J.** *Comparative World Politics.* Belmont: Wadsworth, 1964.

11058 **Lauterpacht, H.** *The Development of International Law by the International Court.* New York: Praeger, 1958.

11059 **Lauterpacht, H.** *Recognition in International Law.* Cambridge, England: Cambridge University Press, 1947.

11060 **Lawson, Ruth C.** *International Regional Organizations: Constitutional Foundations.* New York: Praeger, 1962.

11061 **Lebow, Richard Ned**, and **Stein, Janice Gross.** *We All Lost the Cold War.* Princeton: Princeton University Press, 1994.

11062 **Lerner, Stevan Jay.** *Affective Dynamics of International Relations.* Chapel Hill: University of North Carolina, Ph.D., 1983.

11063 **Lippmann, Walter.** *U.S. Foreign Policy: Shield of the Republic.* Boston, Massachusetts: Little Brown, 1943.

11064 **Lousada, Francisco d'Almo.** *Diplomacia e Geografia.* Rio de Janeiro: Imp. Nacional, 1950.

11065 **Macgridis, Roy C.** *Foreign Policy in World Politics.* Englewood Cliffs, New Jersey: Prentice-Hall, 1962.

11066 **Mangold, Peter.** *National Security and International Relations.* London: Routledge, 1990.

11067 **Maoz, Zeev.** *National Choices and International Processes.* Cambridge: Cambridge University Press, 1990.

11068 **Mason, Kenneth.** *The Geography of Current Affairs.* Oxford: Clarendon Press, 1932.

11069 **Massialas, Byron G., and Zevin, Jack.** *World Order.* Chicago, Illinois: Rand McNally, 1970.

11070 **Mazi-Iheme, Chinenye.** *The Impact of International Cooperation in Education on Ecouwas Nations' Foreign Educational Policy (Relations, United States, Russia, France, United Kingdom.* Minneapolis: University of Minnesota, Ph.D., 1984.

11071 **Mazuri, Ali A., and Patil, Haasu H.,** eds. *Africa in World Affairs: The Next Thirty Years.* New York: The Third Press, 1973.

11072 **McCandless, Raymond James, III.** *A College Classroom History of International Relations (1930-1978).* Bethlehem, Pennsylvania: Lehigh University, Ph.D., 1982.

11073 **Meares, Edward Dickinson.** *The Effects of Participation in an International Relations Simulation on the Decisionmaking Attitudes of the Participants.* Baltimore: University of Maryland, Ph.D., 1978.

11074 **Melanson, Richard Allen.** *The Regional System in International Relations Theory: A Comparative Study and a Conceptual Analysis.* Baltimore, Maryland: Johns Hopkins University Press, Ph.D., 1974.

11075 **Meyer, Alfred H.** *Current Events of Contemporary Geography.* New York: Thomas Y. Crowell, 1944.

11076 **Morgenthau, H.J.** *Dilemmas of Politics.* Chicago, Illinois: University of Chicago Press, 1958.

11077 **Morgenthau, H.J.** *Politics Among Nations.* New York: Vintage, 1973.

11078 **Morgenthau, H.J., and Thomson, K.W.** *Principles and Problems of International Politics.* Lanham, Maryland: University Press of America, 1982.

11079 **Most, B.A. and Starr, Harvey.** *"Inquiry, Logic and International Politics.* Columbia: University of South Carolina Press, 1989.

11080 **Murray, Ronald Charles.** *Towards a New Model of International Maritime Relations: The Contribution of Existential Phenomenology and General Systems Theory.* Kingston, Ontario, Canada: Queen's University at Kingston, Ph.D., 1975.

11081 **Neves, Joao.** *Relacao entre o Estado e a poliitca internacional.* Rio de Janeiro: Min. das Relacoes exteriores, 1948.

11082 **Nevins, Allan.** *The New Deal and World Affairs, A Chronicle of International Affairs, 1933-1945.* New Haven, Connecticut: Yale University Press, 1950.

11083 **Ogburn, William Fielding,** ed. *Technology and International Relations.* Chicago, Illinois: University of Chicago Press, 1949.

11084 **Oppenheim, L.** *International Law.* New York: Longmans, 1955.

11085 **Oren, Nissan,** ed. *When Patterns Change: Turning Points in International Politics.* New York: St. Martin's Press, 1984.

11086 **Pappas, Nicholas John.** *Two Contemporary Christian Thinkers on the Use of Force in International Relations: Paul Ramsey and Mulford Q. Sibley.* Charlottesville: University of Virginia, Ph.D., 1973.

11087 **Patterson, Ernest Minor.** *An Introduction to World Economics.* New York: Macmillan, 1947.

11088 **Pearson, Frederic S., and Rochester, J. Martin.** *International Relations: The Global Condition in the Late Twentieth Century.* 3rd ed. New York: McGraw-Hill, Inc., 1992.

11089 **Pearson, Geoffrey A.H.** *Seize the Day: Lester B. Pearson and Crisis Diplomacy.* Ottawa: Carleton University Press, 1993.

11090 **Plano, J.C., and Olton, R.** *The International Relations Dictionary,* 3rd ed. Santa Barbara, California: ABC-CLIO, 1982.

11091 **Reid, Jack Justice.** *The "New York Times," 1931-1941: An Editorial Response to International Relations.* Lawrence: University of Kansas, Ph.D., 1971.

11092 **Renouvin, Pierre, and Duroselle, Jean-Baptiste.** *Introduction a l'Histoire des Relations Internationales.* Paris: Armand Colin, 1970.

11093 **Robinson, Thomas Webster.** *Hans J. Morgenthau's Theory of International Relations.* New York City: Columbia University, Ph.D., 1970.

11094 **Rosenau, James N.** *The Study of Global Interdependence: Essays on the Transnationalization of World Affairs.* New York: Nichols Publishing, 1980.

11095 **Roussy de Sales, Raoul de.** *The Making of Tomorrow.* New York: Reynal and Hitchcock, 1942.

11096 **Sanchez, G. Walter.** *International Relations between Metropolis and Periphery: Theory and Practice (Spanish Text).* Notre Dame, Indiana: University of Notre Dame, Ph.D., 1978.

11097 **Schechter, Neil.** *Prospects of mathematical Systems Analysis in International Relations Using Differential Equations.* Lawrence: University of Kansas, Ph.D., 1971.

11098 **Schuman, Frederick L.** *International Politics.* New York: McGraw-Hill, 1948.

11099 **Sharp, Walter R., and Kirk, Grayson.** *Contemporary International Politics.* New York: Farrar and Rinehart, 1940.

11100 **Simonds, Frank H., and Emeny, Brooks.** *The Great Powers in World Politics; International Relations and Economic Nationalism.* The new ed. New York: American Book Company, 1939.

11101 **Singer, J. David.** *Quantitative International Politics.* New York: The Free Press, 1967.

11102 **Smith, Michael Joseph.** *Realism as an Approach to International Relations: A Critical Analysis.* Cambridge, Massachusetts: Harvard University, Ph.D., 1982.

11103 **Smith, Sarah Ann.** *A Comparative Analysis of the Views of Three Theologians and Their Relevance to International Relations.* Washington, D.C.: American University, Master's Thesis, 1971.

11104 **Stein, Maran Allan.** *Attitude Change in an Introductory International Relations Class.* Urbana: University of Illinois, Ph.D., 1976.

11105 **Steiner, Ethel Miriam.** *Critique of Applications of Systems Theory to International Relations.* Pittsburgh, Pennsylvania: University of Pittsburgh, Ph.D., 1975.

11106 **Sturdevant, Stephen Leroy.** *Implications of Simulation for Teaching: An International Relations Model.* Kansas City: University of Missouri, Ph.D., 1976.

11107 **Tansill, Charles Callan.** *Canadian-American Relations, 1875-1911.* New Haven, Connecticut: Yale University Press, 1943.

11108 **Temperley, H.W.V., ed.** *A History of the Peace Conference of Paris.* London: Henry Frowde, Hodder & Stoughton, 1920.

11109 **Tharp, Louis Benjayman, Jr.** *Mythological Ethnocentrism and Empathy-Blindness: Constructs Relevant to the Double Standard in International Relations.* Claremont, California: Claremont Graduate School, Ph.D., 1974.

11110 **Tinkelman, Theodore Evan.** *The Cultural Role of Sport in International Relations.* Washington, D.C.: American University, Master's Thesis, 1984.

11111 *Treaties and Alliances of the World: An International Survey Covering Treaties in Force and Communities of States.* New York: Charles Scribner's Sons, 1968.

11112 **U.S. Department of State.** *United States Treaties and Other International Agreements, 1950.* Washington, D.C.: Government Printing Office, 1952.

11113 **Valters, Suzanne Elizabeth.** *The Threat or Use of Force in International Relations and the Right of Self-Determination.* New York City: Columbia University, Ph.D., 1979.

11114 **Van der Wusten, Herman, and O'Loughlin, John.** *A Political Geography of International Relations.* New York: Guildford Publications, 1990.

11115 **Vasquez, John Anthony.** *The Power of Paradigms: An Empirical Evaluation of International Relations Inquiry.* Syracuse, New York: Syracuse University, Ph.D., 1974.

11116 **Vattel, E. de.** *The Law of Nations* (translated of the edition of 1758 by C.G. Fenwick). New York: Oceana, 1964.

11117 **Vernay, Alain.** *Les paradis fiscaux.* Paris: Seuil, 1968.

11118 **Ward, B.** *The International Share-Out.* London: Nelson, 1938.

11119 **Whiteman, Marjorie M.** *Digest of International Law.* Washington, D.C.: Department of State Publication, 1965.

11120 **Woolbert, Robert Gale.** *Foreign Affairs Bibliography; A Selected and Annotated List of Books on International Relations, 1932-1942.* New York: Harper & Brothers for Council on Foreign Relations, 1945.

11121 **Wright, Quincy.** *The Study of International Relations.* New York: Appleton Century Crofts, 1955.

11122 **Young, Robert Arthur.** *Prediction and Forecasting in International Relations: An Exploratory Analysis.* Los Angeles: University of Southern California, Ph.D., 1970.

Journals

11123 **Amaro, Manuel.** "Symbol of Good Will: The Antarctic Treaty." *Americas*, 19, No. 2 (February, 1967), 1-9.

11124 **Andriole, Stephen J.** "The Quiet Revolution in the Scientific Study of International Politics and Foreign Policy." *Policy Sciences*, 14, No. 1 (December, 1981), 1-22.

11125 **Antonwicz, Lech.** "Mapa Polityczna Swiata ze Stanowiska Prau a Miedzynarodowego" [The Political Map of the World from the Viewpoint of International Law]. *Przeglad Geograficzny*, Tome 51, Zeszyt 1 (1979), 27-38.

11126 **Armstrong, Hamilton Fish.** "The World is Round." *Foreign Affairs*. 31, No. 2 (January, 1953), 175-199.

11127 **Atwood, Wallace W.** "Geography in International Relations." *Education*, 58, No. 5 (January, 1938), 258-261.

11128 **Bernstein, Robert A., and Weldon, Peter D.** "A Structural Approach to the Analysis of International Relations." *Journal of Conflict Resolution*, 12, No. 2 (June, 1968), 159-181.

11129 **Beukema, Herman.** "The Geographical Factor in the Study of International Relations." *Professional Geographer*, 7, No. 1 (January, 1948), 21-23.

11130 **Boggs, S. Whittemore.** "Mapping the Changing World: Suggested Developments in Maps." *Annals of the Association of American Geographers*, 31, No. 2 (June, 1941), 119-128.

11131 **Bowett, D.W.** "Estoppel before International Tribunals and Its Relation to Acquiescence." *British Year Book of International Law*, 34 (1957), 176.

11132 **Briggs, H.W.** "New Dimensions in International Law." *American Political Science Review*, 46, No. 3 (September, 1952), 677-698.

11133 **Cox, Robert C.** "Social Forces, States and World Order: Beyond International Relations Theory." *Millennium*, 10, No. 2 (Summer, 1981), 126-155.

11134 **Dahrendorf, Ralf.** "Social Change and International Relations." *Jerusalem Journal of International Relations*, 4, No. 1 (Fall, 1979), 34-47.

11135 **Der, Derian, James.** "The (S)pace of International Relations: Simulation, Surveillance, and Speed." *International Studies Quarterly* [Stoneham], 34, No. 3 (September, 1990), 295-310.

11136 **Dix, Arthur.** "Geographische Abrundungstendenzen in der Weltpolitik." *Geographische Zeitschrift*, 17, No. 1 (March, 1911), 1-18.

11137 **Easterly, Ernest S.** "Global Patterns of Legal Systems: Notes Towards a New Geojuriesprudence." *Geographical Review*, 67, No. 2 (April, 1977), 209-220.

11138 **Edmunds, Charles K.** "Geography as a Factor in the Determination of Foreign Policy." *Proceedings of the Institute of World Affairs*, 16th session, 16 (1939), 13-21 and 36-45.

11139 **Etzioni, Amitai.** "A Paradigm for the Study of Political Unification." *World Politics*, 15, No. 1 (October, 1962), 44–74.

11140 **Fleure, H.J.** "The Geographic Study of Society and World Problems." *Socttish Geographical Magazine*, 48, No. 5 (September 15, 1932), 257-274.

11141 **Gaile, Gary L.** "Review Essay: The Geography of International Development." *Political Geography Quarterly*, 7, No. 4 (October, 1988), 369–373.

11142 **Geldenhuys, Deon.** "International Isolation: Toward a Framework for Analysis." *Jerusalem Journal of International Relations*, 10, No. 2 (June, 1988), 1-25.

11143 **Geutzkow, Harold.** "A Use of Simulation in the Study of Inter-Nation Relations." *Behavioral Science*. 4, No. 3 (July, 1959), 183-191.

11144 **Griffiths, Martin.** "Order and International Society: The Real Realism?" *Review of International Studies* [Cambridge], 18, No. 3 (July, 1992), 217-240.

11145 **Halliday, Fred.** "Three Concepts of Internationalism." *International Affairs*, 64, No. 2 (Spring, 1988), 187–198.

11146 **Hauser, Philip M.** "Demographic Dimensions of World Politics." *Science*, 131, No. 3414 (1960), 1641-1647.

11147 **Holsti, K.J.** "Retreat from Utopia: International Relations Theory, 1945-70." *Canadian Journal of Political Science*, 4, No. 2 (June, 1971), 165-177.

11148 **Hormats, Robert D.** "Making Regionalism Safe." *Foreign Affairs* [New York], 73, No. 2 (March/April, 1994), 97-108.

11149 **Jamieson, Alison.** "Mafia and Political Power, 1943-1989." *International Relations* [London], 10, No. 1 (May, 1990), 13-30.

11150 **Keller, R. Carlos.** "Las bases geograficas de la politica internacional." *Atenea*, Ano 2, Num. 10 (Dicbre 31, 1925), 527-535.

11151 **Kelsen, Hans.** "Principle of Sovereign Equality of States as a Basis for International Organization." *Yale Law Journal*, 53, No. 2 (March, 1944), 207-220.

11152 **Kissinger, Henry.** "Reflections on Containment." *Foreign Affairs* [New York], 73, No. 3 (May/June, 1994), 113-130.

11153 **Koch, Howard E.; North, Robert D.; and Zinnes, Dinna.** "Some Theoretical Notes on Geography and International Conflict." *Journal of Conflict Resolution*, 4, No. 1 (March, 1960), 4-14.

11154 **Kottmann, Jean.** "Geography and International Relations." *World Politics*, 3, No. 2 (January, 1951), 153-173.

11155 **Kozyrev, Andrei.** "The Lagging Partnership." *Foreign Affairs* [New York], 73, No. 3 (May/June, 1994), 59-71.

11156 **Lemarchand, Rene,** ed. *The Green and the Black: Qadhafi's Policies in Africa.* Bloomington: Indiana University Press, 1988.

11157 **Mac Gibbon, I.C.** "The Scope of Acquiescence in International Law." *British Year Book of International Law*, 31 (1954), 143.

11158 **Meinig, Donald W.** "Cultural Blocs and Political Blocs: Emergent Patterns in World Affairs." *Western Humanities Review*, 10, No. 3 (Summer, 1956), 203-222.

11159 **Merritt, Richard L.** "Distance and Interaction Among Political Communities." *General Systems*, 9 (1964), 255-263.

11160 **Midlarsky, Manus I.; Crenshaw, Martha; and Yoshida, Fumihiko.** "Why Violence Spreads the Contagion of International Terrorism." *International Studies Quarterly*, 24, No. 2 (June, 1980), 262-298.

11161 **Millar, T.B.** "On Writing About Foreign Policy." *Australian Outlook*, 21, No. 1 (April, 1967), 71-84.

11162 **Mingst, Karen A.** "National Images in International Relations: Structure, Content, and Source." *Coexistence*, 21, No. 3 (November, 1984), 175-189.

11163 **Nafzinger, J.** "The Development of the International Law: Obstacles and Hopes." *Australian Outlook*, 38, No. 1 (April, 1984), 33-39.

11164 **Natoli, S.J., and Bond, Andrew R.,** eds. *Geography in Internationalizing the Undergraduate Curriculum.* Washington, D.C.: Association of American Geographers, Resource Publications in Geography, 1985.

11165 **Nicrop, Tom.** "Macro-Regions and the Global Institutional Network." *Political Geography Quarterly*, 8, No. 1 (January, 1989), 43-65.

11166 **Nijim, Basheer K.** "The Matter of Scale in International Affairs." *Journal of Geography*, 76, No. 1 (January, 1977), 36-37.

11167 **Osala, E.M.** "Some Current Aspects of International Commodity Policy." *Journal of Agricultural Economics*, 18 (1967), 27-46.

11168 **O'Tuathail, Gearoid, and Luke, Timothy W.** "Present at the (Dis)Integration: Deterritorialization and Reterritorialization in the New Wor(l)d Order." *Association of the American Geographers. Annals*, 84, No. 3 (September, 1994), 381-398.

11169 **Patterson, Ernest Minor.** "Looking Toward One World." *Annals of the American Academy of Political and Social Science*, 258 (July, 1948), 1-123. (Whole issue, multiple authors)

11170 **Pearcy, G. Etzel.** "Geography and Foreign Affairs." *Department of State Bulletin*, 52, No. 1357 (June 28, 1965), 1035-1041.

11171 **Peixoto, Joao Batista.** "Os fatores geograifcos e o Mundo em que vivemos." *A Defesa Nacional*, 530 (Set., 1958), 10-14.

11172 **Peterson, M.J.** "Transnational Activity, International Society and World Politics." *Millennium* [London], 21, No. 3 (Winter, 1992), 371-388.

11173 **Piscatori, James P.** "The Contribution of International Law to International Relations." *International Affairs*, 53, No. 2 (April, 1977), 217-231.

11174 **Pistore, Sergio.** "Introduzione allo Studio Delle Relazioni Internazionali." *Il Politico*, Anno 45, No. 2 (Giugno, 1980), 249-270.

11175 **Reclus, Elisee.** "East and West." *Contemporary Review*, 66 (October, 1894), 475-487.

11176 **Rossler, M.** "1988: Geographie et national-socialisme: remarques sur le processus de construction d'une relation problematique." *L'Espace Geographique*, 17 (1988), 5-12.

11177 **Rummel, R.J.** "Dimensions of Conflict Behaviour Within and Between Nations." *Yearbook of the Society for General Systems*, 8 (1963), 1-50.

11178 **Russett, Bruce M.** "Is There a Long-run Trend Toward Concentration in the International System?" *Comparative Political Studies*. 1, No. 1 (April, 1958), 103-122.

11179 **Sawer, G.** "On Writing About Foreign Policy: Comments." *Australian Outlook*, 21, No. 1 (August, 1967), 235-237.

11180 **Schroeder, Paul W.** "The 19th Century International System: Changes in Structure." *World Politics,* 39, No. 1 (October, 1986), 1-26.

11181 **Schumacher, Rupert Von.** "Der Grosse Weltatlas." *Zeitschrift fur Geopolitik*, 12 Jahrgang, Heft 5 (Mai, 1935), 328–329.

11182 **Sevrin, Robert.** "LeConseil d'Assistance Mutuelle Economique, organe de la division internationale du travail entre les Etats socialistes." *La Geographie*, 64, No. 1 (Janvier, 1965), 1-47.

11183 **Singer, J. David.** "The Relevance of the Behavioral Sciences to the Study of International Relations." *Behavioral Science*, 6, No. 4 (October, 1961), 324-335.

11184 **Sinha, R.N.P.** "Geographical Foundations of International Understanding (Hindi). *Bhu–Vigyan*, 1, No. 1 (1986), 38-41.

11185 **Sprout, Harold H.** and **Sprout, Margaret.** "Geography and International Politics in an Era of Revolutionary Change." *Journal of Conflict Resolution*, 4, No. 1 (March, 1960), 145-161.

11186 **Spykman, Nicholas J.** "Geography and Foreign Policy." *American Political Science Review*, 32, No. 1 (March, 1938), 28-50 and 32, No. 2 (June, 1938), 213-236.

11187 **Spykman, Nicholas J.** "Methods of Approach to the Study of International Relations." In *Proceedings of the Fifth Conference of Teachers of International Law and Related Subjects,* Washington, D.C.: Department of Education, (1933), 60–69.

11188 **Spykman, Nicholas J.,** and **Rollins, Abbie A.** "Geographic Objectives in Foreign Policy."

American Political Science Review, 33, No. 3 (September, 1939), 391-410; No. 4 (December, 1939), 591–614.

11189 **Susumu, Awanohara.** "Yours, Mine and Ours." *Far Eastern Economic Review*, 31 (October, 1980a), 50.

11190 **Taylor, Peter J.** "Editorial Comments, One Worldism." *Political Geography Quarterly*, 8, No. 3 (July, 1989), 211-214.

11191 **Terry, James P.** "State Terrorism: A Juridical Examination in Terms of Existing International Law." *Journal of Palestine Studies*, 10, No. 1, Issue 37 (Autumn, 1980), 94-117.

11192 **Thompson, K.W.** "The Limits of Principle in International Politics." *Journal of Politics*, 20, No. 3 (August, 1958), 437-467.

11193 **Van der Wusten, Herman,** and **Nierop, T.** "Functions, Roles and Form in International Politics." *Political Geography Quarterly,* 9, No. 3 (July, 1990), 213-231.

11194 **Weede, E.** "U.S. Support for Foreign Governments or Domestic Disorder and Imperial Intervention, 1958-1965." *Comparative Political Studies*, 10, No. 4 (January, 1978), 497-528.

11195 **White, Gilbert F.** "The Changing Dimensions of the World Community." *Journal of Geography*, 59, No. 4 (April, 1960), 165-170.

11196 **Wigmore, J.H.** "A Map of the World's Law." *Geographical Review*, 19, No. 1 (January, 1929), 114-120.

11197 **Wolfgang, Marvin E.,** ed. "International Terrorism." *The American Academy of Political and Social Science Annals*, 463 (September, 1982), 1–206. (Complete issue, multiple authors)

11198 **Wright, John K.** "Geography and the Study of Foreign Affairs." *Foreign Affairs*, 27, No. 1 (October, 1938), 153-163.

POLITICAL GEOGRAPHY OF REGIONS

AFRICA

Books and Journals

11199 **Addo, Herbert C.** *Trends and Patterns in African Participation in International Relations, 1960-1970: Toward a Theory of International Development*. Ottawa, Ontario, Canada: Carleton University, Ph.D., 1975.

11200 **Attuquayefio, Re Sumo, Jr.** *The Antecedents of Contemporary African Diplomacy (A Theoretical Study of Intertribal and International Relations in Traditional Africa.* Washington, D.C.: American University, Ph.D., 1969.

11201 **Barber, James, and Barratt, John.** *South Africa's Foreign Policy: The Search for Status and Security 1945-1988.* Cambridge: Cambridge University Press, 1990.

11202 **Boyd, Andrew, and Van Rensburg, Patrick.** *An Atlas of African Affairs.* New York: Praeger, 1966.

11203 **Coker, Christopher.** "The United States and National Liberation in Southern Africa." *African Affairs,* 78, No. 312 (July, 1979), 319-330.

11204 **Diaite, Ibou.** "Les constitutions Africaines et le Droit International." *Annals Africaines, 1971-1972,* (1973), 33-51.

11205 **Fordham, Paul.** *The Geography of African Affairs.* Baltimore, Maryland: Penguin, 1972.

11206 **Henderson, Willie.** "Independent Botswana: A Reappraisal of Foreign Policy Options." *African Affairs,* 73, No. 290 (January, 1974), 37-49.

11207 **Hertslet, Edward.** *The Map of Africa by Treaty.* London: Harrison and Sons, 1909.

11208 **Idang, Gordon J.** *Nigeria: Internal Politics and Foreign Policy.* Ibadan: Ibadan University Press, 1973.

11209 **Ingham, K., ed.** *Foreign Relations of African States.* London: Butterworths, 1974.

11210 **Jackson, Mabel V.** *European Powers and South-east Africa; A Study of International Relations on the South-east Coast of Africa, 1796-1856.* (Royal Empire Society, Imperial Studies, No. 18). London: Longmans, 1942.

11211 **Kempton, Daniel R.** "Africa in the Age of Perestroika." *Africa Today* [Denver], 38, No. 3 (1991), 7-29.

11212 **Kittler, Glenn.** *Mediterranean Africa.* Camden: Thomas Nelson and Sons, 1969.

11213 **Korn, David A.** *Assassination in Khartoum.* Bloomington: Indiana University Press, 1993.

11214 **Lamarchand, Rene, ed.** *The Green and Black: Qadhafi's Policies in Africa.* Bloomington: Indiana University Press, 1988.

11215 **MacMichael, H.** *The Anglo-Egyptian Sudan.* London: Faber & Faber, 1934.

11216 **MacMichael, H.** "Egyptian-Sudanere Relations." *Middle Eastern Affairs,* 10 (1959), 102-108.

11217 **Marlowe, J.** *Anglo-Egyptian Relations, 1800-1956,* 2nd ed. London: Frank Cass, 1965.

11218 **Mbachu, Ozoemenam.** "The Impact of Perestroika and Glastnost in African Politics." *Coexistence* [Dordrecht], 29, No. 3 (September, 1992), 297-304.

11219 **Nusta, Manfred Nenge.** *The African Ideology and Its Relationship to Intra-African and International Relations from 1960-1983.* Washington, D.C.: American University, Master's Thesis, 1984.

11220 **O'Loughlin, John, and Anselin, Luc.** "Bringing Geography Back to the Study of International Relations: Spatial Dependence and Regional Context in Africa, 1966-1978." *International Interactions* [Philadelphia], 17, No. 1 (1991), 29-61.

11221 **Onwuka, Ralth I., and Shaw, Timothy M., eds.** *Africa in World Politics: Into the 1990s.* Houndmills: Macmillan, 1989.

11222 **Osia, Kunirum.** *Choice in African International Relations: Perspectives on Arab and Israeli Influences in Africa, 1967 to 1979.* Washington, D.C.: George Washington University, Ph.D., 1981.

11223 **Patman, Robert G.** *The Soviet Union in the Horn of Africa: The Diplomacy of Intervention and Disengagement.* Cambridge: Cambridge University Press, 1990.

11224 **Pazzanita, Anthony G.** "Mauritania's Foreign Policy: The Search for Protection." *The Journal of Modern African Studies* [Cambridge], 30, No. 2 (June, 1992), 281-304.

11225 **Pazzanita, Anthony G.** "Morocco Versus Polisario: A Political Interpretation." *The Journal of Modern African Studies,* 32, No. 2 (June, 1994), 265-278.

11226 **Schraeder, Peter J.** "The Horn of Africa: US foreign Policy in an Altered Cold War Environment." *The Middle East Journal* [Bloomington], 46, No. 4 (Autumn, 1992), 571-593.

11227 **Seidman, Robert B.** "Law Development and Legislative Drafting in English-Speaking Africa." *Journal of Modern African Studies,* 19, No. 1 (March, 1981), 133-161.

11228 **Strack, Harry Robert.** *The International Relations of Rhodesia Under Sanctions.* Iowa City: University of Iowa, Ph.D., 1974.

11229 **Tekle, Amare.** "The Determinants of the Foreigh Policy of Revolutionary Ethiopia." *Journal of Modern African Studies*, 27, No. 3 (September, 1989), 479-502.

11230 **Viall, J.D.** "South Africa: The Road to the Antarctic Treaty." *South African Journal of Antarctic Research* [Pretoria], 21, No. 2 (1991), 125-128.

11231 **Zacklin, Ralph.** *Challenge of Rhodesia: Toward an International Public Policy.* New York: Carnegie Endowment for International Peace, 1969.

11232 **Zike, Admasu.** *An Application of the Theory of Social Exchange to International Relations: The Kagnew Station as the Linchpin of the Ethiopian-United States Relationship.* DeKalb: Northern Illinois University, Ph.D., 1979.

11233 **Zoubir, Yahia H.,** and **Volman, Daniel,** eds. *International Dimensions of the Western Sahara Conflict.* Westport: Praeger Publishers, 1993.

AMERICAS

Books and Journals

11234 **Abdi, Emily George.** *The Teaching of Selected International Relations Concepts in Georgia Public High Schools.* Atlanta: Georgia State University, College of Education, Ph.D., 1979.

11235 **Adams, D.K.,** and **Rodgers, H.B.** *An Atlas of North American Affairs.* London: Methuen, 1970.

11236 **Agnew, John A.** "An Excess of 'National Exceptionalism': Towards a New Political Geography of American Foreign Policy." *Political Geography Quarterly*, 2, No. 2 (April, 1983), 151-166.

11237 **Alton, Roy.** *Problems of American Foreign Relations in the African Area During the Nineteenth Century.* Medford, Massachusetts: Tufts University, Fletcher School of Law and Diplomacy, 1954.

11238 **Ambrose, Stephen E.** *Rise to Globalism: American Foreign Policy Since 1938.* 7th rev. ed. New York: Penguin Books, 1993.

11239 **Andrade, Roberto.** "Peru y Ecuador." *Boletin de la Sociedad Geografica de Lima*, 34, No. 1 (March 31, 1918), 23-34.

11240 **Atkins, G. Pope,** ed. *South America into the 1990's: Evolving International Relationship in a New Era.* Boulder, Colorado: Westview Press, 1990.

11241 **Bagley, Bruce Michael,** and **Aquayo Quezada, Sergio,** eds. *Mexico: In Search of Security.* New Brunswick: Transaction Publishers, 1993.

11242 **Bailey, Thomas A.** *America's Foreign Policies: Past and Present.* (Headline Books, No. 40.) New York: Foreign Policy Association, 1943.

11243 **Ballantine, Joseph W.** *Formosa; A Problem for United States Foreign Policy.* Washington, D.C.: The Brookings Institute, 1952.

11244 **Bisson, T.A.** *America's Far Eastern Policy.* New York: Macmillan, 1945.

11245 **Black, Lloyd D.** "U.S. Economic Aid to Africa." *Annals of the Association of American Geographers*, (abstract), 53, No. 4 (December, 1963), 579-580.

11246 **Blight, James G.; Allyn, Bruce J.;** and **Welch, David A.** *Cuba on the Brink: Castro, the Missile Crisis, and the Soviet Collapse.* New York: Pantheon Books, 1993.

11247 **Boyer, Harold.** *Canada and Cuba: A Study in International Relations.* Burnaby, British Columbia, Canada: Simon Fraser University, Ph.D., 1972.

11248 **Boyle, Peter G.** *American-Soviet Relations: From the Russian Revolution to hte Fall of Communism.* London: Routledge, 1993.

11249 **Brands, H.W.** *Bound to Empire: The United States and the Philippines.* New York: Oxford University Press, 1992.

11250 **Braveboy-Wagner, Jacqueline A.** *The Caribbean in the Pacific Century: Prospects for Caribbean-Pacific Cooperation.* Boulder: Lynne Rienner Publishers, 1993.

11251 **Buchenau, Jurgen.** "Counter-Intervention Against Uncle Sam: Mexico's Support for Nicaraguan Nationalism, 1903-1910." *The Americas* [Washington, DC], 50, No. 2 (October, 1993), 207-232.

11252 **Burnet, Alastair.** *America, 1843-1993: 150 Years of Reporting the American Connection.* London: The Economist Books, 1993.

11253 **Campbell, John C.,** and the Research Staff of the Council on Foreign Relations. *United States in World Affairs, 1947-48.* New York: Harper & Brothers for the Council on Foreign Relations, 1948.

11254 **Carter, Barry E.** *International Economic Sanctions: Improving the Haphazard U.S. Legal Regime.* Cambridge, Massachusetts: Cambridge University Press, 1988.

11255 **Cerny, P.G.** "Political Entropy of American Decline." *Millennium*, 18 (1989), 47–63.

11256 **Charlesworth, James C.**, ed. "America and a New Asia." *Annals of the American Academy of Political and Social Science.* 294 (July, 1954), 1–243 (whole issue, multiple authors).

11257 **Claxton, Brooke.** "The Place of Canada in Post-war Organization." *Canadian Journal of Economics and Political Science*, 10, No. 4 (November, 1944), 409-421.

11258 **Coatsworth, John H.** *Central America and the United States: The Clients and the Colossus.* New York: Twayne Publishers, 1994.

11259 **Coleman, Kenneth, and Herring, George C.**, eds. *The Central American Crisis: Sources of Conflict and the Failure of U.S. Policy.* Wilmington, Delaware: Scholarly Resources, 1985.

11260 **Coram, Robert.** *Caribbean Time Bomb: The United States Complicity in the Corruption of Antigua.* New York: William Morrow and Company, Inc., 1993.

11261 **Corbridge, S.** "The Assymetry of Interdependence: The United States and the Geopolitics of International Financial Relations." *Studies in Comparative International Development*, 23 (1988a), 3–30.

11262 **Cox, Michael.** "The Necessary Partnership?: The Clinton Presidency and Post-Soviet Russia." *International Affairs*, 70, No. 4 (October, 1994), 635-658.

11263 **Cuff, R.D., and Granastein, J.L.** *Ties that Bind: Canadian-American Relations in Wartime from the Great War to the Cold War.* Toronto: Hakkert, 1977.

11264 **Curtis, Gerald L.**, ed. *The United States, Japan, and Asia.* New York: W. W. Norton & Company, 1994.

11265 **Dallek, R.** *Franklin Roosevelt and American Foreign Policy, 1932-1945.* New York: Oxford University Press, 1979.

11266 **Desch, Michael C.** *When the Third World Matters: Latin America and United States Grand Strategy.* Baltimore: The Johns Hopkins University Press, 1993.

11267 **Divine, R.** *Second Change, The Triumph of Internationalism in America During World War II.* New York: Antheum, 1967.

11268 **Dominguez, Jorge I.** "Cuban Foreign Policy." *Foreign Affairs* (New York), 57, No. 1 (Fall, 1978), 83-108.

11269 **Dominguez, Jorge I.** *To Make a World Safe for Revolution: Cuba's Foreign Policy.* Cambridge, Massachusetts: Harvard University Press, 1989.

11270 **Dreisziger, Nandor Alexander Fred.** *The International Joint Commission of the United States and Canada, 1895-1920: A Study in Canadian-American Relations.* Toronto, Ontario, Canada: University of Toronto, Ph.D., 1974.

11271 **Dulles, Foster Rhea.** *Behind the Open Door; the Story of American Far Eastern Relations.* Marguerite Ann Stewart, ed. St. Louis, Missouri: Webster Publishing, 1944.

11272 **Dunkerley, James.** *The Pacification of Central America: Political Change in the Isthmuas, 1987-1993.* London: Verso, 1994.

11273 **Ealy, Lawrence O.** *The Republic of Panama in World Affairs, 1903-1950.* Philadelphia: University of Pennsylvania Press, 1951.

11274 **Eisenhower, Milton S.** "The United States-Latin American Relations; Report to the President." *Department of State Bulletin*, 29, No. 752 (November 23, 1953), 695-717.

11275 **Erisman, H. Michael.** *Cuba's Internaitonal Relations: The Anatomy of a Nationalistic Foreign Policy.* Boulder, Colorado: Westview Press, 1985.

11276 **Fagen, Richard R.** *Forging Peace: The Challenge of Central America.* New York: Basil Blackwell, 1987.

11277 **Fauriol, Georges, and Loser, Eva**, eds. *Cuba: The International Dimension.* New Brunswick: Transaction Publishers, 1990.

11278 **Feig, Konnilyn Gay.** *The Northwest and America's International Relations, 1919-1941: A Regional Study of the Domestic Formulation of Foreign Policy.* Seattle: University of Washington, Ph.D., 1970.

11279 **Fenwick, C.G.** *The Inter-America Regional System.* New York: D.X. McMullen, 1949.

11280 **Fernandez, Damian J.**, eds. *Central America and the Middle Easts: Internationalization of the Crises.* Miami: Florida International University Press, 1990.

11281 **Foreign Affairs.** *America and the World 1984.* New York: Pergamon Press, 1985.

11282 **Forsythe, David P.** *The Politics of International Law: U.S. Foreign Policy Reconsidered.* Boulder, Colorado: Lynne Rienner Publishers, 1990.

11283 **Friedland, E.; Seabury, P.; and Wildavsky, A.** *The Great Detente Disaster: Oil and the Decline of American Foreign Policy.* New York: Basic Books, 1975.

11284 **Gilbert, F.** *The Beginnings of American Foreign Policy.* Princeton, New Jersey: Princeton University Press, 1961.

11285 **Glassner, Martin Ira.** "The Foreign Relations of Jamaica and Trinidad and Tobago, 1960-1965. Reprint: *Caribbean Studies*, 10, No. 3 (October, 1970), 116-153.

11286 **Hamilton, Edward K.**, ed. *America's Global Interests: A New Agenda.* New York: W.W. Norton, 1989.

11287 **Hartman, Jeffrey, and Vogeler, Ingolf.** "Where in the World Is the U.S. Secretary of State?" *Journal of Geography* [Indiana, PA], 92, No. 1 (January-February, 1993), 2-12.

11288 **Hennelly, Michael J.** "US Policy in El Salvador: Creating Beauty or the Beast?" *Parameters* [Carlisle], 23, No. 1 (Spring, 1993), 59-69.

11289 **Hernandez, Jose M.** *Cuba and the United States: Intervention and Militarism, 1868-1933.* Austin: University of Texas Press, 1993.

11290 **Hey, Jeanne A. K.** "Foreign Policy Options Under Dependence: A Theoretical Evaluation with Evidence from Ecuador." *Journal of Latin American Studies* [Cambridge], 25, Part 2 (October, 1993), 543-574.

11291 **Hillman, Richard S., and D'Agostino, Thomas J.** *Distant Neighbors in the Caribbean: The Dominican Republic and Jamaica in Comparative Perspective.* New York: Praeger Publishers, 1992.

11292 **Hyde, C.C.** *International Law, Chiefly as Interpreted and Applied by the United States*, 3 vols. Boston, Massachusetts: Little Brown, 1947.

11293 **Ikenberry, G. John.** "Rethinking the Origins of American Hegemony." *Political Science Quarterly*, 104, No. 3 (Fall, 1989), 375-400.

11294 **James, Joy.** "US Policyin Panama." *Race and Class* [London], 32, No. 1 (July-September, 1990), 17-32.

11295 **Johnson, Gilbert R.** "United States-Canadian Treaties Affecting Great Lakes Commerce and Navigation." *Inland Seas*, 3, No. 4 (October, 1947), 203-207 and 4, No. 2 (Summer, 1948), 113–119.

11296 **Johnson, Sterling.** *Nation-State and Non-State Nations: The International Relations and Foreign Policies of Black America.* Columbus: Ohio State University, Ph.D., 1979.

11297 **Jones, Joseph M.** *A Modern Foreign Policy for the United States.* New York: Macmillan, 1944.

11298 **Jryzanek, Michale J., and Wiarda, Howard J.** *The Politics of External Influence in the Dominican Republic.* New York: Praeger, 1988.

11299 **Joo-Hong, Nam.** *America's Commitment to South Korea: The First Decade of the Nixon Doctrine.* Cambridge University Press, LSE Monographys in International Studies, 1986.

11300 **Kaplan, Robert D.** *The Arabists: The Romance of an American Elite.* New York: The Free Press, 1993.

11301 **Kaplowitz, Donna Rich**, ed. *Cuba's Ties to a Changing World.* Boulder: Lynne Rienner Publishers, 1993.

11302 **Kimble, George H.T.** "A U.S. of Africa: Not Very Likely." *New York Times Magazine*, Section 6 (March 29, 1964), 10 and 68.

11303 **Kingsbury, Robert C., and Schneider, Ronald M.** *An Atlas of Latin American Affairs.* New York: Praeger, 1970.

11304 **Kodras, J. E.** "Shifting Global Strategies of US Foreign Food Aid, 1955-90." *Political Geography*, 12, No. 3 (May, 1993), 232-246.

11305 **Kumamoto, Robert Dale.** *International Terrorism and American Foreign Relations, 1945-1976.* Berkeley: University of California, Ph.D., 1984.

11306 **Kuzma, Larry Donald.** *The International Relations Thought of Zbigniew Brzezinski: An Intellectual Profile.* West Lafayette, Indiana: Purdue University, Ph.D., 1983.

11307 **Landau, S.** *The Dangerous Doctrine: National Security and U.S. Foreign Policy.* Boulder, Colorado: Westview Press, 1988.

11308 **Langley, Lester D.** *America and the Americas: The United States in the Western Hemisphere.* Athens: University of Georgia Press, 1989.

11309 **Langley, Lester D.** *Central America: The Real Stakes: Understanding Central America Before It's Too Late.* New York: Crown Publishing, 1985.

11310 **Langley, Lester D.** *The United States and the Caribbean in the Twentieth Century*, 4th ed. Athens: University of Georgia Press, 1989.

11311 **Lasater, Martin L.** *U.S. Interests in the New Taiwan.* Boulder: Westview Press, 1993.

11312 Leonard, Thomas M. *Central America and United States Policies, 1820s-1980s*. Claremont: Regina Books, 1985.

11313 Lindenberg, Marc. "World Economic Cycles and Central American Political Instability." *World Politics*, 42, No. 3 (April, 1990), 397-421.

11314 Livingston, Craig. "One Thousand Wings': The United States Air Force Group and the American Mission for Aid to Turkey, 1947-50." *Middle Eastern Studies*, 30, No. 4 (October, 1994), 778-825.

11315 Lloyd, Trevor. "Some International Aspects of Arctic Canada." *International Journal*, 25, No. 4 (Autumn, 1970), 717-725.

11316 Lowenthal, Abraham F., and Treverton, Gregory F., eds. *Latin America in a New World*. Boulder: Westview Press, 1994.

11317 Maira, Luis. "Latin America and the Challenges of the New International Order." *Security Dialogue* [London], 23, No. 3 (September, 1992), 69-80.

11318 Major, John. *Prize Possession: The United States and the Panama Canal, 1903-1979*. Cambridge: Cambridge University Press, 1993.

11319 Mandelbaum, Michael, ed. *The Rise of Nations in the Soviet Union: American Foreign Policy and the Disintegration of the USSR*. New York: Council on Foreign Relations Press, 1991.

11320 Manning, Robert A. "Clinton and China: Beyond Human Rights." *Orbis* [Greenwich, CT], 38, No. 2 (Spring, 1994), 193-205.

11321 Mares, David R. "Mexico's Foreign Policy as a Middle Power: The Nicaragua Connection, 1884-1986." *Latin American Research Review*, 23, No. 3 (1988), 81-107.

11322 Marr, Phebe. "The United States, Europe, and the Middle East: An Uneasy Triangle." *The Middle East Journal*, 48, No. 2 (Spring, 1994), 211-225.

11323 Martin, Wayne Richard. *An Analysis of United States International Relations Before and During Limited War*. Los Angeles: University of Southern California, Ph.D., 1970.

11324 Martinez del Rio, Pablo. "Mexican-American Relations, Past, Present, and Future." *Inter-Americana*, Short Papers, 6 (1945), 17-28.

11325 McDonald, James G., and Others. "Twenty-five Years of U.S. Foreign Policy: A Symposium Celebrating the Twenty-Fifth Anniversary of the Foreign Policy Association." *Foreign Policy Reports*, 19, No. 15 (October 15, 1943), 184-211.

11326 McFadden, David W. "John Quincy Adams, American Commercial Diplomacy, and Russia, 1809-1825." *The New England Quarterly* [Boston], 66, No. 4 (December, 1993), 613-629.

11327 McIntyre, Stuart Hull. *Legal Effect of World War II on Treaties of the United States*. The Hague: Martinus Nijhoff, 1958.

11328 McWilliams, Tennant S. *The New South Faces the World: Foreign Affairs and the Southern Sense of Self, 1877-1950*. Baton Rouge: Louisiana State University Press, 1988.

11329 Menezes, Adolpho Justo Bezerra de. *O Brasil e o mundo Asio-Africano*. Rio de Janeiro, Irmaos Pongetti, 1956.

11330 Miller, Ronnie. *Following the Americans to the Persian Gulf: Canada, Australia, and the Development of the New World Order*. Rutherford: Fairleigh Dickinson University Press, 1994.

11331 Momsen, Janet Henshall. "Canada--Caribbean Relations: Wherein the Special Relationship?" *Political Geography* [Oxford], 11, No. 5 (September, 1992), 501-513.

11332 Montaner, Carlos Alberto. "The Roots of Anti-Americanism in Cuba: Sovereignty in an Age of World Cultural Homogeneity." *Caribbean Review*, 13, No. 2 (Spring, 1984), 13-16 and 42-46.

11333 Moreno, Dario. *The Struggle for Peace in Central America*. Gainesville: University Press of Florida, 1994.

11334 Morley, Morris H. *Washington, Somoza, and the Sandinistas: State and Regime in U.S. Policy toward Nicaragua, 1969-1981*. Cambridge: Cambridge University Press, 1994.

11335 Mujal-Leon, Eusebio, and Gutierrez Bermedo, Hernan. "Central America and the New International Political Order: The Eurosocialist Dimension." *International Journal,*, 43, No. 3 (Summer, 1988), 467-472.

11336 Munro, Dana G. "The Mexico City Conference and the Inter-American System." *Department of State Bulletin*, 12, No. 301 (April 1, 1945), 525-530.

11337 Nish, Ian Hill. *The Anglo-Japanese Alliance; The Diplomacy of Two Island Empires, 1984-1907*. Westport, Connecticut: Greenwood Press, 1976.

11338 Oberdorfer, Don. *The Turn from the Cold War to the New Era: The United States and the Soviet Union, 1983-1990*. New York: Poseidon Press, 1991.

11339 O Tuathail, Gearoid. "The Bush Administration and the 'End' of the Cold War: A Critical Geopolitics of U.S. Foreign Policy in 1989." *Geoforum* [Oxford], 23, No. 4 (November, 1992), 437-452.

11340 O Tuathail, Gearoid. "The Effacement of Place?: U.S. Foreign Policy nad the Spatiality of the Gulf Crisis." *Antipode* [Cambridge, MA], 25, No. 1 (January, 1993), 4-31.

11341 O Tuathail, Gearoid, and Agnew, John. "Geopolitics and Discourse: Practical Geopolitical Reasoning in American Foreign Policy." *Political Geography*, 11, No. 2 (March, 1992), 190-204.

11342 Palmer, Michael A. *Guardians of the Gulf: A History of America's Expanding Role in the Persian Gulf, 1833-1992.* New York: The Free Press, 1992.

11343 Payne, Anthony J. "The Belize Triangle: Relations with Britain, Guatemala and the United States." *Journal of Interamerican Studies and World Affairs,* 32, No. 1 (Spring, 1990), 119-135.

11344 Payne, Anthony, and Sutton, Paul, eds. *Modern Caribbean Politics.* Baltimore: The Johns Hopkins University Press, 1993.

11345 Perez, Louis A., Jr. *Cuba and the United States: Ties of Singular Intimacy.* Athens: The University of Georgia Press, 1990.

11346 Platt, Robert S. "Latin America in World Affairs." *Journal of Geography,* 40, No. 9 (December, 1941), 321-330.

11347 Quijano, Anibal, and Wallerstein, Immanuel. "Americanity as a Concept, or the Americas in the Modern World-System." *International Social Science Journal* [Oxford], No. 134 (November, 1992), 549-557.

11348 Rachwald, Arthur R. "United States Policy in East Europe." *Current History,* 74, No. 436 (April, 1978), 150-153 and 185.

11349 Reitzel, William. *The Mediterranean; Its Role in America's Foreign Policy.* New York: Harcourt, Brace, 1948.

11350 "Report of Fourth Antarctic Treaty Consultative Meeting, Santiago, Chile, 1966." *Polar Record,* 13, No. 86 (May, 1967), 629-649.

11351 Rochlin, James. *Discovering the Americas: The Evolution of Canadian Foreign Policy Towards Latin America.* Vnacouver: UBC Press, 1994.

11352 Royal Institute of International Affairs. London Information Department. *The British Caribbean; A Brief Political and Economic Survey.* London: Royal Institute of International Affairs, 1957.

11353 Rueter, Theodore, ed. *The United States in the World of Political Economy.* New York: McGraw-Hill, Inc., 1994.

11354 Samhaber, E. "Ibero-Amerika un der Pazifik." *Zeitschrfit fur Geopolitik,* Jahrgang 12, Heft 1 (Januar, 1935), 12-19.

11355 Schoonover, T.D. *Dollars and Dominion: The Triumph of Liberalism in Mexican-United States Relations, 1861-1867.* Baton Rouge: Louisiana State University Press, 1978.

11356 Schulz, Donald E., ed. *Cuba and the Future.* Westport: Greenwood Press, 1994.

11357 Schulz, Donald E., and Schulz, Deborah Sundloff. *The United States, Honduras, and the Crisis in Central America.* Boulder: Westview Press, 1994.

11358 Schuurman, N. & Verkonen, O. "Midden-Amerika: eenheid in verscheidenheid." *Nederlandse geografische studies,* 103, 1989, 103-133.

11359 Schwarz, Henry G. "America Faces Asia: The Problem of Image Projection." *Journal of Politics,* 26, No. 3 (August, 1964), 532-549.

11360 Segev, Samuel. *The Iranian Triangle: The Untold Story of Isreal's Role in the Iran-Contra Affair.* New York: The Free Press, 1988.

11361 Serbin, Andres. "The Caribbean: Myths and Realities for the 1990s." *Journal of InterAmerican Studies* [Coral Gables], 32, No. 2 (Summer, 1990), 121-141.

11362 Sergeev, V.M. "Interdependence in a Crisis Situation: A Cognitive Approach to Modeling the Caribbean Crisis." *Journal of Conflict Resolution* [Newbury Park], 34, No. 2 (June, 1990), 179-207.

11363 Smith, Robert Freeman. *The Caribbean World and the United States: Mixing Rum and Coca-Cola.* New York: Twayne Publishers, 1994.

11364 Soucek, Carol Boyce. *The Use of Theatre Abroad in United States Government International Cultural Relations (1949-1975).* Los Angeles: University of Southern California, Ph.D., 1975.

11365 Spanier, J. *American Foreign Policy Since World War II.* New York: Oxford University Press, 1973.

11366 "Status of the Pan American Treaties and Conventions." Rev. to January 1, 1942 by the Juridical Division of the Pan American Union. *Bulletin of the Pan American Union*, 76, No. 4 (April, 1942), 218-223.

11367 "Status of the Pan American Treaties and Conventions." Rev. to July 1, 1941 by the Juridical Division of the Pan American Union. *Handbook of Latin American Studies: 1940*, 6 (1941), 336-338.

11368 **Steinbruner, John D.**, ed. *Restructuring American Foreign Policy*. Washington, D.C.: The Brookings Institute, 1989.

11369 **Sutter, Robert G.**, and **Johnson, William R.**, ed. *Taiwan in World Affairs*. Boulder: Westview Press, 1994.

11370 **Targ, Harry R.** *Cuba and the USA: A New World Order?* New York: International Publishers, 1992.

11371 **Thompson, John Herd**, and **Randall, Stephen J.** *Canada and the United States: Ambivalent Allies*. Athens: The University of Georgia Press, 1994.

11372 **Tomlin, Brian William**, and **Molot, Maureen**, eds. *Canada Among Nations 1984: A Time of Transition*. Toronto: James Lorimer, 1985.

11373 **Trotter, Reginald G.** "Future Canadian-American Relations." *Queens Quarterly*, 52, No. 2 (Summer, 1945), 215-229.

11374 **Trubowitz, P.** "Political Conflict and Foreign Policy in the United States: A Geographical Interpretation." *Political Geography*, 12, No. 2 (March, 1993), 121-135.

11375 **Trubowitz, P.** "Sectionalism and American Foreign Policy: The Political Geography of Consensus and Conflict." *International Studies Quarterly*, 36 (1992), 173-190.

11376 **U.S. Department of State.** *Our Southern Partners; The Story of Our Latin American Relations*. Washington, D.C.: U.S. Department of State, 1954.

11377 **U.S. Department of State.** *Treaties in Force; A List of Treaties and Other International Acts of the United States in Force on December 31, 1941*. Publication 2103. Washington, D.C.: U.S. Department of State, 1944.

11378 **U.S. Department of State.** *Antarctica: Measures in Furtherance of Principles and Objectives of the Antarctic Treaty. Certain Recommendations Adopted at the Fourth Consultative Meeting under Article IX of the Antarctic Treaty, Santiago, November 3-18, 1966*. Washington, D.C.: U.S. Department of State, 1969.

11379 **U.S. Department of State.** Office of Legal Advisor. Treaty Affairs Staff. *Treaties in Force: A List of Treaties and Other International Agreements of the United States in Force on January 1, 1970*. Publication 8513. Washington, D.C.: U.S. Department of State, 1970.

11380 **U.S. Department of State.** *Papers Relating to the Foreign Relations of the United States, 1928*. 3 Vol. Publications 1839-1841. Washington, D.C.: U.S. Department of State, 1942-433.

11381 **U.S. Department of State.** *Papers Relating to the Foreign Relations of the United States. Japan: 1931-1941*. 2 Vol. Publications 2008 and 2016, 1942.

11382 **U.S. Treaties**, etc. *Treaties, Conventions, International Acts, Protocols, and Agreements between the United States of America and Other Powers, 1923-1937. Vol. 4: Continuing Treaties, Conventions, International Acts, Protocols, and Agreements between the United States of America and Other Powers, 1776-1923 to December 31, 1937*. U.S. Congress, 75th, 3rd Session. Senate. Document No. 134. Washington, D.C.: U.S. Congress, 75th, 3rd Session, 1938, 3913-5755.

11383 **Varland, John Robert.** *An Investigation of the Effects of an Experimental Course in United States History on Student Ability to Conceptualize and to Transfer Concepts to Issues in International Relations*. Tallahassee: Florida State University, Ph.D., 1976.

11384 **Volgy, Thomas J.**, and **Kenski, Henry.** "Systems Theory and Foreign Policy Reconstructuring Distance Change in Latin America, 1953-1970." *International Studies Quarterly*, 26, No. 3 (September, 1982), 445-474.

11385 **Walworth, A.** *America's Movement: 1918-American Diplomacy at the End of World War I*. New York: W.W. Norton, 1976.

11386 **Waterman, Peter.** "The New Internationalisms: A More Real Thing Than Big, Big Coke?" *Fernand Braudel Center Review*, 11, No. 3 (Summer, 1988), 289-328.

11387 **Webster, Gerald R.** "A Time-series Analysis of Political Support, Strategic Location and the Geography of the U.S. Foreign Aid to Latin America and the Caribbean, 1966-1987." *Geografiska Annaler* [Oslo], 74B, No. 2 (1992), 125-132.

11388 **Weinstein, Brian**, and **Segal, Aaron.** *Haiti: The Failure of Politics*. New York: Praeger Publishers, 1992.

11389 **Whitaker, Arthur P.** *The Western Hemisphere Idea: Its Rise and Decline.* New York: Oxford University Press, 1964.

11390 **Whittlesey, Derwent S.** "Geographic Factors in the Relation of the United States and Cuba." *Geographical Review*, 12, No. 2 (April, 1922), 241-256.

11391 **Williams, Eric.** "The Foreign Policy of the Caribbean States." *Round Table*, 63, No. 249 (January, 1973), 77-88.

11392 **Windmiller, Marshall.** *The Peace Corps and Pan America.* Washington, D.C.: Public Affairs Press, 1970.

11393 **Wynia, Gary W.** *Argentina: Illusions and Realities.* 2nd ed. New York: Holmes & Meier, 1992.

11394 **Yager, J.A.,** and **Steinberg, Eleanor B.** *Energy and U.S. Foreign Policy.* Cambridge, Massachusetts: Ballinger, 1978.

11395 **Yoder, Amos.** *The Conduct of American Foreign Policy Since World War II.* New York: Pergamon Press, 1986.

11396 **Young, H.F.** *Atlas of United States Foreign Relations.* Washington, D.C.: U.S. Department of State, Bureau of Public Affairs, 1983.

ASIA

Books

11397 **Aitchison, C.** *Collection of Treaties, Engagements and Sanads Relating to India and Neighboring Countries.* Calcutta: Government Printing Press, 1929.

11398 **Akaha, Tsuneo,** and **Langdon, Frank,** eds. *Japan in the Posthegemonic World.* Boulder: Lynne Rienner Publishers, 1993.

11399 **Albaharna, Husain M.** *The Legal Status of the Arabian Gulf States: A Study of Their Treaty Relations and Their International Problems.* Dobbs Ferry, New York: Manchester University Press, 1968.

11400 **Ambedkar, B.R.,** and **Divekar.** *Documents on China's Relations with South and Southeast Asia.* New Delhi: Allied Publishers Private, 1964.

11401 **Amirahmadi, Hooshang,** and **Entessar, Nader,** eds. *Iran and the Arab World.* New York: St. Martin's Press, 1993.

11402 **Armin, J.H.** *Middle East Legal Systems.* Glasgow: Royston Limited, 1985.

11403 **Arnold, Anthony.** *The Fateful Pebble: Afghanistan's Role in the Fall of the Soviet Empire.* Novato, CA: Presidio, 1993.

11404 **Asano, Sueko.** *Japanese Economic and Monetary Policies in International Relations: Yen Forecast and Its Implications.* San Diego, California: United States International University, Ph.D., 1978.

11405 *Aspects of India's Foreign Relations.* New Delhi: Indian Council of World Affairs, 1957.

11406 **Balkir, Canan,** and **Williams, Allan M.,** eds. *Turkey and Europe.* London: Pinter Publishers, Ltd., 1993.

11407 **Baram, Amatzia,** and **Rubin, Barry,** eds. *Iraq's Road to War.* New York: St. Martin's Press, 1993.

11408 **Barzilai, Gad; Klieman, Aharon;** and **Shidlo, Gil,** eds. *The Gulf Crisis and Its Global Aftermath.* London: Routledge, 1993.

11409 **Bailer, Uri.** *Between East and West: Israel's Foreign Policy Orientation 1948-1956.* Cambridge: Cambridge University Press, 1990.

11410 **Bains, J.S.** *India's International Disputes: A Legal Study.* New Delhi: Asia Publishing House, 1962.

11411 **Bajracharya, B.R.; Sharma, S.R.;** and **Bakshi, S.R.,** ed. *Foreign Policy of Nepal.* New Delhi: Anmol Publications, 1993.

11412 **Barnett, A. Doak.** *Communist China and Asia: Challenge to American Policy.* New York: Harper & Row, 1961.

11413 **Beatrice, Nanette A.** *The Dialectic of U.S. Relations with China and the East Asian Subsystem: A Diachronic Analysis of Balance of Power.* New York City: New York University, 1986.

11414 **Ben-Zvi, Abraham.** *The United States and Israel: The Limits of the Special Relationship.* New York: Columbia University Press, 1993.

11415 **Bhatt, G.D.** *Indo-Soviet Relations and Indian Public Opinion.* New Delhi: Pacifier, 1989.

11416 **Brecher, Michael.** *The Foreign Policy System of Israel: Setting, Image and Process.* New Haven, Connecticut: Yale University Press, 1972.

11417 **Brown, Frederick Z.** *Second Chance: The United States and Indo-China in the 1990's.* New York: Council on Foreign Relations Press, 1989.

11418 **Brown, William Norman.** *The United States and India and Pakistan.* Cambridge, Massachusetts: Harvard University Press, 1953.

11419 **Bruzonsky, Mark A.,** ed. *The Middle East: U.S. Policy, Israel and the Arabs*, 3rd ed. Washington, D.C.: Congressional Quarterly, 1977.

11420 **Bueler, William M.** *U.S. China Policy and the Problem of Taiwan.* Boulder, Colorado: Colorado Associated University Press, 1971.

11421 **Buszynski, Leszek.** *Gorbachev and Southeast Asia.* London: Routledge, 1992.

11422 **Butwell, Richard A.** *Southeast Asia Today--and Tomorrow; A Political Analysis.* New York: Praeger, 1961.

11423 **Campbell, Eila M.J.,** and **Shave, D.W.** *Asia and the USSR.* London: G. Philip, 1957.

11424 **Chakravarti, Prithwis Chandra.** *India-China Relations.* Calcutta: Firma K.L. Mukhopadhyay, 1961.

11425 **Chakravarti, Prithwis Chandra.** *India's China Policy.* Bloomington: Indiana University Press, 1962.

11426 **Chaudhuri, Mohammed Ahsen.** *Pakistan and the Great Powers.* Karachi: University of Karachi, Council for Pakistan Studies, 1970.

11427 **Choudhury, G.W.,** and **Hasen, Parvez.** *Pakistan's External Relations.* Karachi: Pakistan Institute of International Affairs, 1958.

11428 **Clements, Kevin,** ed. *Peace and Security in the Asia Pacific Region: Post-Cold War Problems and Prospects.* Tokyo: United Nations University Press, 1993.

11429 **Clough, Ralph N.** *Reaching Across the Taiwan Strait: People-to-People Diplomacy.* Boulder: Westview Press, 1993.

11430 **Cohen, Shaul Ephraim.** *The Politics of Planting: Israeli-Palestinian Competition for Control of Land in the Jerusalem Periphery.* Chicago: The University of Chicago Press, 1993.

11431 **Cook, Ralph Elliot.** *The United States and the Armenian Question, 1894-1924.* Medford, Massachusetts: Tufts University, Fletcher School of Law, Ph.D., 1957.

11432 **Crane, Robert I.** *India's Role in Asia.* Chicago, Illinois: University of Chicago Press, 1955.

11433 **Curtis, Gerald L.,** ed. *Japan's Foreign Policy After the Cold War: Coping with Change.* Armonk: M. E. Sharpe, 1993.

11434 **Damodaran, A.K.,** and **Damodaran, U.S.** *Indian Foreign Policy: The Indira Gandhi Years.* New Delhi: Radiant, 1990.

11435 **Darvich-Kodjouri, Djamchid.** *Image and Perception in International Relations: A Case Study of Relationship between Iran and the Great Powers, 1919-1953.* Oxford, Ohio: Miami University, Ph.D., 1976.

11436 **Das Gupta, Joyoti Bhusan.** *India-Pakistan Relations.* Amsterdam: Uitgenerij De Brug-Djambatan, 1958.

11437 **Das Gupta, Joyoti Bhusan.** *Indo-Pakistan Relations, 1947-1955.* New York: Lounz, 1958.

11438 **Drifte, Reinhard.** *Japan's Foreign Policy.* New York: Council on Foreign Relations Press, 1990.

11439 **Druhe, David N.** *Russo-Indian Relations 1466-1917.* New York: Vantage Press, 1970.

11440 **Dubery, Ravi Kant.** *Indo-Sri Lankan Relations with Special Reference to the Tamirl Problems.* New Delhi: Deep and Deep, 1989.

11441 **Duncan, Peter J.S.** *The Soviet Union and India.* New York: Council on Foreign Policy Press, 1989.

11442 **Dupree, Louis.** *India's Stake in Afghan-Pakistan Relations.* New York: American Universities Field Staff, Reports Service, South Asia Series, 6, No.1, 1962.

11443 **Dutt, V.P.** *India and the World.* New Delhi: Sanchar, 1990.

11444 **Fuller, Graham E.,** and **Lesser, Ian O.** *Turkey's New Geopolitics: From the Balkans to Western China.* Boulder: Westview Pres, 1993.

11445 **Funabashi, Yoichi,** eds. *Japan's International Agenda.* New York: New York University Press, 1994.

11446 **Gaikwad, Sanjay.** *Dynamics of Indo-Soviet Relations: The Era of Indira Gandhi.* New Delhi: Deep & Deep, 1990.

11447 **Garver, John W.** *Foreign Relations of the People's Republic of China.* Englewood Cliffs: Prentice Hall, 1993.

11448 **Gause, F. Gregory, III.** *Oil Monarchies: Domestic and Security Challenges in the Arab Gulf States.* New York: Council on Foreign Relations Press, 1994.

11449 **Georgetown University, Center for Strategic Studies.** *United States-Japanese Political Relations: The Critical Issues Affecting Asia's Future.* Washington, D.C.: Georgetown University, 1968.

11450 **Gibney, Frank.** *The Pacific Century: America and Asia in a Changing World.* New York: Charles Scribner's Sons, 1992.

11451 **Goyal, Narendra.** *Prelude to India; A Study of India's Relations with Himalaya States.* New Delhi: Cambridge Book and Stationery Store, 1964.

11452 **Grant, Richard L.,** ed. *China and Southeast Asia: Into the Twenty-First Century.* Honolulu: Pacific Forum/Center for Strategic and Internaitonal Studies, 1993.

11453 **Gupta, Karunakar.** *Indian Foreign Policy.* Calcutta: World Press, 1956.

11454 **Gupta, Sisir K.** *Kashmir: A Study in India-Pakistan Relations.* New York: Asia Publishing House, 1967.

11455 **Gupta, Vinod.** *Anderson Papers: A Study of Nixon's Blackmail of India.* New Delhi: Indian School Supply Depot, Publication Division, 1972.

11456 **Halpern, A.M.,** ed. *Policies Toward China: Views from Six Continents.* New York: McGraw-Hill, 1963.

11457 **Henessy, Jossleyn.** *India and Pakistan in World Politics.* London: K-H Services, 1949.

11458 **Heper, Metin; Oncu, Ayse; and Kramer, Heinz,** eds. *Turkey and the West: Changing Political and Cultural Identities.* London: I.B. Tauris & Co., Ltd., 1993.

11459 **Hepinstall, Larry Gene.** *The International Relations of Military Rule: South Korea, 1961-1963.* Seattle: University of Washington, Ph.D., 1975.

11460 **Hoskins, Halford L.** *The Middle East: Problem Area in World Politics.* New York: Macmillan, 1954.

11461 **Hunter, Shireen T.** *Iran and the World: Continuity in a Revolutionary Decade.* Bloomington: Indiana University Press, 1990.

11462 **Imam, Z.** *Soviet Russia's Policy Towards India and Its Effect on Anglo-Soviet Relations, 1917-1928.* London: London School of Economics, University of London, Ph.D., 1965.

11463 **India (Republic).** Ministry of External Affairs. *China Disregards the Colombo Proposals; Attempts to Retain GAins of Aggression Against India.* New Delhi: Publication Division, Government of India Press, 1963.

11464 **India (Republic).** Ministry of External Affairs. *India and China—A Brief Survey.* New Delhi: Publication Division, Government of India Press, 1966.

11465 **India (Republic).** Ministry of External Affairs. *Leading Events in India-China Relations, 1947-1962.* New Delhi: Publication Division, Government of India Press, 1962.

11466 **India (Republic).** Ministry of External Affairs. *Prime Minister on Sino-Indian Relations.* New Delhi: Publication Division, Government of India Press, 1961.

11467 **India (Republic).** Ministry of Information and Broadcasting. *India and China: A Brief Survey,* by B.K. Acharya. New Delhi: Publication Division, Government of India Press, 1965.

11468 **Isaacs, Harold R.** *Images of Asia: American Views of China and India.* New York: Capricorn Books, 1962.

11469 *Japan's Future in Southeast Asia.* Kyoto: The Center for Southeast Asian Studies, Kyoto University, 1966.

11470 **Kaplan, Morton A., and Ginsburg, Norton S.,** eds. *Japan, America, and the Future World Order.* New York: The Free Press, 1976.

11471 **Kapur, Harish.** *Distant Neighbours: China and Europe.* London: Pinter Publishers, 1990.

11472 **Kapur, Harish.** *The Soviet Union and the Emerging Nations: A Case Study of Soviet Policy Towards India.* London: Joseph for the Graduate Institute of International Studies (Geneva), 1972.

11473 **Karunakaran, K.P.** *India in World Affairs: August 1947-January, 1950.* London: Oxford University Press, 1952.

11474 **Katz, Joshua D., and Friedman-Lichtschein, Tilly C.,** eds. *Japan's New World Role.* Boulder, Colorado: Westview Press, 1985.

11475 **Keddie, Nikki R. and Gasiorowski, Mark J.** *Neither East nor West: Iran, the Soviet Union, and the United States.* New Haven, Connecticut: Yale University Press, 1990.

11476 **Khair, Mohammed Abul.** *United States Foreign Policy in the Indo-Pakistan Sub-Continent, 1940-1955.* Berkeley: University of California, Ph.D., 1962.

11477 **Kihl, Young Whan,** ed. *Korea and the World: Beyond the Cold War.* Boulder: Westview Press, 1994.

11478 **Kim, Samuel S.**, ed. *China and the World: Chinese Foreign Relations in the Post-Cold War Era.* Boulder: Westview Press, 1994.

11479 **Kim, Samuel S.**, ed. *China and the World: New Directions in Chinese Foreign Relations*, 2nd ed. Boulder, Colorado: Westview Press, 1989.

11480 **Kingsbury, Patricia.** *Afghanistan and The Himalayan States.* Garden City: Doubleday, 1960.

11481 **Kingsbury, Robert C.**, and **Pounds, Norman J.G.** *An Atlas of Middle Eastern Affairs.* New York: Praeger, 1970.

11482 **Klintworth, Gary.** *Taiwan in the Asia Pacific in the 1990s.* Canberra: Allen & Unwin, 1994.

11483 **Lattimore, Owen.** *America and Asia: Problems of Today's War and the Peace of Tomorrow.* Claremont, California: Claremont Colleges, 1943.

11484 **LeBoutillier, John.** *Vietnam Now: A Case for Normalizing Relations with Hanoi.* New York: Praeger, 1989.

11485 **Lorenz, Joseph P.** *Egypt and the Arabs: Foreign Policy and the Search for National Identity.* Boulder: Westview Press, 1990.

11486 **Madani, Nizar Obaid.** *The Islamic Content of the Foreign Policy of Saudia Arabia: King Faisal's Call for Islamic Solidarity: 1965-1975.* Washington, D.C.: American University, Ph.D., 1977.

11487 **Maeno, John Rey.** *Postwar Japanese Policy Toward Communist China, 1952-1972: Japan's Changing International Relations and New Political Culture.* Seattle: University of Washington, Ph.D., 1973.

11488 **Mahan, Alfred Thayer.** *The Problem of Asia and Its Effect Upon International Policies.* Boston, Massachusetts: Little Brown, 1900.

11489 **Mandelbaum, Michael**, ed. *Central Asia and the World: Kazakhstan, Uzbekistan, Tajikistan, Kyrgyzstan, and Turkmenistan.* New York: Council on Foreign Relations Press, 1994.

11490 **Mango, Andrew.** *Turkey: The Challenge of a New Role.* Westport: Praeger Publishers, 1994.

11491 **Marr, Phebe**, and **Lewis, William**, eds. *Riding the Tiger: The Middle East Challenge after the Cold War.* Boulder: Westview Press, 1993.

11492 **Mayer, Ann Elizabeth**, ed. *Property, Social Structure and Law in the Modern Middle East.* Albany: State University of New York Press, 1985.

11493 **Menon, Kumara Padmanabha Sivasundara.** *The Indo-Soviet Treaty: Setting and Meaning.* Delhi: Vikas Publications, 1971.

11494 **Michelson, Mark Charles.** *A Place in the Sun: The Foreign Ministry and Perceptions and Policies in Japan's International Relations, 1931-1941.* Urbana: University of Illinois, Ph.D., 1979.

11495 **Miyoshi, Masao**, and **Harootunian, Harry D.**, eds. *Japan in the World.* Durham: Duke University Press, 1993.

11496 **Mojumdar, K.K.** *Political Relations between India and Nepal, 1877-1923.* London: University of London, Ph.D., 1968.

11497 **Monnankulama, Wimal.** *The External Affairs of a New State: An Analysis of the Foreign Policy of Independent Ceylon, 1948-1966.* Chicago, Illinois: University of Chicago, Master's Thesis, 1966.

11498 **Muni, S.D.** *India and Nepal: A Changing Relationship.* Delhi: Konark Publishers Pvt., Ltd., 1992.

11499 **Naik, J.A.** *Soviet Policy Towards India from Stalin to Brezhnev.* Delhi: Vikas Publications, 1970.

11500 **Neelkant, K.** *Partner in Peace. A Study of Indo-Soviet Relations.* Delhi: Vikas Publications, 1972.

11501 **Neher, Clark D.** *Southeast Asia in the New International Era.* Boulder: Westview Press, 1991.

11502 **Neher, Clark D.** *Southeast Asia in the New International Era.* 2nd ed. Boulder: Westview Press, 1994.

11503 **Nguyen-Trieu-Dan.** *Lew Relations de l'Inde Avec la Chine de 1947 a nos Jours.* Theses Doctorat d'Etat, University de Paris, Paris, 1966.

11504 **Nimmo, William F.** *Japan and Russia: A Reevaluation in the Post-Soviet Era.* Westport: Greenwood Press, 1994.

11505 **O'Mally, L.S.S.**, ed. *Modern India and the West.* London: Oxford University Press, 1941.

11506 **Page, Stanley W.** *The USSR and Arabia.* Toronto: Canadian Institute of International Affairs, 1971.

11507 **Palmer, Norman Dunbar.** *South Asia and United States Policy.* Boston, Massachusetts: Houghton Mifflin, 1966.

11508 **Parker, Richard B.** *The Politics of Miscalculation in the Middle East.* Bloomington: Indiana University Press, 1993.

11509 **Peretz, Don.** *Palestinians, Refugees, and the Middle East Peace Process.* Washington, D.C.: United States Institute of Peace Press, 1993.

11510 **Permanand.** *Political Development in South Asia.* New Delhi: Sterling, 1988.

11511 **Printup, Roger Owen.** *Indo-Pakistan Relations: 1962-1967. An Events-Data Approach to Analyzing Dyadic International Conflict.* Syracuse, New York: Syracuse University, Ph.D., 1976.

11512 **Rai, S.S.** *Red Star and the Lotus: The Political Dynamics of Indo-Soviet Relations.* New Delhi: Konard, 1990.

11513 **Ramachandra Rao, P.R.** *India and Her Neighbours.* Bombay: Orient Longmans, 1954.

11514 **Rezun, Miron,** ed. *Iran at the Crossroads: Global Relations in a Turbulent Decade.* Boulder: Westview Press, 1990.

11515 **Rice, Michael.** *False Inheritance: Israel in Palestine and the Search for a Solution.* London: Kegan Paul International, 1994.

11516 **Rosinger, Lawrence K.** *India and the United States: Political and Economic Relations.* New York: Macmillan, 1950.

11517 **Rowland, John.** *A History of Sino-Indian Relations: Hostile Co-Existence.* Princeton, New Jersey: Van Nostrand, 1967.

11518 **Sajjadur, Rasheed K.B.** *China and India--Two Rimland Nations.* Dacca: University of Dacca, 1964.

11519 **Samuel, C.M.,** comp. *India Treaty Manual, 1966. Giving Citations to the Text of Over 1000 Treaties Binding India in 1966; Arranged Chronologically with a Numerical Part Giving Their Register Numbers in the League and the U.N. Records.* Kozhikode: The Author, 1967.

11520 **Sandler, Shmuel.** *The State of Israel, the Land of Israel: The Statist and Ethnonational Dimensions of Foreign Policy.* Westport: Greenwood Press, 1993.

11521 **Sarwar, Hasan K.,** ed. *Documents on the Foreign Relations of Pakistan-China, India, Pakistan.* Karachi: Pakistan Institute of International Affairs, 1966.

11522 **Schaller, Erhard.** *Indiens Politik in Sud-Und Sudostasien: Triebkrafte, Ziele, und Methoden in d. Aussenpolitik (1947-1962).* Potsdam: Deutsche Akademie fur Staats-Und Rechtswissenschaft, Ph.D., 1967.

11523 **Schaller, Michael.** *The United States and China in the Twentieth Century.* (2nd Edition) New York: Oxford University Press, 1990.

11524 **Segal, Gerald,** ed. *Chinese Politics and Foreign Policy Reform.* London: Kegan Paul International, 1990.

11525 **Shandhye, Vincent K.** *The Political Geography of Dutch New Guinea External Aspects.* Columbus: Ohio State University, M.A., 1953.

11526 **Sharma, J.P.** *The Arab Mind: A Study of Egypt, Arab Unity and the World.* New Delhi: Deep & Deep, 1990.

11527 **Sherwani, Latif Ahmed.** *India, China and Pakistan.* Karachi: Council for Pakistan Studies, 1967.

11528 **Shih, Chih-yu.** *China's Just World: The Morality of Chinese Foreign Policy.* Boulder: Lynne Rienner Publishers, 1993.

11529 **Shin, Jung Hyun.** *Japanese-North Korean Relations: 1953-1977--Linkage Politics in a Changing International System.* New York City: City University of New York, Ph.D., 1979.

11530 *Sino-Pakistan Relations: A Legal Study.* New Delhi: The Indian Society of International Law, 1963.

11531 **Spear, Thomas George Percival.** *India, Pakistan and the West.* 3rd ed. New York: Oxford University Press, 1958.

11532 **Stein, Arthur Benjamin.** *India and the Soviet Union: The Nehru Era.* Chicago, Illinois: University of Chicago Press, 1969.

11533 **Syatauw, J.J.G.** *Some Newly Established Asian States and the Development of International Law.* The Hague: Martinus Nijhoff, 1961.

11534 **Tabibi, Abdul Hakim.** *Aftermath Created by British Policy in Respect to Afghanistan-Pakistan Relations.* Washington, D.C.: American University, Ph.D., 1955.

11535 **Talbot, Phillips.** *Aspects of India-Pakistan Relations, 1947-52.* Chicago, Illinois: University of Chicago, Ph.D., 1955.

11536 **Talbot, Phillips,** and **Popkin, S.L.** *India and America: A Study of Their Relations.* New York: Harper & Row, 1958.

11537 **Thakur, Ramesh,** and **Thayer, Carlyle A.,** eds. *Reshaping Regional Relations: Asia-Pacific and the Former Soviet Union.* Boulder: Westview Press, 1993.

11538 **Thayer, Carlyle A.** "Sino-Vietnamese Relations: The Interplay of Ideology nad National Interests." *Asian Survey* [Berkeley], 34, No. 6 (June, 1994), 513-528.

11539 **Unger, Danny,** and **Blackburn, Pual,** eds. *Japan's Emerging Global Role.* Boulder: Lynne Rienner Publishers, 1993.

11540 **Untawale, Mukund Gajanan.** *Cooperation Within Conflict: International Relations in South Asia.* Berkeley: University of California, Ph.D., 1971.

11541 **U.S. Treaties,** etc. *Treaty of Peace with Japan...Entered into Force April 28, 1952; With Declarations by Japan and Exchange of Notes, Signed at San Francisco September 8, 1951.* Washington, D.C.: Government Printing Office, 1952.

11542 **Vko Xuan Han.** *Oil, the Persian Gulf States, and the United States.* Westport: Praeger Publishers, 1994.

11543 **Wagner, Charles Herald.** *Setting the Pattern of Contemporary International Relations in the Middle East: 1953-1958.* Los Angeles: University of Southern California, Ph.D., 1972.

11544 **Wai Chiao Pu.** *Selected Documents on Sino-Indian Relations (December, 1961-May, 1962).* Peking: Foreign Languages Press, 1962.

11545 **Ward, Barbara.** *India and the West.* New York: W.W. Norton, 1961.

11546 **Ward, Richard Edmund.** *West Asia in Indian Foreign Policy.* Cincinnati, Ohio: University of Cincinnati, Ph.D., 1970.

11547 **Ward, Richard Edmund,** ed. *Five Studies in Japanese Politics.* Ann Arbor: University of Michigan Press, 1957.

11548 **Washington, D.C. Embassy of India.** India-Pakistan Relations by B.K. Nehru. Washington, D.C.: Embassy of India, Information Service, 1965.

11549 **Weinbaum, Marvin G.** *Pakistan and Afghanistan: Resistance and Reconstruction.* Boulder: Westview Press, 1994.

11550 **Weinstein, Martin E.** *Japan: The Risen Sun.* New York: Foreign Policy Association, 1970.

11551 **Whittlesey, Derwent S.** *L'Asie du Sud-Est entre la Chine et le Japon.* Quebec: Centre quebecoise de relations internationales, 1971.

11552 **Wilcox, Wayne Ayres.** *Asia and United States Policy.* Englewood Cliffs, New Jersey: Prentice-Hall, 1967.

11553 **Wilcox, Wayne Ayres.** *India and Pakistan.* Washington, D.C.: Foreign Policy Association, 1967. (Headline Series No. 185)

11554 **Wirsing, Robert G.** *India, Pakistan, and the Kashmir Dispute: On Regional Conflict and Its Resolution.* New York: St. Martin's Press, 1994.

11555 **Wolff, Evelyn J.** *Determinants of Indian Foreign Policy.* New York City: Columbia University, Master's Thesis, 1966.

11556 **Woods, Lawrence T.** *Asia-Pacific Diplomacy: Nongovernmental Organizations and International Relations.* Vancouver: UBC Press, 1993.

11557 **Wu, Aitchen K.** *China and the Soviet Union, A Study of Sino-Soviet Relations.* New York: J. Day, 1950.

11558 **Yousuf, Kaniz F.** *Economic and Political Cooperation of Pakistan, Iran and Afghanistan.* Worcester, Massachusetts: Clark University, Master's Thesis, 1959.

11559 **Zafar, Imam.** *Ideology and Reality in Soviet Policy in Asia: Indo-Soviet Relations.* Delhi: Kalyani Publishers, 1975.

11560 **Ziegler, Charles E.** *Foreign Policy and East Asia: Learning and Adaption in the Gorbachev Era.* Cambridge: Cambridge University Press, 1993.

11561 **Zinkin, Maurice.** *Asia and the West.* London: Chatto and Windus, 1951.

Journals

11562 **Alexandrowicz-Alexander, C.H.** "The Legal Position of Tibet." *American Journal of International Law*, 48, No. 2 (April, 1954), 265-274.

11563 **Bandyopadhyaya, Jayantanuja.** "China, India and Tibet." *Foreign Affairs Reports*, 11, No. 12 (December, 1962), 99-107.

11564 **Bandyopadhyaya, Jayantanuja.** "China, India and Tibet." *India Quarterly*, 18, No. 4 (October-December, 1962), 382-393.

11565 **Banerji, Arun Kumar.** "The Quest for a New Order in Indo-British Relations." *India Quarterly*, 33, No. 3 (July-September, 1977), 292-307.

11566 **Barnett, A. Doak.** "Our China Policy: The Need for Change." *Foreign Policy Association*, Headline Series No.204 (February, 1971), 3-63.

11567 **Barua, Hem.** "India's China Policy." *United Asia*, 15, No. 4 (August, 1963), 540-544.

11568 **Bashir, Abdulaziz, and Wright, Stephen.** "Saudi Arabia: Foreign Policy After the Gulf War." *Middle East Policy* [Washington, DC], 1, No. 1 (1992), 107-116.

11569 **Bedeski, Robert E.** "Japan: Diplomacy of a Developmental State." *Journal of Asian and African Studies* [Leiden], 25, Nos. 1-2 (January-April, 1990), 60-70.

11570 **Belfiglio, Valentine J.** "India's Economic and Political Relations with Bhutan. *Asian Survey*, 12, No. 8 (August, 1972), 676-685.

11571 **Berkes, Ross N.** "Indian-Pakistani Relations." *Current History*, 52, No. 2 (May, 1967), 289-294.

11572 **Blum, Robert.** "U.S. Policy Toward Communist China: the Alternatives." *Foreign Policy Association*. Headline Series No. 180 (December, 1966), complete issue.

11573 **Bozeman, Adda B.** "India's Foreign Policy Today: Reflections Upon Its Sources." *World Politics*, 10,No. 2 (January, 1958), 256-273.

11574 **Brecher, Michael.** "International Relations and Asian Studies: The Subordinate State System of Southern Asia." *World Politics*, 15, No. 1 (January, 1963), 213-235.

11575 **Brown, Mary Alice.** "Some Aspects of India's Foreign Policy." *United Asia*, 12, No. 6 (November-December, 1960), 493-498.

11576 **Burki, S.M.** "Sino-Pakistani Relations." *Orbis*, 8, No. 2 (Summer,1964), 391-404.

11577 **Cardinale, Gerald J.** "Through the Japanese Looking Glass." *Asian Survey* [Berkeley], 32, No. 7 (July, 1992), 635-648.

11578 **Catley, H.E.B.** "Indian and Pakistani Relations with the Middle East." *Asian Review*, 50 (July, 1954), 198-209.

11579 **Chaudhri, Mohammed Ahsen.** "Pakistan's Relations with the Soviet Union." *Asian Survey*, 6, No. 9 (September, 1966), 492-500.

11580 **Chavannes, Ed.** "Les resultats de la guerre entre la Chine et le Japon." *Annales de Geographie*, 5, No. 19 (October 15, 1896), 216-233.

11581 **Choi, Chong-Ko.** "The Reception of Western Law in Korea." *Korea Journal*, 20, No. 5 (May, 1980), 33-44.

11582 **Dai, Shen Yu.** "China and Afghanistan." *China Quarterly*, 25, No. 1 (January-March, 1966), 213-221.

11583 **Das, Taraknath.** *Free India's Role in World Affairs*. University of Hawaii, Occasional Paper No. 59 (May, 1953), 93-111.

11584 **Deliusin, Lev.** "The Influence of China's Domestic Policy on Its Foreign Policy." *The Academy of Political Science, Proceedings* [New York], 38, No. 2 (1991), 53-62.

11585 **Dhar, Panna Lal.** "India's Foreign Policy and Liberation of Goa, Daman and Diu." *Asian Review*, 111 (May, 1962), 376-382.

11586 **Drysdale, Alasdair.** "Syria and Iraq--The Geopathology of a Relationship." *GeoJournal* [Dordrecht], 28, No. 3 (November, 1992), 347-355.

11587 **Dutt, Srikant.** "India and the Himalayan States." *Asian Survey*), 11 (Old Series Vol. 67), Part 1 (February, 1980), 71-81.

11588 **Emmerson, Donald K.** "Power and Pancaroba: Indonesia in a Changing World of States." *International Journal* [Toronto], 46, No. 3 (Summer, 1991), 449-474.

11589 **Foot, Rosemary.** "The Changing Pattern of Afghanistan's Relations with Its Neighbours." *Asian Survey*, 11 (Old Series Vol. 67), Part 1 (February, 19780), 55-62.

11590 **Gandhi, Indira.** "India and the World." *Foreign Affairs*, 51, No. 1 (October, 1972), 65-77.

11591 **Garrett, Banning N., and Glaser, Bonnie S.** "Chinese Assessments of Global Trends and the Emerging Era in International Realtions." *Asian Survey*, 29, No. 4 (April, 1989), 347-362.

11592 **Ginsburg, Norton S.** "No Country is an Island: Problems in Japanese Foreign Policy." *Center Report*, 6, No. 3 (August, 1973), 29-32.

11593 **Gordon, Bernard K.** "Japan, the United States and Southeast Asia." *Foreign Affairs*, 56, No. 3 (April, 1978), 579-600.

11594 **Griffith, Percival, Sir.** "India and Pakistan Today." In *Nineteenth Century and After, No. 163*. London: University of London, 1948, 61-67.

11595 **Griffith, W.E.** "Sino-Soviet Relation 1964-1965." *China Quarterly*, 25, No. 1 (January-March, 1966), 3-143.

11596 **Gupta, Sisir K.** "Indo-Pakistan Relations." *International Studies*, 5, No. 3 (July-October, 1963), 174-179.

11597 **Harding, Harry.** *China and Northeast Asia: The Political Dimension.* Lanham, Maryland: University Press of America, 1988.

11598 **Hatta, Mohammad.** "Indonesia's Foreign Policy." *Foreign Affairs*, 31, No. 3 (April, 1953), 441-452.

11599 **Hyder, Khurshid.** "Recent Trends in the Foreign Policy of Pakistan." *World Today*, 22, No. 11 (November, 1966), 482-491.

11600 **Inoguchi, Takashi.** "Japan's Role in International Affairs." *Survival* [London], 34, No. 2 (Summer, 1992), 71-87.

11601 **Joffe, E.G.H.** "Relations Between the Middle East and the West." *The Middle East Journal*, 48, No. 2 (Spring, 1994), 250-267.

11602 **Johnson, Chalmers.** "The New Trust in China's Foreign Policy." *Foreign Affairs*, 57, No. 1 (Fall, 1978), 125-137.

11603 **Joseph, Ralph.** "Pakistan-Soviet Relations." *Eastern World*, 19, No. 3 (March, 1965), 10, 11 and 13.

11604 **Kapur, Ashok.** "Indo-Soviet Treaty and the Emerging Asian Balance." *Asian Survey*, 12, No. 6 (June, 1972), 463-474.

11605 **Kass, Ilana.** "Moscow and the Lebanese Triangle." *Middle East Journal*, 33, No. 2 (Spring, 1979), 164-187.

11606 **Khalilzad, Zalmay.** "Afghanistan and the Crisis in American Foreign Policy." *Survival*, 22, No. 4 (July-August, 1980), 151-'60.

11607 **Khan, Fazlur R.** "The Geographical Basis of Pakistan's Foreign Policy." *Pakistan Geographical Review*, 7, No. 2 (July, 1952), 90-101.

11608 **Kindermann, Gottfried-Kant.** "Washington Between Beijing and Taipei: The Restructured Triangle 1978-1980." *Asian Survey*, 20, No. 5 (May, 1980), 457-476.

11609 **Kliot, Nurit.** "Lebanon-A Geography of Hostages." *Political Geography Quarterly*, 5, No. 3 (July, 1986), 199-220.

11610 **Leifer, Michael.** "The Outlook for Singapore and Malaysia: Foreign Policies in Divergence." *Round Table*, 63, No. 250 (April, 1973), 205-215.

11611 **Mahendra, King of Nepal.** "Relations Between India and Nepal." In *Foreign Affairs Reports*, No. 11. New Delhi: Government of India Press, 1962, 31-36.

11612 **Manning, Robert A.** "Burdens of the Past, Dilemmas of the Future: Sino-Japanese Relations in the Emerging International System." *The Washington Quaterly* [Washington, DC], 17, No. 1 (Winter, 1994), 45-58.

11613 **Martin, Jurek.** "Japanese Foreign Policy in the 1990s." *Asian Affairs* [London], 21, Part 3 (October, 1990), 268-276.

11614 **Mehra, Parushotam L.** "India, China and Tibet, 1950-54." *India Quarterly*, 12, No. 1 (January-March, 1956), 3-22.

11615 **Metcalfe, Sir Aubrey.** "India's Foreign Relations Now and in the Future." *International Affairs*, 21, No. 4 (October, 1945), 485-496.

11616 **Monroe, Elizabeth.** "Kuwait and Aden; A Contrast in British Policies." *Middle East Journal*, 18, No. 1 (Winter, 1964), 63-74.

11617 **Nayar, Baldev Raj.** "Treat India Seriously." *Foreign Policy*, 18 (Spring, 1975), 133-54.

11618 **Neff, Donald.** "Israel-Syria: Conflict at the Jordan River, 1949-1967." *Journal of Palestine Studies*, 23, No. 4, Issue 92 (Summer, 1994), 26-40.

11619 **Ogata, Sadako.** "Japanese Attitudes toward China." *Asian Survey*, 5, No. 8 (August, 1965), 389-398.

11620 **Palmer, Norman D.** "India's Foreign Policy." *Policy Quarterly*, 33, No. 4 (1962), 391-403.

11621 **Park, Kyung Ae,** and **Lee, Sung-Chull.** "Changes and Prospects in Inter-Korean Relations." *Asian Survey* [Berkeley], 32, No. 5 (May, 1992), 429-447.

11622 **Park, Richard L.** "India's Foreign Policy, 1964-1968." *Current History*, 54, No. 320 (April, 1968), 200-206 and 214.

11623 **Payind, Alam.** "Soviet-Afghan Relations from Cooperation to Occupation." *International Journal of Middle East Studies*), 21, No. 1 (February, 1989), 107-128.

11624 **Pike, Douglas.** "Vietnam in 1991: The Turning Point." *Asian Survey* [Berkeley], 32, No. 1 (January, 1992), 74-81.

11625 **Pipes, Daniel.** "Dealing with Middle Eastern Conspiracy Theories." *Orbis* [Philadelphia], 36, No. 1 (Winter, 1992), 41-56.

11626 **Qureshi, Ishtiaq Husain.** "Relations between Great Britain and the Indo-Pakistan Sub-Continent." *Confluence*, 4, No. 1 (January, 1956), 471-486.

11627 **Ramazani, R.K.** "Iran's Foreign Policy: Both North and South." *The Middle East Journal* [Bloomington], 46, No. 3 (Summer, 1992), 393-412.

11628 **Roberson, B.A.** "Islam and Europe: An Enigma or a Myth?" *The Middle East Journal*, 48, No. 2 (Spring, 1994), 288-308.

11629 **Rose, Leo E.** "India and Sikkim: Redefining the Relationship." *Pacific Affairs*, 42, No. 1 (Spring, 1969), 32-46.

11630 **Rubin, Barry.** "Reshaping the Middle East." *Foreign Affairs*, 69, No. 3 (Summer, 1990), 131-146.

11631 **Sayeed, Khalid B.** "Pakistan and China: The Scope and Limits of Convergent Policies." In *Policies Toward China: Views from Six Continents*, A.M. Halpern, ed. New York: McGraw-Hill, 1963, 229-261.

11632 **Schmiegelow, Henrik, and Schmiegelow, Michele.** "How Japan Affects the International System." *International Organization* [Cambridge, MA], 44, No. 4 (Autumn, 1990), 553-588.

11633 **Schwartz, Benjamin I.** "The Maoist Image of World Order." *International Affairs*, 21, No. 1 (January, 1967), 92-102.

11634 **Segal, Gerald.** "The Challenges to Chinese foreign Policy." *Asian Affairs* [London], 21, Part 3 (October, 1990), 295-311.

11635 **Segal, Gerald.** "China's Changing Shape." *Foreign Affairs* [New York], 73, No. 3 (May/June, 1994), 43-58.

11636 **Shaumian, Tatyana L.** "India's Foreign Policy: Interactions of Global and Regional Aspects." *Asian Survey*, 28, No. 11 (November, 1988), 1161-1169.

11637 **Sheng, Michael M.** "Chinese Communist Policy Toward the United States and the Myth of the Lost Chance, 1948-1950." *Modern Asian Studies*, 28, Part 3 (July, 1994), 475-502.

11638 **Shumshere, Papshupati.** "India and Nepal: The Political Economy of a Relationship." *Asian Survey*, 11, No. 7 (July, 1971), 645-660.

11639 **Sicherman, Harvey.** "Politics of Dependence: Western Europe and the Arab-Israeli Conflict." *Orbis*, 23, No. 4 (Winter, 1980), 845-857.

11640 **Sinha, V.K.** "India, China and the Himalayan

States." *China Report*, 3, No. 2 (February-March, 1967), 27-32.

11641 **Subedi, Surya P.** "India-Nepal Security Relations and the 1950 Treaty." *Asian Survey* [Berkeley], 34, No. 3 (March, 1994), 273-284.

11642 **Trager, Frank N.** "The United States and Pakistan; A Failure of Diplomacy." *Orbis*, 9, No. 3 (Fall, 1965), 613-629.

11643 **Watanabe, Akio.** "Foreign Policy Making Japanese Style. *International Affairs*, 54, No. 1 (January, 1978), 75-88.

11644 **Weinbaum, Marvin G.** "War and Peace in Afghanistan: The Pakistani Role." *The Middle East Journal* [Bloomington], 45, No. 1 (Winter, 1990), 71-85.

11645 **Wem-Jui, Tan.** "Chairman Mao's Analysis of the Three Worlds." *China Reconstructs*, 27, No. 1 (January, 1978), 19-22.

11646 **Whiting, Allen S.** "Chinese Domestic Politics and Foreign Policy in the 1970's." *Michigan Papers in Chinese Studies*, 36 (1979), 1-85.

11647 "The Yemen in Modern Treaty Pattern." *American Perspective*, 1, No. 1 (April, 1947), 41-48.

11648 **Zinkin, Taya.** "India Foreign Policy; An Interpretation of Attitudes." *World Politics*, 7, No. 1 (January, 1955), 179-208.

AUSTRALIA, OCEANIA AND ANTARCTICA

Books and Journals

11649 **Cunningham, J.K.** "A Politico-Geographical Appreciation of New Zealand Foreign Policy." *New Zealand Geographer*, 14, No. 2 (October, 1958), 147-160.

11650 **Dorrance, John C.** "The Soviet Union and the Pacific Islands." *Asian Survey* [Berkeley], 30, No. 9 (September, 1990), 908-925.

11651 **Gilpin, Robert.** "International Politics in the Pacific Rim Era." *American Academy of Political and Social Science. Annals*, 505 (September, 1989), 56-67.

11652 **Grotius, Hugo.** *De Jure Belli ac Pacis*. Oxford: J.B. Scott, 1928.

11653 **Harries, Owen.** "Australia's Foreign Policy Under Whitlam." *Orbis*, 19, No. 3 (Fall, 1974), 1090-101.

11654 **Hasluck, P.** "Australia and Southeast Asia." *Foreign Affairs*, 43, No. 1 (October, 1964), 51-63.

11655 **Howard, Michael.** "The Lonely Antipodes? British Reflections on the Future of Australia and New Zealand." *Round Table*, 62, No. 245 (January, 1972), 77-83.

11656 **Leal, Barry.** "Australian Perspectives on Europe." *Journal of European Studies*, 24, Part 2, No. 94 (June, 1994), 127-139.

11657 **Levi, Werner.** *Australia's Outlook on Asia.* East Lansing: Michigan State University Press, 1958.

11658 **McCraw, David J.** "New Zealand's Foreign Policy Under National and Labour Governments; Variations on the 'Small State' Theme?" *Pacific Affairs* [Vancouver], 67, No. 1 (Spring, 1994), 7-25.

11659 **Munro, L.K.** "Geography and New Zealand's External Relations." *New Zealand Geographer*, 4, No. 1 (April, 1948), 1-14.

11660 **United Nations.** *Systematic Survey of Treaties for the Pacific Settlement of International Disputes (1928-1949).* New York: Lake Success, 1948.

11661 **Vakar, Nicholai P.** "Russia and the Baltic States." *Russian Review*, 3, No. 1 (Autumn, 1943), 45-54.

EUROPE

Books and Journals

11662 **Alexandroff, Alan Sheldon.** *Symmetry in International Relations: An Empirical Analysis of the Behavioral Interaction of the European Powers from 1870 to 1890.* Ithaca, New York: Cornell University, Ph.D., 1979.

11663 **Alexeyeva, Ludmilla.** "Unrest in the Soviet Union." *Washington Quarterly, 13, No. 1 (Winter, 1990), 63-77.*

11664 **Armstrong, John A.** *the Soviet Union: Toward Confrontation or Coexistence?* New York: Foreign Policy Association, 1970.

11665 **Aron, Leon, and Jensen, Kenneth M.,** eds. *The Emergence of Russian Foreign Policy.* Washington, DC: United States Institute of Peace Press, 1994.

11666 *The Baltic States and the Soviet Union.* Stockholm: Estonian Information Centre; Latvian National Foundation; Supreme Committee for Liberation of Lithuania, 1962.

11667 **Baranovsky, Vladimir, and Spanger, Hans-Joachim,** eds. *In From the Cold: Germany, Russia, and the Future of Europe.* Boulder: Westview Press, 1992.

11668 **Beonio Brocchierii, V.** *Europe e oltre.* Pavia: Centro Studi Popoli Extra-Europei, 1967.

11669 **Bischof, Gunter, and Pelinka, Anton,** eds. *Austria in the New Europe.* New Brunswick: Transaction Publishers, 1993.

11670 **Blum, Douglas W.** "The Soviet Foreign Policy Belief System: Beliefs, Politics, and Foreign Policy Outcomes." *International Studies Quarterly* [Oxford], 37, No. 4 (December, 1993), 373-394.

11671 **Brandt, Edward R.** *Confidence and Crises of Confidence in International Relations: A Case Study of West German Political Attitudes Toward the United States During the Postwar Period.* Minneapolis: University of Minnesota, Ph.D., 1970.

11672 **Braun, Aurel,** ed. *The Soviet-East European Relationship in the Gorbachev Era: The Prospects for Adaptation.* Boulder, Colorado: Westview Press, 1990.

11673 **Brun, Ellen, and Hersh, Jacques.** *Soviet-Third World Relations in a Capitalist World: The Political Economy of Broken Promises.* New York: St. Martin's Press, 1990.

11674 **Buschenfeld, Herbert J.** "Jugoslawien in der Zerreibprobe." *Geographische Rundschau*, Jahr 41, Heft 11 (November, 1989), 626-632.

11675 **Cavazza, Fabio Luca, and Pelanda, Carlo.** "Maastricht: Before, During, After." *Daedalus* [Cambridge, MA], 123, No. 2 (Spring, 1994), 53-80.

11676 **Checkel, Jeff.** "Ideas, Institutions, and the Gorbachev Foreign Policy Revolution." *World Politics* [Baltimore], 45, No. 2 (January, 1993), 271-300.

11677 **Crampton, R.J.** "The Balkans as a Factor in German Foreign Policy, 1912-1914." *Slavik and East European Review*, 55, No. 3 (July, 1977), 370-390.

11678 **Crowe, David M.** *The Baltic States and the Great Powers: Foreign Relations, 1938-1940.* Boulder: Westview Press, 1993.

11679 **Diebold, William, Jr.** *The Shuman Plan: A Study in Economic Cooperation.* New York: Praeger, 1959.

11680 **Duncan, W. Raymond,** and **Ekedahl, Carolyn McGiffert.** *Moscow and the Third World Under Gorbachev.* Boulder: Westview Press, 1990.

11681 **Edwards, Lovett.** *Russia and Her Neighbours.* New York: Franklin Watts, 1969.

11682 **Edwards, Sutherland H.** *Russian Projects Against India from the Tsar Peter to General Skobeleff.* London: Remington, 1885.

11683 **Elleman, Bruce A.** "Secret Sino-Soviet Negotiations on Outer Mongolia, 1918-1925." *Pacific Affairs* [Vancouver], 66, No. 4 (Winter, 1993-94), 539-563.

11684 **Endersby, James W.,** and **Thomason, W. David.** "Spotlight on Vermont: Third Party Success in the 1990 Congressional Election." *The Social Science Journal,* 31, No. 3 (1994), 251-262.

11685 **Fagen, Richard R.** "Studying Latin American Politics: Some Implications of a Dependencia Approach." *Latin American Research Review,* 12, No. 2 (1977), 3-26.

11686 **Fisher, Charles A.** "The Britain of the East? A Study in the Geography of Imitation." *Modern Asia Studies,* 2, Part 4 (October, 1968), 343-376.

11687 **Flynn, Gregory,** and **Greene, Richard E.,** eds. *The West and the Soviet Union: Politics and Policy.* New York: St. Martin's Press, 1990.

11688 **Frieder, Steven Edward.** *Edmund Burke: Thoughts on French Affairs (A Study of Theory and Practice in International Relations).* Los Angeles: New School for Social Research, Ph.D., 1971.

11689 **Fulton, Edgar Dewar Jr.** *National Interests in the International Economic Relations of Eastern Europe and the Soviet Union in the 1970's.* Washington, D.C.: American University, Master's Thesis, 1979.

11690 **Gathorne-Hardy, G.M.** *The Scandinavian States and Finland: A Political and Economic Survey.* London: Royal Institute of International Affairs, 1951.

11691 **Ginsburgs, George; Rubinstein, Alvin Z.;** and **Smolansky, Oles M.,** eds. *Russian and America: From Rivalry to Reconciliation.* Armonk: M. E. Sharpe, Inc., 1993.

11692 **Golan, Galia.** *Moscow and the Middle East: New Thinking on Regional Conflict.* London: Pinter Publishers, 1992.

11693 **Golan, Galia.** *Soviet Policies in the Middle East from World War Two to Gorbachev.* Cambridge: Cambridge University Press, 1990.

11694 **Grabendorff, Wolf.** "Germany and Latin America: A Complex Relationship." *Journal of Interamerican Studies and World Affairs* [Miami], 35, No. 4 (Winter, 1993-94), 43-100.

11695 **Greer, Deon Carr.** *Finland and Her Relations with the Soviet Union from 1947 to 1960.* Provo, Utah: Brigham Young University, Master's Thesis, 1961.

11696 **Gutjahr, Lothar.** *German Foreign and Defence Policy After Unification.* Translated from the German by Lothar Gutjahr and Paul Addison. London: Pinter Publishers, 1994.

11697 **Hambro, Edyard.** "Some Notes on the Future of the Atlantic Treaty Collaboration." *American Journal of International Law,* 68, No. 2 (April, 1974), 217-226.

11698 **Harle, Vilho,** and **Iivonen, Jyrki,** eds. *Gorbachev and Europe.* London: Pinter Publishers, 1990.

11699 **Harsanyi, Doina,** and **Harsanyi, Nicolae.** "The Discreet Charm of the Little Sister: France and Romania." *East European Quarterly* [Boulder], 28, No. 2 (Summer, 1994), 183-192.

11700 **Hasegawa, Tsuyoshi,** and **Pravda, Alex,** eds. *Perestroika: Soviet Domestic and Foreign Policies.* London: Sage Publications, Ltd., 1990.

11701 **Hertslet, Sir E.** *The Map of Europe by Treaty,* Vol. 4. London: Her Majesty's Stationery Office, 1875-91.

11702 **Howe, Geoffrey.** "Sovereignty and Interdependence: Britain's Place in the World." *International Affairs* [Cambridge], 66, No. 4 (October, 1990), 675-695.

11703 **James, Alan.** "Sovereignty in Eastern Europe." *Millenium* [London], 20, No. 1 (Spring, 1991), 81-89.

11704 **Jasse, Richard L.** "Great Britain and Palestine Towards the United Nations." *Middle Eastern Studies,* 30, No. 3 (July, 1994), 558-578.

11705 **Keeble, Curtis.** *Britain and the Soviet Union, 1917-89.* New York: St. Martin's Press, 1990.

11706 **Keeble, Curtis,** ed. *The Soviet State: The Domestic Roots of Soviet Foreign Policy.* Aldershot: Gower Publishing, 1985.

11707 **Kennan, G.** "The Sources of Soviet Conduct." *Foreign Affairs,* 24, No. 4 (July, 1947), 566-582.

11708 **Kennan, G.** *Soviet Foreign Policy (1917-41).* Princeton, New Jersey: Van Nostrand, 1960.

11709 Kingsbury, Robert C., and Taaffe, Robert N. *An Atlas of Soviet Affairs*. New York: Praeger, 1968.

11710 Koniaris, Theodore B. *A Century of Greek Trade Unions, 1875-1975. Structure, Behavior and International Relations*. Antwerp, Belgium: Dr., Universitaire Instelling Antwerpen, 1976.

11711 Kramer, Mark. "The Role of the CPSU International Department in Soviet Foreign Relations and National Security Policy." *Soviet Studies* [Glasgow], 42, No. 3 (July, 1990), 429-446.

11712 Krepp, Endel. *The Baltic States: A Survey of the International Relations of Estonia, Latvia and Lithuania*. Stockholm: Exhibition Balticum, 1968.

11713 Kubalkova, Vendulka. "The Post-Cold War Geopolitics of Knowledge: International Studies in the Former Soviet Bloc." *Studies in Comparative Communism* [Oxford], 25, No. 4 (December, 1992), 405-417.

11714 Lederer, Ivo J., and Vucinich, Wayne S., eds. *The Soviet Union and the Middle East: The Post-World War II Era*. Stanford, California: Hoover Institution Press, 1974.

11715 Leiss, Amelia C. *European Peace Treaties after World War II*. Boston: World Peace Foundation, 1954.

11716 *Let the American People Know; The Story of Finland's Tragic Struggle for Survival and Its Significance for American Foreign Policy*. New York: Friends of Finland for Dewey, 1941.

11717 Lighthart, Henk, and Reitsma, Henk. "Portugal's Semi-peripheral Middleman Role in Its Relations with England, 1640-1760." *Political Geography Quarterly*, 7, No. 4 (October, 1988), 353-363.

11718 Likhotal, Alexander. "The New Russia and Eurasia." *Security Dialogue* [London], 23, No. 3 (September, 1992), 9-17.

11719 Lincoln, J.K., and Ferris, E.G., eds. *The Dynamics of Latin American Foreign Policies: Challenges for the 1980s*. Boulder, Colorado: Westview Press, 1984.

11720 Lynch, Allen Charles. *The Soviet Study of International Relations, 1968-1982*. New York City: Columbia University, Ph.D., Massachusetts, 1984.

11721 MacDonald, Scott B. *European Destiny, Atlantic Transformations: Portuguese Foreign Policy Under the Second Republic, 1974-1992*. New Brunswick: Transaction Publishers, 1993.

11722 MacFarlane, S. Neil. "Russian Conceptions of Europe." *Post-Soviet Affairs*, 10, No. 3 (July-September, 1994), 234-269.

11723 Malcolm, Neil, ed. *Russia and Europe: An End to Confrontation?* London: Pinter Publishers, 1994.

11724 Markaovits, Andrei S., and Gorski, Philip S. *The German Left: Red, Green and Beyond*. New York: Oxford University Press, 1993.

11725 Martinez-Fernandez, Luis. *Torn Between Empires: Economy, Society, and Patterns of Political Thought in the Hispanic Caribbean, 1840-1878*. Athens: The University of Georgia Press, 1994.

11726 Mattox, Gale A., and Shingleton, A. Bradley, eds. *Germany at the Crossroads: Foreign and Domestic Policy Issues*. Boulder: Westview Press, 1992.

11727 Maxwell, Kenneth, and Spiegel, Steven. *The New Spain: From Isolation to Influence*. New York: Council on Foreign Relations Press, 1994.

11728 McLaurin, Ronald D. *The Soviet Union and the Middle East*. Washington, D.C.: American Institute for Research, Social Environment Research Center, 1974.

11729 Mead, W. R. "Finland in a Changing Europe." *The Geographical Journal* [London], 157, Part 3 (November, 1991), 307-315.

11730 Mehnert, Klaus. "Soviet-Chinese Relations." *International Affairs*. 35, No. 4 (October, 1959), 417-426.

11731 Miller, Linda B. "The Clinton Years: Reinventing US Foreign Policy." *International Affairs*, 70, No. 4 (October, 1994), 621-634.

11732 Musto, Stefen A., and Pinkala, Carl F., eds. *Europe at the Crossroads: Agendas of the Crisis*. New York: Praeger, 1985.

11733 Necatigil, Zaim M. *The Cyprus Question and the Turkish Position in International Law*. Oxford: Oxford University Press, 1989.

11734 Olson, Robert K. "Europe Returns to the Middle East." *American-Arab Affairs* [Washington, DC], No. 34 (Fall, 1990), 46-52.

11735 Paasche, John H. "Europa und die Islamische Welt." *Zeitschrift fur Geopolitik*, 24 Jahrgang, Heft 9 (September, 1953), 501-502.

11736 Palmer, Thomas W. *Search for a Latin American Policy*. Gainesville: University of Florida Press, 1957.

11737 **Parboni, R.** "U.S. Economic Strategies Against Western Europe: From Nixon to Reagan." *Geoforum*, 19 (1988), 45–54.

11738 **Pipa, Arshi.** *Albanian Stalinism: Ideo-Political Aspects.* Boulder: East European Monographs, 1990.

11739 **Porter, Bruce D., and Saivetz, Carol R.** "The Once and Future Empire: Russia and the 'Near Abroad.'" *The Washington Quarterly* [Washington, DC], 17, No. 3 (Summer, 1994), 75–90.

11740 **Pounds, Norman J.G.** *Europe and the Mediterranean.* New York: McGraw-Hill, 1953.

11741 **Pounds, Norman J.G.** *Europe and the Soviet Union.* New York: McGraw-Hill, 1966.

11742 **Pradetto, August.** "Transformation in Eastern Europe, International Cooperation, and the German Position." *Studies in Comparative Communism* [Oxford], 25, No. 1 (March, 1992), 23-30.

11743 **Ragsdale, Hugh, ed.** *Imperial Russian Foreign Policy.* Translated from the Russian by Hugh Ragsdale. Cambridge: Woodrow Wilson Center Press, 1993.

11744 **Rees, G. Wyn, ed.** *International Politics in Europe: The New Agenda.* London: Routledge, 1993.

11745 **Robertson, George.** "Britain in the New Europe." *International Affairs* [Cambridge], 66, No. 4 (October, 1990), 697-702.

11746 **Ronning, C. Neale.** *Diplomatic Asylum. Legal Norms and Political Reality in Latin American Relations.* The Hague: Martinus Nijhoff, 1965.

11747 **Roucek, Joseph S.** *Balkan Politics; International Relations in No Man's Land.* Stanford, California: Stanford University Press, 1948.

11748 **Royal Institute of International Affairs.** Information Department. *The Baltic States; A Survey of the Political and Economic Structure and the Foreign Relations of Estonia, Latvia, and Lithuania.* London: Oxford University Press, 1938.

11749 **Sahni, Varun.** "Not Quite British: A Study of External Influences on the Argentine Navy." *Journal of Latin American Studies* [Cambridge], 25, Part 2 (October, 1993), 489-513.

11750 **Salame, Ghassan.** "Torn Between the Atlantic and the Mediterranean: Europe and the Middle East in the Post-Cold War Era." *The Middle East Journal* [Washington, DC], 48, No. 2 (Spring, 1994), 226-249.

11751 **Sallnow, John.** "Yugoslavia-Powder Keg of Europe." *Geographical Magazine*, 61, No. 5 (May, 1988), 16-20.

11752 **Schuman, Frederick L.** *Soviet Politics at Home and Abroad.* New York: Alfred A. Knopf, 1946.

11753 **Schwarz, Hans-Peter.** "Germany's National and European Interests." *Daedalus* [Cambridge, MA], 123, No. 2 (Spring, 1994), 81-105.

11754 **Sestanovich, Stephen, ed.** *Rethinking Russia's National Interests.* Washington, DC: Center for Strategic and International Studies, 1994.

11755 **Siegfried, Andre.** *Aspects du XX⁰ siecle.* Paris: Hachette, 1961.

11756 **Smith, Wayne, ed.** *The Russians Aren't Coming: New Soviet Policy in Latin America.* Boulder: Lynne Rienner Publishers, 1992.

11757 **Smyser, W.R.** *Germany and America: New Identities, Fateful Rift?* Boulder: Westview Press, 1993.

11758 **Soustelle, Jacques.** "France and Europe: A Gaulist View." *Foreign Affairs*, 30, No. 3 (April, 1952), 545-553.

11759 **Staar, Richard F.** "Soviet Relations with East Europe." *Current History*, 74, No. 436 (April, 1978), 145-149 and 184-185.

11760 **Taylor, J.R.** "Deep Analysis of the Russian Mind." *New York Times.* Section 3 (January 3, 1962), 1.

11761 **Tiersky, Ronald.** "France in the New Europe." *Foreign Affairs* [New York], 71, No. 2 (Spring, 1992), 131-146.

11762 **Tregendhat, Christopher, and Wallace, William.** *Options for British Foreign Policy.* New York: Council on Foreign Relations Press, 1989.

11763 **U.S. Department of State.** *Making Peace Treaties, 1941-1947. A History of the Making of the Peace Beginning with the Atlantic Charter, the Yalta and Potsdam Conferences, and Culminating in the Drafting of Peace Treaties with Italy, Bulgaria, Hungary, Rumania, and Finland.* Publication 2774. European Series 24. Washington, D.C.: U.S. Department of State, 1947.

11764 **Vanneman, Peter.** *Soviet Strategy in Southern Africa: Gorbachev's Pragmatic Approach.* Stanford: Hoover Institution Press, 1990.

Geography of International Relations

11765 **Verheyen, Dirk, and Soe, Christian,** eds. *The Germans and Their Neighbors.* Boulder: Westview Press, 1993.

11766 **Vernet, Daniel.** "The Dilemma of French Foreign Policy." *International Affairs* [Cambridge], 68, No. 4 (October, 1992), 655-664.

11767 **Vitas, Robert A.** *The United States and Lithuania: The Stimson Doctrine of Nonrecognition.* New York: Praeger Publishers, 1990.

11768 **Vleeschauwer, A. de.** *L'Intergration Europeenne et les Territoires d'Outer-Mer. Traites Internationaun Depuis 1944-1945.* Bruxelles: Institut Royal Colonial Belge, 1953.

11769 **Vlekke, Bernard H.M.** *The Netherlands and the United States.* (America Looks Ahead, No. 10.) Boston: World Peace Foundation, 1945.

11770 **Vogel, Walther.** *Des Neue Europa und Seine Historich-Geographischen Grundlagen.* Bonn: Kurt Schroeder, 1921.

11771 **Vorontsov, Guennadi.** "From East-West Conflict to a Common European Home: Theory and Practice." *International Social Science Journal* [Oxford], No. 131 (February, 1992), 107-114.

11772 **Waever, Ole.** "Nordic Nostalgia: Northern Europe After the Cold War." *International Affairs* [Cambridge], 68, No. 1 (January, 1992), 77-102.

11773 **Waever, Ole.** "Three Competing Europes: German, French, Russian." *International Affairs* [Cambridge], 66, No. 3 (July, 1990), 477-493.

11774 **Wasmund, Klaus.** "The Political Socialization of Terrorist Groups in West Germany." *Journal of Political and Military Sociology*, 11, No. 2 (Fall, 1983), 223-240.

11775 **Weigert, Hans W.** "Iceland, Greenland and the United States." *Foreign Affairs*, 23, No. 1 (October, 1944), 112-122.

11776 **Wettig, Gerhard.** *Changes in Soviet Policy Towards the West.* London: Pinter Publishers, 1991.

11777 **Wettig, Gerhard.** "Stalin and German Reunification: Archival Evidence on Soviet Foreign Policy in Spring 1952." *The Historical Journal* [Cambridge], 37, No. 2 (June, 1994), 411-419.

11778 **Wheeler-Bennett, John W.** *The Treaty of Brest-Litovsk and Germany's Eastern Policy.* New ed., rev. and encl. (Oxford Pamphlets on World Affairs, No. 14) Oxford: Clarendon Press, 1940.

11779 **Wolfe, Bertram.** *Krushchev and Stalin's Ghost.* New York: Praeger, 1957.

11780 **Wolfe, Roy I.** *Soviet-American Relations and World Order: The Two and the Many.* Toronto: The Institute for Strategic Studies, Canadian Institute of International Affairs, 1970.

11781 **Wood, William B.** "Forced Migration: Local Conflicts and International Dilemmas." *Annals of the Association of American Geographers*, 84, No. 4 (December, 1994), 607-634.

11782 **World Peace Foundation.** *European Peace Treaties After World War II. Negotiations and Texts of Treaties with Italy, Bulgaria, Hungary, Rumania, and Finland,* Amelia C. Leiss, ed. Boston: 1954.

11783 **Yokoyama, Shiochi.** "Development of International Relations in European Area." *Political Geography* (Seejichiri). Vol. 1. Tokyo: Kokon-Shion, 1960, 169-200.

11784 **Zimmerman, William.** "Markets, Democracy and Russian Foreign Policy." *Post-Soviet Affairs*, 10, No. 2 (April-June, 1994), 103-126.

CHAPTER XII

POLITICAL GEOGRAPHY OF INTERSTATE AND INTERNATIONAL RIVERS, PORTS, BAYS, STRAITS AND CANALS

GENERAL AND THEORY

Books and Journals

11785 **Ahmed, Sukru Emser.** "The Straits: Crux of World Politics." *Foreign Affairs*, 25, No. 2 (January, 1947), 290-302.

11786 **Alexander, Lewis M.** "Exceptions to the Transit Passage Regime: Straits with Routes of Similar Convenience." *Ocean Development and International Law*, 18, No. 4 (1987), 479–496.

11787 **Beck, J. Mansvelt.** "Dakar: Politik-geografische Aspecten van haar Ontwikkeling" [Dakar: Political-geographic Aspects of Its Development], in *Een Wereld van Staten*, J.M.M. van Amersfoort, ed. Alphen aan den Rijn: Samson Uitgeverij, 1981, 209–220.

11788 **Berber, F.J.** *Rivers in International Law.* London: Stevens and Sons, 1959.

11789 **Bouchez, Leo J.** *The Regime of Bays in International Law.* Leyden: A.W. Sythoff, 1964.

11790 **Bruel, Erik.** *International Straits, A Treatise on International Law.* 2 vol. Copenhagen: Nyt Nordisk Forlag A. Busck, 1947.

11791 **Bruffey, Joseph Alan.** *The Impact of the Super-Carrier Upon Ocean Cargo Flows, Routes, and Port Activity.* Seattle: University of Washington, Ph.D., 1971.

11792 **Butler, William E.** *International Straits of the World: Northeast Arctic Passage.* Alphen aan den Rijn: Sijthoff and Noordhoff, 1978.

11793 **Caponera, D.A.** "Patterns of Cooperation in International Water Law: Principles and Institutions." *Natural Resources Journal*, 25, No. 3 (1985), 563–587.

11794 **Graves, Philip.** *The Question of the Straits.* London: Ernest Benn, 1937.

11795 **Griffin, W.L.** "The Use of International Drainage Basins under Customary International Law." *American Journal of International Law*, 53, No. 1 (January, 1959), 50-80.

11796 **Hargreaves, Reginald.** *The Narrow Seas.* London: Sidgwick and Jackson, 1959.

11797 **Harlow, Rear Admiral Bruce A.** "UNCLOS III and Conflict Management in Straits." *Ocean Development and International Law*, 15, No. 2 (1983), 197-208.

11798 **Hurst, C.K.** "Water in International Affairs." *Behind the Headlines*, 16, No. 3 (September, 1956), 1–16.

11799 *International Rivers: Some Case Studies.* Occasional Paper No. 1. Bloomington: Indiana University, Department of Geography, 1965.

11800 **Kaeckenbeeck, G.** *International Rivers.* London: Grotins Society Publications, 1918.

11801 **Kelso, Harold.** "'Navigable Waters' as a Legal Fiction." *Journal of Land and Public Utility Economics*, 17, No. 4 (November, 1941), 394-405.

11802 **Krenz, F.E.** *International Enclaves in Rights of Passage.* Geneve: Droz, 1961.

11803 **Kumar, Chandra.** "International Waterways: Strategic International Straits." *India Quarterly*, 14, No. 1 (January-March, 1958), 87–94.

11804 **Larson, David L.** "Innocent, Transit, and Archipelagic Sea Lane Passage." *Ocean Development and International Law*, 18, No. 4 (1987), 411–444.

11805 **Laylin, John G., and Bianchi, Rinaldo L.** "The Role of Adjudication in International River Disputes." *American Journal of International Law*, 53, No. 1 (January, 1959), 30-49.

11806 **Leifer, Michael.** *International Straits of the World: Malacca, Singapore and Indonesia.* Alphen aan den Rijn: Sijthoff and Noordhoff, 1978.

11807 **Lepawsky, Albert.** "International Development of River Resources." *International Affairs*, 39, No. 41 (October, 1963), 533-550.

11808 **Macos Lopez, Francisco.** *Quibra y Reintegracion del perecho de Gentes: Gibraltar, Belice, Las Malvinas.* Guatemala: Talleres de Imprenta Hispania, 1958.

11809 **Mahan, Alfred Thayer.** "The Isthmus and Sea Power." *Atlantic Monthly*, 72, No. 432 (October, 1893), 459-472.

11810 **Mance, O.** *International River and Canal Transport.* London: Oxford University Press, 1945.

11811 **Mangone, Gerard J.** "Straits Used for International Navigation." *Ocean Development and International Law*, 18, No. 4 (1987), 391–409.

11812 **Moodie, A.E.** "The Straits and the World." *London Quarterly of World Affairs*, 12, No. 2 (July, 1946), 109–117.

11813 **Morgan, F.W.** *Ports and Harbours.* London: Hutchinson University Library, 1952.

11814 **Murphy, I.L., and Sabadell, J.E.** "International River Basins: A Policy Model for Conflict Resolution." *Resources Policy*, 12, No. 2 (1986), 133–144.

11815 **Sargent, A.J.** *Seaports and Hinterlands.* London: A. & C. Black, 1938.

11816 **Siegfried, Andre.** *Suez, Panama et les routes maritimes mondiales.* Paris: Armand Colin, 1940.

11817 **Smith, H.A.** *The Economic Uses of International Rivers.* London: P.S. King and Sons, 1931.

11818 **Smith, Richard Austin.** "Troubled Oil on Troubled Waters." *Fortune*, 54, No. 6 (December, 1956), 115–1224.

11819 **Strohl, Mitchell P.** *The International Law of Bays.* The Hague: Martinus Nijhoff, 1963.

11820 **Teclaff, Ludwik A.** *The River Basin in History and Law.* The Hague: Martinus Nijhoff, 1967.

11821 **Thoman, R.S.** *Free Ports and Foreign Trade Zones.* Cambridge: Cornell Maritime Press, 1956.

11822 **Zacklin, Ralph, and Caflisch, Lucius, eds.** *The Legal Regime of International Rivers and Lakes.* The Hague: Martinus Nijhoff, 1981.

POLITICAL GEOGRAPHY OF REGIONS

AFRICA

Books and Journals

11823 **Agoro, Idowu Olayimika.** "Cooperation in the Utilization of International Rivers in Africa." In *African Conference on International Law and African Problems, March 14-18, 1967.* Lagos: University of Nigeria, 1967, 32-35, 46-47, 51-52, and 102-103.

11824 **Amoah, Frank Emmanuel Kwame.** *The Growth and Decline of Seaports in Ghana: 1800-1962.* Los Angeles: University of California, Ph.D., 1969.

11825 **Andre, Jean-Claude.** "L'Evolution du Statut des Fleuves Internationaux d'Afrique Noire" [The Evolution of the Statute of the International Rivers of Black Africa]. *Revue Juridique et Politique, Independance et Cooperation*, 19 (1965), 285-310.

11826 **Bazabas, B.** *Le Niger, Fleuve International. Etude su l'Internationalisation du Niger (The Niger, International River. Study on the Internationalization of the Nigher).* Republique du Niger, Ministere des Travaus Publics, des Mines et de l'Urbanisme, June, 1962.

11827 **Bornstein, Ronald.** "The Organization of Senegal River States. *Journal of Modern African Studies*,10, No. 2 (July, 1972), 267-283.

11828 **Brunskill, G.S.** "Navigable Waterways of Africa: Urgent Need for a Co-ordinated International System." *Dock and Harbour Authority*, 30, No. 345 (1949), 75-76.

11829 **Crary, Douglas D.** "Geography and Politics in the Nile Valley." *Middle East Journal*, 3, No. 3 (Summer, 1949), 315-327.

11830 **Farran, C. D.** "The Nile Water Question in the Waters Question in International Law." *Sudan Notes and Records*, 41 (1960), 88–100.

11831 **Jarrett, H.R.** "Bathurst, Port of Gambia River." *Geography*, 36, No. 172 (January, 1951), 98-107.

11832 **Jarrett, H.R.** "The Port and Town of Freetown." *Geography*, 40, No. 188, Part 2 (April, 1955), 108-118.

11833 **Robertson, James W.** *The Kenya Coastal Strip.* London: Her Majesty's Stationery Office, 1961.

11834 **Spinnato, John M.** "Historic and Vital Bays: An Analysis of Libya's Claim to the Gulf of Sidra." *Ocean Development and International Law*, 13, No. 1 (1983), 65-85.

11835 **Waterbury, John.** *Hydropolitics of the Nile Valley.* Syracuse, New York: Syracuse University Press, 1979.

11836 **Whittlesey, Derwent S.** "Lands Athwart the Nile." *World Politics*, 5, No. 2 (January, 1953), 214-241.

11837 **Wolpe, Howard.** *Urban Politics in Nigeria: A Study of Port Harcourt.* Berkeley: University of California Press, 1974.

AMERICAS

Books and Journals

11838 **Alfardo, Olmedo**. *El Canal de Panama en las guerras futuras*. Guayaquil, Imp. Mercantil-Olmedo Monteverde, 1930.

11839 **Augelli, John P.** "The Panama Canal Area." *Focus*, 36, 10. 1 (Spring, 1986), 20-29.

11840 "The Beagle Channel Affair." *American Journal of International Law*, 71, No. 4 (October, 1977), 733-739.

11841 **Bernstein, Harry.** "Power Politics on the Rio de la Plata. How Argentina's Control over Strategic River Plate Waterway Sways Her Foreign Policy." *Inter-America*, 2, No. 9 (September, 1943), 11-13.

11842 **Birken, Arthur M.** "Gulf of Venezuela: Border Dispute." *Lawyer of the Americas*, 6, No. 1 (Winter, 1974), 52-68.

11843 **Bullon, Eloy.** "Las relaciones de Espana con Portugal. Lecciones del pasado y orientaciones para el porvenir." *Estudios Geograficos*, Ano 5, Num. 16 (Agosto, 1944), 467-493.

11844 **Carreras, Alfredo de las.** "International River Boundaries in the Argentine Republic." *International Relations*, 9, No. 1 (May, 1987), 56–63.

11845 **Chile, Government of.** *Relaciones Chileno-Argentinas: La Controversia del Canal Beagle: Algunos Documentos Informativos*. 2nd ed., enlarged. Geneva: F. Impr. Atar., 1979.

11846 **Day, John R.** *Managing the Lower Rio Grande: An Experience in International River Development*. Chicago, Illinois: University of Chicago, Department of Geography Research Paper No. 125, 1970.

11847 **Denz, Ernest J.** "Regulation of Lake Ontario." *Military Engineer*, 54, No. 357 (1962), 22-25.

11848 **Dunkerley, James.** *Power in the Isthmus: A Political History of Modern Central America*. London: Verso, 1988.

11849 **Elgin, Richard L., and Knowles, David R.** "Arkansas Riparian Boundaries." *Surveying and Mapping*, 44, No. 1 (March, 1984), 39-57.

11850 **Esteves, Asdrulal.** "Bacias hydrograficas: Rios Paraguay e Parana." *A Defesa Nacional*, 30, Nos. 588-589 (May-August, 1963), 71–116.

11851 **Ferejohn, John A.** *Pork Barrel Politics: Rivers and Harbors Legislation, 1947-1968*. Stanford, California: Stanford University Press, 1974.

11852 **Figueiredo, Jose de Lima.** "O Rio Parano no roturo da marcha para oeste." *Revista Brasileira de Geografia*, 4, No. 2 (1942), 143-148.

11853 **Gilmore, Voit.** *Inter-state Competition for Water: The Virginia Beach Case*. Chapel Hill: University of North Carolina, Ph.D., 1988.

11854 **Glassner, Martin Ira.** "The Rio Lauca: Dispute Over an International River." *Geographical Review*, 60, No. 2 (April, 1970), 192–207.

11855 **Great Britain Treaties**, etc. *Convention between His Majesty in Respect of the Dominion of Canada and the President of the United States of America Providing for Emergency Regulation of the Level of Rainy Lake and of the Level of Other Boundary Waters in the Rainy Lake Watershed, Ottawa, September 15, 1938. Ratifications Exchanged at Ottawa on October 3, 1940.* Treaty Series No. 12. Cmd. 6276. London: Great Britain Parliament, 1941.

11856 **Grunawalt, Richard J.** "United States Policy on International Straits." *Ocean Development and International Law*, 18, No. 4 (1987), 445–458.

11857 **Hills, T.L.** *The St. Lawrence Seaway*. London: Methuen, 1959.

11858 **Himmelreich, David M.** "The Beagle Channel Affair: A Failure in Judicial Persuasion." *Vanderbilt Journal of Transnational Law*, 12 (1979), 971-998.

11859 **Hundley, Norris.** *Dividing the Waters: A Century of Controversy Between the United States and Mexico*. Berkeley, California: University of California Press, 1966.

11860 **Hunt, H.E.** "How the Great Lakes Became "High Seas" and Their Status Viewed from the Stand Point of International Law." *American Journal of International Law*, 4, No. 2 (April, 1910), 285–313.

11861 **Instituto Panamericano de Geografia e Historia.** *El Territorio del Istmo de Panama, en que se Encuentra la Republica de Panama, Pertenence Geograficamente a America Central o a America del Sur? Resultado de un Estudio Solicitado por el Gobienno de Panama*. Mexico: Instituto Panamericano de Geografia e Historia, 1955.

11862 **Jamail, Milton H., and Mumme, Stephen P.** "The International Boundary and Water Commission as a Conflict Management Agency in the U.S.-Mexico Borderlands." *Social Science Journal*, 19, No. 1 (January, 1982), 45-62.

11863 **Jessup, Philip C.** "Great Lakes-St. Lawrence Deep Waterway Treaty." *American Journal of International Law*, 26, No. 4 (October, 1932), 814-819.

11864 **Johnson, R.W.** "The Canada-United States Controversy over the Columbia River." *University of Washington Law Review*, 41, No. 4 (August, 1966), 676-763.

11865 **Keller, R. Carlos.** "Nuestra Frontera en el Canal Beagle." *Anales de la Universidad de Chile*, 116, No. 1112 (4 Trimestre, 1958), 7-29.

11866 **Krutilla, John V.** *The Columbia River Treaty.* Baltimore, Maryland: Resources for the Future, 1967.

11867 **Lasserre, Jean-Claude.** "Le role d'un fleuve-frontiere: le cas des deux rives du Saint-Laurent superieur." *Canadian Geographer*, 16, No. 3 (September, 1972), 199-210.

11868 **Mahan, Alfred Thayer.** "The Panama Canal and the Distribution of the Fleet." *North American Review*, 200, No. 706 (September, 1941), 406-417.

11869 **Mahan, Alfred Thayer.** "Why Fortify the Panama Canal?" *North American Review*, 193, No. 664 (March, 1911), 331-339.

11870 **Marti, Bruce Edward.** *The Seaport of Miami: Site Development, the Container Revolution, and Waterborne Commerce.* Boca Raton: Florida Atlantic University, Master's Thesis, 1975.

11871 **Martin, Roscoe C.; Birkhead, Guthrie S.; Burkhead, Jesse; and Munger, Frank J.** *River Basin Administration and the Delaware.* Syracuse, New York: Syracuse University Press, 1960.

11872 **Martin-Montero, Homero B.** *El rio Uruguay: Geografia, historia y geopolitica de Sus Aguas y Sus Islas.* Montevideo: Bib. Gen. Artigas de Centro Militar, 1957.

11873 **Miller, E. Willard.** "The Hudson Bay Railway Route: A Geographical Reconnaissance." *Journal of Geography*, 57, No. 4 (April, 1958), 163-173.

11874 **Morris, Michael A.** "The Politics of Caribbean Straits." *Ocean Development and International Law*, 18, No. 4 (1987), 459-477.

11875 "The New Treaty between the United States and Panama." In *Survey of International Affairs* by A.J. Toynbee. London: Oxford University Press, 1937, 872-875.

11876 **Nichols, Susan.** "The Gulf of Maine Boundary Dispute: A Surveying and Mapping Perspective." *Association of Canadian Map Librarie*, Bulletin No. 51 (June, 1984), 4-16.

11877 **Overgaard, Willard Michele.** *Legal Norms and Normative Bases for the Progressive Development of International Law, as Defined in Soviet Treaty Relations, 1945-1964.* Minneapolis: University of Minneapolis, Unpublished Ph.D. Dissertation, 1969.

11878 **Padelford, Norman J.** *The Panama Canal in Peace and War.* New York: Macmillan, 1942.

11879 **Pendle, George.** *Paraguay, a Riverside Nation.* London: Royal Institute of International Affairs, 1954.

11880 **Perejda, Andrew J.** *The St. Clair River: A Study in Political Geography,* Ann Arbor: University of Michigan, Ph.D., 1949.

11881 **Pharand, Donat.** *Canada's Arctic Waters in International Law.* London: Cambridge University Press, 1988.

11882 **Reinhardt, G.F.** "Rectification of the Rio Grande in the El Paso-Juarez Valley." *American Journal of International Law*, 31, No. 1 (January, 1937), 41-54.

11883 **Renner, George T.** "Arizona's Lost Seaport." *Journal of Geography*, 61, No. 2 (February, 1962), 57-59.

11884 **Robinson, Ross.** *Spatial Structure of Port-Linked Flows: The Port of Vancouver, Canada, 1965.* Vancouver, British Columbia, Canada: University of British Columbia, Ph.D., 1969.

11885 **Seeman, Sonia Henrietta Hubner.** *Some Impacts of Containerization on California Port Geography.* Long Beach: California State University, Master's Thesis, 1974.

11886 **Segundo Silioni, Rolando.** *La diplomacia luso-brasilena en la Cuenca del Plata.* Buenos Aires: Circulo Militar, 1964.

11887 **Sewell, W.R.D.** "The Columbia River Treaty: Some Lessons and Implications." *Canadian Geographer*, 10, No. 3 (September, 1966), 145-156.

11888 **Shalowitz, Aaron L.** "Navigability; a New Supreme Court Interpretation." *United States Naval Institute Proceedings*, 67, No. 461 (July, 1941), 932-934.

11889 **Shipton, Robert Walter.** *The Spatial Aspects of Recreational Ports on the American Side of Lake St. Clair.* Detroit, Michigan: Wayne State University, Master's Thesis, 1970.

11890 **Simsarian, James.** "The Division of Waters Affecting the United States and Canada." *American Journal of International Law*, 32, No. 3 (July, 1938), 488-518.

11891 "States's Rights Over Half of Lake Erie Waters Outlined in Opinion." *Pennsylvania Department of Internal Affairs* (Monthly Bulletin), 6, No. 4 (September, 1938), 18-26.

11892 Templer, Otis Worth, Jr. *Geographical Aspects of Water Law in the Nueces River Basin, Texas.* Los Angeles: University of California, Ph.D., 1969.

11893 *Ten Rivers in America's Future.* Washington, D.C.: Report of the President's Water Resources Policy Commission, 2, 1950.

11894 Terrell, J. Upton. *War for the Colorado River.* Glendale, California: Arthur H. Clark, 1965.

11895 Travis, Martin B., and Watkins, James T. "Control of the Panama Canal: An Obsolete Shibboleth?" *Foreign Affairs*, 37, No. 3 (April, 1959), 407-418.

11896 Van Alstyne, Richard W. "The Panama Canal: A Classical Case of an Imperial Hangover." *Journal of Contemporary History*, 5, No. 2 (April, 1980), 299-316.

11897 Veliz, Claudio. "Crisis in Panama." *World Today*, 20, No. 2 (February, 1964), 77-83.

11898 Villalobos R., Sergio. "El Canal de Beagle y las Tierras Aerstrales: su Historia." *Anales de la Universidad de Chile, Santiago*, 117, No. 113 (1st trimestre, 1959), 43-82.

11899 Venin, V.M. *Panama i Panamskii kanal.* Moscow: Gosudarstvennoe Izdatelstvo Geograficheskol Literatury, 1951.

11900 Willacres, Moscoso Jorge W. "Conferencia sobre el tema: la gran via interoceanica ecuatoriana a traves del Amazonas (estudio geopolitico)." *Anales de la universidad de Guayaquil*, 4 (1952), 182-204.

11901 Willacres, Moscoso Jorge W. "Las vias interoceanicas a traves del Amazonas." *Revista Geografica*, 23, No. 49 (Julho-Dezembro de, 1958), 65-74.

11902 William, Jerry Ray. *The Functional Relationship of Manaus of the Amazon Basin.* Tallahassee: University of Florida, Ph.D., 1969.

11903 Zatman, I. William. "The Mediterranean, Bridge or Barrier." *United States Naval Institute Proceedings*, 93, No. 2 (February, 1967), 63-71.

ASIA

Books and Journals

11904 Ahmad, Kazi S. "Some Geographical Aspects of the Indus Water Treaty and Development of Irrigation in West Pakistan." *Pakistan Geographical Review*, 20, No. 1 (January, 1965), 1-30.

11905 Al-Ebraheem, Hassan Ali. *Kuwait and the Gulf: Small States and the International System.* Washington, D.C.: Center for Contemporary Arab Studies, 1984.

11906 Al-Izzi, Khalid. *The Shatt-al-Arab River Dispute in Terms of Law.* Baghdad: Ministry of Information, 1972.

11907 Al-Khashab, W.H. *The Water Budget of the Tigris and Euphrates Basin.* Chicago, Illinois: University of Chicago Press, 1958.

11908 Batra, Satkartar. *The Ports of India.* Revised third edition. Adipur, India: The Kandla Commercial Publications, 1982.

11909 Berreby, J.J. "La Situation Politique des Emirats du golfe Persique." *Politique Etrangere*, 27 annee, No. 6 (December, 1962), 567-580.

11910 Biger, Gideon. "The Shatt-Al-Arab River Boundary: A Note." *Middle Eastern Studies*, 25, No. 2 (April, 1989), 249-252.

11911 Bilsel, Cemil. "The Turkish Straits in the Light of Recent Turkish-Soviet Russian Correspondence." *American Journal of International Law*, 41, 4 (October, 1947), 727-747.

11912 Black, Cyril E. "The Turkish Straits and the Great Powers." *Foreign Policy Reports*, 23, No. 14 (October 1, 1947), 174-182.

11913 Blake, Gerald H. "Coveted Waterway of Bab el Mandeb." *Geography Magazine*, 53, No. 4 (January, 1981), 233-238.

11914 Blake, Gerald H. "Flash-point through which Middle East Oil Must Pass." *Geographical Magazine*, 53, No. 1 (October, 1980), 50-52.

11915 Busch, Briton Cooper. *Britain and the Persian Gulf, 1894-1914.* Berkeley: University of California Press, 1967.

11916 Cagle, Malcolm W. "The Gulf of Aqaba-Trigger for Conflict." *United States Naval Institute Proceedings*, 85, No. 1 (January, 1959), 75-81.

11917 Center for Strategic and International Studies. Georgetown University. *The Gulf: Implications of British Withdrawal.* Washington, D.C.: Georgetown University, 1969.

11918 Chaturvedi, B.N. "Problems of Interstate River Water Management in South India." *Deccan Geographer*, 7, No. 1 (January-June, 1969), 65-70.

11919 Chia, Allan, and Long, Lee Yong. "The Strategic Strait with Special Reference to the Malacca Straits." *Singapore Journal of Tropical Geography*, 8, No. 2 (December, 1987), 97–113.

11920 Cohen, Saul B. *Haifa, Israel's Link to the World: The Political Geography of the Port and Its Environs.* Cambridge, Massachusetts: Harvard University, Ph.D., 1954.

11921 Cooley, John K. "Iran and the Palestinians and the Gulf." *Foreign Affairs*, 57, No. 3 (Summer, 1979), 1017-34.

11922 Dalyell, G. "The Persian Gulf." *Journal of the Royal Central Asian Society*, 25, Part 3 (July, 1938), 349-364.

11923 Davies, Charles E., ed. *Global Interests in the Arab Gulf.* Exeter: University of Exeter Press, 1992.

11924 *Development of Water Resources in the lower Mekong Basin.* Bangkok: Flood Control Series 12, Economic Commission for Asia and the Far East, 1957.

11925 Dickason, David Gordon. *The Efficiency of the Major Indian Seaports.* Bloomington: University of Indiana, Ph.D., 1970.

11926 "Dividing the Waters: The Canal Question in the Punjab." *Round Table*, 44, No. 179 (June, 1955), 240-248.

11927 "The Eastern River Dispute Between India and Pakistan." *World Today*, 13, No. 12 (December, 1957), 536-544.

11928 Eilts, Hermann Frederick. "The Persian Gulf Crisis: Perspectives and Prospects." *The Middle East Journal* [Bloomington], 45, No. 1 (Winter, 1990), 7-22.

11929 Farnie, D.A. *East and West of Suez. The Suez Canal in History 1854-1956.* Oxford: Oxford University Press, 1969.

11930 Foroughi, Mohamoud. "Iran and the Gulf." *Australian Outlook*, 31, No. 1 (April, 1977), 142-146.

11931 Fowler, F.J. "The Indo-Pakistan Water Dispute." In *Yearbook of World Affairs, No. 9.* Washington, D.C.: U.S. Government Printing Office, 1955, 101-124.

11932 "The Future of the Suez Canal Zone." *Round Table*, 44, No. 171 (June, 1953), 220-227.

11933 Gehrke, Ulrich, and Kuhn, Gustav. *Die Grenzen des Irak: Historische und Rechtliche Aspekte des Irakischen Anspruchs auf Kuwait und des Irakisch-Persischen streites um den schalt all-*

Arab, 3d. 2. Stuttgart: W. Kohlhammer Gmbh, 1963.

11934 Giannini, Amedeo. "La nuova fase del problema arabo: la Societs degli State Arabi." *L. Universo,* Anno 28, No. 1 (Gennaio-Febbraio, 1948), 33-48.

11935 Gibb, R.A. "The Channel Tunnel: A Political Geographical Analysis." *Research Paper, University of Oxford School of Geography*, 35 (1986), 1–31.

11936 Giniewski, Paul. "L'Egypte a-t-elle Droit de Controler le Golfe d'Akaba?" *Political Etrangere*, 20, No. 5 (November, 1955), 595-602.

11937 Gross, L. "Passage through the Strait of Tiran and in the Gulf of Aqaba." In *The Middle East Crisis: Test of International Law,* J.W. Halderman, ed. Dobbs Ferry: Oceana, 1969, 1–125.

11938 Hasan, Masuma. "The Farakka Barrage Dispute. Pakistan's Case." *Pakistan Horizon*, 21, No. 4 (Fourth Quarter, 1968), 356-360.

11939 Hirsch, Abraham M. "Utilization of International Rivers in the Middle East: A Study of Conventional International Law." *American Journal of International Law*, 50, No. 1 (January, 1956), 81-100.

11940 Hirsch, Abraham M. "From the Indus to the Jordan: Characteristics on Middle East International River Dispute." *Political Science Quarterly*, 1, No. 2 (June, 1956), 203-222.

11941 Howard, Harry N., ed. "Problem of the Turkish Straits; Principal Treaties and Conventions (1774-1936)." *Department of State Bulletin*, 15, No. 383 (November 3, 1946), 790-807.

11942 Howard, Harry N., ed. "Some Recent Developments in the Problem of Turkish Straits, 1945-1946." *Department of State Bulletin*, 16, No. 395 (January 26, 1947), 143-151+.

11943 Howard, Harry N., ed. "The United States and the Problem of the Turkish Straits." *Middle East Journal*, 1, No. 1 (January, 1947), 59-72.

11944 Huang, Thomas T.F. "Some International and Legal Aspects of the Suez Canal Question." *American Journal of International Law*, 51, No. 2 (April, 1957), 277-307.

11945 Hurewitz, J.C. *The Persian Gulf: Prospects of Stability.* New York: Foreign Policy Association, Headline Series, No. 220, 1974.

11946 Hurst, H.E. *The Nile.* London: Constable, 1957.

11947 *The Indus Basin Development-Fund Agreement.* London: Her Majesty's Stationery Office, 1960.

11948 "Indus Waters Treaty." *American Journal of International Law*, 55, No. 3 (July, 1961), 797-822.

11949 **Ionides, M.G.** "The Disputed Waters of the Jordan." *Middle East Journal*, 7, No. 2 (Spring, 1953), 153-164.

11950 **Jawed, Tufail.** "The World Bank and the Indus Basin Dispute: Mediation by the World Bank, 2." *Pakistan Horizon*, 19, No. 1 (First Quarter, 1966), 34-44; and No. 2 (Second Quarter, 1966), 133-142.

11951 **Karan, Pradyumna P.** "Dividing the Water: A Problem in Political Geography. (Colorado and Indus River Basins)." *Professional Geographer.* 13, No. 1 (January, 1961), 6-11.

11952 **Kelly, J.B.** *Britain and the Persian Gulf, 1790-1880.* Oxford: Clarendon Press, 1968.

11953 **Kelly, J.B.** "The British Position in the Persian Gulf." *World Today*, 20, No. 6 (June, 1964), 238-249.

11954 **Lapidoth-Eschelbacher, R.** *The Red Sea and the Gulf of Aden.* The Hague: Martinus Nijhoff, 1982.

11955 **Leifer, Michael, and Dolliver, Nelson.** "Conflict of Interest in the Straits of Malacca." *International Affairs*, 49, No. 2 (April, 1973), 190-203.

11956 **Levine, I.O.** "Les projets de percement de l'isthme de Kra et leur histoire." *Affairs Etrangers*, 2 (1937), 83-97.

11957 **Lindt, A.R.** "Politics in the Persian Gulf." *Journal of the Royal Central Asian Society*, 26, Part 4 (October, 1939), 619-633.

11958 **Loewy, Karl.** "Die Wasser des Jordan." *Zeitschrift fur Geopolitik*, 24 Jahrgang, Heft 2 (Februar, 1953), 97-99.

11959 **Maclean, Donald.** *British Foreign Policy Since Suez. 1956-1968.* London: Hodder and Stoughton, 1970.

11960 **Melamid, Alexander.** "Legal Status of the Gulf of Aqaba." *American Journal of International Law*, 53, No. 2 (April, 1959), 412-413.

11961 **Melamid, Alexander.** "The Political Geography of the Gulf of Aqaba." *Annals of the Association of American Geographers*, 47, No. 3 (September, 1957), 231-240.

11962 **Michel, Aloys A.** *The Indus Basin: A Study of the Effects of Partition.* New Haven, Connecticut: Yale University Press, 1967.

11963 **Moorthy, K. Krishna.** "The Indus Pact." *Far Eastern Economic Review*, 29, No. 11 (September 15, 1960), 600-603.

11964 **Mountjoy, Alan B.** "The Suez Canal, 1935-1955." *Geography*, 42, Part III (July, 1957), 186-190.

11965 **Mountjoy, Alan B.** "The Suez Canal at Mid-Century." *Economic Geography*, 34, No. 2 (April, 1958), 155-168.

11966 **Mueller, Herbert.** "Dairen und Port Arthur vor, auf und nach der Jalta-Konferenz." *Zeitschrift fur Geopolitik*, 24 Jahrgang, Heft 10 (Oktober, 1953), 541-545.

11967 **Murphy, Patrick J.** "Indus Basin Water Dispute." *New Commonwealth*, 33, No. 12 (June 12, 1957), 570-573.

11968 **Murphy, Patrick J.** *Partition of the Punjab and the Indus Water Dispute.* London: Oxford University Press, 1955-56.

11969 **Nijim, Basheer K.** *The Indus, Nile, and Jordan: International Rivers and Factors in Conflict Potential.* Bloomington: University of Indiana, Ph.D., 1969.

11970 **Nutting, Anthony.** *No End of a Lesson: The Story of Suez.* London: Constable, 1967.

11971 **Osborn, James.** "Malacca in Malaysian National Development." In *Malacca*, Paul Wheatley and K.S. Sandhu, eds. London: Oxford University Press, 1980.

11972 **Padelford, Norman J.** "Solutions to the Problem of the Turkish Straits; a Brief Appraisal." *Middle East Journal*, 2, No. 2 (April, 1948), 175-190.

11973 "The Problem of the Indus and Its Tributaries: An Alternative View." *World Today*, 14, No. 6 (June, 1958), 266-276.

11974 **Rama Rao, T.S.** "Inter-State Water Disputes in the Indian Union." In *Indian Yearbook of International Affairs, Vol. 11.* New Delhi: Indian Institute of International Relations, Government of India Press, 1962, 219-279.

11975 **Ramazani, Rouhollah K.** *The Persian Gulf: Iran's Role.* Charlottesville: University Press of Virginia, 1972.

11976 **Schaaf, C. Hart, and Fifield, Russell H.** *The Lower Mekong: Challenge to Cooperation in Southeast Asia.* Princeton, New Jersey: Van Nostrand, 1963.

11977 Schonfield, H.J. *The Suez Canal in World Affairs*. New York: Philosophical Library, 1953.

11978 Scovazzi, Tuillo. "Bays and Straight Baselines in the Mediterranean." *Ocean Development and International Law*, 19, No. 5 (1988), 401–420.

11979 Selak, Charles B. "A Consideration of the Legal Status of the Gulf of Aqaba." *American Journal of International Law*, 52, No. 4 (October,1958), 660–698.

11980 Shaw, K.E., and Thomson, George C. *The Straits of Malacca: In Relation to the Problems of the Indian Pacific Oceans*. Singapore: University Education Press, 1973.

11981 Shmueli, Aushalom. "The Settlement of the Sinaitic Ayaydah in the Suez Canal Zone." *Palestine Exploration Quarterly*, 109,No. 1 (January–June, 1977), 27–38.

11982 Shotwell, James T., and Deak, Francis. *Turkey at the Straits; a Short History*. New York: Macmillan, 1940.

11983 Smith, C.G. "The Disputed Waters of the Jordan." *Institute of British Geographers, Transactions*, 40 (December, 1966), 111-128.

11984 Smith, C.G. "The Great Ditch Across the Suez Isthmus." *Geographical Magazine*, 41, No. 4 (January, 1969), 259-270.

11985 Smith, H.A. "The Waters of the Jordan: A Problem of International Water Control." *International Affairs*, 25, No. 4 (October, 1949), 415-425.

11986 Sokolnicki, Michael. *The Turkish Straits*. Beirut: American Press, 1950.

11987 Somogyi, Joseph de. "The Question of the Turkish Straits." *Journal of Central European Affairs*, 11, No. 3 (October, 1951), 279-290.

11988 Steinbach, Udo. "Der Persisch/Arabische Golf-Wirtschaftsraum und Krisenherd" [The Persian/Arabian Gulf Centre of Economic Development and Political Crisis]. *Geographische Rundschau*, Jahr 32, Heft 12 (December, 1980), 514–522.

11989 Stevens, G.G. "The Jordan River Valley." *International Conciliation*, 506 (January, 1956), 227–283.

11990 Vertzberger, Yaacov Y.I. *Coastal States Regional Powers, Super Powers and the Malacca-Singapore Straits*. Research Papers and Policy Studies, Vol. 10. Berkeley: Institute of East Asian Studies, 1984.

11991 Washington, D.C. Pakistan Embassy.

Pakistan: The Struggle for Water Existence. Washington, D.C.: Pakistan Embassy, 1953.

11992 Williams, M.H. "Russia and the Turkish Straits." *Untied Nations Naval Institute Proceedings*, 78, No. 5 (May, 1952), 479-485.

11993 Wilson, Arnold. *The Persian Gulf*. London: Allen & Unwin, 1954.

11994 Yehuda, Gradus. "Is the Israeli Negev a Viable Alternative to the Suez Canal?" *Geoforum*, 8, No. 1 (1977), 29-32.

11995 Yehuda, Gradus, and Stern, Eliahu. "New Perspectives on the Negev Continental Bridge." *Geoforum*, 8, No. 5/6 (1977), 311-318.

AUSTRALIA, OCEANIA AND ANTARCTICA

Journals

11996 Loeffler, M. John. "Australian-American Interbasin Water Transfer." *Annals of the Association of American Geographers*, 60, No. 3 (September, 1970), 493-516.

11997 Rosh, Robert M. "Antarctica Increasing Incorporation into the World-System." *Fernand Braudel Center Review*, 12, No. 1 (Winter, 1989), 121-137.

11998 Ryan, K.W., and White, M.W.D. "The Torres Strait Treaty." *Australian Year Book of International Law*, 7 (1981), 87-113.

EUROPE

Books and Journals

11999 Ancel, Jacques. "La ville libre de Danzig, geographie politique regionale." *Annales de Geographie*, 42, No. 237 (Mai 15, 1933), 286-302.

12000 Alexandersson, Gunnar. *The Baltic Straits*. The Hague: Martinus Nijhoff, 1982.

12001 Alexandersson, Gunnar. "International Straits of the World: The Baltic Straits." *International Straits of the World*. Vol. 6. The Hague: Martinus Nijhoff, 1982.

12002 Anchiere, Sttore. *Costantenopoli e gli Stretti nella politica Russa ed Europea Dal trattal di Quciuk Qaenaige alla Convenzione di Montreux Milani A. Guiffre*. Milan: Milani A. Guiffre, 1948.

12003 **Bierman, Don E.** "International Status of the Baltic Sea." *Soviet Geography Review and Translation*, 22, No. 7 (September, 1981), 429-436.

12004 **Bilmanis, Alfred.** "The Struggle for Domination of the Baltic; an Historical Aspect of the Baltic Problem." *Journal of Central European Affairs*, 5, No. 2 (July, 1945), 119-142.

12005 **Bird, James.** *The Geography of the Port of London.* London: Hutchinson Publishing Group, 1957.

12006 **Campbell, John C.** "Diplomacy on the Danube." *Foreign Affairs*, 27, No. 2 (January, 1949), 315-327.

12007 **Carrington, C.E.** *Gibraltar.* London: Royal Institute of International Affairs, 1956.

12008 **Carrington, C.E.** "Gibraltar--the Rock with an Emotional Problem." *Commonwealth Journal*, 9, No. 5 (October, 1966), 187-190.

12009 **Castiella, Fernando M.** *The Gibraltar.* Madrid, Spain: Minister of Foreign Affairs, 1966.

12010 **Cecovini, Manlio.** "The 'Adriatic Route' of Europe and the Port of Trieste." *Osterreischische Zeitschrift fur Aussenpolitik*, 21 Jg., Heft 3 (1981), 268-274.

12011 **de Donno, Alfredo.** "La questione di Trieste." *La Critica Politica*, n.s., Anno 7, Fasc. 5 (Maggi-Giugno, 1945), 142-149.

12012 **East, W. Gordon.** "The Danube Routeway." *An Historical Geography of Europe.* London: Methuen, 1967.

12013 **Fawcett, J.E.S.** "Gibraltar: The Legal Issues." *International Affairs*, 43, No. 2 (April, 1967), 236-251.

12014 **Fuchs, Karl Hans,** ed. *Danzig-What Is It All About?.* Gdabnsk, Poland: Foreign Relations, Government Press, 1939.

12015 **Giannini, Amedeo.** "Il problema del Baltico." *L'Universo*, Anno 32, Num. 3 (Maggio-Giugno, 1952), 317-324.

12016 [Gibraltar, Spain]. *Africa*, Ano 9, Num. 121 (Enero, 1952), 2-18.

12017 **Gorove, Stephen.** *Law and Politics of the Danube, An Interdisciplinary Study.* The Hague: Martinus Nijhoff, 1964.

12018 **Gorski, Karol.** *Polska w zlewisku Baltyku.* (Prace naukowo-informacyjne. Seria: Pomorze.) Gdansk: Wydawnictwa Instytutu Baltyckiego, 1947.

12019 **Govorchin, Gerald G.** "The Struggle for Trieste." *Social Studies*, 46, No. 4 (April, 1955), 123-127.

12020 **Haines, C. Grove.** "Trieste--A Storm Center of Europe." *Foreign Policy Reports*, 22, No. 2 (April 1, 1946), 14-23.

12021 **Hajnal, H.** *The Danube, Its Historical, Political and Economic Importance.* The Hague: Marrtinus Nijhoff, 1920.

12022 **Hamel, J.A. Van.** *Danzig and the Polish Problem.* New York: Carnegie Endowment for International Peace, 1933.

12023 **Haushofer, von Albert.** "Der Staat Danzig." *Zeitschrift der Gesellschaft fur Erdkunde*, 7-8 (1926), 335-350.

12024 **Heasman, D.D.** "The Gibralter Affair." *International Journal*, 22, No. 2 (Spring, 1967), 265-277.

12025 **Howes, H.W.** *The Story of Gibraltar.* London: Philip & Tacey, 1946.

12026 **Joscano, Mario.** "Trieste, Ecran de la Politique Yougoslave?" *Politique Etrangere*, 19, No. 1 (February-March, 1954), 5-10.

12027 **Kish, G.** "TVA on the Danube." *Geographical Review*, 37, No. 2 (April, 1947), 274-302.

12028 **Knatchbull-Hugessen, Sir Hughe.** "Constantinople and the Straits." *United Empire*, 39, No. 2 (March-April, 1948), 63-69.

12029 **Kucherov, Samuel.** "The Problem of Constantinople and the Straits." *Russian Review*, 8, No. 3 (July, 1949), 205-220.

12030 **Kyle, Keith.** *Suez.* London: Weidenfeld and Nicolson, 1991.

12031 **Leonhardt, Hans.** "Why Die for Danzig?" *Journal of Central European Affairs*, 4, No. 3 (October, 1944), 274-280.

12032 **Lohse, Gunter.** *Deutschland und der Korridor.* In Zusammenarbeit mit Gunter Lohse und Waldemar Wucher; hrsg. von Friedrich Heiss. Berlin: Volk und Reich Verlag, 1939.

12033 **Massey, Isabella M.** *The Question of Trieste.* London: The British-Italian Society, 1945.

12034 **Meiksins, Gregory.** "Russian Britain and the Straits." *American Review on the Soviet Union*, 7, No. 3 (May, 1946), 3-15.

12035 **Micklin, Philip Patrick.** *An Inquiry into the Cospian Sea Problem and Proposals for Its Alleviation.* Seattle: University of Washington, Ph.D., 1971.

12036 **Mihelic, Dusan.** *The Political Element in Port Geography of Trieste.* Chicago, Illinois: University of Chicago, Ph.D., 1968.

12037 **Mikolajski, Juliusz.** "Polish Seaports, Their Hinterlands and Forelands." *Geographia Polonica*, 2 (1964), 221-229.

12038 **Morgan, F.W.** "Rotterdam and Waterway Approaches to the Rhine." *Economic Geography*, 24, No. 1 (January, 1948), 1-19.

12039 **Morrison, John A.** "Russia and the Warm Waters." *U.S. Naval Institute Proceedings*, 78 (November, 1952).

12040 **Peterson, Charles Buckley, III.** *Geographical Aspects of Foreign Colonization in Prerevolutionary New Russia.* Seattle: University of Washington, Ph.D., 1969.

12041 "Port Triest Waznym Portem Naftowym" [Port Trieste an Important Oil Port]. *Technika i Gospodarka Morska*, 19, No. 2 (December, 1969), 575-576.

12042 **Pounds, Norman J.G.** "The Political Geography of the Straits of Gibralter." *Journal of Geography*, 51, No. 4 (April, 1952), 165-170.

12043 **Preston, Richard A.** "Don't Sell Gibraltar Short." *United States Naval Institute Proceedings*, 76, No. 12 (December, 1950), 1328-1335.

12044 **Preston, R.A.** "Gibraltar, Colony and Fortress." *Canadian Historical Review*, 27, No. 4 (December, 1946), 402-423.

12045 **Reddaway, William Fiddian.** *Problems of the Baltic.* London: Cambridge University Press, 1940.

12046 **Roletto, Georgio.** *Trieste ed i suoi problemi; situazione, tendenze, prospettive.* Trieste: E. Borsatti, Editore, 1952.

12047 **Routh, D.A.** "The Montreux Convention Regarding the Regime of the Black Sea Straits (20th July, 1936)." In *Survey of International Affairs*, A.J. Toynbee, ed. London: Oxford University Press, 1936, 584-651.

12048 **Rusinow, Denison.** "Ports and Politics in Yugoslavia." Reports of the *American Universities Field Staff; Southeast Europe Series*, 9, No. 3, 1964.

12049 **Salvemini, Gaetano.** "Gorizia, Trieste e l'Istria Occidentale." *La Critica Politica*, n.s, Anno 7, Fasc. 8-9 (Agosto-Settembre, 1945), 283-293.

12050 **Salvemini, Gaetano.** "Il problema de Trieste." *La Critica Politica*, n.s, Anno 7, Fasc. 6 (Giugno-Luglio, 1945), 185-189.

12051 **Sanmann, Horst.** *Die Verkehrsstruktur der Nordwesteuropaischen Seehafen (Antwerpen, Rotterdam, Amsterdam, Bremen und Hamburg) und ihre Wandlungen von der Jahrhundretwende bis zur Gegenwart* [The Traffic Structure of the Northwest European Seaports...and Their Changes from the Turn of the Century to the Present]. Schriften des Verkehrswissenschaftlichen Seminars der Universitat Hamburg. Vol. 4. Hamburg: Schiffahrts-Verlag Hansa C. Schroedter & Co., 1956.

12052 **Schiffrer, Carlo.** *Historic Glance at the Relations between Italians and Slaves (!) in Venezia Giulia.* Trieste: Stabilimento Tipografico Nazionale, 1946.

12053 **Schmollck, Frank H.** "Britische Interessen auf demamerikanischen isthmus." *Zeitschrift fur Geopolitik*, 15, Jahrg, Heft 7 (July, 1938), 533-539.

12054 **Spain, Minister of Foreign Affairs.** *Documents on Gibraltar Presented to the Spanish Cortes by the Minister of Foreign Affairs.* Madrid: Miniester of Foreign Affairs, 1965.

12055 **Toschi, Umberto.** "Gibilterra e la sua funzione." *Bollettino della R. Societa geografica italiana*, Serie 7, Vol. 5, Fasc. 11-12 (November-December, 1940), 593-598.

12056 "Trieste, Background to a Deadlock." *World Today*, 8, No. 10 (October, 1952), 429-439.

12057 "Trieste's New Role in Europe." *World Today*, 5, No. 11 (November, 1949), 471-477.

12058 **Unger, Leonard.** "The Economy of the Free Territory of Trieste." *Geographical Review*, 37, No. 4 (October, 1947), 583-608.

12059 **Weigend, Gujido G.** "The Danube River: An Emerging Regional Bond." *Geoforum*, 6, No. 2 (1975), 151-161.

12060 **Wolf, S.** "Danzig, Poland and Germany." *Contemporary Review*, 822 (June, 1939), 674-680.

CHAPTER XIII

SUPERNATIONALISM, INTERNATIONAL ORGANIZATIONS, POWER BLOCS AND GLOBAL STRUCTURE

GENERAL AND THEORY

Books

12061 **Akzin, Benjamin.** *New States and International Organizations.* Paris: United Nations Educational, Scientific, and Cultural Organization, 1955.

12062 **Alker, Hayward R.,** and **Russett, Bruce M.** *World Politics in the General Assembly.* New Haven, Connecticut: Yale University Press, 1965.

12063 **Andemicael, B.** *Regionalism and the United Nations.* Alphen aan den Rijn: Sijthoff and Noordhoff, for the United Nations Institute for Training and Research, 1979.

12064 **Arangio-Ruiz, Gaetano.** *The UN Declaration on Friendly Relations and the System of the Sources of International Law.* Alphen aan den Rijn: Sijthoff and Noorhoff, 1979.

12065 **Aufricht, Hans.** *World Organization; an Annotated Bibliography.* 5th rev. ed. New York: Woodrow Wilson Foundation, 1946.

12066 **Baer, George W.** *Test Case: Italy, Ethiopia, and the League of Nations.* Stanford, California: Stanford University, Hoover Institution Press Publication No. 159, 1976.

12067 **Bailey, Sydney D.** *The General Assembly of the United Nations.* New York: Praeger, 1964.

12068 **Bergner, Jeffrey T.** *The New Superpowers: Germany, Japan, the U.S. and the New World Order.* New York: St. Martin's Press, 1991.

12069 **Bialer, Seweryn,** and **Mandelbaum, Michael.** *The Global Rivals.* New York: Alfred A. Knopf, 1988.

12070 **Banks, Arthur S.,** ed. *Political Handbook of the World, 1975: Governments and Intergovernmental Organizations as of January 1, 1975.* New York: McGraw-Hill, 1975.

12071 **Bialer, Seweryn,** and **Mandelbaum, Michael.** *The Global Rivals,* (Focus is on United States and Soviet Union.) New York: Alfred A. Knopf, 1988.

12072 **Bonnet, Henri.** *Outlines of the Future; World Organization Emerging from the War.* Chicago, Illinois: World Citizens Association, 1943.

12073 **Bonnet, Henri.** *The United Nations; What They Are, What They May Become.* Chicago, Illinois: World Citizens Association, 1942.

12074 **Bonnet, Henri.** *The United Nations on the Way; Principles and Policies.* Chicago, Illinois: World Citizens Association, 1942.

12075 **Brueckner, Aleksander.** *Die Geschichte der deutsch-polnischen Beziehungen in Lichte Aleksander Brueckeners.* Einleitung, Ubersetzung und Ammerkungen von Bo ko Freiherr von Richthofen. Hrsg. vona "Freiheitsbund Deutch-Polnische Freundschaft." Munchen: 1953.

12076 **Castaneda, J.** *Legal Effects of United Nations Resolutions.* New York and London: Columbia University Press, 1969.

12077 **Commission to Study the Organization of Peace.** *The United Nations and Non-Self Governing Peoples; a Plan for Trusteeship.* New York: Commission to Study the Organization of Peace, 1944.

12078 **Conover, Helen F.,** Comp. *Non-Self-Governance Areas, with Special Emphasis on Mandates and Trusteeships; A Selected List of References,* 2 Vols. Washington, D.C.: U.S. Library of Congress, General Reference and Bibliography Division, 1947.

12079 **Coyle, David Cushman.** *The United Nations and How It Works.* New York: New American Library, 1955.

12080 **Czempiel, Ernst-Otto,** and **Rosenau, James N.,** eds. *Global Changes and Theoretical Challenges: Approaches to World Politics for the 1990s.* Lexington: Lexington Books, 1989.

12081 **Deutsch, Karl W.,** et al. *Political Community and the North Atlantic Area.* Princeton, New Jersey: Princeton University Press, 1957.

12082 *Documents Relating to the Selection of the Site for the Permanent Headquarters of the United Nations in the United States and the Arrangements for the Control of the Area Comprising the Site.* Washington, D.C.: U.S. Department of State, 1946.

12083 **Dumbarton Oaks Conference, 1944.** *Dumbarton Oaks. Propositions relatives a l'etablissement d'une organisation internationale generale.* Ottawa: Commission de l'information en temps de guerre, 1944.

12084 **Eagleton, Clyde.** *Covenant of the League of Nations and Charter of the United Nations: Points of Difference.* Publication 2442. Reprinted from the Department of State Bulletin of August 19, 1945. Washington, D.C.: U.S. Department of State, 1945.

12085 **Eichelberger, Clark W.** *The United Nations Charter; What Was Done at San Francisco.* New York: American Association for the United Nations, Commission to Study the Organization of Peace, 1945.

12086 **Enequist, Gerd Margareta.** *Malarlanens lantbebyggelse enlight det aldre ekonomiska Kartverket.* Stockholm: Almquist and Wiksell International, 1975.

12087 **Farrington, Hugh.** *Strategic Geography: NATO, the Warsaw Pact, and the Superpowers.* New York: Routledge, 1988.

12088 **Fawcett, C.B.** *The Bases of a World Commonwealth.* London: Watts, 1941.

12089 **Fehrenbach, T.R.** *The United Nations in War and Peace.* New York: Random House, 1968.

12090 **Finer, Herman.** *The United Nations Economic and Social Council.* (America Looks Ahead, No. 12.) Boston: World Peace Foundation, 1946.

12091 **Fisher, Harold H.** *America and Russia in the World Community.* Published...for the Three Associated Colleges at Claremont: Pomona College, Scripps College, Claremont College. Claremont, California: Claremont College, 1946.

12092 **Fox, William T.R.** *The Super-Powers: The United States, Britain, and the Soviet Union-Their Responsibility for Peace.* New York: Harcourt Brace, 1944.

12093 **Galtung, Johan,** and **Vincent, Richard.** *Global Glasnost: Toward a New World Information and Communication Order?* Cresskill: Hampton Press, Inc., 1992.

12094 **Goodrich, Leland M.** *United Nations.* London: Stevens, 1960.

12095 **Goodrich, Leland M; Hambro, Edyard;** and **Simons, A.P.** *Charter of the United Nations,* 3rd and revised edition. New York, London: Columbia University Press, 1969.

12096 **Gross, Ernest A.** *The New United Nations.* New York: Foreign Policy Association, 1957.

12097 *Guide to United Nations and Allied Agencies.* New York: United Nations Information Office, 1945.

12098 **Halderman, J.W.** *The United Nations and the Rule of Law.* Dobbs Ferry: Oceana, 1966.

12099 **Hall, Duncan.** *Mandates, Dependencies and Trusteeship.* (Studies in the Administration of International Law and Organization, No. 9.) Washington, D.C.: Carnegie Endowment for International Peace, 1948.

12100 **Higgins, Rosalyn A.** *United Nations Peacekeeping 1946-1967 - Documents and Commentary.* London, New York, Toronto: Oxford University Press, 1969.

12101 **Holborn, Louise W.,** ed. *War and Peace Aims of the United Nations, September 1, 1939-December 31, 1942.* Boston: World Peace Foundation, 1943.

12102 **Hudson, Manley O.** *The Permanent Court of International Justice, 1920-1942; a Treatise.* New York: Macmillan, 1943.

12103 **Hudson, Manley O.** *World Court Reports.* Washington, D.C.: Carnegie Endowment for International Peace (Vol. 1, 1922-26), 1934.

12104 **Kelsen, H.** *The Law of the United Nations.* London: Stevens and Sons, 1950.

12105 **Kunugi, Tatsuro.** *State Succession and Multilateral Treaty Relations in the Framework of International Organizations.* New York City: Columbia University, Ph.D., 1970.

12106 **League of Nations.** *The Mandates System: Origin-Principles-Application.* Geneve: Societe des Nations, 1945.

12107 **Luard, Evan.** *The Globalization of Politics: The Changed Focus of Political Action in the Modern World.* Houndmills: Macmillan, 1990.

12108 **Lyon-Allen, Mary Martha.** *The United Nations Conference on Science and Technology for Development: The International Negotiation of Technological Relations.* Washington, D.C.: George Washington University, Ph.D., 1979.

12109 **Mahamedi, Afsaneh Sepahpour.** *Changes in Power Relations in the International Monetary System and the IMF: A Case Study of Organizational Responses to Environmental Variations.* Philadelphia: University of Pennsylvania, Ph.D., 1981.

12110 **Mance, Sir Osborne.** *Frontiers, Peace Treaties, International Organization.* London: Oxford University Press, 1946.

12111 *The Mandates System; Origin, Principles, Application.* (Publications. VI.A. Mandates. 1945. VI.A. 1.) Geneva: League of Nations, 1945.

12112 **Miller, Lynn H.** *Global Order: Values and Power in International Politics.* Boulder, Colorado: Westview Press, 1990.

12113 **Mitrany, David.** *A Working Peace System: An Argument for the Functional Development of International Organization.* London: The Royal Institute of International Affairs, 1943.

12114 **Modelski, G. and Thompson, W.R.** *Seapower in Global Politics, 1494–1993.* Seattle: University of Washington Press, 1988.

12115 **Moffitt, Leonard Caum.** *Global Positioning for the Twenty First Century: Rethinking Strategic Planning.* East Lansing: Michigan State University Press, 1990.

12116 **Nelsen, Harvey W.** *Power and Insecurity: Beijing, Moscow and Washington 1949-1988.* Boulder, Colorado: Lynne Rienner Publishers, 1989.

12117 **Nicholas, H.G.** *The United Nations as a Political Institution.* London: Oxford University Press, 1968.

12118 **Nijman, Jan.** *The Geopolitics of Power and Conflict: Superpowers in the International System, 1945-1992.* New York: John Wiley and Sons, Inc., 1993.

12119 **Nincic, Djura.** *The Problem of Sovereignty in the Charter and in the Practice of the United Nations.* The Hague: Martinus Nijhoff, 1970.

12120 *Non-self-governing Territories.* 2 vols. Lake Success, New York: United Nations, 1950.

12121 **Parker, W.H.** *The Superpowers: The United States and U.S.S.R. Compared.* London: Macmillan, 1972.

12122 **Pickard, Bertram.** *The Greater United Nations; An Essay Concerning the Place and Significance of International Non-governmental Organizations.* New York: Carnegie Endowment for International Peace, 1956.

12123 **Popke, E. Jeffrey.** *Recasting Geopolitics: The Discursive Scripting of the International Monetary Fund.* Lexington, KY: Master's Thesis, University of Kentucky, 1993.

12124 **Rai, Kul Bhushan.** *The Relationship Between Foreign Policy Indicators and Patterns of Voting in the United Nations General Assembly.* Rochester, New York: University of Rochester, Ph.D., 1970.

12125 **Rajana, Cecil.** *The Lorne Convention and the New International Economic Order: A Critical Appraisal of ACP-EEC Relations.* Kingston Ontario Canada: Queen's University at Kingston, Ph.D., 1981.

12126 *Report of the Secretary-General on the Work of the Organization.* (Document No. A/65.) New York: United Nations, 1946.

12127 **Rothstein, R.L.** *Alliance and Small Powers.* New York: Columbia University Press, 1968.

12128 **Seegers, Kathleen Walker.** *Alliance for Progress.* New York: Coward McCann, 1964.

12129 **Seyersted, F.** *United Nations Forces in the Law of Peace and War.* Leyden: Sijthoff, 1966.

12130 **Shukri, M.A.** *The Concept of Self-Determination in the United Nations.* Damascus: Al Jadidah Press, 1965.

12131 **Straight, Michael.** *Make This the Last War; The Future of the United Nations.* New York: Harcourt Brace, 1943.

12132 **Stuart, Graham H.,** ed. *The Conflict of Two Worlds.* Los Angeles: University of Southern California, 1949.

12133 **Taylor, Alice.** *Egypt and Syria.* Garden City: Doubleday, 1960.

12134 **Taylor, Peter J.,** ed. *World Government.* New York: Oxford University Press, 1990.

12135 **Terverton, G.** *Making the Alliance Work.* Ithaca, New York: Cornell University Press, 1985.

12136 **Tomlin, Brian William.** *United Nations Supra-nationalism: An Analysis of Roll-Call Voting in the General Assembly.* Toronto, Ontario, Canada: York University, Ph.D., 1972.

12137 **Tow, William T.** *Subregional Security Cooperation in the Third World.* Boulder, Colorado: Lynne Rienner Publishers, 1990.

12138 **Travis, Tom Allen.** *A Theoretical and Empirical Study of Communications Relations in the NATO and Warsaw Intrabloc and Interbloc International Systems.* Syracuse, New York: Syracuse University, Ph.D., 1970.

12139 **United Nations.** *Non-self-governing Territories. Summaries of Information Transmitted to the Secretary-General During 1946.* Lake Success, New York: United Nations, 1947.

12140 **United Nations.** Information Office. *War and Peace Aims; Extracts from Statements of United Nations Leaders.* (Special Supplement No. 5 to the United Nations Review, April 15, 1945.) New York: United Nations Information Office, 1945.

12141 **United Nations Institute for Training and Research.** *Small States & Territories: Status and Problems.* A UNITAR study by Jacques Rapaport, Ernest Muteba, and Joseph J. Therattil. New York: Arno Press, 1971.

12142 **United Nations.** Office of Public Information. *Everyman's United Nations; The Structure, Functions, and Work of the Organization and Its Related Agencies During the Years 1945-1958,* 6th ed. New York: Office of Public Information, United Nations, 1959.

12143 **United Nations.** Office of Public Information. *Handbook of the United Nations and the Specialized Agencies.* Lake Success, New York: Office of Public Information, 1949.

12144 **United Nations.** Office of Public Information. *The United Nations and Decolonization; Summary of the Work of the Special Committee of Twenty-Four.* New York: Office of Public Information, 1965.

12145 **United Nations.** Secretary-General. *Annual Report of the Secretary-General on the Work of the Organization 1 July 1949-30 June 1950.* Lake Success, New York: Secretary-General, 1950.

12146 **United Nations.** Secretary-General. *Non-self-governing Territories.* New York: Secretary-General, 1957.

12147 **U.S. Department of State.** Charter of the United Nations. *Report to the President on the Results of the San Francisco Conference, by the Chairman of the United States Delegation, the Secretary of State.* Publication 2349. Conference Series 71. Washington, D.C.: U.S. Department of State, 1945.

12148 **U.S. Department of State.** *Charter of the United Nations, Together with the Statute of International Court of Justice, Signed at the United Nations Conference on International Organization, San Francisco, California, June 26, 1945.* Publication 2353. Conference Series 74. Washington, D.C.: U.S. Department of State, 1945.

12149 **U.S. Department of State.** *Charter of the United Nations and Statute of the International Court of Justice.* Publication 2368. Conference Series 76. San Francisco: U.S. Department of State, 1945.

12150 **U.S. Department of State.** *Dumbarton Oaks Documents on International Organization; Together with Chart and Questions and Answers.*

Publication 2223. Conference Series 60. Washington, D.C.: U.S. Department of State, 1944.

12151 **U.S. Department of State.** *Commonwealth of Nations.* Washington, D.C.: Office of the Geographer, 1968.

12152 **U.S. Department of State.** *Dumbarton Oaks Documents on International Organization.* Publication 2192. Conference Series 56. Washington, D.C.: U.S. Department of State, 1944.

12153 **Vallaux, Camille.** *Les Federations d'Etats et la Societe des Nations.* Paris: Alcan, 1919.

12154 **Von Kleinsmid, Rufus B., and Christensen, Francis,** eds. *Preparedness for World Unity. Proceedings of the Institute of World Affairs, Twenty-Second Session, the University of Southern California, June 25 to 28, 1946.* Los Angeles: University of Southern California for the Institute of World Affairs, 1947.

12155 **Wade, William W.; Riggs, Fred W.; and Gary, Howard C.** *Problems of East-West Settlement.* New York: Office of Public Information, 1953.

12156 **Wright, Quincy.** *Mandates Under the League of Nations.* Chicago, Illinois: University of Chicago Press, 1930.

Journals

12157 **Abuetan, Barid.** "Eritrea: United Nations Problem and Solution." *Middle Eastern Affairs,* 2, No. 2 (February, 1951), 35-53.

12158 **Alger, Chadwick F.** "Perceiving, Analysing and Coping with the Local-Global Nexus." *International Social Science Journal,* 117 (August, 1988), 321-340.

12159 **Alker, Hayward R.** "Dimensions of Conflict in the General Assembly." *American Political Science Review.* 58, No. 3 (September, 1964), 642-657.

12160 **Archer, Clive.** "The North as a Multidimensional Strategic Arena." *The American Academyof Political and Social Science. Annals* [Newbury Park], 512 (November, 1990), 22-32.

12161 **Archibugi, Daniele.** "Models of International Organization in Perpetual Peace Projects." *Review of International Studies* [Cambridge], 18, No. 4 (October, 1992), 295-317.

12162 **Armstrong, Elizabeth H., and Cargo, William I.** "The Inauguration of the Trusteeship System of the United Nations." *U.S. Department of State Bulletin,* 16, No. 403 (March 23, 1947), 511-521.

12163 **Arncoot, Ghassan.** "The Organization of Petroleum-Exporting Countries (OPEC). *Rocky Mountain Social Science Journal*, 11, No. 2 (April, 1974), 11-17.

12164 **Aufricht, Hans.** "General Bibliography on International Organization and Post-War Reconstruction." *Bulletin of the Commission to Study the Organization of Peace*, 5-6 (May-June, 1942), 1-28.

12165 **Ball, George W.** "3 1/2 Super Powers." *Life Magazine*, (March 19, 1968), 74-89.

12166 **Bayliss, John.** "Nato Strategy: The Case for a New Strategic Concept." *International Affairs*, 64, No. 1 (Winter, 1987/88), 43-59.

12167 **Beloff, Max.** "The Balance of Power." *Interplay of European/American Affairs*, 1, No. 2 (August/September, 1967), 14-18.

12168 **Carlsson, Ingvar.** "A New International Order Through the United Nations." *Security Dialogue* [Newbury Park], 23, No. 4 (December, 1992), 7-11.

12169 **Chamberlain, Joseph P.** "International Organization." *International Conciliation*, 385, Section 1, (December, 1942), 459-623.

12170 **Cherne, Leo.** "Ideology and the Balance of Power." *American Academy of Political and Social Science Annals*, 442 (March, 1979), 46-56.

12171 **Cohen, R.,** and **Wilson, P.A.** "Superpowers in Decline: Economic Performance and National Security." *Comparative Strategy*, 7 (1988), 99-132.

12172 **Cox, Robert W.** "The Crisis of World Order and the Problem of International Organization in the 1980's." *International Journal*, 35, No. 2 (Spring, 1980), 370-395.

12173 **Dean, Vera Micheles.** "The San Francisco Conference--with Text of Charter." *Foreign Policy Reports*, 21, No. 9 (July 15, 1945), 110-136.

12174 **East, W. Gordon.** "Political Organizations at Higher Ranks." In *Essays in Political Geography*, Charles A. Fisher, ed. London: Methuen, 1968, 39-60.

12175 **Engelson, S.** "Les petites nations et l'avenir des Nations Unies selon U Thant." *Syntheses*, 17 Annee, No. 196-197 (Septembre-Octobre, 1962), 192-203.

12176 **Fachiri, A.P.** "Judgments and Advisory Opinions of the Permanent Court of International Justice." *British Year Book of International Law*, 7 (1926), 203-205.

12177 **Fox, Annette Baker.** "International Organization for Colonial Development. *World Politics*, 3, No. 3 (April, 1951), 340-368.

12178 **Fox, Annette Baker.** "The United Nations and Colonial Development." *International Organization*, 4, No. 2 (Spring, 1950), 199-218.

12179 **Gardner, Richard N.,** and **Milllikan, Max F.,** eds. "The Global Partnership: International Agencies and Economic Development." *International Organization*, 22, No. 1 (Winter, 1968), 1-475.

12180 **Garvey, J.I.** "United Nations Peacekeeping and Host State Consent." *American Journal of International Law*, 64, No. 2 (April, 1970), 241-269.

12181 **Ghils, Paul.** "International Civil Society: International Nongovernmental Organizations in the International System." *International Social Science Journal* [Oxford], No. 133 (August, 1992), 417-431.

12182 **Glassner, Martin.** "Review Essay: Political Geography in the United Nations." *Political Geography*, 13, No. 6 (November, 1994), 559-567.

12183 **Gregg, Phillip M.,** and **Banks, Arthur S.** "Grouping Political Systems: Q-Factor Analysis of a Cross-Polity Survey." *American Behavioral Scientist*, 9, No. 3 (November, 1965), 3-6.

12184 **Grundy-Warr, Carl E.R.** "Towards a Political Geography of United Nations Peacekeeping: Some Considerations." *GeoJournal*, 34, No. 2 (October, 1994), 177-190.

12185 **Haas, Ernst B.** "Regionalism, Functionalism, and Universal International Organization." *World Politics*, 8, No. 2 (January, 1956), 238-263.

12186 **Hagan, Joe D.** "Domestic Political Regime Changes and Third World Voting Realignments in the United Nations, 1964-1984. *International Organization*, 43, No. 3 (Summer, 1989), 505-541.

12187 **Hardy, J.** "The Interpretation of Plurilingual Treaties by International Courts and Tribunals." *British Year Book of International Law*, 37 (1961), 72.

12188 **Higgins, Rosalyn A.** "The Place of International Law in the Settlement of Disputes by the Security Council. *American Journal of International Law*, 64, No. 1 (January, 1970), 1-18.

12189 **Hill, Gladwin.** "U.N. Parley Plans a Global Environment Conference." *New York Times*, (September 14, 1971), 24.

12190 **Hitchcock, Charles B.** "Westchester-Fairfield: Proposed Site for the Permanent Seat of the United Nations." *Geographical Review*, 36, No. 3 (July, 1946), 351-397.

12191 **Hudson, Manley O.** "The New World Court." *Foreign Affairs*, 24, No. 1 (October, 1945), 75-84.

12192 **Huth, Paul; Bennett, D. Scott; and Gelpi, Christopher.** "System Uncertainty, Risk Propensity, and International Conflict Among the Great Powers." *Journal of Conflict Resolution* [Newbury Park], 36, No. 3 (September, 1992), 478-517.

12193 **International Organization**, 1, No. 1 (February, 1947), 43-183.

12194 **International Conciliation**, 458 (February, 1950), 113-200.

12195 **Jones, Joseph M.** "Half of One World. Dependent Peoples, Through Regional Organization and the Application of New Concepts of Colonial Development, May Reap Great Gains from this War." Excerpt: *Fortune*, 30, No. 10 (October, 1944), 123-131+.

12196 **Joyner, Christopher C., and Joyner, Nancy D.** "Global Eco-management and International Organizations: The Stockholm Conference and Problems of Cooperation." *Natural Resource Journal*, 14, No. 4 (October, 1974), 533-555.

12197 **Katseli, L.** "Devaluation: A Critical Appraisal of the IMF's Policy Prescriptions." *American Economic Review*, 73, No. 2 (May, 1983), 359-363.

12198 **Koslowski, Rey, and Kratochwil, Friedrich V.** "Understanding Change in International Politics: The Soviet Empire's Demise and the International System." *International Organization* [Cambridge, MA], 48, No. 2 (Spring, 1994), 215-247.

12199 **Krout, John A.**, ed. "World Organization--Economic, Political, and Social. A Series of Addresses and Papers Presented at the Semi-Annual Meeting of the Academy of Political Science, April 4-5, 1945." *Proceedings of the Academy of Political Science*, 21, No. 3 (May, 1945), 1-460.

12200 **Lapidoth, R.** "La resolution du Conseil de Securite au 22 novembre 1967 au sujet du Moyen Orient." *Revue Generale de Droit International Public*, (1970), 1-289.

12201 **Mares, David R.** "Middle Powers Under Regional Hegemony: to Challenge or Acquiesce in Hegemonic Enforcement." *International Studies Quarterly*, 32, No. 4 (December, 1988), 453-471.

12202 **McKay, Vernon.** "International Trusteeship--Role of United Nations in the Colonial World." *Foreign Policy Reports*, 22, No. 5 (May 15, 1946), 54-67.

12203 **Morrill, Richard L.** "Views and Opinions: The Geography of Representation in the United Nations." *Professional Geographer*, 24, No. 4 (November, 1972), 297-301.

12204 **Norton, C. McKin.** "The Hunt for a World Headquarters Site. (U.N.O.)." Excerpt: *The American City*, 61, No. 3 (March, 1946), 86-87+.

12205 **Oliver, James K.** "The Balance of Power. Heritage of 'Interdependence' and 'Traditionalism'." *International Studies Quarterly*, 26, No. 3 (September, 1982), 373-396.

12206 **Parker, John J.** "World Organization." *International Conciliation*, 397 (February, 1944), 150-165.

12207 **Parsons, Sir Anthony.** "The United Nations in the Post-Cold War Era." *International Relations* [London], 11, No. 3 (December, 1992), 189-200.

12208 **Patterson, Ernest Minor**, ed. "Making the United Nations Work." *Annals of the American Academy of Political and Social Science*, 246 (July, 1946), 1-142. (Complete issue, multiple authors.)

12209 **Patterson, Ernest Minor**, ed. "Progress and Prospects of the United Nations." *Annals of the American Academy of Political and Social Science*, 252 (July, 1947), 1-183. (Complete issue, multiple authors.)

12210 **Patterson, Ernest Minor**, ed. "World Government." *Annals of the American Academy of Political and Social Science*, 264 (July, 1949), 1-123. (Complete issue, multiple authors.)

12211 **Platig, E. Raymond.** "Crisis, Pretentious Ideologies, and Superpower Behavior." *Orbis*, 25, No. 3 (Fall, 1981), 511-524.

12212 **Raffestin, Claude.** "Geographie et organisations internationales." *Annales de Geographie*, 79, No. 434 (Juillet-Aout, 1970), 470-480.

12213 **Rejai, Mostafa.** "On Superpowers: Global and Regional." *Co-existence*, 16, No. 2 (October, 1979), 129-141.

12214 **Riggs, Fred W.** "Wards of the UN: Trust and Dependent Areas." *Foreign Policy Reports*, 26, No. 6 (June 1, 1950), 54-63.

12215 **Rivlin, Benjamin.** "Regional Arrangements and the UN System for Collective Security and Conflict Resolution: A New Road Ahead?" *International Relations* [London], 11, No. 2 (August, 1992), 95-110.

12216 **Rosecrance, Richard.** "A New Concert of Powers." *Foreign Affairs* [New York], 71, No. 2 (Spring, 1992), 64-82.

12217 **Samuels, Gertrude.** "The U.N.'s 'Thin Blue Line': Fighting for Peace." *New Leader*, 61, No. 23 (November 20, 1978), 10-11.

12218 **Schmidt, Helmut.** "The Search for Global Order: The Problems of Survival." *Security Dialogue* [London], 23, No. 3 (September, 1992), 41-56.

12219 **Schwartzberg, Joseph E.** "Editorial: Towards a More Representative and Effective Security Council." *Political Geography,* 13, No. 6 (November, 1994), 483-491.

12220 **Schwartzberg, Joseph E.** "More on 'The Geography of Representation in the United Nations': An Alternative to the Morrill Proposal." *Professional Geographer*, 25, No. 3 (August, 1973), 205-211.

12221 **Shapira, Amos.** "The Security Council Resolution of November 22, 1967--Its Legal Nature and Implications." *Israel Law Review*, 4, No. 2 (April, 1969), 229-241.

12222 **Sharp, Paul.** "Adieu to the Superpowers?" *International Journal* [Toronto], 47, No. 4 (Autumn, 1992), 818-847.

12223 **Shaw, Martin.** "Global Slociety and Global Responsibility: The Theoretical, Historical and Political Limits of 'International Society.'" *Millennium* [London], 21, No. 3 (WInter, 1992), 421-434.

12224 **Spykman, Nicholas John.** "Frontiers, Security, and International Organization." *Geographical Review*, 32, No. 3 (July, 1942), 436-447.

12225 **Tandy, Sir Edward.** "Regional Organization During and After the War." *Journal of the Royal Society of Arts*, 88, No. 4554 (March 1, 1940), 368-381. Discussion: 381-389.

12226 **Thies, Wallace J.** "The 'Demise' of NATO: A Postmortem." *Parameters* [Carlisle Barracks, PA], 20, No. 2 (June, 1990), 17-30.

12227 "The United Nations: Appraisal at 25 Years." *American Journal of International Law*, 64, No. 4 (September, 1970), 1-358.

12228 "The United Nations and Non-self-governing Territories." *International Conciliation*, 435 (November, 1947), 700-730.

12229 **United Nations.** Department of Public Information. *Research Section.* Lake Success, New York: The International Trusteeship System and the Trusteeship Council, 1949.

12230 **Ward, Michael D.** "Review Essay Recognizing a Hegemon [Robert O. Keohane, "After Hegemony: Cooperation and Discord in the World Political Community, 1984"]. *Political Geography Quarterly*, 4, No. 4 (October, 1985), 343-346.

12231 **Wild, Payson S., Jr.** "Machinery of Collaboration Between the United Nations." *Foreign Policy Reports*, 18, No. 8 (July 1, 1942), 94-108.

POLITICAL GEOGRAPHY OF REGIONS

AFRICA

Books

12232 **Addona, A.F.** *The Organisation of African Unity.* Cleveland: World Publishing, 1969.

12233 **Chabal, Patrick.** *Power in Africa: An Essay in Political Interpretation.* Houndmills: Macmillan, 1992.

12234 **Chanock, Martin.** *Britain, Rhodesia and South Africa, 1900-45: The Unconsummated Union.* Totowa, New Jrsey: Frank Cass, 1977.

12235 **Chidzero, B.T.G.** *Tanganyika and International Trusteeship.* London: Oxford University Press, 1961.

12236 **Clark, John Franklin III.** *Relations Among International Organizations in Africa.* Syracuse, New York: Syracuse University, Ph.D., 1974.

12237 **Dugard, John**, ed. *The South West Africa/Namibia Dispute: Documents and Scholarly Writings on the Controversy between South Africa and the United Nations.* Berkeley: University of California Press, 1973.

12238 **Egyptian Society of International Law.** Study Group on Egypt and the United Nations. *Egypt and the United Nations.* New York: Manhattan Publishing, 1957.

12239 **Franck, Thomas M.** *East African Unity through Law.* New Haven, Connecticut: Yale University Press, 1964.

12240 **Gardinier, David E.** *Cameroon, United Nations Challenge to French Policy.* London: Oxford University Press, 1963.

12241 **Great Britain Colonial Office.** *Trusteeship: Togoland and the Cameroons under United Kingdom Mandate.* Cmd. 6863. London: Great Britain Colonial Office, 1946.

12242 **Great Britain Parliament.** *Basutoland, the Bechuanaland Protectorate and Swaziland; History of Discussion with the Union of South Africa, 1909-1939.* London: Great Britain Parliament, 1952.

12243 **Great Britain Parliament.** *Cameroons under United Kingdom Trusteeship. Text of Trusteeship Agreement as Approved by the General Assembly of the United Nations, New York, 13th December, 1946.* Treaty Series, No. 20, 1947. Cmd. 7082. London: Great Britain Parliament, 1947.

12244 **Great Britain Parliament.** *Togoland under United Kingdom Trusteeship. Text of Trusteeship Agreement as Approved by the General Assembly of the United Nations, New York, 13th December, 1946.* Treaty Series, No. 21, 1947. Cmd. 7083. London: Great Britain Parliament, 1947.

12245 **Hazelwood, Arthur,** ed. *African Integration and Disintegration: Case Studies in Economic and Political Union.* London: Oxford University Press, 1967.

12246 **Imishue, R.W.** *South West Africa; An International Problem.* London: Pall Mall Press, 1965.

12247 **Jalloh, Abdul A.** *Political Integration in French-speaking Africa.* Berkeley: University of California, Institute of International Studies, 1973.

12248 **Logan, Rayford W.** *The African Mandates in World Politics.* Washington, D.C.: Public Affair Press, 1948.1

12249 **Lugard, Lord.** *The Dual Mandate in British Tropical Africa.* Edinburgh: W. Blackwood and Sons, 1922.

12250 **Naldi, Gino J.** *The Organization of African Unity: An Analysis of Its Role.* London: Mansell, 1989.

12251 **Nyangoni, Wellington W.** *Africa in the United Nations System.* Rutherford, New Jersey: Farleigh Dickinson University Press, 1985.

12252 **Nye, J.S.** *Pan-Africanism and East African Integration.* Cambridge, Massachusetts: Harvard University Press, 1965.

12253 **Organization of African Unity.** *Basic Documents of the Organization of African Unity.* Addis Ababa: Provisional Secretariat of the Organization of African Unity, 1964.

12254 **Organization of African Unity.** *Proceedings of the Summit Conference of Independent Africa States.* Organization of African Unity, 1963.

12255 **Orizu, Akweke Abyssinia Nwafor.** *Without Bitterness; Western Nations in Post-War Africa.* New York: Creative Age Press, 1944.

12256 **Padmore, George.** *Pan-Africanism or Communism? The Coming Struggle for Africa.* New York: Roy Publishers, 1956.

12257 **Pondi, Jean-Emmanuel.** *Political Rhetoric and Economic Reality in African International Relations: A Systems Analysis of the Relationships between the OAU and South Africa (Eastonian).* University Park: Pennsylvania State University, Ph.D., 1986.

12258 *South West Africa and the Union of South Africa; the History of a Mandate.* New York: Published by Authority of the Government of the Union of South Africa, 1947.

12259 **Touval, Saadia.** "The Organization of African Unity and African Borders." *International Organization* 21, No. 1 (Winter, 1967), 102-127.

12260 **United Nations.** Trusteeship Council. *Trusteeship Agreement for the Territory of the Cameroons under French Administration, as Approved by the General Assembly on 13 December 1946* Lake Success, New York: United Nations Trusteeship Council, 1947.

12261 **United Nations.** Trusteeship Council. *Trusteeship Agreement for the Territory of the Cameroons under British Administration, as Approved by the General assembly on 13 December 1946.* Lake Success, New York: United Nations Trusteeship Council, 1947.

12262 **United Nations.** Trusteeship Council. *Trusteeship Agreement for the Territory of Ruanda-Urundi, as Approved by the General Assembly on 13 December 1946.* Lake Success, New York: United Nations Trusteeship Council, 1947.

12263 **United Nations.** Trusteeship Council. *Trusteeship Agreement for the Territory of Tanganyika, as Approved by the General Assembly on 13 December 1946.* Lake Success, New York: United Nations Trusteeship Council, 1947.

12264 **United Nations.** Trusteeship Council. *Trusteeship Agreement for the Territory of Togoland under British Administration, as Approved by the General Assembly on 13 December 1946.* Lake Success, New York: United Nations Trusteeship Council, 1947.

12265 **Yohannes, Okbazghi.** *Eritrea, a Pawn in World Politics.* Gainesville: University of Florida Press, 1991.

Journals

12266 **Aderbigde, A.B.** "Symposium on West African Integration." *Nigerian Journal of Economic and Social Studies,*5, No. 1 (March, 1963), 1-40.

12267 **Arden-Clarke, Sir Charles.** South-West Africa, the Union and the United Nations." *African Affairs,* 59, No. 234 (January, 1960), 26-35.

12268 **Arnett, E.J.** The French Mandate in Cameroons." *Journal of the Royal African Society,* 37, No. 147 (April, 1938), 191-198.

12269 **Atyeo, Henry C.** "Morocco, Tunisia, and Algeria before the United Nation." *Middle Eastern Affairs* 6, Nos. 8-9 (August-September, 1955), 229-248.

12270 **Austin, Dennis, and Nagel, Ronald.** "The Organization of African Unity." *World Today* 22, No. 12 (December, 1966), 520-529.

12271 **Boateng, E.A.** "Outlook for African Unity: A Geographical Appraisal." *Bulletin of the Ghana Geographical Association,* 11, No. 2 (July, 1966), 38-50.

12272 **Boutros-Ghali, B.Y.** "The Addis Ababa Charter." *International Conciliation* 546 (January, 1964), 5-62.

12273 **Brayton, Abbott A.** "Soviet Involvement in Africa." The Journal of Modern African Studie, 17, No. 2 (June, 1979), 253-269.

12274 **Church, R.J. Harrison.** "Gambia and Senegal: Senegambia?" The Geographical Magazine 39, No. 5 (September, 1966), 339-350.

12275 **Clark, John Henrick.** "Pan Americanism: A Brief History of an Idea in the African World." *Presence Africaine,* No. 145 (1988), 25-56.

12276 **Coleman, James S.** "Problems of Political Integration in Emergent Africa." *Western Political Quarterly,* 8, No. 1 (Marcy, 1955), 44-57.

12277 **Cooke, Stanley.** "Federation in Central Africa; Stepping Stone to Ultimate Creation of a Great New British Dominion." *African World* (September, 1949), 9-12.

12278 **Damis, John.** "The U.N. Settlement Plan for the Western Sahara: Problems and Prospects." *Middle East Policy* [Washington, DC], 1, No. 2 (1992), 36-46.

12279 **Dikshit, R.D.** "O.A.U.: Promise and Performance." *African Quarterly,*6, No. 1 (April-June 1966), 50-59.

12280 **Gross, Ernest A.** "The South West Africa Case: What Happened?" *Foreign Affairs* 45, No. 1 (October, 1966), 36-48.

12281 **Higgins, Rosalyn A.** "The International Court and South West Africa: The Implications of the Judgement." *International Affairs,* 42, No. 4 (October, 1966), 573-599.

12282 **Hirschmann, David.** "Southern Africa: Detente?" *Journal of Modern African Studies* 14, no. 1 (March, 1976), 107-126.

12283 **Houphouet-Boigny, Felix.** "Black Africa and the French Union." *Foreign Affairs* 35, No. 4 (July, 1957), 593-599.

12284 **Jackson, Barbara Ward.** "Free Africa and the Common Market." *Foreign Affairs,*40, no. 3 (April, 1962), 419-430.

12285 **Jansen, J.P.** "Recent Developments and Trends in Africa: Pan-Africanism." *Journal for Geography* 2, No. 1 (September, 1962), 37-52.

12286 **Johns, David H.** "East African Unity-Problems and Prospects." *World Today* 19, No. 2 (December, 1963), 533-540.

12287 **Kraft, Louis.** "Pan Africanism: Political, Economic, Strategic or Scientific?" *International Affairs* 24, No. 2 (April, 1948), 218-228.

12288 **Kunert, D.T.** "Superpowers in Africa." *African Institute of South Africa Bulletin* 16, No. 6 (1978), 212-215.

12289 **LeMelle, Wilbert J.** "The OAU and Superpower Intervention in Africa." *Africa Today,*Vo. 35, No. 3-4 (1988), 21-26.

12290 **Lewis, I.M.** "Pan-Africanism and Pan-Somalism." *Journal of Modern African Studies* 1, No. 2 (June, 1963), 147-162.

12291 **Louis, W.R.** "African Origins of the Mandates Idea." International Organization,19, No. 1 (Winter, 1965), 20-36.

12292 **Mason, Philip.** "Partnership in Central Africa (Rhodesia and Nyasaland)." *International Affairs* 33, No. 2 (April, 1957), 154-164 and 33, No. 3 (July, 1957), 310-318.

12293 **Mathews, K.** "The Organization of Africa Unity." *India Quarterl,* 33, No. 3 (July-September, 1977), 308-324.

12294 **Mugomba, Agrippah T.** "Regional Organizations and African Underdevelopment: The Collapse of the East African Community." *Journal of Modern African Studies* 16, No. 2 (June, 1978), 261-272.

12295 **Norclau, R.N.** "The South West Africa Case." *World Today,* 22, No. 3 (March, 1966), 122-130.

12296 **Owens, W.H.** "International Roads for West Africa." *New Commonwealth,*40, No. 6 (June, 1962), 363-366.

12297 **Padelford, Norman J.** "Africa and International Organization." *International Organization,* 16, No. 2 (Spring1962), 275-464.

12298 **Pelissier, Rene.** "Ifni: A Pawn in the North African Power Game." *Geographical Magazine* 41, No. 8 (May, 1969), 601-605.

12299 **Pelissier, Rene.** "Mozambique Moves to Africa." *Geographical Magazine,* 46, Nos. 3, 4, 5 (February, 1974: incorporating December, 1973 and January, 1974), 167-177.

12300 **Persuad, Motee.** "Namibia and the International Court of Justice." *Current History* 68, No. 405 (May, 1975), 220-225.

12301 **Sircar, Parbati K.** "Toward a Greater East African Community." *Africa Quarterly,* 16, No. 3 (October-November, 1976), 1-14.

12302 **Uttley, Garrick.** "Globalism or Regionalism? United States Policy Towards South Africa." *Adelphi Paper,* 154 (Winter, 1979/1980).

12303 **Wild, Patricia Berko.** "The Organization of African Unity and the Algerian-Morocco Border of Conflict: A Study of New Machinery for Peacekeeping and for the Peaceful Settlement of Disputes Among African States." *International Organization* 20, No. 1 (Winter, 1966), 18-36.

AMERICAS

Books

12304 **Arend, Anthony Clark.** *John Foster Dulles and International Organization: His Thoughts and Actions (Law, Foreign Policy, Affairs, Relations).* Charlottesville: University of Virginia, Ph.D., 1985.

12305 **Augelli, Enrico,** and **Murphy, Craig N.** *America's Quest for Supremacy and The Third World: A Gramscian Analysis* London: Pinter Publishers, 1988.

12306 **Baker, Richard W.,** ed. *The ANZUS States and Their Region: Regional Policies of Australia, New Zealand, and the United States.* Westport: Praeger Publishers, 1994.

12307 **Brebner, John Bartlett.** *The North American Triangle, The Interplay of Canada, The United States and Great Britain.* New Haven, Connecticut: Yale University Press, 1954.

12308 **Brown, Benjamin H.,** and **Johnson, Joseph E.** *The U.S. and the U.N.* New York: Foreign Policy Assocation, 1954.

12309 **Burr, Robert N.,** and **Hussey, Roland D.** *Documents on Inter-American Cooper* Philadelphia: University of Pennsylvania Press, 1955.

12310 **Chamorro, Diego Manuel.** *La posicion juridica de Nicaragua y de Honduras ante el laudo del Rey de Espana.* Managua, D.N., Nicaragua: Impreso en los Talleres Nacionales, 1937.

12311 **Cole, John P.** *Factor Analysis and Clustering in Brazil and Peru* Nottingham: Nottingham University, Department of Geography, 1970.

12312 **Cromwell, William C.,** ed. *Political Problems of Atlantic Partnership: National Perspectives.* Bruges: College of Europe, 1969.

12313 **Finch, Elizabeth A.** *The Politics of Regional Integration: A Study of Uruguay's Decision to Join LAFTA* (Latin American Free Trade Association). Liverpool: University of Liverpool, Center for Latin American Studies, Monograph Series;, No. 4, 1973.

12314 **Goldenhamer, Herbert.** *The Foreign Powers in Latin America.* Princeton, New Jersey: Princeton University Press, 1972.

12315 **Grosser, A.** *The Western Alliance.* London: Macmillan, 1980.

12316 **Haya de la Torre, Raul.** *Adonde va Indio-America?* Santiago: Ercilla, 1935.

12317 **Healey, David.** *Drive to Hegemony: The United States in the Caribbean 1898-1917.* Madison: University of Wisconsin Press, 1988.

12318 **Herring, H.** *Good Neighbors: Argentina, Brazil, Chile and Seventeen Other Countries.* New Haven, Connecticut: Yale University Press, 1948.

12319 **Jefferson, Mark.** *The Mark Jefferson Paris Peace Conference Diary.* Geoffrey J. Martin, ed. Ann Arbor, Michigan: University Microfilms, 1966.

12320 **Karnes, Thomas L.** *The Failure of Union: Central America, 1824-1960.* Chapel Hill: University of North Carolina Press, 1961.

12321 **La Foy, Margaret.** *The Chaco Dispute and the League of Nations.* Thesis—Bryn Mawr, 1941. Ann Arbor, Michigan: Edwards Brothers, 1946.

12322 **Luft, Hermann.** *Latinamerika: Provinzen der Weltwirtschaft und Weltpolitik.* Leipzig: Bibliographisches Institut, 1930.

12323 **Matus, Ramon Ignacio.** *Jurisdiccion territorial atlantaica de la Republica de Nicaragua, civil, politica y eclesiastica, desde las Bocas del Desaguadero o Rio San Juan del Norte, hasta la medianeria de las aguas navegables del rio Grande o Aguan, hacia el Poniente del Cabo Camaron, en su colindancia con la Republica de Honduras.* Managua, D.N., Nicaragua: Los Talleres Nacionales, 1938.

12324 **Orrego Vicuna, Eugenio.** *Federacion del Pacifico.* Santiago: University de Chile, 1939.

12325 **Poitras, Guy.** *The Ordeal of Hegemony: The United States and Latin America.* Boulder: Westview Press, 1990.

12326 **Soward, F.H., and Mccaulay, A.M.** *Canada and the Pan American System.* (Canadian Institute of International Affairs, Contemporary Affairs, No. 21.) Toronto: Ryerson Press, 1948.

12327 **Travassos, Mario.** *Aspectos geograficos sul-americanos.* Sao Paulo: Comp. Editora Nacional, 1930.

12328 **Travassos, Mario.** *Aspectos geograficos sul-americanos.* Rio de Janeiro: Imp. Militar, 1933.

12329 **Traverso, Antonio.** *Fatores da formacao dos povos sul-americanos.* Rio de Janeiro: Canton Reile, 1941.

12330 *The United States and the International Trusteeship System.* New York: Commission to Study the Organization of Peace, 1945.

12331 **U.S. Department of State.** *Organization of American States.* Washington, D.C.: U.S. Department of State, 1958.

12332 **U.S. Department of State.** *The United States and Non-Self-Governing Territories. A Summary of Information Regarding the United States and Non-Self-Governing Territories with Particular Reference to Chapters XI, XII, and XIII of the Charter of the United Nations.* (Publication 2812.) United States - United Nations Information Series, 18. Washington, D.C.: U.S. Department of State, 1947.

12333 **Vincenes, Vives.** *Les Ameriques latines: terres de feu.* Quebec: Centre quebecois de relations internationales, 1970.

12334 **Weller, George.** *Bases Overseas; an American Trusteeship in Power.* New York: Harcourt Brace, 1944.

Journals

12335 **Augelli, John P.** "Central American Common Market." *Geographical Review,* 53, No. 3, (July, 1963), 449-451.

12336 **Canas Montalva, Ramon.** "Estructuracion geografica de America. Agrupacion o Confederacion del Pacifico." *Revista Geografica de Chile,* 2, No. 2 (Diciembre de, 1949), 15-19.

12337 **Catroux, Georges.** "The French Union: Concept, Reality and Prospects." *International Conciliatio,* 495 (November, 1953), 195-256.

12338 **Dean, Vera Micheles.** "U.S. Plans for World Organization." *Foreign Policy Reports* 20, No. 11 (August 15, 1944), 130-133.

12339 "International Co-operation for Development: The Andean Common Market." *Focus,* 24, No. 3 (November, 1973), 1-8.

12340 **Giannini, Amedeo.** "L'Organizzazione degli Stati de Centro America (ODECA)." *L'Universo* 33, No. 2 (March-April, 1953), 163-172.

12341 **Gigax, William R.** "The Central American Common Market." *Inter-American Economic Affairs,*16, No. 2 (Autumn, 1962), 59-77.

12342 **Glassner, Martin Ira.** "CARICOM: A Community in Trouble." *Focus,*29, No. 2 (November-December, 1978), 13-16.

12343 **Glassner, Martin Ira.** "CARICOM and the Future of the Caribbean." In *International Aspects of Development in Latin America: Geographical Perspectives* Gary S. Elbow, ed. Muncie, Indiana: CLAG Publications, 1977.

12344 **Gomes, Pimentel.** "Pontos dolorosos na America do Sul." *Correio da Manha,*19 (Janeiro 22, 1959), 151-156.

12345 **Hardy, D.** "South America Alliances: Some Political and Geographical Considerations." *Geographical Review,* 4-5 No. 2 (April, 1919), 259-265.

12346 **Hinton, Harold C.** "Die Amerikanische Ostasienpolitik." Zeitschrift fur Geopolitik 24 Jahrgang, Hebb 10 (Oktober, 1953), 524-529.

12347 **Hurrell, Andrew.** "Latin America in the New World Order: A Regional Bloc of the Americas? *International Affairs* [Cambridge], 68, No. 1 (January, 1992), 121-139.

12348 **Jamison, Edward Alden.** "Cuba and the Inter-American System: Exclusion of the Castro's Regime from the Organization of American States." *America*, 36, No. 3 (January, 1980), 317-346.

12349 **Jones, Edwin and Mills, G.E.** "Institutional Innovations and Change in the Commonwealth Caribbean." *Ekistic*, 45, No. 266 (January, 1978), 29-35.

12350 **Karol, K.S.** "Cuba esta sola: Das Insel-Haerland einer Neuen Lateinamerikanischen Hemisphare." *Zeitschrift fur Geopolitik,*Jahrgang, Heft 2 (Marz-April 1968), 82-85.

12351 **Klein, B.S.** "Hegemony and Strategic Culture: American Power Projection and Alliance Defense Politics." *Review of International Stdies* 14 (1988), 133-148.

12352 **Leach, Richard H.** "Changing Caribbean Commonwealth." *World Today,* 29, No. 5 (May, 1973), 216-226.

12353 **Lima, Felicio.** "Panorama sul-Americano." *Revista do instituto de geografia e Historia Militar do Brasil,*17, Ano. 12, No. 5, 23-24 (1 and 2 Semesters, 1953), 77-108.

12354 **Mattos, Carlos de Meira.** "Brasil e o despertar Afro-Asiatico." *Revista da Universidale de Sao Paulo,*18, No. 32 (1959), 459-480.

12355 **Mattos, Carlos de Meira.** "Caribe, O punctum dolens da politica continental." *A Defesa Nacional,*28, No. 563 (Junho, 1961), 73-77.

12356 **Mills, G.E.,** ed. "Problems of Administrative Change in the Common-wealth Caribbean." *Social and Economic Studies* 19, No. 1 (March, 1970), 1-145.

12357 "Nauru and Its Future: A Trusteeship Problem." *United Nations Review* 8, No. 8 (August, 1961), 21-24.

12358 **Nijman, Jan.** "The Limits of Superpower: The United States and the Soviet Union Since World War II." *Association of American Geographers. Annals* [Washington, DC], 82, No. 4 (December, 1992), 681-695.

12359 **Padelford, Norman J.** "Cooperation in the Central American Region; The Organization of Central American States." *International Organization* 11, No. 1 (Winter, 1957), 41-54.

12360 "Pan-Americanism without Argentina: From Rio to Mexico City." *Bulletin of International News* 22, No. 4 (February, 1945), 147-156.

12361 **Pepper, D.M.** "Geographical Dimensions of NATO'S Evolving Military Strategy." *Progress in Human Geography* 12 (1988), 157-178.

12362 **Piccini, R.** "Evoluzione del Panamericanismo." *Comunita Internationale* 15, No. 4 (1960), 293-318.

12363 **Ross, Colin R.** "Zwischen Nord-und Sudamerika." *Zeitschrift fur Geopoliti*, 15, Jahrgang, Heft 10 (Oktober, 1937), 813-823.

12364 **Tasso Fragoso, Augusto.** "A paz com o Paraguai depois de Guerra da Triplice Alianca." *Revista do Instituto historico e geografico brasileiro* 174, No. 1 (January-March, 1939), (1940), 1-334.

12365 **Travis, Martin B.** "The Organization of American States: A Guide to the Future." *Western Political Quarterly* 10, No. 3 (September, 1957), 491-511.

12366 **Webster, Gerald R.** "Support for the United States in the United Nations on Cold War Issues and the Distribution of Foreign Aid to Central American and Caribbean Countries." *TheGeographical Bulletin* [Ypsilanti], 33, No. 2 (November, 1991), 87-97.

12367 **Whitaker, Arthur P.** "Development of American Regionalism. The Organization of American States." *International Conciliation* 469 (March, 1951), 121-164.

12368 **Whitaker, Arthur P.** "The Origin of the Western Hemisphere Idea." *Proceedings of the American Philosophical Society* 98, No. 5 (October 15, 1954), 323-326.

12369 **Zubek, Voytek.** "Societ 'New Thinking' and the Central American Crisis." *Journal of Interamerican Studies and World Affairs* 29, No. 3 (Fall, 1987), 87-106.

ASIA

Books

12370 *The Arab World and the Arab League.* Washington, D.C.: Arab Office, 1945.

12371 **Barnds, William J.** *India, Pakistan, and the Great Powers* New York: Praeger, for the Council on Foreign Relations, 1974.

12372 **Brohi, A.K.** Five Lectures on Asia and the United Nations. Hague: Academy of International Law, Recueil des Cours, 1961.

12373 **Brookes, Jean Ingram.** *International Rivalry in the Pacific Islands, 1800-1875.* Berkeley: University of California Press, 1941.

12374 **Buss, R.** *Wary Partners: The Soviet Union and Arab Socialis.* Toronto: The Institute for Strategic Studies, Canadian Institute of International Affairs, 1970.

12375 **Cameron, Meribeth E.; Mahoney, Thomas, H.D.; and McReynolds, George E.** *China, Japan and the Power.* Foreward by Kenneth Scott Latourette. New York: Ronald Press, 1952.

12376 **Chopra, V.D.,** ed. *Mikhail Gorbchev's New Thinking - Asia-Pacific; A Critical Assessment on Behalf of International Institute for Asia-Pacific Studies.* New Delhi: Continental, 1988.

12377 **Choudhury, G.W.** *India, Pakistan, Bangladesh, and the Major Powers.* New York: The Free Press, 1975.

12378 **Chaudhuri, Mohammed Ahsen.** *Pakistan and the Regional Pacts* New York: Institute of Pacific Relations, 1959.

12379 **Chia, Siow Yue,** ed. ASEAN Economic Cooperation: Proceedings of the ASEAN Economic Research Unit Workshop. Singapore: Institute of Southeast Asian Studies, 1980.

12380 **Clubb, Oliver E.** *The United States and the Sino-Soviet Bloc in Southeast Asia.* Washington, D.C.: Brookings Institution, 1962.

12381 **Dharamdasani, M.D.,** ed. *Cooperation Among South Asian Nations: Studies in Southasian Regional Cooperation.* Varanasi: Shalimar, 1988.

12382 **Ehteshami, Anoushiravan, and Varasteh, Manshour,** eds. *Iran and the International Community.* London: Routledge, 1991.

12383 **Frye, Richard N.,** ed. *The Near East and the Great Powers.* Introduction by Ralph Bunche. Cambridge, Massachusetts: Harvard University Press, 1951.

12384 **Grant, Margaret,** ed. *South Asia Pacific Crisis; National Development and the World Community.* New York: Dodd, Mead, 1964.

12385 **Great Britain Parliament.** *Pacific Islands. Text of Trusteeship Agreement as Approved by the Security Council of the United Nations, New York, 2nd April, 1947* Treaty Series, No. 76, 1947. Cmd. 7233. London: Great Britain Parliament, 1947.

12386 **Gupta, Sisir K.** *India and Regional Integration in Asia.* New York: Asia Publishing House, 1964.

12387 *India in World Affairs.* College Park: University of Maryland, Studies in Business and Economics.

11, No. 1 (1957).

12388 **India (Republic).** Ministry of External Affairs. *India-Pakistan Conflict: Security Council Documents, November, 1965.* New Delhi: Publication Division, Government of India Press, 1965.

12389 **India Ministry of External Affairs.** *Kashmir Papers.* Reports of the United Nations Commission for India and Pakistan. New Delhi: Publication Division, Government of India Press, 1949.

12390 **Indian Council of World Affairs.** Study Group. *India and the United Nations.* New York: Manhattan Publishing, 1957.

12391 *Israel and the United Nations.* New York: Manhattan Publishing, 1956.

12392 **Jennings, W. Ivor, Sir.** *The Commonwealth of Asia.* Oxford: Clarendon Press, 1949.

12393 **Joldersma, Jerry.** *Ceylon and the United Nations.* Lexington: University of Kentucky, Ph.D., 1966.

12394 **Jukes, Geoffrey.** *The Soviet Union in Asia.* Berkeley: University of California Press, 1973.

12395 **Kennan, George F.** *Russia and the West under Lenin and Stali.* Boston, Massachusetts: Little Brown, 1960.

12396 **Khadduri, Majid.** "Towards an Arab Union: The League of Arab States." *American Political Science Review,* 40, No. 1 (February, 1946), 90-100.

12397 **Lall, A.** *The United Nations and the Middle East Crisis, 1967.* New York: Columbia University Press, 1968.

12398 **Lenczowski, George.** *Russia and the West in Iran 1918-1948.* Ithaca, New York: Cornell University Press, 1949.

12399 **Longrigg, S.H.** *Syria and Lebanon under French Mandate.* London: Oxford University Press, 1958.

12400 **Maung, Maung.** *Burma in the Family of Nations.* New York: Institute of Pacific Relations, 1956.

12401 **Meister, Irene W.** *Soviet Policy in Iran, 1917-1950: A Study in Techniques.* Medford, Massachusetts: Tufts University, 1954.

12402 **Murphy, George Gregory S.** *Soviet Mongolia: A Study of the Oldest Political Satellite.* Berkeley: University of California Press, 1966.

12403 **Narain, Jai, and Rakesh, Mukar Datta.** *Economics of Defence: A Study of SAARC Countries.* New Delhi: Lancer, 1989.

12404 **Office of the Chief of Naval Operations.** *Administration Organization and Personnel of the Japanese Mandated Islands.* Civil Affairs Handbook. OPNAV P22-102 (formerly (OPNAV 50E-4). Washington, D.C.: U.S. Navy Department, 1944.

12405 **Pact of the Arab League.** Washington, D.C.: Arab Office, 1945.

12406 **Pannikar, K.M.** *Asia and Western Dominance.* New York: Collier Books, 1969.

12407 **Reddy, T. Ramakrishna.** *India's Policy at the United Nations.* Lexington: University of Kentucky, Ph.D., 1966.

12408 **Sarwar, Hasan K.,** ed. *Pakistan and the United Nations.* New York: Manhattan Publishing, 1961.

12409 **Segal, Gerald,** ed. *The Soviet Union in East Asia: Predicaments of Power.* London: Heinemann, 1984.

12410 **Smolansky, Oles M.** *The Soviet Union and the Arab East Under Kruschev.* Lewisburg, Pennsylvania: Bucknell University, 1974.

12411 **Southeast Asia Treaty Organization.** *The First Annual Report of the Council Representatives, March, 1956.* Washington, D.C., SEATO 1956.

12412 **Southeast Asia Treaty Organization.** *SEATO; Record of Partnership, 1957-58* Bangkok: SEATO Headquarters, Frequin Publishers, 1959.

12413 **United Nations.** *Korea and the United Nations.* New York: Department of Public Information, 1950.

12414 **United Nations.** International Commission of Jurists. *Tibet and the Chinese People's Republic.* Geneva: U.N. Legal Inquiry Committee on Tibet, 1960.

12415 **United Nations.** The Permanent Mission of Pakistan to the United Nations. *The India-Pakistan Question: Kashmir, a Brief Study.* New York: Government of Pakistan, 1962.

12416 **United Nations.** The Permanent Mission of Pakistan. *Kashmir Issue.* New York: Government of Pakistan, 1962.

12417 **United Nations.** The Permanent Mission of Pakistan. *World Opinion on Kashmir, No. 1.* New York: Government of Pakistan, 1967.

12418 **United Nations.** *The Story of Kashmir.* New York: Security Council, 1951.

12419 **United Nations.** Trusteeship Council. *Trusteeship Agreement for the Territory of Western Samoa, as Approved by the General Assembly on 13 December 1946.* Lake Success, New York: United Nations, Trusteeship Council, 1947.

12420 **U.S. Department of State.** *Draft Trusteeship Agreement for the Japanese Mandated Islands,* with article by article comments, and statements by President Truman and the U.S. Representative on the Security Council. Publication 2784. Far Eastern Series, 20. Washington, D.C.: U.S. Department of State, 1947.

12421 **Utley, Freda.** *Will the Middle East Go West?* Chicago, Illinois: H. Regnery, 1957.

12422 **Washington, D.C. Pakistan Embassy.** *Kasmir and the United Nations--1962: Background Notes.* Washington, D.C.: Pakistan Embassy, Information Division, 1962.

12423 **Weatherbee, Donald E.,** ed. *Southeast Asia Divided: The ASEAN-Indochina Crisis.* Boulder, Colorado: Westview Press, 1985.

12424 **Wong, John.** *The ASEAN Economies: Development Outlook for the 1980s.* Singapore: Occasional Paper No. 1, 1977.

Journals

12425 **Ajami, Fouad.** "The End of Pan-Arabism." *Foreign Affairs* 57, No. 2 (Winter, 1978/79), 355-373.

12426 **Alagappa, Muthiah.** "The Major powers and Southeast Asia." *International Journal,* 44, No. 3 (Summer, 1989), 541-597.

12427 **Allman, T.D.** "Turkey's Risky Balancing Act." *Geo,* 2, No. 5 (May, 1980), 8-32.

12428 **Al-Marayati, Abid A.** "United Nations and the Problem of Aden." *India Quarterly* 22, No. 3 (July-September, 1966), 257-278.

12429 **Andel, Horst J.** "China und die Entwicklungslander." *Zeitschrift fur Geopolitik,* 35 Jahrgant, Huft 1 (Januar/Februar, 1964), 5-10.

12430 **Andelman, David A.** "China's Balkan Strategy." *International Security,* 4, No. 3 (Winter, 1979/80), 31-59.

12431 **Anthony, John Duke.** "The Union of Arab Emirates." *Middle East Journal,* 26, No. 3 (Summer, 1972), 271-287.

12432 **Blakeslee, George H.** "Japan's Mandated Islands." *Department of State Bulletin*, 2, No. 286 (December 17, 1944), 764-768.

12433 **Boutros-Ghali, B.Y.** "The Arab League, 1945-1955." *International Conciliation*, 498 (May, 1954), 387-448.

12434 **Brecher, Michael.** "Kashmir; A Case Study in United Nations Mediation." *Pacific Affairs*, 26, No. 3 (September, 1953), 195-207.

12435 **Campbell, Sir Jock.** "The West Indies; Can They Stand Alone?" *International Affairs*, 39, No. 3 (July, 1963), 335-344.

12436 **Das, Taraknath.** "The Kashmir Issue and the United Nations." *Political Science Quarterly*, 26, No. 2 (June, 1950), 264-282.

12437 **Dean, Vera Micheles.** "Soviet Influence in the Non-Western World." *University of Arizona Bulletin*, 29, No. 2 (1958), 31-33.

12438 **Dobell, W.M.** "Pakistan's Relations with the Major Powers and Some Minor Agreements." *Pacific Affairs*, 37, No. 4 (Winter, 1964-65), 384-395.

12439 **Eyre, James K.** "Japanese Expansion Toward the Mandated Islands." *United States Naval Institute Proceedings*, 70, No. 501 (November, 1944), 1321-1331.

12440 **Finkelstein, Lawrence S.** "Indonesia's Record in the United Nations." *International Conciliation*, 475 (November, 1951), 513-546.

12441 **Gelber, Marvin B.** "The Palestine Mandate: Story of a Fumble." *International Journal*, 1, No. 4 (Autumn, 1946), 302-316.

12442 **Gilchrist, Huntington.** "The Japanese Islands: Annexation or Trusteeship?" *Foreign Affairs*, 22, No. 4 (July, 1944), 634-642.

12443 **Green, L.C.** "Korea and the United Nations." *World Affairs*, 4, No. 4 (October, 1950), 414-437.

12444 **Hatta, Mohammad.** "Indonesia between the Power Blocs." *Foreign Affairs*, 36, No. 3 (April, 1958), 480-490.

12445 **Hubel, Helmut.** "Nonregional Powers in the Middle East: New Trends in the Eighties?" *Jerusalem Journal of International Relations*, 10, No. 2 (June, 1988), 52-72.

12446 **Hurewitz, J.C.** "Unity and Disunity in the Middle East." *International Conciliation*, 481 (May, 1952), 197-260.

12447 **Ireland, Philip W.** "The Pact of the League of Arab States." *American Journal of International Law*, 39, No. 4 (October, 1945), 797-800.

12448 **Ismael, Tareq Y.** "The United Arab Republic and the Sudan." *Middle East Journal*, 32, No. 1 (Winter, 1969), 14-28.

12449 **Issawi, Charles.** "The Bases of Arab Unity." *International Affairs*, 31, No. 1 (January, 1955), 36-47.

12450 **Jenkins, A.M. and Cannon, T.** "The Chinese Socialist Experience: From Utopia to Myopia?" *Geography*, 72 (October 4), (1987), 335-340.

12451 **Johnstone, William C.** "Future of the Japanese Mandated Islands." *Foreign Policy Reports*, 21, No. 13 (September 15, 1945), 190-199.

12452 **Khadduri, Majid.** "The Arab League as a Regional Arrangement." *American Journal of International Law*, 40, No. 4 (October, 1946), 756-777.

12453 **Khadduri, Majid.** "Towards an Arab Union: The League of Arab States." *American Political Science Review*, 40, No. 1 (February, 1946), 90-100.

12454 **Karbel, Josef.** "The Kashmir Dispute and the United Nations." *International Organization*, 3, No. 2 (May, 1949), 278-287.

12455 **Lee, Yong Leng.** "Supranationalism in Southeast Asia." *Journal of Tropical Geography*, 46, No. 1 (June, 1978), 27-36.

12456 **Leonard, L. Larry.** "The United Nations and Palestine." *International Conciliation*, 454 (October, 1949), 603-786.

12457 **Leszcycki, S.** "The Development of Geography in the People's Republic of China." *Geography*, 48 No. 2 (July, 1963), 139-154.

12458 **Levi, Werner.** "Struggle for Power in Southeastern Asia." *American Perspective*, 2, No. 9 (February, 1949), 451-464.

12459 **Lillico, Stuart.** "Pan-America or Pan-Malaya. Which Will the Filipino Choose?" *Asia and the Americas*, 43, No. 3 (March, 1943), 148-150.

12460 **Longrigg, S.H.** "New Grouping Among the Arab States." *International Affairs*, 34, No. 3 (July, 1958), 305-317.

12461 **Malhoney, James Waite.** *India in the Commonwealth*. Medford, Massachusetts: Tufts University, Fletcher School of Law and Diplomacy, Thesis Abstract No. 2, 1957.

12462 **McGhee, George C.** "Turkey Joins the West." *Foreign Affairs*, 32 No. 4 (July, 1954), 617-31.

12463 "The Meaning of the United Arab Republic." *World Today*, 14, No. 3 (March, 1958), 93-101.

12464 Mezerik, A.G., ed. "The Crisis in the Middle East. Lebanon, Jordan, Iraq, U.N. Action." *International Review Service*, 4, No. 45 (August, 1958) 1-55.

12465 Mezerik, A.G., ed. "The Middle East; Unification Among Arab States." International Review Service, 4, No. 42 (May, 1958), 1-60.

12466 "The Middle East and the Balance of Power." *Current History*, 33, No. 195 (November, 1957), 257-298.

12467 Millar, T.B. "Kashmir, the Commonwealth and the United Nations." *Australian Outlook*, 17 No. 1 (April, 1963), 54-73.

12468 Milne, R.S. "Malaysia and Singapore in 1974." *Asian Survey*, 15, No. 2 (February, 1975), 166-173.

12469 Milne, R.S. "Singapore's Exit from Malaysia; The Consequences of Ambiguity." *Asian Survey*, 6, No. 3 (March, 1966), 175-184.

12470 Nehru, Jawaharlal. *India and the Commonwealth*. New Delhi: Foreign Relations Society, 1949.

12471 "New Arab Pattern; Federal Union in the Middle East." *Round Table*, 48 No. 191 (June, 1958), 229-237.

12472 Newcombe, S.F. "A Forecast of Arab Unity." *Journal of the Royal Central Asian Society*, 31, Part 2 (May, 1944), 158-164.

12473 Ofuatey-Kodjoe, W. "Third World Perspectives at the United Nations: The Problem for Israel." *Jerusalem Journal of International Relations*, 10, No. 1 (March, 1988), 114-124.

12474 Pannikar, K.M. "Regional Organization for the Indian Ocean Area." *Pacific Affairs*, 18, No. 3 (September, 1945), 246-251.

12475 Pauker, Guy. "The Soviet Challenge in Indonesia." *Foreign Affairs*. 40 , No. 4 (July, 1962), 612-626.

12476 Pollard, Vincent K. "ASA and ASEAN, 1961-1967: Southeast Asian Regionalism." *Asian Survey*, 10, No. 3 (March, 1970), 244-255.

12477 Rajaratham, S. "Conferences for American Business on ASEAN." Address to the Asia Society. *New York*, 4 (October, 1977), 1977a.

12478 Reitsma, Hendrik S. "China in Africa." *Focus*, 26, No. 1 (September-October, 1975), 9-14.

12479 Richardson, M. "Lee Defines the ASEAN Blueprint." Far Eastern Economic Review, 96, No. 23 (June 10, 1977), 40-41.

12480 Rivlin, Benjamin. "Changing Perspectives on Internationalism at the United Nations: The Impact of the Ideological Factor on the Arab-Israeli Dispute." *Jerusalem Journal of Internationl Relations*, 10, No. 1 (March, 1988), 1-11.

12481 Rubinstein, Alvin Z. "Afghanistan and the Great Powers." *United States Naval Institute Proceedings*, 83, No. 1 (January, 1957), 62-68.

12482 Schwartzberg, Joseph E. "The Evolution of Regional Power Configurations in the Indian Subcontinent." In *Realm and Region in Traditional India*, Richard G. Fox, ed., Durham, North Carolina. Duke University Monograph and Occasional Paper Series, 1977. Monograph 14, 197-233.

12483 Seah, Chee-Meow. "Major Powers and the Search for a New Equilibrium in Southeast Asia." *Asia Pacific Community* , 7 (Winter, 1980), 79-93.

12484 Seale, Patrick. "The Break-up of the United Arab Republic." World Today, 17, No. 11 (November, 1961), 471-479.

12485 Simon, Sheldon W. "The Kashmir Dispute in Sino-Soviet Perspective." *Asian Survey*, 7, No. 3 (March, 1967), 176-187.

12486 Solarz, Stephen J. "Cambodia and the International Community." *Foreign Affairs*, 69, No. 2 (Spring, 1990), 99-115.

12487 Steinberg, David I. "International Rivalries in Burma." *Asian Survye* [Berkeley], 30, No. 6 (June, 1990), 587-601.

12488 Steiner, H. Arthur. "Communist China in the World Community." *International Conciliation*, 533 (May, 1961), 387-454.

12489 Susumu, Awanohara. "ASEAN Closes Economic Ranks." *Far Eastern Economic Review*, 31 (October, 1980a), 50.

12490 "Syria and Lebanon. The States of the Levant Under French Mandate." *Bulletin of International News*, 17, No. 14 (July 13, 1940), 841-851.

12491 Thomson, R. Stanley. "The Establishment of the French Protectorate Over Cambodia." *Far Eastern Quarterly*, 4, No. 4 (August, 1945), 313-340.

12492 Tope, T.K. "India-China Border Dispute and the International Court of Justice." *United Asia*, 15, No. 1 (January, 1963), 60-65.

12493 "Transjordan: From Mandate to Kingdom." *American Perspective,* 1, No. 8 (January, 1948), 501-506.

12494 "The United Nations and Indonesia." *International Conciliation,* 458 (February, 1950), 113-120.

12495 "The United Nations Charter; with Explanatory Notes of Its Development at San Francisco by the Executive Officers of the Four Commissions in the Conference: Malcolm W. Davis, Huntington Gilchrist, Grayson Kirk, Norman J. Padelford. The Potsdam Declaration, August 2, 1945." *International Conciliation,* 413, Sec. 1 (September, 1945), 439-557.

12496 **Vanderbosch, Amry.** "The Netherlands-Indonesian Union. the Hague Agreement, Based on Mutual Compromise, Replaces the Old Colonial Relationship with a 'Loose' Union Dependent on the Good Will of Both Parties." *Far Eastern Survey,* 19, No. 1 (January 11, 1950), 1-7.

12497 **Veur, Paul W. Van der.** "The United Nations in West Iran; A Critique." *International Organization,* 18, No. 1 (Winter, 1964), 53-73.

12498 **Weaver, Leon H.** "International Government in the Pacific." *Far Eastern Survey,* 13, No. 25 (December 13, 1944), 238-241.

12499 **Wiedemann, Kent M.** "China in the Vanguard of a New Socialism." *Asian Survey,* 26, No. 7 (July, 1986), 774-792.

AUSTRALIA, OCEANIA AND ANTARCTICA

Books and Journals

12500 "American Trusteeship in the Pacific Islands." *World Today,* 3, No. 7 (July, 1947), 317-322.

12501 **Baum, Allyn.** *Antarctica: The Worst Place in the World.* New York: Macmillan, 1966.

12502 **Beck, Peter J.** "The United Nations and Antarctica 1993: Continuing Controversy About the UN's Role in Antarctica." *Polar Record,* 30, No. 175 (October, 1994), 257-264.

12503 **Fry, Thomas Penberthy.** "Papua and Mandated New Guinea Today." *Pacific Affairs,* 19, No. 2 (June, 1946), 146-164.

12504 **Key, L.C.** "Australia in Commonwealth and World Affairs, 1939 to 1944." *International Affairs,* 21, No. 1 (January, 1945), 60-73.

12505 **Limb, Ben C.** "The Pacific Pact: Looking Forward or Backward?" *Foreign Affairs,* 29, No. 4 (July, 1951), 539-549.

12506 **Robbins, Robert R.** "United States Trusteeship for the Territory of the Pacific Islands." *Department of State Bulletin,* 16, No. 409 (May 4, 1947), 783-790.

12507 **Shackleton, Edward.** "Antarctica; the Continent Everybody Wants and the U.N. Should Get." *United Nation World,* 3, No. 9 (September, 1949), 19-21.

12508 **Stanner, W.E.H.** "New Guinea Under War Conditions." *International Affairs,* 20, No. 4 (October, 1944), 481-494.

12509 **Tomasetti, W.E.** *Australia and the United Nations: New Guinea Trusteeship Issues From 1946 to 1966.* Canberra, A.C.T., Boroko, Papua-New Guinea, Australian National University, New Guinea Research Unit, 1970.

12510 **United Nations.** Trusteeship Council. *Trusteeship Agreement for the Territory of New Guinea, as Approved by the General Assembly on 13 December 1946.* Lake Success, New York: United Nations, Trusteeship Council, 1947.

EUROPE

Books

12511 **Adams, T.W.,** and **Cottrell, Alvin J.** *Cyprus between East and West.* Baltimore, Maryland: Johns Hopkins University Press, 1968.

12512 **Austin, Dennis.** *The Commonwealth and Britain.* London: Routledge, 1988.

12513 **Benoit, Emile.** *Europe at Sixes and Sevens: The Common Market, The Free Trade Association and The United States.* New York: Columbia University Press, 1962.

12514 **Biberaj, Elez.** *Albania and China: A Study of an Unequal Alliance.* Boulder, Colorado: Westview Press, 1986.

12515 **Birdwood, Christopher Bromhead, 2d Baron.** *A Continent Decides; Introducing Two New Members in the Great and Diverse Family of the Commonwealth and Some of the Problems which They Offer for Our Understanding and Solution.* London: R. Hale, 1953.

12516 **Bittman, Ladiolav.** The KGB and Soviet Disinformation: An Insider's View. Washington, D.C.: Pergamon-Brassey's International Defense Publishers, 1985.

12517 **Bonn, M.J.** *Whither Europe--Union or Partnership?* New York: Philosophical Library, 1952.

12518 **Brandt, Karl.** *Will All of Europe Go Neutral? It Depends on the Decisions We Make.* New York: City News Publishing, 1957.

12519 **British Information Services.** *The Commonwealth Association in Brief.* New York: British Information Service, 1958.

12520 **British Information Services.** Reference Division. *Commonwealth in Brief.* New York: British Information Service, 1955.

12521 **Clemens, Walter C., Jr.** *Can Russia Change? The USSR Confronts Global Interdependence.* Boston: Unwin Hyman, 1990.

12522 **Cole, John, and Cole, Francis.** *The Geography of the European Community.* New York: Routledge, 1993.

12523 **DeBois, Jean-Marie.** *Policy Choice, Voting, and Prisoners' Dilemma Game, with an Application to EEC Agricultural Support.* Berkeley: University of California, Ph.D., 1976.

12524 **Dibb, Paul.** *The Soviet Union: The Incomplete Superpower.* London: Macmillan, 1986.

12525 **Florinsky, Michael T.** *Integrated Europe?* New York: Macmillan, 1955.

12526 *The French Union; Political and Administrative Structure.* Paris: Direction de la Documentation, 1950.

12527 **Frost, Richard A.** *The British Commonwealth and the World.* London: Royal Institute of International Affairs, 1945.

12528 **Galtung, Johan.** *Europe in the Making.* New York: Crane Russak, 1989.

12529 **Gati, Charles.** *The Bloc that Failed: Soviet-East European Relations in Transition.* Bloomington: Indiana University Press, 1990.

12530 **Gati, Charles.** *Hungary and the Soviet Bloc.* Durham, North Carolina: Duke University Press, 1986.

12531 **Ginsberg, Roy H.** *Foreign Policy Actions of the European Community: The Politics of Scale.* Boulder, Colorado: Lynne Rienner Publishers, 1990.

12532 **Gleason, John Howes.** *The Genesis of Russophobia in Great Britain.* Cambridge, Massachusetts: Harvard University Press, 1950.

12533 **Gottstein, Klaus,** ed. *Integrated Europe?: Eastern and Western Perceptions of the Future.* Frankfurt am Main: Campus Verlag, 1992.

12534 **Grigg, Sir Edward.** The British Commonwealth; Its Place in the Service of the World. New York: Liveright Publishing Corporation, 1944.

12535 **Groth, Alexander J.** *Eastern Europe after Czechoslovakia.* New York: Foreign Policy Association, 1969.

12536 **Haas, Ernst.** *The Uniting of Europe.* Stanford, California: Stanford University Press, 1957.

12537 **Haines, C. Grove,** ed. *European Integration.* Baltimore, Maryland: Johns Hopkins University Press, 1957.

12538 **Hall, Duncan.** *The British Commonwealth of Nations.* London: Methuen, 1920.

12539 **Hallstein, Walter.** United Europe: Challenge and Opportunity. Cambridge, Massachusetts: Harvard University Press, 1962.

12540 **Harlow, Vincent,** ed. *Origins and Purpose; a Handbook on the British Commonwealth and Empire.* Glasgow: McCorquodale, 1944.

12541 **Hawtrey, R.G.** *Western European Union: Implication for the United Kingdom.* London: Royal Institute of International Affairs, 1949.

12542 **Heater, Derek.** *The Idea of European Unity.* Leicester: Leicester University Press, 1992.

12543 **Hudson, R.; Rhind, D.W.,** and **Mounsey, H.** *An Atlas of EEC Affairs.* London: Methuen, 1984.

12544 **Hurwitz, Leon,** and **LeQuesne,** eds. *The State of the European Community, 1989-90.* Boulder, Colorado: Lynne Rienner Publishers, 1991.

12545 **Institute on World Organization.** Conference, 2d, Washington, D.C., 1943. *Regionalism and World Organization; Post-war Aspects of Europe's Global Relationships.* Washington, D.C.: American Council on Public Affairs, 1944.

12546 **Jelavich, C.** and **Jelavich, B.** *The Balkans.* Englewood Cliffs, New Jersey: Prentice-Hall, 1965.

12547 **Jennings, W. Ivor, Sir.** *The British Commonwealth of Nations.* 2nd ed. London: Hutchinson, 1954, p. 108-14.

12548 **Keating, M.** and **Jones, B.,** eds. *Regions in the European Community.* London: Clarendon Press, 1985.

12549 **Kitzinger, V.W.** The Politics and Economics of European Integration. New York: Praeger, 1963.

12550 **Knorr, Klaus.** *NATO: Past, Present, Prospect.* New York: Foreign Policy Association, 1969.

12551 **Laserson, Max**. *Russia and the Western World; The Place of the Soviet Union in the Community of Nations.* New York: Macmillan, 1945.

12552 **Lerner, Daniel, and Gorden, Morton.** *Euratlantica: Changing Perspectives of the European Elites.* Cambridge: Massachusetts Institute of Technology Press, 1969.

12553 **Lindsay, K.** *Towards a European Parliament.* Strasbourg: Conseil de l'Europe, 1958.

12554 **Mansergh, Nicholas.** *The Commonwealth and the Nations.* London: Royal Institute of International Affairs, 1948.

12555 **Mawson, J.; M.R. Martins; and Gibney, J.R.** *Regions in the European Community.* London: Clarendon Press, 1985.

12556 **Mayne, R.** *The Community of Europe.* London: Gollancz, 1962.

12557 **Menges, Constantine C.** *The Future of Germany and the Atlantic Alliance.* Washington, DC: The AEI Press, 1991.

12558 *NATO after Czechoslovakia.* Washington, D.C.: Georgetown University, Center for Strategic and International Studies, 1969.

12559 **Nicholson, F. and East, R.,** eds. *From the Six to the Twelve: The Enlargement of* European Communities. London: Longman, 1987.

12560 **North Atlantic Treaty Organization.** Information Service. *Facts About NATO.* Paris: NATO, 1957.

12561 **North Atlantic Treaty Organization.** *The North Atlantic Treaty Organization.* Paris: NATO, 1956.

12562 **Nystrom, J. Warren, and Malof, Peter.** *The Common Market: European Community in Action.* Princeton, New Jersey: Van Nostrand, 1962.

12563 **Painchaud, Paul.** *Francophonie: Bibliographie 1960-1969.* Montreal: Presses de l'Universite de Quebec, 1972.

12564 **Parker, Geoffrey.** *An Economic Geography of the Common Market.* New York: Praeger, 1969.

12565 **Pijpers, Alfred,** ed. *The European Community at the Crossroads: Major Issues and Priorities for the EC Presidency.* Dordrecht: Martinus Nijhoff Publishers, 1992.

12566 **Pounds, Norman J.G.** *Poland Between East and West.* Princeton, New Jersey: Van Nostrand, 1964.

12567 **Rivlin, Benjamin.** *The United Nations and the Italian Colonies.* New York: Carnegie Endowment for International Peace, 1950.

12568 **Scott, F.R.** *Cooperation for What? United States and British Commonwealth.* (I.P.R. Pamphlets, No. 11) New York: American Council, Institute of Pacific Relations, 1944.

12569 **Stern, H. Peter.** *The Struggle for Poland.* Washington, D.C.: Public Affairs Press, 1953.

12570 **Stillman, Edmund.** *The Balkans.* New York: Time Life Books, 1964.

12571 **Swedish Institute of International Affairs.** *Sweden and the United Nations.* New York: Manhattan Publishing, 1956.

12572 **Tovias, Alfred.** *Foreign Economic Relations of the European Community: The Impact of Spain and Portugal.* Boulder, Colorado: Lynne Rienner Publishers, 1990.

12573 **Tugendhat, Christopher.** *Making Sense of Europe.* New York: Columbia University Press, 1988.

12574 **United Nations.** Department of Public Information. *Shaping a People's Destiny; The Story of Eritrea and the United Nations.* New York: Department of Public Information, 1953.

12575 **U.S. Department of State.** *East Germany Under Soviet Control.* Washington, D.C.: U.S. Department of State, 1952.

12576 **U.S. Department of State.** *NATO; 1949-1959, The First Ten Years.* Washington, D.C.: U.S. Department of State, 1959.

12577 **U.S. Department of State.** *NATO: North Atlantic Treaty Organization, Its Development and Significance.* Washington, D.C.: U.S. Department of State, 1952.

12578 **U.S. Department of State.** *The United Nations and the Problem of Greece. Publication 2909.* Near Eastern Series, 9. Washington, D.C.: U.S. Department of State, 1947.

12579 **Viatte, Auguste.** *La Francophonie.* Paris: Larousse, 1969.

12580 **Weil, Gordon L.** *A Foreign Policy for Europe? The External Relations of the European Community.* Bruges: College of Europe, 1970.

12581 **Wheare, K.C.** *The Constitutional Structure of the Commonwealth.* Oxford: Oxford University Press, 1960.

12582 **Whelan, James R.**, and **Jaeckle, Franklin A.**
The Soviet Assualt on America's Southern Flank.
Washington, D.C.: Regnelry Gateway, 1988.

Journals

12583 **Arlett, Sara**, and **Sallnow, John.** "European
Centres of Dissent." *Geographical Magazine,* 61,
No. 9 (September, 1989), 6-9.

12584 **Betts, R.R.** "The European Satellite States; Their
War Contribution and Present Position."
International Affairs, 21, No. 1 (January, 1945),
15-29.

12585 **Bonanno. A.** "The Agro-Food Sector and the
Transnational State: The Case of the EC."
Political Geography, 12, No. 4 (July, 1993), 341-
360.

12586 **Brandt, Karl.** "The Unification of Europe."
Vital Speeches of the Day, 19, No. 6 (January 1,
1953), 180-185.

12587 **Buozynowska, O.** "Spoleczno-Przestrzenna
Stauktura Warszawskeigo Zespolu Mie, Skiego
(The Socio-Spatial Structure of the Warsaw
Conurbation)." *Przeglao Geograficzny,* 57, No.
3, (1988), complete volume.

12588 "Britain, the Commonwealth and Europe." *Round
Table,* 61, No. 244 (October, 1971), 431-594
(Complete issue, multiple authors).

12589 **Catroux, Georges.** "The French Union:
Concept, Reality, and Prospects." *International
Conciliation,* 495 (November, 1953), 195-256.

12590 **Cleveland, Harold van B.**, and **Cleveland, Joan
B.** "The Atlantic Alliance: Problems and
Prospectives." *Foreign Policy Association,*
Headline Series. 177 (June, 1966), 1-63.

12591 **Cole, John P.** "Republics of the Former USSR
in the Context of a United Europe and New
World Order." *Soviet Geography* [Silver Spring],
32, No. 9 (November, 1991), 587-603.

12592 "The Commonwealth of Nations." *International
Journal,* 26, No. 2 (Spring, 1971), 291-432.

12593 **Costanzo, G.A.** "The Association of Overseas
Countries and Territories with the Common
Market." *Civilizations.* 8, No. 4 (1958), 505-
526.

12594 **de la Serre, Francoise.** "Communaute
Europeenne en 1989: Des Choix de Plus en Plus
Pressants." *Notes et Etudes Documentaires*
[Paris], No. 4912-13 (1990), 255-279.

12595 **Dedijer, Vladimir.** "Albania, Soviet Pawn."
Foreign Affairs, 30, No. 1 (October, 1951), 103-
111.

12596 **Delors, Jacques.** "European Integration and
Security." *Survival* [London], 33, No. 2
(March/April, 1991), 99-109.

12597 **Demangeon, Albert.** "Relations de l'Irlande avec
la Grande-Baretagne." *Annales de Geographie,*
32, No. 177 (Mai 15, 1923).

12598 **Desmond, Annabelle.** "The Common Market."
Population Bulletin. 18, No. 4 (July, 1962), 65-
90.

12599 **Diebold, William, Jr.** "Britain, the Six, and the
World Economy." *Foreign Affairs,* 40, No. 3
(April, 1962), 407-418.

12600 **Dietzel, Karl H.** "Die english-franzosische
Mandatsgrenze in Kamerun und ihr politischer
Sinn." *Zeitschrift der Gesellschaft fur Erdkunde
zu Berlin,* Heft 9-10 (Dezember, 1937), 321-348.

12601 **Dittler, Eriwn.** "Bundesrepublik Deutschland und
Deutsche Demokratische Republik." *Zeitschrift
fur Geopolitik,* 34 Jahrgang, Heft 1 (Januar,
1963), 12-13.

12602 **Efron, Reuben**, and **Nanes, Allan S.** "The
Common Market and Euratom Treaties:
Supranationality and the Integration of Europe."
International and Comparative Law Quarterly, 6,
No. 4 (1957), 670-684.

12603 **Elliott, A. Randle.** "Portugal: Beleaguered
Neutral." *Foreign Policy Reports,* 17, No. 19
(December 15, 1941), 234-244.

12604 **Farlow, Robert L.** "Romania: The Politics of
Autonomy." *Current History,* 74, No. 436
(April, 1978), 168-171 and 185-186.

12605 **Farogo, Ladislas.** "What Lies Behind the
Transparent Iron Curtain." *United Nation World,*
2, No. 11 (December, 1948), 17-21.

12606 **Fisher, Charles A.** "The Changing Significance
of the Commonwealth in the Political Geography
of Great Britain." *Geography,* 48, Part 2 (April,
1963), 113-129.

12607 **Fleming, Douglas K.** "The Common Market
Today." *Journal of Geography,* 66, No. 8
(November, 1967), 449-453.

12608 "France and the French Union; A New World
Comes to Birth." *Round Table,* 44, No. 170
(March, 1953), 145-152.

12609 **Giordano, C.** "The 'Wine War' Between France
and Italy: Ethno-Anthropoligical Aspects of the
European Community." *Sociologia Ruralis,* 27,
No. 2 (1987) 56-66.

12610 **Gnesotto, Nicole.** "European Union After Minsk and Maastricht." *International Affairs* [Cambridge], 68, No. 2 (April, 1992), 223-231.

12611 **Goldberg, Andrew C.** "Soviet Imperial Decline and the Emerging Balance of Power." *Washington Quarterly,* 13, No. 1 (Winter, 1990), 157-167.

12612 **Goormaghtigh, John.** "European Coal and Steel Community." *International Conciliation,* 503 (May, 1955), 343-408.

12613 **Goormaghtigh, John.** "European Integration." International Conciliation, 488 (February, 1953), 53-109.

12614 **Gubbels, F. and Ugonis, M.** "La Promotion des Investissements ands les Pays en Voie de Developement: Quel Rolle pour lad Communanoe? (What role for the European Community in the Promotion of Investment in Developing Countries?)." *Revue de Marche Commun,* 300 (1986), 463-467.

12615 **Gyorgy, Andrew.** "East Germany-Profile of a Reluctant Satellite." *United States Naval Institute Proceedings,* 87, No. 6 (June, 1961), 50-62.

12616 **Haines, C. Grove.** "Italy's Struggle for Recovery-An Allied Dilemma." *Foreign Policy Reports,* 20, No. 18 (December 1, 1944), 222-235.

12617 **Hambro, John.** "Norway and the Atlantic Pact." *American Perspective,* 2, No. 8 (January, 1949), 431-439.

12618 **Hartley, Anthony.** "Europe between the Superpowers." *Foreign Affairs,* 49, No. 2 (January, 1971), 271-282.

12619 **Harvey, Heather Joan.** "The British Commonwealth: A Pattern of Cooperation." *International Conciliation,* 487 (January, 1953), 1-48.

12620 **Hasna, Bou.** "Structure Administrative du Protectorat Francais en Tunisie." *L'Afrique Francaise,* 47ᵉ anne, No. 10 (October, 1937), 472-476; No. 11 (Novembre, 1937), 545-550; and No. 12 (Decembre, 1937), 575-578.

12621 **Hassner, Pierre.** "Europe Beyond Partition and Unity: Disintegration or Reconstruction?" *International Affairs* [Cambridge], 66, No. 3 (July, 1990), 461-475.

12622 **Heath, Edward.** "European Unity Over the Next Ten Years: From Community to Union." *International Affairs,* 64, No. 2 (Spring, 1988), 199-207.

12623 **Hirsch, V.** "Afrique du Sud: Le Talon d'Achille de la Co-Operation Politique. (South Africa: The Achilles' Heel of Political Cooperation in the European Community)." *Revue du Marche Commun,* 310 1986) 497-498.

12624 **Hoffman, George W.** "The Survival of an Independent Austria." The Geographical Review, 41, No. 4 (October, 1951), 606-621.

12625 **Hoffman, George W.** "Toward Greater Integration in Europe: Transfer of Electric Power Across International Boundaries." *Journal of Geography,* 55, No. 4 (April, 1956), 165-176.

12626 **Holmes, Olive.** "Portugal: Atlantic Pact Ally." *American Perspective,* 4, No. 1 (Winter, 1950), 45-56.

12627 **Hopper, Bruce.** "Sweden: A Case Study in Neutrality." *Foreign Affairs,* 23, No. 3 (April, 1945), 435-449.

12628 **Howard, C.** "External Affairs Power and the Commonwealth." *Current Affairs Bulletin,* 60 (1983), 16-24.

12629 **Hudson, R., and Sadler, D.** "Region, Class and the Politics of Steel Closures in European Community." *Society and Space,* 1 (1983), 405-428.

12630 **Hurrell, Andrew.** "The Politics of South Atlantic Security: A Survey of Proposals for a South Atlantic Treaty Organization." *International Affairs,* 59, No. 2 (April, 1983), 179-193.

12631 "Italian Colonies and Trusteeship." *African Transcripts,* 5 (September, 1945), 134-137.

12632 **Kaeckenbeeck, Georges S.** "Upper Silesia Under the League of Nations." *Annals of the American Academy of Political and Social Science,* 243 (January, 1946), 129-133.

12633 **Kalijarvi, Thorsten V.** "Obstacles to European Unification." *Annals of the American Academy of Politics and Social Science,* 348 (July, 1963), 46-53.

12634 **Kelsen, Hans.** "The Free Territory of Triste Under the United Nations." *Yearbook of World Affairs* (1950), 174-190.

12635 **Kesseli, John E.** "Switzerland Remains Neutral." *Education,* 63, No. 5 (January, 1943), 288-295.

12636 **Khrushchev, Nikita S.** "On Peaceful Coexistence." *Foreign Affairs,* 38, No. 1 (October, 1959), 1-18.

12637 **Kish, George.** "Eastern Europe's Power Grid." *Geographical Review,* 58, No. 1 (January, 1968), 137-140.

12638 **Kitromilides, Paschalis M.** "The Enlightenment East and West: A Comparative Perspective on the Ideological Origins of the Balkan Political Traditions." Canadian Review of Studies in Nationalism, 10, No. 1 (Spring, 1983), 51-70.

12639 **Kitzinger, V.W.** "Europe: The Six and the Sevens." International Organization, 14, No. 1 (February,1960), 20-36.

12640 **Knutsen, Oddbjorn.** "Cleavage Dimensions in Ten West European Countries: A Comparative Empirical Analysis." *Comparative Political Studies,* 21, No. 4 (January, 1989), 495-533.

12641 **Konetzke, Richard.** "Hispanoamerika und Europe." Zeitschrift fur Geopolitik, 25, Jahrgang, Heft 9 (Septbr, 1954), 511-515.

12642 **Krippendorff, E.** "A Critique of Bonn's Ostpolitik." *Survey,* No. 61 (Octobler, 1966), 47-55.

12643 **Lerner, Daniel.** "Will European Union Bring About Merged National Goals?" *Annals of the American Academy of Politics and Social Science,* 348 (July, 1963), 34-45.

12644 **Lester, A.P.** "State Succession to Treaties in the Commonwealth." *International and Comparative Law Quarterly,* 12, No. 3 (July, 1963), 475 and 14, No. 2 (April, 1965), 365.

12645 **Lester, A.P.** "State Succession to Treaties in the Commonwealth." *International and Comparative Law Quarterly,* 12 No. 3 (July, 1963), 475-507.

12646 **Lodgaard, Sverre.** "Competing Schemes for Europe: The CSCE, NATO and the European Union." *Security Dialogue* [London], 23, No. 3 (September, 1992), 57-68.

12647 **Lodge, Juliet.** "The European Community in the 1980s: Towards a Federal Union?" *Australian Outlook,* 41, No. 2 (August, 1987) 95-100.

12648 **Logoreci, Anton.** "Albania: A Chinese Satellite in the Making?" *World Today,* 17, No. 5 (May, 1961), 197-205.

12649 **Lowenthal, Richard.** "The Limits of Intra-Bloc Pluralism: The Changing Threshold of Soviet Intervention." *International Journall,* 37, No. 2 (Spring, 1982), 263-284.

12650 **Luc, Jean-Claude.** "La Francophonie." *Revue francaise d'etudes politiques africaines,* No. 39 (Mars, 1969) 63-85.

12651 **Mander, Linden A.** "The British Commonwealth and Colonial Rivalry in Southeast Asia." *The Pacific Historical Review,* 11, No. 1 (March, 1942), 19-27.

12652 **Mandeville, D.C.** "Fifteen Years of the Colombo Plan and of the British Contribution to It." Royal Central Asia Journal, 53, Pt. 1 (February, 1966), 32-42.

12653 **Mansergh, Nicholas.** "Ireland: The Republic Outside the Commonwealth." *International Affairs,* 28, No. 3 (July, 1952), 277-291.

12654 **Michel, Aloys S.** "The Canalization of the Moselle and West European Integration." *Geographical Review,* 52, No. 4 (October, 1962), 475-491.

12655 **Moulin, Lee.** "L'Italie et la Distribution des Mandats Coloniaux au Lendemain de la Guerre." *Revue Economique Internationale,* 29ᵉ annee, 4, No. 3 (Decembre, 1937), 477-505.

12656 **O'Neill, Robert.** "European Security in the 1990s: A New Organisation for a New Challenge--the Alliance for Development in Europe." *Australian Journal of International Affairs* [Canberra], 44, No. 3 (December, 1990), 211-220.

12657 **Orvik, Nils.** "Scandinavia, NATO, and Northern Security." *International Organization,* 20, No. 3 (Summer, 1966), 380-396.

12658 **Padover, Saul K.** "Europe's Quest for Unity." *Foreign Policy Association. Headline Series,* 97 No. 1 (January-February, 1953), 3-57.

12659 **Patterson, Ernest Minor,** ed. "NATO and World Peace." *Annals of the American Academy of Political and Social Science,* 288 (July, 1953), 1-237 (complete issue, multiple authors).

12660 **Popper, David H.** "NATO After Sixteen Years: An Anniversary Assessment." *Department of State Bulletin,* 52, No. 1346 (April 12, 1965), 518-527.

12661 "Problems of British Colonial Trusteeship." *International Labour Review,* 44, No. 5 (November, 1941), 538-546.

12662 **Roberts, D.T.** "The Dutch-Belgian Economic Union." *Foreign Affairs,* 25, No. 4 (July, 1947), 691-94.

12663 **Roucek, Joseph S.,** ed. "Moscow's European Satellites." *Annals of the American Academy of Political and Social Science,* 271 (September, 1950), 78-93.

12664 **Rudnick, David.** "NATO and the Cyprus Crisis: Pressure Groups Versus Power Politics." *Round Table,* 67, No. 266 (April, 1977), 182-190.

12665 **Severiano Teixeira, Nuno.** "From Neutrality to Alignment: Portugal in the Foundation of the Atlantic Pact." *Luso-Brazilian Review* [Madison], 29, No. 2 (Winter, 1992), 113-126.

12666 **Simon, Jeffrey.** "Does Eastern Europe Belong in NATO? *Orbis* [Greenwich, CT], 37, No. 1 (Winter, 1993), 21-35.

12667 **Singleton, Seth.** "Soviet Policy and Socialist Expansion in Asia and Africa." *Armed Forces and Society*, 6, No. 3 (Spring, 1980), 339-369.

12668 **Skendi, Stevro.** "Albania and the Sino-Soviet Conflict." *Foreign Affairs,* 40, No. 3 (Winter, 1992), 113-126.

12669 **Skubiszewski, Krysztof.** "The Postwar Alliances of Poland and the United Nations Charter." *American Journal of International Law,* 53, No. 3 (July, 1959), 613-634.

12670 **Soppelsa, Jacques.** "La 'Crise' de L'Alliance Atlantique: Analyse de geographie Politique." *L'Information Geographique*, 47, No. 2 (1983), 45-51.

12671 **Sparring, Ake.** "Iceland, Europe and Nato." *World Today,* 28, No. 9 (September, 1972), 393-403.

12672 **Spinelli, Alterio.** "Atlantic Pact or European Unity." *Foreign Affairs,* 40, No. 4 (July, 1962), 542-552.

12673 **Stewart, J.F.** "The Changed Baltic." *Scottish Geographical Magazine,* 56, No. 3 (November, 1940), 115-126.

12674 **Strang, Sir William.** "Germany between East and West." *Foreign Affairs,* 33, No. 3 (April, 1955), 387-401.

12675 **Tammes, K.C.** "Finland. Een Politick-Geografische Beschouwing Met Betrekking tot de Fins-Russische Betrekkingen." *Geografisch Tijdschrift Nieuwe Reeks*, 15, No. 2 (1981), 194-201.

12676 **Taras, Raymond, and Zeringue, Marshal.** "Grand Strategy in a Post-Bipolar World: Interpreting the Final Soviet Response." *Review of International Studies* [Cambridge], 18, No. 4 (October, 1992), 355-375.

12677 **Taylor, Paul.** "British Sovereignty and the European Community: What Is at Risk?" *Millennium* [London], 20, No. 1 (Spring, 1991), 73-80.

12678 **Timmerman, Heinz.** "Die Sowjetunion Und Der Umbruch in Osteuropa: Von Der Moskauer Hegemonie Zu Konstruktiver Partnerschaft?" *Osteuropa* [Suttgart], 41, Heft 1 (Januar, 1991), 3-14.

12679 **Urjewicz, Charles.** "Russie: Un 'Geant Aux Pieds D'argile'" *Herodote* [Paris], No. 58-59 (Juillet-Decembre, 1990), 155-172.

12680 **Valenta, Jiri.** "Revolutionary Change. Soviet Intervention, and 'Normalization' in East-Central Europe." *Comparative Politics*, 16, No. 2 (January, 1984), 127-151.

12681 **Vasile, A.** "L'evoluzione del Commonwealth." *Civitas,* Naova Serie, (Angostc-Settembre, 1960), 61-80.

12682 **Vicenes Vives, J.** "Panispanismo." *Geopolitica*, 2, No. 6-7 (1940), 295.

12683 **Volgyes, Ivan.** "Regional Differences within the Warsaw Pact." *Orbis*, 26, No. 3 (Fall, 1982), 665-679.

12684 **Watt, D.C.** "Towards a Neutral Balkans?" *The World Today,* 27, No. 8 (August, 1971), 359-364.

12685 **Wilcox, Francis O., and Haviland, H. Field,** eds. "The Atlantic Community: Progress and Prospects." *International Organization,* 17, No. 3 (Summer, 1963), 521-812.

12686 **Williamson, J.A.** "The British Commonwealth." *Geographical Magazine,* 12, No. 5 (March, 1941), 322-331, cont.

12687 **Wise, Mark and Gregory, Croyford.** "The European Regional Development Fund: Community Ideals and National Realities." *Political Geography Quarterly,* 7, No. 2 (April, 1988), 161-182.

12688 **Wohlgemuth, Patricia.** "The Portuguese Territories and the United Nations." *International Conciliation,* 545 (November, 1963), 200-265.

12689 **Yokoyama, Shiochi.** "Characteristics and Development Patterns of the East European Economic Integration." *Political Geography.* Tokyo: Kokon-Shoin, (1963, p. 91-114.

CHAPTER XIV

COLONIES, COLONIALISM, AND RESURGENT NATIONALISM

GENERAL AND THEORY

Books

12690 **Ansprenger, Franz.** *The Dissolution of the Colonial Empires.* London: Routledge, 1989.

12691 **Ayittey, George B.N.** *Africa Betrayed.* New York: St. Martin's Press, 1992.

12692 **Carrington, C.E.** *An Exposition of Empire.* New York: Cambridge University Press, 1947.

12693 **Church, R.J. Harrison.** *Modern Colonization.* London: Hutchinson University Library, 1951.

12694 **Clark, G.L.** *The Balance Sheet of Imperialism.* New York: Columbia University Press, 1936.

12695 **Cobban, Alfred.** *National Self-Determination.* London: Oxford University Press, 1944.

12696 **Cook, Chris, and Killingray, David.** *African Political Facts Since 1945.* 2nd ed. London: Macmillan, 1991.

12697 **Dinstein, Yoram**, ed. *Models of Autonomy.* New Brunswick, New Jersey: Transaction Books, Rutgers University, 1981.

12698 **Dirks, Nicholas B.**, ed. *Colonialism and Culture.* Ann Arbor: The University of Michigan Press, 1992.

12699 **Eddy, John and Schreuder, Deryck**, eds. *The Rise of Colonial Nationalism: Australia, New Zealand, Canada and South Africa First Assert Their Nationalities, 1880 1914.* Sydney: Allen & Unwin, 1988

12700 **Einstadt, S.N.** *The Political Systems of Empires.* New York: The Free Press, 1963.

12701 **Emerson, Rupert.** *From Empire to Nation.* Cambridge, Massachusetts: Harvard University Press, 1960.

12702 **Emerson, Rupert.** *Self-Determination Revisited in the Era of Decolonization.* Occasional Papers in International Affairs No. 9, December, 1964. Cambridge, Massachusetts: Center for International Affairs, Harvard University, 1964.

12703 **Fanon, F.** *A Dying Colonialism.* New York: Grove Press, 1965.

12704 **Frankel, S. Herbert.** *The Concept of Colonization.* Oxford: Clarendon Press, 1949.

12705 **Fukuyama, Francis.** *Gorbachev and the New Soviet Agenda in the Third World.* Santa Monica, California: The Rand Corporation, 1989.

12706 **Hailey, William Malcolm, Baron.** *The Future of Colonial Peoples.* Princeton, New Jersey: Princeton University Press, 1944.

12707 **Hancock, W.K.** *The Argument of Empire.* London: Penguin, 1943.

12708 **Hancock, W.K.** *Wealth of Colonies.* Cambridge, England: University Press, 1950.

12709 **Hardy, Georges.** *Geographie et colonisation.* Paris: Gillimard, 1933.

12710 **Harrison-Church, R.J.** *Modern Colonization.* London: Hutchinson, 1951.

12711 **Hobson, J.A.** *Imperialism.* London: Allen & Unwin, 1938.

12712 **Hodson, Henry Vincent.** *Twentieth Century Empire.* London: Faber & Faber, 1948.

12713 **Holcombe, Arthur N.** *Dependent Areas in the Post-War World.* (America Looks Ahead; A Pamphlet Series, No. 4.) Boston: World Peace Foundation, 1941.

12714 **Huxley, Julian**, and **Deane, Phyllis.** *The Future of the Colonies.* (Target for Tomorrow, No. 8.) London: The Pilot Press, 1944.

12715 **International Law Association** (auspices). *The Effect of Independence on Treaties.* London: Stevens, 1965.

12716 **Jsnard, Hildebert.** *Geographie de la decolonisation.* Paris: Presses Universitaires de France, 1971.

12717 **Julien, Charles Andre**, ed. *Les techniciens de la colonisation (XIXᵉ-XXᵉ siecles)* [Colonies et empires; collection internationale de documentation coloniale, 1ᵉ serie: Etudes coloniales, I). Paris: Presses Universitaires de France, 1946.

12718 **King, Anthony B.** *Colonial Urban Development: Culture, Social Power and Environment.* London: Routledge, 1976.

12719 **Kruger, Karl.** *Kolonialanspruch und kontinentale Wirtschaftsplanung. Hrsg. von der Gesellschafat fur europaische Wirtschaftsplanung und Grossraumwirtschaft.* Dresden: Meinhold Verlagsgesellschaft, 1940.

12720 **Labouret, Henri.** *Colonisation, Colonialisme, Decolonisation.* Paris: Larose, 1952.

12721 **MacInnes, C.M.**, comp. and ed. *Principles and Methods of Colonial Administration.* Colston Papers based on a symposium promoted by the Colston Research Society and the University of Bristol in April, 1950. London: Butterworths Scientific Publications, 1950.

12722 **MacMillan, W.M.** *The Road to Self-Rule.* London: Faber and Faber, 1959.

12723 **Memmi, Albert.** *The Colonizer and the Colonized.* Boston: Beacon, 1967.

12724 **Mondaini, G.** *Storia Coloniale dell' epoca contemporanea.* Firenze: Barbera, 1916.

12725 **Monheim, Chr.** *Colonisation: principes et realisations.* Anvers: L'Avenir Belge, 1939.

12726 **Nkrumah, Kwame.** *Neocolonialism, the Last Stage of Imperialism.* London: Nelson, 1965.

12727 **Perham, Margery.** *The Colonial Reckoning.* London: Collins, 1962.

12728 **Ragatz, Lowell,** and **Ragatz, Janet Evans,** comps. *A Bibliography of Articles, Descriptive, Historical, and Scientific, on Colonies and Other Dependent Territories, Appearing in American Geographical and Kindred Journals.* Washington, D.C.: Educational Research Bureau, 1951. 2 vols. Vol. I through 1934, 2d ed. Vol. II 1935-1950.

12729 *Revolution in the Colonies.* London: British Association for Labour Legislation, 1945.

12730 **Shils, Edward.** *Political Development in the New States.* The Hague: Mouton, 1968.

12731 **Smith, T.** *The Pattern of Imperialism: The U.S., Great Britain and the Late Industrializing World Since 1815.* Cambridge: Cambridge University Press, 1981.

12732 **Strachey, John.** *The End of Empire.* London: Gollancz, 1959.

12733 **Strausz-Hupe, Robert,** and **Hazard, Harry W.,** eds. *The Idea of Colonialism.* New York: Praeger, 1958.

12734 **Thompson, Laura.** *Steps Toward Colonial Freedom; Some Long-Range Planning Principles for a Peaceful World Order.* New York: American Council, Institute of Pacific Relations, 1943.

12735 **Twaddle, Michael,** ed. *Imperialism, the State and the Third World.* London: British Academic Press, 1992.

12736 **U.S. Department of State.** *Newly Independent States, Geography Report, No. 3,* April 2, 1962. Washington, D.C.: Department of State, 1962.

12737 **Wainhouse, David Walter.** *Remnants of Empires: The United Nations and the End of Colonialism.* New York: Harper & Row, 1964.

12738 **Walker, Eric A.** *Colonies.* (Current Problems, No. 20.) Cambridge, England: University Press, 1944.

12739 **Ward, Barbara,** and Others. *The Legacy of Imperialism.* Pittsburgh, Pennsylvania: Catham College, 1960.

Journals

12740 **Alam, M.S.** "Colonialism, Decolonialisation and Growth Rates: Theory and Empirical Evidence." *Cambridge Journal of Economics* [London], 18, No. 3 (June, 1994), 235-257.

12741 **Amin, Samir.** "Revolution ov decadence? La Crise du Systeme Imperialiste Contemporain et celle de l'Empire Romain." *Review,* 4, No. 1 (Summer, 1980), 155-167.

12742 **Arden-Clarke, Sir Charles.** "The Problem of the High Commission Territories." *Optima,* 8, No. 4 (December, 1958), 163-170.

12743 **Arneil, Barbara.** "Trade, Plantations, and Property: John Locke and the Economic Defense of Colonialism." *Journal of the History of Ideas,* 55, No. 4 (October, 1994), 591-609.

12744 **Benson, Wilfrid.** "A People's Peace in the Colonies." *International Labour Review,* 47, No. 2 (February, 1943), 141-168.

12745 **Bourdillon, Sir Bernard H.** "Colonial Development and Welfare." *International Affairs,* 20, No. 3 (July, 1944), 369-380.

12746 **Butzin, Bernhard.** "Selbstverwaltung in Gronland: Zwischen Modernisierungszwang und Wohlstandsdiktatur" [Self-Administration in Greenland]. *Geographische Rundschau,* Jahr. 32, Heft. 3 (Marz, 1980), 92-98.

12747 **Capot-Rey, Robert.** "Situation politique et economique des anciennes colonies allemandes." *Annales de Geographie,* 31, No. 172 (Septembre 15, 1922), 509-515.

12748 Carrington, C.E. "Decolonization: The Last Stages." *International Affairs*, 38, No. 1 (January, 1962), 29-40.

12749 Chandra, Bipan. "Colonialism, Stages of Colonialism and the Colonial State." *Journal of Contemporary Asia*, 10, No. 3 (1980), 272-285.

12750 Chase-Dunn, Christopher. "Resistance to Imperialism: Semiperipheral Actors." *Fernand Braudel Center. Review* [Binghamton], 13, No. 1 (Winter, 1990), 1-31.

12751 Cockram, Ben. "The 'Protectorates'-an International Problem." *Optima*, 13, No. 4 (December, 1963), 176-184.

12752 "Colonial Development and Reconstruction." *Nature*, 149, No. 3779 (April 4, 1942), 365-368.

12753 "Colonialism and Colonization in World History." *Journal of Economic History*, 21, No. 4 (December, 1961), 443-651.

12754 Correia Fernandes, Avertano. "Emigracao Indo-Portuguese." *Boletim de Sociedade de Geografia de Lisboa*, Serie 56a, Nos. 7 and 8 (Julho-Agosto, 1938), 277-306.

12755 Crofton, R.H. "Atlantic Charter: Its Colonial Applications." *Crown Colonist*, 13, No. 136 (March, 1943), 165-166.

12756 deSouza, Anthony R. "To Have and to Have Not: Colonialism and Core-periphery Relations." *Focus*, 36, No. 3 (Fall, 1986), 14-19.

12757 "Development of Colonial Dependencies." *Nature*, 151, No. 3832 (April 10, 1943), 399-402.

12758 Dietzel, Karl H. "Imperialismus und Kolonialpolitik." *Zeitschrift fur Geopolitik*, 17, 313-322, and Heft 8 (August, 1940), 372-376.

12759 Dikshit, R.D. "On the Geography of Colonialism: A Third World Perspective." *Transactions of the Institute of Indian Geographers*, 1, No. 1 (1979), 1-15.

12760 Dingelstedt, V. "Ruling Nations: Considerations on Their Characters." *Scottish Geographical Magazine*, 26, No. 3 (December, 1911), 291-306.

12761 Eayro, James, and Spencer, Robert, eds. "Losing an Empire, Binding a Role." *International Journal*, 23, No. 4 (Autumn, 1968), 507-614.

12762 Epstein, Fritz T. "National Socialism and French Colonialism." *Journal of Central European Affairs*, 3, No. 1 (April, 1943), 52-64.

12763 Epstein, Fritz T. "The Question of Colonies." *Geographical Review*, 28, No. 2 (April, 1938), 306-309.

12764 Frank, Andre Gunder. "Dependence is Dead, Long Live Independence and the Class Struggle: An Answer to Critics." *World Development*, 5, No. 4 (April, 1977), 355-370.

12765 "Future of the Colonies." *Round Table*, 33, No. 129 (December, 1942), 8-16.

12766 Ginsburg, Norton S. "From Colonialism to National Development: Geographical Perspectives on Patterns and Policies." *Annals of the Association of American Geographers*, 63, No. 1 (March, 1973), 1-21.

12767 Gotlieb, Yosef. "Retrieving Life-space from Colonized Space: Transcending the Encumbrances of the Post-colonial State." *Political Geography* [Oxford], 11, No. 5 (September, 1992), 461-474.

12768 Hailey, William Malcolm, Baron. "The Scientific Approach to Colonial Development." *Nature*, 148, No. 3759 (November 15, 1941), 584-588.

12769 Hanham, H.J. "The Problem of the Highland Discontent, 1880-1885." *Transactions of the Royal Historical Society, Fifth Series*, 19 (1969), 21-65.

12770 Harris, John. "Colonies and Peace Aims." *Contemporary Review*. 894, No. 6 (June, 1940), 670-677.

12771 Harrison Church, R.J. "The Case for Colonial Geography." *Institute of British Geographers*, 14, Part 2 (1949), 15-25.

12772 Heawood, Edward. "A New Representation of the Colonial Empire." *Crown Colonist*, 12, No. 131 (October, 1942), 649-652.

12773 Hellen, J.A. "Colonialism and Independence: A Reassessment." *Geographical Society Journal* (University of Newcastle Upon Tyne). 19 (1971), 7-18.

12774 Holifield, E. Brooks. "Peace, Conflict, and Ritual in Puritan Congregations." *The Journal of Interdisciplinary History* [Cambridge, MA], 23, No. 3 (Winter, 1993), 551-570.

12775 Horvath, Ronald J. "A Definition of Colonialism." *Current Anthropology*, 13, No. 1 (February, 1972), 45-57.

12776 Houbert, Jean. "Settlers & Seaways in a Decolonised World." *Journal of Modern African Studies*, 23, No. 1 (March, 1985), 1-29.

12777 "The International Interest in Colonies." *Round Table*, 35, No. 137 (December, 1944), 24-39.

12778 **Kautsky, John H.** "The Politics of Traditional Aristocratic Empires and Their Legacy." *International Journal of Comparative Sociology,* 24, Nos. 1-2 (January-April, 1983), 47-60.

12779 **Keesing, Felix M.** "Applied Anthropology in Colonial Administration." In *The Science of Man in the World Crisis,* Linton, Ralph, ed. New York: Octagon Books, 1980, 373-398.

12780 **Kennedy, Raymond.** "The Colonial Crisis and the Future." In *The Science of Man in the World Crisis,* Linton, Ralph, ed. New York: Octagon Books, 1980, 306-346.

12781 **Kimble, George H.T.** "A Handicap for New Nations: Climate." *New York Times Magazine,* Section 6, Part 1 (September 29, 1963), 35 and 106-107.

12782 **Krasner, Stephen D.** "Sovereignty: An Institutional Perspective." *Comparative Political Studies,* Vol. 21, No. 1 (April, 1988), 66-94.

12783 **Marshall, P.J., and Williams, Glyndwr, eds.** "The British Atlantic Empire before the American Revolution." *Journal of Imperial and Commonwealth History,* 8, No. 2 (January, 1980), 1-130.

12784 **Massey, D.** "A Case of Colonial Collaboration: The Hut Tax and Migrant Labour." *Botswana Notes and Records,* 10 (1979), 95-98.

12785 **McKay, Vernon.** "Empires in Transition-- British, French, and Dutch Colonial Plans." *Foreign Policy Reports,* 23, No. 4 (May 1, 1947), 34-47.

12786 **Meyer, William H.** "Dependency and Neoimperialism." *Comparative Political Studies,* 3 (October, 1989), 243-264.

12787 **Moreira, Eduardo.** "Portuguese Colonial Policy." *Africa,* 17, No. 3 (July, 1947), 181-191.

12788 **Murray, Roger.** "No Easy Path to Independence." *Africa Report,* 22, No. 3 (May-June, 1977), 17-20+.

12789 **Nicolson, Harold.** "The Colonial Problem." *International Affairs,* 17, No. 1 (January-February, 1938), 32-50.

12790 **Obst, Eric.** "Wir fordern unsere Kolonien zuruck!" *Zeitschrfit fur Geopolitik,* 3 Jahrgang, Heft 3 (Marz, 1926), 151-160.

12791 **Olson, Ralph E.** "A Geographic Inventory of Newly Independent Nations," in Benson, Oliver, ed., *Emerging Nations,* Monograph No. 1, Norman, Oklahoma: Graduate International Studies Program, University of Oklahoma, 1963, 16-30.

12792 **Passarge, Siegfried.** "Kolonien und Kolonialgeographie." *Afrika Rundschau.* 4, Jahrg, No. 1 (Mai, 1939), 7-8.

12793 **Pistolese, Gennaro E.** "Fondamenti e prospettive di una nuova fase della colonizzazione." *Rassegna economica dell'Africa Italiana,* Anno 29, No. 8 (Agosto, 1941), 561-565.

12794 **Rivlin, Benjamin.** "Self-Determination and Dependent Areas." *International Conciliation,* 501 (January, 1955), 195-271.

12795 **Robinson, Kenneth.** "World Opinion and Colonial Statues." *International Organization,* 8, No. 4 (November, 1954), 468-483.

12796 **Sauer, Carl.** "Destructive Exploitation in Modern Colonial Expansion." *C.r., Amsterdam,* Tome 2 (Section III C. (1938), 494-499.

12797 **Schaffer, B.B.** "The Concept of Preparation: Some Questions about the Transfer of Systems of Government." *World Politics,* 18, No. 1 (October, 1965), 42-67.

12798 **Scheynius, Ignas J.** "Why Can't They Exist as Free Countries?" Baltic Review, 1, No. 2-3 (March, 1946), 65-71.

12799 **Schneider, William.** "Colonies at the 1900 World Fair." *History Today,* 31 (May, 1981), 31-36.

12800 **Scott, F.R.** "The End of Dominion Status." *American Journal of International Law,* 38, No. 1 (January, 1944), 34-49.

12801 **Seton-Watson, Hugh.** "Aftermaths of Empire." *Journal of Contemporary History,* 15, No. 1 (January, 1980), 197-208.

12802 **Ulmer, Henri.** "La statistique dans les pays coloniaux." *Journal de la Societe de statistique de Paris,* 79ᵉ annee, Nos. 8-9 (Aout-Septembere, 1938), 231-250.

12803 **Varenne, Alexandre.** "L'industrialisation des colonies." *C.r., Amsterdam,* Tome 2, Section III c. (1938), 601-604.

12804 **Yokayama, Matajiro.** "Solution of Colonial Problem." *Journal of Geography, Tokyo Geographical Society,* 50, No. 596 (October, 1938), 437-441.

POLITICAL GEOGRAPHY OF REGIONS

AFRICA

Books

12805 **Abbas, Mekki.** *The Sudan Question; The Dispute Over the Anglo-Egyptian Condominium, 1884-1951.* New York: Praeger, 1952.

12806 **Abraham, Kinfe.** *Politics of Black Nationalism: From Harlem to Soweto.* Trenton: Africa World Press, Inc., 1991.

12807 *Africa: Colonial Development to Self-government. Political Structure of Africa Today,* Georg Westermann, Braunschweig, eds. Chicago, Illinois: Denoyer-Geppert, 1966.

12808 **Anstey, R.** *Britain and the Congo in the Nineteenth Century.* Oxford: Clarendon Press, 1962.

12809 **Apter, David E.** *The Gold Coast in Transition.* Princeton, New Jersey: Princeton University Press, 1955.

12810 **Ashford, Douglas E.** *Political Change in Morocco.* Princeton, New Jersey: Princeton University Press, 1961.

12811 **Axelson, E.** *Portugal and the Scramble for Africa 1875-1891.* Johannesburg: Witwatersrand University Press, 1967.

12812 **Barnes, James F.** *Gabon: Beyond the Colonial Legacy.* Boulder: Westview Press, 1992.

12813 **Bennett, George.** *Kenya, A Political History: The Colonial Period.* London: Oxford University Press, 1963.

12814 **Bontinck, Francois.** *Aux Origines de l'Etat Independant du Congo: documents tires d'archives Americaines.* Louvain Editions Nauweaerts; Paris: Beatrice-Nauwelaerts, 1966.

12815 **Brausch, George.** *Belgian Administration in The Congo.* London: Oxford University Press, 1961.

12816 **Bretton, H.L.** *Power and Stability in Nigeria: The Politics of Decolinisation.* New York: Praeger, 1962.

12817 **Carter, Gwendolen M.** *Independence for Africa.* New York: Praeger, 1960.

12818 **Carter, Gwendolen M.; Karis, Thomas; and Stultz, Newell M.** *South Africa's Transkei: The Politics of Domestic Colonialism.* Evanston, Illinois: Northwestern University Press, 1967.

12819 **Carter, Gwendolen M., and O'Meara, Patrick,** eds. *African Independence: The First Twenty-five Years.* Bloomington: Indiana University Press, 1985.

12820 **Charlton, Michael.** *The Last Colony in Africa: Diplomacy and the Independence of Rhodesia.* Oxford: Basil Blackwell, 1990.

12821 **Christopher, A.J.** Colonial Africa. London: Totawa, New Jersey: Barnes and Noble, 1984.

12822 **Collins, Robert O.,** ed. *The Partition of Africa: Illusion or Necessity.* New York: John Wiley & Sons, 1969.

12823 **Cook, Arthur Norton.** *British Enterprise in Nigeria.* Philadelphia: University of Pennsylvania Press, 1943.

12824 **Crowder, Michael.** *Senegal: A Study in French Assimilation Policy.* London: Oxford University Press, 1962.

12825 **Daly, M.W., and Sikainga, Ahmad Alawad,** eds. *Civil War in the Sudan.* London: British Academic Press, 1993.

12826 **DeKlerk, Willem.** *F. W. de Klerk: The Man in His Time.* Johannesburg: Jonathan Ball Publishers, 1991.

12827 **Deng, Francis M., and Zartman, I.** *Conflict Resolution in Africa.* Washington, DC: The Brookings Institution, 1991.

12828 **Di Marzo, Costanzo.** *Origini e sviluppi della colonizzazione belga. Volume I. Dalle origini alla fondazione dell Stato Indipendente del Congo.* Napoli: S.I.E.M., S.G.M. Pignatelli, 1938.

12829 **Duffy, James.** *Portuguese Africa.* Cambridge, Massachusetts: Harvard University Press, 1959.

12830 **Eldredge, Elizabeth A.** *A South African Kingdom: The Pursuit of Security in Nineteenth-Century Lesotho.* Cambridge: Cambridge University Press, 1993.

12831 **Erlich, Haggai.** *Ethiopia and the Challenge of Independence.* Boulder, Colorado: Lynne Rienner Publishers, 1986.

12832 **Fields, Karen E.** *Revival & Rebellion in Colonial Central Africa.* Princeton, New Jersey: Princeton University Press, 1985.

12833 **Fowler, Gary Lane.** *Italian Agricultural Colonization in Tripolitania, Libya.* Syracuse, New York: Syracuse University, Ph.D., 1969.

12834 **Gann, Lewis H., and Duignan, Peter,** eds. *Colonialism in Africa, 1870-1960.* London: Cambridge University Press, 1969.

12835 **Gann, Lewis H., and Duignan, Peter.** *White Settlers in Tropical Africa.* Harmondsworth: Penguin, 1962.

12836 **Gauthier, Emile Felix.** *La Conquete du Sahara: Essai de Psychologie Politique.* Paris: Armand Colin, 1910.

12837 **Gifford, P., and Louis, W.R.,** eds. *Britain and Germany in Africa.* New Haven, Connecticut: Yale University Press, 1967.

12838 **Gifford, P., and Louis, W.R.,** eds. *Decolonization and African Independence: The Transfers of Power, 1960-1980.* New Haven, Connecticut: Yale University Press, 1988.

12839 **Gordon, David F.** *Decolonization and the State of Kenya.* Boulder, Colorado: Westview Press, 1986.

12840 **Graham, Malbone W.** *The Diplomatic Struggle for Africa.* Berkeley: University of California, Committee on International Relations. Africa, the Near East and the War. 1943, 175-212.

12841 **Great Britain.** Treaties, etc. *Agreement between the Government of the United Kingdom of Great Britain and Northern Ireland and the Egyptian Government Concerning Self-government and Self-determination for the Sudan, Cairo, February 12, 1953* (with agreed minutes, exchange of notes, and statute). Presented by the Secretary of State for Foreign Affairs to Parliament. London: 1953.

12842 **Grotpeter, John J., and Weinstein, Warren.** *The Pattern of African Decolonization: A New Interpretation.* Syracuse, New York: Syracuse University, Maxwell School of Citizenship and Public Affairs, Program of Eastern African Studies, No. 10, 1973.

12843 **Gupta, Vijay,** ed. *Independent Namibia Problems and Prospects.* Delhi: Konark Publishers, Pvt., Ltd., 1990.

12844 **Haack, H. Perlet veb Hermann,** ed. *Derzerfall kolonialsystems in Afrika.* Gotha: Geographisch-Kartographische Anstalt, Gotha, 1965.

12845 **Hailey, William Malcolm, Baron.** *Native Administration in the British African Territories* 4 vols. London: Great Britain Colonial Office, 1950-1951.

12846 **Hailey, William Malcolm, Baron.** *The Republic of South Africa and the High Commission Territories.* London: Oxford University Press, 1963.

12847 **Hanna, A.J.** *The Story of the Rhodesias and Nyasaland.* London: Faber and Faber, 1960.

12848 **Hanna, W.J.,** ed. *Independent Black Africa: The Politics of Freedom.* Chicago, Illinois: Rand McNally, 1964.

12849 **Hargreaves, John D.** *Decolonization in Africa.* London: Longman Group, 1988.

12850 **Harris, Norman.** *Intervention and Colonization in Africa.* Boston: Houghton Mifflin, 1914.

12851 **Hodgkin, Thomas.** *Nationalism in Colonial Africa.* New York: New York University Press, 1957.

12852 **Johnston, Sir H.H.** *A History of the Colonization of Africa by Alien Races.* Cambridge: Cambridge University Press, 1913.

12853 **Keltie, J.S.** *The Partition of Africa.* London: Stanford, 1893.

12854 **Northern Frontier District Commission.** *Kenya Report of the Northern Frontier District Commission.* London: Secretary of State for the Colonies, Her Majesty's Stationery Office, 1962.

12855 **Killingray, David.** *A Plague of Europeans: Westerners in Africa Since the Fifteenth Century.* Baltimore, Maryland: Penguin Education, 1973.

12856 **King, Gillian.** *Imperial Outpost-Aden, Its Place in British Strategic Policy.* London: Oxford University Press, 1964.

12857 **Kitchen, Helen,** ed. *South Africa: In Transition to What.* New York: Praeger, 1988.

12858 *Le Congo Independant.* Bruxelles: Infor Congo, 1960.

12859 **Levine, Victor T.** *The Cameroons: From Mandate to Independence.* Berkeley: University of California Press, 1965.

12860 **Liebesny, Herbert J.** *The Government of French North Africa.* (University of Pennsylvania. University Museum. African Handbooks: 1.) Philadelphia: University of Pennsylvania Press, 1943.

12861 **Louw, Eric H.** Changing Continent; South Africa's Role in Africa. New York: Information Service of South Africa, 1959.

12862 **Lucas, C.P.** *The Partition and Colonization of Africa.* Oxford: Clarendon Press, 1922.

12863 **Maddox, Gregory,** ed. *The Colonial Epoch in Africa.* New York: Garland Publishers, Inc., 1993.

12864 **Maddox, Gregory,** ed. *Conquest and Resistance to Colonialism in Africa.* New York: Garland Publishing, Inc., 1993.

12865 **Mashasha, F.** *The Road to Colonialism: Concessions and the Collapse of Swazi Independence.* England: University of Oxford, Ph.D., 1977.

12866 **Maxon, Robert M.** *Struggle for Kenya: The Loss and Reassertion of Imperial Initiative, 1912-1923.* Rutherford: Fairleigh Dickinson University Press, 1993.

12867 **McClintock, N.C.** *Kingdoms in the Sand and Sun: An African Path to Independence.* London: Radcliffe Press, 1992.

12868 **Moore, Martin.** *Fourth Shore. Italy's Mass Colonization of Libya.* London: Routledge, 1940.

12869 **Morrison, Donald G.** *Black Africa: A Comparative Handbook.* New York: The Free Press, 1972.

12870 **Mungazi, Dickson A.** *Colonial Policy and Conflict in Zimbabwe: A Study of Cultures in Collision, 1890-1979.* New York: Crane Russak, 1992.

12871 **Murphy, Jefferson.** *Understanding Africa.* New York: Thomas Y. Crowell, 1969.

12872 **Nasser, Gamal Abdul.** *Egypt's Liberation: The Philosophy of the Revolution.* Washington, D.C.: Public Affairs Press, 1955.

12873 **Nelson, Samuel H.** *Colonialism in the Congo Basin, 1880-1940.* Athens: Oio University Center for International Studies, 1994.

12874 **Noyes, John.** *Colonial Space: Spatiality in the Discourse of German South West Africa 1884-1915.* Chur: Harwood Academic Publishers, 1992.

12875 **Oduho, J., and Deng, William.** *The Problem of the Southern Sudan.* London: Oxford University Press, 1963.

12876 **Padmore, George.** *Africa: Britain's Third Empire.* London: D. Dobson, 1949.

12877 **Pankhurst, E. Sylvia.** *British Policy in Eastern Ethiopia; the Ogaden and the Reserved Area.* Woodford, Essex; The Author, 1945.

12878 **Pankhurst, E. Sylvia.** *Ex-Italian Somaliland.* Foreword by Peter Freeman. London: Watts, 1951.

12879 **Pascal, Roger.** *La Republique Malgache: Pacifique Independence.* Paris: Editions Berger-Levrault, 1965.

12880 **Perham, Margery.** *Africans and British Rule.* London: Oxford University Press, 1941.

12881 **Petchenkine, Youry.** *Ghana: In Search of Stability, 1957-1992.* Westport: Praeger Publishers, 1993.

12882 **Pim, Sir Alan.** *The Financial and Economic History of the African Tropical Territories.* Oxford: Clarendon Press, 1940.

12883 **Pollock, Norman Charles.** *Studies in Emerging Africa.* Stoncham, Massachusettes: Butterworths, 1971.

12884 **Rodney, W.** How Europe Underdeveloped Africa. London and Dar es Salaam: Bogle l'Ouverture Tanzania Publishing House, 1972.

12885 **Rotberg, R.I.** *The Rise of Nationalism in Central Africa.* London: Fontana, 1965.

12886 **Rudin, Harry Rudolph.** *Germans in the Cameroons, 1884-1914: A Case Study in Modern Imperialism.* Hamden, Conn.: Archon Books, 1968.

12887 **Saul, John S.** *Recolonization and Resistance: Southern Africa in the 1990s.* Trenton: Africa World Press, Inc., 1993.

12888 **Sesay, Amandu,** ed. *Africa and Europe: from Partition to Interdependence or Dependence.* London: Croom Helm, 1986.

12889 **Slade, Ruth.** *The Belgian Congo; Some Recent Changes.* London: Oxford University Press, 1960.

12890 **Smock, David R.,** ed. *Making War and Waging Peace: Foreign Intervention in Africa.* Washington, DC: United States Institute of Peace Press, 1993.

12891 **Sparks, Donald L.,** and **Green, December.** *Namibia: The Nation After Independence.* Boulder: Westview Press, 1992.

12892 **Spence, J.E.** Lesotho: The Politics of Dependence. London: Published for the Institute of Race Relations by Oxford University Press, 1968.

12893 **Strayer, Robert W.; Steinhart, Edward I.;** and **Maxon, Robert M.** *Protest Movements in Colonial East Africa: Aspects of Early African Response to European Rule.* Syracuse, New York: Syracuse University, Maxwell School of Citizenship and Public Affairs, Program of East African Studies, No. 12, 1973.

12894 **Tamarkin, M.** *The Making of Zimbabwe: Decolonization in Regional and International Politics.* London: Frank Cass, 1990.

12895 **Thompson, Virginia, and Addolf, Richard.** *French West Africa.* Stanford, California: Stanford University Press, 1958.

12896 **Trevaskis, G.K.N.** *Eritra, A Colony in Transition: 1941-52.* London: Oxford University Press, 1960.

12897 **U.S. Department of State. The Geographer.** *Africa: Pattern of Sovereignty.* Rev. ed. Washington, D.C.: U.S. Department of State, 1968.

12898 **Wallerstein, I.** *Africa: The Politics of Independence.* New York: Random House, 1961.

12899 **Wieschhoff, H.A.** Colonial Policies in Africa. (African Handbooks, 5.) Philadelphia: University of Pennsylvania Press, University Museum, 1944.

12900 **Williams, John Hout.** *Historical Outline and Analysis of the Work of the Survey Department of Kenya Colony.* Nairobi: Government Printer, 1931.

12901 **Wolff, Richard D.** *The Economics of Colonialism: Britain and Kenya, 1870-1930.* New Haven, Connecticut: Yale University Press, 1974.

12902 **Young, Crawford.** *Politics in the Congo: Decolonization and Independence.* Princeton, New Jersey: Princeton University Press, 1965.

Journals

12903 **Apthorpe, Raymond.** "The Introduction of Bureaucracy into African Politics." *Journal of African Administration,* 12, No. 3 (July, 1960) 125-134.

12904 **Arden-Clarke, Sir Charles.** "Gold Coast into Ghana; Some Problems of Transition." *International Affairs,* 34, No. 1 (January, 1958), 49-56.

12905 **Ballinger, R.B.** "Southwest Africa after the Judgement." *Optima,* 14, No. 3 (September, 1964), 142-154.

12906 **Barbosa, Honorio Jose.** "Informacoes juridicas para o conhecimento da organica administrativa da guine Portuguesa." *Boletim Cultural da Guine Portuguesa,*1, No. 4 (Outubro, 1946), 663-705.

12907 **Bates, Margaret L.** "Tanganyika; The Development of a Trust Territory." *International Organization,* 9, No. 1 (February, 195), 32-51.

12908 **Bechtold, Peter K.** "More Turbulence in Sudan: A New Politics This Time? *The Middle East Journal,* 44, N0. 4 (Autumn, 1990), 1990.

12909 **Belfiglio, Valentine J.** "The Issue of Namibian Independence." African Affairs, 78, No. 313 (October, 1979), 507-522.

12910 "The Belgian Congo on the Eve of Independence." Belgian Congo Today, 9, No. 2 (April-May, 1960).

12911 **Bell, J. Franklin.** "The French Colonies of Equatorial Africa." *Military Engineer,* 35, No. 207 (January, 1943), 1-7.

12912 **Bell, J. Franklin.** "Italy's African Empire." *Military Engineer,* 35, No. 209 (March, 1943), 114-119.

12913 **Bergonzi, Angelo.** "I confini terrestri dell'Italia secondo il progetto del trattato di pace." *L'Universo,* Anno 27, N. 1 (Gennaio-Feboraio, 1947), 3-15.

12914 **Berman, B., and Lonsdale, J.** "Crises of Accumulation, Coercion and the Colonial State: The Development of the Labour Control System in Kenya, 1919-1929." *Canadian Journal of African Studies,* No. 14 (1980), 37-54.

12915 **Best, Alan C.G. and de Blij, Harm J.** "Namibia: Political Geography of a Coveted Prize." *Focus,* 26, No. 3 (January/February, 1976).

12916 "The Birth of Ghana; Independence for the Gold Coast." *Round Table,* 47, No. 185 (December, 1956), 48-56.

12917 **Bischoff, Paul-Henri.** "Why Swaziland is different: an explanation of the Kingdom's political position in Southern Africa." *Journal of modern African Studies,* 26, No. 3, September, 1988, 457-471.

12918 **Bourdillon, Sir Bernard.** "Partnership in Nigeria." *Journal of the Royal Society of Arts,* 92, No. 4664 (April 28, 1944), 255-263.

12919 **Bouvier, Paule.** "Aux Sources du Pouvoir Africain." *Academie Royale des Sciences d'Outre-Mer. Bulletin des Seances,* 37e Annee (Jaar. 4, 1991), 519-541.

12920 **Bouvier, Rudolf J.** "Neue Staaten im Kommen Entwicklungen und Fuhrungsfragen im heutigen Afrika." *Zeitschrift fur Geopolitik,* Heft 1 (Januar, 1959), 27-32.

12921 **Brett, Michael.** "The Colonial Period in the Maghrib and Its Aftermath: The Present State of Historical Writing." *Journal of African History,* 17, No. 2 (1976), 291-305.

12922 "The British South African Territories." *African Affairs*, 44, No. 175 (April, 1945), 62-72.

12923 Brunschwig, Henri. "De la Resistance Africaine a l'imperialisme Europeen." *Journal of African History*, 14, No. 1 (1974), 47-64.

12924 Brusa, Alfio. "Una unita coloniale inglese bifronte Unione Sud-Africana e Rhodesie." *Rivista delle colonie*, Anno 14, No. 2 (Febbraio, 1940), 159-178.

12925 Caforio, Giuseppe. "Il Punto Sulla Namibia." *Il Politico (Pavia)*, Anno 45, No. 1 (Marzo, 1980), 131-150.

12926 Cair-Gregg, John R.E. "Self-Rule in Africa: Recent Advances in the Gold Coast." *International Conciliation*, 473 (September, 1951), 319-382.

12927 Campbell, Gwyn. "Currency Crisis, Missionaries, and the French Takeover in Madagascar." 1861-1895. *International Journal of African Historical Studies*, 21, No. 2 (1988), 237-289.

12928 Carter, Gwendolen M. "The Gold Coast: A Future Dominion?" *International Journal*, 9, No. 2 (Spring, 1954), 133-143.

12929 Chick, Joh D. "Uganda: The Quest for Control." *World Today*, 26, No. 1 (January, 1970), 18-28.

12930 Cook, O.F. "A Scientific Approach to African Colonization." *Journal of the Washington Academy of Sciences*, 32, No. 1 (January 15, 1942), 1-17.

12931 Crook, Richard C. "Decolonization, the Colonial State, and Chieftaincy in the Gold Coast." *African Affairs*, 85, No. 338 (January, 1986), 75-106.

12932 Crush, Jonathan S. "The Colonial Division of Space: The Significance of the Swaziland Land Partition." *International Journal of African Historical Studies*, 13, No. 1 (1980), 71-86.

12933 Crush, Jonathan S. "The Genesis of Colonial Land Policy in Swaziland." *South African Geographical Journal*, 62 (April, 1980), 73-88.

12934 Crush, Jonathan S. "Landlords, Tenants, and Colonial Social Engineers: The Farm Labor Question in Early Colonial Swaziland." *Journal of Southern African Studies*, 11, No. 2 (April, 1985), 235-257.

12935 Crush, Jonathan S. "The Parameters of Dependence in Southern Africa: A Case Study of Swaziland." *Journal of Southern African Affairs*, 4, No. 1 (January, 1979), 55-66.

12936 "Das Afrikanische Kolonialproblem." *Zeitschrift der Gesellschaft fur Erdkunde zu Berlin*, Heft 1-4 (Mai, 1941), 1-144.

12937 Dearden, Ann. "Independence for Libya, the Political Problems." *Middle East Journal*, 4, No. 4 (October, 1950), 395-409.

12938 de Blij, Harm J. "Mozambique: Fragile Independence." *Focus*, 27, No. 2 (November-December, 1976), 9-16.

12939 Decalo, Samuel. "The Process, Prospects and Constraints of Democratization in Africa." *African Affairs*, 91, No. 362 (January, 1992), 7-15.

12940 Dellicourt, F. "Les institution politiques et administrative du Congo Belge." *Buletin de la Societe Royale de Geographie d'Anriers*, Tome 62, 1' et 2' (1948), 3-21.

12941 Dias, Jill R. "Black Chiefs, White Traders and Colonial Policy Near the Kwanza: Kabuku Kambilo and the Portuguese, 1873-1896." *Journal of African History*, 17, No. 2 (1976), 245-265.

12942 Donham, Donald L. "Revolution and Modernity in Maale: Ethiopia, 1974-1987." *Comparative Studies in Society and History*, 34, No. 1 (January, 1992), 28-57.

12943 Dresch, J. "Methodes coloniales au Congo Belge et en Afrique equatoriale francaise." *Politique Etrangere*, 12ᵉ, No. 1 (Janvier-Mars, 1947), 77-89.

12944 Drysdale, John. "The Problem of French Somaliland." *Africa Report*, 11, No. 8 (November, 1966), 10-17.

12945 Duffy, James. "Portugal in Africa." *Foreign Affairs*, 39, No. 3 (April, 1961), 481-493.

12946 Dunlop, John Stewart. "The Influence of David Livingstone on Subsequent Political Developments in Africa." *Scottish Geographical Magazine*, 75, No. 3 (1959), 144-152.

12947 Engelborghs-Bertels, Marthe. "La decolonisation et l'Afrique; articles publies par les pays a regime communiste." Belgium. *Academic Royale des Sciences d'Outre-mer Bulletin des Seances*, 4 (1965), 870-922.

12948 Fitzgerald, Richard C. "South Africa and the High Commission Territories." *World Affairs*, 4, No. 3 (July, 1950), 306-320.

12949 Floyd, Barry N. "Pre-European Political Patterns in Sub-Saharan Africa." *Bulletin of the Ghana Geographical Association*, 8, No. 2 (July, 1963), 3-11.

12950 **Fraenkel, Peter.** "Last French Colony in Africa." *Geographical Magazine,* 48, No. 7 (April, 1976), 404-408.

12951 **Francolini, Bruno.** "La Tunisia e il lavoro italiano." *Bollettino della R. Societa geografica italiana,* Serie 7, Vol. 4, Fasc. 3-4 (Marzo-Aprile, 1939), 255-272.

12952 **Frazier, E. Franklin.** "Urbanization and Its Effects Upon the Task of Nation-Building in Africa South of the Sahara." *Journal of Negro Education,* 30, No. 3 (Summer, 1961), 214-222.

12953 *"French Colonial Policy in Africa." Free France,* Special Issue No. 2 (September, 1944), 1-38.

12954 "French North Africa; Empire in Transition." *American Perspective,* 1, No. 5 (October, 1947), 259-285.

12955 "French North Africa Since June 1940." *Bulletin of International News,* 19, No. 25 (December 12, 1942), 1125-1134.

12956 "Future of Ruanda-Urundi; Fourth Committee Considers Commission's Report." *United Nations Review,* 9, No. 2, Sec. 1 (February, 1962), 9-13+.

12957 **Gocking, Roger.** "British Justice and the Native Tribunals of the Southern Gold Coast Colony." *The Journal of African History,* 34, No. 1 (1993), 93-113.

12958 **Guadio, Attilio.** "Rhodesia e Namibia nell'ora dell'independenza." *L'Universo. Firenze,* 58, No. 5 (Settembre-Ottobre, 1978), 1057-1979.

12959 "Ghana: Developments Since Independence." *World Today,* 14, No. 10 (October, 1958), 441-452.

12960 **Gillan, Sir Angus.** "The Sudan: Past, Present and Future." *African Affairs,* 43, No. 172 (July, 1944), 123-128.

12961 **Good, Kenneth.** "Settler Colonialism in Rhodesia." *African Affairs,* 73, No. 290 (January, 1974), 10-36.

12962 **Gorbold, R.** "Tanganyka: The Path to Independence." *Geographical Magazine,* 35, No. 9 (September,1962), 371-384.

12963 **Gould, Peter.** "Tanzania 1920-1963: The Spatial Impress of the Modernization Process." *World Politics,* 22 (January, 1970), 149-170.

12964 **Goulven, J.** "La renaissance de l'empire colonial portugais en Afrique." *Reseignements Coloniaux,* 6 (Supplement a l'Afrique francaise de Juin, 1939), 137-142.

12965 **Gritzner, Charles F.** "French Guiana Penal Colony: Its Role in Colonial Development." *Journal of Geography,* 63, No. 7 (October, 1964), 314-319.

12966 **Guatelli, Mario.** "Profili economici della colonizzazione intensiva demografica in Libia." *Rassegna economica dell'Africa italiana,* Anno 28, No. 1 (Gennaio, 1940), 13-17.

12967 **Hahn, Lorna.** "Last Chance in North Africa." *Foreign Affairs,* 35, No. 2 (January, 1958), 302-314.

12968 **Hailey, William Malcolm, Baron.** "The Foundation of Self-government in the African Colonies." *African Affairs,* 47, No. 188 (July, 1948), 147-153.

12969 **Hailey, William Malcolm, Baron.** "Native Administration in Africa." *International Affairs,* 23, No. 3 (July, 1947), 336-342.

12970 **Hanna, Paul L.** "The Anglo-Egyptian Negotiations, 1950-52." *Middle Eastern Affairs,* 3, Nos. 8-9 (August-September, 1952), 213-233.

12971 **Hargreaves, John D.** "Towards a History of the Partition of Africa." *Journal of African History,* No. 1 (1960), 97-109.

12972 **Harvey, William B., and Dean, W.H.B.** "The Independence of Transkei-A Largely Constitutional Inquiry." *Journal of Modern African Studies,* 16, No. 2 (June, 1978), 189-220.

12973 **Heinemeijer, W.J.** "De Nationale Grenzen van Marokko." *Tijdschrift van Het Koninklijk Nederlandsch Aardrijkskunig Genootschap Amsterdam,* 75, No. 1 (January, 1958), 56-63.

12974 **Henderson, Gavin B.** "German Colonial Projects on the Mosquito Coast, 1844-1848." Excerpt: *English Historical Review,* 59, No. 234 (May, 1944), 257-261.

12975 **Henriques, Julian.** "The Struggle of the Zimbabweans: Conflicts between the Nationalists and with the Rhodesian Regime." *African Affairs,* 76, No. 305 (October, 1977), 495-518.

12976 **Hermens, Edith.** "Vom Leben der Deutschen Siedler in der alten Kolonie Deutsch-Ostafrika." *Geographischer Anzeiger,* 39, Jahrg, Heft 24 (1938), 555-561.

12977 **Hexham, Irving.** "Dutch Calvinism and the Development of Afrikaner Nationalism." *African Affairs,* 79, No. 315 (April, 1980), 195-208.

12978 **Hill, Christopher R.** "Independent Botswana: Myth or Reality?" *The Round Table,* 62, No. 245 (January, 1972), 55-62.

12979 **Hodgkin, Thomas, and Schachter, Ruth.** "French-Speaking West Africa in Transition." *International Conciliation*, 528 (May, 1960), 373-436.

12980 **Hodgkiss, A.G., and Steel, R.W.** "The Changing Face of Africa." *Geography*, 46, No. 211, Part 2 (April, 1961), 156-160.

12981 **Hofmeyr, Jan H.** "Germany's Colonial Claims: A South African View." *Foreign Affairs*, 17, No. 4 (July, 1939), 788-798.

12982 **Holmquist, Frank.** "Defending Peasant Political Space in Independent Africa." *Revue Canadienne des Etudes Africaines*, 14, No. 1 (1980), 157-167.

12983 **Hoskins, Halford L.** "British Policy in Africa, 1873-1877; A Study in Geographical Politics." *Geographical Review*, 32, No. 1 (January, 1942), 140-149.

12984 **Huffman, Robert T.** "Colonialism, Socialism and Destabilization in Mozambique." *Africa Today*, 39, Nos. 1-2 (1992), 9-27.

12985 **Hunter, Guy.** "Independence and Development. Some Comparisons Between Tropical Africa and South-East Asia." *Ekistics*, 104 (1964), 3-6.

12986 **Huxley, Elspeth.** "East Africa and the Future." *Geographical Magazine*, 16, No. 1 (May, 1943), 14-23.

12987 **Ijere, M.O.** "Colonial Policy in Nigerian Agriculture and Its Implementation." *Agricultural History*, 48, No. 2 (April, 1974), 298-304.

12988 "Independencia de Guinea Ecuatorial." *Africa*, 25, No. 323 (Noviembre, 1968), 533-540.

12989 **Ingham, K.** "Uganda's Old Eastern Province: The Transfer to East Africa Protectorate in 1902." *Uganda Journal*, 21, No. 1 (March, 1957), 1-41.

12990 **Isaacman, A., and Isaacman, B.** "Resistance and Collaboration in Southern and Central Africa; c 1850-1920." *International Journal of African Historical Studies*, 10 (1977), 31-62.

12991 **Johnson, Hildegard Binder.** "Die Verteilung der Europaer in Afrika." *Koloniale Rundschau*, 26, No. 3/4 (August/Oktober, 1934), 1-4.

12992 **Jones, N.S.C.** "The Decolonisation of the White Highlands of Kenya." *Geographical Journal*, 131, Part 2 (June, 1965), 186-201.

12993 **Julien, Charles Andre.** "Crisis and Reform in French North Africa." *Foreign Affairs*, 29, No. 3 (April, 1951), 445-455.

12994 **Kabit, Ghislan C.** "Zaire: The Roots of Continuing Crisis." *Journal of Modern African Studies*, 17, No. 3 (September, 1979), 381-407.

12995 **Kimble, George H.T.** "How Free and the New Countries of Africa?" *Optima*, 13, No. 4 (December, 1963), 169-174.

12996 **Knight, Virginia Curtin.** "Namibia's Transition to Independence." *Current History*, 88, No. 538 (May, 1989), 225-228, 241.

12997 "Koloniale Wirtschaft in Afrika." *Afrika Rundschau*, 6, Jahrg, Num. 9 (Januar, 1941), 102-131.

12998 **Laborde, Fernand.** "Francais et Italiens en Tunisie." *Revue Economique Internationale*, 31e annee, 1, No. 1 (Janvier, 1939), 31-52.

12999 **Labouret, Henri.** "France's Colonial Policy in Africa." *Journal of the Royal African Society*, 39, No. 154 (January, 1940), 22-35.

13000 **Langlade, Claude.** "Kjibouti, Escale Imperiale." *L'Europe Nouvelle*, 22e annee, No. 1092 (Janvier 14, 1939), 33-34.

13001 **Laschinger, Michael.** "Roads to Independence: The Case of Swaziland." *The World Today*, 21, No. 11 (November, 1965), 486-494.

13002 **Latham-Koenig, A.L.** "Ruanda-Urundi on the Threshold of Independence." *World Today*, 18, No. 7 (July, 1962), 288-295.

13003 **Longrigg, H.** "Disposal of Italian Africa." *International Affairs*, 21, No. 3 (July, 1945), 363-369.

13004 **Louis, W.R.** "The Anglo-German Hinterland Settlement of 1890 and Uganda." *Uganda Journal*, 27, No. 1 (March, 1963), 71-83.

13005 **Low, D.A.** "Uganda Unhinged." *International Affairs*, 49, No. 2 (April, 1973), 219-228.

13006 **Lutz, James M.** "The Diffusion of Political Phenomena in Sub-Saharan Africa." *Journal of Political and Military Sociology*, 17, No. 1 (Spring, 1989), 93-114.

13007 **Lyne, R.N.** "Germany's Claim to Colonies: The African Mandates." *Journal of the Royal African society*, 38, No. 151 (April, 1939), 273-280.

13008 **Mackintosh, John P.** "Nigeria Since Independence." *World Today*, 20, No. 8 (August, 1964), 328-337.

13009 **MacQueen, Norman.** "Portugal & Africa: The Politics of Re-Engagement." *Journal of Modern African Studies*, 23, No. 1 (March, 1985), 31-51.

13010 McWilliam, M.D. "Economic Problems During the Transfer of Power in Kenya." *World Today,* 18, No. 4 (April, 1962), 164-175.

13011 Martelli, George. "The Portuguese in Guinea." *World Today,* 21, No. 8 (August, 1965), 345-350.

13012 Matznetter, Josef. "Portugiesische Kolonisationstypen am Beispiel von Sudwest-Angola." *Deutscher Geograph entag Bochum,* 8, bis 11 (June, 1965). Tagungsbericht und Wissenschaftliche Adhandlungen. Verhandlungen dis Deutschen Geographentages, Band 35 (1966), 263-275.

13013 McKay, Vernon. "British Rule in West Africa." *Foreign Policy Reports,* 24, No. 7 (June 15, 1948), 70-79.

13014 McKay, Vernon. "France's Future in North Africa." *Middle East Journal,* 2, No. 3 (July, 1948), 293-305.

13015 McKay, Vernon. "Too Slow or Too Fast? Political Change in African Trust Territories." *Foreign Affairs,* 35, No. 2 (January, 1957), 295-310.

13016 Muller, Dietrich O. "Die Sudgrenze Ugandas Entstehungsweise und Bewertujng einer Kolonialen Grenze." *Abhandlungen des 1. Geographischen Instituts der Fieien Universitat Berlin,* Bd. 13 (1970), 493-513.

13017 Murphy, John E. "Legitimation and Paternalism: The Colonial State in Kenya." *African Studies Review,* 29, No. 3 (September, 1986), 55-65.

13018 Mitchell, Sir Philip. "Native Administration in the British Territories in Africa" by Lord Hailey, Review. *Journal of African Administration,* 3, No. 2 (April, 1951), 55-65.

13019 "Nigeria: The African Giant; A Survey on the Even of Independence." *Round Table,* 50, No. 197 (December, 1959), 55-63.

13020 Nyekoy, B. "Prenationalist Resistance to Colonial Rule: Swaziland on the Eve of the Imposition of British Administration." *Trans African Journal of History,* 5, No. 2 (1976), 66-83.

13021 Nyerere, Julius K. "Rhodesia in the Context of Southern Africa." *Foreign Affairs,* 44, No. 3 (April, 1966), 373-386.

13022 O'Brien, Rita Cruise. "Some Problems in the Consolidation of National Independence in Africa: The Case of the French Expatriates in Senegal." *African Affairs,* 73, No. 290 (January, 1974), 85-94.

13023 Orsini, Paolo d'Agostino. "La Colonizzazione Francese in Africa Nella Sua Evoluzione Storico-geografico-politica." *Rivista Delle Colonie,* Anno 14, No. 4 (Aprile, 1940), 461-476.

13024 Pedler, F.J. "Quelques Problemes Administratifs de l'Afrique Occidentale Britannique." *Politique Etrangere,* 11e Annee, No. 4 (Aout, 1946), 339-348.

13025 Palley, Claire. "What Future for Zimbabwe?" *The Political Quarterly,* 51, No. 3 (July-September, 1980), 285-302.

13026 Pelissier, Rene. "Political Movements in Spanish Guinea." *Africa Report,* 9, No. 5 (May, 1964), 3-7.

13027 Perham, Margery. "African Facts and American Criticisms." *Foreign Affairs,* 22, No. 3 (April, 1944), 444-457.

13028 Perham, Margery. "The Rhodesian Crisis: The Background." *International Affairs,* 42, No. 1 (January, 1966), 1-13.

13029 Pfalz, Richard. "Zwei Jahrzehnte Libyen." *Geographischer Anzeiger,* 43, Jahrg, Heft 23-24 (Dezember, 1942), 459-467.

13030 Phiri, Bizeck Jube. "The Capricorn Africa Society Revisited: The Impact of Liberalism in Zambia's Colonial History, 1949-1963." *The International Journal of African Historical Studies,* 24, No. 1 (1991), 65-83.

13031 Pich, Hella. "Independent Mauritania." *World Today,* 17, No. 4 (April, 1961), 149-158.

13032 "Political Development in Basutoland." *International Bulletin,* 2, No. 3 (March, 1964), 69-83.

13033 "Political Development in the Basutoland Protectorate." *International Bulletin,* 2, No. 2 (February, 1964), 42-53.

13034 "Portugal in Africa." *Africa Institute, International Bulletin,* 1, No. 10 (November, 1963), 284-292.

13035 "Portuguese East Africa: The Re-Incorporation of the Territories of the Mozambique Company into Direct State Administration." *Journal of the Royal African Society,* 41, No. 165 (October, 1942), 238-239.

13036 Prenant, Andre. "Algerie: Neo-realisme ou Volontansme < <liberal> >?" *Herode,* No. 45 (Avril-Juin, 1987), 71-106.

13037 Price, R.M. "Pretoria's Southern African Strategy." *African Affairs,* 83, No. 330 (January, 1984), 11-32.

13038 **Rai, K.B.** "Southern Rhodesia." *India Quarterly,* 20, No. 4 (October-December, 1964), 390-402.

13039 **Rennell, Francis James Rennell Rodd, 2d Baron.** "African Colonial Administration." *United Empire,* 36, No. 3 (May-June, 1945), 96-99.

13040 "The Republic of Tanganyika: A Break with the Colonial Past." *Round Table,* 208 (September, 1962), 339-347.

13041 **Reyner, Anthony S.** "Somalia: The Problems of Independence." *Middle East Journal,* 14, No. 3 (1960), 247-255.

13042 **Robert, M.** "La Ligne d'Evolution Suivie par le Katanga." *Institut Royal Colonial Belge. Bulletin des Seances.* Tome 9, No. 3 (1938), 575-594.

13043 **Roberts, Andrew.** "The Evolution of the Uganda Protectorate." *Uganda Journal,* 27, No. 1 (March, 1963), 95-106.

13044 **Roberts, Margaret.** "Political Prospects for the Cameroun." *World Today,* 16, No. 7 (1960), 305-315.

13045 **Rubin, Leslie.** "The High Commission Territories: What Now?" *Africa Report,* 9, No. 4 (April, 1964), 9-10.

13046 **Robertson, James W.** "The Sudan in Transition." *African Affairs,* 52, No. 209 (1953), 317-327.

13047 **Robinson, K.E.** "French West Africa." *African Affairs,* 50, No. 199 (1951), 123-132.

13048 **Robinson, K.E.** "Political Development in French West Africa." In *Africa in the Modern World,* Calvin W. Stillman, ed. Chicago, Illinois: University of Chicago Press, 1955.

13049 **Roothchild, Donald S.** "The Politics of African Separatism." *Journal of International Affairs,* 15 (1961), 18-28.

13050 **St. John, Peter.** "Independent Algeria from Ben Bella to Boumedienne." *The World Today,* 24, No. 7 (July, 1968), 290-296 and 24, No. 8 (August, 1968), 339-345.

13051 **Schultze, J.H.** "Der Gegenwartige Stand Unserer Kenntnisse von den Deutsch-Afrikanischen Kolonien." *Geographischer Anzeiger,* 40 Jahrg, Heft 7 (1939), 145-154.

13052 **Shilling, Nancy A.** "Problems of Political Development in a Ministate: The French Territory of the Afars and the Issas." *The Journal of Developing Areas,* 7, No. 4 (July, 1973), 613-633.

13053 **Scott, Michael.** "The International Status of South African West Africa." *International Affairs,* 34, No. 3 (July, 1958), 318-329.

13054 **Segre, Dan V.** "Colonization and Decolonization: The Case of Zionist and African Elites." *Comparative Studies in Society and History,* 22, No. 1 (January, 1980), 23-41.

13055 **Shaw, Timothy M.** "From Dependence to Self-Reliance: Africa's Prospects for the Next Twenty Years." *International Journal,* 35, No. 4 (Autumn, 1980), 821-844.

13056 **Silvestri, Ubaldo.** "Demografia e Colonizzazione in Africa Orientale Italiana." *Rassegna Economica dell'Africa Italiana,* Anno 28, No. 1 (Gennaio, 1940), 18-21.

13057 **Simon, David.** "Decolonisation and Local Government in Namibia: The Neo-Apartheid Plan, 1977-1983." *Journal of Modern African Studies,* 23, No. 3 (September, 1985), 507-526.

13058 **Smit, P.** "Recent Developments and Trends in Africa: Africa's Changing Political Pattern." *Tydskrif Vir Aardrykskunde, Journal of Geography,* 1, No. 7 (July, 1960), 55-60.

13059 **Smith, Sheila.** "Colonialism in Economic Theory: The Experience of Nigeria." *Journal of Development Studies,* 15, No. 3 (April, 1979), 38-59.

13060 "Somalia Heads Toward Independence." *Africa,* 3, No. 12 (December, 1958), 8-12+.

13061 "South Africa and the High Commission Territories." *Africa Institute, International Bulletin,* 2, No. 1 (January, 1964), 9-24.

13062 **Southall, Roger J.** "The Beneficiaries of Transkeian 'Independence.'" *Journal of Modern African Studies,* 15, No. 1 (March, 1977), 1-23.

13063 **Spence, J.E.** "Basutoland Comes to Independence." *World Today,* 22, No. 10 (October, 1966), 435-446.

13064 "The Status of Tangier." *World Today,* 1, No. 5 (November, 1945), 221-229.

13065 **Steel, R.W.** "Land and Population in British Tropical Africa." *Geography,* 40, No. 187 (1955), 1-17.

13066 **Stuart, Graham H.** "The Future of Tangier." *Foreign Affairs,* 23, No. 4 (July, 1945), 675-679.

13067 "The Sudan for the Sudanese: The Threshold of Self-Determination." *The World Today,* 11, No. 10 (October, 1955), 421-430.

13068 **Taylor, Alan R., and Dvorin, Eugene P.**
"Political Development in British Central Africa
(1890-1956)." *Race,* 1, No. 1 (1959), 61-78.

13069 **Teague, Michael.** "Portugal's Permanence in
Africa." *Geographical Magazine,* 28, No. 9
(September, 1955), 326-336.

13070 **Teye, V.B.** "Liberation Wars and Tourism
Development in Africa--The Case of Zambia."
Annals of Tourism Research, 13, No. 4 (1988),
589-608.

13071 **Touval, Saadia.** "Africa's Frontiers: Reactions
to a Colonial Legacy." *International Affairs,* 42,
No. 4 (October, 1966), 641-654

13072 **Troll, C.** "Koloniale Raumplanung in Afrika."
Zeitschrift der Gesellschaft fur Erdkunde, Nv. 1/2
(April, 1941), 1-41.

13073 "Tunisia - A Convalescent Protectorate." *World
Today,* 4, No. 6 (June, 1948), 261-272.

13074 **Ukpabi, S.C.** "The Beginning of the British
Conquest of Northern Nigeria." *Bulletin de
l'Institut Fondamental d'Afrique. Ser. B:
Sciences Humanities,* Tome 35, No. 3 (Juillet,
1973), 593-613.

13075 **Van Bilsen, A.A.J.** "Some Aspects of the Congo
Problem." *International Affairs,* 38, No. 1
(January, 1962), 41-51.

13076 **Waller, Richard.** "The Maasai and the British,
1895-1905: The Origins of an Alliance." *Journal
of African History,* 17, No. 4 (1976), 529-553.

13077 **Weiss, P.F.D.** "The Question of Rhodesia's
Independence." *Africa Institute Bulletin,* 3, No. 1
(January, 1965), 1-6.

13078 **Weulersee, Jacques.** "Le Probleme Indigene
Dans l'Union Sud-Africaine." *Annales de
Geographie,* 40, No. 233 (Janvier 15, 1931), 47-
61.

13079 **Whittlesey, Derwent S.** "Southern Rhodesia--An
African Compage." *Annals of the Association of
American Geographers,* 46, No. 1 (March, 1956),
1-97.

13080 "Why Belgium Quit the Congo." *Fortune,* 62,
No. 5 (November, 1960), 128-131+.

13081 **Wigny, Pierre.** "The Belgian Plan for
Democracy in Africa." *Optima,* 8, No. 1
(March, 1958), 23-31.

13082 **Yohannes, Okbazghi.** "The Entrean Question:
A Colonial Case?" *Journal of Modern African
Studies,* 25, No. 4 (December, 1987), 643-668.

13083 **Zolberlg, Aristide R.** "The Political Revival of

Mali." *World Today,* 21, No. 4 (April, 1965),
151-160.

AMERICAS

Books

13084 **Alberdi, J.B.** *Reconstruccion Geografica de La
America del Sur.* Buenos Aires: Libreria "La
Facultad" de J. Roldan, 1920.

13085 **Alden, Dauril,** eds. *Colonial Roots of Modern
Brazil: Papers of the Newberry Library
Conference.* Berkeley: University of California
Press, 1973.

13086 **Alvarado, rafael.** *La Cuestion de Belice.*
Guatemala: Secretariat de Imformacion de la
Presidencia de la Republica, 1958.

13087 **Anciaux, Leon.** *La Participation des Belgs a
l'oeuvre Coloniale des Hollandais aux Indes
Orientales.* Bruxelles: Academic Royal des
Sciences d'Outermer, 1955.

13088 **Arnade, Charles W.** *The Emergence of the
Republic of Bolivia.* Gainesville: University of
Florida Press, 1957.

13089 **Ashcraft, Norman.** *Colonialism and
Underdevelopment: Processes of Political
Economic Change in British Honduras.* New
York: Teachers College Pres, 1973.

13090 **Ayearst, Morley.** *The British West Indies: The
Search for Self-Government.* New York: New
York University Pres, 1960.

13091 **Blanshard, Paul.** *Democracy and Empire in the
Caribbean: A Contemporary Review.* New York:
Macmillan, 1947.

13092 **Bousquet, G.H.** *A French View of the
Netherlands Indies.* Translated from Brench by
Philip E. Lilienthal. London: Oxford University
Press, 1940.

13093 **Carr, Raymond.** *Puereto Rico: A Colonial
Experiment.* New York: New York University
Press, 1984.

13094 **Clarke, John I.** *A Geographical Analysis of
Colonial Settlement in the Western District of
Upper Canada, 1788-1850.* London, Ontario,
Canada: University of Western Ontario, Ph.D.,
1970.

13095 Consejo Superior de Investigaciones Cientificas,
Madrid. *La Administracion Espanola en el
Protectorado de Marruecos, Plazas de Soberania
y Colonies de Africa, Por Sabino Alvarex Gendin.*
Madrid: Instituto de Estudio Africanos, 1949.

13096 **Coulter, John Wesley.** *The Pacific Dependencies of the United States.* New York: Macmillan, 1957.

13097 **Da Pena, Ramon.** *Belize: Prospects for Independence and Sovereignty.* Los Angeles: University of California, Ph.D., 1976.

13098 **Davis, William Columbus.** *The Last Conquistadores, the Spanish Intervention in Peru and Chile, 1863-1866.* Athens: University of Georgia Press, 1950.

13099 "Developments Towards Self-Government in the Caribbean." A Symposium Held Under the Auspices of the Netherlands Universities Foundation for International Cooperation at the Hague, September, 1954. The Hague: W. Van Howe, 1955.

13100 **Edie, Carlene J.,** ed. *Democracy in the Caribbean: Myths and Realities.* Westport: Praeger Publishers, 1994.

13101 **Emerson, Rupert,** and others. *America's Pacific Dependencies.* New York: American Institute of Pacific Relations, 1949.

13102 **Fox, Annette Baker.** *Freedom and Welfare in the Caribbean: A ColonialDilemma.* New York: Harcourt Brace, 1949.

13103 **Guatemala.** Ministerio de Relaciones Exteriores. *Belice Pertenence a Guatemala. La Propaganda Britanica Tergiversa la Historia. (Articulos publicados en la prensa de Guatemala.) Belize belongs to Guatemala. The Britannic Propaganda Tergiversates History.* Articles appeared in Guatemala's newspapers. Guatemala: Ministerio de Relaciones Exteriores, 1947.

13104 **Guatemala.** Secretaria de Relaciones Exteriores. *Coleccion de Tratados de Guatemala,* comp. por Jose rodriguez Cerna. Vol. 1. Pactos con el resto de Centro America. Guatemala: Secretaria de Relaciones Exteriores, 1939.

13105 **Haas, William H.,** eds. *The American Empire: A Study of the Outlying Territories of the United States.* Chicago, Illinois: University of Chicago Press, 1940.

13106 **Hurtado Aquilar, Luis.** *Belice es de Guatemala: Tratados, Situacion, Juridica, Actuaciones, Opiniones.* Guatemala: Secretaria de Informatioan de la Precidencia de la Republica, 1958.

13107 **Jagan, Cheddi.** *Forbidden Freedom: The Story of British Guiana.* New York: International Publishers, 1954.

13108 **Kaplan, Amy,** and **Pease, Donald E.,** eds. *Cultures of United States Imperialism.* Durham: Duke University Press, 1993.

13109 **Louis, W.R.** *Imperialism at Bay: The United States and the Decolonization of the British Empire 1941-1945.* New York: Oxford University Press, 1945.

13110 **Lowenthal, David,** and **Comitas, Lombros,** eds. *The Aftermath of Sovereignty: West Indian Perspective.* Garden City, New York: ANchor Press/Doubleday, 1973.

13111 **Madariaga, Salvador de.** *The Rise of the Spanish American Empire.* New York: Macmillan, 1947.

13112 **McNeill, Robert Leonard.** *The United States and Self-Government for Puerto Rico, 1893-1952.* Medford, Masachusetts; Tufts University, 1956.

13113 **Melendex, Edwardo.** *Puerto Rico's Statehood Movement.* New York: Greenwood Press, 1988.

13114 **Miller, Hunter.** *San Juan Archipelagos: Study of the Joint Occupation of San Juan Island.* Bellows Falls, Vermont: Wyndham Press, 1943.

13115 **Mintz, Sidney W.** *Caribbean Transformation.* Chicago, Illinois: Aldine Publishing, 1974.

13116 **Pomeroy, Earl S.** *The Territories and the United States, 1861-1890: Studies in Colonial Administration.* Philadelphia: University of Pennsylvania Press, 1947.

13117 **Pratt, Julius W.** *America's Colonial Experiment, How the United States Gained, Governed, and in Part Gave Away a Colonial Empire.* New York: Prentice-Hall, 1950.

13118 **Reece, Andrew G.** *Colonial Dualism in the Commonwealth Caribbean: A Study of Kingston, Jamaica.* Chapel Hill, NC: Master's thesis, University of North Carolina, 1993.

13119 **Roberts, W. Adolphe.** *The French in the West Indies.* Indianapolis: Bobbs-Merrill, 1942.

13120 **Robertson, William Spence.** *France and Latin-American Independence.* Baltimore, Maryland: Johns Hopkins University Press, 1939.

13121 **Salisbury, Richard V.** *Anti-Imperialism and International Competition in Central America 1920-1929.* Wilmington, Delaware: Scholarly Resources, 1989.

13122 **Sutton, P.K.** *The Caribbean as a Subordinate State System, 1945-1976. Part 1: 1945-1959.* Hull: University of Hull, Hull Papers in Politics, No. 16, 1980.

13123 **Swan, M.** *British Guiana: Land of the Six Peoples.* London: Her Majesty's Stationery Office, 1957.

13124 **Trias, Vivian.** *Imperialismo y Geopolitica en Ameica Latina.* Montevideo: Ed. El Sol, 1967.

13125 **U.S. Congress, 79th, 1st Session.** Senate. *Independence for Puerto Rico. Hearings before the Committee on Territories and Insular Affairs...on S. 227; a Bill to Provide for the Withdrawal of the Sovereignty of the United States Over the Island of Puerto Rico and for the Recognition of Its Independence. Part 1.* Washington, D.C.: U.S. Congress, 79th, 1st Session, 1945.

13126 **U.S. Department of the Interior.** *Territorial Areas Administered by the United States.* Washington, D.C.: U.S. Department of Interior, 1968.

13127 **U.S. Office of War Information.** *Proposals for a Free World.* (Toward New Horizons, No. 2) Washington, D.C.: U.S. Office of War Information, 1943.

13128 **Wagenheim, Olga Himenz de.** *Puerto Rico's Revolt for Independence: El Grito de Lares.* Boulder, Colorado: Westview Press, 1985.

13129 **Weinberg, A.K.** *Manifest Destiny: A Study of Nationalist Expansion in American History.* Baltimore, Maryland: Johns Hopkins University Press, 1935.

13130 **Williams, W.A.** *The Roots of hte Modern American Empire.* New York: Vintage, 1969.

Journals

13131 **Arnold, Edwin G.** "Self-Government in U.S. Territories." *Foreign Affairs,* 25, No. 4 (July, 1947), 655-666.

13132 **Bebelgisler, D.** "Passe Inacahieve de l'Esclavage: Etat Francais, Transnational et Little de Liberation Nationale en Gaudeloupe. (The Incomplete Past of Slavery: The French State, The Transnational Order and Struggle for National Liberation in Guadeloupe)." *Peuples Mediterraneens, Miditerranean Peoples,* 35,36 (1986), 295-307.

13133 **Bell, Philip W.** "Colonialism as a Problem in American Foreign Policy." *World Politics,* 5, No. 1 (October, 1952), 86-109.

13134 **Bernardes, Nilo.** "Condicoes Geograficas da Colonizacao em Alagoes." *Revista Brasileira de Geografia,* 29, No. 2 (Abr.-Jun., 1967), 65-83.

13135 **Burns, W. I.** "The United States as a Colonial Power." *The Contemporary Review,* 889 (January, 1940), 74-83.

13136 **Byroade, Henry A.** "The World's Colonies and Ex-Colonies: A Challenge to America." *Department of State Bulletin,* 29, No. 751 (November 16, 1953), 655-660.

13137 **Carney, James J., Jr.** "Early Spanish Imperialism." *Hispanic American Historical Review,* 19, No. 2 (May, 1939), 138-146.

13138 **Clegern, Wayne M.** "New Light on the Belize Dispute." *The AMerican Journal of International Law,* 52, No. 2 (April, 1958), 280-297.

13139 **Collins, B.A.N.** "Independence for Guyana." *World Today,* 22, No. 6 (June, 1966), 260-268.

13140 "A Colony in Dispute: Past and Future of British Honduras." *Round Table,* 48, No. 190 (March, 1958), 151-159.

13141 **Courtland Penfield, F.** "The Practical Phases of Caribbean Domination." *North American Review,* 178, No. 566 (January, 1904), 75-85.

13142 **Crist, Raymond E.,** and **Chardon, Carlos E.** "Intercultural Colonial Policies in the Americas: Iberians and Britons in the New World." Reprinted from: *American Journal of Economics and Sociology,* 6, No. 3 (April, 1947), 371-385.

13143 **de Azevedo, Aroldo.** "O Imperio Colonial Portugues e o Brasil (um Esboco de Geografia Politica)." *Congresso Brasileiro de Geografia, 9ª, Florianopolis, 1940,* Anais, 5 (1944), 239-246.

13144 **de Blij, Harm J.** "Cultural Pluralism and the Political Geography of Decolonization: The Case of Surinam." *Pennsylvania Geographer,* 7, No. 2 (July, 1970).

13145 **Eidt, R. C.** "Aboriginal Chibcha Settlement in Columbia." *Annals of the Association of American Geographers,* 49, No. 4 (December, 1959), 374-392.

13146 **Elliott, A. Randle.** "American Policy towards Pacific Dependencies." *Pacific Affairs,* 20, No. 3 (September, 1947), 259-275.

13147 **Elliott, A. Randle.** "European Colonies in the Western Hemisphere." *Foreign Policy Reports,* 16, No. 11 (August 15, 1940), 138-148.

13148 **Fawcett, J.E.S.** "The Falklands and the Law." *World Today,* 38, No. 6 (June, 1982), 203-206.

13149 "Federation in the British Caribbean: An Exercise in Colonial Administration." *Round Table,* 39, No. 155 (June, 1949), 234-239.

13150 **Graham, William C.** "Reflections on United States Legal Imperialism: Canadian Sovereignty in the Context of North American Economic Integration." *International Journal,* 40, No. 3 (Summer, 1985), 478-509.

13151 **Greenleaf, Richard E.** "Persistence of Native Values: The Inquisition and the Indians of Colonial Mexico." *The Americas,* 50, No. 3 (January, 1994), 351-376.

13152 **Grunberg, Bernard.** "The Origins of the Conquistadores of Mexico City." *Hispanic American Historical Review,* 74, No. 2 (May, 1994), 259-283.

13153 **Hickey, J.** "Keep the Falklands British? The Principle of Self-determination of Dependent Territories." *Journal of Inter-American Economic Affairs,* 31 (1977), 77-88.

13154 **Hitch, Thomas K.** "The Administration of America's Pacific Islands." *Political Science Quaterly,* 41, No. 3 (Spetember, 1946), 384-407.

13155 **Holmes, Olive.** "Anglo-American Caribbean Commission--Pattern for Colonial Cooperation." *Foreign Policy Reports,* 20, No. 19 (December 15, 1944), 238-247.

13156 **House, J.W.** "Political Geography of Contemporary Events: Unfinished Business in the South Atlantic." *Political Geography Quarterly,* 2, No. 3 (July, 1983), 233-246.

13157 **Howells, William W.** "The Distribution of Man." *Scientific American,* 203, No. 3 (September, 1960), 113-127.

13158 "Imperial Responsibilities in the West Indies." *Round Table,* 28, No. 112 (September, 1938), 692-707.

13159 **Johnson, Casell L.** "Political Unionism and Autonomy in Economies of British Colonial Origin: The Case of Jamaica and Trinidad." *American Journal of Economics and Sociology,* 39, No. 3 (July, 1980), 237-248.

13160 **Johnson, John J.** "The Political Role of the Latin-American Middle Sectors." *Annals of the American Academy of Political and Social Sciences,* 334 (March, 1961), 20-29.

13161 **Jones, David.** "Belize Hovers on the Brink of Independence." *Geographical Magazine,* 3, No. 10 (July, 1971), 708-712.

13162 **Jones, Joseph M.** "Caribbean Laboratory: There We Can Learn the Potentials of U.S. Influence on World Colonial Policy." Reprint: *Fortune,* 29, No. 2 (February, 1944), 124-127+.

13163 **Jones, Joseph M.** "Let's Beign with Puerot Rico. Our Wards Have a Plan for Working Toward Independence." Reprint: *Fortune,* 29, No. 5 (May, 1944), 133-136+.

13164 **Jordan, Terry G.** "Preadaption and European Colonization in Rural North America (Presidential Address)." *Annals of The Association of American Geographers,* 79, No. 4 (December, 1989), 489-500.

13165 **Kiemetz, Alvin.** "Decolonization in the North: Canada and the United States." *Canadian Review of Studies in Nationalism,* 13, No. 1 (Spring, 1986), 57-77.

13166 **Knight, Rudolph H.** "La Planificacion y la Politica en el Caribe Britanico." *Revista de Ciencias Sociales,* 4, No. 1 (March, 1960), 193-213.

13167 "La Isla de Chipre. La Sociedad Mexicana de Geografia y Estadistica Contra el Sistma Colonilista." *Boletin de la Sociedad de Geografia y Estadistica,* 79, No. 1 (January-Februray, 1955).

13168 **Ludlum, David M.** "The Weather of American Independence-2: The Seige and Evacuation of Boston, 1975-76." *Weatherwise,* 27, No. 4 (August, 1974), 162-168.

13169 **Marchiori, Mario.** "La Colonizzazione Russa Dell' Alaska." *L'Universo* [Firenze], Anno 74, No. 1 (Gennaio-Febbraio, 1994), 60-69.

13170 "The Maroons in the 18th Century: A Note on Indirect Rule in Jamaica." *Caribbean Quarterly,* 8, No. 1 (1962), 25-27.

13171 **Mehnert, Klaus.** "USA, Annektiert Pazifische Inseln." *Zeitschrift fur Geopolitik,* Jahrg, 15, Heft 5 (Mai, 1938), 341-347.

13172 **Meinig, Donald W.** "The American Colonial Era: A Geographic Commentary." *Proceedings Royal Geographical Society of Australia,* 59 (1957), 1-22.

13173 **Mendez, J. Ignacio.** "Azul y Rojo: Panama's Independence in 1840." *Hispanic American Review,* 60, No. 2 (May, 1980), 269-293.

13174 **Murkland, Harry B.** "The West Indies Unit: British Colonies Take First Step Toward Independence." *Americas,* 10, No. 7 (July, 1958), 3-9.

13175 **Nicholas, Madaline W.** "Argentine Colonial Economy." In *Hispanic American Essays,* A.C. Wilgus, ed. Chapel Hill: University of North Carolina Press, 1942, 85-98.

13176 **Nicholson, Norman L.** "The Further Partition of the Northwest Territories of Canada: An Aspect of Decolonization in Northernmost North America." In *Essays in Political Geography,* Charles A. Fisher, ed., 1968, 311-324.

13177 **Piel, Jean.** "Rebeliones Agrarias y Supevivencias Coloniales en el Peru del Siglo XIX." *Revista del Musco Nacionall,* Tomo 39 (1973), 301-304.

13178 **Pomeroy, Earl S.** "The American Colonial Office." *Misissippi Valley Historical Review,* 30, No. 4 (March, 1944), 521-532.

13179 **Pomeroy, Earl S.** "The Navy and Colonial Government." *United States Naval Institute Proceedings,* 71, No. 505 (March, 1945), 291-297.

13180 "Recent Political Developments in the British West Indies." *American Perspective,* 1, No. 4 (September, 1947), 236-252.

13181 **Rowcliff, G.J.** "Guam." *United States Naval Institute Proceedings,* 71, No. 509 (July, 1945), 781-793.

13182 **Sandner, Gerhard.** "El Concepto Espacial y los Sistemas Funcionales en la Colonizacion Espontanea Costarricence (Spatial Concept and Function Systms in the Spontaneous Colonization of Costa Rica)." *Rivista Geografiea de America Central,* 15-16 (1981-82), 95-117.

13183 **Schaeffer, Wendell G.** "The Delayed Cession of Spanish Santa Domingo to France, 1795-1801." *Hispanic American Historical Review,* 29, No. 1, Pt. 1 (February, 1949), 46-68.

13184 **Shepard, E. Lee; Pollard, Frances S.; and Schwarz, Janet B.** "'The Love of Liberty Brought Us Here': Virginians and the Colonization of Liberia." *The Virginia Magazine of History and Biography,* 102, No. 1 (January, 1994), 89-100.

13185 "Soberania Argentina en la Antartida." *Informaciones Argentinas,* Num. 109 (Enero-Marzo, 1947), 38-43.

13186 **Strong, John A.** "The Imposition of Colonial Jurisdiction Over the Montauk Indians of Long Island." *Ethnohistory,* 41, No. 4 (Fall, 1994), 561-590.

13187 **Taussig, Charles W.** "A Four-Power Program in the Caribbean." *Foreign Affairs,* 24, No. 4 (July, 1946), 699-710.

13188 **Tomaseh, Robert D.** "British Guiana: A Case Study of British Colonial Policy." *Political Science Quarterly,* 74, No. 3 (September, 1959), 393-411.

13189 **Walker, R.G.** "Brazil: Political and Economic Evolution." *World Affairs,* 3, No. 3 (July, 1949), 300-309.

13190 **Wehling, Franz B.H.** "Imperialismus und Kolonial Politik der USA." *Archiv fur Wanderrungswesen und Auslandkunde,* 9, No. 1-2 (1937), 46-51.

13191 **Zavala, Silvio.** "Los Aspectos Geograficos en la Colonizacion del Nuevo Mundo." *Rivista Geografica,* Tomo 29, No. 55 (Julho-Decembro de, 1961), 51-138.

ASIA

Books

13192 **Adamiyat, Feregdoun.** *Bahrien Islands: A Legal and Diplomataic Study of the British-Iranian Controversy.* New York: Praeger, 1955.

13193 **Ambedkar, B.R.** *Pakistan, or the Partition of India.* 3rd ed. Bombay: Thacker, 1946.

13194 **Amirahmadi, Hooshang, and Parvin, Manoucher,** eds. *Post-revolutionary Iran.* Boulder, Colorado: Westview Press, 1988.

13195 **Arab Information Center, New York.** *The Question of Oman: An Analysis of the British Oman Dispute.* New York: Arab Information Center, 1960.

13196 **Baker, D.E.U.** *Colonialism in an Indian Hinterland: The Central Provinces, 1820-1920.* Delhi: Oxford University Press, 1993.

13197 **Behdad, Ali.** *Belated Travelers: Orientalism in the Age of Colonial Dissolution.* Durham: Duke University Press, 1994.

13198 **Ben Dor, Gabriel.** *State and Conflict in the Middle East: Emergence of the Post Colonial State.* New York: Praeger, 1983.

13199 **Biger, Gideon.** *The Role of the British Administration in Changing the Geography of Palestine, 1918-1929.* London: University College, Department of Geography, Occasional Paper, No. 35, February, 1979.

13200 **Cady, J.F.; Barnett, P.G.; and Jenkins, S.** *The Development of Self-Rule and Independence in Burma, Malaya, and the Philippines.* New York: Institute of Pacific Relations, 1948.

13201 **Choudhury, Deba Prasad.** *British Policy on the Northeast Frontier of India, 1865-1914.* London, England: University of London, Ph.D., 1970.

13202 *Decline of Western Colonialism in Asia, 1954.* Chicago, Illinois: Nystorm, 1954.

13203 **Donnison, F.S.V.** *Public Administration in Burma: A Study in Development During the British Connexian.* London: Royal Institute of International Affairs, 1953.

13204 **Furber, Holden.** *John Company at Work. A Study of European Expansion in India in the Late Eighteenth Century.* Harvard Historical Studies, Vol. 55. Cambridge, Massachusetts: Harvard University Press, 1948.

13205 **Furbringer, Gerhardt.** *Frankreich Kolonisiert Indochina.* (Schriften des Deutschen *Instituts fur Aussenpolitische* Forschung und des Hamburger Instituts fur Ausartige Politik; hrsg. in Gemeinschaft mit dem Deutschen Auslandswissenschaftlichen Institute, Heft 64. Frankreich gegen die Zivilisation, Heft 9. Berlin: Junker und Dunnhaupt Verlag, 1940.

13206 **Furnivall, J.S.** *Netherlands India. A Study of Plural Economy.* Cambridge: Cambridge University Press, 1967.

13207 **Furnivall, J.S.** *Colonial Policy and Practice: A Comparative Study of Burma and Netherlands India.* New York: New York University Press, 1956.

13208 **Gaitonde, Pundlik, and Mani, A.O.** *The Goa Problem.* New Delhi: Indian Council of World Affairs, 1956.

13209 **Goodman, G.T.,** comp. *The American Occupation of Japan: A Retrospective View.* Lawrence: University of Kansas, 1968.

13210 **Great Britain Colonial Office and Great Britain Foreign Office.** *Palestine, Termination of the Mandate, 15th May, 1948.* Reprinted by British Information Services, New York. London: Great Britain Colonial Office, 1948.

13211 **Great Britain Government.** *The Political History of Palestine Under British Administration.* Memorandum by His Brittanic Majesty's Government Presented in 1947 to the United Nations Special Committee on Palestine. First published at Jerusalem, 1947. New York: British Information Services, 1947.

13212 **Gunther, Frances.** *Revolution in India.* New York: Island Press, 1944.

13213 **Hammer, Ellen J.** *The Struggle for Indochina.* Stanford, California: Stanford University Press, 1954.

13214 **Hanna, Paul L.** *British Policy in Palestine.* Washington, D.C.: American Council on Public Affairs, 1942.

13215 **Harvey, G.E.** *British Rule in Burma, 1824-1942.* New York: AMS Press, 1974.

13216 **Hasan, M.** *The Transfer of Power to Pakistan and Its Consequences.* Cambridge: University of Cambridge, 1967.

13217 **Hemery, D.** *Revolutionnaires Vietnamiens et Pouvoir Coloniale en Indochine.* Paris: Maspero, 1975.

13218 **Hope, A. Guy.** *America and Swaraj: The U.S. Role in Indian Independence.* Washington, D.C.: Public Affairs Press, 1968.

13219 **India. Constituent Assembly.** *India's Charter of Freedom.* Delhi: Director of Publicity, Government Printing Office, 1947.

13220 **Institute of Pacific Relations.** *A World on hte Move: A History of Colonialism and Naitonalism and Nationalism in Asia and North Africa from the Turn of the Century to the Bandung Conference.* New York: Institute of Pacific Relations, 1956.

13221 **Khan, Rashid Amhad.** *Government of India Policy Towards Portuguese Possessions in India from 1947-1957.* London, Englnad: London School of Economics, University of London, M.S. Thesis, 1961.

13222 **Khan, Riaz M.** *Untying the Afghan Knot: Negotiating Soviet Withdrawal.* Durham: Duke University Press, 1991.

13223 **Kuno, Yoshi S.** *Japanese Expansion on the Asiatic Continent: A Study in the History of Japan with Special Reference to Her International Relations with China, Korea, and Russia.* Berkeley: University of California Press, 1937.

13224 **Lattimore, Owen.** *Solution in Asia.* Boston: Little Brown, 1945.

13225 **Levy, Roger.** *L'Indochine et ses Traites, 1946.* (Centre d'etudes de politique etrangere, Section d'information, Publication No. 19.) Paris: P. Hartmann, edituer, 1947.

13226 **Lilienthal, Philip E., and Oakie, John H.** *Asia's Captive Colonies.* (Far Eastern Pamphlets No. 6) New York: Institute of Pacific Relations, American Council, 1942.

13227 **Lumby, E.W.R.** *The Transfer of Power to India.* London: Allen & Unwin, 1954.

13228 **Malcom, George A.** *First Malayan Republic: The Story of the Philippines.* boston: Cristopher Publishing House, 1951.

13229 **Marr, D.G.** *Vietnamese Anticolonialism 1885-1925.* Berkeley: University of California Press, 1971.

13230 **Menon, Vapal Pangunni.** *The Transfer of Power in India.* Bombay: Orient Longmans, 1957.

13231 **Mills, Lennox A.** *British Rule in Eastern Asia: A Study of Contemporary Government and Economic Develoopment in British Malaya and Hong Kong.* Minneapolis: University of Minnesota Press, 1942.

13232 **Mills, Lennox A.,** and others. *The New World of Southeast Asia.* Minneapolis: University of Minnesota Press, 1949.

13233 *Muslim Demand for Pakistan by an Indian Muslim Politician.* Indian Paper No. 10. Quebec, Canada: Institute of Pacific Relations, December, 1942.

13234 **Palmier, Leslie H.** *Indonesia and the Dutch.* London: Oxford University Press, 1962.

13235 **Pannikar, K.M.** *Malabar and the Portuguese.* Bombay: D.B. Taraporevala Sons, 1929.

13236 *The Political Events in the Republic of Indonesia: A Review of hte Developments in the Indonesian Republic (Java and Sumatra) Since the Japanese Surrender Together with Statements by the Netherlands and Netherlands Indies Governments, and Complete Text of the Linggadjati Agreement.* New York: Netherlands Information Bureau, 1948.

13237 **Pratt, John T.** *The Expansion of Europe into the Far East.* London: Sylvan Press, 1947.

13238 **Qureshi, M.A.** *British Relations with Pakistan, 1947-1962: A Study of British Policy Towards Pakistan.* Oxford, England: University of Oxford, 1968.

13239 **Rao, R.P.** *Portuguese Rule in India.* New Delhi: Asia Publishing House, 1963.

13240 **Reed, Robert Ronald.** *Origins of the Philippine City: A Comparative Inquiry Concerning Indigenous Southeast Asian Settlement and Spanish Colonial Urbanism.* Berkeley: University of California, Ph.D., 1972.

13241 **Robequain, C.** *The Economic Development of French Indo-China.* London: Oxford University Press, 1944.

13242 **Roth, Andrew.** *Japan Strikes South. The Story of French Indo-China Pasing Under Japanese Domination.* New York: American Council, Institute of Pacific Relations, 1941.

13243 **Robinson, Michael Edson.** *Cultural Nationalism in Colonial Korea, 1920-1925.* Seattle: University of Washington Press, 1988.

13244 **Rowley, Gwyn.** *Israel Into Palestine.* London and New York: Mansell Publishing, 1984.

13245 **Sadik, Muhammad T.,** and **Snavely, William P.** *Bahrain, Quatar, and the United Arab Emirates: Colonial Past, Present Problems, and Future Prospects.* Lexington, Massachusetts: Lexington Book, 1972.

13246 **Scholberg, Henry,** comp. and ed. *A Bibliography on the District Gazetteers of British India.* Zug, Switzerland: Inter Documentation Company A.G., 1970.

13247 **Schwartzberg, Joseph E.** *New India, 1885: British Official Policy and the Emergence of the Indian National Congress.* Berkeley: University of California Press, 1969.

13248 **Seton-William, M.V.** *Britain and the Arab State, 1920-1948.* London: Luz, 1948.

13249 **Sisson, John Richard,** and **Rose, Leo E.** *War and Secession: Pakistan, India, and the Creation of Bangladesh.* Berkeley: University of California Press, 1990.

13250 **Stephens, Ian.** *Pakistan: Old Country New Naiton.* Baltimore, Maryland: Penguin, 1964.

13251 **Stern, Marc I.** *A Comparison of Attitudes Towards the Use of Force and Related Issues of the Participants in the Suez and Goa Situations.* New York City: Columbia University, Master's Thesis, 1966.

13252 **Thompson, Edward** and **Garratt, G.T.** *Rise and Fulfillment of British Rule in India.* New York: AMS Press, 1971.

13253 **Tinker, Hugh.** *Experiment with Freedom: India and Pakistan 1947.* London: Oxford University Press, 1967.

13254 **Tinker, Hugh.** *The Union of Burma: A Study of the First Years of Independence.* London: Oxford University Press, 1957.

13255 **Tinker, Hugh.** *Towards a Free and Sovereign United States of Indonesia.* New York: Netherlands Information Bureau, 1949.

13256 **United Nations.** Research Section. The India-Pakistan Question. Background Paper No. 72. Supersedes Background Paper No. 49. New York: Research Section, U.N., 1949.

13257 **Vandenbosch, Amry.** *The Dutch East Indies: Its Government, Problems, and Politics.* 3rd ed. Berkeley: University of California Press, 1942.

13258 **Viton, Albert.** *American Empire in Asia?* New York: Day, 1943.

13259 **Vlekke, B.H.M.,** ed. *Indonesia's Struggle, 1957-1958.* The Hague: Netherlands Institute of International Affairs, 1959.

13260 **Whiteaway, R.S.** *The Rise of Portuguese Power in India, 1497-1550.* Westminster: Archibald Constable, 1899.

13261 **Wint, G.,** ed. *The British in Asia.* London: Farber and Farber, 1947.

13262 **Wolf, Charles, Jr.** *The Indonesian Story: The Birth, Growth and Structure of the Indonesian Republic.* Issued under the auspices of the American Institute of Pacific Relations. New York: Day, 1948.

Journals

13263 **Amery, L.S.** "La Politique Britannique aux Indes." *Politique Etrangere,* 11e Annee, No. 3 (Juillett, 1946), 237-250.

13264 "Amore di Terra Lontana," pseud. Gli stati indiani prima e dopo la concessione dell'indipendenza all'India. *L'Universo,* Anno 29, Num 4 (Luglio-Agosto, 1949), 417-432.

13265 **Andrus, J. Russell.** "Burma--An Experiment in Self-Government." *Foreign Policy Reports,* 21, No. 19 (December 15, 1945), 258-267.

13266 **Bailey, Sydney D.** "Ceylon's New Status." *Far Eastern Survey,* 17, No. 21 (November 3, 1948), 251-254.

13267 **Bailey, Sydney D.** "The Path to Self-Government in Ceylon." *World Affairs,* 3, No. 2 (April, 1949), 196-206.

13268 **Balachandran, G.** "Towards a Hindoo Marriage: Anglo-Indian Monetary Relations in Interwar India, 1917-35." *Modern Asian Studies,* 28, Part 3 (July, 1994), 615-647.

13269 **Barbour, Nevill.** "Aden and the Arab South." *World Today,* 15, No. 8 (August, 1959), 302-310.

13270 **Batta, K.A.** "Die Raumpolitic der Parteien Indiens." *Zeitschrift fur Geopolitik,* 17 Jahrg, Heft 10 (Oktober, 1940), 470-479.

13271 **Becker, Herbert Theodor.** "Hollandische Kolonialpolitik und das Schulwesen Niederlandisch-Indiens; Eine Kolonialpadagaogische Studie." *Koloniale Rundschau,* 31, Jahrg, Heft 1 (Mai, 1940), 1-37.

13272 **Bennett, G.D.** "The Partition of India." *Trident,* 11 (1949), 56-60.

13273 **Booth, Anne.** "The Burden of Taxation in Colonial Indonesia in the Twentieth Century." *Journal of Southeast Asian Studies,* 11, No. 1 (March, 1980), 91-109.

13274 **Bousquet, G.H.** "The International Position of Netherlands India." *Pacific Affairs,* 12, No. 4 (December, 1939), 379-393.

13275 "Britain's Opportunity in India: A Gulf to be Bridged." *Round Table,* 35, No. 138 (March, 1945), 122-129.

13276 "Britain's Plans for India." *Amerasia,* 9, No. 12 (June 15, 1945), 180-189.

13277 "British Imperial Policy in Asia." *Amerasia,* 9, No. 1 (January 12, 1945), 3-13.

13278 **Brugmans, I.J.** "Trois Siecles et Demi de Relations Hollando-Indonesiennes." *Politique Etrangerre,* 12e annee, No. 4 (Aout-Septembre, 1947), 409-420.

13279 **Brush, John E.** "Divided India." *Journal of Geography,* 47, No. 6 (September, 1948), 209-219.

13280 "Burma: Political Testing Ground." *Amerasia,* 9, No. 13 (June 29, 1945), 195-206.

13281 "Burma: The Struggle for Power." *Round Table,* 37, No. 146 (March, 1947), 146-152.

13282 **Buss, Claude A.** "What Follows Liberation? In the Philippines We Are Pledged to Free and Help Rebuild a Country Whose Independence from Us We Ourselves Have Promised." Reprint: *Fortune,* 30, No. 12 (December, 1944), 126-129+.

13283 **Caroe, Olaf, Sir.** "China in Central Asia: A Challenge to Russia's Empire." *Round Table,* 224 (October, 1966), 379-386.

13284 **Cheng, Joseph Y.S.** "The Post-1997 Government in Hong Kong." *Asian Survey,* 29, No. 8 (August, 1989), 731-748.

13285 **Cima, Ronald J.** "Vietnam in 1988: The Brink of Renewal." *Asian Survey,* 29, No. 1 (January, 1989), 64-72.

13286 **Christian, John L.** "Anglo-French Rivalry in Southeast Asia: Its Historical Geography and Diplomatic Climate." *Geographical Review,* 31, No. 2 (April, 1941), 272-282.

13287 **Christian, John L.** "The Other Side of India." *Pacific Historical Review,* 10, No. 4 (December, 1941), 447-460.

13288 **Crawshaw, Nancy.** "The Republic of Cyprus: From Zurich Agreement to Independence." *World Today,* 16, No. 12 (December, 1960), 526-540.

13289 **Crosbie, A.J.** "Brunei Moves to Independence." *Geographical Magazine,* 51, No. 5 (February, 1979), 329.

13290 **Crowfoot, J.W.** "Greater Syria and the Four Freedoms." *Journal of the Royal Central Asian Society,* 31, Part 2 (May, 1944), 149-157.

13291 **d'Arcy, Jean.** "Confrontation des Theses Francaises et Vietnamiennes." *Politique Etrangere,* 12e annee, No. 3 (Juillet, 1947), 325-344.

13292 **Das, Taraknath.** "The Status of Hyderabad During and After British Rule in India." *American Journal of International Law,* 43, No. 1 (January, 1949), 57-72.

13293 **DeJong, Ellen van Zyll.** "The American Stake in Netherlands India." *Far Eastern Survey,* 9, No. 13 (June 19, 1940), 145-153.

13294 **De la Roche, Jean.** "Indo-China in the New French Colonial Framework." *Pacific Affairs,* 18, No. 1 (March, 1945), 62-75.

13295 **Dennery, Etienne.** "Problemes d'Extreme Orient." *Annales de Geogoraphie,* 46, No. 262 (Juillet 15, 1937), 337-368.

13296 **Dianous, H.J. de.** "Le Tibet et ses Relations Avec la Chine." *Politique Etranger,* 27e annee, No. 1 (February, 1962), 38-72.

13297 **Dutt, Vidya Prakash.** "The Impasse in Indochina." *India Quarterly,* 8, No. 1 (January-March, 1952), 14-31.

13298 **Ellison, Joseph Waldo.** "The Partition of Samoa: A Study in Imperialism and Diplomacy." *Pacific Historical Review,* 8, No. 3 (September, 1939), 259-288.

13299 **Emerson, Rupert.** "The Outlook in Southeast Asia: Netherlands Indies, French Indo-China, British Malaya." *Foreign Policy Reports,* 15, No. 17 (November 15, 1939), 206-216.

13300 "The Empire and the Arab East: Strategy and Its Social Implications." *Round Table,* 138 (March, 1945), 137-142.

13301 "The Empire and the Middle East." *Round Table,* 141 (December, 1945), 26-34.

13302 **Ergil, Dogu.** "Development of Turkish Semi-Colonialism." *Islamic Studies* (Islambad), 18, No. 3 (Autumn, 1979), 183-229.

13303 **Fifield, Russell H.** "The Future of French India." *Far Eastern Survey,* 19, No. 6 (March 22, 1950), 62-64.

13304 **Fisher, Margaret W.** "Goa in Wider Perspective." *Asian Survey,* 2, No. 2 (Apirl, 1962), 3-10.

13305 **Flugal, R.R.** "The Palestine Problem: A Brief Geographical, Historical, and Political Evaluation." *Social Studies,* 48, No. 2 (February, 1957), 43-51.

13306 **Frankel, Joseph.** "The Background in French Indo-China." *World Affairs,* 5, No. 1 (January, 1951), 13-25.

13307 "French Relations with Syria and the Lebanon." *Free France,* Special Issue, 3 (April, 1945), 1-16.

13308 **Furnivall, J.S.** "The Future of Burma, Independence and After." *Pacific Affairs,* 18, No. 2 (June, 1945), 156-168.

13309 **Furnivall, J.S.** "Twilight in Burma: Independence and After." *Pacific Affairs,* 22, No. 2 (June, 1949), 155-172.

13310 "The Future of Burma: A New Balance of East and West." *Round Table,* 139 (June, 1945), 233-239.

13311 **Gassier, Maurice.** "Que Faire en Indochine?" *Politique Etrangere,* 12e annee, No. 2 (Mai, 1947), 132-154.

13312 **Giannini, Amedeo.** "Gli Stati Dell'Indochina Francese." *L'Universo,* 34, No. 5 (September-October, 1954), 677-686; 34, No. 6 (November-December, 1954), 849-860.

13313 **Giannini, Amedeo.** "The Questione di Hong Kong e di Macao." *L'Universo,* 33, No. 1 (January-February, 1953), 1-12.

13314 **Ginsburg, Norton S.** "Should the United States Back the Indochina Settlement." *University of Chicago Round Table,* 850 (July 25, 1954).

13315 "Goa and the Indian Union: Background of the Recent Dispute." *World Today,* 10, No. 12 (December, 1954), 542-550.

13316 **Grajdanzev, Andrew J.** "Formosa (Taiwan) Under Japanese Rule." *Pacific Affairs,* 15, No. 3 (September, 1942), 311-324.

13317 **Green, James Frederick.** "India's Struggle for Independence." *Foreign Policy Reports,* 16, No. 6 (June, 1940), 70-84.

13318 **Grobb, Lorna B.** "Annam Wants Its Freedom." *Asia and the Americas,* 46, No. 10 (October, 1946), 441-444.

13319 **Gutersohn, H.** "Punjab und Die Granze Swischen Indien und Pakistan." *Geographic Helvetica,* 6, No. 1 (Januar, 1951), 16-27.

13320 **Handler, Joseph.** "Indo-China: Eighty Years of French Rule." *Annals of the American Academy of Political and Social Science,* 226 (March, 1943), 129-136.

13321 **Harrison, Tom.** "Sarawak in the Whirlpool of Southeast Asia." *Geographical Magazine,* 31, No. 8 (August, 1958), 378-385.

13322 **Hart, George H.C.** "The Netherlands Indies and Her Neighbors." *Pacific Affairs,* 16, No. 1 (March, 1943), 21-32.

13323 **Hawkins, David C.** "Britian and Malaysia--Another View: Was the Decision to Withdraw Entirely Voluntary or Was Britain Pushed a Little?" *Asian Survey,* 9, No. 7 (July, 1969), 546-562.

13324 **Hendershot, Clarence.** "Burma Compromise." *Far Eastern Survey,* 16, No. 12 (June 18, 1947), 133-138.

13325 **Higa, Mikio.** "Okinawa: Recent Political Developments." *Asian Survey,* 3, No. 9 (September, 1963), 415-426.

13326 **Holland, Sir Robert.** "A British View of India's Problems." *Yale Review,* 31, No. 3 (Spring, 1942), 569-587.

13327 **Homan, Gerlof D.** "The United States and the Netherlands East Indies: The Evolution of American Anticolonialism." *Pacific Historical Review,* 53, No. 4 (November, 1984), 423-446.

13328 **Iimoto, Nobuyuki.** "European Rule of Colonies in South-Eastern Asia: Their History and Their Present Political and Economical Position." *Journal of Geography, Tokyo Geographical Society,* 53, No. 626 (April, 1941), 153-172.

13329 **Ingrams, Harold.** "Aden's Destiny." *Commonwealth Journal,* 6, No. 1 (February, 1963), 11-16.

13330 **Ingrams, Harold.** "The Progress Towards Independence of Aden and the Aden Protectorate." *Journal of the Royal Society for the Encouragement of Arts, Manufactures, and Commerce,* 111, No. 5085 (August, 1963), 756-769.

13331 **Jennings, W. Ivor, Sir.** "The Dominion of Ceylon." *Pacific Affairs,* 22, No. 1 (March, 1949), 21-33.

13332 **Julien, Charles Andre.** "French Difficulties in the Middle East." *Foreign Affairs,* 24, No. 2 (January, 1946), 327-336.

13333 **Kapur, Ashok.** "The Indian Subcontinent: The Contemporary Structure of Power and the Development of Power Relations." *Asian Survey,* 28, No. 7 (July, 1988), 693-710.

13334 **Kattenburg, Paul.** "Political Alignments in Indonesia." *Far Eastern Survey,* 15, No. 19 (September 25, 1946), 289-294.

13335 **Kennedy, Raymond.** "Dutch Plan for the Indies." *Far Eastern Survey,* 15, No. 7 (April 10, 1946), 97-102.

13336 **Kennedy, Raymond.** "Malaya: Colony Without Plan." *Far Eastern Survey,* 14, No. 16 (August 15, 1945), 225-226.

13337 **Kennedy, Raymond.** "Status of British Borneo." *Far Eastern Survey,* 14, No. 17 (August 29, 1945), 243-246.

13338 **Kerr, George H.** "Formosa: Colonial Laboratory." *Far Eastern Survey,* 11, No. 4 (February 23, 1942), 50-55.

13339 **Kerr, George H.** "Sovereignty of the Liuchiu Islands." *Far Eastern Survey,* 14, No. 8 (April 25, 1945), 96-100.

13340 **Khadduri, Majid.** "Iran's Cliam to the Sovereignty of Bahrayn." *American Journal of International Law,* 45, No. 4 (October, 1951), 631-647.

13341 **Khoury, Philips.** "The Tribal Shaykh, French Tribal Policy, and the Nationalist Movement in Syria Between Two World Wars." *Middle Eastern Studies* (London), 18, No. 2 (April, 1982), 180-193.

13342 **Koh, B.C.** "North Korea and Its Quest for Autonomy." *Pacific Affairs,* 38, No. 3-4 (Fall-Winter, 1965-1966), 294-306.

13343 **Kublin, Hyman.** "Okinawa: A Key to the Western Pacific." *United States Naval Institute Proceedings,* 80, No. 12 (December, 1954), 1359-1365.

13344 **Lattimore, Eleanor.** "Indo-China: French Union or Japanese 'Independence'?" *Far Eastern Survey,* 14, No. 10 (May 23, 1945), 132-134.

13345 **Lattimore, Eleanor.** "Report on Sinkiang." *Far Eastern Survey,* 14, No. 7 (April 11, 1945), 77-79.

13346 **Leach, F. Burton.** "The Problem of Burma." *Journal of the Royal Society of Arts,* 93, No. 4695 (July 6, 1945), 409-418.

13347 **Lijphart, A.** "The Indonesian Image of West Iran." *Asian Survey,* 1, No. 5 (July, 1961), 9-15.

13348 **Lo Shiu-hing.** "Decolonization and Political Development in Hong Kong: Citizen Participation." *Asian Survey,* 28, No. 6 (June, 1988), 613-629.

13349 **Lone, Stewart.** "The Japanese Annexation of Korea 1910: The Failure of East Asian Co-Prosperity." *Modern Asian Studies,* 25, Part 1 (February, 1991), 143-173.

13350 **Macfayden, Sir Eric.** "A Political Future for British Malaya." *Pacific Affairs,* 17, No. 1 (March, 1944), 49-55.

13351 **Manners, Ian R.** "The Political Dimension: Colonialism to Nationalism in the Middle East." *Focus,* 22, No. 1 (September, 1971), 6-8.

13352 **May, Jacques M.** "La Politique Coloniale Future et la Situation de l'Indochine." Excerpt: *Renaissance,* 1e annee, Num. 8 (Janvier, 1945), 53-66.

13353 **McClellan, Grant S.** "India's Problems as a Free Nation." *Foreign Policy Reports,* 22, No. 12 (September 1, 1946), 142-155.

13354 **McCune, Shannon.** "Changes in the Sovereignty of the Ryukyu Islands." In University of Florida, Department of Geography, Ryukyu Islands Project. Research and Information Papers, No. 16. Geographical Papers on the s. Gainsville: University of Florida, 1972, 13-29.

13355 **McCune, Shannon.** "The Rhyukyu Islands: Geographic Aspects of a Change in Sovereignty." *Journal of Geography,* 71, No. 6 (September, 1972), 363-369.

13356 **McKay, C.G.R.** "Western Samoa's Independence." *Journal of the Polynesian Society,* 71, No. 1 (March, 1961), 107-110.

13357 **McLeod, John.** "The English Honours System in Princely India, 1925-1947." *Journal of the Royal Asiatic Society,* 4, Part 2 (July, 1994), 237-249.

13358 **Melamid, Alexander.** "Uncertainty in the Sychelles." *Geographical Review,* 68 (April, 1978).

13359 **Merrill, Frederick T.** "The Outlook for Philippine Independence." *Foreign Policy Reports,* 15, No. 13 (September 15, 1939), 154-164.

13360 **Metcalfe, Aubrey, Sir.** "India's Foreign Relations Now and in the Future." *International Affairs,* 21, No. 4 (October, 1945), 485-496.

13361 **Moseley, George V.H.** "New China and Old Macoa." *Pacific Affairs,* 32, No. 3 (September, 1959), 268-276.

13362 **Nath, Paresh.** "Pakistan: Is It God's Gift to the British Empire?" *Asia and the Americas,* 43, No. 10 (October, 1943), 567-570.

13363 **Nelson, Frederick J.,** and **Nelson, Evelyn G.** "Guam-Pacific Outpost." *Asia,* 41, No. 6 (June, 1941), 299-302.

13364 **Netherlands Information Bureau, New York.** *Toward a Free and Sovereign United State of Indonesia.* New York: Netherlands Information Bureau, 1949.

13365 **Nish, Ian.** "Regaining Confidence--Japan After the Loss of Empire." *Journal of Contemporary History,* 15, No. 1 (January, 1980), 181-195.

13366 "The Outlook in India. Can the Present British Plan Solve Britain's Problem?" *Amerasia,* 11, No. 4 (Apirl, 1947), 97-110.

13367 **Owen, G.N.** "The First British Occupation of the Island of Singapore." *Asiatic Review,* 34, No. 117 (January, 1938), 131-139.

13368 **Owen, R.P.** "The British Withdrawal from the Persian Gulf." *World Today,* 28, No. 2 (February, 1972), 75-81.

13369 **Philips, Cyril.** "Was the Partition of India in 1947 Inevitable." *Asian Affairs,* 17, Part 3 (October, 1986), 243-251.

13370 **Phillips, D.R.** "Hong Kong's Edging Towards Local Democracy." *Geography,* 71, No. 2 (1986), 142-146.

13371 **Pillai, A.K.** "A Political Plan for India." *Asiatic Review,* 41, No. 147 (July, 1945), 233-245.

13372 **Porter, Catherine.** "The Future of Philippine-American Relations." *Pacific Affairs,* 16, No. 3 (September, 1943), 261-276.

13373 **Porter, Catherine.** "Japan's Blue-print for the Philippines." *Far Eastern Survey,* 12, No. 11 (May 31, 1943), 109-112.

13374 **Puckle, Sir Frederick.** "The Pakistan Doctrine: Its Origins and Power." *Foreign Affairs,* 24, No. 3 (April, 1946), 526-538.

13375 **Radovanovic, Lyumbomir.** "Liberation of Goa." *Review of International Affairs,* 13 (January 5, 1962), 15-16.

13376 **Rajagopalacharia, Chakravarti.** "Reconciliation in India." *Foreign Affairs,* 23, No. 3 (April, 1945), 422-434.

13377 **Raman, T.A.** "Essentials of an Indian Settlement." *Far Eastern Survey,* 11, No. 20 (October 5, 1942), 205-211.

13378 **Raza, Moonis, and Habeeb, Atiya.** "Characteristics of Colonial Urbanization: A Case Study of the Satellite 'Primacy' of Calcutta, 1850-1921." In *Urbanization in Developing Countries*, S. Manzoor Alam and V.V. Pokshishevsky. Hederabad, India: Osmania University, 1976, 185-218.

13379 **Robequain, Charles.** "Problemes de Colonisation dans les Indes Neerlandaises." *Annales de Geographie*, 37-57 and 49-50, No. 279 (Janvier-Mars, 1940) (Avril-Septembre, 1940), 114-136.

13380 **Rogers, Robert F.** "Guam's Quest for Political Identity." *Pacific Studies*, 12, No. 1 (November, 1988).

13381 **Rosinger, Lawrence K.** "Breaking Up the Japanese Empire." *Foreign Policy Reports*, 20, No. 6 (June 1, 1944), 62-71.

13382 **Rosinger, Lawrence K.** "France and the Future of Indo-China." *Foreign Policy Reports*, 21, No. 5 (May 15, 1945), 54-63.

13383 **Rosinger, Lawrence K.** "Independence for Colonial Asia--The Coast to the Western World." *Foreign Policy Reports*, 19, No. 22 (February 1, 944), 290-303.

13384 **Rosinger, Lawrence K.** "The Philippines--Problems of Independence." *Foreign Policy Reports*, 24, No. 8 (September 1, 1948), 82-95.

13385 **Rueff, Gaston.** "The Future of French Indo-China." *Foreign Affairs*, 23, No. 1 (October, 1944), 140-146.

13386 **Rueff, Gaston.** "Postwar Problems of French Indo-China: Social and Political Aspects." *Pacific Affairs*, 18, No. 3 (September, 1945), 229-245.

13387 **Saint-Mleux, G.** "The French Administration of Indo-China." *Journal of the Royal Central Asian Society*, 33, Part 1 (January, 1946), 25-31.

13388 **Salazar, Oliveira.** "Goa and the Indian Union: The Portuguese View." *Foreign Affairs*, 34, No. 3 (APril, 1956), 418-431.

13389 **Samson, Gerald L.G.** "The Significance of Japan's North Manchurian Colonies." *China Journal*, 30, No. 4 (April, 1939), 191-198.

13390 **Santhanam, K.** "Liberation of Goa." *Indian Review*, 63, No. 1 (January, 1962), 29-30.

13391 **Scammell, G.V.** "INdigenous Assistance in the Establishment of Portuguese Powe in Asia in the Sixteenth Century." *Modern Asian Studies*, 14, Part 1 (February, 1980), 1-11.

13392 **Schiller, A. Arthur.** Autonomy for Indonesia." *Pacific Affairs*, 17, No. 4 (December, 1944), 478-488.

13393 **Selwyn-Clarke, Hilda.** "Hong Kong Dilemma." *Far Eastern Survey*, 16, No. 1 (January 15, 1947), 5-8.

13394 **Sharp, Lauriston.** "French Plan for Indochina." *Far Eastern Survey*, 15, No. 13 (July 3, 1946), 193-197.

13395 **Shiva Rao, B.** "An Indian Report on the Goan Crisis." *Reporter*, 26, No. 2 (January 18, 1962), 26-27.

13396 "Should the United States Stay in the Philippines?" *Asia*, 39, No. 9 (September, 1939), 439-499.

13397 **Singh, Balmiki Prasad.** "Goa and International Law." *Modern Review*, 111, No. 3 (March, 1962), 229-232.

13398 **Singh, Mahendra Prasad.** "The Indian National Movement: A Psycho-Cultural Aapproach." *Indian Political Science Review*, 14, No. 1 (January, 1980), 24-38.

13399 **Smith, R.B.** "The Development of Opposition to French Rule in Southern Vietnam 1880-1940." *Past and Present*, 54 (1972), 94-129.

13400 **Spate, O.H.K.** "Geographical Aspects of the Pakistan Scheme." *Geographical Journal*, 102, No. 3 (September, 1943), 125-136.

13401 **Spry, Graham.** "The Independence of India." *International Journal*, 1, No. 4 (Autumn, 1946), 28-301.

13402 **Srivastava, R.P.** "Politico-Territorial Structure of India During British Period." *National Geographer*, 14, No. 2 (December, 1979), 175-191.

13403 **Stern, Bernard S.** "Cyprus: The British Key to Western Asia." *Social Studies*, 46, No. 2 (February, 1955), 43-49.

13404 **Stewart, John R.** "Japanese Enterprises in North China." *Far Eastern Survey*, 7, No. 9 (May 4, 1938), 99-107.

13405 **Stewart, John R.** "Japan-Manchoukuo Revamp Colonization Schemes." *Far Eastern Survey*, 9, No. 12 (June 5, 1940), 141-142.

13406 **Talbot, Phillips.** "The Independence of India." *Foreign Policy Reports*, 23, No. 7 (June 15, 1947), 74-95.

13407 **Tang, James T.H.** "From Empire Defence to Imperial Retreat: Britain's Postwar China Policy and the Decolonization of Hong Kong." *Modern Asian Studies*, 28, Part 2 (May, 1994), 317-337.

13408 **Thompson, Virginia, and Adloff, Richard.** "Cambodia Moves Toward Independence." *Far Eastern Survye*, 22, No. 9 (August, 1953), 105-111.

13409 **Thompson, Virginia, and Adloff, Richard.** "Empires End in Southeast Asia." *Foreign Policy Associaiton*, 78 (1949), 3-57.

13410 **Ueda, Toshio.** "Legal Status of the British Concession of Tientsin." *Contemporary Japan*, 9, No. 2 (February, 1940), 167-172.

13411 **Vandenbosch, Amry.** "Netherlands Indies: Internal Political Structure." *Department of State Bulletin*, 2, No. 282 (November 19, 1944), 605-609+.

13412 **Van Der Kroef, Justus M.** "Indonesia and the Origins ofDutch Colonial Sovereignty." *Far Eastern Quarterly*, 10, No. 2 (February, 1951), 151-169.

13413 **Van Der Kroef, Justus M.** "Indonesia: Independent in the Cold War." *International Journal*, 7, No. 4 (Autumn, 1952), 283-292.

13414 **van Der Plan, Charles O.** "Some Aspects of Post-war Problems in the Netherlands East Indies: Comparison with Other South-Eastern Asiatic Countries." *Agenda*, 1, No. 4 (October, 1942), 329-338.

13415 **Varma, Lalima.** "Okinawa Before and Since Reversion." *International Studies*, 19, No. 1 (January-March, 1980), 43-57.

13416 **Vinacke, Harold M.** "Implications of Japanese Foreign Policy for the Philippines and Southeastern Asia." *Annals of the American Academy of Political and Social Science*, 226, No. 1 (March, 1943), 50-61.

13417 **Visman, Frans H.** "Provisional Government in the Netherlands East Indies." *Pacific Affairs*, 18, No. 2 (June, 1945), 180-187.

13418 **Wagner, Edward W.** "Failure in Korea." *Foreign Affairs*, 40, No. 1 (October, 1961), 128-136.

13419 **Wallach, Bret.** "Hongkong: Bound and Adrift." *Focus*, 39, No. 3 (Fall, 1989), 17-25.

13420 **Weatherbee, Donald E.** "Portuguese Timor: An Indonesian Dilemma." *Asian Survey*, 6, No. 12 (December, 1966), 683-695.

13421 **Weight, Ernst.** "Pakistan and Indien." In

Universitata Geographisches Institut and Akademie fur Raumforschung und Landsplaung, Festschrift zum 70, Hamburg: Universitat, 1949, 171-183.

13422 **Weulersee, Jacques.** "Problemes d'Irak." *Annales de Geographie*, (Janvier 15, 1934), 49-75.

13423 **White, Oswald.** "Japanese Administration of Korea and Manchuria." *Journal of the Royal Cenral Asian Society*, 30, Part 1 (January, 1943), 19-32; discussion p. 32-36.

13424 **Wilkinson, J.C.** "Britain in the Gulf: Review Article." *Geographical Journal*, 134, No. 4 (December, 1968), 552-554.

13425 **Wilson, Dick.** "The Future of Hong Kong." *World Today*, 20, No. 9 (September, 1964), 395-402.

13426 **Wright, Quincy.** "The Goa Incident." *American Journal of International Law*, 56, No. 3 (July, 1962), 617-632.

13427 **Yanaihara, Tadao.** "Problems of Japanese Administration in Korea." *Pacific Affairs*, 2, No. 2 (June, 1938), 198-207.

AUSTRALIA, OCEANIA AND ANTARCTICA

Books and Journals

13428 **Albinski, Henry S.** "Australia and the Dutch New Guinea Dispute." International Journal, 16, No. 4 (Autumn, 1961), 358-382.

13429 **Asmis, Rudolf.** "Die Farbigenpolitik der Briten auf den Fidji-Inseln." Koloniale Rundschau, 24, Jahrg, Heft 2 (Mai, 1938), 79-96.

13430 "Australia and New Guinea; Trusteeship for a Neolithic Culture." *Round Table*, 195, No. 2 (June, 1959), 240-249.

13431 **Bailey, K.H.** "Dependent Areas of the Pacific." *Foreign Affairs*, 24, No. 3 (April, 1946), 494-512.

13432 **Beaglehole, Ernest.** "Trusteeship and New Zealand's Pacific Dependencies." *Journal of the Polynesian Society, 56, No. 2 (June, 1947), 128-157.*

13433 **Belshau, Cyril S.** Island Administration in the South West Pacific, Government and Reconstruction in New Caledonia, the New Hebrides, and the British Solomon Islands, London: Royal Institute of International Affairs, 1950.

13434 **Belshau, Cyril S.** "Native Administration in South-Eastern Papua." *The Australian Outlook,* 5, No. 2 (June, 1951), 106-115.

13435 **Bhatnagar, A.K.** "West New Guinea." India Quarterly, 7, No. 2 (April-June, 1951), 162-174.

13436 **Bogan, Eugene F.** "Government of the Trust Territory of the Pacific Islands." *The Annals of the American Academy of Political and Social Science,* 267 (January, 1950), 164-174.

13437 **Brookfield, Harold C.** *Colonialism, Development and Independence: The Case of the Melanesian Islands in the South Pacific,* Toronto: Macmillan, 1972.

13438 **Clark, Alan.** "Constitutional Dynamic, Political Risk: Self-determination in New Caledonia, 1986-1987." *Pacific Studies,* 12, No. 1 (November, 1988), 5-22.

13439 **Connell, John.** "Independence, Dependence, and Fragmentation in the South Pacific." *GeoJournal,* 5, No. 6 (1981), 583-588.

13440 **Connell, John.** "The Fight for Kanaky: Decolonisation in South Pacific." *Australian Geographer* (North Ryde, NSW), 18, No. 1 (May, 1987), 57-62.

13441 **Croconbe, R.G.** "Development and Regression in New Zealand's Island Territories." Pacific Viewpoint, 3, No. 2 (September, 1962), 17-32.

13442 **Driver, Marjorie G.** "Cross Sword, and Silver: The Nascent Spanish Colony in the Mariaha Islands." *Pacific Studies,* 11, No. 3 (July, 1988), 21-51.

13443 "Executive Order Placing Certain Islands in the Pacific Ocean Under the Control and Jurisdiction of the Secretary of the Interior. Canton Island and Enderbury Island." Federal Register, 3, No. 46 (March 8, 1938), 609.

13444 **Fisher, Charles A.** "West New Guinea in Its Regional Setting." *Yearbook of World Affairs,* 6 (1952), 189-210.

13445 **Foxcroft, Edmund J.B.** *Australian Native Policy; Its History, Especially in Victoria. Melbourne, London: Melbourne University Press,* in association with Oxford University Press, 1941.

13446 "The Future of West New Guinea, a Dutch Review." World Today, 7, No. 3 (March, 1951), 124-136.

13447 **Gordon, Donald Craigie.** The Australian Frontier in New Guinea, 1870-1885. New York City: Columbia University Press, 1951.

13448 **Gordon, Donald Craigie.** "Beginnings of an Australasian Pacific Policy." Political Science Quarterly, 60, No. 1 (March, 1945), 79-89.

13449 **Griffin, James.** "Papua New Guinea and the British Solomon Islands Protectorate: Fusion or Transfusion?" *Australian Outlook,* 27, No. 3 (December, 1973), 319-328.

13450 **Haas, Anthony.** "Independence Movements in the South Pacific Societies." Pacific View Point, 11, No. 1 (May, 1970), 97-119.

13451 **Hall, Russell E.** "Outposts of Empire in the Southern Pacific." *Far Eastern Survey,* 7, No. 4 (February 16, 1938), 35-43.

13452 **Hasluck, Paul.** Australia's Task in Papua and New Guinea, The Commonwealth Secretary, Melbourne, Victoria: Australian Institute of International Affairs, 1956.

13453 **Hasluck, Paul.** Black Australians; A Survey of Native Policy in Western Australia, 1829-1897, Melbourne: Melbourne University Press, in association with Oxford University Press, 1942.

13454 **Hogbin, H. Ian.** "Local Government for New Guinea." Oceania, 17, No. 1 (September, 1946), 38-66.

13455 **Hudson, W.J.** "New Guinea Mandate: The View from Geneva." Australian Outlook, 22, No. 3 (December, 1968), 302-316.

13456 **Jacobsen, Harold Karan.** "Our 'Colonial' Problem in the Pacific." Foreign Affairs, 39, No. 1 (October, 1960), 56-66.

13457 **Kaplan, Martha.** "Meaning, Agency and Colonial History: Navosavakadua and the *Tuka* Movement in Fiji." *American Ethnologist,* 17, No. 1 (February, 1990), 3-22.

13458 **Kerr, J.R.** "The Political Future of New Guinea." *Australian Outlook,* 13, No. 3 (September, 1959), 181-192.

13459 **Larmour, Peter.** "Alienated Land and Independence in Melanesia." *Pacific Studies,* 8, No. 1 (Fall, 1984), 1-47.

13460 **Lattimore, Eleanor.** *Decline of Empire in the Pacific,* (I.P.R. Pamphlets, No. 25.) New York: American Institute of Pacific Relations, 1947.

13461 **Lavigne, Rene.** "Le statut des iles du Pacifique." *L'Europe Nouvelle,* 21ᵉ annee, No. 1048 (Mars 12, 1938), 258-259.

13462 **Legge, J.D.** *Australian Colonial Policy; A Survey of Native Administration and European Development in Papua.* Sydney: Angus and Robertson, 1956.

13463 Leifer, Michael. "Australia, Trusteeship and New Guinea." *Pacific Affairs*, 36, No. 3 (Fall, 1963), 250-264.

13464 Lowe, W.S., and Airey, W.T.G. "New Zealand Dependencies and the Development of Autonomy." *Pacific Affairs*, 18, No. 3 (September, 1945), 252-272.

13465 Mackie, J.A.C. "The West New Guinea Argument." *Australian Outlook*, 16, No. 1 (April, 1962), 26-46.

13466 Mander, Linden A. "The Future of the Pacific Islands." *Institute of World Affairs*, Interim Proceedings, 21 (1945), 92-102.

13467 Maude, H.E. "South Pacific: Independence and Regionalism in the South Sea Islands." *Round Table*, 243, No. 3 (July, 1971), 369-381.

13468 McDonald, A.H., ed. *Trusteeship in the Pacific.* Published under the auspice of the Australian Institute of International Affairs and the Institute of Pacific Relations. Sydney: ANgus and Robertson, 1949.

13469 Metzemaekers, L. "The Western New Guinea Problem." *Pacific Affairs*, 24, No. 2 (June, 1951), 131-142.

13470 Miller, T.B., ed. *Britain's Withdrawal from Asia. Its Implications for Australia.* Canberra: Strategic nad Defense Studies Centre, Australian National University, 1967.

13471 Morrell, W.P. *Britain in the Pacific Islands.* Oxford: Clarendon Press, 1960.

13472 Munro, L.K. "The Canberra Pact and the Political Geography of the Pacific." *New Zealand Geographical Society*, 1, No. 1 (April, 1945), 48-56.

13473 Murray, J.K. *The Provisional Administration of the Territory of Papua-New Guinea, Its Policy and Its Problems.* Brisbane: Univerity of Queensland, 1949.

13474 Orent, Beatrice, and Reinsch, Pauline. "Sovereignty Over Islands in the Pacific." *American Journal of International Law*, 35, No. 3 (July, 1941), 443-461.

13475 Phillips, P.D. "Australia's Attitude to the Pacific Dependencies." *Pacific Affairs*, 18, No. 1 (March, 1945), 76-83.

13476 Smith, Clifford Neal. "America and the Pacific Islands." *American Perspective*, 2, No. 5 (October. 1948), 243-253.

13477 Southwood, Julie. "Papua New Guinea: The Second Colonisation." *Journal of Contemporary Asia*, 10, Nos. 1-2 (1980), 155-165.

13478 Spencer, Michael, and Connell, Alan Ward John. *New Caledonia: Essays in Nationalism and Dependency.* St. Jucia: University of Queensland Press, 1988.

13479 Taylor, Alastair M. "'Nederlands Nieuw-Guinea' Becomes 'Irian Barat.'" *International Journal*, 17, No. 4 (Autumn, 1962), 429-435.

13480 Van Der Kroef, Justus M. "Australia and the West Irian Problem." *Asian Survey*, 10, No. 6 (June, 1970), 483-500.

13481 Van Der Kroef, Justus M. "Recent Developments in West New Guinea." *Pacific Affairs*, 34, No. 3 (Fall, 1961), 279-291.

13482 Van Der Kroef, Justus M. "West New Guinea in the Crucible." *Political Science Quarterly*, 75, No. 4 (December, 1960), 519-538.

13483 Van Der Kroef, Justus M. "The West New Guinea Problem." *World Today*, 17, No. 11 (November, 1961), 489-502.

13484 Van der Veur, Paul W. "The Political Future of Papua-New Guinea." *Australian Outlook*, 20, No. 2 (August, 1966), 200-203.

13485 Walker, Leslie W. "Guam's Seizure by the United States in 1898." *Pacific Historical Review*, 14, No. 1 (March, 1945), 1-12.

13486 Ward, John M. *British Policy in the South Pacific 1786-1893.* Sydney: Australasu Publishing, 1948.

13487 Ward, R. Gerard, and Ballard, J.A. "In Their Own Image: Australia's Impact on Papua New Guinea and Lessons for Future Aid." *Australian Outlook*, 30, No. 3 (December, 1976), 439-458.

13488 West, F.J. "The New Guinea Question: An Australian View." *Foreign Affairs*, 39, No. 3 (April, 1961), 504-511.

13489 "The West New Guinea Dispute." *Round Table*, 207, No. 2 (June, 1965), 300-305.

13490 Wiens, Herold J. *Pacific Island Bastions of the United States.* Princeton, NJ: Van Nostrand, 1962.

13491 Wolfers, Edward P. "Papua New Guinea on the Verge of Self-Government." *World Today*, 28, No. 7 (July, 1972), 320-326.

EUROPE

Books

13492 **Afonso dos Santos, Alvaro.** Breves conceitos para um ideario de colonizacao portuguesa. Lisboa: Sociedade de geografia de Lisboa. Semana das colonias de I., 1945.

13493 **Bade, Klaus J.,** ed. Imperialismus und Kolonialmission: Kaiserliches Deutschland und Koloniales Imperium. 2. Auf 1. Wiesbaden: Steiner, 1984.

13494 **Berard, Victor.** British Imperialism and Commercial Supremacy. New York: Longmans, 1906.

13495 **Betts, R.F.** Assimilation and Association in French Colonial Theory (1890-1914). New York City: Columbia University Press, 1961.

13496 **Bilmanis, Alfred.** Latvia; Between the Anvil and the Hammer. Washington, D.C.: Latvian Legation, 1945.

13497 **Bilmanis, Alfred,** comp. Latvian-Russian Relations; Documents. Washington, D.C.: Latvian Legation, 1944.

13498 **Brand, Jack.** The National Movement in Scotland. London: Routledge, 1978.

13499 **British Information.** Services Reference Division. Towards Self-Government in the British Colonies; an Account of the Growth of Political Responsibility and of the Steps by which Democratic Institutions are Being Built Up. Rev. (I.D. 598.) New York: British Information Services, 1947.

13500 **British Information.** The V.K. Dependencies in Brief. New York: British Information Service, 1958.

13501 **Brunschwig, Henri.** *La colonisation francaise, du pacte colonial a l'Unkon Francaise.* Paris: Calmann-Levy, Editeurs, 1949.

13502 **Bryce, J.** The Holy Roman Empire. New York: Macmillan, 1919.

13503 **Burns, Sir Allen.** In Defense of Colonies. British Colonial Territories in International Affairs. London: Allen & Unwin, 1957.

13504 **Carrington, C.E.** The British Overseas Exploits of a Nation of Shopkeepers. Cambridge, England: University Press, 1950.

13505 **Carrington, C.E.** The Liquidation of the British Empire. London: George C. Harrap, 1961.

13506 **Chamberlain, M.E.** Decolorization: The Fall of the European Empires. New York: Basil Blackwell, 1985.

13507 **Clarence-Smith, Gervase.** *The Third Portuguese Empire, 1825-1975: A Study in Economic Imperialism.* Manchester: Manchester University Press, 1985.

13508 **Clayton, Anthony.** *The British Empire as a Superpower, 1919-39.* Houndmills: Macmillan, 1986.

13509 **Clemens, Walter C., Jr.** *Baltic Independence and Russian Empire.* New York: St. Martin's Press, 1991.

13510 **Crocker, Walter Russell.** *On Governing Colonies, Being an Outline of the Real Issue and a Comparison of the British, French and Belgian Approach to Them.* London: Allen & Unwin, 1947.

13511 **Crozier, A.J.** *Appeasement and Germany's Lost Bid for Colonies.* New York: St. Martin's Press, 1988.

13512 **de Alamda, Jose,** and Others. Colonial Administration by European Powers. A Series of Papers Read at King's College, London, 14 November to 12 December 1946. London: Royal Institute of International Affairs, 1947.

13513 **de Alamda, Jose,** and Others. Portuguese Colonial Administration. London: Royal Institute of International Affairs, Colonial Administration by European Powers, 1947.

13514 **de Favitski de Probobysz, A.** Repertoire bibliographique de la litterature militaire et coloniale francaise depuis cent ans. Leige, Belgigue: Imp. G. Thone, 1935.

13515 **Demangeon, Albert.** Le declin de l'Europe. Paris: Payot, 1920.

13516 **Demangeon, Albert.** L'Emprire Britannique: Etude de geographie coloniale. Paris: Armand Colin, 1923.

13517 **Deschamps, Hubert.** Les Methodes et les Doctrines Coloniales de la France (du XVIc siecle a nos jaurs). Paris: Armand Colin, 1953.

13518 **Devese, Michel.** *La France de'outre-mer, de l'empire colonial a l'union Francaise, 1938-1947.* Paris: Hachette, 1948.

13519 **Dobie, Edith.** Malteis Road to Independence. Norman, Oklahoma: University of Oklahoma Press, 1967.

13520   *Downing Street and the Colonies.* Report submitted to the Fabian Colonial Bureau. London: Allen & Unwin and the Fabian Society, 1942.

13521   **Drower, George.** *Britain's Dependent Teritories: A Fistful of Islands.* Aldershot: Dartmouth, 1992.

13522   **Easton, Stuart C.** *The Twilight of European Colonialism.* London: Methuen, 1961.

13523   **Fawcett, C.B.** Political Geography of the British Empire. London: Ginn, 1933.

13524   **Fernau, Friedrich Wilhelm.** Imperialismus und arabische Frage. (Arabische Welt.) Heidelberg, etc.: Kurt Vowinckel, 1943.

13525   **Frank, T.M.** Roman Imperialism. New York: Macmillan, 1914.

13526   **Freedman, Lawrence.** *Britain and the Falklands War.* Oxford: Blackwell Scientific Publications, 1988.

13527   **Freyre, Gilberto.** *O mundo que o Portugues criou; aspectos das relacoes sociaes e de cultura do Brasil com Portugal e as colonias poruguesas.* (Colecao Documentos brasileiros, 28.) Rio de Janeiro: Livraria J. Olympio, editora, 1940.

13528   **Freyre, Gilberto.** *The Portuguese and the Tropics: Suggestions inspired by the Portuguese Methods of Integrating Autocthonous Peoples and Cultures Differing from the European in a New, or Lusto-Tropical Complex of Civilization.* Lisbon: Executive Committee for the Commemoration of the 5th Centenary of the Death of Prince Henry the Navigator, 1961.

13529   **Frochot, Michel.** L'empire colonial portugais: organisation constittutionnelle, politique et administrative. Lisbonne: Editions SPN, 1942.

13530   **Goldberg, Harvey.** French Colonialism. Progress of Poverty? New York: Rinehart, 1959.

13531   **Great Britain, Treaties**, etc. State Treaty for the Re-establishment of an Independent and Democratic Austria, Vienna, May 15, 1955. London: Great Britain, Treaties, etc., 1957.

13532   **Great Britain, Treaties**, etc. *Treaty Concerning the Establishment of the Republic of Cyprus with Exchanges of Notes.* London: Great Britain Treaties, etc., 1961.

13533   **Great Britain Treaties**, etc. *Treaty of Peace with Hungary; Treaty Series No. 54, February 10, 1947.* Paris: LMD, 1948.

13534   **Gregory, Robert C.** India and East Africa: A History of Race Relations within the British Empire, 1890-1939. Oxford: Clarendon Press, 1971.

13535   **Hailey, William Malcolm, Baron.** Britain and Her Dependencies. (Longman's pamphlets on the British Commonwealth.) London: Longmans Green, 1943.

13536   **Hardy, Georges.** Histoire Sociale de la Colonisation Francaise. Paris: Larose, 1953.

13537   **Havinden, Michael,** and **Meredith, David.** *Colonialism and Development: Britain and Its Tropical Colonies, 1850-1960.* London: Routledge, 1993.

13538   **Hechter, M.** Internal Colonialism: The Celtic Fringe in British National Development. Berkeley: University of California Press, 1974.

13539   **Heyes, Th.** Les eaux dans l'expansion coloniale belge; contribution bibliographique elaboree sous la direction de Th. Heyse. Bruxelles: Librairie Falk fils, 1939. "Publication editee avec l'appui de la Commission coloniale de la grande saison internationale de l'eau. Leige, 1939."

13540   **Howe, Stephen.** *Anticolonialism in British Politics: The Left and the End of Empire, 1918-1964.* Oxford: Clarendon Press, 1993.

13541   **Johannsen, G. Kurt,** and **Kraft, H.H.** *Germany's Colonial Problem.* London: Butterworth, 1937.

13542   **Knorr, Klaus.** *British Colonial Theories, 1570-1850.* Toronto: University of Toronto Press, 1944.

13543   **Kolarz, Walter.** *Russia and Her Colonies.* London: Philip and Sons, 1952.

13544   **Labaree, Leonard W.** *Royal Government in America: A Study of the British Colonial System Before 1783.* New Haven, Connecticut: Yale University Press, 1930.

13545   **Lantzeff, George V.** *Siberia in the Seventeenth Century; A Study of the Colonial Administration.* (Univ. of California Publications in History, Vol. 30.) Berkeley: Univ. of California Press, 1943.

13546   **Laurentie, H.** *Recent Developments in French Colonial Policy.* Paris: Royal Institute of International Affairs, Colonial Administration by European Powers, 1947.

13547   **MacDonald, Donald C.** *Evolution of Empire: Britain's Plans for Her Colonies.* (Behind the Headlines, 7, No. 5.) Toronto: Canadian Association for Adult Education, and Canadian Institute of International Affairs, 1947.

13548 **Meyer, Richard M.** *Das Deutsche Kolonialreich; eine lander-kunde der deutschen schutz-gebiete.* Leipzig, Wien: Verlag des Bibliographischen Instituts, 1909-1910.

13549 **Pavel, Pavel.** *Transylvania and Danubian Peace.* London: New Europe Publishing, 1943.

13550 **Pinion, Rene.** L'Empire de la Mediterranee. Paris: Perrin, 1904.

13551 **Platt, Raye R.**, and Others. The European Possessions in the Caribbean Area. New York: American Geographical Society, 1941.

13552 **Power, Thomas F., Jr.** Jules Ferry and the Renaissance of French Imperialism. New York: King's Crown Press, 1944.

13553 **Priestley, Herbert Ingram.** France Overseas; a Study of Modern Imperialism. New York: Appleton-Century, 1938.

13554 **Royal Institute of International Affairs.** The French Colonial Empire. Information Department Papers, No. 25. First published in 1940. London: Royal Institute of International Affairs, 1941.

13555 **Royal Institute of International Affairs.** *Great Britain and Palestine, 1915-1939.* The ed. of January 1937 rev. and enl. *Information Department* Papers No. 20a. London: Royal Institute of International Affairs, 1939.

13556 **Royal Institute of International Affairs.** *The Italian Colonial Empire, with Chapters on the Dodecanese and Albania.* Information Department Papers, No. 27. London: Royal Institute of International Affairs, 1940.

13557 **Royal Institute of International Affairs.** *Netherlands Overseas Territories.* Information Department Papers, No. 28. London: Royal Institute of International Affairs, 1941.

13558 *Russischer Kolonialismus in der Ukraine, Berichte und Dokumente.* Munchen: Ukrainischer Verlga in Munchen, 1962.

13559 **Sanders, David.** *Losing an Empire, Finding a Role: British Foreign Policy Since 1945.* Houndmills: Macmillan, 1990.

13560 **Schechter, Stephen L.** International Dependance Relations: A Study of the Transactional Ties of the Former British and French Dependencies. Pittsburgh, Pennsylvania: University of Pittsburgh, Ph.D., 1972.

13561 **Schulte-Althoff, F.J.** Studien zur politischen Wissenschaftsgeschichte der deutschen Geographie im Zeitalter des Imperialismus. Bochumer Geographische Arbeiten 9. Paderborn: Schoningh, 1971.

13562 **Silva, Fernando Emygdio da.** L'essor colonial portugais. (Conference) ("Conference faite a Rio de Janeiro...le 24 Novembre 1939.") Lisbonne: Secretariado da propaganda nacional, 1941.

13563 **Stahl, Kathleen M.** British and Soviet Colonial Systems. London: Faber and Fabu, 1951.

13564 **Thurnwald, Richard.** Koloniale Gestaltung. Methoden und Probleme uberseeischer Ausdehnung. Hamburg: Hoffmann und Campe, 1939.

13565 **U.S. Department of State.** Office of the Geographer. *Portugal and Overseas Provinces.* Washington, D.C.: U.S. Department of State, 1961.

13566 **Vedovato, G.; Moreno, M.M.; and Mangano, G.** *The Question of the Administration of Italian Colonies in Africa Under Trusteeship.* Publication No. 35. Firenze: Florence University, Center of Colonial Studies, 1947.

13567 **Walker, Eric A.** The British Empire: Its Structure and Spirit. London: Oxford University Press, 1943.

13568 **Wauters, Arthur.** *La Nouvelle Politique Coloniale.* Bruxelles: Institute Royal Colonial Belege, Section des Sciences morales et Politiques, Memoires, Collection in-8, Tohu 12, Fase. 2, 1955.

13569 **Western, John.** The End of European Primacy, 1971-1945. London: Blandford Press, 1965 or New York: Harper & Row, Colophon edition, 1967.

13570 **Wheare, K.C.** The Statute of Westminster and Dominion Status. Oxford: Oxford University Press, 1953.

13571 **Williamson, J.A.** Cambridge History of the British Empire. Cambridge: University Press, 1929.

13572 **Williamson, J.A.** *The French Colonial Empire.* London: Royal Institute of International Affairs, 1940.

13573 **Williamson, J.A.** Germany's Claim to Colonies. London: Royal Institute of International Affairs, 1938.

13574 **Williamson, J.A.** Short History of British Expansion. London: Macmillan, 1945.

13575 **Wilson, Thomas,** ed. Ulster Under Home Rule; A Study of the Political and Economic Problems of Northern Ireland. London: Oxford University Press, 1955.

Journals

13576 "Administration of Countries Under German Control. III. Czechoslovakia, Denmark, Norway, Low Countries, and Rumania." *Bulletin of International News*, 18, No. 2 (January 25, 1941), 59-67.

13577 **Amaral, Ilidio do.** "A irrupcao de estados-insulares apos a segunda guerra mundial: um facto novo de geografia politica." *Finisterra* (Lisboa), 22, No. 44 (1987), 297-359.

13578 **Brenner, R.** "The Social Basis of English Colonial Expansion, 1550-1650. *Journal of Economic History*, 32, No. 1 (March, 1972), 361-384.

13579 **Breslauer, George W.** "Observations on Soviet Imperial Disintegration." *Post-Soviet Geography*, 35, No. 4 (April, 1994), 216-220.

13580 **Burpee, Lawrence J.** "Poland's Fight for Freedom." *Canadian Geographical Journal*, 19, No. 4 (October, 1939), 213-227.

13581 **Calchi Novati, G.P.** "Cipro,nuova repubblica indipendente." *Universo*, 41, No. 2 (March-April1961), 231-244.

13582 **Calchi Novati, Giampaolo.** "Italy in the Triangle of the Horn: Too Many Corners for a Half Power." *The Journal of Modern African Studies*, 32, No. 3 (September, 1994), 369-385.

13583 **Chilcote, Ronald H.** "Politics in Portugal and Her Empire." *World Today*, 17, No. 9 (September, 1961), 376-387.

13584 "Colonial Development in the British Empire." *Nature*, 151, No. 3829 (March 20, 1943), 315-317.

13585 **Cora, Giuliano.** "La questione coloniale italiana dopo il trattato di pace." *L'Universo*, Anno 27, No. 3 (Maggio-Giugno, 1947), 261-271.

13586 **Crawshaw, Nancy.** "The Republic of Cyprus: From Zurich Agreement to Independence." *World Today*, 16, No. 12 (1960), 526-540.

13587 **Darwin, John.** "British Decolonization Since 1945: A Pattern or a Puzzle?" *Journal of Imperial and Commonwealth History*, 11, No. 1 (January, 1984), 187-209.

13588 **Demangeon, Albert.** "Problemes britanniques." *Annales de Geographie,* 31, No. 169 (Janvier 15, 1922), 15-36.

13589 **de Passos, Franciso.** "A capacidade colonial dos portugueses." *Boletim da Sociedade de geografia de Lisboa*, Serie 59ª, Nos. 1-2 (Janeiro-Fevereiro, 1941), 59-67.

13590 **Dowdall, J.** "Mintoff's Malta: Problems of Independence." *World Today*, 28, No. 5 (May, 1972), 189-195.

13591 **Dvoichenco-Markow, Demetrius.** "The Ukranian Cossacks in the Early Anti-Ottoman Struggle for Independence of Moldavia." *East European Quarterly*, 14, No. 2 (Summer, 1980), 241-250.

13592 **Foncin, P.** "La France Experieure (1891)." *Annales de Geographie,*(1891), 1-8.

13593 **Frost, Richard A.** "Reflections on British Colonial Policy." *Pacific Affairs*, 18, No. 4 (December, 1945), 309-320.

13594 **Galloway, Patricia.** "'So Many Little Republics': British Negotiations with the Choctaw Confederacy, 1765." *Ethnohistory,* 41, No. 4 (Fall, 1994), 513-537.

13595 **Gore, Rick.** "When the Greeks Went West." *National Geographic*, 186, No. 5 (November, 1994), 2-37.

13596 **Griffin, Joan.** "Germany's First Colony. (Slovakie)." *The Contemporary Review*, 894 (June, 1940), 693-699.

13597 **Hadsel, Winifred N.** "Political Currents in Liberated Europe." *Foreign Policy Reports*, 21, No. 6 (June 1, 1945), 66-80.

13598 **Haines, O. Grove.** "The Problem of the Italian Colonies." *The Middle East Journal*, 1, No. 4 (October, 1947), 417-431.

13599 **Harrison-Church, R.J.** "The Problem of the Italian Colonies." *World Affairs*, 3, N.S. No. 1 (January, 1949), 77-86.

13600 **Hempenstall, Peter J.** "Resistance in the German Pacific Empire: Towards a Theory of Early Colonial Response." *Journal of the Polynesian Society*, 84, No. 1 (March, 1975), 5-24.

13601 **Hogg, Quintin.** "British Policy: A Conservative Forecast." *Foreign Affairs*, 22, No. 1 (October, 1943), 28-44.

13602 **Jones, Howard Mumford.** "Origins of the Colonial Idea in England." *Proceedings of the American Philosophical Society*, 85, No. 5 (September 30, 1942), 448-465.

13603 **Knott, A.J.** "The Problem of the Italian Colonies." *Royal Engineers Journal*, 61, No. 4 (December, 1947), 364-370.

13604 **Kuyper, Dirk.** "Holland's Eastern Empire." *Amerasia*, 5, No. 5 (July, 1941), 202-208.

13605 **Lapie, P.O.** "The New Colonial Policy of France." *Foreign Affairs*, 23, No. 1 (October, 1944), 104-111.

13606 **Lloyd, Trevor.** "Greenland Gains Provincial Home Rule." *Canadian Geographie*, 99, No. 1 (August/September, 1979), 32-37.

13607 **Lugard, Frederick Dealtry, 1st Baron.** "British Colonial Policy." *Britain Today*, 67 (November 28, 1941), 4-9.

13608 **MacLaughlin, James G., and Agnew, John A.** "Hegemony and the Regional Question: The Political Geography of Regional Industrial Policy in Northern Ireland, 1945-1972." *Association of American Geographers Annals*, 76, No. 2 (June, 1986), 246-261.

13609 **Marchiori, Mario.** "La Colonizzazione Russa Dell' Alaska." *L'Universo*, Anno 74, No. 1 (Gennaio-Febbraio, 1994), 60-69.

13610 **Massicot, S.** "Effects su la Nationalite Francaise de l'accession a l'independence des Territoires ayant ete sous las Souverain ete Francaise (The Consequences of Granting Independence to Former French Colonies on French Nationality)." *Population*, 41, No. 3 (1986), 533-546.

13611 **Massicot, S.** "La Nationalite Francaise. Attribution et Acquisition (French Nationality. Acquired or Granted)." *Population*, 41, No. 2 (1986), 349-370.

13612 **Matthews, Lawrence.** "Italian Colonies: Politics and Realities." *American Perspective*, 2, No. 5 (October, 1948), 218-230.

13613 **McKay, Vernon.** "The Future of Italy's Colonies." *Foreign Policy Reports*, 21, No. 20 (January 1, 1946), 270-279.

13614 **Megret, Helene.** "L'Empire britannique et la Conference d'Ottawa." *Annales de Geographie*, 42, No. 237 (May, 1933), 372-390.

13615 **Moskowitz, Moses.** "Three Years of the Protectorate of Bohemia and Moravia." *Political Science Quarterly*, 57, No. 3 (September, 1942), 353-375.

13616 **Oliveira Boleo, Jose de.** "Causas determinantes da autonomia politica de Portugal." *Boletimda Sociedade de geografia de Lisboa*, 57ª serie, Nos. 7 e 8 (Julho e Agosto, 1939), 351-362; Nos. 9-10 (Setembro-Outubro, 1939), 441-457.

13617 **Olmi, M.** "Dall' Unione Francese alla Comunita rinovata." *Civitas*, 11, No. 11 (November, 1960), 31-48.

13618 **Ortlieb, Heinz-Dietrich.** "Die koloniale Wirtschaftspolitik Belgiens." *Wirtschaftsdienst*, 26, Jahrg, Nr. 17 (April 21, 1941), 384-386.

13619 **Pelissier, Rene.** "Spain's Discreet Decolinization." *Foreign Affairs*, 43, No. 3 (April, 1965), 519-527.

13620 **Pfalz, Richard.** "Italien als Kolonialmacht." *Geographischer Anzeiger*, 43, Jahrg, Heft 17-18(September, 1942), 322-334.

13621 **Picard, Roger.** "Les relation commerciales de la France avec sonempire colonial." *L'Actualite Economique*, 21ᵉ annee, 1, No. 4 (Aout-Septembre, 1945), 336-351.

13622 **Pringle, D.G.** "The Northern Ireland Conflict: A Framework for Discussion." *Antipode*, 12, No. 1 (Summer, 1980), 28-38.

13623 **Punnssalo, V.I.** "The Reality of Finlandization-Living Under the Soviet Shadow." *Conflict Series*, 93 (1978), 2-13.

13624 **Quarles, Willem.** "Hollands kolonialvalde." *Jorden Runt*, Arg. 12 (September, 1940), 417-428.

13625 **Read, David.** "Colonialism and Coherence: The Case of Captain John smith's *Generalle Historie of Virginia*." *Modern Philology*, 91, No. 4 (May, 1994), 428-448.

13626 **Robbins, Keith.** "'This Grubby Wreck of Old Glories': The United Kingdom and the End of the British Empire." *Journal of Contemporary History*, 15, No. 1 (January, 1980), 87-95.

13627 **Rubinstein, Alvin Z.** "Soviet Client-States: From Empire to Commonwealth?" *Orbis*, 35, No. 1 (Winter, 1991), 69-78.

13628 **Ryckmans, Pierre.** "Belgian 'Colonialism'." *Foreign Affairs*, 34, No. 1 (October, 1955), 9-101.

13629 **Sallnow, John.** "Baltic Facae of Independence." *Geographical*, 66, No. 12 (December, 1994), 24-26.

13630 **Sallnow, John.** "The Bear Wakes Up." *Geographical*, 66, No. 11 (November, 1994), 38-40.

13631 **Schacht, H.** "Germany's Colonial Demands." *Foreign Affairs*, 15, No. 2 (January, 1937), 223-233.

13632 **Schoenfeld, H.F. Arthur.** "Soviet Imperialism in Hungary." *Foreign Affairs*, 26, No. 3 (April, 1948), 554-566.

13633 **Scramuzza, Vincent M.** "Greek and English Colonization." *The American Historical Review*, 44, No. 2 (January, 1939), 303-315.

13634 **Seton-Watson, Christopher.** "Italy's Imperial Hangover." *Journal of Contemporary History*, 15, No. 1 (January, 1980), 169-179.

13635 **Simnett, W.E.** "Britain's Colonies in the War." *Foreign Affairs*, 19, No. 3 (April, 1941), 655-664.

13636 **Smith, Raymond A.** "The Status of the Kaliningrad Oblast Under International Law." *Lituanus,* 38, No. 1 (1992), 7-52.

13637 **Stewart, J.F.** "The Restitution of the German Colonies." *Scottish Geographical Magazine,* 54, No. 1 (January, 1938), 19-28.

13638 **Stafford, F.E.** "The Ex-Italian Colonies." *International Affairs*, 25, No. 1 (January, 1949), 47-55.

13639 **Shtromas, Alexander.** "Prospects for restoring the Baltic States' Independence: A View on the Prerequisites and possibilities of Their Realization." *Journal of Baltic Studies*, 17, No. 3 (Fall, 1986), 256-279.

13640 **Tate, H.R.** "The Italian Colonial Empire." *Journal of the Royal African Society*, 40, No. 159 (April, 1941), 146-158.

13641 **Townsend, Mary E.** "The German Colonies and the Third Reich." *Political Science Quarterly*, 53, No. 2 (June, 1938), 186-206.

13642 **Treadgold, Donald W.** "Siberian Colonization and the Futureof Asiatic Russia." *Pacific Historical Review*, 25, No. 1 (February, 1956), 47-54.

13643 **Vardys, V. Stanley.** "Soviet Colonialism in the Baltic States: A Note on the Nature of Modern Colonialism." Lituanus, Lithuanian Quarterly, 10, No. 2 (Summer, 1964), 5-23.

13644 **Weseling, H.L.** "Post-Imperial Holland." *Journal of Contemporary History*, 15, No. 1 (January, 1980), 125-142.

CHAPTER XV

INTERNATIONAL POLITICAL GEOGRAPHIC PATTERNS

POLITICAL GEOGRAPHY OF THE THIRD WORLD DEVELOPMENT NATIONS AND NON-ALIGNMENT

Books

13645 **Arhin, Kwame,** ed. *The Life and Work of Kwame Nkrumah: Papers of a Symposium Organized by the Institute of African Studies, University of Ghana, Legon.* Trenton: Africa World Press, Inc., 1993.

13646 **Allison, Roy.** *The Soviet Union and the Strategy of Non-alignment in the Third World.* Cambridge: Cambridge University Press, 1988.

13647 **Almond, Gabriel A.,** and **Coleman, James S.** *The Politics of the Developing Areas.* Princeton, New Jersey: Princeton University Press, 1960.

13648 **Almond, Gabriel A.; Coleman, James S.,** and **Powell, G.B.** *Comparative Politics: A Developmental Approach.* Boston: Little Brown, 1966.

13649 **Andrain, Charles F.** *Political Change in the Third World.* Boston: Unwin Hyman, 1988.

13650 **Balasubramanyam, V.N.** *International Transfer of Technology to India.* New York: Praeger, 1973.

13651 **Banks, A.L.** *The Development of Tropical and Subtropical Countries with Particular Reference to Africa.* London: E. Arnold, 1954.

13652 **Bell, Morag.** *Contemporary Africa: Development, Culture and the State.* White Plains, New York: Longman, 1986.

13653 **Bersch, G.K.; Clark, R.P.;** and **Ward, D.M.** *Comparing Political Systems: Power and Policy in Three Worlds.* New York: John Wiley & Sons, 1978.

13654 **Binder, et al.** *Crises and Sequences in Political Development.* Princeton, New Jersey: Princeton University Press, 1971.

13655 **Brandt, W.** *Common Crisis North-South: Co-operation for World Recovery.* London: Pan, 1983.

13656 **Brandt, W.** *North-South: A Programme for Survival. Report of the Independant Commission of International Development Issues.* London: Pan, 1980.

13657 **Brenner, Philip** and others. *The Cuba Reader: The Making of a Revolutionary Society.* New York: Grove Press, 1989.

13658 **Brown, Lester R.** *The Interdependence of Nations.* New York: Foreign Policy Association, 1972.

13659 **Callard, Keith B.** *Pakistan's Foreign Policy: An Interpretation.* 2nd ed. New York: Institute of Pacific Relations, 1959.

13660 **Calvez, Jean-Yves.** *Politics and Society in the Third World.* Maryknoll, New York: Orbis Books, 1973.

13661 **Cammack, Paul; Pool, David;** and **Tordoff, William.** *Third World Politics: A Comparative Introduction.* Houndmills: Macmillan, 1988.

13662 **Chaliand, Gerard.** *Revolutions in the Third World.* Rev. ed. New York: Viking, 1989.

13663 **Clapham, Christopher.** *Third World Politics: An Introduction.* London: Croom Helm, 1985.

13664 **Clinard, Marshall Barron,** and **Abbott, Daniel J.** *Crime in Developing Countries: A Comparative Perspective.* New York: Wiley-Interscience/Wiley, 1973.

13665 **Coale, A.J.,** and **Hoover, E.M.** *Population Growth and Economic Development in Low Income Countries: A Case of India's Prospects.* Princeton, New Jersey: Princeton University Press, 1958.

13666 **Dale, Edmund H.** *Spotlight on the Caribbean, a Microcosm of the Third World.* Regina, Canada: University of Regina, Department of Geography, Regina Geographical Studies, No. 2, 1977.

13667 **Darkoh, Michael Bernard Kwesi.** *Industrial Location in a Developing Country: A Study of the Distribution of Manufacturing in Ghana in Relation to Selected Socio-Economic Characteristics.* Madison: University of Wisconsin, Ph.D., 1971.

13668 **Dean, Vera Micheles.** *The Nature of the Non-Western World.* New York: New American Library, 1957.

13669 **Demas, W.G.** *The Economics of Development in Small Countries with Special Reference to the Caribbean.* Montreal: McGill University Press, 1965.

13670 **De Mille, John B.** *Strategic Minerals.* New York: McGraw-Hill, 1947.

13671 **De Souza, A.** *The Underdevelopment and Modernization of the Third World.* Comments on College Geography, Paper No. 28. Washington, D.C.: Association of American Geographers, 1974.

13672 **Dharamdasani, M.D.,** ed. *Politics in Contemporary South Asia.* Varanasi: Shalimar, 1988.

13673 **Dodd, C.H.,** ed. *The Political, Social and Economic Development of Northern Cyprus.* Huntington, UK: The Eothen Press, 1993.

13674 **Elim, Rage Sayed.** *An Analytical Approach to the Study of Some Aspects of Neutralism.* Washington, D.C.: American University, Ph.D., 1967.

13675 **Eralp, Atila; Tunay, Muharrem; Yesilada, Birol,** eds. *The Political and Socioeconomic Transformation of Turkey.* Westport: Praeger Publishers, 1993.

13676 **Erb, Guy F., and Kallab, Valeriana,** eds. *Beyond Dependency: The Developing World Speaks Out.* Washington, D.C.: Overseas Development Council, 1975.

13677 **Farms, J., and Smith, F.** *Studies in World Development.* London: Edward Arnold, 1985.

13678 **Fromkin, David.** *The Independence of Nations.* New York: Praeger, 1981.

13679 **Gendzier, Irene L.** *Managing Political Change: Social Scientists and the Third World.* Boulder, Colorado: Westview Press, 1985.

13680 **Golan, Galia.** *The Soviet Union and National Liberation Movements in the Third World.* Boston: Unwin Hyman, 1988.

13681 **Goodman, Melvin A.** *Gorbachev's Retreat: The Third World.* New York: Praeger, 1991.

13682 **Green, L.P., and Fair, T.J.D.** *Development in Africa: A Study in Regional Analysis with Special Reference to Southern Africa.* Johannesburg: Witwatersrand University Press, 1962.

13683 **Hardgrave, R.L., Jr.** *India: Government and Politics in a Developing Nation.* New York: Harcourt Brace and World, 1970.

13684 **Hoffman, Paul G.** *One Hundred Countries—One and One Quarter Billion People.* Washington, D.C.: Committee for International Economic Growth, 1960.

13685 **Hoogvelt, A.** *The Third World in Global Development.* London: Macmillan, 1982.

13686 **Horowitz, Irving Louis.** *Three Worlds of Development: The Theory and Practice of International Stratification.* 2nd ed. New York: Oxford University Press, 1972.

13687 **Hough, Jerry F.** *The Struggle for the Third World: Soviet Debates and American Options.* Washington, D.C.: The Brookings Institute, 1986.

13688 **Howe, James W.** *The United States and the Developing World: Agenda for Action, 1974.* New York: Praeger, 1974.

13689 **Hoyle, B.S.,** ed. *Spatial Aspects of Development.* London: John Wiley & Sons, 1973.

13690 **Hughlett, L.J.** *Industrialization of Latin America.* New York: McGraw-Hill, 1946.

13691 **ILO.** *Lesotho: Options for a Dependent Economy.* Addis Ababa: ILO, 1979.

13692 **Johnson, John J.** *The Role of the Military in Underdeveloped Countries.* Princeton, New Jersey: Princeton University Press, 1962.

13693 **Jones, D.** *Aid and Development in Southern Africa.* London: Croom Helm/ODI, 1977.

13694 **Kamrava, Mehran.** *Politics and Society in the Third World.* London: Routledge, 1993.

13695 **Kanet, Roger E.,** ed. *The Soviet Union and the Developing Nations.* Baltimore, Maryland: Johns Hopkins University Press, 1974.

13696 **Kautsky, John H.** *Political Change in Underdeveloped Countries: Nationalism and Communism.* New York: John Wiley & Sons, 1962.

13697 **Kitching, Gavin.** *Development and Underdevelopment in Historical Perspective.* New York: Routledge, 1989.

13698 **Kolodziej, Edward A., and Kanet, Roger E.,** eds. *The Limits of Soviet Power in lthe Developing World."* Baltimore, Maryland: Johns Hopkins University Press, 1989.

13699 **Lagos, Gustavo.** *International Stratification and Underdeveloped Countries.* Chapel Hill: University of North Carolina Press, 1963.

13700 **Lassassi, Assassi.** *Non-alignment and Algerian Foreign Policy.* Aldershot: Avebury, 1988.

13701 **Leys, C.,** ed. *Politics and Change in Developing Countries: Studies in the Theory and Practice of Development.* Cambridge: University Press, 1969.

13702 **Lyon, Peter.** *Neutralism.* Leicester, England: Leicester University Press, 1963.

13703 **Marcussen, H., and Torp, J.** *Internationalization of Capital: Prospects for the Third World.* London: ZED Press, 1982.

13704 **Martz, John D.** *Central America: The Crisis and the Challenge.* Chapel Hill: University of North Carolina Press, 1959.

13705 **Meyer, Ralph Christian.** *The Political Elite in an Underdeveloped Society, the Case of Uttar Pradesh, India.* Philadelphia: University of Pennsylvania, Ph.D., 1969.

13706 **Miller, J.D.B.** *The Politics of the Third World.* London: Oxford University Press, 1966.

13707 **Miyasato, Seigen.** *American Foreign Policy Toward South Asian Neutralism, 1947-1957.* Columbus: Ohio State University, 1962.

13708 **Myrdal, Gunnar.** *Asian Drama: An Inquiry into the Poverty of Nations.* New York: Twentieth Century Fund, 1968.

13709 **Myrdal, Gunnar.** *Rich Lands and Poor: The Road to World Prosperity.* New York: Harper and Brothers, 1957.

13710 **Nogueira, Franco.** *The Third World.* London: Johnson, 1967.

13711 **Norwine, J., and Gonzalez, A.,** eds. *The Third World: Status of Mind and Being.* Boston: Unwin and Hyman, 1988.

13712 **Ogley, R.** *Neutrality and Mediation.* London: Routledge, 1970.

13713 **Piven, F.F., and Cloward, R.A.** *Poor People's Movements.* New York: Pantheon, 1977.

13714 **Poffenberger, M.** *Patterns of Interaction: Demography, Ecology, and Society in the Nepal Himalayas.* Ann Arbor: University of Michigan, Ph.D., 1976.

13715 **Randall, Vicky, and Theobald, Robin.** *A Critical Introduction to Third World Politics.* Houndmills: Macmillan, 1985.

13716 **Rubinstein, Alvin Z., and Smith, Donald E.,** eds. *Anti-Americanism in the Third World: Implications for U.S. Foreign Policy.* New York: Praeger, 1985.

13717 **Sachs, I.** *Patterns of Public Sector in Underdeveloped Countries.* Delhi: Delhi School of Economics, Ph.D, 1966.

13718 **Sarigianis, Steven.** *A Geographical and Political Analysis of Poverty in Haiti.* University Park: Pennsylvania State University, Master's Thesis, 1985.

13719 **Sen, Lalita.** *Optimization of Plant Location and Transport Operating Decisions: A Set of Viable Models for Developing Nations.* Evanston, Illinois: Northwestern University, Ph.D., 1970.

13720 **Sharma, Shanti Ram.** *British Opinions and Indian Neutralism: An Analysis of India's Foreign Policy in the Light of British Public Relations, 1947-1957.* London, England: London School of Economics, University of London, Ph.D., 1959.

13721 **Simonia, Nodari A.** *Synthesis of Traditional and Modern in the Evolution of Third World Societies.* New York: Greenwood Press, 1992.

13722 **Staley, E., and Morse, R.** *Modern Small-scale Industry for Developed Countries.* Englewood Cliffs, New Jersey: Prentice-Hall, 1965.

13723 **Stamp, L. Dudley.** *Africa, A Study in Tropical Development.* New York: John Wiley & Sons, 1953.

13724 **Stamp, L. Dudley.** *Our Developing World.* London: Faber and Farber, 1968.

13725 **Sullivan, Michael Joseph, III.** *The Attitudes of India Toward the Nuclear Non-Proliferation Treaty.* Charlottesville: University of Virginia, Ph.D., 1969.

13726 **Symons, L.** *Russia and the Third World.* Melbourne: Paper presented to The Thirty-Ninth Congress, at Melbourne, of the Australian and New Zealand Association for the Advancement of cience, Section P, 1967.

13727 **Szulc, Tad.** *The Winds of Revolution; Latin America Today--and Tomorrow.* New York: Praeger, 1963.

13728 **Taylor, J. Clagett.** *The Political Development of Tanganyika.* Stanford, California: Stanford University Press, 1963.

13729 **Theobald, Robert.** *The Rich and the Poor.* New York: Mentor Books, 1961.

13730 **Todaro, M.P.** *Internal Migration in Developing Countries.* Geneva: ILO, 1976.

13731 **Toh, Swee-Hin.** *The Overseas Development Council: An Elite Policy-Planning Group on U.S. Third-World Relations, Its Power Structure and International Development-Education Ideology.* Edmonton, Alberta, Canada: University of Alberta, Ph.D., 1980.

13732 **Valenta, Jiri, and Cibulka, Frank,** eds. *Gorbachev's New Thinking nad Third World Conflicts.* New Brunswick: Transaction Publishers, 1990.

13733 **Whelan, Joseph, and Dixon, Michael J.** *The Soviet Union in the Third World: Threat to World Peace?* Washington, D.C.: Pergamon-Brassey's International Defense Publishers, 1986.

13734 **Williamson, J.A.** *IMF Conditionality.* Washington, D.C.: Institute for International Economics, 1983.

13735 **World Bank.** *Lesotho: A Development Challenge.* Washington, D.C.: World Bank, 1975.

13736 **Zinkin, M.** *Development for Free Asia.* Fairlawn, New Jersey: Essential Books, 1956.

Journals

13737 **Becker, Bertha K.** "Geography in Brazil in the 1980s: Background and Recent Advances." *Progress in Human Geography,*10, No. 2 (June, 1986), 157-183.

13738 **Becker, Bertha K.** "The State Crisis and the Region--Preliminary Thoughts from a Third World Perspective." In *Political Geography: Recent Advances and Future Directions*, P.J. Taylor and J.W. House, eds. Beckenham, United Kingdom: Crom Helm, 1984, 81-97.

13739 **Bennathan, Ezra.** "The Political Economy of Bangladesh: Problems of Development." *Round Table*, 252 (October, 1973), 507-518.

13740 **Berrington, H.** "Decade of Dealignment." *Political Studies*, 32 (1984), 117-120.

13741 **Bird, G.** "Developing Country and Finances, Present and Future." *Futures*, 13, No. 3 (1981), 191-205.

13742 **Bird, Richard M.** "A New Look at Indirect Taxation in Developing Countries." *World Development*, 15, No. 9 (September, 1987), 1151-1161.

13743 **Buchanan, Keith.** "Profiles of the Third World." *Pacific Viewpoint*, 5, No. 2 (September, 1964), 97-126.

13744 **Burghardt, Andrew F.** "Canada and the Third World." *Journal of Geography*, 83, No. 5 (September-October, 1984), 205-211.

13745 **Cheysson, Claude.** "Europe and the Third World After Lome." *World Today*, 31, No. 6 (June, 1975), 232-239.

13746 **Chowdhury, Iftekhar A.** "Strategy of a Small Power in a Subsystem: Bangladesh's External Relations." *Australian Outlook*, 34, No. 1 (April, 1980), 85-98.

13747 **Cobbe, J.H.** "The Changing Nature of Dependence: Economic Problems in Lesotho." *Journal of Modern African Studies*, 21, No. 2 (June, 1983), 293-310.

13748 **Cobbe, J.H.** "Emigration and Development in Southern Africa, with Special Reference to Lesotho." *International Migration Review*,1, No. 4 (Winter, 1982), 837-868.

13749 **Cobbe, J.H.** "Integration Among Unequals: The Southern African Customs Union and Development." *World Development*, 8, No. 4 (April, 1980), 329-336.

13750 **Dale, Edmund H.** "Political Intervention, A third World Strategy in Agricultural Renaissance: The Jamaican Case." In *Spotlight on the Caribbean, A Microcosm of the Third World.* Regina: Regina Geographical Studies No. 2, Department of Geography, University of Regina, 1977, 47-95.

13751 **Evans, Richard.** "Central America's Slide to Ruin." *Geographical Magazine,* 59, No. 12 (December, 1987), 582-591.

13752 **Evers, Hans-Dieter.** "The Bureaucratization of Southeast Asia." *Comparative Studies in Society and History*, 29, No. 4 (October, 1987), 666-685.

13753 **Hoffman, George W.** "The Problem of the Underdeveloped Regions in Southeast Europe: A Comparative Analysis of Romania, Yugoslavia, and Greece." *Annals of the Association of American Geographers*, 57, No. 4 (December, 1967), 637-666.

13754 **Hussain, Karki.** "China's Image of India's Foreign Policy of Non-Alignment." *Indian Journal of Political Science*, 23, No. 3 (July, 1962), 242-251.

13755 **Gonick, Lev S., and Rosh, Robert M.** "The Structural Constraints of the World-Economy on National Political Development." *Comparative Political Studies*, 21, No. 2 (July, 1988), 171-200.

13756 **Kanyeihamba, G.W.** "The Impact of the Received Law on Planning and Development in Anglophonic Africa." *International Journal of Urban and Regional Research*, 4, No. 2 (June, 1980), 239-266.

13757 **Keller, F.L.** "Institutional Barriers to Economic Development. Some Examples from Bolivia." *Economic Geography*, 31, No. 4 (October, - 6761955), 351-363.

13758 **Lal, D.** "Time to Put the Third World Debt into Perspective." *Times*, (May 6, 1983), 18.

13759 **Laufer, Leopold.** "Israel and the Third World." *Political Science Quarterly*, 87, No. 4 (December, 1972), 615-630.

13760 **Legum, Colin.** "The Postcommunist Third World: Focus on Africa." *Problems of Communism* [Washington, DC], 41, Nos. 1-2 (January-April, 1992), 195-206.

13761 **Lucke, Hartmut.** "Korsika-eine unterentwickelte Mittilmeirinsel. Okonomische Moglichkeiten und grenzen ihrer Selbstverwaltung." [Corsica-An Underdeveloped Mediterranean Island. Possibilities and Limits of Its Autonomy.] *Geographische Rundschau*, Jahr. 32, Heft. 10 (Oktober, 1980), 444-452.

13762 **Malecela, John S.W.** "The Place of the Developing Nations in a Changing World." In *A World of Change: Proceedings of the Dedication, Von Kleinsmid Center for International and Public Affairs, University of Southern California, Los Angeles, September 30-October 2, 1966.* Los Angeles: Institute of World Affairs. 44th Session. 43 (1968), 149-153.

13763 **Melamid, Alexander.** "The Economic Geography of Neutral Territories." *Geographical Review*, 45, No. 3 (July, 1955), 359-374.

13764 **Melamid, Alexander.** "Political Geography of Economic Underdevelopment." *Geographical Review*, 56, No. 2 (April, 1966), 293-294.

13765 **Molinari, A.E.** "Estudio de los informes de Terceros estados ante el Tratado Antartico. (Study of the Reports by Third World Nations on the Antarctic Treaty." *Contribucion-Instituto Antarctico Argentino*, 292 (1946), 1-292.

13766 **O'Loughlin, John.** "World Power Competition in the Third World." In *A World in Crisis?*, R.J. Johnston and P.J. Taylor, eds. Oxford: Basil Blackwell, 1986, 131-168.

13767 **Oren, Nissan.** "The Fate of the Small in a World Concerted and in a World Divided." *Jerusalem Journal of International Relations*, 5, No. 1 (Fall, 1980), 111-119.

13768 **Osborn, James.** "The Geography of Development Policy: Reflections on Malaysia and Indonesia." In *Spatial Aspects of Development*, B.S. Hoyle, ed. London: John Wiley & Sons, 1973.

13769 **Palmer, J.** "The Debt Bomb Threat." *Time Magazine*, (January 10, 1983), 4-11.

13770 **Patnaik, Sivananda.** "Sri Lanke and the South Asian Sub-System: A Study of Submacro International Politics." *India Quarterly*, 36, No. 2 (April-June, 1980), 137-158.

13771 **Panitt, Keith.** "Technology, International Competition, and Economic Growth: Some Lessons and Perspectives." *World Politics*, 25, No. 2 (January, 1973), 183-205.

13772 **Perkins, S.E.** "Geolexigraph of the Neutrality Act of 1939." *Commerce Reports*, 8 (February 24, 1940), 182-183.

13773 **Plange, Nii-K.** "'Opportunity Cost' and Labor Migration: A Misinterpretation of Proletarianization in Northern Ghana." *Journal of Modern African Studies*, 17, No. 4 (December, 1979) 6551, No. 9 (September, 1989).

13774 **Portes, Alejandro.** "Migration and Underdevelopment." *Politics & Society*, 8, No. 1 (Spring, 1978),

13775 **Rastogi, B.C.** "Alignment and Non-Alignment in Pakistan's Foreign Policy, 1947-1959." *International Studies*, 3, No. 4 (October, 1961), 159-180.

13776 **Robinson, K.W.** "Political Development in French West Africa." In *Africa in the Modern World*, C.W. Stillman, ed. Chicago, Illinois: University of Chicago Press, 155, 140-181.

13777 **Sallnow, John.** "Non-alignment in a polar world." Geographical Magazine, Six Developed Countries." *Progress in Human Geography*, 12, No. 2 (June, 1988), 179-207.

13778 **Sanchez, Walter.** "Third World Perspectives on Regional Arrangements for Peace and Security: The Latin American Case." *Jerusalem Journal of International Relations*, 5, No. 2 (Winter, 1981), 1-15.

13779 **Schwartzberg, Joseph E.** "Three Approaches to the Mapping of Economic Development in India." *Annals of the Association of American Geographers*, 52 (December, 1962), 455-468.

13780 **Sdasyuk, Galina V.** "Geographical Approach to the Problem of Regional Inequalities and Development in Developing Countries (A Case Study of India)." In *International Geographical Union, Commission on Regional Aspects of Development, Proceedings, Vol. 1: Methodology and Case Studies, Held in Victoria, Brazil, April 12-15, 1971.* Edited by Richard S. Thoman. Montreal: Allister Typesetting and Graphics, 1974, 693-722.

13781 **Shrestha, Nanda R.** "The Political Economy of Economic Underdevelopment and External Migration in Nepal." *Political Geography Quarterly*, 4, No. 4 (October, 1985), 289-306.

13782 **Shrestha, Nanda R.** "A Structural Perspective on Labour Migration in Underdevelopment and External Migration in Nepal." *Political Geography Quarterly*, 4, No. 4 (October, 1985), 289-306.

13783 **Singh, A.** "Foreign Aid for Structural Change in Lesotho." In *Industry and Accumulation in Africa*, M. Fransman, ed. London: Heinemann, 1982, 301-323.

13784 **Smith, D. Drakakis; Doherty, J.; and Thrift, N.J.** "Introduction: What is a Socialist Developing Country?" *Geography*, 72, No. 4 (October, 1987), 333-335.

13785 **Stanley, Timothy W.** "An Orthodox View of the North-South Dialogue." *Atlantic Community Quarterly*, 18, No. 3 (Fall, 1980), 310-322.

13786 **Sukhwal, B.L.** "South Asia: A Region of Conflicts and contradictions." In *The Third World: States of Mind and Being*, by James R. Norwine and Alfonso Gonzalez, eds. Boston: Unwin Hyman, 1988, 209-221.

13787 **Swindell, K.** "Labor Migration in Underdeveloped Countries: The Case of Subsaharan Africa." *Progress in Human Geography*, 3, No. 2 (June, 1979), 239-259.

13788 **Taylor, P.J.** "Political Geography and the World-Economy." In *Political Studies from Spatial Perspectives*, A.D. Burnett and P.J. Taylor, eds. Chichester: John Wiley & Sons, 1981, 157-172.

13789 **Thomas, Dani B.** "Political Development Theory and Africa: Toward a Conceptual Clarification and Comparative Analysis." *Journal of Developing Areas*, 8, No. 3 (April, 1974), 375-393.

13790 **Thornton, William H.** "The Korean Road to Postmodernization and Development." *Asian Pacific Quarterly* [Seoul], 26, No. 1 (Spring, 1994), 1-11.

13791 **Torngren, Ralf.** "THe Neutrality of Finland." *Foreign Affairs*, 39, No. 4 (July, 1961), 601-609.

13792 **Villaneuva, A.B.** "Elite Choices and Constitutional Guarantees of Local Autonomy in the Third World: The Case of the Philippines, 1971-1973." *Modern Asian Studies*, 14, Part 3 (July, 1980), 489-499.

13793 **Wilcox, Wayne Ayers,** ed. "Protagonists, Power, and the Third World: Essays on the Changing International System." *Annals of the American Academy of Political and Social Science*,386 (November, 1969), 1-167 (complete issue, multiple authors).

13794 **Yag'ya, V.S.** "Natural Resources Development and Changes in Political Geography of Developing Countries." *Vsesoyuznoe Geograficheskoe Obshchestvo Izvestiia*, Tom 115, Vyp. 1 (Ianvar'-Fevral' 1983), 52-59.

13795 **Yerasimos, Stephane.** "Turquie: Les Choix Difficiles." *Herodote* [Paris], Nos. 58-59 (Juillet-Decembre, 1990), 111-131.

13796 **Young, Crawford.** "Nationalizing the Third-World: Categorical Imperative or Mission Impossible?" *Polity*, 15, No. 2 (Winter, 1982), 161-181.

INTERNATIONAL POLITICS AND ENVIRONMENT

Books

13797 **Abbasi, Sherie Ann.** *Current Legal Literature on Three Aspects of Ecology: Air, Noise, and Water Pollution: A Selected and Partially Annotated Bibliography, 1969-1974.* Monticello, IL: Council of Planning Librarians, Exchange Bib., No. 740, 1975.

13798 **Allison, L.** *Environmental Planning. A Political and Philosophical Analysis.* London: Allen & Unwin, 1975.

13799 **Barros, James,** and Johnston, Douglas M. *The International Law of Pollution.* New York: The Free Press, 1974.

13800 **Bigham, D. Alastair.** *The Law and Administration Relating to Protection of the Environment.* London: Oyez, 1973.

13801 **Bissell, Harold Preston.** *The Effects of Selected Physical and Cultural Variables on the Population, Land Use, and Vegetation Patterns of Two Pacific Island Ecosystems.* Norman: University of Oklahoma, Ph.D., 1971.

13802 **Brickman, Ronald; Jasanoff, Sheila; and Ilgren, Thomas.** *Controlling Chemicals: The Politics of Regulation in Europe and the United States.* Ithaca, New York: Cornell University Press, 1985.

13803 **Brynielsson, H.** *Radioactive-Waste Disposal into the Sea.* Report of the ad hoc Panel, Safety Series No. 5. New York: International Atomic Energy Agency, 1961.

13804 **Daugherty, Howard Edward.** *Man-Induced Ecologic Change in El Salvador.* Los Angeles: University of California, Ph.D., 1969.

13805 **Doughty, Robin Whitaker.** *Feather Fashions and Bird Presentation: A Study in Nature Protection.* Berkeley: University of California, Ph.D., 1971.

13806 **Ewald, William R., Jr.,** ed. *Environment for Man: The Next Fifty Years.* Bloomington: Indiana University Press, 1967.

13807 **Ericksen, E. Gordon.** *The Territorial Experience: Human Ecology as Symbolic Interaction.* Austin: University of Texas Press, 1980.

13808 **Halme, Kalervo Raymond.** *Environmental Hazards and Urban Development: A Historical, Spatial and Systems View of the City of Long Beach.* Long Beach: California State University, Master's Thesis, 1974.

13809 **Henry, James Albert.** *A Correlation and Regression Analysis of Particulate Pollution and Minimum Temperatures in the Los Angeles Area, 1953-1972.* Long Beach: California State University, Master's Thesis, 1974.

13810 **Johnson, S.P.** *The Politics of Environment.* London: Stacey, 1973.

13811 **Kiss, Alexander-Charles,** ed. *Colloquisim 1973: The Protection of the Environment and International Law, 14-16 August, 1973.* Leiden: Sijthoff, 1975.

13812 **Lirette, Susan Marie.** *Dendroclimatology and Air Pollution in the San Bernardino Mountains of Southern California.* Fullerton: California State University, Master's Thesis, 1975.

13813 **Lowenthal, David,** ed. *Environmental Perception and Behavior.* Chicago, Illinois: University of Chicago, Department of Geography Research Paper No. 109. 1967.

13814 **Manners, Ian R.** *North Sea Oil and Environmental Planning: The United Kingdom Experience.* Austin: University of Texas Press, 1982.

13815 **McCarthy, Jeffrey J.** *Class, Community, and Conflict over the Urban Environment Under Advanced Capitalism* (Social Geography). Columbus: Ohio State University, Ph.D., 1979.

13816 **M'Gonigle, R. Michael, and Zacher, Mark W.** *Pollution, Politics, and International Law: Tankers at Sea.* Berkeley: University of California Press, 1979.

13817 **Mote, Victor Lee.** *The Geography of Air Pollution in the USSR.* Seattle: University of Washington, Ph.D., 1971.

13818 **Myers, Norman.** *Ultimate Security: The Environmental Basis for Political Stability.* New York: W. W. Norton, 1993.

13819 **Norwine, James Randolph.** *Cities, Air Pollution, and Regional Climate: A Quantitative Analysis of the Relationships Between Climatological Parameters and Urban Influences, Primarily Atmospheric Pollution, in the Six-State Region of the United States Gulf of Mexico Coastline.* Terre Haute: Indiana State University, Ph.D., 1971.

13820 **Papadakis, Elim.** *Politics and the Environment: The Australian Experience.* St. Leonards, Australia: Allen & Unwin, 1993.

13821 **Pontecorvo, Giulio,** ed. *The New Order of the Oceans: The Advent of a Managed Environment.* New York City: Columbia University Press, 1986.

13822 **Ross, William Michael.** *Oil Pollution as a Developing International Problem: A Study of the Puget Sound and Straight of Georgia Regions of Washington and British Columbia.* Seattle: University of Washington, Ph.D., 1972.

13823 **Seymour, Priscilla Jane Lee.** *Strategic Planning Methodology to Evaluate Low Probability/High Consequence Tanker Oil Spills, Using the Gulf of Mexico as a Test Area.* Volumes I and II. College Station: Texas A & M University, Ph.D., 1983.

13824 **Springer, Allen L.** *The International Law of Pollution: Protecting the Global Environment in a World of Sovereign States.* Westport, Connecticut: Quorum Books, 1983.

13825 **Sprout, Harold H. and Sprout, Margaret.** *The Ecological Perspective on Human Affairs.* Princeton, New Jersey: Princeton University Press, 1965.

13826 **Thomas, William A.,** ed. *Legal and Scientific Uncertainties of Weather Modification.* Durham, North Carolina: Duke University Press, 1977.

13827 **Usher, Peter Joseph, Jr.** *The Blakslanders: Economy and Ecology of a Frontier Trapping Community*. Vancouver, British Columbia, Canada: University of British Columbia, Ph.D., 1970.

13828 **Utton, Albert E.**, ed. *Pollution and International Boundaries: United States-Mexican Environmental Problems*. Albuquerque: University of New Mexico Press, 1973.

13829 **Vadya, Andrew P.** *War in Ecological Perspective: Persistence, Change, and Adaptive Processes in Oceanian Societies*. New York: Plenum Press, 1976.

13830 **Yandle, Bruce.** *The Political Limits of Environmental Regulations: Tracking the Unicorn*. New York: Quorum Books, 1989.

Journals

13831 **Aniol, Wlodzimierz.** "Global Problems: An Ecological Paradigm." *Coexistence*, 25, No. 2 (June, 1988), 213-255.

13832 **Arkell, Thomas.** "Environmental Determinism and the Balance of World Power." *Geographical Magazine* [London], 62, No. 11 (November, 1990), 18-22.

13833 **Bach, Wilfrid.** "Nuclear War: The Effects of Smoke and Dust on Weather and Climate." *Progress in Physical Geography*, 10, No. 3 (September, 1986), 315-363.

13834 **Bonnemaison, Joel.** "A Propos de l'(affairs) GreenPeace... La-bas a' l'onset de l'occident: L'Australie et la Nouvelle Nelande." *Herodote*, No. 40 (Janvier-Mars, 1986), 126-139.

13835 **Cabouret, Michel.** "Les enjeux strategiques dans le secteur nordique de la zone boreale." *L'espace Geographique*, 16, No. 4 (Octobre/Decembre, 1987), 285-293.

13836 **Clark, M.** "Antarctica: A Wilderness Compromised." *International Studies Notes*, 11, No. 3 (1985), 29-33.

13837 **Cotgrove, S.**, and **Duff, A.** "Environmentalism, Values and Social Change." *British Journal of Sociology*, 32, No. 1 (March, 1981), 92-110.

13838 **Coulter, John Wesley.** "Environment, Race, and Government in South Sea Islands." *Scottish Geographical Magazine*, 63, No. 2 (September, 1947), 49-56.

13839 **Dalby, Simon.** "Ecopolitical Discourse: 'Enviornmental Security' and Political Geography." *Progress in Human Geography* [London], 16, No. 4 (October, 1992), 503-522.

13840 **de Blij, Harm J.**, and **Capone, Donald L.** "Wildlife Conservation in East Africa: An Application of Field Theory in Political Geography." *Southeastern Geographer*, 9, No. 2 (November, 1969).

13841 **Donaldson, S.** "City Fight: Modern Combat in the Urban Environment." *Strategy & Tactics*, 77 (1979), 15-24.

13842 **Johnston, R.J.** "Laws, States and Super-States: International Law and the Environment." *Applied Geography* [Oxford], 12, No. 3 (July, 1992), 211-228.

13843 **Kasperson, Roger E.**, and **Pijawka, K.D.** "Societal Responses to Hazards and Major Hazard Events: Comparing Natural and Technological Hazards." *Public Administration Review*, Special Issue, (1985), 7-18.

13844 **Kates, Robert W.**, and **Wohlwill, Joachim F.**, eds. "Man's Response to the Physical Environment." *Journal of Social Issues*, 22, No. 4 (October, 1966) 15-20.

13845 **Kindt, John Warren.** "The Claims of Limiting Marine Research: Compliance with International Environmental Standards." *Ocean Development and International Law*, 15, No. 1 (1985), 13-35.

13846 **Lyden, Fremont J.**, and **Shipman, George A.** "Public Policy Issues Raised by Weather Modification: Possible Alternative Strategies for Government Action." In *Human Dimensions of Weather Modification*, W.R. Derrick Sewell, ed. Chicago, Illinois: University of Chicago, Department of Geography Research Paper No. 105, 1966, 289-303.

13847 **Lyon, V.** "The Reluctant Party: Ideology Versus Organizationin Canada's Green Movement." *Alternatives*, 13, No. 1 (1985), 3-8.

13848 **Morin, Jacques-Yvan.** "Le Progres Technique, la Pollution et l'Evolution Recente du Droit de la mer au Canada, particulierement a l'egard de l'Arctique." *Canadian Yearbook of International Law*, 8 (1970), 158-248.

13849 **Myers, N.** "The Environmental Dimension to Security Issues." *Environmentalist*, 6, No. 4 (1988), 251-257.

13850 **Ossenbrugge, Jurgen.** "Regional Restructuring and the Ecological Welfare State: Spatial Impacts of Environmental Protection in West Germany." *Geographische Zeitschrift*, 76, No. 1 (Marz, 1988), 78-96.

13851 **Otter, R.J.** Developments in International Legislation (Europe)." *Water Pollution Control*, 85, No. 2 (1986), 216-224.

13852 **Packard, R.** "Maize, Cattle and Mosquitoes: The Political Economy of Malaria Epidemics in Colonial Swaziland." *Journal of African History*, 25, No. 2 (1984), 189-212.

13853 **Pratt, C.** "Chemical Feathers." *Scientific American*, 212, No. 6 (June, 1965), 61-72.

13854 **Ra'anan, Uri.** "Before and After Chernobyl: Stresses in the Soviet Leadership." *Orbis*, 30, No. 2 (Summer, 1986), 249-257.

13855 **Sewell, W.R.D.; Derrick; Kates, Robert W.; and Phillips, Lee E.** "Human Response to Weather and Climate: Geography Contributions." *Geographical Review*, 58, No. 2 (April, 1968), 262-280.

13856 **Schachter, O., and Serwer, D.** "Marine Pollution Problems and Remedies." *American Journal of International Law*, 65, No. 1 (January, 1971), 84-111.

13857 **Siddiqui, M.A.H.** "Politico-Geographic Environment: An Enquiry into Power Relations." *National Association of Geographers, India*, 2, No. 1 (June-December, 1982), 49-52.

13858 **Siddiqui, M.A.H.** "Politico-Geographic Environment of the Indian Ocean Lettoral: A Search for Remedial Aspects." *Geographer*, 31, No. 1 (January, 1984), 62-67.

13859 **Side, J.** "The European Community and Dumping at Sea." *Marine Pollution Bulletin*, 17, No. 7 (1986), 290-294.

13860 **Smith, Robert W.** "The Political Geography of the Marine Environment." *Geographical Bulletin*, 10 (May, 1975), 13-19.

13861 **Sokolov, V.E., and others.** "Ecological and Genetic Consequences of the Chernobyl Atomic Power Plant Accident." *Vegetatio* [Dordrecht], 109, No. 1 (September, 1993), 91-99.

13862 **Solomon, Barry D.** "Review Essay: The Politics of Nuclear Power and Radioactive Waste Disposal: From State Coercion to Procedural Justice?" *Political Geography Quarterly*, 7, No. 3 (July, 1988), 291-299.

13863 **Spiller, Judith, and Hayden, Cynthia.** "Radwaste at Sea: A New ERA of Polarization or a New Basis for Consensus?" *Ocean Development and International Law*, 19, No. 5 (1988), 345-366.

13864 **Sprout, Harold H. and Sprout, Margaret.** "Environmental Factors in the Study of International Politics." *Journal of Conflict Resolution*, 1, No. 2 (June, 1957), 309-328.

13865 **Sukhwal, Bheru L.** "Geostrategie Considerations and the Ecological Devastations of South Vietnam." *National Geographical Journal of India*, 25, Part 1 (March, 1978), 1-20.

13866 **Szekely, A.** "The International Law of Submarine Transboundlary Hydrocarbon Resources: Legal Limits to Behavior and Experiences for the Gulf of Mexico." *Natural Resources Journal*, 26, No. 4 (1986), 733-768.

13867 **Thomas, William L.** "The Use of Herbicides in South Vietnam: Resultant Economic Stress and Settlement Changes." *Pacific Viewpoint*, 16, No. 1 (May, 1975), 1-25.

13868 **Titova, E.L.** "Modern Ecological Movement in the EEC Countries (in Russian." *Vestnik-Leningradskogo Universiteta, Seriya Geologiya i Geografiya*, 1 (1987), 57-63.

13869 **Trotter, Bernard, and Watson, J.W.** "Poland in the European Balance." *Canadian Geographical Journal*, 29, No. 3 (September, 1944), 143-149.

13870 **Van Valkenburg, Samuel.** "Climatology and Political Geography." *Bulletin of the American Meteorological Society*, 20, No. 6 (June, 1939), 253-254.

13871 **Wang, Cheng-Pang.** "A Review of the Enforcement Regime for Vessel-Source Oil Pollution Control." *Ocean Development and International Law*, 16, No. 4 (1980), 305-339.

13872 **Weiner, Jerome B.** "The Green March in Historical Perspective." *Middle East Journal*, 33, No. 1 (Winter, 1979), 20-33.

13873 **Wilkes, Daniel.** "Law for Special Environments: Jurisdiction over Polar Activities." *Polar Record*, 16, No. 104 (May, 1973), 701-705.

POLITICAL GEOGRAPHY OF FOREIGN TRADE, FOREIGN AID, AND CORPORATIONS AND INVESTMENT

Books

13874 **Alvi, Hamza A., and Khusro, Amir.** *Pakistan and the Burden of U.S. Aid*. Karachi: Syed and Syed, 1965.

13875 **Argy, V.** *The Post War International Monetary Crisis*. London: Allen & Unwin, 1981.

13876 **Beamish, Paul W.** *Multinational Joint Ventures in Developing Countries*. New York: Routledge, 1988.

13877 **Beenstock, M.** *The World Economy in Transition*. London: Allen & Unwin, 1983.

13878 **Behrman, Jack N.** *National Interests and Multinational Enterprise.* Englewood Cliffs, New Jersey: Prentice-Hall, 1970.

13879 **Birchfield, Cynthia.** "The Economic Impact of Multinational Marketing and Advertising upon Less Developed Countries." Buffalo: State University of New York, M.A., 1989.

13880 **Brodkin, E.I.** *American Attitudes Towards Foreign Aid, with Special Reference to the Indian Sub-continent.* London, England: London School of Economics, University of London, M.S., 1964.

13881 **Cahn, Anne Hessing; Kruzel, Joseph J.; et al.** *Controlling Future Arms Trade.* New York: McGraw-Hill, 1977.

13882 **Calleo, D.P., and Rowland, B.M.** *America and the World Political Economy: Atlantic Dreams and National Realities.* Bloomington: Indiana University Press, 1973.

13883 **Choudhry, Yusuf Ahmed.** *International Direct Investment Propensity of U.S. Multinational Firms: A Test of Political and Economic Relations (Political Risk, Foreign Direct Investment, United States).* Syracuse, New York: Syracuse University, Ph.D., 1984.

13884 **Clement, W.** *The Canadian Corporate Elite.* Toronto: McClelland and Stewart, 1975.

13885 **Clement, W.** *Continental Corporate Power.* Toronto: McClelland and Stewart, 1977.

13886 **Cohen, Benjamin J.** *The Question of Imperialism: The Political Economy of Dominance and Dependence.* New York: Basic Books, 1973.

13887 **Demack, Gary Clark.** *Demographic Determinants of Senators' Roll-Call Voting Positions on Foreign Aid Legislation, 1947-1974.* Boca Raton: Florida Atlantic University, Master's Thesis, 1976.

13888 **Department of Transport.** *Inland Origins and Destinations of UK International Trade.* London: Department of Transport and National Ports Council, 1980.

13889 **Edisis, Wayne Alan.** *The Hidden Agenda: Negotiations for the Generalized System of Preferences (International Trade, North-South Relations, Tariff).* Waltham, Massachusetts: Brandeis University, Ph.D., 1985.

13890 **Eldridge, P.J.** *Some Political Aspects of Foreign Aid in India: 1947-1966.* London, England: London School of Economics, University of London, Ph.D., 1968.

13891 **Faltas, Nabil Charles Mikhail.** *Methodological and Implementational Issues in the Design of International Economic Relations.* Berkeley: University of California, Ph.D., 1972.

13892 **Farley, Philip J.; Kaplan, Stephan S.; and Lewis, William H.** *Arms Across the Sea.* Washington, D.C.: The Brookings Institute, 1978.

13893 **Feis, Herbert.** *The Changing Pattern of International Economic Affairs.* New York: Harper and Row, 1940; reprinted Port Washington, New York: Kennikat Press, 1971.

13894 **Freeman, Donald Bernard.** *International Trade, Migration, and Capital Flows: A Quantitative Analysis of Spatial Economic Interaction.* Chicago, Illinois: University of Chicago, Ph.D., 1972.

13895 **Gassaway, Alexander Ramsey.** *The Geography of Food Supply of Finnmark Flyke, Northernmost Norway: 1946-1965.* Worcester, Massachusetts: Clark University, Ph.D., 1972.

13896 **Gold, Edgar.** *Maritime Transport: The Evolution of International Marine Policy and Shipping Law.* Lexington, Massachusetts: Lexington Books, 1981.

13897 **Green, Robert T.** *Political Instability as a Determinant of U.S. Foreign Investment.* Austin: University of Texas, Graduate School of Business, Research, Studies in Marketing No. 17, 1972.

13898 **Grosse, Robert.** *Multinationals in Latin America.* New York: Routledge, 1989.

13899 **Gordon, D.L., and Dangerfield, R.** *The Hidden Weapon: The Story of Economic Warfare.* New York: Harper and Row, 1947.

13900 **Hamnett, Brian R.** *Politics and Trade in Southern Mexico, 1750-1821.* Cambridge: University Press, 1971.

13901 **Hartley, Joseph R.** *The Effects of the St. Lawrence Seaway on Grain Movements.* Bloomington, Indiana, Indiana Business Report 24, 1957.

13902 **Harvey, David W.** *The Limits to Capital.* Oxford: Basil Blackwell, 1982.

13903 **Hirschman, A.O.** *National Power and the Structure of Foreign Trade.* Berkeley: University of California Press, 1945.

13904 **Hodgson, R.A.** *Introduction to International Trade and Tariffs.* London: Sir Isaac Pitman & Sons, 1932.

13905 **Hood, N., and Wood, Susan.** *Multinationals in Retreat: The Scottish Experience.* New York City: Columbia University Press, 1982.

13906 **Hyder, Khurshid.** *Equality of Treatment and Trade Discrimination in International Law.* The Hague: Martinus Nijhoft, 1968.

13907 **Jackson, John H.** *Restructuring the GATT System.* New York: Council on Foreign Relations Press, 1990.

13908 **Julius, DeAnne.** *Global Companies and Public Policy: The Growing Challenge of Foreign Direct Investment.* New York: Council on Foreign Policy Press, 1990.

13909 **Jung, Hui, Jonathon.** *The Demand for United States Rice: An Economic-Geographic Analysis.* Seattle: University of Washington, Ph.D., 1971.

13910 **Klare, Michael T.** *Supplying Repression.* New York: Field Foundation, 1977.

13911 **Kodaira, Hiroshi.** *Majority Voting in a Stock Market Economy with Uncertainty.* Rochester, New York: University of Rochester, Ph.D., 1979.

13912 **Kolarik, William Francis, Jr.** *A Model for the Study of International Trade Politics: The United States Business Community and Soviet-American Relations, 1975-1976.* Kent, Ohio: Kent State University, Ph.D., 1981.

13913 **Kronfol, Zouhair A.** *Protection of Foreign Investment: A Study in International Law.* Leiden: A.W. Sijthoft, 1972.

13914 **Kubrian, G.T.** *The Book of World Rankings.* New York: Facts on File, 1979.

13915 **Kurian, Mannakunnil Verughese.** *An Evalution of American Food Aid to India, 1956-1967.* St. Louis, Missouri: University of St. Louis, Ph.D., 1970.

13916 **Levy, Tereza Lucia Halliday.** *Organizational Rhetoric: Multinational Corporations: Legitimation in Brazil, France, and the United States.* Vols. I and II. Baltimore: University of Maryland, Ph.D., 1985.

13917 **Lewis, Cleona.** *Nazi Europe and World Trade.* Washington, D.C.: The Brookings Institute, 1941.

13918 **Lissitzyn, Oliver J.** *International Air Transport and National Policy.* New York: Council on Foreign Relations, 1942.

13919 **MacGregor, R.E.** *Who Owns Whom.* Johannesburg; Purdey, 1982.

13920 **Martech Consultants.** *Britain's Foreign Trade.* London: Port of London Authority, 1964.

13921 **McConnell, James Eakin.** *An Analysis of International Trade Networks: The Examples of EETA and LAFTA.* Columbus: Ohio State University, Ph.D., 1969.

13922 **McKinley, Edward H.** *The Lure of Africa: American Interest in Tropical Africa, 1919-1939.* Indianapolis: Bobbs-Merrill, 1974.

13923 **Meeks, Philip Joseph.** *The Crisis of Governance and Economic Policy in Postindustrial States: The Politics of Corporatism and International Economic Relations in the United Kingdom, West Germany, and France, 1958-1978.* Austin: University of Texas, Ph.D., 1980.

13924 **Mizruchi, M.S.** *The Structure of the American Corporate Network (1904-1974).* Beverly Hills: Sage Publications, 1982.

13925 **Moran, T.H.** *Multinational Corporations and the Politics of Dependence: Copper in Chile.* Princeton, New Jersey: Princeton University Press, 1974.

13926 **Morin, F.** *La Structure Financiere du Capitalism Francaise.* Paris: Calman-Levi, 1974.

13927 **Murphy, Craig N., and Tooze, Roger,** eds. *The New International Political Economy.* Boulder, Colorado: Lynne Rienner Publishers, 1990.

13928 **Nappi, C.** *Commodity Market Controls: A Historical Review.* Lexington, Massachusetts: D.C. Heath, 1979.

13929 **Ocampo-Gaviria, Jose Antonio.** *Capital Accumulation and International Relations.* New Haven, Connecticut: Yale University, Ph.D., 1976.

13930 **Ostrg, Sylvia.** *Governments and Corporations in a Shrinking World: Trade and Innovation Policy in the United States, Europe and Japan.* New York: Council on Foreign Policy Press, 1990.

13931 **Parboni, R.** *The Dollar and Its Rivals: Recession, Inflation and International Finance.* London: Verso, 1981.

13932 **Pennings, J.M.** *Interlocking Directorates.* London: Jossey-Bass, 1980.

13933 **Pierre, Andrew J.,** ed. *Arms Transfers and American Foreign Policy.* New York: New York University Press, 1979.

13934 **Pye, Lucian W.,** ed. *Communications and Political Development.* Princeton, New Jersey: Princeton University Press, 1963.

13935 **Republic of South Africa.** *Report of the Commission of Inquiry into the Regulation of Monopolistic Conditions Act, 1955.* Pretoria: Government Printer RP64/1977, 1977.

13936 **Rolfe, Sidney E.,** and **Damm, Walter,** eds. *The Multinational Corporation in the World Economy.* New York: Praeger, 1970.

13937 **Rothstein, R.L.** *Global Bargaining: UNCTAD and the Quest for a New International Order.* Princeton, New Jersey: Princeton University Press, 1979.

13938 **Rowe, J.W.F.** *Primary Commodities in International Trade.* Cambridge: Cambridge University Press, 1965.

13939 **Roy, Ram Mohan.** *The India Emergency Food Act of 1951: A Study of Foreign Policy Formation in the U.S.* Claremont, California: Claremont Graduate School and University Center, Ph.D., 1969.

13940 **Royal Institute of International Affairs.** *British Interests in the Mediterranean and Middle East: A Report by a Chathan House Study Group.* London, New York: Oxford University Press, 1958.

13941 **Sattar, Mohammed Abdus.** *United States Aid and Pakistan's Economic Development.* Medford, Massachusetts: Tufts University, Ph.D., 1969.

13942 **Schlemmer, L.** *Black Worker Attitudes: Political Options, Capitalism and Investment in South Africa.* Durban: Centre for Applied Social Sciences, University of Natal, 1984.

13943 **Sealey, Kenneth R.** *The Geography of Air Transport;* London: Hutchinson University Library, 1957.

13944 **Smith, William C.; Acuna, Carlos H.; Gamarra, Eduardo A.,** eds. *Democracy, Markets, and Structural Reform in Latin America.* New Brunswick: Transaction Publishers, 1994.

13945 **Solomon, Lewis D.** *Multinational Corporations and the Emerging World Order.* Port Washington, New York: Kenmikat Press, 1978.

13946 **Spicer, James K.** *External Aid in Canadian Foreign Policy: A Political and Administrative Study of Canada's Assistance Under the Colombo Plan.* Toronto, Ontario, Canada: University of Toronto, Ph.D., 1962.

13947 **Stockholm, International Peace Research Institute.** *Arms Trade Register; the Arms Trade with the Third World.* Prepared by Eva Greenback, New York/Cambridge: Massachusetts Institute of Technology Press; Stockholm; Almquist and Wiksell, 1975.

13948 **Swainson, N.** *The Development of Corporate Capitalism in Kenya, 1918-1977.* London: Heinemann, 1980.

13949 **Taylor, M.,** and **Thrift, N.J.** *Finance and Organisations: Towards a Dualistic Interpretation of the Geography of Enterprise.* Canberra: Australian National University, Department of Human Geography, Unpublished Seminar Paper, 1980.

13950 **Thayer, George.** *The War Business: The International Trade in Armaments.* New York: Simon and Schuster, 1969.

13951 **Towle, L.W.** *International Trade and Commercial Policy.* New York: Harper & Row, 1956.

13952 **Ulch, Carol Lorine.** *Communication Processes in a Politico-Spatial Context.* Iowa City: University of Iowa, Ph.D., 1972.

13953 **Ullman, Edward L.** *American Commodity Flow.* Seattle: University of Washington Press, 1957.

13954 **U.S. Congress.** Senate Committee on Foreign Relations. Subcommittee on Multinational Corporations. *Multinational Oil Corporations and United States Foreign Policy.* Washington, D.C.: U.S. Government Printing Office, 1975.

13955 **Vernon, Raymond.** *Sovereignty at Bay: The Multinational Spread of U.S. Enterprises.* New York: Basic Books, 1971.

13956 **Vincent, William.** *The Commerce and Navigation of the Ancients in the Indian Ocean.* London: T. Cadell and W. Davies, 1807.

13957 **Wistrich, Enid.** *The Politics of Transport.* London: Longmans Group Limited, 1983.

13958 **Wolfe, Roy I.** *Transportation and Politics.* Princeton, New Jersey: Van Nostrand, 1963.

13959 **Woytinsky, W.S.,** and **Woytinsky, E.S.** *World Commerce and Government; Trends and Outlook.* New York: Twentieth Century Fund, 1955.

Journals

13960 **Adikibi, Owen T.** "The Multinational Corporation and Monopoly of Patents in Nigeria." *World Development,* 16, No. 4 (April, 1988), 511-526.

13961 **Allen, M.P.** "Economic Interest Groups and the Corporate Elite Structure." *Social Sciences Quarterly,* 58, No. 4 (March, 1978), 597-615.

13962 **Allen, M.P.** "The Structural of Interorganisational Elite Cooptioni Interlocking Corporate Directors." *American Sociological Review,* 39, No. 2 (June, 1974), 393-406.

13963 "America Tries Geopolitics; Complete Control of all Foreign Trade Begins August 15." *Business Week,* 671 (July 11, 1942), 88.

13964 **Bissell, Richard E.** "Geopolitical Implications of the Oil Tanker Industry." *Asia Pacific Community,* 9 (Summer, 1980), 95-106.

13965 **Brodkin, E.I.** "United States Aid to India and Pakistan." *International Affairs,* 43, No. 4 (October, 1967), 664-677.

13966 **Bryan, Anthony T.** "Cuba's Impact in the Caribbean." *International Journal,* 40, No. 2 (Spring, 1985), 331-347.

13967 **Bunting, D., and Barbour, J.** "Interlocking Dictorates in Large American Corporations, 1896-1964." *Business History Review,* 45, No. 3 (Autumn, 1971), 317-335.

13968 **Cawson, A.** "Corporatism and Local Politics." In *The Political Economy of Corporations,* W. Grant, ed. London: Macmillan, 1985, 126-147.

13969 "China's Race Against Time. Her Resurgence in War, in Politics, and in Livelihood Depends Upon the Quantity and Speed of U.S. Aid." Reprint: *Fortune,* 32, No. 8 (August, 1945), 117-122+.

13970 **Clark, Gordon L.** "Political Geography of contemporary Affairs: NAFTA--Clinton's Victory, Organized Labor's Loss." *Political Geography,* 13, No. 4 (July, 1994), 377-384.

13971 "Colonial Tariffs and Quotas." *Round Table,* 109, No. 4 (December, 1937), 92-109.

13972 "Contribucion al Estudio de la Marina Mercante Nacional" [Contribution to the Study of the National Merchant Marine]. Articles with this title or titled "Marina Mercante Nacional" appeared frequently in *Boletin Naval* (Asuncion) written by Aurelio C. Franco, Jose Bozzano, Agustin Rojas Gonzales, Humberto Infante Rivarola and Muguel Cardona. They are: *A.C.F.,* Vol. 1, No. 1 (September, 1944), p. 21-25; *J.B.,* Vol. 1, No. 3 (January, 1945), 17-19; *J.B.,* Vol. 1, No. 5 (May, 1945), 26-34; *J.B.,* Vol. 1, No. 6 (July, 1945), 8-10; *J.B.,* Vol. 1, NO. 7 (September, 1945), 37-44; *A.R.G.,* Vol. 1, No. 7 (September, 1945), 53-55; *J.B.,* Vol. 2, No. 8 (November,1945) 9-17; *H.I.R.,* Vol. 2, No. 10 (March,1 946), 33-38; *H.I.R.,* Vol. 2, No. 11 (May, 1946), 63-64; *H.I.R.,* Vol. 2, No. 12 (July, 1946), 40-55; *M.C.,* Vol. 2, No. 13 (September, 1946), 43-61.

13973 **Corbridge, Stuart.** "The Asymmetry of Interdependence: The United States and the Geopolitics of International Financial Relations." *Studies in Comparative International Development,* 23, No. 1 (Spring, 1988), 3-29.

13974 **Cox, B.A., and Rogerson, C.M.** "The Structure and Geography of Interlocking Corporate Directorates in South Africa." *South African Geographer,* 12, No. 2 (September, 1984), 133-148.

13975 **Crowson, P.C.F.** "Trends and Patterns of International Investment in Nonfuel Minerals." In *Probleme der Robstoffsicherung.* Bonn: Freidrich Ebert Stiftung, 1981, 25-41.

13976 **Crush, Jonathan S.** "Settler-Estate Production, Monopoly Control and the Imperial Response: The Case of the Swaziland Corporation Ltd." *African Economic History,* 8 (Fall, 1979), 183-197.

13977 **Cuyvers, Luc, and Meeusen, W.** "The Structure of Personal Influence of the Belgian Holding Companies." *European Economic Review,* 8, No. 1 (January, 1976), 51-59.

13978 **Curry, R.L.** "U.S.-Aid's Southern African Program." *Journal of Southern African Affairs,* 5, No. 2 (April, 1980), 183-198.

13979 **De Oliver, M.** "The Hegemonic Cycle and Free Trade: The US and Mexico." *Political Geography,* 12, No. 5 (September, 1993), 457-472.

13980 **Dooley, P.** "The Interlocking Directorate." *American Economic Review,* 59, No. 2 (May, 1969), 314-323.

13981 **Dunleavy, P.** "Professions and Policy Change: Notes Towards a Model of Ideological Corporatism." *Public Administration Bulletin,* 36 (1981), 3-16.

13982 **Errington, Frederick, and Gewertz, Deborah.** "The Triumph of Capitalism in East New Britain?: A Contemporary Papua New Guinean Rhetoric of Motives." *Oceania* [Sydney], 64, No. 1 (September, 1993), 1-17.

13983 **Evanson, Robert K.** "Sovient Political Uses of Trade with Latin America." *Journal of Interamerican Studies and World Affairs,* 27, No. 2 (Summer, 1985), 99-127.

13984 **Everett, Guerra.** "Laws Affecting Foreign Commerce." *Commerce Reports,* 46 (November 18, 1939), 1056-1059.

13985 **Feldman, H.** "Aid as Imperialism?" *International Affairs,* 43, No. 2 (April, 1967), 219-235.

13986 **Feldstein, M.** "The World Economy Today: Signs of Recovery." *Economist*, 287, No. 7293 (1983), 43-48.

13987 **Fennema, M., and Schijf, H.** "Analysing Interlocking Directorates: Theory and Method." *Social Networks*, 1 (1978/1979), 297-332.

13988 **Fried, E.R.** "International Trade in Raw Materials: Myths and Realities." *Science*, 191, No. 4228 (Feb. 20, 1976), 641-646.

13989 **Fryer, Donald W.** "The Political Geography of International Lending by Private Banks." *Institute of British Geographers. Transactions.* New Series, 12, No. 4 (1987), 413-432.

13990 **Gallagher, John S., Jr.** "Improving Transport to Expand Exports." *International Trade Forum* (UNCTGAD-GATT International Trade Centre), 15, No. 2 (April-June, 1979), 18-22.

13991 **Gallagher, John S., Jr., and Robinson, Ronald.** "The Imperialism of Free Trade." *Economic History Review*, 2nd Ser. 6, No. 1 (August, 1953), 1-15.

13992 **Gini, Corrado.** "Trade Follows the Flag." *Weltwirtschaftliches Archiv*, 47, Band, Heft 2 (Marz, 1938), 181-227.

13993 **Gogel, R., and Koenig, T.** "Commercial Banks, Interlocking Directorates and Economic Power: An Analysis of the Primary Metals Industry." *Social Problems*, 29, No. 2 (December, 1981), 117-128.

13994 **Grant, R.** "Against the Grain: Agricultural Trade Policies of the US, the European Community and Japan at the Gatt." *Political Geography*, 12, No. 3 (May, 1993), 247-262.

13995 **Green, M.B.** "The Interurban Corporate Interlocking Directorate Network of Canada and the United States: A Spatial Perspective." *Urban Geography*. 4, No. 4 (October-December, 1983), 338-354.

13996 **Green, M.B.** "Regional Preferences for Interlocking Directorates Among the Largest American Corporations." *Environment and Planning*, A 13, No. 7 (July, 1981), 829-839.

13997 **Green, M.B., and Semple, R.K.** "The Corporate Interlocking Directorate as an Urban Spatial Information Network." *Urban Geography*, 2, No. 2 (April-June1981), 148-160.

13998 **Harvey, David W.** "The Geography of Capital Accumulation: A Reconstruction of Marxist Theory," *Antipode,* 7, No. 2 (September, 1975), 9-21.

13999 **Hauser, Philip M.** "Cultural and Personal Obstacles to Economic Development in the Less Developed Areas." *Human Organization,*, 82, No. 2 (Summer, 1959), 78-84.

14000 **Holdar, Sven.** "The Study of Foreign Aid: Unbroken Ground in Geography." *Progress in Human Geography* [London], 17, No. 4 (December, 1993), 453-470.

14001 **Hudson, S.C.** "Role of Commodity Agreements in International Trade." *Journal of Agricultural Economics*, 14 (1961), 507-30.

14002 **Ilchman, Warren F.** "A Political Economy of Foreign Aid: The Case of India." *Asian Survey*, 7, No. 10 (October, 1967), 667-688.

14003 **Jager, J.J.** "Sweden's Iron Ore Exports to Germany, 1933-1944." *Scandinavian Economic History Review*, 15, Nos. 1 and 2 (1967), 139-147.

14004 **Johnson, R.** "The Great Debt Explosion." *New Society,* (January, 1983), 148-149.

14005 **Kaplan, David.** "The Internationalisation of South African Direct Foreign Investment in the Contemporary Period." *African Affairs*, 82, No. 329 (October, 1983), 465-494.

14006 **Kerbo, H.R., and Della Fave, L.R.** "Corporate Linkage and Control of the Corporate Economy: New Evidence and a Reinterpretation." *Sociological Quarterly*, 24, No. 2 (Spring, 1983), 201-218.

14007 **Koenig, T., and Gogel, R.** "Interlocking Corporate Directorates, A Social Network." *American Journal of Economics and Sociology*, 40, No. 1 (January, 1981), 37-50.

14008 **Koenig, T.; Gogel, R.; and Sonquist, J.A.** "Models of the Significance of Interlocking Directorates." *American Journal of Economics and Sociology*, 38, No. 2 (April, 1979), 173-186.

14009 **Lee, Yong Leng.** "Southeast Asia: The Political Geography of Economic Imbalance." *Tijdschrift voor Economisch en Sociale Geografie*, 70, No. 6 (December, 1979), 339-349.

14010 **Letiche, J.M.** "Soviet Foreign Economic Policy: Trade and Assistance Programs." Institute for the Study of the U.S.S.R., Munich." *Report on the Soviet Union in 1956*, (1956), 172-191.

14011 **Levy, Walter J.** "Oil and the Decline of the West." *Foreign Affairs*, 58, No. 5 (Summer, 1980), 999-1015.

14012 **Mariolis, Peter.** "Interlocking Directorates and Control of Corporations." *Social Science Quarterly*, 56, No. 3 (December, 1975), 424-439.

14013 McCarthy, Eugene J. "Against the Grain: Is America the World's Colony?" *Policy Review*, 17 (Summer, 1981), 120-124.

14014 Mintz, Beth, and Schwartz, Michael. "Interlocking Directorates and Interest Group Formation." *American Sociological Review*, 46, No. 4 (December, 1981), 851-869.

14015 Mintz, Beth, and Schwartz, Michael. "The Structure of Intercorporate Unity in American Business." *Social Problems*, 29, No. 2 (December, 1981), 88-103.

14016 Mokken, R.J., and Stokman, F.N. "Corporate-Governmental Networks in the Netherlands." *Social Networks*, 1 (1978/79), 333-358.

14017 Moseley, Paul. "The Politics of Economic Liberalization: USAID and the World Bank in Keneya, 1980-1984." *African Affairs,* 85, No. 338 (January, 1986), 107-119.

14018 Moss, R. "Reaching for Oil: The Soviets' Bold Mideast Strategy." *Saturday Review*, 7, No. 8 (April 12, 1980), 14-22.

14019 Murphy, Rhoads. "Economic Conflicts in South Asia." *Journal of Conflict Resolution*, 4, No. 1 (March, 1960), 83-96.

14020 Norich, S. "Interlocking Directorates, the Control of Large Corporations, and Patterns of Accumulation in the Capitalist Class." In *Classes, Class Conflict and the State: Empirical Studies in Class Analysis.* M. Zeitlin, ed. Cambridge, Massachusetts: Winthrop Publishers, 1980, 83-106.

14021 Nyang'oro, Julius E. "The State of Politics in Africa: The Corporatist Factor." *Studies in Comparative International Development,* 24, No. 1 (Spring, 1989), 5-19.

14022 Ojala, E.M. "Some Current Aspects of International Commodity Policy." *Journal of Agricultural Economics*, 18 (1967), 27-46.

14023 O'Loughlin, John. "Geo-Economic Competition in the Pacific Rim: The Political Geography of Japanese and US Exports, 1966-1988. *Institute of British Geographers. Transactions* [London], New Series, 18, No. 4 (1993), 438-459.

14024 Olson, Ralph E. "The International Wheat Agreement." *Southwestern Social Science Quarterly*, 32, No. 1 (June, 1951), 38-44.

14025 Pankhurst, Richard. "Transport and Communications." In *Economic History of Ethiopia 1800-1935.* Addis Ababa: Haile Selassie University Press, 1968, 280-345.

14026 Poitras, Guy, and Robinson, Raymond. "The Politics of NAFTA in Mexico." *Journal of Interamerican Studies and World Affairs* [Coral Gables], 36, No. 1 (Spring, 1994), 1-35.

14027 Pool, Ithiel de Sola, et al. "The Influence of Foreign Travel on Political Attitudes of American Businessmen." *Public Opinion Quarterly*, 20, No. 1 (Spring, 1956), 161-195.

14028 "Porty Europejskie w Walce oLadunki Trazytowe" [Transit Cargoes as Object of European Ports' Competition]. *Gospodarka Morska*, 1, No. 2 (1948), 155-158.

14029 "Potential for U.S.-China Trade Lies Through Foreign-based Subsidiaries." *Christian Science Monitor*, (November 2, 1971), 1-12.

14030 Ratcliff, R.E.; Gallagher, Michael; and Ratcliff, K.S. "The Civic Involvement of Bankers: An Analysis of the Influence of Economic Power and Social Prominence in the Comman of Civic Policy Positions." *Social Problems*; 26, No. 3 (February, 1979), 298-313.

14031 Roett, Riordan. "Brazil and the United States: Beyond the Debt Crisis." *Journal of International Studies and World Affairs*, 27, No. 1 (February, 1985), 1-15.

14032 Rogerson, C.M. "The Goegraphy of Business-Management in South Africa." *South African Geographical Journal*, 56, No. 1 (April, 1974), 87-93.

14033 Rogerson, C.M. "The Spatial Concentraiton of Corporate Control in South Africa, 1965-1980." *South African Geographical Journal*, 66, No. 1 (April, 1984), 97-100.

14034 Reynolds, Edward. "Economic Imperialism: The Case of the Gold Coast." *Journal of Economic History*, 35, No. 1 (March, 1975), 94-116.

14035 Savage, M. "Interlocking Directorates in South Africa." In *ASSA Sociology Southern Africa: Papers from the First Conference of the Association for Sociologists in Southern Africa.* Durban: University of Natal, 1973, 44-69.

14036 Schmidt, Danna. "Oil Nations Seeking Role in Companies." *New York Times*, (November 3, 1971), 8.

14037 Scott, J., and Hughes, M. "Ownerhsip and Control in a Satellite Economy, A Discussion from Scottish Data." *Sociology*, 10 (1977), 21-41.

14038 **Shonfield, Andrew**. "Changing Commercial Policies in the Soviet Bloc." *International Affairs*, 44, No. 1 (January, 1968), 1-13.

14039 **Sonquist, J.A.**, and **Koenig, T.** "Examining Corporate Interconnections through Interlocking Directorates." In *Power and Control: Social Stsructures and Their Transformation*, T.R. Burns and W. Buckley, eds. Beverly Hills: Sage Publications, 1976, 53-83.

14040 **Sonquist, J.A.**, and **Koenig, T.** "Interlocking Directorates in the Top U.S. Corporations: A Graphy Theory Approach." *Insurgent Sociologist*, 5, No. 3 (Spring, 1975), 196-229.

14041 **Stanworth, P.**, and **Giddens, A.** "The Modern Corporate Economy: Interlocking Directorships in Britain, 1906-1970." *Sociological Review*, 23, No. 1, New Series (February, 1975), 5-28.

14042 **Stephenson, Glenn V.** "The Impact of International Economic Sanctions on the Internal Viability of Rhodesia." *Geographical Review*, 65, No. 3 (July, 1975), 377-389.

14043 **Taylor, M.**, and **Thrift, N.J.** "The Changing Spatial Concentraiton of Large Company Ownership and Control in Australia 1953-1978." *Australian Geographer*, 15 (1981), 98-105.

14044 **Taylor, M.**, and **Thrift, N.J.** "Spatial Variaitons in Australian Enterprise: The Case of Large Firms Headquartered in Melbourne and Sydney." *Environment and Planning*, A 13 , No. 1 (January, 1981), 137-146.

14045 **Terrill, Ross**. "China and the World, Self-reliance or Interdependence." *Foreign Affairs*, 55, No. 2 (January, 1977), 295-305.

14046 **Thrall, Grant Ian**. "Geoinvestment: The Interdendence Among Space, Market Size, and Political Turmoil in Attracting Foreign Direct Investment." *Conflict Management and Peace Science*, 8, No. 1 (Fall, 1984), 17-48.

14047 **Thrift, Nigel**, and **Leyshon, Anadrew**. "A Phantom State? The De-Traditionalization of Money, the International Financial System and International Financial Centres." *Political Geography*, 13, No. 4 (July, 1994), 299-327.

14048 **Tickner, V.** "International-Local Capital: The Ivory Coast Sugar Industry." *Review of African Political Economy*, 14 (1979), 119-121.

14049 **Ufkes, F.M.** "The Globalization of Agriculture." *Political Geography*, 12, No. 3 (May, 1993), 194-197.

14050 **Ufkes, F.M.** "Trade Liberalization, Agro-Food Politics and the Globalization of Agriculture." *Political Geography*, 12, No. 3 (May, 1993), 215-

231.

14051 **Useem, M.** "Classwide Rationality in the Politics of Manager and Directors of Large Corporations in the United States and Great Britain." *Administrative Science Quarterly*, 27, No. 2 (June, 1982), 199-226.

14052 **Useem, M.** "The Inner Group of the Americna Capitalist Class." *Social Problems*, 25 (1978), 225-240.

14053 **van Ommen, J.** "Pros and Cons of Foreign Private Enterprise in Developing Countries." *Progress, The Unilever Quarterly*, 2 (1969), 122-128.

14054 **Wade, Larry L.**, and **Gates, John Boatner**. "A New Tariff Map of the United States House of Representatives." *Political Geography Quarterly*, 9, No. 3 (July, 1990), 284-304.

14055 **Wellings, P.A.** "Aid to Southern African Periphery: The Case of Lesotho." *Applied Geography*, 2, No. 4 (October, 1982), 267-290.

14056 **Whidden, Howard P., Jr.** "Reciprocal Trade Program and Post-War Reconstruction." *Foreign Policy Reports*, 19, No. 2 (April 1, 1943), 14-23.

14057 **Wu, Yu-Shan**. "Marketization of Politics: The Taiwan Experience." *Asian Survey*, 29, No. 4 (April, 1989), 382-400.

MINORITIES

Books

14058 **Ashworth, G.**, ed. *World Minorities*, Vol. 1. London: Quartermaine House, and the Minority Group, 1977; Vol. II, 1978.

14059 **Ashworth, G.**, ed. *World Minorities in the Eighties*. Vol. 3. Sunbury, United Kingdom: Quartermaine House, 1980.

14060 **Beaglehole, J.H.** *Minorities in Southern Asia and Public Policy, with Special Reference to India, Mainly Since 1919*. London, England: London School of Economics, University of London, Ph.D., 1966.

14061 **Bennion, Lowell Colton**. *Flight from the Reich: A Geogaphic Exposition of South-West German Emigraiton, 1683-1815*. Syracuse, New York: Syracuse University, Ph.D., 1971.

14062 **Borrow, George**. *The Zincale; Or an Account of the Gypsies in Spain*. London: John Murray, 1864.

14063 **Boteni, Viorica**. *Les minorities en Transylvanie*. Paris: Pedone, 1983.

14064 **Byczkowski, J.** *Mniejzosci narodowosciowe w Europie (National Minorities in Europe), 1945-1974.* Opole: Instytnt Bsczkowski, 1976.

14065 **Capotorti, F.** *Study on the Rights of Persons Belonging to Ethnic, Religious, and Linguistic Minorities.* New York: United Nations, 1979.

14066 **Chang, Chi-Jen.** *The Minority Groups of Yunnan and Chisese Political Expansion into Southeast Asia.* East Lansing: Michigan State University, Ph.D., 1966.

14067 **Corbeil, Y., and Delude, C.** *Etudes des communautes francophones hors Quebec, des communautes anglophones au Quebec, des francophones au Quebec et des anglophones hors Quebec.* Montreal: CROP, 1982.

14068 **Coughlin, Richard J.** *Double Identity, the Chinese in Modern Thailand.* Hong Kong: Hong Kong University Press, 1960.

14069 **Esman, Milton J., ed.** *Ethnic Conflict in the Western World.* Ithaca, New York: Cornell University Press, 1977.

14070 **Fawcett, James.** *The International Protection of Minorities.* London: Minority Rights Group, Report No. 41, 1979.

14071 **Fischer, Eric.** *Minorities and Minority Problems.* New York: Vantage Press, 1980.

14072 **Fisherman, J., ed.** *Advance in the Study of Societal Multilingualism.* New York: Morton, 1978.

14073 **George, Pierre.** *Geopolitiques des Minorites.* Paris: Presses Universitaires de France, 1984.

14074 **Gurr, Ted Robert.** *Minorities at Risk: A Global View of Ethnopolitical Conflicts.* Washington, DC: United States Institute of Peace Press, 1993.

14075 **Haines, David W., ed.** *Refugees as Migrants: Cambodians, Laotians, and Vietnamese in America.* Savage, Maryland: Rowman and Littlefield Publishers, 1988.

14076 **Han, Sin Fong.** *A Study of the Occupational Patterns and Social Interaction of Overseas Chinese in Sabah, Malaysia.* Ann Arbor: University of Michigan, Ph.D., 1971.

14077 **Hickok, Floyd Clinton.** *The Distribution and Demographic Characer of the Major Minorities in California, 1970.* Fullerton: California State University, Master's Thesis, 1975.

14078 **Hourani, A.H.** *Minorities in the Arab World.* London: Oxford University Press, 1947.

14079 **Janowsky, Oscar I.** *Nationalities and National Minorities.* New York: Macmillan, 1945.

14080 **Kovacik, Charles Frank.** *A Geographical Analysis of the Foreign-Born in Huron, Sanilac, and St. Clair Counties of Michigan with Particular Refernece to Canadians: 1850-1880.* East Lansing: Michigan State University, Ph.D., 1970.

14081 **Ladas, S.P.** *The Exchange of Minorities, Bulgaria, Greece, and Turkey.* New York: Macmillan, 1932.

14082 **Laponce, J.A.** *The Protection of Minorities.* Berkeley: University of California Press, 1961.

14083 **Lessing, O.E.** *Minorities and Boundaries.* New York: Van Riemsdyck, 1931.

14084 **LeVine, R., and Campbell, Donald.** *Ethnocentrism: Theories of Conflict, Ethnic Attitudes, and Group Behavior.* New York: John Wiley & Sons, 1972.

14085 **L'Huillier, Marc-Andre.** "The Metropolitan Concentration of Minorities in the United States and Britain." Seattle: University of Washington, Ph.D., 1988.

14086 **Little, David.** *Sri Lanka: The Inventory of Enmity.* Washington, DC: United States Institute of Peace Press, 1994.

14087 **Lucien-Brun, Jean.** *Le probleme des minorites devant le droit international.* Paris: Spes, 1923.

14088 **Macartney, C.A.** *Naitonal States and National Minorities.* New York: Oxford University Press, 1934.

14089 **Mair, L.P.** *The Protection of Minorities.* Londres: Christopher's, 1928.

14090 **Masud-Piloto, Felix Roberto.** *With Open Arms: Cuban Migration in the United States.* Ithaca, New York: Cornell University Press, 1988.

14091 **Mossa, H.** *The Geographical Distribution of Arab Homeland Refugees in the Galilee Region.* Haifa: University of Haifa, M.A. (in Hebrew), 1988.

14092 **Nasse, George N.** *The Survival of the Albanian Minority in Southern Italy.* Ann Arbor: University of Michigan, Ph.D., 1960.

14093 **Nayar, Baldev Raj.** *Minority Politics in the Punjab.* Princeton, New Jersey: Princeton University Press, 1966.

14094 **Otok, Stanislaw.** *An Analysis of the Territorial Distribution of Americans of Polish Extraction in the United States of America;* American Studies, Vol. 1. Warsaw: Warsaw University Press, 1983.

14095 **Proudfoot, M.J.** *European Refugees, 1939-52: A Study of Forced Popualtion Movement.* Evanston, Illinois: Northwestern University Press, 1956.

14096 **Purcell, Victor.** *The Chinese in Malaya.* London: R.I.I.A., 1952.

14097 **Purcell, Victor.** *The Chinese in Southeast Asia,* 2nd ed. London: R.I.I.A., 1965.

14098 **Rechlin, Alice Theodora Merten.** *The Utilization of Space by the Nappanee, Indiana Old Order Amish: A Minority Group Study.* Ann Arbor: University of Michigan, Ph.D., 1970.

14099 **Ressler, John Quenton.** *Moenkopi: Sequent Occupance, Landscape Change, and the View of the Environment in an Oasis on the Western Navajo Reservation, Arizona.* Eugene: University of Oregon, Ph.D., 1970.

14100 **Richardson, P.** *Chinese Mine Labour in the Transvaal.* London: Macmillan, 1982.

14101 **Robertson, W.** *The Dispossessed Majority.* Cape Canaveral: Howard Allen Enterprises, 1976.

14102 **Sandhu, K.S.** *Indians in Malaya: Some Aspects of Their Immigration and Settlement.* London: Cambridge University Press, 1969.

14103 **Sen, Rakesranjan.** *The Problem of Minorities.* Calcutta: University of Calcutta, Ph.D., 1935.

14104 **The Slovene Carinthia.** *Carinthie Slovene.* Ljubljana: 1946.

14105 **Thompson, Virginia,** and **Adloff, Richard.** *Minority Problems in Southeast Asia,* I.P.R. Stanford, California: Stanford University Press, 1955.

14106 **United Nations.** *Commission on Human Rights.* Lake Success, New York: Sub-commission on Prevention of Discrimination and Protection of Minorities. Definition and Classification of Minorities. Memorandum submitted by the Secretary-General, 1950.

14107 **Wade, M.** *The French Canadians, 1760-1945.* London: Macmillan, 1955.

14108 **Wagley, C.,** and **Harris, M.** *Minorities in the New World.* New York: Columbia University Press, 1958.

14109 **Wickberg, Edgar.** *The Chinese in Philippine Life.* New Haven, Connecticut: Yale University Press, 1965.

14110 **Williams, Lea E.** *The Future of the Overseas Chinese Communities in Southeast Asia.* New York: McGraw-Hill, 1966.

14111 **Willmott, William E.** *The Chinese in Cambodia.* Vancouver: University of British Columbia, 1967.

14112 **Young, Crawford.** *The Politics of Cultural Plurasism.* Madison: University of Wisconsin Press, 1976.

Journals

14113 **Ares, R.** "Les minorites franco-canadiennes, etude statistique." *Royal Society, Transactions, Series 4,* 13 (1975), 123-132.

14114 **Beckett, Jeremy R.** "Australia's Melanesian Minority: Political Development in the Torres Straits Islands." *Human Organization,* 24, No. 2 (Summer, 1965), 152-158.

14115 **Bedr Khan, Kamuran Ali.** "The Kurdish Problem." *Journal of the Royal Central Asian Society,* 36, Parts 3 and 4 (July-October, 1949), 237-48.

14116 **Buchanan, Keith,** and **Hurwitz, N.** "The Asiatic Immigrant Community in the Union of South Africa." *Geographical Review,* 39, No. 3 (July, 1949), 440-450.

14117 **Castonguay, C.** "Exogamie et anglicisation chez les minorites canadiennesfrqancaises." *Canadian Review of Sociology and Anthropology,* 16 (1979), 21-31.

14118 **Chichekian, Garo.** "Armenian Immigrants in Canada and Their Distribution in Montreal." *Cahiers de Geographie de Quebec,* 21, No. 52 (April, 1977), 65-81.

14119 **Condominas, Georges.** "Aspects of a Minority Problem in Indonesia." *Pacific Affairs,* 24, No. 1 (March, 1951), 77-82.

14120 **Connelley, B.P.,** ed. "Political Integration in Multi-National States." *Journal of International Affairs,* 27, No. 1 (Spring, 1973), 1-57; 27, and No. 2 (Fall, 1973), 159-260.

14121 **Edmonds, G.J.** "The Kurdish War in Iraq: A Plan for Peace." *Royal Central Asian Journal,* 54, Part I (February, 1967), 10-22.

14122 **Falk, Karl.** "Strife in Czechoslovakia: The German Minority Question." *Foreign Policy Reports,* 14, No. 1 (March 15, 1938), 1-12.

14123 **Farmer, B.H.** "Ceylon: Some Problems of a Plural Society." *Essays in Political Geography*, Charles A. Fisher, ed. London: Methuen, 1968, 147-160.

14124 **Griffiths, Leuan.** "A Future Uncertain." *Geographic Magazine*, 59, No. 3 (March, 1987), 140-145.

14125 **Heiser, M.O.,** ed. "Ethnic Conflict in the World Today." *Annals of the American Academy of Political and Social Science*, 433 (September, 197), 1-160 (complete issue, multiple authors).

14126 **Held, Colbert Colgate.** "Refugee Industries in West Germany after 1945." *Economic Geography*, 32, No. 4 (October,1956), 316-335.

14127 **Hamelin, Louis-Edmond.** "French Soul in a British Form - Opportunity for Modern Quebec." *Geographical Magazine*, 46, No. 11 (November, 1972), 744-752.

14128 **Hayit, Baymizza.** "Turkestan in der Sowjetunian." *Zeitschrift fur Geopolitik*, 24 Jahrgang, Heft 3 (Marz, 1953), 141-147.

14129 **Jillani, M.S.** "Resettlement Pattern of Displaced Persons in Pakistan." *Geografia*, 2, No. 2 (Winter, 1963), 77-98.

14130 **Joy, R.** "Canada's Official Language Population as Shown by the 1981 Census." *American Review of Canadian Studies*, 15, No. 1 (1985), 90-96.

14131 **Kielczewska-Zaleska, M.,** and **Bonasewicz, A.** "Rozmieszczenie Polakow za granica (Distribution of Polish Abroad)." *Problemy Polonii Zagranicznej*, 1 (1960), 5-19.

14132 **Landon, Kenneth Perry.** "The Problem of the Chinese in Thailand." *Pacific Affairs*, 13, No. 2 (June, 1940), 149-161.

14133 **Libomyr, Y. Luciuk.** "Internal Security and an Ethnic Minority: The Ukranians and Internment Operations in Canada, 1914-1920." *Signum,* (Spring-Summer, 1980), Complete Issue.

14134 **Lucink, Lubomyr Y.** "internal Security and an Ethnic Minority: The Ukrainians and Internment Operations in Canada, 1914-1920." *Signum,* Royal Military College, Kingston (Spring-Summer, 1980), complete issue.

14135 **Maryanski, A.** "Stan i rozmieszczenie mniejszosci polskiej w ZSSR (Distribution of Polish Minorities in Soviet Union)." *Czasopismo Geograficzne*, 45, Part I (1974), 145-146.

14136 **Moseley, George V.H.** "China's Fresh Approach to the National Minority Question." *China Quarterly*, 24, (October-December, 1965)15-27.

14137 **Mrazek, Josef.** "Human Rights: Their International Standards and Protection." *Coexistence* [Dordrecht], 27, No. 4 (December, 1990), 301-335.

14138 **Passaris, C.** "Canada's Demographic Outlook and Multicultural Immigration." *International Migration*, 25, No. 4 (1987), 361-384.

14139 **Sarkar, Subhasa Chandsa.** "China's Policy Towards Minorities." *World Today*, 15, No. 10 (October, 1959), 408-416.

14140 **Seig, L.** "Concepts of Ghetto: A Geography of Minority Group." *Professional Geographer*, 23, No. 1 (January, 1971), 1-4.

14141 **Shmueli, Aushalom.** "The Bedouin of the Land of Israel--Settlement and Changes." *Urban Ecology*, 4 (1980), 253-286.

14142 "The Struggle of the Sudeten Germans for Freedom and the Right of Self-Determination." *Volkerbund*, 7, No. 23 (September 12, 1938), 309-324.

14143 **Thornberry, Patrick.** "Fashions and Rights: Minorities and International Law." *Co-existence*, 16, No. 2 (October, 1979), 145-156.

14144 **Unger, Leonard.** "The Chinese in Southeast Asia." *Geographical Review*, 34, No. 2 (April, 1944), 195-217.

14145 **Vedovato, G.** "Il problema dell' autonomia per la minoranza di lingua tedesca dell' Alto Adige." *Riviste di Studi Politici Internazionali*, 35, No. 1 (January, 1968), 79-93.

14146 **Weerawardana, I.D.S.** "Minority Problems in Ceylon." *Pacific Affairs*, 25, No. 3 (September, 1952), 278-287.

14147 **Wind, B.** "O potrzebie badan nad iloscia Polakow za granica (Requirements of Quantitative Research on Polich Abroad). *Problemy Polonii Zagranicznej*, 2 (1961), 184-191.

14148 **Wood, William B.** "Political Geography of Contemporary Events 11: The Political Geography of Asylum: Two Models and a Case Study." *Political Geography Quarterly*, 8, No. 2 (April, 1989), 181-196.

CAPITALIST, MARXIST, COMMUNIST AND OTHER IDEOLOGICAL PHILOSOPHIES

Books

14149 **Abrams, James,** and Others. *China: From the Long March to Tiananmen Square.* New York: Henry Holt, 1990.

14150 **Althusser, L.** *For Marx*. London: New Left Books, 1977.

14151 **Althusser, L.** *Lenin and Philosophy*. London: New Left Books, 1971.

14152 **Beissinger, Mark R.** *Scientific Management, Socialist Discipline, and Soviet Power*. Cambridge, Massachusetts: Harvard University Press, 1988.

14153 **Bideleux, Robert.** *Communism and Development*. London: Methuen, 1985.

14154 **Blecher, M.D.** *China: Politics, Economics and Society. Iconoclasm and Innovation in a Revolutionary Socialist Country*. London: Pinter, London/Rienner, Boulder Marxist Regimes Series, 1986.

14155 **Braudel, F.** *Afterthoughts on Materialism and Capitalism*. Baltimore, Maryland: Johns Hopkins University Press, 1977.

14156 **Brewer, A.** *Marxist Theories of Imperialism: A Critical Survey*. London: Routledge, 1980.

14157 **Brown, Archie,** ed. *Political Culture and Communist Studies*. London: Macmillan, 1984.

14158 **Brzezinski, Zbigniew.** *The Grand Failure: The Birth and Death of Communism in the Twentieth Century*. New York: Charles Scribner's Sons, 1989.

14159 **Buchanan, Keith.** *The Geography of Imperialism*. London: Book Ends, 1972.

14160 **Bukowski, Charles,** and **Walsh, J. Richard,** eds. *Glasnost, Perestroika, and the Socialist Community*. New York: Praeger, 1990.

14161 **Bunge, W.** *Fitzerald, Geography of a Revolution*. Cambridge, Massachusetts: Schenkman, 1971.

14162 **Buraway, M.** *Manufacturing Consent Changes in the Labour Process Under Monopoly Capitalism*. Chicago, Illinois: University of Chicago Press, 1979.

14163 **Burch, R. Kurt, Jr.** *Late Capitalism and Changing Patterns of International Relations*. Washington, D.C.: American University, Master's Thesis, 1983.

14164 **Burchett, W.** *Catapult to Freedom*. London: Quartet, 1978.

14165 **Burgess, Rod.** *Marxism and Geography*. London: University College London, Department of Geography, Occasional Papers, No. 30, 1976.

14166 **Carman, E. Day.** *Soviet Imperialism; Russia's Drive Toward World Domination*. Washington,

D.C.: Public Affairs Press, (1950).

14167 **Cerny, P.G.,** and **Schain, M.A.,** eds. *Socialism, the State and Public Policy in France*. London: Frances Rinters, 1985.

14168 **Christenson, R.M.,** et al. *Ideologies and Modern Politics*. London: Nelson, 1971.

14169 **Corsino, MacArthur Flores.** *A Conceptual Framework for Studying the International Relations of a Communist Revolutionary Movement: The Partai Komunis Indonesia*. DeKalb: Northern Illinois University, Ph.D., 1977.

14170 **Cox, Kevin R.,** and **Mair, Andrew.** *The Capitalist Space-Economy and the New Spatial Politics*. Columbus: Ohio State University, Department of Geography, unpublished paper, 1985.

14171 **Cromer, Earl.** *Ancient and Modern Imperialism*. London: John Murray, 1910.

14172 **Dean, M.,** and **Scott, A.J.,** eds. *Urbanization and Planning in Capitalist Societies*. New York and London: Methuen, 1980.

14173 **Des Forges, Roger; Luo, Ning;** and **Wu Yen-bo,** eds. *Chinese Democracy and the Crisis of 1989: Chinese and American Reflections*. Albany: State University of New York Press, 1993.

14174 **Dirlik, Arif.** *The Origins of Chinese Communism*. New York: Oxford University Press, 1989.

14175 **Eberstadt, Nick.** *The Poverty of Communism*. New Brunswick, New Jersey: Transaction Books, 1988.

14176 **Engles, F.** *Letter to J. Bloch, 21 September; Marx and Engles, Selected Works*. London: Lawrence and Wishart, 1968.

14177 **Frank, Andre Gunder.** *Capitalism and Underdevelopment in Latin America*. New York: M.R. Press, 1967.

14178 **Frank, Andre Gunder.** *On Capitalist Underdevelopment*. Oxford: Oxford University Press, 1975.

14179 **Friedman, A.** *Industry and Labour, Class Struggle at Work and Monopoly Capitalism*. London: Macmillan, 1977.

14180 **Gans, Herbert J.** *Middle American Individualism: The Future of Liberal Democracy*. New York: The Free Press, 1988.

14181 **Gamble, A.** *The Conservative Nation*. London: Routledge, 1974.

14182 **Goldberg, Richard.** *The International Relations of the French Communist and Socialist Parties: 1968-1975.* Boston: University of Massachusetts, Ph.D., 1982.

14183 **Gorny, Yosef.** *Zionism and the Arabs: 1882-1948: A Study of Ideology.* Oxford: Oxford University Press, 1987.

14184 **Guelke, L.** "Idealism." *Themes in Geographic Thought*, M.E. Harvey and B.P. Holly, eds. London: Croom Helm, 1981, 133-147.

14185 **Halliday, Fred,** and **Alavi, Hamza,** eds. *State and Ideology in the Middle East and Pakistan.* Houndmills: Macmillan, 1988.

14186 **Harris, Richard L.** *Marxism, Socialism and Democracy in Latin America.* Boulder: Westview Press, 1992.

14187 **Hilton, R.H.** *The Transition from Feudalism to Capitalism.* London: Verso, 1978.

14188 **Hobson, Christopher Z.,** and **Tabor, Ronald D.** *Trotskyism and the Dilemma of Socialism.* New York: Greenwood Press, 1988.

14189 **Hollist, W.C.,** and **Rosenau, J.N.** *World System Debates,* World System Structure. Beverly Hills: Sage Publications, 1982.

14190 **Hunt, A.,** ed. *Marxism and Democracy.* London: Lawrence and Wishart, 1980.

14191 **Hutchins, F.G.** *The Illusion of Permanence: British Imperialism in India.* Princeton, New Jersey: Princeton University Press, 1967.

14192 **Jessop, B.** *The Capitalist State.* New York University Press, 1982.

14193 **Kamrava, Mehran.** *The Political History of Modern Iran: Form Tribalism to Theocracy.* Westport: Praeger Publishers, 1992.

14194 **Keene, Francis.** *Neither Liberty Nor Bread: The Meaning and Tragedy of Facism.* New York: Harper & Row, 1940.

14195 **Kiernan, V.G.** *Marxism and Imperialism.* New York: St. Martin's Press, 1974.

14196 **Kitschelt, Herbert,** and **Hellemans, Staf.** *Beyond the European Left: Ideology and Political Action in the Belgian Ecology Parties.* Durham, North Carolina: Duke University Press, 1990.

14197 **Kolakowski, Leszek.** *Main Currents of Marxism: The Founders.* London: Oxford University Press, 1978.

14198 **Kroker, Arthur,** and **Kroker, Marilouise,** eds. *Ideology and Power in the Age of Lenin in Ruins.*

New York: St. Martin's Press, 1991.

14199 **Laqueur, Walter,** and Others. *Soviet Union 2000: Reform or Revolution?* New York: St. Martin's Press, 1990.

14200 **Lenin, V.I.** *On Imperialism and Imperialists.* Moscow: Progress Press, 1973.

14201 **Levine, Alan J.** *The Soviet Union, the Communist Movement, and the World: Prelude to the Cold War, 1917-1941.* New York: Praeger, 1990.

14202 **Lichtheim, G.** *Imperialism.* London: Penguin, 1971.

14203 **Lindberg, L.N.,** et al., eds. *Stress and Contradiction in Modern Capitalism.* Lexington: D.C. Heath, 1975.

14204 **Linden, Ronald H.,** and **Rockman, Bert A.,** eds. *Elite Studies and Communist Politics: Essays in Memory of Carl Beck.* Pittsburgh, Pennsylvania: University of Pittsburgh, University Center for International Studies, 1984.

14205 **Liska, G.** *Imperial America: The International Politics of Privacy.* Baltimore, Maryland: Johns Hopkins University Press, 1967.

14206 **Lojkine, J.** *Le Marxisme, l'Etat et la Question urbaine.* Paris: PUF, 1977.

14207 **Macintyre, S.** *Little Moscows, Communism and Working-Class Militancy in Inter-War Britain.* London: Croom Helm.

14208 **Mackerras, Colin,** and **Knight, Nick.** *Marxism in Asia.* London: Croom Helm, 1985.

14209 **Mandel, E.** *Late Capitalism.* London: Verso, 1978.

14210 **Markovits, Andrei S.,** and **Gorski, Philip S.** *The German Left: Red, Green and Beyond.* New York: Oxford University Press, 1993.

14211 **McCuen, Gary E.** *The Nicaraguan Revolution.* Hudson, Wisconsin: McCuen Publications, 1986.

14212 **Miliband, R.** *The State in Capitalist Society.* London: Quartet Books, 1969.

14213 **Mollenkopf, J.** *Marxism and the Metropolis.* Oxford: Oxford University Press, 1978.

14214 **Montgomery, Michael.** *Imperialist Japan: The Yen to Dominate.* London: Christopher Helm, 1987.

14215 **Moon, P.T.** *Imperialism and World Politics.* New York: Macmillan, 1933.

14216 **Moore, W.G.** *the Geography of Capitalism.* (The New People's Library, Vol. 18) London: V. Gollancz, 1938.

14217 **Mukherjee, A.N.** *Sino-Indian Relations and the Communists.* Calcutta: Institute of Political Studies, 1960.

14218 **Murray, M.J.** *The Development of Capitalism in Colonial Indo-China (1870-1940).* Berkeley: University of California Press, 1980.

14219 **Nathan, K.S.** "Malaysia in 1989: Communists End Armed Struggle." *Asian Survey,* 30, No. 2 (February, 1990), 210-220.

14220 **Nogee, Joseph L.,** ed. *Soviet Politics: Russian After Brezhnev.* New York: Praeger, 1985.

14221 **Offe, C.** *Strukturprobleme des Kapitalistischen Staates: Aufshatze zur Politischen Soziologie.* Frankfurt am Main: Suhrkamp, 1975.

14222 **Ottaway, Marina,** and **Ottaway, David.** *Afrocommunism,* 2nd ed. New York: African Publishing, 1986.

14223 **Passfield, Sidney James Webb, Baron.** *Soviet Communism: A New Civilisation?* 2 v. by Sidney and Beatrice Webb. New York: Charles Scribner's Sons, 1938.

14224 **Peet, Richard.** *Global Capitalism: A Critical Survey of Global Development Through Time.* New York: Rutledge, 1990.

14225 **Peet, Richard.** *Global Capitalism: Theories of Social Development.* New York: Routledge, 1991.

14226 **Perez, Louis A., Jr.** *Cuba: Between Reform and Revolution.* New York: Oxford University Press, 1988.

14227 **Piven, F.F.,** and **Cloward, R.A.** *The New Class War.* New York: Pantheon, 1982.

14228 **Poulanteas, N.** *Classes in Contemporary Capitalism.* London: New Left Books, 1975.

14229 **Quaini, M.P.** *Geography and Marxism.* Oxford: Blackwell, 1982.

14230 **Ra'anan, Uri,** and Others. *Third World Marxist-Leninist Regimes: Strengths, Vulnerabilities, and U.S. Policy.* Washington, D.C.: Pengamon-Brasseys International Defense Publishers, 1985.

14231 **Ramazanoglu, Huseyin.** *Turkey in the World Capitalish System.* Brookfield, Vermont: Gower Publishing, 1986.

14232 **Rees, E.A.** *State Control in Soviet Russia: The Rise and Fall of the Workers' and Peasants' Inspectorate, 1920-34.* Houndmills: Macmillan, 1987.

14233 **Remington, Thomas F.,** ed. *Politics and the Soviet System: Essays in Honour of Frederick C. Barghoorn.* New York: St. Martin's Press, 1989.

14234 **Reynolds, Charles.** *Modes of Imperialism.* Oxford: Martin Robertson, 1981.

14235 **Robbins, Merritt Wesley.** *Cuban-Soviet Relations, 1963-1968: An Asymmetrical Alliance Regime and the Politics of International Communist Gamesmanship.* Cambridge, Massachusetts: Harvard University, Ph.D., 1978.

14236 **Rodd, L.C.** *Australian Imperialism.* (Survey of Australia Series, No. 2.) Sydney: Modern Publishers and Importers, 1938.

14237 **Roucek, Joseph S.** *Contemporary Political Ideologies.* New York: Philosophical Library, 1961.

14238 **Rowen, Henry S.,** and **Wolf, Charles, Jr.,** eds. *The Future of the Soviet Empire.* New York: St. Martin's Press, 1987.

14239 **Rydenfelt, Sven.** *Kommunismen i Sverige; en Samhallsvetenskaplig Studie.* Lund: Gleerupska Universitatsbockhandeln, 1954.

14240 **Sandel, M.** *Liberalism and the Limits of Justice.* Cambridge: Cambridge University Press, 1982.

14241 **Schmidt, Carl T.** *The Plough and the Sword: Labor, Land, and Property in Fascist Italy.* New York: Columbia University Press, 1938.

14242 **Schumpeter, J.** *Capitalism, Socialism and Democracy.* New York: Harper & Row, 1950.

14243 **Scruton, R.** *The Meaning of Conservatism.* London: Macmillan, 1980.

14244 **Seton-Watson, Hugh.** *The Imperialist Revolutionaries: Trends in World Communism in the 1960's and 1970's.* Boulder, Colorado: Westview Press, 1985.

14245 **Sicker, Martin.** *The Bear and the Lion: Soviet Imperialism and Iran.* New York: Praeger, 1988.

14246 **Sombart, W.** *Why is There No Socialism in the United States?* Tubingen, Germany: Mohr, 1906.

14247 **Stedman, Jones G.** *Ideology in Social Science: Readings in Social Theory.* New York: Pantheon, 1973.

14248 Stern, Geoffrey. *The Atlas of Communism.* New York: Macmillan, 1990.

14249 Storper, M. and Walker, R. *The Capitalist Imperative: Territory, Technology and Industrial Growth.* Oxford: Basil Blackwell, 1989.

14250 Szporluk, Roman. *Communism and Naturalism: Karl Marx versus Friedrich List.* New York: Oxford University Press, 1988.

14251 Taras, Ray. *Ideology in Socialist State: Poland, 1956-1983.* Cambridge: Cambridge University Press, 1984.

14252 Therborn, G. *The Ideology of Power and the Power of Ideology.* London: New Left Books, 1980.

14253 Timmerman, Heinz. *The Decline of the World Communist Movement: Moscow, Beijing and Communish Parties in the West.* Translated by Julius W. Friend. Boulder, Colorado: Westview Press, 1987.

14254 Urban, G.R., ed. *Can the Soviet System Survive Reform?* London: Pinter, 1989.

14255 Urry, J. *The Anatomy of Capitalist Societies. The Economy, Civil Society and the State.* London: Macmillan, 1981b.

14256 U.S. Congress, 79th, 2d Session, House. *Communism in Action; a Documented Study and Analysis of Communism in Operation in the Soviet Union.* Prepared at the instance and under the direction of Representative Everett M. Dirksen of Illinois by the Legislative Reference Service of the Library of Congress under the direction of Ernest S. Griffith. Document No. 754. Washington, D.C.: U.S.Congress, 79th, 2d Session, House, 1946.

14257 Verdery, Katherine. *National Ideology Under Socialism: Identity and Cultural Politics in Ceausescu's Romania.* Berkeley: University of California Press, 1991.

14258 Waller, R. *Democracy and Sectarianism.* Liverpool: Liverpool University Press, 1980.

14259 Wallerstein, I. *The Capitalist World Economy.* Cambridge: Cambridge University Press, 1979.

14260 Wallerstein, I. *The Historical Capitalism.* London: Verso, 1983.

14261 Wallerstein, I. *The Modern World-System III: The Second Era of Great Expansion of the Capitalist World-Economy, 1730-1840's.* New York: Academic Press, 1989.

14262 Wauters, Arthur. *Le Communisme et la Decolonisation.* Bruxelles: 1952.

14263 Westergaard, J.H., and Resler, H. *Class in a Capitalist Society: A Study of Contemporary Britain.* London: Heinemann Educational Books, 1975.

14264 Wheelwright, E.L. and Buckley, K., eds. *Essays in the Political Economy of Australian Capitalism*, vol. 5. Sydney: Australia and New Zealand Book Co., 1983.

14265 Wiarda, Howard J., and Others. *The Communish Challenge in the Caribbean and Central America.* Washington, D.C.: American Enterprise Institute for Public Policy Research, 1987.

14266 Wiles, Peter, ed. *The New Communist Third World: An Essay in Political Economy.* London: Croom Helm, 1982.

14267 Wright, E.O. *Class, Crisis and the State.* London: New Left Books, 1978.

14268 Yakovlev, Alexander. *The Fate of Marxism in Russia.* Translated from the Russian by Catherine A. Fitzpatrick. New York: Yale University Press, 1993.

14269 Young, Crawford. *Ideology and Development in Africa.* New Haven and London: Yale University Press, 1982.

Journals

14270 Adam, Heribert. "Survival Politics: Afrikanerdom in Search of a New Ideology." *Journal of Modern African Studies*, 16, No. 4 (December, 1978), 657-669.

14271 Aglietta, M. "World Capitalism in the Eighties." *New Left Review*, 136 (November-December, 1982), 5-41.

14272 Allen, J. "In Search of a Method: Hegel, Marx, and Realism." *Radical Philosophy*, 35 (Autumn, 1983), 26-33.

14273 Amin, Nurul. "Maoism in Bangladesh: The Case of the East Bengal Sarbohara Party." *Asian Survey*, 26, No. 7 (July, 1986), 759-773.

14274 Amin, Nurul. "The Pro-Chinese Communist Movement in Bangladesh." *Journal of Contemporary Asia*, 15, No. 3 (1985), 349-360.

14275 Anzolin, Alexandra, and Di Seo, Gan Lucia. "Les Mafias et le Milieu Politique Italien." *Herodote*, No. 72-73 (Janvier-Juin, 1994), 92-100.

14276 **Baker, Christopher; Johnson, Gordon;** and **Seal, Anil,** eds. "Power, Profit and Politics: Essays on Imperialism, Nationalism, and Change in Twentieth-Century India." *Modern Asian Studies*, 15, Part 3 (July, 1981), 355-721.

14277 **Bilinsky, Yaroslav.** "Nationality Policy in Gorbachev's First Year." *Orbis,* 30, No. 2 (Summer, 1986), 331-342.

14278 **Blake, Charles H.** "Social Pacts and Inflation Control in New Democracies: The Impact of 'Wildcat Cooperation' in Argentina and Uruguay." *Comparative Political Studies*, 27, No. 3 (October, 1994), 381-401.

14279 **Blasier, S. Cole.** "Chile: A Communist Battleground." *Political Science Quarterly*, 65, No. 3 (September, 1950), 353-375.

14280 **Brenner, R.** "The Origins of Capitalist Development: A Critique of Neo-Smithian Marxism." *New Left Review*, 104 (July-August, 1977), 25-92.

14281 **Broden, Eric.** "The Seven Decades of Communist Imperialism." *International Social Science Review*, 63, No. 3 (Summer, 1988), 127-128.

14282 **Brumberg, Abraham.** "Poland: The Demise of Communism." *Foreign Affairs,* 69, No. 1 (1990) 70-88.

14283 **Carr, Graham.** "Imperialism and Nationalism in Revisionalist Historiography: A Critique of Some Recent Trends." *Journal of Canadian Studies*, 17, No. 2 (Summer, 1982), 91-99.

14284 **Cawson, A.,** and **Saunders, P.** "Corporatism, Competitive Politics and Class Struggle." In *Capital and Politics*, R. King, ed. London: Routledge, 1983, 8-27.

14285 **Chao, Linda,** and **Myers, Ramon H.** "The First Chinese Democracy: Political Development of the Republic of China on Taiwan, 1986-1994." *Asian Survey* [Berkeley], 34, No. 3 (March, 1994), 213-230.

14286 **Chouinard, Vera.** "Transformations in the Capitalist State: The Development of Legal Aid and Legal Clinics in Canada." *Institute of British Geographers. Transactions.* New Series, 14, No. 3 (1989), 329-349.

14287 **Clapham, Christopher.** "Revolutionary Socialist Development in Ethiopia." *African Affairs,* 86, No. 343 (April, 1987), 151-165.

14288 **Clark, G.L.** "Capitalism and Regional Disparities." *Annals of the Association of American Geographers*, 70, No. 2, (June, 1980), 226-237.

14289 **Clark, William A.** "Toward the Construction of a Political Mobility Ranking of Oblast' Communist Party Committees." *Soviet Union,* 14, No. 2 (1987), 197-227.

14290 "Competing Ideologies in Korea." *World Today,* 5, No. 6 (June, 1949), 243-250.

14291 **Cousins, Alan.** "State, Ideology, and Power in Rhodesia: 1958-1972." *The International Journal of African Historical Studies* [Boston], 24, No. 1 (1991), 35-64.

14292 **Crush, J.** "Capitalist Homoficence, Frontier and Uneven Development in Southern Africa." *GeoJournal*, 12, No. 2 (1986), 129-136.

14293 **Curzon of Keddleston, Lord.** "The True Imperialism." *Nineteenth Century and After*, 62 (January, 1908), 157-161.

14294 **Cuthbert, A.R.** "Hong Kong 1997: The Transition to Socialism--Ideology, Discourse, and Urban Spatial Structure." *Environment & Planning D: Society & Space*, 5, No. 2 (1987), 123-150.

14295 **Dale, Patrick.** "The Aftermath of the Twenthy-Seventh CPSU Congress: Leadership Conflict and Socio-political Change." *Soviet Union,* 14, No. 1 (1987), 19-64.

14296 **Dean, Vera Micheles.** "Yugoslavia: A New Form of Communism?" *Foreign Policy Reports*, 27, No. 4 (May, 1951), 38-47.

14297 **Duncan, J.,** and **Ley, David.** "Structural Marxism and Human Geography: A Critical Assessment." *Annals of the Association of American Geographers*, 72, No. 1 (March, 1982), 30-54.

14298 **Dziewanowski, M.K.** "The Future of Soviet Russia in Western Sovietology." *Co-Existence*, 19, No. 1 (April, 1982), 93-114.

14299 **Elliot, Philip,** and **Schlesinger, Philip.** "On the Stratification of Political Knowledge: Studying 'Eurocommunism' an Unfolding Ideology." *Sociological Review*, New Series, 27, No. 1 (February, 1979), 55-81.

14300 **Ensalaco, Mark.** "In With the New, Out With the Old?: The Democratising Impact of Constitutional Reform in Chile." *Journal of Latin American Studies* [Cambridge], 26, Part 2 (May, 1994), 409-429.

14301 **Esping-Anderson, G.; Friedland, Roger;** and **Wright, E.O.** "Modes of Class Struggle and the Capitalist State." *Kapitalistate*, 4/5 (1976), 186-220.

14302 **Etherington, Norman.** "Reconsidering Theories of Imperialism." *History and Theory*, 21, No. 1 (February, 1982), 1-36.

14303 **Evans, Alfred B., Jr.** "The New Program of the CPSU: Changes in Soviet Ideology." *Soviet Union*, 14, No. 1 (1987), 1-18.

14304 **Fitzgerald, Frank T.** "The 'Sovietization of Cuba Thesis' Revisited." *Science & Sociology*, 51, No. 4 (Winter, 1987-88), 439-457.

14305 **Franda, Marcus F.** "Communism and Regional Politics in East Pakistan." *Asian Survey*, 10, No. 7 (July, 1970), 588-606.

14306 **Friedman, Edward.** "After Mao: Maoism and Post-Mao China." *Telos*, No. 65 (Fall, 1965), 23-46.

14307 **Garreton, Manuel Antonio.** ""Problems of Democracy in Latin America: On the Processes of Transition and Consolidation." *International Journal*, 43, No. 3 (Summer, 1988), 357-377.

14308 **Geddes, M.** "The Capitalist State and the Local Economy: Restructuring for Labor and Beyond." *Capital and Class*, 35, (Summer, 1988), 85-120.

14309 **George, Francois.** "The Legend of Communism." *Social Research*, 49, No. 2 (Summer, 1982), 339-358.

14310 **Gregory, D.** "The Ideology of Control: Systems Theory and Geography. *Tidjschrift voor Economische en Sociale Geografie*, 71, No. 6 (November-December, 1980), 327-342.

14311 **Gutmann, A.** "Communitarian Critics of Liberalism." *Philosophy and Public Affairs*, 14 (1985), 308-322.

14312 **Harrison, Royden.** "Marxism as Nineteenth-Century Critique and Twentieth Century Ideology." *History*, 66, No. 217 (June, 1981), 208-220.

14313 **Harvey, David W.** "Labour, Capital and Class Struggle Around the Built Environment in Advanced capitalist Societies." In *Urbanisations and Conflict in Market Societies*. London: Methuen, 1978, p. 9-37.

14314 **Heinl, Robert D.** "Hong Kong: Communism and Colonialism in Collisio." *United States Naval Institute Proceedings*, 92, No. 7 (July, 1966), 72-81.

14315 **Heller, Agnes.** "Can Communist Regimes be Reformed?" *Society*, 25, No. 4 (May-June, 1988), 22-24.

14316 **Heywood, Paul.** "Rethinking Socialism in Spain: Programma 2000 and the Social State."

Coexistence [Dordrecht], 30, No. 3 (Spetember, 1993), 167-185.

14317 **Hilton, R.H.,** and Hill, **Christopher R.** "The Transition from Feudalism to Capitalism." *Science and Society*, 18, No. 4 (Fall, 1953), 340-351.

14318 **Horvath, R.I.,** and Gibson, **K.D.** "Abstraction in Marx's Method." *Antipode*, 16, No. 1 (April, 1983), 12-25.

14319 **Hoxie, R.F.** "The Rising Tide of Socialism: A Study." *Journal of Political Economy*, 19, No. 6 (April, 1983), 609-631.

14320 **Innes, D.** "Monopoly Capitalism in South Africa." In *South African Review*, SARS, ed. Johannesburg: Raven Press, 1983, 171-184.

14321 **Jones, S.F.** "Marxism and Peasant Revolt in the Russian Empire: The Case of the Gurian Republic." *Slavonic and East European Review*, 67, No. 3 (July, 1989), 403-434.

14322 **Jordan, Amos A.,** and **Grant, Richard L.** "Explosive Change in China and the Soviet Union: Implications for the West." *Washington Quarterly*, 12, No. 4 (Autumn, 1989), 97-111.

14323 **Jowitt, Ken.** "Soviet Neotraditionalism: The Political Corruption of a Leninist Regime." *Soviet Studies*, 35, No. 3 (July, 1983), 275-297.

14324 **Karner, Tracy X.** "Ideology and Nationalism: The Finnish Move to Independence, 1809-1918." *Ethnic and Racial Studies* [London], 14, No. 2 (April, 1991), 152-169.

14325 **Katona, Paul.** "The Danube--Blue or Red?" *World Today*, 21, No. 2 (February, 1965), 73-83.

14326 **Katz, Yossi.** "Ideology and Urban Development: Zionism and the Origins of Tel-Aviv, 1906-1914." *Journal of Historical Geography*, 12, No. 4 (October, 1986), 402-424.

14327 **Kearney, Robert N.** "The Marxist and the Coalition Government in Ceylon." *Asian Survey*, 5, No. 2 (February, 1965), 120-124.

14328 **Kiernan, Ben.** "Conflict in the Kampuchean Communist Movement." *Journal of Contemporary Asia*, 10, Nos. 1-2 (1980), 7-74.

14329 **Kleinschmager, R.** "Geographie et Ideologie Entre Deux Guerres; La Zeitschrift fur Geopolitik, 1924-1944. *L'Espace Geographique*, 15 (1980), 15-28.

14330 **Koopmans, Ruud.** "The Dynamics of Protest Waves: West Germany, 1965 to 1989." *American Sociological Review* [Washington, DC], 58, No. 5 (October, 1993), 637-658.

14331 **Korolev, Sergei.** "An Ideological Synthesis." *Social Sciences* [Moscow], 22, No. 1 (1991), 71-86.

14332 **Landau, Jacob M.** "Ideologies in the Late Ottoman Empire: A Soviet Perspective." *Middle Eastern Studies,* 25, No. 3 (July, 1989), 405-406.

14333 **Laqueur, Walter Z.** "The End of the Monolith: World Communism in 1962." *Foreign Affairs,* 40, No. 2 (January, 1962), 360-74.

14334 **Lash, S., and Urry, J.** "The New Marxism of Collective Action: A Critical Analysis." *Sociology,* 18, No. 1 (February, 1984), 33-50.

14335 **Lauria, Mickey.** "The Implications of Marxian Rent Theory for Community-Controlled Redevelopment Strategies." *Journal of Planning Education and Research,* 4, No. 1 (August, 1984), 16-24.

14336 **Lecuona, Rafael A.** "Cuba and Nicaragua: The Path to Communism." *International Journal on World Peace,* 4, No. 2 (April-June, 1987), 105-125.

14337 **Linz, Juan J.** "Totalitarian and Authoritarian Regimes." In *Handbook of Political Science.* Vol. 3 *Macropolitical Theory,* F.I. Greenstein and N.W. Polsby, eds. Reading, Massachusetts: Addison-Wesley, 1975, 175-411.

14338 **Lukashev, K.I.** "Imperialisticheskie Konceptsu Sovremennoi Amerikaniskoe Lzhegeografii [Imperialistic Conceptions of Contemporary American Pseudogeography]." *Izvestua Akademu nauk SSSR. Ser. Geograficheskaia* [Bulletin of the Academy of Sciences of the U.S.S.R., Geographical Series]. 2 (1952), 36-46.

14339 **Lynch, Allen Charles.** "Does Gorbachev Matter Anymore?" *Foreign Affairs,* 69, No. 3 (Summer, 1990), 19-29.

14340 **MacLaughlin, James G.** "Industrial Capitalism, Ulster Unionism and Orangeism: An Historical Reappraisal." *Antipode,* 12, No. 1 (April, 1980), 15-28.

14341 **MacLean, Guy R.** "Yugoslavia: The 'Trojan Horse' of Communism." *International Journal,* 13, No. 4 (Autumn, 1958), 287-297.

14342 **Machan, Tibor R.** "The Fantasy of Glasnost." *International Journal of Social Economics,* 16, No. 2 (1989), 46-53.

14343 **McKibbin, Ross.** "Why Was There No Marxism in Great Britain?" *English Historical Review,* 99, No. 391 (April, 1984), 297-331.

14344 **Meinig, D.W.** "A Macrogeography of Western Imperialism: Some Morphologies of Moving Frontiers of Political Control." In *Settlement & Encounter: Geographical Studies Presented to Sir Grenfill Price,* Fay Gale and Graham H. Lawton, eds. Melbourne: Oxford University Press, 1969, 213-240.

14345 **Mills, Charles W.** "Red Peril to the Green Island: The 'Communist Threat' to Jamaica in Genre Fiction, 1955-1969." *Caribbean Studies,* 23, Nos. 1-2 (January-June, 1990), 141-165.

14346 **Nyang'oro, Julius E.** "Reform Politics and the Democratization Process in Africa." *African Studies Review* [Atlanta], 37, No. 1 (April, 1994), 133-149.

14347 **Offe, C.** "The Theory of the Capitalist State and the Problem of Policy Formulation." In *Stress and Contradiction in Modern Capitalism.* Lexington: D.C. Heath, 1975.

14348 **Oh, Kong Dan.** "North Korea in 1989: Touched by Winds of Change?" *Asian Survey,* 30, No. 1 (January, 1990), 74-80.

14349 **Opp, Karl-Dieter, and Gern, Christiane.** "Dissident Groups, Personal Networks, and Spontaneous Cooperation: The East German Revolution of 1989." *American Sociological Review* [Washington, DC], 58, No. 5 (October, 1993), 659-680.

14350 **Oresau, Serban.** "A Structural-Functional Model for the Comparative Study of Communist Systems." *Studies in Comparative Communism,* 16, No. 4 (Winter, 1983), 265-274.

14351 **Ottaway, Marina.** "Mozambique: From Symbolic Socialism to Symbolic Reform." *Journal of African Studies,* 26, No. 2 (June, 1988), 211-226.

14352 **Peet, Richard.** "Spatial Dialectics in Marxist Geography." *Progress in Human Geography,* 5, No. 1 (March, 1981), 105-110.

14353 **Pena, Milagros.** "The Sodalitium Vitae Movement in Peru: A Rewriting of Liberation Theology." *Sociological Analysis* [Washington, DC], 53, No. 2 (Summer, 1992), 159-173.

14354 **Premdas, Ralph R.** "Guyana: Socialism and Destabilization in the Western Hemisphere." *Caribbean Quarterly,* 25, No. 3 (September, 1979), 25-43.

14355 **Rado, Sandor.** "Az Imperializmus es Szocializmus Politikai Foldrajzanak Vazlata; A Vilag O rszagacnak Kosjogi es Tenyleges Status Holyzete." *Geographical Review,* 83, No. 3 (July, 1959), 197-234.

14356 **Rallis, Donald N.** "The Rise and Fall of Apatheid." *Virginia Geographer* [Norfold], 25, No. 2 (Fall-Winter, 1993), 3-21.

14357 **Reclus, Elisee.** "Anarchy: By an Anarchist." *Contemporary Review*, 45 (May, 1884), 627-641.

14358 "Red Star Rising. Although Tormented by Insecurity, Disappointed in World Revolution, Rigid in Theory, Inconsistent in Method, the Soviet Union Grows Larger." Reprint: *Fortune*, 34, No. 7 (July, 1946), 106-111 +.

14359 **Reitsman, Hendrik-Jan A.** "Development Geography, Dependency Relations and the Capitalist Scapegoat." *Professional Geographer*, 34, No. 2 (May, 1982), 125-130.

14360 **Rice, Condoleezza.** "The Party, the Military and Decision Authority in the Soviet Union." *World Politics*, 40, No. 1 (October, 1987), 55-81.

14361 **Rorty, R.** "Postmodernist Bourgeois Liberalism." *Journal of Philosophy*, 80, No. 10 (October, 1983), 583-589.

14362 **Rosenberger, Leif.** "Philippine Communism and the Soviet Union." *Survey*, 29, No. 1 (124) (Spring, 1985), 113-145.

14363 **Ross, Lloyd.** "Communism in Australia." *Far Eastern Survey*, 20, No. 22 (December 26, 1951), 217-222.

14364 **Ruud, Arild Engelsen.** "Land and Power: The Marxist Conquest of Rural Bengal." *Modern Asian Studies* [Cambridge], 28, Part 2 (May, 1994), 357-380.

14365 **St. John, R.B.** "Marxist-Leninist Theory and Organization in South Vietnam." *Asian Survey*, 20, No. 8 (August, 1980), 812-828.

14366 **Sallnow, John, and John, Anna.** "Iberia without Fascism." *Geographical Magazine*, 50, No. 7 (April, 1978), 425-430.

14367 **Scarpaci, Joseph L., and Frazier, Lessie Jo.** "State Terror: Ideology, Protest and the Gendering of Landscapes." *Progress in Human Geography* [London], 17, No. 1 (March, 1993), 1-21.

14368 **Schopflin, George.** "The End of Communism in Eastern Europe." *International Affairs*, 66, No. 1 (January, 1990), 3-16.

14369 **Segal, Gerald.** "China after Tiananmen." *Asian Affairs*, 21, Part 2 (June, 1990), 144-154, New Series.

14370 **Schopflin, George.** "The Political Traditions of Eastern Europe." *Daedalus*, 119, N 1 (Winter, 1990), 55-90.

14371 **Sharma, T.R.** "Dialectics of Polycentrism in the World Communist Movement." *Indian Political Science Review*, 16, No. 1 (January, 1982), 35-48.

14372 **Shavit, Yaacov.** "Ideology, World View, and National Policy: The Case of the Likud Government, 1977-1984." *Jerusalem Journal of International Relations*, 9, No. 2 (June, 1987), 101-115.

14373 **Skocpol, T.** "Wallerstein's World Capitalist System: A Theoretical and Historical Critique." *American Journal of Sociology*, 82, No. 5 (March, 1977), 1075-1090.

14374 **Snyder, Jack.** "The Gorbachev Revolution: A Waning of Soviet Expansion?" *International Security*, 12, No. 3 (Winter, 1987/88), 93-131.

14375 **Soja, E., and Hadjimichalis, C.** "Between Geographical Materialism and Spatial Fetishism: Some Observations on the Development of Marxist Spatial Analysis." *Antipode*, 11, No. 2 (September, 1979), 3-11.

14376 **Southall, Roger J.** "Post-Apartheid South Africa: Constraints on Socialism." *Journal of Modern African Studies*, 25, No. 2 (June, 1987), 345-374.

14377 **Stadelbauer, Jorg.** "Glasnost - Uskorenije - Perestrojka. Die Sowjetunion zu Beginn der Ara Gorbatschow." *Rundschau*, Jahr 40, Heft 9 (September, 1988), 6-8.

14378 **Stalin, J.** "Marxism and the National Question." In *Works*, Vol. 2 (1953), 1707-1717.

14379 **Stavis, Benedict.** "Contradictions in Communist Reform: China Before 4 June 1989." *Political Science Quarterly*, 105, No. 1 (Spring, 1990), 31-52.

14380 **Sutcliffe, M., and Wellings, P.** "Worker Mititancy in South Africa: A Socio-Spatial Analysis of Trade Union Activism in the Manufacturing Sector." *Environment and Planning D: Society and Space, 3, No. 3* (September, 1985), 277-386.

14381 **Taylor, P.J.** "The Paradox of Geographical Scale in Marx's Politics." *Antipode*, 19, No. 4 (March, 1987a), 287-306.

14382 **Taylor, Peter J.** "The Crisis of the Movements: The Enabling State as Quisling." *Antipode* [Oxford], 23, No. 2 (April, 1991), 214-228.

14383 **Thurner, Mark.** "Peasant Politics and Andean Haciendas in the Transition to Capitalism: An Ethnographic History." *Latin American Research Review* [Albuquerque], 28, No. 3 (1993), 41-82.

14384 "Tibet Under Communist Occupation." *World Today*. 13, No. 7 (July, 1957), 286-294.

14385 **Thornburgh, Richard.** "The Soviet Union and the Rule of Law." *Foreign Affairs*, 69, No. 2 (Spring, 1990), 13-27.

14386 **Timmerman, Heinz.** "The CPSU and the International Communist Party System: A Change of Paradigms in Moscow." *Studies in Comparative Communism*, 22, Nos. 2/3 (Summer/Autumn, 1989), 265-277.

14387 **Trescott, Paul B.** "Henry George, Sun Yat-sen and China: More Than Land Policy Was Involved." *The American Journal of Economics and Sociology* [New York], 53, No. 3 (July, 1994), 363-375.

14388 **Walker, R.A.** "Left-Wing Libertarianism, An Academic Disorder: A Reply to David Sibley." *Professional Geographer*, 33, No. 1 (February, 1981), 5-9,

14389 **Wanasinghe, Sydney.** "From Marxist to Communalism." *Young Socialist*, 3, No. 3 (June, 1965), 113-125.

14390 **Webster, Craig.** "The Formation of the DDR Based on the Ashes of Fascism." *Geographical Essays*, 4 (Fall, 1987), SU1-SU8.

14391 **White, Stephen.** "Economic Performance and Communist Legitimacy." *World Politics*, 38, No. 3 (April, 1986), 462-482.

14392 **White, Stephen.** "Political Culture in Communist States: Some Problems of Theory and Method." *Comparative Politics*, 16, No. 3 (April, 1984), 351-365.

14393 **White, Stephen.** "What is a Communist System?" *Studies in Comparative Communism*, 16, No. 4 (Winter, 1983), 247-263.

14394 **Wolfe, A.** "New Directions in the Marxist Theory of the Politcs." *Politics and Society*, 4, No. 2 (Winter, 1974), 131-160.

14395 **Wylie, Raymond F.** "Mao Tse-tung, Ch'en Po-ta and the 'Sinification of Marxism,' 1936-38." *China Quarterly*, 79 (September, 1979), 447-480.

GEOPOLITICS OF RESOURCES

Books

14396 **Adie, W.A.C.** *Oil Politics and Seapower: The Indian Ocean Vortex*. New York: Crane, Russak, 1975.

14397 **Alexander, Lewis M.,** and **Carter, L.,** eds. *Antartic Politics and Marine Resources: Critical Choices for the 1980's: Proceedings of the Eighth Annual Conference*. Kingston: University of Rhode Island, Center for Ocean Management Studies, 1985.

14398 **Ali, Sheikh Rustum.** *South Africa: An American Enigma*. New York: Praeger, 1987.

14399 **Ali, Sheikh Rustum.** *The Uses of Oil as a Weapon of Diplomacy: A Case of Saudi Arabia*. Washington, D.C.: American University, Ph.D., 1975.

14400 **Angell, Norman.** *Raw Materials, Population Pressure and War*. New York: National Peace Conference, 1936.

14401 **Arad, R.W.,** ed. *Sharing Global Resources*. New York: McGraw-Hill, 1979.

14402 **Bennett, James T.,** and **Williams, Walter E.** *Strategic Minerals: The Economic Impact of Supply Disruptions*. Philadelphia: The Heritage Foundation, 1981.

14403 **Beukema, Herman.** *Strategic and Critical Raw Materials as a Factor in American Foreign Policy, Charlottesville, 1940*. Charlottesville: University of Virginia, Institute of Public Affairs. Address delivered June 14, 1940.

14404 **Boveri, Margret.** *Minaret and Pipe-Line: Yesterday and To-day in the Near East*. London: Oxford University Press, 1939.

14405 **Butts, Kent Hughes.** *Resources Geopolitics: U.S. Dependence on South African Chromium*. Seattle: University of Washington, Ph.D., 1985.

14406 **Cameron, Eugene N.,** ed. *The Mineral Position of the United States, 1975-2000*. Madison: University of Wisconsin Press, 1973.

14407 **Castle, E.N.,** and **Price, K.A.,** eds. *Interests and Global Natural Resources: Energy, Minerals, Food*. Washington, D.C.: Resources for the Future, 1983.

14408 **Chouri, Nazli,** and **Ferraro, Vincent.** *International Politics of Energy Interdependence*. Lexington, Massachusetts: Lexington Books, 1976.

14409 **Conant, Melvin A.,** and **Gold, Fern A.** *The Geopolitics of Energy*. Boulder, Colorado: Westview Press, 1978.

14410 **Connelly, P.,** and **Perlman, R.** *The Politics of Scarcity. Resource Conflicts in International Relations*. London: Oxford University Press, 1975.

14411 **Cottrell, A.J.**, and **Burrell, R.M.**, eds. *Politics, Oil and the Western Mediterranean.* Beverly Hills: Sage Publications, 1973.

14412 **DeMille, John G.** *Strategic Minerals.* New York: McGraw-Hill, 1947.

14413 **Denny, L.** *We Fight for Oil.* New York: Alfred A. Knopf, 1928.

14414 **Eckel, Edmund C.** *Coal, Iron and War.* New York: Henry Holt, 1920.

14415 **Eckes, Alfred, Jr.** *The United States and the Global Struggle for Minerals.* Austin: University of Texas Press, 1979.

14416 **Emeny, Brooks.** *The Strategy of Raw Materials: A Study of America in Peace and War.* New York: Macmillan, 1934.

14417 **Erol, Cenzig.** *The Location of Foreign Direct Investment and the Assessment of Political Risk.* Buffalo: State University of New York, Ph.D., 1983.

14418 **Fischman, Leonard L.** *World Mineral Trends and United States Supply Problems.* Washington, D.C.: Resources for the Future, 1980.

14419 **Fulda, Michael.** *Oil and International Relations: Energy Trade, Technology and Politics.* Washington, D.C.: American University, Ph.D., 1970.

14420 **Garvey, Lou Ann Benshoof.** *Ecological Theory and International Relations: The Case of Wheat.* Washington, D.C.: American University, Ph.D., 1975.

14421 **Glassner, Martin Ira,** ed. *Global Resources: Challenges of Interdependence.* New York: Praeger, for the Foreign Policy Association, 1983.

14422 **Harrison, Wilks Douglas.** *Geography of Iron Ore Pellets.* Chapel Hill: University of North Carolina, Ph.D., 1970.

14423 **Hauser, Philip M.** *Population and World Politics.* Glencoe, Illinois: The Free Press, 1958.

14424 **Henderson, H.D.** *Colonies and Raw Materials.* Pamphlets on World Affairs, No. 7. New York: Farrar & Rinehart, 1939.

14425 **Hessell, Mary Stanley; Murphy, W.J.;** and **Hessell, F.A.** *Strategic Materials in Hemispheric Defense.* New York: Hastings House, 1942.

14426 **Hill, Gary Alan.** *Resource Politics: Mineral Resource Leverage in International Relations.* Los Angeles: University of Southern California, Ph.D., 1979.

14427 **Hodgkins, Jordan A.** *Soviet Power: Energy Resources, Production and Potentials.* Englewood Cliffs, New Jersey: Prentice-Hall, 1961.

14428 **International Economic Studies Institute.** *Raw Materials and Foreign Policy.* Washington, D.C.: IESE, 1976.

14429 **Kincaid, Charles V.** *The Energy Crisis and Japan: Future Strategic and Foreign Policy Implications.* Washington, D.C.: National Ware College, Strategic Research Group, 1975.

14430 **Klass, M.W.; Burrows, J.C.;** and **Beggs, S.D.** *International Minerals Cartels and Embargoes: Policy Implications for the United States.* New York: Praeger, 1980.

14431 **Klinghoffer, Arthur Jay.** *The Soviet Union and International Oil Politics.* New York: Columbia University Press, 1977.

14432 **Krasner, Stephen D.** *Defending the National Interest: Raw Materials Investments and U.S. Foreign Policy.* Princeton, New Jersey: Princeton University Press, 1978.

14433 **Leith, Charles K.** *Minerals in the Peace Settlement.* New York: Geological Society of America, 1940.

14434 **Leith, Charles K.; Furness, J.W.;** and **Lewis, Cleona.** *World Minerals and World Peace.* Washington, D.C.: The Brookings Institute, 1943.

14435 **Levy, Walter J.** *Oil Strategy and Politics, 1941-1981.* Boulder, Colorado: Westview Press, 1982.

14436 **Licklider, Roy.** *Political Power and the Arab Oil Weapon: The Experience of Five Industrial Nations.* Berkeley: University of California Press, 1988.

14437 **Longrigg, S.H.** *Oil in the Middle East.* 3rd ed. London: 1967.

14438 **Lovering, T.S.** *Minerals in World Affairs.* New York: Prentice-Hall, 1943.

14439 **Malmgren, H.B.** *The Raw Material and Commodity Controversy.* Washington, D.C.: International Economic Studies Institute, 1975.

14440 **Markham, S.E.** *Climate and the Energy of Nations.* New York: Oxford University Press, 1947.

14441 **Mattox, William Gurney.** *Fishing in West Greenland 1910-1966: The Development of a New Native Industry.* Montreal, Province of Ontario, Canada: McGill University, Ph.D., 1971.

14442 **Mazuri, Ali A.** *The Barrel of the Gun and the Barrel of Oil in the North-South Equation.* New York: Institute for World Order, 1971.

14443 **McDivitt, J.F.** *Minerals and Men: An Exploration of the World of Minerals and Its Effects on the World We Live In.* Baltimore, Maryland: Johns Hopkins University Press, 1965.

14444 **Mikdashi, Zuhayr.** *The International Politics of Natural Resources.* Ithaca, New York: Cornell University Press, 1976.

14445 **Mikesell, R.F.** *New Patterns of World Mineral Development.* London: British-North American Committee, 1979.

14446 **Miller, J.A.; Fine, D.I.; and McMichael, R.D.** *The Resource War in 3-D: Dependency, Diplomacy, Defense.* Pittsburgh, Pennsylvania: World Affairs Council of Pittsburgh, 1980.

14447 **Morgan, John D.** *Future Demands of the United States for Strategic Minerals.* Wilmington, Deleware: Conference on Strategic Minerals and International Economic Assistance, December 9, 1982.

14448 **Mouzon, Olin T.** *International Resources and National Policy.* New York: Harper & Row, 1959.

14449 **Mudd, Stuart,** Editor-in-Chief. *The Population Crisis and Use of World Resources.* Bloomington: Indiana University Press, for World Academy of Arts and Sciences, 1964.

14450 **Naff, Thomas, and Matson, Ruth C.** *Water in the Middle East: Conflict or Cooperation.* Boulder, Colorado: Westview Press, 1984.

14451 **National Strategy Information Center.** *Strategic Minerals: A Resource Crisis.* Washington, D.C.: Council on Economics and National Security, 1981.

14452 **Nore, P., and Turner, T.,** eds. *Oil and Class Struggle.* London: ZED Press, 1980.

14453 **Odell, Peter R.** *Oil and World Power.* 5th ed. New York: Penguin Books, 1979.

14454 **Orchard, John E.** *Resources for Victory.* Pamphlet No. 4. New York: Columbia University Press Series, 1942.

14455 **Pirages, Dennis.** *The New Context for

International Relations: Global Ecopolitics.* North Scituate, Massachusetts: Duxbury Press, 1978.

14456 **Prestwich, Roger.** *America's Dependency of Foreign Sources of Metallic Minerals: Patterns and Policies.* Minneapolis: University of Minnesota, Ph.D., 1971.

14457 **Report of the President's Materials Policy Commission.** *Resources for Freedom,* 5 vols. Washington, D.C.: U.S. Government Printing Press, 1952.

14458 **Roush, G.A.** *Strategic Mineral Supplies.* New York: McMillan, 1939.

14459 **Russell, John C.** *Geopolitics of Natural Gas.* Cambridge, Massachusetts: Ballinger, 1983.

14460 **Scarff, James E.** *The International Management of Whales, Dolphins, and Porpoises: An Interdisciplinary Assessment,* Pt. 1. Berkeley, California: University of California, School of Law, 1977.

14461 **Schneider, William.** *Food, Foreign Policy, and Raw Materials Cartels.* Strategy Paper No. 28. New York: National Strategy Information Center, 1976.

14462 **Shwadran, B.** *The Middle East Oil and the Great Powers.* New York: John Wiley & Sons, 1959.

14463 **Smith, G.O.** *The Strategy of Minerals: A Study of the Mineral Factor in the World Position of America in War and Peace.* New York: Appleton, 1919.

14464 **Stankey, George Henry.** *The Perception of Wilderness Recreation Carrying Capacity: A Geographic Study in Natural Resources Management.* East Lansing: Michigan State University, Ph.D., 1971.

14465 **Stoff, M.B.** *Oil, War, and American Security: The Search for a National Policy on Foreign Oil, 1941-1947.* New Haven, Connecticut: Yale University Press, 1980.

14466 **Sutlov, Alexander.** *Minerals in World Affairs.* Salt Lake City: University of Utah Printing Services, 1973.

14467 **Szuprowicz, B.O.** *How to Avoid Strategic Materials Shortages: Dealing with Cartels, Embargoes, and Supply Disruptions.* New York: John Wiley & Sons, 1981.

14468 **Thomas, Charles M.** *The Strategic Significance of Africa—Raw Materials in United States Planning.* Alabama: Maxwell Air Force Base, 1962.

14469 **Thompson, Lucias P.** *Can Germany Stand the Strain?* Oxford Pamphlets on World Affairs, No. 19. New York: Farrar and Rinehart, 1939.

14470 **Thompson, Warren S.** *Population and Peace in the Pacific.* Chicago, Illinois: University of Chicago Press, 1946.

14471 **Tilton, J.E.** *The Future of Nonfuel Minerals.* Washington, D.C.: Brookings Institution, 1977.

14472 **Tucker, Robert W.** *The Inequality of Nations.* New York: Basic Books, 1977.

14473 **Tufte, E.R.** *Political Control of the Economy.* Princeton, New Jersey: Princeton University Press, 1978.

14474 **U.S. Congress.** Senate Committee on Energy and Natural Resources. Staff Report. *Geopolitics of Oil.* Publication No. 96-119. Washington, D.C.: U.S. Government Printing Office, 1980.

14475 **U.S. Congress.** Office of Technology Assessment. *Strategic Materials: Technologies to Reduce US Import Vulnerability.* Washington, D.C.: U.S. Government Printing Office, 1985.

14476 **U.S. Congressional Budget Office.** *Resources of Defense: A Review of Key Issues for Fiscal Years 1982-1986.* Washington, D.C.: U.S. Government Printing Office, 1981.

14477 **U.S. Congressional Budget Office.** *Strategic and Critical Nonfuel Minerals: Problems and Policy Alternatives.* Washington, D.C.: U.S. Government Printing Office, 1983.

14478 **U.S. Department of the Navy.** *U.S. Lifelines: Imports of Essential Materials--1967, 1971, 1975--and the Impact of Waterborne Commerce on the Nation.* Washington, D.C.: U.S. Government Printing Office, 1978.

14479 **U.S. House Committee on Foreign Affairs.** *The Possibility of a Resource War in Southern Africa.* Washington, D.C.: U.S. Government Printing Office, 1981.

14480 **U.S. Library of Congress.** *United States: Economic Dependence on Six Imported Strategic Non-Fuel Minerals.* Washington, D.C.: U.S. Government Printing Office, 1982.

14481 **U.S. Library of Congress.** Congressional Research Service. *United States Materials Report Dependency/Vulnerability.* Washington, D.C.: U.S. Government Printing Office, 1981.

14482 **Van Royen, William,** and **Bowels, Oliver.** *The Mineral Resources of the World,* Vol. 2 of *Atlas of the World Resources.* Englewood Cliffs, New Jersey: Prentice-Hall, 1952.

14483 **Wales, Don,** ed. *The Law of the Sea: Issues in Ocean Resource Management.* New York: Praeger, 1977.

14484 **Wallerstein, I.** *The Modern World System: Mercantilism and the Consolidation of the European World-Economy, 1600-1750.* New York: Academic Press, 1980.

14485 **Warren, Kenneth.** *Mineral Resources.* New York: John Wiley & Sons, 1973.

14486 **Wengert, Norman.** *Natural Resources and the Political Struggle.* New York: Doubleday, 1955.

14487 **Westing, Arthur H.,** ed. *Global Resources and International Conflict: Environmental Factors in Strategic Policy and Action.* Oxford: Oxford University Press, 1986.

14488 **Wilrich, Mason.** *Global Politics of Nuclear Energy.* New York: Praeger, 1971.

14489 **Wilrich, Mason,** and Others. *Energy and World Politics.* Princeton, New Jersey: Van Nostrand, 1963.

14490 **Woytinsky, W.S.,** and **Woytinsky, E.S.** *World Population and Production: Trends and Outlook.* New York: Twentieth Century Fund, 1953.

14491 **Wu, Yuan-li.** *Raw Material Supply in a Multipolar World.* New York: Crane, Russak, 1973.

14492 **Wyer, Samuel S.,** and **Burkhart, Roy A.** *How to Win the Peace; a Discussional Outline with Resource Material.* Columbus, Ohio: The First Community Church, 1943.

Journals

14493 **Arad, R.W.,** and **Arad, U.B.** "Scarce Natural Resources and Potential Conflict." In *Sharing Global Resources,* R.W. Arad, ed. New York: McGraw-Hill, 1979, p. 25-104.

14494 **Behre, Charles H., Jr.** "Mineral Economics and World Politics." *Geographical Review,* 30, No. 4 (October, 1940), 676-678.

14495 **Bose, S.C.** "The Sindhu-Ganga Water Parting." *Geographical Thought,* 3, No. 1 (1967), 1-14.

14496 **Buckley, Robert J.** "Critical Materials for Industry: A Predicament That Need Not Become a Crisis." *Vital Speeches,* 47, No. 10, (March 1, June, 1981), 517-520.

14497 **Bullard, Sir Reader.** "Behind the Oil Dispute in Iran: A British View." *Foreign Affairs,* 31, No. 3 (April, 1953), 460-71.

14498 **Campbell, John C.** "Oil Power in the Middle East." *Foreign Affairs*, 56, No. 1 (October, 1977), 89-110.

14499 **Choucri, N., and North, R.C.** "Dynamics of International Conflict: Some Policy Implications of Population, Resources, and Technology." In *Theory and Policy in International Relations*, R. Tanter and R.H. Ullman, eds. Princeton, New Jersey: Princeton University Press, 1972, 80-122.

14500 "Colonies and Raw Materials. The Position of the International Discussion." *Volkerbund*, 7th year, No. 5 (December 1, 1937), 65-79.

14501 **Cooke, H.J.** "The Kalahari Today: A Case of Conflict Over Resource Use." *Geographical Journal*, 151, No. 1 (March, 1985), 75-85.

14502 **Courtenay, P.P.** "International Tin Restriction and Its Effects on the Malayan Tin Mining Industry." *Geography*, 46, No. 212, Part 3 (July, 1961), 223-231.

14503 **Dore, M.H.I.** "Mineral Taxation in Jamaica: An Oligopoly Confronts Taxes on Resource Rent - and Prevails." *American Journal of Economics and Sociology*, 46, No. 2 (April, 1987), 179-204.

14504 **Doulman, D.J.** "Licensing Distant-Water Tuna Fleets in Papua New Guinea." *Marine Policy*, 11, No. 1 (1987), 16-28.

14505 **Dunn, John M.** "American Dependence on Material Imports: The World-Wide Resource Base." *Journal of Conflict Resolution*, 4, No. 1 (March, 1960), 106-122.

14506 **Earney, Fillmore C.F.** "The Geopolitics of Minerals." *Focus*, 31, No. 5 (May-June, 1981), 1-16.

14507 **Erickson, Edward W.** "The Strategic-Military Importance of Oil." *Current History*, 75, No. 4 (July-August, 1978), 5-8.

14508 **Feis, Herbert.** "Raw Materials and Foreign Policy." *Foreign Affairs*, 16, No. 4 (July, 1938), 574-586.

14509 **Freementh, M.H.; Hulings, Neil C.; Mulqi, M.; and Watton, E.C.** "Calcium and Phosphate in the Jordan Gulf of Aquaba." *Marine Pollution Bulletin*, 9, No. 3 (1978), 79-80.

14510 **Goldwater, Barry.** "United States Dependency on Foreign Sources for Critical Material: The Military Industrial Base." *Vital Speeches of the Day*, 47, No. 17 (June 15, 1981), 517-523.

14511 **Gustafson, T.** "Energy and the Soviet Bloc." *International Security*, 6, No. 3 (Winter, 1981/82), 65-89.

14512 **Gwyer, G.D.** "Three International Commodity Agreements: The Experience of East Africa." *Economic Development and Cultural Change*, 21, No. 3 (April, 1972), 465-476.

14513 **Haglund, David G.** "The New Geopolitics of Minerals: An Inquiry Into the Changing International Significance of Strategic Minerals." *Political Geography Quarterly*, 5, No. 3 (July, 1986), 221-240.

14514 **Haglund, David G.** "The Question of Persian Gulf Oil and US 'Vital' Interests." *Middle East Focus*, 7, No. 3 (1984b), 7-11ff.

14515 **Haglund, David G.** "Strategic Minerals: A Conceptual Analysis." *Resources Policy*, 10 (1984a), 146-152.

14516 **Haglund, David G.** "The West's Dependence on Imported Strategic Minerals: Implications for Canada." In *Canada and International Trade: Conference Papers.* Montreal: Institute for Research on Public Policy, Vol. 1, 1985, 379-413.

14517 **Head, Simon.** "The Monarchs of the Persian Gulf." *New York Review of Books*, (March 12, 1974), 29-36.

14518 **Hoffman, George W.** "The Role of Nuclear Power in Europe's Future Energy Balance." *Annals of the Association of American Geographers*, 47, No. 1 (March, 1957), 15-40.

14519 **Holland, Sir Thomas.** "Relation of Mineral Resources to World Peace." *Nature*, 150, No. 3804 (September 26, 1942), 364-366.

14520 **Hulings, Neil C.** "The Uranium Content of Sediments from the Jordan Gulf of Aquaba." *Marine Pollution Bulletin*, 13, No. 2 (February, 1982), 47-49.

14521 **Hurtsfield, J.** "The Control of British Raw Material Supplies, 1919-1939. *Economic History Review*, 14, No. 1 (February, 1944), 1-31.

14522 **Klinghoffer, Arthur Jay.** "The Soviet Union and the Arab Oil Embargo of 1973-74." *International Relations*, 5, No. 1 (May, 1976), 1011-23.

14523 **Kliot, Nurit.** "Israel vs. Palestine: Competition for Resources." *Focus, 38, No. 3* (Fall, 1988), 30-33.

14524 **King, John Kerby.** "Rice Politics." *Foreign Affairs*, 31, No. 3 (April, 1953), 453-461.

14525 **Kretzmann, Edwin M.J.** "Oil, Water and Nationalism." *Institute of World Affairs Proceedings*, 33 (1959), 175-183.

14526 **Krishnan, Radha**. "Geopolitics of Petroleum." *Indian Geographer*, 6, No. 1 (August, 1961), 90-110.

14527 **Lathrop, H.O.** "The Struggle for Water Resources as a Cause of the European War." *Journal of Geography*, 39, No. 9 (December, 1940), 351-355.

14528 **Leal, J.** "Algo mas sobre el petroles y la Antartida (Additional Notes on Petroleum and Antarctica)." *Geosur*, 21 (1981), 39-45.

14529 **Leith, Charles Kenneth**. "Mineral Resources and Peace." *Foreign Affairs*, 16, No. 3 (April, 1938), 515-524.

14530 **Leith, Charles Kenneth**. "The Role of Minerals in the Present International Situation." *Bulletin of the Geological Society of America*, 50, No. 3 (March 1, 1939), 433-442.

14531 **Leith, Charles Kenneth**. "Strategic Minerals in War and Peace." *Science*, 93, No. 2411 (March 14, 1941), 244-246.

14532 **Lenczowski, George**. "The Persian Gulf Crisis and Global Oil." *Current History*, 20, No. 1 (January, 1981), 10-13.

14533 **Livermore, Shaw**. "International Control of Raw Materials." *Annals of the American Academy of Political and Social Science*, 278 (November, 1951), 157-165.

14534 **Longrigg, S.H.** "Economics and Politics of Oil in the Middle East." *Jour. Intern. Affairs*, 19, No. 1 (Spring, 1965), 111-122.

14535 **Lonsdale, Richard E.** "The Political Burden of Sparseland: Some International Consistences." *Geographical Research Forum*, 6 (September, 1983), 72-77.

14536 **Lovering, T.S.** "Non-Fuel Mineral Resources in the Next Century." *Texas Quarterly*, 11 (1968), 127-147.

14537 **Mason, E.S.** "American Security and Access to Raw Materials." *World Politics*, 1, No. 2 (January, 1949), 147-160.

14538 **Massey, D.** "Spatial Labour Markets in an International Context." *Tijdschrift voor Economische en Sociale Geografie,* 78, No. 5 (1987), 374-379.

14539 **McNee, Robert B.** "Centrigufal-Centripetal Forces in International Petroleum Company Regions." *Annals of the Association of American Geographer*, 51, No. 1 (March, 1961), 124-138.

14540 **Meyer, John W.** "Political Structure and the World Economy." *Contemporary Sociology*, 11, No. 3 (May, 1982), 263-266.

14541 **Meyerhoff, Arthur** A. "Economic Impact and Geopolitical Implications of Giant Petroleum Fields." *American Scientist*, 64, No. 5 (May, 1976), 530-540.

14542 **Milward, A.S.** "Could Sweden Have Stopped the Second World War? *Scandinavian Economic History Review*, 15, Nos. 1 and 2 (1967), 127-138.

14543 "Mineral Resources and the Atlantic Charter." *Advancement of Science*, 2, No. 8 (August, 1943), 339-345.

14544 **Mussett, Rene**. "La crise de Suez et le petrole, ses enseignements." *Annals de Geographie*, 68, No. 366 (March-April, 1959), 161-167.

14545 **North, R.C.** "Toward a Framework for the Analysis of Scarcity and Conflict." *International Studies Quarterly*, 21, No. 4 (December, 1977), 569-591.

14546 **Odell, Clarence B.** "Significance of Population Studies in International Problems." *Abstract: Annals of the Association of American Geographers*, 37, No. 1 (March,1 947), 56.

14547 **Odell, Peter R.** "The Future of Oil: A Rejoinder." *Geographical Journal*, 139,Part 3 (October, 1973), 436-454.

14548 **Olson, Ralph E.** "Geographers and the Immigration Problem." *Professional Geographer*, 7, No. 1 (April, 1948), 31-32.

14549 **Pehrson, Elmer W.** "Problems of United States Mineral Supply." *Annals of the American Academy of Political and Social Science*, 228 (November, 1951), 16-78.

14550 **Pfaltzgraff, R.L.** "Resource Issues and the Atlantic Community." In *Atlantic Community in Crisis: A Redefinition of the Transatlantic Relationship*, W.F. Hahn and R.L. Pfaltzgraff, eds. New York: Pergamon Press, 1979, 298-314.

14551 **Rabl, H.** "Das Ol und die kleinen Nationen." *Zeitschrift fur Geopolitik*, 11 Jahrgang, Heft 7 (Juli, 1934), 423-429 and Heft 8 (August, 1934), 489-495.

14552 **Rothschild, Emma**. "Food Politics." *Foreign Affairs*, 54, No. 2 (January, 1976), 285-307.

14553 **Rustow, Dankwart A.** "U.S.-Saudi Relations and the Oil Crisis of the 1980's." *Foreign Affairs*, 55, No. 3 (April, 1977), 495-516.

14554 **Salmon, P.** "British Plans for Economic Warfare Against Germany, 1937-1939: The Problem of Swedish Iron Ore." In *The Second World War: Essays in Military and Political History*, W. Laqueur, ed. London: Sage Publications, 1982, p. 31-49.

14555 **Sambunaris, Georgia.** "Strategic Minerals and the Third World." *Agenda*, 4, No. 6 (July-August, 1981), 11-15.

14556 **Schmidhauser, John R.** "Whales and Salmon: The Interface of Pacific Ocean and Cross-international Policy Making." In *The Law of the Sea: Issues in Ocean Resource Management.* Edited by Don Wales. New York: Praeger, 1977, 144-171.

14557 **Schultze, C.L.** "The Economic Content of National Security Police." *Foreign Affairs*, 51, No. 3 (April, 1973), 522-540.

14558 **Shafer, Michael.** "Mineral Myths." *Foreign Policy*, 47 (Summer, 1982), 154-171.

14559 **Shuichi, Miyoshi.** "Oil Shock." *Japan Quarterly*, 21, No. 2 (April-June, 1974), 20-28.

14560 **Sinha, R.P.** "Japan and the Oil Crisis." *World Today*, 30, No. 8 (August, 1974), 335-44.

14561 **Slay, Alton D.** "Minerals and National Security." *Mining Congress Journal*, 66 (November, 1980), 22-26.

14562 **Smith, G.H.** "International Resources and National Policy." *Economic Geography*, 36, No. 4 (October, 1960), 375-376.

14563 **Sollie, Finn.** "Polar Politics: Old Games in New Territories, or New Patterns in Political Development?" *International Journal*, 39, No. 4 (Autumn, 1984), 695-720.

14564 "Southern Africa: Problems and U.S. Alternatives, a Guide to Discussion, Study and Resources." *Intercom,* 70, No. 9 (September, 1972), 2-70.

14565 **Strausz-Hupe, Robert.** "Raw Materials and Power." Part Three. *The Balance of Tomorrow.* New York: Putnam, 1945, 17-235.

14566 **Taylor, M., and Kissling, C.** "Resource Dependence, Power Networks and the Airline System of the South Pacific." *Regional Studies*, 17 (1983), 237-250.

14567 **Taylor, P.J., and Johnston, R.J.** "Population Distributions and Political Power in the European Parliament." *Regional Studies*, 12, No. 1 (February, 1978), 61-68.

14568 **Thomas, Trevor M.** "World Energy Resources:

Survey and Review." *Geographical Review*, 63, No. 2 (April, 1973), 246-258.

14569 **Tilton, J.E., and Landsberg, H.H.** "Nonfuel Minerals--the Fear of Shortages and the Search for Policies." In *US Interests and Global Natural Resources: Energy, Minerals, Food*, E.N. Castle and K.A. Price, eds. Washington, D.C.: Resources for the Future, 1983, 48-80.

14570 **Tucker, Robert W.** "Oil: The Issue of American Intervention." *Commentary*, 59, No. 1 (January, 1975), 21-31.

14571 **Voskuil, Walter H.** "Coal and Political Power in Europe." *Economic Geography*, 18, No. 3 (July, 1942), 247-258.

14572 **Warman, H.R.** "The Future of Oil." *Geographical Journal*, 138, No. 3 (September, 1972), 287-297.

14573 **Zumberge, James H.** "Mineral Resources and Geopolitics in Antarctica." *American Scientists*, 67, No. 1 (January-February, 1979), 68-77.

INTERNATIONAL REGIONAL CONFLICTS AND COOPERATION

Books

14574 **Abu-Lughod, Ibrahim**, ed. *The Transformation of Palestine: Essays on the Origin and Development of the Arab-Israeli Conflict.* 2nd ed. Evanston, Illinois: Northwestern University Press, 1987.

14575 **Ahmed, Aziz.** *Challenge to Free Asia's Survival: The Kashmir Dispute.* Washington, D.C.: Information Division, Embassy of Pakistan, 1959.

14576 **American Zionist Council, New York.** *Israel and the Arab States. The Issues in Dispute: Israel's Frontiers, the Status of Jerusalem, the Arab Refugees.* New York: American Zionist Council, 1951.

14577 **Andersen, Roy R.; Seibert, Robert F.; and Wagner, Jon G.** *Politics and Change in the Middle East: Sources of Conflict and Accommodation.* 3rd ed. Englewood Cliffs: Prentice-Hall, 1990.

14578 **Anderson, Ewan W., and Rashidian, Khalil H.** *Iraq and the Continuing Middle East Crisis.* London: Inter Publishers, 1991.

14579 **Arab Office.** *Palestine: The Solution. The Arab Proposals and the Case on Which They Rest.* Washington, D.C.: Arab Office, 1947.

14580 *The Background of the Kashmir Problem.* London: Vernon Lock, 1949.

14581 **Beck, Peter.** *The Falkland Islands as an International Problem.* London: Routledge, 1988.

14582 **Beg, Aziz.** *Captive Kashmir.* Lahore: Allied Business Corporation, 1957.

14583 **Beg, Aziz.** *Pakistan Faces India.* Lahore: Baur and Amer Publications, 1966.

14584 **Brines, Russell.** *The Indo-Pakistan Conflict.* London: Pall Mall, 1968.

14585 **Brogan, Patrick.** *World Conflicts: Why and Where They Are Happening.* London: Bloomsbury Publishing, Ltd., 1992.

14586 **Burton, John A., Jr.; Groom, Margot; Light, C.R.; Mitchell, Dennis; and Samdole, J.D.** *Territorial Power Domains, Southeast Asia, and China.* Brookfield, Vermont: Gower Publishing, 1985.

14587 **Cattan, Henry.** *The Palestine Question.* London: Croom Helm, 1988.

14588 **Chagla, M.C.** *Kashmir, 1947-1965.* New Delhi: Publication Division, Government of India Press, 1965.

14589 **Child, Jack,** ed. *Conflict in Central America: Approaches to Peace and Security.* London: C. Hurst, 1986.

14590 **Christaller, W.** *Die zentralen Orte in Suddeutschland.* Jena: Diss, 1933.

14591 **Cohen, Shaul Ephraim.** *The Politics of Planting: Israeli-Palestinian Competition for Control of Land in the Jerusalem Pheriphery.* Chicago: University of Chicago Press, 1993.

14592 **Davis, E.E., and Sinnot, R.** *Attitudes in the Republic of Ireland Relevant to the Northern Ireland Problem,* Vol. 1. *Descriptive Analysis and Some Comparisons with Attitudes in Northern Ireland and Great Britain.* Dublin: Economic and Social Research Institute, 1979.

14593 **Drysdale, Alsdair Duncan.** *Obstacles to Regional Integration in the Arab Middle East.* Durham, England: University of Durham, Master's Thesis, 1972.

14594 **Fabian, Larry L., and Schift, Ze'ev,** eds. *Israel's Speak About Themselves and the Palestinians.* New York: Carnegie Endowment for International Peace, 1977.

14595 **Fawcett, Louise L'Estrange.** *Iran and the Cold War: The Azerbaijan Crisis of 1946.* Cambridge: Cambridge University Press, 1992.

14596 **Fritsch-Bournazel, Renata.** *Confronting the German Question: Germans on the East-West Divide."* Translated by Caroline Bray. Oxford: Berg Publishers, 1988.

14597 **Gainsborough, J.R.** *The Arab-Israeli Conflict: A Politico-legal Analysis.* Aldershot: Gower Publishing, 1986.

14598 **Gajendragadkar, P.B.** *Kashmir: Prospect and Retrospect.* Bombay: University of Bombay, 1967.

14599 **Garner, William R.** *The Chaco Dispute; A Study of Prestige Diplomacy.* Washington, D.C.: Public Affairs Press, 1966.

14600 **Gauhar, Altaf.** *Regional Integration: The Latin American Experience.* London: Third World Foundation for Social and Economic Studies, 1985.

14601 **Gentilli, J.** *Australia--India or Pacific.* Sydney: New Century Press, 1949.

14602 **Gordon, Bernard K.** *The Dimensions of Conflict in South-East Asia,* New York, 1966. *Toward Disengagement in Asia,* Englewood Cliffs, New Jersey: Prentice-Hall, 1969.

14603 **Gordon, Haim, and Gordon, Rivca,** eds. *Israel/Palestine: Quest for Dialogue.* Maryknoll, NY: Orbis Books, 1991.

14604 **Gururaj Rao, H.S.** *Legal Aspects of the Kashmir Study.* Bombay: Asia Publishing House, 1967.

14605 **Harris, William Wilson.** *Taking Root: Israeli Settlement in the West Bank, the Golan and Gaza-Sinai, 1967-1980.* Chinchester and New York: Research Studies Press, John Wiley & Sons, 1980.

14606 **Houghton, Nancy E.** *The Kashmir Dispute.* Ithaca, New York: Cornell University, Master's Thesis, 1956.

14607 **India (Republic).** Ministry of External Affairs. *Extract from the Note Containing the Agreement of September 10, 1958, Between the Government of India and the Government of Pakistan.* New Delhi: Publication Division, Government of India Press, 1958.

14608 **India (Republic).** Ministry of External Affairs. *World Opinion on Kashmir, No. 1.* New Delhi: Publication Division, Government of India Press, 1951.

14609 **India (Republic).** Ministry of External Affairs. *World Press on Chinese Aggression.* New Delhi: Publication Division, Government of India Press, 1962.

14610 **India (Republic).** Ministry of Information and Broadcasting. *China's Betrayal of India: Background to the Invasion.* New Delhi: Publication Division, Government of India Press, 1962.

14611 **India (Republic).** Ministry of Information and Broadcasting. *Kashmir, 1947-1965, by M.C. Chagla.* New Delhi: Publication Division, Government of India Press, 1965.

14612 **India (Republic).** Ministry of Information and Broadcasting. *The Kashmir Story.* Delhi: Publication Division, Government of India Press, 1948.

14613 **Institute of Arab American Affairs, New York.** *Papers on Palestine; A Collection of Statements, Articles and Letters Dealing with the Palestine Problem.* New York: Institute of Arab American Affairs, 1945.

14614 **Islamic Republic of Pakistan.** Department of Films and Publications. *Story of Kashmir, 1947-1949.* Karachi: Pakistan Government Printing Press, 1968.

14615 **Islamic Republic of Pakistan.** Department of Films and Publications. *Tragedy of Kashmir.* Karachi: Pakistan Government Printing Press, 1958.

14616 **Islamic Republic of Pakistan.** Ministry of Information and Broadcasting. *White Paper on the Crisis in East Pakistan.* Islamabad: Pakistan Government Printing Press, 1971.

14617 **Islamic Republic of Pakistan.** Prime Minister of Pakistan. *Kashmir: What Now?* Karachi: Pakistan Government Printing Press, 1951.

14618 **Kadian, Rajesh.** *The Kashmir Tangle: Issues and Options.* Boulder: Westview Press, 1993.

14619 **Karnik, V.B.,** ed. *China Invades India.* Bombay: Allied Publishers, 1963.

14620 *The Kashmir Issue.* New York: Information Division, Pakistan Mission to the United Nations, 1962.

14621 **Keller, Edmond J.,** and **Pickard, Louis, A.,** eds. *South Africa in Southern Africa: Domestic Change and International Conflict.* Boulder, Colorado: Lynne Rienner Publishers, 1989.

14622 **Khalaf, Samir.** *Lebanon's Predicament.* New York City: Columbia University Press, 1987.

14623 **Khan, Daultana,** and **Mian, Mumtaz Muhammad.** *Kashmir Dispute in Present-day Perspective.* Lahore: Punjab Literary League, 1965.

14624 **Kodikara, S.U.** *Indo-Ceylon Relations Since Independence.* London, England: University of London, London School of Economics, Ph.D., 1963.

14625 **Korbel, Josef.** *Danger in Kashmir.* Rev. ed. Princeton, New Jersey: Princeton University Press, 1966.

14626 **Lal, John.** *Aksaichin and Sino-Indian Conflict.* New Delhi: Allied Publishers, 1989.

14627 **Lamb, Alastair.** *Crisis in Kashmir, 1947-1966.* London: Routledge, 1966.

14628 **Lamb, Alastair.** *The Kashmir Problem: A Historical Survey.* New York: Praeger, 1967.

14629 **Little, Tom.** *South Arabia; Area of Conflict.* London: Pall Mall Press, 1968.

14630 **Loshak, David.** *Pakistan Crisis.* London: Heinemann, Educational Publishers, 1971.

14631 **Mahncke, Dieter.** *Konfikt in Sudafrika: die Politische Problematic Sudafrikas in ihren innen- und auBenpolitischen Dimensionen.* Paderborn: Ferdinant Schoningh, 1989.

14632 **Mangope, Lukas.** *Will Bophuthastswana join Botswana?* Pasadena: California Institute of Technology, Munger African Library, 1973.

14633 **McDowall, David.** *Palestine and Israel: The Uprisings and Beyond.* London: I.B. Tauris, 1989.

14634 **Melman, Yossi,** and **Raviv, Dan.** *Behind the Uprising: Israelis, Jordanians, and Palestinians.* New York: Greenwood Press, 1989.

14635 **Muni, S.D.** *Pangs of Proximity: India and Sri Lanka's Ethnic Crisis.* Oslo: International Peace Research Institute, 1993.

14636 **Nassar, Jamil R.,** and **Heacock, Roger,** eds. *Intifada: Palestine at the Crossroads.* New York: Praeger, 1990.

14637 **Nehru, Jawaharlal.** *We Accept China's Challenge: Speeches in the Lok Sabha on India's Resolve to Drive Out the Aggressor.* New Delhi: Publications Division, Government of India Press, 1962.

14638 **Nijim, Basheer K.** *Toward the De-Arabization of Palestine/Israel 1945-1977.* Dubuque, Iowa: Kendall-Hunt, 1984.

14639 **Noorani, A.G.** *The Kashmir Question.* Bombay: Manaktalas, 1964.

14640 Nuechterlein, Donald E. *Iceland, Reluctant Ally.* Ithaca, New York: Cornell University Press, 1961.

14641 Nuccio, Richard A. *What's Wrong, Who's Right in Central America?* 2nd ed. New York: Holmes & Meier, 1989.

14642 Pakistan. Embassy. Washington, D.C. Information Division. *Peril and Opportunity in Kashmir; Background Report.* Washington, D.C.: Pakistan Embassy, 1961.

14643 Peretz, Don. *Intifada: The Palestinian Uprising.* Boulder, Colorado: Westview Press, 1990.

14644 Posner, Steve. *Israel Undercover: Secret Warfare and Hidden Diplomacy in the Middle East.* Syracuse, New York: Syracuse University Press, 1987.

14645 Pringle, D.G. *One Island, Two Nations? A Political Geographical Analysis of the National Conflict in Ireland.* Letchworth, England: Research Studies Press, 1985.

14646 Quandt, William B., ed. *The Middle East: Ten years After Camp David.* Washington, D.C.: The Brookings Institute, 1988.

14647 Ramazani, B.K. *Revolutionary Iran: Challenge and Response in the Middle East.* Baltimore, Maryland: Johns Hopkins University Press, 1986.

14648 Roche, Patrick J., and Barton, Brian, eds. *The Northern Ireland Question: Myth and Reality.* Aldershot: Avebury, 1991.

14649 Rotberg, Robert I., and Others. *South Africa and Its Neighbors: Regional Security & Self-Interest.* Lexington, Massachusetts: Lexington Books, 1985.

14650 Samara, Adel, and Others. *Palestine: Profile of an Occupation.* London: Zed Books, 1989.

14651 Sandhu, Bhim. *Unresolved Conflict--China and India.* New Delhi: Radiant, 1988.

14652 Sharma, Brij Lal. *The Kashmir Story.* Bombay: Asia Publishing House, 1967.

14653 Sharma, Brij Lal. *The Pakistan-China Axis.* Bombay: Asia Publishing House, 1967.

14654 Shemesh, Moshe. *The Palestinian Entity 1959-1974: Arab Politics and the PLO.* London: Frank Cass, 1988.

14655 Smith, Charles D. *Palestine and the Arab-Israeli Conflict.* 2nd ed. New York: St. Martin's Press, 1992.

14656 Stephenson, Glenn V. *Western Europe: The Search for Regional Cohesion.* 1978.

14657 Tadjbakhche, Gholam Reza. *La Question des Iles Bahrein.* Paris: Editions A. Pedone, 1960.

14658 Tekle, Amare. *Eritrea and Ethiopia: From Conflict to Cooperation.* Lawrenceville: The Red Sea Press, 1994.

14659 Tessler, Mark. *A History of the Israeli-Palestinian Conflict.* Bloomington: Indiana University Press, 1994.

14660 Thomas, Raju G.,C., ed. *Perspectives on Kashmir: The Roots of Conflict in South Asia.* Boulder: Westview Press, 1992.

14661 *Tragedy of Kashmir.* Karachi: Pakistan, Department of Advertising, Films and Publications, 1958.

14662 Voss, Carl Herman. *The Palestine Problem Today: Israel and the Its Neighbors.* Boston, Massachusetts: Beacon Press, 1953.

14663 Pakistan Embassy. *Challenge to Free Asia's Survival: The Kashmir Dispute,* Aziz Ahmad, ed. Washington, D.C.: Pakistan Embassy, Information Division, 1959.

14664 Pakistan Embassy. *Dispute--Rann of Kutch: Background Report.* Washington, D.C.: Pakistan Embassy, 1965.

14665 Wichert, Sabine. *Northern Ireland Since 1945.* London: Longman Group, 1991.

14666 Wilson, Andrew, ed. *The Observer Atlas of World Affairs: A Guide to Major Tensions and Conflicts.* London: George Philip and Son, 1971.

14667 Zasloff, Joseph J., and Goodman, Allen E., eds. *Indochina in Conflict: A Political Assessment.* Lexington, Massachusetts: Lexington Books, 1972.

Journals

14668 Abdullah, Sheikh Mohammad. "Kashmir, India and Pakistan." *Foreign Affairs.* 43, No. 2 (April, 1965), 528-535.

14669 Ali, S. Amjad. "Indian Vandalism on Pakistan Territory." *Pakistan Quarterly,* 14, No. 2 (Autumn, 1966), 69-78.

14670 Allon, Yigal. "The Arab-Israel Conflict." *International Affairs,* 40, No. 2 (April, 1964), 205-218.

14671 **Anglin, Douglas G.** "Southern Africa Under Seige: Options for the Frontline States." *Journal of Modern African Studies*, 20, No. 4 (December, 1989), 549-565.

14672 **Axelgard, Frederick W.** "Iraq: The Postwar Political Setting." *American-Arab Affairs*, No. 28 (Spring, 1989), 30-37.

14673 **Babcock, F. Lawrence.** "The Explosive Middle East." Reprint: *Fortune*, 30, No. 9 (September, 1944), 113-116+.

14674 **Balta, Paul.** "La Conflit Irak-Iran: de La 'guerre-eclaire' a la 'drole-de guerre' Maghreb." *Machrek*, No. 113 (Juillet-Aout-Septembre, 1986), 47-72.

14675 **Baroody, Jamil M.** "Arab Upheaval." *Asia and the Americas*, 45, No. 6 (June, 1945), 290-294.

14676 **Barston, Ronald P.** "Cyprus: The Unresolved Problem 1963-70." *India Quarterly*, 27, No. 2 (April-June, 1971), 114-121.

14677 **Bartels, D.** "Das Problem der Gemeinde-Typisierung." *Geographische Rundschau*, 17, No. 1 (January, 1965), 22-25.

14678 **Bataillon, Gilles.** "Amerique Centrale: Entre Violence et Democratie." *Herodote* [Paris], No. 57 (Avril-Juin, 1990), 211-238.

14679 **Berger, Kurt Martin.** "Indien und China, Order Die Torheit der Alternative." *Gemeinschaft und Politik*, 10 (April-May, 1962), 133-136.

14680 **Birdwood, Christopher Bromhead, 2nd Baron.** "Kashmir." *International Affairs*, 28, No. 3 (July, 1952), 299-309.

14681 **Bokhari, Imtiaz H.** "Evolution of a Dual Negotiation Process: Afghanistan." *The American Academy of Political and Social Science. The Annals* [Newbury Park], 518 (November, 1991), 58-68.

14682 **Braine, Bernard.** "Storm Clouds Over the Horn of Africa." *International Affairs*, 34, No. 4 (October, 1958), 435-443.

14683 **Braun, Gerald.** "Sudafrika: Zwischen Erster und Dritter Welt." *Geographische Rundschau*, Jahr, 40, Heft 12 (Dezember, 1988), 14-21.

14684 **Brown, William Norman.** "India-Pakistan Issue." In *Proceedings of the American Philosophical Society*, Vol. 91, No. 2. Philadelphia: American Philosophical Society, 1947, 162-180.

14685 **Bueno de Mesquita, Bruce.** "Multilateral Negotiations: A Spatial Analysis of the Arab-Israeli Dispute." *International Organization*, 44, No. 3 (Summer, 1990), 317-340.

14686 **Cable, James.** "The Falklands Conflict." *U.S. Naval Institute Proceedings*, 108, No. 955 (September, 1982), 70-76.

14687 **Campbell, John C.** "Insecurity and Cooperation: Yugoslavia and the Balkans." *Foreign Affairs*, 51, No. 4 (July, 1973), 778-793.

14688 **Carlson, Fred A.** "Geography in Inter-American Cooperation." *Journal of Geography*, 40, No. 5 (May, 1941), 161-168.

14689 **Castagno, A.A.** "The Somali-Kenyan Controversy: Implications for the Future." *Journal of Modern African Studies*, 2, No. 2 (July, 1964), 165-188.

14690 **Chabry, Laurent, and Chabry, Annie.** "Le Conflit Irako-Iranien: de l'Anthime Au Comprimis?" *Maghreb, Machrek, Monde Arabe*, 95, No. 1 (Janvier-Mars, 1982), 5-29.

14691 **Chang, Li.** "The Soviet Grip on Sinkiang." *Foreign Affairs*, 32, No. 3 (April, 1954), 491-503.

14692 **Cobban, Helena.** "The PLO and the Intifada." *Middle East Journal*, 44, No. 2 (Spring, 1990), 207-238.

14693 **Collins, J.** "Foreign Conflict Behavior and Domestic Disorder in Africa." In *Conflict Behavior and Linkage Politics*, J. Wilkenfeld, ed. New York: David McKay, 251-293.

14694 **Cox, Kevin R., and Agnew, J.A.** "Optimal and Non-Optimal Territorial Partitions: A Possible Approach Toward Conflict." *Peace Science Society Papers*, 23 (1974), 123-158.

14695 **Craig, James.** "What's Wrong with the Middle East? *Asian Affairs* [London], 23, Part 2 (June, 1992), 131-141.

14696 **Deeb, Mary-Jane, and Deeb, Marius K.** "Regional Conflict and Regional Solutions: Lebanon." *The American Academy of Political and Social Science. The Annals* [Newbury Park], 518 (November, 1991), 82-94.

14697 **Diehl, Paul F., and Goertz, Gary.** "Interstate Conflict Over Exchanges of Homeland Territory, 1816-1980." *Political Geography Quarterly* [Oxford], 10, No. 4 (October, 1991), 342-355.

14698 **Dollot, Rene.** "Situation de l'Afghanistan." *Politique Entrangere*, 23, No. 4 (1958), 352-364.

14699 **Diubaldo, Richard J.** "Wrangling Over Wiangel Island." *Canadian Historical Review*, 48, No. 3 (September, 1967), 201-226.

14700 **Dow, Maynard Weston.** "Assimilate or Accommodate? The Case of the Hoa Hao and Vietnam." *Professional Geographer*, 22, No. 6 (November, 1970), 317-320.

14701 **Duncan, Constance.** "Korea--Source of Conflict." *Australian Outlook*, 4, No. 3 (September, 1950), 147-161.

14702 **Earney, Fillmore C.F.** "Conflict for Western Sahara." *Focus*, 32, No. 5 (May-June, 1982), 13-16.

14703 **East, G.** "The Concept and Political Status of the Shatter Zone." In *Geographical Essay on Eastern Europe*, N.J.G. Pounds, ed. Bloomington: Indiana University Press, 1961, 1-27.

14704 **Eckhardt, W., and Azar, E.** "Major World Conflicts and Intervention, 1945 to 1975." *International Interactions*, 5, No. 1 (1979), 75-110..

14705 **Edwards, Michael.** "Tashkent and After." *International Affairs*, 42, No. 3 (July, 1966), 381-389.

14706 **Eitner, Hans Jurgen.** "Unkampfte Grenze: der Indisch-Chinesische Streit." *Politische Meinung*, 7, No. 4 (October, 1962), 79-82.

14707 **Eppel, Michael.** "The Iraqi Domestic Scene and Its Bearing on the Question of Palestine, 1947." *Asian and African Studies* [Haifa], 24, No. 1 (March, 1990), 51-73.

14708 **Eppel, Michael.** "Iraqi Politics and Regional Policies, 1945-49." *Middle Eastern Studies* [London], 28, No. 1 (January, 1992), 108-119.

14709 **Evans, Trefor.** "The New Libya: Coming to Terms with Revolutions in the Arab World." *Round Table*, 239, No. 3 (July, 1970), 265-273.

14710 **Evensen, Bruce J.** "Truman, Palestine and the Cold War." *Middle Eastern Studies* [London], 28, No. 1 (January, 1992), 120-156.

14711 **Gause, F. Gregory III.** "Yemeni Unity: Past and Future." *Middle East Journal*, 42, No. 1 (Winter, 1988), 33-47.

14712 **Gentilli, J.** *Australia--India or Pacific.* Sydney: New Century Press, 1949.

14713 **Giniewski, Paul.** "Le 'Retour a 1947' Peut-il Resoudre le Probleme Israelo-Arabe?" *Political Etrangere*, 23, No. 1 (1958), 87-95.

14714 **Glassner, Martin Ira.** "The Bedouin of Southern Sinai Under Israeli Administration." *Geographical Review*, 64, No. 1 (January, 1974) 31-60.

14715 **Gonzalez, F. Garchiahuidobro.** "Relationships Between Chile and Bolivia." *Revista Chilena de Geopolitica.* 2 (1985), 65-95.

14716 **Gordon, Edward.** "Resolution of the Bahrain Dispute." *American Journal of International Law*, 65, No. 3 (July, 1971), 560-568.

14717 **Graves, Norman J.** "The Falklands or Las Malvinas: An Issue in Political Geography." *Journal of Geography*, 82, No. 3 (May-June, 1983), 123-125.

14718 **Green, Murray.** "Kashmir: Valley of Indecision." In *United States Naval Institute Proceedings*, Vol. 81, No. 12. Washington, D.C.: Government Printing Office, 1953, 1339-1349.

14719 **Groom, A.J.B.** "Cyprus: Back in the Doldrums." *Round Table,* 300, No. 3 (July, 1986), 362-383.

14720 **Guynne, R.N.** "Conflict in South America." *Geographical Magazine*, 51, No. 6 (March, 1979), 398-402.

14721 **Hansen, Niles M.** "International Cooperation in Border Regions: An Overview and Research Agenda." *International Regional Science Review*, 8, No. 3 (December, 1983), 225-270.

14722 **Harding, Sir John.** "The Cyprus Problem in Relation to the Middle East." *International Affairs*, 34, No. 3 (July, 1958), 291-296.

14723 **Harris, William Wilson.** "War and Settlement Change: The Golan Heights and the Jordan Rift, 1967-77." *Transactions of the Institute of British Geographers*, New Series, 3, No. 3, (1978), 309-330.

14724 **Heineitz, G., and Lichtenberger, E.** "Munich and Vienna--A Cross National Comparison." *Erdkundliches Wissen*, 76 (1986), 1-26.

14725 **Hervouet, Gerard.** "The Cambodian Conflict: The Difficulties of Intervention and Compromise." *International Journal,* 45, No. 2 (Spring, 1990), 258-291.

14726 **Hill, Christopher R.** "Regional Co-Operation in Southern Africa." *African Affairs*, 82, No. 327 (April, 1983), 215-239.

14727 **Hirschmann, David.** "Changes in Lesotho's Policy Towards South Africa." *African Affairs*, 78, No. 311 (April, 1979), 177-196.

14728 **Hodges, Tony.** "Western Sahara: The Escalating Confrontation." *Africa Report*, 23, No. 2 (March-April, 1978), 4-9.

14729 **Hoffman, G.W.** "The Shatterbelt in Relation to the East-West Conflict." *Journal of Geography,* 51, No. 7 (October, 1952), 265-275.

14730 **Hoffman, Stanley.** "Perceptions, Reality and the Franco-American Conflict." *Journal of International Affairs,* 21, No. 1 (Spring, 1967), 57-71.

14731 **Hudson, Michael C.** "Fedayeen are Facing Lebanon's Hand: A New Flash Point in the Middle East Conflict." *Mid East,* 10, No. 1 (February, 1970), 7-14.

14732 **Hurewitz, J.C.** "The Israeli-Syrian Arises in the Light of the Arab-Israel Armistice System." *International Organization,* 5, No. 3 (August, 1951), 459-479.

14733 **Husain, Ita'at.** "The Ordeal of Kashmir." *Pakistan Quarterly,* 13, Nos. 2 and 3 (Autumn-Winter, 1965), 26-32.

14734 "India: The Indian Approach to Kashmir." *Round Table,* 51, No. 21 (December, 1965), 67-74.

14735 "Indo-China: the Unfinished Struggle." *World Today,* 12, No. 1 (January, 1956), 17-26.

14736 **Ingrams, Harold.** "Aden and the Situation in South-West Arabia." *United Empire.* 48, No. 3 (May-June, 1957), 113-117.

14737 **Jabber, Paul.** "Forces of Change in the Middle East." *Middle East Journal,* 42, No. 1 (Winter, 1988), 7-15.

14738 **Jain, Girilal.** "India Faces Hostile China." *New Commonwealth,* 40, No. 8 (August, 1962), 486-489.

14739 **Jenkins, A.M.** "Territorial Issues in the sino-Soviet Conflict." *Tijdschrift voor Economische en Sociale Geografie,* 65, No. 1 (1974), 35-47.

14740 **Johnson, Richard.** "The Future of the Falkland Islands." *World Today,* 33, No. 6 (June, 1977), 223-231.

14741 **Kahin, Audrey R.** "Crisis on the Periphery: The Rift Between Kuala Lumpur and Sabah." *Pacific Affairs* [Vancouver], 65, No. 1 (Spring, 1992), 30-49.

14742 **Kahin, George McTurnan.** "Malaysia and Indonesia." *Pacific Affairs,* 37, No. 3 (Fall, 1964), 253-270.

14743 **Kamen, C.S.** "After the Catostrophe I: The Arabs in Israel, 1948-1951." *Middle East Studies,* 24, No. 1 (1988), 68-109.

14744 **Kamrany, Nake M.** "The Continuing Soviet War in Afghanistan." *Current History,* 85, No. 513 (October, 1986), 333-336.

14745 **Kapur, Ashok.** "India and China: Adversaries or Potential Partners?" *World Today,* 30, No. 3 (March, 1974), 129-134.

14746 **Karsh, Efraim.** "Military Power and Foreign Policy Goals: The Iran-Iraq War Revisited." *International Affairs,* 64, No. 1 (Winter, 1987/88), 83-95.

14747 **Karumaratne, Victor.** "The Indo-Ceylonese Issue." *Eastern World,* 16, No. 10 (October, 1962), 13-14.

14748 "Kashmir and the North-West Frontier Province." *Central Asian Review.* 5, No. 3 (September, 1957), 286-328.

14749 "The Kashmir Dispute After Ten Years." *World Today.* 14, No. 2 (February, 1958), 61-70.

14750 **Kelly, Philip L.** "Escalation of Regional Conflict: Testing the Shatterbelt Concept." *Political Geography Quarterly,* 5, No. 2 (April, 1986), 161-180.

14751 **Kelly, Philip L., and Boardman, T.** "Intervention and the Caribbean: Latin American Responses Toward United Nations Peacekeeping." *Revista/Review Interamericana,* 6 (1976), 403-411.

14752 **Kende, Istvan.** "Twenty-five Years of Local Wars." *Journal of Peace Research,* 8, No. 1 (1971), 5-22.

14753 **Khadduri, Majid.** "The Franco-Lebanese Dispute and the Crisis of November, 1943." *American Journal of International Law,* 38, No. 4 (October, 1944), 601-620.

14754 **Khalilzad, Zalmay.** "The War in Afghanistan." *International Journal,* 41, No. 2 (Spring, 1986), 271-299.

14755 **Khouri, Fred J.** "Friction and Conflict on the Israeli-Syrian Front." *Middle East Journal,* 17, Nos. 1-2 (Winter-Spring, 1963), 14-34.

14756 **Kliot, Nurit.** "Sense of Place Lost: The Evacuation of Israeli Settlements from the Sinai." In *Contemporary Problems in Political Geography: An international Seminar.* Eds., S. Waterman and N. Kliot. Haifa: University of Haifa, Department of Geography, 1982, 70-75.

14757 **Kim, Joungwon Alexander.** "Divided Korea 1969: Consolidating for Transition." *Asian Survey,* 10, No. 1 (January, 1970), 30-42.

14758 **King, Gillian.** "The Problem of Aden." *World Today,* 18, No. 12 (December, 1962), 498-503.

14759 **King, Russell, and Gradus, Yehuda.** "Negev Becomes a Front-Line Again." *Geographical Magazine*, 53, No. 14 (November, 1981), 902-909.

14760 **Kipnis, B.** "Geopolitical Ideologies and Regional Strategies in Israel." *Tijdschrift Voor Economische en Sociale Geografie*, 78, No. 2 (1987), 125-138.

14761 **Klieman, Aaron S.** "The Resolution of Conflicts through Territorial Partition: The Palestine Experience." *Comparative Studies in Society and History*, 22, No. 2 (April, 1980), 281-300.

14762 **Korbel, Josef.** "The Kasmir Dispute After Six Years." *International Organization*, 7, No. 4 (November, 1953), 498-510.

14763 **Kumar, Satish.** "Chinese Aggression and Indo-Nepalese Relations." *United Asia*, 15 (November, 1963), 740-744.

14764 **La Foy, Margaret.** "India's Role in the World Conflict." *Foreign Policy Reports*, 18, No. 4 (May 1, 1942), 38-47.

14765 **Latynski, Maya, and Wimbush, S. Enders.** "The Mujahideen and the Russian Empire." *National Interest*, No. 11 (Spring, 1988), 30-42.

14766 **Lawson, Fred H.** "The Iranian Crisis of 1945-1946 and the Spiral Model of International Conflict." *International Journal of Middle East Studies*, 21, No. 3 (August, 1989), 307-326.

14767 **Leguizamon Pondal, Martiniano.** "Derechos de la Argentina a las Islas Malvenias Basados en Autores Ingleses." *Boletin de la Academia Nacional de Ciencias, Cordoba*, 39, No. 4 (1956), 417-431.

14768 **Leifer, Michael.** "Conflict and Regional Order in South-east Asia." *Adelphi Papers*, 163 (Winter, 1980), 1-39.

14769 **Leifer, Michael.** "The Stakes of Conflict in Cambodia." *Asian Affairs*, 21, Part 2 (June, 1990), 155-161, New Series.

14770 **Little, Walter.** "International Conflict in Latin America." *International Affairs*, 63, No. 4 (Autumn, 1987), 589-601.

14771 **Mace, Gordon.** "Regional Integration in Latin America: A Long and Winding Road." *International Journal*, 43, No. 3 (Summer, 1988), 404-427.

14772 **Mahbubani, Kishore.** "The Kampuchian Problem: A Southeast Asian Perception." *Foreign Affairs*, 62, No. 2 (Winter, 1983/1984), 407-425.

14773 **Mansfield, Peter.** "The Arab Gulf States: End of the Status Quo?" *Asian Affairs* [London], 22, Part 3 (October, 1991), 284-292.

14774 **Maxwell, Neville.** "Why the Russians Lifted the Blockade at Bear Island?" *Foreign Affairs*, 57, No. 1 (Fall, 1978), 138-145.

14775 **Mayfield, Robert C.** "A Geographical Study of the Kashmir Issue." *Geographical Review*, 45, No. 2 (April, 1955), 181-196.

14776 **McLachian, Keith.** "Iran and the Continuing Crisis in the Persian Gulf." *GeoJournal* [Dordrecht], 28, No. 3 (November, 1992), 357-363.

14777 **McLaurin, Ronald D.** "Lebanon: Into or Out of Oblivion? *Current History* [Philadelphia], 91, No. 561 (January, 1992), 29-33.

14778 **McLeish, Alexander.** "The Kashmir Dispute." *World Affairs*, 4, No. 1 (January, 1950), 60-71.

14779 **Melamid, Alexander.** "The Shatt el Arab Dispute." *Middle East Journal*, 22, No. 3 (Summer, 1968), 350-357.

14780 **Metford, J.C.J.** "Falklands or Malvinas? The Background to the Dispute." *International Affairs*, 44, No. 3 (July, 1968), 463-481.

14781 **Mezerik, A.G., ed.** "The Algerian-French Conflict. International Impacts, U.N. Action." *International Review Service*, 4, No. 43 (June, 1958), 39.

14782 **Michaelson, J.M.** "Sakhalin Island Shared by Russia and Japan." *Indian Geographical Journal*, 17, No. 4 (October-December, 1942), 271-282.

14783 **Milivojevic, Marko.** "Zone of Escalating Conflict." *Geographical Magazine*, 62, No. 3 (March, 1990), 22-27.

14784 **Miller, Aaron David.** "The Arab-Israeli Conflict, 1967-1987, A Retrospect." *Middle East Journal*, 41, No. 3 (Summer, 1987), 349-360.

14785 **Miller, Aaron David.** "The Arab-Israeli Conflict: The Shape of Things to Come." *Washington Quarterly*, 11, No. 4 (Autumn, 1988), 159-170.

14786 **Mills, Lennox A.** "Some Problems of Southeastern Asia and the Philippines." *Amerasia*, 6, No. 13 (January 25, 1943), 530-540.

14787 **Momsen, J.H.** "Political Geography of Contemporary Events III: Caribbean Conflict: Cold War in the Sun." *Political Geography Quarterly*, 3, No. 2 (April, 1984), 145-159.

14788 **Morris, Michael A.** "The 1984 Argentine-Chilean Pact of Peace and Friendship." *Oceanus*, 28, No. 2 (1985), 93-96.

14789 **Mukerji, A.B.** "Kashmir: A Study in Political Geography." *Geographical Review of India*, 19, No. 1 (March, 1956), 15-29.

14790 **Mujnslow, B., and O'Keefe, P.** "Energy and Southern African Regional Confrontation." *Third World Quarterly*, 6 (1984), 25-42.

14791 **Nachtigall, H.** "Zur Politischen Volkerkunde von Kaschmir." *Geographische Zeitschrift*, 555 Jahrg, Heft 1 (Marz, 1967), 62-69.

14792 **Nag, B.C.** "The Kashmir Dispute: India's Position." *Modern Review*, 111, No. 4 (April, 1962), 318-320.

14793 **Neff, Donald.** "Struggle Over Jerusalem." *American-Arab Affairs*, No. 23 (Winter, 1977-78), 15-23.

14794 **Nevo, Joseph.** "The Arabs of Palestine 1947-48: Military and Political Activity." *Middle Eastern Studies*, 23, No. 1 (January, 1987), 3-38.

14795 **Newman, David.** "Civilian and Military Presence as Strategin of Territorial Control: The Arab Israel Conflict." *Political Geography Quarterly*, 8, No. 3 (July, 1989), 215-227.

14796 **Newman, David, and Portugali, Juval.** "Israeli-Palestinian Relations as Reflected in Human Geography. *Progress in Human Geography*, 11, No. 3 (September, 1987), 315-332.

14797 **Nijim, Basheer K.** "Israel and the Potential for Conflict." *Professional Geographer*, 21, No. 5 (September, 1969), 319-323.

14798 **Nijim, Basheer K.** "Israeli Jewish Settlements in the West Bank, 1967-1980." *Asian Profile*, 12, No. 3 (June, 1984), 257-269.

14799 **Nijim, Basheer K.** "Myths and the Arab-Israeli Conflict." *North American Review*, 254, No. 4 (Winter, 1969), 42-45.

14800 **Oltmans, William L.** "India-Pakistan Dispute: Rising Concern in Washington." *United Asia*, 15 (November, 1963), 779-780.

14801 **Ottaway, Marina.** "Mediation in a Transitional Conflict: Eritrea." *The American Academy of Political and Social Science. The Annals* [Newbury Park], 518 (November, 1991), 69-81.

14802 **Padelford, Norman J.** "Regional Cooperation in Scandanavia." *International Organization*, 11, No. 4 (Autumn, 1957), 597-614.

14803 "Pakistan: Crisis in Kashmir." *Round Table*, 53, No. 215 (June, 1964), 289-292.

14804 "Pakistan: Pakistan's Case in Kashmir." *Round Table*, 54, No. 221 (December, 1965), 75-78.

14805 **Palmer, Norman D.** "Trans-Himalayan Confrontation." *Orbis*. 6, No. 3 (Fall, 1963), 513-527.

14806 **Patrick, Richard A.** "Geography's Contribution to Conflict Research." In *Political Geography and the Cyprus Conflict, 1963-1971*. Waterloo, Ontario: Department of Geography Faculty of Environmental Studies, University of Waterloo, 1976, 400-412.

14807 **Peters, William.** "The Unresolved Problem of Tibet." *Asian Affairs*, 19, Part 2 (June, 1988), 140-153.

14808 **Phadnis, Urmila.** "The Indo-Ceylon Pact and the Stateless Indians in Ceylon." *Asian Survey*, 7, No. 4 (April, 1967), 226-236.

14809 **Philip, George.** "Belize: The Troubled Regional Context." *World Today*, 40, Nos. 8-9 (August-September, 1984), 370-376.

14810 **Plummer, Mark.** "Taiwan: Toward a Second Generation of Mainland Rule." *Asian Survey*, 10, No. 1 (January, 1970), 18-24.

14811 **Porter, Gareth.** "The Sino-Vietnamese Conflict in Southeast Asia." *Current History*, 75, No. 442 (December, 1978), 193-196, 226 and 230.

14812 **Pringsheim, Klaus H.** "The Conflict in Tibet." *Contemporary China*, 4 (1959-60), 70-86.

14813 "Problems of European Integration." *Proceedings of the Institute of World Affairs*, 43rd Session. 42 (1966), Complete Volume, Multiple Authors.

14814 "The Problem of Palestine; Review of Developments Since the Peel Report; Summary of the White Paper; Attitude of Arabs and Jews." *Bulletin of International News*, 16, No. 11 (June 3, 1939), 537-549.

14815 **Ramazani, R.K.** "Iran and the Arab-Israeli Conflict." *Middle East Journal*, 32, No. 4 (Autumn, 1978), 413-428.

14816 **Reilly, J.** "Israel in Lebanon 1975-1982." *MERIP Reports*, 108/109 (1982), 16-20.

14817 **Rey, Violette.** "Apres L'Europe de L'Est?" *L'Espace Geographique* [Paris], 19-20, No. 1 (1990-1991), 79-90.

14818 **Roberts, Adam.** "Decline of Illusions: The Status of the Israeli-occupied Territories over 21 Years." *International Affairs*, 64, No. 3 (Summer, 1988), 345-359.

14819 **Rowley, Gwyn.** "Israel and the Potential for Conflict." A Rejoinder." *Professional Geographer*, 22, No. 5 (September, 1970), 248-251.

14820 **Rundle, Christopher.** "The Iran/Iraq Conflict." *Asian Affairs*, 17, Old Series, 73, Part 2 (June, 1986), 128-133.

14821 **Saikal, Amin.** "The Persian Gulf Crisis: Regional Implications." *Australian Journal of International Affairs* [Canberra], 44, No. 3 (December, 1990), 237-246.

14822 **Sakwa, George.** "The Politsh Ultimatum to Lithuania in March, 1938." *Slavonik and East European Review*, 55, No. 2 (April, 1977), 204-226.

14823 **Salisbury, Howard Graves III.** "The Israeli-Syrian Demilitarized Zone: An Examination of Unresolved Conflict." *Journal of Geography*, 71, No. 2 (February, 1972), 109-116.

14824 **Salisbury, Howard Graves III.** "The Vietnamese Demilitarized Zone: A Behavioral Analysis of Unresolved Conflict." Presented at the 16th Annual Meeting of the Arizona Academy of Science, May 1972, Prescott Arizona. Abstract in the *Journal of the Arizona Academy of Science*, 17 (April, 1972), 33-34.

14825 **Samad, Paridah Abd., and Abu Bakar, Darusalam.** "Malaysia-Philippines Relations: The Issue of Sabah." *Asian Survey* [Berkeley], 32, No. 6 (June, 1992), 554-567.

14826 **Sanders, Lena.** "L'Europe S'arrete-t-elle a la Baltique? La Suede Face a la Communautre Europeenne." *L'Espace Geographique* [Paris], 19-20, No. 2 (1990-1991), 97-104.

14827 **Schweinfurth, Ulrich.** "Nagaland und die Invasion der Chinesen." *Aussenpolitik*,13, No. 2 (December, 1962), 853-857.

14828 **Shahak, Israel.** "Israeli Land Seizure in the Occupied Territories." *Middle East Policy* [Washington, DC], 1 (No. 2 (1992), 96-105.

14829 **Sheffer, Gabriel.** "Appeasement and the Problem of Palestine." *International Journal of Middle East Studies*, 11, No. 3 (May, 1980), 377-399.

14830 **Sigler, John H.** "The Iran-Iraq Conflict: The Tragedy of Limited Conventional War." *International Journal*, 41, No. 2 (Spring, 1986), 424-456.

14831 **Silberman, Leo.** "Change and Conflict in the Horn of Africa." *Foreign Affairs*, 37, No. 4 (July, 1959), 649-659.

14832 **Simon, Sheldon W.** "Cambodia: Barbarism in a Small State under Siege." *Current History*, 75, No. 442 (December, 1978), 197-201 and 227-228.

14833 **Sloan, T.J.** "The Association Between Domestic and International Conflict Hypothesis Revisited." *International Interaction*, 4, No. 1 (January, 1977), 3-32.

14834 "South-West Africa: The Crisis and Its Background." *Round Table*, 206, No. 1 (March, 1962), 155-161.

14835 "The Soviet Attitude to Pushtunistan." *Central Asian Review*, 13, No. 3 (July, 1960), 310-315.

14836 **Springer, Neil A.** "Conflict Over Western Sahara." *Focus*, 29, No. 4 (March-April, 1979), 10-16.

14837 **Srivastava, R.P.** "Kashmir: A Geo-Political Problem." *National Geographer*, 1 (1958), 19-23.

14838 **Sussman, Gerald.** "Macapagal, the Sabah Claim and Maphilindo: The Politics of Penetration." *Journal of Contemporary Asia*, 13, No. 2 (1983), 210-228.

14839 **Tarzi, Shah M.** "Politics of the Afaghan Resistance Movement." *Asian Survey* [Berkeley], 31, No. 6 (June, 1991), 479-495.

14840 **Taylor, Edmond.** "Tortured Kashmir, 1: The Smoke and Fire." *Reporter*, 33, No. 3 (November 4, 1965), 24-27.

14841 **Taylor, Richard Bingham.** "Amhara Cloud Over Eritrea." *Geographical Magazine*, 46, Nos. 3, 4, 5 (February, 1974): Incorporating December, 1973 and January, 1974, 196-201.

14842 **Tessler, Mark A.** "Center and Periphery within Regional International Systems: The Case of the Arab World." *Jerusalem Journal of International Relations,* 11, No. 3 (September, 1989), 74-89.

14843 **Thian-Hok, Li.** "The China Impasse: A Formosan View." *Foreign Affairs,* 36, No. 3 (April, 1958), 437-448.

14844 **Thompson, D.** "China and Tibet, 1911-1961." *Journal of the Royal Central Asian Society*, 49, No. 3-4 (July-October, 1962), 266-276.

14845 **Traband, Andre.** "Grenzprobleme und Raumordnung am Oberrhein." *Geographische Zeitschrift*, 58 Jahrg, Heft 2 (August, 1970), 124-137.

14846 **Van De Vliert, Evert.** "Siding and Other Reactions to a Conflict." *Journal of Conflict Resolution*, 25, No. 3 (September, 1981), 495-520.

14847 **Waller, Harold M.** "Israel's Continuing Dilemma." *Current History*, 89, No. 544 (February, 1990), 86-88.

14848 **Walsh, Abdul H.** "Pakhtun's Inevitable Destiny: Self-Determination." *Eastern World*, 16, No. 1 (January, 1962), 16 and 23.

14849 **Washbourne, John.** "The Soviet Invasion and Presence in Afghanistan." *Geographical Essays*, 4 (Fall, 1987), SB1-SB6.

14850 **Waterfield, Gordon.** "Trouble in the Horn of Africa? The British Somali Case." *International Affairs*, 32, No. 1 (January, 1956), 52-60.

14851 **Watson, J.W.** "North America in the Changing World." *Journal of Geography*, 57, No. 8 (November, 1958), 381-389.

14852 **Weed, Charles F.** "Tunisia: The Calm Before the Storm?" *New England-St. Lawrence Valley Geographical Society. Proceedings* [Montreal], 19 (September, 1990), 43-51.

14853 **Wheeler, G.E.** "Russia and China in Central Asia." *Royal Central Asian Journal*, 54, Part 3 (October, 1967), 254-263.

14854 **Whitton, Douglas.** "The Problem of Palestine." *Australian Outlook*, 10, No. 3 (September, 1956), 46-54.

14855 **Wilson, Dick.** "Where the World's Roof End." *Far Eastern Economic Review*, 47, No. 10 (March 12, 1965), 442 and 456-459.

14856 **Wilson, Dick.** "Who's Right in the Himalayas." *Far Eastern Economic Review*, 47, No. 11 (March 18, 1965), 485-487.

14857 **Wiskemann, Elizabeth.** "Czechs and Germans After Munich." *Foreign Affairs*, 17, No. 2 (January, 1939), 291-304.

14858 **Zobler, L.** "Decision Making in Regional Construction." *Annals of the Association of American Geographers*, 48, No. 2 (June, 1958), 140-148.

POLITICAL GEOGRAPHY OF SPACE

Books

14859 **Bloomfield, Lincoln P.** *Outer Space: Prospects for Man and Society.* Englewood Cliffs: Prentice-Hall, 1962.

14860 **Cooper, John C.** *Explorations in Aerospace Law.* Montreal: I.A. Vlasic, 1968.

14861 **Cooper, John C..** *The Right to Fly.* New York: Holt Rinehart Winston, 1947.

14862 **Fuller, R. Buckminster.** *Operating Manual for Spaceship Earth.* Carbondale: Southern Illinois University Press, 1961.

14863 **Goldsen, Joseph M.** *Outer Space in World Politics.* New York: Praeger, 1963.

14864 **Goodwin, H.L.** *Space: Frontier Unlimited.* Princeton, New Jersey: Van Nostrand, 1962.

14865 **Haley, Andrew G.** *Space Law and Government.* New York: Appleton-Century-Crofts, 1963.

14866 **Heppenheimer, T.A.** *Colonies in Space.* Harrisburg, Pennsylvania: Stackpole Books, 1977.

14867 **Jessup, Philip C.**, and **Taubenfeld, Howard J.** *Controls for Outer Space and the Antarctic Analogy.* New York: Columbia University Press, 1959.

14868 **Just, Ole.** *Au-dessus des mers et des frontieres.* Rio de Janeiro: Organ Cultural Vida, 1948.

14869 **Kirby, Stephen**, and **Robson, Gordon**, eds. *The Militariasation of Space.* Boulder, Colorado: Lynne Rienner Publishers, 1987.

14870 **Kish, John.** *The Law of International Spaces.* The Hague: A.W. Sijthoff and Leiden, 1973.

14871 **Kuczynski, Robert Rene.** *"Living-Space" and Population Problems.* Oxford: Clarendon Press, 1939.

14872 **Lapalme-Roy, Lise-Aurore.** *Space Boundaries: A Geopolitical Analysis.* Boulder, Colorado: University of Colorado, Ph.D., 1987.

14873 **McDougal, Myres S.; Lasswell, Harold D.;** and **Vlasic, Ivan A.** *Law and Public Order in Space.* New Haven, Connecticut: Yale University Press, 1963.

14874 **Morenus, R.** *Dewline: Distant Early Warning, The Miracle of America's Pivot Line of Defense.* New York: Rand McNally, 1957.

14875 **Peebles, Curtis.** *Battle for Space.* New York: Beaufort Books, 1983.

14876 **Peterson, Robert W.** *Space: From Gemini to the Moon and Beyond.* New York: Facts on File, 1972.

14877 **Renner, George T.** *Human Geography in the Air Age.* New York: Macmillan, 1942.

14878 **Smith, H.B.** *The Use of Polar Ice in Interhemispheric Air Operations.* Washington, D.C.: Georgetown University, 1956.

14879 *Survey of Space Law: Staff Report of the Select Committee on Astronautics and Space Exploration.* Washington, D.C.: House Document 89, 86th Congress, 1st Session, 1959.

14880 **White, Irving L.** *Decision-making for Space: Law and Politics in Air, Sea, and Outer Space.* West Lafayette, Indiana: Purdue Research Foundation, 1970.

Journals

14881 **Agar, William.** "Aviation Prophet." *Commonweal*, 36, No. 22 (September 18, 1942), 521-522.

14882 **Alberts, D.J.** "An Alternative View of Air Interdiction." *Air University Review*, 32, No. 5 (1981), 31-44.

14883 **Cheng, Bin.** "The Legal Regime of Airspace and Outer Space: The Boundary Problem— Functionalism Versus Spatialism: The Major Premises." *Annals of Air and Space Law*, 5 (1980), 323-361.

14884 **Cleveland, Harlan.** "The Politics of Outer Space." *Department of State Bulletin*, 52, No. 1356 (June 21, 1956), 1007-1013.

14885 **Cohen, Saul B.** "The Oblique Plane Air Boundary." *Professional Geographer*, 10, No. 6 (November, 1958), 11-15.

14886 **Denaro, J.M.** "'States' Jurisdiction in Aerospace Under International Law." *Journal of Air Law and Commerce*, 36, No. 4 (Autumn, 1970), 697.

14887 **Ferrer, Manuel Augusto, Jr.** "The Establishment of a Boundary Between Airspace and Outer Space." In *Bangkok World Conference on World Peace Through Law.* Bangkok: Bangkok University, 1969, 507-515.

14888 **Foders, F.** "Exploitation Regime for the Antarctic and Outer Space in the Shadow of the Recent Law of the Sea." *Weltwirtschaft*, 1 (1985), 146-159.

14889 **Gardner, Richard N.** "Cooperation in Outer Space." *Foreign Affairs*, 41, No. 2 (January, 1963), 344-359.

14890 **Goedhuis, D.** "The Present State of International Relations in Outer Space." *International Relations*, 7, No. 5 (May, 1983), 2284-2303.

14891 **Hart, C.A.** "Air Survey: The Modern Aspect." *Geographical Journal*, 108, No. 4-6 (October-December, 1946), 179-197.

14892 **Jessup, Philip C.,** and **Taubenfeld, Howard J.** "Outer Space, Antarctica, and the United Nations." *International Organization*, 13, No. 3 (Summer, 1959), 363-379.

14893 **Moon, Albert I., Jr.** "A Look at Airspace Sovereignty." *Journal of Air Law and Commerce*, 29, No. 4 (Autumn, 1963), 328-345.

14894 **Mott, P.G.** "Airborne Surveying in the Antarctic." *Geographical Journal*, 124, No. 1 (March, 1958), 1-19.

14895 **Neunan, S.** "Fashions in Space." *Foreign Affairs*, 21, No. 2 (January, 1943), 276-288.

14896 **Perek, Lubos.** "Scientific Criteria for the Delimitation of Outer Space." *Journal of Space Law*, 5, Nos. 1-2 (Spring and Fall, 1977), 111-124.

14897 **Quigg, Philip W.** "Open Skies and Open Space." *Foreign Affairs*, 37, No. 1 (October, 1958), 95-107.

14898 **Rosenfield, Stanley B.** "Where Air Space Ends and Outer Space Begins." *Journal of Space Law*, 7, Nos. 1 and 2 (Spring and Fall,1979), 137-148.

14899 **Sanguin, Andre-Louis.** "Geographie Politique, espace aerien et cosmos." *Annales de Geographie*, 86ᵉ Annee, No. 475 (Mai-Juin, 1977), 257-278.

14900 **Santis, Arenas, H.** "La Geopolitica del and 2000: el Poder Espacial. (Geopolitics in the Year 2000: The Outer Space Thesis)." *Revista Chilena de Geopolitica*, 2, No. 1 (1985), 5-22.

14901 **Schneider, A.R.H.** "Remote Sensing of the Earth from Space. Can it be Effectively Regulated?" *Environmental Policy & Law*, 16, No. 2 (1986), 50-59.

14902 **Simsarian, James.** "Outer Space Cooperation in the United Nations." *American Journal of International Law*, 57, No. 4 (October, 1963), 854-867.

14903 **Williams, Maureen.** "The Problem of Demarcation is Back in the Limelight." In *Proceedings of the Twenty-Second Colloquium of the Law of Outer Space.* Munich: 1979, 245-249.

CHAPTER XVI

MILITARY GEOGRAPHY AND GEOSTRATEGY

GENERAL AND THEORY

Books

14904 **Ackland, L., and McGuire, S.,** eds. *Assessing the Nuclear Age.* Chicago, Illinois: Educational Foundation for Nuclear Science, 1986.

14905 **Adams, G.** *The Politics of Defense Contracting: The Iron Triangle.* New Brunswick: Transaction Books, 1981.

14906 **Aiyar, S.K.** *Law and Practice of Arms and Explosives with Rules and Other Allied Laws.* 10th ed. Allahabad: Law Book Co., 1988.

14907 **Alford, Jonathan,** ed. *Sea Power and Influence: Old Issues and New Challenges.* Farnborough: Gower Publishing/Montclair, New Jersey: Allanheld, Osmun & Co. The Adelphi Library. Vol. 2 (1980).

14908 **Arkin, William M., and Fieldhouse, Richard W.** *Global Links in the Arms Race.* New York: Harper & Row, 1985.

14909 **Arkin, William M., and Fieldhouse, Richard W.** *Nuclear Battlefields: Global Links in the Arms Race.* Cambridge, Massachusetts: Ballinger Publishing, 1985.

14910 **Arnold, G.L.** *The Pattern of World Conflict.* New York: Dial, 1955.

14911 **Arquill, John, and Davis, Paul K.** *Extended Deterrence, Compellence nad the 'Old World Order.'* Santa Monica: RAND, 1992.

14912 **Ashcrift, G.** *Military Logistic Systems in NATO: The Goal of Integration: Military Aspects.* Toronto: The Institute for Strategic Studies, Canadian Institute of International Affairs, 1970.

14913 **Asprey, R.B.** *War in the Shadows.* Garden City, New York: Doubleday, 1975.

14914 **Aufricht, Hans.** *War, Peace, and Reconstruction; a Classified Bibliography.* Revised and enlarged edition of the *General Bibliography on International Organization and Postwar Reconstruction,* published by the Commission in its May-June 1942 Bulletin and supplemented in the January-February 1943 Bulletin. New York: Commission to Study the Organization of Peace, pref. 1943.

14915 **Baker, J.N.L.,** ed. *An Atlas of the War. Oxford Pamphlets on World Affairs, No. 22.* New York: Farrar and Rinehart, 1940.

14916 **Balbo, Italo.** *My Air Armada.* Translated by G. Griffen. Garden City, New York: Doubleday, 1934.

14917 **Baldwin, Hanson W.** *Strategy for Victory.* New York: W.W. Norton, 1942.

14918 **Ball, D.** *Targeting for Strategic Deterrence.* Adelphi Papers No. 185, Summer. London: IISS, 1983.

14919 **Barclay, C.N.** *The New Warfare.* New York: Philosophical Library, 1954.

14920 **Barnaby, Frank.** *Defence Without the Bomb: Report of the Alternative Defence Commission.* London: Taylor and Francis, 1983.

14921 **Barnaby, Frank, and Windass, S.** *What Is Just Defence?* Blagdon, Oxford: Just Defence, 1983.

14922 **Barreto, Castro.** *Populacao, riqueza e seguranca.* Rio de Janeiro: Biblioteca do exercito, 1961.

14923 **Bateman, Michael, and Riley, Raymond Charles,** eds. *The Geography of Defence.* Totowa, New Jersey: Barnes and Noble, 1987.

14924 **Becker, Abraham S.** *Military Expenditure Limitations for Arms Control: Problems and Prospects.* Cambridge, Massachusetts: Ballinger, 1977.

14925 **Bellamy, C.** *The Future of Land Warfare.* London and Dover, New Hampshire: Croom Helm, 1987.

14926 **Benoit, Emile.** *Defense and Economic Growth in Developing Countries.* Lexington, Massachusetts: Lexington Books/D.C. Heath, 1973.

14927 **Berg, P., and Heroff, G.** *The Arms Race and Arms Control: The Shorter SIPRI Yearbook.* London: Taylor and Francis, 1984.

14928 **Blechman, Barry M.,** ed. *Rethinking of U.S. Strategic Posture: A Report from the Aspen Consortium on Arms Control and Security Issues.* Cambridge, Massachusetts: Ballinger, 1982.

14929 **Boggs, S. Whittemore.** *This Hemisphere.* Washington, D.C.: U.S. Department of State, 1945.

14930 **Bolton, Roger E.** *Defense Purchases and Regional Growth.* Washington, D.C.: The Brookings Institute, 1966.

14931 **Boulding, E.,** ed. *New Agenda for Peace Research: Conflict and Security* Boulder: Lynne Rienner, 1992.

14932 **Boulding, Kenneth E.** *Conflict and Defense: A General Theory.* New York: Harper & Row, 1963.

14933 **Bowett, D.W.** *Self-Defence in International Law.* Manchester: Manchester University Press, 1958.

14934 **Bradford, Ernb.** *The Sword and the Scimitar: The Saga of the Crusades.* New York: G.P. Putnam's Sons, 1974.

14935 **Brodie, Bernard.** *The Absolute Weapon: Atomic Power and World Order.* New York: Harcourt Brace, 1946.

14936 **Brodie, Fawn M.,** comp. *Peace Aims and Post-War Planning; a Bibliography, Selected and Annotated.* Boston: World Peace Foundation, 1942.

14937 **Brown, Francis,** and **Herlin, Emil.** *The War in Maps: An Atlas of "The New York Times."* New York: Oxford University Press, 1942 and 1944.

14938 **Brown, James,** and **Snyder, William P.,** eds. *The Regionalization of Warfare: The Falkland/Malvinas Islands, Lebanon, and the Iran-Iraq Conflict.* New Brunswick, New Jersey: Transaction Books, 1985.

14939 **Brown, Neville.** *The Future Global Challenge: A Predictive Study of World Security, 1977-1990.* Whitehall, London: Royal United Services Institute for Defence Studies/New York: Crane Russak and Company, 1977.

14940 **Brunk, G.G.; Cohen, J.E.;** and **Hardee, B.** *Predicting Attitudes Toward Nuclear Power.* Birmingham: University of Alabama, 1983.

14941 **Bunge, William W.** *The Nuclear War Atlas.* Oxford: Basil Blackwell, 1988.

14942 **Burlingame, Roger.** *General Billy Mitchell: Champion of Defense.* New York: McGraw-Hill, 1952.

14943 **Burnett, Alan.** *Geography as the Queen of the Peace Sciences.* Unpublished manuscript, mimeographed, East Lansing: Michigan State University, 1986.

14944 **Burton, John W.** *Global Conflict: The Domestic Sources of International Crisis.* College Park: University of Maryland, Center for International Development, 1984.

14945 **Caldwell, Cyril C.** *Air Power and Total War. The Capacity of Air Power to Strike at Industrial Targets.* New York: Coward-McCann, 1943.

14946 **Cannizzo, Cynthia,** ed. *The Gun Merchants: Politics and Policies of the Major Arms Suppliers.* Elmsford, New York: Pergamon Press, 1980.

14947 **Chamberlain, James.** *Air Age Geography and Society.* Philadelphia: Lippincott, 1945.

14948 **Cioffi-ReVilla, Claudio.** *The Scientific Measurement of International Conflicts: Handbook of Datasets on Crises and Wars, 1495-1988 A.D.* Boulder, Colorado: Lynne Rienner Publishers, 1990.

14949 **Clark, Ian.** *Limited Nuclear War: Political Theory and War Conventions.* Princeton, New Jersey: Princeton University Press, 1982.

14950 **Clark, Ian.** *Waging War: A Philosophical Introduction.* Oxford: Clarendon Press, 1988.

14951 **Clarkson, Jesse D.,** and **Cochran, Thomas C.,** eds. *War as a Social Institution; the Historian's Perspective.* New York: Columbia University Press, 1941.

14952 **Clutterbuck, Richard.** *Terrorism and Guerrilla Warfare: Forecasts and Remedies.* London: Routledge, 1990.

14953 **Cochran, A.T.; Arkin, W.B.;** and **Hoening, M.M.** *Nuclear Weapons Databook, vol. 1.* Cambridge, Massachusetts: Ballinger, 1984.

14954 **Coffey, Joseph I.** *Strategic Power and National Security.* Pittsburgh, Pennsylvania: University of Pittsburgh Press, 1971.

14955 **Cole, D.H.** *Imperial Military Geography.* London: Sifton Praed, 1956.

14956 **Cook, A.,** and **Kirk, Grayson.** *Greenham Women Everywhere: Dreams, Ideas and Actions from the Women's Peace Movement.* Boston and London: South End Press/Pluto Press, 1983.

14957 **Copson, Raymond W.** *Africa's Wars and Prospects for Peace.* Armonk: M.E. Sharpe, 1994.

14958 **Council for National Parks.** *Military Use of National Parks.* London: Mimeo, available from CNP, 45 Shelton Street, London WC2H 9HJ, 1985.

14959 **Cornish, Vaughan.** *A Geography of Imperial Defence.* London: Sifton Praed, 1922.

14960 **Cox, J.** *Overkill: The Story of Modern Weapons.* London: Penguin, 1981.

14961 **Curry, M.G.** *After Nuclear War: Possible Worlds and the Cult of Experience.* Minneapolis: University of Minnesota, Ph.D., 1984.

14962 **Cutter, Susan L.,** and **Solecki, W.D.** *Geography, Nuclear War, and Peace.* Unpublished manuscript, mimiographed, New Brunswick, New Jersey: Rutgers-The State University, 1986.

14963 **Dalby, Wilfrid Simon.** *Creating the Second Cold War: The Discourse of Politics.* New York: Guildford Publications, 1990.

14964 **DeHuszar, George B.,** ed. *New Perspectives on Peace.* Chicago, Illinois: University of Chicago Press, 1944.

14965 **de Seversky, Alexander P.** *Air Power, Key to Survival.* New York: Simon & Schuster, 1950.

14966 **de Seversky, Alexander P.** *Victory Through Air Power.* Baltimore: Williams and Wilkins, 1941.

14967 **Deutscher, Isaac.** *Marxism, Wars and Revolutions: Essays from Four Decades.* London: Verso, 1984.

14968 **Dotto, L.** *Planet Earth in Jeopardy. Environmental Consequences of Nuclear War.* New York: John Wiley & Sons, 1986.

14969 **Douhet, Giulio.** *The Command of the Air.* New York: Coward-McCann, 1942.

14970 **Doyle, Adrian Conan.** *Heaven has Claws.* New York: Random House, 1953.

14971 **Durch, William J.,** ed. *National Interests and the Military Use of Space.* Cambridge, Massachusetts: Ballinger, 1984.

14972 **Earle, Edward Mead,** ed. *Makers of Modern Strategy: Machiavelli to Hitler.* Princeton, New Jersey: Princeton University Press, 1944.

14973 **Eliot, George Fielding.** *Bombs Bursting in Air: The Influence of Air Power on International Relations.* New York: Reynal and Hitchcock, 1939.

14974 **Emme, Eugene M.,** ed. *The Impact of Air Power, National Security and World Politics.* Princeton, New Jersey: Van Nostrand, 1959.

14975 **Farington, Hugh.** *Strategic Geography: NATO, Warsaw Pact and the Superpowers.* 2nd ed. New York: Routledge, 1989.

14976 **Flenley, R.** *Post-War Problems - A Reading List; A Select Bibliography on Post-War Settlement and Reconstruction.* Toronto: The Canadian Institute of International Affairs, 1943.

14977 **Fraser, Niall M.,** and **Hipel, Keith W.** *Conflict Analysis: Models and Resolutions.* New York: North-Holland, 1984.

14978 **Freedman, Lawrence.** *Atlas of Global Strategy.* London: Macmillan, 1985.

14979 **Freedman, Lawrence.** *The Evolution of Nuclear Strategy.* New York: St. Martin's Press, 1983.

14980 **Fuller, J.F.C.** *The Decisive Battles of the Western.* London: Paladin, 1970.

14981 **Fullerton, William Morton.** *Problems of Power: A Study of International Politics from Sadowa to Kir-Kilisse.* New York: Charles Scribner's Sons, 1913.

14982 **Gansler, J.S.** *The Defense Industry.* Cambridge, Massachusetts: Massachusetts Institute of Technology Press, 1980.

14983 **Gardner, L.C.; Schlesinger, A., Jr.;** and **Morgenthau, H.J.** *The Origin of the Cold War.* Boston: Ginn, 1970.

14984 **Gavreau, Emile.** *The Wild Blue Yonder.* New York: Doubleday, 1946.

14985 **Gavreau, Emile,** and **Cohen, Lester.** *Billy Mitchell: Founder of Our Air Force and Prophet Without Honor.* New York: Dutton, 1942.

14986 **George, James J.,** ed. *Problems of Sea Power as We Approach the Twenty-First Century.* Washington, D.C.: American Enterprise Institute for Public Policy Research, 1978.

14987 **Germany. Foreign Office.** *Documents on the Events Preceding the Outbreak of War.* Berlin: German Foreign Office, 1939; New York: German Library of Information, 1940.

14988 **Gideonese, Harry D.,** and **Others.** *The Politics of Atomic Energy.* New York: Woodrow Wilson Foundation, 1946.

14989 **Goldstein, J.** *Long Cycles: Prosperity and War in the Modern Age.* New Haven, Connecticut: Yale University Press, 1988.

14990 **Goodenough, Simon.** *War Maps: World War II, From September 1939 to August 1945; Air, Sea, and Land, Battle by Battle.* New York: St. Martin's Press, 1982.

14991 **Gorgol, J.F.** *The Military-Industrial Firm: A Practical Theory and Model.* New York: Praeger, 1972.

14992 Gorshkov, Sergei G. *The Sea Power of the State*. New York: Pergamon Press, 1979.

14993 Gray, Colin S. *The Leverage of Sea Power: The Strategic Advantage of Navies in War*. New York: The Free Press, 1992.

14994 Green, J.B. *Military Geography: Tactical Terrain Analysis*. Tallahassee: Florida State University, M.A., 1979.

14995 Hackel, E. *Military Manpower and Political Purpose*. Toronto: THe Institute for Strategic Studies, Canadian Institute of International Affairs, 1970.

14996 Hackett, J. *The Third World War*. London: Sphere, 1978.

14997 Hall, A. Hamer. *The Fundamentals of World Peace*. New York: Philosophical Library, 1953.

14998 Halle, L.J. *The Cold War as History*. New York: Harper & Row, 1967.

14999 Harkavy, Robert E., and Neuman, Stephanie, eds. *International Arms Transfers*. New York: Praeger, 1979.

15000 Harrison, Joseph B.; Mander, Linden A.; and Engle, Nathanael H., eds. *If Men Want Peace; The Mandates of World Order, By Members of the Faculty of the University of Washington*. New York: Macmillan, 1946.

15001 Harwell, M.A., and Hutchinson, T.C. *Environmental Consequences of Nuclear War*. SCOPE 28, Volume 11. New York: John Wiley & Sons, 1985.

15002 Haskins, Homer, and Lord, Howard. *Some Problems of the Peace Conference*. Cambridge, Massachusetts: Harvard University Press, 1920.

15003 Haya de la Torre, Raul. *La Defensa Continental*. Buenos Aires: Americalee, 1942.

15004 Higham, R. *Air Power: A Concise History*. New York: St. Martin's Press, 1972.

15005 Hinsley, F.H. *Power and the Pursuit of Peace*. London: Cambridge University Press, 1963.

15006 Hurley, Alfred F. *Billy Mitchell: Crusader for Air Power*. New York: F. Watts, 1964.

15007 Independent Commission on Disarmament and Security Issues. *Common Security*. London: Pan, 1982.

15008 Ingram, Kenneth. *History of the Cold War*. New York: Philosophical Library, 1955.

15009 Isard, Walter. *Arms Race, Arms Control, and Conflict Analysis: Contributions from Peace Science and Peace Economics*. New York: Cambridge University Press, 1988.

15010 Janowitz, M. *The Military in the Political Development of New Nations*. Chicago, Illinois: University of Chicago Press, 1964.

15011 Johnson, Douglas Wilson. *Battlefields of the World War: A Study in Military Geography*. New York: Oxford University Press, 1921.

15012 Johnson, Douglas Wilson. *Topography and Strategy in the War*. New York: Henry Hold, 1917.

15013 Jones, Rodney W., and Hildreth, Steven A. *Emerging Powers: Defense and Security in the Third World*. New York: Praeger, 1986.

15014 Jones, Stephen B. *The Conditions of War Limitation*. New Haven, Connecticut: Yale University Press, 1955.

15015 Kaplan, S. *The Diplomacy of Power*. Washington, D.C.: The Brookings Institute, 1981.

15016 Kapur, Harish. *The Embattled Triangle, Moscow-Peking-New Delhi*. New York: Humanities Press, 1973.

15017 Keegan, John, and Wheatcroft, Andrew. *Zones of Conflict: An Atlas of Future Wars*. London: Jonathan Cape, 1986.

15018 Kelleher, Cathrine McArdle, ed. *Political-Military Systems: Comparative Perspectives*. Beverly Hills, California: Sage Publications, 1974.

15019 Kemp, Geoffrey; Pfaltzgraff, Robert L., Jr.; Ra'anan, Uri, et al. *The Superpowers in a Multinuclear World*. Lexington, Massachusetts: Lexington Books, 1974.

15020 Kennedy, G. *The Military in the Third World*. London: Duckworth, 1974.

15021 Keynes, J.M. *The Economic Consequences of the Peace*. London: Macmillan, 1919.

15022 Kidron, Michael. *The War Atlas: Armed Conflict-Armed Peace*. New York: Simon and Schuster, 1983.

15023 Kissinger, Henry A. *Nuclear Weapons and Foreign Policy*. New York: Harper and Brothers, 1957.

15024 Klare, Michael T., and Kornbluh, P., eds. *Low Intensity Warfare; Counterinsurgency, Proinsurgency and Anti Terrorism in the 1980's*. New York: Pantheon, 1988.

15025 **Knorr, Klaus.** *Military Power and Potential.* Lexington, Massachusetts: D.C. Heath, 1970.

15026 **Knorr, Klaus.** *The War Potential of Nations.* Princeton, New Jersey: Princeton University Press, 1956.

15027 **La Feber, Walter.** *America, Russia and the Cold War, 1945-1966.* New York: John Wiley & Sons, 1967.

15028 **Lackey, D.P.** *The Ethics of War and Peace.* Englewood Cliffs, New Jersey: Prentice-Hall, 1989.

15029 **Lacoste, Y.** *La Geographie, Ca Sert, d'abord, a Faire la Guerre.* Paris: Editions Francois Maspero, 1976.

15030 **Laffin, John.** *The World in Conflict 1989. War Annual 3: Contemporary Warfare Described and Analysed.* London: Brassey's Defence Publishers, 1989.

15031 **Leaning, J., and Keyes, L., eds.** *The Counterfeit Ark: Crisis Relocation for Nuclear War.* Cambridge, Massachusetts: Ballinger, 1984.

15032 **Lee, Fitzgerald.** *Imperial Military Geography.* London: William Clowes and Sons, 1922.

15033 **Levine, Isaac Don.** *Mitchell: Pioneer of Air Power.* New York: Duell, Sloan and Pearce, 1943.

15034 **Liska, G.** *War and Order.* Baltimore, Maryland: Johns Hopkins University Press, 1968.

15035 **Litton, R.J., and Falk, R.** *Indefensible Weapons: The Political and Psychological Case Against Nuclearism.* New York: Basic Books, 1982.

15036 **London, J., and White, G.F., eds.** *The Environmental Effects of Nuclear War.* AAAS Selected Symposium No. 98. Boulder, Colorado: Westview Press, 1984.

15037 **Lubow, Robert E.** *The War Animals.* Garden City, New York: Doubleday, 1977.

15038 **Luttwak, Edward N.** *The Political Use of Sea Power.* Studies in International Affairs, No. 23. Baltimore, Maryland: Johns Hopkins University Press, 1974.

15039 **Luttwak, Edward N.** *The Strategic Balance.* New York: Library Press, 1972.

15040 **Luttwak, Edward N.** *Strategic Power: Military Capabilities and Political Utility.* Beverly Hills, California: Published for the Center for Strategic and International Studies by Sage Publications, 1976.

15041 **Luttwak, Edward N.** *The US-USSR Nuclear Weapons Balance.* Beverly Hills, California: Sage Publications, 1974.

15042 **MacDonnell, A.C.** *Outlines of Military Geography.* London: H. Rees, 1911.

15043 **Macguire, T.M.** *Outlines of Military Geography.* Cambridge: Cambridge University Press, 1900.

15044 **Mandelbaum, Michael.** *The Nuclear Revolution.* Cambridge: Cambridge University Press, 1981.

15045 **Mann, Michael.** *States, War and Capitalism: Studies in Political Sociology.* Oxford: Basil Blackwell, 1988.

15046 **Maoz, Zeev.** *Paradoxes of War: On the Art of National Self-Entrapment.* Boston, Massachusetts: Unwin Hyman, 1990.

15047 **Marshall-Cornwall, J.H.** *Geographic Disarmament: A Study of Regional Demilitarization.* London: Cambridge University Press, 1935.

15048 **Martin, Charles E., and Von Kleinsmid, Rufus B., eds.** *Problems of the Peace.* Institute of World Affairs. Interim Proceedings, Vol. 21. Los Angeles: University of Southern California, 1945.

15049 **Martin, Laurence W.** *Arms and Strategy: The World Power Structure Today.* New York: D. McKay, 1973.

15050 **May, E.S.** *An Introduction to Military Geography.* London: Hugh Rees, 1909.

15051 **McLuhan, Marshall, and Fiore, Quentin.** *War and Peace in the Global Village.* New York: McGraw-Hill, 1968.

15052 **Melman, S.** *The Demilitarized Society: Disarmament and Conversion.* Nottingham: Spokesman, 1988.

15053 **Midlarsky, M., ed.** *Handbook of War Studies.* Boston, Massachusetts: Unwin and Hyman, 1989.

15054 **Miksche, F.O.** *Atomic Weapons and Armies.* New York: Praeger, 1955.

15055 *Military Aspects of World Political Geography.* 2 Vols. Montgomery, Alabama: Maxwell Air Force Base, 1959.

15056 **Miller, Steven E., ed.** *Strategy and Nuclear Deterrence.* Princeton, New Jersey: Princeton University Press, 1984.

15057 **Ministry of Defence.** *Statement on the Report of Defence Lands Committee 1971-73.* London: Her Majesty's Stationery Office, 1974.

15058 **Mitchell, William.** *Winged Defense: The Development and Possibilities of Modern Air Power--Economic and Military.* New York: Putnam, 1925.

15059 **Moodie, Michael.** *Sovereignty, Security, and Arms.* The Washington Papers, No. 67. Beverly Hills, California: Sage Publications, 1979.

15060 **Moulton, Harold G.,** and **Marlio, Louis.** *The Control of Germany and Japan.* Washington, D.C.: The Brookings Institute, 1944.

15061 **Mowrer, Edgar Ansel,** and **Rajchman, Marthe.** *Global War, An Atlas of World Strategy.* New York: William Morrow, 1942.

15062 **Murray, Williamson.** *Strategy for Defeat: The Luftwaffe, 1933-1945.* Montgomery, Alabama: Air University Press, 1983.

15063 **NATO.** *NATO and the Warsaw Pact: Force Comparison*, Figure 1. Brussels: NATO Information Service, 1984.

15064 **Neumann, William L.,** ed. *Making the Peace, 1941-1945; The Diploma of the Wartime Conference.* Washington, D.C.: Foundation for Foreign Affairs, 1950.

15065 **New York Times.** *Documents on World Security.* New York: Promotion Department, New York Times, 1945.

15066 **Newbigin, M.J.** *Aftermach: A Geographical Study of the Peace Terms.* Edinburg: Johnston, 1920.

15067 **Nugent (Lord).** *Report of the Defence Lands Committee.* Cmd 5714. London: Her Majesty's Stationery Office, 1973.

15068 **Oglesby, A.J.** *The Effects of Geographical Mobility on the Naval Rating's Family Unit.* Southampton: Defence Fellowship, University of Southampton, 1974.

15069 **Olvey, L.O.,** et al., eds. *Industrial Capacity and Defense Planning.* Lexington, Massachusetts: Lexington Books, 1983.

15070 **Oppenheim, L.** *Peace.* New York: Longmans, 1955.

15071 **Oppenheim, L.** *Disputes, War and Neutrality.* New York: Longmans, 1955.

15072 **Oppenheimer, M.** *Urban Guerrilla.* Harmondsworth: Penguin, 1969.

15073 **O'Sullivan, Patrick,** and **Miller, Jesse W. Jr.** *The Geography of Warfare.* New York: St. Martin's Press, 1983.

15074 **Owen, Wilfred.** *Strategy for Mobility.* Washington, D.C.: The Brookings Institute, 1964.

15075 **Parker, H.M.D.** *Manpower: A Study of Wartime Policy and Administration.* London: Her Majesty's Stationery Office, 1957.

15076 **Payne, Keith B.,** ed. *Laser Weapons in Space: Policy and Doctrine.* Boulder, Colorado: Westview Press, 1983.

15077 **Peltier, Louis C.,** and **Pearcy, G. Etzel.** *Military Geography.* Princeton, New Jersey: Van Nostrand, 1966.

15078 **Pepper, D.M.,** and **Jenkins, A.M.,** eds. *The Geography of Peace and War.* Oxford: Basil Blackwell, 1985.

15079 **Pierre, Andrew J.** *The Global Politics of Arms Sales.* Princeton, New Jersey: Princeton University Press, 1982.

15080 **Pigou, A.C.** *The Political Economy of War.* London: Macmillan, 1939.

15081 **Pittock, A. Barrie,** and Others. *Environmental Consequences of Nuclear War, vol. 1. Physical and Atmospheric Effects.* Chichester: John Wiley & Sons, 1986.

15082 **Possony, Stefan T.** *Strategic Air Power: The Pattern of Dynamic Security.* Washington, D.C.: Infantry Journal Press, 1949.

15083 **Pratt, Eric K.** *Selling Strategic Defence: Interests, Ideologies, and the Arms Race.* Boulder, Colorado: Lynne Rienner Publishers, 1990.

15084 **Renwick, H.L.** *The Post-nuclear Landscape: How Science Fiction Compares with Official and Scientific Scenarios.* Discussion Paper No. 24. New Brunswick, New Jersey; Rutgers-The State University, Department of Geography, 1986.

15085 **Riordan, Michael.** *The Day After Midnight: The Effects of Nuclear War.* Palo Alto, California: Cheshire Books, 1982.

15086 **Roberts, Adam,** and **Guedff, Richard.** *Documents on the Laws of War,* 2nd ed. New York: Oxford University Press, 1989.

15087 **Roberts, Philip J.** *Nuclear Winter: Implications for U.S. and Soviet Strategy.* Santa Monica: The Rand Corporation, The Rand Paper Series, No. P-7009, 1984.

15088 **Sageret, Jules.** *Philosophie de la guerre et de la paix.* Paris: Alcan, 1919.

15089 **Salisbury, Howard Graves, III.** *The Demilitarized Zones.* Los Angeles: University of California, Ph.D., 1972.

15090 **Sampson, Anthony.** *The Arms Bazaar: From Lebanon to Lockheed.* New York: Viking Press, 1977; Bantam, 1978.

15091 **Sanjian, Gregory.** *Arms Transfers to the Third World: Probability Models of Superpower Decisionmaking.* Boulder, Colorado: Lynne Rienner Publishers, 1987.

15092 **Schultz, Barry M.,** and **Slater, Robert O.,** eds. *Revolution and Political Change in the Third World.* Boulder, Colorado: Lynne Rienner Publishers, 1990.

15093 **Segal, Gerald; Moreton, E.; Freedman, Lawrence;** and **Baylis, J.** *Nuclear War and Nuclear Peace.* London: Macmillan, 1983.

15094 **Seton-Watson, Hugh.** *Neither War Nor Peace.* New York: Praeger, 1960.

15095 **Shotwell, James T.** *Lesson of the Last World War.* New York: American Institute of Consulting Engineers, 1942.

15096 **Signaud, Louis A.** *Air Power and Unification.* Harisburg, Pennsylvania: Military Services Press, 1949.

15097 **Silva, Golbery do Couto e.** *Planejamento estrategico.* Rio de Janeiro: Biblioteca do exercito, 1955.

15098 **Simon, Jerry,** ed. *NATO-Warsaw Pact Force Mobilization.* Washington, D.C., The National Defense University Press, 1988.

15099 **Sivard, R.L.** *World Military and Social Expenditures.* Washington, D.C.: World Priorities, 1983.

15100 **Siverson, Randolph M.,** and **Starr, Harvey.** *The Diffusion of War: A Study of Opportunity and Willingness.* Ann Arbor: The University of Michigan Press, 1991.

15101 **Slessor, Sir John C.** *Air Power and Armies.* London: Oxford University Press, 1936.

15102 **Slessor, Sir John C.** *Command and Control of Allied Nuclear Forces: A British View.* London: Adelphia Papers No. 22, 1965.

15103 **Slessor, Sir John C.** *The Greatest Deterrent.* New York: Praeger, 1957.

15104 **Slick, Tom.** *Permanent Peace; A Check and Balance Plan.* Englewood Cliffs, New Jersey: Prentice-Hall, 1958.

15105 **Soppelsa, Jacques.** *Geographie des armements.* Paris: Masson, 1980.

15106 **Spaight, James M.** *The Beginnings of Organised Air Power.* London: Longmans, Green, 1927.

15107 **Spaight, James M.** *Air Power in the Next War.* London: G. Bles, 1938.

15108 **Speiser, Stuart M.** *How to End the Nuclear Nightmare.* Croton on Hudson, New York: North River Press, 1984.

15109 **Spykman, Nicholas J.** *The Geography of the Peace.* New York: Harcourt Brace and World, 1944.

15110 **Stoessinger, J.C.** *The Might of Nations.* New York: Random House, 1963.

15111 **Stokesbury, James L.** *Navy and Empire.* New York: William Morrow, 1983.

15112 **Stone, J.** *Legal Controls of International Conflict.* Sydney: Maitland Publications, 1954.

15113 **Strassoldo, Raimondo.** *Sviluppo Regionale e Difesa Nazionale.* Trieste: Lint, 1972.

15114 **Strieber, W.,** and **Kunetka, J.** *Warday.* New York: Warner Books, 1985.

15115 **Sturgill, Claude C.** *The Military History of the Third World Since 1945: A Reference Guide.* Westport: Greenwood Press, 1994.

15116 **Thomas, Caroline.** *In Search of Security: The Third World in International Relations.* Boulder, Colorado: Lynne Rienner Publishers, 1987.

15117 **Thompson, W.R.** *On Global War: Historical-Structural Approaches to World Politics.* Columbia: University of South Carolina Press, 1989.

15118 **Todd, Daniel.** *Defence Industries: A Global Perspective.* New York: Routledge, 1988.

15119 **U.S. Air Force Reserve Officers Training Corps.** Air University, Maxwell Air Force Base, Alabama. *Military Aspects of World Political Geography.* Alabama: Maxwell Air Force Base, 1959.

15120 **United States. War Department.** *A Graphic History of the War: September 1, 1939 to May 10, 1942.* Washington, D.C.: United States War Department, 1942.

15121 **Unsworth, Michael E.**, ed. *Military Periodicals: United States nad Selected International Journals and Newspapers*. New York: Greenwood Press, 1990.

15122 **Van Valkenburg, Samuel.** *Peace Atlas of Europe*. Published in cooperation with the Foreign Policy Association. New York: Duell, Sloan and Pearce, 1946.

15123 **Villate, Robert.** *Les conditions geographiques de la guerre*. Paris: Payot, 1925.

15124 **Vlahos, Olivia.** *The Battle-Ax People*. New York: Viking Press, 1968.

15125 **Walker, R.B.J.** *One World/Many Worlds: Struggle for a Just World Peace*. Boulder, Colorado: Lynne Rienner Publishers, 1988.

15126 **Wallensteen, Peter,** and Others, eds. *Global Militarization*. Boulder, Colorado: Westview Press, 1985.

15127 **Walters, R.E.** *Sea Power and the Nuclear Fallacy: A Reevaluation of Global Strategy*. New York: Holmes and Meier, 1975.

15128 **Welles, Summer,** ed. *An Intelligent American's Guide to the Peace*. New York: The Dryden Press, 1945.

15129 **Westing, Arthur H.,** ed. *Environmental Warfare: A Technical, Legal and Policy Appraisal*. London: Taylor & Francis, 1984.

15130 **Westing, Arthur H.,** ed. *Explosive Remnants of War: Mitigating the Environmental Effects*. London: Taylor & Francis, 1985.

15131 **Westing, Arthur H.** *Warfare in a Fragile World: Military Impact on the Human Environment*. London: Taylor & Francis, 1980.

15132 **Wiberg, Hakan; Petersen, Ib Ddamgaard;** and **Paul, Smoker.** *Inadvertent Nuclear War*. New York: Elsevier Science, 1993.

15133 **Williams, Shelton L.** *The US, India, and the Bomb*. Baltimore, Maryland: Johns Hopkins University Press, 1969.

15134 **Willow Run Laboratories.** *Peaceful Uses of Earth Observation Spacecrafts*. 3 vols. Ann Arbor: University of Michigan Press, 1966.

15135 **Wilson, A.** *The Bomb and the Computer*. London: Barrie and Rockliff, 1968.

15136 **Wirsing, Giselher.** *The War in Maps, 1939-40*. New York: German Library of Information, 1941.

15137 **Woolsey, R. James,** ed. *Nuclear Arms: Ethnics, Strategy, Politics*. San Francisco: Institute for Contemporary Studies (ICS) Press, 1984.

15138 **Wright, Quincy.** *The Role of International Law in the Elimination of War*. Manchester: Manchester University Press, 1961.

15139 **Wright, Quincy.** *A Study of War*. 2 Vol. Chicago, Illinois: University of Chicago Press, 1942.

15140 **Wriston, Henry M.** *Strategy of Peace*. Boston: World Peace Foundation, 1944.

15141 **Yashpe, H.B.,** and **Brown, F.R.** *The Economics of National Security: Transportation, the Nation's Lifelines*. Washington, D.C.: Government Printing Office, 1961.

15142 **Yashpe, H.B.,** and **Brown, P.R.** *Survey of Strategic Studies*. Toronto: The Institute for Strategic Studies, Canadian Institute of International Affairs, 1970.

15143 **Young, E.** *The Control of Proliferation: The 1968 Treaty in Hindsight and Forecast*. Toronto: The Institute for Strategic Studies, Canadian Institute of International Affairs, 1969.

15144 **Young, E.** *The Military Balance*. Toronto: The Institute for Strategic Studies, Canadian Institute of International Affairs, 1971.

15145 **Zabriskie, Edward H.** *American-Russian Rivalry in the Far East; a Study in Diplomacy and Power Politics, 1895-1914*. Philadelphia: University of Pennsylvania Press, 1946.

15146 **Ziff, William B.** *Two Worlds; a Realistic Approach to the Problem of Keeping the Peace*. New York: Harper and Brothers, 1946.

Journals

15147 **Abel, Christopher A.** "Forgotten Lessons of Riverine Warfare." *U.S. Naval Institute Proceedings*, 108, No. 1 (January, 1982), 64-68.

15148 **Abrams, H.L.,** and **von Kaenel, W.E.** "Special Report: Medical Problems of Survivors of Nuclear War." *New England Journal of Medicine*, 305 (1981), 1226-1232.

15149 **Adragna, Steven.** "Doctrine and Strategy." *Orbis*, 33, No. 2 (Spring, 1989), 165-179.

15150 "Airpower: An Airman's View of the Role It Can Play in Winning the War." *Life*, 13, No. 24 (December 14, 1942), 124-138.

15151 **Alford, Johathan.** "Security Dilemmas of Small States." *The World Today* (London). 40, Nos. 8-9 (August-September, 1984), 363-369.

15152 **Alford, Jonathan.** "Some Reflections on Technology and Seapower." *International Journal*, 38, No. 3 (Summer, 1983), 397-408.

15153 **Anderson, Ewan W.** "Disaster Management and the Military." *GeoJournal*, 34, No. 2 (October, 1994), 201-205.

15154 **Anderson, Ewan W.** "The Geopolitics of Military Material Supply." *Geojournal* [Dordrecht], 31, No. 2 (October, 1993), 207-214.

15155 **Anderton, C.H., and Isard, W.** "The Geography of Arms Manufacture." In *The Geography of Peace and War*, D. Pepper and A. Jenkins, eds. Oxford: Basil Blackwell, 1985, 90-104.

15156 **Anderton, Charles H.** "Toward a Mathematical Theory of the Offensive/Defensive Balance." *International Studies Quarterly* [Cambridge], 36, No. 1 (March, 1992), 75-99.

15157 "The Arctic. It Has Become the Key to World Strategy." *Life*. 22, No. 3 (January 20, 1947), 55-62. Contains: "The Polar Concept; It is Revolutionizing American Strategy" by Charles J.V. Murphy, 61-62.

15158 **Barang, Marcel.** "Unity in a Divided Power Vacuum." *South: The Third World Magazine*, No. 15 (January, 1982), 16-17.

15159 **Barbera, Henry.** "On the Frequency of War: Toward a Reconciliation of State Sovereignty and World Order." *Journal of Political and Military Sociology*, 8, No. 2 (Fall, 1980), 257-268.

15160 **Barkey, Jenri J.** "Why Military Regimes Fail: The Perils of Transition. *Armed Forces & Society*, 16, No. 2 (winter, 1990), 169-192.

15161 **Barnaby, Frank.** "Strategic Submarines and Anti-Submarine Warfare." In *Ocean Yearbook*, Vol. 1, edited by Elisabeth Mann Borgese and Norton Ginsburg. Chicago, Illinois: University of Chicago Press, 1978, p. 376-379.

15162 **Bekef, G.** "Particle Beam Weapons-A Technical Assessment." *Nature*, 284, No. 5753 (March 20, 1980), 219-225.

15163 **Berg, P., and Lodgaard, S.** "Disengagement Zones: A Step Towards Meaningful Defence?" *Journal of Peace and Research*, 20, No. 1 (1983), 5-15.

15164 **Bernades, Lysias M.C.** "Geografia e poder nacional." *Revista Brasileira de Geografia*, Ano 28 No 3 (Julho-Septembro de, 1966), 267-281.

15165 **Betts, Richard K.** "Surprise Attack: NATO's Political Vulnerability." *International Security*, 5, No. 4 (Spring, 1981), 117-149.

15166 **Beukema, Herman.** "School for Statesmen." *Fortune*, 27, No. 1 (January, 1943), 108-109+.

15167 **Bezdek, Roger H.** "The 1980 Economic Impact-Regional and Occupational-of Compensated Shifts in Defence Spending." *Journal of Regional Science*, 15, No. 2 (August, 1975), 183-198.

15168 **Bialer, Seweryn.** "Socialist Stagnation and Communist Encirclement." *The Soviet Union in the 1980's*, 35, No. 3 (1984), 160-176.

15169 **Borgese, Elisabeth Mann, and Ginsburg, Norton S., eds.** "The ASW Problem: ASW Detection and Weapon Systems." In *Ocean Yearbook*, Vol. 1, Elisabeth Mann Borgese and Norton Ginsburg, eds. Chicago, Illinois: University of Chicago Press, 1978, 380-385.

15170 **Bracken, Paul, and Shubik, Martin.** "Strategic War: What Are the Questions and Who Should Ask Them?" *Technology in Society*, 1, No. 4 (1982), 155-179.

15171 **Bradshaw, Mary E.** "Military Control of Zone A in Venezia Giulia." *Department of State Bulletin*, 16, No. 417 (June, 1947), 1257-1272.

15172 **Brams, Steven J., and Hessel, Marek P.** "Threat Power in Sequential Games." *International Studies Quarterly*, 28, No. 1 (March, 1984), 23-44.

15173 **Bruce-Biggs, B.** "Suburban Warfare." *Military Review*, 54, No. 6 (June, 1974), 3-10.

15174 **Brunn, Stanley D.** "The Geography of Peace Movements." In *The Geography of Peace and War*. D. Pepper and A. Jenkins, eds. Oxford: Basil Blackwell, 1985, 178-91.

15175 **Brunn, Stanley D.** "A World Peace and Military Landscape." *The Journal of Geography*, 86, No. 6 (November-December, 1987), 253-262.

15176 **Brush, John E.** "Peace Research and Geography." *Professional Geographer*, 16, No. 4 (July, 1964), 49.

15177 **Brzezinski, Zbigniew.** "Ending the Cold War." *Washington Quarterly*, 12, No. 4 (Autumn, 1989), 29-34.

15178 **Burnett, Alan.** "Propaganda Cartography." In *The Geography of Peace and War*. D. Pepper and A. Jenkins, eds. Oxford: Basil Blackwell, 1985, 60-89.

15179 **Cannizzo, Cynthia.** "Quantitative International Conflict Studies: A Look at the Record." *Armed Forces and Society*, 6, No. 1 (Fall, 1979), 111-121.

15180 **Cohen, P.** "The Erosion of Surface Naval Power." *Foreign Affairs*, 49, No. 2 (January, 1971), 330-341.

15181 **Conrad, V.** "World Climate and World War." *Bulletin of the American Meteorological Society*, 23, No. 6 (June, 1942), 262-273.

15182 **Cooper, Dale F., and Klein, Jonathan.** "Board Wargames for Decision Making Research." *European Journal of Operational Research*, 5, No. 1 (July, 1980), 36-41.

15183 **Corney, A.** "The Portsmouth Fortress." *Journal of the Royal Society of Arts*, 131, No. 5326 (September, 1983), 578-586.

15184 **Coyle, R.G.** "A System Description of Counter Insurgency Warfare." *Policy Sciences*, 18, No. 1 (March, 1985), 55-78.

15185 **Crutzen, P.** "The Global Environment After Nuclear War." *Environment*, 27, No. 8 (October, 1985), 6-37.

15186 **Curry, M.** "In the Wake of Nuclear War-- Possible Worlds in an Age of Scientific Expertise." *Environment and Planning D*, 3, No. 3 (September, 1985), 309-21.

15187 **Cutler, Susan; Holcomb, H. Brianel; and Shatin, Dianne.** "Spatial Patterns of Support for Nuclear Weapons Freeze." *Professional Geographer*, 38, No. 1 (February, 1986), 42-52.

15188 **Cutter, Susan L.** "Geographers and Nuclear War: Why We Lack Influence on Public Policy." *Annals of the Association of American Geographers*. Annals, 78, No. 1 (March, 1988), 132-143.

15189 **Daniel, Donald C.** "Antisubmarine Warfare in the Nuclear Age." *Orbis*, 28, No. 3 (Fall, 1984), 527-552.

15190 **Davidson, L.S.** "The Impact of Precision-Guided Munitions on War. *RUSI and Brassey's Defence Yearbook*. Oxford: Brassey's, 1984, 237-252.

15191 **Deese, David A.** "Oil, War, and Grand Strategy." *Orbis*, 25, No. 3 (Fall, 1981), 525-555.

15192 **DeGrasse, R.W.** "Military Spending and Jobs." *Challenge*, 26, No. 3 (July-August), 4-15.

15193 **Deibel, Terry L.** "Strategies Before Containment: Patterns for the Future." *International Security* [Cambridge, MA], 16, No. 4 (Spring, 1992), 79-108.

15194 **Deitchman, Seymour J.** "The Future of Tactical Air Power in Land Warfare." *Astronautics & Aeronautics*, 18, No. 7-8 (July-August, 1980), 34-45, 53.

15195 **Delmas, Claude.** "Geopolitique de l'age nucleaire." *L'Espace Geographique,* 16, No. 4 (Octobre/Decembre, 1987), 277-284.

15196 **Dempsey, R., and Schmude, D.** "Occupational Impact of Defense Expenditures." *Monthly Labor Review*, 94, No. 12 (December, 1971), 12-15.

15197 **Desai, Raj, and Eckstein, Harry.** "Insurgency: The Transformation of Peasant Rebellion." *World Politics,* 42, No. 4 (July, 1990), 441-465.

15198 **Deshpande, C.D.** "A Suggested Syllabus in Military Geography and Map Reading in lthe University Studies." *The Indian Geographical Journal*, 18, No. 1 (January-March, 1943), 37-52.

15199 **de Seversky, Alexander P.** "Air Power Ends Isolation." *Atlantic Monthly,*168, No. 10 (October, 1941), 407-416.

15200 **de Seversky, Alexander P.** "Air Power to Rule the World." *Science Digest*, 12, No. 4 (October, 1942), 33-36.

15201 **de Seversky, Alexander P.** "The Twilight of Sea Power." *American Mercury*, 52, No. 210 (June, 1941), 647-658.

15202 **Deutsch, Karl W., and Singer, J. David.** "Multipolar Power Systems and International Stability." *World Politics*, 16, No. 3 (April, 1964), 390-406.

15203 **Diehl, Paul F.** "Contiguity and Military Escalation in Major Power Rivalries, 1816-1980." *Journal of Politics*, 47, No. 4 (November, 1985), 1203-1211.

15204 **Diehl, Paul F.** "Geography and War: A Review and Assessment of the Empirical Literature." *International Interactions* [Philadelphia], 17, No. 1 (1991), 11-27.

15205 **Dittmer, Lowell.** "The Strategic Triangle: An Elementary Game-Theoretical Analysis." *World Politics*, 33, No. 4 (July, 1981), 485-515.

15206 **Dix, Robert H.** "The Varieties of Revolution." *Comparative Politics*, 15, No. 3 (April, 1983), 281-294.

15207 **Doerfel, S.** "Meeting the Strategic Challenge." *International Defense Review*, 17, No. 3 (1984), 251-255.

15208 **Doran, Charles F.** "War and Power Dynamics: Economic Underpinnings." *International Studies Quarterly*, 27, No. 4 (December, 1983),419-441.

15209 **Douglas, J.D.** "Strategic Planning and Nuclear Insecurity." *Orbis*, 27, No. 3 (Fall, 1983), 667-694.

15210 **Drew, Dennis M.** "Strategy Process and Principles: Back to the Basics." *Air University Review*, 31, No. 4 (May-June, 1980), 38-45.

15211 **Dunn, Lewis A.** "U.S. Strategic Force Requirements in a Nuclear-Proliferated World." *Air University Review*, 31, No. 5 (July-August, 1980), 26-33.

15212 **Dupuy, T.N.** "The Influence of Technology on War." *Marine Corps Gazette*, 67, No. 9 (September, 1983), 50-59.

15213 **Elliot, S.R., and Lee, Ian.** "Guns and Geography." *The Geographical Magazine*, 52, No. 9 (June, 1980), 640-646.

15214 **Ehrlich, A.** "Nuclear Winter." *Bulletin of the Atomic Scientists*, 40, No. 4 (April, 1984), 1s-15s.

15215 **Ellis, Mark; Barf, Richard; and Markusen, Ann R.** "Defense Spending and Interregional Labor Migration." *Economic Geography* [Worcester], 69, No. 2 (April, 1993), 182-203.

15216 **Emeny, Brooks.** "The Economic Basis of Peace and War." *Proceedings of the Institute of World Affairs*, 15th Session, 1937. (1938), 206-217.

15217 **Emme, Eugene M.** "Some Fallacies Concerning Air Power." *The Annals of the American Academy of Political and Social Science*, 299 (May, 1955), 12-24.

15218 "The Environmental Consequences of Nuclear War." *Environment*, 30 (June, 1988), Special issue.

15219 **Epstein, J.M.** "Horizontal Escalation." *International Security*, 8, No. 3 (Winter, 1983/4), 19-31.

15220 **Etter, James P.** "Military Geography: The Common Meeting Ground for all Military Activity." *Papers and Proceedings of Applied Geography Conferences* [Binghamton], 13 (September, 1990), 233-237.

15221 **Etzold, Thomas H.** "Clawsewitzian Lessons for Modern Strategists." *Air University Review*, 31, No. 4 (May-June, 1980), 24-28.

15222 **Fabyanic, Thomas A.** "The Grammar and Logic of Conflict: Differing Concepts by Statesman and Soldiers." *Air University Review*, 32, No. 3 (March-April, 1981), 22-31.

15223 **Fairweather, Jr., Robert S.** "A New Model for Land Warfare: The Firepower Dominance Concept." *Air University Review*, 32, No. 1 (November-December, 1980), 79-87.

15224 **Falls, Cyril.** "Geography and War Strategy." *Geographical Journal*, 112, Nos. 1-3 (July-December, 1948), 4-18.

15225 **Fauvet, Paul.** "Roots of Counter Revolution: The MNR." *Review of African Political Economy*, 29 (1984), 108-121.

15226 **Feiveson, Harold A., and Dufied, John.** "Stopping the Sea-Based Counterforce Threat." *International Security*, 38, No. 3 (Summer, 1984), 451-458.

15227 **Feld, Bernard T., and Tsipis, Kosta.** "Land-Based Intercontinental Ballistic Missiles." *Scientific American*, 241, No. 5 (November, 1979), 50-61.

15228 **Feng, Peiyue, and Shen, Weillie.** "An Approach to Some Problems of Military Geography." *Scientia Geographica Sinica*, 4, No. 2 (1984), 183-187.

15229 **Fetter, Steve.** "Ballistic Missiles and Weapons of Mass Destruction: What Is the Threat? What Should Be Done?" *International Security* [Cambridge, MA], 16, No. 1 (Summer, 1991), 5-42.

15230 **Fifield, Russell H.** "The Geostrategy of Location." *Journal of Geography*, 43, No. 8 (November, 1944), 297-303.

15231 **Fisher, Allan G.B.** "Economic Appeasement as a Means to Political Understanding and Peace." *Survey of International Affairs 1937*, 1 (1938), 56-109.

15232 **Freedman, Lawrence.** "Indignation, Influence and Strategic Studies." *International Affairs*, 60, No. 2 (Spring, 1984), 207-219.

15233 **Fritchey, Clayton.** "The Navy We Need vs.the Navy We've Got." *Washington Monthly*, 9, No. 1 (March, 1977), 38-44.

15234 **Fulton, J.F.** "Employment Impact of Changing Defense Programs." *Monthly Labor Review*, (May, 1954), 508-516.

15235 **Furlong, Raymond B.** "The Utility of Military Forces." *Air University Review*, 33, No. 1 (November-December, 1981), 29-33.

15236 **Gallois, Pierre M.** "The Soviet Global Threat and the West." *Orbis*, 25, No. 3 (Fall, 1981), 649-662.

15237 **Garn, Jake.** "Exploitable Strategic Nuclear Superiority." *International Security Review*, 5, No. 2 (Summer, 1980), 173-192.

15238 **Garnham, D.** "Dyadic International War, 1816-1965: The Role of Power Parity and Geographic Proximity." *Western Political Quarterly*, 29, No. 2 (June, 1976), 231-242.

15239 **Garwin, R.L., and Bethe, H .A.** "Anti-Ballistic-Missile Systems." *Scientific American*, 218, No. 3 (March, 1968), 21-31.

15240 **Geiselman, Ralph E., and Sanet, Michael G.** "Summarizing Military Information: An Application of Schema Theory." *Human Factors*, 22, No. 6 (December, 1980), 693-705.

15241 **Gentles, R.G.** "The Rogers Plan: A New Direction for NATO?" *Canadian Defence Quarterly*, 13, No. 2 (1983), 15-23.

15242 **Gessert, R.** "The AirLand Battle and NATO's New Doctrinal Debate." *RUSI Journal for Defence Studies*, 129, No. 2 (1984), 52-60.

15243 **Gleditsch, D., and Singer, J.D.** "Distance and International War, 1816-1965." *Proceedings of the International Peace Research Association*, (1975), 481-506.

15244 **Gochman, Charles S., and Moaz, Zuz.** "Militarized Interstate Disputes, 1816-1976: Procedures, Patterns, and Insights." *The Journal of Conflict Resolution*. 28, No. 4 (December, 1984), 585-616.

15245 **Goldgeier, James M., and McFaul, Michael.** "A Tale of Two Worlds: Core and Periphery in the Post-Cold War Era." *International Organization* [Cambridge, MA], 46, No. 2 (Spring, 1992), 467-491.

15246 **Goodwin, C.** "War and Peace: Time for a New Role for Scientists." *Computing*, (July 5, 1984), 22-23.

15247 **Goure, Daniel, and Cooper, Jeffrey R.** "Conventional Deep Strike: A Critical Look." *Comparative Strategy*, 4, No. 3 (1984), 215-248.

15248 **Goure, Daniel, and McCormick, Gordon H.** "Soviet Strategic Defense: The Neglected Dimension of the U.S.-Soviet Balance." *Orbis*, 24, No. 1 (Spring, 1980), 103-127.

15249 **Graubard, Morlie H., and Builder, Carl H.** "New Methods for Strategic Analysis: Automating the Wargame." *Policy Sciences*, 15, No. 1 (November, 1982), 71-84.

15250 **Greenwood, D.** "Strengthening Conventional Deterrence." *NATO Review*, 34, No. 2 (April, 1984), 8-12.

15251 **Grotte, Jeffrey H.** "Measuring Strategic Stability with Two-Strike Nuclear Exchange Models." *Journal of Conflict Resolution*, 24, No. 2 (June,

1980), 213-239.

15252 **Guertner, Gary L.** "Nuclear War in Suburbia." *Orbis*, 26, No. 1 (Spring, 1982), 49-69.

15253 **Guimaraes, Fabio de Macedo Soares.** "Os factores politicos no condicionamento do conceito estrategico nacional." *A Defesa Nacional*, 26, 359 (Junho, 1959), 103-106.

15254 **Gupta, Amit.** "Third World Militaries: New Suppliers, Deadlier Weapons." *Orbis* [Greenwich, CT], 37, No. 1 (Winter, 1993), 57-68.

15255 **Gustavson, C.G.** "Historical Maps and Seapower." *Journal of Geography*, 55, No. 8 (November, 1946), 317-321.

15256 **Haas, Ernst B.** "The Balance of Power: Prescription, Concept or Propaganda?" *World Politics*, 5, No. 4 (July, 1953), 442-477.

15257 **Halperin, Martin.** "Nuclear Weapons and Limited War. *Journal of Conflict Resolution*, 5, No. 2 (June, 1961), 146-166.

15258 **Hamilton, Kingsley W.** "Aspects of the Coming Postwar Settlement." *International Conciliation*, 393 (October, 1943), 540-563.

15259 **Hanks, Robert J.** "Rapid Deployment in Perspective." *Strategic Review*, 9, No. 2 (Spring, 1981), 17-23.

15260 **Hanne, W.G.** "AirLand Battle--Doctrine Not Dogma." *International Defence Review*, 16, No. 8 (August, 1983), 1035-1040.

15261 **Harbeson, Robert W.** "Transportation: Achilles Heel of National Security." *Political Science Quarterly*, 74, No. 1 (March1959), 1-20.

15262 **Hargreaves, Reginald.** "War Aims, the Real Answer." *National Review*, 116, No. 700 (June, 1941), 703-706.

15263 **Harrison, Richard Edes.** "The War of the Maps." *Saturday Review of Literature*, 26, No. 2 (August 7, 1943), 24-27.

15264 **Harvey, John R.** "Regional Ballistic Missiles and Advanced Strike Aircraft: Comparing Military Effectiveness." *International Security* [Cambridge, MA], 17, No. 2 (Fall, 1992), 41-83.

15265 **Herlin, Emil.** "Over There: Penetration, Intervention and Conquest in the 1930's." *Survey Graphic*, 28, No. 2 (February, 1939), 54.

15266 **Heseltine, M.** "Oral Answer." *Hansard*, (May 22, 1984), 819-820.

15267 **Hewitt, Kenneth.** "Place Annihilation: Area Bombing and Fate of Urban Places." *Association of Annals of the American Geographers*, 73, No. 2 (June, 1983), 257-284.

15268 **Hinder, Rolf.** "Koexisenze in der Krise." *Zeitschrift fur Geopolitik*, 38, Jahr gang, Heft 3 (Juli-August, 1967), 154-159.

15269 **Hirsch, Rudolf,** comp. "Plans for the Organization of International Peace, 1306-1789; A List of Thirty-six Peace Proposals." *Bulletin of the New York Public Library*, 47, No. 8 (August, 1943), 569-580.

15270 **Hofman, W.** "Is NATO's Defence Policy Facing a Crisis?" *NATO Review*, 32, No. 4 (1984), 1-7.

15271 **Hooker, Richard D., Jr.** "The Mythology Surrounding Maneuver Warfare." *Parameters* [Carlisle], 23, No. 1 (Spring, 1993), 27-38.

15272 **Howard, Michael E.** "On Fighting Nuclear War." *International Security*, 4, No.4 (Spring, 1901), 3-17.

15273 **Huff, Anne Sigismund.** "Strategic Intelligence Systems." *Information & Management*, 2, No. 5 (November, 1979), 187-196.

15274 **Hughes, J.J.** "Disarmament and Regional Unemployment." *Journal of Regional Science*, 5, No. 1 (April, 1964), 37-49.

15275 **Huisken, Ronald.** "Naval Forces." In *Ocean Yearbook*, Vol.1, Elisabeth Mann Borgese and Norton Ginsburg, eds. Chicago, Illinois: University of Chicago Press, 1978, 412-435.

15276 **Huntington, Thomas W.** "When the Army Governs: The Literature of Military Government." *Wilson Library Bulletin*, 17, No. 10 (June, 1943), 816-819.

15277 **Husbands, Jo. L.** "A World in Arms: Geography of the Weapons Trade." *Focus*, 30, No. 4 (March-April, 1980), 1-16.

15278 **Ikle, Fred Charles.** "Nuclear Strategy: Can there Be a Happy Ending?" *Foreign Affairs*, 63, No. 4 (Spring, 1985), 810-826.

15279 **Ives, T.** "The Geography of Arms Dispersal." In *The Geography of Peace and War*, D. Pepper and A. Jenkins, eds. Oxford: Basil Blackwell, 1985, 42-59.

15280 **Jackman, Albert H.** "The Nature of Military Geography." *Professional Geographer*, 14, No. 1 (January, 1962), 7-12.

15281 **Jasani, Bhupendra,** and **Lunderius, Maria A.** "Peaceful Uses of Outer Space: Legal Fiction and Military Reality." *Bulletin of Peace Proposals,* 11, No. 1 (March, 1980), 57-70.

15282 **Jencks, Harlan W.** "People's War Under Modern Conditions: Wishful Thinking, National Suicide, or Effective Deterrent?" *China Quarterly*, 98, No. 2 (June, 1984), 305-319.

15283 **Jenkins, A.M.** "Peace Education and the Geography Curriculum." In *The Geography of Peace and War*, D. Pepper and A. Jenkins, eds. Oxford: Basil Blackwell, 1985, 202-213.

15284 **Joffe, Ellis.** "People's War Under Modern Conditions: A Doctrine for Modern War." *China Quarterly*, No. 112 (December, 1987), 555-571.

15285 **Johnson, Douglas Wilson.** "A Geographer at the Front and at the Peace Conference." *Natural History*, 19 (1919), 511-521.

15286 **Kaldor, M.** "A Dangerous Hoax." *End Journal*, 9, No. 2 (April-May, 1984), 14-16.

15287 **Kaldor, M.; Borosage, B.; Pianta, M.; Winther, J.; Phillips, S.; Vilanova, P.;** and **Statz, A.** "NATO at the Crossroads." *End Journal*, 18 (1985), 14-17.

15288 **Kalijarvi, Thorsten V.,** ed. "Peace Settlements of World War II." *The Annals of the American Academy of Political and Social Science*, 257 (May, 1948), 1-271, (complete issue, multiple authors).

15289 **Kapur, Ashok.** "Indo-Soviet Military Relations: Dependency, Inter-Dependency and Uncertainties." *India Quarterly*, 33, No. 3 (July-September, 1977), 263-280.

15290 **Kaufman, Joyce.** "The Social Consequences of War: The Social Development of Four Nations." *Armed Forces and Society*, 9, No. 2 (Winter, 1983), 245-264.

15291 **Kegley, Charles W., Jr.,** and **Raymond, Gregory A.** "Must We Fear a Post-Cold War Multipolar System?" *Journal of Conflict Resolution* [Newbury Park], 36, No. 3 (September, 1992), 573-585.

15292 **Kelly, P.M.,** and **Karas, J.H.W.** "The consequences of Nuclear War." *Contemporary Issues in Geography & Education*, 2, No. 3 (1987), 3-15.

15293 **Kemp, Geoffrey.** "Scarcity and Strategy." *Foreign Affairs*, 56, No. 2 (January, 1978), 396-414.

15294 **Kick, Edward L.** "World-System Properties and Military Intervention-Internal War Linkages." *Journal of Political and Military Sociology*, 11, No. 2 (Fall, 1983), 185-222.

15295 **Kirsch, Guy.** "International vs. Intranational Conflicts." *The Jerusalem Journal of International Relations*, 4, No. 3 (Spring, 1980), 82-104.

15296 **Kish, George,** and **Singer, J. David,** eds. "The Geography of Conflict." *The Journal of Conflict Resolution*, 4, No. 1 (March, 1960), 1-3.

15297 **Klein, B.S.** "After Strategy: The Search for a Post-Modern Politics of Peace." *Alternatives*, 13, No. 4 (December, 1988), 293-318.

15298 **Knorr, Klaus.** "The Concept of Economic Potential for War." *World Politics*, 10, No. 1 (October, 1957), 49-62.

15299 **Koch, Howard E.** "Some Theoretical Notes on Geography and International Conflict." *Journal of Conflict Resolution*, 4, No. 1 (March, 1960), 4-14.

15300 **Kofman, Eleanor.** "Information and Nuclear Issues: The Role of the Academic." *Area*, 16, No. 2 (July, 1984), 166.

15301 **Kouba, Leonard J.** "Is Military Geography a Part of Political Geography?" *Virginia Geographer*, 4, No. 1 (Spring, 1969), 13-15.

15302 **Kumar, Ashok.** "The Concept of Military Geography.' In *Recent Trends and Concepts in Geography*, Vol. 3. Ram Buhadur Mandal and Vishwa Nath Prasad Sinha, eds. New Delhi: Concept Publishing, 1980, 389-397.

15303 **Kurth, J.R.** "The Political Economy of Weapons and Procurement: The Follow-On Imperataie." *American Economic Review Papers and Proceedings*, 62 (1972), 304-311.

15304 **Lagrange, D.M.** "The Military Family Syndrome." *American Journal of Psychiatry*, 135 (1978), 1040-1043.

15305 **Lambeth, Benjamin S.,** and **Lewis, Kevin N.** "Economic Targeting in Nuclear War: U.S. and Soviet Approaches." *Orbis*, 27, No. 1 (Spring, 1983), 127-149.

15306 **Landheer, B.** "Interstate Competition and Survival Potential." *Journal of Conflict and Resolution*, 3, No. 2 (June, 1959), 162-171.

15307 **Larson, David L.** "Naval Weaponry and the Law of the Sea." *Ocean Development and International Law.* 18, No. 2 (1987), 125-198.

15308 **Lautenschlager, Karl.** "Technology and the Evolution of Naval Warfare." *International Security*, 8, No. 2 (Fall, 1983), 3-51.

15309 **Lebow, Richard Ned,** and **Stein, Janice Gross.** "Deterrence: The Elusive Dependent Variable."

World Politics, 42, No. 3 (April, 1990), 336-369.

15310 **Lepotier, A.** "Geostrategie de la Coree." *Geographia*, 16 (January, 1953), 8-12.

15311 **Levy, Jack S.** "Declining Power and the Preventive Motivation for War." *World Politics*, 40, No. 1 (October, 1987), 82-107.

15312 **Levy, Jack S.** "Historical Trends in Great Powers War, 1495-1975." *International Studies Quarterly*, 26, No. 2 (June, 1982), 278-300.

15313 **Levy, Jack S.** Misperception and the Causes of War: Theoretical Linkages and Analytical Problems." *World Politics*, 36, No. 1 (October, 1983), 76-99.

15314 **Levy, Jack S.** "The Offensive/Defensive Balance of Military Technology: A Theoretical and Historical Analysis." *International Studies Quarterly*, 28, No. 2 (June, 1984), 219-238.

15315 **Levy, Jack S.,** and **Morgan, T. Cliften.** "The Frequency and Seriousness of War: An Inverse Relationship?" *Journal of Conflict and Resolution*, 28, No. 4 (December, 1984), 731-749.

15316 **Lewis, Kevin N.** "Surprise, Perceptions, and Military Style." *Orbis*, 26, No. 4 (Winter, 1983), 833-847.

15317 **Lichbach, Mark Irving,** and **Gurr, Ted Robert.** "The Conflict Process: A Formal Model." *Journal of Conflict Resolution*, 25, No. 1 (March, 1981), 3-29.

15318 "The Logic of the Air." *Fortune*, 27, No. 4 (April, 1943), 70-74; 188-194.

15319 **Lodal, Jan M.** "Deterrence and Nuclear Strategy." *Daedalus*, 109, No. 4 (Fall, 1980), 155-175.

15320 **Looney, Robert E.** "Militarization, Military Regimes, and the General Quality of Life in the Third World." *Armed Forces & Society* [New Brunswick], 17, No. 1 (Fall, 1990), 127-139.

15321 **Lopez, R.** "The Air-Land Battle 2000 Controversy." *International Defence Review*, 16, No. 11 (November, 1983), 1551-1556.

15322 **Lovins, Amory B.; Lovins, L. Hunter;** and **Ross, Leonard.** "Nuclear Power and Nuclear Bombs." *Foreign Affairs*, 58, No. 5 (Summer, 1980), 1137-1177.

15323 **Mackinder, Halford J.** "The Round World and the Winning of the Peace." *Foreign Affairs*, 21, No. 4 (July, 1943), 595-605.

15324 **Mahnken, Thomas G.** "Why Third World Space Systems Matter." *Orbis* [Philadelphia], 35, No. 4 (Fall, 1991), 563-579.

15325 **Mallery, Otto Tod.** "Typical Plans for Postwar World Peace." *International Conciliation*, 384 (November, 1942), 431-451.

15326 "Maps: Global War Teaches Global Cartography." *Life*, 13, No. 5 (August 3, 1942), 57-65.

15327 **Martin, J.J.** "Nuclear Weapons in NATO's Deterrent Strategy." *Orbis*, 22, No. 4 (Winter, 1979), 875-895.

15328 **Mason, Charles H.** "The Role of the Geographer in Military Planning." *Professional Geographer*, 7, No. 1 (January, 1948), 4-6.

15329 **Maynard, Wayne K.** "Spears vs. Rifles: The New Equation of Military Power." *Parameters* [Carlisle], 23, No. 1 (Spring, 1993), 49-58.

15330 **Mazuri, Ali A.** "Changing the Guards from Hindus to Muslims: Collective Third World Security in a Cultural Perspective." *International Affairs*, 57, No. 1 (Winter, 1980-81), 1-20.

15331 **Mathews, J.T.** "Redefining Security." *Foreign Affairs*, 68, No. 2 (January, 1989), 162-177.

15332 **McColl, R.W.** "Guerrilla War and Insurrections: A Classroom Simulation of Their Political and Geographical Realities." *Journal of Geography*, 73, No. 8 (November, 1974), 15-28.

15333 **McColl, Robert W.** "The Creation and Consequences of International Refugees: Politics, Military and Geography." *GeoJournal* [Dordrecht], 31, No. 2 (October, 1993), 169-177.

15334 **McDowell, T.** "The Air Land Battle." *Radiator*, 30, No. 7 (July, 1984), 8-10.

15335 **McManners, Hugh.** "The Geography of War." *Geographical Magazine*, 59, No. 11 (November, 1987), 548-553.

15336 **Meacham, James.** "NATO: A Two-Step Approach to Deep Strike." *World Today*, 40, No. 7 (July, 1984), 286-291.

15337 **Melman, S.** "Swords into Plowshares." *Technology Review*, (January, 1986), 63-71.

15338 **Mercado, J.** "Algo sobre geografia militar." *Boletin del Ejercito*, 4, No. 1 (1917), 45-58.

15339 **Mesquita, Bruce Bueno de and Lalman, David.** "Empirical Support for Systemic and Dyadic Explanations of International Conflict." *World Politics*, 41, No. 1 (October, 1988), 1-20.

15340 **Mewes, H.** "The Green Party Comes of Age." *Environment*, 27, No. 5 (June, 1985), 13-17 & 33-39.

15341 **Miettinen, Jorma.** "Maapallon Geopolitinenja Strateginen tilanne- Pelastaako varustelu Ihmiskunan Kolmannelta Maailmansodalta? [The Geopolitical and Strategical Situation in the World. Is the Rearmament Able to Protect Mankind from the Third World War?]" *Terra*, 95, No. 1 (1983), 25-31.

15342 **Mills, Lennox A.** "Some Problems of Postwar Reconstruction." *Annals of the American Academy of Political and Social Science*, 226 (March, 1943), 137-150.

15343 **Morgan, Arthur E.** "The Conditions of Enduring Peace." *Common Ground*, 4, No. 3 (Spring, 1944), 61-68.

15344 **Morrill, R.L.** "The Responsibility of Geography." *Annals of the Association of American Geographers*, 74, No. 1 (March, 1984), 1-8.

15345 **Most, Benjamin A., and Starr, Harvey.** "Conceptualizing 'War': Consequences for Theory and Research." *Journal of Conflict Resolution*, 27, No. 1 (March, 1983), 137-159.

15346 **Nijman, Jan.** "The Dynamics of Superpower Spheres of Influence: U.S. and Soviet Military Activities, 1948-1978." *International Interactions* [Philadelphia], 17, No. 1 (1991), 63-91.

15347 **Nuri, Maqsud N.** "The Rapid Deployment Force." *Strategic Studies*, 5 (Summer, 1982), 26-44.

15348 **Nye, Joseph S., Jr.** "The Changing Nature of World Power." *Political Science Quarterly* [New York], 105, No. 2 (Summer, 1990), 177-192.

15349 **O'Loughlin, John.** "Spatial Models of International Conflicts: Extending Current Theories of War Behavior." *Annals of the Association of American Geographers*, 76, No. 1 (March, 1986), 63-80.

15350 **O'Loughlin, John.** "Superpower Competition and the Militarization of the Third World." *Journal of Geography*, 86, No. 6 (November-December, 1987), 269-275.

15351 **O'Loughlin, John, and van der Wusten, H.** "Geography, War and Peace: Notes for a Contribution to a Revived Political Geography." *Progress in Human Geography*, 10, No. 4 (December, 1986), 484-510.

15352 **Openshaw, Stan,** and **Steadman, Philip.** "The Bomb: Where will the Survivors be?" *Geographical Magazine,* 55, No. 6 (June, 1983), 293-296.

15353 **O'Sullivan, Patrick.** "A Geographical Analysis of Guerilla Warfare." *Political Geography Quarterly,* 2, No. 2 (April, 1983), 139-150.

15354 **O'Sullivan, Patrick.** "The Geopolitics of Deterrence." In *The Geography of Peace and War,* D. Pepper and A. Jenkins, eds. Oxford: Basil Blackwell, 1985, 29-41.

15355 **O'Sullivan, Patrick.** "A Theory of Revolutionary War." *Papers and Proceedings of Applied Geography Conferences,* 11 (1988).

15356 **O'Sullivan, Patrick.** "War in Cities." *Papers and Proceedings of Applied Geography Conferences* [Binghamton], 13 (September, 1990), 255-262.

15357 **Otok, S.** "Problems of War and Social Situation in the World." *Miscellanea Geographica,* (1986), 165-169.

15358 **Parks, W. Hays.** "Rolling Thunder and the Law of War." *Air University Review,* 33, No. 2 (January-February, 1982), 2-23.

15359 **Patterson, Ernest Minor,** ed. "Winning Both the War and the Peace." *Annals of the American Academy of Political and Social Science,* 222 (July, 1942), 1-132 (Complete issue, multiple authors).

15360 **Pearson, F.S.** "Geographic Proximity and Foreign Military Intervention." *Journal of Conflict Resolution,* 18, No. 3 (September, 1974), 432-460.

15361 **Pelig, Ilan.** "Arms Supply to the Third World: Models and Explanations." *Journal of Modern African Studies,* 15, No. 1 (March, 1977), 91-103.

15362 **Peltier, Louis C.** "The Potential of Military Geography." *Professional Geographer,* 13, No. 6 (November, 1961), 1-5.

15363 **Pengelly, P.** "Air Land Battle: A Hollow Charge?" *Defence Attache,* 3 (1983), 7-15.

15364 **Pepper, David.** "Geographical Dimensions of NATO's Evolving Military Strategy." *Progress in Human Geography,* 12, No. 2 (June, 1988), 157-178.

15365 **Pepper, David.** "Political Geography of Contemporary Events IX: Spatial Aspects of the West's 'Deep Strike' Doctrine." *Political Geography Quarterly,* 5, No. 3 (July, 1986), 253-266.

15366 **Pepper, David,** and **Jenkins. Alan.** "A Call to Arms: Geography and Peace Studies." *Area,* 15, No. 3 (September, 1983), 202-208.

15367 **Pepper, David,** and **Jenkins. Alan.** "Reversing the Nuclear Arms Race: Geopolitical Bases for Permission." *Professional Geographer,* 36, No. 4 (November, 1984), 419-427.

15368 **Perry, A.M.** "The Nuclear Winter Controversy." *Progress in Physical Geography,* 9, No. 1 (March, 1985), 76-81.

15369 **Petrie, C.** "The Strategic Concept of Modern Diplomacy." *Quarterly Review,* 290, No. 593 (July, 1952), 289-301.

15370 **Platt, R.H.** "The Planner and Nuclear Crisis Relocation." *Journal of American Planning Association,* 50, No. 3 (July, 1984), 259-60.

15371 **Plesch, D.T.** "Air-Land Battle and NATO's Military Posture." *ADIU Report,* 7, No. 2 (1985), 7-11.

15372 **Popper, David H.** "Hemisphere Solidarity in the War Crisis." *Foreign Policy Reports,* 18, No. 5 (May 15, 1942), 50-63.

15373 **Posen, Barry R.** "The Security Dilemma and Ethnic Conflicts." *Survival* [London], 35, No. 1 (Spring, 1993), 27-47.

15374 **Possony, Stefan T.,** and **Rosenzweig, Leslie.** "The Geography of the Air." *Annals of the American Academy of Political and Social Science.* 299 (May, 1955), 1-11.

15375 **Quester, George H.** "Trouble in the Islands: Defending the Micro-States." *International Security,* 8, No. 2 (Fall, 1983), 160-175.

15376 **Quick, John,** and **O'Sullivan, Patrick.** "Military Analysis of Urban Terrain." *Professional Geographer,* 38, No. 3 (August, 1986), 286-290.

15377 **Rathjens, G.W.,** and **Kistiakowsky, G.B.** "The Limitation of Strategic Arms." *Scientific American,* 222, No. 1 (January, 1970), 19-29.

15378 **Richelson, Jeffrey T.** "Static Indicators and the Ranking of Strategic Forces." *Journal of Conflict Resolution,* 26, No. 2 (June, 1982), 265-282.

15379 **Ringler, D.** "Nuclear War: A Teaching Guide." *Bulletin of the Atomic Scientists,* 40, No. 10 (October, 1985), 2s-32s.

15380 **Ristow, Walter W.** "Maps for Global War." *Library Journal,* 68, No. 8 (April 15, 1943), 324-325.

15381 **Ropp, Theodore.** "The Strategic Dimensions of Global War." *Air University Review*, 31, No. 5 (July-August, 1980), 58-64.

15382 **Rose, A.J.** "Strategic Geography and the Northern Approaches." *Australian Outlook*, 13, No. 4 (December, 1959), 304-314.

15383 **Sabrosky, Alan Ned.** "Allies, Clients, and Encumbrances." *International Security Review*, 5, No. 2 (Summer, 1980), 117-149.

15384 **Salisbury, Howard Graves III,** and **Worthington, Wayne.** "The Insurgency to End All Insurgency: Studying the Insurgent Environment." *Military Intelligence*, 6, No. 1 (1976), 40-45.

15385 **Sanders, R.T.** "Is AirLand Battle a Paper Tiger?" *Armor*, (November-December, 1983), 49-50.

15386 **Sarwar, Ghulam.** "Thoughts on Defense of the Muslim World." *Pakistan Horizon*, 33, No. 1-2 (First and Second Quarter, 1980), 23-30.

15387 **Schepe, G.** "The Rogers Plan and the Concept of 'Deep Battle' on the Central Front." *Canadian Defence Quarterly*, 13, No. 1 (1983), 30-33.

15388 **Schultz, J.B.** "AirLand Battle 2000: The Force Multiplier." *Defense Electronics*, 15, No. 2 (1983), 48-67.

15389 **Schultz, H.D.** "Pax Geographica. Spatial concepts of War and Peace in the Geographical Tradition." *Geographische Zeitschrift*, 75, No. 1 (1987), 1-22.

15390 **Schuman, Frederick L.** "War for Time and Space." *Saturday Review of Literature*, 25, No. 26 (June 27, 1942), 3-5.

15391 **Schuman, Frederick L.** "Are We Guarding the Crossroads?" *Independent Woman*, 21, No. 10 (October, 1942), 291-292+.

15392 **Schwarzenberger, Georg.** "Peace and War in International Society." *United Nations. Economic, Social, and Cultural Organization. International Social Science Bulletin*, 1, No. 3-4 (1949), 61-68.

15393 **Segal, Gerald.** "Defence Culture and Sino-Soviet Relations." *Journal of Strategic Studies*, 8, No. 2 (June, 1985), 180-198.

15394 **Segal, Gerald.** "Strategy and 'Ethnic Chic'." *International Affairs*, 60, No. 1 (Winter, 1983/4), 15-30.

15395 **Sharma, R.C.** "Geopolitics of Strategic Bases." *National Geographer*, 10 (1975), 59-75.

15396 **Sherwin, Ronald G.,** and **Laurence, Edward J.** "Arms Transfers and Military Capability: Measuring and Evaluating Conventional Arms Transfers." *International Studies Quarterly*, 23, No. 3 (September, 1979), 360-389.

15397 **Shimshoni, Jonathan.** "Technology, Military Advantage, and World War I: A Case for Military Entrepreneurship." *International Security* [Cambridge], 15, No. 3 (Winter, 1990-91), 187-215.

15398 **Shugart, Matthew Soberg.** "Patterns of Revolution." *Theory and Society*, 18, No. 2 (March, 1989), 249-271.

15399 **Siverson, Randolph M.,** and **Sullivan, Michael P.** "The Distribution of Power and the Onset of War." *Journal of Conflict Resolution*, 27, No. 3 (September, 1983), 473-494.

15400 **Slessor, Sir John.** "Air Power and World Strategy." *Foreign Affairs*, 33, No. 1 (October, 1954), 43-53.

15401 **Smart, Christopher.** "Amid the Ruins, Arms Makers Raise New Threats." *Orbis* [Philadelphia], 36, No. 3 (Summer, 1992), 349-364.

15402 **Smernoff, Barry J.** "The Strategic Value of Space-based Laser Weapons." *Air University Review*, 33, No. 3 (March-April, 1982), 2-17.

15403 **Smith, H.A.** "Modern Weapons and Modern War," *Yearbook of World Affairs 1955*, 222-247.

15404 **Smith, Neil.** "History and Philosophy of Geography: Real Wars, Theory Wars." *Progress in Human Geography* [London], 16, No. 2 (June, 1992), 257-271.

15405 **Smith, Robert H.** "Mine Warfare: Promise Deferred." *United States Naval Institute Proceedings*, 106, No. 4-926 (April, 1980), 23-33.

15406 **Smith, Theresa Clair.** "Arms Race Instability and War." *Journal of Conflict Resolution*, 24, No. 2 (June, 1980), 253-284.

15407 **Snow, Donald M.** "Current Nuclear Deterrence Thinking: An Overview and Review." *International Studies Quarterly*, 23, No. 3 (September, 1979), 445-486.

15408 **Solecki, William D.,** and **Cutter, Susan L.** "Living in the Nuclear Age: Teaching About Nuclear War and Peace." *Journal of Geography*, 86, No. 3 (May-June, 1987), 114-120.

15409 **Solzhenitsyn, Aleksandr.** "Misconceptions about Russia are a Threat to America." *Foreign Affairs*, 58, No. 4 (Spring, 1980), 797-834.

15410 **Sommer, Robert.** "Leadership and Group Geography." *Sociometry*, 24, No. 10 (March, 1961), 99-110.

15411 **Steinberg, Gerald M.** "Non-Proliferation: Time for Regional Approaches?" *Orbis* [Greenwich, CT], 38, No. 3 (Summer, 1994), 409-423.

15412 **Steinbruner, John.** "Launch Under Attack." *Scientific American*, 250, No. 1 (January, 1984), 37-47.

15413 **Stepan, A.** "The New Professionalism of Internal Warfare and Military Role Expansion." *Authoritarian Brazil*, (1973), 47-65.

15414 **Stephenson, C.M.** "The Need for Alternative Forms of Security: Crises and Opportunities." *Alternatives*, 13, No. 1 (March, 1988).

15415 **Stolberg, Irving.** "Geography and Peace Research." *Professional Geographer*, 17, No. 4 (July, 1965), 9-12.

15416 **Stone, J.** "De Victoribus Victis: The International Law Commission and Imposed Peace Treaties." *Virginia Journal of International Law*, 8 (1967-8), 1-356 (whole issue, multiple authors).

15417 **Stone, Kirk H.** "Geography's Wartime Service." *Annals of the Association of American Geographers*, 69, No. 1 (March, 1979), 89-96.

15418 **Subrahmanyam, K.** "Regional Conflicts and Nuclear Fears." *Bulletin of the Atomic Scientists*, 40, No. 5 (May, 1984), 16-19.

15419 **Supino, Paolo.** "Geografia Militare, Geopolitica e Strategia Politica." *L'Universo*, 35, No.3 (May-June, 1955), 387-396.

15420 **Szafranski, Richard.** "Thinking About Small Wars." *Parameters* [Carlisle, PA], 20, No. 3 (September, 1990), 39-49.

15421 **Taylor, Griffith.** "How Geography May Promote World Peace." *Geographical Outlook*, 4 (1962).

15422 **Thompson, Barry L.** "'Directed Energy' Weapons and the Strategic Balance." *Orbis*, 23, No. 3 (Fall, 197), 697-709.

15423 **Thompson, Kenneth W.** "The Coming of the Third World War: A Review Essay." *Political Science Quarterly*, 94, No. 4 (Winter, 1979-80), 669-677.

15424 **Todd, D.** "The Defence Sector in Regional Development." *Area*, 12, No. 2 (July, 1980), 115-21.

15425 **Todd, William R.**, and **Rasler, Karen A.** "War and Systemic Capability Reconcentration." *Journal of Conflict Resolution*, 32, No. 2 (June, 1988), 325-366.

15426 **Trachtenberg, Marc.** "The Meaning of Mobilization in 1914." *International Security* [Cambridge], 15, No. 3 (Winter, 1990-91), 120-150.

15427 **Travassos, Mario.** "O Poder nacional: seus fundamentos geograficos." *A Defesa Nacional*, 539-540 (Junho-August,1959), 87-102 and 117-130.

15428 **Tsipis, Kosta.** "Laser Weapons." *Scientific American*, 245, No. 6 (December, 1981), 51-57.

15429 **Udis, B.** "Random Thoughts on the Consequences of a Reduction in Military Expenditures." *Papers of the Regional Science Association.* 23 (1969), 177-199.

15430 **Valle, James E.** "The Navy's Battle Doctrine in the War of 1812." *American Neptune*, 44, No. 3 (Summer, 1984), 171-178.

15431 **van der Wusten, H.** "The Geography of Conflict Since 1945." In *The Geography of Peace and War*, D. Pepper and A. Jenkins, eds. Oxford: Basil Blackwell, 1985, 13-28.

15432 **van der Wusten, H.** "Geography and War/Peace Studies." In *Political Geography: Recent Advances and Future Directions*, P.J. Taylor and J. House, eds. London: Croom Helm, 1984, 191-201.

15433 **van der Wusten, H.**, and **O'Loughlin, J.** "Claiming New Territory for a Stable Peace: How Geography Can Contribute." *Professional Geographer.* 38, No. 1 (February, 1986), 18-28.

15434 **Vayrynen, Raimo.** "Economic Cycles. Power Transitions, Political Management and Wars Between Major Powers." *International Studies Quarterly*, 27, No. 4 (December, 1983), 389-418.

15435 **Vertzberger, Yaacov Y.I.** "National Capabilities and Foreign Military Intervention: A Policy-Relevant Theoretical Analysis." *International Interactions* [Philadelphia], 17, No. 4 (1992), 349-373.

15436 **Vick, Alan J.** "Post-Attack Strategic Command and Control Survival: Options for the Future." *Orbis*, 29, No. 1 (Spring, 1985), 95-117.

15437 **Vollmer, C.D.** "The Future Defense Industrial Environment." *Washington Quarterly*, 13, No. 2 (Spring, 1990), 93-109.

15438 **Waltz, Kenneth N.** "A Strategy for the Rapid Deployment Force." *International Security*, 5, No. 4 (Spring, 1981), 49-73.

15439 "War and Peace Aims; Extracts from Statements of United Nations Leaders." *United Nations Review.* Special Supplement. 4 (October 31, 1944), 1-124.

15440 **Warner, Edward.** "Douhet, Mitchell, Seversky: Theories of Air Warfare." In *Makers of Modern Strategy: Machiavelli to Hitler,* ed. by Edward Mead Earle. Princeton, New Jersey: Princeton University Press, 1944, 485-503.

15441 **Watt, Donald Cameron.** "1939 Revisited: On Theories of the Origins of Wars." *International Affairs,* 65, No. 4 (Autumn, 1989), 685-692.

15442 **Wayman, Frank Whelon.** "Bipolarity and War: The Role of Capability Concentration and Alliance Patterns Among Major Powers, 1816-1965." *Journal of Peace Research,* 21, No. 1 (1984), 61-78.

15443 **Wayman, Frank Whelon; Singer, J. David; and Goertz, Gary.** "Capabilities, Allocations, and Success in Militarized Disputes and Wars, 1816-1976." *International Studies Quarterly,* 27, No. 4 (December, 1983), 497-515.

15444 **Weidenbaum, M.L.** "The Economic Impact of an Arms Cut: Comment. *Review of Economics and Statistics,* 49, No. 4 (November, 1967), 612-13.

15445 **Weidenbaum, M.L.** "Measurements of the Economic Impact of Defense and Space Programs." *American Journal of Economics and Sociology,* 25, No. 4 (October, 1966), 415-426.

15446 **Weigert, Hans W.** "Maps are Weapons." *Survey Graphic,* 30, No. 10 (October, 1941), 528-530.

15447 **Wells, II, Linton.** "Maneuver in Naval Warfare." *United States Naval Institute Proceedings,* 106, No. 12 (934) (December, 1980), 34-41.

15448 **Weltman, John J.** "Nuclear Devolution and World Order." *World Politics,* 32, No. 2 (January, 1980), 169-193.

15449 **Wesley, J.P.** "Frequency of War and Geographic Opportunity." *Journal of Conflict Resolution,* 6, No. 4 (December, 1962), 387-389.

15450 **Westing, Arthur H.** "The Ecological Dimension of Nuclear War." *Environmental Conservation,* 14, No. 4 (Winter, 1987), 295-306.

15451 **Westing, Arthur H.** "Military Impact on Ocean Ecology." In *Ocean Yearbook,* Vol. 1, Elisabeth Mann Borgese and Norton Ginsburg, eds. Chicago, Illinois: University of Chicago Press, 1978, 436-466.

15452 **White, C. Langdon.** "Geography in a World at War." Reprinted from *Denison University Bulletin, Journal of the Scientific Laboratories,* 37, No. 4 (December, 1942), 133-139.

15453 **White, G.F.** "Notes on Geographers and the Threat of Nuclear War." *Transition,* 14, No. 1 (1984), 2-4.

15454 **Williams, Stephen Wyn.** "Arms for the Poor? The International Arms Trade." *Contemporary Issues in Geography and Education,* 2, No. 3 (1987), 16-27.

15455 **Wisner, B.** "Geographers in a Periously Changing World." *Annals of the Association of American Geographers,* 75, No. 1 (March, 1986), 10-16.

15456 **Wisner, B.** "Geography: War on Peace Studies." *Antipode,* 18, No. 2 (September, 1986), 212-217.

15457 **Wiesner, J.B., and York, H.F.** "The Test Ban." *Scientific American,* 211, No. 4 (October, 1964), 27-35.

15458 **Williams, Benjamin H., ed.** "The Search for National Security." *Annals of the American Academy of Political and Social Science,* 278 (November, 1951), 1-190 (complete issue, multiple authors).

15459 **Williams, Jr., Robin M.** "Resolving and Restricting International Conflicts." *Armed Forces and Society,* 7, No. 3 (Spring, 1981), 367-382.

15460 **Williams, Stephen Wyn.** "Pieces in the Global War Game." *Geographical Magazine,* 54, No. 7 (July, 1982), 372-375.

15461 **Williams, Sylvia Maureen.** "International Law and the Military Uses of Outer Space." *International Relations,* 9, No. 5 (May, 1989), 407-418.

15462 **Wimperis, Harry E.** "Air Power." *International Affairs,* 15, No. 3 (July, 1939), 497-505.

15463 **Wit, Joel S.** "Advances in Antisubmarine Warfare." *Scientific American,* 244, No. 2 (February, 1981), 31-41.

15464 **Woo, Jung Ju.** "Nature of the Cold War." *Asian Profile,* 9, No. 1 (February, 1981), 71-79.

15465 "The World in Crisis." *Proceedings of the Institute of World Affairs,* 1947. 24 (1948), 1-229.

15466 **Wright, John K.** "Geography for War and for Peace." Excerpt: *American Scholar,* 12, No. 1 (Winter, 1943-43, 118-123.

15467 **Wright, Quincy.** "The Historic Circumstances of Enduring Peace." *American Historical Association.* 38, No. 4 (October, 1944), 533-545.

15468 **Wright, Quincy.** "Peace Problems of Today and Yesterday." *American Political Science Review,* 38, No. 3 (June, 1944), 512-530.

15469 **Yamamoto, Y., and Bremer, S.A.** "Wider Wars and Restless Nights: Major Power intervention in Ongoing Wars." In *The Correlates of War II: Testing Some Realpolitik Models,* J.D. Singer, ed. New York: Free Press, 1980, 199-229.

15470 **Yost, David S.** "The Delegitimization of Nuclear Deterrence?" *Armed Forces & Society* [New Brunswick], 16, No. 4 (Summer, 1990), 487-508.

15471 **Zinnes, Dina A., and Muncaster, Robert G.** "The Dynamics of Hostile Activity and the Prediction of War." *Journal of Conflict Resolution,* 28, No. 2 (June, 1984), 187-229.

POLITICAL GEOGRAPHY OF REGIONS

AFRICA

Books and Journals

15472 **Abate, Yohannis.** "Civil-Military Relations in Ethiopia." *Armed Forces and Society,* 10, No. 3 (Spring, 1984), 380-400.

15473 **Adelman, Kenneth, and Bender, Gerald J.** "Conflict in Southern Africa: A Debate." *International Security,* 3, No. 2 (Fall, 1978), 67-122.

15474 **Agyeman-Duah, Baffour.** "Military Coups, Regime Change, and Interstate Conflicts in West Africa." *Armed Forces and Society* [New Brunswick], 16, No. 4 (Summer, 1990), 547-570.

15475 *The Atlantic Charter and Africa from an American Standpoint; A Study.* New York: Committee on Africa, the War, and Peace Aims, 1942.

15476 **Avery, William P., and Picard, Louis A.** "Pull Factors in the Transfer of Conventional Armaments to Africa." *Journal of Political & Military Sociology,* 8, No. 1 (Spring, 1980), 55-70.

15477 **Bell, J. Bowyer.** "Strategic Implications of the Soviet Presence in Somalia." *Orbis,* 1999, No. 2 (Summer, 1975), 402-411.

15478 **Bienen, Henry.** "Perspectives on Soviet Intervention in Africa." *Political Science Quarterly,* 95, No. 1 (Spring, 1980), 29-42.

15479 **Booth, Alan R.** *The Armed Forces of African States.* Toronto: The Institute for Strategic Studies, Canadian Institute of International Affairs, 1970.

15480 **Booth, Alan R.** "South Africa's Hinterland: Swaziland's Role in Strategies for Sanctions-breaking." *Africa Today,* 36, No. 1 (1989), 41-50.

15481 **Bourgey, Andre.** "La Guerre et ses Consequences Geographiques au Liban." *Annales de Geographie,* 94ᵉ Annee, No. 521 (Janvier-Fevrier, 1985), 1-37.

15482 **Braca, Giovanni.** "I rilevamenti topografici della Missione dell'Institute geografico militare per la delimitzione confine tra la Somalia Francese e l'Africa Italiana." *L'Universo,* Anno 20, No. 3 (Marzo, 1939), 165-185.

15483 **Bradbury, Mark.** "The Case of the Yellow Settee: Experiences of Doing Development in Post-War Somaliland." *Community Development Journal* [Oxford], 29, No. 2 (April, 1994), 113-122.

15484 **Butts, Kent Hughes.** "Geographic Factors in Zimbabwe's Low Intensity Conflict." *Papers and Proceedings of Applied Geography Conferences* [Binghamton], 13 (September, 1990), 238-246.

15485 **Chaliand, Gerard.** "The Horn of Africa's Dilemma." *Foreign Policy,* 30 (Spring, 1978), 116-131.

15486 **Charlton, Roger.** "Diffusion and Political Change in Post-Colonial Africa. Perspectives on Unipartism and Military Intervention." *Cultures et Developpment,* 11, No. 3 (1979), 439-456.

15487 **Cook, Weston F., Jr.** *The Hundred Years War for Morocco: Gunpowder and the Military Revolution in the Early Modern Muslim World.* Boulder: Westview Press, 1994.

15488 **Crozier, Brian.** *The Soviet Presence in Somalia.* London: Institute for the Study of Conflict, 1975.

15489 **David, Steven.** "Realignment in the Horn: The Soviet Advantage." *International Security,* 4, No. 2 (Fall, 1979), 69-90.

15490 **Davies, R.H., and O'Meara, D.** "The State of Analysis of the Southern African Region: Issues Raised by the South African Strategy." *Review of African Political Economy,* 29 (1984), 64-76.

15491 **Dessouki, Ali E. Hillal.** "Domestic Variables in the Inter-State Conflict: A Case Study of the Sahara." *Armed Forces and Society,* 7, No. 3 (Spring, 1981), 409-422.

15492 **Farer, Thomas.** *War Clouds on the Horn of Africa.* New York: Carnegie Endowment for International Peace, 1976.

15493 **Finnegan, William.** *A Complicated War: The Harrowing of Mozambique.* Berkeley: University of California Press, 1992.

15494 **Gorman, Robert F.** *Political Conflict on the Horn of Africa.* New York: Praeger, 1981.

15495 **Grabendorff, Wolf.** "Cuba's Involvement in Africa: An Interpretation of Objectives, Reactions, and Limitations." *Journal of Interamerican Studies and World Affairs,* 22, No. 1 (February, 1980), 3-29.

15496 **Griffiths, Ievan.** "War in Angola." *The Geographical Magazine.* 56, No. 3 (March, 1984), 114-115.

15497 **Grundy, Kenneth W.** "The Social Costs of Armed Struggle in Southern Africa." *Armed Forces and Society,* 7, No. 3 (Spring, 1981), 445-466.

15498 **Henze, Paul B.** *The Horn of Africa: From War to Peace.* Houndmills: Macmillan, 1991.

15499 **Imobighe, T.A.** "An African High Command: The Search for a Feasible Strategy of Continental Defense." *African Affairs,* 79, No. 315 (April, 1980), 241-254.

15500 **Jaster, Robert,** ed. *Southern Africa: Regional Security Problems and Prospects.* Aldershot: Gower Publishing, 1985.

15501 **Jones, Stephen B.** *Africa and American Security.* New Haven, Connecticut: Yale Institute of International Studies, Yale University, 1945.

15502 **Kun, Joseph.** *Sino-Soviet Competition in Africa: The Crucial Role of Military Assistance.* Munich: Radio Liberty Research, 1976.

15503 **Legum, Colin,** and **Lee, Bill.** *Conflict in the Horn of Africa.* New York: Africana Publishing, 1977.

15504 **MacFarlane, S. Neil.** "Africa's Decaying Security System and the Rise of Intervention." *International Security,* 8, No. 4 (Spring, 1984), 127-151.

15505 **Marcum, John A.** "Lessons of Angola." *Foreign Affairs,* 54, No. 3 (April, 1976), 407-25.

15506 **Marks, S.** *Reluctant Rebellion: The 1906-1908 Disturbances in Natal.* Oxford: Clarendon Press, 1970.

15507 **Mattos, Carlos de Meira.** "Problemas estrategicos da Africa e em particular Africa do Norte." *A Defesa Nacional,* 28, Nos. 535-536 (1959), 111-121 and 125-131.

15508 **Maxwell, David J.** "Local Politics and the War of Liberation in North-East Zimbabwe." *Journal of Southern African Studies* [Oxford], 19, No. 3 (September, 1993), 361-386.

15509 **Michael, Alazar Tesfa.** *Eritrea To-day. Fascist Oppression Under Nose of British Military.* Woodford, Essex: New Time Book Department, 1946.

15510 **Miller, Charles.** *Battle for the Bundu: The First World War in East Africa.* New York: Macmillan, 1974.

15511 **Mohammed, Nadir A.L.** "Militarization in Sudan: Trends and Determinants." *Armed Forces and Society* (New Brunswick], 19, No. 3 (Spring, 1993), 411-433.

15512 **Page, Melvin E.,** ed. *Africa and the First World War.* Houndmills: Macmillan, 1987.

15513 **Papp, Daniel S.** "The Soviet Union and Cuba in Ethiopia." *Current History,* 18, No. 3 (March, 1979), 110-13.

15514 **Patemen, Roy.** "The Eritrean War." *Armed Forces and Society* [New Brunswick], 17, No. 1 (Fall, 1990), 81-98.

15515 **Pearson, Frederic S.,** and **Baumann, Robert A.** "International Military Intervention in the Sub-Saharan African Subsystems." *Journal of Political and Military Sociology,* 17, No. 1 (Spring, 1989), 115-150.

15516 **Ranger, T.** "The People in African Resistance: A Review." *Journal of Southern African Studies,* 4, No. 1 (October, 1977), 125-146.

15517 **Ranger, T.** *Revolt in Southern Rhodesia: A Study in African Resistance.* London: Heinemann, 1967.

15518 **Rogerson, C.M.** "Defending Apatheid: Armscor and the Geography of Military Production in South Africa." *GeoJournal* [Dordrecht], 22, No. 3 (November, 1990), 241-250.

15519 **Seegers, Annette.** "Current Trends in South Africa's Security Establishment." *Armed Forces and Society* [New Brunswick], 18, No. 2 (Winter, 1992), 159-174.

15520 **Segal, Aaron.** "Rwanda/the Underlying Causes; a Behind-the-Headlines Report on Bahutu-Batutsi Warfare." *Africa Report,* 9, No. 4 (April, 1964), 3-6.

15521 **Selassie, Bereket Habte.** "The OAU and Regional Conflicts: Focus on the Eritrean War." *Africa Today,* 35, Nos. 3-4 (1988), 61-67.

15522 **Smaldone, Joseph P.** "Bibliographic Sources for African Military Studies." *A Current Bibliography on African Affairs*, 11, No. 2 (1978-79), 101-109.

15523 **Somerville, Keith.** *Foreign Military Intervention in Africa.* London: Pinter Publishers, 1990.

15524 **Spence, John Edward.** *The Strategic Significance of Southern Africa.* London: Royal United Services Institution, 1970.

15525 **Starr, Harvey, and Most, Benjamin A.** "Contagion and Border Effects on Contemporary African Conflict." *Comparative Political Studies*, 16, No. 1 (April, 1983), 92-117.

15526 **Vale, Peter.** "The Search for Southern Africa's Security." *International Affairs* [Cambridge], 67, No. 4 (October, 1991), 697-708.

15527 **Valenta, Jiri.** "The Soviet-Cuban Intervention in Angola." *United States Naval Institute Proceedings*, 106, No. 4-926 (April, 1980), 51-57.

15528 **Vanneman, Peter, and James, Martin.** "The Soviet Intervention in Angola: Intentions and Implications." *Strategic Review*, 4, No. 3 (Summer, 1976), 92-103.

15529 **Vengroff, Richard.** "Domestic Instability and Foreign Conflict Behavior in Black Africa." *African Studies Review*, 23, No. 3 (December, 1980), 101-114.

15530 **Virpsha, E.S.** "Strategic Importance of South Africa." *NATO's Fifteen Nations*, 12, No. 1 (March, 1967), 36-43.

15531 **Warwick, P.** *Black People and the South African War, 1899-1902.* Johannesburg: Ravan Press, 1983.

15532 **Yhedgo, Michael, and Gotlieb, Philip.** "Konflikten pa Afrikas Horn: Eritrea og Ethiopien." *Geografisk Magasin*, Nr. 132 (June, 1983), 20-23.

AMERICAS

Books

15533 **Adkin, Major Mark.** *Urgent Fury: The Battle for Grenada.* Lexington, Massachusetts: Lexington Books, 1989.

15534 **Aulich, James,** ed. *Framing the Falklands War: Nationhood, Culture and Identity.* Milton Keynes: Open University Press, 1992.

15535 **Bacchus, Wilfred A.** *Mission in Mufti: Brazil's Military Regimes, 1964-1985.* New York: Greenwood Press, 1990.

15536 **Barnett, Frank R.; Tovar, B. Hugh; and Schultz, Richard H.,** eds. *Special Operations in U.S. Strategy.* Washington, D.C.: National Defense University Press in Cooperation with National Strategy Information Center, 1984.

15537 **Barrett, Jeffrey W.** *Impulse to Revolution in Latin America.* New York: Praeger, 1985.

15538 **Bloomfield, Richard J.,** and **Treverton, Gregory F.,** eds. *Alternative to Intervention: A New U.S.-Latin America Security Relationship.* Boulder, Colorado: Lynne Rienner Publishers, 1990.

15539 **Boretsky, M.** *The Threat to U.S. High Technology Industries: Economic and National Security Implications.* Draft Report. Washington, D.C.: International Trade Administration, U.S. Department of Commerce, 1982.

15540 **Buchan, Alastair.** *American Assembly. A World of Nuclear Powers?* Englewood Cliffs, New Jersey: Prentice-Hall, 1966.

15541 **Builder, Carl H.** *The Masks of War: American Military Styles in Strategy and Analysis.* Baltimore, Maryland: Johns Hopkins University Press, 1989.

15542 **Burns, A.L.** *Ethics and Deterrence (A Nuclear Balance Without Hostage Cities?).* Toronto: The Institute of Strategic Studies, Canadian Institute of International Affairs, 1970.

15543 **Calvert, Peter,** ed. *The Central American Security System: North-South or East-West?* Cambridge: Cambridge University Press, 1988.

15544 **Calvert, Peter.** *The Falklands Crisis: The Rights and the Wrongs.* London: Printer, 1982.

15545 **Chase, J.,** and **Carr, C.** *America Invulnerable: The Quest for Absolute Security, 1812 to Star Wars.* New York: Summit, 1988.

15546 **Cherdame, Andre.** *Defense of the Americas.* New York: Doubleday, 1941.

15547 **Child, Jack.** *The Central American Peace Process, 1983-1991: Sheathing Swords, Building Confidence.* Boulder: Lynne Rienner Publishers, 1992.

15548 **Cidade, Francisco de Paula.** *Notas de geografia militar sul-americana.* Rio de Janeiro: Biblioteca Militar, 1940.

15549 **Clarfield, G.H.,** and **Wiecek, W.M.** *Nuclear America: Military and Civilian Nuclear Power in the United States 1940-1980.* New York: Harper & Row, 1984.

15550 **Coll, Alberto R., and Arend, Anthony C.,** eds. *The Falklands War: Lessons for Strategy, Diplomacy, and International Law.* Boston: Allen and Unwin, 1985.

15551 **Cordier, Sherwood S.** *U.S. Military Power and Rapid Deployment Requirements in the 1980's.* Boulder, Colorado: Westview Press, 1983.

15552 **Dabat, Alejandro, and Lorenzano, Luis.** *Argentina: The Malvinas and the End of Military Rule.* London: Verso Editions, 1984.

15553 **DeGrasse, R.W.** *Military Expansion Economic Decline: The Impact of Military Spending on U.S. Economic Performance.* New York: M.E. Sharpe, 1983.

15554 **de Seversky, Alexander P.** *America: Too Young to Die.* New York: McGraw-Hill, 1961.

15555 **de Souza, Antonio.** *O Brasil e a terceira guerra mundial.* Rio de Janeiro: Biblioteca do exercito, 1959.

15556 **Duggan, Laurance.** *The Americas, The Search for Hemisphere Security.* New York: Holt, c1949.

15557 **Dunn, Peter M., and Watson, Bruce W.,** eds. *American Intervention in Grenada: The Implications & Operation "Urgent Fury."* Boulder, Colorado: Westview Press, 1985.

15558 **Engelmann, Karsten G.** *The Correlation Between Military Base Location and the Distribution of War.* Fairfax, VA: Master's thesis, George Mason University, 1993.

15559 **Evans, Luther Harris.** *The Virgin Islands, From Naval Base to New Deal.* Ann Arbor: J.W. Edwards, 1945.

15560 **Fox, Richard Allen, Jr.** *Archaeology, History, and Custer's Last Battle: The Little Big Horn Reexamined.* Norman: University of Oklahoma Press, 1993.

15561 **Futrell, Robert F.** *Ideas, Concepts, and Doctrines: A History of Basic Thinking in the United States Air Force, 1907-1964.* Montgomery: Air University Press, 1971.

15562 **Gaddis, J.L.** *Strategies of Containment. A Critical Appraisal of Postwar American National Security Policy.* New York: Oxford University Press, 1982.

15563 **Gervasi, Tom.** *Arsenal of Democracy: American Weapons Available for Export.* New York: Grove Press, 1977.

15564 **Gettleman, Marvin E., and Others,** eds. *El Salvador: Central America in the New Cold War.*

New York: Grove Press, 1987.

15565 **Gough, Barry.** *The Falkland Islands/Malvinas: The Contest for Empire in the South Atlantic.* London: The Athlone Press, 1992.

15566 **Goytia, Victor Florencio.** *Unidad y poder en la Paz de America.* Panama: Ed. Imp. Hernandez, 1950.

15567 **Griffith, Ivelaw L.,** ed. *Strategy and Security in the Caribbean.* New York: Praeger Publishers, 1991.

15568 **Hartman, Frederick A, and Wendzel, Robert L.** *Defending America's Security.* 2nd ed. McLean, Virginia: Brassey's, 1990.

15569 **Herring, George C.** *LBJ and Vietnam: A Different Kind of War.* Austin: University of Texas Press, 1994.

15570 **Isaacs, Anita.** *Military Rule and Transition in Ecuador, 1972-92.* Pittsburgh: University of Pittsburgh Press, 1993.

15571 **Isenberg, Michael T.** *Shield of the Republic: The United States Navy in an Era of Cold War and Violent Peace, Vol 1: 1945-1962.* New York: St. Martin's Press, 1993.

15572 **Johnson, John J.** *The Military and Society in Latin America.* Stanford, California: Stanford University Press, 1964.

15573 **Johnsrud, Judith Ann Hays.** *A Political Geography of the Nuclear Power Controversy: The Peaceful Atom in Pennsylvania.* University Park: Pennsylvania State University, Ph.D., 1977.

15574 **Katz, Arthur M.** *Life After Nuclear War: The Economic and Social Impacts of Nuclear Attacks on the United States.* Cambridge, Massachusetts: Ballinger, 1982.

15575 **Kaufman, W.W.** *Glasnot, Perestroika, and U.S. Defense Spending.* Washington, DC: Brookings Institute, 1990.

15576 **Kent, S.** *Strategic Intelligence for American World Policy.* Princeton, New Jersey: Princeton University Press, 1966.

15577 **Kimble, George H.T.** *Canadian Military Geography.* Ottawa: Queen's Printer, 1949.

15578 **Leckie, Robert.** *From Sea to Shining Sea: From the War of 1812 to the Mexican War, the Saga of America's Expansion.* New York: Harper Collins Publishers, 1993.

15579 **Luttwak, E.** *The Pentagon and the Art of War.* New York: Simon and Schuster, 1985.

15580 **Lloyd Jones, C.** *Caribbean Interests of the United States*. New York: Appleton, 1916.

15581 **Lyra Tavares, A.**, ed. *Seguranca Nacional: Antagonismos e Vulnerabilidades*. Rio de Janeiro: Biblioteca do Exercito, 1958.

15582 **MacKay, R.A.**, ed. *Newfoundland; Economic Diplomatic, and Strategic Studies*. Issued under the auspices of the Royal Institute of International Affairs. Toronto: Oxford University Press, 1946.

15583 **Mallin, Maurice A.** *Tanks Fighters and Ships: Conventional Force Planning Since W.W. II.* McLean, Virginia: Brassey's, 1990.

15584 **Mayers, Teena Karsa.** *Understanding Weapons and Arms Control.* 4 McLean, Virgina: Brassey's, 1990.

15585 **Melman, S.** *The Permanent War Economy: American Capitalism in Decline.* New York: Simon and Schuster, 1985.

15586 **Mendez, J.** *Realidad del equilibrio hispano-americano y necessidad de la neutralizacion perpetua de Bolivia.* Lima: Imp. de La Patria, 1874.

15587 **Milicki, E.J.** *The Economic and Regional Consequences of Military Innovation.* Berkeley: Working Paper No. 442, Institute of Urban and Regional Development, University of California, 1985b.

15588 **More, F.** *La proxima conflagracion suramericana.* La Paz: Gonzalez y Medina, 1918.

15589 **Musicant, Ivan.** *The Banana Wars: A History of the United States Military Intervention in Latin America From the Spanish-American War to the Invasion of Panama.* New York: Macmillan Publishing Company, 1990.

15590 **Nebenzahl, Kenneth.** *A Bibliography of Printed Battle Plans of the American Revolution, 1775-1795.* Chicago, Illinois: University of Chicago Press, 1975.

15591 **Nye, Joseph S., Jr.** *Bond to Lead: The Changing Nature of American Power.* New York: Basic Books, 1990.

15592 **Office of the Chief of Naval Operations.** *Marshall Islands.* Military Government Handbook. OPNAV P22-1. (Formerly OPNAV 50E-1). Washington, D.C.: U.S. Navy Department, 1944.

15593 **Parrott, William.** *The Military Legacy of the Second World War on the Newfoundland Landscape.* St. John's, Newfoundland: Master's thesis, Memorial University of Newfoundland, 1993.

15594 **Pierre, Andrew J.**, ed. *Arms Transfers and American Foreign Policy.* New York: New York University Press, 1979.

15595 **Potter, E.B.** *The United States and World Sea Power.* Englewood Cliffs, New Jersey: Prentice-Hall, 1955.

15596 **Rable, George C.** *The Confederate Republic: A Revolution Against Politics.* Chapel Hill: The University of North Carolina Press, 1994.

15597 **Ramierz, Eugenio.** *La republica de los E.U. del Brasil: Su poder militar nuestras fronteras.* Buenos Aires: s.e., 1917.

15598 **Ramierz, Eugenio.** *La Republic de los Estados Unidos del Brasil; Su Poder Militar, Importancia Economica-Requezas Industrias.* Buenos Aires: Neustras Fronteras, 1917.

15599 **Rasor, Eugene L.** *The Falklands/Malvinas Campaign: A Bibliography.* New York: Greenwood Press, 1992.

15600 **Regehr, E.** *Making a Killing: Canada;s Arms Industry.* Toronto: McClelland and Stewart, 1975.

15601 **Reston, Jr., James.** *Sherman's March and Vietnam.* New York: Macmillan, 1984.

15602 **Rogers, James Grafton.** *World Policing and the Constitution; an Inquiry into the Powers of the President and Congress, Nine Wars and a Hundred Military Operations, 1789-1945.* (America Looks Ahead, No. 11.) Boston: World Peace Foundation, 1945.

15603 **Sarkesian, Sam C.** *America's Forgotten Wars: The Counter-Revolutionary Past and Lessons for the Future.* Westport: Greenwood Press, 1984.

15604 **Sarkesian, Sam C.** *U.S. National Security: Policymakers, Processes and Politics.* Boulder, Colorado: Lynne Rienner Publishers, 1989.

15605 **Sarkesian, Sam C.**, and **Williams, John Allen**, eds. *The U.S. Army in a New Security Era.* Boulder, Colorado: Lynne Rienner Publishers, 1990.

15606 **Schilling, Warner R.**, et al. *American Arms and a Changing Europe: Dilemmas of Deterrence and Disarmament.* New York City: Columbia University Press, 1973.

15607 **Schocnhals, Kai P., and McLanson, Richard A.** *Revolution and Intervention in Grenada: The New Jewel Movement, the United States, and the Caribbean.* Boulder, Colorado: Westview Press, 1985.

15608 **Serbin, Andres.** *Caribbean Geopolitics: Toward Security Through Peace.* Translated by Sebet Ramirez. Boulder, Colorado: Lynne Rienner Publishers, 1990.

15609 **Shatin, Dianne.** "The Spatial Pattern of Support for the Nuclear Weapon Freeze in the United States, 1982-84." New Brunswick, New Jersey: Rutgers-The State University, M.A., 1988.

15610 **Sheehan, Edward R.F.** Agony in the Garden: A Stranger in Central America. Boston: Houghton Mifflin, 1988.

15611 **Slessor, John.** *Strategy for the West.* New York: Morrow, 1954.

15612 **Sloan, G.R.** *Geopolitics in the United States Strategic Policy, 1890-1987.* New York: St. Martin's Press, 1988.

15613 **Stepan, A.** *The Military in Politics. Changing Patterns in Brazil.* Princeton, New Jersey: Princeton University Press, 1971.

15614 **Tammes, Rolf.** *The United States and the Cold War in the High North.* Aldershot: Dartmouth, 1991.

15615 **Tavares, Aurelio de Lyra.** *Seguranca nacional: antagonismo e vulnerabilidades.* Rio de Janeiro: Bibliotecado exercito, 1958.

15616 **Travassos, Mario.** *As Condicoes geograficas e o problema militar brasileiro.* Rio de Janeiro: Ed. a Defesa Nacional, 1941.

15617 **United States.** *Arms Control and Disarmament Agency. Defense Program and Analysis Division. World Military Expenditures and Arms Transfer, 1971-1980.* Washington, D.C.: ACDA Publication, No. 115, 1983.

15618 **United States Army.** *Combat in Built-up Areas.* Fort Benning, Georgia: Field Manual No. ST 31-51-171, Infantry School, 1972.

15619 **U.S. Department of State.** *The Chaco Peace Conference. Report of the Delegation of the United States of America to the Peace Conference Held at Buenos Aires, July 1, 1935-January 23, 1939.* Publication 1466, Conference Series 46. Washington, D.C.: Government Printing Office, 1940.

15620 **U.S. Department of State.** *Peace and War. United States Foreign Policy, 1931-1941.* Publication 1983. Documented edition.

Washington, D.C.: U.S. Department of State, 1943.

15621 **United States.** Library of Congress, Foreign Affairs and National Defense Division. *United States Arms Transfers and Security Assistance Programs.* Washington, D.C.: United States Government Printing Office, 1978.

15622 **United States.** Office of War Information. *A War Atlas for Americans.* New York: Simon and Schuster, 1944.

15623 **Villar, Rodger.** *Merchant Ships of War: The Falklands Experience.* London: Conway Maritime Press, 1984.

15624 **Warden, John A., III.** *The Air Campaign: Planning for Combat.* Washington, D.C.: National Defense University Press, 1988.

15625 **Wedemeyer, Austin C., and Others.** *Essay on Strategy: Selections from the 1983 Joint Chiefs on Staff Essay Competition.* Washington, D.C.: National Defense University Press, 1984.

15626 **Wildavsky, Aaron, ed.** *Beyond Containment: Alternative American Politics Toward the Soviet Union.* San Francisco: ICS Press, 1983.

15627 **Wirls, D.** *Build-up: The Politics of Defense in the Reagan Era.* Ithaka, NY: Cornell University Press, 1992.

15628 **Wittner, L.S.** *Rebels Against War: The American Peace Movement 1933-1983.* Philadelphia, Pennsylvania: Temple University Press, 1984.

15629 **Wolfe, Roy I.** *Political and Strategic Interests of the United Kingdom.* New York: Oxford University Press, 1939.

15630 **Young, Louise B.** *Power Over People.* London: Oxford University Press, 1973.

Journals

15631 **Acharya, Amitav.** "The Rapid Deployment Force and the U.S. Military Build-Up in the Persian Gulf Region: A Critical Perspective." *Australian Outlook*, 38, No. 2 (August, 1984), 90-98.

15632 **Akatiff, Clark.** "The March on the Pentagon." *Annals of the Association of American Geographers*, 64, No. 1 (March, 1974), 26-33.

15633 **Alencar, Carlos Ramos de.** "O Sentido Militar da transferencia da Capital." *A Defesa Nacional*, 29, Nos. 574-575 (Maio, 1962), 47-50.

15634   **Alpert, Annie.** "Alaska's New Deal Colonists."
American History [Harrisburg], 27, No. 1
(March/April, 1992), 50-53.

15635   **Alvares Noll, Darcy.** "Estudios geografico-
militar do Rio Grande do Sul." *A Defesa
Nacional*, 30, No. 582 (Maio, 1963), 5-76.

15636   **Aquino, Tasso Villar.** "A Amazonia brasileira
sob o angulo militar." *A Defesa Nacional*, 73,
No. 504 (Maio, 1956), 59-64.

15637   **Art, R.J.** "A Defensible Defense: America's
Grand Strategy After the Cold War."
International Security, 15 (1991), 5-53.

15638   **Barnett, Anthony.** "Iron Britannica: War Over
the Falklands." *New Left Review*, 134 (July,
1982), 1-96.

15639   **Baucom, Donald R.** "Technological War:
Reality and the American Myth." *Air University
Review*, 32, No. 6 (September-October, 1981),
56-66.

15640   **Beck, Peter J.** "Cooperative Confrontation in the
Falkland Islands Dispute." *Journal of Inter-
American Studies and World Affairs*, 24, No. 1
(February, 1982), 37-58.

15641   **Birch, B.P.** "Winning Land from the Sea at
Portsmouth." *Geography*, 58, Part 2 (April,
1973), 152-154.

15642   **Bittner, Donald F.** "Canadian
Militiamobilization and Deployment for War:
The Iceland Experience of 1940." *Armed Forces
and Society* [New Brunswick], 18, No. 3 (Spring,
1992), 343-361.

15643   **Bowman, Isaiah.** "The Military Geography of
the Atacama." *Educational Bi-monthly*, 6 (1911),
1-21.

15644   **Bryan, G.S.** "La geografia y la defensa del
Caribe y del Canal de Panama." *Revista de la
Sociedade Geografica de Cuba*, Ano 14, Numero
2 (Abril, 1941), 50-61.

15645   **Bryan, G.S.** "Geography and the Defense of the
Caribbean and the Panama Canal." *Annals of the
Association of American Geographers*, 31, No. 2
(June, 1941), 83-94.

15646   **Bueno Ortiz, Armando.** "Algunos aspectos
geopoliticos del Peru en la deensa nacional."
Peruanidad, (1944), 1539-1548.

15647   **Burghardt, Andrew F.** "The Economic Impact
of War: The Case of the U.S. Civil War."
Journal of Geography, 72, No. 1 (January, 1973),
7-10.

15648   **Burk, James.** "National Attachments and the

Decline of the Mass and Armed Force." *Journal
of Political and Military Sociology*, 17, No. 1
(Spring, 1989), 65-81.

15649   **Cambiasso, Juan A.** "A Defesa da Paz." *A
Defesa Nacional*,20, No. 465 (Junho, 1953), 77-
78.

15650   **Castel, Albert.** "Prevaricating Through Georgia:
Sherman's *Memoirs* as a Source on the Atlanta
Campaign." *Civil War History* [Kent], 40, No. 1
(March, 1994), 48-71.

15651   **De Castro, Therezinha.** "O Mundo Atlantico e
seus imperativos estrategicos." *A Defesa
Nacional*, 35, No. 622 (Junho, 1968), 61-65.

15652   **Child, John.** "From 'Color' to 'Rainbow': U.S.
Strategic Planning for Latin America, 1919-
1945." *Journal of Interamerican Studies and
World Affairs*, 21, No. 2 (May, 1979), 233-259.

15653   **Child, John.** "Strategic Concepts of Latin
America: An Update." *Inter-American Economic
Affairs*, 34, No. 1 (Summer, 1980), 61-82.

15654   **Clodfelter, Mark.** "Pinpointing Devastation:
American Air Campaign Planning Before Pearl
Harbor." *The Journal of Military History*
[Lexington], 58, No. 1 (January, 1994), 75-101.

15655   **Colburn, Forrest D.** "The Fading of the
Revolutionary Era in Central America." *Current
History* [Philadelphia], 91, No. 562 (February,
1992), 70-73.

15656   **Collihan, Kathleen M., and Danopoulos,
Constantine P.** "Copu D'etat Attempt in
Trinidad: Its Causes and Failure." *Armed Forces
and Society* [New Brunswick], 19, No. 3 (Spring,
1993), 435-450.

15657   **Conant, Melvin.** "Canada's Role in Western
Defense." *Foreign Affairs*, 40, No. 3 (April,
1962), 431-443.

15658   **Couffignal, Georges.** "L'intervention de
Decembre 1989 a Panama: 'Big Stick,' Bulletin
de Vote et 'Mare Nostrum.'" *Herodote* [Paris],
No. 57 (Avril-Juin, 1990), 76-86.

15659   **Crist, George B.** "A U.S. Military Strategy for a
Changing World." *Strategic Review*, 18, No. 1
(Winter, 1990), 16-24.

15660   **Crowley, William, and Griffin, Ernst C.**
"Political Upheaval in Central America." *Focus*,
34, No. 1 (September-October, 1983), 1-15.

15661   **Crump, J.R., and Clark Archer, J.** "Spatial
and Temporal Variability in the Geography of
American Defense Outlays." *Political
Geography*, 12, No. 1 (January, 1993), 38-63.

15662 **Crump, Jeff R.** "Sectoral Composition and Spatial Distribution of Department of Defense Services Procurement." *The Professional Geographer*, 43, No. 3 (August, 1993), 286-296.

15663 **Cutler, Robert M.; Despres, Laure; and Karp, Aaron.** "The Political Economy of East-South Military Transfers." *International Studies Quarterly*, 31, No.3 (September, 1987), 273-299.

15664 **Cutter, S.L., et al.** "From Grass to Roots to Partisan Politics: Nuclear Freeze Referenda in New Jersey and South Dakota." *Political Geography Quarterly*, 6, No. 4 (October, 1987), 287-300.

15665 **Dalby, Simon.** "American Security Discourse: The Persistence of Geopolitics." *Political Geography Quarterly*, 9, No. 2 (April, 1990), 171-188.

15666 **Davis, John W.** "Anglo-American Relations and Sea Power." *Foreign Affairs*, 7, No. 3 (April, 1929), 345-355.

15667 **de Seversky, Alexander P.** "The Ordeal of American Air Power." *American Mercury*, 53, No. 211 (July, 1941), 7-14 and 127.

15668 **del Aguila, Juan M.** "Central American Vulnerability to Soviet/Cuban Penetration." *Journal of Interamerican Studies*, 27, No. 2 (Summer, 1985), 77-98.

15669 **Dietz, Henry A., and Schmitt, Karl.** "Militarization in Latin America: For What? And Why?" *Inter-American Economic Affairs*, 38, No. 1 (Summer, 1984), 44-46.

15670 **Dix, Robert H.** "Military Coups and Military Rule in Latin America." *Armed Forces and Society* [New Brunswick], 20, No. 3 (Spring, 1994), 439-456.

15671 **Doherty, Tom.** "Buna: The Red Arrow Division's Heart of Darkness." *Wisconsin Magazine of History* [Madiosn], 77, No. 2 (Winter, 1993-94), 109-138.

15672 **Edrington, Thomas S.** "Military Influence on the Texas-New Mexico Boundary Settlement." *New Mexico Historical Journal*, 59, No. 4 (October, 1984), 371-393.

15673 **Elliott, Bob.** "The Long Distance War." *The Geographical Magazine*, 55, No. 1 (January, 1983), 35-37. (Focus is on the recent Falkland Islands conflict.)

15674 **Etzold, Thomas H.** "From Far East to Middle East: Overextension in American Strategy Since World War II." *US Naval Institute Proceedings*, 107 (May, 1981), 66-77.

15675 **Fensterwald, Bernard.** "The Anatomy of American Isolationism and Expansionism." *Journal of Conflict Resolution*, 2, No. 2 (June, 1958), 111-139.

15676 **Fischer, LeRoy H.,** ed. "The Western Territories in the Civil War." *Journal of the West*, 16, No. 2 (April, 1977), 3-120.

15677 **Fiske, S.T.; Pratto, F.; and Pavelchak, M.A.** "Citizens Images of Nuclear War: Contents and Consequences." *Journal of Social Issues*, 39, No. 1 (January, 1983), 41-66.

15678 **Friedberg, Aaron L.** "A History of the US Strategic 'Doctrine' - 1945 to 1980." *The Journal of Strategic Studies*, 3, No. 3 (December, 1980), 37-71.

15679 **Frieberg, Aaron L.** "Why Didn't the United States Become a Garrison State?" *International Security* [Cambridge, MA], 16, No. 4 (Spring, 1992), 109-142.

15680 **Friedman, Norman.** "The Falklands War: Lessons Learned and Mislearned." *Orbis*, 26, No. 4 (Winter, 1983), 907-940.

15681 **Galbraith, K.D., and Wakefield, J.C.** "National Defense Spending: A Review of Appropriations and Real Purchases." *Survey of Current Business*, 64, No. 11 (November, 1984), 11-16.

15682 **Ganasegui, Marco A., Jr.** "The Military Regimes of Panama." *Journal of Interamerican Studies and World Affairs* [Coral Gables], 35, No. 3 (Fall, 1993), 1-17.

15683 **Goin, Peter.** "Ground Zero: Nevada Test Site." *Landscape*, 30, No. 1 (Fall, 1988), 24-29.

15684 **Gonzalez, Edward.** "The Cuban & Soviet Challenge in the Caribbean Basin." *Orbis*, 29, No. 1 (Spring, 1985), 73-94.

15685 **Gouvea Neto, Raul de.** "How Brazil Competes in the Global Defense Industry." *Latin American Research Review* [Albuquerque], 26, No. 3 (1991), 83-107.

15686 **Gurley, Franklin Louis.** "Policy Versus Strategy: The Defense of Strasbourg in Winter 1944-1945." *The Journal of Military History* [Lexington], 58, No. 3 (July, 1994), 481-514.

15687 **Harper, Gilbert S.** "Logistics in Grenada: Supporting No-Plan Wars." *Parameters* [Carlisle Barracks, PA], 20, No. 2 (June, 1990), 50-63.

15688 **Hayes, Margaret Daly.** "Security to the South: U.S. Interests in Latin America." *International Security*, 5, No. 1 (Summer,1980), 130-151.

15689 **Hipel, Keith W.; Wang, Muhong; and Fraser, Niall M.** "Hypergame Analysis of the Falkland Malvinas Vonflict." *International Studies Quarterly*, 32, No. 3 (September, 1988), 335-358.

15690 **Hochberg, Leonard.** "The English Civil War in Geographical Perspective." *Journal of Interdisciplinary History*, 14, No. 4 (Spring, 1984), 729-750.

15691 **Hooker, Richard D., Jr.** "Presidential Decisionmaking and Use of Force: Case Study in Grenada." *Parameters* [Carlisle], 21, No. 2 (Summer, 1991), 61-72.

15692 **Hoopes, Townsend.** "Overseas Bases in American Strategy." *Foreign Affairs*, 37, No. 1 (October, 1958), 69-83.

15693 **Hopple, Gerald W.** "Intelligence and Warning: Implications and Lessons of the Falkland Islands War." *World Politics*, 36, No. 3 (April, 1984), 339-361.

15694 **Howe, Herbert M.** "The South African Defence Force and Political Reform." *The Journal of Modern African Studies* [Cambridge], 32, No. 1 (March, 1994), 29-51.

15695 **Hutchison, Bruce.** "'The Linchpin of Peace'...Canada's Historic Opportunity." Reprint: *Fortune*, 28, No. 1 (July, 1943), 108-116+.

15696 **Jackson, Lon.** "Our Billion Dollar Rock. Oahu, Key of the Hawaiian Islands, Has Become Uncle Sam's Strategic Fort in the Pacific Ocean." *Current History*, 51, No. 7 (March, 1940), 36-38.

15697 **Jockel, Joseph T.** "Canada in the Post-Cold War World." *Current History* [Philadelphia], 90, No. 560 (December, 1991), 405-410.

15698 **Johnston, R.J.** "Congressional Committees and the Inter-State Distribution of Military Spending." *Geoforum*, 10, No. 2 (1979), 151-162.

15699 **Jordan, Weymouth T., Jr.** "'North Carolinians...Must Bear the Blame': Calumny, an Affaire D'honneur, and Expiation for the Fifty-fifth Regiment North Carolina Troops at the Siege of Suffolk, April-May 1863." *The North Carolina Historical Review* [Raleigh], 71, No. 3 (July, 1994), 306-330.

15700 **Judson, W.V.** "The Strategy Value of Her West Indian Possession to the United States." *Annals of the American Academy of Political and Social Science*, 19, No. 2 (1902), 383-391.

15701 **Karaska, G.J.** "Inter-Regional Flows of Defense-space Awards: The Role of Subcontracting in an Impact Analysis of Changes in the Levels of Defense Awards Upon the Philadelphia Economy. *Papers, Peace Research Society*, 5 (1966), 45-62.

15702 **Krasmo, Jean.** "Non-Proliferation: Brazil's Secret Nuclear Program." *Orbis* [Greenwich, CT], 38, No. 3 (Summer, 1994), 425-439.

15703 **Laird, Robbin F.** "The Latin American Arms Market: Soviet Perceptions and Arms Transfers, 1972-82." *Soviet Union*, 12, No. 3 (1985), 277-304.

15704 **Lefebvre, Jeffrey A.** "Globalism and Regionalism: U.S. Arms Transfers to Sudan." *Armed Forces and Society* [New Brunswick], 17, No. 2 (Winter, 1991), 211-227.

15705 **Leonard, Thomas M.** "Search for Security: The United States and Central America in the Twentieth Century." *The Americas* [Washington, DC], 47, No. 4 (April, 1991), 477-490.

15706 **Lernre, Victoria.** "Espias Mexicanos en Tierras Norteamericanas." *New Mexico Historical Review* [Albuquerque], 69, No. 3 (July, 1994), 230, 247.

15707 **Lerwill, I.** "The Lifestyle of the Serviceman and His Family Problems." *Proceedings of the Triservice Multidisciplinary Conference*, 3 (1975), 3-14.

15708 **Lloyd, Trevor.** "Canada's Strategic North." *International Journal*, 2, No. 2 (Spring, 1947), 144-149.

15709 **Lyon, Eugene.** "Pedro Menendez's Strategic Plan for the Florida Peninsula." *Florida Historical Quarterly*, 67, No.1 (July, 1988), 1-14.

15710 **Mackinder, Halford J.** "O mundo redondo e a Conquista da paz." *Boletim Geografico*, 12, No. 118 (1954), 80-84.

15711 **Mahaffey, F.K.** "C3I in the AirLand Battle." *Defence Update International*, 39 (1983), 2-9 and 60-63.

15712 **Malan, Alfredo Souto.** "Geopolitica e seguranca nacional." *Boletim Geografico*, 28, No. 183 (1964), 445-451.

15713 **Malecki, E.J.** "Military Spending and the U.S. Defense Industry: Regional Patterns of Military Contracts and Subcontracts." *Environment and Planning*. C 2, No. 1 (January, 1984), 31-44.

15714 **Markoff, J., and Baretta, S.R.D.** "Professional Ideology and Military Activism in Brazil: Critique of a Thesis of Alfred Stepan." *Comparative Politics*,17, No. 2 (January, 1985), 175-191.

15715 **Markusen, A.R.** "The Military Remapping of the United States." *Built Environment.* 11, No. 3 (1985), 171-180.

15716 **Martin, L.** "The Geography of the Monroe Doctrine and the Limits of the Western Hemisphere." *Geographical Review*, 30, No. 3 (July, 1940), 525-528.

15717 **Mauceri, Philip.** "Military Politics and Counter-Insurgency in Peru." *Journal of Interamerican Studies and World Affairs* [Coral Gables], 33, No. 4 (Winter, 1991), 83-109.

15718 **McAndrew, W.** "The Early Days of Aircraft Acquisition in Canadian Military Action." *Defence Quarterly*, 12, No. 2 (1982), 35-43.

15719 **McElfresh, Earl B.** "Richmond Is a Hard Road to Travel: Maps and Map Makers of the Civil War." *Special Libraries Association. Geography and Map Division, Bulletin*, No. 178 (December, 1994), 2-12.

15720 **McLean, Ephraim R., Jr.** "The Caribbean - An American Lake." *United States Naval Institute Proceedings*, 67, No. 461 (July, 1941), 947-952.

15721 **Meyer, Walter dos Santos.** "Estudios geograficos militares: Rio Grande so Dul e fronteiras meridionais." *A Defesa Nacional*, 28, Nos. 556-567 (Maio-Junho, 1961), 23-28.

15722 **Milenky, Edward S.** "Arms Production and National Security in Argentina." *Journal of Interamerican Studies and World Affairs*, 22, No. 3 (August, 1980), 267-288.

15723 **Momsen, Janet Henshall.** "Caribbean Conflict Cold War in the Sun." *Political Geography Quarterly*, 3, No. 2 (April, 1984), 145-151.

15724 **Morrison, D.C.** "Pentagon's on a Downward Glide Path." *National Journal*, 24 (1992), 279-280.

15725 **Muniz, Humberto Garcia.** "Defense Policy and Planning in the Caribbean: An Assessment of the Case of Jamaica on its 25th Independence Anniversary." *Caribbean Studies*, 21, Nos. 1-2 (Enero-Junio, 1988), 67-123.

15726 **Nacht, Michael.** "Toward an American Conception of Regional Security." *Daedalus*, 110, No. 1 (Winter, 1981), 1-22.

15727 **National Research Council.** "Lessons from the War-Time Experience for Improving Graduate Training for Geographic Research." *Annals of the Association of American Geographers*, 36, No. 2 (June, 1946), 195-214.

15728 **Needler, Martin C.** "The Military Withdrawal from Power in South America." *Armed Forces and Society*, 6, No. 4 (Summer, 1980), 614-624.

15729 **Nolan, John S.** "The Militarization of the Elizabethan State." *The Journal of Military History* [Lexington], 58, No. 3 (July, 1994), 391-420.

15730 **North, Liisa, and Draimin, Tim.** "The Decay of the Security Regime in Central America." *International Journal*, 45, No. 2 (Spring, 1990), 224-257.

15731 **O'hUallachain, Breandan.** "Regional and Technological Implications of the Recent Buildup in American Defense Spending." *Annals of the Association of American Geographers*, 77, No. 2 (June, 1987), 208-223.

15732 **O'Keefe, Phil; Soussan, J.; and Susman, P.** "A Sad Note for Grenada." *Political Geography Quarterly*, 3, No. 2 (April, 1984), 152-159. (Book review)

15733 **Pablo Parto, Luis M. de.** "La posicion geografica de la Argentina como factor en su politica exterior." *Revista del Instituto de Derecho Internacional*, 2, No. 6 (Juno, 1949), 205-215.

15734 **Parks, E. Taylor, and Rippy, J. Fred.** "The Galapagos Islands, A Neglected Phase of American Strategy Diplomacy." *Pacific Historical Review*, 9, No. 1 (March, 1940), 37-45.

15735 **Perez Tort, Miguel.** "El potencial economico-industrial Argentino y la defensa nacional." *Ejercito*, 9, No. 107 (1948), 31-36.

15736 **Platt, R.H.** "Nuclear Crisis Relocation: Issues for a Host Community-The Case of Greenfield, Massachusetts, USA." *Environmental Management.* 10, No. 2 (1986), 189-198.

15737 **Rogers, B.** "Follow-on-Forces Attack (FOFA): Myths and Realities." *NATO Review*, 6, No. (December, 1984), 1-9.

15738 **Ropp, Steve C.** "Military Retrenchment and Decay in Panama." *Current History*, 89, No. 543 (January, 1990), 17-20.

15739 **Rosenberg, David Alan.** "'A Smoking Radiating Ruin at the End of Two Hours': Documents on American Plans for Nuclear War with the Soviet Union, 1954-1955." *International Security*, 6, No. 3 (Winter, 1981/1982), 3-38.

15740 **Sahni, Varun.** "Not Quite British: A Study of External Influences on the Argentine Navy." *Journal of Latin American Studies* [Cambridge], 25, Part 2 (October, 1993), 489-513.

15741 **Sauers, Richard A.** "The Confederate Congress and the Loss of Roanoke Island." *Civil War History* [Kent], 40, No. 2 (June, 1994), 134-150.

15742 **Schneider, J., and Patton, W.** "Urban and Regional Effects of Military Spending: A Case Study of Vallejo, California and Mare Island Shipyard." *Built Environment*, 11, No. 3, (1985), 207-218.

15743 **Scott, A.J., and Gauthier, D.J.** "The U.S. Missile and Space Industry." *National Geogrpahic Research and Exploration*, 7 (1991), 472-489.

15744 **Scott, J.T.** "The Frederica Homefront in 1742." *The Georgia Historical Quarterly*, 75, No. 3 (Fall, 1994), 493-508.

15745 **Shatin, Dianne.** "The Spatial Pattern of Support for the Nuclear Weapon Freeze in the United States, 1982-84." New Brunswick, New Jersey: Rutgers-The State University, M.A., 1988.

15746 **Sheehan, Edward R.F., and Dorrance, John C.** "The Pacific Islands and U.S. Security Interests: A New Era Poses New Challenges." *Asian Survey*, 29, No. 7 (July, 1989), 698-715.

15747 **Silva, Golbery do Couto e.** "O Brasil e a Defesa do Ocidente." *A Defesa Nacional*. 534 (Jan. 1959), 87-88; 535 (Fev., 1959), 123-128; 536 (Marco, 1959), 133-134; 537 (Abril, 1959), 105-114; 538 (Maio, 1959), 139-141.

15748 **Silva, Golbery do Couto e.** "O Problema vital da seguranca nacional." *A Defesa Nacional*, 539 (Junho, 1959), 129-135.

15749 **Simmons, David A.** "Militarization of the Caribbean: Concerns for National & Regional Security." *International Journal*, 40, No. 2 (Spring, 1985), 348-376.

15750 **Snyder, Richard C., and Paige, Glenn D.** "The United States Decision to Resist Aggression in Korea: The Application of an Analytical Scheme." *Administrative Science Quarterly*, 3, No. 3 (September, 1958), 341-378.

15751 **Soppelsa, J.** "Le Complexe Militaro-Industriel Americain. Etude Geographique." *L'Information Geographique*, 44, No. 3 (1980), 97-103.

15752 **Sprout, Harold H.** "America's Strategy in World Politics." *American Political Science Review*, 36, No. 5 (October, 1942), 956-958.

15753 **Staley, E.** "America's Strategy in World Politics." *American Economic Review*, 32, No. 2 (May, 1942), 457-461.

15754 **Stubbs, B.B.** "The US Coast Guard: A Unique Instrument of US National Security." *Marine Policy*, 18, No. 6 (November, 1994), 506-520.

15755 **Sun, James M.S.** "Monte Carlo Simulation of the Survivability of Minutemen Deployed in a Soft-Rock Geophysical Environment." *New Mexico Journal of Science*, 19, No. 1 (June, 1979), 15-22.

15756 **Tracy, Nicholas.** "Why does Canada want Nuclear Aubmarines?" *International Journal*, 43, No. 3 (Summer, 1988), 499-518.

15757 **Travassos, Mario.** "Estrutura geo-militar do Brasil." *Cultura Politica*, 1, No. 9 (September, 1941), 17-25.

15758 **Trubowitz, Peter, and Roberts, Brian E.** "Regional Interests and the Reagan Military Buildup." *Regional Studies* [Abingdon], 26, No. 6 (1991), 555-567.

15759 **Tubbs, William B.,** comp. "A Bibliography of Illinois Civil War Regimental Sources in the Illinois State Historical Library." *Illinois Historical Journal*, 87, No. 3 (Autumn, 1994), 185-232.

15760 **Wickham-Crowley, Timothy P.** "Terror and Guerrilla Warfare in Latin America, 1956-1970." *Comparative Studies in Society and History*, 32, No. 2 (April, 1990), 201-237.

15761 **Wolf, Barney, and Cox, Joseph C.** "Military Prime Contracts and Taxes in the New York Metropolitan Region: A Short-Run Analysis. *Regional Studies*, 23, No. 3 (June, 1989), 241-251.

15762 "Watch Morocco, Political Trouble Brewing Behind U.S. Air Bases." Reprint: *Fortune*, 44, No. 3 (September, 1951), 95+.

15763 **Wickoff, Theodore.** "A localizacao estrategica da America do sul." *Military Review*, 36, No. 4 (April, 1956), 14-18.

15764 **Winkler, A.M.** "A 40-year History of Civil Defense." *Bulletin of the Atomic Scientists*, 40, No. 6 (June-July, 1984), 16-22.

15765 **Wynne, M.A.** "The Long-Run Effects of a Permanent Change in Defense Purchases." *Federal Reserve Bank of Dallas: Economic Review*, (January, 1991), 1-16.

15766 **Zeigler, D.J.** "Evacuation from a Nuclear Attack: Prospects for Population Protection in Hampton Roads." *Virginia Social Science Journal*, 21, No. 1 (April, 1986), 22-31.

15767 **Zhu, Liping.** "From Ruins to a National Monument: Fort Union, New Mexico, 1891-1956." *New Mexico Historical Review* [Albuquerque], 69, No. 1 (January, 1994), 1-17.

ASIA

Books

15768 **Ahrari, Mohammed E., and Noyes, James H.,** eds. *The Persian Gulf After the Cold War.* Westport: Praeger Publishers, 1993.

15769 **Alpher, Joseph,** ed. *War in the Gulf: Implications for Israel.* Boulder: Westview Press, 1992.

15770 **Amos, Deborah.** *Lines in the Sand: Desert Storm and the Remaking of the Arab World.* New York: Simon & Schuster, 1992.

15771 **Anwar, Raja.** *The Tragedy of Afghanistan: A First-Hand Account.* London: Verso, 1988.

15772 **Arnold, Anthony.** *Afghanistan: The Soviet Invasion in Perspective.* Stanford, California: Hoover Institution Press, 1985.

15773 **Atkinson, Rick.** *Crusade: The Untold Story of the Persian Gulf War.* Boston: Houghton Mifflin Company, 1993.

15774 **Bandyopadhyaya, Jayantanuja, and Others,** eds. *Dimensions of Strategy; Some Indian Perspectives (School of International Relations and Strategic Studies).* New Delhi: Minerva, 1989.

15775 **Barker, A.J.** *Suez: The Seven Day War.* New York: Praeger, 1965.

15776 **Blackwell, James.** *Thunder in the Desert: The Strategy and Tactics of the Persian Gulf War.* New York: Bantam Books, 1991.

15777 **Bresheeth, Haim, and Yuval-Davis, Nira,** eds. *The Gulf War and the New World Order.* London: Zed Books, Ltd., 1991.

15778 **Brigot, Andre, and Roy, Oliver.** *The War in Afghanistan: An Account and Analysis of the Country.* New York: Harvester-Wheatsheaf, 1988.

15779 **Brown, T. Louise.** *War and Aftermath in Vietnam.* London: Routledge, 1991.

15780 **Bulloch, John, and Morris, Harvey.** *Saddam's War: The Origins of the Kuwait Conflict and the International Response.* London: Faber and Faber, 1991.

15781 **Campbell, J.C.** *Defense of the Middle East, Problems of American Policy.* New York: Praeger, 1960.

15782 **Chapin, William.** *The Asian Balance of Power: An American View.* Adelphi Paper No. 35. London: Institute for Strategic Studies, April, 1967.

15783 **Chisti, Raiz Ali.** *Betrayals of Another Kind: Islam, Democracy and the Army in Pakistan.* Karachi: Tricolor Publishers, 1989.

15784 **Choudhury, Golam W.** *Brezhnev's Collective Security Plan for Asia.* Durham: North Carolina Central University, Center for Strategic and International Studies, 1976.

15785 **Chubi, Chahram.** *Soviet Policy Towards Iran and the Gulf."* Adelphi Papers. No. 157. London: Institute for Strategic Studies, Spring, 1980.

15786 **Collins, Joseph J.** *The Soviet Invasion of Afghanistan: A Study in the Use of Force in Soviet Foreign Policy.* Lexington, Massachusetts: Lexington Books, 1986.

15787 **Dawisha, Adud.** *Saudi Arabia's Search for Security.* Adelphi Papers. No. 158. London: Institute for Strategic Studies, Winter, 1979-1980.

15788 **DePotter, Aimee.** *Postwar Reconstruction in the Far East; A Selective Bibliography.* Institute of Pacific Relations, 8th Conference, Mont Tremblant, Quebec, Canada, December, 1942. American Council Paper No. 9. New York: American Council, Institute of Pacific Relations, 1942.

15789 **Dil, Shaheen, Fatemah.** *Great Power Interaction in Local Crisis: Soviet, American, and Chinese Participation in South Asia.* Princeton, New Jersey: Princeton University, Ph.D., 1974.

15790 **Donaldson, Robert Herschel.** *The Soviet Approach to India: Doctrinal Assessment and Operational Strategy.* Cambridge, Massachusetts: Harvard University, Ph.D., 1969.

15791 **Donaldson, Robert Herschel.** *Soviet Policy Toward India: Ideology and Strategy.* Cambridge, Massachusetts: Harvard University Press, 1974.

15792 **Doran, Charles F., and Buck, Stephen W.,** eds. *The Gulf, Energy, and Global Security: Political and Economic Issues.* Boulder, Colorado: Lynne Rienner Publishers, 1991.

15793 **Drifte, Reinhard.** *Japan's Rise to International Responsibilities: The Case of Arms Control.* London: The Athlone Press, 1990.

15794 **Elegant, Robert S.** *The Dragon's Seed: Peking and Overseas Chinese.* New York: St. Martin's Press, 1959.

15795 **Fall, B.** *The Two Viet-nams. A Political and Military Analysis.* London: Pall Mall Press, 1967.

15796 **Farr, Grant M.,** and **Merriam, John G.,** eds. *Afghan Resistance: The Politics of Survival.* Boulder, Colorado: Westview Press, 1987.

15797 **Faour, Muhammad.** *The Arab World After Desert Storm.* Washington, DC: United States Institute of Peace Press, 1993.

15798 **Feldman, Shai,** and **Rechnitz-Kijner, Heda.** *Deceptions Consensus, and War: Israel and Lebanon.* Tel Aviv: Tel Aviv University, 1984.

15799 **Fitzgerald, F.** *Fire in the Lake: THe Vietnamese and the Americans in Vietnam.* Boston, Massachusetts: Little Brown, 1972.

15800 **Freedman, Robert O.,** ed. *The Middle East After Iraq's Invasion of Kuwait.* Gainesville: University Press of Florida, 1993.

15801 **Gall, Sandy.** *Afghanistan: Agony of a Nation.* London: The Bodley Heat, 1988.

15802 **Girardet, Edward.** *Afghanistan: The Soviet War.* London: Croom Helm, 1985.

15803 **Greene, Fred,** ed. *The Philippines Bases: Negotiating for the Future—American and Philippine Perspective.* New York: Council on Foreign Relations Press, 1988.

15804 **Gresh, Alain,** and **Vidal, Dominique.** *The Middle East: War Without End?* Translated by Simon Medaney with Henriette Bardel. London: Lawrence and Wishart, 1988.

15805 **Gupta, Rakesh,** ed. *India's Security Problems in the Nineties.* New Delhi: Patriot, 1989.

15806 **Hahskar, P.N.,** ed. *Nehru's Vision of Peace and Security in Nuclear Age.* New Delhi: Patriot, 1989.

15807 **Hale, William.** *Turkish Politics and the Military.* London: Routledge, 1994.

15808 **Hallion, Richard P.** *Storm Over Iraq: Air Power and the Gulf War.* Washington D.C.: Smithsonian Institution Press, 1992.

15809 **Harkabi, Yehoshafat.** *Israel's Fateful Decisions.* Translated by Lenn Schramm. London: L.B. Tauris, 1986.

15810 **Harkabi, Yehoshafat.** *Israel's Fateful Hour.* Translated from the Hebrew by Lenn Schramm. New York: Harper & Row, 1988.

15811 **Hauner, Milan,** and **Canfield, Robert L.,** eds. *Afghanistan and the Soviet Union: Collision and Transformation.* Boulder, Colorado: Westview Press, 1989.

15812 **Hiro, Dilip.** *Desert Shield to Desert Storm: The Second Gulf War.* New York: Routledge, 1992.

15813 **Holstein, James J.** *The Japanese Power Game: What It Means for America.* New York: Charles Scribner's Sons, 1990.

15814 **Hoyt, Edwin P.** *The Day the Chinese Attacked: Korea, 1950: The Story of the Failure of America's China Policy.* New York: McGraw-Hill Publishing Co., 1990.

15815 **Hunter, Robert T.** *The Soviet Dilemma in the Middle East.* Part I. Problems of Commitment. London: Institute for Strategic Problems, 1969.

15816 **Hutchison, E.H.** *Violent Truce; A Military Observer Looks at the Arab-Israeli Conflict, 1951-1955.* New York: Devin-Adair, 1956.

15817 **Hyman, Anthony.** *Afghanistan Under Soviet Domination, 1964-1981.* London: MacMillan, 1982.

15818 **Inbar, Efraim.** *War and Peace in Israeli Politics: Labor Party Positions on National Security.* Boulder, Colorado: Lynne Rienner Publishers, 1991.

15819 **Jalal, Ayesha.** *The State of Martial Rule: The Origins of Pakistan's Political Economy of Defence.* Cambridge: Cambridge University Press, 1990.

15820 **Joo-Dock, J.** *Geo-Strategy in the South China Sea Basin.* Singapore: Singapore University Press, 1979.

15821 **Joyner, Christopher C.,** ed. *The Persian Gulf War: Lessons for Strategy, Law, and Diplomacy.* New York: Greenwood Press, 1990.

15822 **Karsh, Efraim,** ed. *The Iran-Iraq War: Impact and Implications.* Houndmills: Macmillan, 1989.

15823 **Keeton, George W.** *Some Factors in a Far Eastern Peace Settlement.* Institute of Pacific Relations, 8th Conference, Mont Tremblant, Quebec, Canada, December, 1942. Secretariat Paper No. 6. New York: International Secretariat, Institute of Pacific Relations, 1942.

15824 **Kennedy, D.F.** *The Security of Southern Asia.* London: Institute for Strategic Studies, 1965.

15825 **Khalidi, W.** *Conflict and Violence in Lebanon.* Cambridge, Massachusetts: Harvard University Press, 1979.

15826 **Kihl, Young Whan,** and **Grinter, Lawrence E.,** eds. *Security, Strategy, and Pacific Responses in the Pacific Rin.* Boulder, Colorado: Lynne Rienner Publishers, 1989.

15827 **Klieman, Aaron S.** *Israel and the World After 40 Years.* Washington, D.C.: Pergamon-Brassey's International Defense Publishers, 1990.

15828 **Kodikara, Shelton,** ed. *South Asian Strategic Issues: Sri Lankan Perspectives.* New Delhi: Sage Publications, 1990.

15829 **Kuehl, Kenneth J.** Patterns of Foreign Influence on Korean Settlements Near Military Installations. Honolulu: University of Hawaii, Master's Thesis, 1976.

15830 **Kureishy, K.U.** *Pakistan: A Geomilitary Study.* Chandigash: University of the Punjab, Ph.D., 1955.

15831 **Laqueur, W.,** ed. *The Israel-Arab Reader - A Documentary History of the Middle East Conflict,* Revised Edition. London, New York, Toronto: Bantam Books, 1970.

15832 **Laqueur, W.,** ed. *The Road to War - The Origin and Aftermath of the Arab-Israeli Conflict 1967-68.* London: Penguin, 1970.

15833 **Lim Joo-Jock.** *Territorial Power Domains, Southeast Asia and China.* Singapore, Regional Strategic Programme, Institute of Southeast Asian Studies. Canberra: Strategic and Defense Studies Centre, Research School of Pacific Studies, Australian National University.

15834 **Lyon, Peter.** *War and Peace in South-east Asia.* London: R.I.I.A., 1969.

15835 **Manguo, Ralph H.,** ed. *Afghan Alternatives: Issues, Options, & Policies.* New Brunswick: Transaction Books, 1985.

15836 **Marwah, Onkar,** and **Pollack, Jonathan D.,** eds. *Military Power and Policy in Asian States: China, India and Japan.* Boulder, Colorado: Westview Press, 1980.

15837 **Menashri, David.** *Iran: A Decade of War and Revolution.* New York: Holmes and Meier, 1990.

15838 *Military Situation in the Far East.* 4 volumes. Washington, D.C.: U.S. Senate, Armed Services and Foreign Relations Committees, 82d Congress, 1st Session, 1951.

15839 **Monroe, Elizabeth.** *The Changing Balance of Power in the Persian Gulf: The Report of an International Seminar at the Center for Mediterranean Studies, Rome,* June 26th to July 1st, 1972. New York: American Universities Field Staff, 1972.

15840 **Morris, Benny.** *Israel's Border War, 1949-1956: Arab Infiltration, Israeli Retaliation, and the Countdown to the Suez War.* Oxford: Clarendon Press, 1993.

15841 **Naga, K.S.,** and **Sharma, Gautam,** eds. *India's Security; Super Power Threat.* New Delhi: Reliance, 1990.

15842 **Nath, Rajendra.** *Military Leadership in India; Vedic Period to Indo-Pak Wars.* New Delhi: Lancers, 1990.

15843 **Newman, David.** *Civilian Settlement and Military Presence as Alternative Strategies of Territorial Control in the Arab-Israel Conflict.* Ben Gurion University, Ph.D., 1988.

15844 **O'Ballance, Edgar.** *The Cyanide War: Tamil Insurrection in Sri Lanka.* London: Brassey's, 1989.

15845 **Office of the Chief of Naval Operations.** *Ryukyu (Loochoo) Islands.* (Civil Affairs Handbook). OPNAV 13-31. Washington, D.C.: U.S. Navy Department, 1944.

15846 **Owen, R.,** ed. *Essays on the Crisis in Lebanon.* London: Ithaca Press, 1976.

15847 **Palmer, Bruce, Jr.** *The 25-Year War: America's Military Role in Vietnam.* Lexington: University Press of Kentucky, 1984.

15848 **Pannikar, K.M.** *India and the Indian Ocean; an Essay on the Influence of Sea Power on Indian History.* London: Allen & Unwin, 1945.

15849 **Pannikar, K.M.** *Problems of Indian Defense.* Bombay: Asia Publishing House, 1960.

15850 **Patel, H.M.** *The Defense of India.* Poona: Gokhle Institute of Politics and Economics, 1963.

15851 **Peffer, Nathaniel.** *Basis for Peace in the Far East.* New York: Harper and Brothers, 1942.

15852 **Pelletiere, Stephen C.** *The Iran-Iraq War: Chaos in a Vacuum.* New York: Praeger Publishers, 1992.

15853 **Platt, Alan,** ed. *Arms Control and Confidence Building in the Middle East.* Washington, DC: United States Institute of Peace Press, 1992.

15854 **Porter, D. Gareth.** *Interest, Alliance, and Military Aid: The Case of Pakistan.* Chicago, Illinois: University of Chicago, Master's Thesis, 1966.

15855 **Pryer, Melvyn.** *A View from the Rimland: An Appraisal of Soviet Interests and Involvement in the Gulf.* Durham: University of North Carolina. Centre for Middle Eastern and Islamic Studies, Occasional Paper Series, No. 8, 1981.

15856 **Race, J.** *War Comes to Long An Revolutionary Conflict in a Vietnamese Province.* Berkeley: University of California Press, 1972.

15857 **Rajaee, Farhang,** ed. *The Iran-Iraq War: The Politics of Aggression.* Gainesville: University Press of Florida, 1993.

15858 **Riley, R.C.** *The Growth of Southsea as a Naval Satellite and Victorian Resort,* Portsmouth Paper No. 16. Portsmouth, England: Portsmouth City Council, 1972.

15859 **Rosenne, Sh.** *Israel's Armistice Agreements with the Arab States.* Tel-Aviv, International Law Association, Israeli Branch, 1951.

15860 **Sakamoto, Yoshikazu,** ed. *Asia: Militarization and Regional Conflict.* Tokyo: United Nations University, 1988.

15861 **Samuels, Marwyn S.** *Contest for the South China Sea.* New York and London: Methuen, 1982.

15862 **Segal, G.,** ed. *Arms Control in Asia.* London: Macmillan, 1986.

15863 **Sen, Surendra Nath.** *The Military System of the Marathas.* Bombay: Longmans, 1958.

15864 **Shah, Shafqat Ali.** *The Political and Strategic Foundations of International Arms Transfers: A Case Study of American Arms Supplies to and Purchase by Iran and Saudi Arabia, 1968-76.* Charlottesville: University of Virginia, Ph.D., 1978.

15865 **Shaleu, Arych.** *The West Bank: Line of Defense.* New York: Praeger, 1985.

15866 **Sharma, V.B.L.** *Strategic Aspects of India's Foreign Policy.* London: London School of Economics, University of London, Ph.D., 1958.

15867 **Sicker, Martin.** *Israel's Quest for Security.* New York: Praeger, 1989.

15868 **Stone, J.** *The Middle East Under Cease-Fire.* Sydney: A Bridge Publication, 1967.

15869 **Stone, J.** *No Peace - No War in the Middle East.* Sydney: Maitland Publications, 1970.

15870 **Stone, J.** *Peace in the Middle East.* Sydney: A Bridge Publication, 1967.

15871 **Tan Tsou.** *China's Policies in Asia and America's Alternatives.* Chicago, Illinois: University of Chicago Press, 1968.

15872 **Thomas, Methew,** ed. *Indian Defence Review, 1989.* New Delhi: Lancer, 1989.

15873 **Tondel, L.M.** *The Southeast Asia Crisis.* Dobbs Ferry: Oceana Publications, 1966.

15874 **Toni, Y.T.** *Spatial Aspects of Justice in the Middle East Peace Processes.* Occasional Paper No. 3. Sudbury, Ontario : Department of Geography, Laurentian University, 1979.

15875 **Urban, Mark.** *War in Afghanistan.* Houndmills: Macmillan, 1988.

15876 **U.S. Department of the Army.** *South Asia: A Strategic Survey.* Washington, D.C.: Government Printing Press, 1966.

15877 **Vertzberger, Yaacov Y.I.** *China's Southwestern Strategy: Encirclement and Counterencirclement.* New York: Praeger, 1985.

15878 **Wilcox, Wayne Ayres.** *Nuclear Weapon Options and the Strategic Environment in South Asia: Arms Control Implications for India.* Santa Monica: Southern California Arms Control and Foreign Policy Seminar, 1972.

15879 **Yaniv, Avner,** ed. *National Security and Democracy in Israel.* Boulder: Lynne Rienner Publishers, 1993.

15880 **Zimmerman, Cullen Caswell.** *The Indian Army, 1917-1941: A Study in the Control of a Native Army.* Durham, North Carolina: Duke University, Master's Thesis, 1968.

Journals

15881 **Abraham, Itty.** "India's 'Strategic Enclave': Civilian Scientists and Military Technologies." *Armed Forces and Society* [New Brunswich], 18, No. 2 (Winter, 1992), 231-252.

15882 **Adelman, Jonathan R.** "The Soviet and Chinese Armies: Their Post-Civil War Roles." *Survey,* 24, No. 1 (106) (Winter, 1979), 57-81.

15883 **Ahmad, Samina.** "Pakistan's Proposal for a Nuclear-Weapon-Free Zone in South Asia." *Pakistan Horizon,* 32, Nos. 1 and 2 (1st and 2nd Quarters, 1979), 92-141.

15884 **Ahrari, M.E.,** and **Khalidi, Omar.** "The Emerging Shape of Strategic Competition in the Persian Gulf." *Strategic Review* [Washington, DC], 18, No. 4 (Fall, 1990), 23-29.

15885 **Alagappa, Muthiah.** "The Dynamics of International Security in Southeast Asia: Change and Continuity." *Australian Journal of International Affairs* [Canberra], 45, No. 1 (May, 1991), 1-37.

15886 **Algappa, Muthiah.** "A Nuclear-Weapons-Free Zone in Southeast Asia: Problems and Prospects." *Australian Outlook,* 41, No. 3 (December, 1987), 173-180.

15887 **Ali, Mehrunnisa.** "The Impact of the Iran-Iraq War." *Pakistan Horizon,* 33, No. 4 (Fourth Quarter, 1980), 21-34.

15888 **Allan, Pierrre, and Stahel, Albert A.** "Tribal Guerrilla Warfare Against a Colonial Power: Analyzing the War in Afghanistan." *The Journal of Conflict Resolution,* 27, No. 1 (December, 1983), 560-617.

15889 **Allen, Robert C.** "Regional Security in the Persian Gulf." *Military Review,* 63, No. 12 (December, 1983), 2-11.

15890 **Amin, Tahir.** "Afghan Resistance: Past, Present, and Future." *Asian Survey,* 24, No. 4 (April, 1984), 373-399.

15891 **Anderson, Walter K.** "Soviets in the Indian Ocean: Much Ado About Something, But What?" *Asian Survey,* 24, No. 9 (September, 1984), 910-930.

15892 "Arabia Felix and the Indian Ocean, A Study of Political Strategy." *The Round Table,* 216, No. 3 (September, 1964), 343-353.

15893 **Baldry, John.** "The Yamani Island of Kamaran During the Napoleonic Wars." *Middle Eastern Studies,* 16, No. 3 (October, 1980), 246-266.

15894 **Baldwin, Hanson W.** "Strategy of the Middle East." *Foreign Affairs,* 35, No. 4 (July, 1957), 655-665.

15895 **Ball, Desmond.** "Arms and Affluence: Military Acquisitions in the Asia-Pacific Region." *International Security* [Cambridge, MA], 18, No. 3 (Winter, 1993-94), 78-112.

15896 **Balta, Paul.** "La Nouvelle Crise du Golfe et Ses Antecedents." *Herodote* [Paris], No. 58-59 (Juillet-Decembre, 1990), 46-58.

15897 **Banks, Mike.** "Aden: Strategic Crossroads." *The Geographical Magazine,* 37, No. 5 (September, 1964), 359-371.

15898 **Baram, Amatzia.** "Israeli Deterrence, Iraqi Responses." *Orbis* [Philadelphia], 36, No. 3 (Summer, 1992), 397-409.

15899 **Barr, John.** "The Ryuku Islands: A U.S. Bastion in the Pacific." *The World Today,* 17, No. 5 (May, 1961), 187-197.

15900 **Bennett, Andrew; Lepgold, Joseph; and Unger, Danny.** "Burden-Sharing in the Persian Gulf War." *International Organization* [Cambridge,

MA], 48, No. 1 (Winter, 1994), 39-75.

15901 **Beres, Louis Rene.** "Israeli Security in a Changing World." *Strategic Review* [Washington, DC], 18, No. 4 (Flal, 1990), 10-22.

15902 **Beugel, Ernest van der.** "After Afghanistan." *Survival,* 22, No. 6 (November-December, 1980), 242-7.

15903 **Bhagat, G.** "Retrenchment of American Power and Regionalism in Asia." *Indian Political Science Review,* 8, No. 2 (July, 1974), 129-150.

15904 **Bhattacharyya, N.N.** "Geopolitical Setting of North East India." *The Journal of North East India Geographical Society,* 15, Nosd. 1 and 2 (1984), 39-41.

15905 **Blumberg, Herbert H., and French, Christopher C.,** eds. *The Persian Gulf War: Views from the Social and Behavioral Sciences.* Lanham: University Press of America, 1994.

15906 **Bou-Nacklie, N.E.** "The 1941 Invasion of Syria and Lebanon: The Role of the Local Paramilitary." *Middle Eastern Studies,* 30, No. 3 (July, 1994), 512-529.

15907 **Brown, Frederick Z.** "Security Issues in Southeast Asia." *The Academy of Political Proceedings* [New York], 38, No. 2 (1991), 120-130.

15908 **Brown, James.** "The Military and Society: The Turkish Case." *Middle Eastern Studies,* 25, No. 3 (July, 1989), 387-404.

15909 **Bunbongkarn, Suchit.** "Thailand in 1991: Coping with Military Guardianship." *Asian Survey* [Berkeley], 32, No. 2 (February, 1992), 131-139.

15910 **Camp, Glen D.** "Greek-Turkish Conflict Over Cyprus." *Political Science Quarterly,* 95, No. 1 (Spring, 1980), 43-70.

15911 **Carrington, Lord.** "A World Changed by the Soviet Invasion of Afghanistan." *Atlantic Community Quarterly,* 18, No. 1 (Spring, 1980), 20-26.

15912 **Casper, Gretchen.** "Theories of Military Intervention in the Third World: Lessons from the Philippines." *Armed Forces and Society* [New Brunswick], 17, No. 2 (Winter, 1991), 191-210.

15913 **Chang, Pao-Min.** "Some Reflections on the Sino-Vietnamese Conflict over Kampuchea." *International Affairs,* 59, No. 3 (Summer, 1983), 381-389.

15914 "China and the Asian Triangle; An Appraisal of the Sino-Indian Border War." *India Quarterly*, 23, No. 2 (April-June, 1967), 87-105.

15915 **Choi Chang-Yoon.** "Korea: Security and Strategic Issues." *Asian Survey*, 20, No. 11 (November, 1980), 1123-1139.

15916 **Chubin, Shahram.** "Post-War Gulf Security." *Survival* [London], 33, No. 2 (March/April, 1991), 140-157.

15917 **Cioffi-Revilla, Claudio.** "On the Unlikely Magnitude, Extent, and Duration of an Iraq-UN War." *Journal of Conflict Resolution* [Newbur Park], 35, No. 3 (September, 1991), 387-411.

15918 **Clark, Ian.** "Soviet Conceptions of Asian Security: From Balance 'Between' to Balance Within." *Pacific Community*, 7, No. 1 (January, 1976), 162-78.

15919 **Chopra, Maharaj K.** "The Himalayan Border War: An Indian Military Review." *Military Review*, 43, No. 5 (May, 1963), 8-16.

15920 **Columbe, Marcel.** "LaTurquie, les etats arabes et la defense du Moyen-Orient. *Politique Etrangere*, 16e annee, No. 4-5 (Aout-Decembre, 1951), 365-378.

15921 **Corning, Gregory P.** "The Philippine Bases and U.S. Pacific Strategy." *Pacific Affairs*, 63, No. 1 (Spring, 1990), 6-23.

15922 **Cottam, Richard.** "The Iran-Iraq War." *Current History*, 83, No. 489 (January, 1984), 9-12 and 40-41.

15923 **Cummins, Ian.** "Afghanistan: 'The Great Game' or the Domino Theory." *Australian Outlook*, 34, No. 2 (August, 1980), 141-147.

15924 **Danziger, Raphael.** "The Naval Race in the Persian Gulf." *U.S. Naval Institute Proceedings*, 108, No. 3 (March, 1982), 92-98.

15925 **Da Lage, Olivier.** "L'Invasion du Koweit: Quelques Reperes." *Herodote* [Paris], No. 58-59 (Juillet-Decembre, 1990), 29-45.

15926 **Denker, Debra.** "Along Afghanistan's War-Torn Frontier." *National Geographic*, 167, No. 6 (June, 1985), 772-797.

15927 **Desai, Raj, and Eckstein, Harry.** "Insurgency: The Transofrmation of Peasant Rebellion." *World Politics* [Baltimore], 42, No. 4 (July, 1990), 441-465.

15928 **Dinstein, Yoram.** "The Legal Issues of 'Para-War' and Peace in the Middle East." *St. John's Law Review*, 44, No. 2 (October, 1969), 466-482.

15929 **Donaldson, Robert H.** "India: The Soviet Stake in Stability." *Asian Survey*, 12, No. 6 (June, 1972), 475-492.

15930 **Dowdy, William L., and Trood, Russell B.** "The Indian Ocean: An Emerging Geostrategic Region." *International Journal*, 38, No. 3 (Summer, 1983), 432-458.

15931 **Dreyer, June Teufel.** "Deng Xiaoping and Modernization of the Chinese Military." *Armed Forces and Society*, 14, No. 2 (Winter, 1988), 215-231.

15932 **Dreyer, June Teufel.** "The Military in China." *Current History* [Philadelphia], 89, No. 548 (September, 1990), 261-264, 277-279.

15933 **Dunn, Keith A.** "Constraints on the USSR in Southwest Asia: A Military Analysis." *Orbis*, 25, No. 3 (Fall, 1981), 607-629.

15934 **Dunn, Keith A.** "Soviet Strategy, Opportunities and Constraints in Southwester Asia." *Soviet Union/Sovietique Union*, 11, Part 2 (1984), 182-211.

15935 **Dupree, Nancy Hatch.** "The Question of Jaladabad During the First Anglo-Afghan War." *Asian Affairs, Journal of the Royal Asian Society*, 62, Part 1 (February, 1975), 44-60.

15936 **Eberstadt, Nicholas, and Banister, Judith.** "Military Buildup in the DPRK: Some New Indications from North Korean Data." *Asian Survey* [Berkeley], 31, No. 11 (November, 1991), 1095-1115.

15937 **Edwards, Michael.** "India, Pakistan and Nuclear Weapons." *International Affairs*, 43, No. 4 (October, 1967), 655-663.

15938 **Eiland, Michael D.** "Military Modernization and China's Economy." *Asian Survey*, 17, No. 12 (December, 1977), 1143-1157.

15939 **Elegant, Robert S.** "China, the US and Soviet Expansion." *Commentary*, 61, No. 2 (February, 1976), 39-46.

15940 **Elits, Hermann F.** "Security Considerations in the Persian Gulf." *International Security*, 5, No. 2 (Fall, 1980), 79-113.

15941 **Fairbank, John K.** "The Chinese World Order." *Encounter*, 27, No. 6 (December, 1966), 14-20.

15942 **Farago, Ladislas.** "The Defenses North of India." *Asia*, 40, No. 5 (May, 1940), 243-246.

15943 **Farley, Jonathan.** "The Gulf War and the Littoral States." *The World Today*, 40, No. 7 (July, 1984), 269-276.

15944 Field, A.R. "Strategic Development in Sinkiang." *Foreign Affairs*, 39, No. 2 (January, 1961), 312-319.

15945 Fisher, Charles A. "The Chinese Threat to South East Asia: Fact or Fiction?" *Royal Central Asian Journal*, 51, No. 2 (April, 1964), 251-267.

15946 Fisher, Charles A. "The Vietnamese Problem in its Geographical Context." *Geographical Journal*, 131, No. 4 (December, 1965), 502-515.

15947 Forester, Richard. "Die strategische Lage Japans an der Kuste Asiens." *Zeitschrift der Gesellschaft fur Erdkunde zu Berlin*, Heft 9/10 (Dezember, 1942), 301-314.

15948 Foot, Rosemary. "The Sino-American Conflict in Korea: The U.S. Assessment of China's Ability to Intervene in the War." *Asian Affairs*, 14, Part II (June, 1983), 160-166.

15949 Freadman, Paul. "The Strategic Background to Middle East and African Policies." *Australian Outlook*, 3, No. 4 (December, 1949), 268-279.

15950 Freistetter, Franz. "The Battle in Afghanistan." *Strategic Review*, 9, No. 1 (Winter, 1981), 36-43.

15951 Friedgut, Theodore H. "The Middle East in Soviet Global Strategy." *Jerusalem Journal of International Relations*, 5, No. 1 (Fall, 1980), 66-93.

15952 Fromkin, David. "The Great Game in Asia." *Foreign Affairs*, 58, No. 4 (Spring, 1980), 936-951.

15953 Gallagher, Joseph P. "China's Military Industrial Complex: Its Approach to the Acquisition of Modern Military Technology." *Asian Survey*, 27, No. 9 (September, 1987), 991-1002.

15954 Garrett, W.E. "Mountaintop War in Remote Ladakh." *National Geographic Magazine*, 123, No. 5 (May, 1963), 664-687.

15955 Garver, John W. "China-India Rivalry in Nepal: The Clash Over Chinese Arms Sales." *Asian Survey* [Berkeley], 31, No. 10 (October, 1991), 956-975.

15956 Gelich, Fernando. "Corea: sguardo geografico, politico e strategico; le operazioni militari, ammaestiamenti e deduzioni." *L'Universo*, Anno 30, N.S. (Settembre-Ottobre, 1950), 631-654.

15957 Gill, R. Bates. "Curbing Beijing's Arms Sales." *Orbis* [Philadelphia], 36, No. 3 (Summer, 1992), 379-396.

15958 Glubb, J.B. "Transjordan and the War." *Journal of the Royal Central Asian Society*, 32, Part 1 (January, 1945), 24-33.

15959 "Goa as a Naval Base." *Indian Review*, 64, No. 1 (March, 1965), 127-128.

15960 Godwin, Paul H.B. "Changing Concepts of Doctrine, Strategy and Operations in the Chinese People's Liberation Army 1978-87." *China Quarterly*, No. 112 (December, 1987), 572-590.

15961 Goddberg, Jacob. "The Saudi Military Buildup: Strategy and Risks." *Middle East Review*, 21, No. 3 (Spring, 1989).

15962 Goldman, Minton F. "Soviet Military Intervention in Afghanistan: Root & Causes." *Polity*, 16, No. 3 (Spring, 1984), 384-403.

15963 Gordon, Bernard K. "The Third Indochina Conflict." *Foreign Affairs*, 65, No. 1 (Fall, 1986), 66-85.

15964 Grayson, Kirk. "Strategic Communications in the Middle East." *Foreign Affairs*, 20, No. 4 (July, 1942), 762-766.

15965 Griffith, William G. "Super-Power Relations after Afghanistan." *Survival*, 22, No. 4 (July-August, 1980), 18-24.

15966 Gupta, Amit. "The Indian Arms Industry: A Lumbering Giant?" *Asian Survey* [Berkeley], 30, No. 9 (September, 1990), 846-861.

15967 Ha, Joseph M., and Guinasso, John. "Japan's Rearmament Dilemma: The Paradox of Recovery." *Pacific Affairs*, 53, No. 2 (Summer, 1980), 245-269.

15968 Haines, Milan. "Seizing the Third Parallel: Geopolitics and the Soviet Advance into Central Asia." *Orbis*, 29, No. 1 (Spring, 1985), 5-31.

15969 Halliday, Fred. "The Gulf War and Its Aftermath: First Reflections." *International Affairs* [Cambridge], 67, No. 2 (April, 1991), 223-234.

15970 Harding, John, Sir. "The India and Pakistan Armies of Today." *Asian Review*, 51, No. 7 (July, 1955), 175-187.

15971 Hervouet, Gerard. "The Cambodian Conflict: The Difficulties of Intervention and Compromise." *Internaitonal Journal* [Toronto], 45, No. 2 (Spring, 1990), 258-291.

15972 Hewison, Kevin J. "Revolutionary Warfare in Thailand: A Comment." *Australian Outlook*, 34, No. 2 (August, 1980), 197-208.

15973 Hollis, Rosemary. "Israel's Search for Security." *Asian Affairs* [London], 22, Part 3 (October, 1991), 272-283.

15974 House, John. "War, Peace and Conflict Resolution: Towards and Indian Ocean Model." *Institute of British Geographers Transactions. New Series*, 9, No. 1 (1984), 3-21.

15975 Howland, Felix. "Sea Power and Central Asia." *United States Naval Institute Proceedings*, 66, No. 6 (June, 1940), 779-789.

15976 Hu, Shih. "China in Stalin's Grand Strategy." *Foreign Affairs*, 29, No. 1 (October, 1950), 11-40.

15977 Hyman, Anthony. "The Struggle for Afghanistan." *World Today*, 40, No. 7 (July, 1984), 276-284.

15978 Ikle, Fred Charles, and Nakanishi, Terumasa. "Japan's Grand Strategy." *Foreign Affairs* [New York], 69, No. 3 (Summer, 1990), 81-95.

15979 "India and the Cold War." *Middle East Journal*, 9, No. 3 (Summer, 1955), 256-268.

15980 Kaihara, Osamu. "Japan's Defense Structure and Capability." *Asia Pacific Community*, 12 (Spring, 1981), 52-61.

15981 Kamlin, Muhammad. "Russia in Afghanistan: 'Piercing a Window,' or Bursting the Floodgates?" *Asia Pacific Community*, 8 (Spring, 1980), 67-93.

15982 Karsh, Efraim. "Military Lessons of the Iran-Iraq War." *Orbis*, 33, No. 2 (Spring, 1989), 209-223.

15983 Karsh, Efraim. "Geopolitical Determinism: The Origins of the Iran-Iraq War." *Middle East Journal*, 44, No. 2 (Spring, 1990), 257-268.

15984 Katz, Mark N. "Yemeni Unity and Saudi Security." *Middle East Policy* [Washington, DC], 1, No. 1 (1992), 117-135.

15985 Katzenbach, Edward L. "Indo-China: A Military-Political Appreciation." *World Politics*, 4, No. 2 (January, 1952), 186-218.

15986 Kaul, Ravi. "The Indo-Pakistani War and the Changing Balance of Power in the Indian Ocean." *US Naval Institute Proceedings*, 98 (May, 1973), 172-95.

15987 Kelly, III, Clinton W.; Andriole, Stephen, J.; and Daly, Judith Ayres. "Computer-based Decision Analysis: An Application to a Middle East Evacuation Problem." *Jerusalem Journal of International Relations*, 5, No. 2 (Winter, 1981), 62-84.

15988 Kolb, Albert. "Der Fernostliche Konfliktraum Zwischen Sowjetunion, Volksrepublik China und Japan." *Geographische Rundschau*, Jahr. 35, Heft 11 (November, 1983), 544-552.

15989 Kureishy, K.U. "Strategical Importance of Kashmir to Pakistan." *Pakistan Geographical Review*, 6, No. 2 (July, 1951), 10-18.

15990 Lal, Baha. "The North-West Frontier in the First World War." *Asian Affairs*, 57, Part 1 (February, 1970), 29-37.

15991 Lawson, Fred H. "Syria's Intervention in the Lebanese Civil War, 1976: A Domestic Conflict Explanation." *International Organization*, 38, No. 3 (Summer, 1984), 451-458.

15992 Levi, Werner. "The Sino-Indian Border War." *Current History*, 45, No. 3 (September, 1963), 136-143.

15993 Lewis, John Wilson. "Communist China's Invasion of the Indian Frontier: The Framework of Motivation." *Current Scene*, 2, No. 7 (January 2, 1963), 1-10.

15994 Lewis, John Wilson, and Hua Di. "China's Ballistic Missile Programs: Technologies, Strategies, Goals." *International Security* [Cambridge, MA], 17, No. 2 (Fall, 1992), 5-40.

15995 Lewis, John Wilson, and Xue, Litai. "Strategic Weapons and Chinese Power: The Formation Years." *China Quarterly*, No. 112 (December, 1987), 541-554.

15996 Lho, Kyongsoo. "The Military Balance in the Korean Peninsula." *Asian Affairs*, 19, No. 1 (February, 1988), 36-44.

15997 Looney, Robert E. "Budgetary Dilemmas in Pakistan: Costs and Benefits of Sustained Defense Expenditures." *Asian Survey* [Berkeley], 34, No. 5 (May, 1994), 417-429.

15998 Loya, A. "Radio Propaganda of the United Arab Republic An Analysis." *Middle East Affairs*, 13, No. 4 (April, 1962), 98-110.

15999 Mackenzie, Richard. "Afghanistan's Uneasy Peace." *National Geographic* [Washington, DC], 184, No. 4 (October, 1993), 58-89.

16000 Maksoud, Clovis. "Twenty Years Later: The 1967 War and Its Aftermath." *American-Arab Affairs*, No. 21 (Summer, 1987), 27-39.

16001 Mandelbaum, Michael. "Israel's Security Dilemma." *Orbis*, 32, No. 3 (Summer, 1988), 355-368.

16002 Mansvetov, Fedor S. "Strategic Mongolia." *Asia and the Americas*, 45, No. 4 (April, 1945), 202-205.

16003 **Markusen, Ann,** and **Park, Sam Ock.** "The State as Industrial Locator nad District Builder: The Case of Changwon, South Korea." *Economic Geography,* 69, No. 2 (April, 1993), 157-181.

16004 **Marwah, Onkar.** "India's Military Intervention in East Pakistan, 1971-1972." *Modern Asian Studies,* 13, Part 4 (October, 1979), 549-580.

16005 **McColl, Robert W.** "A Political Geography of Revolution: China, Vietnam, and Thailand." *Journal of Conflict Resolution,* 11, No. 2 (June, 1967), 153-167.

16006 **Meron, Th.** "The Demilitarization of Mount Scopus: A Regime That Was." *Israel Law Review,* 3, No. 4 (October, 1968), 501-525.

16007 "The Middle East. I. Political and Strategic Position." *Bulletin of International News,* 17, No. 3 (February 10, 1940), 143-155.

16008 **Misra, K.P.** "Paramilitary Forces in India." *Armed Forces and Society,* 6, No. 3 (Spring, 1980), 371-388.

16009 **Monroe, Elizabeth.** "The West Bank, Palestinian or Israeli?" *Middle East Journal,* 31, No. 4 (Autumn, 1977), 397-412.

16010 **Murarka, Dev.** "Afghanistan: The Russian Intervention: A Moscow Analysis." *Round Table,* 282, No. 1 (April, 1981), 122-39.

16011 **Murphey, Rhoads.** "China and the Dominoes." *Asian Survey,* 6, No. 9 (September, 1966), 510-515.

16012 **Mylroie, Laurie A.** "After the Guns Fell Silent: Iraq in the Middle East." *Middle East Journal,* 43, No. 1 (Winter, 1989), 51-67.

16013 **Mylroie, Laurie.** "Why Saddam Hussein Invaded Kuwait." *Orbis* [Greenwich, CT], 37, No. 1 (Winter, 1993), 123-134.

16014 **Nagaoka, Masatoshi.** "Record and History of Operaetional Mapping Project in Japan Before and During the World War II: Viewed From the Indexes and Catalogues of the Army Land Survey and the General Staff Office of the Japanese Imperial Army." *Map* [Tokyo], 31, No. 4 (1993), 12-29.

16015 **Nazer, Hisham M.** "Saudi Arabia's Contribution to Security and Peace in the Middle East." *American-Arab Affairs,* 32 (Spring, 1990), 43-48.

16016 **Neumann, Robert G.** "The Iraq Crisis--and What Then?" *American-Arab Affairs* [Washington, DC], No. 34 (Fall, 1990), 1-7.

16017 "A New American Posture Toward Asia." *Annals of the American Academy of Political and Social Science,* 390 (July, 1970), 1-119. (Complete issue, multiple authors.)

16018 **Newell, Richard S.** "International Responses to the Afghanistan Crisis." *World Today,* 37, No. 5 (May, 1981), 172-81.

16019 **Newell, Richard S.** "Soviet Intervention in Afghanistan." *World Today,* 36, No. 7 (July, 1980), 250-258.

16020 **Niu, Sien-chong.** "New Strategic Outlook of the Indian Subcontinent." *NATO's Fifteen Nations,* 19 (October-November, 1974), 62-65.

16021 **Oren, Ido.** "The Indo-Pakistani Arms Competition: A Deductive and Statistical Analysis." *Journal of Conflict Resolution* [London], 38, No. 2 (June, 1994), 185-214.

16022 **Owen, R.P.** "The Rebellion in Dhofar - A Threat to Western Interests in the Gulf." *World Today,* 29, No. 6 (June, 1973), 266-272.

16023 **Page, Stephen.** "Patterns of Soviet Activity in Southwest Asia." *International Journal,* 41, No. 2 (Spring, 1986), 301-323.

16024 "Pakistan: America in the India Ocean." *Round Table,* 53, No. 214 (March, 1964), 175-179.

16025 **Parker, Richard B.** "The June 1967 War: Some Mysteries Explored." *The Middle East Journal* [Washington, DC], 46, No. 2 (Spring, 1992), 177-197.

16026 **Patterson, George N.** "The Five Fingers of China." *Indian Review,* 64, No. 2 (February, 1965), 57-59.

16027 **Pickard, Cyril, Sir.** "Afghanistan: Difficult Decisions for the West." *Round Table,* 278, No. 1 (April, 1980), 132-7.

16028 "Political Reconstruction in Postwar Burma." *Pacific Affairs,* 16, No. 3 (September, 1943), 277-300.

16029 **Porter, Gareth.** "Hanoi's Strategic Perspective and the Sino-Vietnamese Conflict." *Pacific Affairs,* 57, No. 1 (Spring, 1984), 7-25.

16030 **Price, Willard.** "Japan Faces Russia in Manchuria." *National Geographic Magazine,* 82, No. 5 (November, 1942), 603-634.

16031 **Rais, Rasul B.** "Afghanistan and Regional Security After the Cold War." *Problems of Communism* [Washington, DC], 41, No. 3 (May-June, 1992), 82-94.

16032 **Rand, Christopher C.** "Li Ch'uan and Chinese Military Thought." *Harvard Journal of Asiatic Studies,* 39, No. 1 (June, 1979), 107-137.

16033 **Rasler, Karen.** "Internationalized Civil War: A Dynamic Analysis of the Syrian Intervention in Lebanon." *Journal of Conflict Resolution*, 27, No. 3 (September, 1983), 421-456.

16034 **Rassam, Ghassan.** "How Geology Affects War in Iran, Iraq." *Geotimes*, 25, No. 12 (December, 1980), 20-22.

16035 **Razvi, Mujtaba.** "Politico-Strategic Impact of Soviet Intervention in Afghanistan." *Pakistan Horizon*, 33, No. 3 (Third Quarter, 1980), 12-30.

16036 **Robertson, Horace B., Jr.** "Interdiction of Iraqi Maritime Commerce in the 1990-1991 Persian Gulf Conflict." *Ocean Development and International Law*, 22, No. 3 (July-Sept., 1991), 289-299.

16037 **Role, Maurice.** "La Strategie Navale Japonaise Dans L'ocean Indien au Printempts 1942." *Guerres Mondiales et Conflits Contemporains* [Pais], No. 159 (Juillet, 1990), 53-71.

16038 **Rosen, Stephen Peter.** "Vietnam and the American Theory of Limited War." *International Security*, 7, No. 2 (Fall, 1982), 83-113.

16039 **Rostow, E.V.** "Legal Aspects in the Search for Peace in the Middle East." *Proceedings of the American Society of International Law*, 64 (1970), 1-64.

16040 **Rubinstein, Alvin Z.** "Perspectives on the Iran-Iraq War." *Orbis*, 29, No. 3 (Fall, 1985), 597-608.

16041 **Rubinstein, Alvin Z.** "Soviet Imperialism in Afghanistan." *Current History*, 79, No. 459 (October, 1980), 80-83 and 103-104.

16042 **Russo, Francis V., Jr.** "Neutrality at Sea in Transition: State Practice in the Gulf War as Emerging International Customary Law." *Ocean Development and International Law*, 19, No. 5 (1988), 381-400.

16043 **Said, E.** "Palestinians in the Aftermath of Beirut: A Preliminary Stocktaking." *Arab Studies Quarterly*, 4, No. 3 (Summer, 1982), 301-308.

16044 **Saint Brides, Lord.** "Afghanistan: The Empire that Plays to Win." *Orbis*, 24, No. 3 (Fall, 1980), 533-540.

16045 **Saint Brides, Lord.** "New Perspectives South of the Hindu Kush." *International Security*, 5, No. 3 (Winter, 1980-1), 164-170.

16046 **Sakanaka, Tomohisa.** "Military Threats and Japan's Defense Capability." *Asian Survey*, 20, No. 7 (July, 1980), 762-775.

16047 **Sayari, Sabri.** "Turkey: The Changing European Security Environment and the Gulf Crisis." *The Middle East Journal* [Bloomington], 46, No. 1 (Winter, 1992), 9-21.

16048 **Schiff, Ze'ev.** "The Spectre of Civil War in Israel." *Middle East Journal*, 39, No. 2 (Spring, 1985), 231-245.

16049 **Schweinfurth, Ulrich.** "Ladakhdas Streitobjekt Zwischen Indien und China." *Aussenpolitik*, 13, No. 9 (September, 1962), 626-629.

16050 **Scobell, Andrew.** "Why the People's Army Fired on the People: The Chinese Military and Tiananmen." *Armed Forces and Society* [New Brunswick], 18, No. 2 (Winter, 1992), 193-213.

16051 **Segal, G.** "China and Arms Control." *World Today*, 41, Nos. 8-9(Aug-Sept, 1985), 162-167.

16052 **Seshadri, B.** "Kalimpong, Strategic Indo-Sikkimese Border Town." *Canadian Geographical Journal*, 66, No. 1 (January, 1963), 18-23.

16053 **Shah, Shafqut Ali.** "Southwest Asia: Can the US Learn from Past Mistakes?" *Strategic Review*, 9, No. 1 (Winter, 1981), 27-35.

16054 **Shambaugh, David.** "China's Security Policy in the Post-Cold War Era." *Survival* [London], 34, No. 2 (Summer, 1992), 88-106.

16055 **Shapira, Amos.** "The Six-Day War and the Right of Self-Defence." *Israel Law Review*, 6, No. 1 (January, 1971), 65-80.

16056 **Shawcross, William.** "The Devastation of Cambodia: Millions die in Cockpit of International Rivalry." *Round Table*, 277, No. 1 (January, 1980), 33-38.

16057 **Sick, Gary.** "Trial by Error: Reflections on the Iran-Iraq War." *Middle East Journal*, 43, No. 2 (Spring, 1989), 230-245.

16058 **Singh, K.R.** "Conflict and Cooperation in the Gulf." *International Studies*, 15, No. 1 (October-December, 1976), 487-508.

16059 **Sirriyyeh, H.** "The Palestinian Armed Presence in Lebanon." In *Essays on the Crisis in Lebanon*, R. Owen, ed. London: Ithaca Press, 1976, 73-89.

16060 **Sliwinski, Marek.** "Afghanistan: The Decimation of a People." *Orbis*, 33, No. 1 (Winter, 1989), 39-56.

16061 **Slonim, Shlomo.** "Suez and the Soviets." *United States Naval Institute Proceedings*, 101, No. 4 (April, 1975), 37-41.

16062 **Smith, C.G.** "Israel After the June War." *Geography*, 53, Part 3 (July, 1968), 315-319.

16063 **Soffer, Arnon, and Minghi, Julian V.** "Israel's Security Landscapes: The Impact of Military Considerations on Land Uses." *Professional Geographer*, 38, No. 1 (February, 1986), 28-41.

16064 **Soustelle, Jacques.** "Indo-China and Korea: One Front." *Foreign Affairs*, 29, No. 1 (October, 1950), 56-66.

16065 **Spain, James W.** "Military Assistance to Pakistan." *American Political Science Review*, 48, No. 3 (September, 1954), 738-751.

16066 **Sterner, Michael.** "The Iran-Iraq War." *Foreign Affairs* , 63, No. 1 (Fall, 1984), 128-143.

16067 **Sullivan, Michael J., III.** "Reorientation of Indian Arms Control Policy, 1969-1972." *Asian Survey*, 13, No. 7 (July, 1973), 691-706.

16068 **Swann, Robert.** "Laos, Pawn in the Cold War." *Geographical Magazine*, 32, No. 8 (August, 1960), 365-375.

16069 **Tai Yong Yan.** "Maintaining the Military Districts: Civil-Military Integration and District Soldiers' Boards in the Punjab, 1919-1939." *Modern Asian Studies*, 28, Part 4 (October, 1994), 833-874.

16070 **Tarpey, John F.** "A Strategic Analysis of Northeast Asia and the Northwest Pacific." *United States Naval Institute Proceedings* , 106, No. 51, 927 (May, 1980), 106-125.

16071 **Thompson, Virginia.** "Undeclared War Along the Mekong." *Far Eastern Survey*, 10, No. 1 (January 29, 1941), 4-9.

16072 **Thompson, W.Scott.** "The Persian Gulf and the Correlation of Forces." *International Security*, 7, No. 1 (Summer, 1982), 157-180.

16073 **Townshend, Charles.** "The Defence of Palestine: Insurrection and Public Security, 1936-1939." *English Historical Review*, 103, No. 409 (October, 1988), 917-949.

16074 **Tretiak, Daniel.** "China's Vietnam War and Its Consequences." *China Quarter*, 80, No. 4 (December, 1979), 740-767.

16075 **Trice, Robert H.** "The American Elite Press and the Arab-Israeli Conflict." *Middle East Journal*, 33, No. 3 (Summer, 1979), 304-325.

16076 **Tucker, R.W.** "American Power and the Persian Gulf." *Commentary*, 70, No. 5 (November, 1980), 25-41.

16077 **Van der Kroef, Justus M.** "The Cambodian Conflict in Southeast Asia's Strategic Considerations." *Asian Profile,* 8, No. 2 (April, 1980), 181-196.

16078 **van der Kroef, Justus M.** "Kampuchea: Protracted Conflict, Suspended Compromise." *Asian Survey*, 24, No. 3 (March, 1984), 314-334.

16079 **Wanandi, Jusuf.** "Politico-Security Dimensions of Southeast Asia." *Asian Survey*, 17, No. 8 (August, 1977), 771-792.

16080 **Wang Chi-wu.** "Military Preparedness and Security Needs: Perceptions from the Republic of China on Taiwan." *Asian Survey*, 21, No. 6 (June, 1981), 651, 663.

16081 **Wang, Robert S.** "China's Evolving Strategic Doctrine." *Asian Survey*, 24, No. 10 (October, 1984), 1040-1055.

16082 **Weland, James.** "Misguided Intelligence: Japanese Military Intelligence Officers in the Manchurian Incident, September 1931." *The Journal of Military History* [Lexington], 58, No. 3 (July, 1994), 445-460.

16083 **Wright, Qu.** "The Middle East Crisis." *Proceedings of the American Society of International Law*, 64 (1970), 1-71.

16084 **Wrong, Denis H.; Harrington, Michael; Brand, H.; and Clark, Joseph.** "After Afghanistan." *Dissent*, 27, No. 2 (Spring, 1980), 135-143.

16085 **Yamiv, Avner, and Lieber, Robert J.** "Personal Whim or Strategic Imperative? The Israeli Invasion of Lebanon." *International Security*, 8, No. 2 (Fall, 1983), 117-142.

16086 **Yorke, Valerie.** "Security in the Gulf: A Strategy of Pre-emption." *World Today*, 36, No. 7 (July, 1980), 239-250.

16087 **Zagoria, Donald S.** "The End of the Cold War in Asia: Its Impact on China." *The Academy of Political Science. Proceedings* [New York], 38, No. 2 (1991), 1-11.

16088 **Zagoria, Donald S.** "The Strategic Situation on the Korean Peninsula." *Korea & World Affairs*, 3, No. 4 (Winter, 1979), 435-438.

AUSTRALIA, OCEANIA AND ANTARCTICA

Books and Journals

16089 **Alves, Dora.** "The Changing New Zealand Defense Posture." *Asian Survey*, 29, No. 4 (April, 1989), 363-381.

16090 **Babbage, Ross.** "Australian Defense Planning Force Structure and Equipment: The American Effect." *Australian Outlook*, 38, No. 3 (December, 1984), 163-168.

16091 **Ball, Desmond.** "American Bases in Australia: The Strategic Implications." *Current Affairs Bulletin*, 51 (March, 1975), 4-17.

16092 **Buesst, T.N.M.**, et al. *Security Problems in the Pacific Region.* Part Five: Eastern Asia and Australia. New York: Institute of Pacific Relations, 1949.

16093 **Bywater, Hector Charles.** *Sea Power in the Pacific: A Study of the American-Japanese Naval Problem.* Boston: Houghton Mifflin, 1921.

16094 **Cheeseman, Graeme.** "Australia's Defence: White Paper in the Red." *Australian Journal of International Affairs* [Canberra], 44, No. 2 (August, 1990), 101-118.

16095 **Child, Jack.** *Antarctica and South American Geopolitics: Frozen Lebensraum.* New York: Praeger, 1988.

16096 **Chow, S.R.** "The Pacific After the War." *Foreign Affairs*, 21, No. 1 (October, 1942), 71-86.

16097 "The Cold War Reaches the Antarctic." *Fortune*, 50, No. 5 (November, 1954), 111+.

16098 **Conant, Melvin A.** "Polar Strategic Concerns." *Oceanus*, 28, No. 2 (Summer, 1985), 62-66.

16099 **Fox, James W.** "New Zealand and the Pacific: Some Strategic Implications." *New Zealand Geographer*, 4, No. 1 (April, 1948), 15-28.

16100 **Freire Lavenee-Wanderley, N.**, et al. "Atlantico Sur: tres visiones de una estrategia." *Geopolitica*, 3, No. 5 (Mai, 1978), 15-26.

16101 **Gould, Laurence M.** "Strategy and Politics in the Polar Areas." *Annals of the American Academy of Political and Social Science*, 255 (January, 1948), 105-114.

16102 **Harris, William W.** "New Zealand Defence Policy: A Geostrategic Appreciation." *New Zealand Geographer* [Dunedin], 47, No. 2 (October, 1991), 72-79.

16103 **Henningham, Stephen.** "The French Administration, the Local Population, and the American Presence in New Caledonia, 1943-44." *Societe des Oceanistes. Journal*, 98, No. 1 (1994), 21-41.

16104 **Holland, W.L.** "War Aims and Peace Aims in the Pacific." *Pacific Affairs*, 15, No. 4 (December, 1942), 410-427.

16105 **Jones, Stephen B.** *The Arctic: Problems and Possibilities.* New Haven, Connecticut: Yale Institute of International Studies, 1948.

16106 **Lee, S.H.** "Antarctic Regime and the International Community: Future Policy Implications for Korea." *Korea & World Affairs*, 9, No. 2 (1985), 338-359.

16107 **Mitchell, B.**, and **Kimball, L.** "Conflict Over the Cold Continent." *Foreign Policy*, 35 (Summer, 1979),124-141.

16108 **Moneta, C.J.** "Antartida Argentina: los problemas de 1975-1990." *Estrategia*, Nos. 31-32, (Enero-Febrero, 1973), 5-35.

16109 "The Pacific Islands in the Peace." *Round Table*, 141, No. 4 (December, 1945), 35-39.

16110 "Problems of War and Peace in the Pacific." *Austral-Asiatic Bulletin*, Special Number (February, 1943), 1-105.

16111 **Rawlins, D.** "Evaluating Claim of North Polar Priority." *Norks Geografisk Tidsskrift*, Bind 26, Hefte 3 (1972), 135-140.

16112 **Scobell, Andrew.** "Politics, Professionalism, and Peacekeeping: An Analysis of the 1987 Military Coup in Fiji." *Comparative Politics* [New York], 26, No. 2 (January, 1994), 187-201.

16113 **Sullivan, Walter.** "Antarctica in a Two-Power World." *Foreign Affairs*, 36, No. 1 (October, 1957), 154-166.

16114 **Sweeney, Edward C.** "Admiral Richard E. Byrd's Assessment of the South Pacific Islands." *Explorers Journal*, 45, No. 3 (September, 1967), 156-164.

16115 **Touzet du Vigier, Alain.** "Introduction a l'Examen des Problems Geostrategiques du Pacifique Sud." *Journal de la Societe des Oceanistes*, 87 Annee, No. 2 (1989), 3-9.

16116 **Useem, John.** "The American Pattern of Military Government in Micronesia." *American Journal of Sociology*, 51, No. 2 (September, 1945), 93-102.

16117 **Van der Kroef, Justus M.** *Australian Security Policies and Problems.* New York: National Strategy Information Center, 1970.

16118 *War and Peace in the Pacific. A Preliminary Report of the Eighth Conference of the Institute of Pacific Relations on Wartime and Post-war Cooperation of the United Nations in the Pacific and the Far East, Mont Tremblant, Quebec, December 4-14, 1942.* London: The Royal Institute of International Affairs, 1943.

EUROPE

Books

16119 **Agulhon, M.** *Marianne into Battle; Republican Imagery and Symbolism in France, 1789-1880.* Cambridge: Cambridge University Press, 1980.

16120 **Alexander, Arthur J.** *Decision-Making in Soviet Weapons Procurement. A Delphi Papers,147 & 148.* London: Institute for Strategic Studies, Winter 1978/1979.

16121 **Alexiev, Alexander R., and Nurick, Robert C.** *The Soviet Military Under Gorbachev: Report on a RAND Workshop.* Santa Monica: The RAND Corporation, Feburary 1990.

16122 **Alford, Jonathan, ed.** *The Soviet Union: Security Policies & Constraints.* Aldershot, England: Gower Publishing, 1985.

16123 **Amundsen, Kirsten.** *Soviet Strategic Interests in the North.* London: Pinter Publishers, 1990.

16124 **Archer, Clive, ed.** *The Soviet Union and Northern Waters.* London: Routledge, 1988.

16125 **"The Baltic States During the War."** *The Bulletin of International News.* 21, No. 24 (November 25, 1944), 991-1000.

16126 **Banse, Ewald.** *Germany Prepares for War: A Nazi Theory of national Defense.* New York: Harcourt Brace, 1941.

16127 **Beard, C.A., and Radin, George.** *The Balkan Pivot: Yugoslavia.* New York: Macmillan, 1929.

16128 **Bilmanis, Alfred.** *Baltic States and World Peace and Security Organization. Facts in Review.* Washington, D.C.: Latvian Legation, 1945.

16129 **Bluth, Christopher.** *New Thinking in Soviet Military Policy.* New York: Council on Foreign Policy Press, 1990.

16130 **Bonjour, Edgar.** *Swiss Neutrality.* London: Allen & Unwin, 1946.

16131 **Booth, Ken.** *The Military Instrument in Soviet Foreign Policy 1917-1972.* London: Royal United Services Institute for Defense Studies, 1973.

16132 **Borkin, Joseph, and Welsh, C.A.** *Germany's Master Plan: The Story of Industrial Offensive.* New York: Duell, Sloan and Pearce, 1943.

16133 *British Security.* New York: Oxford University Press for the Royal Institute of International Affairs, 1946.

16134 **Campbell, Brian.** *The Roman Army, 31 BC - AD 337: A Sourcebook.* London: Routledge, 1994.

16135 **Carr, William.** *The Origins of the Wars of German Unification.* London Longman, 1991.

16136 **Chabot, Georges.** *La Geographie Appliques a la Conference de la Paix en 1919.* Saint-Brieuc: La Pensce Geographique Francaise Contemporaine, Presses Universitaires de Britague, 1972.

16137 **Charlton, Michael.** *The Eagle and the Small Birds: Crisis in the Soviet Empire: From Yalta to Solidarity.* Chicago, Illinois: University of Chicago Press, 1984.

16138 **Clayton, Anthony.** *France, Soldiers and Africa.* London: Brassey's, 1988.

16139 **Cressey, George.** *How Strong Is Russia?* Syracuse, New York: Syracuse University Press, 1954.

16140 **Curtis, Monica, eds.** *Norway and the War, September 1939-December 1940.* London: Oxford University Press, 1941.

16141 **da Cunha, Derek.** *Soviet Naval Power in the Pacific.* Boulder, Colorado: Lynne Rienner Publishers, 1990.

16142 **Darby, Phillip.** *British Defence Policy East of Suez 1947-1968.* London: Oxford University Press, 1973.

16143 **East, William Gordon.** *Mediterranean Problems.* London: T. Nelson and Son, 1940.

16144 **Erickson, John.** *Soviet Military Power.* Washington, D.C.: United States Strategic Institute, 1973.

16145 **European Security Study.** *Strengthening Conventional Deterrence in Europe.* London: Macmillan, 1983.

16146 **Fitzgerald, Mary C.** "The Russian Military's Strategy for 'Sixth Generation' Warfare." *Orbis* [Greenwich, CT], 38, No. 3 (Summer, 1994), 457-476.

16147 **Fontanella, Sharon K.** "The Impact of Regional Development on the Soviet's Military Posture in Siberia and the Far East." East Lansing: Michigan State University, M.A., 1989.

16148 **Gillette, Philip S., and Frank, Willard C., Jr., eds.** *The Sources of Soviet Naval Conduct.* Lexington, MA: Lexington Books, 1990.

16149 **Goldstein, Walter.** *The Dilemma of British Defense: The Imbalance Between Commitments and Resources.* Columbus: Ohio State University Press, 1966.

16150 **Green, Howard.** *Guide to the Battlefield of Britain and Ireland.* London: Constable, 1973.

16151 **Greene, O.** *Europe's Folly.* London: CNP Publications, 1983.

16152 **Greene, O. ; Rubin, B.; Turok, N.; and Webber, P.** *London After the Bomb. What a Nuclear Attack Really Means.* New York: Oxford University Press, 1982.

16153 **Hammond, Thomas Taylor.** *Yugoslavia - Between East and West.* New York: Foreign Policy Association, 1954.

16154 **Haselkorn, Avigdor.** *The Evolution of Soviet Security Strategy, 1965-1975.* New York: Crane, Russak and Company,/National Strategy Information Center, 1978.

16155 **Hayes, Carlton, J.H.** *Wartime Mission in Spain, 1942-1945.* New York: Macmillan, 1945.

16156 **Henningham, Stephen.** "The Uneasy Peace: New Caledonia's Matignon Accords at Mid-Term." *Pacific Affairs* [Vancouver], 66, No. 4 (Winter, 1993-94), 519-537.

16157 **Howard, M.** *The Franco-Prussian War: The German Invasion of France, 1870-1871.* New York: Macmillan, 1961.

16158 **Jackson, Robert J.,** ed. *Europe in Transition: The Management of Security After the Cold War.* New York: Praeger Publishers, 1992.

16159 **Johnson, A. Ross; Dean, Robert W.; and Alexiev, Alexander.** *East European Military Establishments: The Warsaw Pact Northern Tier.* New York: Crane Russak, 1982.

16160 **Keith, A.B.** *War Government of the British Dominions.* Oxford: Clarendon Press, 1921.

16161 **Kemler, John H.** *The Struggle for Wolfram in the Iberian Peninsula (June 42 - June 44): A Study in Political and Economic Geography in Wartime.* Chicago, Illinois: University of Chicago, Ph.D., 1949.

16162 **Kantorowicz, H.U.** *The Spirit of British Policy and the Myth of the Encirclement of Germany.* New York: Oxford University Press, 1932.

16163 **Laird, Robbin F.,** and **Herspring, Dale R.** *The Soviet Union and Strategic Arms.* Boulder, Colorado: Westview Press, 1984.

16164 **Lambi, Ivo Nikolai.** *The Navy & German Power Politics 1862-1914.* Boston, Massachusetts: Allen & Unwin, 1984.

16165 **Leebaert, Derek,** and **Dickinson, Timothy,** ed. *Soviet Strategy and New Military Thinking.* New York: Cambridge University Press, 1992.

16166 **Leites, Nathan.** *Soviet Style in War.* New York: Crane Russak, 1982.

16167 **Linz, Susan J.,** ed. *The Impact of WWII on The Soviet Union.* Totowa: Rowman & Allanheld, 1985.

16168 **Lockwood, Jonathan Samuel,** and **Lockwood, Kathleen O'Brien.** *The Russian View of U.S. Strategy: Its Past, Its Future.* New Brunswick: Transaction Publishers, 1993.

16169 **Luke, Sir Harry.** *Britain and the South Seas.* London: Longmans, Green, 1945.

16170 **Luttwak, Edward N.** *Sea Power in the Mediterranean: Political Utility and Military Constraints.* Beverly Hills, California: Published for the Center for Strategic and International Studies, Georgetown University, by Sage Publications, 1979.

16171 **MacDiarmid, S.M.J.** *The Use of Land by the Ministry of Defence within the National Parks of England and Wales.* London: Unpublished BSc Field Study, Wye College, University of London, 1985.

16172 **Macdonald, Hugh.** *The Soviet Challenge and the Structure of European Society.* Aldershot: Edward Elgar, 1990.

16173 **Malleret, Thierry.** *Conversion of the Defense Industry in the Former Soviet Union.* New York: Institute for East-West Security Studies, 1992.

16174 **Mandelbaum, Michael,** ed. *The Other Side of the Table: The Soviet Approach to Arms Control.* New York: Council on Foreign Policy Press, 1989.

16175 **Martin, L.W.** *British Defence Policy: The Long Recessional.* Toronto: The Institute for Strategic Studies, Canadian Institute for Strategic Studies, Canadian Institute of International Affairs, 1969.

16176 **Mazour, Anatole Grigorevich.** *Finland Between East and West.* Princeton, New Jersey: Van Nostrand, 1956.

16177 **Meiksins, Gregory.** *The Baltic Riddle. Finland, Estonia, Latvia, Lithuania--Key-Points of European Peace.* New York: L.B. Fischer, 1943.

16178 **Menon, Rajan,** and **Nelson, Daniel N.,** eds. *Limits to Soviet Power.* Lexington, Massachusetts: Lexington Books, 1989.

16179 **Millman, Brock.** "Toward War With Russia: British Naval and Air Planning for Conflict in the Near East, 1939-40." *Journal of Contemporary History* [London], 29, No. 2 (April, 1994), 261-283.

16180 **Morrow, J.H.** *Building German Airpower, 1909-1914.* Knoxville: University of Tennessee Press, 1976.

16181 **Nelson, Dnaiel N.** *Balkan Imbroglio: Politics and Security in Southeastern Europe.* Boulder: Westview Press, 1991.

16182 **Nicolson, Harold.** *Why Britain is at War.* Harmondsworth, England: Penguin, 1939.

16183 **Ogilvie, Alan Grant.** *La securite europeenne dans les annees 1970-1980.* Quebec: Centre Quebecois de Relations Internationales, 1973.

16184 **Openshaw, S.; Steadman, P.; and Green, O.** *Doomsday: Britain After Nuclear Attack.* Oxford: Basil Blackwell, 1983.

16185 **Pratt, Clayton Arthur, Lt. Col., U.S. Army.** *Military Use by Warsaw Treaty Organization Forces of 20th Century Operational Forces in the Benelux and Northern Germany.* Laramie: University of Wyoming, Department of Geography and International Studies, M.A., April, 1977. (Also abstracted in *Military Review,* 58 (June, 1978), 2-8.)

16186 **Rosecrance, Richard N.** *Defense of the Realm: British Strategy in the Nuclear Epoch.* New York City: Columbia University Press, 1968.

16187 **Roucek, Joseph S., and Others.** *Central-Eastern Europe, Crucible of World Wars.* New York: Prentice-Hall, 1946.

16188 **Rowen, Henry S., and Charles, Jr., eds.** *The Impoverished Superpower: Prestroika and the Soviet Military Burden.* San Francisco: Institute for Contemporary Studies, 1990.

16189 **Schmid, Alex P.** *Soviet Military Interventions Since 1945.* New Brunswick, New Jersey: Transaction Books, 1985.

16190 **Schweitzer, Carl-Christoph, ed.** *The Changing Western Analysis of the Soviet Threat.* London: Pinter Publishers, 1990.

16191 **Scott, Harriet Fast, and Scott, William F.** *The Armed Forces and the USSR.* 3rd Rev. ed. Boulder, Colorado: Westview Press, 1984.

16192 **Scott, William F.** *Soviet Sources of Military Doctrine and Strategy.* New York: Crane Russak, 1975.

16193 **Seton-Watson, Hugh.** *Eastern Europe Between the Wars, 1918-1941.* First edition, 1945; second edition, 1946. Cambridge: Cambridge University Press, 1946.

16194 **Shansab, Nasir.** *Soviet Expansion in the Third World: Afghanistan: A Case Study.* Silver Spring, Maryland: Bartleby Press, 1986.

16195 **Simon, Jeffrey.** *Warsaw Pact Forces: Problems of Command and Control.* Boulder, Colorado: Westview Press, 1985.

16196 **Shultz, Richard H., Jr.** *The Soviet Union and Revolutionary Warfare: Principles, Practices, and Regional Comparisons.* Stanford, California: Hoover Institutional Press, 1988.

16197 **Smith, M.L., and Stirk, Peter M.R., eds.** *Making the New Europe: European Unity and the Second World War.* London: Pinter Publishers, 1990.

16198 **Snyder, William P.** *The Politics of British Defense Policy, 1945-1962.* Columbus: Ohio State University Press, 1964.

16199 **Stavrou, Nikolaos A., ed.** *Greece Under Socialism: A NATO Ally Adrift.* New Rochelle, New York: Aristide D. Caratzas, 1988.

16200 **Tannenberg, O.R.** *Gross Deutchland: Die Arbeit des 20 Jahrunderts.* Leipsig: Volger, 1911.

16201 **Taylor, Peter J.** *Britain and the Cold War: 1945 as Geopolitical Transition.* New York: Guilford Publications, 1990.

16202 **Taylor, Trevor.** *European Defence Cooperation;* Chatham House Papers, No. 24. London: Routledge, 1984.

16203 **Tunstall, Graydon A., Jr.** *Planning for War Against Russia and Serbia: Austro-Hungarian and German Military Strategies, 1871-1914.* Boulder: Social Science Monographs, 1993.

16204 **Vincent, W.T.** *The Records of the Woolwich District.* London: J.S. Virtue, 1890.

16205 **Werth, A.** *Russia at War 1941-1945.* London: Pan Books, 1964.

16206 **Wolfe, Roy I.** *La securite europeenne dans les annees 1970-1980.* Quebec: Centre Quebecois des Relations Internationales, 1973.

16207 **Wolfe, Roy I.** *Soviet-American Relations and World Order: Arms Limitations and Policy.* Toronto: The Institute for Strategic Studies, Canadian Institute of International Affairs, 1970.

16208 **Wynfred, Joshua.** *Soviet Penetration into the Middle East.* Strategy Paper No. 4. New York: National Strategy Information Center, 1971.

Journals

16209 "Agreement Relating to the Defense of Greenland. (Signed by the United States April 9, 1941)." *Polar Record*, 3, No. 23 (January, 1942), 476-479.

16210 **Anderson, Albin T.** "The Soviets and Northern Europe." *World Politics*, 4, No. 4 (July, 1952), 468-487.

16211 **Andrews, William R.** "The Azerbaijan Incident: The Soviet Union in Iran, 1941-6." *Military Review*, 54, No. 8 (August, 1974), 74-85.

16212 "Armistice with Finland." *Department of State Bulletin*, 12, No. 295 (February, 1945), 261-268.

16213 **Aspaturian, Vernon V.** "Soviet Global Power and the Correlation of Forces." *Problems of Communism*, 29, No. 3 (May-June, 1980), 1-18.

16214 **Baldwin, Hansen N.** "The Soviet Navy." *Foreign Affairs*, 33, No. 4 (July, 1955), 587-604.

16215 **Ball, Desmond.** "Soviet Strategic Planning and the Control of Nuclear War." *Soviet Union/Union Sovietique*, 10, Parts 2-3 (1983), 201-217.

16216 "The Baltic States During the War." *Bulletin of International News*, 21, No. 24 (November, 1944), 991-1000.

16217 **Banac, Ivo.** "The Fearful Asymmetry of War: The Causes and Consequences of Yugoslavia's Demise." *Daedalus* [Cambridge, MA], 121, No. 2 (Spring, 1992), 141-174.

16218 **Barany, Zoltan D.** "East European Armed Forces in Transitions and Beyond." *East European Quarterly* [Boulder], 26, No. 1 (Spring, 1992), 1-30.

16219 **Barlow, William J.** "Soviet Damage-Denial: Strategy, Systems, SALT, and Solution." *Air University Review*, 32, No. 6 (September-October, 1981), 2-20.

16220 **Basov, A.V.** "The Soviet Union's Struggle for the Change in Balance of Forces in the Course of War." *Istoriia SSSR*, 6 (November-December, 1984), 3-16.

16221 **Bellamy, Christopher D.** "Solider of Fortune: Britain's New Military Role." *International Affairs* [Cambridge], 68, No. 3 (July, 1992), 443-456.

16222 **Bellamy, Christopher D., and Lahnstein, Joseph S.** "The New Soviet Defensive Policy: Khalkhin Gol 1939 as Case Study." *Parameters* [Carlisle, PA], 20, No. 3 (September, 1990), 19-32.

16223 **Betts, Richard K.** "Systems for Peace or Causes of War?: Collective Security, Arms Control, and the New Europe." *International Security* [Cambridge, MA], 17, No. 1 (Summer, 1992), 5-43.

16224 **Bilmanis, Alfred.** "The Legend of the Baltic Barrier States." *Journal of Central European Affairs*, 6, No. 2 (July, 1946), 126-146.

16225 **Birch, B.P.** "Winning Land from the Sea at Portsmouth." *Geography*, 58, Part 2 (April, 1973), 152-154.

16226 **Bjorkman, Thomas N., and Zamostny, Thomas J.** "Soviet Politics and Strategy Toward the West: Three Cases." *World Politics*, 36, No. 2 (January, 1984), 189-214.

16227 **Bodie, William C.** "Anarchy and Cold War in Moscow's 'Near Abroad.'" *Strategic Review* [Washington, DC], 21, No. 1 (Winter, 1993), 40-53.

16228 **Bradley, Margaret.** "Bonaparte's Plans to Invade England in 1801: The Fortunes of Pierre Forfait." *Annals of Science*, 51, No. 5 (September, 1994), 453-475.

16229 **Bradshaw, Nicholas F.** "The Role and Disposition of Military Forces in the Russian Federation." *GeoJournal*, 34, No. 2 (October, 1994), 155-166.

16230 **Burg, Steven L.** "Soviet Policy and the Central Asian Problem." *Survey*, 24, No. 3 (108) (Summer, 1979), 65-82.

16231 **Burke, David P.** "Defense and Mass Mobilization in Romania." *Armed Forces and Society*, 7, No. 1 (Fall, 1980), 31-49.

16232 **Callan, P.** "The Irish Soldier: A Propaganda Paper for Ireland." *Irish Sword*, 25, No. 59 (1982), 67-75.

16233 **Canby, Steven L.** "Territorial Defense in Central Europe." *Armed Forces and Society*, 7, No. 1 (Fall, 1980), 51-67.

16234 **Chevrier, Bruno.** "The International Status of the Baltic States." *Baltic Review*, 1, No. 6 (Novembler, 1946), 270-276.

16235 **Chipman, Donald.** "Admiral Gorshkov and the Soviet Navy." *Air University Review*, 33, No. 5 (July-August, 1982), 28-47.

16236 **Critchley, W. Harriet.** "Polar Deployment of Soviet Submarines." *International Journal*, 39, No. 4 (Autumn, 1984), 828-865.

16237 **Crook, Paul.** "Science and War: Radical Scientists and the Tizard-Cherwell Area Bombing Debate in Britain." *War and Society*, 12, No. 2 (October, 1994), 69-101.

16238 **Dandeker, Christopher.** "National Security and Democracy: The United Kingdom Experience." *Armed Forces and Society* [New Brunswick], 20, No. 3 (Spring, 1994), 353-374.

16239 **Danopoulos, Constantine P., and Gerston, Larry N.** "Democratic Currents in Authoritarian Seas: The Military in Greece and the Philippines." *Armed Forces and Society* [New Brunswick], 16, No. 4 (Summer, 1990), 529-545.

16240 **Dawisha, Karen.** "Soviet Security and the Role of the Military: The 1968 Czechoslovakia Crisis." *British Journal of Political Science*, 10, Part 3 (July, 1980), 341-363.

16241 **Deroc, M.** "Demise of the Yugoslav Army." *East European Quarterly*, 24, No. 1 (Spring, 1990), 57-64.

16242 **Dicks, Brian.** "Conflict in Khuzestan." *Geographical Magazine*, 53, No. 6 (March, 1981), 372-373.

16243 **Donelly, C.** "The Development of the Soviet Concept of Echeloning." *NATO Review*, 6, No. 6 (December, 1984), 9-17.

16244 **Dunnigan, J.F., et al.** "Berlin '85: The Enemy at the Gates." *Strategy and Tactics*, 79 (1980), 4-14.

16245 **Dupuy, T.N.** "The Soviet Second Echelon: Is This a Red Herring?" *Armed Forces Journal International*, (August, 1982), 60.

16246 **East, W. Gordon.** "The Mediterranean: Pivot of Peace and War." *Foreign Affairs*, 31, No. 4 (July, 1953), 619-633.

16247 **East, W. Gordon.** "The Mediterranean Problem." *Geographical Review*, 28, No. 1 (January, 1938), 83-101.

16248 **Edney, Matthew H.** "British Military Education, Mapmaking, and Military Map-Mindness' in the Later Enlightenment." *The Cartographic Journal* [Edinburgh], 31, No. 1 (June, 1994), 14-20.

16249 **Erickson, John.** "Red Alert: The Soviet Military and Military Power." *Political Quarterly*, 51, No. 3 (July-September, 1980), 274-284.

16250 **Erickson, John.** "Soviet Military Policy in the 1980's." *Current History*, 75, No. 440 (October, 1978), 97-99 and 135-138.

16251 **Fane, Daria.** "After Afghanistan: The Decline of Soviet Military Prestige." *Washington Quarterly*, 13, No. 2 (Spring, 1990), 5-16.

16252 **Fullerton, John.** "Projecting Soviet Power." *South African Journal of African Affairs*, 9, No. 2 (1979), 56-62.

16253 **Garthoff, Raymond L.** "New Thinking in Soviet Military Doctrine." *Washington Quarterly*, 11, No. 3 (Summer, 1988), 131-158.

16254 **Gasteyger, Curt.** "European Defence Supplement." *Times*, 8 (February, 1974), complete volume.

16255 **Gerasimov, I.P.** "Geography of Peace and War: A Soviet View." In *The Geography of Peace and War*, D. Pepper and A. Jenkins, eds. Oxford: Basil Blackwell, 1985, 192-201.

16256 **Glantz, David M.** "Soviet Offensive Ground Doctrine Since 1945: Historical Overview." *Air University Review*, 34, No. 3 (March-April, 1983), 24-35.

16257 **Goda, Norman J.W.** "Hitler's Demand for Casablanca in 1940: Incident or Policy? *The International History Review*, 16, No. 3 (August, 1994), 491-510.

16258 **Goumley, Dennism.** "A New Dimension to Soviet Theater Strategy." *Orbis*, 29, No. 3 (Fall, 1985), 537-569.

16259 **Grizold, Anton.** "Military Intervention in Slovenia." *International Social Science Review* [Winfield, KS], 67, No. 1 (Winter, 1992), 8-14.

16260 **Gross, Natalie.** "Youth and the Army in the USSR in the 1980s." *Soviet Studies* [Glasgow], 42, No. 3 (July, 1990), 481-498.

16261 **Guertner, Gary L.** "Strategic Vulnerability of a Multinational State: Deterring the Soviet Union." *Political Science Quarterly*, 96, No. 2 (Summer, 1981), 209-223.

16262 **Haas, Hans-Dieter.** "The German Armament Industry with Specific Regard to Military Air- and Space-Crafts." *Zeitschrift fur Wirtschaftsgeographie*, Jahr, 32, Heft 3 (1988), 192-208.

16263 **Hadsel, Winifred N.** "Allied Military Rule in Germany." *Foreign Policy Reports*, 21, No. 16 (November 1, 1945), 222-231.

16264 **Hall, Christopher D.** "The Royal Navy and the Peninsular War." *The Mariner's Mirror* [London], 79, No. 4 (November, 1993), 403-418.

16265 **Haltiner, Karl, and Meyer, Ruth.** "Aspects of the Relationship Between Military and Society in Switzerland." *Armed Forces and Society*, 6, No. 1 (Fall, 1979), 49-81.

16266 **Harsch, Joseph C.** "The 'Unbelievable' Nazi Blueprint." *New York Times Magazine*, Section 7 (May , 1941), 3-4, 26 and 31.

16267 **Heinisch, Emanuel, and Ullrich, Seigfried.** "Verantwortung fur den weltfrieden: Globale Auswirkungen eines nuklearean Infernos." *Geographische Berichte*, 31 Jahr, Heft 4 (1986), 217-228.

16268 **Herspring, Dale R.** "The Soviet Military in the Aftermath of the 27th Party Congress. *Orbis*, 30, No. 2 (Summer, 1986), 297-315.

16269 **Herspring, Dale R., and Volgyes, Ivan.** "Political Reliability in the Eastern European Warsaw Pact Armies." *Armed Forces and Society*, 6, No. 2 (Winter, 1980), 270-296.

16270 **Hewitt, Kenneth.** "Our Cities Bombarded." *Geographical Magazine*, 62, No. 5 (May, 1990), 10-13.

16271 **Hohn, Uta.** "The Bomber's Baedeker--Target Book for Strategic Bombing in the Economic Warfare Against German Towns, 1943-45." *GeoJournal*, 34, No. 2 (October, 1994), 213-230.

16272 **Huber, Reiner K.** "Parity and Stability: Some Conclusions from Geometricl Models of Military Operations in Central Europe." *International Interactions* [New York], 16, No. 4 (1991), 225-238.

16273 "Iceland, Its Importance in an Air Age." *World Today*, 4, No. 7 (July, 1948), 297-307.

16274 **Issawi, Charles.** "Europe, the Middle East and the Shift in Power: Reflections on a Theme by Marshall Hodgson." *Comparative Studies in Society and History*, 22, No. 4 (October, 1980), 487-504.

16275 **James, Alan.** "The UN Force in Cyprus." *International Affairs*, 65, No. 3 (Summer, 1989), 481-500.

16276 **Jones, Christopher.** "The Warsaw Pact: Military Exercises and Military Interventions." *Armed Forces and Society*, 7, No. 1 (Fall, 1980), 5-30.

16277 **King, Peter.** "Two Eyes for a Tooth: The State of Soviet Strategic Doctrine." *Survey*, 24, No. 1-106 (Winter, 1979), 45-56.

16278 **Kissinger, Henry A.** "The Unsolved Problems of European Defense." *Foreign Affairs*, 40, No. 4 (July, 1962), 515-542.

16279 **Kunzmann, K.R.** "Military Production and Regional Development in the Federal Republic of Germany." *Built Environment*, 11, No. 3 (1985), 181-192.

16280 **Lacoste, Yves.** "L'Allemagne et le probleme des euromissiles." *Herodote*, 28 (Janvier-Mars, 1983), 6-22.

16281 **Law, C.M.** "The Defence Sector in British Regional Development." *Geoforum*, 14, No. 2 (1983), 169-184.

16282 **Lepotier, A.** "L'importance strategique du Groenland." *Geographia*, 6 (1956), 29-35.

16283 **Levi, Barbara G.; von Hippel, Frank N.; and Daugherty, William H.** "Civilian Casualties from "Limited" Nuclear Attacks on the USSR. *International Security*, 12, No. 3 (Winter, 1987/88), 168-189.

16284 **Lovering, J.** "Defence Expenditure and the Regions: The Case of Bristol." *Built Environment*, 11, No. 3 (1985), 193-206.

16285 **MacGwire, Michael.** "Update: Soviet Military Objectives." *World Policy Journal*, 4, No. 4 (Summer, 1987), 723-731.

16286 **Maconochie, Alexander K.** "Across or Along: Soviet Amphibious Options in Northwestern Europe." *United States Naval Institute Proceedings*, 106, No. 4-926 (April, 1980), 46-50.

16287 **Mahoney, Shane E.** "Defensive Doctrine: The Crisis in Soviet Military Thought." *Slavic Review* [Stanford], 49, No. 3 (Fall, 1990), 398-408.

16288 **Manigart, Philippe, and Marlier, Eric.** "European Public Opinion on the Future of Its Security." *Armed Forces and Society* [New Brunswick], 19, No. 3 (Spring, 1993), 335-352.

16289 **Manthorpe, Jr., William H.J.** "The Soviet Navy in 1979: Part I." *United States Naval Institute Proceedings*, 106, No. 4-926 (April, 1980), 113-119.

16290 **Martin, Michel Louis.** "National Security and Democracy: The Dilemma from a French Perspective." *Armed Forces and Society* [New Brunswick], 20, No. 3 (Spring, 1994), 395-421.

16291 **Mason, Michael.** "Killing Time: The British Army and Its Antagonists in Egypt, 1945-1954." *War and Society*, 12, No. 2 (October, 1994), 103-126.

16292 **Maurer, John H., and McCormick, Gordon H.** "Surprise Attack and Conventional Defense in Europe." *Orbis*, 27, No. 1 (Spring, 1983), 107-126.

16293 **McClellan, Grant S.** "Britain's Search for Security." *Foreign Policy Reports*, 21, No. 1 (March 15, 1945), 1-14.

16294 **McKernan, Anne.** "War, Gender, and Industrial Innovation: Recruiting Women Weavers in Early Nineteenth-Century Ireland." *Journal of Social History*, 28, No. 1 (Fall, 1994), 109-124.

16295 **Mead, W.R.** "The Finnish Outlook, East and West." *Geographical Journal*, 113, Part 1 (January-June, 1949), 9-20.

16296 **Milijan, Toivo.** "East vs. West: Political and Military Strategy and the Baltic Littoral." *Journal of Baltic Studies*, 12, No. 3 (Fall, 1981), 209-233.

16297 **Miller, John H.** "The Geographical Disposition of the Soviet Armed Forces." *Soviet Studies*, 40, No. 3 (July, 1988), 406-433.

16298 **Mookerjee, Girija.** "Peace Settlements in Europe Since 1945." *India Quarterly*, 5, No. 4 (October-December, 1949), 304-317.

16299 **Moravec, Emmanuel.** "L'importance de la Tchecoslovaquie et ses forces." *Le Monde Slave*, 15ᵉ annee, Tome 11 (Avril, 1938), 1-31, cont.

16300 **Morrison, John A.** "Russia and Warm Water." *United States Naval Institute Proceedings*, 78 (1952), 1169-1179.

16301 **Morsy, Laila Amin.** "Indicative Cases of Britain's Wartime Policy in Egypt, 1942-44." *Middle Eastern Studies* [London], 30, No. 1 (January, 1994), 91-122.

16302 **Nelson, Daniel N.** "A Balkan Perspesctive." *Strategic Review* [Washington, DC], 21, No. 1 (Winter, 1993), 26-39.

16303 **Odom, William E.** "Soviet Military Doctrine." *Foreign Affairs*, 67, No. 2 (Winter, 1988/89), 114-134.

16304 **Openshaw, S.,** and **Steadman, P.** "Doomsday Revisited." In *The Geography of Peace and War*, D. Pepper and A. Jenkins, eds. Oxford: Basil Blackwell, 1985, 107-25.

16305 **Openshaw, S.,** and **Steadman, P.** "The Geography of Two Hypothetical Nuclear Attacks on Britain." *Area*, 15, No. 3 (September, 1983), 193-210.

16306 **Openshaw, S.,** and **Steadman, P.** "Predicting the Consequences of a Nuclear Attack on Britain: Models, Results, and Implications for Public Policy." *Environment and Planning* C1, No. 2 (April, 1983), 205-228.

16307 **Peck, F.,** and **Townsend, A.** "Contrasting Experience of Recession and Spatial Restructuring: British Shipbuilders, Plessey and Metal Box." *Regional Studies*, 18, No. 4 (August, 1984), 319-38.

16308 **Perjes, Geza.** "Game Theory and the Rationality of War: The Battles of Mohacs and the Disintegration of Medieval Hungary." *East European Quarterly*, 15, No. 2 (Summer, 1981), 153-162.

16309 **Perry, Nicholas.** "Nationality in the Irish Infantry Regiments in the First World War." *War and Society* [Canberra], 12, No. 1 (May, 1994), 65-95.

16310 **Pipes, Richard.** "Militarism and the Soviet State." *Daedalus*, 109, No. 4 (Fall, 1980), 1-12.

16311 **Pollitt, Ronald.** "Contingency Planning and the Defeat of the Spanish Armada." *American Neptune*, 44, No. 1 (Winter, 1984), 25-32.

16312 **Polmar, Norman,** and **Others.** "Soviet Navy Issue." *U.S. Naval Institute Proceedings*, 108, No. 956 (Octobre, 1982), 11-176.

16313 **Possony, Stefan T.** "Political and Military Geography of Central, Balkan, and Eastern Europe." *Annals of the American Academy of Political and Social Science*, 232 (March, 1944), 1-8.

16314 **Radvanyi, Jean.** "Les Republiques Baltes et la Nouvelle Strategie Sovietique des Marges Occidentales." *Annales de Geographie*, 93ᵉ Annee, No. 515 (Janvier-Fevrier, 1984), 44-65.

16315 **Ravenhill, William.** "The Honourable Robert Edward Clifford, 1767-1817: A Cartographer's Response to Napoleon." *The Geographical Journal* [London], 160, Part 2 (July, 1994), 159-172.

16316 **Richelson, Jeffrey T.** "Social Choice Theory and Soviet National Security Decisionmaking." *Soviet Union/Union Sovietique*, 11, Part 3 (1984), 257-284.

16317 **Ruiz Palmer, Diego A.** "Spain's Security Policy and Army in the 1990s." *Parameters* [Carlisle Barracks, PA], 20, No. 2 (June, 1990), 90-98.

16318 **Schlor, Wolfgang.** "Barrier Defense in Europe: An Option for the 1990s? *Parameters*, 20, No. 1 (March, 1990), 20-37.

16319 **Short, John R.** "Defence Spending in the UK Regions." *Regional Studies*, 15, No. 2 (1981), 101-110.

16320 **Showalter, Dennis E.** "The Political Solidiers of Bismarck's Germany: Myths and Realities." *German Studies Review* [Tempe], 17, No. 1 (February, 1994), 59-81.

16321 **Simes, Dimitri K.** "The Military and Militarism in Soviet Society." *International Security*, 6, No. 3 (Winter 1981/1982), 123-143.

16322 **Smith, Thomas R., and Black, Lloyd D.** "German Geography: War Work and Present." *Geographical Review*, 36, No. 3 (July, 1946), 398-408.

16323 **Smolka, H.P.** "Soviet Strategy in the Arctic." *Foreign Affairs*, 16, No. 2 (January, 1938), 272-278.

16324 **Smyth, Denis.** "The Dispatch of the Spanish Blue Division to the Russian Front: Reasons and Repercussions." *European History Quarterly*, 24, No. 4 (October, 1994), 537-553.

16325 **Sorenson, David S.** "Getting Back to Europe: Strategic Lift Needed Now More Than Ever." *Parameters* [Carlisle Barracks, PA], 20, No. 2 (June, 1990), 64-74.

16326 **Stavrianos, L.S.** "Greece: The War and Aftermath." *Foreign Policy Reports*, 21, No. 12 (September 1, 1945), 174-188.

16327 **Stoll, Richard J.** "The Russians are Coming: A Computer Simulation." *Armed Forces & Society*, 16, No. 2 (Winter, 1990), 193-213.

16328 **Storkel, Arno.** "The Defenders of Mayence in 1792: A Portrait of a Small European Army at the Outbreak of the French Revolutionary Wars." *War and Society*, 12, No. 2 (October, 1994), 1-21.

16329 "Strategic Concepts for Europe." *Defence Update International*, 44 (1984), 12-24.

16330 **Swan, Guy C., III.** "Theater Campaign Planning for NATO's Northern Region." *Parameters*, 20, No. 1 (March, 1990), 48-63.

16331 **Torrey, Glenn E.** "The Redemption of an Army: The Romanian Campaign of 1917." *War and Society*, 12, No. 2 (October, 1994), 23-42.

16332 **Ule, Otto.** "The 'Normalization' of Post-Invasion Czechoslovakia." *Survey*, 24, No. 3 (Summer, 108) (Summer, 1979), 201-213.

16333 **Uller, Lennart.** "The Nordic Reach of Soviet Forces in the Leningrad and Baltic Military Districts." *Journal of Baltic Studies*, 17, No. 3 (Fall, 1986), 220-230.

16334 **Valenta, Jiri.** "From Prague to Kabul: The Soviet Style of Invasion." *International Security*, 5, No. 2 (Fall, 1980), 114-141.

16335 **Van Evera, Stephen.** "Primed for Peace: Europe After the Cold War." *International Security* [Cambridge], 15, No. 3 (Winter, 1990-91), 7-57.

16336 **Venkataraman, V.** "The Political Geography of the Italo-Abyssinian War." *Indian Geographical Journal*, 10, No. 4 (January, 1936), 223-233.

16337 **Waever, Ole.** "Three Competing Europes: German, French, Russian." *International Affairs*, 66, No. 3 (July 1990), 447-493.

16338 **Walker, William.** "Nuclear Weapons and the Former Soviet Republics." *International Affiars* [Cambridge], 68, No. 2 (April, 1992), 255-277.

16339 **Wallander, Celeste A.** "Third World Conflict in Soviet Military Thought: Does the 'New Thinking' Grow Prematurely Grey." *World Politics*, 42, No. 1 (October, 1989), 31-63.

16340 **Walters, William D., Jr.** "The Geography of the European *Dreadnought* Race: 1884-1919." *The Geographical Bulletin* [Ypsilanti], 34, No. 1 (May, 1992), 45-58.

16341 **Wessell, Nils H.** "Soviet Views of Multipolarity and the Emerging Balance of Power." *Orbis*, 22, No. 4 (Winter, 1979), 785-813.

16342 **Whitby, Michael.** "The Seaward Defence of the British Assault Area, 6-14 June 1944." *The Mariner's Mirror* [London], 80, No. 2 (May, 1994), 191-207.

CHAPTER XVII

POLITICAL GEOGRAPHY OF OCEANS

GENERAL AND THEORY

Books

16343 **Alexander, Lewis M.**, ed. *The Law of the Sea: Offshore Boundaries and Zones.* Columbus: Ohio State University Press, 1967.

16344 **Anand, R.P.**, ed. *Law of the Sea: Caracas and Beyond.* Boston, Massachusetts: Martinus Nijhoff, 1980.

16345 **Anderson, John William.** *The Law of the Sea: A Proposal for Projecting State Voting Behavior.* Atlanta, Georgia: Emory University, Ph.D., 1979.

16346 **Bowett, Derek W.** *The Law of the Sea.* Dobbs Ferry, New York: Oceania Publications, 1967.

16347 **Bowett, Derek W.** *The Legal Regime of Islands in International Law.* Dobbs Ferry, New York: Oceana Publications, 1979.

16348 **Bringe, Ruth.** *The Rise and Fall of the Seas.* New York: Harcourt Brace and World, 1964.

16349 **Brown, E.D.** *The Legal Regime of Hydrospace.* London: Stevens and Sons, 1971.

16350 **Buzan, Barry.** *Seabed Politics.* New York: Praeger, 1976.

16351 **Bywater, H.C.** *Navies and Nations.* Boston, Massachusetts: Houghton Mifflin, 1927.

16352 **Churchill, R.R.**, and **Lowe, A.V.** *The Law of the Sea.* Manchester, England: Manchester University Press, 1983.

16353 **Coker, R.D.** *This Great and Wide Sea.* Chapel Hill: University of North Carolina Press, 1947.

16354 **Colombos, C. John.** *The International Law of the Sea*, 6th ed. London: Longmans, 1967.

16355 **Couper, Alastair D.** *The Geography of Sea Transport.* London: Hutchinson University Library, 1972.

16356 **Couper, Alastair D.**, ed. *The Times Atlas of the Oceans.* New York: Van Nostrand, 1983.

16357 **Dupuy, Rene-Jean.** *L'Ocean Partage.* Paris: Editions A. Pedone, 1979.

16358 **Fulton, T.W.** *The Sovereignty of the Sea.* Edinburgh: Blackwood and Sons, 1911.

16359 **Glassner, Martin Ira.** *Naptune's Domain: A Political Geography of the Sea.* New Haven, Connecticut: Southern Connecticut State University, 1990.

16360 **Hodgson, Robert D.**, and **Alexander, Lewis M.** *Towards an Objective Analysis of Special Circumstances.* Kingston, Rhode Island: Law of the Sea Institute, 1972.

16361 **Jessup, Philip C.** *The Law of Territorial Waters and Maritime Jurisdiction.* New York: G.A. Jennings, 1927.

16362 **Johnston, Douglas M.** and **Saunders, P.**, eds. *Ocean Boundary Making: Regional Issues and Developments.* London: Croom Helm, 1988.

16363 **Kazemi, Ali-Asghar.** *Toward a Regional Sea Concept in a New Maritime Environment: Problems, Prospects, and Implications for International Relations.* Medford, Massachusetts: Tufts University, Fletcher School of Law and Diplomacy, Ph.D., 1978.

16364 **Keesing, Felix M.** *The South Seas in the Modern World.* (Institute of Pacific Relations. International Research Series.) New York: John Day, 1941.

16365 **McDougal, Myres S.**, and **Burke, William T.** *Public Order of the Oceans.* New Haven, Connecticut: Yale University Press, 1962.

16366 **McFee, W.** *The Law of the Sea.* Philadelphia: Lippincott, 1950.

16367 **Mendoza, Jaime.** *El Mar del Sur.* Sucre: Imp. Bolivar, 1926.

16368 **Moore, S.A.** *History and Law of the Foreshore, and the Law Relationg Thereto*, 3rd ed. London: Stevens and Haynes, 1988.

16369 **O'Connell, D.P.** *The Law of the Sea in Our Time-The United Nations Seabed Committee, 1968-1973.* The Hague: Sijthoff and Leiden, 1977.

16370 **Papadakis, Nikos.** *International Law of the Sea: A Bibliography.* Alphen aan den Rijn, Netherlands: Sijthoff and Noordhoff, 1980.

16371 **Prescott, J.R.V.** *The Political Geography of the Oceans: Problems in Modern Geography.* New York: John Wiley & Sons, A Halsted Press Book, 1975.

16372 **Shalowitz, Aaron L.** *Shore and Sea Boundaries.* Washington, D.C.: U.S. Government Printing Office, Vol. 1, 1962; Vol. 2, 1964.

16373 **Smith, H.A.** *The Law and Custom of the Sea.* London: Stevens, 1984.

16374 **Stewart, Harris B., Jr.** *The Global Sea.* Princeton, New Jersey: Van Nostrand, 1963.

16375 **United Nations.** *Conference on the Law of the Sea,* Vol. 1 and Vol. 3. New York: United Nations, 1958.

16376 **United Nations.** *Official Records of the Second United Nations Conference on the Law of the Sea,* Vol. 3. New York: United Nations, 1962.

16377 **U.S. Department of State.** *Sovereignty of the Sea.* Washington, D.C.: Office of the Geographer, 1969.

16378 **Vukas, Budislav,** ed. *Essays on the New Law of the Sea.* Zegrab: Prinosiza Poredbeno Provoavan je Prava id Medunarodno Pravo, 18, No. 21, 1985.

16379 **Watts, H.D.** *The Branch of Plant Economy: A Study of External Control.* London: Longman, 1981.

16380 **Wirsing, Robert G.,** ed. *International Relations and the Future of Ocean Space.* Columbia: University of South Carolina Press, Studies in International Affairs, No. 10 (Symposium on International Relations and the Future of Ocean Space, University of South Carolina, 1972.), 1974.

Journals

16381 **Abrahamsson, Bernhard J.** "The Law of the Sea Convention and Shipping." *Political Geography Quarterly,* 5, No. 1 (January, 1986), 13-17.

16382 **Alexander, Lewis M.** "Geography and the Law of the Sea." *Annals of the Association of American Geographers,* 58, No. 1 (March, 1968), 177-197.

16383 **Alexander, Lewis M.** "The New Geography of the World's Oceans Before and After Law of the Sea." *Columbia Journal of World Business,* 15, No. 4 (Winter, 1980), 6-16.

16384 **Alexander, Lewis M.** "Uncertanties in the Aftermath of UNCLOSIII: The Case for Navigational Freedom." *Ocean Development and Inlernational Law,* 18, No. 3 (1987), 333-342.

16385 **Allott, Philip.** "Making the New International Law: Law of the Sea as Law of the Future." *International Journal,* 40, No. 3 (Summer, 1985), 442-460.

16386 **Bascom, Willard.** "Technology and the Ocean." *Scientific American,* 221, No. 3 (September, 1969), 198-217.

16387 **Beck, Peter J.** "Antarctic Treaty System After 25 Years." *World Today,* 42, No. 11 (November, 1986), 196-199.

16388 **Blacksell, Mark.** "Frontiers at Sea." *Geographical Magazine,* 51, No. 8 (May, 1979), 521-524.

16389 **Bowett, Derek W.** "The Second U.N. Conference on the Law of the Sea." *International and Comparative Law Quarterly,* 9, No. 3 (July, 1960), 415-435.

16390 **Bravender-Coyle, Paul.** "The Emerging Legal Principles and Equitable Criteria Governing the Delimitation of Marine Boundaries Between States." *Ocean Development and International Law,* 19, No. 3 (1988), 171-228.

16391 **Bucholz, H.** "Ozeane als Nationale Territorien. (Oceans as National Territories)." *Geographische Rundschau,* 38, No. 12 (1986), 614-620.

16392 **Burpee, Lawrence J.** "From Sea to Sea." *Canadian Geographical Journal,* 16, No. 1 (January, 1938), 3-32.

16393 **Burke, William T.** "Critical Changes in the law of the Sea." *Columbia Journal of World Business,* 15, No. 4 (Winter, 1980), 17-21.

16394 **Burke, William T.** "National Legislation on Ocean Authority Zones and the Contemporary Law of the Sea." *Ocean Development and International Law,* 9, No. 3/4 (1981), 289-322.

16395 **Clark, Harold F.,** and **Renner, George T.** "We Should Annex 50,000,000 Square Miles of Ocean." *Saturday Evening Post,* 218, No. 4 (May 4, 1946), 16-17+.

16396 **Colwell, Rita R.,** and **Greer, Jack R.** "Biotechnology and the Sea." *Ocean Development and International Law,* 17, Nos. 1, 2 and 3 (1986), 163-189.

16397 **Couper, Alastair.** "Who Owns the Oceans?" *Geographical Magazine,* 55, No. 9 (September, 1983), 450-457.

16398 **D'Amato, Anthony.** "The Authoritativeness of Custom in International Law." *Rivista di Diritto Internazionale,* 53 (1970), 491-505.

16399 **Dean, Arthur H.** "Freedom of the Seas." *Foreign Affairs*, 37, No. 1 (October, 1958), 83-94.

16400 **Dean, Arthur H.** "The Geneva Conference on the Law of the Sea: What Was Accomplished." *American Journal of International Law*, 52, No. 4 (October, 1958), 607-628.

16401 **Dean, Arthur H.** "The Law of the Sea." *Department of State Bulletin*, 38, 980 (April, 1958), 574-581.

16402 **Dean, Arthur H.** "The Law of the Sea Conference, 1958-60, and Its Aftermath." In *The Law of the Sea: Offshore Boundaries and Zones*, Lewis M. Alexander, ed. Columbus: Ohio State University Press, 1967, 244-264.

16403 **Dean, Arthur H.** "The Second Geneva Conference on the Law of the Sea: The Fight for Freedom of the Seas." *American Journal of International Law*, 54, No. 4 (October, 1960), 751-789.

16404 **Fawcett, J.E.S.** "How Free are the Seas?" *International Affairs*, 49, No. 1 (January, 1973), 14-22.

16405 **Fitzmaurice, G.** "Some Results of the Geneva Conference on the Law of the Sea." *International and Comparative Law Quarterly*, 8, No. 1 (January, 1959), 73-121.

16406 **Gambe, Jr., John King.** "Where Trends the Law of the Sea?" *Ocean Development and International Law*, 10, No. 1/2 (1982), 61-91.

16407 **Glassner, Martin Ira.** "Geographers and the Law of the Sea," *Geographical Survey*, 6, No. 3 (July, 1977), 9-13.

16408 **Glassner, Martin Ira.** "The Law of the Sea." *Focus*, Special Issue, (March-April, 1978), 1-24.

16409 **Glassner, Martin Ira.** "The New Political Geography of the Sea." *Political Geography Quarterly*, 5, No. 1 (January, 1986), 6-8.

16410 **Gold, Edgar.** "Vessel Traffic Services: The New Law of the Sea." *Journal of Navigation*, 38, No. 1 (January, 1985), 71-84.

16411 **Goldblat, Josef.** "The Seabed Treaty." In *Ocean Yearbook*, Vol. I, Elisabeth Mann Borgese and Norton Ginsburg, eds. Chicago, Illinois: University of Chicago Press, 1978, 386-411.

16412 **Griffin, William L.** "The Emerging Law of Ocean Space." *International Lawyer*, 1, No. 4 (July, 1966), 548-587.

16413 **Guill, James H.** "The Regimen of the Seas." *U.S. Naval Institute Proceedings*, 83, No. 12 (December, 1957), 1308-1319.

16414 **Hayton, Robert D.** "Polar Region Problems and International Law." *American Journal of International Law*, 52, No. 4 (October, 1958), 746-765.

16415 **Henkin, Louis.** "Politics and the Changing Law of the Sea." *Political Science Quarterly*, 89, No. 1 (March, 1974), 47-67.

16416 **Hudson, H.** "The First Conference for the Codification of International Law." *American Journal of International Law*, 24, No. 3 (July, 1930), 447-466.

16417 **Hodgson, Robert D.** "Islands: Normal and Special Circumstances." In *Law of the Sea: The Emerging Regime of the Oceans*, John King Gamble, Jr. and Giulio Pontercorvo, eds. Cambridge, Massachusetts: Ballinger, 1974, 137-199.

16418 **Hodgson, Robert D., and Cooper, E. John.** "The Technical Delimitation of a Modern Equidistant Boundary." *Ocean Development and International Law*, 3, No. 4 (1976), 361-388.

16419 **Hodgson, Robert D., and Smith, Robert W.** "The Informal Single Negotiating Text (Committee II): A Geographical Perspective." *Ocean Development and International Law*, 3, No. 3 (1976), 225-259.

16420 **Jacovides, Andreas J.** "Three Aspects of the Law of the Sea." *Marine Policy*, 3, No. 4 (October, 1979), 278-288.

16421 **Janaki, V.A.** "Indian Ocean Policies." *Faculty of Science Magazine*, (1974-75), 29-37.

16422 **Janaki, V.A.** "Sea Power and the Law of the Sea." *Faculty of Science Magazine*, (1975), 1-8.

16423 **Joesten, Joachim.** "The Second U.N. Conference on the Law of the Sea." *World Today*, 16, No. 6 (June, 1960), 249-257.

16424 **Johnson, D.H.N.** "Minquiers and Ecrehos Case." *International and Comparative Law Quarterly*, 3, No. 2 (April, 1954), 189-216.

16425 **Joyner, Christopher C.** "Normative Evolution and Policy Process in the Law of the Sea." *Ocean Development and International Law*, 15, No. 1 (1985), 61-76.

16426 **Kimball, Lee A.** "International Law and Institutions: The Oceans and Beyond." *Ocean Development and International Law* [New York], 21, No. 2 (1990), 147-165.

16427 **Klemm, Ulf-Dieter**. "Allgemeine Abgrenzungsprobleme verschiedener seerechtlich definierter Raume." *Zeitschrift fur auslandisches offentliches Recht und Volkerrecht*, 38 (1978), 512-567.

16428 **Knight, H. Gary**. "The Draft United Nations Convention on the International Seabed Area: Background, Description, and Some Preliminary Thoughts." *San Diego Law Review*, 8, No. 3 (May, 1971), 459-550.

16429 **Kruger-Sprengel, Friedhelm**. "Die Seerechtskonferenz der Vereinten Nationen und die neven Meereszonen." *Die Erde*, 114 Jahr, Heft 1 (July, 1983), 11-18.

16430 **Larson, David L**. "When Will the UN Convention on the Law of the Sea Come into Effect?" *Ocean Development and International Law,* 20, No. 2 (1989), 175-202.

16431 **Luard, Evan**. "The Law of the Sea Conference." *International Affairs*, 50, 2 (April, 1974), 268-278.

16432 **Mahmoudi, Said**. "Customary International Law and Transit Passage." *Ocean Development and International Law,* 20, No. 2 (1989), 157-174.

16433 **Manin, Philippe**. "Le Juge International et la Regle Generale." *Revue Generale de Droit International Public*, 80 (1976), 7-54.

16434 "The Marine Scientific Research Issue in the Law of the Sea Negotiations. Ocean Policy Committee of the Commission on International Relations." *Science*, 197, No. 4300 (July 15, 1977), 230-233.

16435 **McWethy, R.D**. "Significance of the Nautilus Polar Cruise." *Proceedings U.S. Naval Institute*, 84, No. 5 (1958), 32-35.

16436 **Medeiros Querejazu, Gustavo**. "III Conferenceia de las Naciones Unidas sobre el Derecho al Mar [The Third United Nations Conference on the Law of the Sea]." *Kollasuyo*, 88 (First Semester, 1975), 76-93.

16437 **Menon, P.K**. "The Commonwealth Caribbean and the Development of the Law of the Sea: An Overview." *Revue de Droit International de Sciences Diplomatiques et Politiques*, 58,No. 1 (Janvier-Mars, 1980), 39-72.

16438 **Miles, Edward L**. "Preparation for UNCLOS IV." *International Law*, 19, No. 5 (1988), 421+.

16439 **Navaretta, Stephen**. "Part V, Chapter III, Restatement of the Foreign Relations Law of the United States: An Analysis of Tentative Draft No. 6." *Ocean Development and International Law*, 18, No. 3 (1987), 343-390.

16440 **Nelson, L.D.M**. "The Patrimonial Sea." *International and Comparative Law Quarterly*, 22, No. 4 (October, 1973), 668-686.

16441 **Noel, H.S**. "The Law of the Sea?" No! The Law of Survival." *World Fishing*, 7, No. 7 (July, 1958), 30-38.

16442 **Oxman, Bernard H**. "The Third United Nations Conference on the Law of the Sea: The 1976 New York Sessions." *American Journal of International Law*, 71, No. 2 (April, 1977), 247-269.

16443 **Oxman, Bernard H**. "The Third United Nations Conference on the Law of the Sea: The 1977 New York Session." *American Journal of International Law*, 72, No. 1 (January, 1978), 57-83.

16444 **Oxman, Bernard H**. "The Third United Nations Conference on the Law of the Sea: The Eighth Session (1979)." *American Journal of International Law*, 74, No. 1 (January, 1980), 1-47.

16445 **Oxman, Bernard H**. "The Third United Nations Conference on the Law of the Sea: The Ninth Session (1980)." *American Journal of International Law*, 75, No. 2 (April, 1981), 211-256.

16446 **Oxman, Bernard H**. "The Third United Nations Conference on the Law of the Sea: The Seventh Session (1978)." *American Journal of International Law*, 73, No. 1 (January, 1979), 1-41.

16447 **Pardo, Arvid**. "The Evolving Law of the Sea: A Critique of the Informal Composite Negotiating Text, 1977." In *Ocean Yearbook*, Vol. 1, Elisabeth Mann Borgese and Norton Ginsburg, eds. Chicago, Illinois: University of Chicago Press, 1978, 9-37.

16448 **Pardo, Arvid**. "Who Will Control the Seabed?" *Foreign Affairs*, 47, 1 (October, 1968), 123-137.

16449 **Pardo, Arvid**. "Sovereignty Under the Sea: The Threat of National Occupation." *Round Table*, 58, No. 232 (October, 1968), 341-355.

16450 **Pardo, Arvid., and Young, R**. "The Legal Regime of the Deep Sea Floor." *American Journal of International Law*, 62, No. 3 (July, 1968), 641-653.

16451 **Peterson, M.J**. "Antarctic Implications of the New Law of the Sea." *Ocean Development and International Law*, 16, No. 2 (1986), 137-181.

16452 "Preliminary Documents of the Conference for the Codification The International Law, The Hague, March-April, 1930." *American Journal of International Law*, 30, Nos. 1-4 (January-October, 1930), 1-238 (supplement).

16453 **Quester, George H.** "Maritime Issues in Avoiding Nuclear War." *Armed Forces and Society*, 13, No. 2 (Winter, 1987), 189-214.

16454 **Richardson, Elliot L.** "Power, Mobility and the Law of the Sea." *Foreign Affairs*, 58, No. 4 (Spring, 1980), 902-919.

16455 **Romano, Ferdinando.** "Il fattore geografico nel diritto maritimo internazionale." *Universo*, 50, No. 2 (Marzo-Aprile, 1970), 429-444.

16456 **Ross, David A.** "A Changing Ocean Policy Horizon for Marine Science." *Ocean Development and International Law*, 15, Nos. 3 and 4 (1983), 221-232.

16457 **Schachte, William L., Jr.** "The Value of the 1982 UN Convention on the Law of the Sea: Preserving Our Freedoms and Protecting the Environment." *Ocean Development and International Law* [Washington, DC], 23, No. 1 (January-March, 1992), 55-69.

16458 **Sebenius, James K.** "The Computer as Mediator: Law of the Sea and Beyond." *Journal of Policy Analysis and Management*, 1, No. 1 (Fall, 1981), 77-95.

16459 **Sloz, P.J.** "The International Legal Regime for Navigation." *Ocean Development and International Law*, 15, No. 1 (1985), 89-98.

16460 **Smith, Robert W.** "Unilateralism: The Wave of the Future?" With Robert D. Hodgson in *Law of the Sea: Conference Outcomes and Problems of Implementation*, Edward Miles and John K. Gamble, eds. Cambridge, Massachusetts: Ballinger, 1977, 137-152.

16461 **Sorensen, Max.** "Law of the Sea." *International Conciliation*, 520 (November, 1958), 195-256.

16462 **Stevenson, John R., and Oxman, Bernard H.** "The Preparations for the Law of the Sea Conference." *American Journal of International Law*, 68, No. 1 (January, 1974), 1-32.

16463 **Stevenson, John R., and Oxman, Bernard H.** "The Third United Nations Conference on the Law of the Sea: The 1974 Caracas Session." *American Journal of International Law*, 69, No. 1 (January, 1975), 1-30.

16464 **Stevenson, John R., and Oxman, Bernard H.** "The Third United Nations Conference on the Law of the Sea: The 1975 Geneva Session." *American Journal of International Law*, 69, No. 4

(October, 1975), 763-797.

16465 **Swing, John Temple.** "Who Will Own the Oceans?" *Foreign Affairs*, 54, 3 (April, 1976), 527-546.

16466 **Vorbach, Joseph E.** "The Law of the Sea Regime and Ocean Law Enforcement: New Challenges for Technology." *Ocean Development and International Law*, 9, No. 3/4 (1981), 323-333.

16467 **Wahiche, Jean Dominique.** "Artificial Structures and Traditional Uses of the Sea: The Field of Conflict." *Marine Policy*, 7, No. 1 (January, 1983), 37-52.

16468 **Whiteman, M.M.** "Conference on the Law of the Sea: Convention on the Continental Shelf." *American Journal of International Law*, 52, No. 4 (October, 1958), 629-659.

16469 **Wilder, Robert J.** "Is This Holistic Ecology or Just Muddling Through?: The Theory and Practice of Marine Policy." *Coastal Management* [London], 21, No. 3 (July-September, 1993), 209-224.

16470 **Young, Oran R.** "Artic Waters': The Politics of Regime Formation." *Ocean Development and International Law*, 18, No. 1 (1987), 101-124.

16471 **Young, Richard.** "The Legal Status of Submarine Areas Beneath the High Seas." *American Journal of International Law*, 45, No. 2 (April, 1951), 225-239.

POLITICAL GEOGRAPHY OF REGIONS

Books and Journals

16472 **Adar, Korua Gombe.** "A Note on the Role of African States in Committee I of UNCLOS III." *Ocean Development and International Law*, 18, No. 6 (1987), 665-681.

16473 **Alexander, Lewis M.**, ed. *The Law of the Sea: National Policy Recommendations.* Kingston: University of Rhode Island, 1970.

16474 **Alexander, Lewis M.** *Offshore Geography of Northwestern Europe.* Chicago, Illinois: Rand McNally, 1963.

16475 **Allison, Anthony P.** "The Soviet Union and UNCLOS III: Pragmatism and Policy Evolution." *Ocean Development and International Law*, 16, No. 2 (1986), 109-136.

16476 **Anon (ICSU).** "Report of the Thirteenth Antarctic Treaty Consultative Meeting, Brussels 1985," *SCAR Bulletin*, 83 (1986), 19-50.

16477 **Aquarone, Marie-Christine.** "French Marine Policy in the 1970s and 1980s." *Ocean Development and International Law,* 19, No. 4 (1988), 267-286.

16478 **Armstrong, Terence; Rogers, George;** and **Rowley, Graham.** *Circumpolar North: A Political and Economic Geography of the Arctic and Sub-Arctic.* London: Methuen, 1978.

16479 **Baginski, Hennryk.** *Poland's Freedom of the Sea,* 4th ed. Kirkcaldy, Scotland: Allen Lithographic, 1944.

16480 **Barsegov, Yuri G.** "The USSR and the International Law of the Sea." *Oceanus* [Woods Hole], 34, No. 2 (Summer, 1991), 35-40.

16481 **Bassin, Mark.** *A Russian Mississippi, A Political-Geographical Inquiry into the Vision of Russia on the Pacific, 1840-1865.* Berkley: University of California, Ph.D., 1983.

16482 **Bergin, A.** "Australian Ocean Policy--The Need for Review." *Marine Policy,* 10, No. 2 (April, 1986), 155-158.

16483 **Brouwer, L.E.J.** "The North Sea." *World Land Use Survey,* Occasional Papers, No. 5. London: Cambridge University Press, 1964.

16484 **Butler, William E.** *The Soviet Union and the Law of the Sea.* Baltimore and London: Johns Hopkins University Press, 1971.

16485 **Buzan, Barry.** "Maritime Issues in North-East Asia." *Marine Policy,* 3, No. 3 (July, 1979),190-200.

16486 **Cagle, Malcolm W.** "The Neglected Ocean (The Indian Ocean)." *United States Naval Institute Proceedings,* 84, No. 11 (November, 1958), 54-61.

16487 **Cardoso de Menezes, E.** "A Antarctica e os desafios da Era Oceanica." *A Defesa Nacional,* 68, No. 695 (Julho-Augusto, 1981), 121-129.

16488 **Chiu, Hungdah.** "Political Geography in the Western Pacific After the Adoption of the 1982 United Nations Convention of the Law of the Sea." *Political Geography Quarterly,* 5, No. 1 (January, 1986), 25-32.

16489 **Costa, E.F.** "Peru and the Law of the Sea Convlention." *Marine Policy,* 11, 1 (January, 1987), 45-57.

16490 **Darman, Richard G.** "The Law of the Sea: Rethinking U.S. Interests." *Foreign Affairs,* 56, No. 2 (January, 1978), 373-395.

16491 **Das Gupta, Ashin,** and **Pearson, M.N.,** eds. *India and the Indian Ocean, 1500-1800.* New

Delhi: Oxford University Press, 1987.

16492 **de Blij, Harm J.** "A Regional Geography of Antarctica and the Southern Ocean." *University of Miami Law Review.* 3e, No. 2 (December, 1978), 229-314.

16493 **Drascher, W.** *Das Vordrigen der Vereinigten Staaten in Westindischen Mittlemeergebiet.* Hamburg: Friederichsen, 1918.

16494 **Dubosq, Andre.** *Le probleme du Pacifique.* Paris: Delagrave, 1927.

16495 "The East China Sea: The Role of International Law in the Settlement of Disputes." *Duke Law Journal,* 90, No. 4 (September, 1973), 823-865.

16496 **El Hakim, Ali A.** *The Middle Eastern States and the Law of the Sea.* Syracuse, New York: Syracuse University Press, 1979.

16497 **Franklin, C.M.** *The Law of the Sea. Some Recent Developments, with Particular Reference to the United Nations Conference of 1958.* Washington, D.C.: U.S. Printing Office, 1961.

16498 "Geopolitique et geostratigie dans l'ocean Pacifique." *Bulletin de l'Association des Geographes Francaises,* 64 (1988), 97-137, (special issue)

16499 **Ghelardoni, Paolo.** "Le Nuove Norme del Diritto del Mare e la Situazione Italiana nel Mediterraneo [The New Regulations of the Laws of the Sea and the Italian Situation in the Mediterranean]." *Rivista Geografica Italiana,* Annata 86, Fasc. 2 (Givgno, 1979), 153-171.

16500 **Greenfield, Jeanette.** *China and the Law of the Sea, Air, and Environment.* The Hague: Sijthoff and Noordhoff, 1979.

16501 **Grolin, Jesper.** "The Question of Antarctica and the Problem of Sovereignty." *International Relations,* 9, NO. 1 (May, 1987), 39-55.

16502 **Gross, Leo.** "The Geneva Conference on the Law of the Sea and the Right of Innocent Passage Through the Gulf of Aqaba." *American Journal of International Law,* 53, No. 3 (July, 1959), 564-594.

16503 **Herrick, Carl H.** *The Indian Ocean: The End of an Era.* Report No. 3928, March 23, 1970. Air War College, Air University, Alabama: Maxwell Air Force Base, 1970.

16504 **Herrick, Robert W.** *The USSR's "Blue Belt Defense" Concept.* Arlington, Virginia: Center for Naval Analysis, 1973.

16505 **Hollick, Ann L.** *U.S. Foreign Policy and the Law of the Sea.* Princeton, New Jersey: Princeton University Press, 1981.

16506 **Hourani, George Fadio.** *Arab Seafaring in the Indian Ocean in Ancient and Early Medieval Times.* New York: Octagon Books, 1975.

16507 **Ibler, Vladimir.** "The Changing Law of the Sea as Affecting the Adriatic." *German Yearbook of International Law*, 20 (1977), 174-195.

16508 **Jones, Stephen B.** *The Arctic: Problems and Possibilities.* New Haven, Connecticut: Yale Institute of International Studies, 1948.

16509 **Kawagami, Kenzo.** *Le probleme du Pacifique et la politique japonaise.* Paris: Bossard, 1923.

16510 **Kent, George, and Valencia, Mark J.,** eds. *Marine Policy in Southeast Asia.* Berkeley: University of California Press, 1985.

16511 **Kimball, Lee.** "Whiter Antarctica." *International Studies Notes*, 11, No. 3 (1985), 16-22.

16512 **Kirk, William.** "Indian Ocean Community." *Scottish Geographical Magazine*, 67, Nos. 3-4 (December, 1951), 161-177.

16513 **Kittredge, G.W.** "Under the Polar Cap: A Voyage that Must be Made." *Proceedings U.S. Naval Institute*, 84, No. 2 (February, 1958), 61-65.

16514 **Kizer, Benjamin H.** *The North Pacific International Planning Project.* 39 mimeographed 1. Institute of Pacific Relations, 8th Conference, Mont Tremblant, Quebec, Canada, December, 1942. American Council Paper No. 2. New York: American Council, Institute of Pacific Relations, 1942.

16515 **Knecht, Robert W.; Cicin-Sain, Biliana; and Archer, Jack H.** National Ocean Policy: A Window of Opportunity." *Ocean Development and International Law*, 19, No. 2(1988), 113-142.

16516 **Lee, Roy S.** "The New Law of the Sea and the Pacific Basin." *Ocean Development and International Law*,12, Nos. 3/4 (1983), 247-264.

16517 **Lee, Yong Leng.** *Southeast Asia and the Law of the Sea. Some Preliminary Observations on the Political Geography of Southeast Asian Seas.* Rev. ed. Singapore: University Press, 1980.

16518 **Lloyd, Trevor.** "Aben himmal i Artic." *Gronland*, (1959), 353-360.

16519 **Logan, Roderick M.** *Canada, the United States, and the Third Law of the Sea Conference.* Montreal: C.D. Howe Research Institute, 1974.

16520 **Macdonald, Charles Gordon.** *Iran and Saudi Arabia in the Persian Gulf: A Study of the Law of the Sea.* Charlottesville, Virginia: University of Virginia, Ph.D., 1976.

16521 **MacDonald, Charles G.** *Iran, Saudi Arabia, and the Law of the Sea: Political Interaction and Legal Development in the Persian Gulf.* Westport: Greenwood Press Contributions in Political Science, 48, 1980.

16522 **McDorman, Ted L.** "Implementation of the LOS Convention: Options, Impediments, and the ASEAN States." *Ocean Development and International Law*, 18, No. 3 (1987), 279-303.

16523 **Massi, Ernesto.** "Problemi mediterranei." *Geopolitica*, Anno 2, Num. 12 (Dicembre 31, 1940), 531-540.

16524 **Meredith, Brian.** "A Plan for the Artic: Mr. Trudeau's International Regime." *Round Table*, 238 (April, 1970), 177-182.

16525 **Miller, Francis Pickens.** "The Atlantic Area." *Foreign Affairs*, 19, No. 4 (July, 1941), 727-728.

16526 **Morell, James B.** *The Law of the Sea: An Historical Anlaysis of the 1982 Treaty and Its Rejection by the United States.* Jefferson: McFarland and Company, Inc., 1992.

16527 **Oxman, Bernard H.; Caron, David D.; and Buderi, Charles L.O.,** eds. *Law of the Sea: U.S. Policy Dilemma.* San Francisco: Institute for Contemporary Studies, 1983.

16528 **Payne, Richard J.** "The Caribbean and the Law of the Sea." *Round Table* (London), Issue 279, No. 3 (July, 1980), 322-329.

16529 **Pharand, Donat.** *The Law of the Sea of the Arctic with Special Reference to Canada.* Ottawa, Ontario, Canada: University of Ottawa, 1973.

16530 **Rembe, Nasila S.** *Africa and the International Law of the Sea: A Study of the Contribution of the African States to the Third United Nations Conference on the Law of the Sea,* vol. 6. The Hague: Alphen aan den Rijn; Sijthoff and Noordhoff: Sijthoff Publications on Ocean Development, 1980.

16531 "Report of Fifth Antarctic Treaty Consultative Meeting, Paris, 1968." *Polar Record*, 14, No. 92 (May, 1969), 663-675.

16532 **Rothwell, Donald R., and Kaye, Stuart.** "Law of the Sea and the Polar Regions: Reconsidering the Traditional Norms." *Marine Policy* [Oxford], 18, No. 1 (January, 1994), 41-58.

16533 **Roucek, Joseph S.** "The Indian Ocean." *Social Studies*, 44, No. 3 (March, 1953), 103-104.

16534 "The Role of the Sea in the Political Geography of Scotland." *Scottish Geographical Magazine,* 100, No. 3 (December, 1984), 138-150.

16535 **Shannon, W. Wayne, and Palmer, David D.** "Academic Marine Scientists and the Federal Funding System." *Ocean Development and International Law,* 17, Nos. 1, 2, and 3 (1986), 9-35.

16536 **Smith, Roger C.** "The Maritime Geography of the Cayman Islands." *Caribbean Geography,* 1, No. 4 (November, 1984), 247-255.

16537 **Sullivan, William J., Jr.** "Is there a National Ocean Policy?" *Ocean Development and International Law,* 15, No. 1 (1985), 77-88.

16538 **Svarlien, O.** "The Legal Status of Artic." *Proceedings, American Society of International Law,* (April 24-26, 1958), 136-144.

16539 **Thorpe, Captain A.G.Y.** "Mine Warfare at Sea- -Some Legal Aspects of the Future." *Ocean Development and International Law,* 18, No. 2 (1987), 255-278.

16540 **Toussaint, August.** *History of the Indian Ocean.* Chicago, Illinois: University of Chicago Press, 1966.

16541 **U.S. Department of State.** Washington, D.C. "Denmark." *Limits in the Sea, The Geographer.* 19 (1970), 8, pamphlet.

16542 **U.S. Department of State.** Washington, D.C. "Finland." *Limits in the Sea, The Geographer. The Geographer.* 48 (1972), pamphlet.

16543 **U.S. Department of State.** Washington, D.C. "Ireland." *Limits in the Sea, The Geographer.* 3 (1970), pamphlet.

16544 **U.S. Department of State.** Washington, D.C. The Maritime Boundary Between the United States and Mexico." *Limits in the Sea, The Geographer.* 45 (1972), pamphlet.

16545 **U.S. Department of State.** Washington, D.C. "Mauritania." *Limits in the Sea, The Geographer.* 8 (1970), 1, pamphlet.

16546 **U.S. Department of State.** Washington, D.C. "The People's Republic of China." *Limits in the Sea, The Geographer.* 43 (1972), 2, pamphlet.

16547 **Volckaert, I.** "Formulation of National Marine Police: The Case of Belgium." *Marine Policy,* 10, No. 2 (April, 1986), 90-100.

16548 **Villiers, Alan.** *The Indian Ocean.* London: Museum Press, 1952.

CONTINENTAL SHELF, TERRITORIAL SEA AND MARITIME BOUNDARIES

GENERAL AND THEORY

Books

16549 **Alexander, Lewis M.** *Alternative Methods for Delimiting the Outer Boundary of the Continental Shelf.* Washington, D.C.: U.S. Department of State, Office of External Research, 1970.

16550 **Anninos, P.C.L.** *The Continental Shelf and Public International Law.* La Haye: Imprimerie H.P. De Swart et Fils, 1953.

16551 **Auguste, B.B.L.** *The Continental Shelf. Practice and Policy of Latin American States with Special Reference to Chile, Ecuador, and Peru; A Study in International Relations.* Geneve: Libraire E. Droz, 1960.

16552 **Barster, R.P., and Birni, Patricia, eds.** *Maritime Dimensions.* London: Allen & Unwin, 1980.

16553 **Blake, Gerald.** *Maritime Boundaries and Ocean Resources.* London: Croom Helm, 1987.

16554 **Clingham, Thomas A., ed.** *Law of the Sea: State Practice in Zones of Special Jurisdiction.* Honolulu: Law of the Sea Institute, 1982.

16555 **Crocker, Henry G.** *The Extent of the Marginal Sea.* Washington, D.C.: Government Printing Office, 1919.

16556 **Day, E.E.D., ed.** *Public Policy and the Coastal Zone.* Halifax: Saint Malry's University, Department of Geography, Studies in Marine Coastal Geography, No. 5, 1986a.

16557 **Dubner, Barry Hart.** *The Law of Territorial Waters of Mid-Ocean Archipelagoes and Archipelagic States.* The Hague: Martinus Nijhoff, 1976.

16558 *The Frontier of the Seas: The Problems of Delimitation.* Tokyo: The Ocean Association of Japan, 1981. (Proceedings and Papers of the Fifth Annual International Ocean Symposium held in Tokyo, November 26-27, 1980.)

16559 **Friedheim, Robert L.** *The Continental Shelf Issue at the United Nations: A Quantitative Content Analysis.* Arlington, Virginia: Center for Naval Analyses, 1970.

16560 **Hall, Arthur R.** *Ballistics in the Seventeenth Century.* Cambridge: Cambridge University Press, 1952.

16561 **Hedberg, Hollis D.** *National-International Jurisdictional Boundary on the Ocean Floor.* Kingston, Rhode Island: Law of the Sea Institute, 1972.

16562 **Johnston, Douglas M.** *The Theory and History of Ocean Boundlary Making.* Montreal: McGill University Press, 1988.

16563 **Johnston, Douglas M., and Saunders, P.** *Ocean Boundary Making: Regional Issues and Development.* London: Croom Helm, 1988.

16564 *Laws and Regulations on the Regime of the Territorial Sea.* New York: United Nations Legislative Series, ST/LEG/SER. B/6, 1957.

16565 *Legal Foundations of the Ocean Regime.* Malta: Royal University of Malta Press, 1971.

16566 **Marz, Josef.** *Landmachte und Seemachte.* Berlin: Zentralverlag, 1928.

16567 **Masterson, William E.** *Jurisdiction in Marginal Seas.* New York: Macmillan, 1929.

16568 **McDorman, Ted L.; Beauchamp, Kenneth P.; and Johnston, Douglas M.** *Maritime Boundary Delimitation: An Annotated Bibliography.* Lexington, Massachusetts: Lexington Books, 1983.

16569 **Meijer, C.B.V.** *The Extent of Jurisdiction in Coastal Waters.* Leiden: A.W. Sijthoff's Vitgevers Maatschappij, N.V., 1937.

16570 **Mouton, M.W.** *The Continental Shelf.* The Hague: Martinus Nijhoff, 1952.

16571 **Park, Choon-Ho.** *Continental Shelf Issues in the Yellow Sea and the East China Sea.* Kingston, Rhode Island: Law of the Sea Institute, 1972.

16572 **Prescott, J.R.V.** *The Maritime Political Boundaries of the World.* London and New York: Methuen, 1985.

16573 **Raested, Arnold Christopher.** *La Mer Territoriale.* Paris: A. Pedone, 1913.

16574 **Reynaud, Andre.** *La Volonte la Nature, et de Droit: Les Differends du Plateau Continental de la Mer du Nord devant la Court Internationale de Justice. Bibliotheque de Droit International, Vol. 78.* Paris: Librairie Generale de Droit et de Jurisprudence, 1986.

16575 **Rubio Y Munoz-Bocanegra, Angel.** *Las plataformas Continentales como problema geopolitico.* Panama: University de Panama, 1955.

16576 **Slouka, Zdenek J.** *International Custom and the Continental Shelf.* The Hague: Martinus Nijhoff, 1968.

16577 **Swarztrauber, Sayre A.** *The Three Mile Limit of Territorial Seas.* Annapolis, Maryland: Naval Institute Press, 1972.

16578 **Symmons, Clive Ralph.** *The Maritime Zones of Islands in International Law.* The Hague: Martinus Nijhoff. Developments in International Law, Vol. 1, 1979.

16579 **Tobar Donoso, J. and Luna Tobar, A.** *Derecho Territorial Ecuatoriano,* 3rd ed. Quito: Ministerio de Relaciones Exteriores, 1982.

16580 **U.S. Department of State.** Washington, D.C. *Map Showing Theoretical Division of the Continental Shelf and Seabed. The Geographer.* Washington, D.C.: U.S. Department of State, 1971.

16581 **U.S. Department of State.** *National Claims to Maritime Jurisdictions.* Washington, D.C.: Office of the Geographer, 1973.

16582 **U.S. Department of State.** *Theoretical Areal Allocations of Seabed to Coastal States.* Washington, D.C.: Office of the Geographer, 1972.

16583 **Yates, G.T. III. and Young, J.H.,** eds. *Limits to National Jurisdiction over the Sea.* Charlottesville: University Press of Virginia, 1974.

Journals

16584 **Adede, A.O.** "Toward the Formulation of the Rule of Delimitation of Sea Boundaries Between States with Adjacent or Opposite Coasts." *Virginia Journal of International Law,* 19, No. 2 (Winter, 1979), 207-255.

16585 **Alexander, Lewis M.** "Alternative Regimes for the Continental Shelf." In *Legal Foundations of the Ocean Regime.* Malta: Royal University of Malta Press, 1971, 31-43.

16586 **Alexander, Lewis M.** "The Delimitation of Maritime Boundaries." *Political Geography Quarterly,* 5, No. 1 (January, 1986), 19-24.

16587 **Alexander, Lewis M.** "The Expanding Territorial Sea." *Professional Geographer,* 11, No. 4 (July, 1959), 6-8.

16588 **Allen, Edward W.** "Territorial Waters and Extraterritorial Rights." *American Journal of International Law,* 47, No. 3 (July, 1953), 478-480.

16589 **Archdale, H.E.** "Territorial Waters: What are They?" *Australian Outlook*, 10, No. 1 (March, 1956), 42-45.

16590 **Auburn, F.M.** "The 1973 Conference on the Law of the Sea in the Light of Current Trends in State Seabed Practice." *Canadian Bar Review*, 50, No. 1 (March, 1972), 87-109.

16591 **Barry, F.J.** "The Administration of the Outer Continental Lands Act." *Natural Resources Lawyer*, 1, No. 3 (July, 1968), 38-48.

16592 **Baty, Thomas.** "The Three Mile Limit." *American Journal of International Law*, 22, No. 3 (July, 1928), 503-537.

16593 **Beazley, P.B.** "Developments in Maritime Delimitation." *Hydrographic Journal*, 39 (1986), 5-9.

16594 **Beazley, P.B.** "Maritime Boundaries." *International Hydrographic Review*, 59, No. 1 (January,1982), 149-159.

16595 **Berry, K.B.** "Delimitation and the Anglo-French Arbitration." *Australian Year Book of International Law*, 6 (1978), 139-152.

16596 **Birnie, P.W.** "Contemporary Maritime Legal Problems." In *The Maritime Dimension*, R.P. Barstor and Patricia Birni, eds. London: Allen & Unwin, 1980, 169-189.

16597 **Blecher, M.D.** "Equitable Delimitation of Continental Shelf." *American Journal of International Law*, 73, No. 1 (January, 1979), 60-88.

16598 **Boggs, S. Whittemore.** "Delimitation of Seaward Areas Under National Jurisdiction." *American Journal of International Law*, 45, No. 1 (January, 1951), 240-266.

16599 **Boggs, S. Whittemore.** "Delimitation of the Territorial Sea." *American Journal of International Law*, 24, No. 3 (July, 1930), 541-555.

16600 **Boggs, S. Whittemore.** "National Claims in Adjacent Seas." *Geographical Review*, 41, No. 2 (April, 1951), 185-209.

16601 **Boggs, S. Whittemore.** "Problems of Water-Boundary Definition: Median Lines and International Boundaries through Territorial Waters." *Geographical Review*, 27, No. 3 (July, 1937), 445-456.

16602 **Borchard, Edwin.** "Jurisdiction Over the Littoral Bed of the Sea." *American Journal of International Law*, 35, No. 3 (July, 1941), 515-519.

16603 **Bouchez, Leo J.** "The Outer Boundary of National Jurisdiction." In *Legal Foundations of the Ocean Regime*. Malta: Royal University of Malta Press, 1971, 50-60.

16604 **Bowen, Robert E., and Hennessey, Timothy M.** "Adjacent State Issues for the United States in Establishing an Exclusive Economic Zone: The Case of Canada and Mexico." *Ocean Development and International Law*, 15, Nos. 3 and 4 (1985), 355-375.

16605 **Brownlie, Ian.** "Recommendations on the Limits of the Continental Shelf and Related Matters: A Contemporary View." In *The Law of the Sea: National Policy Recommendations*, ed. by Lewis M. Alexander. Kingston: University of Rhode Island, 1970, 133-158.

16606 **Brown, E.D.** "Delimitation of Offshore Areas: Hard Labour and Bitter Fruits at UNCLOS III." *Marine Policy*, 5, No. 2 (April, 1981), 172-184.

16607 **Brown, E.D.** "The Outer Limit of the Continental Shelf." *Juridical Review*, 13 (1968), 111-146.

16608 **Brown, P.M.** "Address on Three-Mile Limit." *American Journal of International Law*, 17, No. 3 (July, 1923), 528-533.

16609 **Brown, P.M.** "The Marginal Sea." *American Journal of International Law*, 17, No. 1 (January, 1923), 89-95.

16610 **Caflisch, Lucius.** "Les Zones Maritimes sous Juridiction Nationale, leurs Limites et leur Delimitation." *Reveue Generale de Droit International Public*, 84 (1980), 68-119.

16611 **Carter, Jared G.** "The Seabed Beyond the Limits of National Jurisdiction." *Stanford Journal of International Studies*, 4 (June, 1969), 1-31.

16612 **Cataudella, M.** "Suilimiti delle acque territoriali." *Geografia nel scuole*, 15, 5 (1970), 165-174.

16613 **Chaney, Jonathan I.** "The Delimitation of Ocean Boundaries." *Ocean Development and International Law*, 18, No. 5 (1987), 497-531.

16614 **Chaney, Jonathan I.** "The Exclusive Economic Zone and Public International Law." *Ocean Development and International Law*, 15, Nos. 3 and 4 (1985), 233-288.

16615 **Chng, Yi-ting.** "Delimitation of the Continental Shelf." *Annals of the Chinese Society of International Law*, 6 (1969), 39-50.

16616 **Clemison, H.M.** "Laws of Maritime Jurisdiction in Time of Peace." *British Year Book of International Law*, 6 (1925), 1-144.

16617 **Codding, C.A., and Rubenstein, Alvin Z.** "How Wide the Territorial Sea?" *U.S. Naval Institute Proceedings*, 87, No. 2 (February, 1961), 74-77.

16618 **Colombos, C. John.** "Territorial Waters." *Transactions Grotins Society*, 9 (1923), 89.

16619 **Cosford, Edwin J., Jr.** "The Continental Shelf 1910-1945." *McGill Law Journal*, 4, No. 4 (December, 1958), 245-266.

16620 **Christy, Francis T.** "Property Rights in the World Oceans." *Natural Resources Journal*, 15, No. 4 (October, 1975), 695-712.

16621 **Dean, Arthur H.** "Geneva Convention on the Continental Shelf." *Tulane Law Review*, 41, No. 2 (February, 1967), 419-432.

16622 **Delin, Lars.** "Shall Islands be Taken into Account when Drawing the Median Line According to Art. 6 of the Convention on the Continental Shelf?" *Nordisk Tidsskrift for International Ret*, 41, Fase 1-4 (1971), 205-219.

16623 **Dellapenna, Joseph W., and Wang, Ar-Young.** "The Republic of China's Claims Relating to the Territorial Sea, Continental Shelf, and Exclusive Economic Zones: Legal and Economic Aspects." *Boston College International and Comparative Law Review*, 3, No. 2 (Summer, 1980), 353-376.

16624 **Denorme, Roger.** "The Seaward Limit of the Continental Shelf." In *The Law of the Sea: National Policy Recommendations*, Lewis M. Alexander, ed. Kingston: University of Rhode Island, 1970, 263-274. (Proceedings and Papers of the Fourth Law of the Sea Institute Conference held in Kingston, Rhode Island, June 23-26, 1969.)

16625 **Durante, Francesco.** "Norme Generali e Regole Convenzionali per la Delimitazione della Piattaforma Continentale." *Rivista di Diritto Internazionale*, 53 (1970), 5-20.

16626 **Ely, Northcutt.** "Seabed Boundaries Between Coastal States: The Effect to be Given Islets as 'Special Circumstances.'" *International Lawyer*, 6, No. 2 (April, 1972), 219-236.

16627 **Emery, K.O.** "The Continental Shelf." *Scientific American*, 221, No. 3 (September, 1969), 106-125.

16628 **Emery, K.O.** "Geological Aspects of Sea-floor Sovereignty." In *The Law of the Sea: Offshore Boundaries and Zones*, Lewis M. Alexander, ed. Columbus: Ohio State University Press, 1967, 139-159. (Proceedings and Papers of the First Law of the Sea Institute Conference held in Kingston, Rhode Island, June 27-July 1, 1966.)

16629 **Emery, K.O.** "Geological Limits of the 'Continental Shelf.'" *Ocean Development and International Law*, 10, Nos. 1 and 2 (1982), 1-11.

16630 **Eustis, Frederic A., III.** "Method and Basis of Seaward Delimitation of Continental Shelf Jurisdiction." *Virginia Journal of International Law*, 17, No. 1 (Fall, 1976), 107-130.

16631 **Fenn, P.T.** "Origins of the Theory of Territorial Waters." *American Journal of International Law*, 10, No. 3 (July, 1926), 465-482.

16632 **Feulner, Gary R.** "Delimitation of Continental Shelf Jurisdiction Between States: The Effect of Physical Irregularities in the Natural Continental Shelf." *Virginia Journal of International Law*, 17, No. 1 (Fall, 1976), 77-105.

16633 **Finlay, Luke W.** "The Outer Limit of the Continental Shelf: A Rejoinder to Professor Louis Henkin." *American Journal of International Law*, 64 (1970), 42-61.

16634 **Finlay, Luke W.** "Realism vs. Idealism as the Key to the Determination of the Limits of National Jurisdiction Over the Continental Shelf. In *Limits to National Jurisdiction Over the Sea*, G.T. Yates, III and J.H. Young, eds. Charlottesville: University Press of Virginia, 1974, 75-99.

16635 **Fleischer, Carl August.** "The Northern Waters and the New Maritime Zones." *German Yearbook of International Law*, 22 (1979), 100-118.

16636 **Friedmann, Wolfgang.** "Selden Redivivus-Towards a Partition of the Seas?" *American Journal of International Law*, 65, No. 5 (October, 1971), 757-770.

16637 **Gihl, Torsten.** "The Baseline of the Territorial Sea." *Scandinavian Studies in Law*, 11 (1967), 119-174.

16638 **Glantz, Michael H.** "Man, State, and Fisheries: An Inquiry into Some Societal Constraints that Affect Fisheries Management." *Ocean Development and International Law*, 17, Nos. 1, 2, and 3 (1986), 192-270.

16639 **Goldie, L.F.E.** "The Continental Shelf's Outer Boundary-A Postscript." *Journal of Maritime Law and Commerce*, 2, No. 1 (October, 1970), 173-177.

16640 **Goldie, L.F.E.** "Delimiting Continental Shelf Boundaries." In *Limits to National Jurisdiction Over the Sea*, G.T. Yate, III, and J.H. Young, eds. Charlottesville: University Press of Virginia, 1974, 3-74.

16641 **Goldie, L.F.E.** "The International Court of Justice's 'Natural Prolongation' and the Continental Shelf Problem of Islands." *Netherlands Yearbook of International Law*, 4 (1973), 237-261.

16642 **Goldie, L.F.E.** "A Lexicographical Controversy-The World 'Adjacent' in Article I of the Continental Shelf Convention." *American Journal of International Law*, 66, No. 5 (October, 1972), 829-835.

16643 **Goldie, L.F.E.** "Where is the Continental Shelf's Outer Boundary?" *Journal of Maritime Law and Commerce*, 1, No. 3 (April, 1970), 461-472.

16644 **Goncalves, Maria Eduarda.** "Concepts of Marine Regions and the New Law of the Sea." *Marine Policy*, 3, No. 4 (October, 1979), 255-263.

16645 **Gormley, W. Paul.** "The Unilateral Extension of Territorial Waters: The Failure of the United Nations to Protect Freedom of the Seas." *University of Detroit Law Journal*, 43, No. 5 (June, 1966), 695-730.

16646 **Green, L.C.** "The Continental Shelf." *Current Legal Problems*, 4 (April, 1951), 54-80.

16647 **Grex, T.** "Territorial Waters." *Law Quarterly Review*, 42, No. 3 (July, 1926), 350-367.

16648 **Gutteridge, J.A.C.** "The 1958 Geneva Convention on the Continental Shelf." *British Year Book of International Law*, 35 (1959), 102-123.

16649 **Haight, G. Winthrop.** "The Seabed and the Ocean Floor." *International Lawyer*, 3, No. 3 (April, 1969), 642-673.

16650 **Hedberg, Hollis D.** "The National-International Jurisdictional Boundary on the Ocean Floor." *Ocean Management*, 1, No 1 (March, 1973), 83-118.

16651 **Hedberg, Hollis D.** "Relation of Political Boundaries on the Ocean Floor to the Continental Margin." *Virginia Journal of International Law*, 17, No. 1 (Fall, 1976), 57-75.

16652 **Henkin, Louis.** "The Extent of the Legal Continental Shelf." In *Legal Foundations of the Ocean Regime.* Malta: Royal University of Malta Press, 1971, 15-30.

16653 **Henkin, Louis.** "International Law and 'the Interests': the Law of the Seabed." *American Journal of International Law*, 63, No. 3 (July, 1969), 504-510.

16654 **Hilbert, W.E.** "The Three-Mile Limit of Territorial Waters." *United States Naval Institute*

Proceedings, 64, No. 424 (June, 1938), 804-812.

16655 **Hodgson, Robert D., and Smith, Robert W.** "Boundary Issues Created by Extended National Marine Jurisdiction." *Geographical Review*, 69, No. 4 (October, 1979), 423-433.

16656 **Holland, Henry F.** "The Juridical Status of the Continental Shelf." *Texas Law Review*, 30, No. 5 (May, 1952), 586-598.

16657 **Hosni, Sayed M.** "The Partition of the Neutral Zone." *American Journal of International Law*, 60, No. 4 (October, 1966), 735-749.

16658 **Hurst, Sir Cecil C.** "The Continental Shelf." *Transactions of the Grotius Society*, 34 (1949), 153-169.

16659 **Hurst, Sir Cecil C.** "The Territoriality of Bays." *British Year Book of International Law*, 3 (1922-1923), 1-42.

16660 **Hurst, Sir Cecil C.** "Whose is the Bed of the Sea?" *British Yearbook of International Law*, (1953-54), 34-43.

16661 **Irwin, Paul C.** "Settlement of Maritime Boundary Disputes: An Analysis of the law of the Sea Negotiations." *Ocean Development and International Law*, 8, No. 2 (1980), 105-148.

16662 **Jain, H.M.** "Continental Shelf-Some Geological Aspects." *Indian Journal of International Law*, 12, No. 4 (October-December, 1972), 564-580.

16663 **Johnston, Douglas M., and Gold, Edgar.** "Extended Jurisdiction: UNCLOS III on Coastal State Practice." In *Law of the Sea: State Practice in Zones of Special Jurisdiction*, Thomas A. Clinghan, ed. Honolulu: Law of the Sea Institute, 1982, 3-56. (Proceedings and Papers of the Thirteenth Annual Law of the Sea Institute Conference held in Mexico City, October 15-18, 1979.)

16664 **Jones, Lawrence, R., Jr.** "International Law-The Three Mile Limit or More-It's Anyone's Guess." *Journal of Air Law and Commerce*, 33, No. 2 (Spring, 1967), 356-361.

16665 **Juda, Lawrence.** "The Exclusive Economic Zone: Compatibility of National Claims and the U.N. Convention onl the Law of the Sea." *Ocean Development and International Law*, 16, No. 1 (1986), 1-58.

16666 **Juda, Lawrence.** "The Exclusive Economic Zone and Ocean Management." *Ocean Development and International Law*, 18, No. 3 (1987), 305-331.

16667 **Kamat, D.A.** "Recent Developments in the Law Relating to the Seabed." *Indian Journal of International Law*, 11, No. 1 (January-March, 1971), 9-19.

16668 **Karl, Donald E.** "Islands and the Delimitation of the Continental Shelf: A Framework for Analysis." *American Journal of International Law*, 71, No. 4 (October, 1977), 642-673.

16669 **Kawakami, Kenzo.** "The Continental Shelf and Its Geographically Controversial Points." *Journal of Geography of Tokyo*, 63, No. 2 (692) (1954), 53-59.

16670 **Kent, H.S.K.** "The Historical Origins of the Three Mile Limit." *American Journal of International Law*, 48, No. 4 (October, 1954), 537-553.

16671 **King, John.** "Beyond the Shoreline: The Marine Estate." *Marine Policy*, 18, No. 6 (November, 1994), 457-463.

16672 **Knauss, John A.** "Creeping Jurisdiction and Customary International Law." *Ocean Development and International Law*, 15, No. 2 (1985), 209-216.

16673 **Koh, Kwang Lim.** "The Continental Shelf and the International Law Commission." *Boston University Law Review*, 35, No. 4 (November, 1955), 522-540.

16674 **Kunz, Josef L.** "Continental Shelf and International Law: Confusion and Abuse." *American Journal of International Law*, 50,No. 4 (October, 1956), 828-853.

16675 **Kwiatkowska, Barbara.** "Creeping Jurisdiction Beyond 200 Miles in the Light of the 1982 Law of the Sea Convention and State Practice." *Ocean Development and International Law* [New York], 22, No. 2 (April-June, 1991), 153-187.

16676 **Laurent, Francis W.** "Judicial Definitions of Navigable Waters." *Military Engineer*, 30, No. 173 (September-October, 1938), 332-336.

16677 **Leach, Warren B., Jr.** "Locating the Baseline in Determining Territorial Jurisdiction Over Natural Resources in the Ocean Floor." *South Texas Law Journal*, 9, No. 2 (1967), 45-64.

16678 **Leardi, Eraldo.** "Utilizzazione die fondi marini e mare territoriale: note di geografia politica ed economica [Utilization of the Sea Bottoms and Territorial Sea: Notes of Economic and Political Geography]." *Bollettino della Societa Geografica Italiana*. Ser. 10, Vol. 6, Fasc. 1-3 (Gennaio-Marzo, 1977), 1-24.

16679 **Lee, Yong Leng.** "Some Geopolitical Implications of UNCLOS III Continental Shelf Problems." *Singapore Journal of Tropical Geography*, 2, No. 1 (June, 1981), 32-39.

16680 **Leversen, Michael A.** "The Problems of Delimitations of Base Lines for Outlying Archipelagoes." *San Diego Law Review*, 9, No. 3 (May, 1971), 733-746.

16681 **Lewis, Austin W.** "Offshore Boundary and Title Issues." *Natural Resources Lawyer*, 4, No. 4 (December, 1971), 737-746.

16682 **Limitone, Anthony, Jr.** "The Interaction of Law and Technology: The Continental Shelf Problem." *Cornell International Law Journal*, 1, (Spring, 1968), 49-65.

16683 **Long, M.J.** "Defining Offshore Boundaries." *Land & Minerals Surveying*, 4 , No. 3 (1986), 141-145.

16684 **Lowe, A.V.** "International Law and Federal Offshore Lands Disputes." *Marine Policy*, 1, No. 4 (October, 1977), 311-317.

16685 **Macdonald, Roderick.** "Marine Order and the New Law of the Sea." *International Hydrographic Review*, 60, No. 2 (July, 1983), 121-126.

16686 **Mani, V.S.** "National Jurisdiction: Islands and Archipelagoes." In *Law of the Sea: Caracas and Beyond*, R.P. Anand, ed. Boston, Massachusetts: Martinus Nijhoff, 1980, 82-110.

16687 **Manner, E.J.** "Some Basic Viewpoints on Delimitation of Marine Areas Between Neighbouring States." In *The Frontier of the Seas: The Problems of Delimitation*. Tokyo: The Ocean Association of Japan, 1981, 7-17. (Proceedings and Papers of the Fifth Annual International Ocean Symposium held in Tokyo, November 26-27, 1980.)

16688 **Marston, Geoffrey.** "Low-Tide Elevations and Straight Baselines." *British Year Book of International Law*, 46 (1972-1973), 405-423.

16689 **McDougal, Myres S., and Burke, William T.** "The Community Interest in a Narrow Territorial Sea: Inclusive Versus Exclusive Competence Over the Oceans." *Cornell Law Quarterly*, 45, No. 2 (Winter, 1960), 171-253.

16690 **Melamid, Alexander.** "Artificial Islands on Continental Shelves." *Professional Geographer*, 9, No. 1 (January, 1957), 16-17.

16691 **Moodie, A.E.** "The Continental Shelf: Some Territorial Problems Associated with the Continental Shelf." *Advancement of Science*, 11, No. 41 (June, 1954), 42-48.

16692 **Morales Paul, Isidro.** "El Regimen de la Alta Mar [The Regime of the High Seas]." In *Tendencias del derecho del mar Contemporaneo,* Francisco Orrego Vicuna, ed. Buenos Aires: Libreria El Ateneo Editorial (For UNITAR), 1974, 130-134.

16693 **Munkman, A.L.W.** "Adjudication and Adjustment-International Judicial Decision and the Settlement of Territorial Boundary Disputes." *British Yearbook of International Law,* 46 (1972-1973), 1-116.

16694 **Nawaz, M.K.** "Alternative Criteria for Delimiting the Continental Shelf." *Indian Journal of International Law,* 13, No. 1 (January-March, 1973), 25-40.

16695 **Nelso, L.D.M.** "Equity and the Delimitation of Maritime Boundaries." *Revue Iranienne des relations Internationales,* 11/12 (1978), 197-218.

16696 **Oda, Shigeru.** "Boundary of the Continental Shelf." *Japanese Annual of International Law,* 12 (1968), 264-284.

16697 **Oda, Shigeru.** "The Concept of the Contiguous Zone." *International and Comparative Law Quarterly,* 11, No. 1 (January, 1962), 131-153.

16698 **Oda, Shigeru.** "Proposals for Revising the Convention on the Continental Shelf." *Columbia Journal of Transnational Law,* 7, No. 1 (Spring, 1968), 1-31.

16699 **Orlin, Hyman.** "Offshore Boundaries: Engineering and Economic Aspects." *Ocean Development and International Law,* 3, No. 1 (1975), 87-96.

16700 **Oxman, Bernard H.** "The Preparation of Article 1 of the Convention on the Continental Shelf." *Journal of Maritime Law and Commerce,* 3, No. 2 (January, 1972), 245-305; 3, No. 3 (April, 1972), 445-472; and 3, No. 4 (July, 1972), 683-723.

16701 **Pawda, David J.** "Submarine Boundaries." *International and Comparative Law Quarterly,* 9, No. 4 (October, 1960), 628-653.

16702 **Pearcy, G. Etzel.** "The Continental Shelf: Physical Versus Legal Definitions." *Canadian Geographer,* 5, No. 3 (Fall, 1961), 26-29.

16703 "Petroleum (Submerged Lands), Second Schedule, Areas Adjacent to States and Territories," *Government Gazette, Canberra,* No. 118 (1967), 958-963.

16704 **Powers, R.D., Jr., and Hardy, Leonard R.** "How Wide the Territorial Sea." *U.S. Naval Institute Proceedings,* 87, No. 2 (February, 1961), 68-73.

16705 **Puri, Rama.** "Exclusive Economic Zone: A New Dimension in the Law of the Sea." *Indian Political Science Review,* 14, No. 1 (January,1980), 39-54.

16706 **Puri, Rama.** "The Law of the Continental Shelf: A New Perspective." *Indian Political Science Review,* 12, No. 2 (July, 1978), 200-216.

16707 **Rahman, M.Habiur.** "Coastal States, the Continental Shelf, and International Law." *Mazingira,* 8, No. 6 (1985), 19-21.

16708 **Rahman, M. Habiur.** "Delimination of Maritime Boundaries." *Asian Survey,* 24, No.12 (December, 1984), 1302-1317.

16709 **Reeves, J.S.** "The Codification of the Law of Territorial Waters." *American Journal of International Law,* 24, No. 3 (July, 1930), 486-499.

16710 **Rembe, Nasila S.** "Law of the Sea: Conflicts Over Limits of National Jurisdiction." *Eastern Africa Law Review,* 7, No. 1 (1974), 65-106.

16711 **Reyes, Roger Z.** "The Continental Shelf." *Philippine Law Journal,* 49, No. 4 (September, 1974), 488-504.

16712 **Sinjela, Andrew Mpazi.** "Land-locked States Rights in the Exclusive Economic Zone from the Perspective of the UN Convention on the Law of the Sea: An Historical Evaluation." *Ocean Development and International Law,* 20, No. 1 (1989), 63-81.

16713 **Smith, Robert W.** "Global Maritime Claims." *Ocean Development and International Law,* 20, No. 1 (1989), 83-103.

16714 **Sutherland, Paul.** "The Lagging Law of the Continental Shelf: Some Problems and Proposals." *Catholic University of America Law Review,* 22, No. 1 (Fall, 1972), 131-155.

16715 **Teclaff, Ludwik A.** "Shrinking the High Seas by Technical Methods-From the 1930 Hague Conference to the 1958 Geneva Conference." *University of Detroit Law Journal,* 39,No. 5 (June, 1962), 660-684.

16716 **Tuori, Heikki.** "On the Technical Delimitation of Territorial Waters." *Soumen Geodecttisen Laitoksen Julkaisuja,* 946 (1955), 157-170.

16717 **U.S. Department of State.** Washington, D.C. "Claims to National Jurisdiction." *Limits in the Sea, The Geographer,* 36 (1973), pamphlet.

16718 **U.S. Department of State.** U.S. Department of State, Washington, D.C. "Limits in the Sea." *International Boundary Study. The Geographer,* Washington, D.C.: Bureau of Intelligence and Research, State Department, Since January, 1970, pamphlet.

16719 **U.S. Department of State.** Washington, D.C. "Theoretical Areal Allocation of the Seabed to Coastal States." *Limits in the Sea, The Geographer,* 46 (1972), pamphlet.

16720 **Voelckel, Michael.** "Apercu de Quelques Problemes Techniques Concernant la Delimitation des Frontieres Martimes." *Annuaire Francais de Droit International,* 25 (1979), 693-711.

16721 **Voelckel, Michael.** "Les Lignes de Base dans la Convention de Geneve sur la Mer Territoriale." *Annuaire Francais de Droit International,* 19 (1973), 820-836.

16722 **Walker, W.L.** "Territorial Waters: The Cannot Shot Rule." *British Yearbook of International Law,* 22 (1945), 210-231.

16723 **Yates, George Talmadege, III.** "International Law and the Delimitation of Bays." *North Carolina Law Review,* 49 (1971), 943-963.

16724 **Young, Richard.** "The Geneva Convention on the Continental Shelf: A First Impression." *American Journal of Internaitonal Law,* 52, No. 4 (October, 1958), 733-738.

16725 **Young, Richard.** "The Limits of the Continental Shelf and Beyond." *Proceedings of the American Society of International Law,* 62, (1968), 229-236.

16726 **Young, Richard.** "The Overextension of the Continental Shelf." *American Journal of International Law,* 47, No. 3 (July, 1953), 454-456.

16727 **Young, Richard.** "Recent Developments with Respect to the Continental Shelf." *American Journal of International Law,* 42, No. 4 (October, 1948), 849-857.

POLITICAL GEOGRAPHY OF REGIONS

AFRICA

Books and Journals

16728 **Feldman, Mark B.** "The Tunisia-Libya Continental Shelf Case: Geographic Justice or Judicial Compromise?" *American Journal of International Law,* 77, No. 2 (April, 1983), 219-238.

16729 **The Geographer.** U.S. Department of State. "Limits in the Sea." *Straight Baseline: Guinea,* Ser. A. 40 (1972), complete issue.

16730 **The Geographer.** U.S. Department of State. *Straight Baselines: Mauritania.* Washington, D.C.: Office of the Geographer, 1970.

16731 **Kibola, Hamisi S.** "A Note on Africa and the Exclusive Economic Zone." *Ocean Development and International Law,* 16, No. 4 (1986), 369-380.

16732 **Melamid, Alexander.** "The Kenya Coastal Strip." *Geographical Review,* 53, No. 3 (July, 1963), 457-459.

16733 **Nwogugu, E.I.** "Problems of Nigerian Off-shore Jurisdiction." *International and Comparative Law Quarterly,* 22, No. 2 (April, 1973), 349-363.

AMERICAS

Books and Journals

16734 **Allen, Philip A., III.** "Law of the Sea: The Delimitation of the Maritime Boundary Between the United States and the Bahamas." *University of Florida Law Review,* 33, No. 2 (Winter, 1981), 207-239.

16735 **Antinori, Camille M.** "The Bering Sea: A Maritime Delimitation Dispute Between the United States and the Soviet Union." *Ocean Development and International Law,* 18, No. 1 (1987), 1-47.

16736 **Arenas, H. Santis.** "Frontiers and Maritime Limits inl the Concept of Territoriality: The Chilean Case." *Revista Chilena de Geopolitica,* 2, No. 3 (1986), 13-30.

16737 **Azambuja, P.** "Brasil y su derecho a la Antartida. (Brazil's Right to Antarctica)." *Geosur,* 23 (1981), 36-40.

16738 **Beauchamp, Kenneth P.; Crommelin, M.; and Thompson, A.R.** "Jurisdictional Problems in Canada's Offshore." *Alberta Law Review,* 11 (1973), 431-470 (Petroleum Law Supplement, 431-458).

16739 **Biggs, Gonzalo.** *Seismic Studies Project in the Continental Shelves of Latin America and the Caribbean and the Law of the Sea.* Washington, D.C.: Inter-American Development Bank, Legal Department, 1981.

16740 **Bourne, C.B., and McRae, D.M.** "Maritime Jurisdiction in the Dixon Entrance: The Alaska Boundary Re-examined." *Canadian Yearbook of International Law,* 14 (1976), 175-223.

16741 **Brittin, B.H.** "International Law Aspects of the Acquisition of the Continental Shelf by the United States." *U.S. Naval Institute Proceedings*, 74, No. 550 (1948), 1541-1543.

16742 **Charney, Jonathan I.** "The Delimitation of Lateral Seaward Boundaries Between States in a Domestic Context." *American Journal of International Law*, 75, No. 1 (January, 1981), 28-68.

16743 **Cooper, John.** "Delimitation of the Maritime Boundary in the Gulf of Maine Area." *Ocean Development and International Law*, 16, NO. 1 (1986), 59-90.

16744 **Cuyvers, Luc.** "Maritime Boundaries: Canada versus United States." *Marine Policy Reports*, 2 (1979), 1-5.

16745 **Done, P.** "Trinidad's Marine Boundaries." *Hydrographic Journal*, 44 (1987), 37-43.

16746 **Dubner, Bary Hart; Hanks, Peter; and Pryles, Michael.** "Demarcation of Authority Over Coastal Waters and Submerged Lands in the United States and Australia." *Stetson Law Review*, 10, No. 2 (Winter, 1981), 228-271.

16747 **Easterly, Ernest S., III.** "The Role of Geoforensic Experts in Marine Boundary Delimitation: The Case of the Lake Pontchartrain Basin." *Papers and Proceedings of Applied Geography Conferences*, 11 (1988), 118-124.

16748 **Fahrney, Richard L., II.** "Status of an Island's Continental Shelf Jurisdiction: A Case Study of the Falkland Islands." *Journal of Maritime Law and Commerce*, 10, No. 4 (July, 1979), 539-555.

16749 **Feldman, Mark B., and Colson, David A.** "The Maritime Boundaries of the United States." *American Journal of International Law*, 75, No. 4 (October, 1981), 729-763.

16750 **Gass, James D.** "The French Claim to the Eastern North American Continental Shelf." *JAG Journal*, 17 (1973), 367-391.

16751 **Greig, D.W.** "The Beagle Channel Arbitration." *Australian Year Book of International Law*, 7 (1981), 332-385.

16752 **Gross, Avrum M.** "The Maritime Boundaries of the States." *Michigan Law Review*, 64, No. 4 (February, 1966), 639-670.

16753 **Gushue, Raymond.** "The Territorial Waters of Newfoundland." *Canadian Journal of Economic and Political Science*, 15, No. 3 (August, 1949), 344-352.

16754 **Harrison, Rowland J.** "Jurisdiction Over the Canadian Offshore: A Sea of Confusion." *Osgoode Hall Law Journal*, 17, No. 3 (December, 1979), 469-505.

16755 **Hershman, Marc J.** "The Seaward Extension of States: A Boundary for New Jersey Under the Submerged Lands Act." *Temple Law Quarterly*, 40, No. 1 (Fall, 1966), 66-101.

16756 **Hodgson, Robert D., and McIntyre, Terry V.** "National Seabed Boundary Options." In *Limits to National Jurisdiction Over the Sea*, G.T. Yates, III and J.H. Young, eds. Charlottesville: University Press of Virginia, 1974, 152-173.

16757 **Hollick, Ann L.** "U.S. Oceans Policy: The Truman Proclamations." *Virginia Journal of International Law*, 17, No. 1 (Fall, 1976), 23-55.

16758 **Holser, A.F.** "Offshore Lands of the USA: The US Exclusive Economic Zone, Continental Shelf and Water Continental Shelf." *Marine Policy*, 12, No. 1 (January, 1988), 2-8.

16759 **House, J.W.** "Unfinished Business in the South Atlantic." *Political Geography Quarterly*, 2, No. 3 (June, 1983), 233-246.

16760 **Inions, Noela J.** "Newfoundland Offshore Claims." *Alberta Law Review*, 19, No. 3 (1981), 461-482.

16761 **Jaramillo, R. Riesco.** "Chilean Geopolitics and Frontiers in the Southern Pacific Ocean and in the Antarctic Continent." *Revista Chilena de Geopolitica*, 2 (1985), 17-34.

16762 **Jhabvala, Farrokh.** "Two Hundred Islands of Soledad: International Law of the South Atlantic." *Caribbean Review*, 11, No. 3 (Summer, 1982), 8-11 and 42-43.

16763 **Kaelin, Jeffrey H.** "The Gulf of Maine Dispute: The Attempts of the United States and Canada to Delimit the Northwest Atlantic Continental Shelf." *Marine Affairs Journal*, 7 (1981), 1-17.

16764 **Klock, Roberto D.** "Gulf of Venezuela: A Proposed Delimitation." *Lawyer of the Americas*, 12, No. 1 (Winter, 1980), 93-108.

16765 **LaForest, G.V.** "Boundary Waters Problems in the East." In *Canada-United States Treaty Relations*, David R. Deener, ed. Durham, North Carolina: Duke University Press, 1963, 28-50.

16766 **Labrecque, Georges.** "La dilimitation de la frontiere maritime dans la region du Golfe du Maine." Quebec, Province of Quebec, Canada: Universite Laval, M.A., 1988.

16767 **Lamson, Cynthia, and Zwaan, David Vander.** "Artic Waters: Needs and Options for Canadian-American Cooperation." *Ocean Development and International Law*, 18, No. 1 (1987), 47-99.

16768 **Legault, L.H.** "A Line for All Uses: The Gulf of Maine Boundary Revisited." *International Journal*, 40, No. 3 (Summer, 1985), 461-477.

16769 **Lewis, Vaughan.** "The Bahamas in International Politics: Issues Arising for an Archipelago State." *Journal of Inter-American Studies and World Affairs*, 16, No. 2 (May, 1974), 131-152.

16770 **Long, John W.** "The Origin and Development of the San Juan Island Water Boundary Controversy." *Pacific Northwest Quarterly*, 43, No. 3 (July, 1952), 187-213.

16771 **Martz, Mary Jeanne Reid.** "Delimitation of Marine and Submarine Areas: The Gulf of Venezuela." *Lawyer of the Americas*, 9, No. 2 (June, 1977), 301-317.

16772 **McDorman, Ted L.** "In the Wake of the Povar Sea: Canadian Jurisdiction and the Northwest Passage." *Marine Policy*, 10, No. 4 (October, 1986), 243-257.

16773 **McLaughlin, Richard J.** Classification of Multi-Beam Bathymetric Mapping of the U.S. EEZ: Is a New U.S. marine Scientific Research Policy in Order?" *Ocean Development and International Law*, 19, No. 1 (1988), 1-34.

16774 **McRae, D.M.** "Adjudication of the Maritime Boundary in the Gulf of Maine." *Canadian Yearbook of International Law*, 17 (1979), 292-303.

16775 **Nielsen, F.K.** "Is the Jurisdiction of the United States Exclusive Within the Three Mile Limit? Does It Extend Beyond This Limit for any Purpose?" *American Society of International Law Proceedings*, (April 26-28, 1923), 32-39.

16776 **Nweihed, Kaldone G.** *Delimitation Principles and Problems in the Caribbean.* Caracas: Universidad Simon Boliver, 1981.

16777 **Nweihed, Kaldone G.** *El Golfo de Venezuela: Ayer Y Hoy.* Caracas: Coleccion Historia de Nuestras Fronteras, No. 2. 1981.

16778 **Nweihed, Kaldone G.** "Delimitation in the Semi-enclosed Caribbean Sea: Recent Agreements Between Venezuela and Her Neighbours." *Ocean Development and International Law*, 8, No. 1 (1980), 1-33.

16779 **Osterng, Willy.** "The Continental Shelf-Issues in the 'Eastern' Arctic Oceans. Implications of UNCLOS III, with Special Reference to the Informal Composite Negotiating Text (ICNT)." In *Law of the Sea: Neglected Issues*, John King Gamble, Jr., ed. Hawaii: Law of the Sea Institute, 1979, 165-182. (Proceedings and Papers of the Twelfth Annual Law of the Sea Institute Conference Held in The Hague, October 23-26, 1979.)

16780 **Pearcy, G. Etzel.** "Hawaii's Territorial Sea." *Professional Geographer*, 11, No. 6 (November, 1959), 2-6.

16781 **Pearcy, G. Etzel.** "Measurement of the U.S. Territorial Sea." *U.S. Department of State Bulletin*, 40, No. 1044 (June, 1959), 963-971.

16782 **Pharand, Donat.** "The Continental Shelf Redefinition, with Special Reference to the Arctic." *McGill Law Journal*, 18, No. 4 (December, 1972), 536-559.

16783 **Price, Richard L.,** and **Vaucher, Marc E.** "Prospective Maritime Jurisdiction in the Polar Seas." *Annals of the Association of American Geographers*, 73, No. 4 (December, 1983), 617-618.

16784 **Ramakrishna, K.; Bowen, Robert E.,** and **Archer, J.H.** "Outer Limits of Continental Shelf. A Legal Analysis of Chilean and Equadorian Island Claims and U.S. Response." *Marine Policy*, 11, No. 1 (January, 1987), 58-68.

16785 **Rekhopf, Donald G., Jr.** "The Law of the Sea: An Analysis of the Scientific Justifications for Boundary Extensions in South America." *Air Force Law Review*, 18, No. 2 (Summer, 1976), 35-56.

16786 **Rey Caro, Ernesto J.** "Aspectos de Derecho Internacional Maritimo en el Tratado sobre el rio de la Plata." *Anuario de Derecho Internacional*, 1 (1974), 317-334.

16787 **Rhee, Sang-Myon.** "Equitable Solutions to the Maritime Boundary Dispute Between the United States and Canada in the Gulf of Maine." *American Journal of International Law*, 75, No. 3 (July, 1981), 590-628.

16788 **Ricketts, Peter.** "Geography and International Law: The Case of the 1984 Gulf of Maine Boundary Dispute." *Canadian Geographer*, 30, No. 3 (Fall, 1986), 194-205.

16789 **Rivas, Pedro.** *Limits entre Honduras y Nicaragua en el Atlantico. Historia cartografica documentado (1508 a 1821).* Tegucigalpa, Honduras: Talleres Tipograficos Nacionales, 1938.

16790 **Schmitt, Karl M.** "The Problem of Maritime Boundaries in the U.S.-Mexican Relations." *Natural Resources Journal*, 22, No. 1 (January, 1982), 139-153.

16791 **Schroder, Peter.** "Der Vertrag von Tordesillas 1494: Machtpolitik und Europaische Expansion Nach Ubersee." *Geographische Rundschau* [Braunschweig], 46, Heft 6 (Juni, 1994), 368-371.

16792 **Scott, Munford, J., Jr.** "The Continental Shelf and the United States." *South Carolina Law Review*, 22 , No. 1 (1970), 34-49.

16793 **Shalowitz, Aaron L.** "Boundary Problems Raised by the Submerged Lands Act." *Columbia Law Review*, 54, No. 7 (November, 1954), 1021-1048.

16794 **Shalowitz, Aaron L.** "Where are Our Seaward Boundaries?" *U.S. Naval Institute Proceedings*, 83, No. 6 (June, 1957), 616-627.

16795 **Shaw, Malcolm.** "The Beagle Channel Arbitration Award." *International Relations*, 6, No. 2 (November, 1978), 415-445.

16796 **Silva, Maynard, and Westermeyer, William.** "The Law of the Sea and the U.S. Exclusive Economic Zone: Perspectives on Marine Transportation and Fisheries." *Ocean Development and International Law*, 15, Nos. 3 and 4 (1985), 321-353.

16797 **Smith, Robert W.** "The Maritime Boundaries of the United States." *Geographical Review*, 71, No. 4 (October, 1981), 395-410.

16798 **Swan, George Steven.** "The Gulf of Maine Dispute: Canada and the United States Delimit the Atlantic Continental Shelf." *Natural Resources Lawyer*, 10, No. 2 (June, 1977), 405-456.

16799 **Swan, George Steven.** "The Newfoundland Offshore Claims: Interface of Constitutional Federalism and International Law." *McGill Law Journal*, 22, No. 4 (Winter, 1976), 541-573.

16800 **Swan, George Steven.** "Remembering Maine: Offshore Federalism in the United States and Canada." *California Western International Law Journal*, 6, No. 2 (Spring, 1976), 296-322.

16801 **U.S. Department of State.** "Maritime Boundaries: Columbia-Cominican Republic and Netherlands (Netherlands Antilles)--Venezuela." *Limits in the Seas--U.S. Department of State*, 105 (1986), 1-23.

16802 **U.S. Department of State.** "Maritime Boundary: Cuba-Mexico." *Limits in the Seas--U.S. Department of State*, 104 (1985), 1-6.

16803 **U.S. Department of State.** *Straight Baselines: Dominican Republic.* Washington, D.C.: Office of the Geographer, 1970.

16804 **U.S. Department of State.** *Straight Baselines: Mexico.* Washington, D.C.: Office of the Geographer, 1970.

16805 **U.S. Department of State.** *Maritime Boundary: Mexico-United States.* Washington, D.C.: Office of the Geographer, 1972.

16806 **U.S. Department of State.** *Continental Shelf Boundary: Trinidad Tobago-Venezuela.* Washington, D.C.: Office of the Geographer, 1970.

16807 **U.S. Department of State.** *Swan Islands: Honduran Sovereignty Recognized by the United States.* Washington, D.C.: Office of the Geographer, 1972.

16808 **U.S. Department of State.** Washington, D.C. "Venezuela-Trinidad and Tobago." *Limits in the Sea, The Geographer*, 11 (1970), pamphlet.

16809 **Vorsey, Louis de.** "Florida Seaward Boundary." *Professional Geographer*, 25, No. 3 (August, 1973), 214-220.

16810 **Walz, Kathleen L.** "The United States Supreme Court and Article VII of the 1958 Convention on the Territorial Sea and Contiguous Zone." *University of San Francisco Law Review*, 11, No. 1 (Fall, 1976), 1-51.

16811 **Wulf, Norman A.** "Freezing the Boundary Dividing Federal and State Interests in Offshore Submerged Lands." *San Diego Law Review*, 8, No. 3 (May, 1971), 584-605.

ASIA

Books and Journals

16812 **Allen, Donald R., and Mitchell, Patrick H.** "The Legal Status of the Continental Shelf of the East China Sea." *Oregon Law Review*, 51, No. 4, Part II (Summer, 1972), 789-812.

16813 **Amin, S.H.** "Customary Rules of Delimitation of the Continental Shelf: The Gulf States Practice." *Journal of Maritime Law and Commerce*, 11, No. 4 (July, 1980), 509-526.

16814 **Australia, Government of.** *Maritime Boundaries in the Western Indian Ocean Region.* Canberra: Office of National Assessments, 1981.

16815 **Bloomfield, L.M.** *Egypt, Israel and the Gulf of Akaba.* Toronto: Carswell, 1957.

16816 **Chiu, Hungdah.** "China and the Question of Territorial Sea." *International Trade Law Journal*, 1, No. 1 (Spring, 1975), 29-77.

16817 **Chiu, Hungdah.** *Chinese Attitude Toward Continental Shelf and Its Implication on Delimiting Seabed in Southeast Asia.* Reprint Series in Contemporary Asian Studies. College Park: University of Maryland Press, 1977.

16818 **Chiu, Hungdah.** "Some Problems Concerning the Delimitation of the Maritime Boundary Between the Republic of China (Taiwan) and the Philippines." *Ocean Development and the International Law*, 14, No. 1 (1984), 79-105.

16819 **Cosford, Edwin J., Jr.** "The Continental Shelf and the Abu Dhabi Award." *McGill Law Journal*, 1, No. 1 (March, 1953), 109-127.

16820 **Ely, Northcutt, and Marcoux, J. Michael.** "National Seabed Jurisdiction in the Marginal Sea: The South China Sea." In *Limits to National Jurisdiction Over the Sea*, George T. Yates, III, and John Hardin Young, eds. Charlottesville: University Press of Virginia, 1974, 103-151.

16821 **Ely, Northcutt, and Pietrowski, Robert F., Jr.** "Boundaries of Seabed Jurisdiction Off the Pacific Coast of Asia." *Natural Resources Lawyer*, 8, No. 4 (December, 1975), 611-629.

16822 **Emmerson, Donald K.** "The Case for a Maritime Perspective on Southeast Asia." *Journal of Southeast Asian Studies*, 11, No. 1 (March, 1980), 139-145.

16823 **Fairbridge, Rhodes W.** *Report on Limits of the Indian Ocean.* Perth, Western Australia: Pan Indian Ocean Science Congress, 2d, 1954. Proceedings. Sec. F: Geography and Oceanography, 1954, 18-28.

16824 **Feeney, William R.** "Dispute Settlement, the Emerging Law of the Sea, and East Asian Maritime Boundary Conflicts." *Asian Profile*, 8, No. 6 (December, 1980), 573-595.

16825 **Glassner, Martin Ira.** "Israel's Maritime Boundaries." *Ocean Development and International Law.* No. 4 (1974).

16826 **Kassim, Anis F.** "Conflicting Claims in the Persian Gulf." *Journal of Law and Economic Development*, 4, No. 2 (Fall, 1969), 282-337.

16827 **Kikuchi, Tadashi.** "Delimitation of the Continental Shelf of the East China Sea." *Meijo Law Review*, 22 (1973-1974), 1-51.

16828 **Kim, Dong Hi.** "Accord entre la Coree du Sud et le Japon sur le Developpement Commun de la Partie Sud du Plateau Continental adjacent aux Deux Pays." *Korean Journal of Comparative Law*, 2, No. 2 (December, 1974), 103-129.

16829 **Lee, Wei-Chin.** "Trouble Under the Water: Sino-Japanese Conflict of Sovereignty on the Continental Shelf in the East China Sea." *Ocean Development and International Law*, 18, No. 5 (1987), 585-611.

16830 **Lee, Yong Leng.** "Offshore Boundary Disputes in Southeast Asia." *Journal of Southeast Asian Studies*, 10, No. 1 (March, 1979), 175-189.

16831 **Lee, Yong Leng.** "The Archipelagic Concept and Its Impact on Southeast Asia." *Singapore Journal of Tropical Geography*, 4, No. 1 (June, 1983), 34-39.

16832 **Lentz, Wolfgang.** "Der Iranische Fischfang im Kaspischen Meer." *Zeitschrift fur Geopolitik*, 24 Jahrgang, Heft 3 (Maz, 1953), 171-172.

16833 **Lumb, R.D.** *The Law of the Sea and Australian Off-Shore Areas.* 2nd ed. St. Lucia, Queensland: University of Queensland Press, 1978.

16834 **Lumb, R.D.** "The Delimitation of Maritime Boundaries in the Timor Sea." *Australian Year Book of International Law*, 7 (1981), 72-86.

16835 **Nakauchi, Kiyofumi.** "Problems of Delimitation in the East China Sea and the Sea of Japan." *Ocean Development and International Law*, 6, No. 4 (1979), 305-316.

16836 **Oda, Shigeru.** "The Delimitation of the Continental Shelf in Southeast Asia and the Far East." *Ocean Management*, 1, No. 4 (December, 1973), 327-346.

16837 **Okuhara, Toshio.** "The Territorial Sovereignty Over the Senkaku Islands and Problems on the Surrounding Continental Shelf." *Japanese Annual of International Law*, 15 (1971), 97-106.

16838 **Park, Choon-Ho.** "China and Maritime Jurisdiction: Some Boundary Issues." *German Yearbook of International Law*, 22 (1979), 119-141.

16839 **Park, Choon-Ho.** "The 50-Mile Military Boundary Zone of North Korea." *American Journal of International Law*, 72, No. 4 (October, 1978), 866-875.

16840 **Prescott, J.R.V.** *Maritime Jurisdiction in Southeast Asia: A Commentary and Map.* Honolulu: East-West Environment and Policy Institute, 1981.

16841 **Prescott, J.R.V.** "Maritime Jurisdictional Issues." In *Marine Policy in Southeast Asia*, G. Kent and M.J. Valencia, eds. Berkeley: University of California Press, 1985, p. 58-97.

16842 **Sundstrom, Harold W.** "Exploring Korea's Seashores." *Korean Report*, 1, No. 3 (August, 1961), 3-6.

16843 **U.S. Department of State.** *Continental Shelf Boundary: Abu Dhabi-Qatar.* Washington, D.C.: Office of the Geographer, 1970.

16844 **U.S. Department of State.** *Continental Shelf Boundary: Bahrain-Saudi Arabia.* Washington, D.C.: Office of the Geographer, 1970.

16845 **U.S. Department of State.** *Continental Shelf Boundary: Indonesia-Malaysia.* Washington, D.C.: Office of the Geographer, 1970 and 1973.

16846 **U.S. Department of State.** *Continental Shelf Boundary: Iran-Saudi Arabia.* Washington, D.C.: Office of the Geographer, 1970.

16847 **U.S. Department of State.** *Continental Shelf Boundary: Iran-Qatar.* Washington, D.C.: Office of the Geographer, 1970.

16848 **U.S. Department of State.** Washington, D.C. "Bahrain-Saudi Arabia." *Limits in the Sea, The Geographer,* 12 (1970), pamphlet.

16849 **U.S. Department of State.** Washington, D.C. "Iran-Qatar." *Limits in the Sea, The Geographer,* 25 (1970), pamphlet.

16850 **U.S. Department of State.** Washington, D.C. "Iran-Saudi Arabia." *Limits in the Sea, The Geographer,* 24 (1970), pamphlet.4

16851 **Valencia, Mark J., and Jaffar, A.B.** "Malaysia and Extended Maritime Jurisdiction: The Foreign Policy Issues." *Malaysian Journal of Tropical Geography,* 10 (1984), 56-87.

16852 **Valencia, Mark J., and Miyoshi, Masahiro.** "Southwest Asia Seas: Joint Development of Hydrocarbons in Overlapping Claim Areas?" *Ocean Development and International Law,* 16, No. 2 (1986), 211-254.

16853 **Young, Richard.** "Equitable Solutions for Offshore Boundaries: The 1968 Saudi Arabia-Iran Agreement." *American Journal of International Law,* 64, No. 1 (January, 1970), 152-157.

AUSTRALIA, OCEANIA AND ANTARCTICA

Books and Journals

16854 **Forbes, V.L.** "Australia's International Obligation to Maritime Boundary Determination." *Cartography* [Canberra], 20, No. 2 (December, 1991), 19-28.

16855 **Goldsworthy, Peter.** "Ownership of the Territorial Sea and Continental Shelf of Australia: An Analysis of the Seas and Submerged Lands Act Case (State of New South Wales and Ors vs. The Commonwealth of Australia)." *Australian Law Journal,* 50, No. 4 (April, 1976), 175-184.

16856 **Ihl C., Pablo.** "Delimitacion Natural Entro el Oceano Pacifico y Atlantico, en resguardo de Nuestra Soberania Sobre la Antartica y Navarino." *Revista Geographico de Chile,* 6, No. 9 (June, 1953), 45-51.

16857 **Lee, H.C.** "An Archipelagic Claim for Papua New Guinea." *Melanesian Law Journal,* 2 (1974), 91-107.

16858 **Lumb, R.D.** *The Maritime Boundaries of Queensland and New South Wales.* St. Lucia: University of Queensland Press, 1964.

16859 **Lumb, R.D.** "Sovereignty and Jurisdiction Over Australian Coastal Waters." *Australian Law Journal,* 43, No. 9 (October, 1969), 421-449.

16860 **O'Connell, D.P.** "The Australian Maritime Domain." *Australian Law Journal,* 44, No. 5 (May, 1970), 192-208.

16861 **Prescott, J.R.V.,** ed. *Australia's Continental Shelf.* Melbourne: T. Nelson Australia, 1979.

16862 **Prescott, J.R.V.** *Australia's Maritime Boundaries.* Canberra: Australian National University, Department of International Relations. Canberra Studies in World Affairs. 16 (1985).

16863 **Prescott, J.R.V.** "Australia's Maritime Claims and the Great Barrier Reef." *Australian Geographical Studies,* 19, No. 1 (April, 1981), 99-106.

16864 **Prescott, J.R.V.** "Existing and Potential Maritime Claims in the Southwest Pacific Ocean." *Ocean Yearbook,* 2 (1980), 317-345.

16865 **Prescott, J.R.V.** "The International Limits of Australia's Continental Shelf." In *Australia's Continental Shelf,* J.R.V. Prescott, ed. Melbourne: T. Nelson Australia, 1979, 22-49.

16866 **U.S. Department of State.** *Oceania and Miscellaneous Insular Areas: Civil Divisions.* Washington, D.C.: Office of the Geographer, 1971.

16867 **Young, Richard.** "Problems of Australian Coastal Jurisdiction." *Australian Law Journal,* 42, No. 2 (June, 1968), 39-51.

EUROPE

Books and Journals

16868 **Ahnish, Faraj Abdullah.** *The International Law of Maritime Boundaries and the Practice of States in the Mediterranean Sea.* Oxford: Clarendon Press, 1993.

16869 **Alexander, Lewis M.** *A Comparative Study of Offshore Claims in Northwestern Europe.* Washington, D.C.: Office of Naval Research, 1960.

16870 **Alexander, Lewis M.** *Offshore Geography of Northwestern Europe: The Political and Economic Problems of Delimitation and Control.* Chicago, Illinois: Rand McNally, 1963.

16871 **Andrassy, Juraj.** "Application of the Geneva Convention, 1958, in Delimiting the Continental Shelf of the North Sea Area." *Revue Egyptienne de Droit International*, 23 (1967), 1-19.

16872 **Auburn, F.M.** "The North Sea Continental Shelf Boundary Settlement." *Archiv des Volkerrechts*, 16 Band, No. 1 (1974), 28-36.

16873 **Azcarraga, Jose Luis de.** "Espana Subscribe, con Francia e Italia, dos Conveniossobre Delimitacion de sus Plataformas Submarinas Comunes." *Revista Espanola de Derecho Internacional*, 28 (1975), 131-138.

16874 **Bettati, Mario.** "L'Affaire du Plateau Continental de la Mer Egee devant la Cour Internationale de Justice-Competence (arret du 19 Decembre 1978)." *Annuaire Francais de Droit International*, 24 (1978), 303-320.

16875 **Bettati, Mario.** "L'Affaire du Plateau Continental de la Mer Egee devant la Cour Internationale de Justice. Demande en Indication de Mesures Conservatores, Ordonnance 11 Septembre 1976." *Annuaire Francais de Droit International*, 22 (1976), 99-115.

16876 **Bindoff, S.T.** *The Sheldt Question.* London: Allen & Unwin, 1945.

16877 **Birnie, Patricia.** "Maritime Policy and Legal Issues: Impact of the LOS Convention and UNCED on UK Maritime Law and Policy." *Marine Policy*, 18, No. 6 (Novemer, 1994), 483-493.

16878 **Bouchez, Leo J.** "The North Sea Continental Shelf Case." *Journal of Maritime Law and Commerce*, 1, No. 1 (October, 1969), 113-121.

16879 **Bowett, Derek W.** "The Arbitration Between the United Kingdom and France Concerning the Continental Shelf Boundary in the English Channel and South-Western Approaches." *British Year Book of International Law*, 49 (1978), 1-29.

16880 **Brown, E.D.** "The Anglo-French Continental Shelf Case." *San Diego Law Review*, 16, No. 3 (April, 1979), 461-530.

16881 **Brown, E.D.** "The Anglo-French Continental Shelf Case." *Year Book of World Affairs*, (1979), 304-327.

16882 **Brown, E.D.** "Delimitation of Maritime Frontiers: Radio Stations in the Thames Estuary." *Australian Year Book of International Law*, (1966), 19-113.

16883 **Brown, E.D.** "The North Sea Continental Shelf Cases." *Current Legal Problems*, 23 (April, 1970), 187-215.

16884 **Brown, E.D.** "Rockall and the Limits of National Jurisdiction of the UK." *Marine Policy*, 2, (July, 1978), 181-211 and 275-303.

16885 **Cable, James.** "Closing the British Seas." *Marine Policy*, 11, No. 2 (April, 1987), 90-96.

16886 **Chao, John K.T.** "The Aegean Sea Continental Shelf Dispute." *Annals of the Chinese Society of International Law*, 16 (1979), 7-21.

16887 **Chaturvedi, S.C.** "The North Sea Continental Shelf Case Analyzed." *Indian Journal of International Law*, 13, No. 4 (October-December, 1973), 481-493.

16888 **Colson, David A.** "The United Kingdom-France Continental Shelf Arbitration." *American Journal of International Law*, 72, No. 1 (January, 1978), 95-112.

16889 **Colson, David A.** "The United Kingdom-France Continental Shelf Arbitration: Interpretive Decision of March 1978." *American Journal of International Law*, 73, No. 1 (January, 1979), 112-120.

16890 **Couper, Alastair D.** "The Maritime Boundaries of the United Kingdom and the Law of the Sea." *Geographical Journal*, 151, No. 2 (July, 1985), 228-236.

16891 **Digovic, Pero.** *La Dalmatie et les problemes de l'Adriatique.* Lausanne: F. Rouge & Cie, 1944.

16892 **Eustache, Francois.** "L'Affaire du Plateau Continental de la Mer du Nord devant la Cour Internationale de Justice." *Revue Generale de Droit International Public*, 74 (1970), 590-639.

16893 **Florio, Franco.** "Problemi della Frontiera Marritima nel Golfo di Trieste." *Rivista di Diritto Internazionale*, 60 (1977), 467-484.

16894 **Franckx, Erik.** "'New' Soviet Delimitation Agreement with Its Neighbors in the Baltic Sea." *Ocean Development and International Law*, 19, No. 2 (1988), 143-158.

16895 **Friedmann, Wolfgang.** "The North Sea Continental Shelf Cases-A Critique." *American Journal of International Law*, 64, No. 2 (April, 1970), 229-240.

16896 **Georgacopoulos, John.** "The Aegean Sea Continental Shelf Problem: Presentation of the Greek Case." *International Business Lawyer*, 6 (1978), 479-494.

16897 **Goldie, L.F.E.** "The North Sea Continental Shelf Case: A Postscript." *New York Law Forum*, 18, No. 2 (Fall, 1972), 411-434.

16898 **Goldie, L.F.E.** "The North Sea Continental Shelf Case-A Ray of Hope for the International Court?" *New York Law Forum*, 16, No. 2 (Summer, 1970), 325-377.

16899 **Green, L.C.** "The Territorial Sea and the Anglo-Icelandic Dispute." *Journal of Public Law*, 9 (1960), 53-72.

16900 **Grisel, Etienne.** "The Lateral Boundaries of the Continental Shelf and the Judgment of the International Court of Justice in the North Sea Continental Shelf Cases." *American Journal of International Law*, 64, No. 3 (July, 1970), 562-593.

16901 **Gross, Leo.** "The Dispute Between Greece and Turkey Concerning the Continental Shelf in the Aegean." *American Journal of International Law*, 71, No. 1 (January, 1977), 31-59.

16902 **Hanks, Robert J.** "Maritime Doctrines and Capabilities: The United States and the Soviet Union." *American Academy of Political and Social Science Annals*, 457 (September, 1981), 121-130.

16903 **Imbert, Pierre-Henri.** "La Question des Reserves dans la Decision Arbitrale du 30 Juin 1977 relative a la delimitation du Plateau Continentale entre la Republique Francaise et le Royaume-Uni de Grande-Bretagne et d'Irlande du Nord." *Annuaire Francais de Droit International*, 24 (1978), 29-58.

16904 **International Court of Justice.** *North Sea Continental Shelf Cases*, Vol. 1. The Hague: International Court of Justice, 1968, complete issue.

16905 **International Court of Justice.** "The North Sea Continental Shelf Cases." *Reports of Judgements, Advisory Opinions and Orders*, The Hague: International Court of Justice, 1969, 53-54.

16906 **Jennings, R.Y.** "The Limits of Continental Shelf Jurisdiction: Some Possible Implications of the North Sea Case Judgment." *International and Comparative Law Quarterly*, 18, No. 4 (October, 1969), 819-832.

16907 **Johnson, D.H.N.** "The North Sea Continental Shelf Cases." *International Relations*, 3, No. 8 (November, 1969), 522-540.

16908 **Joyner, Christopher C.** "Security Issues and the Law of the Sea: The Southern Ocean." *Ocean Development and International Law*, 15, No. 2 (1985), 171-195.

16909 **Kobayashi, Teruo.** *The Anglo-Norwegian Fisheries Case of 1951 and the Changing Law of the Territorial Sea.* Coral Gables: University of Florida Monographs, Social Sciences, No. 26. University of Florida Press, 1965.

16910 **Koymen, Avukat Feridun.** "The Aegean Sea Continental Shelf Problem: Presentation of the Turkish Case." *International Business Lawyer*, 6 (1978), 495-507.

16911 **Lang, Jack.** *Le Plateau Continentalde la Mer du Nord.* Biblioteque de Droit International, Vol. 58. Paris: Librairie Generale de Droit et de Jurisprudence, 1970.

16912 **Larson, David L.** "Security Issues and the Law of the Sea: A General Framework." *Ocean Development and International Law*, 15, No. 2 (1985), 99-166.

16913 **Lowe, A.V.** "Some Legal Problems Arising from the Use of the Seas for Military Purposes." *Marine Policy*, 10, No. 3 (July, 1986), 171-184.

16914 **Malintoppi, Antonio.** "La Delimitazione della Piattaforma Continentale Adriatica e l'Art. 80 della Costituzione." *Rivista di Diritto Internazionale*, 53 (1970), 506-525.

16915 **Manin, Philippe.** "Le Traite de Frigg." *Annuaire Francais de Droit International*, 24 (1978), 792-809.

16916 **Marek, Krystyna.** "Le Probleme des Sources du Droit International dans l'Arret sur le Plateau Continental da la Mer du Nord." *Revue Belge de Droit International*, 6 (1970), 44-78.

16917 **Marston, Geoffrey.** *The Marginal Seabed: United Kingdom Legal Practice.* Oxford: Clarendon Press, 1981.

16918 **McRae, D.M.** "Delimitation of the Continental Shelf Between the United Kingdom and France: The Channel Arbitration." *Canadian Yearbook of International Law*, 15 (1977), 173-197.

16919 **Merrills, J.G.** "The United Kingdom-France Continental Shelf Arbitration." *California Western International Law Journal*, 10, No. 2 (Spring, 1980), 314-364.

16920 **Monconduit, Francois.** "Affaire du Plateau Continentale de la Mer du Nord." *Annuaire Francais de Droit International*, 15 (1969), 213-244.

16921 **Munch, Fritz**. "Das Urteil des Internationalen Gerichtshofes vom 20. Februar 1969 uber den deutschen Anteil am Festlandsockel in der Nordsee." *Zeitschrift fur auslandisches offentliches Recht und Volkerrecht*, 29 (1969), 455-475.

16922 **Murray, Stephen J.** "The North Sea Continental Shelf Cases: A Critique." *JAG Journal (Navy)*, 24 (1969-1970), 87-98.

16923 **Nawaz, M.K.** "The North Sea Continental Shelf Cases Revisited." *Indian Journal of International Law*, 15, No. 4 (October-December, 1975), 506-520.

16924 **Nelson, L.D.M.** "The North Sea Continental Shelf Cases and Law-Making Conventions." *Modern Law Review*, 35, No. 1 (January, 1972), 52-56.

16925 **Nordquist, Myron H.** "The Legal Status of Articles 1-3 of the Continental Shelf Convention According to the North Sea Caes." *California Western International Law Journal*, 1, No. 1 (Fall, 1970), 60-79.

16926 *North Sea Continental Shelf Cases, 1968, Vol. 1.* The Hague: International Court of Justice, 1968.

16927 "The Norwegian Claim in the Atlantic Sector of the Antarctic." *Polar Record*, 18 (July, 1939), 169-173.

16928 **Oellers-Frahm, Karin.** "Der Beschluss des Internationalen Gerichtshofs im griechisch-turkischen Streit um den Festlandsockel in der Agais." *Zeitschrift fur auslandisches offentliches Recht und volkerrecht*, 37 (1977), 620-639.

16929 **Oellers-Frahm, Karin.** "Die Entscheidung des Internationalen Gerichtshofes im griechisch-turkischen Streit um den Festlandsockel in der Agais." *Archiv des Volokerrechts*, 18, Band, No. 4 (1980), 377-392.

16930 **Olenicoff, S.M.** *Territorial Waters in the Arctic: The Soviet Position.* Santa Monica, California: The Rand Corporation, 1972.

16931 **Queneudec, Jean-Pierre.** "L'Affaire de la Delimitation du Plateau Continental entre la France et le Royaume-Uni." *Revue Generale de Droit International Public*, 83 (1979), 53-103.

16932 **Phylactopoulous, Alexis.** "Mediterranean Discord: Conflicting Greek-Turkish Claims on the Aegean Seabed." *International Lawyer*, 8, No. 3 (July, 1974), 431-441.

16933 **Przetacznik, Franciszek.** "La Declaration sur le Plateau Continental de la Mer Baltique et le Droit International." *Revue Belge de Droit International*, 6 (1970), 462-483.

16934 **Rigaldies, Francis.** "L'Affaire de la Delimitation du Plateau Continental entre la Republique Francaise et la Royaume-Uni de Grande-Bretagne et d'Irlande du Nord." *Journal du Droit International*, 106 Anne, No. 3 (Juiliet-Aout-Septembre, 1979), 506-531.

16935 **Robol, Richard T.** "The Agean Sea Continental Shelf Case." *Harvard International Law Journal*, 18, No. 3 (Summer, 1977), 649-675.

16936 **Rothpfeffer, Tomas.** "Equity in the North Sea Continental Shelf Cases." *Nordisk Tidsskrift for International Ret*, 42 Fasc.1-4 (1972), 81-137.

16937 **Rozakis, Christos L.** *The Greek-Turkish Dispute Over the Aegean continental Shelf.* Kingston, Rhode Island: Law of the Sea Institute, 1975.

16938 **Saguirian, Artemy A.** "Russia and Some Pending Law of the Sea Issues in the North Pacific: Cntroversies Over Higher Seas Fisheries Regulation and Delimitation of Marine Spaces." *Ocean Development and International Law* [Washington, DC], 23, No. 1 (January-March, 1992), 1-16.

16939 **Sambrailo, Branko.** "Contribution of the Yugoslav-Italian Agreement on Delimitation of the Continental Shelf in the Adriatic Sea to the Settlement of Dispute in the North Sea Continental Shelf Cases." *Jugoslovenska Revija Za Medunarodno Pravo*, 17, Nos. 2 and 3 (1970), 247-255.

16940 **Sluiter, Engel.** "Dutch Maritime Power and the Colonial Status Quo, 1585-1641." *Pacific Historical Review*, 11, No. 1 (March, 1942), 29-41.

16941 **Smith, Robert W.** *A Geographical Analysis of the North Sea Continental Shelf.* Chapel Hill: University of North Carolina, Ph.D., 1980.

16942 **Symmons, Clive Ralph.** "Legal Aspects of the Anglo-Irish Dispute Over Rockall." *Northern Ireland Legal Quarterly*, 26, No. 2 (Summer, 1975), 65-93.

16943 **Symmons, Clive Ralph.** "The Rockall Dispute." *Irish Geography*, 8 (1975), 122-126.

16944 **Tammes, K.C.** "Svalbard: Politieke Geografie van an gedeelde Archipel." *Geografisch Tidjschrift*, 17, No. 3 (1983), 179-186.

16945 **Tullio, Leopoldo.** "L'Accordo Italo-Jugoslavo per la delimitazione della Piattaforma Continentale del l'Ardriatico." *Rivista del Dritto della Navigazione*, 35 (1969), 300-319.

16946 **U.S. Department of State.** *Continental Shelf Boundary: Finland-Soviet Union.* Washington, D.C.: Office of the Geographer, 1970.

16947 **U.S. Department of State.** *Continental Shelf Boundary: Italy-Yugoslavia.* Washington, D.C.: Office of the Geographer, 1970.

16948 **U.S. Department of State.** *Continental Shelf Boundary: Norway-Soviet Union.* Washington, D.C.: Office of the Geographer, 1970.

16949 **U.S. Department of State.** *Continental Shelf Boundary: Norway-Sweden.* Washington, D.C.: Office of the Geographer, 1970.

16950 **U.S. Department of State.** *Continental Shelf Boundary: The North Sea.* Washington, D.C.: Office of the Geographer, 1970.

16951 **U.S. Department of State,** International Boundary Study, Ser. A. "Straight Base Line: Germany." *Limits in the Sea, The Geographer,* 38 (1972), pamphlet.

16952 **U.S. Department of State.** "Italy-Yugoslavia." *Limits in the Sea, The Geographer,* 9 (1970), pamphlet.

16953 **U.S. Department of State.** *Straight Baselines: Albania.* Washington, D.C.: Office of the Geographer, 1970.

16954 **U.S. Department of State.** *Straight Baselines: Ireland.* Washington, D.C.: Office of the Geographer, 1970.

16955 **U.S. Department of State.** *Straight Baselines: Yugoslavia.* Washington, D.C.: Office of the Geographer, 1970.

16956 **U.S. Department of State.** *Territorial Sea Boundary: Cyprus-Sovereign Base Area (United Kingdom).* Washington, D.C.: Office of the Geographer, 1972.

16957 **U.S. Department of State.** *Territorial Sea Boundary: Denmark-Sweden.* Washington, D.C.: Office of the Geographer, 1970.

16958 **Urtecho, J. Andres.** *Nuestro derecho territorial en la Costa Atlantica y el laudo del Rey de Espana.* Managa, D.N.: Los Talleres Nacionales, 1937.

16959 **Young, Richard.** "Offshore Claims and Problems in the North Sea." *American Journal of International Law,* 59, No. 2 (April, 1965), 505-522.

16960 **Zoller, Elisabeth.** "L'Affaire de la Delimitation du Plateau Continental entre la Republique Francaise et le Royaume-Uni de Grande Bretagne et D'Irlande du Nord." *Annuaire Francais de Droit International,* 23 (1977), 359-407.

STRATEGIC ASPECTS OF THE OCEANS

GENERAL AND THEORY

Books and Journals

16961 **Bacon, Reginald,** and **McMurtrie, Francie E.** *Modern Naval Strategy.* New York: Chemical Publishing, 1941.

16962 **Barralt, Glynn.** "Joseph-Fidele Bernard on the Bering Sea Frontier, 1921-1922." *Polar Record,* 18, No. 115 (January, 1977), 341-349.

16963 **Batcheller, Gordon D.** "Maritime Strategy." *Marine Corps Gazette,* 65, No. 7 (July, 1981), 43-45.

16964 **Bathurst, Robert B.** "The Patterns of Naval Analysis." *Naval War College Review,* 27, No. 6 (November-December, 1974), 16-27.

16965 **Booth, Ken.** "Naval Strategy and the Spread of Psycho-legal Boundaries at Sea." *International Journal,* 38, No. 3 (Summer, 1983), 373-396.

16966 **Brezina, Dennis W.** "The Blue Water Strategy." *Sea Power,* 14 (May, 1971), 24-28.

16967 **Brodie, Bernard.** *Strategy and National Interests: Reflections for the Future.* New York: National Strategy Information Center, 1971.

16968 **Brown, Neville.** "Deterrence from the Sea." *Survival,* 12, No. 6 (June, 1970), 194-198.

16969 **Cable, James.** *Gunboat Diplomacy: Political Application of Limited Naval Force.* New York: Praeger, 1971.

16970 **Chubin, Shahram.** "The Northern Tier in Disarray." *World Today,* 35, No. 12 (December, 1979), 474-482.

16971 **Cohen, Maxwell.** "The Arctic and the National Interest." *International Journal,* 26, No. 1 (Winter, 1970-1), 52-81.

16972 **Corbett, Julian S.** *Some Principles of Maritime Strategy.* New York: Longmans, Green, 1911.

16973 **Cranwell, John Philips.** *The Destiny of Sea Power and Its Influence on Land Power and Air Power.* New York: W.W. Norton, 1941.

16974 **Eldridge, Frank B.** *The Background of Eastern Sea Power.* London: Phoenix House, 1948.

16975 **Etzold, Thomas H.** "Is Mahan Still Valid?" *United States Naval Institute Proceedings,* 106, No. 8/930 (August, 1980), 38-43.

16976 **Gorshkov, S.G.** "Navies in War and Peace." *US Naval Institute Proceedings*, 100 (January-November, 1974), 19-26.

16977 **Gorshkov, S.G.** *The Sea Power of the State.* Annapolis, Maryland: Naval Institute Press, 1976.

16978 **Hamilton, C.I.** "Naval Power and Diplomacy in the Nineteenth Century." *Journal of Strategic Studies*, 3, No. 1 (May, 1980), 74-88.

16979 **Hazen, David C.** "Nine Prejudices About Future Naval Systems." *US Naval Institute Proceedings*, 106, No. 7 (July, 1980), 26-32.

16980 **Klare, Michael T.** "Superpower Rivalry at Sea." *Foreign Policy*, 86-96 and 160-7.

16981 **Komer, Robert W.** "Maritime Strategy vs. Coalition Defense." *Foreign Affairs*, 60, No. 4 (Summer, 1982), 1124-44.

16982 **Lalor, W.G.** "Submarine Through the North Pole." *National Geographic Magazine*, 115, No. 1 (January, 1959), 1-20.

16983 **Laursen, Finn.** *Superpower at Sea: U.S. Ocean Policy.* New York: Praeger, 1983.

16984 **Lauterpacht, H.** "Sovereignty Over Submarine Areas." *British Year Book of International Law*, 27 (1950), 376-433.

16985 **Lenczowski, George.** "The Arc of Crisis: Its Central Sector." *Foreign Affairs*, 57, No. 3 (Spring, 1979), 796-820.

16986 **Martin, Laurence W.** *The Sea in Modern Strategy.* London: Chatto & Windus, 1967.

16987 **Mendoza, Jaime.** *La ruta atlantica.* Sucre: Imp. Bolivar, 1927.

16988 **Meyers, H.** *The Nationality of Ships.* The Hague: Martinus Nijhoff, 1967.

16989 "The Persian/Arabian Gulf Tanker War: International Law or International Chaos." *Ocean Development and International Law,* 19, No. 4 (1988), 299-322.

16990 **Rohwer, Jurgen.** *Superpower Confrontation on the Seas: Naval Development and Strategy Since 1945.* Beverly Hills, California: Sage Publications, 1975.

16991 **Shyam, Manjula R.** "The U.N. Convlention on the Law of the Sea and Military Interests in the Indian Ocean." *Ocean Development and International Law*, 15, No. 2 (1985), 147-170.

16992 **Siddiqui, M.A.H.** "Politico-Geographic Environment of the Indian Ocean Littoral: An Enquiry into Power Relations." *Annales*, 11, No. 1 (1982), 49-52.

16993 **Siddiqui, M.A.H.** "Politico-Geographic Environment of the Indian Ocean Littoral: A Search for Remedial Aspect." *Geographer*, 31, No. 1 (January, 1984), 62-67.

16994 **Sprout, Harold H.** and **Sprout, Margaret.** "Command of the Atlantic Ocean." *Encyclopedia Britannica*, 2 (1946), 637.

16995 **Troebst, Cord Christian.** *Conquest of the Sea.* London: Hodder & Stoughton, 1963.

16996 **Vego, Milan.** "The Potential Influence of Third World Navies on Ocean Shipping." *US Naval Institute Proceedings*, 107, No. 5 (May, 1981), 94-113.

16997 **Wegner, Edward.** "Theory of Naval Strategy in the Nuclear Age." *US Naval Institute Proceedings*, 98, No. 5 (May, 1972), 192-207.

16998 **Winokur, Robert S.,** and **Gonzalez, Jr., Rene E.** "Ocean Science and Military Uses of the Oceans." *Oceanus*, 25, No. 4 (Winter 1982/83), 58-66.

POLITICAL GEOGRAPHY OF REGIONS

AFRICA

Journals

16999 **Ispahani, Mahnaz Zehra.** "Alone Together: Regional Security Arrangements in Southern Africa and Arabian Peninsula." *International Security*, 8, No. 4 (Spring, 1984), 152-75.

17000 **Marks, Thomas A.** "Djibouti: France's Strategic Toehold in Africa." *African Affairs*, 73, No. 290 (January, 1974), 95-104.

17001 **Rensburg, van W.C.J.** "Africa and Western Lifelines." *Strategic Review*, 6, No. 2 (Spring, 1978), 41-50.

17002 **Spence, J.E.** "South Africa and the Defence of the West." *Round Table*, 241, No. 1 (January, 1971), 15-23.

AMERICAS

Books and Journals

17003 **Barnett, Roger W.** "U.S. Sstrategy, Freedom of the Seas, Sovereignty and Crisis Management." *Strategic Review* [Washington, DC], 20, No. 1 (Winter, 1992), 32-41.

17004 **Beck, Peter.** *The International Politics of Antartica.* London: Croom Helm, 1986.

17005 **Bezboruah, Monoranjan.** *US Strategy in the Indian Ocean: The International Response.* New York: Praeger, 1977.

17006 **Blechman, Barry M.** *The Control of Naval Armaments: Prospects and Possibilities.* Studies in Defense Policy. Washington, D.C.: The Brookings Institute, 1975.

17007 **Botto, Carlo Penna.** "Importancia das rotes maritimas para o Brasil." *A Defesa Nacional*, 18, No. 446 (1951), 177-178.

17008 **Bunster, Enrique.** "Penetracion de Chile en el Pacifico." *Mar*, 22, No. 139 (1951), 3-4.

17009 **Hanks, Robert J.** *American Sea Power and Global Strategy.* Washington, D.C.: Pergamon-Brassey's, 1985.

17010 **Hattendorf, John B.** "Some Concepts in Amerian Naal Strategic Thought, 1940-1970." In *The Yankee Mariner and Sea Power: America's Challenge of Ocean Space.* Los Angeles: University of Southern California Press, 1982.

17011 **Hayward, Thomas B.** "The Future of US Sea Power." *US Naval Institute Proceedings*, 105, No. 5 (May, 1979), 66-71.

17012 **LaRocque, Gene.** "An Island Paradise for the Admirals." *Washington Monthly*, 6, No. 5 (May, 1974), 49-51.

17013 **Luttwak, Edward.** *American Naval Power in the Mediterranean.* Part I. The Political Application of Naval Force. Newport, Rhode Island: Naval War College, 1973.

17014 **Mahan, Alfred Thayer.** "The Panama Canal and Sea Power in the Pacific." *Century Magazine*, 82, No. 2 (June, 1911), 240-248.

17015 **Mahan, Alfred Thayer.** "Strategic Features of the Caribbean Sea and the Gulf of Mexico." *Harper's New Monthly Magazine*, 95 (1911), 680-691.

17016 **McKinley, Charles.** *Uncle Sam in the Pacific Northwest.* Berkeley: University of California Press, 1952.

17017 **Middendorf, J. William II.** "American Maritime Strategy and Soviet Naval Expansion." *Strategic Review*, 4, No. 1 (Winter, 1976), 16-25.

17018 **Riesco, R.** "Chile y sus perspectivas geograficas frente al Pacifico y la Antartida." *Revista de Geografia Norte Grande*, 7 (1980), 49-56.

17019 **Schmollck, Frank H.** "Das Amerikanische Mittelmeer." *Zeitschrift fur Geopolitik*, 16 Jahrgang, Heft 8/9 (August-Septber, 1939), 581-587.

17020 **Seaga, Edward.** "The Importance of the Caribbean." *World Affairs*, 143, 2 (Fall, 1980), 136-144.

17021 **Simmons, Henry T.** "The US Navy-Countering the Soviet Building." *International Defense Review*, 7, No. 8 (August, 1974), 443-447.

17022 **Stivers, William.** "Doves, Hawks, and Detente." *Foreign Policy*, 45 (Winter, 1981-82), 126-144.

17023 **Tucker, Robert W.** "The Purpose of American Power." *Foreign Affairs*, 59, No. 2 (January, 1980), 241-276.

17024 **Turner, Stansfield.** "Missions of the US Navy." *Naval War College Review*, (March-April, 1974), 14-19.

17025 **Turner, Stansfield.** "Thinking About the Future of the Navy." *US Naval Institute Proceedings*, 106, No. 8 (August, 1980), 66-69.

17026 **Venin, V.M.** "Canada's Sovereignty in the Arctic." *Royal Canadian Mounted Police Quarterly*, 10 (1945), 273-274.

ASIA

Books and Journals

17027 **Adhikari, Sudeepta; and Kumar, A.** "Geopolitics of the Indian Ocean." *Indian Geographical Studies Bulletin, Patna*, 9 (September, 1977).

17028 **Adie, W.A.C.** "The Indian Ocean-Seen From Australia." *Iranian Review of International Relations*, 8, No. 3 (Fall, 1976), 119-161.

17029 **Adie, W.A.C.** *Oil, Politics, and Seapower: The Indian Ocean Vortex.* New York: Crane, Russak, 1975.

17030 **Agnihotri, S.P.** "Some Strategic Models: A Critical Study of Indian Ocean." *Indian Geographical Studies Bulletin, Patna*, No. 12 (March, 1979).

17031 **Ahmad, Samina.** "Australia and the Indian Ocean." *Pakistan Horizon*, 35, No. 3 (Third Quarter, 1982), 67-85.

17032 **Akaha, Tsureo.** *Japan in Global Ocean Politics*, Honolulu: University of Hawaii Press, 1985.

17033 **Alford, Jonathan.** "Strategic Developments in the Indian Ocean Area." *Asian Affairs*, 68 (June, 1979), 141-149.

17034 **Amirie, Abbas,** ed. *The Persian Gulf and Indian Ocean in International Politics.* Tehran: Institute of International Political and Economic Studies, 1975.

17035 **Anand, R.P.** "Big Powers and the Indian Ocean." *Institute for Defence Studies and Analysis Journal*, 8, No. 2 (April-June, 1976), 569-602.

17036 **Atkinson, James D.** "Who Will Dominate the Strategic Indian Ocean Area in the 1970's?" *Sea Power*, 11, No. 9 (September, 1968), 22-6.

17037 **Ballard, G.A.** *Rulers of the Indian Ocean.* New York: Houghton Mifflin, 1928.

17038 **Beazley, K.C.,** and **Clark, J.** *Politics of Intrusion: The Superpowers and the Indian Ocean.* Sydney: Alternative Publishing Cooperative, 1979.

17039 **Bindra, A.P.S.** "The Indian Ocean as Seen by an Indian." *United States Naval Institute Proceedings*, 96, No. 5/807 (May, 1970), 178-203.

17040 **Bowman, Larry W.,** and **Clark, Ian,** eds. *The Indian Ocean in Global Politics.* Boulder, Colorado: Westview Press/Nedlands: University of Western Australia, 1981.

17041 **Braun, Dieter.** "The Indian Ocean in Afro-Asian Perspective." *World Today*, 28, No. 2 (June, 1972), 249-256.

17042 **Braun, Dieter.** *The Indian Ocean: Region of Conflict or 'Peace Zone.'* London: C. Hurst, 1983.

17043 **Burkaramber, Bukar.** "Zone of Peace or Strategic Primacy: Politics of Security in the Indian Ocean." *Bulletin of Peace Proposals*, 16, No. 1 (1985), 51-60.

17044 **Burt, Richard.** "Strategic Politics and the Indian Ocean." *Pacific Affairs*, 47 (Winter, 1975-76), 509-54.

17045 **Centre d'etude du Sud-Est asiatique et de l'Extreme Orient,** ed. *The Politics of the Great Powers in the Indian Ocean.* Brussels: Free University of Brussels, 1971.

17046 **Chari, P.R.** "The Indian Ocean: An Indian Viewpoint." *Iranian Review of International Relations*, 8, No. 2 (Fall, 1976), 163-184.

17047 **Chari, P.R.** "The Indian Ocean: Strategic Issues." *International Studies*, 18, No. 2 (April-June, 1979), 163-76.

17048 **Chelhardt, Alexander O.** "Soviet and US Interests in the Indian Ocean." *Asian Survey*, 15, No. 8 (August, 1975), 672-83.

17049 **Cottrell, Alvin J.** "Indian Ocean of Tomorrow." *Sea Power*, 25, No. 3 (March, 1971), 10-16.

17050 **Cottrell, Alvin J.,** and **Burrell, R.M.,** eds. *The Indian Ocean: Its Political, Economic, and Military Importance.* New York: Praeger, 1972.

17051 **Cottrell, Alvin,** and **Hahn, Walter F.** *Indian Ocean Naval Limitations: Regional Issues and Global Implications.* New York: National Strategy Information Center, 1976.

17052 **Cottrell, Alvin J.,** and **Burrell, R.M.** "The Soviet Navy and the Indian Ocean." *Strategic Review*, 2 (Fall, 1974), 25-35.

17053 **Cottrell, A.,** et al. *Sea Power and Strategy in the Indian Ocean.* Beverly Hills, California: Sage Publications, 1981.

17054 **Darby, Phillip.** "Beyond East of Suez." *International Affairs*, 46, No. 4 (October, 1970), 655-669.

17055 **Das, D.P.** "India and the Indian Ocean: A Study of Past and Future Strategy." *China Report*, 10, No. 1 (January-April, 1974), 55-70.

17056 **Devare, Sudhir T.** "Indian Ocean: Politico and Strategy." *Bombay Geographical Magazine*, 14, No. 1 (December, 1966), 33-38.

17057 **Dikshit, R.D.** "Political Stability in the Indian Ocean Area and the Strategic Significance of the Remote Islands of Mauritius, Seychelles, etc." *Geographical Thought*, 3, 1 (June, 1967), 15-22.

17058 **Dowdy, William L.,** and **Trood, Russell B.,** eds. *The Indian Ocean: Perspectives on a Strategic Arena.* Durham, North Carolina: Duke University Press, 1985.

17059 **Eilersten, James T.** *The Soviet Versus United States Naval Presence in the Indian Ocean.* Research Study No. 0870-73. Air War College, Air University, Alabama: Maxwell Air Force Base, 1973.

17060 **Franda, Marcus F.** "The Indian Ocean: A Delhi Perspective." *American Universities Field Staff. Southeast Asia Series*, 19, No. 1 (1975), complete issue.

17061 **Fuler, Jack.** "Dateline Diego Garcia: Paved-over Paradise." *Foreign Policy*, 28 (Fall, 1977), 175-186.

17062 **Furlong, R.D.M.** "Strategic Power in the Indian Ocean." *International Defense Review*, 5, No. 4 (April, 1972), 133-140.

17063 **Gerosa, Guide.** "Will the Indian Ocean Become a Soviet Pond." *Atlas*, 19, No. 11 (November, 1970), 20-21.

17064 **Ghebhardt, Alexander O.** "Soviet and US Interests in the Indian Ocean." *Asian Survey*, 15, No. 8 (August, 1977), 2153-2160.

17065 **Graham, Gerald S.** *Great Britain in the Indian Ocean: A Study of Maritime Enterprise 1810-1850.* Oxford: Oxford University Press, 1967.

17066 **Griffith, William E.** "The Great Powers, the Indian Ocean, and the Persian Gulf." *Jerusalem Journal of International Relations*, 1, No. 2 (Winter, 1975), 5-19.

17067 **Hanks, Robert J.** "The Indian Ocean Negotiations: Rocks and Schoals." *Strategic Review*, 6, No. 1 (Winter, 1978), 18-27.

17068 **Harrison, Kirkby.** "Pictorial-Diego Garcia: The Seabees at Work." *US Naval Institute Proceedings*, 105, No. 8 (August, 1979), 53-61.

17069 **Hickman, William F.** "Soviet Naval Policy in the Indian Ocean." *US Naval Institute Proceedings*, 105/8/918 (August, 1979), 42-52.

17070 **Houbert, Jean.** "The Indian Ocean Creole Islands: Geo-Politics and Decolonisation." *The Journal of Modern African Studies* [Cambridge], 30, No. 3 (September, 1992), 465-484.

17071 **Hurewitz, J.C.** "The Persian Gulf: British Withdrawal and Western Security." *Annals of the Academy of Political and Social Science*, 401 (May, 1972), 106-115.

17072 **Hutchinson, Alaister, G.L.** *The Strategic Significance of the Indian Ocean.* Professional Study No. 4619, Air War College, Air University. Alabama: Maxwell Air Force Base, April, 1972.

17073 **Hutchison, Alan.** "Indian Ocean: The Island Viewpoint." *Africa Report*, 20, No. 1 (January-February, 1975), 52-4.

17074 **Indian International Centre.** *Seminar on Indian Ocean as a Zone of Peace*, New Delhi: IIC, 1980.

17075 **Jacobs, G.** "The Pakistan Navy." *Asian Defence Journal*, (September, 1981), 143-152.

17076 **Jukes, Geoffrey.** "The Soviet Union and the Indian Ocean." *Survival*, 13, No. 11 (November, 1971), 370-375.

17077 **Katchen, Martin H.** "The Spratly Islands and the Law of the Sea: 'Dangerous Ground' for Asian Peace." *Asian Survey*, 17, No. 12 (December, 1977), 1167-1181.

17078 **Kaushik, Devendra.** *The Indian Ocean: Towards a Peace Zone.* Delhi: Vikas Publications, 1972.

17079 **Kerr, Alex.** *The Indian Ocean Region.* Boulder, Colorado: Westview Press, 1981.

17080 **Khan, Rashid Ahmad.** "India's Indian Ocean Policy: Origins and Development." *Strategic Studies*, 6, No. 4 (Summer, 1983), 50-61.

17081 **Khan, Rashid Ahmad.** *Scramble for the Indian Ocean*, Lahore: Progressive Publishers, 1973.

17082 **Kist, F.J.** "The Geo-Political and Strategic Importance of the Waterways in the Netherlands Indies." *Bulletin of the Colonial Institute of Amsterdam*, 1, No.4 (August, 1938), 252-262.

17083 **Kline, Hibberd V.B.** "Diego Garcia and the Need for a Continuous American Presence in the Indian Ocean." *Marine Corps Gazette*, 59 (April, 1975), 29-34.

17084 **Kumar, Chandra.** "The Indian Ocean: Arc of Crisis or Zone of Peace?" *International Affairs*, 60, No. 2 (Spring, 1984), 233-246.

17085 **Lacouture, John E.** "Seapower in the Indian Ocean: A Requirement for Western Security." *US Naval Institute Proceedings*, 105, No. 8 (August, 1979), 30-41.

17086 **Larus, Joel.** "The End of Naval Detente in the Indian Ocean." *World Today*, 36, No. 4 (April, 1980), 126-132.

17087 **Lavretyev, Alexander.** "Indian Ocean: The Soviet Perspective." *Africa Report*, 20, No. 1 (January-February), 46-49.

17088 **Lebedev, Igor A.** "Soviet Policy Considerations Regarding the Indian Ocean." *Australian Outlook*, 31, No. 1 (April, 1977), 133-42.

17089 **Lewein, Terence.** "The Indian Ocean and Beyond: British Interests Yesterday and Today." *Asian Affairs*, 9 (Old Series, Vol. 65), Pt. 3 (October, 1978), 247-259.

17090 **Lim, Joo-Jock.** *Geo-strategy and the South China Sea Basin.* Singapore: Singapore University Press, 1977a.

17091 **MacDonald, Charles G.** "Iran's Strategic Interests and the Law of the Sea." *Middle East Journal*, 34, No. 3 (Summer, 1980), 302-322.

17092 **Macleod, Alexander.** "Shah of the Indian Ocean?" *Pacific Community*, 7, 3 (April, 1976), 423-432.

17093 **Madeley, John.** "Diego Garcia: An Indian Ocean Storm-Centre." *Round Table*, 283, No. 2 (July, 1981), 253-257.

17094 **MccGwire, Michael.** "The Geopolitical Importance of Strategic Waterways in the Asia-Pacific Region." *ORBIS*, 19, No. 3 (Fall, 1975), 1058-1076.

17095 **Millar, T.B.** *The Indian and Pacific Oceans: Some Strategic Considerations.* Toronto: THe Institute for Strategic Studies, Canadian Institute of International Affairs, 1969.

17096 **Millar, T.B.** "Control of the Indian Ocean." *Survival*, 9, No. 10 (October, 1976), 323-326.

17097 **Mishra, Binaya Ranjan.** "US Strategy in the Indian Ocean: India's Perception and Response." *Asia Pacific Community*, 18 (Fall, 1982), 64-79.

17098 **Misra, K.P.** "Developments in the Indian Ocean Area: The Littoral Response." *International Studies*, 16, No. 3 (January-March, 1977), 17-34.

17099 **Misra, K.P.** "International Politics in the Indian Ocean." *ORBIS*, 18, 4 (Winter, 1975), 1088-1089.

17100 **Moorer, Thomas H., and Cottrell, Alvin J.** "The Search for US Bases in the Indian Ocean: A Last Chance." *Strategic Review*, 8, No. 2 (Spring, 1980), 30-38.

17101 **Mugomba, Agrippah T.** "Indian Ocean as a Zone of Peace: An African Perspective." *Alternatives*, 4, No. 1 (July, 1979), 115-133.

17102 **Namboodiri, P.K.S., et al.** *Intervention in the Indian Ocean.* New Delhi: ABC Publishing House, 1982.

17103 **Paone, R.M.** "The Big Three and the Indian Ocean." *Sea Power*, 18, No. 8 (August, 1975), 28-34.

17104 **Parker, J.A.** "Indian Ocean: A New Soviet Lake?" *New Guard*, 15 (March, 1975), 7-10.

17105 **Pavlovsky, V.** "Imperialist Plans in the Indian Ocean." *New Times*, 2 (January, 1971), 8-9.

17106 **Pavlovsky, V., and Tomilin, Y.** "Indian Ocean: Confrontation or Security?" *New Times*, 10 (March, 1974), 4-5.

17107 **Poulose, T.T., ed.** *Indian Ocean Power Rivalry.* New Delhi: Young Asia Publications, 1974.

17108 **Poulose, T.T.** "Indian Ocean: Prospects of a Nuclear-free Peace Zone." *Pacific Community*, 5, No. 2 (January, 1974), 319-334.

17109 **Prina, L. Edgar.** "At Last, A Base in the Indian Ocean." *Sea Power*, 14, No. 1 (January, 1971), 26-8.

17110 **Ragland, Thomas R.** "A Harbinger: The Senkaku Islands." *San Diego Law Review*, 10, No. 3 (May, 1973), 664-691.

17111 **Rais, Rasul B.** "An Appraisal of US Strategy in the Indian Ocean." *Asian Survey*, 23, No. 9 (September, 1983), 1043-51.

17112 **Rais, Rasul B.** *The Indian Ocean and the Super Powers.* Totowa, New Jersey: Barnes and Noble, 1987.

17113 **Ramazani, R.K.** "Security in the Gulf." *Foreign Affairs*, 57, No. 3 (April, 1979), 821-835.

17114 **Ramchandani, R.R.** "Superpower Rivalry in Africa and the Indian Ocean." *Foreign Affairs Reports*, 31, No. 2 (February, 1982), 39-47.

17115 **Rao, R. Rama.** "A Strategy for the Indian Ocean." *Indian & Foreign Review*, 12, No. 11 (March 15, 1974), 16-18.

17116 **Richard, Jr., A. Best.** "Indian Ocean Arms Control." *US Naval Institute Proceedings*, 106/2/924 (February, 1980), 42-48.

17117 **Riedl, Harold A.** *The Indian Ocean Power Vacuum.* Report No. 4701, April, 1972. Air War College, Air University. Alabama: Maxwell Air Force Base, 1972.

17118 **Rossi, Georges.** "Une Ville de Colonisation Francaise dans l'ocean Indien: Diego-Suarez [A French Colonization Town in the Indian Ocean: Diego Suarez]." *Les Cahiers d'Outre-mer*, 26 Annee, No. 104 (Octobre-Decembre, 1973), 410-426.

17119 **Satpathi, D.D.P.P.** "Geopolitical Significance of the Diego Garcia." *Geographical Outlook*, 16 (1980-81).

17120 **Scham, Alan M.** "Perim on the Red Sea: Geo-Stategic Flashpoint." *U.S. Naval Institute Proceedings*, 108, No. 3 (March, 1982), 143-145.

17121 **Seth, S.P.** "The Indian Ocean and the Indo-American Relations." *Asian Survey*, 15, No. 7 (August, 1975), 645-55.

17122 **Shanti, Sadiq Ali.** "India and the Indian Ocean." *Foreign Affairs Reports*, 31, No. 2 (February, 1982), 22-28.

17123 **Sharma, R.C.** "International and Regional Focus on the Indian Ocean." *Pacific Community*, 7, No. 3 (April, 1976), 433-457.

17124 **Shepherd, George W.** "Developing Collective Self-reliance in the Zone of Peace." *IDSA Journal*, 15, No. 3 (July-September, 1982), 19-33.

17125 **Sinha, R.N.P.** "Diego Garcia: A Geostrategic Viewpoint." *Geographical Outlook*, 15 (1979-1980).

17126 **Smolansky, O.M.** "Moscow and the Persian Gulf: An Analysis of Soviet Ambitions and Potential." *ORBIS*, 14, No. 1 (Spring, 1970), 92-108.

17127 **Song, Yann-Huei (Billy).** "China and the Military Use of the Ocean." *Ocean Development and International Law* [New York], 21, No. 1 (1990), 213-235.

17128 **Speed, F.W.** "Indian Ocean Rivalry." *Army Quarterly and Defence Journal*, 105, No. 4 (October, 1975), 457-62.

17129 **Sreedhar.** "Buying Security in the Gulf." *IDSA Journal*, 14, No. 1 (January-March, 1982), 358-382.

17130 **Stone, Norman L.** "An Indian Ocean Fleet-The Case and the Cost." *US Naval Institute Proceedings*, 107, No. 7 (July, 1981), 54-57.

17131 **Subrahmanyam, K.** "Indian Ocean." *IDSA Journal*, 14, No. 1 (January-March, 1982), 329-357.

17132 **Subrahmanyam, K., and Amand, J.P.** "Indian Ocean as an Area of Peace." *India Quarterly*, 27, No. 4 (October-December, 1971), 289-315.

17133 **Sukhwal, B.L.** "Geopolitical and Geostrategic Importance of the Superpower Rivalry in the Indian Ocean." *Asian Profile: Asia's International Journal*, 10, No. 1 (February, 1982), 25-46.

17134 **Tahtinen, Dale R.** *Arms in the Indian Ocean: Interests and Challenges.* Washington, D.C.: American Enterprise Institute for Public Policy Research, 1977.

17135 **Teplinsky, B.** "The Persian Gulf in Imperialist Plans." *New Times*, 36 (September, 1972), 23-24.

17136 **Thomson, George C.** *Problems of Strategy in the Pacific and Indian Oceans.* New York: National Strategy Information Center, 1970.

17137 **Towle, Philip.** *Naval Power in the Indian Ocean Threats, Bluffs, and Fantasies.* Canberra: Strategic and Defense Studies Centre, Australian National University, 1979.

17138 **Vaidya, K.B.** *The Naval Defence of India.* Bombay: Thacker, 1949.

17139 **Valencia, Mark J.** "The South China Sea: Prospects for Marine Regionalism." *Marine Policy*, 2, No. 1 (January, 1978), 87-104.

17140 **Vali, Ference A.** *Politics of the Indian Ocean: The Balance of Power.* New York: The Free Press, 1976.

17141 **Van Der Kroef, Justus M.** "The American Soviet Confrontation in the Waters of Asian Rim." *Strategic Studies*, 6, No. 1 (Autumn, 19820, 25-40.

17142 **Vichakar, Jagdish.** *Afro-Asian Security and the Indian Ocean.* New Delhi: Sterling Publishers, 1974.

17143 **Vivekanandan, B.** "The Indian Ocean as a Zone of Peace: Problems and Prospects." *Asian Survey*, 21, No. 6 (June, 1981), 1237-49.

17144 **Wall, Patrick, ed.** *The Indian Ocean and the Threat to the West: Four Studies in Global Strategy.* London: Stacey International, 1975.

17145 **Wheeler, Geoffrey.** "The Indian Ocean Area: Soviet Aims and Interests." *Asian Affairs*, 59 (October, 1972), 270-274.

17146 **Wingerter, Rex.** "The United States, the Soviet Union, and the Indian Ocean: The Competition for the Third World." *Bulletin of Concerned Asian Scholars*, 9, No. 3 (July-September, 1977), 52-64.

17147 **Yefremov, V.** "The Indian Ocean: Confrontation Arena or Peace Zone?" *Soviet Military Review*, 4, No. 2 (April, 1981), 50-1.

17148 **Zakheim, Dov. S.** "Towards a Western Approach to the Indian Ocean." *Survival*, 22, No. 1 (January-February, 1980), 7-14.

AUSTRALIA, OCEANIA AND ANTARCTICA

Books and Journals

17149 Antarctic Treaty System: An Assessment. Proceedings of a Workshop Held at Beardmore Glacier South Camp, Antarctic, January 1985. Washington, D.C.: National Academy Press, 1986.

17150 "Australian Policy and Programs in the Antarctic." *Ascent*, 8 (1985), 30-31.

17151 **Barreda Laos, F.** *La Antartida Sudamericana ante el Derecho Internacional.* Buenos Aires: Impresores Linari y Cia, 1948.

17152 **Brookfield, Harold C.** *The Pacific in Transition: Geographical Perspectives on Adaptation and Change.* Toronto: Macmillan, 1974.

17153 **Glassner, Martin Ira.** "The View from the Near North: South Americans View Antarctica and the Southern Ocean Geopolitically." *Political Geography Quarterly,* 4, No. 4 (October, 1985), 329-342.

17154 **Joyner, Christopher C.** "Antarctica and the Indian Ocean States: The Interplay of Law, Interests, and Geopolitics." *Ocean Development and International Law* [New York], 21, No. 1 (1990), 41-70.

17155 **Kaye, Stuart, and Rothwell, Donald R.** "Australian Law in Antarctica." *Polar Record* [Cambridge], 29, No. 170 (July, 1993), 215-218.

17156 **Keesing, Felix M.** "The South Sea Islands Now." *Asia and the Americas,* 45, No. 2 (February, 1945), 77-80.

17157 **Lattimore, Eleanor.** "Pacific Ocean or American Lake?" *Far Eastern Survey,* 14, No. 22 (November 7, 1945), 313-316.

17158 **Livermore, Seward W.** "American Strategy Diplomacy in the South Pacific, 1890-1914." *Pacific Historical Review,* 12, No. 1 (March, 1943), 33-51.

17159 *The Pattern of Pacific Security.* A report by a Chatham House Study Group. London: Royal Institute of International Affairs, 1946.

17160 **Snider, Anthony G.** "Antartica: A Geopolitical Analysis." Burlington: University of Vermont, M.A., 1988.

17161 **Tellez, Indalicio.** "Signification del mar Pacifico." *Revista Geografica de Chile,* Ano 2, No. 2 (Decembre de, 1949), 21-24.

17162 **Tow, William T.** "ANZUS: A Strategic Role in the Indian Ocean?" *World Today,* 34, No. 10 (October, 1978), 401-8.

17163 **Zamora, L.A.** "Proyeccion permana a la Antartida. (Peru's Projection of Antarctica)." *Geosur,* 23 (1981), 41-43.

EUROPE

Books and Journals

17164 **Araldsen, O.P.** "The Soviet Union and the Arctic." *United States Naval Institute Proceedings,* 93, No. 6 (June, 1967), 49-57.

17165 **Armstrong, Terence.** *The Northern Sea Route.* Cambridge: 1952 and *Russian Settlement in the North.* Cambridge: Cambridge University Press, 1965.

17166 **Bathurst, Robert B.** *Understanding the Soviet Navy: A Handbook.* Newport, Rhode Island: Naval War College Press, 1979.

17167 **Bilmanis, Alfred.** *The Baltic States and the Problem of the Freedom of the Baltic Sea.* Washington, D.C.: Press Bureau of the Latvian Legation, 1943.

17168 **Blechman, Barry M.** *The Changing Soviet Navy: Studies in Defense Policy.* Washington, D.C.: Brookings Institute, 1973.

17169 **Brown, R.N. Rudmose.** "Spitsbergen terra nullius." *Geographical Review,* 7, No. 2 (April, 1917), 311-321.

17170 **Burt, Richard.** "Soviet Sea-based Forces and SALT." *Survival,* 17, No. 1 (January-February, 1975), 9-13.

17171 **Cottrell, Alvin J., and Theberge, James D.,** eds. *The Western Mediterranean: Its Political, Economic, and Strategic Importance.* New York: Praeger, 1974.

17172 **Dowrick, F.W.** "Submarine Areas Around Great Britain." *Public Law,* (Spring, 1977), 10-28.

17173 **Edwards, Mickey.** "Soviet Expansion and Control of the Sea-Lanes." *US Naval Institute Proceedings,* 106, No. 9 (September, 1980), 46-51.

17174 **Gill, Graeme F.** "The Soviet Union, Detente and the Indian Ocean." *Australian Outlook,* 31, No. 2 (August, 1977), 253-60.

17175 **Graham, Gerald S.** *The Politics of Naval Supremacy: Studies in British maritime Ascendancy.* Cambridge: University Press, 1965.

17176 **Grzybowski, Kazimierz.** "The Soviet Doctrine of Mare Clausum and Policies in Black and Baltic Seas." *Journal of Central European Affairs,* 14, No. 4 (January, 1955), 339-353.

17177 **Guill, James H.** "The Lenin and the Soviet Design for the Arctic." *Proceedings U.S. Naval Institute,* 84, No. 7 (July, 1958), 88-93.

17178 **Herrick, Robert W.** *Soviet Naval Strategy: Fifty Years of Theory and Practice.* Annapolis, Maryland: US Naval Institute, 1968.

17179 **Hopker, Wolfgang.** "Soviet Global Strategy: The Great Challenge to the West Sea." *US Naval Institute Proceedings*, 101, No. 12 (December, 1975), 24-29.

17180 **Hudson, George E.** "Soviet Naval Doctrine Under Lenin and Stalin." *Soviet Studies*, 28, No. 1 (January, 1976), 42-65.

17181 **Hudson, George E.** "Soviet Naval Doctrine and Soviet Politics, 1953-1975." *World Politics*, 29, No. 1 (October, 1976), 90-113.

17182 **Kerner, Robert J.** *The Urge to the Sea: The Course of Russian History.* Berkeley: University of California Press, 1942.

17183 **Kilmarx, Robert A.,** ed. *Soviet-United States Naval Balance.* Washington, D.C.: Center for Strategic and International Studies, 1975.

17184 **Laursen, Finn.** "Security Aspects of Danish and Norwegian Law of the Sea Policies." *Ocean Development and International Law,* 18, No. 2 (1987), 199-233.

17185 **Lenczowski, George.** "The Soviet Union and the Persian Gulf: An Encircling Strategy." *International Journal*, 37, No. 2 (Spring, 1982), 307-327.

17186 **McConnell, James,** ed. *Soviet Naval Diplomacy.* New York: Pergamon, 1979.

17187 **MccGwire, Michael.** "Naval Power and Soviet Global Strategy." *International Security*, 3, No. 4 (Spring, 1979), 134-89.

17188 **MccGwire, Michael.** "The Rationale for the Development of Soviet Seapower." *U.S. Naval Institute Proceedings*, 106, No. 5 (May, 1980), 154-183.

17189 **MccGwire, Michael; Booth, Ken;** and **McDonnell, John,** eds. *Soviet Naval Developments: Context and Capability.* Halifax: Center for Foreign Policy Studies, Dalhousie University, 1973.

17190 **MccGwire, Michael, and McDonnell, John,** eds. *Soviet Naval Indulgence, Domestic and Foreign Dimensions.* New York: Praeger, 1977.

17191 **MccGwire, Michael, and McDonnell, John,** eds. *Soviet Naval Policy: Objectives and Constraints.* New York: Praeger, 1975.

17192 **Millar, T.B.** *Soviet Policies in the Indian Ocean Area.* Canberra Papers on Strategy and Defence, No. 7. Canberra: Australian National University Press, 1970.

17193 **Mitchell, Donald W.** "The Soviet Naval Challenge." *ORBIS*, 14, No. 1 (Spring, 1970), 129-153.

17194 **Morris, Michael A.** "Southern Cone Maritime Security after the 1984 Argentine-Chilean Treaty of Peace and Friendship." *Ocean Development and International Law,* 18, No. 2 (1987), 235-254.

17195 **Moulton, J.L.** *British Maritime Strategy in the 1970s.* London: Royal United Service Institution, 1969.

17196 **Nitze, Paul H.,** et al. *Securing the Seas: The Soviet Naval Challenge and Western Alliance Options.* Boulder, Colorado: Westview Press, 1979.

17197 **O'Connor, Raymond G.,** and **Vladimir P. Prokofieff.** "The Soviet Navy in the Mediterranean and Indian Ocean." *Virginia Quarterly Review*, 49, No. 4 (Autumn, 1973), 481-493.

17198 **Oddvar, B.** *The Soviet Union in International Shipping.* Bergen, Norway: Institute for Shipping Research, 1970.

17199 **Pandolfe, Frank C.** "Soviet Seapower in Light of Mahan's Principles." *United States Naval Institute Proceedings*, 106, No. 8 (August, 1980), 44-46.

17200 **Polmar, Norman.** *Soviet Naval Power: Challenge for the 1970s.* Revised edition, New York: National Strategy Information Center, 1974.

17201 **Price, David Lynn.** "Moscow and the Persian Gulf." *Problems of Communism*, 28, No. 2 (March-April, 1979), 1-13.

17202 **Ra'anan, Uri.** "The Soviet View of Navies in Peacetime." *Naval War College Review*, 29, No. 2 (Summer, 1976), 30-38.

17203 **Rohwer, Jurgen.** "Admiral Gorshkov and the Influence of History Upon Sea Power." *US Naval Institute Proceedings*, 107, No. 51 (May, 1981), 150-173.

17204 **Rollins, Patrick J.** "Russia's Fictitious Naval Tradition." *US Naval Institute Proceedings*, 99, No. 1 (January, 1973), 65-71.

17205 **Romano, Sergio.** "Italy's New Course in the Mediterranean." *Australian Outlook,* 41, No. 2 (August, 1987), 101-103.

17206 **Schofield, Brian B.** *British Sea Power: Naval Policy in the Twentieth Century.* London: B.T. Batsford, 1967.

17207 **Seebohm, Lord,** ed. *Report of the Naval Warfare Committee.* London: Her Majesty's Stationery Office, 1974.

17208 **Sim, J.P.** "Soviet Naval Presence in the Indian Ocean." *Australian Outlook,* 31, No. 1 (April, 1977), 185-192.

17209 **Skogan, John Kristen,** and **Brundtland, Arne Olav,** eds. *Soviet Seapower in Northern Waters: Facts, Motivation, Impact and Responses.* New York: St. Martin's Press, 1990.

17210 **Smith, Clyde A.** "Constraints of Naval Geography on Soviet Naval Power." *Naval War College Review,* 27, No. 5 (September-October, 1974), 46-57.

17211 **Svyatov, G.,** and **Kokoshin, A.** "Naval Power in the US Strategic Plans." *International Affairs,* 49, No. 2 (April, 1973), 56-62.

17212 **Synhorst, Gerald E.** "Soviet Strategic Interest in the Maritime Arctic." *United States Naval Institute Proceedings,* 99, No. 843 (May, 1973), 89-111.

17213 **Taft, Jr., Robert.** "Meeting the Soviet Naval Challenge." *Journal of Social and Political Affairs,* 1, No. 3 (July, 1976), 195-201.

17214 **Timtchenko, Leonid.** "The Legal Status of the Northern Sea Route." *Polar Record* [Cambridge], 30, No. 174 (July, 1994), 193-200.

17215 **Traavik, Kim,** and **Ostreng, Willy.** "Security and Ocean Law: Norway and the Soviet Union in the Barents Sea." *Ocean Developments and International Law,* 4, No. 4 (1977), 343-367.

17216 **Vanneman, Peter,** and **Janus, Martin.** "Soviet Thrust into the Horn of Africa: 'The Next Targets.'" *Strategic Review,* 6, No. 2 (Spring, 1978), 33-40.

17217 **Vigor, P.H.** "Admiral S.G. Gorshkov's Views on Seapower." *Journal of the Royal United Services Institute for Defence Studies,* 119, No. 1 (March, 1974), 53-60.

17218 **Weinland, Robert G.; Herrick, Robert W.; MccGwire, Michael;** and **McConnell, James M.** "Admiral Gorshkov's' Navies in Ware and Peace." *Survival,* 17, No. 2 (March-April, 1975), 54-63.

17219 **Wooldridge, E.T.** "The Gorshkov Papers: Soviet Naval Doctrine for the Nuclear Age." *ORBIS,* 18, No. 4 (Winter, 1975), 1153-75.

17220 **Zagoria, Donald S.** "Into the Breach: New Soviet Alliances in the Third World." *Foreign Affairs,* 57, No. 3 (April, 1979), 733-754.

17221 **Zumwalt, Jr., Elmo R.** "Gorshkov and His Navy." *ORBIS,* 24, No. 3 (Fall, 1980), 491-510.

EXPLORATION AND CONTROL OVER THE RESOURCES OF THE OCEANS

GENERAL AND THEORY

Books and Journals

17222 **Alexander, Lewis M.** "National Jurisdiction and the Use of the Sea." *Natural Resources Journal,* 8, No. 3 (July, 1968), 373-400.

17223 **Alexander, Lewis M.,** and **Hanson, L.C.,** eds. *Antarctic Politics and Marine Resources: Critical Choices for the 1980's.* Kingston: Center for Ocean Management Studies, University of Rhode Island, 1984.

17224 **Alexander, Lewis M.,** and **Hodgson, Robert D.** "The Impact of the 200-Mile Economic Zone on the Law of the Sea." *San Diego Law Review,* 12, No. 3 (April, 1975), 569-599.

17225 **Amador, F.V. Garcia.** *The Exploitation and Conservation of the Resources of the Sea.* Leiden: Sijthoff, 1959.

17226 **Becker, Loftus.** "The Breadth of the Territorial Sea and Fisheries Jurisdiction." *U.S. Department of State Bulletin,* 40 , No. 1029 (March, 1959), 369-375.

17227 **Birnie, P.** "The Role of Law in Protecting Marine Mammals." *Ambio,* 15, No. 3 (1986), 137-143.

17228 "Boundary Delimitation in the Economic Zone: The Gulf of Maine Dispute." *Maine Law Review,* 30, No. 2 (1979), 207-245.

17229 **Briggs, H.W.** "Jurisdiction Over the Sea Bed and Subsoil Beyond Territorial Waters." *American Journal of International Law,* 45, No. 4 (October, 1951), 338-342.

17230 **Brown, E.D.** "The Continental Shelf and the Exclusive Economic Zone: The Problem of Delimitation at UNCLOS III." *Maritime Policy and Management,* 4 (1977), 377-408.

17231 **Brown, E.D.** "The Present Regime of the Exploration and Exploitation of Sea-Bed Resources in International Law and in National Legislation: An Evaluation." In *Symposium on the International Regime of the Sea-Bed*, Jerzy Sztucki, ed. Rome: Accademia Nazionale dei Lincei, 1970, 241-278.

17232 **Bubier, Jill L.** "Internatioanl Management of Atlantic Salmon: Equitable Sharing and Building Consensus." *Ocean Development and International Law*, 19, No. 1 (1988), 35-58.

17233 **Burke, William T.** "Anadromous Species and the New International Law of the Sea." *Ocean Development and International Law* [New York], 22, No. 2 (April-June, 1991), 95-131.

17234 **Butlin, J.A.** "The Political Economy of International Marine Resources Management." *Resources Policy*, 2, No. 2 (June, 1976), 128-135.

17235 **Carritt, D.E.** (Chairman). *Desalination Research and the Water Problem*, Pub. 901. Washington D.C.: National Academy of Sciences-National Research Council, 1962.

17236 **Christy, Francis T.** "Maritime Wealth: How Much? For How Long?" *Economic Impact*, 4 (1973), 43-44.

17237 **Cobbe, J.H.** *Government and Mining Companies in Developing Countries*. Boulder, Colorado: Westview Press, 1979.

17238 **Colborn, Paul A.** "National Jurisdiction Over Resources of the Continental Shelf." *Bulletin of Pan American Union*, 82, No. 1 (1948), 38-40.

17239 **Cruikshank, M.J.** *The Exploration and Exploitation of Off-shore Mineral Deposits*. Boulder, Colorado: University of Colorado, M.S., 1962.

17240 **Doumani, George A.** *Ocean Wealth: Policy and Potential*. Rochelle Park, New Jersey: Hayden Book Company, 1973.

17241 **Durante, Francesco.** "The Present Regime of the Exploration and Exploitation of the Sea-bed Resources in International Law and in National Legislation." In *Symposium on the International Regime of the Sea-bed*, Jerzy Sztucki, ed. Rome: 1970, p. 279-294.

17242 **Earney, Fillmore C.F.** "Law of the Sea, Resource Use, and International Understanding." *Journal of Geography*, 84, No. 3 (May-June, 1985), 105-110.

17243 **Earney, Fillmore C.F.** *Ocean Mining: Geographic Perspectives*. Bergen: Meddelelser

Fra Geografrisk Institutt, Universiteset i Bergen, No. 70, 1982.

17244 **Earney, Fillmore C.F.** "Ocean Space and Seabed Mining." *Journal of Geography*, 74, No. 9 (December, 1975), 539-547.

17245 **Earney, Fillmore C.F.** *Petroleum and Hard Minerals from the Sea*. Washington, D.C.: Winston & Sons with John Wiley & Sons in the Halsted Press Series, 1980.

17246 **Eckert, Ross D.** *The Enclosure of Ocean Resources: Economics and the Law of the Sea*. Stanford, California: Stanford University, Hoover Institute Publication, No. 210, 1979.

17247 **Extavour, Winston Conrad.** *The Exclusive Economic Zone*. Geneva: Institut universitaire de hautes etudes internationales, 1979.

17248 **Felando, August.** "Problems Confronting Distant-Water Fisheries in the New Law of the Sea Environment." In *The Law of the Sea: Issues in Ocean Resource Management*, Don Walsh, ed. New York: Praeger, 1977, 129-143.

17249 **Garcia-Amador, F.V.** *The Exploitation and Conservation of the Resources of the Sea*. The Hague: Sijthoff and Leiden, 1963.

17250 **Garcia, S.J.A. Gulland**, and **Miles, E.** "The New Law of the Sea, and the Access to Surplus Fish Resources: Bioeconomic Reality and Scientific Collaboration." *Marine Policy*, 10, No. 3 (June, 1986), 192-200.

17251 **Gardiner, Piers R.R.** "Reasons and Methods for Fixing the Outer Limit of the Legal Continental Shelf Beyond 200 Nautical Miles." *Revue Iranienne des Relations Internationales*, 11/12 (1978), 145-177.

17252 **Gold, Edgar.** "Legal Aspects of the Transportation of Dangerous Goods at Sea." *Marine Policy*, 10, No. 3 (June, 1986), 185-191.

17253 **Goldie, L.F.E.** "The Exploitability Test-Interpretation and Potentialities." *Natural Resources Journal*, 8, No. 3 (July, 1968), 434-477.

17254 **Gregory, H .E.**, and **Barnes, K.** *The North Pacific Fisheries*. New York: Milwood, Krause Reprint Company, 1976, 225-242.

17255 **Grunawalt, Richard J.** "The Acquisition of the Resources of the Bottom of the Sea-A New Frontier International Law." *Military Law Review*, 34 , Pamphlet No. 27-100-34 (October, 1966), 101-133.

17256 **Hardy, A.C.** *The Open Sea, Its Natural History, The World of Plankton.* Boston, Massachusetts: Houghton Mifflin, 1959.

17257 **Hedberg, Hollis D.** "Limits of National Jurisdiction Over Natural Resources of the Ocean Bottom." In *The Law of the Sea: National Policy Recommendations.* Kingston: University of Rhode Island, 1970. (Proceedings and Papers of the Fourth Law of the Sea Institute Conference held in Kingston, Rhode Island, June 23-26, 1969.)

17258 **Henkin, Louis.** *Law of the Sea's Mineral Resources.* New York; Institute for the Study of Sciences in Human Affairs, 1968.

17259 **Hodgson, Robert D.** "National Maritime Limits: The Economic Zone and the Seabed." In *Law of the Sea: Caracas and Beyond*, Francis T. Christy, Jr., and others, eds. Cambridge, Massachusetts: Ballinger Publishing, 1975, p. 183-192. (Proceedings and Papers of the Ninth Annual Law of the Sea Institute Conference held in Kingston, Rhode Island, January 6-9, 1975.)

17260 **Hodgson, Robert D., and Smith, Robert W.** "Boundaries of the Economic Zone." In *Law of the Sea: Conference Outcomes and Problems of Implementation*, Edward Miles and John King Gamble, Jr., eds. Cambridge, Massachusetts: Ballinger Publishing, 1977, 183-206. (Proceedings and Papers of the Tenth Annual Law of the Sea Institute Conference held in Kingston, Rhode Island, June 22-25, 1976.)

17261 **Johnston, Douglas M.** *The International Law of Fisheries: A Framework for Policy Oriented Inquiries.* New Haven, Connecticut: Yale University Press, 1965.

17262 **Johnston, Douglas M., and Gold, Edgar.** *The Economic Zone in the Law of the Sea: Survey, Analysis and Appraisal of Current Trends.* Kingston, Rhode Island: Law of the Sea Institute, 1973.

17263 **Jones, William B.** "Risk Assessment: Corporate Ventures in Deep Seabed Mining Outside the Framework of the U.N. Convention on the Laws of the Sea." *Ocean Development and International Law,* 16, No. 4 (1986), 341-351.

17264 **Joyner, Christopher C.** "The Antarctic Legal Regime and the Law of the Sea." *Oceanus*, 31, No. 2 (Summer, 1988), 22-27.

17265 **Kimball, Lee.** "Turning Points in the Future of Deep Seabed Mining." *Ocean Development and International Law,* 17, No. 4 (1986), 367-398.

17266 **King, Lavriston R.** "Introduction: Science, Technology, and the Marine Resource." *Ocean Development and International Law,* 17, Nos. 1, 2, and 3 (1986), 1-8.

17267 **Krueger, Robert B., and Nordquist, Myron H.** "The Evolution of the 200-Mile Exclusive Economic Zone: State Practice in the Pacific Basin." *Virginia Journal of International Law,* 19, NO. 2 (Winter, 1979), 321-399.

17268 **Lagoni, Rainer.** "Oil and Gas Deposits Across National Frontiers." *American Journal of International Law,* 73, No. 2 (April, 1979), 215-243.

17269 **Larson, David L.** "Deep Seabed Mining: A Definition of the Problem." *Ocean Development and International Law,* 17, No. 4 (1986), 271-308.

17270 **Leonard, L. Larry.** *International Regulation of Fisheries.* Washington, D.C.: Carnegie Endowment for International Peace, 1944.

17271 **Levy, Jean-Pierre, and Odunton, Nii Allotey.** "Economic Impact of Sea-bed Mineral Resources Development in Light of the Convention on the Law of the Sea." *Natural Resources Forum,* 8, No. 2 (April, 1984), 147-161.

17272 **Logan, Roderick M.** "Geography and Salmon." *Journal of the West*, 8 (1969), 438-446.

17273 **Luard, Evan.** *The Control of the Sea-bed; Who Owns the Resources of the Oceans?* Revised edition, London: Heinemann, 1977.

17274 **Marz, Josef.** *Die Ozeane in der Politik und Staatenbildung.* Breslan: Ferdinand Hirt, 1931.

17275 **McKelvey, V.E.** "Seabed Minerals and the Law of the Sea." *Science*, 209, No. 4455 (July 25, 1980), 464-472.

17276 **Meese, Sally A.** "The Legal Regime Governing Seafloor Polymetallic Sufide Deposits." *Ocean Development and International Law,* 17, Nos. 1, 2, and 3 (1986), 131-162.

17277 **Merrals, J.D.** "Problems in Commonwealth-State Relations Concerning Offshore Resources." In *Australia's Continental Shelf*, J.R.V. Prescott, ed. Melbourne: T. Nelson Australia Pty, 1979, 50-65.

17278 **Morgan, R.** *World Sea Fisheries.* London: Methuen, 1956.

17279 **Nawaz, M.K.** "On the Limits of the Coastal State Jurisdiction: Continental Shelf, Fisheries and Economic Zone." *Indian Journal of International Law,* 14, No. 2 (April-June, 1974), 261-279.

17280 **Oda, Shigeru**. *International Law of the Resources of the Sea*. Alphen aan den Rijn: Sijthoff and Noorhoff, 1979.

17281 **Oda, Shigeru**. "The Territorial Sea and Natural Resources." *International and Comparative Law Quarterly*, 4, No. 3 (July, 1955), 415-425.

17282 **Oxman, Bernard H.** "Conflicting Approaches to the Control and Exploitation of the Oceans." *American Journal of International Law*, 65, No. 4 (September, 1971), 121-123.

17283 "Preventing a Scramble for the Sea." *Australian Foreign Affairs Record*, 44, No. 10 (October, 1973), 642-658.

17284 **Riessenfeld, Stephan A.** *Protection of Coastal Fisheries Under International Law*. Washington, D.C.: Carnegie Endowment for International Peace, 1942.

17285 **Slade, David C.** "Back to the Drawing Board: Fourth Amendment Rights and the Marine Mammal Protection Act." *Ocean Development and International Law*, 16, 1 (1986), 91-101.

17286 **Smith, Robert W.** "Boundaries of the Economic Zone," with Robert D. Hodgson. In *Law of the Sea: Conference Outcomes and Problems of Implementation*, Edward Miles and John K. Gamble, Jr., eds. Cambridge, Massachusetts: Ballinger, 1977, 183-207.

17287 **Stone, Oliver L.** "Some Aspects of Jurisdiction Over Natural Resources Under the Ocean Floor." *Natural Resources Lawyer*, 3, No. 2 (June, 1970), 155-194.

17288 **Sztucki, Jerzy**, ed. *Symposium on the International Regime of the Sea-bed*. Rome: Accademia Nazionale dei Lincie, 1970.

17289 **Tomasevich, Jozo**. *International Agreements on Conservation of Marine Resources*. Stanford, California: Food Research Institute of Stanford University, 1943.

17290 **Treby, Elliott.** "The Role of the Political Idiom in Jurisdictional Conflicts Over Offshore Oil and Gas." *Journal of Maritime Law and Commerce*, 5, No. 2 (January, 1974), 281-297.

17291 **Ulfstein, Geir.** "The Conflict Between Petroleum Production, Navigation, and Fisheries in International Law." *Ocean Development and International Law*, 19, No. 3 (1988), 229-262.

17292 **Walsh, Don**, ed. *The Law of the Sea: Issues on Ocean Resource Management*. New York: Praeger, 1977.

17293 **Young, Richard.** "Sedentary Fisheries and the Convention on the Continental Shelf." *American*

Journal of International Law, 55, No. 2 (April, 1961), 359-373.

17294 **Zacher, Mark W.**, and **McConnell, James G.** "Down to the Sea with Stakes: The Evolving Law of the Sea and the Future of the Deep Seabed Regime." *Ocean Development and International Law* [New York], 21, No. 1 (1990), 71-103.

POLITICAL GEOGRAPHY OF REGIONS

Books and Journals

17295 **Ahern, William R., Jr.** *Oil and the Outer Continental Shelf: The Georges Bank Case.* Cambridge, Massachusetts: Ballinger, 1973.

17296 **Alexander, Lewis M.** "Offshore Claims and Fisheries in the North Pacific." *Pacific Viewpoint*, 2, No. 1 (March, 1961), 59-86.

17297 **Allen, Edward W.** "Fishery Geography of the North Pacific Ocean." *Geographical Review*, 43, No. 4 (October, 1953), 558-563.

17298 **Beeby, C.D.** "Antarctic Treaty System and a Minerals Regime." *New Zealand Foreign Affairs Review*, (January-March, 1985), 18-26.

17299 **Bernhardt, J. Peter A.** "Spitzbergen: Jurisdictional Friction Over Unexplored Oil Reserves." *California Western International Law Journal*, 4 (1973), 61-120.

17300 **Black, W.A.** "The Labrador Codfishery." *Annals of the Association of American Geography*, 50, No. 3 (September, 1960), 267-295.

17301 **Blake, Gerald H.** "Offshore Politics and Resources in the Middle East." In *Change and Development in the Middle East*, J.I. Clarke and H. Bowden-Jones, eds. London: Methuen, 1981, 113-129.

17302 **Broadus, James M.**, and **Bowen, Robert E.** "Developing a U.S. Research Strategy for Marine Polymetallic Sulfides." *Ocean Development and International Law*, 17, Nos. 1, 2, and 3 (1986), 91-130.

17303 **Brown, E.D.** "It's Scotland's Oil? Hypothetical Boundaries in the North Sea-A Case Study." *Marine Policy*, 2, No. 1 (January, 1978), 3-21.

17304 **Chen, P.** "Heavy Mineral Deposits of Western Taiwan." *Bulletin of the Geological Society of Taiwan*, 4 (1963), 13-21.

17305 **Christie, Donna R.** "Coastal Energy Impact Program Boundaries on the Atlantic Coast: A Case Study of the Law Applicable to Lateral Seaward Boundaries." *Virginia Journal of International Law*, 19, No. 4 (Summer, 1979) 841-882.

17306 **Churchill, Robin, and Ulfstein, Geir.** *Marine Management in Disputed Areas: The Case of the Barents Sea.* London: Routledge, 1992.

17307 **Cicin-Sain, Biliana, and Knecht, Robert W.** "The Problem of Governance of U.S. Ocean Resources and the New Exclusive Economic Zone." *Ocean Development and International Law*, 15, Nos. 3 and 4 (1985), 289-320.

17308 **Cook, B.A., and McGraw, Richard L.** "Interdependence in the Bay of Fundy Herring Fishery." *Ocean Development and International Law*, 19, No. 5 (1988), 367-380.

17309 **Day, D.** "The Political Geography of Offshore Hydrocarbon Exploration in Eastern Canada." *Studies in Marine & Costal Geography-Saint Mary's University*, 6 (1986), 1-11.

17310 **Dietz, R.S.; Emery, K.O.; and Shepard, F.P.** "Phosphorite Deposits on the Sea Floor Off Southern California." *Bulletin of the Geological Society of America*, 53, No. 6 (June, 1942), 815-48.

17311 **Douglas, Colin.** "Conflicting Claims to Oil and Natural Gas Resources Off the Eastern Coast of Canada." *Alberta Law Review*, 18, Supplement Edition (1980), 54-69.

17312 **Emanuelli, Claude C.** "Modes de Reglement des Differends entre la Canada et les Etats-Unis en Matiere de Frontieres et de Ressources Maritimes." *Revue de Droit Universite de Sherbrooke*, 7 (1977), 319-356.

17313 **Espenshade, Ada.** "A Program for Japanese Fisheries." *Geographical Review*, 39, No. 1 (January, 1949), 76-85.

17314 **Evensen, Jens.** "The Anglo-Norwegian Fisheries Case and Its Legal Consequences." *American Journal of International Law*, 46, No. 4 (October, 1952), 609-630.

17315 **Fischer, David W.** "Hard Mineral Resource Development Policy in the U.S. Exclusive Economic Zone: A Review of the Role of the Costal States." *Ocean Development and International Law*, 19, No. 2 (1986), 100-112.

17316 **Fischer, David W.** "Structuring a U.S. Offshore Hard Mineral Development Policy: Reflections on a Seabed Tenure System." *Ocean Development and International Law*, 19, No. 1 (1988), 59-72.

17317 **Fischer, David W.** "Two Alternatives in National Governance of Marine Hard Minerals in the U.S. Exclusive Economic Zone." *Ocean Development and International Law*, 19, No. 4 (1988), 287-298.

17318 **Fleischer, Carl August.** "Le Regime d'Exploitation du Spitsberg (Svalbard)." *Annuaire Francais de Droit International*, 24 (1978), 275-300.

17319 **Foley, Edward C.** "Nova Scotia's Case for Coastal and Offshore Resources." *Ottawa Law Review*, 13, No. 2 (Spring, 1981), 281-308.

17320 **Goldie, L.F.E.** "The Contents of Davy Jones's Locker-A Proposed Regime for the Seabed and Subsoil." *Rutgers Law Review*, 22, No. 1 (Winter, 1967), 1-66.

17321 **Hall, H. Robert.** "The 'Open Door' into Antarctica: An Explanation of the Hughes Doctrine. *Polar Record*, 25, No. 153 (April, 1989), 137-140.

17322 **Harders, C.W.** "The Sea-Bed." *Federal Law Review*, 3, No. 2 (December, 1969), 202-220.

17323 **Hardy, Michael.** "The Law of the Sea and the Prospects for Deep Seabed Mining: The Position of the European Community." *Ocean Development and International Law*, 17, No. 4 (1986), 309-323.

17324 **Harrison, Selig S.** *China, Oil, and Asia: Conflict Ahead?* New York: Columbia University Press, 1977.

17325 **Hayashi, Moritaka.** "Japan and Deep Seabed Mining." *Ocean Development and International Law*, 17, No. 4 (1986), 351-365.

17326 **Helin, Ronald A.** "Soviet Fishing in the Barents and the North Atlantic." *Geographical Review*, 54, No. 3 (July, 1964), 386-409.

17327 **Horigan, James E.** "Unitization of Petroleum Reservoirs Extending Across Sub-Sea Boundary Lines of Bordering States in the North Sea." *Natural Resources Lawyer*, 7, No. 1 (January, 1974), 67-76.

17328 **Ippolito, Joseph T.** "Newfoundland and the Continental Shelf: From Cod to Oil and Gas." *Columbia Journal of Transnational Law*, 15, No. 1 (Spring, 1976), 138-162.

17329 **International Court of Justice.** "Fisheries Case-Judgement of 18 December 1951." *Reports of Judgements, Advisory Opinions and Orders*, (1951), 129, 133, and 140-2.

17330 **Johnson, D.H.N.** "The Anglo-Norwegian Fisheries Case." *International and Comparative Law Quarterly*, 1, Part 2 (April, 1952), 145-180.

17331 **Johnston, Douglas M.** "The Economic Zone in North America: Scenarios and Options." *Ocean Development and International Law*, 3, No. 1 (1975), 53-68.

17332 **Jonsson, Hannes.** *Friends in Conflict: The Anglo-Icelandic Cold Wars and the law of the Sea.* London: C. Hurst & Company/Hamden, Connecticut: Archon Books, 1982.

17333 **Joyner, Christopher C.** "The Evolving Antartic Minerals Regime." *Ocean Development and International Law*, 19, No. 1 (1988), 73-96.

17334 **Kexser, C. Frank.** *Tidelandsd: Selected References on the Question of Ownership and Development of Resources Thereof.* Washington, D.C.: Library of Congress Legal Reference Service, 1957.

17335 **Leistikow, Gunner.** "The Fisheries Dispute in the North Atlantic." *American Scandinavian Review*, 47, No. 1 (March, 1959), 15-24.

17336 **Li, Victor H.** "China and Off-Shore Oil: The Tiao-yu Tai Dispute." *Stanford Journal of International Studies*, 10 (Spring, 1975), 143-162.

17337 **Marcoux, J. Michael.** "Natural Resources Jurisdiction on the Antarctic Continental Margin." *Virginia Journal of International Law*, 11, No. 3 (May, 1971), 374-405.

17338 **Marts, Marion, and Sewell, W.R.D.** "Conflict Between Fish and Power Resources in the Pacific Northwest." *Annals of the Association of American Geographers*, 50, 1 (March, 1960), 42-50.

17339 **Martin, Cabot.** "Newfoundland's Case on Offshore Minerals: A Brief Outline." *Ottawa Law Review*, 7, No. 1 (Winter, 1975), 34-61.

17340 **McCloskey, William, Jr.** "The 200-Mile Fishing Limit: United States Grids for Jurisdiction." *Oceans*, 9, No. 5 (September-October, 1976), 60-63.

17341 **McDorman, Ted L.** "Thailand's Fisheries: A Victim of 200 Mile Zones." *Ocean Development and International Law*, 16, No. 2 (1986), 183-209.

17342 **Merrills, J.G.** "Oil Exploration in the Aegean." *Law Quarterly Review*, 93, No. 1 (January, 1977), 29-33.

17343 **Mills, Hal.** "Eastern Canada's Offshore Resources and Boundaries." *Journal of Canadian Studies*, 6 (1971), 36-50.

17344 **Minghi, Julian V.** *The Conflict of Salmon Fishing Policies in the North Pacific.* Seattle: University of Washington, M.A., 1959.

17345 **Minghi, Julian V.** "The Conflict of Salmon Fishing Policies in the North Pacific." *Pacific Viewpoint*, 11, No. 1 (March, 1961), 59-84.

17346 **Morris, Joseph W.** "The North Sea Continental Shelf: Oil and Gas Legal Problems." *International Lawyer*, 2 (1968), 191-214.

17347 **Moss, Phillip, and Terkla, David.** "Income and Employment Change in lthe New England Fishing Industry." *Ocean Development and International Law,* 15, No. 1 (1985), 37-59.

17348 **Murray, Stephen J.** "A Discussion of the World Court's North Sea Judgment." *American University Law Review*, 19, Nos. 3 and 4 (June-August, 1970), 470-49.

17349 **Nanda, J.N.** *Development of the Resources of the Sea: India.* New Delhi: Concept Publishers, 1988.

17350 **O'Connell, D.P.** "Sedentary Fisheries and the Australian Continental Shelf." *American Journal of International Law*, 49, No. 2 (April, 1955), 185-209.

17351 **Ostreng, W.** "Delimitation Arrangements in Arctic Seas: Cases of Precedence or Securing of Strategic/Economic Interests?" *Marine Policy*, 10, No. 2 (April, 1986), 132-154.

17352 **Park, Choon-Ho.** "Offshore Oil Development in the China Seas: Some Legal and Territorial Issues." *Ocean Yearbook*, 2 (1980), 302-316.

17353 **Park, Choon-Ho.** "Oil Under Troubled Waters: The Northeast Asia Seabed Controversy." *Harvard International Law Journal*, 14, No. 2 (Spring, 1973), 212-260.

17354 **Park, Choon-Ho.** "The Sino-Japanese-Korean Sea Resources Controversy and the Hypothesis of a 200-Mile Economic Zone." *Harvard International Law Journal*, 16, 1 (Winter, 1975), 27-46.

17355 **Park, Choon-Ho.** "The South China Sea Disputes: Who Owns the Islands and the Natural Resources?" *Ocean Development and International Law*, 5, No. 1 (1978), 27-59.

17356 **Peterson, M.J.** *Managing the Frozen South: The Creation and Evolution of the Antarctic Treaty System.* Berkeley: University of California Press, 1988.

17357 **Phillips, Alan G.** *Jurisdictional Conflicts in Resource Management: Perspectives on the Canadian West Coast Commercial Fishing Industry*. Victoria, British Columbia, Canada: University of Victoria, M.A., 1984.

17358 **Ranke, W.** "Die Agglomerationsraume der atlantischen Fernfishereien." *Petermann's Geographische Mitteilungen*, 113 Jahr, No. 4 (July, 1969), 269-73.

17359 **Rhee, Sang-Myon.** "The Application of Equitable Principles to Resolve the United States-Canada Dispute Over East Coast Fishery Resources." *Harvard International Law Journal*, 21, No. 3 (Fall, 1980), 667-683.

17360 **Ritterbush, Stephen W.** "Marine Resources and the Potential for Conflict in the South China Sea." *Fletcher Forum*, 2 (1978), 64-85.

17361 **Schrank, William E.; Skoda, Blanch; Roy, Noal; and Tsoa, Eugene.** "Canadian Government Financial Intervention in a Marine Fishery: The Case of Newfoundland 1972/73-1980/81." *Ocean Development and International Law*, 18, No. 5 (1987), 533-584.

17362 **Sharma, R.C.** "Codwar Between Iceland and U.K. and Its Impact on International Politics." *International Geography*. XXII International Geographical Congress, Geography of the Ocean, Section 3, Moscow, 1976, 59-63.

17363 **Shyam, Manjula R.** "Deap Seabed Mining: An Indian Perspective." *Ocean Development and International Law*, 17, No. 4 (1986), 325-349.

17364 **Shyam, Manjula R., and Sundler, S.** "International Seabed Regime: India's Interests and Policy Options." *Indian Political Science Review*, 10, No. 1 (January, 1976), 1-18.

17365 **Siddayao, Corazon Morales.** *The Off-Shore Petroleum Resources of South-East Asia: Potential Conflict Situations and Related Economic Considerations*. New York: Oxford University Press, 1978.

17366 **Siddiquie, H.N., and Rao, P.S.** "Exploration and Polymetallic Nodules in the Indian Ocean." *Ocean Development and International Law*, 19, No. 4 (1988), 323-336.

17367 **Sollie, Finn.** "Norway's Continental Shelf and Boundary Question on the Seabed." In *The Challenge of New Territories*, F. Sollie, ed. Oslo: Universitets Forlaget, 1974, 101-113.

17368 **Song, Yann-Huei.** "The British 150-Mile Fishery Conservation and Management Zone Around the Flakland (Malrinas) Islands." *Political Geography Quarterly*, 7, No. 2 (April, 1988), 183-196.

17369 **Sukhwal, B.L.** "The Global Geopolitics of Seabed Mining of Polymetallic Nodules and the Third World." *Scandinavian Journal of Development Alternatives*, 2, No. 2 (June, 1983), 9-24.

17370 **Sukhwal, B.L.** "India's Role in Recovering the Polymetallic Nodules From the Ocean Floor and the Law of the Sea Treaty." *Indian Geographical Journal*, 52, No. 2 (December, 1982), 47-57.

17371 **Suter, Keith.** *Antarctica: Private Property or Public Heritage?* London: Zed Books, 1991.

17372 **Sutherland, William M.** "Management conservation and Cooperation in EEZ Fishing: The Law of the Sea Convention and the South Pacific Forum Fisheries Agency." *Ocean Development and International Law*, 18, No. 6 (1987), 613-640.

17373 **Symmons, Clive Ralph.** "British Off-Shore Continental Shelf and Fishery Limit Boundaries: An Analysis of Overlapping Zones." *International and Comparative Law Quarterly*, 28, No. 4 (October, 1979), 703-733.

17374 **Symmons, Clive Ralph.** "The Canadian 200-Mile Fishery Limit and the Delimitation of Maritime Zones Around St. Pierre and Miquelon." *Ottawa Law Review*, 12, No. 1 (Winter, 1980), 145-165.

17375 **Terr, Leonard B.** "The 'Distance Plus Joint Development Zone' Formula: A Proposal for the Speedy and Practical Resolution of the East China and Yellow Seas Continental Shelf Oil Controversy." *Cornell International Law Journal*, 7, No. 1 (December, 1973), 49-71.

17376 **Thompson, W.F.** "Fishing Treaties and Salmon in the North Pacific." *Science*, 50, No. 3705 (1965), 1786-1789.

17377 **Valencia, Mark J.** "South China Sea: Present and Potential Coastal Area Resource Use Conflicts." *Ocean Management*, 5, No. 1 (April, 1979), 1-38.

17378 **Vinnenow, J.** "The Soviet Fishing Fleet." *Geographical Review*, 53, No. 2 (April, 1963), 310-312.

17379 **Vosper, William J.** *A Fishing Zone Delimitation of the Alaskan Coast: Introducing Fishery Baselines*. Coral Gables, Florida: University of Miami Sea Grant Program, 1971.

17380 **Waldock, C.H.M.** "The Anglo-Norwegian Fisheries Case." *British Year Book of International Law*, 28 (1951), 114-171.

17381 **Wang, Erik B.** "Canada-United States Fisheries
       and Maritime Boundary Negotiations: Diplomacy
       in Deep Water." *Behind the Headlines*, 38, No. 6
       and 39, No. 1 (April, 1981), 1-47.

17382 **Wilkes, Daniel.** "Legal Implications of the
       Stratton Commission Report." *Journal of
       Maritime Law and Commerce*, 1, No. 2 (January,
       1970), 291-311.

AUTHOR INDEX

Beonio Brocchierii, V. 11668
Berard, Victor 13494
Berber, F.J. 11788
Berberoglu, Berch 3396
Berelson, Bernard R. 9231, 9522
Beres, Anemone 2092
Beres, Louis Rene 15901
Berezkin, A.V. 10754
Berezowski, Stanislaw 4053
Berg, Dale A. 10233
Berg, John A. 9523
Berg, P. 14927, 15163
Berg-Schlosser, Dirk 342
Berger, B.M. 5142
Berger, Kurt Martin 6597, 8185,
    14679
Berger, R. 4906
Bergin, A. 16482
Bergman, Edward Fisher 6, 67,
    4907
Bergner, Jeffrey T. 12068
Bergonzi, Angelo 12913
Beriault, Yvon 7442
Berker, Jonathan 2730
Berkes, Ross N. 11571
Berkowitz, Leonard 7371
Berman, B. 3349, 4388, 12914
Berman, David R. 10023
Bermeo, Nancy 4869
Bernades, Lysias M.C. 15164
Bernard, Augustin 7831
Bernard, Georges 8615
Bernard, Marie–Claire 10755, 10756
Bernardes, Lysia M.C. 3547
Bernardes, Nilo 13134
Berner, William Sherman 9524
Bernhardt, J. Peter A. 17299
Bernheim, Roger 7622
Bernier, Lynne Louise 5545
Bernstein, Harry 11841
Bernstein, Marverll 4783
Bernstein, Robert A. 11128
Berra, Angel Carlos 1404
Berreby, J.J. 11909
Berrington, H. 13740
Berry, Brian J.L. 1941, 4984,
    5143, 5240, 9323
Berry, C.J. 1942
Berry, David 4985
Berry, K.B. 16595
Berry, W. 5310
Bersch, G.K. 3665, 13653
Bertlin and Partners 8445-8447
Bertram, Christoph 3183
Bertrand, A. 6969
Bertrand, Jean-Rene 10828
Besancon, Alain 4054
Bessone, Juan B. 1405
Best, Alan C.G. 2093, 3486, 3487,
    4389, 4390, 6205, 8448, 8616,
    12915
Best, Harry 2503
Best, Judy 6750
Beth, Loren P. 9265

Bethe, H.A. 15239
Bettati, Mario 7557, 16874, 16875
Betts, Dianne C. 7443
Betts, R.F. 13495
Betts, R.R. 12584
Betts, Richard K. 1576, 15165,
    16223
Betz, Hans-George 4055
Beugel, Ernest van der 15902
Beukema, Herman 11129, 14403,
    15166
Bezboruah, Monoranjan 17005
Bezdek, Roger H. 15167
Bhadraj, Vijai Sen 2334
Bhagat, G. 1523, 15903
Bhagat, K.P. 10359
Bhagwati, J.N. 3289
Bhalla, G.S. 6402
Bhardwaj, Surinder Mohan 6403
Bhargava, G.S. 2266
Bhargava, Pradeep 3397
Bhat, Budhi Prasad 6837
Bhat, L.S. 5858, 5859
Bhatnagar, A.K. 13435
Bhatt, G.D. 5359, 11415
Bhatta, Pandit K.A. 3084
Bhattacharjee, Tarun Kumar 7372,
    7788
Bhattacharya, B.K. 2335, 2336
Bhattacharya, S.S. 6838, 7104
Bhattacharyya, N.N. 1577, 7631,
    15904
Bialer, Seweryn 4056, 5546,
    12069, 12071, 15168
Bian, Teshale Engliz 9525
Bianchi, Rinaldo L. 11805
Bianchi, William J. 7444
Biberaj, Elez 4391, 12514
Bibes, G. 10757
Bicik, Ivan 7729
Bicker, William Elmer 9526
BID 8979
Biddiss, Michael 4057
Bideleux, Robert 14153
Bidinger, Jerome R. 9527
Bidwell, Percy W. 5645
Biechler, Michael Joseph 3366
Biegeleisen, Joseph Alan 9528
Biel, H.S. 10758
Bienen, Henry 15478
Bierly, Robert Foust 9529
Bierman, Don E. 12003
Biersteker, Thomas J. 548
Biesinger, Joseph Anton 10640
Biger, Gideon 6906, 11910, 13199
Biggs, Gonzalo 16739
Bigham, D. Alastair 13800
Bildt, Carl 1756
Bilinsky, Yaroslav 14277
Billeb, Eberhard 980, 981
Billelt, H. 10759
Billet, Bret L. 10464
Billington, Monroe 7445
Billington, R.A. 7864

Billman, Christine W. 6970
Bilmanis, Alfred 2576, 12004,
    13496, 13497, 16128, 16224,
    17167
Bilocerkowycz, Jaroslaw 4058
Bilsel, Cemil 11911
Bilzin, M.D. 10024
Binder 13654
Bindoff, S.T. 16876
Bindra, A.P.S. 17039
Bing, John Howard 6146
Binkley, Clark S. 5241
Binyan, Liu 3013
Birch, A.H. 3184
Birch, Brian P. 7989, 15641, 16225
Birchfield, Cynthia 13879
Bird, Annie Laurie 3548
Bird, G. 13741
Bird, James 3633, 12005
Bird, Richard M. 13742
Birdwood, Christopher Bromhead,
    2nd Baron 7558, 12515, 14680
Birge, John R. 6776
Birken, Arthur M. 11842
Birkhead, Guthrie S. 11871
Birnbaum, Pierre 4059
Birni, Patricia 16552
Birnie, P.W. 16596, 17227
Birnie, Patricia 16877
Birtles, Terry G. 3634
Bischof, Gunter 11669
Bischoff, Paul-Henri 12917
Bish and Partners Ltd. 8220
Bishop, W.W. Jr. 7373
Biskupski, M. B. 3185
Bissell, Harold Preston 13801
Bissell, Richard E. 13964
Bisson, T.A. 11244
Bittman, Ladiolav 12516
Bittner, Donald F. 15642
Biyela, Mlandu 6206
Bizberg, Ilan 10019
Bjorklund, Ulf 3915
Bjorkman, Thomas N. 16226
Bjornlund, Eric 9454
Black, Cyril E. 11912
Black, Jan Knippers 4710
Black, Jeremy 693
Black, Jerome Harold 9530
Black, Lloyd D. 11245, 16322
Black, W.A. 17300
Blackburn, Paul 11539
Blackburn, William Herman 9531
Blackford, M.G. 10025
Blackman, Tim 2577
Blacksell, Mark 168, 460, 1943,
    2578, 4986, 16388
Blackwell, James 15776
Bladen, Wildred A. 2337
Blaikie, Peter Rutherford 10986
Blainey, G. 4845
Blair, Harry Wallace 4275
Blair, Leon B. 1757
Blair, Patricia Wohlgemuth 1847,

Carroll, Glenn R. 3551
Carroll, John J. 5207
Carroll, Marie J. 11032
Carroll, Susan Jane 9573
Carroll, Terrance G. 6077
Carroll, William K. 4715
Carroue, Laurent. 1760, 5557
Carstairs, A.M. 10658
Carsten, F.L. 3191
Cartaxo, Octacilio 1335
Carter, Barry E. 11254
Carter, F.W. 2510, 2585
Carter, G.F. 6527
Carter, Gwendolen M. 584, 2586,
    6149, 12817, 12818, 12819,
    12928
Carter, Jared G. 16611
Carter, L. 14397
Cartledge, Bryan 4403
Cartwright, D.G. 6275, 6348, 6349
Carvalho, Carlos Miguel Delgado de
    23, 24, 1421
Carvalho, Juvenal de 2843
Casetti, Emilio 3292
Cashdan, Elizabeth 2098
Casper, Dale E. 9574
Casper, Gretchen 15912
Cassirer, Ernst 1852
Castagno, A.A. 14689
Castaingts, Jean-Pierre 1973
Castaneda, Jorge 4404, 12076
Castel, Albert 15650
Castelli, Joseph Roy 6276
Castells, M. 4915-4918, 4995,
    5149
Castiella, Fernando M. 12009
Castigiano, L. 6528
Castilhos Goicocheia, Luiz Filipe de
    6786
Castillo, P. 9022
Castle, E.N. 14407
Castonguay, C. 14117
Castro, Christovam Leite de 3552
Castro, Eugenio de 5972
Castro, Josue de 761, 762
Castro Martinez, P.F. 1336
Cataudella, M. 16612
Catley, H.E.B. 11578
Catley, R. 4787
CATRAM 8455
Catroux, Georges 12337, 12589
Catsiapis, Jean 10774
Cattan, Henry 14587
Cattaneo, Atilio E. 763
Catterberg, Edgardo. 4405
Catudal, Honore M. 2587, 8187
Cauvin, C. 10776
Cavalcanti, Temistoctes 5252
Cavalla, A. 764
Cavanagh, T.E. 10055
Cavazza, Fabio Luca 11675
Caviedes, Cesar N. 4406, 9575,
    9576
Cawson, A. 13968, 14284

Cebreros, Francisco 6978
Cecovini, Manlio 12010
Celerier, J. 6601
Celerier, Paul 765
Centeno, Miguel Angel 10056
Center for Strategic and
    International Studies 11917
Centre d'etude du Sud-Est asiatique
    et de l'Extreme Orient 17045
Centre for Economic Development
    and Administration (CEDA)
    9084
CEPAL 8928, 8929, 8979-8983
Cerami, Charles A. 6602
Cermakian, Jean 2964, 5253, 5254
Cerny, P.G. 11255, 14167
Cervenka, Zdenek 8456, 8629-8632
Cervin, Vladimir 2350
Chabal, Patrick 12233
Chabat, Jorge 10057
Chabod, F. 1853
Chabot, Georges 16136
Chabry, Annie 14690
Chabry, Laurent 14690
Chadjipadelis, Theodore 10777
Chadwick, H.M. 1736, 1737
Chadwick, Thomas Timothy 9241
Chafetz, Glenn R. 4407
Chaffee, Eugene B. 3553
Chagla, M.C. 14588
Chai, Trong R. 10469
Chakravarti, Prithwis Chandra
    6843, 11424, 11425
Chalapathi Rau, M. 4279
Chaliand, Gerard 766, 13662,
    15485
Chalothorn, Supannee 10362
Chamberlain, James Franklin 5973,
    14947
Chamberlain, Joseph P. 12169
Chamberlain, M.E. 13506
Chamberlin, William Henry 2511
Chamorro, Diego Manuel 6787,
    12310
Champaud, Jacques 8633
Champier, Laurent 998
Champion, A.G. 5494
Champion, A.M. 6212
Chan, Steve 3611
Chanaiwa, David Shingirai 2099
Chander, N. Jose 5360
Chandidas, R. 10363
Chandler, Andrea 4102
Chandra, Bipan 3919, 12749
Chandrasekhar, S. 1581
Chaney, Jonathan I. 16613, 16614
Chang, Chi-Jen 14066
Chang, King-yuh 4408
Chang, Li 14691
Chang, Maria Hsia 3920
Chang, Pao-Min 7563, 7627, 15913
Chang, Sen-dou 3612, 3613
Chang, Stephen Sin-Tak 5748
Channa, V. C. 6520

Chanock, Martin 12234
Chao, John K.T. 16886
Chao, Kuo-Chun 3398
Chao, Linda 14285
Chapin, F. Stuart 10058
Chapin, Helen B. 3614
Chapin, William 15782
Chapman, Abraham 2200
Chapman, Brian 3646, 7457
Chapman, Murray Thomas 6547
Chapman, Shirley 4919
Chappell, H.W. 9327
Charbonneau, Randall J. 5749
Chardon, Carlos E. 13142
Chari, P.R. 17046, 17047
Charles C. Colby 960
Charles, J.L. 8634
Charles, Jr. 16188
Charlesworth, James C. 11256
Charlet, M. 8635
Charley, R.J. 8
Charlton, Michael 12820, 16137
Charlton, Roger 15486
Charney, Jonathan I. 16742
Charpentier, Jean 8188
Charpin, F. 5974
Chase-Dunn, Christopher 1958,
    12750
Chase, J. 15545
Chataigneau, Y. 2588
Chatan, Naomi 6189
Chateaus, J. 764
Chatelain, Abel 3675, 9328, 10778,
    10779
Chatterjee, S.P. 519, 1582
Chatterji, Amiya 4788
Chatterji, Suniti K. 6407
Chaturvedi, B.N. 5861, 11918
Chaturvedi, S.C. 16887
Chau, Phan Thien 3088
Chaudhri, Mohammed Ahsen 7628,
    11579
Chaudhuri, Manoranjan 183, 999,
    5874
Chaudhuri, Mohammed Ahsen
    11426, 12378
Chauhan, Balbir R. 8296
Chaunu, Pierre 1422
Chavannes, Ed 11580
Chavenatto, J.J. 767
Chaves, Omar Emir 1423
Chay, John 3676
Checkel, Jeff 11676
Chee, Chan Hing 4326
Cheeseman, Graeme 16094
Chelhardt, Alexander O. 17048
Chen, Cheng-Siang 3015, 3016
Chen, P. 17304
Chen, Shih-Tsai 3089
Chen Yi 7629
Chen, Yi-Fong 1524
Cheng, Bin 7376, 14883
Cheng, Joseph Y.S. 10470, 13284
Cheng, Peter P. 10471

Author Index

Goldman, Minton F. 15962
Goldman, Robert Michael 9257, 9667
Goldmann, Nahum 3106
Goldschmidt, Arthur, Jr. 2283
Goldschmidt, V. 6559
Goldsen, Joseph M. 14863
Goldsmith, F.B. 5709
Goldsmith, M. 5661
Goldstein, J. 14989
Goldstein, Joel Harris 9668
Goldstein, Julius 5991
Goldstein, Michael 3107
Goldstein, Walter 16149
Goldsworthy, Peter 16855
Goldwater, Barry 14510
Goldwin, Robert A. 1870
Golitsyn, Vladimir Vladimirovich 8238, 8330
Golovin, N. 684
Gomer, Hilaire 8682
Gomes, Pimentel 12344
Gomez, Leopoldo 10017
Goncalves, Maria Eduarda 16644
Goncalves Mariano, Alfredo 8336
Gong, Gerrit W. 3108
Gonick, Lev S. 13755
Gonzalez, A. 13711
Gonzalez, Edward 15684
Gonzalez, F. Garchiahuidobro 14715
Gonzalez, Jr., Rene E. 16998
Gonzalez, Luis J. 8952
Gonzalez Salinas, Edmundo 2976
Good, David F. 4193
Good, Kenneth 2908, 5726, 12961
Goodchild, M.F. 5282
Goodenough, Simon 14990
Goodey, Brian R. 472, 9258
Goodin, R.E. 10119
Gooding, John 4452
Goodman, Allen E. 14667
Goodman, G.T. 13209
Goodman, Melvin A. 13681
Goodno, James B. 4809
Goodrich, Leland M. 11032, 12094, 12095
Goodrich, M.F. 5041
Goodsell, Charles T. 5015
Goodway, D. 5499
Goodwin, C. 15246
Goodwin-Gill, G.S. 6101
Goodwin, H.L. 14864
Goodwin, M. 1977, 2215, 4926, 4929, 4930, 5010, 5270
Goormaghtigh, John 12612, 12613
Gopal, Madan 1534
Gopalachari, K. 7643, 7644
Gopalkrishnan, Ramamorthy 415
Gopian, James David 9669
Gorban, N.V. 705
Gorbatsevich, R.A. 218
Gorbold, R. 12962
Gordejuela, Amando 1054

Gorden, Morton 12552
Gordon, Bernard K. 11593, 14602, 15963
Gordon, D.L. 2284, 5992, 6158, 13899
Gordon, David F. 12839
Gordon, Dennis R. 9035
Gordon, Donald Craigie 13447, 13448
Gordon, Edward 14716
Gordon, Haim 14603
Gordon, Joel 10491
Gordon, Lincoln 3305
Gordon, Rivca 14603
Gore-Browne, Sir Stewart 6754
Gore, Rick 13595
Gorer, Geoffrey 3856
Gorgol, J.F. 14991
Goria, Wade R. 3032
Gorlich, Ernst Josef 2619
Gorman, Robert F. 15494
Gorman, Stephen M. 1452, 1453
Gormley, W. Paul 16645
Gorner, Alexander 2620
Gorny, Yosef 14183
Gorove, Stephen 12017
Gorshkov, S.G. 14992, 16976, 16977
Gorski, Karol 12018
Gorski, Philip S. 11724, 14210
Gosar, Anton 6624
Gosnell, Harold F. 10120, 10121
Gotlieb, Philip 15532
Gotlieb, Yosef 12767
Gottlieb, Gidon 3694
Gottmann, Jean 56, 219-222, 1055, 1056, 1871, 3494, 4939, 10676
Gottstein, Klaus 12533
Goudinoff, Peter Alexis 9670
Goudoever, Albert P. van 3211
Gough, Barry M. 7483, 15565
Goulbourne, Harry 6616
Gould, Harold A. 10372
Gould, Laurence M. 1689, 16101
Gould, Peter 12963
Goulven, J. 12964
Goumley, Dennis 16258
Goure, Daniel 15247, 15248
Gourevitch, P.A. 3695
Gourou, Pierre 4810, 6102, 8683
Gouvea Neto, Raul de. 15685
Government of India 5864, 7947
Government of Lesotho 3342
Government of Madhya Pradesh 5865
Govett, G.J.S. 5662
Govett, M.H. 5662
Govindaraj, V.C. 8337-8339, 9141
Govorchin, Gerald G. 12019
Gow, D.J. 10122
Gow, James 1535, 4453
Gow, Neil 10602
Goyal, Narendra 11451
Goyal, O.P. 3109, 6470

Goyder, J. 5680
Goytia, Victor Florencio 15566
Grabendorff, Wolf 1454, 11033, 11694, 15495
Grabonsky, A. 794
Graca, Jayme Ribeiro da 795
Grada, Carmac 706
Gradus, Yehuda 4454, 5426, 5866, 14759
Graff, Henry F. 6287
Graham, B. D. 3940
Graham, Gerald S. 17065, 17175
Graham, James D. 1057, 8684
Graham, Malbone W. 2621, 12840
Graham, William C. 13150
Grajdanzev, Andrew J. 2379, 13316
Granados, Carlos 2168
Granastein, J.L. 11263
Grande, J.C. Pedro 5283
Grande, John W. 9671
Grange, Jean 10819
Grant, Christina Phelps 2380
Grant, George 3857
Grant, Margaret 12384
Grant, Philip 1528
Grant, R.M. 5993, 13994
Grant, Richard L. 389, 11452, 14322
Grantham, Dewey W. 610
Grasland, Claude 2719
Grasmuck, Sherri 4111
Graubard, Morlie H. 15249
Grauhan, R.R. 5495
Graves, Norman J. 14717
Graves, Philip 11794
Gravier, Gaston 8073
Gray, Colin S. 796, 797, 14993
Gray, F. 4926
Gray, Hugh 2381, 10492
Gray, W.A.H. 3406
Grayson, John Paul 3306, 9672
Grayson, Kirk 15964
Graz, Liesl. 416
Grazynski, M. 4879
Great Britain 3033, 6755, 6925, 6936-6938, 6997, 6998, 7114-7116, 7183, 7840, 7841, 7949, 8074, 12841
Great Britain Colonial Office 4811, 12241, 13210
Great Britain Foreign Office 6996, 7948, 13210
Great Britain Government 5497, 13211
Great Britain Parliament 4689, 12242-12244, 12385
Great Britain Treaties 11855, 13531, 13532, 13533
Greater Rhodesia 4642
Greca, Alcides 3566
Green, December 12891
Green, Howard 16150
Green, J.B. 14994

Gupta, Vinod 11455
Gupte, Pranay 6676
Gurdon, Charles 57
Gurevich, Avon 527
Gurley, Franklin Louis 15686
Gurr, Ted Robert 14074, 15317
Gursoy, C. 1773
Gururaj Rao, H.S. 14604
Guseyn-Zade, S.M. 5573
Gushue, Raymond 16753
Gustafson, T. 14511
Gustavson, C.G. 15255
Gutersohn, H. 13319
Guth, Gloria Jean Anne 10677
Guthier, Steven L. 2788
Gutierrez Bermedo, Hernan 11335
Gutierrez Gutierrez, Mario R.
    8954, 8955
Gutjahr, Lothar 11696
Gutkind, Peter C.W. 6159
Gutmann, A. 14311
Gutteridge, J.A.C. 16648
Guyer, Jane I. 9462
Guynne, R.N. 14720
Guzman, Raul P. de 5368
Gwyer, G.D. 14512
Gwynn, C.W. 7842
Gyamfi-Fenteng, Lord Justice 8483
Gyford, J. 5500, 10678
Gyorgy, Andrew 801, 1064-1066,
    12615
Gyori, Kenneth A. 3568, 3569
Ha, Joseph M. 2383, 15967
Ha-Lim, F. 2386
Haack, H. Perlet veb Hermann
    12844
Haas, Anthony 13450
Haas, Ernst B. 3699, 12185,
    12536, 15256
Haas, Hans-Dieter 16262
Haas, Michael 2384, 3034
Haas, Peter J. 5281
Haas, William H. 13105
Haataja, Kyosti 8108
Habeeb, Atiya 13378
Habicht, M. 7722
Hachey, Thomas E. 4117
Hackel, E. 14995
Hacker, A. 9676
Hackett, Charles Wilson 7001
Hackett, J. 14996
Hackey, Robert B. 10128
Hadar, Leon T. 10493
Hadawi, Sami 2285, 2385
Haddad, Mahmoud 3941
Hadjeres, Sadek 2909
Hadjimichalis, C. 14375
Hadley, David Jeffery 9677
Hadsel, Winifred N. 2625, 13597,
    16263
Haefele, Edwin T. 8484
Haegen, H. Vander 5930
Hafner, Gerhard 8240, 8241, 8341,
    9175, 9198

Hafner, James Allan 5868
Hag, S. Moinul 666
Hagan, Joe D. 12186
Haggard, J. Villasana 8160
Haggard, M.T. 1593, 8161
Haggard, Stephan 4789
Haggett, P. 8
Haglund, David G. 14513-14516
Hahn, Dwight R. 3859
Hahn, Harlan 3109, 9354
Hahn, Joon-Woo 10375
Hahn, Lorna 3806, 12967
Hahn, Walter F. 835, 17051
Hahskar, P.N. 15806
Haight, G. Winthrop 16649
Haile, Getatchew 5018
Hailey, William Malcolm, Baron
    3495, 12706, 12768, 12845,
    12846, 12968, 12969, 13535
Hailsham, Lord 4252
Haimson, Leopold H. 5574
Haine, Edgar A. 8956
Haines, C. Grove 12020, 12537,
    12616
Haines, David W. 14075
Haines, Milan 15968
Haines, O. Grove 13598
Hainsworth, P. 3472
Hais, Michael David 9678
Hajdu, Joseph 287, 7761
Hajdu, Zoltan 5019
Hajnal, H. 12021
Hakli, Jouni 1986
Halbach, Uwe 4118
Halderman, J.W. 1536, 12098
Haldipeir, R.N. 8009
Hale, Richard W. 6799
Hale, William 10494, 15807
Halebsky, Sandor 4459
Haley, Andrew G. 14865
Halford, Susan 9325, 10823
Halkin, J. 1067
Hall, A. Hamer 14997
Hall, Andrew 10495
Hall, Arthur R. 1068, 7382, 16560
Hall, Christopher D. 16264
Hall, Duncan 1774, 7805, 7806,
    12099, 12538
Hall, Eugene C. 9679
Hall, G.H. 5665
Hall, H. Robert 17321
Hall, Henrique R. 1069
Hall, J.A. 1872
Hall, John Stuart 9680
Hall, Kermit L. 5285
Hall, P. 5501, 5581
Hall, Raymond L. 5996
Hall, Richard 8485, 8692
Hall, Robert A. 6533
Hall, Robert Burnett 2387, 5829
Hall, Russell E. 13451
Hall, Thomas D. 6103
Hall, W.E. 11035
Hall, William Keeny 9681

Hallaj, Mohammad 3942
Halle, Louis J. 1873, 14998
Haller, Hans Rudolf 9176, 9177
Halliday, Fred 11145, 14185,
    15969
Halligan, J.R. 6534
Hallion, Richard P. 15808
Halloway, J. 3496
Hallowell, A.I. 6288, 10129
Hallstein, Walter. 12539
Hallsworth, Alan G. 2626
Halme, Kalervo Raymond 13808
Halperin, Martin 15257
Halpern, A.M. 11456
Halpin, S.A., Jr. 9682, 10130
Haltenberger, Michael 1070, 1071
Haltiner, Karl 16265
Haltom, W. 9322
Haltzel, Michael H. 4139
Halverson, F. Douglas 5169
Ham, C. 5666
Ham-Chande, Roberto 7544
Hambro, Edyard 11697, 12095
Hambro, John 12617
Hamburg, James Fredric 5766
Hamdan, G. 348, 1311, 3525
Hamdani, Abbas 6472
Hamel, J.A. Van 12022
Hamelin, Jean 10131
Hamelin, Louis-Edmond
    5286-5288, 6289, 14127
Hamelin, Marcel 10131
Hamilton, B.M. 10603
Hamilton, C.I. 16978
Hamilton, Daniel 3213
Hamilton, David Napier 6940
Hamilton, Edward K. 11286
Hamilton, Howard D. 9683, 9684,
    10132
Hamilton, J. 2978
Hamilton, Kingsley W. 15258
Hamilton, Richard 2239
Hamilton, Thomas J. 2388
Hamm, K.E. 10133
Hammer, Ellen J. 13213
Hammond, Thomas Taylor 16153
Hamnett, Brian R. 13900
Hamnett, C. 5575
Hampton, C.R. 5027
Hampton, W. 9355
Hamrin, Carol Lee 3035
Han, Sin Fong 14076
Han, Sung-Joo 3943
Hance, William A. 4690, 8693-
    8697, 8890
Hancock, I.R. 2910
Hancock, M. Donald 2524
Hancock, W.K. 12707, 12708
Hand, S.B. 10043
Handelman, Howard 5289
Handelman, John Robert 9263
Handler, Joseph 13320
Handler, Richard 3860, 3861
Handley, Charles D. 10282

Husain, Sohail 8013
Husainn, Majid 10528
Husbands, C.T. 4291, 6564, 9359
Husbands, J.L. 15277
Hussain, Ijaz 9146
Hussain, Karki 13754
Hussey, Gemma 2526
Hussey, Roland D. 12309
Hustich, I. 2635
Huszar, George B. 1355
Hutcheson, J.D. 9997
Hutchins, F.G. 14191
Hutchins, Wells A. 3310
Hutchinson, Alaister, G.L. 17072
Hutchinson, John 2527, 3711
Hutchinson, P. 1102, 1103
Hutchinson, T.C. 15001
Hutchison, Alan 17073
Hutchison, Bruce 7383, 15695
Hutchison, E.H. 15816
Huth, Paul 12192
Hutt, Michael 4473
Huttenback, Robert A. 7570, 7653
Huxley, Elspeth 6165, 12986
Huxley, Julian 12714
Huxley, Tim 10500
Hveem, Helge 8728
Hwang, Su-Ik 9711
Hyamson, Albert Montefiore 2286
Hybel, Alex Roberto 11046
Hyde, C.C. 6684, 6685, 7384,
    7491, 11292
Hyden, Goran 6229
Hyder, Khurshid 11599, 13906
Hyma, Balasubramanyam I. 5370
Hyman, Anthony 15817, 15977
Hymes, Dell 6363
Hynning, Clifford J. 9467
Hynson, Lawrence McKee, Jr.
    9712
Hyun, Min Chong 9272
Ibler, Vladimir 8345, 16507
Ibragimov, A. I. 234
Ibrahim, Saad E. 1528
Idang, Gordon J. 11208
Iheduru, Okecukwu C. 3810
Ihl C., Pablo 1465, 16856
Ihonvbere, Julius O. 3347
Iimoto, Nobuyuki 479, 13328
Iirtha, Ranjit 3409
Iivonen, Jyrki 11698
Ijere, Joseph A. 4694
Ijere, M.O. 12987
Ikenberry, G. John 11293
Ikle, Fred Charles 15278, 15978
Ikporukpo, C.O. 2914
Ilchman, Warren F. 14002
Ilgren, Thomas 13802
Illanes Fernandez, Javier 8346
Illich, I. 5671
Illinois 5297
ILO 13691
Imai, Haruo 9713
Imam, Z. 11462

Imbert, Pierre-Henri 16903
Imbright, Gastone 6004
Imishue, R.W. 12246
Imnaischwili, N. 2636
Imobighe, T.A. 15499
Imus, Merla E. 9096
Inbar, Efraim 6477, 15818
Independent Commission on
    Disarmament and Security Issues
    15007
India (Republic) 2287, 4474, 5371-
    5376, 7121, 7122, 7574-7587,
    10384-10393, 11463-11467,
    12388, 14607, 14608,
    14609-14612
India Embassy 4299
India Ministry of External Affairs
    12389
India. Constituent Assembly. 13219
Indian Council of World Affairs
    12390
Indian International Centre 17074
Indorf, Hans M. 10501
Infante Caffi, Maria Teresa 8958,
    9027
Informe Final 8959
Ingalls, Gerald L. 9714, 10013,
    10014, 10042, 10141-10143
Ingecot (Abidjian) for CILSS 8778
Ingham, K. 11209, 12989
Ingham, Kenneth 6166
Inglehart, Ronald 710
Ingram, Edward 1781, 1782, 3040
Ingram, Kenneth 15008
Ingrams, Harold 2119, 13329,
    13330, 14736
Inions, Noela J. 16760
Inlow, E. Burke 2395, 7654
Inman, Samuel Guy 1356
Innes, D. 1314, 14320
Innes, F.M. 3120
Innis, Donald K. 6296
Innis, Harold A. 3311, 7911
Inoguchi, Takashi 11600
Institute of Arab American Affairs,
    New York 14613
Institute of Pacific Relations. 13220
Institute on World Organization
    12545
Instituto de Investigaciones
Historicas y Culturales de La Paz
    8960
Instituto Panamericano de Geografia
    e Historia 11861
International Boundary Commission
    (U.S. and Canada) 7011, 7012
International Conciliation 12194
International Court of Justice 1700,
    16904, 16905, 17329
International Economic Studies
    Institute 14428
International Geographical Congress
    667
International Law Association

12715
International Organization 12193
Ionides, M.G. 11949
Ippolito, Joseph T. 17328
Iran 6686
Iraq 6686
Ireland, Gordon 7492, 7493
Ireland, Philip W. 12447
Ireland, Willard E. 6800
Ironside, R.G. 5832
Irvine, Jill A. 4126
Irvine, W.P. 5028
Irwin, Paul C. 16661
Irwin, William Joseph, Jr. 9715
Isaac, Barry L. 1466
Isaac, Erich 6106, 6107
Isaacman, A. 12990
Isaacman, B. 12990
Isaacs, Anita 15570
Isaacs, Harold R. 11468
Isajiw, Wsevolod W. 1998
Isard, Walter 4947, 6108, 6109,
    15009, 15155
Isenberg, Michael T. 15571
Ishibashi, Michihiro 10502
Ishida, Takeshi 10394
Ishow, Habib 3408
Islam, Nasir 6478
Islamic Republic of Pakistan
    10395-10398, 14614-14617
Ismael, Jacqueline S. 5377
Ismael, Tareq Y. 5377, 12448
Ispahani, Mahnaz Zehra 16999
Israel, Jerold 10144
Isreal, Michael Louis 9716
Issawi, Charles 12449, 16274
Istituto Studie Ricerche Cattaneo
    10688
Iturriza, Jorge E. 8347, 8961
Ivanicka, Koloman 5580
Ives, T. 15279
Iwata, Kozo 235
Iyer, Raghavan 1604
Izmirlian, Harry, Jr. 10503
Jabber, Paul 14737
Jack, Ernest 1545, 6893
Jackman, Albert H. 15280
Jackman, R.W. 10145
Jackson, Alan 9717
Jackson, Barbara Ward 12284
Jackson, Jesse Jefferson 9718
Jackson, John Edgar 9719
Jackson, John H. 13907
Jackson, Lon 15696
Jackson, Mabel V. 11210
Jackson, Peter 3712, 6005, 6006,
    6364
Jackson, Richard H. 616
Jackson, Robert H. 3348, 6230
Jackson, Robert J. 16158
Jackson, W.A. Douglas 66-69, 236,
    1104, 1499, 7123, 7589
Jacob, Gerald R. 5771
Jacob, H. 9360

16984
Laux, H.D. 10881
Laux, Jeanne K. 3741
Lavalle, Eduard Marcus 5383
Lavallee, E.M. 8078
Laver, M. 6632, 6633, 10882, 10883
Laverde Goubert, Luis 7914
Lavergne, Bernard 1887
Laves, Walter H.C. 850
Lavigne, Rene 13461
Lavin, Jose Domingo 254, 255
Lavrencic, Karl 8757
Lavretyev, Alexander 17087
Law, C.M. 16281
Lawrence, David Gilbert 9761
Lawrence, F. 2921
Lawrence, Henry 7499
Lawrence, Roderick 5055
Laws, J.B. 6945
Lawson, Fred H. 4490, 14766, 15991
Lawson, Ruth C. 11060
Lawson, Stephanie 6536, 10614
Lawson, Steven Fred 9762
Lawuyi, Olatunde Bayo 6946
Laylin, John G. 11805
Lazarsfeld, Paul F. 9522, 9763
Lazarus-Black, Mindie 5306
Lazerwitz, Bernard 6370
Le Bras, Gabriel 6113, 6565, 6634, 9252
Le Duc, Thomas 7500
Le Fur, Lorris 6017
Le Lannon, Maurice 487
Le Lannou, Maurice 1888
Le Roux, Gabriel A. 352
Lea, A.C. 5038
Leach, E.R. 422
Leach, F. Burton 13346
Leach, Richard H. 12352
Leach, Warren B., Jr. 16677
Leaf, Murray J. 3125
League of Nations 7596, 8027, 8112-8114, 12106
Leal, Barry 11656
Leal, J. 14528
Leaney, Joseph Robert 10695
Leaning, J. 15031
Leardi, Eraldo 16678
Learmonth, A.T.A. 1562
Lebedev, Igor A. 17088
LeBoutillier, John 11484
Lebow, Richard Ned 11061, 15309
Lechner, Norberto 4491
Leckie, Robert 15578
Lecuona, Rafael A. 14336
Lederer, Ivo J. 8079, 11714
Leduc, L. 9581
Lee, Bill 15503
Lee, C.S. 6851
Lee, Calvin B.T. 9281
Lee, Chong-Sik 2405
Lee, Fitzgerald 15032

Lee, H.C. 16857
Lee, Ian 15213
Lee, Raymond L.M. 3974
Lee, Robin 4492
Lee, Roy S. 16516
Lee, S.H. 16106
Lee, Su-Hoon 1889
Lee, Sung-Chull 11621
Lee, Wei-Chin 16829
Lee, William Charles 9282
Lee, Yong Leng 423, 6487, 7598, 9152, 12455, 14009, 16517, 16679, 16830, 16831
Lee, Yuk 5180
Leebaert, Derek 16165
Leech, John 8758
Leeds, Patricia Giles 9764
Leedy, Frederick A. 2794
Lefeber, L. 5874
Lefebvre, Andre 6016, 6566
Lefebvre, Jeffrey A. 15704
Lefevre, Vlademar 7028
Leff, Carol Skalnik 2538
Legare, Ann 4737
Legault, L.H. 16768
Legge, J.D. 2493, 13462
LeGloannec, Anne-Marie 3723
Legorreta, Omar Martinez 1616
Legrain, Jean-Francois 2406
Leguizamon Pondal, Martiniano 14767
Legum, Colin 1127, 2125, 8759, 13760, 15503
Legvold, Robert 1795, 3197
Lehman-Wilzig, Sam N. 10407
Lehmann, Josef A. 9101
Lehne, Richard 10175
Lehrer, A. 5434
Lehtinen, A. 4146
Leib, Jonathan I. 9765
Leiblinger, Walter Francisco 1128, 1129
Leibundgut, Hans 2786
Leiden, Carl 2407, 2922
Leifer, Michael 2409, 3047, 7597, 11610, 11806, 11955, 13463, 14768, 14769
Leifer, Walter 7962
Leighton, Marian K. 4493, 7668
Leimbruber, W. 486
Leinbach, Thomas Raymond 3048
Leiss, Amelia C. 11715
Leistikow, Gunner 17335
Leites, Nathan 16166
Leith, Charles K. 14433, 14434, 14529-14531
Leitner, Helga 5039
Leiva, Fernando Ignacio 9862
Leltore, G. 10696
Lemarchand, Rene 2127, 11156
LeMelle, Wilbert J. 12289
Lemon, A. 6172
Lemon, Donald P. 6696
Lencek, Rado L. 6635

Lenchner, Paul 9766
Lenczowski, George 1547, 12398, 14532, 16985, 17185
Lendvai, Paul 2652
Lengelle, Jean G. 3512
Lengyel, Peter 11
Lenin, V.I. 2822, 14200
Lennert, James W. 5508
Lenski, Gerhard 6018
Lentacker, Firmin 8080, 8115
Lentz, Wolfgang 16832
Leonard, L. Larry 12456, 17270
Leonard, Thomas M. 11312, 15705
Leonhardt, Hans 12031
Leopold, W.F. 6019
Lepage, R.B. 6020
Lepawsky, Albert 11807
Lepgold, Joseph 15900
Lepotier, A. 1130, 15310, 16282
Lepotier, R. 1703
Lepsius, M. Ranier 4147
LeQuesne 12544
Lerner, Daniel 12552, 12643
Lerner, Stevan Jay 11062
Lernre, Victoria 15706
Leroy, Frederick E. 9767
Leruez, Jacque. 10884
Lerwill, I. 15707
Lesch, Ann 3126
Lesiak, Jerzy 9205
Leslie, Shane 2653
Leslie, Winsome J. 3813, 4494
Lesser, Ian O. 11444
Lessing, O.E. 14083
Lester, A.P. 12644, 12645
Leszcycki, S. 12457
Letarte, Jacques 10131
Letiche, J.M. 14010
Letiner, H. 6636
Lettke, Kazimierz 9206
Leuchtenburg, W.E. 5782
Leupold, Werner 1890
Lever, Henry 9473
Leversen, Michael A. 16680
Leverson, J.J. 6947
Levesque, Rene 2750
Levesque, T.J. 10069
Levi, Barbara G. 16283
Levi, M. 6104
Levi, Werner 1548, 1617, 3127, 3128, 8167, 11657, 12458, 15992
Levin, Michael D. 3724, 6021
Levine, Alan J. 14201
Levine, B.B. 1474
Levine, Daniel H. 6305
Levine, I.O. 11956
Levine, Isaac Don 15033
Levine, Victor T. 12859
LeVine, R. 14084
Levitt, Joseph 3874
Levy, Jack S. 5085, 15311-15315
Levy, Jacques 9353
Levy, Jean-Pierre 17271

Meijer, C.B.V. 16569
Meijide Pardo, Antonio 3655
Meiksins, Gregory 12034, 16177
Meile, Pierre 2417
Meillet, A. 6027
Meinig, Donald W. 628, 1151, 1152, 6375, 11158, 13172, 14344
Meir, Avinoam 6493
Meira Matos, Aderbal 8380
Meira Mattos, C. de 872, 873, 1153
Meisel, J. 386, 9803, 9804
Meisler, Stanley 4310
Meissner, Boris 4509
Meister, Irene W. 12401
Melamed, Assia. 10897
Melamid, Alexander 430, 2033, 2662, 6703, 7433, 7434, 7674, 8198, 11960, 11961, 13358, 13763, 13764, 14779, 16690, 16732
Melanoer, G. 6117
Melanson, Richard Allen 11074
Melbourne, W.H. 7033
Melendex, Edwardo 13113
Melik, Anton 2663
Mellema, R.L. 4311
Meller, Norman. 4854
Meller, Patricio 7881
Meller, Roy 1899
Mellor, John W. 3420
Mellor, Roy 5599
Melman, S. 15052, 15337, 15585
Melman, Yossi 14634
Melo, Mario 3502
Melon, Amando 5600
Meltzner, A. 4258
Melvin, M.E. 6807
Memmi, Albert 12723
Mencken, H.L. 6311
Mendels, Doron 3735
Mendelsohn, Oliver 5438
Mendenhall 8935, 9102
Mendez, J. 15586
Mendez, J. Ignacio 13173
Mendlovitz, Saul H. 92
Mendoza, Jaime 2229, 7512, 16367, 16987
Menefee, Selden C. 1622
Menendez-Carrion, Amparo 9805
Meneses, Romulo 1361, 8970, 9053
Menezes, Adolpho Justo Bezerra de. 11329
Menges, Constantine C. 12557
Menon, Kumara Padmanabha Sivasundara 11493
Menon, P.K. 7389, 7513, 9054, 16437
Menon, Rajan 16178
Menon, Vapal Pangunni 3054, 13230

Menz, Yves 5514
Menzel, Eberhard 8381
Meow, Seah Chee 4326
Merani, Pritam T. 7600, 7675
Mercado, J. 15338
Mercer, D.C. 5687
Mercer, David 3174, 4855, 6537
Mercer, J. A. 3736
Mercer, John 5, 1804, 3316, 10898
Meredith, Brian 16524
Meredith, David 13537
Merelman, Richard M. 2034
Merenne, Emile 9208
Meriaudeau, Robert 5601
Merkl, P.H. 508, 3239, 10703
Mermelstein, D. 5136
Merom, Gil 10202
Meron, T. 16006
Merrals, J.D. 17277
Merrett, Christopher D. 6239, 7034, 7035
Merriam, John G. 15796
Merridale, Catherine 4510
Merrill, Frederick T. 13359
Merrill, Gordon C. 629, 3737, 4746
Merrills, J.G. 16919, 17342
Merrin, Mary Beth 9806
Merritt, Richard L. 2035, 8199, 8200, 11159
Merryman, John H. 8971
Merton, R.K. 93
Meserve, Peter 7036
Mesquita, Bruce Bueno de 15339
Mess, Henry A. 2863
Messenger, Lewis Clement, Jr. 6312
Mestrovic, Stjepan G. 4511, 4512
Metcalfe, Sir Aubrey 11615, 13360
Metford, J.C.J. 14780
Methol Ferre, Alberto 7514
Metlay, D.S. 5677
Metz, Allan 3881
Metz, W.C. 5834
Metzemaekers, L. 13469
Meulemans, Williams Charles 9807
Mewes, H. 15340
Mexico 5190
Meyer, Alfred H. 11075
Meyer, C. Kenneth 9808
Meyer, David Ralph 6313
Meyer, Douglas Kermit 6314
Meyer, Eric 3981
Meyer, H.C. 491
Meyer, John W. 3551, 14540
Meyer, Milton Walter 7601
Meyer, Peggy Falkenheim 7752
Meyer, Ralph Christian 13705
Meyer, Richard M. 13548
Meyer, Ruth 16265
Meyer, Walter dos Santos 15721
Meyer, William H. 5043, 12786
Meyerhoff, Arthur 14541
Meyers, Dee Dee 10203

Meyers, H. 16988
Meyerson, Martin 3738
Meynaud, J. 10704
Mezerik, A.G. 12464, 12465, 14781
Miaja de la Meula, Adolfo 8382
Mian, Mumtaz Muhammad 14623
Mianecki, Pawel 9184, 9209
Michael, Alazar Tesfa 15509
Michael, Franz 4513, 7964
Michaels, Daniel W. 1154
Michaelson, J.M. 14782
Michel, Aloys A. 9154, 11962
Michel, Aloys S. 12654
Michell, Earl L. 8529
Michels, R. 9289
Michelson, Mark Charles 11494
Michnik, Adam 3739
Michta, Andrew A. 4514
Micklewright, Malcolm Algernon 5941
Micklin, Philip Patrick 12035
Middendorf, J. William II 17017
Midlarsky, Manus I. 11160, 15053
Mielonen, Mauno 3240
Miettinen, Jorma 15341
Migdail, Carl J. 2992
Migdal, Joel S. 3319
Migliorini, E. 94
Migranyan, Adnranit 9393
Migvens, A. Pires 1155
Mihalya, Louis J. 8530, 8791
Mihelic, Dusan 12036
Mijere, Nsolo 5727
Mikdashi, Zuhayr 14444
Mikesell, Marvin W. 2036, 3740, 6060, 7810
Mikesell, R.F. 14445
Mikolajski, Juliusz 12037
Miksche, F.O. 15054
Milani, Mohsen M. 4364
Milbrath, L.W. 9290
Milder, D.N. 9394
Milenky, Edward S. 15722
Miles, Afton Olson 9809
Miles, Edward J. 5191
Miles, Edward L. 16438, 17250
Miles, William F.S. 3350, 10705
Miliband, R. 4259, 14212
Milic, Milenko 8248-8250, 8383, 8384
Milicki, E.J. 15587
Milijan, Toivo 16296
Milivojevic, Marko 671, 3132, 14783
Millar, T.B. 11161, 12467, 17095, 17096, 17192
Millar, Willard 5785
Miller, Aaron David 14784, 14785
Miller, Anthony John 9810
Miller, Arthur H. 9395, 9811, 10899
Miller, Byron 5321
Miller, Charles 15510

Morell, James B. 16526
Morelli Pando, Jorge 9055
Moreno, Dario 11333
Moreno, M.M. 13566
Morenus, R. 14874
Moreton, E. 15093
Morfit, Michael 3133
Morgan, Arthur E. 15343
Morgan, F.W. 11813, 12038
Morgan, J. De 1901
Morgan, J.C. 8036
Morgan, John D. 14447
Morgan, K.O. 2547, 4313
Morgan, R. 17278
Morgan, T. Cliften 15315
Morgenthau, H.J. 877, 2864,
    11076-11078, 14983
Moriarty, B.M. 5837
Morill, R. 9540
Morin, F. 13926
Morin, Jacques-Yvan 13848
Morinigo, Victor 8387
Morisett, Jean 6378
Morison, Samuel Eliot 2175
Morkill, A.G. 4821
Morley, Morris H. 9863, 11334
Morner, Magnus 5193
Moro, R.O. 1158
Morrell, W.P. 13471
Morrill, Richard L. 3384, 7040,
    9293, 9397, 9398, 10210-10212,
    12203, 15344
Morrill, Robert W. 213, 271, 5323,
    5324, 9822
Morris, A.S. 3883
Morris, Benny 15840
Morris, Elizabeth 3245
Morris, Harvey 15780
Morris, James 6430
Morris, James A. 4385
Morris-Jones, W.H. 10529, 10530
Morris, Joseph W. 17346
Morris, Michael A. 11874, 14788,
    17194
Morrison, D.C. 15724
Morrison, Donald G. 12869
Morrison, John A. 5602, 12039,
    16300
Morrison, Peter A. 6921
Morrison, Phoebe 2230
Morrison, William Robert 2176
Morrissey, M. 10213
Morrow, J.H. 16180
Morse, R. 13722
Morse, S.J. 2930
Morsy, Laila Amin 16301
Mortara, Giorgio 4314
Mortimer, Robert. 9475
Morton, Rebecca Bradford 9399,
    9823
Morton, William Lewis 4658, 4749
Morzone, Luis Antonio 8974
Moscosocardenas, Alphonso 3581
Moseley, George V.H. 7965,

13361, 14136
Moseley, M. 4954
Moseley, Paul 14017
Mosely, Philip E. 8119
Moses, Joel C. 4162, 4350
Moskowitz, D.H. 4955
Moskowitz, Jay Henry 9824
Moskowitz, Moses 13615
Mosotho, Jeremiah 2931
Moss, David 6759
Moss, Phillip 17347
Moss, R. 2754, 2826, 9825, 14018
Mossa, H. 14091
Mosse, George L. 4163
Most, B.A. 1159, 7932, 11079
Most, Benjamin A. 15345, 15525
Mostyn, Trevor 672
Mote, Victor Lee 13817
Moten, A. Rashid 3983
Mott, P.G. 14894
Mottola, Karid 1362
Motyl, Alexander J. 4164, 4517,
    4518
Moufflet, Raphele 8251
Moulin, H.A. 7517
Moulin, Lee 12655
Moulton, Harold G. 15060
Moulton, J.L. 17195
Moultrie, William Anthony 5792
Mounsey, H. 12543
Mountjoy, Alan B. 11964, 11965
Mouton, M.W. 16570
Mouzon, Olin T. 14448
Mowrer, Edgar Ansel 15061
Moya Dominguez, Maria Teresa
    8388
Moya Quiroga, Victor 8975
Moyer, Henry Wayne, Jr. 9826
Mozick, R. 2827
Mozier, Jeanne M. 10414
Mrazek, Josef 14137
Mtshali, Benedict Vulindela 8533
Mucghan, A. 10806
Muckelston, Keith Way 5793,
    5838, 10214
Mudd, Stuart 14449
Mueller, Herbert 11966
Mughan, Anthony 4157, 6622,
    10906
Mugomba, Agrippah T. 12294,
    17101
Muir, Richard 98, 99, 5325
Muise, Delphin Andrew 9827
Mujal-Leon, Eusebio 11335
Mujnslow, B. 14790
Mukerjee, Dilip 2418
Mukerjee, Radhakamal 3424
Mukerji, A.B. 3423, 14789
Mukerji, D. 5838, 10214
Mukerji, Krishna Prasada 5384
Mukherjee, A.N. 14217
Mukhopadhyay, Syamal 3134
Mukonoweshuro, Eliphas G. 6495
Mukundan, Rangaswamy 9294

Mulcahy, Patrick Herbert 9828
Muller, Dietrich O. 13016
Muller, Edward N. 2249
Muller, Heribert 10907
Muller, Walter 9210
Muller-Wille, Wilhelm 1160
Mulligan, Jean E. 9295
Mulliner, K. 5883
Mulqi, M. 14509
Mumme, Stephen P. 11862
Muncaster, Robert G. 15471
Munch, Fritz 16921
Munch, Ronnie 4165
Munchow, Sabine 5603
Munck, Ronaldo 9829
Mungazi, Dickson A. 12870
Munger, Edwin S. 3819, 6705,
    8534
Munger, Frank J. 11871
Muni, S.D. 4822, 11498, 14635
Munita Contreras, Herman 1488
Muniz, Humberto Garcia 15725
Munkman, A.L.W. 16693
Munn, Andrew 5263
Munoz, Julio H. 1363
Munoz, Louis J. 2932
Munro, Dana G. 11336
Munro, David M. 4315
Munro, K. 6379
Munro, L.K. 11659, 13472
Munroe, Trevor 6380
Munson, Henry, Jr. 6180
Muraauskas, G. Thomas 10286
Murarka, Dev 16010
Murashimi, Eiji 10531
Murauskas, G. Thomas 5794,
    5839, 10009, 10215
Murawski, Klaus Eberhard 6706
Murdoch, Richard K. 7882
Murdock. G.P. 588
Murgatroyd, L. 5516, 6570
Murkland, Harry B. 13174
Murphey, Rhoads 3622, 16011
Murphy, Alexander B. 2724, 3740,
    6118, 6571
Murphy, Craig N. 12305, 13927
Murphy, George Gregory S. 12402
Murphy, I.L. 11814
Murphy, Jefferson 12871
Murphy, John E. 13017
Murphy, M.F. 76
Murphy, Marion Fisher 3503, 3582
Murphy, Patrick J. 11967, 11968
Murphy, Raymond E. 5326
Murphy, Rhoads 14019
Murphy, T.P. 4659
Murphy, W.J. 14425
Murphy, William Thomas, Jr. 9830
Murray, C. 589
Murray, J.K. 13473
Murray, L. 3352
Murray, M.J. 14218
Murray, R. 2231
Murray, Roger 12788

Schattkowsky, Ralph 2683
Schatz, Gerald S. 904
Schatzberg, Michael G. 2139
Schechter, Neil 11097
Schechter, Stephen L. 13560
Scheele, Raymond Harold 9908
Scheer, Gunter 216
Schellenberg, James A. 9909
Scheman, L. Ronald 396
Schepe, G. 15387
Scheynius, Ignas J. 12798
Schiff, Ze'ev. 16048
Schiffrer, Carlo 6901, 8135, 12052
Schift, Ze'ev 14594
Schijf, H. 13987
Schildhaus, Salomon 9910
Schiller, A. Arthur 4831, 13392
Schilling, P. 905
Schilling, Warner R. 15606
Schilz, Gordon B. 9133
Schinz, A. 3627
Schlee, Gunther 3261
Schlemmer, Lawrence 4492, 13942
Schlesinger, A., Jr. 14983
Schlesinger, James R. 1204
Schlesinger, Mildred 10945
Schlesinger, Philip 14299
Schlesinger, Philip R. 1830
Schlesser, Norman Dennis 8087
Schlichting, Kurt 10959
Schlier, O. 7218
Schlor, Wolfgang 16318
Schmahl, Wolfgang 2442
Schmeckebier, Laurence F. 9911
Schmid, Alex P. 16189
Schmidhauser, John R. 14556
Schmidt, C. 1205, 14241
Schmidt, Danna 14036
Schmidt-Haack 906
Schmidt, Helmut 12218
Schmidt, John D. 3387
Schmidt, Robert H. 8847
Schmieder, Oscar 6385
Schmiegelow, Henrik 11632
Schmiegelow, Michele 11632
Schmitt, Carl M. 9913
Schmitt, Karl M. 15669, 16790
Schmitz, G. 3354
Schmollck, Frank H. 12053, 17019
Schmude, D. 15196
Schnabel, Fritz 3754
Schnapper, Bernard 737
Schneider, A.R.H. 14901
Schneider, F. 3466
Schneider, J. 15742
Schneider, Ronald M. 4563, 11303
Schneider, William 12799, 14461
Schnitzer, E.W. 907
Schnitzer, Ewald W. 1206
Schocnhals, Kai P. 15607
Schoeller, P. 567
Schoenfeld, H.F. Arthur 13632
Schoenrich, Otto 7528
Schofield, Brian B. 17206

Schofield, Richard N. 2310, 6856
Scholberg, Henry 13246
Scholler, Peter 304, 738, 1207-1210, 2684, 4895, 8210
Scholz, Fred 2443
Scholz, John 10488
Schomisch, Thomas Paul 9914
Schone, Emil 128
Schonfield, H.J. 11977
Schoolmaster, F.A. 10272
Schoonover, T.D. 11355
Schopflin, George 4197, 4564, 4565, 10645, 14368, 14370
Schoyer, George 10273
Schraeder, Peter J. 11226
Schram, S.R. 3439
Schrank, William E. 17361
Schreiber, E.M. 10274
Schreiber, Marc 8848
Schreiber, Thomas 4198
Schrepfer, Von Hans 1211
Schreuder, Deryck 12699
Schrieke, J.J. 5341
Schroder, Dieter 8263
Schroder, Peter 16791
Schroeder, Klaus 8211
Schroeder, Paul W. 11180
Schubert, Glendon 9912, 10275
Schulte-Althoff, F.J. 13561
Schultz, Barry M. 15092
Schultz, Hans-Dietrich 739, 740, 15389
Schultz, J.B. 15388
Schultz, Lothar 5619
Schultz, Richard H. 15536
Schultze, C.L. 14557
Schultze, J.H. 505, 1503, 13051
Schultze, Rainer-Olaf 1904
Schulz, Deborah Sundloff 11357
Schulz, Donald E. 11356, 11357
Schulz, Eberhard 2685
Schulz, G. 2804
Schulz, Peter 2556, 5065
Schulze, Hagen. 4199
Schumacher, Rupert Von 1212-1215, 11181
Schuman, Frederick L. 1216, 11098, 11752, 15390, 15391
Schumpeter, J. 14242
Schurmann, Franz H. 908
Schurtz, Heinrich 6046, 6047
Schuttel, L. 6644
Schutz, Barry M. 921
Schuurman, N. 11358
Schwab, George 541
Schwab, L. 10276
Schwalm, Eberhardt 305, 2060, 3262
Schwartz, Alan Jerry 9915
Schwartz, Benjamin I. 11633
Schwartz, Herman 4566
Schwartz, Michael 14014, 14015
Schwartz, Mildred A. 3001
Schwartz, Walter 6258

Schwartzberg, Joseph E. 681, 909, 4763, 10277, 12219, 12220, 12482, 13247, 13779
Schwarz, Hans-Peter 11753
Schwarz, Henry G. 11359
Schwarz, Janet B. 13184
Schwarzenberger, Georg 910, 15392
Schweinfurth, Ulrich 2444, 8039, 14827, 16049
Schweisfurth, Hans–Theodor 8406
Schweitzer, Carl-Christoph 16190
Schwind, M. 306
Schwind, Paul J. 5806
Scigliano, Robert 6511
Scobell, Andrew 16050, 16112
Scofield, J. 3628
Scott, A.J. 4925, 14172, 15743
Scott, A.M. 911
Scott, Allen 5066
Scott, E. Keith, Jr. 4966
Scott, F.R. 12568, 12800
Scott, Harriet Fast 16191
Scott, J. 4858, 14037
Scott, J.B. 7529
Scott, J.C. 3440
Scott, J.T. 15744
Scott, James William 5951
Scott, John 7852
Scott, Marvin B. 2025
Scott, Michael. 13053
Scott, Munford J., Jr. 16792
Scott, P. 6259
Scott, R. 1916, 5483
Scott, William F. 16191, 16192
Scovazzi, Tuillo 11978
Scramuzza, Vincent M. 13633
Scranton, Margaret E. 10278
Scruton, R. 14243
Sdasyuk, Galina V. 13780
Seabury, P. 11283
Seaga, Edward 17020
Seah, Chee-Meow 12483
Seal, Anil 14276
Seale, Patrick 12484
Sealey, Kenneth R. 13943
Searing, James 3834
Searls, Guy 2445
Sebba, Rachel 2061
Sebenius, James K. 16458
Seck, Assane 8849
Seckler, D.W. 5728
Secretariat General 8850, 8851
Secretariat General de l'U.D.E.A.C. 8852
Sedes 8560
Seebohm, Lord 17207
Seegers, Annette. 15519
Seegers, Kathleen Walker 12128
Seeman, Sonia Henrietta Hubner 11885
Seers, Dudley 3755
Seethal, Cecil 5122, 5123
Segal, Aaron 8853, 8854, 11388,